The 1997 Baseball Encyclopedia® Update

Complete Career Records for All Players Who Played in the 1996 Season

Macmillan • USA

Editorial And Research Staff
Ken Samelson, Editorial Director
Seiji Ogata
Chris Dreyer
Bill Deane
Bob Kerler
Richard Topp
Special thanks to Steve Moyer and STATS, Inc.

Macmillan
A Simon & Schuster Macmillan Company
1633 Broadway
New York, NY 10019

ISBN: 0-02-861512-3

10 9 8 7 6 5 4 3 2 1

Printed in the United States of America

Contents

The Teams and
Their Players

The Teams and Their Players lists, for the 1996 season, each team, along with its manager and record, the regulars at each position, as well as the pitchers and the leading substitutes. The teams are presented in the order of the standings of the division. Substitutes are listed if they had at least 162 at-bats or 20 runs batted in; pitchers are listed if they pitched 162 innings or had 10 or more decisions (including saves).

Fielding statistics listed for regulars are for the indicated position only. The position listed for substitutes may vary. If a substitute played 70% of his games at one position, that is the only position listed for him. If he did not play 70% of his games at one position, but played 90% of his games at two positions, he is listed with a combination position, such as "S2" for shortstop and second base, or "CO" for catcher and outfield. In such cases, the fielding statistics listed are combined for both positions. All outfield positions are considered one position for these purposes. If a player failed to meet either the 70% or 90% requirement listed above, he is listed as a utility player ("UT").

Any statistic that appears in boldfaced print is a league-leading total for that category. An asterisk (*) next to a particular statistic indicates that the player led the league, but since he was traded during the season, the figure listed there is not necessarily his league-leading final total or average. For batting averages or percentages, a batter must have 502 plate appearances to qualify for the title. Pitchers must have pitched 162 innings to qualify in any pitching category. Fielders must have appeared in 100 games at the position to qualify.

NATIONAL LEAGUE 1996

East — Atlanta — W-96 L-66 — Bobby Cox

POS	Player	AB	BA	HR	RBI	PO	A	E	DP	TC/G	FA	Pitcher	G	IP	W	L	SV	ERA
1B	F. McGriff	617	.295	28	107	1415	121	12	118	9.8	.992	J. Smoltz	35	254	24	8	0	2.94
2B	M. Lemke	498	.255	5	37	228	408	15	70	4.9	.977	G. Maddux	35	245	15	11	0	2.72
SS	J. Blauser	265	.245	10	35	84	207	23	41	4.0	.927	T. Glavine	36	235	15	10	0	2.98
3B	C. Jones	598	.309	30	110	48	184	13	9	2.1	.947	S. Avery	24	131	7	10	0	4.47
RF	J. Dye	292	.281	12	37	150	2	8	1	1.7	.950	G. McMichael	73	87	5	3	2	3.22
CF	M. Grissom	671	.308	23	74	338	10	1	1	2.2	.997	B. Clontz	81	81	6	3	1	5.69
LF	R. Klesko	528	.282	34	93	190	6	5	1	1.4	.975	M. Wohlers	77	77	2	4	39	3.03
C	J. Lopez	489	.282	23	69	993	81	6	9	8.0	.994							
3B	T. Pendleton	162	.204	4	17	27*	78	7	5	2.7	.938							
OF	D. Justice	140	.321	6	25	88	3	0	1	2.3	1.000							

Montreal — W-88 L-74 — Felipe Alou

POS	Player	AB	BA	HR	RBI	PO	A	E	DP	TC/G	FA	Pitcher	G	IP	W	L	SV	ERA
1B	D. Segui	416	.286	11	58	943	89	7	79	9.1	.993	J. Fassero	34	232	15	11	0	3.30
2B	M. Lansing	641	.285	11	53	347	391	11	84	4.7	.985	P. Martinez	33	217	13	10	0	3.70
SS	M. Grudzielanek	657	.306	6	49	181	454	27	78	4.3	.959	R. Cormier	33	160	7	10	0	4.17
3B	S. Andrews	375	.227	19	64	64	256	15	13	2.7	.955	U. Urbina	33	114	10	5	0	3.71
RF	M. Alou	540	.281	21	96	259	8	3	2	1.9	.989	M. Rojas	74	81	7	4	36	3.22
CF	R. White	334	.293	6	41	185	5	2	0	2.2	.990	K. Rueter	16	79	5	6	0	4.58
LF	H. Rodriguez	532	.276	36	103	102	5	6	0	1.3	.947	D. Veres	68	78	6	3	4	4.17
C	D. Fletcher	394	.266	12	57	722	30	6	5	6.8	.992	M. Dyer	70	76	5	5	2	4.40
OF	F. Santangelo	393	.277	7	56	231	4	4	1	1.9	.983							
OF	C. Floyd	227	.242	6	26	93	2	4	0	1.2	.960							
OF	S. Obando	178	.247	8	22	74	2	3	0	1.7	.962							
C	L. Webster	174	.230	2	17	390	25	1	3	6.6	.998							
3B	D. Silvestri	162	.204	1	17	20	84	10	5	2.4	.912							

Florida — W-80 L-82 — Rene Lachemann W-39 L-47 — Cookie Rojas W-1 L-0 — John Boles W-40 L-35

POS	Player	AB	BA	HR	RBI	PO	A	E	DP	TC/G	FA	Pitcher	G	IP	W	L	SV	ERA
1B	G. Colbrunn	511	.286	16	69	1168	102	6	130	9.5	.995	K. Brown	32	233	17	11	0	1.89
2B	Q. Veras	253	.253	4	14	173	192	5	54	5.5	.986	A. Leiter	33	215	16	12	0	2.93
SS	E. Renteria	431	.309	5	31	162	344	11	76	4.9	.979	P. Rapp	30	162	8	16	0	5.10
3B	T. Pendleton	406	.251	7	58	82*	214	12	20	2.9	.961	J. Burkett	24	154	6	10	0	4.32
RF	G. Sheffield	519	.314	42	120	238	7	6	0	1.6	.976	R. Nen	75	83	5	1	35	1.95
CF	D. White	552	.274	17	84	296	5	4	1	2.2	.989	C. Hammond	38	81	5	8	0	6.56
LF	J. Conine	597	.293	26	95	187	8	5	2	1.6	.975	T. Mathews	57	55	2	4	4	4.91
C	C. Johnson	386	.218	13	37	751	70	4	11	6.9	.995							
UT	K. Abbott	320	.253	8	33	124	205	12	43		.965							
3B	A. Arias	224	.277	3	26	21	67	4	8	1.6	.957							
OF	J. Orsulak	217	.221	2	19	80	6	4	0	1.5	.956							
2B	L. Castillo	164	.262	1	8	99	118	3	36	5.4	.986							

New York — W-71 L-91 — Dallas Green W-59 L-72 — Bobby Valentine W-12 L-19

POS	Player	AB	BA	HR	RBI	PO	A	E	DP	TC/G	FA	Pitcher	G	IP	W	L	SV	ERA
1B	B. Huskey	414	.278	15	60	570	42	10	55	8.3	.984	M. Clark	32	212	14	11	0	3.43
2B	J. Vizcaino	363	.303	1	32	178	257	6	68	4.7	.986	B. Jones	31	196	12	8	0	4.42
SS	R. Ordonez	502	.257	1	30	230	452	27	103	4.7	.962	P. Harnisch	31	195	8	12	0	4.21
3B	J. Kent	335	.290	9	39	75	183	21	17	3.1	.925	J. Isringhausen	27	172	6	14	0	4.77
RF	A. Ochoa	282	.294	4	33	135	8	5	3	1.9	.966	P. Wilson	26	149	5	12	0	5.38
CF	L. Johnson	682	.333	9	69	390	9	12	3	2.6	.971	D. Mlicki	51	90	6	7	1	3.30
LF	B. Gilkey	571	.317	30	117	310	18	6	2	2.2	.982	D. Henry	58	75	2	8	9	4.68
C	T. Hundley	540	.259	41	112	911	72	8	7	6.6	.992	J. Franco	51	54	4	3	28	1.83
UT	E. Alfonzo	368	.261	4	40	146	246	11	52		.973							
OF	C. Everett	192	.240	1	16	95	4	7	1	1.9	.934							
1B	R. Brogna	188	.255	7	30	439	32	2	47	9.1	.996							

Philadelphia — W-67 L-95 — Jim Fregosi

POS	Player	AB	BA	HR	RBI	PO	A	E	DP	TC/G	FA	Pitcher	G	IP	W	L	SV	ERA
1B	G. Jefferies	404	.292	7	51	411	38	1	38	8.5	.998	C. Schilling	26	183	9	10	0	3.19
2B	M. Morandini	539	.250	3	32	286	352	12	87	4.7	.982	M. Williams	32	167	6	14	0	5.44
SS	K. Stocker	394	.254	5	41	165	352	13	79	4.5	.975	T. Mulholland	21	133	8	7	0	4.66
3B	T. Zeile	500	.268	20	80	72	179	10	13	2.5	.962	M. Mimbs	21	99	3	9	0	5.53
RF	J. Eisenreich	338	.361	3	41	167	3	4	1	1.9	.977	R. Springer	51	97	5	3	0	4.66
CF	R. Otero	411	.273	2	32	247	8	4	2	2.6	.985	T. Borland	69	91	7	3	0	4.07
LF	P. Incaviglia	269	.234	16	42	91	4	3	0	1.4	.969	K. Ryan	62	89	3	5	8	2.43
C	B. Santiago	481	.264	30	85	722	61	10	5	7.0	.987	R. Hunter	14	69	3	7	0	6.49
OF	M. Whiten	182	.236	7	21	97	6	6	1	2.1	.945	R. Bottalico	61	68	4	5	34	3.19
C	M. Lieberthal	166	.253	7	23	285	19	3	4	7.1	.990							

Central — St. Louis — W-88 L-74 — Tony La Russa

POS	Player	AB	BA	HR	RBI	PO	A	E	DP	TC/G	FA	Pitcher	G	IP	W	L	SV	ERA
1B	J. Mabry	543	.297	13	74	1172	75	8	107	8.6	.994	An. Benes	36	230	18	10	1	3.83
2B	L. Alicea	380	.258	5	42	242	289	24	70	4.4	.957	T. Stottlemyre	34	223	14	11	0	3.87
SS	R. Clayton	491	.277	6	35	170	346	15	67	4.7	.953	D. Osborne	30	199	13	9	0	3.53
3B	G. Gaetti	522	.274	23	80	63	222	9	16	2.2	.969	Al. Benes	34	191	13	10	0	4.90
RF	B. Jordan	513	.310	17	104	309	9	2	0	2.4	.994	M. Morgan	18	103	4	8	0	5.24
CF	R. Lankford	545	.275	21	86	356	9	1	0	2.5	.997	M. Petkovsek	48	89	11	2	0	3.55
LF	R. Gant	419	.246	30	82	216	4	5	2	1.9	.978	T. Mathews	67	84	2	6	6	3.01
C	T. Pagnozzi	407	.270	13	55	716	48	8	6	6.7	.990	D. Eckersley	63	60	0	6	30	3.30
OF	W. McGee	309	.307	5	41	118	6	5	2	1.6	.961							
SS	O. Smith	227	.282	2	18	90	162	6	36	5.0	.969							
UT	D. Sheaffer	198	.227	2	20	277	42	6	4		.982							
OF	M. Sweeney	170	.265	3	22	59	1	1	0	1.4	.984							

Houston — W-82 L-80 — Terry Collins

POS	Player	AB	BA	HR	RBI	PO	A	E	DP	TC/G	FA	Pitcher	G	IP	W	L	SV	ERA
1B	J. Bagwell	568	.315	31	120	1336	136	16	115	9.2	.989	S. Reynolds	35	239	16	10	0	3.65
2B	C. Biggio	605	.288	15	75	361	442	10	75	5.0	.988	D. Kile	35	219	12	11	0	4.19
SS	O. Miller	468	.256	15	58	133	296	19	59	3.9	.958	D. Drabek	30	175	7	9	0	4.57
3B	S. Berry	431	.281	17	95	67	194	22	13	2.6	.922	M. Hampton	27	160	10	10	0	3.59
RF	D. Bell	627	.263	17	113	284	16	7	4	2.0	.977	D. Wall	26	150	9	8	0	4.56
CF	B. Hunter	526	.276	5	35	279	11	12	0	2.4	.960	X. Hernandez	58	75	5	5	6	4.22
LF	J. Mouton	300	.263	3	34	157	7	5	1	1.6	.970	T. Jones	51	57	6	3	17	4.40
C	R. Wilkins	254	.213	6	23	550	39	6	2	7.3	.990	B. Wagner	37	52	2	2	9	2.44
OF	J. Cangelosi	262	.263	1	16	113	5	3	0	1.6	.975							
OF	D. May	259	.251	5	33	125	5	4	0	1.9	.970							
3B	B. Spiers	218	.252	6	26	22	93	5	8	1.6	.958							
SS	R. Gutierrez	218	.284	1	15	82	140	11	32	3.1	.953							

NATIONAL LEAGUE 1996, *cont.*

Cincinnati
W-81 L-81
Ray Knight

POS	Player	AB	BA	HR	RBI	PO	A	E	DP	TC/G	FA	Pitcher	G	IP	W	L	SV	ERA
1B	H. Morris	528	.313	16	80	1128	92	8	102	8.8	.993	J. Smiley	35	217	13	14	0	3.64
2B	B. Boone	520	.233	12	69	316	381	6	84	5.0	.991	D. Burba	34	195	11	13	0	3.83
SS	B. Larkin	517	.298	33	89	231	426	17	80	4.5	.975	M. Portugal	27	156	8	9	0	3.98
3B	W. Greene	287	.244	19	63	45	145	15	13	2.8	.927	K. Jarvis	24	120	8	9	0	5.98
RF	R. Sanders	287	.251	14	33	160	7	2	1	2.1	.988	R. Salkeld	29	116	8	5	0	5.20
CF	E. Davis	415	.287	26	83	273	4	3	0	2.2	.989	J. Shaw	78	105	8	6	4	2.49
LF	T. Howard	360	.272	6	42	160	6	3	1	1.6	.982	J. Brantley	66	71	1	2	44	2.41
C	J. Oliver	289	.242	11	46	572	43	5	7	6.4	.992							
C	E. Taubensee	327	.291	12	48	538	42	11	7	6.3	.981							
UT	J. Branson	311	.244	9	37	97	201	14	40		.955							
UT	L. Harris	302	.285	5	32	198	65	6	16		.978							
OF	E. Owens	205	.200	0	9	65	3	1	1	1.3	.986							
OF	K. Mitchell	114	.325	6	26	44	0	1	0	1.5	.978							

Chicago
W-76 L-86
Jim Riggleman

POS	Player	AB	BA	HR	RBI	PO	A	E	DP	TC/G	FA	Pitcher	G	IP	W	L	SV	ERA
1B	M. Grace	547	.331	9	75	1259	107	4	119	9.7	.997	J. Navarro	35	237	15	12	0	3.92
2B	R. Sandberg	554	.244	25	92	228	421	6	81	4.5	.991	S. Trachsel	31	205	13	9	0	3.03
SS	R. Sanchez	289	.211	1	12	152	309	11	55	5.1	.977	F. Castillo	33	182	7	16	0	5.28
3B	L. Gomez	362	.238	17	56	69	174	7	16	2.0	.972	J. Bullinger	37	129	6	10	1	6.54
RF	S. Sosa	498	.273	40	100	255	15	10	1	2.3	.964	T. Adams	69	101	3	6	4	2.94
CF	B. McRae	624	.276	17	66	343	2	5	1	2.3	.986	A. Telemaco	25	97	5	7	0	5.46
LF	L. Gonzalez	483	.271	15	79	231	6	3	1	1.7	.988	K. Foster	17	87	7	6	0	6.21
C	S. Servais	445	.265	11	63	797	71	11	11	6.9	.987	T. Wendell	70	79	4	5	18	2.84
S3	J. Hernandez	331	.242	10	41	147	246	20	52		.952	B. Patterson	79	55	3	3	8	3.13
3B	D. Magadan	169	.254	3	17	16	64	3	4	1.6	.964							
OF	S. Bullett	165	.212	3	16	70	2	1	1	1.3	.986							

Pittsburgh
W-73 L-89
Jim Leyland

POS	Player	AB	BA	HR	RBI	PO	A	E	DP	TC/G	FA	Pitcher	G	IP	W	L	SV	ERA
1B	M. Johnson	343	.274	13	47	775	72	5	64	8.5	.994	D. Neagle	27	183	14	6	0	3.05
2B	C. Garcia	390	.285	6	44	131	199	5	35	4.4	.985	J. Lieber	51	142	9	5	1	3.99
SS	J. Bell	527	.250	13	71	215	477	10	78	4.6	.986	D. Darwin	19	122	7	9	0	3.02
3B	C. Hayes	459	.248	10	62	66	273	18	25	2.9	.950	F. Cordova	59	99	4	7	12	4.09
RF	O. Merced	453	.287	17	80	241	14	3	5	2.2	.988	D. Miceli	44	86	2	10	1	5.78
CF	M. Kingery	276	.246	3	27	133	2	2	0	1.7	.985	Z. Smith	16	83	4	6	0	5.08
LF	A. Martin	630	.300	18	72	216	5	8	1	1.5	.965	P. Wagner	16	82	4	8	0	5.40
C	J. Kendall	414	.300	3	42	797	70	18	10	6.9	.980	D. Plesac	73	70	6	5	11	4.09
12	J. King	591	.271	30	111	891	226	9	101		.992	J. Ericks	28	47	4	5	8	5.79
OF	J. Allensworth	229	.262	4	19	139	4	3	0	2.4	.979							
2B	N. Liriano	217	.267	3	30	50	73	2	14	3.5	.984							
OF	D. Clark	211	.275	8	35	81	3	1	1	1.4	.988							

West

San Diego
W-91 L-71
Bruce Bochy

POS	Player	AB	BA	HR	RBI	PO	A	E	DP	TC/G	FA	Pitcher	G	IP	W	L	SV	ERA
1B	W. Joyner	433	.277	8	65	1059	88	3	86	9.7	.997	J. Hamilton	34	212	15	9	0	4.17
2B	J. Reed	495	.244	2	49	274	412	9	87	4.8	.987	B. Tewksbury	36	207	10	10	0	4.31
SS	C. Gomez	328	.262	3	29	126	261	13	54	4.5	.968	F. Valenzuela	33	172	13	8	0	3.62
3B	K. Caminiti	546	.326	40	130	103	310	20	28	3.0	.954	A. Ashby	24	151	9	5	0	3.23
RF	T. Gwynn	451	.353	3	50	182	2	1	1	1.7	.994	S. Sanders	46	144	9	5	0	3.38
CF	S. Finley	655	.298	30	95	384	7	7	2	2.5	.982	T. Worrell	50	121	9	7	1	3.05
LF	R. Henderson	465	.241	9	29	228	3	6	0	1.8	.975	S. Bergman	41	113	6	8	0	4.37
C	J. Flaherty	264	.303	9	41	471	28	5	3	7.0	.990	T. Hoffman	70	88	9	5	42	2.25
C	B. Johnson	243	.272	8	35	451	21	5	3	7.2	.990							
UT	A. Cianfrocco	192	.281	2	32	195	51	3	18		.988							
OF	M. Newfield	191	.251	5	26	64	0	2	0	1.3	.970							
13	S. Livingstone	172	.297	2	20	143	34	2	17		.989							
OF	G. Vaughn	141	.206	10	22	74	2	2	0	2.0	.974							

Los Angeles
W-90 L-72
Tom Lasorda
W-41 L-35
Bill Russell
W-49 L-37

POS	Player	AB	BA	HR	RBI	PO	A	E	DP	TC/G	FA	Pitcher	G	IP	W	L	SV	ERA
1B	E. Karros	608	.260	34	111	1314	118	15	131	9.4	.990	H. Nomo	33	228	16	11	0	3.19
2B	D. DeShields	581	.224	5	41	273	400	17	78	4.5	.975	I. Valdes	33	225	15	7	0	3.32
SS	G. Gagne	428	.255	10	55	184	404	21	86	4.8	.966	P. Astacio	35	212	9	8	0	3.44
3B	M. Blowers	317	.265	6	38	56	120	9	6	2.1	.951	R. Martinez	28	169	15	6	0	3.42
RF	R. Mondesi	634	.297	24	88	338	11	12	3	2.3	.967	T. Candiotti	28	152	9	11	0	4.49
CF	R. Cedeno	211	.246	2	18	117	2	2	0	1.7	.983	C. Park	48	109	5	5	0	3.64
LF	T. Hollandsworth	478	.291	12	59	216	7	5	0	1.6	.978	A. Osuna	73	84	9	6	4	3.00
C	M. Piazza	547	.336	36	105	1056	70	9	6	7.7	.992	T. Worrell	72	65	4	6	44	3.03
UT	C. Fonville	201	.204	0	13	84	71	6	14		.963							
OF	W. Kirby	188	.271	1	11	93	2	3	0	1.8	.969							
3B	T. Wallach	162	.228	4	22	38	62	3	3	2.3	.971							
OF	B. Ashley	110	.200	9	25	38	1	2	1	1.1	.952							

Colorado
W-83 L-79
Don Baylor

POS	Player	AB	BA	HR	RBI	PO	A	E	DP	TC/G	FA	Pitcher	G	IP	W	L	SV	ERA
1B	A. Galarraga	626	.304	47	150	1528	115	14	151	10.4	.992	K. Ritz	35	213	17	11	0	5.28
2B	E. Young	568	.324	8	74	340	429	12	108	5.6	.985	M. Thompson	34	170	9	11	0	5.30
SS	W. Weiss	517	.282	8	48	220	449	30	89	4.5	.957	A. Reynoso	30	169	8	9	0	4.96
3B	V. Castilla	629	.304	40	113	96	389	20	43	3.2	.960	M. Freeman	26	130	7	9	0	6.04
RF	D. Bichette	633	.313	31	141	255	5	9	1	1.7	.967	D. Holmes	62	77	5	4	1	3.97
CF	Q. McCracken	283	.290	3	40	131	3	6	0	1.5	.957	C. Leskanic	70	74	7	5	6	6.23
LF	E. Burks	613	.344	40	128	280	6	5	2	1.9	.983	B. Ruffin	71	70	7	5	24	4.00
C	J. Reed	341	.284	8	37	546	50	11	5	5.5	.982							
OF	L. Walker	272	.276	18	58	152	4	1	0	1.9	.994							
C	J. Owens	180	.239	4	17	312	27	9	3	5.1	.974							
OF	J. Vander Wal	151	.252	5	31	34	0	0	0	1.3	1.000							

NATIONAL LEAGUE 1996, *cont.*

	POS	Player	AB	BA	HR	RBI	PO	A	E	DP	TC/G	FA	Pitcher	G	IP	W	L	SV	ERA
San Francisco	1B	M. Carreon	292	.260	9	51	533	37	8	65	7.9	.986	A. Watson	29	186	8	12	0	4.61
	2B	S. Scarsone	283	.219	5	23	162	162	9	45	4.5	.973	W. VanLandingham	32	182	9	14	0	5.40
W-68 L-94	SS	R. Aurilia	318	.239	3	26	126	227	10	44	3.9	.972	M. Gardner	30	179	12	7	0	4.42
	3B	M. Williams	404	.302	22	85	74	176	13	18	2.9	.951	O. Fernandez	30	172	7	13	0	4.61
Dusty Baker	RF	G. Hill	379	.280	19	67	159	6	7	3	1.8	.959	M. Leiter	23	135	4	10	0	5.19
	CF	M. Benard	488	.248	5	27	309	7	5	0	2.4	.984	R. Beck	63	62	0	9	35	3.34
	LF	B. Bonds	517	.308	42	129	287	10	6	2	2.0	.980							
	C	T. Lampkin	177	.232	6	29	342	25	3	4	7.0	.992							
	SS	S. Dunston	287	.300	5	25	116	218	15	51	4.5	.957							
	OF	S. Javier	274	.270	2	22	180	2	3	0	2.6	.984							
	2B	R. Thompson	227	.211	5	21	124	155	7	39	4.6	.976							
	3B	B. Mueller	200	.330	0	19	34	79	4	10	2.6	.966							
	1B	D. McCarty	175	.217	6	24	269	15	3	29	5.6	.990							
	C	R. Wilkins	157	.293	8	36	188	29	2	4	5.2	.991							

BATTING AND BASE RUNNING LEADERS

Batting Average
- T. Gwynn, SD — .353
- E. Burks, CLR — .344
- M. Piazza, LA — .336
- L. Johnson, NY — .333
- M. Grace, CHI — .331

Slugging Average
- E. Burks, CLR — .639
- G. Sheffield, FLA — .624
- K. Caminiti, SD — .621
- B. Bonds, SF — .615
- A. Galarraga, CLR — .601

Home Runs
- A. Galarraga, CLR — 47
- B. Bonds, SF — 42
- G. Sheffield, FLA — 42
- T. Hundley, NY — 41

Winning Percentage
- J. Smoltz, ATL — .750
- R. Martinez, LA — .714
- I. Valdes, LA — .682
- An. Benes, STL — .643
- D. Neagle, PIT, ATL — .640

PITCHING LEADERS

Earned Run Average
- K. Brown, FLA — 1.89
- G. Maddux, ATL — 2.72
- A. Leiter, FLA — 2.93
- J. Smoltz, ATL — 2.94
- T. Glavine, ATL — 2.98

Wins
- J. Smoltz, ATL — 24
- An. Benes, STL — 18
- K. Ritz, CLR — 17
- K. Brown, FLA — 17

Total Bases
- E. Burks, CLR — 392
- A. Galarraga, CLR — 376
- S. Finley, SD — 348
- V. Castilla, CLR — 345
- K. Caminiti, SD — 339

Runs Batted In
- A. Galarraga, CLR — 150
- D. Bichette, CLR — 141
- K. Caminiti, SD — 130
- B. Bonds, SF — 129
- E. Burks, CLR — 128

Stolen Bases
- E. Young, CLR — 53
- L. Johnson, NY — 50
- D. DeShields, LA — 48
- B. Bonds, SF — 40
- A. Martin, PIT — 38

Saves
- J. Brantley, CIN — 44
- T. Worrell, LA — 44
- T. Hoffman, SD — 42
- M. Wohlers, ATL — 39
- M. Rojas, MON — 36

Strikeouts
- J. Smoltz, ATL — 276
- H. Nomo, LA — 234
- P. Martinez, MON — 222
- J. Fassero, MON — 222
- D. Kile, HOU — 219

Complete Games
- C. Schilling, PHI — 8
- J. Smoltz, ATL — 6
- K. Brown, FLA — 5
- T. Stottlemyre, STL — 5
- J. Fassero, MON — 5
- G. Maddux, ATL — 5

Hits
- L. Johnson, NY — 227
- E. Burks, CLR — 211
- M. Grissom, ATL — 207
- M. Grudzielanek, MON — 201

Base on Balls
- B. Bonds, SF — 151
- G. Sheffield, FLA — 142
- J. Bagwell, HOU — 135
- R. Henderson, SD — 125

Home Run Percentage
- B. Bonds, SF — 8.1
- G. Sheffield, FLA — 8.1
- S. Sosa, CHI — 8.0
- T. Hundley, NY — 7.6

Fewest Hits/9 Innings
- A. Leiter, FLA — 6.39
- J. Smoltz, ATL — 7.06
- H. Nomo, LA — 7.09
- K. Brown, FLA — 7.22

Shutouts
- K. Brown, FLA — 3

Fewest Walks/9 Innings
- G. Maddux, ATL — 1.03
- K. Brown, FLA — 1.27
- D. Darwin, PIT, HOU — 1.48
- S. Reynolds, HOU — 1.66

Runs
- E. Burks, CLR — 142
- S. Finley, SD — 126
- B. Bonds, SF — 122
- A. Galarraga, CLR — 119

Doubles
- J. Bagwell, HOU — 48
- E. Burks, CLR — 45
- S. Finley, SD — 45
- B. Gilkey, NY — 44

Triples
- L. Johnson, NY — 21
- T. Howard, CIN — 10
- M. Grissom, ATL — 10
- S. Finley, SD — 9

Most Strikeouts/9 Inn.
- J. Smoltz, ATL — 9.79
- H. Nomo, LA — 9.22
- P. Martinez, MON — 9.22
- D. Kile, HOU — 9.00

Innings
- J. Smoltz, ATL — 254
- G. Maddux, ATL — 245
- S. Reynolds, HOU — 239
- J. Navarro, CHI — 237

Games Pitched
- B. Clontz, ATL — 81
- B. Patterson, CHI — 79
- M. Dewey, SF — 78
- J. Shaw, CIN — 78

		W	L	PCT	GB	R	OR	2B	3B	HR	BA	SA	SB	E	DP	FA	CG	BB	SO	ShO	SV	ERA
East	Atlanta	96	66	.593		773	648	264	28	197	.270	.432	83	130	143	.979	14	451	1245	9	46	3.52
	Montreal	88	74	.543	8	741	668	297	27	148	.262	.406	108	126	120	.980	11	482	1206	7	43	3.78
	Florida	80	82	.494	16	688	703	240	30	150	.257	.393	99	111	185	.982	8	598	1050	13	41	3.95
	New York	71	91	.438	25	746	779	267	47	147	.270	.412	97	159	160	.974	10	532	999	10	41	4.22
	Philadelphia	67	95	.414	29	650	790	249	39	132	.256	.387	117	116	145	.981	12	510	1044	6	42	4.48
Central	St. Louis	88	74	.543		759	706	281	31	142	.267	.407	149	125	139	.980	13	539	1050	11	43	3.97
	Houston	82	80	.506	6	753	792	297	29	129	.262	.397	180	138	128	.978	13	539	1163	4	35	4.37
	Cincinnati	81	81	.500	7	778	773	259	36	191	.256	.422	171	121	144	.980	6	591	1089	8	52	4.32
	Chicago	76	86	.469	12	772	771	267	19	175	.251	.401	108	104	145	.983	10	546	1027	10	34	4.36
	Pittsburgh	73	89	.451	15	776	833	319	33	138	.266	.407	126	128	145	.980	5	479	1044	7	37	4.61
West	San Diego	91	71	.562		771	682	285	24	147	.265	.402	109	118	137	.981	5	506	1194	11	47	3.72
	Los Angeles	90	72	.556	1	703	652	215	33	150	.252	.384	124	125	140	.980	6	534	1213	9	50	3.46
	Colorado	83	79	.512	8	961	964	297	37	221	.287	.472	201	149	165	.976	5	624	932	4	34	5.59
	San Francisco	68	94	.420	23	752	862	245	21	153	.253	.388	113	136	166	.978	9	570	997	8	35	4.71
						10623	10623	3782	434	2220	.262	.408	1785	1786	2062	.979	127	7501	15253	117	580	4.22

AMERICAN LEAGUE 1996

		POS	Player	AB	BA	HR	RBI	PO	A	E	DP	TC/G	FA	Pitcher	G	IP	W	L	SV	ERA
East	**New York**	1B	T. Martinez	595	.292	25	117	1238	84	5	119	8.8	**.996**	A. Pettitte	35	221	21	8	0	3.87
		2B	M. Duncan	400	.340	8	56	182	239	11	58	4.2	.975	K. Rogers	30	179	12	8	0	4.68
	W-92 L-70	SS	D. Jeter	582	.314	10	78	245	443	22	85	4.5	.969	D. Gooden	29	171	11	7	0	5.01
		3B	W. Boggs	501	.311	2	41	60	202	7	24	2.2	.974	J. Key	30	169	12	11	0	4.68
	Joe Torre	RF	P. O'Neill	546	.302	19	91	294	7	0	3	2.1	1.000	M. Rivera	61	108	8	3	5	2.09
		CF	B. Williams	551	.305	29	102	334	10	5	3	2.5	.986	J. Nelson	73	74	4	4	2	4.36
		LF	G. Williams	233	.270	5	30	131	1	3	1	1.5	.978	J. Wetteland	62	64	2	3	**43**	2.83
		C	J. Girardi	422	.294	2	45	803	45	3	8	7.1	.996							
		DH	R. Sierra	360	.258	11	52													
		UT	J. Leyritz	265	.264	7	40	387	30	6	5		.986							
		OD	D. Strawberry	202	.262	11	36	45	1	0	0		1.000							
		OF	T. Raines	201	.284	9	33	78	3	1	0	1.6	.988							
		DH	C. Fielder	200	.260	13	37													
		UT	A. Fox	189	.196	3	13	94	158	12	27		.955							
	Baltimore	1B	R. Palmeiro	626	.289	39	142	**1383**	**116**	8	**157**	**9.5**	.995	M. Mussina	36	243	19	11	0	4.81
		2B	R. Alomar	588	.328	22	94	279	445	11	107	5.2	.985	D. Wells	34	224	11	14	0	5.14
	W-88 L-74	SS	C. Ripken	640	.278	26	102	229	466	14	109	4.5	.980	S. Erickson	34	222	13	12	0	5.02
		3B	B. Surhoff	537	.292	21	82	80	174	14	22	2.5	.948	R. Coppinger	23	125	10	6	0	5.18
	Davey Johnson	RF	B. Bonilla	595	.287	28	116	184	8	5	1	1.8	.975	J. Haynes	26	89	3	6	1	8.29
		CF	B. Anderson	579	.297	50	110	343	10	3	1	2.5	.992	R. Myers	62	59	4	4	31	3.53
		LF	J. Hammonds	248	.226	9	27	145	3	3	0	2.2	.980	A. Rhodes	28	53	9	1	1	4.08
		C	C. Hoiles	407	.258	25	73	777	41	7	3	6.5	.992							
		DH	E. Murray	230	.257	10	34													
		OF	M. Devereaux	323	.229	8	34	170	7	3	3	1.6	.983							
		OD	L. Polonia	175	.240	2	14	56	1	1	0		.983							
	Boston	1B	M. Vaughn	635	.326	44	143	1208	71	**15**	123	8.9	.988	R. Clemens	34	243	10	13	0	3.63
		2B	J. Frye	419	.286	4	41	201	318	9	70	5.3	.983	T. Gordon	34	216	12	9	0	5.59
	W-85 L-77	SS	J. Valentin	527	.296	13	59	194	349	16	87	4.7	.971	T. Wakefield	32	212	14	13	0	5.14
		3B	T. Naehring	430	.288	17	65	81	206	11	17	2.6	.963	A. Sele	29	157	7	11	0	5.32
	Kevin Kennedy	RF	T. O'Leary	497	.260	15	81	227	8	7	0	1.7	.971	H. Slocumb	75	83	5	5	31	3.02
		CF	L. Tinsley	192	.245	3	14	132	8	1	1	1.7	.993							
		LF	M. Greenwell	295	.295	7	44	137	9	4	2	2.0	.973							
		C	M. Stanley	397	.270	24	69	654	19	**10**	2	6.5	.985							
		DH	J. Canseco	360	.289	28	82													
		UT	R. Jefferson	386	.347	19	74	178	17	3	8		.985							
		C	B. Haselman	237	.274	8	34	495	32	3	6	7.7	.994							
		OF	D. Bragg	222	.252	3	22	136	5	2	2	2.5	.986							
		2B	W. Cordero	198	.288	3	37	75	109	10	18	5.2	.948							
	Toronto	1B	J. Olerud	398	.274	18	61	782	55	2	107	8.3	.998	P. Hentgen	35	266	20	10	0	3.22
		2B	T. Perez	295	.251	1	19	133	226	11	64	4.9	.970	E. Hanson	35	215	13	17	0	5.41
	W-74 L-88	SS	A. Gonzalez	527	.235	14	64	280	465	21	**123**	**5.2**	.973	J. Guzman	27	188	11	8	0	2.93
		3B	E. Sprague	591	.247	36	101	108	217	15	30	2.3	.956	P. Quantrill	38	134	5	14	0	5.43
	Cito Gaston	RF	S. Green	422	.280	11	45	254	10	2	3	2.1	.992	M. Janzen	15	74	4	6	0	7.33
		CF	O. Nixon	496	.286	1	29	341	5	2	1	2.8	.994	M. Timlin	59	57	1	6	31	3.65
		LF	J. Carter	625	.253	30	107	167	7	7	1	1.6	.961							
		C	C. O'Brien	324	.238	13	44	613	37	3	5	6.2	.995							
		DH	C. Delgado	488	.270	25	92													
		OF	J. Brumfield	308	.256	12	52	160	8	3	0	2.1	.982							
		2B	D. Cedeno	282	.280	2	17	109	169	9	47	4.6	.969							
		C	S. Martinez	229	.227	3	18	413	33	3	9	6.0	.993							
		OF	R. Perez	202	.327	2	21	114	3	2	0	1.5	.983							
		UT	J. Samuel	188	.255	8	26	117	3	2	7		.984							
	Detroit	1B	T. Clark	376	.250	27	72	766	53	6	82	9.6	.993	F. Lira	32	195	6	14	0	5.22
		2B	M. Lewis	545	.270	11	55	265	412	9	94	4.8	.987	O. Olivares	25	160	7	11	0	4.89
	W-53 L-109	SS	A. Cedeno	179	.196	7	20	67	147	12	27	4.4	.947	B. Williams	40	121	3	10	2	6.77
		3B	T. Fryman	616	.268	22	100	97	**275**	8	24	3.0	**.979**	G. Gohr	17	92	4	8	0	7.17
	Buddy Bell	RF	M. Nieves	431	.246	24	60	207	9	13	2	2.2	.943	R. Lewis	72	90	4	6	2	4.18
		CF	K. Bartee	217	.253	1	14	217	1	2	0	2.2	.991	J. Lima	39	73	5	6	3	5.70
		LF	B. Higginson	440	.320	26	81	227	9	9	1	2.0	.963	M. Myers	83	65	1	5	6	5.01
		C	B. Ausmus	226	.248	4	22	452	34	4	4	6.7	.992	G. Olson	43	43	3	0	8	5.02
		DH	E. Williams	215	.200	6	26													
		OF	C. Curtis	400	.263	10	37	243	6	9	1	2.5	.965							
		1D	C. Fielder	391	.248	26	80	588	59	7	50		.989							
		OD	C. Pride	267	.300	10	31	89	0	3	0		.967							
		UT	A. Trammell	193	.233	1	16	75	144	6	22		.973							
		OD	R. Sierra	158	.222	1	20	52	1	5	1		.914							
		C	J. Flaherty	152	.250	4	23	243	12	5	1	5.7	.981							
Central	**Cleveland**	1B	J. Franco	432	.322	14	76	851	74	9	90	9.6	.990	C. Nagy	32	222	17	5	0	3.41
		2B	C. Baerga	424	.267	10	55	191	308	15	63	5.1	.971	O. Hershiser	33	206	15	9	0	4.24
	W-99 L-62	SS	O. Vizquel	542	.297	9	64	227	446	20	92	4.6	.971	J. McDowell	30	192	13	9	0	5.11
		3B	J. Thome	505	.311	38	116	86	261	17	24	2.4	.953	C. Ogea	29	147	10	6	0	4.79
	Mike Hargrove	RF	M. Ramirez	550	.309	33	112	272	19	6	4	2.0	.970	D. Martinez	20	112	9	6	0	4.50
		CF	K. Lofton	**662**	.317	14	67	375	13	10	3	2.6	.975	J. Tavarez	51	81	4	7	0	5.36
		LF	A. Belle	602	.311	48	**148**	308	11	6	0	2.2	.970	J. Mesa	69	72	2	7	39	3.73
		C	S. Alomar	418	.263	11	50	724	48	9	6	6.3	.988	P. Shuey	42	54	5	2	4	2.85
		DH	E. Murray	336	.262	12	45													
		2B	J. Vizcaino	179	.285	0	13	80	125	4	27	4.6	.981							
		C	T. Pena	174	.195	1	27	337	26	3	6	5.5	.992							
		OD	J. Burnitz	128	.281	7	26	44	0	0	0		1.000							
		DO	B. Giles	121	.355	5	27	26	0	0	0		1.000							

AMERICAN LEAGUE 1996, *cont.*

Chicago
W-85 L-77

Terry Bevington

POS	Player	AB	BA	HR	RBI	PO	A	E	DP	TC/G	FA	Pitcher	G	IP	W	L	SV	ERA
1B	F. Thomas	527	.349	40	134	1097	84	9	111	8.6	.992	A. Fernandez	35	258	16	10	0	3.45
2B	R. Durham	557	.275	10	65	236	423	11	87	4.5	.984	K. Tapani	34	225	13	10	0	4.59
SS	O. Guillen	499	.263	4	45	221	348	11	69	4.0	.981	W. Alvarez	35	217	15	10	0	4.22
3B	R. Ventura	586	.287	34	105	133	238	10	35	2.5	.974	J. Baldwin	28	169	11	6	0	4.42
RF	D. Tartabull	472	.254	27	101	253	4	7	1	2.2	.973	R. Hernandez	72	85	6	5	38	1.91
CF	D. Lewis	337	.228	4	53	287	0	3	0	2.1	.990	B. Simas	64	73	2	8	2	4.58
LF	T. Phillips	581	.277	12	63	344	13	7	3	2.4	.981	M. Karchner	50	59	7	4	1	5.76
C	R. Karkovice	355	.220	10	38	680	45	5	6	6.6	.993	K. McCaskill	29	52	5	5	0	6.97
DH	H. Baines	495	.311	22	95													
OF	D. Martinez	440	.318	10	53	235	4	3	1	2.0	.988							
OD	L. Mouton	214	.294	7	39	65	1	2	0		.971							

Milwaukee
W-80 L-82

Phil Garner

POS	Player	AB	BA	HR	RBI	PO	A	E	DP	TC/G	FA	Pitcher	G	IP	W	L	SV	ERA
1B	J. Jaha	543	.300	34	118	675	59	6	84	8.7	.992	B. McDonald	35	221	12	10	0	3.90
2B	F. Vina	554	.283	7	46	331	413	16	115	5.5	.979	S. Karl	32	207	13	9	0	4.86
SS	J. Valentin	552	.259	24	95	247	460	37	114	4.9	.950	R. Bones	32	145	7	14	0	5.83
3B	J. Cirillo	566	.325	15	83	105	239	18	18	2.4	.950	A. Miranda	46	109	7	6	1	4.94
RF	M. Mieske	374	.278	14	64	249	7	1	1	2.1	.996	S. Sparks	20	89	4	7	0	6.60
CF	P. Listach	317	.240	1	33	160	6	3	1	2.5	.982	J. D'Amico	17	86	6	6	0	5.44
LF	G. Vaughn	375	.280	31	95	191	5	4	1	2.0	.980	R. Garcia	37	76	4	4	4	6.66
C	M. Matheny	313	.204	8	46	476	40	8	5	5.0	.985	M. Fetters	61	61	3	3	32	3.38
DH	K. Seitzer	490	.316	12	62													
UT	D. Nilsson	453	.331	17	84	251	19	7	16		.975							
C	J. Levis	233	.236	1	21	372	27	1	4	4.4	.998							
OF	M. Newfield	179	.307	7	31	96	3	1	1	2.0	.990							

Minnesota
W-78 L-84

Tom Kelly

POS	Player	AB	BA	HR	RBI	PO	A	E	DP	TC/G	FA	Pitcher	G	IP	W	L	SV	ERA
1B	S. Stahoviak	405	.284	13	61	800	90	5	78	7.9	.994	B. Radke	35	232	11	16	0	4.46
2B	C. Knoblauch	578	.341	13	72	274	389	8	94	4.4	.988	F. Rodriguez	38	207	13	14	2	5.05
SS	P. Meares	517	.267	8	67	257	344	22	85	4.2	.965	R. Robertson	36	186	7	17	0	5.12
3B	D. Hollins	422	.242	13	53	81	206	14	15	2.6	.953	S. Aldred	25	122	6	5	0	5.09
RF	R. Kelly	322	.323	6	47	203	4	2	0	2.2	.990	R. Aguilera	19	111	8	6	0	5.42
CF	R. Becker	525	.291	12	71	390	19	3	9	2.8	.993	E. Guardado	83	74	6	5	4	5.25
LF	M. Cordova	569	.309	16	111	327	9	3	0	2.3	.991	J. Parra	27	70	5	5	0	6.04
C	G. Myers	329	.286	6	47	488	26	8	5	5.8	.985	M. Trombley	43	69	5	1	6	3.01
DH	P. Molitor	660	.341	9	113							D. Stevens	49	58	3	3	11	4.66
OF	M. Lawton	252	.258	6	42	196	4	3	0	2.7	.985							
UT	J. Reboulet	234	.222	0	23	139	114	2	29		.992							
UT	R. Coomer	233	.296	12	41	274	42	4	27		.988							
C	M. Walbeck	215	.223	2	24	326	18	2	2	5.7	.994							

Kansas City
W-75 L-86

Bob Boone

POS	Player	AB	BA	HR	RBI	PO	A	E	DP	TC/G	FA	Pitcher	G	IP	W	L	SV	ERA
1B	J. Offerman	561	.303	5	47	796	68	5	82	9.1	.994	T. Belcher	35	239	15	11	0	3.92
2B	K. Lockhart	433	.273	7	55	111	207	8	54	3.9	.975	C. Haney	35	228	10	14	0	4.70
SS	D. Howard	420	.219	4	48	196	403	11	109	4.5	.982	K. Appier	32	211	14	11	0	3.62
3B	J. Randa	337	.303	6	47	44	131	9	11	2.0	.951	M. Gubicza	19	119	4	12	0	5.13
RF	M. Tucker	339	.260	12	53	183	5	2	1	1.9	.989	J. Rosado	16	107	8	6	0	3.21
CF	J. Damon	517	.271	6	50	349	5	6	3	2.5	.983	D. Linton	21	104	7	9	0	5.02
LF	T. Goodwin	524	.282	1	35	304	7	5	1	2.3	.984	H. Pichardo	57	68	3	5	3	5.43
C	M. Macfarlane	379	.274	19	54	511	35	4	2	5.6	.993	J. Montgomery	48	63	4	6	24	4.26
DH	J. Vitiello	257	.241	8	40													
UT	C. Paquette	429	.259	22	67	261	101	14	35		.963							
2B	B. Roberts	339	.283	0	52	101	188	4	41	4.7	.986							
D1	B. Hamelin	239	.255	9	40	233	19	4	26		.984							
CD	M. Sweeney	165	.279	4	24	158	7	1	3		.994							
UT	K. Young	132	.242	8	23	200	18	1	25		.995							

West

Texas
W-90 L-72

Johnny Oates

POS	Player	AB	BA	HR	RBI	PO	A	E	DP	TC/G	FA	Pitcher	G	IP	W	L	SV	ERA
1B	W. Clark	436	.284	13	72	954	70	4	89	8.8	.996	K. Hill	35	251	16	10	0	3.63
2B	M. McLemore	517	.290	5	46	312	471	12	114	5.4	.985	R. Pavlik	34	201	15	8	0	5.19
SS	K. Elster	515	.252	24	99	287	441	14	104	4.7	.981	B. Witt	33	200	16	12	0	5.41
3B	D. Palmer	582	.280	38	107	105	218	16	17	2.2	.953	D. Oliver	30	174	14	6	0	4.66
RF	J. Gonzalez	541	.314	47	144	164	6	2	0	1.7	.988	K. Gross	28	129	11	8	0	5.22
CF	D. Hamilton	627	.293	6	51	388	2	0	2	2.7	1.000	E. Vosberg	52	44	1	1	8	3.27
LF	R. Greer	542	.332	18	100	303	6	5	0	2.3	.984	M. Henneman	49	42	0	7	31	5.79
C	I. Rodriguez	639	.300	19	86	850	80	10	11	6.4	.989							
DH	M. Tettleton	491	.246	24	83													
OF	W. Newson	235	.255	10	31	122	5	1	2	1.9	.992							
OF	D. Buford	145	.283	6	20	93	3	0	0	1.2	1.000							

Seattle
W-85 L-76

Lou Piniella

POS	Player	AB	BA	HR	RBI	PO	A	E	DP	TC/G	FA	Pitcher	G	IP	W	L	SV	ERA
1B	P. Sorrento	471	.289	23	93	955	80	11	112	7.6	.989	S. Hitchcock	35	197	13	9	0	5.35
2B	J. Cora	530	.291	6	45	299	311	13	88	4.4	.979	B. Wolcott	30	149	7	10	0	5.73
SS	A. Rodriguez	601	.358	36	123	239	403	15	92	4.5	.977	B. Wells	36	131	12	7	0	5.30
3B	R. Davis	167	.234	5	18	31	67	7	5	2.1	.933	R. Carmona	53	90	8	3	1	4.28
RF	J. Buhner	564	.271	44	138	251	10	3	1	1.9	.989	N. Charlton	70	76	4	7	20	4.04
CF	K. Griffey	545	.303	49	140	374	10	4	1	2.8	.990	B. Ayala	50	42	6	3	3	5.88
LF	R. Amaral	312	.292	1	29	168	3	0	0	1.9	1.000							
C	D. Wilson	491	.285	18	83	835	57	4	5	6.6	.996							
DH	E. Martinez	499	.327	26	103													
UT	L. Sojo	247	.211	1	16	96	159	8	32		.970							
1O	B. Hunter	198	.268	7	28	280	10	5	19		.983							
OF	D. Bragg	195	.272	7	25	117	6	1	1	2.0	.992							
UT	D. Strange	183	.235	3	23	26	39	2	4		.970							
OF	M. Whiten	140	.300	12	33	90	4	3	0	2.5	.969							
3B	D. Hollins	94	.351	3	25	21	54	3	6	2.8	.962							

AMERICAN LEAGUE 1996, *cont.*

	POS	Player	AB	BA	HR	RBI	PO	A	E	DP	TC/G	FA	Pitcher	G	IP	W	L	SV	ERA
Oakland	1B	M. McGwire	423	.312	52	113	913	59	10	117	9.0	.990	D. Wengert	36	161	7	11	0	5.58
	2B	B. Gates	247	.263	2	30	140	183	9	48	5.2	.973	D. Johns	40	158	6	12	1	5.98
	SS	M. Bordick	525	.240	5	54	266	**474**	16	121	4.9	.979	J. Wasdin	25	131	8	7	0	5.96
W-78 L-84	3B	S. Brosius	428	.304	22	71	83	231	10	25	**3.0**	.969	A. Prieto	21	126	6	7	0	4.15
	RF	J. Herrera	320	.269	6	30	190	2	6	0	2.0	.970	C. Reyes	46	122	7	10	0	4.78
Art Howe	CF	E. Young	462	.242	19	64	352	8	1	4	2.6	.997	M. Mohler	72	81	6	3	7	3.67
	LF	P. Plantier	231	.212	7	31	137	8	4	2	2.2	.973	S. Wojciechowski	16	80	5	5	0	5.65
	C	T. Steinbach	514	.272	35	100	732	45	7	7	5.7	.991	D. Telgheder	16	79	4	7	0	4.65
	DH	G. Berroa	586	.290	36	106							B. Taylor	55	60	6	3	17	4.33
	UT	J. Giambi	536	.291	20	79	477	119	11	49		.982							
	2B	R. Bournigal	252	.242	0	18	114	175	2	40	4.5	.993							
	UT	T. Batista	238	.298	6	25	97	191	5	40		.983							
	OF	M. Stairs	137	.277	10	23	58	8	1	3	1.5	.985							
California	1B	J. Snow	575	.257	17	67	1274	105	10	136	9.0	.993	C. Finley	35	238	15	16	0	4.16
	2B	R. Velarde	530	.285	14	54	236	252	9	80	4.4	.982	S. Boskie	37	189	12	11	0	5.32
	SS	G. DiSarcina	536	.256	5	48	212	460	20	94	4.6	.971	J. Abbott	27	142	2	18	0	7.48
W-70 L-91	3B	G. Arias	252	.238	6	28	50	189	10	19	3.0	.960	J. Grimsley	35	130	5	7	0	6.84
	RF	T. Salmon	581	.286	30	98	299	13	8	0	2.1	.975	M. Langston	18	123	6	5	0	4.82
Marcel Lachemann	CF	J. Edmonds	431	.304	27	66	280	6	1	2	2.6	.997	D. Springer	20	95	5	6	0	5.51
W-52 L-59	LF	G. Anderson	607	.285	12	72	316	5	7	1	2.2	.979	M. James	69	81	5	5	1	2.67
	C	J. Fabregas	254	.287	2	26	502	45	6	3	6.2	.989	T. Percival	62	74	0	2	36	2.31
John McNamara	DH	C. Davis	530	.292	28	95													
W-18 L-32																			
	UT	R. Hudler	302	.311	16	40	172	116	6	38		.980							
	OF	D. Erstad	208	.284	4	20	121	2	3	0	2.6	.976							
	C	D. Slaught	207	.324	6	32	338	27	3	1	6.2	.992							
	3B	T. Wallach	190	.237	8	20	27	84	7	5	2.6	.941							
	3B	J. Howell	126	.270	8	21	17	44	8	4	1.6	.884							

BATTING AND BASE RUNNING LEADERS

Batting Average
A. Rodriguez, SEA .358
F. Thomas, CHI .349
P. Molitor, MIN .341
C. Knoblauch, MIN .341
R. Greer, TEX .332

Slugging Average
M. McGwire, OAK .730
J. Gonzalez, TEX .643
B. Anderson, BAL .637
A. Rodriguez, SEA .631
K. Griffey, SEA .628

Home Runs
M. McGwire, OAK 52
B. Anderson, BAL 50
K. Griffey, SEA 49
A. Belle, CLE 48
J. Gonzalez, TEX 47

Total Bases
A. Rodriguez, SEA 379
A. Belle, CLE 375
M. Vaughn, BOS 370
B. Anderson, BAL 369
J. Gonzalez, TEX 348

Runs Batted In
A. Belle, CLE 148
J. Gonzalez, TEX 144
M. Vaughn, BOS 143
R. Palmeiro, BAL 142
K. Griffey, SEA 140

Stolen Bases
K. Lofton, CLE 75
T. Goodwin, KC 66
O. Nixon, TOR 54
C. Knoblauch, MIN 45
O. Vizquel, CLE 35

Hits
P. Molitor, MIN 225
A. Rodriguez, SEA 215
K. Lofton, CLE 210
M. Vaughn, BOS 207

Base on Balls
T. Phillips, CHI 125
E. Martinez, SEA 123
J. Thome, CLE 123
M. McGwire, OAK 116

Home Run Percentage
M. McGwire, OAK 12.3
K. Griffey, SEA 9.0
J. Gonzalez, TEX 8.7
B. Anderson, BAL 8.6

Runs
A. Rodriguez, SEA 141
C. Knoblauch, MIN 140
R. Alomar, BAL 132
K. Lofton, CLE 132

Doubles
A. Rodriguez, SEA 54
E. Martinez, SEA 52
I. Rodriguez, TEX 47
J. Cirillo, MIL 46
M. Cordova, MIN 46

Triples
C. Knoblauch, MIN 14
F. Vina, MIL 10

PITCHING LEADERS

Winning Percentage
C. Nagy, CLE .773
A. Pettitte, NY .724
P. Hentgen, TOR .667
R. Pavlik, TEX .652
M. Mussina, BAL .633

Earned Run Average
J. Guzman, TOR 2.93
P. Hentgen, TOR 3.22
C. Nagy, CLE 3.41
A. Fernandez, CHI 3.45
K. Appier, KC 3.62

Wins
A. Pettitte, NY 21
P. Hentgen, TOR 20
M. Mussina, BAL 19
C. Nagy, CLE 17

Saves
J. Wetteland, NY 43
J. Mesa, CLE 39
R. Hernandez, CHI 38
T. Percival, CAL 36
M. Fetters, MIL 32

Strikeouts
R. Clemens, BOS 257
C. Finley, CAL 215
K. Appier, KC 207
M. Mussina, BAL 204
A. Fernandez, CHI 200

Complete Games
P. Hentgen, TOR 10
R. Pavlik, TEX 7
K. Hill, TEX 7

Fewest Hits/9 Innings
J. Guzman, TOR 7.58
R. Clemens, BOS 8.01
P. Hentgen, TOR 8.06
K. Appier, KC 8.18

Shutouts
R. Robertson, MIN 3
K. Hill, TEX 3
P. Hentgen, TOR 3
F. Lira, DET 2
R. Clemens, BOS 2

Fewest Walks/9 Innings
C. Haney, KC 2.01
D. Wells, BAL 2.05
B. Radke, MIN 2.21
C. Nagy, CLE 2.47

Most Strikeouts/9 Inn.
R. Clemens, BOS 9.53
K. Appier, KC 8.82
C. Finley, CAL 8.13
J. Guzman, TOR 7.91

Innings
P. Hentgen, TOR 266
A. Fernandez, CHI 258
K. Hill, TEX 251
R. Clemens, BOS 243
M. Mussina, BAL 243

Games Pitched
E. Guardado, MIN 83
M. Myers, DET 83
M. Stanton, BOS, TEX 81
H. Slocumb, BOS 75

		W	L	PCT	GB	R	OR	Batting						Fielding			Pitching					
								2B	3B	HR	BA	SA	SB	E	DP	FA	CG	BB	SO	ShO	SV	ERA
East	New York	92	70	.568		871	787	293	28	162	.288	.436	96	91	148	.985	6	610	1139	**9**	**52**	4.65
	Baltimore	88	74	.543	4	949	903	299	29	**257**	.274	.472	76	97	173	.984	1	597	1047	1	44	5.14
	Boston	85	77	.525	7	928	921	308	31	209	.283	.457	91	135	151	.978	17	722	**1165**	5	37	4.98
	Toronto	74	88	.457	18	766	809	302	35	177	.259	.420	116	110	189	.982	**19**	610	1033	7	35	4.57
	Detroit	53	109	.327	39	783	1103	257	21	204	.256	.420	87	137	156	.978	10	784	957	4	22	6.38
Central	Cleveland	99	62	.615		952	**769**	335	23	218	**.293**	.475	160	124	157	.980	13	484	1033	9	46	**4.34**
	Chicago	85	77	.525	14.5	898	794	284	33	195	.281	.447	105	109	147	.982	7	616	1039	4	43	4.52
	Milwaukee	80	82	.494	19.5	894	899	304	40	178	.279	.441	101	134	179	.978	6	635	846	4	42	5.14
	Minnesota	78	84	.481	21.5	877	900	332	**47**	118	.288	.425	143	94	141	.984	13	581	959	5	31	5.28
	Kansas City	75	86	.466	24	746	786	286	38	123	.267	.398	**195**	111	183	.982	17	**460**	926	8	35	4.55
West	Texas	90	72	.556		928	799	323	32	221	.284	.469	83	**87**	150	**.986**	**19**	582	976	6	43	4.65
	Seattle	85	76	.528	4.5	**993**	895	**343**	19	245	.287	**.484**	90	110	155	.981	4	605	1000	4	34	5.21
	Oakland	78	84	.481	12	861	900	283	21	243	.265	.452	58	103	**194**	.984	7	644	884	5	34	5.20
	California	70	91	.435	19.5	762	943	256	24	192	.276	.431	53	128	156	.979	12	662	1052	8	38	5.30
						12208	12208	4205	421	2742	.277	.445	1454	1570	2279	.982	163	8592	14056	79	536	4.99

Player Register

The Player Register is an alphabetical listing of the career batting and fielding records of every man who appeared in a game in the 1996 season, with the exception of players who are primarily pitchers. Pitchers who have appeared in a minimum of 25 non-pitching games (pinch-hitting, pinch-running, or playing other positions) are listed in this section; all others have abbreviated batting records listed in the Pitcher Register.

Statistics that appear in boldfaced type indicate that the player led his league in that category that year. Where there is a tie for the league lead, all tied leaders are listed with boldfaced figures. If a superscript "1" appears next to a statistic, as with Rickey Henderson's stolen base total in 1982, it indicates that he is the all-time single season leader in the category. Figures appearing in bold beneath a player's career totals mean that the player ranks in the top ten in baseball history in that category. (Rickey Henderson, naturally, has a "1st" beneath his career stolen base total.) Career leaders are also highlighted underneath the League Championship Series and World Series totals.

Year	Team	Games	BA	SA	AB	H	2B	3B	HR	HR%	R	RBI	BB	SO	SB	Pinch Hit AB	H	PO	A	E	DP	TC/G	FA	G by Pos

Kurt Abbott — ABBOTT, KURT THOMAS. B. June 2, 1969, Zanesville, Ohio. BR TR 5'11" 180 lbs.

Year	Team	Games	BA	SA	AB	H	2B	3B	HR	HR%	R	RBI	BB	SO	SB	PH AB	PH H	PO	A	E	DP	TC/G	FA	G by Pos
1993	OAK A	20	.246	.410	61	15	1	0	3	4.9	11	9	3	20	2	2	1	36	13	2	2	2.4	.961	OF-13, SS-6, 2B-2
1994	FLA N	101	.249	.394	345	86	17	3	9	2.6	41	33	16	98	3	3	2	165	258	15	57	4.4	.966	SS-99
1995		120	.255	.452	420	107	18	7	17	4.0	60	60	36	110	4	5	0	149	290	19	64	4.0	.959	SS-115
1996		109	.253	.428	320	81	18	7	8	2.5	37	37	22	99	3	15	5	124	205	12	43	3.5	.965	SS-44, 3B-33, 2B-20
4 yrs.		350	.252	.426	1146	289	54	17	37	3.2	149	135	77	327	12	25	8	474	766	48	166	3.9	.963	SS-264, 3B-33, 2B-22, OF-13

Bob Abreu — ABREU, BOB KELLY. B. Mar. 11, 1974, Aragua, Venezuela. BL TR 6' 160 lbs.

Year	Team	Games	BA	SA	AB	H	2B	3B	HR	HR%	R	RBI	BB	SO	SB	PH AB	PH H	PO	A	E	DP	TC/G	FA	G by Pos
1996	HOU N	15	.227	.273	22	5	1	0	0	0.0	1	1	2	3	0	7	1	6	0	0	0	0.9	1.000	OF-7

Mike Aldrete — ALDRETE, MICHAEL PETER. B. Jan. 29, 1961, Carmel, Calif. BL TL 5'11" 180 lbs.

Year	Team	Games	BA	SA	AB	H	2B	3B	HR	HR%	R	RBI	BB	SO	SB	PH AB	PH H	PO	A	E	DP	TC/G	FA	G by Pos
1986	SF N	84	.250	.389	216	54	18	3	2	0.9	27	25	33	34	1	16	4	317	36	1	34	5.2	.997	1B-37, OF-31
1987		126	.325	.462	357	116	18	2	9	2.5	50	51	43	50	6	25	6	328	18	3	21	3.1	.991	OF-79, 1B-33
1988		139	.267	.329	389	104	15	0	3	0.8	44	50	56	65	6	29	11	272	8	4	3	2.3	.986	OF-115, 1B-10
1989	MON N	76	.221	.316	136	30	8	1	1	0.7	12	12	19	30	1	26	8	109	9	1	8	2.5	.992	OF-37, 1B-18
1990		96	.242	.317	161	39	7	1	1	0.6	22	18	37	31	1	36	9	160	12	1	16	3.1	.994	OF-38, 1B-18
1991	2 teams	SD N (12G –.000)	CLE A (85G –.262)																					
"	total	97	.242	.298	198	48	6	1	1	0.5	24	20	39	41	1	20	2	341	24	2	31	4.9	.995	1B-47, OF-21, DH-7
1993	OAK A	95	.267	.443	255	68	13	1	10	3.9	40	33	34	45	1	17	7	407	28	2	39	5.1	.995	1B-59, OF-20, DH-6
1994		76	.242	.337	178	43	5	0	4	2.2	23	18	20	35	2	25	3	207	14	1	15	3.5	.995	OF-35, 1B-27, DH-1
1995	2 teams	OAK A (60G –.272)	CAL A (18G –.250)																					
"	total	78	.268	.403	149	40	8	0	4	2.7	19	24	19	31	0	31	11	199	10	3	16	3.8	.986	1B-36, OF-18, DH-2
1996	2 teams	CAL A (31G –.150)	NY A (32G –.250)																					
"	total	63	.213	.435	108	23	6	0	6	5.6	16	20	14	19	0	27	4	48	0	1	4	1.2	.980	DH-15, OF-15, 1B-9, P-1
10 yrs.		930	.263	.377	2147	565	104	9	41	1.9	277	271	314	381	19	252	65	2388	159	19	187	3.5	.993	OF-409, 1B-286, DH-31, P-1

LEAGUE CHAMPIONSHIP SERIES

Year	Team	Games	BA	SA	AB	H	2B	3B	HR	HR%	R	RBI	BB	SO	SB	PH AB	PH H	PO	A	E	DP	TC/G	FA	G by Pos
1987	SF N	5	.100	.100	10	1	0	0	0	0.0	0	0	1	2	0	2	0	5	0	0	0	1.7	1.000	OF-3
1996	NY A	1	—	—	0	0	0	0	0	—	0	1	0	0	0	0	0	0	0	0	0	0.0	—	
2 yrs.		6	.100	.100	10	1	0	0	0	0.0	0	1	1	2	0	2	0	5	0	0	0	1.7	1.000	OF-3

WORLD SERIES

Year	Team	Games	BA	SA	AB	H	2B	3B	HR	HR%	R	RBI	BB	SO	SB	PH AB	PH H	PO	A	E	DP	TC/G	FA	G by Pos
1996	NY A	2	.000	.000	1	0	0	0	0	0.0	0	0	0	0	0	1	0	0	0	0	0	0.0	.000	OF-1

Manny Alexander — ALEXANDER, MANUEL. Born Manuel DeJesus (Alexander). B. Mar. 20, 1971, San Pedro de Macoris, Dominican Republic. BR TR 5'10" 150 lbs.

Year	Team	Games	BA	SA	AB	H	2B	3B	HR	HR%	R	RBI	BB	SO	SB	PH AB	PH H	PO	A	E	DP	TC/G	FA	G by Pos
1992	BAL A	4	.200	.200	5	1	0	0	0	0.0	1	0	0	3	0	0	0	3	3	0	1	2.0	1.000	SS-3
1993		3	—	—	0	0	0	0	0	—	1	0	0	0	0	0	0	0	0	0	0	0.0	.000	DH-1
1995		94	.236	.318	242	57	9	1	3	1.2	35	23	20	30	11	7	1	140	170	10	45	3.5	.969	2B-82, SS-7, 3B-2, DH-1
1996		53	.103	.103	68	7	0	0	0	0.0	6	4	3	27	3	4	0	26	47	5	8	2.0	.936	SS-21, 2B-7, 3B-7, OF-3, DH-1, P-1
4 yrs.		154	.206	.270	315	65	9	1	3	1.0	43	27	23	60	14	11	1	169	220	15	54	3.0	.963	2B-89, SS-31, 3B-9, OF-3, DH-3, P-1

DIVISIONAL PLAYOFF SERIES

Year	Team	Games	BA	SA	AB	H	2B	3B	HR	HR%	R	RBI	BB	SO	SB	PH AB	PH H	PO	A	E	DP	TC/G	FA	G by Pos
1996	BAL A	3	—	—	0	0	0	0	0	—	2	0	0	0	0	0	0	0	0	0	0	0.0	.000	DH-1

Edgardo Alfonzo — ALFONZO, EDGARDO ANTONIO. B. Aug. 11, 1973, Santa Teresa, Venezuela. BR TR 5'11" 185 lbs.

Year	Team	Games	BA	SA	AB	H	2B	3B	HR	HR%	R	RBI	BB	SO	SB	PH AB	PH H	PO	A	E	DP	TC/G	FA	G by Pos
1995	NY N	101	.278	.382	335	93	13	5	4	1.2	26	41	12	37	1	10	2	81	170	7	19	2.8	.973	3B-58, 2B-29, SS-6
1996		123	.261	.345	368	96	15	2	4	1.1	36	40	25	56	2	13	6	146	246	11	52	3.4	.973	2B-66, 3B-36, SS-15
2 yrs.		224	.269	.363	703	189	28	7	8	1.1	62	81	37	93	3	23	8	227	416	18	71	3.1	.973	2B-95, 3B-94, SS-21

Luis Alicea — ALICEA, LUIS RENE. Born Luis Rene Alicea (DeJesus). B. July 29, 1965, Santurce, Puerto Rico. BB TR 5'9" 165 lbs.

Year	Team	Games	BA	SA	AB	H	2B	3B	HR	HR%	R	RBI	BB	SO	SB	PH AB	PH H	PO	A	E	DP	TC/G	FA	G by Pos
1988	STL N	93	.212	.283	297	63	10	4	1	0.3	20	24	25	32	1	5	1	206	240	14	52	5.1	.970	2B-91
1991		56	.191	.235	68	13	3	0	0	0.0	5	0	8	19	0	39	8	19	23	0	4	3.0	1.000	2B-11, 3B-2, SS-1
1992		85	.245	.385	265	65	9	11	2	0.8	26	32	27	40	2	6	0	136	233	7	38	4.8	.981	2B-75, SS-4
1993		115	.279	.373	362	101	19	3	3	0.8	50	46	47	54	11	17	6	210	281	11	61	5.0	.978	2B-96, OF-4, 3B-1
1994		88	.278	.459	205	57	12	5	5	2.4	32	29	30	38	4	34	8	126	148	4	38	5.1	.986	2B-53, OF-2
1995	BOS A	132	.270	.375	419	113	20	3	6	1.4	64	44	63	61	13	0	0	255	429	16	98	5.3	.977	2B-132
1996	STL N	129	.258	.382	380	98	26	3	5	1.3	54	42	52	78	11	10	2	242	289	24	70	4.4	.957	2B-125
7 yrs.		698	.256	.367	1996	510	99	29	22	1.1	251	217	252	322	42	111	25	1194	1643	76	361	4.9	.974	2B-583, OF-6, SS-5, 3B-3

DIVISIONAL PLAYOFF SERIES

Year	Team	Games	BA	SA	AB	H	2B	3B	HR	HR%	R	RBI	BB	SO	SB	PH AB	PH H	PO	A	E	DP	TC/G	FA	G by Pos
1995	BOS A	3	.600	1.000	10	6	1	0	1	10.0	1	1	2	2	0	0	0	6	11	1	0	6.0	.944	2B-3
1996	STL N	3	.182	.364	11	2	2	0	0	0.0	1	0	1	4	0	0	0	2	5	1	0	2.7	.875	2B-3
2 yrs.		6	.381	.667	21	8	3	0	1	4.8	2	1	3	6	0	0	0	8	16	2	0	4.3	.923	2B-6

LEAGUE CHAMPIONSHIP SERIES

Year	Team	Games	BA	SA	AB	H	2B	3B	HR	HR%	R	RBI	BB	SO	SB	PH AB	PH H	PO	A	E	DP	TC/G	FA	G by Pos
1996	STL N	5	.000	.000	8	0	0	0	0	0.0	0	2	1	0	2	0	5	7	1	1	3.3	.923	2B-4

Jermaine Allensworth — ALLENSWORTH, JERMAINE LAMONT. B. Jan. 11, 1972, Anderson, Ind. BR TR 6' 178 lbs.

Year	Team	Games	BA	SA	AB	H	2B	3B	HR	HR%	R	RBI	BB	SO	SB	PH AB	PH H	PO	A	E	DP	TC/G	FA	G by Pos
1996	PIT N	61	.262	.380	229	60	9	3	4	1.7	32	31	23	50	11	0	0	139	4	3	0	2.4	.979	OF-61

Year	Team	Games	BA	SA	AB	H	2B	3B	HR	HR%	R	RBI	BB	SO	SB	Pinch Hit AB	H	PO	A	E	DP	TC/G	FA	G by Pos

Roberto Alomar

ALOMAR, ROBERTO   BB TR 6'   184 lbs.
Born Roberto Alomar (Velazquez).
Brother of Sandy Alomar. Son of Sandy Alomar.
B. Feb. 5, 1968, Ponce, Puerto Rico

Year	Team	Games	BA	SA	AB	H	2B	3B	HR	HR%	R	RBI	BB	SO	SB	Pinch Hit AB	H	PO	A	E	DP	TC/G	FA	G by Pos
1988	SD N	143	.266	.382	545	145	24	6	9	1.7	84	41	47	83	24	0	0	319	459	16	88	5.6	.980	2B-143
1989		158	.295	.376	623	184	27	1	7	1.1	82	56	53	76	42	1	0	341	472	28	91	5.4	.967	2B-157
1990		147	.287	.381	586	168	27	5	6	1.0	80	60	48	72	24	3	0	316	404	19	77	5.2	.974	2B-137, SS-5
1991	TOR A	161	.295	.436	637	188	41	11	9	1.4	88	69	57	86	53	1	0	333	447	15	79	5.0	.981	2B-160
1992		152	.310	.427	571	177	27	8	8	1.4	105	76	87	52	49	0	0	287	378	5	66	4.4	.993	2B-150, DH-1
1993		153	.326	.492	589	192	35	6	17	2.9	109	93	80	67	55	2	1	254	439	14	92	4.7	.980	2B-151
1994		107	.306	.452	392	120	25	4	8	2.0	78	38	51	41	19	4	0	176	275	4	69	4.3	.991	2B-106
1995		130	.300	.449	517	155	24	7	13	2.5	71	66	47	45	30	2	0	273	365	4	84	5.0	.994	2B-128
1996	BAL A	153	.328	.527	588	193	43	4	22	3.7	132	94	90	65	17	2	1	279	445	11	107	4.8	.985	2B-142, DH-10
9 yrs.		1304	.302	.435	5048	1522	273	52	99	2.0	829	593	560	587	313	15	2	2578	3684	116	753	4.9	.982	2B-1274, DH-11, SS-5

DIVISIONAL PLAYOFF SERIES

Year	Team	Games	BA	SA	AB	H	2B	3B	HR	HR%	R	RBI	BB	SO	SB	Pinch Hit AB	H	PO	A	E	DP	TC/G	FA	G by Pos
1996	BAL A	4	.294	.471	17	5	0	0	1	5.9	2	4	2	3	0	0	0	10	6	0	2	4.0	1.000	2B-4

LEAGUE CHAMPIONSHIP SERIES

Year	Team	Games	BA	SA	AB	H	2B	3B	HR	HR%	R	RBI	BB	SO	SB	Pinch Hit AB	H	PO	A	E	DP	TC/G	FA	G by Pos
1991	TOR A	5	.474	.474	19	9	0	0	0	0.0	3	4	2	3	2	0	0	14	9	0	2	4.6	1.000	2B-5
1992		6	.423	.692	26	11	1	0	2	7.7	4	4	2	1	5	0	0	16	15	0	5	5.2	1.000	2B-6
1993		6	.292	.333	24	7	1	0	0	0.0	3	4	4	3	4	0	0	14	19	0	5	5.5	1.000	2B-6
1996	BAL A	5	.217	.304	23	5	2	0	0	0.0	2	1	0	4	0	0	0	15	26	2	7	8.6	.953	2B-5
4 yrs.		22	.348 7th	.457	92 9th	32	4 4th	0	2	2.2	12	13	8	11	11 2nd	0	0	59	69	2	19	5.9	.985	2B-22

WORLD SERIES

Year	Team	Games	BA	SA	AB	H	2B	3B	HR	HR%	R	RBI	BB	SO	SB	Pinch Hit AB	H	PO	A	E	DP	TC/G	FA	G by Pos
1992	TOR A	6	.208	.250	24	5	1	0	0	0.0	3	0	3	3	3	0	0	5	12	0	0	2.8	1.000	2B-6
1993		6	.480	.640	25	12	2	1	0	0.0	5	6	2	3	4	0	0	9	21	2	2	5.3	.938	2B-6
2 yrs.		12	.347	.449	49	17	3	1	0	0.0	8	6	5	6	7 9th	0	0	14	33	2	2	4.1	.959	2B-12

Sandy Alomar

ALOMAR, SANTOS, JR.   BR TR 6'5"   200 lbs.
Born Santos Alomar (Velazquez).
Brother of Roberto Alomar. Son of Sandy Alomar.
B. June 18, 1966, Salinas, Puerto Rico

Year	Team	Games	BA	SA	AB	H	2B	3B	HR	HR%	R	RBI	BB	SO	SB	Pinch Hit AB	H	PO	A	E	DP	TC/G	FA	G by Pos
1988	SD N	1	.000	.000	1	0	0	0	0	0.0	0	0	0	1	0	1	0	0	0	0	0	0.0	—	
1989		7	.211	.421	19	4	1	0	1	5.3	1	6	3	3	0	1	0	33	1	0	1	5.7	1.000	C-6
1990	CLE A	132	.290	.418	445	129	26	2	9	2.0	60	66	25	46	4	9	2	686	46	14	6	5.8	.981	C-129
1991		51	.217	.266	184	40	9	0	0	0.0	10	7	8	24	0	1	0	280	19	4	4	6.1	.987	C-46, DH-4
1992		89	.251	.324	299	75	16	0	2	0.7	22	26	13	32	3	1	0	477	39	2	6	5.8	.996	C-88, DH-1
1993		64	.270	.395	215	58	7	1	6	2.8	24	32	11	28	3	2	1	342	25	6	4	5.8	.984	C-64
1994		80	.288	.490	292	84	15	1	14	4.8	44	43	25	31	8	2	0	453	40	2	6	6.3	.996	C-78
1995		66	.300	.478	203	61	6	0	10	4.9	32	35	7	26	3	10	1	364	22	2	3	6.4	.995	C-61
1996		127	.263	.397	418	110	23	0	11	2.6	53	50	19	42	1	4	1	724	48	9	6	6.2	.988	C-124, 1B-1
9 yrs.		617	.270	.400	2076	561	103	4	53	2.6	246	265	111	233	22	31	5	3359	240	39	30	6.0	.989	C-596, DH-5, 1B-1

DIVISIONAL PLAYOFF SERIES

Year	Team	Games	BA	SA	AB	H	2B	3B	HR	HR%	R	RBI	BB	SO	SB	Pinch Hit AB	H	PO	A	E	DP	TC/G	FA	G by Pos
1995	CLE A	3	.182	.273	11	2	1	0	0	0.0	1	1	0	1	0	0	0	22	1	0	0	7.7	1.000	C-3
1996		4	.125	.125	16	2	0	0	0	0.0	0	3	0	2	0	0	0	40	4	1	0	11.3	.978	C-4
2 yrs.		7	.148	.185	27	4	1	0	0	0.0	1	4	0	3	0	0	0	62	5	1	0	9.7	.985	C-7

LEAGUE CHAMPIONSHIP SERIES

Year	Team	Games	BA	SA	AB	H	2B	3B	HR	HR%	R	RBI	BB	SO	SB	Pinch Hit AB	H	PO	A	E	DP	TC/G	FA	G by Pos
1995	CLE A	5	.267	.467	15	4	1	1	0	0.0	0	1	1	1	0	0	0	30	3	1	0	6.8	.971	C-5

WORLD SERIES

Year	Team	Games	BA	SA	AB	H	2B	3B	HR	HR%	R	RBI	BB	SO	SB	Pinch Hit AB	H	PO	A	E	DP	TC/G	FA	G by Pos
1995	CLE A	5	.200	.333	15	3	2	0	0	0.0	0	1	0	2	0	0	0	28	0	0	0	5.6	1.000	C-5

Moises Alou

ALOU, MOISES ROJAS   BR TR 6'3"   185 lbs.
Son of Felipe Alou.
B. July 3, 1966, Atlanta, Ga.

Year	Team	Games	BA	SA	AB	H	2B	3B	HR	HR%	R	RBI	BB	SO	SB	Pinch Hit AB	H	PO	A	E	DP	TC/G	FA	G by Pos
1990	2 teams	PIT N (2G –.200)		MON N (14G –.200)																				
"	total	16	.200	.300	20	4	0	1	0	0.0	4	0	0	3	0	5	1	9	1	0	0	1.4	1.000	OF-7
1992	MON N	115	.282	.455	341	96	28	2	9	2.6	53	56	25	46	16	15	7	170	6	4	1	1.8	.978	OF-100
1993		136	.286	.483	482	138	29	6	18	3.7	70	85	38	53	17	3	1	254	11	4	2	2.0	.985	OF-136
1994		107	.339	.592	422	143	31	5	22	5.2	81	78	42	63	7	1	0	201	4	3	0	2.0	.986	OF-106
1995		93	.273	.459	344	94	22	0	14	4.1	48	58	29	56	4	0	0	148	5	3	0	1.7	.981	OF-92
1996		143	.281	.457	540	152	28	2	21	3.9	87	96	49	83	9	1	1	259	8	3	2	1.9	.989	OF-142
6 yrs.		610	.292	.488	2149	627	138	16	84	3.9	343	373	183	304	53	25	10	1041	35	17	5	1.9	.984	OF-583

Rich Amaral

AMARAL, RICHARD LOUIS   BR TR 6'   175 lbs.
B. Apr. 1, 1962, Visalia, Calif.

Year	Team	Games	BA	SA	AB	H	2B	3B	HR	HR%	R	RBI	BB	SO	SB	Pinch Hit AB	H	PO	A	E	DP	TC/G	FA	G by Pos
1991	SEA A	14	.063	.063	16	1	0	0	0	0.0	2	0	1	5	0	2	0	13	16	2	6	2.6	.935	2B-5, 3B-2, SS-2, DH-2, 1B-1
1992		35	.240	.300	100	24	3	0	1	1.0	9	7	5	16	4	2	0	33	68	3	10	2.6	.971	SS-17, 3B-17, OF-3, 1B-2, 2B-1
1993		110	.290	.367	373	108	24	1	1	0.3	53	44	33	54	19	5	3	180	270	10	71	3.8	.978	2B-77, 3B-19, SS-14, DH-9, 1B-3
1994		77	.263	.377	228	60	10	2	4	1.8	37	18	24	28	5	6	2	108	117	15	24	3.3	.938	2B-42, OF-16, SS-7, DH-5, 1B-2
1995		90	.282	.382	238	67	14	2	1	0.4	45	19	21	33	21	10	2	121	6	1	0	1.7	.992	OF-73, DH-1
1996		118	.292	.356	312	91	11	3	1	0.3	69	29	47	55	25	9	2	195	24	0	4	1.8	1.000	OF-91, 2B-15, 1B-10, DH-4, 3B-1
6 yrs.		444	.277	.360	1267	351	62	8	9	0.7	215	117	131	191	74	34	9	650	501	31	115	2.7	.974	OF-183, 2B-140, SS-40, 3B-39, DH-21, 1B-18

Year	Team	Games	BA	SA	AB	H	2B	3B	HR	HR%	R	RBI	BB	SO	SB	Pinch Hit AB	H	PO	A	E	DP	TC/G	FA	G by Pos

Rich Amaral *continued*

LEAGUE CHAMPIONSHIP SERIES

| 1995 | SEA A | 2 | .000 | .000 | 2 | 0 | 0 | 0 | 0 | 0.0 | 0 | 0 | 0 | 1 | 0 | 2 | 0 | 0 | 0 | 0 | 0 | 0.0 | — | |

Ruben Amaro

AMARO, RUBEN, JR.
Son of Ruben Amaro.
B. Feb. 12, 1965, Philadelphia, Pa.

BB TR 5'10" 170 lbs.

1991	CAL A	10	.217	.261	23	5	1	0	0	0.0	0	2	3	3	0	2	0	9	6	1	1	1.6	.938	OF-5, 2B-4, DH-1
1992	PHI N	126	.219	.348	374	82	15	6	7	1.9	43	34	37	54	11	14	2	232	5	2	1	2.1	.992	OF-113
1993		25	.333	.521	48	16	2	2	1	2.1	7	6	6	5	0	8	0	25	1	1	1	1.7	.963	OF-16
1994	CLE A	26	.217	.522	23	5	1	0	2	8.7	5	5	2	3	2	11	1	10	0	1	0	0.7	.909	OF-12, DH-3
1995		28	.200	.300	60	12	3	0	1	1.7	5	7	4	6	1	9	2	35	0	0	0	1.4	1.000	OF-22, DH-3
1996	PHI N	61	.316	.453	117	37	10	0	2	1.7	14	15	9	18	0	31	12	50	0	0	0	1.4	1.000	OF-35, 1B-1
6 yrs.		276	.243	.378	645	157	32	8	13	2.0	74	69	61	89	14	75	17	361	12	5	3	1.8	.987	OF-203, DH-7, 2B-4, 1B-1

LEAGUE CHAMPIONSHIP SERIES

| 1995 | CLE A | 3 | .000 | .000 | 1 | 0 | 0 | 0 | 0 | 0.0 | 1 | 0 | 0 | 0 | 0 | 0 | 0 | 0 | 0 | 0 | 0 | 0.0 | .000 | DH-1 |

WORLD SERIES

| 1995 | CLE A | 2 | .000 | .000 | 2 | 0 | 0 | 0 | 0 | 0.0 | 0 | 0 | 0 | 1 | 0 | 1 | 0 | 0 | 0 | 0 | 0 | 0.0 | .000 | OF-1 |

Brady Anderson

ANDERSON, BRADY KEVIN
B. Jan. 18, 1964, Silver Spring, Md.

BL TL 6'1" 170 lbs.

1988	2 teams	BOS A	(41G –.230)	BAL A	(53G –.198)																			
"	total	94	.212	.286	325	69	13	4	1	0.3	31	21	23	75	10	7	0	243	4	4	1	2.8	.984	OF-90
1989	BAL A	94	.207	.312	266	55	12	2	4	1.5	44	16	43	45	16	6	1	191	3	3	0	2.3	.985	OF-79, DH-8
1990		89	.231	.308	234	54	5	2	3	1.3	24	24	31	46	15	18	6	149	3	2	1	2.1	.987	OF-63, DH-11
1991		113	.230	.324	256	59	12	3	2	0.8	40	27	38	44	12	14	4	150	3	3	0	1.5	.981	OF-101, DH-3
1992		159	.271	.449	623	169	28	10	21	3.4	100	80	98	98	53	1	0	382	10	8	6	2.5	.980	OF-158
1993		142	.263	.425	560	147	36	8	13	2.3	87	66	82	99	24	7	2	296	7	2	0	2.1	.993	OF-140, DH-2
1994		111	.263	.419	453	119	25	5	12	2.6	78	48	57	75	31	1	0	247	4	1	0	2.3	.996	OF-109
1995		143	.262	.444	554	145	33	10	16	2.9	108	64	87	111	26	0	0	268	1	3	0	1.9	.989	OF-142
1996		149	.297	.637	579	172	37	5	50	8.6	117	110	76	106	21	3	1	343	10	3	1	2.5	.992	OF-143, DH-2
9 yrs.		1094	.257	.430	3850	989	201	49	122	3.2	629	456	535	699	208	51	12	2269	45	29	9	2.2	.988	OF-1025, DH-26

DIVISIONAL PLAYOFF SERIES

| 1996 | BAL A | 4 | .294 | .647 | 17 | 5 | 0 | 0 | 2 | 11.8 | 3 | 4 | 2 | 3 | 0 | 0 | 0 | 7 | 0 | 0 | 0 | 1.8 | 1.000 | OF-4 |

LEAGUE CHAMPIONSHIP SERIES

| 1996 | BAL A | 5 | .190 | .381 | 21 | 4 | 1 | 0 | 1 | 4.8 | 5 | 1 | 3 | 5 | 0 | 0 | 0 | 8 | 0 | 0 | 0 | 1.6 | 1.000 | OF-5 |

Garret Anderson

ANDERSON, GARRET JOSEPH
B. June 30, 1972, Los Angeles, Calif.

BL TL 6'3" 190 lbs.

1994	CAL A	5	.385	.385	13	5	0	0	0	0.0	0	1	0	2	0	1	1	10	0	0	0	2.5	1.000	OF-4
1995		106	.321	.505	374	120	19	1	16	4.3	50	69	19	65	6	6	1	213	7	5	0	2.2	.978	OF-100, DH-1
1996		150	.285	.405	607	173	33	2	12	2.0	79	72	27	84	7	3	2	316	5	7	1	2.2	.979	OF-146, DH-1
3 yrs.		261	.300	.443	994	298	52	3	28	2.8	129	142	46	151	13	10	4	539	12	12	1	2.2	.979	OF-250, DH-2

Shane Andrews

ANDREWS, DARRELL SHANE
B. Aug. 28, 1971, Dallas, Tex.

BR TR 6'1" 215 lbs.

1995	MON N	84	.214	.377	220	47	10	1	8	3.6	27	31	17	68	1	11	1	182	97	7	13	3.6	.976	3B-51, 1B-29
1996		127	.227	.429	375	85	15	2	19	5.1	43	64	35	119	3	5	2	64	256	15	13	2.7	.955	3B-123
2 yrs.		211	.222	.410	595	132	25	3	27	4.5	70	95	52	187	4	16	3	246	353	22	26	3.1	.965	3B-174, 1B-29

Eric Anthony

ANTHONY, ERIC TODD
B. Nov. 8, 1967, San Diego, Calif.

BL TL 6'2" 195 lbs.

1989	HOU N	25	.180	.410	61	11	2	0	4	6.6	7	7	9	16	0	5	2	34	1	0	0	1.7	1.000	OF-21
1990		84	.192	.351	239	46	8	0	10	4.2	26	29	29	78	5	11	1	124	5	4	0	1.9	.970	OF-71
1991		39	.153	.229	118	18	6	0	1	0.8	11	7	12	41	1	2	0	64	5	1	1	1.9	.986	OF-37
1992		137	.239	.407	440	105	15	1	19	4.3	45	80	38	98	5	22	5	173	6	5	0	1.6	.973	OF-115
1993		145	.249	.397	486	121	19	4	15	3.1	70	66	49	88	3	16	2	233	6	3	0	1.8	.988	OF-131
1994	SEA A	79	.237	.412	262	62	14	1	10	3.8	31	30	23	66	6	9	1	126	4	2	0	1.8	.985	OF-71, DH-4
1995	CIN N	47	.269	.425	134	36	6	0	5	3.7	19	23	13	30	2	9	3	141	12	4	11	3.8	.975	OF-24, 1B-17
1996	2 teams	CIN N	(47G –.244)	CLR N	(32G –.242)																			
"	total	79	.243	.481	185	45	8	0	12	6.5	32	22	32	56	0	2	0	55	4	2	0	1.1	.967	OF-56
8 yrs.		635	.231	.396	1925	444	78	6	76	3.9	241	264	205	473	22	92	16	950	43	21	12	1.9	.979	OF-526, 1B-17, DH-4

LEAGUE CHAMPIONSHIP SERIES

| 1995 | CIN N | 2 | .000 | .000 | 1 | 0 | 0 | 0 | 0 | 0.0 | 0 | 0 | 1 | 1 | 0 | 1 | 0 | 0 | 0 | 0 | 0 | 0.0 | — | |

Alex Arias

ARIAS, ALEJANDRO
B. Nov. 20, 1967, New York, N.Y.

BR TR 6'3" 185 lbs.

1992	CHI N	32	.293	.354	99	29	6	0	0	0.0	14	7	11	13	0	0	0	43	74	4	8	4.0	.967	SS-30
1993	FLA N	96	.269	.321	249	67	5	1	2	0.8	27	20	27	18	1	25	4	94	144	6	25	3.5	.975	2B-30, 3B-22, SS-18
1994		59	.239	.283	113	27	5	0	0	0.0	4	15	9	19	0	27	9	37	52	2	9	2.6	.978	SS-20, 3B-15
1995		94	.269	.370	216	58	9	2	3	1.4	22	26	22	20	1	38	12	57	127	9	21	3.1	.953	SS-36, 3B-21, 2B-6
1996		100	.277	.384	224	62	11	2	3	1.3	27	26	17	28	1	28	10	48	129	7	23	2.3	.962	3B-59, SS-20, 2B-1, 1B-1
5 yrs.		381	.270	.347	901	243	36	5	8	0.9	94	94	86	98	4	118	35	279	526	28	86	3.0	.966	SS-124, 3B-117, 2B-37, 1B-1

Year	Team	Games	BA	SA	AB	H	2B	3B	HR	HR%	R	RBI	BB	SO	SB	Pinch Hit AB	Pinch Hit H	PO	A	E	DP	TC/G	FA	G by Pos

George Arias

ARIAS, GEORGE ALBERTO
B. Mar. 12, 1972, Tucson, Ariz.
BR TR 5'11" 190 lbs.

Year	Team	Games	BA	SA	AB	H	2B	3B	HR	HR%	R	RBI	BB	SO	SB	PH AB	PH H	PO	A	E	DP	TC/G	FA	G by Pos
1996	CAL A	84	.238	.349	252	60	8	1	6	2.4	19	28	16	50	2	2	1	50	189	10	19	3.0	.960	3B-83, DH-1

Billy Ashley

ASHLEY, BILLY MANUAL
B. July 11, 1970, Trenton, Mich.
BR TR 6'7" 220 lbs.

Year	Team	Games	BA	SA	AB	H	2B	3B	HR	HR%	R	RBI	BB	SO	SB	PH AB	PH H	PO	A	E	DP	TC/G	FA	G by Pos
1992	LA N	29	.221	.337	95	21	5	0	2	2.1	6	6	5	34	0	4	2	34	2	6	0	1.6	.857	OF-27
1993		14	.243	.243	37	9	0	0	0	0.0	0	0	2	11	0	3	1	11	3	0	0	1.3	1.000	OF-11
1994		2	.333	.500	6	2	1	0	0	0.0	0	0	0	2	0	0	0	3	0	0	0	1.5	1.000	OF-2
1995		81	.237	.372	215	51	5	0	8	3.7	17	27	25	88	0	14	2	102	2	3	0	1.6	.972	OF-69
1996		71	.200	.482	110	22	2	1	9	8.2	18	25	21	44	0	29	10	38	2	2	1	1.1	.952	OF-38
5 yrs.		197	.227	.382	463	105	13	1	19	4.1	41	58	53	179	0	50	15	188	9	11	1	1.4	.947	OF-147

DIVISIONAL PLAYOFF SERIES

Year	Team	Games	BA	SA	AB	H	2B	3B	HR	HR%	R	RBI	BB	SO	SB	PH AB	PH H	PO	A	E	DP	TC/G	FA	G by Pos
1995	LA N	1	—	—	0	0	0	0	0	—	0	0	1	0	0	0	0	0	0	0	0	0.0	—	
1996		2	.000	.000	2	0	0	0	0	0.0	0	0	0	2	0	2	0	0	0	0	0	0.0	—	
2 yrs.		3	.000	.000	2	0	0	0	0	0.0	0	0	1	2	0	2	0							

Rich Aude

AUDE, RICHARD THOMAS
B. July 13, 1971, Van Nuys, Calif.
BR TR 6'5" 180 lbs.

Year	Team	Games	BA	SA	AB	H	2B	3B	HR	HR%	R	RBI	BB	SO	SB	PH AB	PH H	PO	A	E	DP	TC/G	FA	G by Pos
1993	PIT N	13	.115	.154	26	3	1	0	0	0.0	1	4	1	7	0	6	1	47	3	1	6	6.4	.980	1B-7, OF-1
1995		42	.248	.376	109	27	8	0	2	1.8	10	19	6	20	1	14	4	223	11	1	27	7.3	.996	1B-32
1996		7	.250	.250	16	4	0	0	0	0.0	0	1	0	8	0	3	1	28	3	1	3	8.0	.969	1B-4
3 yrs.		62	.225	.325	151	34	9	0	2	1.3	11	24	7	35	1	23	6	298	17	3	36	7.2	.991	1B-43, OF-1

Rich Aurilia

AURILIA, RICHARD SANTO
B. Sept. 2, 1971, Brooklyn, N.Y.
BR TR 6' 170 lbs.

Year	Team	Games	BA	SA	AB	H	2B	3B	HR	HR%	R	RBI	BB	SO	SB	PH AB	PH H	PO	A	E	DP	TC/G	FA	G by Pos
1995	SF N	9	.474	.947	19	9	3	0	2	10.5	4	4	1	2	1	2	0	8	16	0	4	4.0	1.000	SS-6
1996		105	.239	.296	318	76	7	1	3	0.9	27	26	25	52	4	2	0	142	245	10	52	3.8	.975	SS-93, 2B-11
2 yrs.		114	.252	.332	337	85	10	1	5	1.5	31	30	26	54	5	4	0	150	261	10	56	3.8	.976	SS-99, 2B-11

Brad Ausmus

AUSMUS, BRADLEY DAVID
B. Apr. 14, 1969, New Haven, Conn.
BR TR 5'11" 190 lbs.

Year	Team	Games	BA	SA	AB	H	2B	3B	HR	HR%	R	RBI	BB	SO	SB	PH AB	PH H	PO	A	E	DP	TC/G	FA	G by Pos
1993	SD N	49	.256	.412	160	41	8	1	5	3.1	18	12	6	28	2	0	0	272	34	8	5	6.4	.975	C-49
1994		101	.251	.358	327	82	12	1	7	2.1	45	24	30	63	5	0	0	687	59	7	2	7.5	.991	C-99, 1B-1
1995		103	.293	.412	328	96	16	4	5	1.5	44	34	31	56	16	1	0	657	60	6	8	7.2	.992	C-100, 1B-1
1996	2 teams	SD N (50G –.181)			DET A (75G –.248)																			
"	total	125	.221	.304	375	83	16	0	5	1.3	46	35	39	72	4	4	1	752	56	10	4	6.9	.988	C-119
4 yrs.		378	.254	.363	1190	302	52	6	22	1.8	153	105	106	219	27	5	1	2368	209	31	19	7.1	.988	C-367, 1B-2

Joe Ayrault

AYRAULT, JOSEPH ALLEN
B. Oct. 8, 1971, Rochester, Mich.
BR TR 6'3" 190 lbs.

Year	Team	Games	BA	SA	AB	H	2B	3B	HR	HR%	R	RBI	BB	SO	SB	PH AB	PH H	PO	A	E	DP	TC/G	FA	G by Pos
1996	ATL N	7	.200	.200	5	1	0	0	0	0.0	0	0	0	1	0	0	0	14	0	0	0	2.0	1.000	C-7

Carlos Baerga

BAERGA, CARLOS OBED
Born Carlos Obed Baerga (Ortiz).
B. Nov. 4, 1968, Santurce, Puerto Rico
BR TR 5'11" 165 lbs.

Year	Team	Games	BA	SA	AB	H	2B	3B	HR	HR%	R	RBI	BB	SO	SB	PH AB	PH H	PO	A	E	DP	TC/G	FA	G by Pos
1990	CLE A	108	.260	.394	312	81	17	2	7	2.2	46	47	16	57	0	31	11	79	164	17	27	2.5	.935	3B-50, SS-48, 2B-8
1991		158	.288	.398	593	171	28	2	11	1.9	80	69	48	74	3	4	1	217	421	27	73	4.0	.959	3B-89, 2B-75, SS-2
1992		161	.312	.455	657	205	32	1	20	3.0	92	105	35	76	10	0	0	400	475	19	138	5.6	.979	2B-160, DH-1
1993		154	.321	.486	624	200	28	6	21	3.4	105	114	34	68	15	1	0	347	445	17	108	5.3	.979	2B-150, DH-4
1994		103	.314	.525	442	139	32	2	19	4.3	81	80	10	45	8	0	0	205	334	15	70	5.4	.973	2B-102, DH-1
1995		135	.314	.452	557	175	28	2	15	2.7	87	90	35	31	11	0	0	230	444	19	97	5.1	.973	2B-134, DH-1
1996	2 teams	CLE A (100G –.267)			NY N (26G –.193)																			
"	total	126	.254	.381	507	129	28	0	12	2.4	59	66	21	27	1	5	3	294	320	19	72	5.1	.970	2B-101, 1B-16, 3B-6
7 yrs.		945	.298	.444	3692	1100	193	15	105	2.8	550	571	199	378	48	41	15	1772	2603	133	585	4.8	.970	2B-730, 3B-145, SS-50, 1B-16, DH-7

DIVISIONAL PLAYOFF SERIES

Year	Team	Games	BA	SA	AB	H	2B	3B	HR	HR%	R	RBI	BB	SO	SB	PH AB	PH H	PO	A	E	DP	TC/G	FA	G by Pos
1995	CLE A	3	.286	.357	14	4	1	0	0	0.0	2	1	0	1	0	0	0	8	5	1	1	4.7	.929	2B-3

LEAGUE CHAMPIONSHIP SERIES

Year	Team	Games	BA	SA	AB	H	2B	3B	HR	HR%	R	RBI	BB	SO	SB	PH AB	PH H	PO	A	E	DP	TC/G	FA	G by Pos
1995	CLE A	6	.400	.520	25	10	0	0	1	4.0	3	4	2	3	0	0	0	12	22	0	2	5.7	1.000	2B-6

WORLD SERIES

Year	Team	Games	BA	SA	AB	H	2B	3B	HR	HR%	R	RBI	BB	SO	SB	PH AB	PH H	PO	A	E	DP	TC/G	FA	G by Pos
1995	CLE A	6	.192	.269	26	5	2	0	0	0.0	1	4	1	1	0	0	0	15	24	1	7	6.7	.975	2B-6

Jeff Bagwell

BAGWELL, JEFFREY ROBERT
B. May 27, 1968, Boston, Mass.
BR TR 6' 195 lbs.

Year	Team	Games	BA	SA	AB	H	2B	3B	HR	HR%	R	RBI	BB	SO	SB	PH AB	PH H	PO	A	E	DP	TC/G	FA	G by Pos
1991	HOU N	156	.294	.437	554	163	26	4	15	2.7	79	82	75	116	7	4	2	1270	106	12	97	9.0	.991	1B-155
1992		162	.273	.444	586	160	34	6	18	3.1	87	96	84	97	10	4	2	1334	133	7	110	9.3	.995	1B-159
1993		142	.320	.516	535	171	37	4	20	3.7	76	88	62	73	13	2	1	1200	133	9	106	9.4	.993	1B-140
1994		110	.367	.750	400	147	32	2	39	9.8	104	116	65	65	15	1	0	924	118	9	93	9.6	.991	1B-109, OF-1
1995		114	.290	.496	448	130	29	0	21	4.7	88	87	79	102	12	0	0	1004	129	7	78	10.0	.994	1B-114
1996		162	.315	.570	568	179	48	2	31	5.5	111	120	135	114	21	0	0	1336	136	16	115	9.2	.989	1B-162
6 yrs.		846	.307	.525	3091	950	206	18	144	4.7	545	589	500	567	78	11	5	7068	735	60	599	9.4	.992	1B-839, OF-1

Year	Team	Games	BA	SA	AB	H	2B	3B	HR	HR%	R	RBI	BB	SO	SB	Pinch Hit AB	Pinch Hit H	PO	A	E	DP	TC/G	FA	G by Pos

Harold Baines

BAINES, HAROLD DOUGLAS
B. Mar. 15, 1959, Easton, Md.
BL TL 6'2" 175 lbs.

Year	Team	Games	BA	SA	AB	H	2B	3B	HR	HR%	R	RBI	BB	SO	SB	PH AB	PH H	PO	A	E	DP	TC/G	FA	G by Pos
1980	CHI A	141	.255	.405	491	125	23	6	13	2.6	55	49	19	65	2	9	1	229	6	9	1	1.8	.963	OF-137, DH-1
1981		82	.286	.482	280	80	11	7	10	3.6	42	41	12	41	6	5	1	120	10	2	1	1.6	.985	OF-80, DH-1
1982		161	.271	.469	608	165	29	8	25	4.1	89	105	49	95	10	1	0	326	10	7	4	2.1	.980	OF-161
1983		156	.280	.443	596	167	33	2	20	3.4	76	99	49	85	7	1	1	312	10	9	3	2.1	.973	OF-155
1984		147	.304	.541	569	173	28	10	29	5.1	72	94	54	75	1	1	0	307	8	6	1	2.2	.981	OF-147
1985		160	.309	.467	640	198	29	3	22	3.4	86	113	42	89	1	1	0	318	8	2	2	2.0	.994	OF-159, DH-1
1986		145	.296	.465	570	169	29	2	21	3.7	72	88	38	89	2	1	0	295	15	5	5	2.2	.984	OF-141, DH-3
1987		132	.293	.479	505	148	26	4	20	4.0	59	93	46	82	0	9	3	13	0	0	0	0.1	1.000	DH-117, OF-8
1988		158	.277	.411	599	166	39	1	13	2.2	55	81	67	109	0	4	2	14	1	2	0	0.1	.882	DH-147, OF-9
1989	2 teams CHI A (96G –.321)															TEX A (50G –.285)								
"	total	146	.309	.465	505	156	29	1	16	3.2	73	72	73	79	0	8	1	54	0	2	0	0.4	.964	DH-116, OF-26
1990	2 teams TEX A (103G –.290)															OAK A (32G –.266)								
"	total	135	.284	.441	415	118	15	1	16	3.9	52	65	67	80	0	13	4	5	0	1	0	0.0	.833	DH-125, OF-2
1991	OAK A	141	.295	.473	488	144	25	1	20	4.1	76	90	72	67	0	11	5	11	1	1	0	0.1	.923	DH-125, OF-12
1992		140	.253	.391	478	121	18	0	16	3.3	58	76	59	61	1	9	3	27	0	1	0	0.2	.964	DH-116, OF-23
1993	BAL A	118	.313	.510	416	130	22	0	20	4.8	64	78	57	52	0	6	2	0	0	0	0	0.0	.000	DH-116
1994		94	.294	.485	326	96	12	1	16	4.9	44	54	30	49	0	10	4	0	0	0	0	0.0	.000	DH-91
1995		127	.299	.540	385	115	19	1	24	6.2	60	63	70	45	0	9	5	0	0	0	0	0.0	.000	DH-122
1996	CHI A	143	.311	.503	495	154	29	0	22	4.4	80	95	73	62	3	13	6	0	0	0	0	0.0	.000	DH-141
17 yrs.		2326	.290	.467	8366	2425	416	48	323	3.9	1113	1356	877	1225	33	111	38	2031	69	47	17	0.9	.978	DH-1222, OF-1060

LEAGUE CHAMPIONSHIP SERIES

Year	Team	Games	BA	SA	AB	H	2B	3B	HR	HR%	R	RBI	BB	SO	SB	PH AB	PH H	PO	A	E	DP	TC/G	FA	G by Pos
1983	CHI A	4	.125	.125	16	2	0	0	0	0.0	0	0	1	3	0	0	0	6	1	0	0	1.8	1.000	OF-4
1990	OAK A	4	.357	.429	14	5	1	0	0	0.0	2	3	2	1	1	0	0	0	0	0	0	0.0	.000	DH-4
1992		6	.440	.640	25	11	2	0	1	4.0	6	4	0	3	0	0	0	0	0	0	0	0.0	.000	DH-6
3 yrs.		14	.327	.436	55	18	3	0	1	1.8	8	7	3	7	1	0	0	6	1	0	0	0.5	1.000	DH-10, OF-4

WORLD SERIES

Year	Team	Games	BA	SA	AB	H	2B	3B	HR	HR%	R	RBI	BB	SO	SB	PH AB	PH H	PO	A	E	DP	TC/G	FA	G by Pos
1990	OAK A	3	.143	.571	7	1	0	0	1	14.3	1	2	1	2	1	0	1	0	0	0	0	0.0	.000	DH-2

Brian Banks

BANKS, BRIAN GLEN
B. Sept. 28, 1970, Mesa, Ariz.
BB TR 6'3" 200 lbs.

Year	Team	Games	BA	SA	AB	H	2B	3B	HR	HR%	R	RBI	BB	SO	SB	PH AB	PH H	PO	A	E	DP	TC/G	FA	G by Pos
1996	MIL A	4	.571	1.286	7	4	2	0	1	14.3	2	2	1	2	0	1	0	15	1	0	0	4.0	1.000	OF-3, 1B-1

Bret Barberie

BARBERIE, BRET EDWARD
B. Aug. 16, 1967, Long Beach, Calif.
BB TR 5'11" 185 lbs.

Year	Team	Games	BA	SA	AB	H	2B	3B	HR	HR%	R	RBI	BB	SO	SB	PH AB	PH H	PO	A	E	DP	TC/G	FA	G by Pos
1991	MON N	57	.353	.515	136	48	12	2	2	1.5	16	18	20	22	0	16	1	53	90	5	15	3.7	.966	SS-19, 3B-10, 2B-10, 1B-1
1992		111	.232	.281	285	66	11	0	1	0.4	26	24	47	62	9	22	8	66	188	13	18	3.0	.951	3B-63, 2B-26, SS-1
1993	FLA N	99	.277	.371	375	104	16	2	5	1.3	45	33	33	58	2	2	0	201	303	9	62	5.3	.982	2B-97
1994		107	.301	.406	372	112	20	2	5	1.3	40	31	23	65	2	5	2	223	320	14	61	5.3	.975	2B-106
1995	BAL A	90	.241	.325	237	57	14	0	2	0.8	32	25	36	50	3	15	5	115	187	7	45	3.8	.977	2B-74, DH-5, 3B-3
1996	CHI N	15	.034	.138	29	1	0	0	1	3.4	4	2	5	11	0	5	1	6	19	0	1	2.8	1.000	2B-6, 3B-2, SS-1
6 yrs.		479	.271	.363	1434	388	73	6	16	1.1	163	133	164	268	16	65	17	664	1107	48	202	4.3	.974	2B-319, 3B-78, SS-21, DH-5, 1B-1

Tony Barron

BARRON, ANTHONY DIRK
B. Aug. 17, 1966, Portland, Or.
BR TR 6' 185 lbs.

Year	Team	Games	BA	SA	AB	H	2B	3B	HR	HR%	R	RBI	BB	SO	SB	PH AB	PH H	PO	A	E	DP	TC/G	FA	G by Pos
1996	MON N	1	.000	.000	1	0	0	0	0	0.0	0	0	0	1	0	1	0	0	0	0	0	0.0	—	

Kimera Bartee

BARTEE, KIMERA ANOTCHI
B. Jul. 21, 1972, Omaha, Ne.
BB TR 6' 175 lbs.

Year	Team	Games	BA	SA	AB	H	2B	3B	HR	HR%	R	RBI	BB	SO	SB	PH AB	PH H	PO	A	E	DP	TC/G	FA	G by Pos
1996	DET A	110	.253	.304	217	55	6	1	1	0.5	32	14	17	77	20	5	0	217	1	2	0	2.2	.991	OF-99, DH-2

Jason Bates

BATES, JASON CHARLES
B. Jan. 5, 1971, Downey, Calif.
BB TR 5'11" 170 lbs.

Year	Team	Games	BA	SA	AB	H	2B	3B	HR	HR%	R	RBI	BB	SO	SB	PH AB	PH H	PO	A	E	DP	TC/G	FA	G by Pos
1995	CLR N	116	.267	.419	322	86	17	4	8	2.5	42	46	42	70	3	9	3	168	255	5	53	3.7	.988	2B-81, SS-20, 3B-15
1996		88	.206	.287	160	33	8	1	1	0.6	19	9	23	34	2	33	6	66	110	7	18	2.7	.962	2B-37, SS-18, 3B-12
2 yrs.		204	.247	.376	482	119	25	5	9	1.9	61	55	65	104	5	42	9	234	365	12	71	3.3	.980	2B-118, SS-38, 3B-27

DIVISIONAL PLAYOFF SERIES

Year	Team	Games	BA	SA	AB	H	2B	3B	HR	HR%	R	RBI	BB	SO	SB	PH AB	PH H	PO	A	E	DP	TC/G	FA	G by Pos
1995	CLR N	4	.250	.250	4	1	0	0	0	0.0	0	0	0	0	0	0	0	1	3	0	0	2.0	1.000	3B-1, 2B-1

Tony Batista

BATISTA, LEOCADIO FRANCISCO
B. Dec. 9, 1973 Pyerto Plata, Dominican Republic
BR TR 6' 180 lbs.

Year	Team	Games	BA	SA	AB	H	2B	3B	HR	HR%	R	RBI	BB	SO	SB	PH AB	PH H	PO	A	E	DP	TC/G	FA	G by Pos
1996	OAK A	74	.298	.433	238	71	10	2	6	2.5	38	25	19	49	7	4	0	97	191	5	40	4.0	.983	2B-52, 3B-18, SS-4, DH-4

Kim Batiste

BATISTE, KIMOTHY EMIL
B. Mar. 15, 1968, New Orleans, La.
BR TR 6' 175 lbs.

Year	Team	Games	BA	SA	AB	H	2B	3B	HR	HR%	R	RBI	BB	SO	SB	PH AB	PH H	PO	A	E	DP	TC/G	FA	G by Pos
1991	PHI N	10	.222	.222	27	6	0	0	0	0.0	2	1	1	8	0	2	0	10	22	1	4	4.7	.970	SS-7
1992		44	.206	.257	136	28	4	0	1	0.7	9	10	4	18	0	2	0	69	85	13	17	4.1	.922	SS-41
1993		79	.282	.436	156	44	7	1	5	3.2	14	29	3	29	0	0	0	72	108	10	15	2.3	.947	3B-58, SS-24
1994		64	.234	.278	209	49	6	0	1	0.5	17	13	1	32	1	7	2	52	116	12	13	3.1	.933	3B-42, SS-17
1996	SF N	54	.208	.323	130	27	6	0	3	2.3	17	11	5	33	3	23	4	35	41	11	11	2.7	.874	3B-25, SS-7
5 yrs.		251	.234	.318	658	154	23	1	10	1.5	59	64	14	120	4	34	6	238	372	47	60	3.0	.928	3B-125, SS-96

LEAGUE CHAMPIONSHIP SERIES

Year	Team	Games	BA	SA	AB	H	2B	3B	HR	HR%	R	RBI	BB	SO	SB	PH AB	PH H	PO	A	E	DP	TC/G	FA	G by Pos
1993	PHI N	4	1.000	1.000	1	1	0	0	0	0.0	0	1	0	0	0	0	0	2	0	2	0	1.0	.500	3B-4

Year	Team	Games	BA	SA	AB	H	2B	3B	HR	HR%	R	RBI	BB	SO	SB	Pinch Hit AB	H	PO	A	E	DP	TC/G	FA	G by Pos

Kim Batiste continued

WORLD SERIES

Year	Team	Games	BA	SA	AB	H	2B	3B	HR	HR%	R	RBI	BB	SO	SB	AB	H	PO	A	E	DP	TC/G	FA	G by Pos
1993	PHI N	3	—	—	0	0	0	0	0	—	0	0	0	0	0	0	0	0	1	0	0	0.3	1.000	3B-3

Allen Battle

BATTLE, ALLEN ZELMO
B. Nov. 29, 1968, Grantham, N. C.
BR TR 6' 170 lbs.

Year	Team	Games	BA	SA	AB	H	2B	3B	HR	HR%	R	RBI	BB	SO	SB	AB	H	PO	A	E	DP	TC/G	FA	G by Pos
1995	STL N	61	.271	.314	118	32	5	0	0	0.0	13	2	15	26	3	21	3	60	0	1	0	1.9	.984	OF-32
1996	OAK A	47	.192	.238	130	25	3	0	1	0.8	20	5	17	26	10	2	0	82	2	1	1	1.8	.988	OF-47
2 yrs.		108	.230	.274	248	57	8	0	1	0.4	33	7	32	52	13	23	3	142	2	2	1	1.8	.986	OF-79

Howard Battle

BATTLE, HOWARD DION
B. Mar. 25, 1972, Biloxi, Miss.
BR TR 6' 210 lbs.

Year	Team	Games	BA	SA	AB	H	2B	3B	HR	HR%	R	RBI	BB	SO	SB	AB	H	PO	A	E	DP	TC/G	FA	G by Pos
1995	TOR A	9	.200	.200	15	3	0	0	0	0.0	3	0	4	8	1	1	0	1	6	0	0	1.0	1.000	3B-6, DH-1
1996	PHI N	5	.000	.000	5	0	0	0	0	0.0	0	0	0	2	0	4	0	0	0	0	0	0.0	.000	3B-1
2 yrs.		14	.150	.150	20	3	0	0	0	0.0	3	0	4	10	1	5	0	1	6	0	0	0.9	1.000	3B-7, DH-1

Danny Bautista

BAUTISTA, DANIEL
Born Daniel Bautista (Alcantara).
B. May 24, 1972, Santo Domingo, Dominican Republic
BR TR 5'11" 170 lbs.

Year	Team	Games	BA	SA	AB	H	2B	3B	HR	HR%	R	RBI	BB	SO	SB	AB	H	PO	A	E	DP	TC/G	FA	G by Pos
1993	DET A	17	.311	.410	61	19	3	0	1	1.6	6	9	1	10	3	0	0	38	2	0	0	2.4	1.000	OF-16, DH-1
1994		31	.232	.414	99	23	4	0	4	4.0	12	15	3	18	1	3	1	66	0	0	0	2.1	1.000	OF-30, DH-1
1995		89	.203	.314	271	55	9	0	7	2.6	28	27	12	68	4	6	3	164	3	2	0	2.0	.988	OF-86
1996	2 teams DET A	(25G −.250)		ATL N	(17G −.150)																			
"	total	42	.226	.321	84	19	2	0	2	2.4	13	9	11	20	1	6	1	48	0	1	0	1.3	.980	OF-36, DH-1
4 yrs.		179	.225	.346	515	116	18	1	14	2.7	59	60	27	116	9	15	5	316	5	3	0	1.9	.991	OF-168, DH-3

Trey Beamon

BEAMON, CLIFFORD
B. Feb. 11, 1974, Dallas, Tex.
BL TR 6'3" 195 lbs.

Year	Team	Games	BA	SA	AB	H	2B	3B	HR	HR%	R	RBI	BB	SO	SB	AB	H	PO	A	E	DP	TC/G	FA	G by Pos
1996	PIT N	24	.216	.255	51	11	2	0	0	0.0	7	6	4	6	1	7	1	24	0	1	0	1.7	.960	OF-15

Rich Becker

BECKER, RICHARD GODHARD
B. Feb. 1, 1972, Aurora, Ill.
BL TL 5'10" 180 lbs.
BB 1993–1995

Year	Team	Games	BA	SA	AB	H	2B	3B	HR	HR%	R	RBI	BB	SO	SB	AB	H	PO	A	E	DP	TC/G	FA	G by Pos
1993	MIN A	3	.286	.571	7	2	0	0	0	0.0	3	0	5	4	1	0	0	7	0	1	0	2.7	.875	OF-3
1994		28	.265	.327	98	26	3	0	1	1.0	12	8	13	25	6	2	1	87	2	1	1	3.3	.989	OF-26, DH-1
1995		106	.237	.296	392	93	15	1	2	0.5	45	33	34	95	8	1	1	275	12	4	3	2.8	.986	OF-105
1996		148	.291	.434	525	153	31	4	12	2.3	92	71	68	118	19	7	2	390	19	3	9	2.8	.993	OF-146
4 yrs.		285	.268	.372	1022	274	51	5	15	1.5	152	112	120	242	34	10	4	759	33	9	13	2.9	.989	OF-280, DH-1

Tim Belk

BELK, TIMOTHY WILLIAM
B. Apr. 6, 1970, Cincinnati, Ohio
BR TR 6'3" 200 lbs.

Year	Team	Games	BA	SA	AB	H	2B	3B	HR	HR%	R	RBI	BB	SO	SB	AB	H	PO	A	E	DP	TC/G	FA	G by Pos
1996	CIN N	7	.200	.200	15	3	0	0	0	0.0	2	0	1	2	0	2	0	28	0	0	2	4.7	1.000	1B-6

David Bell

BELL, DAVID MICHAEL
Son of Buddy Bell.
B. Sept. 14, 1972, Cincinnati, Ohio
BR TR 5'10" 170 lbs.

Year	Team	Games	BA	SA	AB	H	2B	3B	HR	HR%	R	RBI	BB	SO	SB	AB	H	PO	A	E	DP	TC/G	FA	G by Pos
1995	2 teams CLE A	(2G −.000)		STL N	(39G −.250)																			
"	total	41	.247	.363	146	36	7	2	2	1.4	13	19	4	25	1	2	0	77	110	4	27	4.6	.964	2B-37, 3B-3
1996	STL N	62	.214	.276	145	31	6	0	1	0.7	12	9	10	22	1	6	2	44	113	5	10	2.5	.969	3B-45, 2B-20, SS-1
2 yrs.		103	.230	.320	291	67	13	2	3	1.0	25	28	14	47	2	8	2	121	223	12	37	3.3	.966	2B-57, 3B-50, SS-1

Derek Bell

BELL, DEREK NATHANIEL
B. Dec. 11, 1968, Tampa, Fla.
BR TR 6'2" 200 lbs.

Year	Team	Games	BA	SA	AB	H	2B	3B	HR	HR%	R	RBI	BB	SO	SB	AB	H	PO	A	E	DP	TC/G	FA	G by Pos
1991	TOR A	18	.143	.143	28	4	0	0	0	0.0	5	1	6	5	3	0	0	16	0	2	0	1.4	.889	OF-13
1992		61	.242	.354	161	39	6	3	2	1.2	23	15	15	34	7	2	0	105	4	0	1	1.9	1.000	OF-56, DH-1
1993	SD N	150	.262	.417	542	142	19	1	21	3.9	73	72	23	122	26	8	0	334	37	17	7	2.7	.956	OF-125, 3B-19
1994		108	.311	.454	434	135	20	0	14	3.2	54	54	29	88	24	1	0	247	3	10	0	2.4	.962	OF-108
1995	HOU N	112	.334	.442	452	151	21	2	8	1.8	63	86	33	71	27	2	1	201	10	8	2	2.0	.963	OF-110
1996		158	.263	.418	627	165	40	3	17	2.7	84	113	40	123	29	1	0	284	16	7	4	2.0	.977	OF-157
6 yrs.		607	.283	.422	2244	636	106	9	62	2.8	302	341	146	443	116	14	1	1187	70	44	14	2.2	.966	OF-569, 3B-19, DH-1

LEAGUE CHAMPIONSHIP SERIES

Year	Team	Games	BA	SA	AB	H	2B	3B	HR	HR%	R	RBI	BB	SO	SB	AB	H	PO	A	E	DP	TC/G	FA	G by Pos
1992	TOR A	2	—	—	0	0	0	0	0	—	0	1	1	0	0	0	0	1	0	0	0	0.5	1.000	OF-2

WORLD SERIES

Year	Team	Games	BA	SA	AB	H	2B	3B	HR	HR%	R	RBI	BB	SO	SB	AB	H	PO	A	E	DP	TC/G	FA	G by Pos
1992	TOR A	2	.000	.000	1	0	0	0	0	0.0	1	0	1	0	0	1	0	0	0	0	0	0.0	—	

Jay Bell

BELL, JAY STUART
B. Dec. 11, 1965, Eglin Air Force Base, Fla.
BR TR 6'1" 180 lbs.

Year	Team	Games	BA	SA	AB	H	2B	3B	HR	HR%	R	RBI	BB	SO	SB	AB	H	PO	A	E	DP	TC/G	FA	G by Pos
1986	CLE A	5	.357	.714	14	5	2	0	1	7.1	4	3	2	3	0	1	0	9	13	4	2	2.3	.778	2B-2, DH-2
1987		38	.216	.352	125	27	9	1	2	1.6	14	13	8	31	2	0	0	67	93	9	22	4.4	.947	SS-38
1988		73	.218	.280	211	46	5	1	2	0.9	23	21	21	53	4	0	0	103	170	10	37	3.9	.965	SS-72
1989	PIT N	78	.258	.351	271	70	13	3	2	0.7	33	27	19	47	5	3	1	109	197	10	41	4.1	.968	SS-78
1990		159	.254	.362	583	148	28	7	7	1.2	93	52	65	109	10	2	1	260	459	22	85	4.7	.970	SS-159
1991		157	.270	.428	608	164	32	8	16	2.6	96	67	52	99	10	2	0	239	491	24	78	4.8	.968	SS-156
1992		159	.264	.383	632	167	36	6	9	1.4	87	55	55	103	7	2	0	268	526	22	94	5.1	.973	SS-159

Year	Team	Games	BA	SA	AB	H	2B	3B	HR	HR%	R	RBI	BB	SO	SB	Pinch Hit AB	H	PO	A	E	DP	TC/G	FA	G by Pos

Jay Bell *continued*

Year	Team	Games	BA	SA	AB	H	2B	3B	HR	HR%	R	RBI	BB	SO	SB	AB	H	PO	A	E	DP	TC/G	FA	G by Pos
1993		154	.310	.437	604	187	32	9	9	1.5	102	51	77	122	16	0	0	256	527	11	100	5.2	.986	SS-154
1994		110	.276	.441	424	117	35	4	9	2.1	68	45	49	82	2	1	0	152	380	15	67	5.0	.973	SS-110
1995		138	.262	.404	530	139	28	4	13	2.5	79	55	55	110	2	1	0	206	414	14	90	4.6	.978	SS-136, 3B-3
1996		151	.250	.391	527	132	29	3	13	2.5	65	71	54	108	6	1	1	215	477	10	78	4.6	.986	SS-151
11 yrs.		1222	.265	.396	4529	1202	249	46	83	1.8	663	461	457	867	64	11	3	1876	3740	149	693	4.7	.974	SS-1213, 3B-3, 2B-2, DH-2

LEAGUE CHAMPIONSHIP SERIES
Year	Team	Games	BA	SA	AB	H	2B	3B	HR	HR%	R	RBI	BB	SO	SB	AB	H	PO	A	E	DP	TC/G	FA	G by Pos
1990	PIT N	6	.250	.450	20	5	1	0	1	5.0	3	1	4	3	0	0	0	4	22	1	2	4.5	.963	SS-6
1991		7	.414	.586	29	12	2	0	1	3.4	2	1	0	10	0	0	0	13	19	1	2	4.7	.970	SS-7
1992		7	.172	.345	29	5	2	0	1	3.4	3	4	3	4	0	0	0	6	8	1	0	2.1	.933	SS-7
3 yrs.		20	.282	.462	78	22	5	0	3	3.8	8	6	7	17	0	0	0	23	49	3	4	3.8	.960	SS-20

Albert Belle

BELLE, ALBERT JOJUAN
B. Aug. 25, 1966, Shreveport, La.

BR TR 6'1" 190 lbs.

Year	Team	Games	BA	SA	AB	H	2B	3B	HR	HR%	R	RBI	BB	SO	SB	AB	H	PO	A	E	DP	TC/G	FA	G by Pos
1989	CLE A	62	.225	.394	218	49	8	4	7	3.2	22	37	12	55	2	2	1	92	3	2	1	1.6	.979	OF-44, DH-17
1990		9	.174	.304	23	4	0	0	1	4.3	1	3	1	6	0	2	0	0	0	0	0	0.0		DH-6, OF-1
1991		123	.282	.540	461	130	31	2	28	6.1	60	95	25	99	3	4	1	170	8	9	1	1.5	.952	OF-89, DH-32
1992		153	.260	.477	585	152	23	1	34	5.8	81	112	52	128	8	1	0	94	1	3	0	0.6	.969	DH-100, OF-52
1993		159	.290	.552	594	172	36	3	38	6.4	93	129	76	96	23	1	0	338	16	5	7	2.3	.986	OF-150, DH-9
1994		106	.357	.714	412	147	35	2	36	8.7	90	101	58	71	9	0	0	205	8	6	0	2.1	.973	OF-104, DH-2
1995		143	.317	.690	546	173	52	1	50	9.2	121	126	73	80	5	0	0	304	7	6	1	2.2	.981	OF-142, DH-1
1996		158	.311	.623	602	187	38	3	48	8.0	124	148	99	87	11	0	0	308	11	10	0	2.1	.970	OF-152, DH-6
8 yrs.		913	.295	.580	3441	1014	223	16	242	7.0	592	751	396	622	61	10	2	1511	54	41	10	1.8	.974	OF-734, DH-173

DIVISIONAL PLAYOFF SERIES
Year	Team	Games	BA	SA	AB	H	2B	3B	HR	HR%	R	RBI	BB	SO	SB	AB	H	PO	A	E	DP	TC/G	FA	G by Pos
1995	CLE A	3	.273	.636	11	3	1	0	1	9.1	3	3	4	3	0	0	0	7	0	1	0	2.7	.875	OF-3
1996		4	.200	.600	15	3	0	0	2	13.3	2	6	3	2	1	0	0	11	1	0	0	3.0	1.000	OF-4
2 yrs.		7	.231	.615	26	6	1	0	3	11.5	5	9	7	5	1	0	0	18	1	1	0	2.9	.950	OF-7

LEAGUE CHAMPIONSHIP SERIES
Year	Team	Games	BA	SA	AB	H	2B	3B	HR	HR%	R	RBI	BB	SO	SB	AB	H	PO	A	E	DP	TC/G	FA	G by Pos
1995	CLE A	5	.222	.444	18	4	1	0	1	5.6	1	1	3	5	0	0	0	4	0	2	0	1.2	.667	OF-5

WORLD SERIES
Year	Team	Games	BA	SA	AB	H	2B	3B	HR	HR%	R	RBI	BB	SO	SB	AB	H	PO	A	E	DP	TC/G	FA	G by Pos
1995	CLE A	6	.235	.588	17	4	0	0	2	11.8	4	4	7	5	0	0	0	10	0	0	0	1.8	.909	OF-6

Rafael Belliard

BELLIARD, RAFAEL LEONIDAS
Born Rafael Leonidas Belliard (Matias).
B. Oct. 24, 1961, Puerto Nuevo Mao, Dominican Republic

BR TR 5'6" 160 lbs.
BB 1982

Year	Team	Games	BA	SA	AB	H	2B	3B	HR	HR%	R	RBI	BB	SO	SB	AB	H	PO	A	E	DP	TC/G	FA	G by Pos
1982	PIT N	9	.500	.500	2	1	0	0	0	0.0	3	0	0	1	1	1	1	2	2	0	0	1.0	1.000	SS-4
1983		4	.000	.000	1	0	0	0	0	0.0	0	0	0	1	0	0	0	1	3	0	1	1.3	1.000	SS-3
1984		20	.227	.227	22	5	0	0	0	0.0	3	0	0	1	4	0	0	12	13	3	4	2.2	.893	SS-12, 2B-1
1985		17	.200	.200	20	4	0	0	0	0.0	1	1	0	5	0	2	0	13	23	2	3	3.2	.947	SS-12
1986		117	.233	.262	309	72	5	2	0	0.0	33	31	26	54	12	4	0	147	317	12	50	4.0	.975	SS-96, 2B-23
1987		81	.207	.271	203	42	4	3	1	0.5	26	15	20	25	5	1	0	113	191	6	31	4.0	.981	SS-71, 2B-7
1988		122	.213	.241	286	61	0	4	0	0.0	28	11	26	47	7	1	0	134	261	9	51	3.4	.978	SS-117, 2B-3
1989		67	.214	.240	154	33	4	0	0	0.0	10	8	8	22	5	1	0	71	138	3	20	3.2	.986	SS-40, 2B-20, 3B-6
1990		47	.204	.259	54	11	3	0	0	0.0	10	6	5	13	1	10	2	37	36	2	8	2.1	.973	2B-21, SS-10, 3B-5
1991	ATL N	149	.249	.286	353	88	9	2	0	0.0	36	27	22	63	3	3	0	168	361	18	53	3.8	.967	SS-145
1992		144	.211	.239	285	60	6	1	0	0.0	20	14	14	43	0	1	0	152	291	14	48	3.3	.969	SS-139, 2B-1
1993		91	.228	.291	79	18	5	0	0	0.0	6	6	4	13	0	4	2	53	99	1	18	1.9	.993	SS-58, 2B-24
1994		46	.242	.317	120	29	7	1	0	0.0	9	9	2	29	0	3	0	45	86	1	16	3.0	.992	SS-26, 2B-18
1995		75	.222	.244	180	40	2	1	0	0.0	12	7	6	28	2	0	0	74	178	1	23	3.5	.996	SS-40, 2B-32
1996		87	.169	.218	142	24	7	0	0	0.0	9	3	2	22	3	4	1	65	150	5	32	2.8	.977	SS-63, 2B-15
15 yrs.		1076	.221	.258	2210	488	52	14	1	0.0	207	138	135	366	43	35	6	1087	2149	77	358	3.3	.977	SS-836, 2B-165, 3B-11

DIVISIONAL PLAYOFF SERIES
Year	Team	Games	BA	SA	AB	H	2B	3B	HR	HR%	R	RBI	BB	SO	SB	AB	H	PO	A	E	DP	TC/G	FA	G by Pos
1995	ATL N	4	.000	.000	5	0	0	0	0	0.0	1	0	0	1	0	0	0	2	5	0	1	1.8	1.000	SS-4
1996		3	—	—	0	0	0	0	0	0.0	0	0	0	0	0	0	0	0	0	0	0	0.0	.000	SS-3
2 yrs.		7	.000	.000	5	0	0	0	0	0.0	1	0	0	1	0	0	0	2	5	0	1	1.0	1.000	SS-7

LEAGUE CHAMPIONSHIP SERIES
Year	Team	Games	BA	SA	AB	H	2B	3B	HR	HR%	R	RBI	BB	SO	SB	AB	H	PO	A	E	DP	TC/G	FA	G by Pos
1991	ATL N	7	.211	.211	19	4	0	0	0	0.0	0	1	3	3	0	0	0	9	15	1	4	3.6	.960	SS-7
1992		4	.000	.000	2	0	0	0	0	0.0	1	0	1	0	0	0	0	2	3	0	1	1.3	1.000	SS-3, 2B-1
1993		2	.000	.000	1	0	0	0	0	0.0	1	0	0	0	0	0	0	0	0	0	0			SS-1, 2B-1
1995		4	.273	.273	11	3	0	0	0	0.0	1	0	0	0	0	0	0	6	7	1	3	3.5	.929	SS-4
1996		4	.667	.667	6	4	0	0	0	0.0	0	2	0	0	0	0	0	2	5	0	0	1.8	1.000	SS-3, 2B-1
5 yrs.		21	.282	.282	39	11	0	0	0	0.0	3	3	4	7	0	0	0	19	30	2	7	2.4	.961	SS-18, 2B-3

WORLD SERIES
Year	Team	Games	BA	SA	AB	H	2B	3B	HR	HR%	R	RBI	BB	SO	SB	AB	H	PO	A	E	DP	TC/G	FA	G by Pos
1991	ATL N	7	.375	.438	16	6	1	0	0	0.0	0	4	1	2	0	0	0	8	21	0	4	4.1	1.000	SS-7
1992		4	—	—	0	0	0	0	0	0.0	0	0	0	0	0	0	0	2	2	0	1	1.0	1.000	SS-3, 2B-1
1995		6	.000	.000	16	0	0	0	0	0.0	0	1	0	4	0	0	0	3	11	2	0	2.7	.875	SS-6
1996		4	—	—	0	0	0	0	0	0.0	0	0	0	0	0	0	0	0	3	0	0	1.0	1.000	SS-3
4 yrs.		21	.188	.219	32	6	1	0	0	0.0	0	5	1	6	0	0	0	13	37	2	5	2.6	.962	SS-19, 2B-1

Esteban Beltre

BELTRE, ESTEBAN
Born Esteban Beltre (Valera).
B. Dec. 26, 1967, Ingenio Quesqueya, Dominican Republic

BR TR 5'10" 155 lbs.

Year	Team	Games	BA	SA	AB	H	2B	3B	HR	HR%	R	RBI	BB	SO	SB	AB	H	PO	A	E	DP	TC/G	FA	G by Pos
1991	CHI A	8	.167	.167	6	1	0	0	0	0.0	0	0	1	1	1	0	0	1	5	0	1	0.8	1.000	SS-8
1992		49	.191	.236	110	21	2	0	1	0.9	21	10	3	18	1	0	0	53	92	12	12	3.3	.924	SS-43, DH-4
1994	TEX A	48	.282	.321	131	37	5	0	0	0.0	12	12	16	25	2	1	0	59	132	9	23	4.3	.955	SS-41, 3B-5, 2B-1

Year	Team	Games	BA	SA	AB	H	2B	3B	HR	HR%	R	RBI	BB	SO	SB	Pinch Hit AB	H	PO	A	E	DP	TC/G	FA	G by Pos

Esteban Beltre continued

Year	Team	Games	BA	SA	AB	H	2B	3B	HR	HR%	R	RBI	BB	SO	SB	AB	H	PO	A	E	DP	TC/G	FA	G by Pos
1995		54	.217	.304	92	20	8	0	0	0.0	7	7	4	15	0	2	2	55	79	5	19	2.7	.964	SS-36, 2B-15, 3B-1
1996	BOS A	27	.258	.290	62	16	2	0	0	0.0	6	6	4	14	1	2	1	31	26	1	5	2.1	.983	3B-13, 2B-8, SS-6, DH-1
5 yrs.		186	.237	.287	401	95	17	0	1	0.2	46	35	28	73	5	5	3	199	334	27	60	3.1	.952	SS-134, 2B-24, 3B-19, DH-5

Marvin Benard

BENARD, MARVIN LARRY
B. Jan. 20, 1971, Bluefields, Nicaragua

BL TL 5'10" 180 lbs.

Year	Team	Games	BA	SA	AB	H	2B	3B	HR	HR%	R	RBI	BB	SO	SB	AB	H	PO	A	E	DP	TC/G	FA	G by Pos
1995	SF N	13	.382	.529	34	13	2	0	1	2.9	5	4	1	7	1	5	1	19	0	0	0	2.7	1.000	OF-7
1996		135	.248	.330	488	121	17	4	5	1.0	89	27	59	84	25	5	1	309	7	5	0	2.4	.984	OF-132
2 yrs.		148	.257	.343	522	134	19	4	6	1.1	94	31	60	91	26	10	2	328	7	5	0	2.4	.985	OF-139

Yamil Benitez

BENITEZ, YAMIL ANTONIO
B. Oct. 5, 1972, San Juan, Puerto Rico

BR TR 6'2" 195 lbs.

Year	Team	Games	BA	SA	AB	H	2B	3B	HR	HR%	R	RBI	BB	SO	SB	AB	H	PO	A	E	DP	TC/G	FA	G by Pos
1995	MON N	14	.385	.641	39	15	2	1	2	5.1	8	7	1	7	0	2	0	18	1	1	0	1.4	.950	OF-14
1996		11	.167	.167	12	2	0	0	0	0.0	0	2	0	4	0	7	1	1	0	1	0	0.5	.500	OF-4
2 yrs.		25	.333	.529	51	17	2	1	2	3.9	8	9	1	11	0	9	1	19	1	2	0	1.2	.909	OF-18

Mike Benjamin

BENJAMIN, MICHAEL PAUL
B. Nov. 22, 1965, Euclid, Ohio

BR TR 6'3" 195 lbs.

Year	Team	Games	BA	SA	AB	H	2B	3B	HR	HR%	R	RBI	BB	SO	SB	AB	H	PO	A	E	DP	TC/G	FA	G by Pos
1989	SF N	14	.167	.167	6	1	0	0	0	0.0	6	0	0	1	0	1	1	4	4	0	0	1.0	1.000	SS-8
1990		22	.214	.411	56	12	3	1	2	3.6	7	3	3	10	1	2	0	29	53	1	10	4.0	.988	SS-21
1991		54	.123	.208	106	13	3	0	2	1.9	12	8	7	26	3	1	0	64	123	3	23	3.7	.984	SS-51, 3B-1
1992		40	.173	.267	75	13	2	1	1	1.3	4	3	4	15	1	2	0	34	71	1	13	3.0	.991	SS-33, 3B-2
1993		63	.199	.329	146	29	7	0	4	2.7	22	16	9	23	0	0	0	74	133	5	33	3.4	.976	2B-23, SS-23, 3B-16
1994		38	.258	.419	62	16	5	1	1	1.6	9	9	5	16	5	0	0	33	69	3	14	3.2	.971	SS-18, 2B-10, 3B-5
1995		68	.220	.301	186	41	6	0	3	1.6	19	12	8	51	11	4	0	51	121	4	9	2.6	.977	3B-43, SS-16, 2B-8
1996	PHI N	35	.223	.408	103	23	5	1	4	3.9	13	13	12	21	1	3	1	38	87	6	14	4.1	.954	SS-31, 2B-1
8 yrs.		334	.200	.322	740	148	31	4	17	2.3	92	64	48	163	24	13	3	327	661	23	116	3.3	.977	SS-201, 3B-67, 2B-42

Gary Bennett

BENNETT, GARY DAVID
B. Apr. 17, 1972, Waukegan, Ill.

BR TR 6' 190 lbs.

Year	Team	Games	BA	SA	AB	H	2B	3B	HR	HR%	R	RBI	BB	SO	SB	AB	H	PO	A	E	DP	TC/G	FA	G by Pos
1995	PHI N	1	.000	.000	1	0	0	0	0	0.0	0	0	0	1	0	1	0	0	0	0	0	0.0	—	
1996		6	.250	.250	16	4	0	0	0	0.0	0	1	2	6	0	1	0	35	5	0	0	8.0	1.000	C-5
2 yrs.		7	.235	.235	17	4	0	0	0	0.0	0	1	2	7	0	2	0	35	5	0	0	8.0	1.000	C-5

Geronimo Berroa

BERROA, GERONIMO EMILIANO
Born Geronimo Emiliano Letta (Berroa).
B. Mar. 18, 1965, Santo Domingo, Dominican Republic

BR TR 6' 165 lbs.

Year	Team	Games	BA	SA	AB	H	2B	3B	HR	HR%	R	RBI	BB	SO	SB	AB	H	PO	A	E	DP	TC/G	FA	G by Pos
1989	ATL N	81	.265	.338	136	36	4	0	2	1.5	7	9	7	32	0	47	11	67	1	2	0	2.1	.971	OF-34
1990		7	.000	.000	4	0	0	0	0	0.0	0	0	1	1	0	3	0	1	0	0	0	0.3	1.000	OF-3
1992	CIN N	13	.267	.333	15	4	1	0	0	0.0	2	0	2	1	0	9	1	2	1	0	0	1.0	1.000	OF-3
1993	FLA N	14	.118	.147	34	4	1	0	0	0.0	3	0	2	7	0	5	0	9	1	2	0	1.3	.833	OF-9
1994	OAK A	96	.306	.485	340	104	18	2	13	3.8	55	65	41	62	7	8	1	131	5	1	6	1.4	.993	DH-44, OF-42, 1B-9
1995		141	.278	.451	546	152	22	3	22	4.0	87	88	63	98	7	2	0	130	5	4	1	1.0	.971	DH-72, OF-71
1996		153	.290	.532	586	170	32	1	36	6.1	101	106	47	122	0	7	1	91	6	2	1	0.7	.980	DH-91, OF-61
7 yrs.		505	.283	.469	1661	470	78	6	73	4.4	255	268	163	323	14	81	14	431	19	11	8	1.1	.976	OF-223, DH-207, 1B-9

Sean Berry

BERRY, SEAN ROBERT
B. Mar. 22, 1966, Santa Monica, Calif.

BR TR 5'11" 200 lbs.

Year	Team	Games	BA	SA	AB	H	2B	3B	HR	HR%	R	RBI	BB	SO	SB	AB	H	PO	A	E	DP	TC/G	FA	G by Pos
1990	KC A	8	.217	.348	23	5	1	1	0	0.0	2	4	2	5	0	0	0	7	10	1	2	2.3	.944	3B-8
1991		31	.133	.183	60	8	3	0	0	0.0	5	1	5	23	0	1	0	13	52	2	3	2.2	.970	3B-30
1992	MON N	24	.333	.404	57	19	1	0	1	1.8	5	4	1	11	2	5	3	10	19	4	1	1.6	.879	3B-20
1993		122	.261	.465	299	78	15	2	14	4.7	50	49	41	70	12	30	7	66	153	15	13	2.4	.936	3B-96
1994		103	.278	.453	320	89	19	2	11	3.4	43	41	32	50	14	3	0	66	147	14	8	2.3	.938	3B-100
1995		103	.318	.529	314	100	22	1	14	4.5	38	55	25	53	3	18	5	76	167	12	18	3.0	.953	3B-83, 1B-3
1996	HOU N	132	.281	.492	431	121	38	1	17	3.9	55	95	23	58	12	21	7	67	194	22	13	2.6	.922	3B-110
7 yrs.		523	.279	.468	1504	420	99	7	57	3.8	198	249	129	270	43	78	22	305	742	70	58	2.5	.937	3B-447, 1B-3

Dante Bichette

BICHETTE, ALPHONSE DANTE
B. Nov. 18, 1963, West Palm Beach, Fla.

BR TR 6'3" 215 lbs.

Year	Team	Games	BA	SA	AB	H	2B	3B	HR	HR%	R	RBI	BB	SO	SB	AB	H	PO	A	E	DP	TC/G	FA	G by Pos
1988	CAL A	21	.261	.304	46	12	2	0	0	0.0	1	8	0	7	0	0	0	44	2	1	0	2.2	.979	OF-21
1989		48	.210	.326	138	29	7	0	3	2.2	13	15	6	24	3	9	0	95	6	1	2	2.5	.990	OF-40, DH-1
1990		109	.255	.433	349	89	15	1	15	4.3	40	53	16	79	5	8	2	183	12	7	5	1.9	.965	OF-105
1991	MIL A	134	.238	.393	445	106	18	3	15	3.4	53	59	22	107	14	10	4	270	14	7	7	2.3	.976	OF-127, 3B-1
1992		112	.287	.406	387	111	27	2	5	1.3	37	41	16	74	18	10	1	188	6	2	4	1.9	.990	OF-101, DH-4
1993	CLR N	141	.310	.526	538	167	43	5	21	3.9	93	89	28	99	14	4	0	308	14	9	3	2.4	.973	OF-137
1994		116	.304	.548	484	147	33	2	27	5.6	74	95	19	70	21	2	1	210	10	2	3	1.9	.991	OF-116
1995		139	.340	.620	579	197	38	2	40	6.9	102	128	22	96	13	3	1	208	9	3	0	1.6	.986	OF-136
1996		159	.313	.531	633	198	39	3	31	4.9	114	141	45	105	31	3	0	255	5	9	1	1.7	.967	OF-156
9 yrs.		979	.293	.496	3599	1056	222	18	157	4.4	527	629	174	661	119	49	9	1761	78	41	23	2.0	.978	OF-939, DH-5, 3B-1

Year	Team	Games	BA	SA	AB	H	2B	3B	HR	HR%	R	RBI	BB	SO	SB	Pinch Hit AB	H	PO	A	E	DP	TC/G	FA	G by Pos

Dante Bichette continued

DIVISIONAL PLAYOFF SERIES
| 1995 | CLR N | 4 | .588 | .941 | 17 | 10 | 3 | 0 | 1 | 5.9 | 6 | 3 | 1 | 3 | 0 | 0 | 0 | 9 | 0 | 0 | 0 | 2.3 | 1.000 | OF-4 |

Craig Biggio
BIGGIO, CRAIG ALAN
B. Dec. 14, 1965, Smithtown, N. Y.
BR TR 5'11" 185 lbs.

1988	HOU N	50	.211	.350	123	26	6	1	3	2.4	14	5	7	29	6	0	0	292	28	3	0	6.5	.991	C-50
1989		134	.257	.402	443	114	21	2	13	2.9	64	60	49	64	21	4	3	742	56	9	6	6.2	.989	C-125, OF-5
1990		150	.276	.348	555	153	24	2	4	0.7	53	42	53	79	25	3	2	657	60	13	4	6.2	.982	C-113, OF-50
1991		149	.295	.374	546	161	23	4	4	0.7	79	46	53	71	19	9	3	894	73	11	11	6.8	.989	C-139, 2B-3, OF-2
1992		162	.277	.369	613	170	32	3	6	1.0	96	39	94	95	38	1	0	344	413	12	81	4.8	.984	2B-161
1993		155	.287	.474	610	175	41	5	21	3.4	98	64	77	93	15	0	0	306	447	14	90	4.9	.982	2B-155
1994		114	.318	.483	437	139	44	5	6	1.4	88	56	62	58	39	2	0	225	339	7	63	5.1	.988	2B-113
1995		141	.302	.483	553	167	30	2	22	4.0	123	77	80	85	33	1	0	297	418	10	74	5.1	.986	2B-141
1996		162	.288	.415	605	174	24	4	15	2.5	113	75	75	72	25	0	0	361	442	10	75	5.0	.988	2B-162
9 yrs.		1217	.285	.415	4485	1279	245	28	94	2.1	728	464	550	646	221	20	8	4118	2276	89	404	5.3	.986	2B-735, C-427, OF-57

Jeff Blauser
BLAUSER, JEFFREY MICHAEL
B. Nov. 8, 1965, Los Gatos, Calif.
BR TR 6' 170 lbs.

1987	ATL N	51	.242	.352	165	40	6	3	2	1.2	11	15	18	34	7	1	0	65	166	9	28	4.8	.963	SS-50
1988		18	.239	.403	67	16	3	1	2	3.0	7	7	2	11	0	1	0	35	59	4	8	5.8	.959	2B-9, SS-8
1989		142	.270	.410	456	123	24	2	12	2.6	63	46	38	101	5	9	4	137	254	21	28	2.8	.949	3B-78, 2B-39, SS-30, OF-2
1990		115	.269	.410	386	104	24	3	8	2.1	46	39	35	70	3	4	2	169	288	16	54	4.0	.966	SS-93, 2B-14, 3B-9, OF-1
1991		129	.259	.409	352	91	14	3	11	3.1	49	54	54	59	5	26	6	136	219	17	37	2.8	.954	SS-85, 2B-32, 3B-18
1992		123	.262	.458	343	90	19	3	14	4.1	61	46	46	82	5	16	2	119	225	14	34	2.8	.961	SS-106, 2B-21, 3B-1
1993		161	.305	.436	597	182	29	2	15	2.5	110	73	85	109	16	2	0	189	426	19	86	3.9	.970	SS-161
1994		96	.258	.382	380	98	21	4	6	1.6	56	45	38	64	1	0	0	126	289	13	44	4.5	.970	SS-96
1995		115	.211	.341	431	91	16	2	12	2.8	60	31	57	107	8	0	0	150	335	15	60	4.3	.970	SS-115
1996		83	.245	.419	265	65	14	1	10	3.8	48	35	40	54	6	1	0	84	207	23	41	4.0	.927	SS-79
10 yrs.		1033	.261	.405	3442	900	170	24	92	2.7	511	391	413	691	56	60	14	1210	2468	151	420	3.7	.961	SS-823, 2B-115, 3B-106, OF-3

DIVISIONAL PLAYOFF SERIES
1995	ATL N	3	.000	.000	6	0	0	0	0	0.0	0	0	1	3	0	0	0	5	11	1	3	5.7	.941	SS-3
1996		3	.111	.111	9	1	0	0	0	0.0	0	0	1	3	0	0	0	0	7	0	1	2.3	1.000	SS-3
2 yrs.		6	.067	.067	15	1	0	0	0	0.0	0	0	2	6	0	0	0	5	18	1	4	4.0	.958	SS-6

LEAGUE CHAMPIONSHIP SERIES
1991	ATL N	2	.000	.000	2	0	0	0	0	0.0	0	0	0	0	0	1	0	0	1	1	0	1.0	.500	SS-2
1992		7	.208	.417	24	5	0	1	1	4.2	3	4	3	2	0	0	0	7	15	2	1	3.4	.917	SS-7
1993		6	.280	.560	25	7	1	0	2	8.0	5	4	4	7	0	0	0	6	14	0	0	3.3	1.000	SS-6
1995		1	.000	.000	4	0	0	0	0	0.0	0	0	1	2	0	0	0	4	6	0	3	10.0	1.000	SS-1
1996		7	.176	.294	17	3	0	1	0	0.0	5	2	4	6	0	0	0	5	9	1	2	2.1	.933	SS-7
5 yrs.		23	.208	.403	72	15	1	2 4th	3	4.2	13	10	12	17 10th	0	1	0	22	45	4	6	3.1	.944	SS-23

WORLD SERIES
1991	ATL N	5	.167	.167	6	1	0	0	0	0.0	0	0	1	1	0	4	0	3	3	0	1	1.2	1.000	SS-5
1992		6	.250	.250	24	6	0	0	0	0.0	2	0	1	9	2	0	0	7	22	0	5	4.8	1.000	SS-6
1996		6	.167	.222	18	3	1	0	0	0.0	2	1	1	4	0	0	0	9	15	1	3	4.2	.960	SS-6
3 yrs.		17	.208	.229	48	10	1	0	0	0.0	4	1	3	14	2	4	0	19	40	1	9	3.5	.983	SS-17

Mike Blowers
BLOWERS, MICHAEL ROY
B. Apr. 24, 1965, Wurzburg, West Germany
BR TR 6'2" 190 lbs.

1989	NY A	13	.263	.263	38	10	0	0	0	0.0	2	3	3	13	0	1	0	9	14	4	3	2.1	.852	3B-13
1990		48	.188	.319	144	27	4	0	5	3.5	16	21	12	50	1	3	0	26	63	10	4	2.1	.899	3B-45, DH-2
1991		15	.200	.286	35	7	0	0	1	2.9	3	1	4	3	0	1	0	4	16	3	1	1.6	.870	3B-14
1992	SEA A	31	.192	.274	73	14	3	0	1	1.4	7	2	6	20	0	1	0	28	44	1	8	2.3	.986	3B-29, 1B-3
1993		127	.280	.475	379	106	23	3	15	4.0	55	57	44	98	1	6	2	70	225	15	14	2.5	.952	3B-117, OF-2, DH-2, 1B-1, C-1
1994		85	.289	.437	270	78	13	0	9	3.3	37	49	25	60	2	14	4	141	108	9	15	3.0	.965	3B-48, 1B-20, OF-9, DH-9
1995		134	.257	.474	439	113	24	1	23	5.2	59	96	53	128	2	10	2	117	172	16	16	2.2	.948	3B-126, 1B-7, OF-5
1996	LA N	92	.265	.394	317	84	19	2	6	1.9	31	38	37	77	0	1	0	76	122	9	6	2.1	.957	3B-90, 1B-6, SS-1
8 yrs.		545	.259	.423	1695	439	86	6	60	3.5	210	267	184	449	6	37	8	471	764	67	67	2.4	.949	3B-482, 1B-37, OF-16, DH-13, SS-1, C-1

DIVISIONAL PLAYOFF SERIES
| 1995 | SEA A | 5 | .167 | .167 | 18 | 3 | 0 | 0 | 0 | 0.0 | 0 | 1 | 3 | 7 | 0 | 0 | 0 | 2 | 6 | 0 | 0 | 1.3 | 1.000 | 3B-5, 1B-1 |

LEAGUE CHAMPIONSHIP SERIES
| 1995 | SEA A | 6 | .222 | .389 | 18 | 4 | 0 | 0 | 1 | 5.6 | 1 | 2 | 0 | 4 | 0 | 0 | 0 | 5 | 9 | 0 | 0 | 2.3 | 1.000 | 3B-6 |

Tim Bogar
BOGAR, TIMOTHY PAUL
B. Oct. 28, 1966, Indianapolis, Ind.
BR TR 6'2" 198 lbs.

1993	NY N	78	.244	.351	205	50	13	0	3	1.5	19	25	14	29	0	4	0	105	217	9	42	4.2	.973	SS-66, 3B-7, 2B-6
1994		50	.154	.269	52	8	0	0	2	3.8	5	5	4	11	1	5	1	77	37	1	16	2.6	.991	3B-22, 1B-14, SS-7, 2B-1, OF-1
1995		78	.290	.359	145	42	7	0	1	0.7	17	21	9	25	1	12	3	82	100	6	21	2.7	.968	SS-27, 3B-25, 1B-10, 2B-7, OF-1
1996		91	.213	.258	89	19	4	0	0	0.0	17	6	8	20	1	6	2	104	60	1	17	2.0	.994	1B-32, 3B-25, SS-19, 2B-8
4 yrs.		297	.242	.328	491	119	24	0	6	1.2	58	57	35	85	3	27	6	368	414	17	96	2.9	.979	SS-119, 3B-79, 1B-56, 2B-22, OF-2

Year	Team	Games	BA	SA	AB	H	2B	3B	HR	HR%	R	RBI	BB	SO	SB	Pinch Hit AB	Pinch Hit H	PO	A	E	DP	TC/G	FA	G by Pos

Wade Boggs

BOGGS, WADE ANTHONY
B. June 15, 1958, Omaha, Neb.
BL TR 6'2" 190 lbs.

Year	Team	Games	BA	SA	AB	H	2B	3B	HR	HR%	R	RBI	BB	SO	SB	PH AB	PH H	PO	A	E	DP	TC/G	FA	G by Pos
1982	BOS A	104	.349	.441	338	118	14	1	5	1.5	51	44	35	21	1	13	4	489	168	8	51	6.9	.988	1B-49, 3B-44, DH-3, OF-1
1983		153	.361	.486	582	210	44	7	5	0.9	100	74	92	36	3	0	0	118	368	27	40	3.4	.947	3B-153
1984		158	.325	.416	625	203	31	4	6	1.0	109	55	89	44	3	1	0	141	330	20	30	3.1	.959	3B-155, DH-2
1985		161	.368	.478	653	240	42	3	8	1.2	107	78	96	61	2	0	0	134	335	17	30	3.0	.965	3B-161
1986		149	.357	.486	580	207	47	2	8	1.4	107	71	105	44	0	0	0	121	267	19	30	2.7	.953	3B-149
1987		147	.363	.588	551	200	40	6	24	4.4	108	89	105	48	1	1	0	112	277	14	37	2.7	.965	3B-145, 1B-1, DH-1
1988		155	.366	.490	584	214	45	6	5	0.9	128	58	125	34	2	1	1	122	250	11	17	2.5	.971	3B-151, DH-3
1989		156	.330	.449	621	205	51	7	3	0.5	113	54	107	51	2	1	0	123	264	17	29	2.6	.958	3B-152, DH-3
1990		155	.302	.418	619	187	44	5	6	1.0	89	63	87	68	0	0	0	108	241	20	18	2.4	.946	3B-152, DH-3
1991		144	.332	.460	546	181	42	2	8	1.5	93	51	89	32	1	3	2	89	276	12	34	2.7	.968	3B-140
1992		143	.259	.358	514	133	22	4	7	1.4	62	50	74	31	1	4	0	70	229	15	23	2.3	.952	3B-117, DH-21
1993	NY A	143	.302	.362	560	169	26	1	2	0.4	83	59	74	49	0	6	1	75	311	12	29	2.8	.970	3B-134, DH-8
1994		97	.342	.489	366	125	19	1	11	3.0	61	55	61	29	2	5	1	66	217	10	21	3.0	.966	3B-93, 1B-4
1995		126	.324	.422	460	149	22	4	5	1.1	76	63	74	50	1	11	4	114	197	5	14	2.5	.984	3B-117, 1B-9
1996		132	.311	.389	501	156	29	2	2	0.4	80	41	67	32	1	7	2	60	202	7	24	2.1	.974	3B-123, DH-4
15 yrs.		2123	.333	.449	8100	2697	518	55	105	1.3	1367	905	1280	630	20	53	15	1942	3932	214	427	2.9	.965	3B-1986, 1B-63, DH-48, OF-1

DIVISIONAL PLAYOFF SERIES

Year	Team	Games	BA	SA	AB	H	2B	3B	HR	HR%	R	RBI	BB	SO	SB	PH AB	PH H	PO	A	E	DP	TC/G	FA	G by Pos
1995	NY A	4	.263	.526	19	5	2	0	1	5.3	4	3	3	5	0	0	0	4	8	0	1	3.0	1.000	3B-4
1996		3	.083	.167	12	1	1	0	0	0.0	0	0	0	2	0	0	0	2	1	0	0	1.0	1.000	3B-3
2 yrs.		7	.194	.387	31	6	3	0	1	3.2	4	3	3	7	0	0	0	6	9	0	1	2.1	1.000	3B-7

LEAGUE CHAMPIONSHIP SERIES

Year	Team	Games	BA	SA	AB	H	2B	3B	HR	HR%	R	RBI	BB	SO	SB	PH AB	PH H	PO	A	E	DP	TC/G	FA	G by Pos
1986	BOS A	7	.233	.333	30	7	1	1	0	0.0	3	2	4	1	0	0	0	7	14	2	1	3.3	.913	3B-7
1988		4	.385	.385	13	5	0	0	0	0.0	2	3	3	4	0	0	0	6	6	0	1	3.0	1.000	3B-4
1990		4	.438	.688	16	7	1	0	1	6.3	1	1	0	3	0	0	0	6	10	0	2	4.0	1.000	3B-4
1996	NY A	3	.133	.133	15	2	0	0	0	0.0	1	0	1	3	0	0	0	2	11	0	0	4.3	1.000	3B-3
4 yrs.		18	.284	.378	74	21	2	1	1	1.4	7	6	8	11	0	0	0	21	41	2	4	3.6	.969	3B-18

WORLD SERIES

Year	Team	Games	BA	SA	AB	H	2B	3B	HR	HR%	R	RBI	BB	SO	SB	PH AB	PH H	PO	A	E	DP	TC/G	FA	G by Pos
1986	BOS A	7	.290	.387	31	9	3	0	0	0.0	3	3	3	2	0	0	0	4	15	0	1	2.7	1.000	3B-7
1996	NY A	4	.273	.364	11	3	1	0	0	0.0	0	2	1	0	0	0	0	0	0	0	0	0.0	.000	3B-4
2 yrs.		11	.286	.381	42	12	4	0	0	0.0	3	5	4	2	0	0	0	4	15	0	1	1.7	1.000	3B-11

Barry Bonds

BONDS, BARRY LAMAR
Son of Bobby Bonds.
B. July 24, 1964, Riverside, Calif.
BL TL 6'1" 185 lbs.

Year	Team	Games	BA	SA	AB	H	2B	3B	HR	HR%	R	RBI	BB	SO	SB	PH AB	PH H	PO	A	E	DP	TC/G	FA	G by Pos
1986	PIT N	113	.223	.416	413	92	26	3	16	3.9	72	48	65	102	36	3	1	280	9	5	2	2.7	.983	OF-110
1987		150	.261	.492	551	144	34	9	25	4.5	99	59	54	88	32	7	1	330	15	5	3	2.4	.986	OF-145
1988		144	.283	.491	538	152	30	5	24	4.5	97	58	72	82	17	11	2	292	5	6	0	2.2	.980	OF-136
1989		159	.248	.426	580	144	34	6	19	3.3	96	58	93	93	32	8	3	365	14	6	1	2.5	.984	OF-156
1990		151	.301	.565	519	156	32	3	33	6.4	104	114	93	83	52	2	0	338	14	6	2	2.4	.983	OF-150
1991		153	.292	.514	510	149	28	5	25	4.9	95	116	107	73	43	3	1	321	13	3	1	2.2	.991	OF-150
1992		140	.311	.624	473	147	36	5	34	7.2	109	103	127	69	39	2	0	310	4	3	0	2.3	.991	OF-139
1993	SF N	159	.336	.677	539	181	38	4	46	8.5	129	123	126	79	29	3	0	310	7	5	0	2.1	.984	OF-157
1994		112	.312	.647	391	122	18	1	37	9.5	89	81	74	43	29	0	0	198	10	3	0	1.9	.986	OF-112
1995		144	.294	.577	506	149	30	7	33	6.5	109	104	120	83	31	1	0	279	12	6	1	2.1	.980	OF-143
1996		158	.308	.615	517	159	27	3	42	8.1	122	129	151	76	40	6	1	287	10	6	2	2.0	.980	OF-152
11 yrs.		1583	.288	.548	5537	1595	333	51	334	6.0	1121	993	1082	871	380	46	9	3310	113	54	12	2.2	.984	OF-1550

LEAGUE CHAMPIONSHIP SERIES

Year	Team	Games	BA	SA	AB	H	2B	3B	HR	HR%	R	RBI	BB	SO	SB	PH AB	PH H	PO	A	E	DP	TC/G	FA	G by Pos
1990	PIT N	6	.167	.167	18	3	0	0	0	0.0	4	1	6	5	2	0	0	13	0	0	0	2.2	1.000	OF-6
1991		7	.148	.185	27	4	1	0	0	0.0	1	0	2	4	3	0	0	14	1	1	0	2.3	.938	OF-7
1992		7	.261	.435	23	6	1	0	1	4.3	5	2	6	4	1	0	0	17	0	0	0	2.4	1.000	OF-7
3 yrs.		20	.191	.265	68	13	2	0	1	1.5	10	3	14 (6th)	13 (8th)	6	0	0	44	1	1	0	2.3	.978	OF-20

Bobby Bonilla

BONILLA, ROBERTO MARTIN ANTONIO
B. Feb. 23, 1963, Bronx, N.Y.
BB TR 6'3" 210 lbs.

Year	Team	Games	BA	SA	AB	H	2B	3B	HR	HR%	R	RBI	BB	SO	SB	PH AB	PH H	PO	A	E	DP	TC/G	FA	G by Pos
1986	2 teams	CHI A	(75G –.269)	PIT N	(63G –.240)																			
"	total	138	.256	.333	426	109	16	4	3	0.7	55	43	62	88	8	19	2	451	38	5	29	3.7	.990	OF-94, 1B-34, 3B-4
1987	PIT N	141	.300	.481	466	140	33	3	15	3.2	58	77	39	64	3	17	6	142	139	16	13	2.1	.946	3B-89, OF-46, 1B-6
1988		159	.274	.476	584	160	32	7	24	4.1	87	100	85	82	3	1	0	121	336	32	17	3.1	.935	3B-159
1989		163	.281	.490	616	173	37	10	24	3.9	96	86	76	93	8	1	0	190	334	35	37	3.4	.937	3B-156, 1B-8, OF-1
1990		160	.280	.518	625	175	39	7	32	5.1	112	120	45	103	4	1	0	315	35	15	2	2.2	.959	OF-149, 3B-14, 1B-3
1991		157	.302	.492	577	174	44	6	18	3.1	102	100	90	67	2	2	0	247	144	15	19	2.3	.963	OF-104, 3B-67, 1B-4
1992	NY N	128	.249	.432	438	109	23	0	19	4.3	62	70	66	73	4	5	2	277	9	4	3	2.3	.986	OF-121, 1B-6
1993		139	.265	.522	502	133	21	3	34	6.8	81	87	72	96	3	0	0	238	112	17	11	2.6	.954	OF-85, 3B-52, 1B-6
1994		108	.290	.504	403	117	24	1	20	5.0	60	67	55	101	1	0	0	77	217	18	24	2.9	.942	3B-107
1995	2 teams	NY N	(80G –.325)	BAL A	(61G –.333)																			
"	total	141	.329	.576	554	182	37	8	28	5.1	96	99	54	79	0	1	0	244	128	19	16	2.6	.951	OF-70, 3B-70, 1B-10
1996	BAL A	159	.287	.491	595	171	27	5	28	4.7	107	116	75	85	1	0	0	212	12	6	5	1.4	.974	OF-108, DH-44, 1B-9, 3B-4
11 yrs.		1593	.284	.487	5786	1643	333	54	245	4.2	916	965	719	931	37	46	10	2514	1504	182	176	2.6	.957	OF-778, 3B-722, 1B-86, DH-44

DIVISIONAL PLAYOFF SERIES

Year	Team	Games	BA	SA	AB	H	2B	3B	HR	HR%	R	RBI	BB	SO	SB	PH AB	PH H	PO	A	E	DP	TC/G	FA	G by Pos
1996	BAL A	4	.200	.600	15	3	0	0	2	13.3	4	5	4	6	0	0	0	9	0	1	0	2.5	.900	OF-4

Year	Team	Games	BA	SA	AB	H	2B	3B	HR	HR%	R	RBI	BB	SO	SB	Pinch Hit AB	Pinch Hit H	PO	A	E	DP	TC/G	FA	G by Pos

Bobby Bonilla *continued*

LEAGUE CHAMPIONSHIP SERIES

Year	Team	Games	BA	SA	AB	H	2B	3B	HR	HR%	R	RBI	BB	SO	SB	PH AB	PH H	PO	A	E	DP	TC/G	FA	G by Pos
1990	PIT N	6	.190	.238	21	4	1	0	0	0.0	0	1	3	1	0	0	0	4	5	1	1	1.3	.900	OF-5, 3B-3
1991		7	.304	.391	23	7	2	0	0	0.0	2	1	6	2	0	0	0	12	1	0	0	1.9	1.000	OF-7
1996	BAL A	5	.050	.200	20	1	0	0	1	5.0	1	2	1	4	0	0	0	11	0	0	0	2.2	1.000	OF-5
3 yrs.		18	.188	.281	64	12	3	0	1	1.6	3	4	10	7	0	0	0	27	6	1	1	1.7	.971	OF-17, 3B-3

Bret Boone

BOONE, BRET ROBERT
Son of Bob Boone.
B. Apr. 6, 1969, El Cajon, Calif.

BR TR 5'10" 180 lbs.

Year	Team	Games	BA	SA	AB	H	2B	3B	HR	HR%	R	RBI	BB	SO	SB	PH AB	PH H	PO	A	E	DP	TC/G	FA	G by Pos
1992	SEA A	33	.194	.318	129	25	4	0	4	3.1	15	15	4	34	1	1	0	72	96	6	22	4.6	.966	2B-32, 3B-6
1993		76	.251	.443	271	68	12	2	12	4.4	31	38	17	52	2	0	0	140	177	3	55	4.3	.991	2B-74, DH-1
1994	CIN N	108	.320	.491	381	122	25	2	12	3.1	59	68	24	74	3	2	1	192	269	12	57	4.4	.975	2B-106, 3B-2
1995		138	.267	.429	513	137	34	2	15	2.9	63	68	41	84	5	0	0	312	362	4	106	4.9	.994	2B-138
1996		142	.233	.354	520	121	21	3	12	2.3	56	69	31	100	3	1	0	316	381	6	84	5.0	.991	2B-141
5 yrs.		497	.261	.415	1814	473	96	9	55	3.0	224	258	117	344	14	4	1	1032	1285	31	324	4.7	.987	2B-491, 3B-8, DH-1

DIVISIONAL PLAYOFF SERIES

Year	Team	Games	BA	SA	AB	H	2B	3B	HR	HR%	R	RBI	BB	SO	SB	PH AB	PH H	PO	A	E	DP	TC/G	FA	G by Pos
1995	CIN N	3	.300	.700	10	3	1	0	1	10.0	4	1	0	3	1	0	0	7	5	0	0	4.0	1.000	2B-3

LEAGUE CHAMPIONSHIP SERIES

Year	Team	Games	BA	SA	AB	H	2B	3B	HR	HR%	R	RBI	BB	SO	SB	PH AB	PH H	PO	A	E	DP	TC/G	FA	G by Pos
1995	CIN N	4	.214	.214	14	3	0	0	0	0.0	1	0	1	2	0	0	0	9	13	0	3	5.5	1.000	2B-4

Josh Booty

BOOTY, JOSHUA GIBSON
B. Apr. 29, 1975, Starkville, Miss.

BR TR 6'3" 210 lbs.

Year	Team	Games	BA	SA	AB	H	2B	3B	HR	HR%	R	RBI	BB	SO	SB	PH AB	PH H	PO	A	E	DP	TC/G	FA	G by Pos
1996	FLA N	2	.500	.500	2	1	0	0	1	0	1	0	3	0	0	2	1	0	0	0	0	—	—	3B-1

Pat Borders

BORDERS, PATRICK LANCE
B. May 14, 1963, Columbus, Ohio

BR TR 6'2" 190 lbs.

Year	Team	Games	BA	SA	AB	H	2B	3B	HR	HR%	R	RBI	BB	SO	SB	PH AB	PH H	PO	A	E	DP	TC/G	FA	G by Pos
1988	TOR A	56	.273	.448	154	42	6	3	5	3.2	15	21	3	24	0	15	5	205	19	7	0	5.1	.970	C-43, 3B-1, 2B-1
1989		94	.257	.349	241	62	11	1	3	1.2	22	29	11	45	2	20	5	261	27	6	1	3.4	.980	C-68, DH-18
1990		125	.286	.497	346	99	24	2	15	4.3	36	49	18	57	0	25	5	515	46	4	6	4.9	.993	C-115, DH-1
1991		105	.244	.354	291	71	17	0	5	1.7	22	36	11	45	0	18	5	505	48	4	4	5.5	.993	C-102
1992		138	.242	.385	480	116	26	2	13	2.7	47	53	33	75	1	3	3	784	88	8	7	6.4	.991	C-137
1993		138	.254	.371	488	124	30	0	9	1.8	38	55	20	66	2	0	0	869	80	13	12	7.0	.986	C-138
1994		85	.247	.329	295	73	13	1	3	1.0	24	26	15	50	1	0	0	583	59	8	2	7.6	.988	C-85
1995	2 teams KC A (52G –.231) HOU N (11G –.114)																							
"	total	63	.208	.331	178	37	8	1	4	2.2	15	13	9	29	0	8	2	252	23	1	4	4.7	.996	C-56, DH-3
1996	3 teams STL N (26G –.319) CAL A (19G –.228) CHI A (31G –.277)																							
"	total	76	.277	.377	220	61	7	0	5	2.3	15	18	9	43	0	8	1	372	39	8	3	6.2	.981	C-66, DH-1, 1B-1
9 yrs.		880	.254	.384	2693	685	142	10	62	2.3	234	300	129	434	6	97	26	4346	429	59	39	5.8	.988	C-810, DH-23, 3B-1, 1B-1, 2B-1

LEAGUE CHAMPIONSHIP SERIES

Year	Team	Games	BA	SA	AB	H	2B	3B	HR	HR%	R	RBI	BB	SO	SB	PH AB	PH H	PO	A	E	DP	TC/G	FA	G by Pos
1989	TOR A	1	1.000	1.000	1	1	0	0	0	0.0	0	1	0	0	0	1	1	1	0	0	0	1.0	1.000	C-1
1991		5	.263	.316	19	5	1	0	0	0.0	0	2	0	0	0	0	0	38	3	2	0	8.6	.953	C-5
1992		6	.318	.455	22	7	0	0	1	4.5	3	3	1	1	0	0	0	38	3	1	1	7.0	.976	C-6
1993		6	.250	.292	24	6	1	0	0	0.0	1	3	0	6	1	0	0	41	4	0	1	7.5	1.000	C-6
4 yrs.		18	.288	.364	66	19	2	0	1	1.5	4	9	1	7	1	1	1	118	10	3	2	7.3	.977	C-18

WORLD SERIES

Year	Team	Games	BA	SA	AB	H	2B	3B	HR	HR%	R	RBI	BB	SO	SB	PH AB	PH H	PO	A	E	DP	TC/G	FA	G by Pos
1992	TOR A	6	.450	.750	20	9	3	0	1	5.0	2	3	2	1	0	0	0	48	5	1	2	9.0	.981	C-6
1993		6	.304	.304	23	7	0	0	0	0.0	2	1	2	1	0	0	0	50	2	1	0	8.8	.981	C-6
2 yrs.		12	.372	.512	43	16	3	0	1	2.3	4	4	4	2	0	0	0	98	7	2	2	8.9	.981	C-12

Mike Bordick

BORDICK, MICHAEL TODD
B. July 21, 1965, Marquette, Mich.

BR TR 5'11" 170 lbs.

Year	Team	Games	BA	SA	AB	H	2B	3B	HR	HR%	R	RBI	BB	SO	SB	PH AB	PH H	PO	A	E	DP	TC/G	FA	G by Pos
1990	OAK A	25	.071	.071	14	1	0	0	0	0.0	0	0	1	4	0	4	1	9	8	0	0	0.7	1.000	3B-10, SS-9, 2B-7
1991		90	.238	.268	235	56	5	1	0	0.0	21	21	14	37	3	2	0	146	213	11	46	4.1	.970	SS-84, 2B-5, 3B-1
1992		154	.300	.371	504	151	19	4	3	0.6	62	48	40	59	12	1	0	311	449	16	107	4.7	.979	2B-95, SS-70
1993		159	.249	.311	546	136	21	2	3	0.5	60	48	60	58	10	2	0	285	420	13	110	4.5	.982	SS-159, 2B-1
1994		114	.253	.335	391	99	18	4	2	0.5	38	37	38	44	7	0	0	190	320	14	67	4.5	.973	SS-112, 2B-4
1995		126	.264	.350	428	113	13	0	8	1.9	46	44	35	48	11	1	0	246	338	10	92	4.7	.983	SS-126, DH-1
1996		155	.240	.318	525	126	18	4	5	1.0	46	54	52	59	5	1	1	266	474	16	121	4.9	.979	SS-155
7 yrs.		823	.258	.329	2643	682	94	15	21	0.8	273	252	240	309	48	11	2	1453	2222	80	543	4.5	.979	SS-715, 2B-112, 3B-11, DH-1

LEAGUE CHAMPIONSHIP SERIES

Year	Team	Games	BA	SA	AB	H	2B	3B	HR	HR%	R	RBI	BB	SO	SB	PH AB	PH H	PO	A	E	DP	TC/G	FA	G by Pos
1992	OAK A	6	.053	.053	19	1	0	0	0	0.0	1	0	1	2	1	0	0	15	14	0	4	4.8	1.000	SS-4, 2B-2

WORLD SERIES

Year	Team	Games	BA	SA	AB	H	2B	3B	HR	HR%	R	RBI	BB	SO	SB	PH AB	PH H	PO	A	E	DP	TC/G	FA	G by Pos
1990	OAK A	3	—	—	0	0	0	0	0	—	0	0	0	0	0	0	0	0	2	0	0	0.7	1.000	SS-3

Rafael Bournigal

BOURNIGAL, RAFAEL ANTONIO
Born Rafael Antonio Bournigal (Pelletier).
B. May 12, 1966, Azua, Dominican Republic

BR TR 5'11" 160 lbs.

Year	Team	Games	BA	SA	AB	H	2B	3B	HR	HR%	R	RBI	BB	SO	SB	PH AB	PH H	PO	A	E	DP	TC/G	FA	G by Pos
1992	LA N	10	.150	.200	20	3	1	0	0	0.0	1	0	1	2	0	1	0	12	17	1	6	3.3	.967	SS-9
1993		8	.500	.556	18	9	1	0	0	0.0	0	3	0	2	0	2	1	5	14	0	3	2.4	1.000	SS-4, 2B-4
1994		40	.224	.267	116	26	3	1	0	0.0	2	11	9	5	0	0	0	56	97	3	19	3.9	.981	SS-40
1996	OAK A	88	.242	.313	252	61	14	2	0	0.0	33	18	16	19	4	5	1	127	208	2	46	3.9	.994	2B-64, SS-23
4 yrs.		146	.244	.305	406	99	19	3	0	0.0	36	32	26	28	4	8	2	200	336	6	74	3.8	.989	SS-76, 2B-68

Year	Team	Games	BA	SA	AB	H	2B	3B	HR	HR%	R	RBI	BB	SO	SB	Pinch Hit AB	Pinch Hit H	PO	A	E	DP	TC/G	FA	G by Pos

Brent Bowers

BOWERS, BRENT RAYMOND
B. May 2, 1971, Bridgeview, Ill.
BL TR 6'3" 200 lbs.

Year	Team	Games	BA	SA	AB	H	2B	3B	HR	HR%	R	RBI	BB	SO	SB	PH AB	PH H	PO	A	E	DP	TC/G	FA	G by Pos
1996	BAL A	21	.308	.359	39	12	2	0	0	0.0	6	3	0	7	0	0	0	22	1	0	0	1.1	1.000	OF-21

Terry Bradshaw

BRADSHAW, TERRY LEON
B. Feb. 3, 1969, Franklin, Va.
BL TR 6' 180 lbs.

Year	Team	Games	BA	SA	AB	H	2B	3B	HR	HR%	R	RBI	BB	SO	SB	PH AB	PH H	PO	A	E	DP	TC/G	FA	G by Pos
1995	STL N	19	.227	.295	44	10	1	0	0	0.0	6	2	2	10	1	8	3	19	1	1	0	2.1	.952	OF-10
1996		15	.333	.381	21	7	1	0	0	0.0	4	3	3	2	0	7	3	4	0	0	0	0.6	1.000	OF-7
2 yrs.		34	.262	.323	65	17	2	1	0	0.0	10	5	5	12	1	15	6	23	1	1	0	1.5	.960	OF-17

Darren Bragg

BRAGG, DARREN WILLIAM
B. Sept. 7, 1969, Waterbury, Conn.
BL TR 5'9" 180 lbs.

Year	Team	Games	BA	SA	AB	H	2B	3B	HR	HR%	R	RBI	BB	SO	SB	PH AB	PH H	PO	A	E	DP	TC/G	FA	G by Pos
1994	SEA A	8	.158	.211	19	3	1	0	0	0.0	4	2	2	5	0	1	0	1	0	0	0	0.2	1.000	OF-3, DH-3
1995		52	.234	.345	145	34	5	1	3	2.1	20	12	18	37	9	6	2	83	7	1	1	1.9	.989	OF-47, DH-1
1996	2 teams	SEA A	(69G –.272)		BOS A	(58G –.252)																		
"	total	127	.261	.405	417	109	26	2	10	2.4	74	47	69	74	14	7	3	253	11	3	3	2.2	.989	OF-121
3 yrs.		187	.251	.384	581	146	32	3	13	2.2	98	61	89	116	23	14	5	337	18	4	4	2.1	.989	OF-171, DH-4

Jeff Branson

BRANSON, JEFFERY GLENN
B. Jan. 26, 1967, Waynesboro, Miss.
BL TR 6' 180 lbs.

Year	Team	Games	BA	SA	AB	H	2B	3B	HR	HR%	R	RBI	BB	SO	SB	PH AB	PH H	PO	A	E	DP	TC/G	FA	G by Pos
1992	CIN N	72	.296	.374	115	34	7	1	0	0.0	12	15	5	16	0	34	13	46	63	7	19	2.8	.940	2B-33, 3B-8, SS-1
1993		125	.241	.310	381	92	15	1	3	0.8	40	22	19	73	4	17	6	185	260	11	56	3.8	.976	SS-59, 2B-45, 3B-14, 1B-1
1994		58	.284	.505	109	31	4	1	6	5.5	18	16	5	16	0	19	5	39	52	1	6	2.0	.989	2B-19, 3B-18, SS-8, 1B-2
1995		122	.260	.435	331	86	18	2	12	3.6	43	45	44	69	2	11	1	84	241	9	37	2.4	.973	3B-98, SS-32, 2B-6, 1B-1
1996		129	.244	.408	311	76	16	4	9	2.9	34	37	31	67	2	20	3	97	201	14	40	2.3	.955	3B-64, SS-38, 2B-31
5 yrs.		506	.256	.391	1247	319	60	9	30	2.4	147	135	104	241	8	101	28	451	817	42	158	2.7	.968	3B-202, SS-138, 2B-134, 1B-4

DIVISIONAL PLAYOFF SERIES

Year	Team	Games	BA	SA	AB	H	2B	3B	HR	HR%	R	RBI	BB	SO	SB	PH AB	PH H	PO	A	E	DP	TC/G	FA	G by Pos
1995	CIN N	3	.286	.429	7	2	1	0	0	0.0	0	2	2	0	0	0	0	1	8	0	0	3.0	1.000	3B-3

LEAGUE CHAMPIONSHIP SERIES

Year	Team	Games	BA	SA	AB	H	2B	3B	HR	HR%	R	RBI	BB	SO	SB	PH AB	PH H	PO	A	E	DP	TC/G	FA	G by Pos
1995	CIN N	4	.111	.222	9	1	1	0	0	0.0	2	0	1	2	1	2	0	1	3	0	1	1.0	1.000	3B-4

Brent Brede

BREDE, BRENT DAVID
B. Sept. 13, 1971, Belleville, Ill.
BL TL 6'4" 190 lbs.

Year	Team	Games	BA	SA	AB	H	2B	3B	HR	HR%	R	RBI	BB	SO	SB	PH AB	PH H	PO	A	E	DP	TC/G	FA	G by Pos
1996	MIN A	10	.300	.400	20	6	0	1	0	0.0	2	2	1	5	0	3	1	12	1	0	0	1.9	1.000	OF-7

Jorge Brito

BRITO, JORGE MANUEL
Born Jorge Manuel Brito (Uceta).
B. June 22, 1966, Moncion, Dominican Republic
BR TR 6'1" 190 lbs.

Year	Team	Games	BA	SA	AB	H	2B	3B	HR	HR%	R	RBI	BB	SO	SB	PH AB	PH H	PO	A	E	DP	TC/G	FA	G by Pos
1995	CLR N	18	.216	.275	51	11	3	0	0	0.0	5	7	2	17	1	0	0	109	6	1	0	6.4	.991	C-18
1996		8	.071	.071	14	1	0	0	0	0.0	1	0	1	8	0	1	0	36	7	0	1	5.4	1.000	C-8
2 yrs.		26	.185	.231	65	12	3	0	0	0.0	6	7	3	25	1	1	0	145	13	1	1	6.1	.994	C-26

Tilson Brito

BRITO, TILSON MANUEL
Born Tilson Manuel Brito (Jiminez).
B. May 28, 1972, Santo Domingo, Dominican Republic
BR TR 6' 170 lbs.

Year	Team	Games	BA	SA	AB	H	2B	3B	HR	HR%	R	RBI	BB	SO	SB	PH AB	PH H	PO	A	E	DP	TC/G	FA	G by Pos
1996	TOR A	26	.237	.362	80	19	7	0	1	1.3	10	7	10	18	1	0	0	42	60	4	17	4.6	.962	2B-18, SS-5, DH-2

Rico Brogna

BROGNA, RICO JOSEPH
B. Apr. 18, 1970, Turners Falls, Mass.
BL TL 6'2" 190 lbs.

Year	Team	Games	BA	SA	AB	H	2B	3B	HR	HR%	R	RBI	BB	SO	SB	PH AB	PH H	PO	A	E	DP	TC/G	FA	G by Pos
1992	DET A	9	.192	.346	26	5	1	0	1	3.8	3	3	3	5	0	0	0	48	6	1	9	5.5	.982	1B-8, DH-2
1994	NY N	39	.351	.626	131	46	11	2	7	5.3	16	20	6	29	1	4	1	308	28	1	29	9.6	.997	1B-35
1995		134	.289	.485	495	143	27	2	22	4.4	72	76	39	111	0	9	2	1113	92	3	93	9.2	.998	1B-131
1996		55	.255	.431	188	48	10	1	7	3.7	18	30	19	50	0	4	0	439	32	2	47	9.1	.996	1B-52
4 yrs.		237	.288	.490	840	242	49	5	37	4.4	109	129	67	195	1	17	3	1908	158	7	178	9.1	.997	1B-226, DH-2

Jerry Brooks

BROOKS, JEROME EDWARD
B. Mar. 23, 1967, Syracuse, N.Y.
BR TR 6' 195 lbs.

Year	Team	Games	BA	SA	AB	H	2B	3B	HR	HR%	R	RBI	BB	SO	SB	PH AB	PH H	PO	A	E	DP	TC/G	FA	G by Pos
1993	LA N	9	.222	.667	9	2	1	0	1	11.1	2	1	0	2	0	8	1	0	0	0	0	0.0	.000	OF-2
1996	FLA N	8	.400	.800	5	2	0	1	0	0.0	2	3	1	1	0	4	1	2	0	1	0	1.0	.667	OF-2, 1B-1
2 yrs.		17	.286	.714	14	4	1	1	1	7.1	4	4	1	3	0	12	2	2	0	1	0	0.6	.667	OF-4, 1B-1

Scott Brosius

BROSIUS, SCOTT DAVID
B. Aug. 15, 1966, Hillsboro, Ore.
BR TR 6'1" 185 lbs.

Year	Team	Games	BA	SA	AB	H	2B	3B	HR	HR%	R	RBI	BB	SO	SB	PH AB	PH H	PO	A	E	DP	TC/G	FA	G by Pos
1991	OAK A	36	.235	.397	68	16	5	0	2	2.9	9	4	3	11	3	4	2	31	16	0	3	1.2	1.000	2B-18, OF-13, 3B-7, DH-1
1992		38	.218	.379	87	19	2	0	4	4.6	13	13	3	13	3	2	0	68	15	1	2	2.3	.988	OF-20, 3B-12, 1B-3, SS-1, DH-1
1993		70	.249	.390	213	53	10	1	6	2.8	26	25	14	37	6	6	2	173	29	2	11	2.7	.990	OF-46, 1B-11, 3B-10, SS-6, DH-2
1994		96	.238	.417	324	77	14	1	14	4.3	31	49	24	57	2	0	0	81	154	13	19	2.5	.948	3B-93, OF-7, 1B-1
1995		123	.262	.452	389	102	19	2	17	4.4	69	46	41	67	4	4	0	207	121	15	35	2.5	.956	3B-60, OF-49, 1B-18, SS-3, 2B-3, DH-2
1996		114	.304	.516	428	130	25	0	22	5.1	73	71	59	85	7	1	1	128	233	10	26	3.0	.973	3B-109, 1B-10, OF-4
6 yrs.		477	.263	.447	1509	397	75	4	65	4.3	221	208	144	270	25	17	5	688	568	41	96	2.5	.968	3B-291, OF-139, 1B-43, 2B-21, SS-10, DH-6

Year	Team	Games	BA	SA	AB	H	2B	3B	HR	HR%	R	RBI	BB	SO	SB	Pinch Hit AB	Pinch Hit H	PO	A	E	DP	TC/G	FA	G by Pos

Brant Brown

BROWN, BRANT MICHAEL
B. June 22, 1971, Porterville, Calif.
BL TL 6'3" 220 lbs.

Year	Team	Games	BA	SA	AB	H	2B	3B	HR	HR%	R	RBI	BB	SO	SB	PH AB	PH H	PO	A	E	DP	TC/G	FA	G by Pos
1996	CHI N	29	.304	.536	69	21	1	0	5	7.2	11	9	2	17	3	11	2	126	15	0	4	7.8	1.000	1B-18

Kevin Brown

BROWN, KEVIN LEE
B. Apr. 21, 1973, Valpariso, Ind.
BR TR 6'2" 200 lbs.

Year	Team	Games	BA	SA	AB	H	2B	3B	HR	HR%	R	RBI	BB	SO	SB	PH AB	PH H	PO	A	E	DP	TC/G	FA	G by Pos
1996	TEX A	3	.000	.000	4	0	0	0	0	0.0	1	1	2	2	0	2	0	11	1	0	0	6.0	1.000	C-2, DH-1

Jacob Brumfield

BRUMFIELD, JACOB DONNELL
B. May 27, 1965, Bogalusa, La.
BR TR 6' 170 lbs.

Year	Team	Games	BA	SA	AB	H	2B	3B	HR	HR%	R	RBI	BB	SO	SB	PH AB	PH H	PO	A	E	DP	TC/G	FA	G by Pos
1992	CIN N	24	.133	.133	30	4	0	0	0	0.0	6	2	2	4	6	5	1	20	1	0	0	1.3	1.000	OF-16
1993		103	.268	.419	272	73	17	3	6	2.2	40	23	21	47	20	5	0	178	16	7	4	2.0	.965	OF-96, 2B-4
1994		68	.311	.525	122	38	10	2	4	3.3	36	11	15	18	6	19	2	74	1	1	0	1.8	.987	OF-43
1995	PIT N	116	.271	.368	402	109	23	2	4	1.0	64	26	37	71	22	18	7	241	8	8	1	2.5	.969	OF-104
1996	2 teams PIT N (29G –.250) TOR A (90G –.256)																							
"	total	119	.255	.446	388	99	28	2	14	3.6	63	60	29	75	15	22	3	194	9	5	1	1.9	.976	OF-105, DH-5
5 yrs.		430	.266	.414	1214	323	78	9	28	2.3	209	122	104	215	69	69	13	707	35	21	6	2.0	.972	OF-364, DH-5, 2B-4

Damon Buford

BUFORD, DAMON JACKSON
Son of Don Buford.
B. June 12, 1970, Baltimore, Md.
BR TR 5'10" 170 lbs.

Year	Team	Games	BA	SA	AB	H	2B	3B	HR	HR%	R	RBI	BB	SO	SB	PH AB	PH H	PO	A	E	DP	TC/G	FA	G by Pos
1993	BAL A	53	.228	.367	79	18	5	0	2	2.5	18	9	9	19	2	3	1	61	2	1	2	1.4	.984	OF-30, DH-16
1994		4	.500	.500	2	1	0	0	0	0.0	2	0	0	1	0	0	0	0	0	0	0	0.0		OF-1, DH-1
1995	2 teams BAL A (24G –.063) NY N (44G –.235)																							
"	total	68	.202	.304	168	34	5	0	4	2.4	30	14	25	35	10	4	2	107	2	2	0	1.8	.982	OF-63
1996	TEX A	90	.283	.469	145	41	9	0	6	4.1	30	20	15	34	8	12	0	93	3	0	0	1.2	1.000	OF-80, DH-3
4 yrs.		215	.239	.378	394	94	19	0	12	3.0	80	43	49	89	20	19	3	261	7	3	2	1.4	.989	OF-174, DH-20

DIVISIONAL PLAYOFF SERIES

Year	Team	Games	BA	SA	AB	H	2B	3B	HR	HR%	R	RBI	BB	SO	SB	PH AB	PH H	PO	A	E	DP	TC/G	FA	G by Pos
1996	TEX A	2	—	—	0	0	0	0	0	—	0	0	0	0	0	0	0	0	0	0	0	0.0	—	

Jay Buhner

BUHNER, JAY CAMPBELL
B. Aug. 13, 1964, Louisville, Ky.
BR TR 6'3" 205 lbs.

Year	Team	Games	BA	SA	AB	H	2B	3B	HR	HR%	R	RBI	BB	SO	SB	PH AB	PH H	PO	A	E	DP	TC/G	FA	G by Pos
1987	NY A	7	.227	.318	22	5	2	0	0	0.0	0	1	1	6	0	0	0	11	1	0	1	1.7	1.000	OF-7
1988	2 teams NY A (25G –.188) SEA A (60G –.224)																							
"	total	85	.215	.421	261	56	13	1	13	5.0	36	38	28	93	1	4	1	186	9	3	3	2.4	.985	OF-81
1989	SEA A	58	.275	.490	204	56	15	1	9	4.4	27	33	19	55	1	0	0	106	6	4	3	2.0	.966	OF-57
1990		51	.276	.479	163	45	12	0	7	4.3	16	33	17	50	2	3	0	55	1	2	0	1.2	.966	OF-40, DH-10
1991		137	.244	.498	406	99	14	4	27	6.7	64	77	53	117	0	10	1	244	15	5	4	2.0	.981	OF-131
1992		152	.243	.422	543	132	16	3	25	4.6	69	79	71	146	0	3	1	314	14	2	4	2.2	.994	OF-150
1993		158	.272	.476	563	153	28	3	27	4.8	91	98	100	144	2	2	1	263	8	6	2	1.8	.978	OF-148, DH-10
1994		101	.279	.542	358	100	23	4	21	5.9	74	68	66	63	0	3	1	179	11	2	2	1.9	.990	OF-96, DH-4
1995		126	.262	.566	470	123	23	0	40	8.5	86	121	60	120	0	0	0	177	5	2	0	1.5	.989	OF-120, DH-4
1996		150	.271	.557	564	153	29	0	44	7.8	107	138	84	**159**	0	0	0	251	10	3	1	1.8	.989	OF-142, DH-8
10 yrs.		1025	.259	.497	3554	922	175	16	213	6.0	570	686	499	953	6	25	5	1786	80	29	20	1.9	.985	OF-972, DH-36

DIVISIONAL PLAYOFF SERIES

Year	Team	Games	BA	SA	AB	H	2B	3B	HR	HR%	R	RBI	BB	SO	SB	PH AB	PH H	PO	A	E	DP	TC/G	FA	G by Pos
1995	SEA A	5	.458	.625	24	11	1	0	1	4.2	2	3	2	4	0	0	0	11	1	0	0	2.4	1.000	OF-5

LEAGUE CHAMPIONSHIP SERIES

Year	Team	Games	BA	SA	AB	H	2B	3B	HR	HR%	R	RBI	BB	SO	SB	PH AB	PH H	PO	A	E	DP	TC/G	FA	G by Pos
1995	SEA A	6	.304	.783	23	7	2	0	3	13.0	5	5	2	8	0	0	0	15	0	1	0	2.7	.938	OF-6

Scott Bullett

BULLETT, SCOTT DOUGLAS
B. Dec. 25, 1968, Martinsburg, W. Va.
BB TL 6'2" 200 lbs.

Year	Team	Games	BA	SA	AB	H	2B	3B	HR	HR%	R	RBI	BB	SO	SB	PH AB	PH H	PO	A	E	DP	TC/G	FA	G by Pos
1991	PIT N	11	.000	.000	4	0	0	0	0	0.0	2	0	0	3	1	1	0	2	0	0	0	0.7	1.000	OF-3
1993		23	.200	.273	55	11	0	2	0	0.0	2	4	3	15	3	4	2	35	1	0	0	1.9	1.000	OF-19
1995	CHI N	104	.273	.460	150	41	5	7	3	2.0	19	22	12	30	8	37	12	59	1	2	0	1.0	.968	OF-64
1996		109	.212	.297	165	35	5	0	3	1.8	26	16	10	54	7	59	12	70	2	1	1	1.3	.986	OF-58
4 yrs.		247	.233	.356	374	87	10	9	6	1.6	49	42	25	102	19	101	26	166	4	3	1	1.2	.983	OF-144

Ellis Burks

BURKS, ELLIS RENA
B. Sept. 11, 1964, Vicksburg, Miss.
BR TR 6'2" 175 lbs.

Year	Team	Games	BA	SA	AB	H	2B	3B	HR	HR%	R	RBI	BB	SO	SB	PH AB	PH H	PO	A	E	DP	TC/G	FA	G by Pos
1987	BOS A	133	.272	.441	558	152	30	2	20	3.6	94	59	41	98	27	0	0	320	15	4	2	2.6	.988	OF-132
1988		144	.294	.481	540	159	37	5	18	3.3	93	92	62	89	25	0	0	370	9	9	0	2.7	.977	OF-142, DH-2
1989		97	.303	.471	399	121	19	6	12	3.0	73	61	36	52	21	0	0	245	7	6	3	2.7	.977	OF-95, DH-1
1990		152	.296	.486	588	174	33	8	21	3.6	89	89	48	82	9	3	1	324	7	2	0	2.2	.994	OF-143, DH-6
1991		130	.251	.422	474	119	33	3	14	3.0	56	56	39	81	6	2	0	283	2	2	1	2.2	.993	OF-126, DH-2
1992		66	.255	.417	235	60	8	3	8	3.4	35	30	25	48	5	3	0	120	3	2	0	2.0	.984	OF-63, DH-1
1993	CHI A	146	.275	.441	499	137	24	4	17	3.4	75	74	60	97	6	5	2	313	6	6	1	2.2	.982	OF-146
1994	CLR N	42	.322	.678	149	48	8	3	13	8.7	33	24	16	39	3	3	0	79	2	3	0	2.2	.964	OF-39
1995		103	.266	.496	278	74	10	6	14	5.0	41	49	39	72	7	29	6	158	3	5	0	2.1	.970	OF-80
1996		156	.344	**.639**	613	211	45	8	40	6.5	**142**	128	61	114	32	5	1	280	6	5	4	1.9	.983	OF-152
10 yrs.		1169	.290	.491	4333	1255	247	48	177	4.1	731	662	427	772	141	50	10	2492	60	44	9	2.3	.983	OF-1118, DH-12

DIVISIONAL PLAYOFF SERIES

Year	Team	Games	BA	SA	AB	H	2B	3B	HR	HR%	R	RBI	BB	SO	SB	PH AB	PH H	PO	A	E	DP	TC/G	FA	G by Pos
1995	CLR N	2	.333	.500	6	2	1	0	0	0.0	1	2	0	1	0	0	0	4	0	1	0	2.5	.800	OF-2

LEAGUE CHAMPIONSHIP SERIES

Year	Team	Games	BA	SA	AB	H	2B	3B	HR	HR%	R	RBI	BB	SO	SB	PH AB	PH H	PO	A	E	DP	TC/G	FA	G by Pos
1988	BOS A	4	.235	.294	17	4	1	0	0	0.0	2	1	0	3	0	0	0	10	0	0	0	2.5	1.000	OF-4
1990		4	.267	.400	15	4	2	0	0	0.0	1	0	1	1	1	0	0	9	1	0	0	2.5	1.000	OF-4
1993	CHI A	6	.304	.478	23	7	1	0	1	4.3	4	3	3	5	0	0	0	15	0	0	0	2.5	1.000	OF-6
3 yrs.		14	.273	.400	55	15	4	0	1	1.8	7	4	4	9	1	0	0	34	1	0	0	2.5	1.000	OF-14

Year	Team	Games	BA	SA	AB	H	2B	3B	HR	HR%	R	RBI	BB	SO	SB	Pinch Hit AB	Pinch Hit H	PO	A	E	DP	TC/G	FA	G by Pos

Jeromy Burnitz

BURNITZ, JEROMY NEAL
B. Apr. 15, 1969, Westminster, Calif. — BL TR 6' 190 lbs.

Year	Team	Games	BA	SA	AB	H	2B	3B	HR	HR%	R	RBI	BB	SO	SB	PH AB	PH H	PO	A	E	DP	TC/G	FA	G by Pos
1993	NY N	86	.243	.475	263	64	10	6	13	4.9	49	38	38	66	3	10	3	165	6	4	2	2.2	.977	OF-79
1994		45	.238	.329	143	34	4	0	3	2.1	26	15	23	45	1	3	1	63	1	2	0	1.6	.970	OF-42
1995	CLE A	9	.571	.714	7	4	1	0	0	0.0	4	0	0	0	0	0	0	10	0	0	0	1.3	1.000	OF-6, DH-2
1996	2 teams	CLE A (71G –.281)		MIL A (23G –.236)																				
"	total	94	.265	.470	200	53	14	0	9	4.5	38	40	33	47	4	26	4	82	1	1	0	1.3	.988	OF-52, DH-15
	4 yrs.	234	.253	.442	613	155	29	6	25	4.1	117	93	94	158	8	39	8	320	8	7	2	1.7	.979	OF-179, DH-17

Mike Busch

BUSCH, MICHAEL ANTHONY
B. July 7, 1968, Davenport, Iowa — BR TR 6'5" 241 lbs.

Year	Team	Games	BA	SA	AB	H	2B	3B	HR	HR%	R	RBI	BB	SO	SB	PH AB	PH H	PO	A	E	DP	TC/G	FA	G by Pos
1995	LA N	13	.235	.765	17	4	0	0	3	17.6	3	6	0	7	0	7	1	10	6	1	2	1.4	.941	3B-10, 1B-2
1996		38	.217	.410	83	18	4	0	4	4.8	8	17	5	33	0	14	3	18	25	3	1	1.9	.935	3B-23, 1B-1
	2 yrs.	51	.220	.470	100	22	4	0	7	7.0	11	23	5	40	0	21	5	28	31	4	3	1.8	.937	3B-33, 1B-3

Brett Butler

BUTLER, BRETT MORGAN
B. June 15, 1957, Los Angeles, Calif. — BL TL 5'10" 160 lbs.

Year	Team	Games	BA	SA	AB	H	2B	3B	HR	HR%	R	RBI	BB	SO	SB	PH AB	PH H	PO	A	E	DP	TC/G	FA	G by Pos
1981	ATL N	40	.254	.317	126	32	2	3	0	0.0	17	4	19	17	9	2	1	76	2	1	0	2.1	.987	OF-37
1982		89	.217	.225	240	52	2	0	0	0.0	35	7	25	35	21	6	1	129	2	0	0	1.7	1.000	OF-77
1983		151	.281	.393	549	154	21	13	5	0.9	84	37	54	56	39	6	1	284	13	4	4	2.1	.987	OF-143
1984	CLE A	159	.269	.355	602	162	25	9	3	0.5	108	49	86	62	52	3	0	448	13	4	3	3.0	.991	OF-156
1985		152	.311	.431	591	184	28	14	5	0.8	106	50	63	42	47	1	0	437	19	1	5	3.0	.998	OF-150, DH-1
1986		161	.278	.375	587	163	17	14	4	0.7	92	51	70	65	32	1	0	434	9	3	3	2.8	.993	OF-159
1987		137	.295	.425	522	154	25	8	9	1.7	91	41	91	55	33	0	0	393	4	4	2	2.9	.990	OF-136
1988	SF N	157	.287	.398	568	163	27	9	6	1.1	109	43	97	64	43	2	0	395	3	5	1	2.6	.988	OF-155
1989		154	.283	.354	594	168	22	4	4	0.7	100	36	59	69	31	0	0	407	11	6	3	2.8	.986	OF-152
1990		160	.309	.384	622	192	20	9	3	0.5	108	44	90	62	51	1	0	420	4	6	0	2.7	.986	OF-159
1991	LA N	161	.296	.343	615	182	13	5	2	0.3	112	38	108	79	38	1	0	372	8	0	3	2.4	1.000	OF-161
1992		157	.309	.391	553	171	14	11	3	0.5	86	39	95	67	41	3	1	353	9	2	3	2.3	.995	OF-155
1993		156	.298	.371	607	181	21	10	1	0.2	80	42	86	69	39	1	0	369	6	0	0	2.4	1.000	OF-155
1994		111	.314	.446	417	131	13	9	8	1.9	79	33	68	52	27	0	0	260	8	2	1	2.4	.993	OF-111
1995	2 teams	NY N (90G –.311)		LA N (39G –.274)																				
"	total	129	.300	.376	513	154	18	9	1	0.2	78	38	67	51	32	1	1	282	6	2	1	2.2	.993	OF-129
1996	LA N	34	.267	.290	131	35	1	1	0	0.0	22	8	9	22	8	0	0	74	1	1	0	2.2	.987	OF-34
	16 yrs.	2108	.291	.378	7837	2278	269	128	54	0.7	1307	560	1087	867	543	28	5	5133	118	41	29	2.6	.992	OF-2069, DH-1

DIVISIONAL PLAYOFF SERIES

Year	Team	Games	BA	SA	AB	H	2B	3B	HR	HR%	R	RBI	BB	SO	SB	PH AB	PH H	PO	A	E	DP	TC/G	FA	G by Pos
1995	LA N	3	.267	.267	15	4	0	0	0	0.0	1	1	0	3	1	0	0	7	0	0	0	2.3	1.000	OF-3

LEAGUE CHAMPIONSHIP SERIES

Year	Team	Games	BA	SA	AB	H	2B	3B	HR	HR%	R	RBI	BB	SO	SB	PH AB	PH H	PO	A	E	DP	TC/G	FA	G by Pos
1982	ATL N	2	.000	.000	1	0	0	0	0	0.0	0	0	0	0	0	1	0	0	0	0	0	0.0	.000	OF-1
1989	SF N	5	.211	.211	19	4	0	0	0	0.0	6	0	3	3	0	0	0	9	0	0	0	1.8	1.000	OF-5
	2 yrs.	7	.200	.200	20	4	0	0	0	0.0	6	0	3	3	0	1	0	9	0	0	0	1.5	1.000	OF-6

WORLD SERIES

Year	Team	Games	BA	SA	AB	H	2B	3B	HR	HR%	R	RBI	BB	SO	SB	PH AB	PH H	PO	A	E	DP	TC/G	FA	G by Pos
1989	SF N	4	.286	.357	14	4	1	0	0	0.0	1	1	2	1	2	0	0	9	0	0	0	2.3	1.000	OF-4

Miguel Cairo

CAIRO, MIGUEL JESUS
B. Jan. 8, 1973, La Grange, Ga. — BR TR 6' 160 lbs.

Year	Team	Games	BA	SA	AB	H	2B	3B	HR	HR%	R	RBI	BB	SO	SB	PH AB	PH H	PO	A	E	DP	TC/G	FA	G by Pos
1996	TOR A	9	.222	.296	27	6	2	0	0	0.0	5	1	2	9	0	0	0	22	18	0	5	4.4	1.000	2B-9

Mike Cameron

CAMERON, MICHAEL TERRANCE
B. Jan. 8, 1973, La Grange, Ga. — BR TR 6'1" 170 lbs.

Year	Team	Games	BA	SA	AB	H	2B	3B	HR	HR%	R	RBI	BB	SO	SB	PH AB	PH H	PO	A	E	DP	TC/G	FA	G by Pos
1995	CHI A	28	.184	.316	38	7	2	0	1	2.6	4	2	3	15	0	0	0	33	1	0	0	1.2	1.000	OF-28
1996		11	.091	.091	11	1	0	0	0	0.0	1	0	1	3	0	1	0	7	0	0	0	0.8	1.000	OF-8, DH-1
	2 yrs.	39	.163	.265	49	8	2	0	1	2.0	5	2	4	18	0	1	0	40	1	0	0	1.1	1.000	OF-36, DH-1

Ken Caminiti

CAMINITI, KENNETH GENE
B. Apr. 21, 1963, Hanford, Calif. — BB TR 6' 200 lbs.

Year	Team	Games	BA	SA	AB	H	2B	3B	HR	HR%	R	RBI	BB	SO	SB	PH AB	PH H	PO	A	E	DP	TC/G	FA	G by Pos
1987	HOU N	63	.246	.335	203	50	7	1	3	1.5	10	23	12	44	0	9	2	50	98	8	11	2.6	.949	3B-61
1988		30	.181	.241	83	15	2	0	1	1.2	5	7	5	18	0	5	0	12	43	3	2	2.1	.948	3B-28
1989		161	.255	.369	585	149	31	3	10	1.7	71	72	51	93	4	2	0	126	335	22	27	3.0	.954	3B-160
1990		153	.242	.309	541	131	20	2	4	0.7	52	51	48	97	9	10	1	118	243	21	22	2.6	.945	3B-149
1991		152	.253	.383	574	145	30	3	13	2.3	65	80	46	85	4	2	0	129	293	23	29	2.9	.948	3B-152
1992		135	.294	.441	506	149	31	2	13	2.6	68	62	44	68	10	6	1	102	210	11	19	2.5	.966	3B-129
1993		143	.262	.390	543	142	31	0	13	2.4	75	75	49	88	8	1	0	123	264	24	23	2.9	.942	3B-143
1994		111	.283	.495	406	115	28	2	18	4.4	63	75	43	71	4	6	0	79	201	9	17	2.7	.969	3B-108
1995	SD N	143	.302	.513	526	159	33	0	26	4.9	74	94	69	94	12	0	0	102	293	27	24	3.0	.936	3B-143
1996		146	.326	.621	546	178	37	2	40	7.3	109	130	78	99	11	2	0	103	310	20	28	3.0	.954	3B-145
	10 yrs.	1237	.273	.429	4513	1233	250	15	141	3.1	592	669	445	757	62	43	4	944	2290	168	202	2.8	.951	3B-1218

DIVISIONAL PLAYOFF SERIES

Year	Team	Games	BA	SA	AB	H	2B	3B	HR	HR%	R	RBI	BB	SO	SB	PH AB	PH H	PO	A	E	DP	TC/G	FA	G by Pos
1996	SD N	3	.300	1.200	10	3	0	0	3	30.0	3	3	2	5	0	0	0	0	5	3	0	2.7	.625	3B-3

Casey Candaele

CANDAELE, CASEY TODD
B. Jan. 12, 1961, Lompoc, Calif. — BB TR 5'9" 160 lbs.

Year	Team	Games	BA	SA	AB	H	2B	3B	HR	HR%	R	RBI	BB	SO	SB	PH AB	PH H	PO	A	E	DP	TC/G	FA	G by Pos
1986	MON N	30	.231	.288	104	24	4	1	0	0.0	9	6	5	15	3	3	1	45	74	2	13	4.3	.983	2B-24, 3B-4
1987		138	.272	.347	449	122	23	4	1	0.2	62	23	38	28	7	12	3	237	176	8	28	2.6	.981	2B-68, OF-67, SS-25, 1B-1
1988	2 teams	MON N (36G –.172)		HOU N (21G –.161)																				
"	total	57	.170	.238	147	25	8	1	0	0.0	11	5	11	17	1	7	1	79	126	2	21	4.1	.990	2B-45, OF-5, 3B-1

Casey Candaele *continued*

Year	Team	Games	BA	SA	AB	H	2B	3B	HR	HR%	R	RBI	BB	SO	SB	Pinch Hit AB	Pinch Hit H	PO	A	E	DP	TC/G	FA	G by Pos
1990	HOU N	130	.286	.397	262	75	8	6	3	1.1	30	22	31	42	7	30	10	147	120	3	20	2.2	.989	OF-58, 2B-49, SS-13, 3B-1
1991		151	.262	.362	461	121	20	7	4	0.9	44	50	40	49	9	19	3	244	318	10	53	3.9	.983	2B-109, OF-26, 3B-11
1992		135	.212	.266	320	68	12	1	1	0.3	19	18	24	36	7	25	3	130	196	11	34	2.7	.967	SS-65, 3B-29, OF-21, 2B-9
1993		75	.240	.331	121	29	8	0	1	0.8	18	7	10	14	2	36	7	46	40	3	4	1.6	.966	2B-19, OF-17, SS-14, 3B-4
1996	CLE A	24	.250	.364	44	11	2	0	1	2.3	8	4	1	9	0	9	2	22	33	0	12	3.7	1.000	2B-11, 3B-3, SS-1
8 yrs.		740	.249	.332	1908	475	85	20	11	0.6	201	135	160	210	36	141	30	950	1083	39	185	3.0	.981	2B-334, OF-194, SS-118, 3B-53, 1B-1

DIVISIONAL PLAYOFF SERIES

Year	Team	Games	BA	SA	AB	H	2B	3B	HR	HR%	R	RBI	BB	SO	SB	Pinch Hit AB	Pinch Hit H	PO	A	E	DP	TC/G	FA	G by Pos
1996	CLE A	2	—	—	0	0	0	0	0	—	1	0	1	0	0	0	0	0	0	0	0	0.0	.000	DH-1

John Cangelosi

CANGELOSI, JOHN ANTHONY
B. Mar. 10, 1963, Brooklyn, N.Y.
BB TL 5'8" 150 lbs.

Year	Team	Games	BA	SA	AB	H	2B	3B	HR	HR%	R	RBI	BB	SO	SB	Pinch Hit AB	Pinch Hit H	PO	A	E	DP	TC/G	FA	G by Pos
1985	CHI A	5	.000	.000	2	0	0	0	0	0.0	2	0	0	1	0	0	0	1	0	0	0	0.2	1.000	OF-3, DH-2
1986		137	.235	.299	438	103	16	3	2	0.5	65	32	71	61	50	1	0	276	7	9	1	2.2	.969	OF-129, DH-3
1987	PIT N	104	.275	.418	182	50	8	3	4	2.2	44	18	46	33	21	50	10	74	3	3	0	1.7	.963	OF-47
1988		75	.254	.305	118	30	4	1	0	0.0	18	8	17	16	9	42	12	52	0	2	0	2.2	.963	OF-24, P-1
1989		112	.219	.269	160	35	4	2	0	0.0	18	9	35	20	11	68	12	71	1	2	0	1.6	.973	OF-46
1990		58	.197	.224	76	15	2	0	0	0.0	13	1	11	12	7	36	8	24	0	0	0	2.0	1.000	OF-12
1992	TEX N	73	.188	.247	85	16	2	0	1	1.2	12	6	18	16	6	5	2	76	4	3	1	1.2	.964	OF-65, DH-6
1994	NY N	62	.252	.288	111	28	4	0	0	0.0	14	4	19	20	5	19	5	64	5	0	1	1.4	1.000	OF-50
1995	HOU N	90	.318	.393	201	64	5	2	2	1.0	46	18	48	42	21	29	8	92	4	5	0	1.7	.950	OF-59, P-1
1996		108	.263	.347	262	69	11	4	1	0.4	49	16	44	41	17	28	1	113	5	3	0	1.6	.975	OF-78
10 yrs.		824	.251	.322	1635	410	66	15	10	0.6	281	112	309	262	147	278	58	843	29	27	3	1.7	.970	OF-513, DH-11, P-2

Jay Canizaro

CANIZARO, JASON KYLE
B. Jul. 4, 1973, Beaumont, Tex.
BR TR 5'9" 170 lbs.

Year	Team	Games	BA	SA	AB	H	2B	3B	HR	HR%	R	RBI	BB	SO	SB	Pinch Hit AB	Pinch Hit H	PO	A	E	DP	TC/G	FA	G by Pos
1996	SF N	43	.200	.300	120	24	4	1	2	1.7	11	8	9	38	10	3	1	64	91	6	19	3.8	.963	2B-35, SS-7

Jose Canseco

CANSECO, JOSE
Born Jose Canseco (Capas).
Brother of Ozzie Canseco.
B. July 2, 1964, Havana, Cuba
BR TR 6'3" 185 lbs.

Year	Team	Games	BA	SA	AB	H	2B	3B	HR	HR%	R	RBI	BB	SO	SB	Pinch Hit AB	Pinch Hit H	PO	A	E	DP	TC/G	FA	G by Pos
1985	OAK A	29	.302	.490	96	29	3	0	5	5.2	16	13	4	31	1	4	1	56	2	3	1	2.3	.951	OF-26
1986		157	.240	.457	600	144	29	1	33	5.5	85	117	65	175	15	1	1	319	4	14	1	2.2	.958	OF-155, DH-1
1987		159	.257	.470	630	162	35	3	31	4.9	81	113	50	157	15	1	0	263	12	7	3	1.8	.975	OF-130, DH-30
1988		158	.307	**.569**	610	187	34	0	**42**	6.9	120	**124**	78	128	40	1	0	304	11	7	3	2.1	.978	OF-144, DH-13
1989		65	.269	.542	227	61	9	1	17	7.5	40	57	23	69	6	3	1	119	5	3	2	2.1	.976	OF-56, DH-5
1990		131	.274	.543	481	132	14	2	37	7.7	83	101	72	158	19	2	1	182	7	1	2	1.5	.995	OF-88, DH-43
1991		154	.266	.556	572	152	32	1	**44**	7.7	115	122	78	152	26	6	2	245	5	9	0	1.7	.965	OF-131, DH-24
1992	2 teams	OAK A (97G –.246)		TEX A (22G –.233)																				
"	total	119	.244	.456	439	107	15	2	26	5.9	74	87	63	128	6	3	0	195	5	3	3	1.7	.985	OF-90, DH-28
1993	TEX A	60	.255	.455	231	59	14	1	10	4.3	30	46	16	62	6	3	0	94	4	3	2	1.7	.970	OF-49, DH-9, P-1
1994		111	.282	.552	429	121	19	2	31	7.2	88	90	69	114	15	0	0	0	0	0	0	0.0	.000	DH-111
1995	BOS A	102	.306	.556	396	121	25	1	24	6.1	64	81	42	93	4	1	0	1	0	0	0	0.0	1.000	DH-101, OF-1
1996		96	.289	.589	360	104	22	1	28	7.8	68	82	63	82	3	4	0	17	1	0	0	0.2	1.000	DH-84, OF-11
12 yrs.		1341	.272	.521	5071	1379	251	13	328	6.5	864	1033	623	1349	156	28	6	1795	56	50	17	1.4	.974	OF-881, DH-449, P-1

DIVISIONAL PLAYOFF SERIES

Year	Team	Games	BA	SA	AB	H	2B	3B	HR	HR%	R	RBI	BB	SO	SB	Pinch Hit AB	Pinch Hit H	PO	A	E	DP	TC/G	FA	G by Pos
1995	BOS A	3	.000	.000	13	0	0	0	0	0.0	0	0	2	2	0	0	0	4	0	0	0	1.3	1.000	DH-2, OF-1

LEAGUE CHAMPIONSHIP SERIES

Year	Team	Games	BA	SA	AB	H	2B	3B	HR	HR%	R	RBI	BB	SO	SB	Pinch Hit AB	Pinch Hit H	PO	A	E	DP	TC/G	FA	G by Pos
1988	OAK A	4	.313	.938	16	5	1	0	3	18.8	4	4	1	2	1	0	0	6	0	0	0	1.5	1.000	OF-4
1989		5	.294	.471	17	5	0	0	1	5.9	1	3	3	7	0	1	0	6	1	1	0	1.6	.875	OF-5
1990		4	.182	.182	11	2	0	0	0	0.0	3	1	5	5	2	0	0	14	0	0	0	3.5	1.000	OF-4
3 yrs.		13	.273	.568	44	12	1	0	4	9.1	8	8	9	14	3	1	0	26	1	1	0	2.2	.964	OF-13

WORLD SERIES

Year	Team	Games	BA	SA	AB	H	2B	3B	HR	HR%	R	RBI	BB	SO	SB	Pinch Hit AB	Pinch Hit H	PO	A	E	DP	TC/G	FA	G by Pos
1988	OAK A	5	.053	.211	19	1	0	0	1	5.3	1	5	2	5	1	0	0	8	0	0	0	1.6	1.000	OF-5
1989		4	.357	.571	14	5	0	0	1	7.1	5	3	4	3	1	0	0	6	0	0	0	1.5	1.000	OF-4
1990		4	.083	.333	12	1	0	0	1	8.3	2	2	2	3	0	1	0	4	0	0	0	1.3	1.000	OF-3
3 yrs.		13	.156	.356	45	7	0	0	3	6.7	7	10	8	11	2	1	0	18	0	0	0	1.5	1.000	OF-12

Mark Carreon

CARREON, MARK STEVEN
Son of Camilo Carreon.
B. July 19, 1963, Chicago, Ill.
BR TL 6' 170 lbs.

Year	Team	Games	BA	SA	AB	H	2B	3B	HR	HR%	R	RBI	BB	SO	SB	Pinch Hit AB	Pinch Hit H	PO	A	E	DP	TC/G	FA	G by Pos
1987	NY N	9	.250	.250	12	3	0	0	0	0.0	1	1	1	1	0	5	1	4	0	1	0	1.0	.800	OF-5
1988		7	.556	1.111	9	5	2	0	1	11.1	5	1	2	1	0	2	0	1	0	0	0	0.3	1.000	OF-4
1989		68	.308	.489	133	41	6	0	6	4.5	20	16	12	17	2	27	10	57	0	1	0	1.5	.983	OF-39
1990		82	.250	.473	188	47	12	0	10	5.3	30	26	15	29	1	24	4	87	1	0	0	1.5	1.000	OF-60
1991		106	.260	.331	254	66	6	0	4	1.6	18	21	12	26	2	35	12	96	4	3	1	1.3	.971	OF-77
1992	DET A	101	.232	.360	336	78	11	1	10	3.0	34	41	22	57	3	8	2	178	5	4	2	1.9	.979	OF-83, DH-13
1993	SF N	78	.327	.540	150	49	9	1	7	4.7	22	33	13	16	1	35	10	54	4	1	1	1.4	.951	OF-41, 1B-3
1994		51	.270	.400	100	27	4	0	3	3.0	8	20	7	20	0	21	6	44	0	1	0	1.4	.978	OF-33
1995		117	.301	.490	396	119	24	0	17	4.3	53	65	23	37	0	15	4	732	45	7	65	7.6	.991	1B-81, OF-22
1996	2 teams	SF N (81G –.260)		CLE A (38G –.324)																				
"	total	119	.281	.449	434	122	34	3	11	2.5	56	65	33	42	3	8	6	849	57	10	88	7.7	.989	1B-107, OF-10, DH-2
10 yrs.		738	.277	.438	2012	557	108	5	69	3.4	246	289	140	246	12	180	55	2102	116	30	157	3.9	.987	OF-374, 1B-191, DH-15

Year	Team	Games	BA	SA	AB	H	2B	3B	HR	HR%	R	RBI	BB	SO	SB	Pinch Hit AB	Pinch Hit H	PO	A	E	DP	TC/G	FA	G by Pos

Joe Carter

CARTER, JOSEPH CHRIS
B. Mar. 7, 1960, Oklahoma City, Okla.

BR TR 6'3" 210 lbs.

Year	Team	Games	BA	SA	AB	H	2B	3B	HR	HR%	R	RBI	BB	SO	SB	PH AB	PH H	PO	A	E	DP	TC/G	FA	G by Pos
1983	CHI N	23	.176	.235	51	9	1	1	0	0.0	6	1	0	21	1	5	1	26	0	0	0	1.6	1.000	OF-16
1984	CLE A	66	.275	.467	244	67	6	1	13	5.3	32	41	11	48	2	7	5	169	11	6	4	2.8	.968	OF-59, 1B-7
1985		143	.262	.409	489	128	27	0	15	3.1	64	59	25	74	24	4	0	311	17	6	4	2.2	.982	OF-135, 1B-11, DH-7, 2B-1, 3B-1
1986		162	.302	.514	663	200	36	9	29	4.4	108	**121**	32	95	29	1	1	800	55	10	52	5.0	.988	OF-104, 1B-70
1987		149	.264	.480	588	155	27	2	32	5.4	83	106	27	105	31	2	0	782	46	17	61	5.6	.980	1B-84, OF-62, DH-5
1988		157	.271	.478	621	168	36	6	27	4.3	85	98	35	82	27	1	0	444	8	7	3	2.9	.985	OF-156
1989		162	.243	.465	**651**	158	32	4	35	5.4	84	105	39	112	13	0	0	443	20	9	7	2.9	.981	OF-146, 1B-11, DH-8
1990	SD N	162	.232	.391	**634**	147	27	1	24	3.8	79	115	48	93	22	1	0	492	16	11	19	3.2	.979	OF-150, 1B-14
1991	TOR A	162	.273	.503	638	174	42	3	33	5.2	89	108	49	112	20	0	0	283	13	8	2	1.9	.974	OF-151, DH-11
1992		158	.264	.498	622	164	30	7	34	5.5	97	119	36	109	12	1	0	284	13	9	3	1.9	.971	OF-129, DH-24, 1B-4
1993		155	.254	.489	603	153	33	5	33	5.5	92	121	47	113	8	1	0	289	7	8	0	2.0	.974	OF-151, DH-3
1994		111	.271	.524	435	118	25	2	27	6.2	70	103	33	64	11	0	0	205	4	2	1	1.9	.991	OF-110, DH-1
1995		139	.253	.495	558	141	23	0	25	4.5	70	76	37	87	12	0	0	315	12	7	3	2.4	.979	OF-128, 1B-7, DH-5
1996		157	.253	.475	625	158	35	7	30	4.8	84	107	44	106	7	0	0	416	23	9	33	2.6	.980	OF-115, 1B-41, DH-15
14 yrs.		1906	.261	.470	7422	1940	380	48	357	4.8	1043	1280	463	1221	219	23	7	5259	245	109	192	2.9	.981	OF-1612, 1B-249, DH-79, 2B-1, 3B-1

LEAGUE CHAMPIONSHIP SERIES

Year	Team	Games	BA	SA	AB	H	2B	3B	HR	HR%	R	RBI	BB	SO	SB	PH AB	PH H	PO	A	E	DP	TC/G	FA	G by Pos
1991	TOR A	5	.263	.526	19	5	2	0	1	5.3	3	4	1	5	0	0	0	4	1	0	0	1.0	1.000	OF-3, DH-2
1992		6	.192	.308	26	5	0	0	1	3.8	2	3	2	4	2	0	0	16	1	1	1	2.3	.944	OF-6, 1B-2
1993		6	.259	.259	27	7	0	0	0	0.0	2	2	1	5	0	0	0	12	1	0	0	2.2	1.000	OF-6
3 yrs.		17	.236	.347	72	17	2	0	2	2.8	7	9	4	14	2	0	0	32	3	1	1	1.9	.972	OF-15, 1B-2, DH-2

WORLD SERIES

Year	Team	Games	BA	SA	AB	H	2B	3B	HR	HR%	R	RBI	BB	SO	SB	PH AB	PH H	PO	A	E	DP	TC/G	FA	G by Pos
1992	TOR A	6	.273	.636	22	6	2	0	2	9.1	2	3	3	2	0	0	0	27	1	0	0	4.7	1.000	OF-4, 1B-2
1993		6	.280	.560	25	7	1	0	2	8.0	6	8	0	4	0	0	0	13	0	2	0	2.5	.867	OF-6
2 yrs.		12	.277	.596	47	13	3	0	4	8.5 5th	8	11	3	6	0	0	0	40	1	2	0	3.6	.953	OF-10, 1B-2

Raul Casanova

CASANOVA, RAUL
B. Aug. 23, 1972, Humacao, Puerto Rico

BB TR 6' 200 lbs.

Year	Team	Games	BA	SA	AB	H	2B	3B	HR	HR%	R	RBI	BB	SO	SB	PH AB	PH H	PO	A	E	DP	TC/G	FA	G by Pos
1996	DET A	25	.188	.341	85	16	1	0	4	4.7	6	9	6	18	0	2	0	123	14	3	0	6.1	.979	C-22, DH-3, 3B-1

Pedro Castellano

CASTELLANO, PEDRO ORLANDO
Born Pedro Orlando Castellano (Arrieta).
B. Mar. 11, 1970, Barquisimeto, Venezuela

BR TR 6'1" 194 lbs.

Year	Team	Games	BA	SA	AB	H	2B	3B	HR	HR%	R	RBI	BB	SO	SB	PH AB	PH H	PO	A	E	DP	TC/G	FA	G by Pos
1993	CLR N	34	.183	.338	71	13	2	0	3	4.2	12	7	8	16	1	6	1	55	33	4	10	2.9	.957	3B-13, 1B-10, SS-5, 2B-4
1995		4	.000	.000	5	0	0	0	0	0.0	0	0	2	3	0	1	0	1	0	0	0	0.3	1.000	3B-3
1996		13	.118	.118	17	2	0	0	0	0.0	1	2	3	6	0	8	1	4	11	0	2	3.0	1.000	2B-3, 3B-1, OF-1
3 yrs.		51	.161	.280	93	15	2	0	3	3.2	13	9	13	25	1	15	2	60	44	4	12	2.7	.963	3B-17, 1B-10, 2B-7, SS-5, OF-1

Vinny Castilla

CASTILLA, VINICIO
Born Vinicio Castilla (Soria).
B. July 4, 1967, Oaxaca, Mexico

BR TR 6'1" 175 lbs.

Year	Team	Games	BA	SA	AB	H	2B	3B	HR	HR%	R	RBI	BB	SO	SB	PH AB	PH H	PO	A	E	DP	TC/G	FA	G by Pos
1991	ATL N	12	.200	.200	5	1	0	0	0	0.0	1	0	0	2	0	0	0	6	6	0	0	1.0	1.000	SS-12
1992		9	.250	.313	16	4	1	0	0	0.0	1	1	1	4	0	0	0	2	12	1	1	1.9	.933	SS-4, 3B-4
1993	CLR N	105	.255	.404	337	86	9	7	9	2.7	36	30	13	45	2	2	0	141	282	11	67	4.2	.975	SS-104
1994		52	.331	.500	130	43	11	1	3	2.3	16	18	7	23	2	10	3	67	78	2	23	3.4	.986	SS-18, 2B-14, 3B-9, 1B-2
1995		139	.309	.564	527	163	34	2	32	6.1	82	90	30	87	2	1	0	89	262	15	21	2.6	.959	3B-136, SS-5
1996		160	.304	.548	629	191	34	0	40	6.4	97	113	35	88	7	2	2	96	389	20	43	3.2	.960	3B-160
6 yrs.		477	.297	.516	1644	488	89	10	84	5.1	233	252	86	249	13	15	5	401	1029	49	155	3.2	.967	3B-309, SS-143, 2B-14, 1B-2

DIVISIONAL PLAYOFF SERIES

Year	Team	Games	BA	SA	AB	H	2B	3B	HR	HR%	R	RBI	BB	SO	SB	PH AB	PH H	PO	A	E	DP	TC/G	FA	G by Pos
1995	CLR N	4	.467	1.133	15	7	1	0	3	20.0	3	6	0	1	0	0	0	3	13	1	1	4.3	.941	3B-4

Alberto Castillo

CASTILLO, ALBERTO TERRERO
B. Feb. 10, 1970, San Juan de la Maguana, Dominican Republic

BR TR 6' 184 lbs.

Year	Team	Games	BA	SA	AB	H	2B	3B	HR	HR%	R	RBI	BB	SO	SB	PH AB	PH H	PO	A	E	DP	TC/G	FA	G by Pos
1995	NY N	13	.103	.103	29	3	0	0	0	0.0	2	0	3	9	1	0	0	66	10	2	0	6.5	.974	C-12
1996		6	.364	.364	11	4	0	0	0	0.0	1	0	0	4	0	0	0	23	0	0	0	3.8	1.000	C-6
2 yrs.		19	.175	.175	40	7	0	0	0	0.0	3	0	3	13	1	0	0	89	10	2	0	5.6	.980	C-18

Luis Castillo

CASTILLO, LUIS ANTONIO
Born Luis Antonio Castillo (Donato).
B. Sept. 4, 1975, San Pedro de Macoris, Dominican Republic

BB TR 5'11" 145 lbs.

Year	Team	Games	BA	SA	AB	H	2B	3B	HR	HR%	R	RBI	BB	SO	SB	PH AB	PH H	PO	A	E	DP	TC/G	FA	G by Pos
1996	FLA N	41	.262	.305	164	43	2	1	1	0.1	26	8	14	46	17	0	0	99	118	3	36	5.4	.986	2B-41

Juan Castro

CASTRO, JUAN GABRIEL
B. June 20, 1972, Los Mochis, Mexico

BR TR 5'10" 163 lbs.

Year	Team	Games	BA	SA	AB	H	2B	3B	HR	HR%	R	RBI	BB	SO	SB	PH AB	PH H	PO	A	E	DP	TC/G	FA	G by Pos
1995	LA N	11	.250	.250	4	1	0	0	0	0.0	0	0	1	1	0	0	0	3	7	0	2	0.9	1.000	3B-7, SS-4
1996		70	.197	.280	132	26	5	3	0	0.0	16	5	10	27	1	11	0	54	84	3	23	2.2	.979	SS-30, 3B-23, 2B-9, OF-1
2 yrs.		81	.199	.279	136	27	5	3	0	0.0	16	5	11	28	1	11	0	57	91	3	25	2.0	.980	SS-34, 3B-30, 2B-9, OF-1

DIVISIONAL PLAYOFF SERIES

Year	Team	Games	BA	SA	AB	H	2B	3B	HR	HR%	R	RBI	BB	SO	SB	PH AB	PH H	PO	A	E	DP	TC/G	FA	G by Pos
1996	LA N	2	.200	.400	5	1	1	0	0	0.0	0	1	1	1	0	0	0	4	3	0	1	3.5	1.000	2B-2

Year	Team	Games	BA	SA	AB	H	2B	3B	HR	HR%	R	RBI	BB	SO	SB	Pinch Hit AB	H	PO	A	E	DP	TC/G	FA	G by Pos

Andujar Cedeno

CEDENO, ANDUJAR
Born Andujar Cedeno (Donastorg).
Brother of Domingo Cedeno.
B. Aug. 21, 1969, La Romana, Dominican Republic

BR TR 6'1" 170 lbs.

Year	Team	Games	BA	SA	AB	H	2B	3B	HR	HR%	R	RBI	BB	SO	SB	PH AB	PH H	PO	A	E	DP	TC/G	FA	G by Pos
1990	HOU N	7	.000	.000	8	0	0	0	0	0.0	0	0	0	5	0	2	0	3	2	1	0	2.0	.833	SS-3
1991		67	.243	.418	251	61	13	2	9	3.6	27	36	9	74	4	1	0	88	151	18	36	3.9	.930	SS-66
1992		71	.173	.277	220	38	13	2	2	0.9	15	13	14	71	2	1	0	82	175	11	27	3.8	.959	SS-70
1993		149	.283	.412	505	143	24	4	11	2.2	69	56	48	97	9	1	1	155	376	25	78	3.7	.955	SS-149, 3B-1
1994		98	.263	.418	342	90	26	0	9	2.6	38	49	29	79	1	3	1	130	280	23	69	4.6	.947	SS-95
1995	SD N	120	.210	.308	390	82	16	2	6	1.5	42	31	28	92	5	1	1	139	305	17	58	3.9	.963	SS-116, 3B-1
1996	3 teams	SD N (49G –.234)			DET A (52G –.196)			HOU N (3G –.000)																
"	total	104	.212	.337	335	71	6	3	10	3.0	30	38	15	70	3	1	1	114	289	22	58	4.1	.948	SS-100, 3B-4
	7 yrs.	616	.236	.366	2051	485	98	13	47	2.3	221	223	143	488	26	12	4	711	1578	117	326	4.0	.951	SS-599, 3B-6

Domingo Cedeno

CEDENO, DOMINGO ANTONIO
Born Domingo Antonio Cedeno (Donastorg).
Brother of Andujar Cedeno.
B. Nov. 4, 1968, La Romana, Dominican Republic

BB TR 6'1" 170 lbs.

Year	Team	Games	BA	SA	AB	H	2B	3B	HR	HR%	R	RBI	BB	SO	SB	PH AB	PH H	PO	A	E	DP	TC/G	FA	G by Pos
1993	TOR A	15	.174	.174	46	8	0	0	0	0.0	5	7	1	10	1	1	0	10	39	1	5	3.3	.980	SS-10, 2B-5
1994		47	.196	.278	97	19	2	3	0	0.0	14	10	10	31	1	3	0	40	64	8	11	2.6	.929	2B-28, SS-8, 3B-6, OF-1
1995		51	.236	.360	161	38	6	1	4	2.5	18	14	10	35	0	1	0	85	131	3	25	4.3	.986	SS-30, 2B-20, 3B-1
1996	2 teams	TOR A (77G –.280)			CHI A (12G –.158)																			
"	total	89	.272	.346	301	82	12	2	2	0.7	46	20	15	64	6	9	2	132	202	10	55	4.4	.971	2B-64, SS-7, 3B-6, DH-1
	4 yrs.	202	.243	.326	605	147	20	6	6	1.0	83	51	36	140	8	14	2	267	436	22	96	3.9	.970	2B-117, SS-55, 3B-13, DH-1, OF-1

Roger Cedeno

CEDENO, ROGER LEANDRO
B. Aug. 16, 1974, Valencia, Venezuela

BB TR 6'1" 165 lbs.

Year	Team	Games	BA	SA	AB	H	2B	3B	HR	HR%	R	RBI	BB	SO	SB	PH AB	PH H	PO	A	E	DP	TC/G	FA	G by Pos
1995	LA N	40	.238	.286	42	10	2	0	0	0.0	4	3	3	10	1	5	1	43	0	1	0	1.2	.977	OF-36
1996		86	.246	.336	211	52	11	1	2	0.9	26	18	24	47	5	17	1	117	2	2	0	1.7	.983	OF-71
	2 yrs.	126	.245	.328	253	62	13	1	2	0.8	30	21	27	57	6	22	2	160	2	3	0	1.5	.982	OF-107

Raul Chavez

CHAVEZ, RAUL ALEXANDER
B. Mar. 1, 1879, Sedalia, Mo. D. June 25, 1956, Paramus, N.J.

BR TR 5'11" 175 lbs.

Year	Team	Games	BA	SA	AB	H	2B	3B	HR	HR%	R	RBI	BB	SO	SB	PH AB	PH H	PO	A	E	DP	TC/G	FA	G by Pos
1996	MON N	3	.200	.200	5	1	0	0	0	0.0	1	0	1	1	1	1	1	13	0	0	0	6.5	1.000	C-2

Archi Cianfrocco

CIANFROCCO, ANGELO DOMINIC
B. Oct. 6, 1966, Rome, N.Y.

BR TR 6'5" 200 lbs.

Year	Team	Games	BA	SA	AB	H	2B	3B	HR	HR%	R	RBI	BB	SO	SB	PH AB	PH H	PO	A	E	DP	TC/G	FA	G by Pos
1992	MON N	86	.241	.358	232	56	5	2	6	2.6	25	30	11	66	3	10	2	387	66	8	26	5.8	.983	1B-56, 3B-19, OF-5
1993	2 teams	MON N (12G –.235)			SD N (84G –.244)																			
"	total	96	.243	.416	296	72	11	2	12	4.1	30	48	17	69	2	2	2	243	97	10	29	3.3	.971	3B-64, 1B-42
1994	SD N	59	.219	.356	146	32	8	0	4	2.7	9	13	3	39	2	12	2	58	67	7	7	2.4	.947	1B-37, 1B-16, SS-1
1995		51	.263	.449	118	31	7	0	5	4.2	22	31	11	28	0	10	4	112	50	3	15	2.8	.982	1B-30, SS-15, OF-7, 3B-3, 2B-3
1996		79	.281	.411	192	54	13	3	2	1.0	21	32	8	56	1	21	2	195	51	3	18	3.6	.988	1B-33, 3B-11, SS-10, OF-8, 2B-6, C-1
	5 yrs.	371	.249	.396	984	245	44	7	29	2.9	107	154	50	258	8	55	12	995	331	31	95	3.7	.977	1B-177, 3B-134, SS-26, OF-20, 2B-9, C-1

DIVISIONAL PLAYOFF SERIES

Year	Team	Games	BA	SA	AB	H	2B	3B	HR	HR%	R	RBI	BB	SO	SB	PH AB	PH H	PO	A	E	DP	TC/G	FA	G by Pos
1996	SD N	3	.333	.333	3	1	0	0	0	0.0	1	0	0	1	0	0	0	8	2	0	1	3.3	1.000	1B-3

Jeff Cirillo

CIRILLO, JEFFREY HOWARD
B. Sept. 23, 1969, Pasadena, Calif.

BR TR 6'2" 190 lbs.

Year	Team	Games	BA	SA	AB	H	2B	3B	HR	HR%	R	RBI	BB	SO	SB	PH AB	PH H	PO	A	E	DP	TC/G	FA	G by Pos
1994	MIL A	39	.238	.381	126	30	9	0	3	2.4	17	12	11	16	0	3	1	23	60	3	7	2.3	.965	3B-37, 2B-1
1995		125	.277	.442	328	91	19	4	9	2.7	57	39	47	42	7	4	0	114	230	15	38	2.6	.958	3B-108, 2B-25, 1B-3, SS-2
1996		158	.325	.504	566	184	46	5	15	2.7	101	83	58	69	4	3	1	112	243	18	19	2.3	.952	3B-154, DH-3, 1B-2, 2B-1
	3 yrs.	322	.299	.469	1020	305	74	9	27	2.6	175	134	116	127	11	10	2	249	533	36	64	2.4	.956	3B-299, 2B-27, 1B-5, DH-3, SS-2

Dave Clark

CLARK, DAVID EARL
B. Sept. 3, 1962, Tupelo, Miss.

BL TR 6'2" 200 lbs.

Year	Team	Games	BA	SA	AB	H	2B	3B	HR	HR%	R	RBI	BB	SO	SB	PH AB	PH H	PO	A	E	DP	TC/G	FA	G by Pos
1986	CLE A	18	.276	.448	58	16	1	0	3	5.2	10	9	7	11	1	0	0	26	0	0	0	1.5	1.000	OF-10, DH-7
1987		29	.207	.368	87	18	5	0	3	3.4	11	12	2	24	1	6	0	24	1	0	0	1.0	1.000	OF-13, DH-12
1988		63	.263	.359	156	41	4	1	3	1.9	11	18	17	28	0	19	4	36	0	2	0	0.8	.947	DH-27, OF-23
1989		102	.237	.379	253	60	12	0	8	3.2	21	29	30	63	0	29	7	27	0	1	0	0.4	.964	DH-55, OF-21
1990	CHI N	84	.275	.409	171	47	4	2	5	2.9	22	20	8	40	7	42	11	60	2	0	0	1.6	1.000	OF-39
1991	KC A	11	.200	.200	10	2	0	0	0	0.0	1	1	1	1	0	10	2	0	0	0	0	0.0		OF-1, DH-1
1992	PIT N	23	.212	.394	33	7	0	0	2	6.1	3	7	6	8	0	11	2	10	0	0	0	1.3	1.000	OF-8
1993		110	.271	.444	277	75	11	2	11	4.0	43	46	38	58	1	22	3	132	3	6	1	1.5	.957	OF-91
1994		86	.296	.489	223	66	11	1	10	4.5	37	46	22	38	0	24	8	107	5	3	1	2.0	.974	OF-57
1995		77	.281	.372	196	55	6	0	4	2.0	30	24	24	38	3	26	9	98	1	4	0	1.7	.961	OF-61
1996	2 teams	PIT N (92G –.275)			LA N (15G –.200)																			
"	total	107	.270	.447	226	61	12	2	8	3.5	28	36	34	53	2	47	13	81	3	1	1	1.4	.988	OF-62
	11 yrs.	710	.265	.415	1690	448	66	8	57	3.4	217	248	189	372	17	236	59	601	15	17	3	1.3	.973	OF-386, DH-102

DIVISIONAL PLAYOFF SERIES

Year	Team	Games	BA	SA	AB	H	2B	3B	HR	HR%	R	RBI	BB	SO	SB	PH AB	PH H	PO	A	E	DP	TC/G	FA	G by Pos
1996	LA N	2	.000	.000	2	0	0	0	0	0.0	0	0	0	2	0	2	0	0	0	0	0	0.0	—	

Year	Team	Games	BA	SA	AB	H	2B	3B	HR	HR%	R	RBI	BB	SO	SB	Pinch Hit AB	H	PO	A	E	DP	TC/G	FA	G by Pos

Phil Clark

CLARK, PHILLIP BENJAMIN
Brother of Jerald Clark.
B. May 6, 1968, Crockett, Tex.

BR TR 6′ 180 lbs.

Year	Team	Games	BA	SA	AB	H	2B	3B	HR	HR%	R	RBI	BB	SO	SB	Pinch Hit AB	H	PO	A	E	DP	TC/G	FA	G by Pos
1992	DET A	23	.407	.537	54	22	4	0	1	1.9	3	5	6	9	1	6	3	27	0	2	0	1.5	.931	OF-13, DH-7
1993	SD N	102	.313	.496	240	75	17	0	9	3.8	33	33	8	31	2	37	13	243	35	8	14	3.8	.972	OF-36, 1B-24, C-11, 3B-5
1994		61	.215	.356	149	32	6	0	5	3.4	14	20	5	17	1	20	4	148	14	4	14	3.5	.976	1B-24, OF-17, C-5, 3B-1
1995		75	.216	.309	97	21	3	0	2	2.1	12	7	8	18	0	38	8	32	0	0	1	0.9	1.000	OF-34, 1B-2
1996	BOS A	3	.000	.000	3	0	0	0	0	0.0	0	0	0	1	0	2	0	2	1	0	0	1.0	1.000	1B-1, 3B-1, DH-1
5 yrs.		264	.276	.425	543	150	30	0	17	3.1	62	65	27	76	4	103	28	452	50	14	29	2.8	.973	OF-100, 1B-51, C-16, DH-8, 3B-7

Tony Clark

CLARK, ANTHONY CHRISTOPHER
B. June 15, 1972, Newton, Kans.

BB TR 6′8″ 205 lbs.

Year	Team	Games	BA	SA	AB	H	2B	3B	HR	HR%	R	RBI	BB	SO	SB	Pinch Hit AB	H	PO	A	E	DP	TC/G	FA	G by Pos
1995	DET A	27	.238	.396	101	24	5	1	3	3.0	10	11	8	30	0	0	0	252	18	4	25	10.1	.985	1B-27
1996		100	.250	.503	376	94	14	0	27	7.2	56	72	29	127	0	2	0	766	53	6	82	8.4	.993	1B-86, DH-12
2 yrs.		127	.247	.480	477	118	19	1	30	6.3	66	83	37	157	0	2	0	1018	71	10	107	8.8	.991	1B-113, DH-12

Will Clark

CLARK, WILLIAM NUSCHLER (The Thrill)
B. Mar. 13, 1964, New Orleans, La.

BL TL 6′2″ 190 lbs.

Year	Team	Games	BA	SA	AB	H	2B	3B	HR	HR%	R	RBI	BB	SO	SB	Pinch Hit AB	H	PO	A	E	DP	TC/G	FA	G by Pos
1986	SF N	111	.287	.444	408	117	27	2	11	2.7	66	41	34	76	4	9	6	942	72	11	76	10.0	.989	1B-102
1987		150	.308	.580	529	163	29	5	35	6.6	89	91	49	98	5	11	3	1253	103	13	130	9.8	.991	1B-139
1988		162	.282	.508	575	162	31	6	29	5.0	102	109	100	129	9	5	0	1492	104	12	126	10.2	.993	1B-158
1989		159	.333	.546	588	196	38	9	23	3.9	104	111	74	103	8	1	0	1445	111	10	117	9.9	.994	1B-158
1990		154	.295	.448	600	177	25	5	19	3.2	91	95	62	97	8	1	0	1456	119	12	118	10.4	.992	1B-153
1991		148	.301	**.536**	565	170	32	7	29	5.1	84	116	51	91	4	3	1	1273	110	4	115	9.6	.997	1B-144
1992		144	.300	.476	513	154	40	1	16	3.1	69	73	73	82	12	2	1	1275	105	10	130	9.9	.993	1B-141
1993		132	.283	.432	491	139	27	2	14	2.9	82	73	63	68	2	2	0	1078	88	14	113	9.1	.988	1B-129
1994	TEX A	110	.329	.501	389	128	24	2	13	3.3	73	80	71	59	5	2	0	968	73	10	85	9.7	.990	1B-107, DH-1
1995		123	.302	.480	454	137	27	3	16	3.5	85	92	68	50	0	1	0	1077	87	7	120	9.5	.994	1B-122, DH-1
1996		117	.284	.436	436	124	25	1	13	3.0	69	72	64	67	2	0	0	954	70	4	89	8.8	.996	1B-117
11 yrs.		1510	.300	.492	5548	1667	325	43	218	3.9	914	953	709	920	59	36	11	13213	1042	107	1219	9.8	.993	1B-1470, DH-2

DIVISIONAL PLAYOFF SERIES

Year	Team	Games	BA	SA	AB	H	2B	3B	HR	HR%	R	RBI	BB	SO	SB	Pinch Hit AB	H	PO	A	E	DP	TC/G	FA	G by Pos
1996	TEX A	4	.125	.125	16	2	0	0	0	0.0	1	0	3	2	0	0	0	35	6	0	5	9.8	1.000	1B-4

LEAGUE CHAMPIONSHIP SERIES

Year	Team	Games	BA	SA	AB	H	2B	3B	HR	HR%	R	RBI	BB	SO	SB	Pinch Hit AB	H	PO	A	E	DP	TC/G	FA	G by Pos
1987	SF N	7	.360	.560	25	9	2	0	1	4.0	3	3	3	6	1	0	0	63	7	1	10	10.1	.986	1B-7
1989		5	.650	1.200	20	13	3	1	2	10.0	8	8	2	2	0	0	0	43	6	0	6	9.8	1.000	1B-5
2 yrs.		12	.489 1st	.844 1st	45	22	5	1	3	6.7 8th	11	11	5	8	1	0	0	106	13	1	16	10.0	.992	1B-12

WORLD SERIES

Year	Team	Games	BA	SA	AB	H	2B	3B	HR	HR%	R	RBI	BB	SO	SB	Pinch Hit AB	H	PO	A	E	DP	TC/G	FA	G by Pos
1989	SF N	4	.250	.313	16	4	1	0	0	0.0	2	0	1	3	0	0	0	40	2	0	2	10.5	1.000	1B-4

Royce Clayton

CLAYTON, ROYCE SPENCER
B. Jan. 2, 1970, Burbank, Calif.

BR TR 6′ 175 lbs.

Year	Team	Games	BA	SA	AB	H	2B	3B	HR	HR%	R	RBI	BB	SO	SB	Pinch Hit AB	H	PO	A	E	DP	TC/G	FA	G by Pos
1991	SF N	9	.115	.154	26	3	1	0	0	0.0	0	2	1	6	0	0	0	16	6	3	1	3.1	.880	SS-8
1992		98	.224	.308	321	72	7	4	4	1.2	31	24	26	63	8	1	0	142	257	11	51	4.3	.973	SS-94, 3B-1
1993		153	.282	.372	549	155	21	5	6	1.1	54	70	38	91	11	1	0	251	449	27	103	4.8	.963	SS-153
1994		108	.236	.327	385	91	14	6	3	0.8	38	30	30	74	23	1	0	178	331	14	62	4.8	.973	SS-108
1995		138	.244	.342	509	124	29	3	5	1.0	56	58	38	109	24	1	0	223	412	20	91	4.8	.969	SS-136
1996	STL N	129	.277	.371	491	136	20	4	6	1.2	64	35	33	89	33	13	3	170	346	15	67	4.7	.972	SS-113
6 yrs.		635	.255	.346	2281	581	92	22	24	1.1	243	219	166	432	99	18	3	980	1801	90	375	4.7	.969	SS-612, 3B-1

DIVISIONAL PLAYOFF SERIES

Year	Team	Games	BA	SA	AB	H	2B	3B	HR	HR%	R	RBI	BB	SO	SB	Pinch Hit AB	H	PO	A	E	DP	TC/G	FA	G by Pos
1996	STL N	2	.333	.333	6	2	0	0	0	0.0	1	0	3	1	0	0	0	4	5	0	0	4.5	1.000	SS-2

LEAGUE CHAMPIONSHIP SERIES

Year	Team	Games	BA	SA	AB	H	2B	3B	HR	HR%	R	RBI	BB	SO	SB	Pinch Hit AB	H	PO	A	E	DP	TC/G	FA	G by Pos
1996	STL N	5	.350	.350	20	7	0	0	0	0.0	4	1	1	4	1	0	0	5	16	2	2	4.6	.913	SS-5

Alan Cockrell

COCKRELL, ATLEE ALAN
B. Dec. 5, 1962, Kansas City, Kans.

BR TR 6′2″ 210 lbs.

Year	Team	Games	BA	SA	AB	H	2B	3B	HR	HR%	R	RBI	BB	SO	SB	Pinch Hit AB	H	PO	A	E	DP	TC/G	FA	G by Pos
1996	CLR N	9	.250	.375	8	2	1	0	0	0.0	0	2	0	4	0	8	2	0	0	0	0	—	—	OF-1

Greg Colbrunn

COLBRUNN, GREGORY JOSEPH
B. July 26, 1969, Fontana, Calif.

BR TR 6′ 190 lbs.

Year	Team	Games	BA	SA	AB	H	2B	3B	HR	HR%	R	RBI	BB	SO	SB	Pinch Hit AB	H	PO	A	E	DP	TC/G	FA	G by Pos
1992	MON N	52	.268	.351	168	45	8	0	2	1.2	12	18	6	34	3	5	0	363	29	3	24	8.4	.992	1B-47
1993		70	.255	.392	153	39	9	0	4	2.6	15	23	6	33	4	10	4	372	27	2	31	6.6	.995	1B-61
1994	FLA N	47	.303	.484	155	47	10	0	6	3.9	17	31	9	27	1	5	2	303	26	4	28	8.1	.988	1B-41
1995		138	.277	.453	528	146	22	1	23	4.4	70	89	22	69	11	4	2	1070	88	5	107	8.7	.996	1B-134
1996		141	.286	.438	511	146	26	2	16	3.1	60	69	25	76	4	8	2	1168	102	6	130	9.5	.995	1B-134
5 yrs.		448	.279	.434	1515	423	75	3	51	3.4	174	230	68	239	23	32	10	3276	272	20	320	8.6	.994	1B-417

Alex Cole

COLE, ALEXANDER, JR.
B. Aug. 17, 1965, Fayetteville, N. C.

BL TL 6′2″ 170 lbs.

Year	Team	Games	BA	SA	AB	H	2B	3B	HR	HR%	R	RBI	BB	SO	SB	Pinch Hit AB	H	PO	A	E	DP	TC/G	FA	G by Pos
1990	CLE A	63	.300	.357	227	68	5	4	0	0.0	43	13	28	38	40	1	0	145	3	6	1	2.6	.961	OF-59, DH-1
1991		122	.295	.354	387	114	17	3	0	0.0	58	21	58	47	27	7	1	256	6	8	1	2.4	.970	OF-107, DH-6
1992	2 teams	CLE A (41G –.206)		PIT N (64G –.278)																				
"	total	105	.255	.315	302	77	4	7	0	0.0	44	15	28	67	16	30	4	118	6	2	1	1.6	.984	OF-77, DH-3

Year	Team	Games	BA	SA	AB	H	2B	3B	HR	HR%	R	RBI	BB	SO	SB	Pinch Hit AB	Pinch Hit H	PO	A	E	DP	TC/G	FA	G by Pos

Alex Cole *continued*

Year	Team	Games	BA	SA	AB	H	2B	3B	HR	HR%	R	RBI	BB	SO	SB	AB	H	PO	A	E	DP	TC/G	FA	G by Pos
1993	CLR N	126	.256	.305	348	89	9	4	0	0.0	50	24	43	58	30	28	6	219	5	4	1	2.5	.982	OF-93
1994	MIN A	105	.296	.403	345	102	15	5	4	1.2	68	23	44	60	29	9	2	245	4	8	0	2.5	.969	OF-100, DH-1
1995		28	.342	.468	79	27	3	2	1	1.3	10	14	8	15	1	9	3	44	1	3	0	1.9	.938	OF-23, DH-2
1996	BOS A	24	.222	.319	72	16	5	1	0	0.0	13	7	8	11	5	2	0	37	1	1	1	1.6	.974	OF-24
7 yrs.		573	.280	.351	1760	493	58	26	5	0.3	286	117	217	296	148	85	16	1064	26	32	5	2.3	.971	OF-483, DH-13

LEAGUE CHAMPIONSHIP SERIES

Year	Team	Games	BA	SA	AB	H	2B	3B	HR	HR%	R	RBI	BB	SO	SB	AB	H	PO	A	E	DP	TC/G	FA	G by Pos
1992	PIT N	4	.200	.200	10	2	0	0	0	0.0	2	1	3	2	1	0	0	7	1	0	1	2.0	1.000	OF-4

Vince Coleman

COLEMAN, VINCENT MAURICE (Vincent Van Go)
B. Sept. 22, 1961, Jacksonville, Fla.   BB TR 6′   170 lbs.

Year	Team	Games	BA	SA	AB	H	2B	3B	HR	HR%	R	RBI	BB	SO	SB	AB	H	PO	A	E	DP	TC/G	FA	G by Pos
1985	STL N	151	.267	.335	636	170	20	10	1	0.2	107	40	50	115	110	1	0	305	16	7	1	2.2	.979	OF-150
1986		154	.232	.280	600	139	13	8	0	0.0	94	29	60	98	107	2	1	300	12	9	2	2.2	.972	OF-149
1987		151	.289	.358	623	180	14	10	3	0.5	121	43	70	126	109	1	0	274	16	9	3	2.0	.970	OF-150
1988		153	.260	.339	616	160	20	10	3	0.5	77	38	49	111	81	2	0	290	14	9	1	2.1	.971	OF-150
1989		145	.254	.334	563	143	21	9	2	0.4	94	28	50	90	65	5	2	247	5	10	1	1.8	.962	OF-142
1990		124	.292	.400	497	145	18	9	6	1.2	73	39	35	88	77	5	0	244	12	5	2	2.2	.981	OF-120
1991	NY N	72	.255	.327	278	71	7	5	1	0.4	45	17	39	47	37	2	0	132	5	3	0	2.0	.979	OF-70
1992		71	.275	.358	229	63	11	1	2	0.9	37	21	27	41	24	8	3	112	2	1	2	1.9	.991	OF-61
1993		92	.279	.375	373	104	14	8	2	0.5	64	25	21	58	38	3	1	162	5	3	0	1.9	.982	OF-90
1994	KC A	104	.240	.340	438	105	14	12	2	0.5	61	33	29	72	50	0	0	163	11	7	1	1.8	.961	OF-99, DH-4
1995	2 teams KC A (75G –.287) SEA A (40G –.290)																							
"	total	115	.288	.398	455	131	23	6	5	1.1	66	29	37	80	42	2	1	190	9	4	1	1.8	.980	OF-107, DH-4
1996	CIN N	33	.155	.226	84	13	1	1	1	1.2	10	4	9	31	12	10	2	28	2	1	0	1.5	.968	OF-20
12 yrs.		1365	.264	.345	5392	1424	176	89	28	0.5	849	346	476	957	752 5th	41	10	2447	109	68	14	2.0	.974	OF-1308, DH-8

DIVISIONAL PLAYOFF SERIES

Year	Team	Games	BA	SA	AB	H	2B	3B	HR	HR%	R	RBI	BB	SO	SB	AB	H	PO	A	E	DP	TC/G	FA	G by Pos
1995	SEA A	5	.217	.435	23	5	0	1	1	4.3	6	1	2	4	1	0	0	14	0	0	0	2.8	1.000	OF-5

LEAGUE CHAMPIONSHIP SERIES

Year	Team	Games	BA	SA	AB	H	2B	3B	HR	HR%	R	RBI	BB	SO	SB	AB	H	PO	A	E	DP	TC/G	FA	G by Pos
1985	STL N	3	.286	.286	14	4	0	0	0	0.0	2	1	0	2	1	0	0	8	0	0	0	2.7	1.000	OF-3
1987		7	.269	.308	26	7	1	0	0	0.0	3	4	4	6	1	0	0	9	1	0	0	1.4	1.000	OF-7
1995	SEA A	6	.100	.100	20	2	0	0	0	0.0	0	0	2	6	4	0	0	12	0	0	0	2.4	1.000	OF-5
3 yrs.		16	.217	.233	60	13	1	0	0	0.0	5	5	6	14	6 8th	0	0	29	1	0	0	2.0	1.000	OF-15

WORLD SERIES

Year	Team	Games	BA	SA	AB	H	2B	3B	HR	HR%	R	RBI	BB	SO	SB	AB	H	PO	A	E	DP	TC/G	FA	G by Pos
1987	STL N	7	.143	.214	28	4	2	0	0	0.0	5	2	2	10	6	0	0	10	2	0	0	1.7	1.000	OF-7

Jeff Conine

CONINE, JEFFREY GUY
B. June 27, 1966, Tacoma, Wash.   BR TR 6′1″   205 lbs.

Year	Team	Games	BA	SA	AB	H	2B	3B	HR	HR%	R	RBI	BB	SO	SB	AB	H	PO	A	E	DP	TC/G	FA	G by Pos
1990	KC A	9	.250	.350	20	5	2	0	0	0.0	3	2	5	2	0	0	0	39	4	1	7	4.9	.977	1B-9
1992		28	.253	.352	91	23	5	2	0	0.0	10	9	8	23	0	0	0	75	3	0	1	2.8	1.000	OF-23, 1B-4, DH-1
1993	FLA N	162	.292	.403	595	174	24	3	12	2.0	75	79	52	135	2	4	1	403	25	2	11	2.3	.995	OF-147, 1B-43
1994		115	.319	.525	451	144	27	6	18	4.0	60	82	40	92	1	1	0	409	24	6	19	3.1	.986	OF-97, 1B-46
1995		133	.302	.520	483	146	26	2	25	5.2	72	105	66	94	2	7	1	292	18	6	11	2.4	.981	OF-118, 1B-14
1996		157	.293	.484	597	175	32	2	26	4.4	84	95	62	121	1	1	0	479	48	8	35	3.0	.985	OF-128, 1B-48
6 yrs.		604	.298	.472	2237	667	116	15	81	3.6	304	372	230	470	6	13	2	1697	122	23	84	2.7	.988	OF-513, 1B-164, DH-1

Ron Coomer

COOMER, RONALD BRYAN
B. Nov. 18, 1966, Crest Hill, Ill.   BR TR 5′11″   195 lbs.

Year	Team	Games	BA	SA	AB	H	2B	3B	HR	HR%	R	RBI	BB	SO	SB	AB	H	PO	A	E	DP	TC/G	FA	G by Pos
1995	MIN A	37	.257	.455	101	26	3	1	5	5.0	15	19	9	11	0	5	0	138	33	2	14	4.3	.988	1B-22, 3B-13, DH-4, OF-1
1996		95	.296	.511	233	69	12	1	12	5.2	34	41	17	24	3	27	10	274	42	4	27	3.5	.988	1B-57, OF-23, 3B-9, DH-3
2 yrs.		132	.284	.494	334	95	15	2	17	5.1	49	60	26	35	3	32	10	412	75	6	41	3.7	.988	1B-79, OF-24, 3B-22, DH-7

Joey Cora

CORA, JOSE MANUEL
Born Jose Manuel Cora (Amaro).
B. May 14, 1965, Caguas, Puerto Rico   BB TR 5′7″   150 lbs.

Year	Team	Games	BA	SA	AB	H	2B	3B	HR	HR%	R	RBI	BB	SO	SB	AB	H	PO	A	E	DP	TC/G	FA	G by Pos
1987	SD N	77	.237	.282	241	57	7	2	0	0.0	23	13	28	26	15	8	2	123	200	10	32	4.6	.970	2B-66, SS-6
1989		12	.316	.368	19	6	1	0	0	0.0	5	1	1	0	1	0	0	11	15	2	3	2.8	.929	SS-7, 3B-2, 2B-1
1990		51	.270	.300	100	27	3	0	0	0.0	12	2	6	9	8	8	0	59	49	11	15	3.2	.908	SS-21, 2B-15, C-1
1991	CHI A	100	.241	.276	228	55	2	3	0	0.0	37	18	20	21	11	7	1	107	192	10	36	3.6	.968	2B-80, SS-5, DH-2
1992		68	.246	.320	122	30	7	1	0	0.0	27	9	22	13	10	9	2	60	84	3	22	2.7	.980	2B-28, DH-16, SS-6, 3B-5
1993		153	.268	.349	579	155	15	13	2	0.3	95	51	67	63	20	3	0	296	413	19	85	4.7	.974	2B-151, 3B-3
1994		90	.276	.362	312	86	13	4	2	0.6	55	30	38	32	8	6	2	161	195	8	47	4.3	.978	2B-84
1995	SEA A	120	.297	.372	427	127	19	2	3	0.7	64	39	37	31	18	9	2	206	261	23	51	4.3	.953	2B-112, SS-1
1996		144	.291	.417	530	154	37	6	6	1.1	90	45	35	32	5	17	4	299	311	13	88	4.4	.979	2B-140, SS-2
9 yrs.		815	.272	.353	2558	697	104	31	13	0.5	408	208	254	227	96	67	13	1322	1720	99	379	4.2	.968	2B-677, SS-46, DH-18, 3B-11, C-1

DIVISIONAL PLAYOFF SERIES

Year	Team	Games	BA	SA	AB	H	2B	3B	HR	HR%	R	RBI	BB	SO	SB	AB	H	PO	A	E	DP	TC/G	FA	G by Pos
1995	SEA A	5	.316	.526	19	6	1	0	1	5.3	7	1	3	0	1	0	0	10	12	1	2	4.6	.957	2B-5

LEAGUE CHAMPIONSHIP SERIES

Year	Team	Games	BA	SA	AB	H	2B	3B	HR	HR%	R	RBI	BB	SO	SB	AB	H	PO	A	E	DP	TC/G	FA	G by Pos
1993	CHI A	6	.136	.136	22	3	0	0	0	0.0	1	1	3	6	0	0	0	18	20	3	2	6.8	.927	2B-6
1995	SEA A	6	.174	.217	23	4	1	0	0	0.0	3	0	1	0	2	0	0	15	12	1	3	4.7	.964	2B-6
2 yrs.		12	.156	.178	45	7	1	0	0	0.0	4	1	4	6	2	0	0	33	32	4	5	5.8	.942	2B-12

Year	Team	Games	BA	SA	AB	H	2B	3B	HR	HR%	R	RBI	BB	SO	SB	Pinch Hit AB	Pinch Hit H	PO	A	E	DP	TC/G	FA	G by Pos

Marty Cordova

CORDOVA, MARTIN KEEVIN
B. July 10, 1969, Las Vegas, Nev.
BR TR 6' 200 lbs.

Year	Team	Games	BA	SA	AB	H	2B	3B	HR	HR%	R	RBI	BB	SO	SB	PH AB	PH H	PO	A	E	DP	TC/G	FA	G by Pos
1995	MIN A	137	.277	.486	512	142	27	4	24	4.7	81	84	52	111	20	0	0	345	12	5	1	2.6	.986	OF-137
1996		145	.309	.478	569	176	46	1	16	2.8	97	111	53	96	11	1	0	327	9	3	0	2.3	.991	OF-145
2 yrs.		282	.294	.482	1081	318	73	5	40	3.7	178	195	105	207	31	1	0	672	21	8	1	2.5	.989	OF-282

Felipe Crespo

CRESPO, FELIPE JAVIER
Born Felipe Javier Crespo (Clausio)
B. Mar. 5, 1973, Rio Piedras, Puerto Rico
BB TR 5'11" 195 lbs.

Year	Team	Games	BA	SA	AB	H	2B	3B	HR	HR%	R	RBI	BB	SO	SB	PH AB	PH H	PO	A	E	DP	TC/G	FA	G by Pos
1996	TOR A	22	.184	.265	49	9	4	0	0	0.0	6	4	12	13	1	3	0	34	38	1	10	4.1	.986	2B-10, 3B-6, 1B-2

Fausto Cruz

CRUZ, FAUSTO SANTIAGO
B. May 1, 1972, Monte Cristi, Dominican Republic
BR TR 5'10" 165 lbs.

Year	Team	Games	BA	SA	AB	H	2B	3B	HR	HR%	R	RBI	BB	SO	SB	PH AB	PH H	PO	A	E	DP	TC/G	FA	G by Pos
1994	OAK A	17	.107	.107	28	3	0	0	0	0.0	2	0	4	6	0	4	0	17	23	2	3	2.8	.952	SS-10, 3B-4, 2B-1
1995		8	.217	.217	23	5	0	0	0	0.0	0	5	3	5	1	0	0	9	24	1	2	4.3	.971	SS-8
1996	DET A	14	.237	.289	38	9	2	0	0	0.0	5	0	1	11	0	2	0	13	30	6	5	3.8	.878	2B-8, SS-4, DH-1
3 yrs.		39	.191	.213	89	17	2	0	0	0.0	7	5	8	22	1	6	0	39	77	9	10	3.5	.928	SS-22, 2B-9, 3B-4, DH-1

Jacob Cruz

CRUZ, JACOB
B. Jan. 28, 1973, Oxnard, Calif.
BL TL 6' 175 lbs.

Year	Team	Games	BA	SA	AB	H	2B	3B	HR	HR%	R	RBI	BB	SO	SB	PH AB	PH H	PO	A	E	DP	TC/G	FA	G by Pos
1996	SF N	33	.234	.390	77	18	3	0	3	3.9	10	10	12	24	0	8	1	41	1	1	0	1.9	.977	OF-23

Midre Cummings

CUMMINGS, MIDRE ALMERIC
B. Oct. 14, 1971, St. Croix, Virgin Islands
BB TR 6'1" 190 lbs.

Year	Team	Games	BA	SA	AB	H	2B	3B	HR	HR%	R	RBI	BB	SO	SB	PH AB	PH H	PO	A	E	DP	TC/G	FA	G by Pos
1993	PIT N	13	.111	.139	36	4	1	0	0	0.0	5	3	4	9	0	2	0	21	0	0	0	1.9	1.000	OF-11
1994		24	.244	.326	86	21	4	0	1	1.2	11	12	4	18	0	0	0	48	1	2	1	2.1	.961	OF-24
1995		59	.243	.342	152	37	7	1	2	1.3	13	15	13	30	1	23	8	79	2	1	0	2.0	.988	OF-41
1996		24	.224	.388	85	19	3	1	3	3.5	11	7	0	16	0	4	0	49	0	1	0	2.4	.980	OF-21
4 yrs.		120	.226	.329	359	81	15	2	6	1.7	40	37	21	73	1	29	8	197	3	4	1	2.1	.980	OF-97

Chad Curtis

CURTIS, CHAD DAVID
B. Nov. 6, 1968, Marion, Ind.
BR TR 5'10" 175 lbs.

Year	Team	Games	BA	SA	AB	H	2B	3B	HR	HR%	R	RBI	BB	SO	SB	PH AB	PH H	PO	A	E	DP	TC/G	FA	G by Pos
1992	CAL A	139	.259	.372	441	114	16	2	10	2.3	59	46	51	71	43	5	0	250	16	6	3	2.0	.978	OF-135, DH-1
1993		152	.285	.369	583	166	25	3	6	1.0	94	59	70	89	48	2	1	428	14	9	6	2.9	.980	OF-151, 2B-3
1994		114	.256	.397	453	116	23	4	11	2.4	67	50	37	69	25	0	0	331	9	4	0	3.0	.988	OF-114
1995	DET A	144	.268	.435	586	157	29	3	21	3.6	96	67	70	93	27	0	0	361	5	3	0	2.6	.992	OF-144
1996	2 teams DET A (104G –.263)																							LA N (43G –.212)
"	total	147	.252	.377	504	127	25	1	12	2.4	85	46	70	88	18	12	2	305	8	10	2	2.2	.969	OF-144
5 yrs.		696	.265	.391	2567	680	118	13	60	2.3	401	268	298	410	161	19	3	1675	52	32	11	2.5	.982	OF-688, 2B-3, DH-1

DIVISIONAL PLAYOFF SERIES

Year	Team	Games	BA	SA	AB	H	2B	3B	HR	HR%	R	RBI	BB	SO	SB	PH AB	PH H	PO	A	E	DP	TC/G	FA	G by Pos
1996	LA N	1	.000	.000	2	0	0	0	0	0.0	0	0	1	1	0	0	0	2	0	0	0	2.0	1.000	OF-1

Milt Cuyler

CUYLER, MILTON
B. Oct. 7, 1968, Macon, Ga.
BB TR 5'10" 175 lbs.

Year	Team	Games	BA	SA	AB	H	2B	3B	HR	HR%	R	RBI	BB	SO	SB	PH AB	PH H	PO	A	E	DP	TC/G	FA	G by Pos
1990	DET A	19	.255	.353	51	13	3	1	0	0.0	8	8	5	10	1	0	0	38	2	1	0	2.4	.976	OF-17
1991		154	.257	.337	475	122	15	7	3	0.6	77	33	52	92	41	1	0	411	7	6	3	2.8	.986	OF-151
1992		89	.241	.316	291	70	11	1	3	1.0	39	28	10	62	8	0	0	232	4	4	1	2.7	.983	OF-89
1993		82	.213	.313	249	53	11	7	0	0.0	46	19	19	53	13	2	0	211	2	7	1	2.8	.968	OF-80
1994		48	.241	.310	116	28	3	1	1	0.9	20	11	13	21	5	0	0	78	1	2	0	1.8	.975	OF-46
1995		41	.205	.307	88	18	1	4	0	0.0	15	5	8	16	2	2	0	51	2	4	0	1.5	.930	OF-36, DH-2
1996	BOS A	50	.200	.300	110	22	1	2	2	1.8	19	12	13	19	7	3	0	104	0	3	0	2.3	.972	OF-45, DH-2
7 yrs.		483	.236	.322	1380	326	45	23	9	0.7	224	116	120	273	77	8	0	1125	18	27	5	2.5	.977	OF-464, DH-3

Johnny Damon

DAMON, JOHNNY DAVID
B. Nov. 5, 1973, Fort Riley, Kans.
BL TL 6' 175 lbs.

Year	Team	Games	BA	SA	AB	H	2B	3B	HR	HR%	R	RBI	BB	SO	SB	PH AB	PH H	PO	A	E	DP	TC/G	FA	G by Pos
1995	KC A	47	.282	.441	188	53	11	5	3	1.6	32	23	12	22	7	1	0	110	0	1	0	2.4	.991	OF-47
1996		145	.271	.368	517	140	22	5	6	1.2	61	50	31	64	25	8	2	349	5	6	3	2.5	.983	OF-144, DH-1
2 yrs.		192	.274	.387	705	193	33	10	9	1.3	93	73	43	86	32	9	2	459	5	7	3	2.5	.985	OF-191, DH-1

Doug Dascenzo

DASCENZO, DOUGLAS CRAIG
B. June 30, 1964, Cleveland, Ohio
BB TL 5'7" 150 lbs.

Year	Team	Games	BA	SA	AB	H	2B	3B	HR	HR%	R	RBI	BB	SO	SB	PH AB	PH H	PO	A	E	DP	TC/G	FA	G by Pos
1988	CHI N	26	.213	.253	75	16	3	0	0	0.0	9	4	9	4	6	5	0	55	0	0	0	2.8	1.000	OF-20
1989		47	.165	.194	139	23	1	0	1	0.7	20	12	13	13	6	0	0	96	0	0	0	2.1	1.000	OF-45
1990		113	.253	.344	241	61	9	5	1	0.4	27	26	21	18	15	6	0	174	2	0	1	1.6	1.000	OF-107, P-1
1991		118	.255	.314	239	61	11	0	1	0.4	40	18	24	26	14	28	3	134	0	2	0	1.5	.985	OF-86, P-3
1992		139	.255	.311	376	96	13	4	0	0.0	37	20	27	32	6	21	9	221	2	5	0	1.9	.978	OF-122
1993	TEX A	76	.199	.288	146	29	5	1	2	1.4	20	10	8	22	2	11	6	91	5	1	2	1.4	.990	OF-68, DH-2
1996	SD N	21	.111	.111	9	1	0	0	0	0.0	3	0	1	2	0	5	1	3	0	0	0	0.3	1.000	OF-10
7 yrs.		540	.234	.297	1225	287	42	10	5	0.4	156	90	103	117	49	76	19	774	10	8	3	1.7	.990	OF-458, P-4, DH-2

Darren Daulton

DAULTON, DARREN ARTHUR
B. Jan. 3, 1962, Arkansas City, Kans.
BL TR 6'2" 195 lbs.

Year	Team	Games	BA	SA	AB	H	2B	3B	HR	HR%	R	RBI	BB	SO	SB	PH AB	PH H	PO	A	E	DP	TC/G	FA	G by Pos
1983	PHI N	2	.333	.333	3	1	0	0	0	0.0	1	1	1	1	0	0	0	8	0	0	0	4.0	1.000	C-2
1985		36	.204	.369	103	21	3	1	4	3.9	14	11	16	37	3	5	0	160	15	1	1	6.3	.994	C-28
1986		49	.225	.428	138	31	4	0	8	5.8	18	21	38	41	2	1	0	244	21	4	6	5.6	.985	C-48

Year	Team	Games	BA	SA	AB	H	2B	3B	HR	HR%	R	RBI	BB	SO	SB	Pinch Hit AB	Pinch Hit H	PO	A	E	DP	TC/G	FA	G by Pos

Darren Daulton *continued*

Year	Team	Games	BA	SA	AB	H	2B	3B	HR	HR%	R	RBI	BB	SO	SB	AB	H	PO	A	E	DP	TC/G	FA	G by Pos
1987		53	.194	.310	129	25	6	0	3	2.3	10	13	16	37	0	12	3	210	13	2	6	5.5	.991	C-40, 1B-1
1988		58	.208	.271	144	30	6	0	1	0.7	13	12	17	26	2	15	4	205	15	6	1	5.0	.973	C-44, 1B-1
1989		131	.201	.310	368	74	12	2	8	2.2	29	44	52	58	2	11	2	627	56	11	8	5.5	.984	C-126
1990		143	.268	.416	459	123	30	1	12	2.6	62	57	72	72	7	10	2	683	70	8	10	5.5	.989	C-139
1991		89	.196	.365	285	56	12	0	12	4.2	36	42	41	66	5	4	1	493	33	8	5	6.1	.985	C-88
1992		145	.270	.524	485	131	32	5	27	5.6	80	**109**	88	103	11	5	1	760	69	11	8	6.0	.987	C-141
1993		147	.257	.482	510	131	35	4	24	4.7	90	105	117	111	5	2	1	981	67	9	19	7.2	.991	C-146
1994		69	.300	.549	257	77	17	1	15	5.8	43	56	33	43	4	1	0	435	41	3	2	7.0	.994	C-68
1995		98	.249	.401	342	85	19	3	9	2.6	44	55	55	52	3	4	0	632	45	4	5	7.2	.994	C-95
1996		5	.167	.167	12	2	0	0	0	0.0	3	0	7	5	0	0	0	6	0	0	0	1.2	1.000	OF-5
13 yrs.		1025	.243	.422	3235	787	176	17	123	3.8	443	525	553	652	44	70	14	5444	445	67	71	6.1	.989	C-965, OF-5, 1B-2

LEAGUE CHAMPIONSHIP SERIES

| 1993 | PHI N | 6 | .263 | .474 | 19 | 5 | 1 | 0 | 1 | 5.3 | 2 | 3 | 6 | 3 | 0 | 0 | 0 | 54 | 3 | 0 | 0 | 9.5 | 1.000 | C-6 |

WORLD SERIES

| 1993 | PHI N | 6 | .217 | .435 | 23 | 5 | 2 | 0 | 1 | 4.3 | 4 | 4 | 4 | 5 | 0 | 0 | 0 | 31 | 4 | 0 | 1 | 5.8 | 1.000 | C-6 |

Chili Davis

DAVIS, CHARLES THEODORE
B. Jan. 17, 1960, Kingston, Jamaica — BB TR 6'3" 195 lbs.

Year	Team	Games	BA	SA	AB	H	2B	3B	HR	HR%	R	RBI	BB	SO	SB	AB	H	PO	A	E	DP	TC/G	FA	G by Pos
1981	SF N	8	.133	.133	15	2	0	0	0	0.0	1	0	1	2	2	3	1	7	0	0	0	1.2	1.000	OF-6
1982		154	.261	.410	641	167	27	6	19	3.0	86	76	45	115	24	1	1	404	16	12	4	2.8	.972	OF-153
1983		137	.233	.352	486	113	21	2	11	2.3	54	59	55	108	10	4	1	357	7	9	1	2.8	.976	OF-133
1984		137	.315	.507	499	157	21	6	21	4.2	87	81	42	74	12	15	6	292	9	9	2	2.5	.971	OF-123
1985		136	.270	.412	481	130	25	2	13	2.7	53	56	62	74	15	9	2	279	10	6	2	2.3	.980	OF-126
1986		153	.278	.416	526	146	28	3	13	2.5	71	70	84	96	16	7	1	303	9	9	2	2.2	.972	OF-148
1987		149	.250	.442	500	125	22	1	24	4.8	80	76	72	109	16	20	3	265	6	7	2	2.1	.975	OF-135
1988	CAL A	158	.268	.432	600	161	29	3	21	3.5	81	93	56	118	9	1	0	299	10	19	1	2.1	.942	OF-153, DH-3
1989		154	.271	.436	560	152	24	1	22	3.9	81	90	61	109	3	2	0	270	5	6	0	1.8	.979	OF-147, DH-6
1990		113	.265	.398	412	109	17	1	12	2.9	58	58	61	89	1	2	0	77	5	3	1	0.8	.965	DH-60, OF-52
1991	MIN A	153	.277	.507	534	148	34	1	29	5.4	84	93	95	117	5	2	0	2	0	0	0	0.0	1.000	DH-150, OF-2
1992		138	.288	.439	444	128	27	2	12	2.7	63	66	73	76	4	16	5	6	0	0	0	0.0	1.000	DH-125, OF-4, 1B-1
1993	CAL A	152	.243	.440	573	139	32	0	27	4.7	74	112	71	135	4	1	0	0	0	0	0	0.0		DH-150, P-1
1994		108	.311	.561	392	122	18	1	26	6.6	72	84	69	84	3	0	0	5	0	0	0	0.0	1.000	DH-106, OF-2
1995		119	.318	.514	424	135	23	0	20	4.7	81	86	89	79	3	0	0	0	0	0	0	0.0	.000	DH-119
1996		145	.292	.496	530	155	24	0	28	5.3	73	95	86	99	5	2	0	0	0	0	0	0.0	.000	DH-143
16 yrs.		2114	.274	.448	7617	2089	372	29	298	3.9	1099	1195	1022	1484	132	85	20	2566	77	80	15	1.3	.971	OF-1184, DH-862, P-1, 1B-1

LEAGUE CHAMPIONSHIP SERIES

1987	SF N	6	.150	.200	20	3	1	0	0	0.0	2	0	1	4	0	0	0	11	1	1	1	2.2	.923	OF-6
1991	MIN A	5	.294	.412	17	5	2	0	0	0.0	3	2	5	8	1	0	0	0	0	0	0	0.0	.000	DH-5
2 yrs.		11	.216	.297	37	8	3	0	0	0.0	5	2	6	12	1	0	0	11	1	1	1	1.2	.923	OF-6, DH-5

WORLD SERIES

| 1991 | MIN A | 6 | .222 | .556 | 18 | 4 | 0 | 0 | 2 | 11.1 | 4 | 4 | 2 | 3 | 0 | 1 | 1 | 1 | 0 | 0 | 0 | 0.2 | 1.000 | DH-4, OF-1 |

Eric Davis

DAVIS, ERIC KEITH
B. May 29, 1962, Los Angeles, Calif. — BR TR 6'3" 175 lbs.

Year	Team	Games	BA	SA	AB	H	2B	3B	HR	HR%	R	RBI	BB	SO	SB	AB	H	PO	A	E	DP	TC/G	FA	G by Pos
1984	CIN N	57	.224	.466	174	39	10	1	10	5.7	33	30	24	48	10	6	1	125	4	1	2	2.5	.992	OF-51
1985		56	.246	.516	122	30	3	3	8	6.6	26	18	7	39	16	8	1	75	3	1	1	1.7	.987	OF-47
1986		132	.277	.523	415	115	15	3	27	6.5	97	71	68	100	80	4	0	274	2	7	0	2.3	.975	OF-121
1987		129	.293	.593	474	139	23	4	37	7.8	120	100	84	134	50	1	0	380	10	4	4	3.1	.990	OF-128
1988		135	.273	.489	472	129	18	3	26	5.5	81	93	65	124	35	3	1	300	2	6	0	2.4	.981	OF-130
1989		131	.281	.541	462	130	14	2	34	7.4	74	101	68	116	21	3	1	298	2	5	1	2.4	.984	OF-125
1990		127	.260	.486	453	118	26	2	24	5.3	84	86	60	100	21	6	1	257	11	2	1	2.2	.993	OF-122
1991		89	.235	.386	285	67	10	0	11	3.9	39	33	48	92	14	8	2	190	5	3	2	2.4	.985	OF-82
1992	LA N	76	.228	.322	267	61	8	1	5	1.9	21	32	36	71	19	0	0	123	0	5	0	1.7	.961	OF-74
1993	2 teams LA N (108G –.234) DET A (23G –.253)																							
"	total	131	.237	.415	451	107	18	0	20	4.4	71	68	55	106	35	4	0	273	7	3	2	2.2	.989	OF-121, DH-5
1994	DET A	37	.183	.292	120	22	4	0	3	2.5	19	13	18	45	5	2	0	85	1	1	1	2.5	.989	OF-35
1996	CIN N	129	.287	.523	415	119	20	0	26	6.3	81	83	70	121	23	4	0	280	4	3	0	2.3	.990	OF-126, 1B-1
12 yrs.		1229	.262	.481	4110	1076	169	20	231	5.6	746	728	603	1096	329	49	7	2660	51	41	14	2.4	.985	OF-1162, DH-5, 1B-1

LEAGUE CHAMPIONSHIP SERIES

| 1990 | CIN N | 6 | .174 | .217 | 23 | 4 | 1 | 0 | 0 | 0.0 | 2 | 2 | 1 | 9 | 0 | 0 | 0 | 12 | 1 | 0 | 0 | 2.2 | 1.000 | OF-6 |

WORLD SERIES

| 1990 | CIN N | 4 | .286 | .500 | 14 | 4 | 0 | 0 | 1 | 7.1 | 3 | 5 | 0 | 0 | 0 | 0 | 0 | 4 | 0 | 0 | 0 | 1.0 | 1.000 | OF-4 |

Russ Davis

DAVIS, RUSSELL STUART
B. Sept. 13, 1969, Birmingham, Ala. — BR TR 6' 170 lbs.

Year	Team	Games	BA	SA	AB	H	2B	3B	HR	HR%	R	RBI	BB	SO	SB	AB	H	PO	A	E	DP	TC/G	FA	G by Pos
1994	NY A	4	.143	.143	14	2	0	0	0	0.0	0	1	0	4	0	0	0	2	6	0	0	2.0	1.000	3B-4
1995		40	.276	.429	98	27	5	2	2	2.0	14	12	10	26	0	3	2	16	45	2	1	1.6	.968	3B-34, DH-4, 1B-2
1996	SEA A	51	.234	.377	167	39	9	0	5	3.0	24	18	17	50	2	2	0	31	67	7	5	2.1	.933	3B-51
3 yrs.		95	.244	.384	279	68	14	2	7	2.5	38	31	27	80	2	5	2	49	118	9	6	1.9	.949	3B-89, DH-4, 1B-2

DIVISIONAL PLAYOFF SERIES

| 1995 | NY A | 2 | .200 | .200 | 5 | 1 | 0 | 0 | 0 | 0.0 | 0 | 0 | 0 | 2 | 0 | 0 | 0 | 0 | 1 | 0 | 0 | 0.5 | 1.000 | 3B-2 |

Year	Team	Games	BA	SA	AB	H	2B	3B	HR	HR%	R	RBI	BB	SO	SB	Pinch Hit AB	Pinch Hit H	PO	A	E	DP	TC/G	FA	G by Pos

Andre Dawson

DAWSON, ANDRE NOLAN (The Hawk)
B. July 10, 1954, Miami, Fla.
BR TR 6'3" 180 lbs.

Year	Team	Games	BA	SA	AB	H	2B	3B	HR	HR%	R	RBI	BB	SO	SB	PH AB	PH H	PO	A	E	DP	TC/G	FA	G by Pos
1976	MON N	24	.235	.306	85	20	4	1	0	0.0	9	7	5	13	1	0	0	61	1	2	1	2.7	.969	OF-24
1977		139	.282	.474	525	148	26	9	19	3.6	64	65	34	93	21	5	0	352	9	4	1	2.7	.989	OF-136
1978		157	.253	.442	609	154	24	8	25	4.1	84	72	30	128	28	5	2	411	17	5	2	2.8	.988	OF-153
1979		155	.275	.468	639	176	24	12	25	3.9	90	92	27	115	35	0	0	394	7	5	1	2.7	.988	OF-153
1980		151	.308	.492	577	178	41	7	17	2.9	96	87	44	69	34	3	1	410	14	6	3	2.9	.986	OF-147
1981		103	.302	.553	394	119	21	3	24	6.1	71	64	35	50	26	0	0	327	10	7	1	3.3	.980	OF-103
1982		148	.301	.498	608	183	37	7	23	3.8	107	83	34	96	39	0	0	419	8	8	2	3.0	.982	OF-147
1983		159	.299	.539	633	**189**	36	10	32	5.1	104	113	38	81	25	1	1	435	6	9	2	2.9	.980	OF-157
1984		138	.248	.409	533	132	23	6	17	3.2	73	86	41	80	13	4	0	297	11	8	2	2.4	.975	OF-134
1985		139	.255	.444	529	135	27	2	23	4.3	65	91	29	92	13	9	3	248	9	7	1	2.0	.973	OF-131
1986		130	.284	.478	496	141	32	2	20	4.0	65	78	37	79	18	3	1	200	11	3	2	1.7	.986	OF-127
1987	CHI N	153	.287	.568	621	178	24	2	**49**	7.9	90	**137**	32	103	11	2	1	271	12	4	0	1.9	.986	OF-152
1988		157	.303	.504	591	179	31	8	24	4.1	78	79	37	73	12	8	2	267	7	3	1	1.9	.989	OF-147
1989		118	.252	.476	416	105	18	6	21	5.0	62	77	35	62	8	5	2	227	4	3	0	2.1	.987	OF-112
1990		147	.310	.535	529	164	28	5	27	5.1	72	100	42	65	16	7	2	250	10	5	4	1.9	.981	OF-139
1991		149	.272	.488	563	153	21	4	31	5.5	69	104	22	80	4	12	4	243	7	3	2	1.8	.988	OF-137
1992		143	.277	.456	542	150	27	2	22	4.1	60	90	30	70	6	6	1	223	11	2	3	1.7	.992	OF-139
1993	BOS A	121	.273	.425	461	126	29	1	13	2.8	44	67	17	49	2	4	2	42	0	0	0	0.4	1.000	DH-97, OF-20
1994		75	.240	.466	292	70	18	0	16	5.5	34	48	9	53	2	2	1	0	0	0	0	0.0	.000	DH-74
1995	FLA N	79	.257	.434	226	58	10	3	8	3.5	30	37	9	45	0	19	4	75	3	8	2	1.5	.907	OF-59
1996		42	.276	.414	58	16	2	0	2	3.4	6	14	2	13	0	34	8	5	0	1	0	1.0	.833	OF-6
21 yrs.		2627	.279	.482	9927	2774	503	98	438	4.4	1373	1591	589	1509	314	129	33	5157	157	93	30	2.2	.983	OF-2323, DH-171

DIVISIONAL PLAYOFF SERIES

| 1981 | MON N | 5 | .300 | .400 | 20 | 6 | 0 | 1 | 0 | 0.0 | 1 | 0 | 1 | 6 | 2 | 0 | 0 | 12 | 1 | 1 | 0 | 2.8 | .929 | OF-5 |

LEAGUE CHAMPIONSHIP SERIES

1981	MON N	5	.150	.150	20	3	0	0	0	0.0	2	0	2	4	0	0	0	12	0	0	0	2.4	1.000	OF-5
1989	CHI N	5	.105	.158	19	2	1	0	0	0.0	0	3	2	6	0	0	0	4	0	0	0	0.8	1.000	OF-5
2 yrs.		10	.128	.154	39	5	1	0	0	0.0	2	3	2	10	0	0	0	16	0	0	0	1.6	1.000	OF-10

Steve Decker

DECKER, STEVEN MICHAEL
B. Oct. 25, 1965, Rock Island, Ill.
BR TR 6'3" 205 lbs.

Year	Team	Games	BA	SA	AB	H	2B	3B	HR	HR%	R	RBI	BB	SO	SB	PH AB	PH H	PO	A	E	DP	TC/G	FA	G by Pos
1990	SF N	15	.296	.500	54	16	2	0	3	5.6	5	8	1	10	0	0	0	75	11	1	2	5.8	.989	C-15
1991		79	.206	.309	233	48	7	1	5	2.1	11	24	16	44	0	4	1	385	41	7	5	5.6	.984	C-78
1992		15	.163	.186	43	7	1	0	0	0.0	3	1	6	7	0	4	0	94	4	0	1	6.5	1.000	C-15
1993	FLA N	8	.000	.000	15	0	0	0	0	0.0	0	1	3	3	0	2	0	28	2	1	0	6.2	.968	C-5
1995		51	.226	.323	133	30	2	1	3	2.3	12	13	19	22	1	5	1	298	25	5	2	6.8	.985	C-46, 1B-2
1996	2 teams	SF N (57G −.230)								CLR N (10G −.320)														
"	total	67	.245	.306	147	36	3	0	2	1.4	24	20	18	29	1	20	4	254	23	0	5	6.2	1.000	C-40, 1B-3, 3B-2
6 yrs.		235	.219	.312	625	137	15	2	13	2.1	55	67	63	115	2	31	6	1134	106	14	15	6.1	.989	C-199, 1B-5, 3B-2

Rob Deer

DEER, ROBERT GEORGE
B. Sept. 29, 1960, Orange, Calif.
BR TR 6'3" 215 lbs.

Year	Team	Games	BA	SA	AB	H	2B	3B	HR	HR%	R	RBI	BB	SO	SB	PH AB	PH H	PO	A	E	DP	TC/G	FA	G by Pos
1984	SF N	13	.167	.542	24	4	0	0	3	12.5	5	3	7	10	1	3	0	19	0	2	0	2.3	.905	OF-9
1985		78	.185	.377	162	30	5	1	8	4.9	22	20	23	71	0	30	5	127	2	2	4	2.8	.985	OF-37, 1B-10
1986	MIL A	134	.232	.494	466	108	17	3	33	7.1	75	86	72	179	5	1	1	312	8	8	3	2.4	.976	OF-131, 1B-4
1987		134	.238	.456	474	113	15	2	28	5.9	71	80	86	**186**	12	2	0	304	16	8	7	2.4	.976	OF-123, 1B-12, DH-4
1988		135	.252	.441	492	124	24	0	23	4.7	71	85	51	**153**	9	1	0	284	10	3	3	2.2	.990	OF-133, DH-1
1989		130	.210	.425	466	98	18	2	26	5.6	72	65	60	158	4	1	1	267	10	8	1	2.2	.972	OF-125, DH-5
1990		134	.209	.432	440	92	15	1	27	6.1	57	69	64	147	2	6	1	373	25	10	19	2.9	.975	OF-117, 1B-21, DH-1
1991	DET A	134	.179	.386	448	80	14	2	25	5.6	64	64	89	**175**	1	1	0	310	8	7	4	2.4	.978	OF-132, DH-2
1992		110	.247	.547	393	97	20	1	32	8.1	66	64	51	131	4	3	0	229	8	4	1	2.2	.983	OF-106, DH-2
1993	2 teams	DET A (90G −.217)								BOS A (38G −.196)														
"	total	128	.210	.386	466	98	17	1	21	4.5	66	55	58	**169**	5	8	2	286	7	8	3	2.4	.973	OF-122, DH-6
1996	SD N	25	.180	.480	50	9	3	0	4	8.0	9	9	14	30	0	9	2	26	0	0	0	1.4	1.000	OF-18
11 yrs.		1155	.220	.442	3881	853	148	13	230	5.9	578	600	575	1409	43	65	12	2537	94	60	45	2.4	.978	OF-1053, 1B-47, DH-21

Alex Delgado

DELGADO, ALEXANDER
B. Jan. 11, 1971, Palmerejo, Venezuela
BR TR 6' 160 lbs.

Year	Team	Games	BA	SA	AB	H	2B	3B	HR	HR%	R	RBI	BB	SO	SB	PH AB	PH H	PO	A	E	DP	TC/G	FA	G by Pos
1996	BOS A	26	.250	.250	20	5	0	0	0	0.0	5	1	3	3	0	6	1	22	3	2	1	1.0	.926	C-14, OF-6, 3B-4, 1B-1, 2B-1

Carlos Delgado

DELGADO, CARLOS JUAN
Born Carlos Juan Delgado (Hernandez).
B. June 25, 1972, Mayaguez, Puerto Rico
BL TR 6'3" 215 lbs.

Year	Team	Games	BA	SA	AB	H	2B	3B	HR	HR%	R	RBI	BB	SO	SB	PH AB	PH H	PO	A	E	DP	TC/G	FA	G by Pos
1993	TOR A	2	.000	.000	1	0	0	0	0	0.0	0	0	1	0	0	1	0	2	0	0	0	1.0	1.000	C-1, DH-1
1994		43	.215	.438	130	28	2	0	9	6.9	17	24	25	46	1	3	0	56	2	2	0	1.4	.967	OF-41, C-1
1995		37	.165	.297	91	15	3	0	3	3.3	7	11	6	26	0	13	1	54	2	0	3	2.0	1.000	OF-17, DH-7, 1B-4
1996		138	.270	.490	488	132	28	2	25	5.1	68	92	58	139	0	11	1	221	13	4	22	1.8	.983	DH-108, 1B-27
4 yrs.		220	.246	.455	710	175	33	2	37	5.2	92	127	90	211	1	28	2	333	17	6	25	1.7	.983	DH-116, OF-58, 1B-31, C-2

Wilson Delgado

DELGADO, WILSON
Born Wilson Delgado (Duran).
B. Jul. 15, 1975, San Cristobal, Dominican Republic
BB TR 5'11" 145 lbs.

Year	Team	Games	BA	SA	AB	H	2B	3B	HR	HR%	R	RBI	BB	SO	SB	PH AB	PH H	PO	A	E	DP	TC/G	FA	G by Pos
1996	SF A	6	.364	.364	8	8	0	0	0	0.0	3	2	1	5	1	0	0	12	12	1	3	4.2	.960	SS-6

Year	Team	Games	BA	SA	AB	H	2B	3B	HR	HR%	R	RBI	BB	SO	SB	Pinch Hit AB	H	PO	A	E	DP	TC/G	FA	G by Pos

Delino DeShields — DeSHIELDS, DELINO LAMONT. B. Jan. 15, 1969, Seaford, Del. — BL TR 6'1" 170 lbs.

1990	MON N	129	.289	.393	499	144	28	6	4	0.8	69	45	66	96	42	4	0	236	371	12	65	4.8	.981	2B-128
1991		151	.238	.332	563	134	15	4	10	1.8	83	51	95	151	56	5	0	285	405	27	72	4.8	.962	2B-148
1992		135	.292	.398	530	155	19	8	7	1.3	82	56	54	108	46	0	0	251	360	15	71	4.7	.976	2B-134
1993		123	.295	.372	481	142	17	7	2	0.4	75	29	72	64	43	0	0	243	381	11	74	5.2	.983	2B-123
1994	LA N	89	.250	.322	320	80	11	3	2	0.6	51	33	54	53	27	2	1	156	282	7	48	4.5	.984	2B-88, SS-10
1995		127	.256	.369	425	109	18	3	8	1.9	66	37	63	83	39	10	3	203	330	11	54	4.8	.980	2B-114
1996		154	.224	.298	581	130	12	8	5	0.9	75	41	53	124	48	2	0	273	400	17	78	4.5	.975	2B-154
7 yrs.		908	.263	.355	3399	894	120	39	38	1.1	501	292	457	679	301	23	4	1647	2529	100	462	4.8	.977	2B-889, SS-10

DIVISIONAL PLAYOFF SERIES
1995	LA N	3	.250	.250	12	3	0	0	0	0.0	1	0	1	3	0	0	0	8	7	0	2	5.0	1.000	2B-3
1996		2	.000	.000	4	0	0	0	0	0.0	0	0	0	1	0	0	0	3	2	0	2	2.5	1.000	2B-2
2 yrs.		5	.188	.188	16	3	0	0	0	0.0	1	0	1	4	0	0	0	11	9	0	4	4.0	1.000	2B-5

Cesar Devarez — DEVAREZ, CESAR SALVATORE. Born Cesar Salvatore Devarez (Santana). B. Sept. 22, 1969, San Francisco de Macoris, Dominican Republic — BR TR 5'10" 175 lbs.

1995	BAL A	6	.000	.000	4	0	0	0	0	0.0	0	0	0	0	0	0	1	14	0	0	0	2.3	1.000	C-6
1996		10	.111	.222	18	2	0	1	0	0.0	0	3	0	1	3	0	1	0	38	1	0	0	3.9	1.000	C-10
2 yrs.		16	.091	.182	22	2	0	1	0	0.0	0	3	0	1	3	0	2	0	52	1	0	0	3.3	1.000	C-16

Mike Devereaux — DEVEREAUX, MICHAEL. B. Apr. 10, 1963, Casper, Wyo. — BR TR 6' 195 lbs.

1987	LA N	19	.222	.278	54	12	3	0	0	0.0	7	4	3	10	3	5	0	21	1	0	0	1.2	1.000	OF-18
1988		30	.116	.140	43	5	1	0	0	0.0	4	2	2	10	0	7	1	29	0	0	0	1.1	1.000	OF-26
1989	BAL A	122	.266	.379	391	104	14	3	8	2.0	55	46	36	60	22	14	0	288	1	5	0	2.5	.983	OF-112, DH-5
1990		108	.240	.392	367	88	18	1	12	3.3	48	49	28	48	13	6	3	281	4	5	1	2.7	.983	OF-104, DH-3
1991		149	.260	.431	608	158	27	10	19	3.1	82	59	47	115	16	8	2	399	10	3	1	2.8	.993	OF-149
1992		156	.276	.464	653	180	29	11	24	3.7	76	107	44	94	10	1	1	431	5	5	3	2.8	.989	OF-155
1993		131	.250	.400	527	132	31	3	14	2.7	72	75	43	99	3	0	0	311	8	4	3	2.5	.988	OF-130
1994		85	.203	.332	301	61	8	2	9	3.0	35	33	22	72	1	2	1	203	3	1	1	2.4	.995	OF-84, DH-1
1995	2 teams CHI A (92G –.306) ATL N (29G –.255)																							
" total		121	.299	.451	388	116	24	1	11	2.8	55	63	27	62	8	1	0	229	4	3	2	2.0	.987	OF-117
1996	BAL A	127	.229	.350	323	74	11	2	8	2.5	49	34	34	53	8	17	7	170	7	3	3	1.5	.983	OF-112, DH-10
10 yrs.		1048	.254	.404	3655	930	166	33	105	2.9	483	472	286	623	84	73	18	2362	43	29	13	2.4	.988	OF-1007, DH-19

DIVISIONAL PLAYOFF SERIES
1995	ATL N	4	.200	.200	5	1	0	0	0	0.0	1	0	0	0	0	3	0	2	0	0	0	0.7	1.000	OF-3
1996	BAL A	4	.000	.000	1	0	0	0	0	0.0	0	0	0	0	0	0	0	2	0	0	0	0.7	1.000	OF-3
2 yrs.		8	.167	.167	6	1	0	0	0	0.0	1	0	0	0	0	3	0	4	0	0	0	0.7	1.000	OF-6

LEAGUE CHAMPIONSHIP SERIES
1995	ATL N	4	.308	.615	13	4	1	0	1	7.7	2	5	1	2	1	0	0	2	0	0	0	0.5	1.000	OF-4
1996	BAL A	3	.000	.000	2	0	0	0	0	0.0	0	0	0	1	0	0	0	1	0	0	0	0.3	1.000	OF-3
2 yrs.		7	.267	.533	15	4	1	0	1	6.7	2	5	1	3	1	0	0	3	0	0	0	0.4	1.000	OF-7

WORLD SERIES
| 1995 | ATL N | 5 | .250 | .250 | 4 | 1 | 0 | 0 | 0 | 0.0 | 0 | 1 | 2 | 1 | 0 | 0 | 0 | 1 | 0 | 1 | 0 | 0.2 | .000 | OF-4, DH-1 |

Alex Diaz — DIAZ, ALEXIS. B. Oct. 5, 1968, Brooklyn, N. Y. — BB TR 5'11" 175 lbs.

1992	MIL A	22	.111	.111	9	1	0	0	0	0.0	5	1	0	3	3	0	0	10	0	0	0	0.8	1.000	OF-11, DH-2
1993		32	.319	.348	69	22	2	0	0	0.0	9	1	0	12	5	4	1	46	1	1	0	1.7	.979	OF-28, DH-1
1994		79	.251	.369	187	47	5	7	1	0.5	17	17	10	19	5	1	1	138	11	2	0	2.0	.987	OF-73, 2B-2, DH-1
1995	SEA A	103	.248	.333	270	67	14	0	3	1.1	44	27	13	27	18	20	6	146	4	2	1	1.7	.987	OF-88
1996		38	.241	.304	79	19	2	0	1	1.3	11	5	2	8	6	7	3	55	1	1	0	2.0	.982	OF-28, DH-1
5 yrs.		274	.254	.339	614	156	23	7	5	0.8	86	51	25	66	37	32	11	395	17	6	1	1.8	.986	OF-228, DH-5, 2B-2

DIVISIONAL PLAYOFF SERIES
| 1995 | SEA A | 2 | .333 | .333 | 3 | 1 | 0 | 0 | 0 | 0.0 | 0 | 0 | 1 | 1 | 0 | 1 | 1 | 1 | 0 | 0 | 0 | 2.0 | 1.000 | OF-1 |

LEAGUE CHAMPIONSHIP SERIES
| 1995 | SEA A | 4 | .429 | .571 | 7 | 3 | 1 | 0 | 0 | 0.0 | 1 | 1 | 0 | 0 | 1 | 0 | 3 | 1 | 1 | 0 | 0 | 0.3 | 1.000 | OF-3 |

Einar Diaz — DIAZ, EINAR ANTONIO. B. Dec. 28, 1972, Chiriqui, Panama — BR TR 5'10" 165 lbs.

| 1996 | CLE A | 4 | .000 | .000 | 1 | 0 | 0 | 0 | 0 | 0.0 | 0 | 0 | 0 | 0 | 0 | 0 | 0 | 4 | 0 | 0 | 0 | 1.0 | 1.000 | C-4 |

Mike Difelice — DIFELICE, MICHAEL WILLIAM. B. May 28, 1969, Philadelphia, Pa. — BR TR 6'2" 205 lbs.

| 1996 | STL N | 4 | .286 | .429 | 7 | 2 | 1 | 0 | 0 | 0.0 | 0 | 2 | 0 | 1 | 0 | 0 | 0 | 15 | 1 | 0 | 0 | 4.0 | 1.000 | C-4 |

Gary DiSarcina — DiSARCINA, GARY THOMAS. B. Nov. 19, 1967, Malden, Mass. — BR TR 6'1" 170 lbs.

1989	CAL A	2	—	—	0	0	0	0	0	—	0	0	0	0	0	0	0	0	0	0	0	0.0	.000	SS-1
1990		18	.140	.193	57	8	1	1	0	0.0	8	0	3	10	1	1	0	17	57	4	9	4.6	.949	SS-14, 2B-3
1991		18	.211	.246	57	12	2	0	0	0.0	5	3	3	4	0	0	0	29	45	4	5	4.1	.949	SS-10, 2B-7, 3B-2
1992		157	.247	.301	518	128	19	0	3	0.6	48	42	20	50	9	1	0	250	486	25	109	4.8	.967	SS-157
1993		126	.238	.313	416	99	20	1	3	0.7	44	45	15	38	5	1	0	193	362	14	77	4.5	.975	SS-126
1994		112	.260	.329	389	101	14	2	3	0.8	53	33	18	28	3	2	1	160	359	9	66	4.8	.983	SS-110
1995		99	.307	.459	362	111	28	6	5	1.4	61	41	20	25	7	0	0	146	275	6	46	4.4	.986	SS-98
1996		150	.256	.347	536	137	26	4	5	0.9	62	48	21	36	2	0	0	212	460	20	94	4.6	.971	SS-150
8 yrs.		682	.255	.339	2335	596	110	14	19	0.8	281	212	100	191	27	5	1	1007	2044	82	406	4.6	.974	SS-666, 2B-10, 3B-2

Year	Team	Games	BA	SA	AB	H	2B	3B	HR	HR%	R	RBI	BB	SO	SB	Pinch Hit AB	Pinch Hit H	PO	A	E	DP	TC/G	FA	G by Pos

Brian Dorsett
DORSETT, BRIAN RICHARD
B. Apr. 9, 1961, Terre Haute, Ind.
BR TR 5'10" 185 lbs.

Year	Team	Games	BA	SA	AB	H	2B	3B	HR	HR%	R	RBI	BB	SO	SB	PH AB	PH H	PO	A	E	DP	TC/G	FA	G by Pos
1987	CLE A	5	.273	.545	11	3	0	0	1	9.1	2	3	0	3	0	2	1	12	0	0	0	3.0	1.000	C-4
1988	CAL A	7	.091	.091	11	1	0	0	0	0.0	0	2	1	5	0	0	0	19	3	0	1	3.1	1.000	C-7
1989	NY A	8	.364	.409	22	8	1	0	0	0.0	3	4	1	3	0	0	0	29	3	0	1	4.0	1.000	C-8
1990		14	.143	.200	35	5	2	0	0	0.0	2	0	2	4	0	2	0	31	0	0	1	2.2	1.000	C-9, DH-5
1991	SD N	11	.083	.083	12	1	0	0	0	0.0	0	1	0	3	0	10	1	4	1	0	0	2.5	1.000	1B-2
1993	CIN N	25	.254	.413	63	16	4	0	2	3.2	7	12	3	14	0	8	2	119	5	0	0	5.9	1.000	C-18, 1B-3
1994		76	.245	.352	216	53	8	0	5	2.3	21	26	21	33	0	8	3	413	34	4	2	6.1	.991	C-73, 1B-1
1996	CHI N	17	.122	.195	41	5	0	0	1	2.4	3	3	4	8	0	2	0	79	5	0	1	5.6	1.000	C-15
8 yrs.		163	.224	.326	411	92	15	0	9	2.2	38	51	32	73	0	32	7	706	51	4	6	5.2	.995	C-134, 1B-6, DH-5

David Doster
DOSTER, DAVID ERIC
B. Oct. 8, 1970, Fort Wayne, Ind.
BL TL 5'11" 175 lbs.

Year	Team	Games	BA	SA	AB	H	2B	3B	HR	HR%	R	RBI	BB	SO	SB	PH AB	PH H	PO	A	E	DP	TC/G	FA	G by Pos
1996	PHI N	39	.267	.371	105	28	8	0	1	0.1	14	8	7	21	0	13	4	51	57	3	12	4.4	.973	2B-24, 3B-1

Mariano Duncan
DUNCAN, MARIANO
Born Mariano Duncan (Nolasco).
B. Mar. 13, 1963, San Pedro de Macoris, Dominican Republic
BR TR 6' 165 lbs.
BB 1985–1987

Year	Team	Games	BA	SA	AB	H	2B	3B	HR	HR%	R	RBI	BB	SO	SB	PH AB	PH H	PO	A	E	DP	TC/G	FA	G by Pos
1985	LA N	142	.244	.340	562	137	24	6	6	1.1	74	39	38	113	38	2	1	224	430	30	64	4.8	.956	SS-123, 2B-19
1986		109	.229	.305	407	93	7	0	8	2.0	47	30	30	78	48	2	0	172	317	25	46	4.8	.951	SS-106
1987		76	.215	.322	261	56	8	1	6	2.3	31	18	17	62	11	1	0	101	213	21	40	4.4	.937	SS-67, 2B-7, OF-2
1989	2 teams	LA N (49G –.250)			CIN N (45G –.247)																			
"	total	94	.248	.357	258	64	15	2	3	1.2	32	21	8	51	9	18	7	101	155	14	30	3.4	.948	SS-60, 2B-13, OF-7
1990	CIN N	125	.306	.476	435	133	22	11	10	2.3	67	55	24	67	13	5	0	265	303	18	55	4.6	.969	2B-115, SS-12, OF-1
1991		100	.258	.411	333	86	7	4	12	3.6	46	40	12	57	5	8	2	169	212	9	41	3.9	.977	2B-62, SS-32, OF-7
1992	PHI N	142	.267	.389	574	153	40	3	8	1.4	71	50	17	108	23	3	1	256	210	16	43	3.4	.967	OF-65, 2B-52, SS-42, 3B-4
1993		124	.282	.417	496	140	26	4	11	2.2	68	73	12	88	6	10	4	180	304	21	50	4.1	.958	2B-65, SS-59
1994		88	.268	.406	347	93	22	1	8	2.3	49	48	17	72	10	3	2	148	188	12	38	3.9	.966	2B-37, 3B-28, SS-19, 1B-6
1995	2 teams	PHI N (52G –.286)			CIN N (29G –.290)																			
"	total	81	.287	.423	265	76	14	2	6	2.3	36	36	5	62	1	18	1	215	145	11	42	5.1	.970	2B-31, SS-20, 1B-18, OF-3, 3B-1
1996	NY A	109	.340	.500	400	136	34	3	8	2.0	62	56	9	77	4	4	2	187	240	12	59	3.9	.973	2B-104, OF-3, 3B-3, DH-2
11 yrs.		1190	.269	.396	4338	1167	219	37	86	2.0	583	466	189	835	168	74	26	2018	2717	189	508	4.1	.962	SS-540, 2B-505, OF-88, 3B-36, 1B-24, DH-2

DIVISIONAL PLAYOFF SERIES

Year	Team	Games	BA	SA	AB	H	2B	3B	HR	HR%	R	RBI	BB	SO	SB	PH AB	PH H	PO	A	E	DP	TC/G	FA	G by Pos
1995	CIN N	2	.667	.667	3	2	0	0	0	0.0	1	1	0	0	1	1	0	0	1	0	0	1.0	1.000	2B-1
1996	NY A	4	.313	.313	16	5	0	0	0	0.0	0	3	0	4	0	0	0	9	13	0	2	5.5	1.000	2B-4
2 yrs.		6	.368	.368	19	7	0	0	0	0.0	1	4	0	4	1	1	0	9	14	0	2	4.6	1.000	2B-5

LEAGUE CHAMPIONSHIP SERIES

Year	Team	Games	BA	SA	AB	H	2B	3B	HR	HR%	R	RBI	BB	SO	SB	PH AB	PH H	PO	A	E	DP	TC/G	FA	G by Pos
1985	LA N	5	.222	.444	18	4	2	1	0	0.0	2	1	1	3	1	0	0	7	16	1	3	4.8	.958	SS-5
1990	CIN N	6	.300	.450	20	6	0	0	1	5.0	1	4	0	8	0	0	0	6	11	1	0	3.0	.944	2B-6
1993	PHI N	3	.267	.533	15	4	0	2	0	0.0	3	0	0	0	0	0	0	5	6	1	0	4.0	.917	2B-3
1995	CIN N	3	.000	.000	3	0	0	0	0	0.0	0	0	1	1	0	0	0	9	0	0	1	9.0	1.000	1B-1
1996	NY A	4	.200	.333	15	3	2	0	0	0.0	0	0	0	3	0	0	0	5	7	1	0	3.3	.923	2B-4
5 yrs.		21	.239	.423	71	17	4 (2nd)	3	1	1.4	6	5	2	20 (6th)	1	1	0	32	40	4	4	4.0	.947	2B-13, SS-5, 1B-1

WORLD SERIES

Year	Team	Games	BA	SA	AB	H	2B	3B	HR	HR%	R	RBI	BB	SO	SB	PH AB	PH H	PO	A	E	DP	TC/G	FA	G by Pos
1990	CIN N	4	.143	.143	14	2	0	0	0	0.0	1	1	2	1	2	0	0	9	9	0	2	4.5	1.000	2B-4
1993	PHI N	6	.345	.414	29	10	0	1	0	0.0	5	2	1	7	3	0	0	11	17	1	5	4.8	.966	2B-5, DH-1
1996	NY A	6	.053	.053	19	1	0	0	0	0.0	1	0	0	4	1	0	0	9	14	2	5	4.2	.920	2B-6
3 yrs.		16	.210	.242	62	13	0	1	0	0.0	7	3	3	13	5	0	0	29	40	3	12	4.5	.958	2B-15, DH-1

Todd Dunn
DUNN, TODD KENT
B. Jul. 29, 1970, Tulsa, Okla. .
BR TR 6'5" 220 lbs.

Year	Team	Games	BA	SA	AB	H	2B	3B	HR	HR%	R	RBI	BB	SO	SB	PH AB	PH H	PO	A	E	DP	TC/G	FA	G by Pos
1996	MIL A	6	.300	.400	10	3	1	0	0	0.0	2	1	0	3	0	1	1	6	0	0	0	1.0	1.000	OF-6

Shawon Dunston
DUNSTON, SHAWON DONNELL
B. Mar. 21, 1963, Brooklyn, N.Y.
BR TR 6'1" 175 lbs.

Year	Team	Games	BA	SA	AB	H	2B	3B	HR	HR%	R	RBI	BB	SO	SB	PH AB	PH H	PO	A	E	DP	TC/G	FA	G by Pos
1985	CHI N	74	.260	.388	250	65	12	4	4	1.6	40	18	19	42	11	0	0	144	248	17	39	5.6	.958	SS-73
1986		150	.250	.410	581	145	36	3	17	2.9	66	68	21	114	13	2	1	320	465	32	96	5.5	.961	SS-149
1987		95	.246	.358	346	85	18	3	5	1.4	40	22	10	68	12	1	0	160	271	14	54	4.7	.969	SS-94
1988		155	.249	.357	575	143	23	6	9	1.6	69	56	16	108	30	3	0	257	455	20	76	4.8	.973	SS-151
1989		138	.278	.403	471	131	20	6	9	1.9	52	60	30	86	19	1	0	213	379	17	76	4.4	.972	SS-138
1990		146	.262	.426	545	143	22	8	17	3.1	73	66	15	87	25	0	0	255	392	20	77	4.6	.970	SS-144
1991		142	.260	.407	492	128	22	7	12	2.4	59	50	23	64	21	2	1	261	383	21	69	4.7	.968	SS-142
1992		18	.315	.384	73	23	3	1	0	0.0	8	2	3	13	2	0	0	28	42	1	9	3.9	.986	SS-18
1993		7	.400	.600	10	4	2	0	0	0.0	3	2	0	1	0	5	2	5	0	0	0	2.5	1.000	SS-2
1994		88	.278	.435	331	92	19	0	11	3.3	38	35	16	48	3	3	2	121	219	12	47	4.2	.966	SS-84
1995		127	.296	.472	477	141	30	6	14	2.9	58	69	10	75	10	1	0	188	336	17	50	4.3	.969	SS-125
1996	SF N	82	.300	.408	287	86	12	2	5	1.7	27	25	13	40	8	3	3	116	218	15	51	4.5	.957	SS-78
12 yrs.		1222	.267	.407	4438	1186	219	46	103	2.3	533	473	176	746	154	21	9	2068	3408	186	644	4.7	.967	SS-1198

LEAGUE CHAMPIONSHIP SERIES

Year	Team	Games	BA	SA	AB	H	2B	3B	HR	HR%	R	RBI	BB	SO	SB	PH AB	PH H	PO	A	E	DP	TC/G	FA	G by Pos
1989	CHI N	5	.316	.316	19	6	0	0	0	0.0	2	0	1	1	1	0	0	10	14	1	1	5.0	.960	SS-5

Year	Team	Games	BA	SA	AB	H	2B	3B	HR	HR%	R	RBI	BB	SO	SB	Pinch Hit AB	Pinch Hit H	PO	A	E	DP	TC/G	FA	G by Pos

Mike Durant
DURANT, MICHAEL JOSEPH
B. Sept. 14, 1969, Columbus, Oh.
BR TR 6'2" 200 lbs.

| 1996 | MIN A | 40 | .210 | .247 | 81 | 17 | 3 | 0 | 0 | 0.0 | 15 | 5 | 10 | 15 | 3 | 1 | 0 | 183 | 13 | 5 | 1 | 5.4 | .975 | C-37 |

Ray Durham
DURHAM, RAY
B. Nov. 30, 1971, Charlotte, N. C.
BB TR 5'8" 170 lbs.

1995	CHI A	125	.257	.384	471	121	27	6	7	1.5	68	51	31	83	18	4	1	245	299	15	66	4.5	.973	2B-122, DH-1
1996		156	.275	.406	557	153	33	5	10	1.8	79	65	58	95	30	1	0	236	423	11	87	4.4	.984	2B-150, DH-3
2 yrs.		281	.267	.396	1028	274	60	11	17	1.7	147	116	89	178	48	5	1	481	722	26	153	4.5	.979	2B-272, DH-4

Jermaine Dye
DYE, JERMAINE TERRELL
B. Jan. 28, 1974, Oakland, Calif.
BR TR 6'4" 210 lbs.
BB 1928

1996	ATL N	98	.281	.459	292	82	16	0	12	4.3	32	37	8	67	1	7	4	150	2	8	1	1.7	.950	OF-92
DIVISIONAL PLAYOFF SERIES																								
1996	ATL N	3	.182	.455	11	2	0	0	1	9.1	1	1	0	6	1	0	0	11	1	0	0	4.0	1.000	OF-3
LEAGUE CHAMPIONSHIP SERIES																								
1996	ATL N	7	.214	.250	28	6	1	0	0	0.0	2	4	1	7	0	0	0	14	0	0	0	2.0	1.000	OF-7
WORLD SERIES																								
1996	ATL N	5	.118	.118	17	2	0	0	0	0.0	0	1	1	1	0	0	0	15	0	1	0	3.2	.938	OF-5

Len Dykstra
DYKSTRA, LEONARD KYLE (Nails)
B. Feb. 10, 1963, Santa Ana, Calif.
BL TL 5'10" 160 lbs.

1985	NY N	83	.254	.331	236	60	9	3	1	0.4	40	19	30	24	15	9	3	165	6	1	2	2.3	.994	OF-74
1986		147	.295	.445	431	127	27	7	8	1.9	77	45	58	55	31	14	4	283	8	3	2	2.1	.990	OF-139
1987		132	.285	.455	431	123	37	3	10	2.3	86	43	40	67	27	18	5	239	4	3	1	2.1	.988	OF-118
1988		126	.270	.385	429	116	19	3	8	1.9	57	33	30	43	30	12	5	270	3	1	0	2.4	.996	OF-112
1989	2 teams NY N (56G –.270) PHI N (90G –.222)																							
"	total	146	.237	.356	511	121	32	4	7	1.4	66	32	60	53	30	9	3	332	10	4	0	2.5	.988	OF-139
1990	PHI N	149	.325	.441	590	192	35	3	9	1.5	106	60	89	48	33	1	0	439	7	6	5	3.0	.987	OF-149
1991		63	.297	.427	246	73	13	5	3	1.2	48	12	37	20	24	1	1	167	3	4	2	2.8	.977	OF-63
1992		85	.301	.406	345	104	18	0	6	1.7	53	39	40	32	30	0	0	253	6	3	4	3.1	.989	OF-85
1993		161	.305	.482	637	194	44	6	19	3.0	143	66	129	64	37	1	0	469	2	10	0	3.0	.979	OF-160
1994		84	.273	.435	315	86	26	5	5	1.6	68	24	68	44	15	1	1	235	4	4	0	2.9	.984	OF-83
1995		62	.264	.354	254	67	15	1	2	0.8	37	18	33	28	10	1	0	152	2	2	1	2.6	.987	OF-61
1996		40	.261	.418	134	35	6	3	3	2.2	21	13	26	25	3	3	1	103	3	0	1	2.7	1.000	OF-39
12 yrs.		1278	.285	.419	4559	1298	281	43	81	1.8	802	404	640	503	285	70	23	3107	58	41	18	2.6	.987	OF-1222
LEAGUE CHAMPIONSHIP SERIES																								
1986	NY N	6	.304	.565	23	7	1	1	1	4.3	3	3	2	4	1	2	1	10	0	0	0	1.7	1.000	OF-6
1988		7	.429	.857	14	6	3	0	1	7.1	6	3	4	0	0	0	0	9	0	0	0	1.3	1.000	OF-7
1993	PHI N	6	.280	.560	25	7	1	0	2	8.0	5	2	5	8	0	0	0	13	0	0	0	2.2	1.000	OF-6
3 yrs.		19	.323 4th	.629	62	20	5	1	4	6.5 10th	14 9th	8	11	12	1	2	1	32	0	0	0	1.7	1.000	OF-19
WORLD SERIES																								
1986	NY N	7	.296	.519	27	8	0	0	2	7.4	4	3	2	7	0	1	0	14	0	0	0	2.0	1.000	OF-7
1993	PHI N	6	.348	.913	23	8	1	0	4	17.4	9	8	7	4	4	0	0	18	1	0	0	3.2	1.000	OF-6
2 yrs.		13	.320 4th	.700	50	16	1	0	6	12.0 1st	13	11	9	11	4	1	1	32	1	0	0	2.5	1.000	OF-13

Damion Easley
EASLEY, JACINTO DAMION
B. Nov. 11, 1969, New York, N. Y.
BR TR 5'11" 155 lbs.

1992	CAL A	47	.258	.311	151	39	5	0	1	0.7	14	12	8	26	9	4	1	30	102	5	13	2.9	.964	3B-45, SS-3
1993		73	.313	.413	230	72	13	2	2	0.9	33	22	28	35	6	3	1	111	157	6	29	4.0	.978	2B-54, 3B-14, DH-1
1994		88	.215	.329	316	68	16	1	6	1.9	41	30	29	48	4	3	1	122	178	7	34	3.5	.977	3B-47, 2B-40
1995		114	.216	.300	357	77	14	2	4	1.1	35	35	32	47	5	0	0	186	276	10	60	4.2	.979	2B-88, SS-25
1996	2 teams CAL A (28G –.156) DET A (21G –.343)																							
"	total	49	.268	.393	112	30	2	0	4	3.6	14	17	10	25	3	3	0	44	86	6	24	2.8	.956	SS-21, 2B-17, 3B-5, DH-3, OF-2
5 yrs.		371	.245	.340	1166	286	50	5	17	1.5	137	116	107	181	27	13	3	493	799	34	160	3.6	.974	2B-199, 3B-111, SS-49, DH-4, OF-2

Angel Echevarria
ECHEVARRIA, ANGEL SANTOS
B. May 25, 1971, Bridgeport, Conn.
BR TR 6'4" 215 lbs.

| 1996 | CLR N | 26 | .286 | .286 | 21 | 6 | 0 | 0 | 0 | 0.0 | 0 | 2 | 0 | 4 | 0 | 14 | 4 | 1 | 0 | 0 | 0 | 0.1 | 1.000 | OF-11 |

Jim Edmonds
EDMONDS, JAMES PATRICK
B. June 27, 1970, Fullerton, Calif.
BL TL 6'1" 190 lbs.

1993	CAL A	18	.246	.344	61	15	4	1	0	0.0	5	4	2	16	0	1	1	47	4	1	2	3.1	.981	OF-17
1994		94	.273	.377	289	79	13	1	5	1.7	35	37	30	72	4	4	0	301	20	3	10	3.3	.991	OF-77, 1B-22
1995		141	.290	.536	558	162	30	4	33	5.9	120	107	51	130	1	3	0	402	8	1	2	3.0	.998	OF-139
1996		114	.304	.571	431	131	28	3	27	6.3	73	66	46	101	4	6	3	280	6	1	2	2.6	.997	OF-111, DH-1
4 yrs.		367	.289	.504	1339	387	75	9	65	4.9	233	214	129	319	9	14	4	1030	38	6	16	2.9	.994	OF-344, 1B-22, DH-1

Year	Team	Games	BA	SA	AB	H	2B	3B	HR	HR%	R	RBI	BB	SO	SB	Pinch Hit AB	Pinch Hit H	PO	A	E	DP	TC/G	FA	G by Pos

Robert Eenhoorn
EENHOORN, ROBERT
B. Feb. 9, 1968, Rotterdam, Netherlands
BR TR 6'3" 170 lbs.

Year	Team	Games	BA	SA	AB	H	2B	3B	HR	HR%	R	RBI	BB	SO	SB	AB	H	PO	A	E	DP	TC/G	FA	G by Pos
1994	NY A	3	.500	.750	4	2	1	0	0	0.0	1	0	0	0	0	2	0	0	1	0	1	0.3	1.000	SS-3
1995		5	.143	.214	14	2	1	0	0	0.0	1	2	1	3	0	1	0	12	8	1	2	4.2	.952	2B-3, SS-2
1996	2 teams NY A	(12G –.071)	**CAL A**	(6G –.267)																				
"	total	18	.172	.172	29	5	0	0	0	0.0	3	2	2	5	0	3	0	21	23	2	7	2.6	.957	2B-12, SS-4, 3B-2
3 yrs.		26	.191	.234	47	9	2	0	0	0.0	5	4	3	8	0	3	0	33	32	3	10	2.6	.956	2B-15, SS-9, 3B-2

Jim Eisenreich
EISENREICH, JAMES MICHAEL
B. Apr. 18, 1959, St. Cloud, Minn.
BL TL 5'11" 175 lbs.

Year	Team	Games	BA	SA	AB	H	2B	3B	HR	HR%	R	RBI	BB	SO	SB	AB	H	PO	A	E	DP	TC/G	FA	G by Pos
1982	MIN A	34	.303	.424	99	30	6	0	2	2.0	10	9	11	13	0	3	1	72	0	2	0	2.5	.973	OF-30
1983		2	.286	.429	7	2	1	0	0	0.0	1	0	1	1	0	0	0	6	1	0	0	3.5	1.000	OF-2
1984		12	.219	.250	32	7	1	0	0	0.0	1	3	2	4	2	3	1	5	0	0	0	0.6	1.000	DH-6, OF-3
1987	KC A	44	.238	.467	105	25	8	2	4	3.8	10	21	7	13	1	15	5	0	0	0	0	0.0	.000	DH-26
1988		82	.218	.282	202	44	8	1	1	0.5	26	19	6	31	9	9	1	109	0	4	0	1.5	.965	OF-64, DH-13
1989		134	.293	.448	475	139	33	7	9	1.9	64	59	37	44	27	6	2	273	4	3	0	2.1	.989	OF-123, DH-10
1990		142	.280	.397	496	139	29	7	5	1.0	61	51	42	51	12	8	4	261	6	1	3	1.9	.996	OF-138, DH-2
1991		135	.301	.392	375	113	22	3	2	0.5	47	47	20	35	5	32	7	243	12	5	12	2.1	.981	OF-105, 1B-15, DH-1
1992		113	.269	.340	353	95	13	3	2	0.6	31	28	24	36	11	27	10	180	1	1	0	1.9	.995	OF-88, DH-8
1993	PHI N	153	.318	.445	362	115	17	4	7	1.9	51	54	26	36	5	21	3	223	6	1	0	1.7	.996	OF-137, 1B-1
1994		104	.300	.421	290	87	15	4	4	1.4	42	43	33	31	6	17	4	178	4	2	2	2.0	.989	OF-93
1995		129	.316	.464	377	119	22	2	10	2.7	46	55	38	44	10	20	4	205	2	0	1	1.9	1.000	OF-111
1996		113	.361	.476	338	122	24	3	3	0.9	45	41	31	32	11	22	3	167	3	4	1	1.9	.977	OF-91
13 yrs.		1197	.295	.414	3511	1037	199	36	49	1.4	435	430	278	371	99	183	45	1922	39	23	19	1.9	.988	OF-985, DH-66, 1B-16

LEAGUE CHAMPIONSHIP SERIES

Year	Team	Games	BA	SA	AB	H	2B	3B	HR	HR%	R	RBI	BB	SO	SB	AB	H	PO	A	E	DP	TC/G	FA	G by Pos
1993	PHI N	6	.133	.200	15	2	1	0	0	0.0	0	1	0	2	0	1	1	6	0	0	0	1.2	1.000	OF-5

WORLD SERIES

Year	Team	Games	BA	SA	AB	H	2B	3B	HR	HR%	R	RBI	BB	SO	SB	AB	H	PO	A	E	DP	TC/G	FA	G by Pos
1993	PHI N	6	.231	.346	26	6	0	0	1	3.8	3	7	2	4	0	0	0	18	0	0	0	3.0	1.000	OF-6

Kevin Elster
ELSTER, KEVIN DANIEL
B. Aug. 3, 1964, San Pedro, Calif.
BR TR 6'2" 180 lbs.

Year	Team	Games	BA	SA	AB	H	2B	3B	HR	HR%	R	RBI	BB	SO	SB	AB	H	PO	A	E	DP	TC/G	FA	G by Pos
1986	NY N	19	.167	.200	30	5	1	0	0	0.0	3	0	3	8	0	0	0	16	35	2	6	2.8	.962	SS-19
1987		5	.400	.600	10	4	2	0	0	0.0	1	1	0	1	0	2	2	4	6	1	0	3.7	.909	SS-3
1988		149	.214	.313	406	87	11	1	9	2.2	41	37	35	47	2	1	0	196	345	13	61	3.7	.977	SS-148
1989		151	.231	.360	458	106	25	2	10	2.2	52	55	34	77	4	0	0	235	374	15	63	4.2	.976	SS-150
1990		92	.207	.363	314	65	20	1	9	2.9	36	45	30	54	2	0	0	159	251	17	42	4.6	.960	SS-92
1991		115	.241	.351	348	84	16	2	6	1.7	33	36	40	53	2	9	2	149	299	14	39	4.3	.970	SS-107
1992		6	.222	.222	18	4	0	0	0	0.0	0	0	0	2	0	1	0	8	10	0	3	3.6	1.000	SS-5
1994	NY A	7	.000	.000	20	0	0	0	0	0.0	0	0	1	6	0	0	0	5	27	0	7	4.6	1.000	SS-7
1995	2 teams NY A	(10G –.118)	**PHI N**	(26G –.208)																				
"	total	36	.186	.329	70	13	5	1	1	1.4	11	9	8	19	0	3	1	47	52	1	14	2.8	.990	SS-29, 1B-4, 3B-2, 2B-1
1996	TEX A	157	.252	.462	515	130	32	2	24	4.7	79	99	52	138	4	0	0	287	441	14	104	4.7	.981	SS-157
10 yrs.		737	.228	.368	2189	498	112	9	59	2.7	256	282	203	405	14	16	5	1106	1840	77	339	4.2	.975	SS-717, 1B-4, 3B-2, 2B-1

DIVISIONAL PLAYOFF SERIES

Year	Team	Games	BA	SA	AB	H	2B	3B	HR	HR%	R	RBI	BB	SO	SB	AB	H	PO	A	E	DP	TC/G	FA	G by Pos
1996	TEX A	4	.333	.500	12	4	2	0	0	0.0	2	0	3	2	1	0	0	6	7	1	4	3.5	.929	SS-4

LEAGUE CHAMPIONSHIP SERIES

Year	Team	Games	BA	SA	AB	H	2B	3B	HR	HR%	R	RBI	BB	SO	SB	AB	H	PO	A	E	DP	TC/G	FA	G by Pos
1986	NY N	4	.000	.000	3	0	0	0	0	0.0	0	0	0	0	0	0	0	2	3	0	0	1.3	1.000	SS-4
1988		5	.250	.375	8	2	1	0	0	0.0	1	1	3	0	0	0	0	7	7	2	2	3.2	.875	SS-5
2 yrs.		9	.182	.273	11	2	1	0	0	0.0	1	1	3	0	0	0	0	9	10	2	2	2.3	.905	SS-9

WORLD SERIES

Year	Team	Games	BA	SA	AB	H	2B	3B	HR	HR%	R	RBI	BB	SO	SB	AB	H	PO	A	E	DP	TC/G	FA	G by Pos
1986	NY N	1	.000	.000	1	0	0	0	0	0.0	0	0	0	0	0	0	0	3	3	1	1	7.0	.857	SS-1

Angelo Encarnacion
ENCARNACION, ANGELO BENJAMIN
B. Apr. 18, 1973, Santo Domingo, Dominican Republic
BR TR 5'8" 180 lbs.

Year	Team	Games	BA	SA	AB	H	2B	3B	HR	HR%	R	RBI	BB	SO	SB	AB	H	PO	A	E	DP	TC/G	FA	G by Pos
1995	PIT N	58	.226	.333	159	36	7	2	2	1.3	18	10	13	28	1	5	1	278	42	7	2	5.9	.979	C-55
1996		7	.318	.409	22	7	2	0	0	0.0	3	1	0	5	0	0	0	36	3	2	0	5.9	.951	C-7
2 yrs.		65	.238	.343	181	43	9	2	2	1.1	21	11	13	33	1	5	1	314	45	9	2	5.9	.976	C-62

Darin Erstad
ERSTAD, DARIN CHARLES
B. June 4, 1974, Baton Rouge, La.
BL TL 6'2" 195 lbs.

Year	Team	Games	BA	SA	AB	H	2B	3B	HR	HR%	R	RBI	BB	SO	SB	AB	H	PO	A	E	DP	TC/G	FA	G by Pos
1996	CAL A	57	.284	.375	208	59	5	1	4	1.9	34	20	174	29	3	9	2	121	2	3	0	2.6	.976	OF-48

Alvaro Espinoza
ESPINOZA, ALVARO ALBERTO
Born Alvaro Alberto Espinoza (Ramirez).
B. Feb. 19, 1962, Valencia, Venezuela
BR TR 6' 160 lbs.

Year	Team	Games	BA	SA	AB	H	2B	3B	HR	HR%	R	RBI	BB	SO	SB	AB	H	PO	A	E	DP	TC/G	FA	G by Pos
1984	MIN A	1	—	—	0	0	0	0	0		0	0	0	0	0	0	0	0	0	0	0	0.0	.000	SS-1
1985		32	.263	.298	57	15	2	0	0	0.0	5	9	1	9	0	0	0	25	69	5	15	3.2	.949	SS-31
1986		37	.214	.238	42	9	1	0	0	0.0	4	1	1	10	0	1	0	23	52	4	11	2.1	.949	2B-19, SS-18
1988	NY A	3	.000	.000	3	0	0	0	0	0.0	0	0	0	0	0	0	0	5	2	0	1	2.3	1.000	2B-2, SS-1
1989		146	.282	.332	503	142	23	1	0	0.0	51	41	14	60	3	0	0	237	471	22	114	5.0	.970	SS-146
1990		150	.224	.274	438	98	12	2	2	0.5	31	20	16	54	1	0	0	268	447	17	100	4.9	.977	SS-150
1991		148	.256	.344	480	123	23	2	5	1.0	51	33	16	57	4	1	0	225	441	21	113	4.6	.969	SS-147, 3B-2, P-1
1993	CLE A	129	.278	.380	263	73	15	0	4	1.5	34	27	8	36	2	9	3	66	157	12	24	1.7	.949	3B-99, SS-35, 2B-2

Year	Team	Games	BA	SA	AB	H	2B	3B	HR	HR%	R	RBI	BB	SO	SB	Pinch Hit AB	Pinch Hit H	PO	A	E	DP	TC/G	FA	G by Pos

Alvaro Espinoza continued

Year	Team	Games	BA	SA	AB	H	2B	3B	HR	HR%	R	RBI	BB	SO	SB	PH AB	PH H	PO	A	E	DP	TC/G	FA	G by Pos
1994		90	.238	.307	231	55	13	0	1	0.4	27	19	6	33	1	1	0	93	209	10	42	3.3	.968	3B-37, SS-36, 2B-20, 1B-3
1995		66	.252	.322	143	36	4	0	2	1.4	15	17	2	16	0	2	0	50	99	5	17	2.3	.968	2B-22, 3B-22, SS-19, 1B-2, DH-1
1996	2 teams CLE A (59G –.223) NY N (48G –.306)																							
"	total	107	.268	.443	246	66	11	4	8	3.3	31	27	10	37	1	6	4	149	126	11	33	2.6	.962	3B-58, SS-23, 1B-19, 2B-7, DH-1
11 yrs.		909	.256	.335	2406	617	104	9	22	0.9	249	194	74	312	12	20	7	1141	2073	107	470	3.6	.968	SS-607, 3B-218, 2B-72, 1B-24, DH-2, P-1

DIVISIONAL PLAYOFF SERIES

| 1995 | CLE A | 1 | .000 | .000 | 1 | 0 | 0 | 0 | 0 | 0.0 | 0 | 0 | 0 | 0 | 0 | 0 | 0 | 0 | 0 | 0 | 0 | 0.0 | .000 | 3B-1 |

LEAGUE CHAMPIONSHIP SERIES

| 1995 | CLE A | 4 | .125 | .125 | 8 | 1 | 0 | 0 | 0 | 0.0 | 1 | 0 | 0 | 3 | 0 | 0 | 0 | 0 | 3 | 1 | 0 | 1.0 | .750 | 3B-4 |

WORLD SERIES

| 1995 | CLE A | 2 | .500 | .500 | 2 | 1 | 0 | 0 | 0 | 0.0 | 1 | 0 | 0 | 0 | 0 | 0 | 0 | 1 | 1 | 0 | 0 | 2.0 | 1.000 | 3B-1 |

Bobby Estalella

ESTALELLA, ROBERT M.
B. Aug. 23, 1974, Hialeah, Fla.
BR TR 6'1" 200 lbs.

| 1996 | PHI N | 7 | .353 | .706 | 17 | 6 | 0 | 0 | 2 | 11.8 | 5 | 4 | 1 | 6 | 1 | 3 | 0 | 24 | 1 | 0 | 0 | 6.3 | 1.000 | C-4 |

Tony Eusebio

EUSEBIO, RAUL ANTONIO
Born Raul Antonio Bare (Eusebio).
B. Apr. 27, 1967, San Jose de Los Llamos, Dominican Republic
BR TR 6'2" 180 lbs.

1991	HOU N	10	.105	.158	19	2	1	0	0	0.0	4	0	6	8	0	1	0	49	4	1	0	6.0	.981	C-9
1994		55	.296	.459	159	47	9	1	5	3.1	18	30	8	33	0	3	1	263	24	2	1	5.6	.993	C-52
1995		113	.299	.410	368	110	21	1	6	1.6	46	58	31	59	0	18	7	644	50	5	6	6.8	.993	C-103
1996		58	.270	.362	152	41	7	2	1	0.7	15	19	18	20	0	13	3	255	24	1	1	5.8	.996	C-48
4 yrs.		236	.287	.404	698	200	38	4	12	1.7	83	107	63	120	0	35	11	1211	102	9	8	6.2	.993	C-212

Carl Everett

EVERETT, CARL EDWARD
B. June 3, 1970, Tampa, Fla.
BB TR 6' 180 lbs.

1993	FLA N	11	.105	.105	19	2	0	0	0	0.0	0	0	1	9	1	3	0	6	0	1	0	0.9	.857	OF-8
1994		16	.216	.353	51	11	1	0	2	3.9	7	6	3	15	4	1	0	28	2	0	0	1.9	1.000	OF-16
1995	NY N	79	.260	.436	289	75	13	1	12	4.2	48	54	39	67	2	2	0	147	10	3	1	2.1	.981	OF-77
1996		101	.240	.307	192	46	8	1	1	0.5	29	16	21	53	6	43	11	95	4	7	1	1.9	.934	OF-55
4 yrs.		207	.243	.372	551	134	22	2	15	2.7	84	76	64	144	13	49	11	276	16	11	2	1.9	.964	OF-156

Jorge Fabregas

FABREGAS, JORGE
B. Mar. 13, 1970, Miami, Fla.
BL TR 6'3" 205 lbs.

1994	CAL A	43	.283	.307	127	36	3	0	0	0.0	12	16	7	18	2	7	3	217	16	3	1	5.8	.987	C-41
1995		73	.247	.304	227	56	10	0	1	0.4	24	22	17	28	0	3	1	391	36	6	1	5.9	.986	C-73
1996		90	.287	.335	254	73	6	0	2	0.8	18	26	17	27	0	2	1	502	45	6	3	6.1	.989	C-89, DH-1
3 yrs.		206	.271	.317	608	165	19	0	3	0.5	54	64	41	73	2	12	5	1110	97	15	5	6.0	.988	C-203, DH-1

Rikkert Faneyte

FANEYTE, RIKKERT
B. May 31, 1969, Amsterdam, Netherlands
BR TR 6' 170 lbs.

1993	SF N	7	.133	.133	15	2	0	0	0	0.0	2	0	2	4	0	1	0	10	0	0	0	1.7	1.000	OF-6
1994		19	.115	.231	26	3	3	0	0	0.0	1	4	3	11	0	12	1	9	0	1	0	1.7	.900	OF-6
1995		46	.198	.267	86	17	4	1	0	0.0	7	4	11	27	1	10	2	49	3	1	0	1.6	.981	OF-34
1996	TEX A	8	.200	.200	5	1	0	0	0	0.0	0	1	0	0	0	2	0	11	0	0	0	1.4	1.000	OF-6, DH-2
4 yrs.		80	.174	.242	132	23	7	1	0	0.0	10	9	16	42	1	25	3	79	3	2	0	1.6	.976	OF-52, DH-2

Sal Fasano

FASANO, SALVATORE FRANK
B. Aug. 10, 1971, Chicago, Ill.
BL TR 6'2" 220 lbs.

| 1996 | KC A | 51 | .203 | .343 | 143 | 29 | 2 | 0 | 6 | 4.2 | 20 | 19 | 14 | 25 | 1 | 0 | 0 | 291 | 13 | 5 | 2 | 6.1 | .984 | C-51 |

Felix Fermin

FERMIN, FELIX JOSE
Born Felix Jose Fermin (Minaya).
B. Oct. 9, 1963, Mao Valverde, Dominican Republic
BR TR 5'11" 160 lbs.

1987	PIT N	23	.250	.250	68	17	0	0	0	0.0	6	4	4	9	0	0	0	36	62	2	13	4.3	.980	SS-23
1988		43	.276	.322	87	24	0	2	0	0.0	9	2	8	10	3	1	0	51	76	6	14	3.1	.955	SS-43
1989	CLE A	156	.238	.260	484	115	9	1	0	0.0	50	21	41	27	6	0	0	253	517	26	84	5.1	.967	SS-153, 2B-2
1990		148	.256	.304	414	106	13	2	1	0.2	47	40	26	22	3	0	0	214	423	16	81	4.4	.975	SS-147, 2B-1
1991		129	.262	.302	424	111	13	2	0	0.0	30	31	26	27	5	0	0	214	372	12	74	4.6	.980	SS-129
1992		79	.270	.321	215	58	7	2	0	0.0	27	13	18	10	0	2	1	79	168	8	42	3.1	.969	SS-55, 3B-17, 2B-7, 1B-2
1993		140	.263	.317	480	126	16	2	2	0.4	48	45	24	14	4	0	0	211	346	23	87	4.1	.960	SS-140
1994	SEA A	101	.317	.380	379	120	21	0	1	0.3	52	35	11	22	4	0	0	168	251	10	57	4.2	.977	SS-77, 2B-25
1995		73	.195	.225	200	39	6	0	0	0.0	21	15	6	6	2	0	0	107	168	6	41	3.7	.979	SS-46, 2B-29
1996	CHI N	11	.125	.188	16	2	1	0	0	0.0	4	1	2	0	0	5	0	5	1	1	1	1.6	.923	2B-6, SS-2
10 yrs.		903	.259	.303	2767	718	86	11	4	0.1	294	207	166	147	27	8	1	1338	2390	110	494	4.2	.971	SS-815, 2B-70, 3B-17, 1B-2

DIVISIONAL PLAYOFF SERIES

| 1995 | SEA A | 3 | .000 | .000 | 1 | 0 | 0 | 0 | 0 | 0.0 | 0 | 0 | 0 | 1 | 0 | 0 | 0 | 3 | 3 | 0 | 1 | 2.0 | 1.000 | SS-2, 2B-1 |

Year	Team	Games	BA	SA	AB	H	2B	3B	HR	HR%	R	RBI	BB	SO	SB	Pinch Hit AB	H	PO	A	E	DP	TC/G	FA	G by Pos

Felix Fermin continued

LEAGUE CHAMPIONSHIP SERIES

| 1995 | SEA A | 2 | — | — | 0 | 0 | 0 | 0 | 0 | — | 0 | 0 | 0 | 0 | 0 | 0 | 0 | 0 | 0 | 0 | 0 | 0.0 | | SS-1, 2B-1 |

Cecil Fielder

FIELDER, CECIL GRANT (Big Daddy)
B. Sept. 21, 1963, Los Angeles, Calif.

BR TR 6'3" 230 lbs.

1985	TOR A	30	.311	.527	74	23	4	0	4	5.4	6	16	6	16	0	4	1	171	17	4	21	7.7	.979	1B-25
1986		34	.157	.325	83	13	2	0	4	4.8	7	13	6	27	0	9	1	37	4	1	3	1.3	.976	DH-22, 1B-7, 3B-2, OF-1
1987		82	.269	.560	175	47	7	1	14	8.0	30	32	20	48	0	19	4	98	6	0	12	1.4	1.000	DH-55, 1B-16, 3B-2
1988		74	.230	.431	174	40	6	1	9	5.2	24	23	14	53	0	21	5	101	12	1	10	1.6	.991	DH-50, 1B-17, 3B-3, 2B-2
1990	DET A	159	.277	**.592**	573	159	25	1	**51**	**8.9**	104	**132**	90	**182**	0	3	0	1190	111	14	137	8.3	.989	1B-143, DH-15
1991		162	.261	.513	624	163	25	0	**44**	7.1	102	**133**	78	151	0	0	0	1055	83	8	110	7.0	.993	1B-122, DH-42
1992		155	.244	.458	594	145	22	0	35	5.9	80	**124**	73	151	0	0	0	957	92	10	98	6.7	.991	1B-114, DH-43
1993		154	.267	.464	573	153	23	0	30	5.2	80	117	90	125	0	1	0	971	78	10	84	6.8	.991	1B-119, DH-36
1994		109	.259	.504	425	110	16	2	28	6.6	67	90	50	110	0	0	0	887	108	7	72	9.2	.993	1B-102, DH-7
1995		136	.243	.472	494	120	18	1	31	6.3	70	82	75	116	0	1	0	631	73	5	65	5.3	.993	1B-77, DH-58
1996	**2 teams**		DET A (107G –.248)		NY A (53G –.260)																			
"	**total**	160	.252	.484	591	149	20	0	39	6.6	85	117	87	139	2	1	0	662	63	7	59	4.6	.990	1B-80, DH-79
11 yrs.		1255	.256	.495	4380	1122	168	6	289	6.6 **8th**	655	879	589	1118	2	60	12	6760	647	67	671	6.0	.991	1B-822, DH-407, 3B-7, 2B-2, OF-1

DIVISIONAL PLAYOFF SERIES

| 1996 | NY A | 3 | .364 | .636 | 11 | 4 | 0 | 0 | 1 | 9.1 | 2 | 4 | 1 | 2 | 0 | 0 | 0 | 0 | 0 | 0 | 0 | 0.0 | .000 | DH-3 |

LEAGUE CHAMPIONSHIP SERIES

1985	TOR A	3	.333	.667	3	1	1	0	0	0.0	0	0	0	1	0	3	1	0	0	0	0	0.0	—	
1996	NY A	5	.167	.500	18	3	0	0	2	11.1	3	8	4	5	0	0	0	0	0	0	0	0.0	.000	DH-5
2 yrs.		8	.190	.524	21	4	1	0	2	9.5	3	8	4	6	0	3	1	0	0	0	0	0.0		DH-5

WORLD SERIES

| 1996 | NY A | 6 | .391 | .478 | 23 | 9 | 2 | 0 | 0 | 0.0 | 1 | 2 | 2 | 2 | 0 | 0 | 0 | 21 | 5 | 0 | 3 | 4.3 | 1.000 | 1B-3, DH-3 |

Steve Finley

FINLEY, STEVEN ALLEN
B. Mar. 12, 1965, Paducah, Tenn.

BL TL 6'2" 175 lbs.

1989	BAL A	81	.249	.318	217	54	5	2	2	0.9	35	25	15	30	17	5	1	144	1	2	0	1.9	.986	OF-76, DH-3
1990		142	.256	.328	464	119	16	4	3	0.6	46	37	32	53	22	12	0	298	4	7	1	2.3	.977	OF-133, DH-2
1991	HOU N	159	.285	.406	596	170	28	10	8	1.3	84	54	42	65	34	9	2	323	13	5	2	2.2	.985	OF-153
1992		162	.292	.407	607	177	29	13	5	0.8	84	55	58	63	44	2	0	417	8	3	3	2.7	.993	OF-160
1993		142	.266	.385	545	145	15	13	8	1.5	69	44	28	65	19	3	2	329	12	4	4	2.5	.988	OF-140
1994		94	.276	.434	373	103	16	5	11	2.9	64	33	28	52	13	2	0	214	9	4	0	2.5	.982	OF-92
1995	SD N	139	.297	.420	562	167	23	8	10	1.8	104	44	59	62	36	1	1	289	8	7	0	2.2	.977	OF-138
1996		161	.298	.531	655	195	45	9	30	4.6	126	95	56	88	22	2	1	384	7	7	2	2.5	.982	OF-160
8 yrs.		1080	.281	.415	4019	1130	177	64	77	1.9	612	387	318	478	207	36	7	2398	62	39	12	2.4	.984	OF-1052, DH-5

DIVISIONAL PLAYOFF SERIES

| 1996 | SD N | 3 | .083 | .083 | 12 | 1 | 0 | 0 | 0 | 0.0 | 0 | 1 | 0 | 4 | 1 | 0 | 0 | 10 | 0 | 0 | 0 | 3.3 | 1.000 | OF-3 |

John Flaherty

FLAHERTY, JOHN TIMOTHY
B. Oct. 21, 1967, New York, N. Y.

BR TR 6'1" 195 lbs.

1992	BOS A	35	.197	.227	66	13	2	0	0	0.0	3	2	3	7	0	1	0	102	7	2	2	3.3	.982	C-34
1993		13	.120	.200	25	3	2	0	0	0.0	3	2	2	6	0	0	0	35	9	0	0	3.4	1.000	C-13
1994	DET A	34	.150	.175	40	6	1	0	0	0.0	2	4	1	11	0	1	0	78	9	0	0	2.6	1.000	C-33, DH-1
1995		112	.243	.404	354	86	22	1	11	3.1	39	40	18	47	0	1	0	570	33	11	4	5.5	.982	C-112
1996	**2 teams**		DET A (47G –.250)		SD N (72G –.303)																			
"	**total**	119	.284	.435	416	118	24	0	13	3.1	40	64	17	61	3	4	2	714	40	10	4	6.5	.987	C-118
5 yrs.		313	.251	.390	901	226	51	1	24	2.7	87	112	41	132	3	8	2	1499	98	23	10	5.2	.986	C-310, DH-1

DIVISIONAL PLAYOFF SERIES

| 1996 | SD N | 2 | .000 | .000 | 4 | 0 | 0 | 0 | 0 | 0.0 | 0 | 0 | 0 | 1 | 0 | 0 | 0 | 9 | 0 | 0 | 0 | 4.5 | 1.000 | C-2 |

Darrin Fletcher

FLETCHER, DARRIN GLEN
Son of Tom Fletcher.
B. Oct. 3, 1966, Elmhurst, Ill.

BL TR 6'2" 195 lbs.

1989	LA N	5	.500	.875	8	4	0	0	1	12.5	1	2	1	0	0	2	1	16	1	0	0	3.4	1.000	C-5
1990	**2 teams**		LA N (2G –.000)		PHI N (9G –.136)																			
"	**total**	11	.130	.174	23	3	1	0	0	0.0	3	1	1	6	0	4	0	30	3	0	0	4.7	1.000	C-7
1991	PHI N	46	.228	.309	136	31	8	0	1	0.7	5	12	5	15	0	1	0	242	22	2	1	5.9	.992	C-45
1992	MON N	83	.243	.333	222	54	10	2	2	0.9	13	26	14	28	0	16	4	360	33	2	3	5.7	.995	C-69
1993		133	.255	.379	396	101	20	1	9	2.3	33	60	34	40	0	16	7	620	41	8	3	5.3	.988	C-127
1994		94	.260	.435	285	74	18	1	10	3.5	28	57	25	23	0	12	2	479	20	2	2	6.2	.996	C-81
1995		110	.286	.446	350	100	21	1	11	3.1	42	45	32	23	0	11	4	612	45	4	5	6.7	.994	C-98
1996		127	.266	.414	394	105	22	0	12	3.0	41	57	27	42	0	18	4	722	30	6	5	6.8	.992	C-112
8 yrs.		609	.260	.397	1814	472	100	5	46	2.5	166	260	139	177	0	80	22	3081	195	24	19	6.1	.993	C-544

Cliff Floyd

FLOYD, CORNELIUS CLIFFORD
B. Dec. 5, 1972, Chicago, Ill.

BL TL 6'5" 220 lbs.

1993	MON N	10	.226	.323	31	7	0	0	1	3.2	3	2	0	9	0	2	0	79	4	0	5	8.3	1.000	1B-10
1994		100	.281	.398	334	94	19	4	4	1.2	43	41	24	63	10	6	3	565	41	6	43	5.9	.990	1B-77, OF-26
1995		29	.130	.188	69	9	1	0	1	1.4	6	8	7	22	3	8	0	146	12	3	13	7.3	.981	1B-18, OF-4
1996		117	.242	.423	227	55	15	4	6	2.6	29	26	30	52	7	33	10	109	2	5	1	1.3	.957	OF-85, 1B-2
4 yrs.		256	.250	.381	661	165	35	8	12	1.8	81	77	61	146	20	49	13	899	59	14	62	4.4	.986	OF-115, 1B-107

38

Year	Team		Games	BA	SA	AB	H	2B	3B	HR	HR%	R	RBI	BB	SO	SB	Pinch Hit AB	Pinch Hit H	PO	A	E	DP	TC/G	FA	G by Pos

Chad Fonville
FONVILLE, CHAD EVERETTE
B. Mar. 5, 1971, Jacksonville, N. C. — BB TR 5'6" 155 lbs.

Year	Team		Games	BA	SA	AB	H	2B	3B	HR	HR%	R	RBI	BB	SO	SB	PH AB	PH H	PO	A	E	DP	TC/G	FA	G by Pos
1995	2 teams	MON N (14G –.333) LA N (88G –.276)																							
"	total		102	.278	.303	320	89	6	1	0	0.0	43	16	23	42	20	16	4	125	195	11	28	3.8	.967	SS-38, 2B-38, OF-11
1996	LA	N	103	.204	.234	201	41	4	1	0	0.0	34	13	17	31	7	19	4	84	71	6	14	2.0	.963	OF-35, 2B-23, SS-20, 3B-2
2 yrs.			205	.250	.276	521	130	10	2	0	0.0	77	29	40	73	27	35	8	209	266	17	42	2.9	.965	2B-61, SS-58, OF-46, 3B-2

DIVISIONAL PLAYOFF SERIES

1995	LA	N	3	.500	.500	12	6	0	0	0	0.0	1	0	0	1	0	0	0	1	7	1	2	3.0	.889	SS-3

Brook Fordyce
FORDYCE, BROOK ALEXANDER
B. May 7, 1970, New London, Conn. — BR TR 6'1" 185 lbs.

1995	NY	N	4	.500	1.000	2	1	1	0	0	0.0	1	0	1	0	0	2	1	0	0	0	0	0.0	—	
1996	CIN	N	4	.286	.429	7	2	1	0	0	0.0	0	1	3	1	0	0	0	18	0	0	0	4.5	1.000	C-4
2 yrs.			8	.333	.556	9	3	2	0	0	0.0	1	1	4	1	0	2	1	18	0	0	0	4.5	1.000	C-4

Andy Fox
FOX, ANDREW JUNIPERO
B. Jan. 12, 1971, Sacramento, Calif. — BL TR 6'4" 205 lbs.

1996	NY	A	113	.196	.265	189	37	4	0	3	1.6	26	13	20	28	11	4	1	94	158	12	27	2.3	.955	2B-72, 3B-31, SS-9, DH-3, OF-1

DIVISIONAL PLAYOFF SERIES

1996	NY	A	2	—	—	0	0	0	0	0	0.0	0	0	0	0	0	0	0	0	0	0	0	0.0	—	DH-2

LEAGUE CHAMPIONSHIP SERIES

1996	NY	A	2	—	—	0	0	0	0	0	0.0	0	0	0	0	0	0	0	0	0	0	0	0.0	—	DH-2

WORLD SERIES

1996	NY	A	4	—	—	0	0	0	0	0	0.0	1	0	0	0	0	0	0	1	0	0	0	0.5	—	2B--1, 3B-1

Julio Franco
FRANCO, JULIO CESAR
Born Julio Cesar Robles (Franco).
B. Aug. 23, 1958, Hato Mayor, Dominican Republic — BR TR 6' 160 lbs.

1982	PHI	N	16	.276	.310	29	8	1	0	0	0.0	3	3	2	4	0	0	0	8	25	0	2	2.5	1.000	SS-11, 3B-2
1983	CLE	A	149	.273	.388	560	153	24	8	8	1.4	68	80	27	50	32	0	0	247	438	28	92	4.8	.961	SS-149
1984			160	.286	.348	658	188	22	5	3	0.5	82	79	43	68	19	0	0	280	481	36	116	5.0	.955	SS-159, DH-1
1985			160	.288	.381	636	183	33	4	6	0.9	97	90	54	74	13	2	0	252	437	36	99	4.5	.950	SS-151, 2B-8, DH-1
1986			149	.306	.422	599	183	30	5	10	1.7	80	74	32	66	10	1	0	248	413	19	90	4.5	.972	SS-134, 2B-13, DH-3
1987			128	.319	.428	495	158	24	3	8	1.6	86	52	57	56	32	1	1	175	313	18	56	4.0	.964	SS-111, 2B-9, DH-8
1988			152	.303	.409	613	186	23	6	10	1.6	88	54	56	72	25	0	0	310	434	14	87	5.0	.982	2B-151, DH-1
1989	TEX	A	150	.316	.462	548	173	31	5	13	2.4	80	92	66	69	21	1	1	256	386	13	70	4.4	.980	2B-140, DH-10
1990			157	.296	.402	582	172	27	1	11	1.9	96	69	82	83	31	1	1	310	444	19	101	5.0	.975	2B-152, DH-3
1991			146	.341	.474	589	201	27	3	15	2.5	108	78	65	78	36	2	1	294	372	14	80	4.7	.979	2B-146
1992			35	.234	.355	107	25	7	0	2	1.9	19	8	15	17	1	7	3	21	17	3	2	1.5	.927	DH-15, 2B-9, OF-4
1993			144	.289	.438	532	154	31	3	14	2.6	85	84	62	95	9	3	1	0	0	0	0	0.0	.000	DH-140
1994	CHI	A	112	.319	.510	433	138	19	2	20	4.6	72	98	62	75	8	0	0	88	7	3	9	0.9	.969	DH-99, 1B-14
1996	CLE	A	112	.322	.470	432	139	20	1	14	3.2	72	76	61	82	8	3	1	851	74	9	90	8.5	.990	1B-97, DH-13
14 yrs.			1770	.303	.422	6813	2061	319	46	134	2.0	1036	937	684	889	245	21	9	3340	3841	212	894	4.2	.971	SS-715, 2B-628, DH-294, 1B-111, OF-4, 3B-2

DIVISIONAL PLAYOFF SERIES

1996	CLE	A	4	.133	.133	15	2	0	0	1		1	1	1	6	0	0	0	18	1	0	1	4.8	1.000	1B-3, DH-1

Matt Franco
FRANCO, MATTHEW NEIL
B. Aug. 19, 1969, Santa Monica, Calif. — BL TR 6'2" 200 lbs.

1995	CHI	N	16	.294	.353	17	5	1	0	0	0.0	3	1	0	4	0	11	3	2	2	0	0	0.8	1.000	2B-3, 1B-1, 3B-1
1996	NY	N	14	.194	.323	31	6	1	0	1	3.2	3	2	1	5	0	5	1	15	12	3	1	3.0	.900	3B-8, 1B-2
2 yrs.			30	.229	.333	48	11	2	0	1	2.1	6	3	1	9	0	16	4	17	14	3	1	2.3	.912	3B-9, 2B-3, 1B-3

Lou Frazier
FRAZIER, ARTHUR LOUIS
B. Jan. 26, 1965, St. Louis, Mo. — BB TR 6'2" 175 lbs.

1993	MON	N	112	.286	.349	189	54	7	1	1	0.5	27	16	16	24	17	48	12	98	9	2	1	1.6	.982	OF-60, 1B-8, 2B-1
1994			76	.271	.307	140	38	3	1	0	0.0	25	14	18	23	20	24	5	61	4	1	1	1.5	.985	OF-36, 2B-6, 1B-1
1995	2 teams	MON N (35G –.190) TEX A (49G –.212)																							
"	total		84	.204	.228	162	33	4	0	0	0.0	25	11	15	32	13	10	0	105	3	3	0	1.5	.973	OF-72, DH-2, 2B-1
1996	TEX	A	30	.260	.340	50	13	2	1	0	0.0	5	5	8	10	4	3	1	31	3	2	0	1.3	.944	OF-15, DH-11, 2B-1
4 yrs.			302	.255	.301	541	138	16	3	1	0.2	82	46	57	89	54	85	18	295	19	8	2	1.5	.975	OF-183, DH-13, 1B-9, 2B-9

Jeff Frye
FRYE, JEFFREY DUSTIN
B. Aug. 31, 1966, Oakland, Calif. — BR TR 5'9" 180 lbs.

1992	TEX	A	67	.256	.327	199	51	9	1	1	0.5	24	12	16	27	1	0	0	120	196	7	43	4.8	.978	2B-67
1994			57	.327	.454	205	67	20	3	0	0.0	37	18	29	23	6	2	1	89	135	4	28	4.1	.982	2B-54, DH-1, 3B-1
1995			90	.278	.377	313	87	15	2	4	1.3	38	29	24	45	3	6	0	172	246	11	51	5.2	.974	2B-83
1996	BOS	A	105	.286	.389	419	120	27	2	4	1.0	74	41	54	57	18	0	0	212	318	9	70	4.9	.983	2B-100, OF-5, SS-3, DH-1
4 yrs.			319	.286	.386	1136	325	71	8	9	0.8	173	100	123	152	28	8	2	593	895	31	192	4.8	.980	2B-304, OF-5, SS-3, DH-2, 3B-1

Travis Fryman
FRYMAN, DAVID TRAVIS
B. Mar. 25, 1969, Lexington, Ky. — BR TR 6'1" 180 lbs.

1990	DET	A	66	.297	.470	232	69	11	1	9	3.9	32	27	17	51	3	1	0	47	145	14	21	3.1	.932	3B-48, SS-17, DH-1
1991			149	.259	.447	557	144	36	3	21	3.8	65	91	40	149	12	1	1	153	354	23	61	3.4	.957	3B-86, SS-71

Year	Team	Games	BA	SA	AB	H	2B	3B	HR	HR%	R	RBI	BB	SO	SB	Pinch Hit AB	Pinch Hit H	PO	A	E	DP	TC/G	FA	G by Pos

Travis Fryman *continued*

Year	Team	Games	BA	SA	AB	H	2B	3B	HR	HR%	R	RBI	BB	SO	SB	AB	H	PO	A	E	DP	TC/G	FA	G by Pos
1992		161	.266	.416	659	175	31	4	20	3.0	87	96	45	144	8	0	0	220	489	22	95	4.5	.970	SS-137, 3B-26
1993		151	.300	.486	607	182	37	5	22	3.6	98	97	77	128	9	0	0	169	382	23	70	3.8	.960	SS-81, 3B-69, DH-1
1994		114	.263	.474	464	122	34	5	18	3.9	66	85	45	128	2	0	0	78	222	14	12	2.8	.955	3B-114
1995		144	.275	.409	567	156	21	5	15	2.6	79	81	63	100	4	0	0	106	335	14	38	3.2	.969	3B-144
1996		157	.268	.437	616	165	32	3	22	3.6	90	100	57	118	4	0	0	150	358	10	42	3.3	.981	3B-128, SS-29
7 yrs.		942	.274	.445	3702	1013	202	26	127	3.4	517	577	344	818	42	2	1	923	2285	120	339	3.5	.964	3B-615, SS-335, DH-2

Gary Gaetti

GAETTI, GARY JOSEPH
B. Aug. 19, 1958, Centralia, Ill.

BR TR 6' 180 lbs.

Year	Team	Games	BA	SA	AB	H	2B	3B	HR	HR%	R	RBI	BB	SO	SB	AB	H	PO	A	E	DP	TC/G	FA	G by Pos
1981	MIN A	9	.192	.423	26	5	0	0	2	7.7	4	3	0	6	0	0	0	5	17	0	1	2.4	1.000	3B-8, DH-1
1982		145	.230	.443	508	117	25	4	25	4.9	59	84	37	107	0	1	0	106	291	17	36	2.9	.959	3B-142, SS-2
1983		157	.245	.414	584	143	30	3	21	3.6	81	78	54	121	7	2	1	131	361	17	46	3.2	.967	3B-154, SS-3, DH-1
1984		162	.262	.350	588	154	29	4	5	0.9	55	65	44	81	11	0	0	163	335	21	27	3.2	.960	3B-154, OF-8, SS-2
1985		160	.246	.409	560	138	31	0	20	3.6	71	63	37	89	13	1	0	162	316	18	31	3.1	.964	3B-156, OF-4, DH-1, 1B-1
1986		157	.287	.518	596	171	34	1	34	5.7	91	108	52	108	14	1	0	120	335	21	36	3.0	.956	3B-156, SS-2, OF-1, 2B-1
1987		154	.257	.485	584	150	36	2	31	5.3	95	109	37	92	10	3	2	134	261	11	28	2.7	.973	3B-150, DH-2
1988		133	.301	.551	468	141	29	2	28	6.0	66	88	36	85	7	14	4	105	191	7	24	2.5	.977	3B-115, DH-5, SS-2
1989		130	.251	.404	498	125	11	4	19	3.8	63	75	25	87	6	3	1	115	253	10	24	2.9	.974	3B-125, DH-3, 1B-2
1990		154	.229	.376	577	132	27	5	16	2.8	61	85	36	101	6	2	0	125	319	18	36	3.0	.961	3B-151, SS-2, 1B-2
1991	CAL A	152	.246	.379	586	144	22	1	18	3.1	58	66	33	104	5	1	1	111	353	17	39	3.2	.965	3B-152
1992		130	.226	.342	456	103	13	2	12	2.6	41	48	21	79	3	7	2	423	196	22	53	5.0	.966	3B-67, 1B-44, DH-17
1993	2 teams CAL A (20G –.180) KC A (82G –.256)																							
"	total	102	.245	.438	331	81	20	1	14	4.2	40	52	21	87	1	8	1	185	153	7	29	3.2	.980	3B-79, 1B-24, DH-6
1994	KC A	90	.287	.462	327	94	15	3	12	3.7	53	57	19	63	0	2	1	99	166	4	20	2.9	.985	3B-85, 1B-9
1995		137	.261	.518	514	134	27	0	35	6.8	76	96	47	91	3	5	1	182	230	16	30	3.1	.963	3B-123, 1B-11, DH-6
1996	STL N	141	.274	.473	522	143	27	4	23	4.4	71	80	35	97	2	1	1	148	228	10	22	2.6	.974	3B-133, 1B-14
16 yrs.		2113	.256	.436	7725	1975	376	36	315	4.1	985	1155	534	1398	88	51	15	2314	4005	216	482	3.1	.967	3B-1950, 1B-107, DH-42, OF-13, SS-13, 2B-1

DIVISIONAL PLAYOFF SERIES

Year	Team	Games	BA	SA	AB	H	2B	3B	HR	HR%	R	RBI	BB	SO	SB	AB	H	PO	A	E	DP	TC/G	FA	G by Pos
1996	STL N	3	.091	.364	11	1	0	0	1	9.1	1	3	0	3	0	0	0	1	3	0	0	1.3	1.000	3B-3

LEAGUE CHAMPIONSHIP SERIES

Year	Team	Games	BA	SA	AB	H	2B	3B	HR	HR%	R	RBI	BB	SO	SB	AB	H	PO	A	E	DP	TC/G	FA	G by Pos
1987	MIN A	5	.300	.650	20	6	1	0	2	10.0	5	5	1	3	0	0	0	8	7	0	1	3.0	1.000	3B-5
1996	STL N	7	.292	.417	24	7	0	0	1	4.2	1	4	1	5	0	0	0	4	12	0	1	2.3	1.000	3B-7
2 yrs.		12	.295	.523	44	13	1	0	3	6.8	6	9	2	8	0	0	0	12	19	0	2	2.6	1.000	3B-12

WORLD SERIES

Year	Team	Games	BA	SA	AB	H	2B	3B	HR	HR%	R	RBI	BB	SO	SB	AB	H	PO	A	E	DP	TC/G	FA	G by Pos
1987	MIN A	7	.259	.519	27	7	2	1	1	3.7	4	4	2	5	2	0	0	6	15	0	2	3.0	1.000	3B-7

Greg Gagne

GAGNE, GREGORY CHRISTOPHER
B. Nov. 12, 1961, Fall River, Mass.

BR TR 5'11" 175 lbs.

Year	Team	Games	BA	SA	AB	H	2B	3B	HR	HR%	R	RBI	BB	SO	SB	AB	H	PO	A	E	DP	TC/G	FA	G by Pos
1983	MIN A	10	.111	.148	27	3	1	0	0	0.0	2	3	0	6	0	0	0	10	14	2	2	2.6	.923	SS-10
1984		2	.000	.000	1	0	0	0	0	0.0	0	0	0	0	0	1	0	0	0	0	0	0.0	—	
1985		114	.225	.317	293	66	15	3	2	0.7	37	23	20	57	10	4	1	149	269	14	48	3.9	.968	SS-106, DH-5
1986		156	.250	.398	472	118	22	6	12	2.5	63	54	30	108	12	0	0	228	381	26	96	4.0	.959	SS-155, 2B-4
1987		137	.265	.430	437	116	28	7	10	2.3	68	40	25	84	6	0	0	196	391	18	75	4.3	.970	SS-136, OF-4, 2B-1
1988		149	.236	.397	461	109	20	6	14	3.0	70	48	27	110	15	1	0	202	373	18	79	4.0	.970	SS-146, OF-2, 3B-1, 2B-1
1989		149	.272	.424	460	125	29	7	9	2.0	69	48	17	80	11	5	0	218	389	18	66	4.3	.971	SS-146, OF-1
1990		138	.235	.361	388	91	22	3	7	1.8	38	38	24	76	8	2	0	184	377	14	62	4.2	.976	SS-135, DH-2, OF-1
1991		139	.265	.395	408	108	23	3	8	2.0	52	42	26	72	11	2	0	181	377	9	69	4.1	.984	SS-137, DH-1
1992		146	.246	.346	439	108	23	0	7	1.6	53	39	19	83	6	1	0	208	438	18	83	4.7	.973	SS-141
1993	KC A	159	.280	.406	540	151	32	3	10	1.9	66	57	33	93	10	1	0	266	451	10	93	4.6	.986	SS-159
1994		107	.259	.392	375	97	23	3	7	1.9	39	51	27	79	10	0	0	189	323	12	63	4.9	.977	SS-106
1995		120	.256	.374	430	110	25	4	6	1.4	58	49	38	60	3	6	3	175	387	18	87	4.8	.969	SS-118, DH-2
1996	LA N	128	.255	.364	428	109	13	2	10	2.3	48	55	50	93	4	0	0	184	404	21	86	4.8	.966	SS-127
14 yrs.		1654	.254	.385	5159	1311	276	47	102	2.0	663	547	336	1001	106	23	5	2390	4574	198	909	4.3	.972	SS-1622, DH-10, OF-8, 2B-6, 3B-1

DIVISIONAL PLAYOFF SERIES

Year	Team	Games	BA	SA	AB	H	2B	3B	HR	HR%	R	RBI	BB	SO	SB	AB	H	PO	A	E	DP	TC/G	FA	G by Pos
1996	LA N	3	.273	.364	11	3	1	0	0	0.0	2	0	0	5	0	0	0	3	9	0	0	4.0	1.000	SS-3

LEAGUE CHAMPIONSHIP SERIES

Year	Team	Games	BA	SA	AB	H	2B	3B	HR	HR%	R	RBI	BB	SO	SB	AB	H	PO	A	E	DP	TC/G	FA	G by Pos
1987	MIN A	5	.278	.778	18	5	3	0	2	11.1	5	3	3	4	0	0	0	9	13	2	2	4.8	.917	SS-5
1991		5	.235	.235	17	4	0	0	0	0.0	1	1	1	5	0	0	0	9	9	2	1	4.0	.900	SS-5
2 yrs.		10	.257	.514	35	9	3	0	2	5.7	6	4	4	9	0	0	0	18	22	4	3	4.4	.909	SS-10

WORLD SERIES

Year	Team	Games	BA	SA	AB	H	2B	3B	HR	HR%	R	RBI	BB	SO	SB	AB	H	PO	A	E	DP	TC/G	FA	G by Pos
1987	MIN A	7	.200	.333	30	6	1	0	1	3.3	3	1	6	0	0	0	0	6	20	2	4	4.0	.929	SS-7
1991		7	.167	.333	24	4	1	0	1	4.2	1	3	0	7	0	0	0	13	24	0	5	5.3	1.000	SS-7
2 yrs.		14	.185	.333	54	10	2	0	2	3.7	6	6	1	13	0	0	0	19	44	2	7	4.6	.969	SS-14

Andres Galarraga

GALARRAGA, ANDRES JOSE (Big Cat)
Born Andres Jose Padovani (Galarraga).
B. June 18, 1961, Caracas, Venezuela

BR TR 6'3" 235 lbs.

Year	Team	Games	BA	SA	AB	H	2B	3B	HR	HR%	R	RBI	BB	SO	SB	AB	H	PO	A	E	DP	TC/G	FA	G by Pos
1985	MON N	24	.187	.280	75	14	1	0	2	2.7	9	4	3	18	6	2	1	173	22	0	14	8.5	.995	1B-23
1986		105	.271	.405	321	87	13	0	10	3.1	39	42	30	79	6	7	1	805	40	4	59	8.3	.995	1B-102
1987		147	.305	.459	551	168	40	3	13	2.4	72	90	41	127	7	1	0	1300	103	10	96	9.7	.993	1B-146
1988		157	.302	.540	609	184	42	8	29	4.8	99	92	39	153	13	2	1	1464	103	15	124	10.1	.991	1B-156
1989		152	.257	.434	572	147	30	1	23	4.0	76	85	48	158	12	6	1	1335	91	11	97	9.8	.992	1B-147

Year	Team	Games	BA	SA	AB	H	2B	3B	HR	HR%	R	RBI	BB	SO	SB	Pinch Hit AB	Pinch Hit H	PO	A	E	DP	TC/G	FA	G by Pos

Andres Galarraga *continued*

Year	Team	Games	BA	SA	AB	H	2B	3B	HR	HR%	R	RBI	BB	SO	SB	AB	H	PO	A	E	DP	TC/G	FA	G by Pos
1990		155	.256	.409	579	148	29	0	20	3.5	65	87	40	**169**	10	7	0	1300	94	10	93	9.1	.993	1B-154
1991		107	.219	.336	375	82	13	2	9	2.4	34	33	23	86	5	2	0	887	80	9	68	9.3	.991	1B-105
1992	STL N	95	.243	.391	325	79	14	2	10	3.1	38	39	11	69	5	6	0	777	62	8	71	9.4	.991	1B-90
1993	CLR N	120	**.370**	.602	470	174	35	4	22	4.7	71	98	24	73	2	1	0	1018	103	11	88	9.5	.990	1B-119
1994		103	.319	.592	417	133	21	0	31	7.4	77	85	19	93	8	0	0	954	64	8	89	10.0	.992	1B-103
1995		143	.280	.511	554	155	29	3	31	5.6	89	106	32	**146**	12	1	0	1300	119	13	128	10.1	.991	1B-142
1996		159	.304	.601	626	190	39	3	**47**	7.5	119	**150**	40	157	18	0	0	1528	115	14	151	10.4	.992	1B-159, 3B-1
12 yrs.		1467	.285	.486	5474	1561	306	26	247	4.5	788	911	350	1328	99	35	4	12841	996	114	1078	9.6	.992	1B-1446, 3B-1

DIVISIONAL PLAYOFF SERIES
Year	Team	Games	BA	SA	AB	H	2B	3B	HR	HR%	R	RBI	BB	SO	SB	AB	H	PO	A	E	DP	TC/G	FA	G by Pos
1995	CLR N	4	.278	.333	18	5	1	0	0	0.0	1	2	0	6	0	0	0	41	2	0	4	10.8	1.000	1B-4

Mike Gallego

GALLEGO, MICHAEL ANTHONY
B. Oct. 31, 1960, Whittier, Calif.

BR TR 5'8" 160 lbs.

Year	Team	Games	BA	SA	AB	H	2B	3B	HR	HR%	R	RBI	BB	SO	SB	AB	H	PO	A	E	DP	TC/G	FA	G by Pos
1985	OAK A	76	.208	.338	77	16	5	1	1	1.3	13	9	12	14	1	2	0	57	94	1	25	2.0	.993	2B-42, SS-21, 3B-12
1986		20	.270	.324	37	10	2	0	0	0.0	2	4	1	6	0	0	0	24	51	1	6	3.5	.987	2B-19, 3B-2, SS-1
1987		72	.250	.347	124	31	6	0	2	1.6	18	14	12	21	0	4	1	75	122	8	29	2.8	.961	2B-31, 3B-24, SS-17
1988		129	.209	.260	277	58	8	0	2	0.7	38	20	34	53	2	3	0	155	254	8	49	3.0	.981	2B-83, SS-42, 3B-16
1989		133	.252	.328	357	90	14	2	3	0.8	45	30	35	43	7	2	0	211	363	19	86	4.3	.968	SS-94, 2B-41, 3B-3, DH-1
1990		140	.206	.272	389	80	13	2	3	0.8	36	34	35	50	5	2	1	207	379	13	78	4.0	.978	2B-83, SS-38, 3B-27, OF-1, DH-1
1991		159	.247	.369	482	119	15	4	12	2.5	67	49	67	84	6	0	0	283	446	12	90	3.9	.984	2B-135, SS-55
1992	NY A	53	.254	.358	173	44	7	1	3	1.7	24	14	20	22	0	0	0	112	153	6	41	5.0	.978	2B-40, SS-14
1993		119	.283	.412	403	114	20	1	10	2.5	63	54	50	65	3	1	0	169	368	13	76	4.1	.976	SS-55, 2B-52, 3B-27, DH-1
1994		89	.239	.359	306	73	17	1	6	2.0	39	41	38	46	0	0	0	141	311	11	69	4.7	.976	SS-72, 2B-26
1995	OAK A	43	.233	.233	120	28	0	0	0	0.0	11	8	9	24	0	1	1	46	90	5	15	3.2	.965	2B-18, SS-14, 3B-12
1996	STL N	51	.210	.224	143	30	2	0	0	0.0	12	4	12	31	0	4	1	91	126	3	32	4.3	.986	2B-43, 3B-7, SS-1
12 yrs.		1084	.240	.330	2888	693	109	12	42	1.5	368	281	325	459	24	19	4	1571	2757	100	596	3.8	.977	2B-613, SS-424, 3B-130, DH-3, OF-1

DIVISIONAL PLAYOFF SERIES
Year	Team	Games	BA	SA	AB	H	2B	3B	HR	HR%	R	RBI	BB	SO	SB	AB	H	PO	A	E	DP	TC/G	FA	G by Pos
1996	STL N	2	.000	.000	1	0	0	0	0	0.0	0	0	0	1	0	0	0	0	0	0	0	0.0		3B-1, 2B-1

LEAGUE CHAMPIONSHIP SERIES
Year	Team	Games	BA	SA	AB	H	2B	3B	HR	HR%	R	RBI	BB	SO	SB	AB	H	PO	A	E	DP	TC/G	FA	G by Pos
1988	OAK A	4	.083	.083	12	1	0	0	0	0.0	1	0	0	3	0	0	0	7	6	0	4	3.3	1.000	2B-4
1989		4	.273	.364	11	3	1	0	0	0.0	3	1	0	2	0	0	0	6	14	0	2	5.0	1.000	SS-2, 2B-2
1990		4	.400	.500	10	4	1	0	0	0.0	1	2	1	1	0	0	0	8	9	0	2	3.4	1.000	SS-3, 2B-2
1996	STL N	7	.143	.143	14	2	0	0	0	0.0	1	0	1	3	0	0	0	8	12	1	2	3.0	.952	2B-5, 3B-2
4 yrs.		19	.213	.255	47	10	2	0	0	0.0	6	3	2	9	0	0	0	29	41	1	10	3.5	.986	2B-13, SS-5, 3B-2

WORLD SERIES
Year	Team	Games	BA	SA	AB	H	2B	3B	HR	HR%	R	RBI	BB	SO	SB	AB	H	PO	A	E	DP	TC/G	FA	G by Pos
1988	OAK A	1	—	—	0	0	0	0	0	0.0	0	0	0	0	0	0	0	0	0	0	0	0.0	.000	2B-1
1989		2	.000	.000	1	0	0	0	0	0.0	0	0	0	0	1	0	0	0	0	0	0	0.0	.000	3B-1, 2B-1
1990		4	.091	.091	11	1	0	0	0	0.0	0	1	1	3	0	0	0	7	10	1	3	4.5	.944	SS-4
3 yrs.		7	.083	.083	12	1	0	0	0	0.0	0	1	1	3	1	0	0	7	10	1	3	2.6	.944	SS-4, 2B-2, 3B-1

Ron Gant

GANT, RONALD EDWIN
B. Mar. 2, 1965, Victoria, Tex.

BR TR 6' 200 lbs.

Year	Team	Games	BA	SA	AB	H	2B	3B	HR	HR%	R	RBI	BB	SO	SB	AB	H	PO	A	E	DP	TC/G	FA	G by Pos
1987	ATL N	21	.265	.386	83	22	4	0	2	2.4	9	9	1	11	4	1	0	45	59	3	17	5.3	.972	2B-20
1988		146	.259	.439	563	146	28	8	19	3.4	85	60	46	118	19	2	0	316	417	31	88	5.3	.959	2B-122, 3B-22
1989		75	.177	.335	260	46	8	3	9	3.5	26	25	20	63	9	8	1	70	103	17	8	2.8	.911	3B-53, OF-14
1990		152	.303	.539	575	174	34	3	32	5.6	107	84	50	86	33	10	2	357	7	8	2	2.5	.978	OF-146
1991		154	.251	.496	561	141	35	3	32	5.7	101	105	71	104	34	6	0	338	7	6	1	2.4	.983	OF-148
1992		153	.259	.415	544	141	22	6	17	3.1	74	80	45	101	32	9	2	277	5	4	0	1.9	.986	OF-147
1993		157	.274	.510	606	166	27	4	36	5.9	113	117	67	117	26	1	0	271	5	11	1	1.9	.962	OF-155
1995	CIN N	119	.276	.554	410	113	19	4	29	7.1	79	88	74	108	23	1	0	191	7	3	0	1.7	.985	OF-117
1996	STL N	122	.246	.504	419	103	14	2	30	7.2	74	82	73	98	13	6	1	216	4	5	2	1.9	.978	OF-116
9 yrs.		1099	.262	.479	4021	1052	191	33	206	5.1	668	650	447	806	193	44	6	2081	614	88	120	2.6	.968	OF-843, 2B-142, 3B-75

DIVISIONAL PLAYOFF SERIES
Year	Team	Games	BA	SA	AB	H	2B	3B	HR	HR%	R	RBI	BB	SO	SB	AB	H	PO	A	E	DP	TC/G	FA	G by Pos
1995	CIN N	3	.231	.462	13	3	0	0	1	7.7	3	2	0	0	0	0	0	8	1	0	0	3.0	1.000	OF-3
1996	STL N	3	.400	.800	10	4	1	0	1	10.0	3	4	2	0	2	0	0	5	0	0	0	1.7	1.000	OF-3
2 yrs.		6	.304	.609	23	7	1	0	2	8.7	6	6	2	3	2	0	0	13	1	0	0	2.3	1.000	OF-6

LEAGUE CHAMPIONSHIP SERIES
Year	Team	Games	BA	SA	AB	H	2B	3B	HR	HR%	R	RBI	BB	SO	SB	AB	H	PO	A	E	DP	TC/G	FA	G by Pos
1991	ATL N	7	.259	.407	27	7	1	0	1	3.7	4	3	2	4	7	0	0	15	2	0	0	2.4	1.000	OF-7
1992		7	.182	.455	22	4	0	0	2	9.1	5	6	4	4	1	0	0	16	0	0	0	2.3	1.000	OF-7
1993		6	.185	.296	27	5	3	0	0	0.0	4	3	2	9	0	0	0	10	1	1	0	2.0	.917	OF-6
1995	CIN N	4	.188	.188	16	3	0	0	0	0.0	1	1	0	3	0	0	0	9	0	0	0	2.3	1.000	OF-4
1996	STL N	7	.240	.520	25	6	1	0	2	8.0	3	4	2	6	0	0	0	12	0	0	0	1.7	1.000	OF-7
5 yrs.		31 3rd	.214	.385 4th	117	25	5	0	5 5th	4.3	17 4th	17 5th	10	26 2nd	8 4th	0	0	62	3	1	0	2.1	.985	OF-31

WORLD SERIES
Year	Team	Games	BA	SA	AB	H	2B	3B	HR	HR%	R	RBI	BB	SO	SB	AB	H	PO	A	E	DP	TC/G	FA	G by Pos
1991	ATL N	7	.267	.333	30	8	0	1	0	0.0	3	4	2	3	1	0	0	19	0	0	0	2.7	1.000	OF-7
1992		4	.125	.250	8	1	1	0	0	0.0	2	0	1	2	2	0	0	3	1	0	0	1.3	1.000	OF-3
2 yrs.		11	.237	.316	38	9	1	1	0	0.0	5	4	3	5	3	0	0	22	1	0	0	2.3	1.000	OF-10

Carlos Garcia

GARCIA, CARLOS JESUS
Born Carlos Jesus Garcia (Guerrero).
B. Oct. 15, 1967, Tachira, Venezuela

BR TR 6'1" 185 lbs.

Year	Team	Games	BA	SA	AB	H	2B	3B	HR	HR%	R	RBI	BB	SO	SB	AB	H	PO	A	E	DP	TC/G	FA	G by Pos
1990	PIT N	4	.500	.500	4	2	0	0	0	0.0	1	0	0	2	0	1	1	0	2	0	1	1.3	1.000	SS-3
1991		12	.250	.417	24	6	0	2	0	0.0	2	1	1	8	0	1	0	11	18	1	3	2.5	.967	SS-9, 3B-2, 2B-1
1992		22	.205	.231	39	8	1	0	0	0.0	4	4	0	9	0	3	1	25	35	2	11	2.8	.968	2B-14, SS-8

Year	Team	Games	BA	SA	AB	H	2B	3B	HR	HR%	R	RBI	BB	SO	SB	Pinch Hit AB	Pinch Hit H	PO	A	E	DP	TC/G	FA	G by Pos

Carlos Garcia *continued*

Year	Team	Games	BA	SA	AB	H	2B	3B	HR	HR%	R	RBI	BB	SO	SB	AB	H	PO	A	E	DP	TC/G	FA	G by Pos
1993		141	.269	.399	546	147	25	5	12	2.2	77	47	31	67	18	2	1	299	347	11	87	4.6	.983	2B-140, SS-3
1994		98	.277	.367	412	114	15	2	6	1.5	49	28	16	67	18	0	0	226	316	12	78	5.7	.978	2B-98
1995		104	.294	.420	367	108	24	2	6	1.6	41	50	25	55	8	0	0	235	298	15	75	5.1	.973	2B-92, SS-15
1996		101	.285	.397	390	111	18	4	6	1.5	66	44	23	58	16	2	0	160	284	11	53	4.1	.976	2B-77, SS-19, 3B-14
7 yrs.		482	.278	.392	1782	496	83	15	30	1.7	240	174	96	266	60	9	3	956	1302	52	308	4.7	.977	2B-422, SS-57, 3B-16
LEAGUE CHAMPIONSHIP SERIES																								
1992	PIT N	1	.000	.000	1	0	0	0	0	0.0	0	0	0	0	0	0	0	0	0	0	0	0.0	.000	2B-1

Karim Garcia

GARCIA, GUSTAVO KARIM
B. Oct. 29, 1975, Ciudad Obregon, Mexico

BL TL 6' 200 lbs.

Year	Team	Games	BA	SA	AB	H	2B	3B	HR	HR%	R	RBI	BB	SO	SB	AB	H	PO	A	E	DP	TC/G	FA	G by Pos
1995	LA N	13	.200	.200	20	4	0	0	0	0.0	1	0	0	4	0	8	2	5	2	0	1	1.4	1.000	OF-5
1996		1	.000	.000	1	0	0	0	0	0.0	0	0	0	1	0	1	0	0	0	0	0	0.0	—	
2 yrs.		14	.190	.190	21	4	0	0	0	0.0	1	0	0	5	0	9	2	5	2	0	1	1.4	1.000	OF-5

Nomar Garciaparra

GARCIAPARRA, ANTHONY NOMAR
B. Jul. 23, 1973, Whittier, Calif.

BR TR 6'0" 165 lbs.

Year	Team	Games	BA	SA	AB	H	2B	3B	HR	HR%	R	RBI	BB	SO	SB	AB	H	PO	A	E	DP	TC/G	FA	G by Pos
1996	BOS A	24	.241	.471	87	21	2	3	4	4.6	11	16	4	14	5	1	1	37	51	1	11	3.9	.989	SS-27, 2B-1, DH-1

Webster Garrison

GARRISON, WEBSTER LEOTIS
B. Aug. 24, 1965, Marrero, La.

BR TR 5'11" 170 lbs.

Year	Team	Games	BA	SA	AB	H	2B	3B	HR	HR%	R	RBI	BB	SO	SB	AB	H	PO	A	E	DP	TC/G	FA	G by Pos
1996	OAK A	5	.000	.000	9	0	0	0	0	0.0	0	0	0	0	0	1	0	4	5	1	1	2.5	.900	2B-3, 1B-1

Brent Gates

GATES, BRENT ROBERT
B. Mar. 14, 1970, Grand Rapids, Mich.

BB TR 6'1" 180 lbs.

Year	Team	Games	BA	SA	AB	H	2B	3B	HR	HR%	R	RBI	BB	SO	SB	AB	H	PO	A	E	DP	TC/G	FA	G by Pos
1993	OAK A	139	.290	.391	535	155	29	2	7	1.3	64	69	56	75	7	3	1	281	431	14	88	5.2	.981	2B-139
1994		64	.283	.365	233	66	11	1	2	0.9	29	24	21	32	3	2	1	112	160	8	28	4.4	.971	2B-63, 1B-1
1995		136	.254	.344	524	133	24	4	5	1.0	60	56	46	84	3	1	0	240	427	12	80	5.0	.982	2B-132, DH-3, 1B-1
1996		64	.263	.381	247	65	19	2	2	0.8	26	30	18	35	1	1	0	140	183	9	48	5.2	.973	2B-64
4 yrs.		403	.272	.369	1539	419	83	9	16	1.0	179	179	141	226	14	7	2	773	1201	43	244	5.0	.979	2B-398, DH-3, 1B-2

Jason Giambi

GIAMBI, JASON GILBERT
B. Jan. 8, 1971, West Covina, Calif.

BL TR 6'2" 200 lbs.

Year	Team	Games	BA	SA	AB	H	2B	3B	HR	HR%	R	RBI	BB	SO	SB	AB	H	PO	A	E	DP	TC/G	FA	G by Pos
1995	OAK A	54	.256	.398	176	45	7	0	6	3.4	27	25	28	31	2	3	0	195	55	4	24	4.4	.984	3B-30, 1B-26, DH-2
1996		140	.291	.481	536	156	40	1	20	3.7	84	79	51	95	0	4	1	477	119	11	49	4.3	.982	1B-45, OF-45, 3B-39, DH-12
2 yrs.		194	.282	.461	712	201	47	1	26	3.7	111	104	79	126	2	7	1	672	174	15	73	4.3	.983	1B-71, 3B-69, OF-45, DH-14

Steve Gibralter

GIBRALTER, STEPHAN BENSON
B. Oct. 9, 1972, Dallas, Tex.

BR TR 6' 185 lbs.

Year	Team	Games	BA	SA	AB	H	2B	3B	HR	HR%	R	RBI	BB	SO	SB	AB	H	PO	A	E	DP	TC/G	FA	G by Pos
1995	CIN N	4	.333	.333	3	1	0	0	0	0.0	0	0	0	0	0	2	1	1	0	0	0	0.5	1.000	OF-2
1996		2	.000	.000	2	0	0	0	0	0.0	0	0	0	2	0	0	0	0	0	1	0	0.5	.000	OF-2
2 yrs.		6	.200	.200	5	1	0	0	0	0.0	0	0	0	2	0	2	1	1	0	1	0	0.5	.500	OF-4

Benji Gil

GIL, ROMAR BENJAMIN
Born Romar Benjamin Gil (Aguilar).
B. Oct. 6, 1972, Tijuana, Mexico

BR TR 6'2" 180 lbs.

Year	Team	Games	BA	SA	AB	H	2B	3B	HR	HR%	R	RBI	BB	SO	SB	AB	H	PO	A	E	DP	TC/G	FA	G by Pos
1993	TEX A	22	.123	.123	57	7	0	0	0	0.0	3	2	5	22	1	0	0	27	76	5	10	4.9	.954	SS-22
1995		130	.219	.347	415	91	20	3	9	2.2	36	46	26	147	2	0	0	228	409	17	92	5.0	.974	SS-130
1996		5	.400	.400	5	2	0	0	0	0.0	0	1	1	1	0	0	0	5	7	1	0	2.6	.923	SS-5
3 yrs.		157	.210	.321	477	100	20	3	9	1.9	39	49	32	170	3	0	0	260	492	23	102	4.9	.970	SS-157

Brian Giles

GILES, BRIAN STEPHEN
B. Jan. 21, 1971, El Cajon, Calif.

BL TL 5'11" 195 lbs.

Year	Team	Games	BA	SA	AB	H	2B	3B	HR	HR%	R	RBI	BB	SO	SB	AB	H	PO	A	E	DP	TC/G	FA	G by Pos
1995	CLE A	6	.556	.889	9	5	0	0	1	11.1	6	3	0	1	0	2	2	2	1	0	0	0.8	1.000	OF-3, DH-1
1996		51	.355	.612	121	43	14	1	5	4.1	26	27	19	13	3	14	4	26	0	0	0	0.7	1.000	DH-21, OF-16
2 yrs.		57	.369	.631	130	48	14	1	6	4.6	32	30	19	14	3	16	6	28	1	0	0	0.7	1.000	DH-22, OF-19
DIVISIONAL PLAYOFF SERIES																								
1996	CLE A	1	.000	.000	1	0	0	0	0	0.0	0	0	0	1	0	1	0	0	0	0	0	0.0	—	

Bernard Gilkey

GILKEY, OTIS BERNARD
B. Sept. 24, 1966, St. Louis, Mo.

BR TR 6' 170 lbs.

Year	Team	Games	BA	SA	AB	H	2B	3B	HR	HR%	R	RBI	BB	SO	SB	AB	H	PO	A	E	DP	TC/G	FA	G by Pos
1990	STL N	18	.297	.484	64	19	5	2	1	1.6	11	3	8	5	6	0	0	47	2	2	0	2.8	.961	OF-18
1991		81	.216	.313	268	58	7	2	5	1.9	28	20	39	33	14	7	1	164	6	1	1	2.3	.994	OF-74
1992		131	.302	.427	384	116	19	4	7	1.8	56	43	39	52	18	20	4	217	9	5	3	2.1	.978	OF-111
1993		137	.305	.481	557	170	40	5	16	2.9	99	70	56	66	15	1	1	251	20	8	4	2.0	.971	OF-134, 1B-3
1994		105	.253	.363	380	96	22	1	6	1.6	52	45	39	65	15	4	2	168	9	3	3	1.8	.983	OF-102
1995		121	.298	.490	480	143	33	4	17	3.5	73	69	42	70	12	3	1	206	10	3	4	1.9	.986	OF-118
1996	NY N	153	.317	.562	571	181	44	3	30	5.3	108	117	73	125	17	2	1	310	18	6	2	2.2	.982	OF-151
7 yrs.		746	.290	.459	2704	783	170	21	82	3.0	427	367	296	416	97	37	10	1363	74	28	17	2.1	.981	OF-708, 1B-3

Year	Team	Games	BA	SA	AB	H	2B	3B	HR	HR%	R	RBI	BB	SO	SB	Pinch Hit AB	Pinch Hit H	PO	A	E	DP	TC/G	FA	G by Pos

Ed Giovanola — GIOVANOLA, EDWARD THOMAS — B. Mar. 4, 1969, Los Gatos, Calif. — BL TR 5'10" 170 lbs.

Year	Team	Games	BA	SA	AB	H	2B	3B	HR	HR%	R	RBI	BB	SO	SB	PH AB	PH H	PO	A	E	DP	TC/G	FA	G by Pos
1995	ATL N	13	.071	.071	14	1	0	0	0	0.0	2	0	3	5	0	2	0	9	7	0	1	1.5	1.000	2B-7, 3B-3, SS-1
1996		43	.232	.256	82	19	2	0	0	0.0	10	7	8	13	1	14	5	24	55	1	12	2.2	.988	SS-25, 3B-6, 2B-5
2 yrs.		56	.208	.229	96	20	2	0	0	0.0	12	7	11	18	1	16	5	33	62	1	13	2.0	.990	SS-26, 2B-12, 3B-9

Joe Girardi — GIRARDI, JOSEPH ELLIOTT — B. Oct. 14, 1964, Peoria, Ill. — BR TR 5'11" 195 lbs.

Year	Team	Games	BA	SA	AB	H	2B	3B	HR	HR%	R	RBI	BB	SO	SB	PH AB	PH H	PO	A	E	DP	TC/G	FA	G by Pos
1989	CHI N	59	.248	.331	157	39	10	0	1	0.6	15	14	11	26	2	0	0	332	28	7	1	6.2	.981	C-59
1990		133	.270	.344	419	113	24	2	1	0.2	36	38	17	50	8	0	0	653	61	11	5	5.5	.985	C-133
1991		21	.191	.234	47	9	2	0	0	0.0	3	6	6	6	0	1	1	95	11	3	1	5.2	.972	C-21
1992		91	.270	.300	270	73	3	1	1	0.4	19	12	19	38	0	10	5	369	51	4	6	4.9	.991	C-86
1993	CLR N	86	.290	.397	310	90	14	5	3	1.0	35	31	24	41	6	2	0	478	46	6	7	6.3	.989	C-84
1994		93	.276	.364	330	91	9	4	4	1.2	47	34	21	48	3	0	0	548	55	5	5	6.5	.992	C-93
1995		125	.262	.359	462	121	17	2	8	1.7	63	55	29	76	3	4	2	729	61	10	3	6.6	.988	C-122
1996	NY A	124	.294	.374	422	124	22	3	2	0.5	55	45	30	55	13	4	1	803	45	3	8	7.0	.996	C-120, DH-2
8 yrs.		732	.273	.354	2417	660	101	17	20	0.8	273	235	157	340	35	21	9	4007	358	49	36	6.1	.989	C-718, DH-2

DIVISIONAL PLAYOFF SERIES

1995	CLR N	4	.125	.125	16	2	0	0	0	0.0	0	0	0	2	0	0	0	25	3	1	2	7.3	.966	C-4
1996	NY A	4	.222	.222	9	2	0	0	0	0.0	1	0	4	1	0	0	0	28	1	0	1	7.3	1.000	C-4
2 yrs.		8	.160	.160	25	4	0	0	0	0.0	1	0	4	3	0	0	0	53	4	1	3	7.3	.983	C-8

LEAGUE CHAMPIONSHIP SERIES

1989	CHI N	4	.100	.100	10	1	0	0	0	0.0	0	1	0	2	0	0	0	20	0	0	0	5.0	1.000	C-4
1996	NY A	4	.250	.417	12	3	0	1	0	0.0	2	1	2	3	0	1	0	22	0	0	0	5.5	1.000	C-4
2 yrs.		8	.182	.273	22	4	0	1	0	0.0	2	2	2	5	0	1	0	42	0	0	0	5.3	1.000	C-8

WORLD SERIES

| 1996 | NY A | 4 | .200 | .400 | 10 | 2 | 0 | 1 | 0 | 0.0 | 1 | 1 | 1 | 2 | 0 | 0 | 0 | 23 | 4 | 0 | 0 | 6.8 | 1.000 | C-4 |

Doug Glanville — GLANVILLE, DOUGLAS METUNWA — B. Aug. 25, 1970, Hackensack, N. J. — BR TR 6'2" 170 lbs.

| 1996 | CHI N | 49 | .241 | .361 | 83 | 20 | 5 | 1 | 1 | 1.2 | 10 | 10 | 3 | 11 | 2 | 19 | 6 | 35 | 1 | 1 | 0 | 1.1 | .973 | OF-35 |

Jerry Goff — GOFF, JERRY LEROY — B. Apr. 12, 1964, San Rafael, Calif. — BL TR 6'3" 205 lbs.

1990	MON N	52	.227	.311	119	27	1	0	3	2.5	14	7	21	36	0	6	3	216	17	9	3	5.5	.963	C-38, 3B-3, 1B-3
1992		3	.000	.000	3	0	0	0	0	0.0	0	0	0	3	0	3	0	0	0	0	0	0.0	—	
1993	PIT N	14	.297	.514	37	11	2	0	2	5.4	5	6	8	9	0	2	1	54	7	1	0	4.4	.984	C-14
1994		8	.080	.080	25	2	0	0	0	0.0	0	1	0	11	0	1	0	34	4	2	0	5.7	.950	C-7
1995	HOU N	12	.154	.346	26	4	0	0	1	3.8	2	3	4	13	0	1	0	80	5	0	1	7.7	1.000	C-11
1996		1	.500	1.250	4	2	0	0	1	25.0	1	2	0	1	0	0	0	11	0	0	1	11.0	1.000	C-1
6 yrs.		90	.215	.336	214	46	5	0	7	3.3	22	19	33	73	0	13	4	395	33	12	5	5.7	.973	C-71, 3B-3, 1B-3

Chris Gomez — GOMEZ, CHRISTOPHER CORY — B. June 16, 1971, Los Angeles, Calif. — BR TR 6'1" 183 lbs.

1993	DET A	46	.250	.320	128	32	7	1	0	0.0	11	11	9	17	2	0	0	69	118	5	23	4.1	.974	SS-29, 2B-17, DH-1
1994		84	.257	.402	296	76	19	0	8	2.7	32	53	33	64	5	0	0	141	210	8	39	4.1	.978	SS-57, 2B-30
1995		123	.223	.355	431	96	20	2	11	2.6	49	50	41	96	4	3	1	210	362	15	78	4.6	.974	SS-97, 2B-31, DH-1
1996	2 teams	DET A (48G –.242)		SD N (89G –.262)																				
"	total	137	.257	.333	456	117	21	1	4	0.9	53	45	57	84	3	1	0	203	375	19	88	4.4	.968	SS-136
4 yrs.		390	.245	.355	1311	321	67	4	23	1.8	145	159	140	261	14	4	1	623	1065	47	228	4.3	.973	SS-319, 2B-78, DH-2

DIVISIONAL PLAYOFF SERIES

| 1996 | SD N | 3 | .167 | .167 | 12 | 2 | 0 | 0 | 0 | 0.0 | 0 | 1 | 0 | 4 | 0 | 0 | 0 | 8 | 5 | 0 | 3 | 4.3 | 1.000 | SS-3 |

Leo Gomez — GOMEZ, LEONARDO — Born Leonardo Gomez (Velez). — B. Mar. 2, 1966, Canovanas, Puerto Rico — BR TR 6' 180 lbs.

1990	BAL A	12	.231	.231	39	9	0	0	0	0.0	3	1	8	7	0	0	0	11	20	4	2	2.9	.886	3B-12
1991		118	.233	.409	391	91	17	2	16	4.1	40	45	40	82	1	5	0	78	184	7	20	2.3	.974	3B-105, DH-10, 1B-3
1992		137	.265	.425	468	124	24	0	17	3.6	62	64	63	78	2	0	0	106	246	18	19	2.7	.951	3B-137
1993		71	.197	.348	244	48	7	0	10	4.1	30	25	32	60	0	0	0	48	145	10	16	2.9	.951	3B-70, DH-1
1994		84	.274	.502	285	78	20	0	15	5.3	46	56	41	55	0	2	0	56	141	5	12	2.4	.975	3B-78, DH-5, 1B-1
1995		53	.236	.370	127	30	5	0	4	3.1	16	12	18	23	0	9	3	28	68	2	3	1.9	.980	3B-44, DH-5, 1B-3
1996	CHI N	136	.238	.431	362	86	19	0	17	4.7	44	56	53	94	1	15	3	110	180	7	18	2.2	.976	3B-124, 1B-8, SS-1
7 yrs.		611	.243	.417	1916	466	92	2	79	4.1	241	259	255	399	4	31	6	437	984	53	90	2.4	.964	3B-570, DH-21, 1B-15, SS-1

Rene Gonzales — GONZALES, RENE ADRIAN — B. Sept. 23, 1960, Austin, Tex. — BR TR 6'3" 180 lbs.

1984	MON N	29	.233	.267	30	7	1	0	0	0.0	5	2	2	5	0	0	0	17	28	2	5	1.7	.957	SS-27
1986		11	.115	.115	26	3	0	0	0	0.0	1	0	2	7	0	0	0	7	19	0	3	2.4	1.000	SS-6, 3B-5
1987	BAL A	37	.267	.383	60	16	2	1	1	1.7	14	7	3	11	1	0	0	22	43	2	5	1.9	.970	3B-29, 2B-6, SS-1
1988		92	.215	.266	237	51	6	0	2	0.8	13	15	13	32	1	0	0	66	185	8	26	2.6	.969	3B-80, 2B-14, SS-2, OF-1, 1B-1
1989		71	.217	.259	166	36	4	0	1	0.6	16	11	12	30	5	2	0	103	146	7	37	3.6	.973	2B-54, 3B-17, SS-1
1990		67	.214	.291	103	22	3	1	1	1.0	13	12	12	14	1	0	0	68	114	2	23	2.7	.989	2B-43, 3B-16, SS-9, OF-1
1991	TOR A	71	.195	.246	118	23	3	0	1	0.8	16	6	12	21	0	2	1	61	118	7	17	2.5	.962	SS-36, 3B-26, 2B-11, 1B-2
1992	CAL A	104	.277	.398	329	91	17	1	7	2.1	47	38	41	46	7	2	1	191	229	9	49	3.7	.979	3B-53, 2B-42, 1B-13, SS-8

Year	Team	Games	BA	SA	AB	H	2B	3B	HR	HR%	R	RBI	BB	SO	SB	Pinch Hit AB	H	PO	A	E	DP	TC/G	FA	G by Pos

Rene Gonzales *continued*

Year	Team	Games	BA	SA	AB	H	2B	3B	HR	HR%	R	RBI	BB	SO	SB	AB	H	PO	A	E	DP	TC/G	FA	G by Pos
1993		117	.251	.319	335	84	17	0	2	0.6	34	31	49	45	5	5	2	234	170	12	46	3.5	.971	3B-79, 1B-31, SS-5, 2B-4, P-1
1994	CLE A	22	.348	.609	23	8	1	1	1	4.3	6	5	5	3	2	3	1	17	21	1	2	1.8	.974	3B-13, SS-4, 1B-4, 2B-1
1995	CAL A	30	.333	.556	18	6	1	0	1	5.6	1	3	0	4	0	5	2	6	12	0	0	0.7	1.000	3B-18, 2B-6, SS-1
1996	TEX A	51	.217	.326	92	20	4	0	2	2.2	19	5	10	11	0	4	0	109	61	2	20	3.2	.988	1B-23, 3B-15, SS-10, 2B-5, OF-1
12 yrs.		702	.239	.319	1537	367	59	4	19	1.2	185	135	161	230	23	23	7	901	1146	52	233	2.9	.975	3B-351, 2B-186, SS-110, 1B-74, OF-3, P-1

DIVISIONAL PLAYOFF SERIES

1996	TEX A	1	—	—	0	0	0	0	0	—	0	0	0	0	0	0	0	0	0	0	0	0.0	.000	SS-1

LEAGUE CHAMPIONSHIP SERIES

1991	TOR A	2	—	—	0	0	0	0	0	—	0	0	0	0	0	0	0	2	0	0	0	1.0	1.000	1B-1, SS-1

Alex Gonzalez

GONZALEZ, ALEXANDER SCOTT
B. Apr. 8, 1973, Miami, Fla.   BR TR 6' 180 lbs.

Year	Team	Games	BA	SA	AB	H	2B	3B	HR	HR%	R	RBI	BB	SO	SB	AB	H	PO	A	E	DP	TC/G	FA	G by Pos
1994	TOR A	15	.151	.245	53	8	3	1	0	0.0	7	1	4	17	3	0	0	18	49	6	5	4.9	.918	SS-15
1995		111	.243	.398	367	89	19	4	10	2.7	51	42	44	114	4	3	0	164	227	19	45	3.8	.954	SS-97, 3B-9, DH-3
1996		147	.235	.391	527	124	30	5	14	2.7	64	64	45	127	16	0	0	280	465	21	123	5.2	.973	SS-147
3 yrs.		273	.233	.385	947	221	52	10	24	2.5	122	107	93	258	23	3	0	462	741	46	173	4.6	.963	SS-259, 3B-9, DH-3

Juan Gonzalez

GONZALEZ, JUAN ALBERTO
Born Juan Alberto Gonzalez (Vasquez).
B. Oct. 16, 1969, Vega Baja, Puerto Rico   BR TR 6'3" 175 lbs.

Year	Team	Games	BA	SA	AB	H	2B	3B	HR	HR%	R	RBI	BB	SO	SB	AB	H	PO	A	E	DP	TC/G	FA	G by Pos
1989	TEX A	24	.150	.250	60	9	3	0	1	1.7	6	7	6	17	0	1	0	53	0	2	0	2.3	.964	OF-24
1990		25	.289	.522	90	26	7	1	4	4.4	11	12	2	18	0	3	1	33	0	0	0	1.3	1.000	OF-16, DH-9
1991		142	.264	.479	545	144	34	1	27	5.0	78	102	42	118	4	3	0	310	6	6	1	2.3	.981	OF-136, DH-4
1992		155	.260	.529	584	152	24	2	43	7.4	77	109	35	143	0	6	1	379	9	10	2	2.6	.975	OF-148, DH-4
1993		140	.310	**.632**	536	166	33	1	46	8.6	105	118	37	99	4	1	1	265	5	4	0	2.0	.985	OF-129, DH-10
1994		107	.275	.472	422	116	18	4	19	4.5	57	85	30	66	6	0	0	223	9	2	1	2.2	.991	OF-107
1995		90	.295	.594	352	104	20	2	27	7.7	57	82	17	66	0	3	0	6	1	0	0	0.1	1.000	DH-83, OF-5
1996		134	.314	.643	541	170	33	2	47	8.7	89	144	45	82	2	0	0	164	6	2	0	1.3	.988	OF-102, DH-32
8 yrs.		817	.283	.552	3130	887	172	13	214	6.8	480	659	214	609	16	17	3	1433	36	26	4	1.8	.983	OF-667, DH-142

DIVISIONAL PLAYOFF SERIES

1996	TEX A	4	.438	1.375	16	7	0	0	5	31.3	5	9	3	2	0	0	0	8	0	0	0	2.0	1.000	OF-4

Luis Gonzalez

GONZALEZ, LUIS EMILIO
B. Sept. 3, 1967, Tampa, Fla.   BL TR 6' 180 lbs.

Year	Team	Games	BA	SA	AB	H	2B	3B	HR	HR%	R	RBI	BB	SO	SB	AB	H	PO	A	E	DP	TC/G	FA	G by Pos
1990	HOU N	12	.190	.286	21	4	2	0	0	0.0	1	0	2	5	0	5	1	22	10	0	1	5.3	1.000	3B-4, 1B-2
1991		137	.254	.433	473	120	28	9	13	2.7	51	69	40	101	10	5	1	294	6	5	1	2.3	.984	OF-133
1992		122	.243	.385	387	94	19	3	10	2.6	40	55	24	52	7	17	5	261	5	2	1	2.4	.993	OF-111
1993		154	.300	.457	540	162	34	3	15	2.8	82	72	47	83	20	6	3	347	10	8	2	2.4	.978	OF-149
1994		112	.273	.429	392	107	29	4	8	2.0	57	67	49	57	15	2	1	228	5	2	1	2.1	.991	OF-111
1995	2 teams	HOU N (56G –.258)				CHI N (77G –.290)																		
"	total	133	.276	.454	471	130	29	4	13	2.8	69	69	57	63	6	4	3	266	7	6	0	2.1	.978	OF-131
1996	CHI N	146	.271	.443	483	131	30	4	15	3.1	70	79	61	49	9	9	1	244	7	3	1	1.8	.988	OF-139, 1B-2
7 yrs.		816	.270	.435	2767	748	171	31	74	2.7	370	411	280	410	67	48	15	1662	50	26	7	2.2	.985	OF-774, 3B-4, 1B-4

Curtis Goodwin

GOODWIN, CURTIS LaMAR
B. Sept. 30, 1972, Oakland, Calif.   BL TL 5'11" 180 lbs.

Year	Team	Games	BA	SA	AB	H	2B	3B	HR	HR%	R	RBI	BB	SO	SB	AB	H	PO	A	E	DP	TC/G	FA	G by Pos
1995	BAL A	87	.263	.332	289	76	11	3	1	0.3	40	24	15	53	22	2	1	202	1	2	1	2.4	.990	OF-84, DH-2
1996	CIN N	49	.228	.250	136	31	3	0	0	0.0	20	5	19	34	15	8	0	64	0	2	0	1.6	.970	OF-42
2 yrs.		136	.252	.306	425	107	14	3	1	0.2	60	29	34	87	37	10	1	266	1	4	1	2.1	.985	OF-126, DH-2

Tom Goodwin

GOODWIN, THOMAS JONES
B. July 27, 1968, Fresno, Calif.   BL TR 6'1" 165 lbs.

Year	Team	Games	BA	SA	AB	H	2B	3B	HR	HR%	R	RBI	BB	SO	SB	AB	H	PO	A	E	DP	TC/G	FA	G by Pos
1991	LA N	16	.143	.143	7	1	0	0	0	0.0	3	0	0	1	1	1	0	8	0	0	0	1.6	1.000	OF-5
1992		57	.233	.274	73	17	1	1	0	0.0	15	3	6	10	7	5	2	43	0	0	0	1.0	1.000	OF-45
1993		30	.294	.353	17	5	1	0	0	0.0	6	1	1	4	1	5	1	8	0	0	0	0.7	1.000	OF-12
1994	KC A	2	.000	.000	2	0	0	0	0	0.0	0	0	0	1	0	0	0	1	0	0	0	0.5	1.000	OF-1, DH-1
1995		133	.287	.358	480	138	16	3	4	0.8	72	28	38	72	50	0	0	290	6	3	1	2.3	.990	OF-130, DH-2
1996		143	.282	.330	524	148	14	4	1	0.2	80	35	39	79	66	2	1	304	7	5	1	2.2	.984	OF-136, DH-5
6 yrs.		381	.280	.337	1103	309	32	8	5	0.5	176	67	84	166	125	13	4	654	13	8	2	2.0	.988	OF-329, DH-8

Mark Grace

GRACE, MARK EUGENE
B. June 28, 1964, Winston-Salem, N. C.   BL TL 6'2" 190 lbs.

Year	Team	Games	BA	SA	AB	H	2B	3B	HR	HR%	R	RBI	BB	SO	SB	AB	H	PO	A	E	DP	TC/G	FA	G by Pos
1988	CHI N	134	.296	.403	486	144	23	4	7	1.4	65	57	60	43	3	7	3	1182	87	17	91	9.7	.987	1B-133
1989		142	.314	.457	510	160	28	3	13	2.5	74	79	80	42	14	1	1	1230	126	6	93	9.6	.996	1B-142
1990		157	.309	.413	589	182	32	1	9	1.5	72	82	59	54	15	7	2	1324	180	12	116	9.9	.992	1B-153
1991		160	.273	.373	619	169	28	5	8	1.3	87	58	70	53	3	4	0	1520	167	8	106	10.6	.995	1B-160
1992		158	.307	.430	603	185	37	5	9	1.5	72	79	72	36	6	1	0	1580	141	4	119	11.0	.998	1B-157
1993		155	.325	.475	594	193	39	4	14	2.4	86	98	71	32	8	1	0	1456	112	5	134	10.2	.997	1B-154
1994		106	.298	.414	403	120	23	3	6	1.5	55	44	48	41	0	5	2	925	76	7	90	9.8	.993	1B-103
1995		143	.326	.516	552	180	51	3	16	2.9	97	92	65	46	6	0	0	1211	115	7	91	9.3	.995	1B-143
1996		142	.331	.455	547	181	39	1	9	1.6	88	75	62	41	2	1	0	1259	107	4	119	10.0	.997	1B-141
9 yrs.		1297	.309	.437	4903	1514	300	29	91	1.9	696	664	587	388	57	27	8	11687	1111	70	959	10.0	.995	1B-1286

Year	Team	Games	BA	SA	AB	H	2B	3B	HR	HR%	R	RBI	BB	SO	SB	Pinch Hit AB	Pinch Hit H	PO	A	E	DP	TC/G	FA	G by Pos

Mark Grace *continued*

LEAGUE CHAMPIONSHIP SERIES

| 1989 | CHI | N | 5 | .647 | 1.118 | 17 | 11 | 3 | 1 | 1 | 5.9 | 3 | 8 | 4 | 1 | 1 | 0 | 0 | 44 | 3 | 0 | 1 | 9.4 | 1.000 | 1B-5 |

Tony Graffanino

GRAFFANINO, ANTHONY JOSEPH
B. Jun. 6, 1972, Amityville, N.Y.
BR TR 6'1" 175 lbs.

| 1996 | ATL | N | 22 | .174 | .239 | 46 | 8 | 1 | 1 | 0 | 0.0 | 7 | 2 | 4 | 13 | 0 | 5 | 0 | 24 | 39 | 2 | 9 | 3.6 | .969 | 2B-18 |

Craig Grebeck

GREBECK, CRAIG ALLEN
B. Dec. 29, 1964, Johnstown, Pa.
BR TR 5'8" 160 lbs.

1990	CHI	A	59	.168	.235	119	20	3	1	1	0.8	7	9	8	24	0	4	1	36	98	3	10	2.4	.978	3B-35, SS-16, 2B-6, DH-1
1991			107	.281	.460	224	63	16	3	6	2.7	37	31	38	40	1	14	3	104	183	10	34	2.7	.966	3B-49, 2B-36, SS-26
1992			88	.268	.387	287	77	21	2	3	1.0	24	35	30	34	0	0	0	112	283	8	47	4.3	.980	SS-85, 3B-7, OF-2
1993			72	.226	.268	190	43	5	0	1	0.5	25	12	26	26	1	3	0	91	185	5	40	3.7	.982	SS-46, 2B-16, 3B-14
1994			35	.309	.361	97	30	5	0	0	0.0	17	5	12	5	0	1	0	44	65	2	13	3.2	.982	2B-14, SS-14, 3B-7
1995			53	.260	.357	154	40	12	0	1	0.6	19	18	21	23	0	2	1	77	127	7	25	3.7	.967	SS-31, 3B-18, 2B-8
1996	FLA	N	50	.211	.253	95	20	1	0	1	1.1	8	9	4	14	0	17	5	68	66	2	24	4.3	.985	2B-29, SS-12, 3B-1
7 yrs.			464	.251	.349	1166	293	63	6	13	1.1	137	119	139	166	2	41	11	532	1007	37	193	3.4	.977	SS-220, 3B-131, 2B-109, OF-2, DH-1

LEAGUE CHAMPIONSHIP SERIES

| 1993 | CHI | A | 1 | 1.000 | 1.000 | 1 | 1 | 0 | 0 | 0 | 0.0 | 0 | 0 | 0 | 0 | 0 | 1 | 1 | 0 | 0 | 0 | 0 | 0.0 | .000 | 3B-1 |

Shawn Green

GREEN, SHAWN DAVID
B. Nov. 10, 1972, Des Plaines, Ill.
BL TL 6'4" 190 lbs.

1993	TOR	A	3	.000	.000	6	0	0	0	0	0.0	0	1	0	0	0	0	0	1	0	0	0	0.3	1.000	OF-2, DH-1
1994			14	.091	.121	33	3	1	0	0	0.0	1	1	1	8	1	0	0	12	2	0	0	1.0	1.000	OF-14
1995			121	.288	.509	379	109	31	4	15	4.0	52	54	20	68	1	15	3	207	9	6	2	2.0	.973	OF-109
1996			132	.280	.448	422	118	32	3	11	2.6	52	45	33	75	5	13	3	254	10	2	3	2.1	.992	OF-127, DH-1
4 yrs.			270	.274	.460	840	230	64	7	26	3.1	105	100	54	152	7	28	6	474	21	8	5	2.0	.984	OF-252, DH-2

Charlie Greene

GREENE, CHARLES PATRICK
B. Jan. 23, 1971, Miami, Fla.
BR TR 6'1" 170 lbs.

| 1996 | NY | N | 2 | .000 | .000 | 0 | 0 | 0 | 0 | 0 | 0.0 | 0 | 0 | 0 | 0 | 0 | 0 | 0 | 1 | 0 | 0 | 0 | 1.0 | 1.000 | C-1 |

Todd Greene

GREENE, TODD ANTHONY
B. Nov. 9, 1954, Detroit, Mich.
BR TR 5'10" 195 lbs.

| 1996 | CAL | A | 29 | .190 | .278 | 79 | 15 | 1 | 0 | 2 | 2.5 | 9 | 9 | 4 | 11 | 2 | 3 | 0 | 119 | 19 | 0 | 1 | 5.3 | 1.000 | C-26, DH-1 |

Willie Greene

GREENE, WILLIE LOUIS
B. Sept. 23, 1971, Milledgeville, Ga.
BL TR 5'11" 180 lbs.

1992	CIN	N	29	.269	.430	93	25	5	2	2	2.2	10	13	10	23	0	4	0	15	40	3	6	2.3	.948	3B-25
1993			15	.160	.340	50	8	1	1	2	4.0	7	5	2	19	0	1	0	19	37	1	8	3.8	.982	SS-10, 3B-5
1994			16	.216	.270	37	8	2	0	0	0.0	5	3	6	14	0	4	1	2	21	1	1	1.7	.958	3B-13, OF-1
1995			8	.105	.105	19	2	0	0	0	0.0	1	0	3	7	0	1	0	1	13	0	1	2.0	1.000	3B-7
1996			115	.244	.495	287	70	5	5	19	6.6	48	63	36	88	0	34	8	56	147	16	13	2.5	.927	3B-74, OF-10, 1B-2, SS-1
5 yrs.			183	.233	.434	486	113	13	8	23	4.7	71	84	57	151	0	44	9	93	258	21	29	2.5	.944	3B-124, OF-11, SS-11, 1B-2

Mike Greenwell

GREENWELL, MICHAEL LEWIS
B. July 18, 1963, Louisville, Ky.
BL TR 6' 170 lbs.

1985	BOS	A	17	.323	.742	31	10	1	0	4	12.9	7	8	3	4	1	1	0	14	0	0	0	0.8	1.000	OF-17
1986			31	.314	.371	35	11	2	0	0	0.0	4	4	5	7	0	12	2	18	1	0	1	1.1	1.000	OF-15, DH-3
1987			125	.328	.570	412	135	31	6	19	4.6	71	89	35	40	5	17	5	165	8	6	0	1.7	.966	OF-91, DH-15, C-1
1988			158	.325	.531	590	192	39	8	22	3.7	86	119	87	38	16	0	0	302	6	6	2	2.0	.981	OF-147, DH-11
1989			145	.308	.443	578	178	36	0	14	2.4	87	95	56	44	13	1	1	220	11	8	1	1.7	.967	OF-139, DH-5
1990			159	.297	.434	610	181	30	6	14	2.3	71	73	65	43	8	1	0	287	13	7	1	1.9	.977	OF-159
1991			147	.300	.419	544	163	26	6	9	1.7	76	83	43	35	15	4	1	263	9	3	3	1.9	.989	OF-143, DH-1
1992			49	.233	.278	180	42	2	0	2	1.1	16	18	18	19	2	2	2	85	1	0	0	1.8	1.000	OF-41, DH-6
1993			146	.315	.480	540	170	38	6	13	2.4	77	72	54	46	5	3	0	261	6	2	1	1.9	.993	OF-134, DH-10
1994			95	.269	.453	327	88	25	1	11	3.4	60	45	38	26	2	7	2	141	10	1	1	1.7	.993	OF-84, DH-6
1995			120	.297	.459	481	143	25	4	15	3.1	67	76	38	35	9	0	0	202	10	6	1	1.8	.972	OF-118, DH-2
1996			77	.295	.441	295	87	20	1	7	2.4	35	44	18	27	4	2	0	137	9	4	2	2.0	.973	OF-76
12 yrs.			1269	.303	.463	4623	1400	275	38	130	2.8	657	726	460	364	80	50	13	2095	84	43	13	1.8	.981	OF-1164, DH-59, C-1

DIVISIONAL PLAYOFF SERIES

| 1995 | BOS | A | 3 | .200 | .200 | 15 | 3 | 0 | 0 | 0 | 0.0 | 0 | 0 | 0 | 1 | 0 | 0 | 0 | 8 | 0 | 0 | 0 | 2.7 | 1.000 | OF-3 |

LEAGUE CHAMPIONSHIP SERIES

1986	BOS	A	2	.500	.500	2	1	0	0	0	0.0	0	0	0	0	0	2	1	0	0	0	0	0.0	—	OF-4
1988			4	.214	.500	14	3	1	0	1	7.1	2	3	3	0	0	0	0	4	0	0	0	1.0	1.000	OF-4
1990			4	.000	.000	14	0	0	0	0	0.0	1	0	2	2	0	0	0	3	0	1	0	1.0	.750	OF-4
3 yrs.			10	.133	.267	30	4	1	0	1	3.3	3	3	5	2	0	2	1	7	0	1	0	1.0	.875	OF-8

Year	Team	Games	BA	SA	AB	H	2B	3B	HR	HR%	R	RBI	BB	SO	SB	Pinch Hit AB	Pinch Hit H	PO	A	E	DP	TC/G	FA	G by Pos

Mike Greenwell *continued*

WORLD SERIES

| 1986 | BOS A | 4 | .000 | .000 | 3 | 0 | 0 | 0 | 0 | 0.0 | 0 | 0 | 1 | 2 | 0 | 3 | 0 | 0 | 0 | 0 | 0 | 0.0 | — | |

Rusty Greer

GREER, THURMAN CLYDE III
B. Jan. 21, 1969, Fort Rucker, Ala.

BL TL 6' 190 lbs.

1994	TEX A	80	.314	.487	277	87	16	1	10	3.6	36	46	46	46	0	2	0	216	4	6	10	2.8	.973	OF-73, 1B-9
1995		131	.271	.424	417	113	21	2	13	3.1	58	61	55	66	3	15	6	241	9	6	3	2.0	.977	OF-125, 1B-3
1996		139	.332	.530	542	180	41	6	18	3.3	96	100	62	86	9	0	0	303	6	5	0	2.3	.984	OF-137, DH-1, 1B-1
3 yrs.		350	.307	.485	1236	380	78	9	41	3.3	190	207	163	198	12	17	6	760	19	17	13	2.3	.979	OF-335, 1B-13, DH-1

DIVISIONAL PLAYOFF SERIES

| 1996 | TEX A | 4 | .125 | .125 | 16 | 2 | 0 | 0 | 0 | 0.0 | 2 | 0 | 3 | 3 | 0 | 0 | 0 | 12 | 0 | 0 | 0 | 3.0 | 1.000 | OF-4 |

Ken Griffey

GRIFFEY, GEORGE KENNETH, JR.
Son of Ken Griffey.
B. Nov. 21, 1969, Donora, Pa.

BL TL 6'3" 195 lbs.

1989	SEA A	127	.264	.420	455	120	23	0	16	3.5	61	61	44	83	16	3	1	302	12	10	6	2.6	.969	OF-127
1990		155	.300	.481	597	179	28	7	22	3.7	91	80	63	81	16	3	1	330	8	7	1	2.3	.980	OF-151, DH-2
1991		154	.327	.527	548	179	42	1	22	4.0	76	100	71	82	18	4	1	360	15	4	4	2.5	.989	OF-152, DH-1
1992		142	.308	.535	565	174	39	4	27	4.8	83	103	44	67	10	3	1	359	8	1	4	2.6	.997	OF-137, DH-3
1993		156	.309	.617	582	180	38	3	45	7.7	113	109	96	91	17	0	0	317	8	3	3	2.1	.991	OF-139, DH-19, 1B-1
1994		111	.323	.674	433	140	24	4	**40**	9.2	94	90	56	73	11	0	0	225	12	4	1	2.2	.983	OF-103, DH-9
1995		72	.258	.481	260	67	7	0	17	6.5	52	42	52	53	4	0	0	190	5	2	1	2.7	.990	OF-70, DH-2
1996		140	.303	.628	545	165	26	2	49	9.0	125	140	78	104	16	0	0	374	10	4	1	2.7	.990	OF-137, DH-5
8 yrs.		1057	.302	.549	3985	1204	227	21	238	6.0	695	725	504	634	108	13	4	2457	78	35	21	2.4	.986	OF-1016, DH-41, 1B-1

DIVISIONAL PLAYOFF SERIES

| 1995 | SEA A | 5 | .391 | 1.043 | 23 | 9 | 0 | 0 | 5 | 21.7 | 9 | 7 | 2 | 4 | 1 | 0 | 0 | 15 | 1 | 0 | 0 | 3.2 | 1.000 | OF-5 |

LEAGUE CHAMPIONSHIP SERIES

| 1995 | SEA A | 6 | .333 | .571 | 21 | 7 | 2 | 0 | 1 | 4.8 | 2 | 2 | 4 | 4 | 2 | 0 | 0 | 13 | 0 | 1 | 0 | 2.3 | .929 | OF-6 |

Marquis Grissom

GRISSOM, MARQUIS DEON
B. Apr. 17, 1967, Atlanta, Ga.

BR TR 5'11" 190 lbs.

1989	MON N	26	.257	.324	74	19	2	0	1	1.4	16	2	12	21	1	3	0	32	1	2	0	1.5	.943	OF-23
1990		98	.257	.351	288	74	14	2	3	1.0	42	29	27	40	22	21	6	165	5	2	0	2.0	.988	OF-87
1991		148	.267	.373	558	149	23	9	6	1.1	73	39	34	89	76	8	1	350	15	6	2	2.7	.984	OF-138
1992		159	.276	.418	653	180	39	6	14	2.1	99	66	42	81	78	1	0	401	7	7	2	2.6	.983	OF-157
1993		157	.298	.438	630	188	27	2	19	3.0	104	95	52	76	53	1	0	416	8	7	3	2.7	.984	OF-157
1994		110	.288	.427	475	137	25	4	11	2.3	96	45	41	66	36	1	1	321	7	5	0	3.1	.985	OF-109
1995	ATL N	139	.258	.376	551	142	23	3	12	2.2	80	42	47	61	29	4	0	309	9	2	1	2.4	.994	OF-136
1996		158	.308	.489	671	207	32	10	23	3.4	106	74	41	73	28	0	0	338	10	1	1	2.2	.997	OF-158
8 yrs.		995	.281	.415	3900	1096	185	36	89	2.3	616	392	296	507	323	39	8	2332	62	32	9	2.5	.987	OF-965

DIVISIONAL PLAYOFF SERIES

1995	ATL N	4	.524	1.048	21	11	2	0	3	14.3	5	4	0	3	2	0	0	9	0	0	0	2.3	1.000	OF-4
1996		3	.083	.083	12	1	0	0	0	0.0	2	0	1	2	1	0	0	4	0	1	0	1.7	.800	OF-3
2 yrs.		7	.364	.697	33	12	2	0	3	9.1	7	4	1	5	3	0	0	13	0	1	0	2.0	.929	OF-7

LEAGUE CHAMPIONSHIP SERIES

1995	ATL N	4	.263	.368	19	5	0	1	0	0.0	2	0	1	4	0	0	0	8	0	1	0	2.3	.889	OF-4
1996		7	.286	.400	35	10	1	0	1	2.9	7	3	0	8	2	0	0	17	0	1	0	2.6	.944	OF-7
2 yrs.		11	.278	.389	54	15	1	1	1	1.9	9	3	1	12	2	0	0	25	0	2	0	2.5	.926	OF-11

WORLD SERIES

1995	ATL N	6	.360	.400	25	9	1	0	0	0.0	3	1	1	3	3	0	0	13	0	0	0	2.2	1.000	OF-6
1996		6	.444	.593	27	12	2	1	0	0.0	4	5	1	2	1	0	0	7	0	1	0	1.3	.875	OF-6
2 yrs.		12	.404 3rd	.500	52	21	3	1	0	0.0	7	6	2	5	4	0	0	20	0	1	0	1.8	.952	OF-12

Mark Grudzielanek

GRUDZIELANEK, MARK JAMES
B. June 30, 1970, Milwaukee, Wis.

BR TR 6'1" 185 lbs.

1995	MON N	78	.245	.316	269	66	12	2	1	0.4	27	20	14	47	8	3	0	94	197	10	25	3.9	.967	SS-34, 3B-31, 2B-13
1996		153	.306	.397	657	201	34	4	6	0.9	99	49	26	83	33	0	0	181	454	27	78	4.3	.959	SS-153
2 yrs.		231	.288	.374	926	267	46	6	7	0.8	126	69	40	130	41	3	0	275	651	37	103	4.2	.962	SS-187, 3B-31, 2B-13

Vladimir Guerrero

GUERRERO, VLADIMIR
B. Feb. 9, 1976, Nizao Bani, Dominican Republic

BR TR 6'2" 158 lbs.

| 1996 | MON N | 9 | .185 | .286 | 27 | 5 | 0 | 0 | 1 | 3.7 | 2 | 1 | 0 | 3 | 0 | 1 | 0 | 11 | 0 | 0 | 0 | 1.4 | 1.000 | OF-8 |

Wilton Guerrero

GUERRERO, WILTON
B. Oct. 24, 1974, Don Gregorio, Dominican Republic

BR TR 5'11" 145 lbs.

| 1996 | LA N | 5 | .000 | .000 | 2 | 0 | 0 | 0 | 0 | 0.8 | 1 | 0 | 0 | 2 | 0 | 2 | 0 | 0 | 0 | 0 | 0 | 0.0 | — | |

Ozzie Guillen

GUILLEN, OSWALDO JOSE
Born Oswaldo Jose Guillen (Barrios).
B. Jan. 20, 1964, Oculare del Tuy, Venezuela

BL TR 5'11" 160 lbs.

| 1985 | CHI A | 150 | .273 | .358 | 491 | 134 | 21 | 9 | 1 | 0.2 | 71 | 33 | 12 | 36 | 7 | 13 | 1 | 220 | 382 | 12 | 80 | 4.1 | .980 | SS-150 |
| 1986 | | 159 | .250 | .311 | 547 | 137 | 19 | 4 | 2 | 0.4 | 58 | 47 | 12 | 52 | 8 | 2 | 0 | 261 | 459 | 22 | 93 | 4.7 | .970 | SS-157, DH-1 |

Year	Team	Games	BA	SA	AB	H	2B	3B	HR	HR%	R	RBI	BB	SO	SB	Pinch Hit AB	H	PO	A	E	DP	TC/G	FA	G by Pos

Ozzie Guillen *continued*

Year	Team	Games	BA	SA	AB	H	2B	3B	HR	HR%	R	RBI	BB	SO	SB	AB	H	PO	A	E	DP	TC/G	FA	G by Pos
1987		149	.279	.354	560	156	22	7	2	0.4	64	51	22	52	25	2	1	266	475	19	105	5.1	.975	SS-149
1988		156	.261	.314	566	148	16	7	0	0.0	58	39	25	40	25	0	0	273	570	20	115	5.5	.977	SS-156
1989		155	.253	.318	597	151	20	8	1	0.2	63	54	15	48	36	0	0	272	512	22	106	5.2	.973	SS-155
1990		160	.279	.341	516	144	21	4	1	0.2	61	58	26	37	13	2	0	252	474	17	100	4.7	.977	SS-159
1991		154	.273	.340	524	143	20	3	3	0.6	52	49	11	38	21	6	1	249	439	21	88	4.8	.970	SS-149
1992		12	.200	.300	40	8	4	0	0	0.0	5	7	1	5	1	0	0	20	39	0	7	4.9	1.000	SS-12
1993		134	.280	.374	457	128	23	4	4	0.9	44	50	10	41	5	3	1	189	361	16	82	4.3	.972	SS-133
1994		100	.288	.348	365	105	9	5	1	0.3	46	39	14	35	5	2	0	141	235	16	44	4.0	.959	SS-99
1995		122	.248	.318	415	103	20	3	1	0.2	50	41	13	25	6	8	3	167	318	12	55	4.1	.976	SS-120, DH-1
1996		150	.263	.367	499	131	24	8	4	0.8	62	45	10	27	6	7	0	223	348	11	69	3.9	.981	SS-146, OF-2
12 yrs.		1601	.267	.339	5577	1488	219	62	20	0.4	634	513	171	436	158	45	7	2533	4612	188	944	4.6	.974	SS-1585, OF-2, DH-2

LEAGUE CHAMPIONSHIP SERIES
| 1993 | CHI A | 6 | .273 | .318 | 22 | 6 | 1 | 0 | 0 | 0.0 | 4 | 2 | 0 | 2 | 1 | 0 | 0 | 12 | 14 | 0 | 4 | 4.3 | 1.000 | SS-6 |

Ricky Gutierrez — GUTIERREZ, RICARDO. B. May 23, 1970, Miami, Fla. BR TR 6'1" 175 lbs.

Year	Team	Games	BA	SA	AB	H	2B	3B	HR	HR%	R	RBI	BB	SO	SB	AB	H	PO	A	E	DP	TC/G	FA	G by Pos
1993	SD N	133	.251	.331	438	110	10	5	5	1.1	76	26	50	97	4	8	2	194	305	14	55	3.9	.973	SS-117, 2B-6, OF-5, 3B-4
1994		90	.240	.305	275	66	11	2	1	0.4	27	28	32	54	2	6	1	93	202	22	34	3.7	.931	SS-78, 2B-7
1995	HOU N	52	.276	.314	156	43	6	0	0	0.0	22	12	10	33	5	4	1	64	107	8	17	3.9	.955	SS-44, 3B-2
1996		89	.284	.344	218	62	8	1	1	0.5	28	15	23	42	6	6	0	86	148	12	33	2.9	.951	SS-74, 3B-6, 2B-5
4 yrs.		364	.259	.325	1087	281	35	8	7	0.6	153	81	115	226	17	24	4	437	762	56	139	3.6	.955	SS-313, 2B-18, 3B-12, OF-5

Chris Gwynn — GWYNN, CHRISTOPHER KARLTON. Brother of Tony Gwynn. B. Oct. 13, 1964, Los Angeles, Calif. BL TL 6' 200 lbs.

Year	Team	Games	BA	SA	AB	H	2B	3B	HR	HR%	R	RBI	BB	SO	SB	AB	H	PO	A	E	DP	TC/G	FA	G by Pos
1987	LA N	17	.219	.250	32	7	1	0	0	0.0	2	2	1	7	0	6	0	12	0	0	0	1.2	1.000	OF-10
1988		12	.182	.182	11	2	0	0	0	0.0	1	0	1	2	0	9	2	0	0	0	0	0.0	.000	OF-4
1989		32	.235	.324	68	16	4	1	0	0.0	8	7	2	9	1	14	3	26	1	0	1	1.4	1.000	OF-19
1990		101	.284	.418	141	40	2	1	5	3.5	19	22	7	28	0	56	13	39	1	0	0	0.9	1.000	OF-44
1991		94	.252	.410	139	35	5	1	5	3.6	18	22	10	23	1	56	13	37	2	0	0	1.0	1.000	OF-41
1992	KC A	34	.286	.405	84	24	3	2	1	1.2	10	7	3	10	0	10	2	33	0	0	0	1.6	1.000	OF-19, DH-2
1993		103	.300	.387	287	86	14	4	1	0.3	36	25	24	34	0	16	6	161	7	1	1	1.9	.994	OF-83, DH-5, 1B-1
1994	LA N	58	.268	.394	71	19	0	0	3	4.2	9	13	7	7	0	35	11	14	0	0	0	0.7	1.000	OF-20
1995		67	.214	.333	84	18	3	2	1	1.2	8	10	6	23	0	43	10	26	1	0	2	1.4	1.000	OF-17, 1B-2
1996	SD N	81	.178	.256	90	16	4	0	1	1.1	8	10	10	28	0	53	8	20	1	0	0	0.7	1.000	OF-29, 1B-1
10 yrs.		599	.261	.369	1007	263	36	11	17	1.7	119	118	71	171	2	298	68	368	13	1	4	1.3	.997	OF-286, DH-7, 1B-4

DIVISIONAL PLAYOFF SERIES
1995	LA N	1	.000	.000	1	0	0	0	0	0.0	0	0	0	1	0	1	0	0	0	0	0	0.0	—	
1996	SD N	2	1.000	1.000	2	2	0	0	0	0.0	1	0	0	0	0	2	2	0	0	0	0	0.0	—	
2 yrs.		3	.667	.667	3	2	0	0	0	0.0	1	0	0	1	0	3	2							

Tony Gwynn — GWYNN, ANTHONY KEITH. Brother of Chris Gwynn. B. May 9, 1960, Los Angeles, Calif. BL TL 5'11" 185 lbs.

Year	Team	Games	BA	SA	AB	H	2B	3B	HR	HR%	R	RBI	BB	SO	SB	AB	H	PO	A	E	DP	TC/G	FA	G by Pos
1982	SD N	54	.289	.389	190	55	12	2	1	0.5	33	17	14	16	8	4	1	110	1	1	0	2.2	.991	OF-52
1983		86	.309	.372	304	94	12	2	1	0.3	34	37	23	21	7	6	1	163	9	1	1	2.1	.994	OF-81
1984		158	.351	.444	606	213	21	10	5	0.8	88	71	59	23	33	2	1	345	11	4	4	2.3	.989	OF-156
1985		154	.317	.408	622	197	29	5	6	1.0	90	46	45	33	14	2	0	337	14	4	2	2.3	.989	OF-152
1986		160	.329	.467	642	211	33	7	14	2.2	107	59	52	35	37	1	0	337	19	4	3	2.3	.989	OF-160
1987		157	.370	.511	589	218	36	13	7	1.2	119	54	82	35	56	2	1	298	13	6	1	2.0	.981	OF-156
1988		133	.313	.415	521	163	22	5	7	1.3	64	70	51	40	26	0	0	264	8	5	1	2.1	.982	OF-133
1989		158	.336	.424	604	203	27	7	4	0.7	82	62	56	30	40	0	0	353	13	6	1	2.4	.984	OF-157
1990		141	.309	.415	573	177	29	10	4	0.7	79	72	44	23	17	0	0	327	11	5	2	2.4	.985	OF-141
1991		134	.317	.432	530	168	27	11	4	0.8	69	62	34	19	8	1	0	291	8	3	2	2.3	.990	OF-134
1992		128	.317	.415	520	165	27	3	6	1.2	77	41	46	16	3	1	0	270	9	5	2	2.2	.982	OF-127
1993		122	.358	.497	489	175	41	3	7	1.4	70	59	36	19	14	2	0	244	8	5	2	2.1	.981	OF-121
1994		110	.394	.568	419	165	35	1	12	2.9	79	64	48	19	5	5	1	191	6	3	1	1.9	.985	OF-106
1995		135	.368	.484	535	197	33	1	9	1.7	82	90	35	15	17	2	1	245	8	2	1	1.9	.992	OF-133
1996		116	.353	.441	451	159	27	2	3	0.7	67	50	39	17	11	5	2	182	2	2	0	1.7	.989	OF-111
15 yrs.		1946	.337	.448	7595	2560	411	82	90	1.2	1140	854	664	361	296	33	8	3957	140	56	23	2.2	.987	OF-1920

DIVISIONAL PLAYOFF SERIES
| 1996 | SD N | 3 | .308 | .385 | 13 | 4 | 1 | 0 | 0 | 0.0 | 0 | 1 | 0 | 0 | 2 | 0 | 0 | 2 | 0 | 0 | 0 | 0.7 | 1.000 | OF-3 |

LEAGUE CHAMPIONSHIP SERIES
| 1984 | SD N | 5 | .368 | .526 | 19 | 7 | 3 | 0 | 0 | 0.0 | 6 | 3 | 1 | 2 | 0 | 0 | 0 | 9 | 0 | 0 | 0 | 1.8 | 1.000 | OF-5 |

WORLD SERIES
| 1984 | SD N | 5 | .263 | .263 | 19 | 5 | 0 | 0 | 0 | 0.0 | 1 | 0 | 1 | 1 | 0 | 0 | 0 | 12 | 1 | 1 | 1 | 2.8 | .929 | OF-5 |

David Hajek — HAJEK, DAVID VINCENT. B. Oct. 14, 1967, Roseville, Calif. BR TR 5'10" 165 lbs.

Year	Team	Games	BA	SA	AB	H	2B	3B	HR	HR%	R	RBI	BB	SO	SB	AB	H	PO	A	E	DP	TC/G	FA	G by Pos
1995	HOU N	5	.000	.000	2	0	0	0	0	0.0	0	0	1	1	1	2	0	0	0	0	0	0.0	—	
1996		8	.300	.400	10	3	1	0	0	0.0	3	0	2	0	0	2	1	3	7	0	0	2.0	1.000	3B-3, 2B-2
2 yrs.		13	.250	.333	12	3	1	0	0	0.0	3	0	3	1	1	4	1	3	7	0	0	2.0	1.000	3B-3, 2B-2

Chip Hale
HALE, WALTER WILLIAM B. Dec. 2, 1964, Santa Clara, Calif. — BL TR 5'11" 180 lbs.

Year	Team	Games	BA	SA	AB	H	2B	3B	HR	HR%	R	RBI	BB	SO	SB	Pinch Hit AB	H	PO	A	E	DP	TC/G	FA	G by Pos
1989	MIN A	28	.209	.254	67	14	3	0	0	0.0	6	4	1	6	0	8	0	15	40	1	8	2.1	.982	2B-16, 3B-9, DH-2
1990		1	.000	.000	2	0	0	0	0	0.0	0	2	0	1	0	0	0	2	6	0	2	8.0	1.000	2B-1
1993		69	.333	.425	186	62	6	1	3	1.6	25	27	18	17	2	17	7	39	63	4	11	1.7	.962	2B-21, 3B-19, DH-19, 1B-1, SS-1
1994		67	.263	.364	118	31	9	0	1	0.8	13	11	16	14	0	**31**	**11**	45	51	3	7	2.3	.970	3B-21, DH-10, 1B-7, 2B-5, OF-1
1995		69	.262	.359	103	27	4	0	2	1.9	10	18	11	20	0	**47**	**14**	16	6	0	2	0.5	1.000	DH-27, 2B-7, 3B-5, 1B-3
1996		85	.276	.368	87	24	5	0	1	1.1	8	16	10	6	0	**65**	**19**	16	16	0	4	0.9	1.000	2B-14, DH-10, 1B-6, 3B-3, OF-3
6 yrs.		319	.281	.369	563	158	27	1	7	1.2	62	78	56	64	2	168	51	133	182	8	34	1.5	.975	DH-68, 2B-64, 3B-57, 1B-17, OF-4, SS-1

Mel Hall
HALL, MELVIN, JR. B. Sept. 16, 1960, Lyons, N.Y. — BL TL 6' 185 lbs.

Year	Team	Games	BA	SA	AB	H	2B	3B	HR	HR%	R	RBI	BB	SO	SB	Pinch Hit AB	H	PO	A	E	DP	TC/G	FA	G by Pos
1981	CHI N	10	.091	.364	11	1	0	0	1	9.1	1	2	1	4	0	7	1	0	0	0	0	0.0	.000	OF-3
1982		24	.263	.350	80	21	3	2	0	0.0	6	4	5	17	0	1	0	42	4	3	1	2.2	.939	OF-22
1983		112	.283	.488	410	116	23	5	17	4.1	60	56	42	101	6	2	1	239	8	3	2	2.2	.988	OF-112
1984	2 teams CHI N (48G –.280) CLE A (83G –.257)																							
"	total	131	.265	.425	407	108	24	4	11	2.7	68	52	47	78	3	14	3	212	8	4	2	1.8	.982	OF-115, DH-9
1985	CLE A	23	.318	.409	66	21	6	0	0	0.0	7	12	8	12	0	6	2	18	0	0	0	0.9	1.000	OF-15, DH-5
1986		140	.296	.493	442	131	29	2	18	4.1	68	77	33	65	6	19	6	233	7	7	1	1.9	.972	OF-126, DH-7
1987		142	.280	.439	485	136	21	1	18	3.7	57	76	20	68	5	17	2	264	3	3	2	2.0	.989	OF-122, DH-14
1988		150	.280	.392	515	144	32	4	6	1.2	69	71	28	50	7	11	4	288	5	10	1	2.0	.967	OF-141, DH-6
1989	NY A	113	.260	.427	361	94	9	0	17	4.7	54	58	21	37	0	16	4	141	3	1	2	1.3	.993	OF-75, DH-34
1990		113	.258	.433	360	93	23	2	12	3.3	41	46	6	46	0	15	3	70	2	2	0	0.7	.973	DH-54, OF-50
1991		141	.285	.455	492	140	23	2	19	3.9	67	80	26	40	0	14	4	221	8	3	2	1.8	.987	OF-120, DH-10
1992		152	.280	.429	583	163	36	3	15	2.6	67	81	29	53	4	12	4	283	10	3	2	2.0	.990	OF-136, DH-11
1996	SF N	25	.120	.120	25	3	0	0	0	0.0	3	5	1	4	0	19	2	0	0	0	0	0.0	.000	OF-4
13 yrs.		1276	.276	.437	4237	1171	229	25	134	3.2	568	620	267	575	31	153	36	2011	56	39	15	1.8	.981	OF-1041, DH-150

Bob Hamelin
HAMELIN, ROBERT JAMES III (The Hammer) B. Nov. 29, 1967, Elizabeth, N.J. — BL TL 6'1" 240 lbs.

Year	Team	Games	BA	SA	AB	H	2B	3B	HR	HR%	R	RBI	BB	SO	SB	Pinch Hit AB	H	PO	A	E	DP	TC/G	FA	G by Pos
1993	KC A	16	.224	.408	49	11	3	0	2	4.1	2	5	6	15	0	1	0	129	9	2	10	9.3	.986	1B-15
1994		101	.282	.599	312	88	25	1	24	7.7	64	65	56	62	4	6	2	234	18	2	11	2.7	.992	DH-70, 1B-24
1995		72	.168	.313	208	35	7	1	7	3.4	20	25	26	56	0	9	3	66	9	0	11	1.2	1.000	DH-56, 1B-8
1996		89	.255	.435	239	61	14	1	9	3.8	31	40	54	58	5	16	3	233	19	4	26	3.2	.984	DH-47, 1B-33
4 yrs.		278	.241	.465	808	195	49	3	42	5.2	117	135	142	191	9	32	8	662	55	8	58	2.9	.989	DH-173, 1B-80

Darryl Hamilton
HAMILTON, DARRYL QUINN B. Dec. 3, 1963, Baton Rouge, La. — BL TR 6'1" 180 lbs.

Year	Team	Games	BA	SA	AB	H	2B	3B	HR	HR%	R	RBI	BB	SO	SB	Pinch Hit AB	H	PO	A	E	DP	TC/G	FA	G by Pos
1988	MIL A	44	.184	.252	103	19	4	0	1	1.0	14	11	12	9	7	3	1	75	1	0	0	1.9	1.000	OF-37, DH-3
1990		89	.295	.346	156	46	5	0	1	0.6	27	18	9	12	10	5	1	120	1	1	0	1.5	.992	OF-72, DH-9
1991		122	.311	.385	405	126	15	6	1	0.2	64	57	33	38	16	3	3	234	3	1	0	2.0	.996	OF-117
1992		128	.298	.400	470	140	19	7	5	1.1	67	62	45	42	41	3	1	279	10	0	0	2.3	1.000	OF-124
1993		135	.310	.406	520	161	21	1	9	1.7	74	48	45	62	21	5	0	340	10	3	1	2.7	.992	OF-129
1994		36	.262	.369	141	37	10	1	1	0.7	23	13	15	17	3	0	0	60	2	0	1	1.8	1.000	OF-32, DH-3
1995		112	.271	.389	398	108	20	6	5	1.3	54	44	47	35	11	8	1	262	4	3	0	2.4	.989	OF-109, DH-2
1996	TEX A	148	.293	.381	627	184	29	4	6	1.0	94	51	54	66	15	1	0	388	2	0	0	2.7	1.000	OF-147
8 yrs.		814	.291	.383	2820	821	123	25	29	1.0	417	304	260	281	124	28	7	1758	33	8	2	2.3	.996	OF-767, DH-17

DIVISIONAL PLAYOFF SERIES

Year	Team	Games	BA	SA	AB	H	2B	3B	HR	HR%	R	RBI	BB	SO	SB	Pinch Hit AB	H	PO	A	E	DP	TC/G	FA	G by Pos
1996	TEX A	4	.158	.158	19	3	0	0	0	0.0	0	2	0	0	0	0	0	16	1	0	1	4.3	1.000	OF-4

Jeffrey Hammonds
HAMMONDS, JEFFREY BRYAN B. Mar. 5, 1971, Plainfield, N.J. — BR TR 6' 195 lbs.

Year	Team	Games	BA	SA	AB	H	2B	3B	HR	HR%	R	RBI	BB	SO	SB	Pinch Hit AB	H	PO	A	E	DP	TC/G	FA	G by Pos
1993	BAL A	33	.305	.467	105	32	8	0	3	2.9	10	19	2	16	4	2	2	47	2	2	0	1.7	.961	OF-23, DH-7
1994		68	.296	.480	250	74	18	2	8	3.2	45	31	17	39	5	0	0	147	5	6	0	2.4	.962	OF-67
1995		57	.242	.371	178	43	9	1	4	2.2	18	23	9	30	4	6	1	88	1	1	0	1.8	.989	OF-46, DH-5
1996		71	.226	.383	248	56	10	1	9	3.6	38	27	23	53	3	2	1	145	3	3	0	2.1	.980	OF-70, DH-1
4 yrs.		229	.262	.423	781	205	45	4	24	3.1	111	100	51	138	16	10	4	427	11	12	0	2.1	.973	OF-206, DH-13

Todd Haney
HANEY, TODD MICHAEL B. July 30, 1965, Galveston, Tex. — BR TR 5'9" 165 lbs.

Year	Team	Games	BA	SA	AB	H	2B	3B	HR	HR%	R	RBI	BB	SO	SB	Pinch Hit AB	H	PO	A	E	DP	TC/G	FA	G by Pos
1992	MON N	7	.300	.400	10	3	1	0	0	0.0	0	0	0	0	0	1	0	2	6	0	1	1.6	1.000	2B-5
1994	CHI N	17	.162	.243	37	6	0	0	1	2.7	6	2	3	3	2	1	0	20	28	1	8	3.5	.980	2B-11, 3B-3
1995		25	.411	.603	73	30	8	0	2	2.7	11	6	7	11	0	2	1	34	61	2	16	4.6	.979	2B-17, 3B-4
1996		49	.134	.146	82	11	1	0	0	0.0	11	3	7	15	1	17	2	32	64	3	12	3.3	.970	2B-23, 3B-4, SS-3
4 yrs.		98	.248	.342	202	50	10	0	3	1.5	28	12	17	29	3	22	4	88	159	6	33	3.6	.976	2B-56, 3B-11, SS-3

Dave Hansen
HANSEN, DAVID ANDREW B. Nov. 24, 1968, Long Beach, Calif. — BL TR 6' 180 lbs.

Year	Team	Games	BA	SA	AB	H	2B	3B	HR	HR%	R	RBI	BB	SO	SB	Pinch Hit AB	H	PO	A	E	DP	TC/G	FA	G by Pos
1990	LA N	5	.143	.143	7	1	0	0	0	0.0	0	1	0	3	0	3	0	0	1	1	0	1.0	.500	3B-2
1991		53	.268	.393	56	15	4	0	1	1.8	3	5	2	12	1	32	10	5	19	0	2	1.1	1.000	3B-21, SS-1
1992		132	.214	.299	341	73	11	0	6	1.8	30	22	34	49	0	25	5	61	183	8	13	2.3	.968	3B-108
1993		84	.362	.505	105	38	3	0	4	3.8	13	30	21	13	0	55	18	11	27	3	1	2.3	.927	3B-18
1994		40	.341	.409	44	15	3	0	0	0.0	3	5	5	5	0	31	8	0	6	1	0	1.0	.857	3B-7

Year	Team	Games	BA	SA	AB	H	2B	3B	HR	HR%	R	RBI	BB	SO	SB	Pinch Hit AB	H	PO	A	E	DP	TC/G	FA	G by Pos

Dave Hansen *continued*

Year	Team	Games	BA	SA	AB	H	2B	3B	HR	HR%	R	RBI	BB	SO	SB	PH AB	PH H	PO	A	E	DP	TC/G	FA	G by Pos
1995		100	.287	.359	181	52	10	0	1	0.6	19	14	28	28	0	35	11	27	70	7	6	1.8	.933	3B-58
1996		80	.221	.231	104	23	1	0	0	0.0	7	6	11	22	0	43	11	60	23	1	4	3.1	.988	3B-19, 1B-8
7 yrs.		494	.259	.340	838	217	32	0	12	1.4	75	83	101	132	1	224	63	164	329	21	26	2.1	.959	3B-233, 1B-8, SS-1

DIVISIONAL PLAYOFF SERIES

Year	Team	Games	BA	SA	AB	H	2B	3B	HR	HR%	R	RBI	BB	SO	SB	PH AB	PH H	PO	A	E	DP	TC/G	FA	G by Pos
1995	LA N	3	.667	.667	3	2	0	0	0	0.0	0	0	0	0	0	3	2	0	0	0	0	0.0	—	
1996		2	.000	.000	2	0	0	0	0	0.0	0	0	0	0	0	1	0	0	0	0	0	0.0	—	
2 yrs.		5	.400	.400	5	2	0	0	0	0.0	0	0	0	0	0	4	2	1	0	0	1	1.0	1.000	3B-1

Jason Hardtke

HARDTKE, JASON ROBERT
B. Sept. 15, 1971, Milwaukee, Wisc.

BB TR 5'10" 175 lbs.

Year	Team	Games	BA	SA	AB	H	2B	3B	HR	HR%	R	RBI	BB	SO	SB	PH AB	PH H	PO	A	E	DP	TC/G	FA	G by Pos
1996	NY N	19	.193	.281	57	11	5	0	0	0.0	3	6	2	12	0	5	1	26	34	0	9	3.3	1.000	2B-18

Lenny Harris

HARRIS, LEONARD ANTHONY
B. Oct. 28, 1964, Miami, Fla.

BL TR 5'10" 195 lbs.

Year	Team	Games	BA	SA	AB	H	2B	3B	HR	HR%	R	RBI	BB	SO	SB	PH AB	PH H	PO	A	E	DP	TC/G	FA	G by Pos
1988	CIN N	16	.372	.395	43	16	1	0	0	0.0	7	8	5	4	4	0	0	14	33	1	2	3.0	.979	3B-10, 2B-6
1989	2 teams	CIN N (61G –.223)		LA N (54G –.252)																				
"	total	115	.236	.299	335	79	10	1	3	0.9	36	26	20	33	14	20	8	147	168	15	32	3.0	.955	2B-46, 3B-24, OF-21, SS-18
1990	LA N	137	.304	.374	431	131	16	4	2	0.5	61	29	29	31	15	23	3	140	205	11	24	2.5	.969	3B-94, 2B-44, OF-2, SS-1
1991		145	.287	.350	429	123	16	1	3	0.7	59	38	37	32	12	24	3	125	250	20	35	2.5	.949	3B-113, 2B-27, SS-20, OF-1
1992		135	.271	.303	347	94	11	0	0	0.0	28	30	24	24	19	29	6	199	248	27	48	3.4	.943	2B-81, 3B-33, OF-15, SS-10
1993		107	.237	.325	160	38	6	1	2	1.3	20	11	15	15	3	45	8	61	99	3	11	2.9	.982	2B-35, 3B-17, SS-3, OF-2
1994	CIN N	66	.310	.360	100	31	3	1	0	0.0	13	14	5	13	7	45	12	27	29	6	2	2.6	.903	3B-15, 1B-4, OF-3, 2B-2
1995		101	.208	.310	197	41	8	3	2	1.0	32	16	14	20	10	50	11	147	68	4	14	3.9	.982	3B-24, 1B-23, OF-8, 2B-1
1996		125	.285	.404	302	86	17	2	5	1.7	33	32	21	31	14	49	17	198	65	6	16	3.2	.978	OF-37, 3B-24, 1B-16, 2B-8
9 yrs.		947	.273	.343	2344	639	88	13	17	0.7	289	204	170	203	98	285	68	1058	1165	93	184	2.9	.960	3B-354, 2B-250, OF-89, SS-52, 1B-43

LEAGUE CHAMPIONSHIP SERIES

Year	Team	Games	BA	SA	AB	H	2B	3B	HR	HR%	R	RBI	BB	SO	SB	PH AB	PH H	PO	A	E	DP	TC/G	FA	G by Pos
1995	CIN N	3	1.000	1.000	2	2	0	0	0	0.0	0	1	0	0	1	2	2	0	0	0	0	0.0	—	

Bill Haselman

HASELMAN, WILLIAM JOSEPH
B. May 25, 1966, Long Branch, N. J.

BR TR 6'3" 205 lbs.

Year	Team	Games	BA	SA	AB	H	2B	3B	HR	HR%	R	RBI	BB	SO	SB	PH AB	PH H	PO	A	E	DP	TC/G	FA	G by Pos
1990	TEX A	7	.154	.154	13	2	0	0	0	0.0	0	3	1	5	0	3	1	8	0	0	0	2.0	1.000	DH-3, C-1
1992	SEA A	8	.263	.263	19	5	0	0	0	0.0	1	0	0	7	0	1	1	19	2	0	0	3.0	1.000	C-5, OF-2
1993		58	.255	.423	137	35	8	0	5	3.6	21	16	12	19	2	6	1	236	17	2	1	4.6	.992	C-49, DH-4, OF-2
1994		38	.193	.337	83	16	7	1	1	1.2	11	8	3	11	1	3	1	157	5	3	0	4.5	.982	C-33, OF-2, DH-2
1995	BOS A	64	.243	.395	152	37	6	1	5	3.3	22	23	17	30	0	9	1	259	16	3	0	4.6	.989	C-48, DH-11, 1B-1, 3B-1
1996		77	.274	.439	237	65	13	1	8	3.4	33	34	19	52	4	6	1	508	32	3	8	7.4	.994	C-69, 1B-2, DH-2
6 yrs.		252	.250	.401	641	160	34	3	19	3.0	88	84	52	124	7	28	6	1187	72	11	9	5.4	.991	C-205, DH-22, OF-6, 1B-3, 3B-1

DIVISIONAL PLAYOFF SERIES

Year	Team	Games	BA	SA	AB	H	2B	3B	HR	HR%	R	RBI	BB	SO	SB	PH AB	PH H	PO	A	E	DP	TC/G	FA	G by Pos
1995	BOS A	1	.000	.000	2	0	0	0	0	0.0	0	0	0	0	0	0	0	6	0	0	0	6.0	1.000	C-1

Scott Hatteberg

HATTEBERG, SCOTT ALLEN
B. Dec. 14, 1969, Salem, Ore.

BL TR 6'1" 192 lbs.

Year	Team	Games	BA	SA	AB	H	2B	3B	HR	HR%	R	RBI	BB	SO	SB	PH AB	PH H	PO	A	E	DP	TC/G	FA	G by Pos
1995	BOS A	2	.500	.500	2	1	0	0	0	0.0	1	0	0	0	0	1	1	4	0	0	0	2.0	1.000	C-2
1996		10	.182	.273	11	2	1	0	0	0.0	3	0	3	2	0	2	0	32	1	0	0	3.3	1.000	C-10
2 yrs.		12	.231	.308	13	3	1	0	0	0.0	4	0	3	2	0	3	1	36	1	0	0	3.1	1.000	C-12

Charlie Hayes

HAYES, CHARLES DEWAYNE
B. May 29, 1965, Hattiesburg, Miss.

BR TR 6' 224 lbs.

Year	Team	Games	BA	SA	AB	H	2B	3B	HR	HR%	R	RBI	BB	SO	SB	PH AB	PH H	PO	A	E	DP	TC/G	FA	G by Pos
1988	SF N	7	.091	.091	11	1	0	0	0	0.0	0	0	0	3	0	2	0	5	0	0	0	0.7	1.000	OF-4, 3B-3
1989	2 teams	SF N (3G –.200)		PHI N (84G –.258)																				
"	total	87	.257	.391	304	78	15	1	8	2.6	26	43	11	50	3	5	2	51	174	22	15	2.9	.911	3B-85
1990	PHI N	152	.258	.348	561	145	20	0	10	1.8	56	57	28	91	4	6	2	151	329	20	31	3.3	.960	3B-146, 1B-4, 2B-1
1991		142	.230	.363	460	106	23	1	12	2.6	34	53	16	75	3	8	4	88	240	15	25	2.5	.956	3B-138, SS-2
1992	NY A	142	.257	.409	509	131	19	2	18	3.5	52	66	28	100	3	1	0	125	249	13	32	2.7	.966	3B-139, 1B-4
1993	CLR N	157	.305	.522	573	175	45	2	25	4.4	89	98	43	82	11	6	1	123	292	20	22	2.8	.954	3B-154, SS-1
1994		113	.288	.433	423	122	23	4	10	2.4	46	50	36	71	3	3	1	72	216	17	19	2.8	.944	3B-110
1995	PHI N	141	.276	.406	529	146	30	3	11	2.1	58	85	50	88	5	0	0	104	262	14	25	2.7	.963	3B-141
1996	2 teams	PIT N (128G –.248)		NY A (20G –.284)																				
"	total	148	.253	.375	526	133	24	2	12	2.3	58	75	37	90	6	10	4	80	303	18	29	2.8	.955	3B-143
9 yrs.		1089	.266	.407	3896	1037	199	15	106	2.7	419	527	249	650	38	41	14	799	2065	139	198	2.8	.954	3B-1059, 1B-8, OF-4, SS-3, 2B-1

DIVISIONAL PLAYOFF SERIES

Year	Team	Games	BA	SA	AB	H	2B	3B	HR	HR%	R	RBI	BB	SO	SB	PH AB	PH H	PO	A	E	DP	TC/G	FA	G by Pos
1996	NY A	3	.200	.200	5	1	0	0	0	0.0	0	1	0	0	0	1	1	1	3	0	0	2.0	1.000	3B-2

LEAGUE CHAMPIONSHIP SERIES

Year	Team	Games	BA	SA	AB	H	2B	3B	HR	HR%	R	RBI	BB	SO	SB	PH AB	PH H	PO	A	E	DP	TC/G	FA	G by Pos
1996	NY A	4	.143	.143	7	1	0	0	0	0.0	0	0	2	2	0	1	0	0	3	0	0	1.0	1.000	3B-2, DH-1

Year	Team	Games	BA	SA	AB	H	2B	3B	HR	HR%	R	RBI	BB	SO	SB	Pinch Hit AB	H	PO	A	E	DP	TC/G	FA	G by Pos

Charlie Hayes continued

WORLD SERIES

Year	Team	Games	BA	SA	AB	H	2B	3B	HR	HR%	R	RBI	BB	SO	SB	Pinch Hit AB	H	PO	A	E	DP	TC/G	FA	G by Pos
1996	NY A	5	.188	.188	16	3	0	0	0	0.0	2	1	1	5	0	1	0	3	6	0	1	1.8	1.000	3B-4, 1B-1

Rickey Henderson

HENDERSON, RICKEY HENLEY
B. Dec. 25, 1957, Chicago, Ill.

BR TL 5'10" 180 lbs.

Year	Team	Games	BA	SA	AB	H	2B	3B	HR	HR%	R	RBI	BB	SO	SB	Pinch Hit AB	H	PO	A	E	DP	TC/G	FA	G by Pos
1979	OAK A	89	.274	.336	351	96	13	3	1	0.3	49	26	34	39	33	0	0	215	5	6	0	2.6	.973	OF-88
1980		158	.303	.399	591	179	22	4	9	1.5	111	53	117	54	100	0	0	407	15	7	1	2.7	.984	OF-157, DH-1
1981		108	.319	.437	423	135	18	7	6	1.4	89	35	64	68	56	1	0	327	7	7	0	3.2	.979	OF-107
1982		149	.267	.382	536	143	24	4	10	1.9	119	51	116	94	130[1]	0	0	379	2	9	0	2.6	.977	OF-144, DH-4
1983		145	.292	.421	513	150	25	7	9	1.8	105	48	103	80	108	6	1	349	9	3	1	2.5	.992	OF-142, DH-1
1984		142	.293	.458	502	147	27	4	16	3.2	113	58	86	81	66	2	0	341	7	11	1	2.6	.969	OF-140
1985	NY A	143	.314	.516	547	172	28	5	24	4.4	146	72	99	65	80	1	0	439	7	9	3	3.2	.980	OF-141, DH-1
1986		153	.263	.469	608	160	31	5	28	4.6	130	74	89	81	87	3	0	426	4	6	0	2.9	.986	OF-146, DH-5
1987		95	.291	.497	358	104	17	3	17	4.7	78	37	80	52	41	2	0	189	3	4	1	2.1	.980	OF-69, DH-24
1988		140	.305	.399	554	169	30	2	6	1.1	118	50	82	54	93	0	0	320	7	12	5	2.4	.965	OF-136, DH-3
1989	2 teams	NY A (65G –.247)			OAK A (85G –.294)																			
"	total	150	.274	.399	541	148	26	3	12	2.2	113	57	126	68	77	2	2	335	6	4	1	2.3	.988	OF-147, DH-3
1990	OAK A	136	.325	.577	489	159	33	3	28	5.7	119	61	97	60	65	1	0	289	5	5	0	2.2	.983	OF-118, DH-15
1991		134	.268	.423	470	126	17	1	18	3.8	105	57	98	73	58	6	1	249	10	8	1	2.1	.970	OF-119, DH-10
1992		117	.283	.457	396	112	18	3	15	3.8	77	46	95	56	48	3	1	231	9	4	2	2.1	.984	OF-108, DH-6
1993	2 teams	OAK A (90G –.327)			TOR A (44G –.215)																			
"	total	134	.289	.474	481	139	22	2	21	4.4	114	59	120	65	53	0	0	258	6	7	0	2.0	.974	OF-118, DH-16
1994	OAK A	87	.260	.365	296	77	13	0	6	2.0	66	20	72	45	22	3	0	166	4	4	0	2.1	.977	OF-71, DH-13
1995		112	.300	.447	407	122	31	1	9	2.2	67	54	72	66	32	5	2	161	5	2	1	1.5	.988	OF-90, DH-19
1996	SD N	148	.241	.344	465	112	17	2	9	1.9	110	29	125	90	37	8	2	228	3	6	0	1.8	.975	OF-134
18 yrs.		2340	.287	.435	8528	2450	412	59	244	2.9	1829 10th	887	1675 7th	1191	1186 1st	45	9	5309	114	114	17	2.4	.979	OF-2175, DH-121

DIVISIONAL PLAYOFF SERIES

Year	Team	Games	BA	SA	AB	H	2B	3B	HR	HR%	R	RBI	BB	SO	SB	Pinch Hit AB	H	PO	A	E	DP	TC/G	FA	G by Pos
1981	OAK A	3	.182	.182	11	2	0	0	0	0.0	0	0	2	0	2	0	0	8	0	0	0	2.7	1.000	OF-3
1996	SD N	3	.333	.583	12	4	0	0	1	8.3	2	1	2	3	0	0	0	4	0	0	0	1.3	1.000	OF-3
2 yrs.		6	.261	.391	23	6	0	0	1	4.3	5	1	4	3	2	0	0	12	0	0	0	2.0	1.000	OF-6

LEAGUE CHAMPIONSHIP SERIES

Year	Team	Games	BA	SA	AB	H	2B	3B	HR	HR%	R	RBI	BB	SO	SB	Pinch Hit AB	H	PO	A	E	DP	TC/G	FA	G by Pos
1981	OAK A	3	.364	.727	11	4	2	1	0	0.0	0	1	1	2	2	0	0	6	0	1	0	2.3	.857	OF-3
1989		5	.400	1.000	15	6	1	1	2	13.3	8	5	7	0	8	0	0	13	0	1	0	2.8	.929	OF-5
1990		4	.294	.294	17	5	0	0	0	0.0	1	3	1	2	2	0	0	10	0	0	0	2.5	1.000	OF-4
1992		6	.261	.261	23	6	0	0	0	0.0	5	1	4	4	2	0	0	15	0	3	0	3.0	.833	OF-6
1993	TOR A	6	.120	.200	25	3	2	0	0	0.0	4	0	4	5	2	0	0	9	0	1	0	1.7	.900	OF-6
5 yrs.		24	.264	.429	91 10th	24	5	2 4th	2	2.2	18 2nd	10	17 2nd	13	16 1st	0	0	53	0	6	0	2.5	.898	OF-24

WORLD SERIES

Year	Team	Games	BA	SA	AB	H	2B	3B	HR	HR%	R	RBI	BB	SO	SB	Pinch Hit AB	H	PO	A	E	DP	TC/G	FA	G by Pos
1989	OAK A	4	.474	.895	19	9	1	2	1	5.3	4	3	2	2	3	0	0	9	0	0	0	2.3	1.000	OF-4
1990		4	.333	.667	15	5	2	0	1	6.7	2	1	3	4	3	0	0	12	1	0	0	3.3	1.000	OF-4
1993	TOR A	6	.227	.318	22	5	2	0	0	0.0	6	2	5	2	1	0	0	8	0	0	0	1.3	1.000	OF-6
3 yrs.		14	.339	.607	56	19	5	2	2	3.6	12	6	10	8	7 9th	0	0	29	1	0	0	2.1	1.000	OF-14

Carlos Hernandez

HERNANDEZ, CARLOS ALBERTO
Born Carlos Alberto Hernandez (Almeida).
B. May 24, 1967, San Felix, Venezuela

BR TR 5'11" 185 lbs.

Year	Team	Games	BA	SA	AB	H	2B	3B	HR	HR%	R	RBI	BB	SO	SB	Pinch Hit AB	H	PO	A	E	DP	TC/G	FA	G by Pos
1990	LA N	10	.200	.250	20	4	1	0	0	0.0	2	1	0	2	0	0	0	37	2	0	0	3.9	1.000	C-10
1991		15	.214	.286	14	3	1	0	0	0.0	1	1	0	5	1	2	0	24	4	1	0	2.1	.966	C-13, 3B-1
1992		69	.260	.335	173	45	4	0	3	1.7	11	17	11	21	0	10	0	295	37	7	4	5.4	.979	C-63
1993		50	.253	.364	99	25	5	0	2	2.0	6	7	2	11	0	11	2	181	15	7	0	4.7	.966	C-43
1994		32	.219	.344	64	14	2	0	2	3.1	6	6	1	14	0	6	0	104	12	0	0	4.3	1.000	C-27
1995		45	.149	.223	94	14	1	0	2	2.1	3	8	7	25	0	5	2	210	24	4	2	5.8	.983	C-41
1996		13	.286	.286	14	4	0	0	0	0.0	1	0	2	2	0	4	2	31	1	0	0	3.6	1.000	C-9
7 yrs.		234	.228	.314	478	109	14	0	9	1.9	30	40	23	80	1	38	6	882	95	19	6	4.8	.981	C-206, 3B-1

Jose Hernandez

HERNANDEZ, JOSE ANTONIO
Born Jose Antonio Hernandez (Figueroa).
B. July 14, 1969, Rio Piedras, Puerto Rico

BR TR 6'1" 180 lbs.

Year	Team	Games	BA	SA	AB	H	2B	3B	HR	HR%	R	RBI	BB	SO	SB	Pinch Hit AB	H	PO	A	E	DP	TC/G	FA	G by Pos
1991	TEX A	45	.184	.224	98	18	2	1	0	0.0	8	4	3	31	0	0	0	49	111	4	18	3.6	.976	SS-44, 3B-1
1992	CLE A	3	.000	.000	4	0	0	0	0	0.0	0	0	0	2	0	0	0	3	3	1	0	2.3	.857	SS-3
1994	CHI N	56	.242	.326	132	32	2	3	1	0.8	18	9	8	29	2	8	2	46	85	4	15	2.3	.970	3B-28, SS-21, 2B-8, OF-1
1995		93	.245	.482	245	60	11	4	13	5.3	37	40	13	69	1	10	3	112	189	9	35	3.4	.971	SS-43, 2B-29, 3B-20
1996		131	.242	.381	331	80	14	1	10	3.0	52	41	24	97	4	6	1	148	247	20	52	3.1	.952	SS-87, 3B-43, OF-1, 2B-1
5 yrs.		328	.235	.381	810	190	29	9	24	3.0	115	94	48	228	7	24	6	358	635	38	120	3.1	.963	SS-198, 3B-92, 2B-38, OF-2

Jose Herrera

HERRERA, JOSE RAMON
Born Jose Ramon Herrera (Catalino).
B. Aug. 30, 1972, Santo Domingo, Dominican Republic

BL TL 6' 165 lbs.

Year	Team	Games	BA	SA	AB	H	2B	3B	HR	HR%	R	RBI	BB	SO	SB	Pinch Hit AB	H	PO	A	E	DP	TC/G	FA	G by Pos
1995	OAK A	33	.243	.314	70	17	1	2	0	0.0	9	2	6	11	1	7	2	41	2	2	1	1.5	.956	OF-25, DH-5
1996		108	.269	.378	320	86	15	1	6	1.9	44	30	20	59	8	12	2	190	2	6	0	1.9	.970	OF-101, DH-1
2 yrs.		141	.264	.367	390	103	16	3	6	1.5	53	32	26	70	9	19	4	231	4	8	1	1.8	.967	OF-126, DH-6

Year	Team	Games	BA	SA	AB	H	2B	3B	HR	HR%	R	RBI	BB	SO	SB	Pinch Hit AB	H	PO	A	E	DP	TC/G	FA	G by Pos

Phil Hiatt
HIATT, PHILIP FARRELL   B. May 1, 1969, Pensacola, Fla.   BR TR 6'3" 200 lbs.

Year	Team	Games	BA	SA	AB	H	2B	3B	HR	HR%	R	RBI	BB	SO	SB	AB	H	PO	A	E	DP	TC/G	FA	G by Pos
1993	KC A	81	.218	.366	238	52	12	1	7	2.9	30	36	16	82	6	2	0	45	114	16	6	2.2	.909	3B-70, DH-9
1995		52	.204	.363	113	23	6	0	4	3.5	11	12	9	37	1	16	4	62	4	3	1	1.4	.957	OF-47, DH-2
1996	DET A	7	.190	.286	21	4	0	1	0	0.0	3	1	2	11	0	1	0	3	8	0	1	1.8	1.000	3B-3, OF-2, DH-1
3 yrs.		140	.212	.360	372	79	18	2	11	3.0	44	49	27	130	7	19	4	110	126	19	8	1.9	.925	3B-73, OF-49, DH-12

Bobby Higginson
HIGGINSON, ROBERT LEIGH   B. Aug. 18, 1970, Philadelphia, Pa.   BL TR 5'11" 180 lbs.

Year	Team	Games	BA	SA	AB	H	2B	3B	HR	HR%	R	RBI	BB	SO	SB	AB	H	PO	A	E	DP	TC/G	FA	G by Pos
1995	DET A	131	.224	.393	410	92	17	5	14	3.4	61	43	62	107	6	14	3	247	13	4	2	2.1	.985	OF-123, DH-2
1996		130	.320	.577	440	141	35	0	26	5.9	75	81	65	66	6	9	3	227	9	9	1	1.9	.963	OF-123, DH-4
2 yrs.		261	.274	.488	850	233	52	5	40	4.7	136	124	127	173	12	23	6	474	22	13	3	2.0	.974	OF-246, DH-6

Glenallen Hill
HILL, GLENALLEN   B. Mar. 22, 1965, Santa Cruz, Calif.   BR TR 6'3" 210 lbs.

Year	Team	Games	BA	SA	AB	H	2B	3B	HR	HR%	R	RBI	BB	SO	SB	AB	H	PO	A	E	DP	TC/G	FA	G by Pos
1989	TOR A	19	.288	.346	52	15	0	0	1	1.9	4	7	3	12	2	0	0	27	0	1	0	1.5	.964	OF-16, DH-3
1990		84	.231	.435	260	60	11	3	12	4.6	47	32	18	62	8	7	2	115	4	2	0	1.5	.983	OF-60, DH-20
1991	2 teams	TOR A (35G –.253)			CLE A (37G –.262)																			
"	total	72	.258	.421	221	57	8	2	8	3.6	29	25	23	54	6	2	0	118	0	3	0	1.9	.975	OF-46, DH-17
1992	CLE A	102	.241	.436	369	89	16	1	18	4.9	38	49	20	73	9	9	1	126	5	6	1	1.5	.956	OF-59, DH-34
1993	2 teams	CLE A (66G –.224)			CHI N (31G –.345)																			
"	total	97	.264	.506	261	69	14	2	15	5.7	33	47	17	71	8	19	6	104	3	6	1	1.4	.947	OF-60, DH-18
1994	CHI N	89	.297	.461	269	80	12	1	10	3.7	48	38	29	57	19	20	5	150	0	2	0	1.9	.987	OF-78
1995	SF N	132	.264	.483	497	131	29	4	24	4.8	71	86	39	98	25	7	5	226	10	10	1	2.0	.959	OF-125
1996		98	.280	.499	379	106	26	0	19	5.0	56	67	33	95	6	0	0	159	6	7	3	1.8	.959	OF-98
8 yrs.		693	.263	.464	2308	607	116	13	107	4.6	326	351	182	522	83	64	19	1025	28	37	6	1.7	.966	OF-542, DH-92

Denny Hocking
HOCKING, DENNIS LEE   B. Apr. 2, 1970, Torrance, Calif.   BB TR 5'10" 180 lbs.

Year	Team	Games	BA	SA	AB	H	2B	3B	HR	HR%	R	RBI	BB	SO	SB	AB	H	PO	A	E	DP	TC/G	FA	G by Pos
1993	MIN A	15	.139	.167	36	5	1	0	0	0.0	7	0	6	8	1	5	0	19	23	1	11	3.3	.977	SS-12, 2B-1
1994		11	.323	.419	31	10	3	0	0	0.0	3	2	0	4	2	1	1	11	27	0	5	3.8	1.000	SS-10
1995		9	.200	.360	25	5	0	2	0	0.0	4	3	2	2	1	1	0	13	20	1	4	5.7	.971	SS-6
1996		49	.197	.268	127	25	6	0	1	0.8	16	10	8	24	3	5	0	67	9	1	1	1.8	.987	OF-33, SS-6, 2B-2, 1B-1, DH-1
4 yrs.		84	.205	.283	219	45	10	2	1	0.5	30	15	16	38	7	12	1	110	79	3	21	2.7	.984	SS-34, OF-33, 2B-3, 1B-1, DH-1

Chris Hoiles
HOILES, CHRISTOPHER ALLEN   B. Mar. 20, 1965, Bowling Green, Ohio   BR TR 6' 195 lbs.

Year	Team	Games	BA	SA	AB	H	2B	3B	HR	HR%	R	RBI	BB	SO	SB	AB	H	PO	A	E	DP	TC/G	FA	G by Pos
1989	BAL A	6	.111	.222	9	1	0	0	0	0.0	0	0	1	3	0	2	0	11	0	0	0	1.8	1.000	C-3, DH-3
1990		23	.190	.286	63	12	3	0	1	1.6	7	6	5	12	0	3	0	62	6	0	6	3.4	1.000	C-7, DH-7, 1B-6
1991		107	.243	.384	341	83	15	0	11	3.2	36	31	29	61	0	6	1	443	44	1	6	4.7	.998	C-89, DH-13, 1B-2
1992		96	.274	.506	310	85	10	1	20	6.5	49	40	55	60	0	0	0	500	31	3	6	5.6	.994	C-95, DH-1
1993		126	.310	.585	419	130	28	0	29	6.9	80	82	69	94	1	3	0	696	64	5	11	6.1	.993	C-124, DH-2
1994		99	.247	.449	332	82	10	0	19	5.7	45	53	63	73	2	3	0	615	36	7	2	6.7	.989	C-98
1995		114	.250	.460	352	88	15	1	19	5.4	53	58	67	80	1	8	2	658	34	3	3	6.2	.996	C-107, DH-6
1996		127	.258	.474	407	105	13	0	25	6.1	64	73	57	97	0	1	0	777	41	7	3	6.5	.992	C-126, 1B-1
8 yrs.		698	.262	.473	2233	586	95	2	124	5.6	334	344	346	480	4	26	3	3762	256	26	37	5.9	.994	C-649, DH-32, 1B-9

DIVISIONAL PLAYOFF SERIES

Year	Team	Games	BA	SA	AB	H	2B	3B	HR	HR%	R	RBI	BB	SO	SB	AB	H	PO	A	E	DP	TC/G	FA	G by Pos
1996	BAL A	4	.143	.143	7	1	0	0	0	0.0	1	0	3	3	0	0	0	14	3	0	0	4.3	1.000	C-4

LEAGUE CHAMPIONSHIP SERIES

Year	Team	Games	BA	SA	AB	H	2B	3B	HR	HR%	R	RBI	BB	SO	SB	AB	H	PO	A	E	DP	TC/G	FA	G by Pos
1996	BAL A	4	.167	.417	12	2	0	0	1	8.3	1	2	1	3	0	1	0	23	2	0	0	6.3	1.000	C-4

Aaron Holbert
HOLBERT, AARON KEITH   B. Jan. 9, 1973, Torrance, Calif.   BR TR 6' 160 lbs.

Year	Team	Games	BA	SA	AB	H	2B	3B	HR	HR%	R	RBI	BB	SO	SB	AB	H	PO	A	E	DP	TC/G	FA	G by Pos
1996	STL N	1	.000	.000	3	0	0	0	0	0.0	0	0	0	0	0	0	0	1	0	0	0	1.0	1.000	2B-1

Todd Hollandsworth
HOLLANDSWORTH, TODD MATTHEW   B. Apr. 20, 1973, Dayton, Ohio   BL TL 6'2" 193 lbs.

Year	Team	Games	BA	SA	AB	H	2B	3B	HR	HR%	R	RBI	BB	SO	SB	AB	H	PO	A	E	DP	TC/G	FA	G by Pos
1995	LA N	41	.233	.398	103	24	2	0	5	4.9	16	13	10	29	2	4	0	60	1	4	0	1.8	.938	OF-37
1996		149	.291	.437	478	139	26	4	12	2.5	64	59	41	93	21	14	6	216	7	5	0	1.6	.978	OF-142
2 yrs.		190	.281	.430	581	163	28	4	17	2.9	80	72	51	122	23	18	6	276	8	9	0	1.6	.969	OF-179

DIVISIONAL PLAYOFF SERIES

Year	Team	Games	BA	SA	AB	H	2B	3B	HR	HR%	R	RBI	BB	SO	SB	AB	H	PO	A	E	DP	TC/G	FA	G by Pos
1995	LA N	2	.000	.000	2	0	0	0	0	0.0	0	0	0	0	0	1	0	0	0	0	0	0.0	.000	OF-2
1996		3	.333	.583	12	4	3	0	0	0.0	1	1	0	3	0	0	0	4	0	0	0	1.3	1.000	OF-3
2 yrs.		5	.286	.500	14	4	3	0	0	0.0	1	1	0	3	0	1	0	4	0	0	0	0.8	1.000	OF-5

Dave Hollins
HOLLINS, DAVID MICHAEL   B. May 25, 1966, Buffalo, N.Y.   BB TR 6'1" 195 lbs.

Year	Team	Games	BA	SA	AB	H	2B	3B	HR	HR%	R	RBI	BB	SO	SB	AB	H	PO	A	E	DP	TC/G	FA	G by Pos
1990	PHI N	72	.184	.316	114	21	0	0	5	4.4	14	15	10	28	0	37	8	27	37	4	0	2.2	.941	3B-30, 1B-1
1991		56	.298	.510	151	45	10	2	6	4.0	18	21	17	26	1	14	3	67	62	8	6	3.3	.942	3B-36, 1B-6
1992		156	.270	.469	586	158	28	4	27	4.6	104	93	76	110	9	0	0	120	253	18	22	2.5	.954	3B-156, 1B-1
1993		143	.273	.442	543	148	30	4	18	3.3	104	93	85	109	2	0	0	73	215	27	9	2.2	.914	3B-143
1994		44	.222	.352	162	36	7	1	4	2.5	28	26	23	32	1	0	0	38	47	11	1	2.2	.885	3B-43, OF-1

Year	Team	Games	BA	SA	AB	H	2B	3B	HR	HR%	R	RBI	BB	SO	SB	Pinch Hit AB	Pinch Hit H	PO	A	E	DP	TC/G	FA	G by Pos

Dave Hollins *continued*

Year	Team	Games	BA	SA	AB	H	2B	3B	HR	HR%	R	RBI	BB	SO	SB	AB	H	PO	A	E	DP	TC/G	FA	G by Pos
1995	2 teams PHI N (65G −.229) BOS A (5G −.154)																							
"	total	70	.225	.394	218	49	12	2	7	3.2	48	26	57	45	1	6	1	536	30	7	53	8.7	.988	1B-61, DH-3, OF-2
1996	2 teams MIN A (121G −.242) SEA A (28G −.351)																							
"	total	149	.262	.411	516	135	29	0	16	3.1	88	78	84	117	6	4	0	102	260	18	21	2.6	.953	3B-144, DH-3, 1B-1, SS-1
	7 yrs.	690	.259	.429	2290	592	116	13	83	3.6	404	352	352	467	20	61	12	963	904	93	112	3.1	.953	3B-552, 1B-70, DH-6, OF-3, SS-1

LEAGUE CHAMPIONSHIP SERIES

Year	Team	Games	BA	SA	AB	H	2B	3B	HR	HR%	R	RBI	BB	SO	SB	AB	H	PO	A	E	DP	TC/G	FA	G by Pos
1993	PHI N	6	.200	.550	20	4	1	0	2	10.0	2	4	5	4	1	0	0	5	4	0	0	1.5	1.000	3B-6

WORLD SERIES

Year	Team	Games	BA	SA	AB	H	2B	3B	HR	HR%	R	RBI	BB	SO	SB	AB	H	PO	A	E	DP	TC/G	FA	G by Pos
1993	PHI N	6	.261	.304	23	6	1	0	0	0.0	5	2	6	5	0	0	0	9	9	0	0	3.0	1.000	3B-6

Dwayne Hosey

HOSEY, DWAYNE SAMUEL
B. Mar. 11, 1967, Sharon, Pa.
BB TR 5'10" 175 lbs.

Year	Team	Games	BA	SA	AB	H	2B	3B	HR	HR%	R	RBI	BB	SO	SB	AB	H	PO	A	E	DP	TC/G	FA	G by Pos
1995	BOS A	24	.338	.618	68	23	8	1	3	4.4	20	7	8	16	6	2	0	46	1	0	0	2.1	1.000	OF-21, DH-1
1996		28	.218	.333	78	17	2	2	1	1.3	13	3	7	17	6	3	1	60	2	1	1	2.3	.984	OF-26, DH-1
	2 yrs.	52	.274	.466	146	40	10	3	4	2.7	33	10	15	33	12	5	1	106	3	1	1	2.2	.991	OF-47, DH-2

DIVISIONAL PLAYOFF SERIES

Year	Team	Games	BA	SA	AB	H	2B	3B	HR	HR%	R	RBI	BB	SO	SB	AB	H	PO	A	E	DP	TC/G	FA	G by Pos
1995	BOS A	3	.000	.000	12	0	0	0	0	0.0	1	0	2	3	1	0	0	7	0	0	0	2.3	1.000	OF-3

Tyler Houston

HOUSTON, TYLER SAM
B. Jan. 17, 1971, Las Vegas, Nev.
BL TR 6'2" 210 lbs.

Year	Team	Games	BA	SA	AB	H	2B	3B	HR	HR%	R	RBI	BB	SO	SB	AB	H	PO	A	E	DP	TC/G	FA	G by Pos
1996	ATL N	33	.222	.481	27	6	2	1	1	3.7	3	8	1	9	0	21	4	15	1	0	1	1.3	1.000	1B-10, 3B-1, OF-1

Dave Howard

HOWARD, DAVID WAYNE
Son of Bruce Howard.
B. Feb. 26, 1967, Sarasota, Fla.
BB TR 6' 165 lbs.

Year	Team	Games	BA	SA	AB	H	2B	3B	HR	HR%	R	RBI	BB	SO	SB	AB	H	PO	A	E	DP	TC/G	FA	G by Pos
1991	KC A	94	.216	.258	236	51	7	0	1	0.4	20	17	16	45	3	1	0	129	248	12	40	4.2	.969	SS-63, 2B-26, OF-1, DH-1, 3B-1
1992		74	.224	.283	219	49	6	2	1	0.5	19	18	15	43	3	0	0	124	204	8	52	4.4	.976	SS-74, OF-2
1993		15	.333	.417	24	8	0	1	0	0.0	5	2	2	5	1	0	0	17	28	3	2	3.7	.938	2B-7, SS-3, 3B-2, OF-1
1994		46	.229	.313	83	19	4	0	1	1.2	9	13	11	23	3	0	0	27	79	1	7	2.3	.991	3B-25, SS-15, 2B-3, DH-2, OF-1, P-1
1995		95	.243	.325	255	62	13	4	0	0.0	23	19	24	41	3	0	0	168	195	6	44	3.5	.984	2B-41, SS-33, OF-30, 1B-1, DH-1
1996		143	.219	.305	420	92	14	5	4	1.0	51	48	40	74	5	4	1	209	412	11	112	4.5	.983	SS-135, 2B-3, 1B-2, OF-1, DH-1
	6 yrs.	467	.227	.299	1237	281	44	12	7	0.6	127	117	108	231	21	9	2	674	1166	41	257	4.0	.978	SS-323, 2B-80, OF-36, 3B-28, DH-5, 1B-3, P-1

Matt Howard

HOWARD, MATTHEW CHRISTOPHER
B. Sept. 22, 1967, Fall River, Mass.
BR TR 5'10" 165 lbs.

Year	Team	Games	BA	SA	AB	H	2B	3B	HR	HR%	R	RBI	BB	SO	SB	AB	H	PO	A	E	DP	TC/G	FA	G by Pos
1996	NY A	35	.204	.278	54	11	1	0	1	1.9	9	9	2	8	1	3	1	20	30	1	5	1.4	.980	2B-30, 3B-6

Thomas Howard

HOWARD, THOMAS SYLVESTER
B. Dec. 11, 1964, Middletown, Ohio
BB TR 6'2" 200 lbs.

Year	Team	Games	BA	SA	AB	H	2B	3B	HR	HR%	R	RBI	BB	SO	SB	AB	H	PO	A	E	DP	TC/G	FA	G by Pos
1990	SD N	20	.273	.318	44	12	2	0	0	0.0	4	0	0	11	0	8	1	19	0	1	0	1.5	.950	OF-13
1991		106	.249	.356	281	70	12	3	4	1.4	30	22	24	57	10	26	3	182	4	1	1	2.2	.995	OF-86
1992	2 teams SD N (5G −.333) CLE A (117G −.277)																							
"	total	122	.277	.346	361	100	15	2	2	0.6	37	32	17	60	15	22	7	185	5	2	0	1.9	.990	OF-97, DH-2
1993	2 teams CLE A (74G −.236) CIN N (38G −.277)																							
"	total	112	.254	.386	319	81	15	3	7	2.2	48	36	24	63	10	29	6	154	7	3	2	1.8	.982	OF-84, DH-7
1994	CIN N	83	.264	.410	178	47	11	0	5	2.8	24	24	10	30	4	32	9	80	2	3	1	1.5	.965	OF-57
1995		113	.302	.402	281	85	15	2	3	1.1	42	26	20	37	17	36	13	127	2	2	0	1.6	.985	OF-82
1996		121	.272	.431	360	98	19	10	6	1.7	50	42	17	51	6	28	11	160	6	3	1	1.6	.982	OF-103
	7 yrs.	677	.270	.385	1824	493	89	20	27	1.5	235	182	112	309	62	181	50	907	26	15	5	1.8	.984	OF-522, DH-9

DIVISIONAL PLAYOFF SERIES

Year	Team	Games	BA	SA	AB	H	2B	3B	HR	HR%	R	RBI	BB	SO	SB	AB	H	PO	A	E	DP	TC/G	FA	G by Pos
1995	CIN N	3	.100	.200	10	1	1	0	0	0.0	0	0	0	2	0	0	0	5	0	0	0	1.7	1.000	OF-3

LEAGUE CHAMPIONSHIP SERIES

Year	Team	Games	BA	SA	AB	H	2B	3B	HR	HR%	R	RBI	BB	SO	SB	AB	H	PO	A	E	DP	TC/G	FA	G by Pos
1995	CIN N	4	.250	.375	8	2	1	0	0	0.0	0	1	2	0	0	2	1	2	0	0	0	0.7	1.000	OF-3

Jack Howell

HOWELL, JACK ROBERT
B. Aug. 18, 1961, Tucson, Ariz.
BL TR 6' 185 lbs.

Year	Team	Games	BA	SA	AB	H	2B	3B	HR	HR%	R	RBI	BB	SO	SB	AB	H	PO	A	E	DP	TC/G	FA	G by Pos
1985	CAL A	43	.197	.336	137	27	4	0	5	3.6	19	18	16	33	1	2	1	33	75	8	10	2.8	.931	3B-42
1986		63	.272	.470	151	41	14	2	4	2.6	26	21	19	28	2	16	4	38	57	2	5	2.0	.979	3B-39, OF-8, DH-2
1987		138	.245	.461	449	110	18	5	23	5.1	64	64	57	118	4	18	6	185	95	7	15	1.9	.976	OF-89, 3B-48, 2B-13
1988		154	.254	.422	500	127	32	2	16	3.2	59	63	46	130	2	4	1	97	249	17	19	2.4	.953	3B-152, OF-2
1989		144	.228	.411	474	108	19	4	20	4.2	56	52	52	125	0	3	1	97	322	11	27	2.9	.974	3B-142, OF-4
1990		105	.228	.370	316	72	19	1	8	2.5	35	33	46	61	3	2	0	76	196	18	18	2.8	.938	3B-102, SS-1, 1B-1
1991	2 teams CAL A (32G −.210) SD N (58G −.206)																							
"	total	90	.207	.336	241	50	5	1	8	3.3	35	23	29	44	1	15	4	86	153	4	14	2.9	.984	3B-62, 2B-12, OF-5, 1B-3, DH-1
1996	CAL A	66	.270	.508	126	34	4	1	8	6.3	20	21	10	30	0	34	10	28	44	9	5	1.6	.889	3B-43, DH-4, 1B-2, 2B-1
	8 yrs.	803	.238	.414	2394	569	115	16	92	3.8	314	295	275	569	13	98	29	640	1191	76	113	2.5	.960	3B-630, OF-108, 2B-26, DH-7, 1B-6, SS-1

Year	Team	Games	BA	SA	AB	H	2B	3B	HR	HR%	R	RBI	BB	SO	SB	Pinch Hit AB	H	PO	A	E	DP	TC/G	FA	G by Pos

Jack Howell *continued*

LEAGUE CHAMPIONSHIP SERIES

Year	Team	Games	BA	SA	AB	H	2B	3B	HR	HR%	R	RBI	BB	SO	SB	AB	H	PO	A	E	DP	TC/G	FA	G by Pos
1986	CAL A	2	.000	.000	1	0	0	0	0	0.0	0	0	1	1	0	1	0	0	0	0	0	0.0	—	

Mike Hubbard

HUBBARD, MICHAEL WAYNE
B. Feb. 16, 1971, Lynchburg, Va.　　　　　BR TR 6'1" 180 lbs.

Year	Team	Games	BA	SA	AB	H	2B	3B	HR	HR%	R	RBI	BB	SO	SB	AB	H	PO	A	E	DP	TC/G	FA	G by Pos
1995	CHI N	15	.174	.174	23	4	0	0	0	0.0	2	1	2	2	0	6	1	33	0	1	0	3.8	.971	C-9
1996		21	.105	.184	38	4	0	0	1	2.6	1	4	0	15	0	9	1	53	3	0	1	4.0	1.000	C-14
2 yrs.		36	.131	.180	61	8	0	0	1	1.6	3	5	2	17	0	15	2	86	3	1	1	3.9	.989	C-23

Trenidad Hubbard

HUBBARD, TRENIDAD AVIEL (Trent)
B. May 11, 1964, Chicago, Ill.　　　　　BR TR 5'8" 180 lbs.

Year	Team	Games	BA	SA	AB	H	2B	3B	HR	HR%	R	RBI	BB	SO	SB	AB	H	PO	A	E	DP	TC/G	FA	G by Pos
1994	CLR N	18	.280	.520	25	7	1	1	1	4.0	3	3	3	4	0	12	5	4	0	0	0	0.8	1.000	OF-5
1995		24	.310	.534	58	18	4	0	3	5.2	13	9	8	6	2	10	3	16	1	0	0	1.1	1.000	OF-16
1996	2 teams CLR N (45G –.217) SF N (10G –.207)																							
"	total	55	.213	.382	89	19	5	2	2	2.2	15	14	11	27	2	25	4	51	0	0	0	1.9	1.000	OF-28
3 yrs.		97	.256	.453	172	44	10	3	6	3.5	31	26	22	37	4	47	12	71	2	0	0	1.5	1.000	OF-49

DIVISIONAL PLAYOFF SERIES

Year	Team	Games	BA	SA	AB	H	2B	3B	HR	HR%	R	RBI	BB	SO	SB	AB	H	PO	A	E	DP	TC/G	FA	G by Pos
1995	CLR N	3	.000	.000	2	0	0	0	0	0.0	0	0	0	2	0	0	0	0	0	0	0	0.0	—	

Rex Hudler

HUDLER, REX ALLEN (The Wonder Dog)
B. Sept. 2, 1960, Tempe, Ariz.　　　　　BR TR 6'1" 180 lbs.

Year	Team	Games	BA	SA	AB	H	2B	3B	HR	HR%	R	RBI	BB	SO	SB	AB	H	PO	A	E	DP	TC/G	FA	G by Pos
1984	NY A	9	.143	.286	7	1	1	0	0	0.0	2	0	1	5	0	0	0	4	7	0	1	1.2	1.000	2B-9
1985		20	.157	.196	51	8	0	1	0	0.0	4	1	1	9	0	0	0	42	51	2	14	5.3	.979	2B-16, SS-1, 1B-1
1986	BAL A	14	.000	.000	1	0	0	0	0	0.0	1	0	0	0	0	0	0	2	3	1	0	0.4	.833	2B-13, 3B-1
1988	MON N	77	.273	.412	216	59	14	2	4	1.9	38	14	10	34	29	3	0	116	168	10	30	4.1	.966	2B-41, SS-27, OF-4
1989		92	.245	.406	155	38	7	0	6	3.9	21	13	6	23	15	27	4	59	59	7	13	1.6	.944	2B-38, OF-23, SS-18
1990	2 teams MON N (4G –.333) STL N (89G –.281)																							
"	total	93	.282	.445	220	62	11	2	7	3.2	31	22	12	32	18	21	4	158	42	5	9	3.0	.976	OF-45, 2B-10, 3B-6, 1B-6, SS-1
1991	STL N	101	.227	.309	207	47	10	2	1	0.5	21	15	10	29	12	27	4	130	6	2	6	1.8	.986	OF-58, 1B-12, 2B-5
1992		61	.245	.378	98	24	4	0	3	3.1	17	5	2	23	2	29	7	44	39	3	6	2.4	.965	2B-16, OF-12, 1B-8
1994	CAL A	56	.298	.556	124	37	8	0	8	6.5	17	20	6	28	2	10	0	71	61	5	20	2.8	.964	2B-22, OF-18, 3B-4, DH-4, 1B-1
1995		84	.265	.417	223	59	16	0	6	2.7	30	27	10	48	13	14	2	122	114	4	33	3.0	.983	2B-52, OF-22, DH-3, 1B-2
1996		92	.311	.556	302	94	20	3	16	5.3	60	40	9	54	14	9	2	172	116	6	38	3.3	.980	2B-53, OF-21, 1B-7, DH-7
11 yrs.		699	.267	.432	1604	429	91	10	51	3.2	242	157	67	285	106	140	23	920	666	45	170	2.8	.972	2B-275, OF-203, SS-47, 1B-37, DH-14, 3B-11

Mike Huff

HUFF, MICHAEL KALE
B. Aug. 11, 1963, Honolulu, Hawaii　　　　　BR TR 6'1" 180 lbs.

Year	Team	Games	BA	SA	AB	H	2B	3B	HR	HR%	R	RBI	BB	SO	SB	AB	H	PO	A	E	DP	TC/G	FA	G by Pos
1989	LA N	12	.200	.360	25	5	1	0	1	4.0	4	2	3	6	0	3	1	18	0	0	0	2.0	1.000	OF-9
1991	2 teams CLE A (51G –.240) CHI A (51G –.268)																							
"	total	102	.251	.346	243	61	10	2	3	1.2	42	25	37	48	14	12	0	168	7	2	1	1.7	.989	OF-96, 2B-4, DH-2
1992	CHI A	60	.209	.252	115	24	5	0	0	0.0	13	8	10	24	1	16	5	68	2	0	0	1.2	1.000	OF-56, DH-1
1993		43	.182	.295	44	8	2	0	1	2.3	4	6	9	15	1	2	0	40	0	0	0	0.9	1.000	OF-43
1994	TOR A	80	.304	.449	207	63	15	3	3	1.4	31	25	27	27	2	9	3	126	4	1	1	1.7	.992	OF-76
1995		61	.232	.333	138	32	9	1	1	0.7	14	14	22	21	1	14	4	95	3	2	0	1.8	.980	OF-55
1996		11	.172	.241	29	5	0	1	0	0.0	5	0	1	5	0	2	1	13	2	0	1	1.3	1.000	OF-9, 3B-3
7 yrs.		369	.247	.351	801	198	42	7	9	1.1	113	75	109	146	19	58	14	528	18	5	3	1.6	.991	OF-344, 2B-4, 3B-3, DH-3

David Hulse

HULSE, DAVID LINDSEY
B. Feb. 25, 1968, San Angelo, Texas　　　　　BL TL 5'11" 170 lbs.

Year	Team	Games	BA	SA	AB	H	2B	3B	HR	HR%	R	RBI	BB	SO	SB	AB	H	PO	A	E	DP	TC/G	FA	G by Pos
1992	TEX A	32	.304	.348	92	28	4	0	0	0.0	14	2	3	18	3	0	0	61	0	1	0	1.9	.984	OF-31, DH-1
1993		114	.290	.369	407	118	9	10	1	0.2	71	29	26	57	29	6	5	244	3	3	1	2.2	.988	OF-112, DH-2
1994		77	.255	.316	310	79	8	4	1	0.3	58	19	21	53	18	0	0	179	0	4	0	2.4	.978	OF-76
1995	MIL A	119	.251	.345	339	85	11	6	3	0.9	46	47	18	60	15	7	2	180	2	3	1	1.6	.984	OF-115
1996		81	.222	.248	117	26	3	0	0	0.0	18	6	8	16	4	2	0	95	1	1	1	1.4	.990	OF-68, DH-3
5 yrs.		423	.266	.337	1265	336	35	20	5	0.4	207	103	76	204	69	15	7	759	6	12	3	1.9	.985	OF-402, DH-6

Todd Hundley

HUNDLEY, TODD RANDOLPH
Son of Randy Hundley.
B. May 27, 1969, Martinsville, Va.　　　　　BB TR 5'11" 170 lbs.

Year	Team	Games	BA	SA	AB	H	2B	3B	HR	HR%	R	RBI	BB	SO	SB	AB	H	PO	A	E	DP	TC/G	FA	G by Pos
1990	NY N	36	.209	.299	67	14	6	0	0	0.0	8	2	6	18	0	3	0	162	8	2	2	4.8	.988	C-36
1991		21	.133	.217	60	8	0	1	1	1.7	5	7	6	14	0	3	1	85	11	0	1	4.8	1.000	C-20
1992		123	.209	.316	358	75	17	0	7	2.0	32	32	19	76	3	7	1	700	48	3	2	6.2	.996	C-121
1993		130	.228	.357	417	95	17	2	11	2.6	40	53	23	62	1	15	3	592	63	8	6	5.4	.988	C-123
1994		91	.237	.443	291	69	10	1	16	5.5	45	42	25	73	2	15	4	448	28	5	0	5.9	.990	C-82
1995		90	.280	.484	275	77	11	0	15	5.5	39	51	42	64	1	12	3	487	28	7	2	5.9	.987	C-89
1996		153	.259	.550	540	140	32	1	41	7.6	85	112	79	146	1	8	1	911	72	8	7	6.6	.992	C-150
7 yrs.		644	.238	.425	2008	478	93	5	91	4.5	254	299	200	453	8	63	13	3385	258	33	20	5.9	.991	C-621

Year	Team	Games	BA	SA	AB	H	2B	3B	HR	HR%	R	RBI	BB	SO	SB	Pinch Hit AB	Pinch Hit H	PO	A	E	DP	TC/G	FA	G by Pos

Brian Hunter

HUNTER, BRIAN LEE
B. Mar. 5, 1971, Portland, Ore.
BR TR 6'4" 180 lbs.

Year	Team	Games	BA	SA	AB	H	2B	3B	HR	HR%	R	RBI	BB	SO	SB	AB	H	PO	A	E	DP	TC/G	FA	G by Pos
1994	HOU N	6	.250	.292	24	6	1	0	0	0.0	2	0	1	6	2	0	0	13	1	1	1	2.5	.933	OF-6
1995		78	.302	.396	321	97	14	5	2	0.6	52	28	21	52	24	3	2	182	8	9	1	2.7	.955	OF-74
1996		132	.276	.363	526	145	27	2	5	1.0	74	35	17	92	35	8	1	279	11	12	0	2.4	.960	OF-127
3 yrs.		216	.285	.373	871	248	42	7	7	0.8	128	63	39	150	61	11	3	474	20	22	2	2.5	.957	OF-207

Brian Hunter

HUNTER, BRIAN RAYNOLD
B. Mar. 4, 1968, Torrance, Calif.
BR TL 6' 195 lbs.

Year	Team	Games	BA	SA	AB	H	2B	3B	HR	HR%	R	RBI	BB	SO	SB	AB	H	PO	A	E	DP	TC/G	FA	G by Pos
1991	ATL N	97	.251	.450	271	68	16	1	12	4.4	32	50	17	48	0	18	3	624	46	8	42	7.5	.988	1B-85, OF-6
1992		102	.239	.487	238	57	13	2	14	5.9	34	41	21	50	1	21	5	542	50	4	35	6.1	.993	1B-92, OF-6
1993		37	.138	.200	80	11	3	1	0	0.0	4	8	2	15	0	11	1	168	13	1	19	5.9	.995	1B-29, OF-2
1994	2 teams PIT N (76G –.227) CIN N (9G –.304)																							
"	total	85	.234	.480	256	60	16	1	15	5.9	34	57	17	56	0	17	5	515	39	5	48	8.0	.991	1B-60, OF-10
1995	CIN N	40	.215	.329	79	17	6	0	1	1.3	9	9	11	21	2	11	5	171	12	3	19	6.9	.984	1B-23, OF-4
1996	SEA A	75	.268	.424	198	53	10	0	7	3.5	21	28	15	43	0	19	4	280	10	5	19	4.1	.983	1B-41, OF-29, DH-2
6 yrs.		436	.237	.434	1122	266	64	5	49	4.4	134	193	83	233	3	97	23	2300	170	26	182	6.4	.990	1B-330, OF-57, DH-2

LEAGUE CHAMPIONSHIP SERIES

Year	Team	Games	BA	SA	AB	H	2B	3B	HR	HR%	R	RBI	BB	SO	SB	AB	H	PO	A	E	DP	TC/G	FA	G by Pos
1991	ATL N	5	.333	.611	18	6	2	0	1	5.6	2	4	0	2	0	0	0	30	4	0	3	6.8	1.000	1B-5
1992		3	.200	.200	5	1	0	0	0	0.0	1	0	0	1	0	2	0	7	0	0	0	3.5	1.000	1B-2
2 yrs.		8	.304	.522	23	7	2	0	1	4.3	3	4	0	3	0	2	0	37	4	0	3	5.9	1.000	1B-7

WORLD SERIES

Year	Team	Games	BA	SA	AB	H	2B	3B	HR	HR%	R	RBI	BB	SO	SB	AB	H	PO	A	E	DP	TC/G	FA	G by Pos
1991	ATL N	7	.190	.381	21	4	1	0	1	4.8	2	3	0	2	0	3	1	6	1	1	1	1.0	.875	OF-4, 1B-4
1992		4	.200	.200	5	1	0	0	0	0.0	0	2	0	1	0	1	0	14	1	0	2	5.0	1.000	1B-3
2 yrs.		11	.192	.346	26	5	1	0	1	3.8	2	5	0	3	0	4	1	20	2	1	3	2.1	.957	1B-7, OF-4

Butch Huskey

HUSKEY, ROBERT LEON
B. Nov. 10, 1971, Anadarko, Okla.
BR TR 6'3" 244 lbs.

Year	Team	Games	BA	SA	AB	H	2B	3B	HR	HR%	R	RBI	BB	SO	SB	AB	H	PO	A	E	DP	TC/G	FA	G by Pos
1993	NY N	13	.146	.171	41	6	1	0	0	0.0	2	3	1	13	0	0	0	9	27	3	2	3.0	.923	3B-13
1995		28	.189	.300	90	17	1	0	3	3.3	8	11	10	16	1	0	0	16	59	6	2	2.9	.926	3B-27, OF-1
1996		118	.278	.435	414	115	16	2	15	3.6	43	60	27	77	1	4	1	639	52	15	58	5.8	.979	1B-75, OF-40, 3B-6
3 yrs.		159	.253	.393	545	138	18	2	18	3.3	53	74	38	106	2	4	1	664	138	24	62	5.1	.971	1B-75, 3B-46, OF-41

Jeff Huson

HUSON, JEFFREY KENT (Huey)
B. Aug. 15, 1964, Scottsdale, Ariz.
BL TR 6'3" 180 lbs.

Year	Team	Games	BA	SA	AB	H	2B	3B	HR	HR%	R	RBI	BB	SO	SB	AB	H	PO	A	E	DP	TC/G	FA	G by Pos
1988	MON N	20	.310	.357	42	13	2	0	0	0.0	7	3	2	2	2	2	1	18	41	4	5	3.3	.937	SS-15, 2B-3, 3B-1, OF-1
1989		32	.162	.230	74	12	5	0	0	0.0	1	2	6	6	3	4	1	40	65	8	11	3.8	.929	SS-20, 2B-9, 3B-1
1990	TEX A	145	.240	.280	396	95	12	2	0	0.0	57	28	46	54	12	18	3	183	304	19	76	3.0	.962	SS-119, 3B-36, 2B-12
1991		119	.213	.287	268	57	8	3	2	0.7	36	26	39	32	8	12	0	141	269	15	43	3.6	.965	SS-116, 2B-2, 3B-1
1992		123	.261	.362	318	83	14	3	4	1.3	49	24	41	43	18	12	1	178	250	9	66	3.3	.979	SS-82, 2B-47, OF-2, DH-1
1993		23	.133	.200	45	6	1	1	0	0.0	3	2	0	10	0	3	0	25	42	6	10	3.5	.918	SS-12, 2B-5, 3B-2, DH-2
1995	BAL A	66	.248	.317	161	40	4	2	1	0.6	24	19	15	20	5	7	2	59	90	1	19	2.6	.993	3B-33, 2B-21, DH-2, SS-1
1996		17	.321	.357	28	9	1	0	0	0.0	5	2	1	3	0	3	1	20	17	1	6	2.4	.974	2B-12, 3B-3, OF-1
8 yrs.		545	.236	.304	1332	315	47	11	7	0.5	182	106	152	171	48	61	10	664	1078	63	236	3.2	.965	SS-365, 2B-110, 3B-77, DH-5, OF-4

Tim Hyers

HYERS, TIMOTHY JAMES
B. Oct. 3, 1971, Atlanta, Ga.
BL TL 6'1" 185 lbs.

Year	Team	Games	BA	SA	AB	H	2B	3B	HR	HR%	R	RBI	BB	SO	SB	AB	H	PO	A	E	DP	TC/G	FA	G by Pos
1994	SD N	52	.254	.280	118	30	3	0	0	0.0	13	7	9	15	3	9	3	258	23	4	19	6.6	.986	1B-41, OF-2
1995		6	.000	.000	5	0	0	0	0	0.0	0	0	0	1	0	5	0	1	1	0	0	2.0	1.000	1B-1
1996	DET A	17	.077	.115	26	2	1	0	0	0.0	1	0	4	5	0	9	0	33	1	0	6	2.8	1.000	1B-9, DH-2, OF-1
3 yrs.		75	.215	.242	149	32	4	0	0	0.0	14	7	13	21	3	23	3	292	25	4	25	5.7	.988	1B-51, OF-3, DH-2

Raul Ibanez

IBANEZ, RAUL JAVIER
B. June 2, 1972, New York, N.Y
BL TR 6'2" 200 lbs.

Year	Team	Games	BA	SA	AB	H	2B	3B	HR	HR%	R	RBI	BB	SO	SB	AB	H	PO	A	E	DP	TC/G	FA	G by Pos
1996	SEA A	4	.000	.000	5	0	0	0	0	0.0	0	0	0	1	0	2	0	0	0	0	0	0.0	—	DH-2

Pete Incaviglia

INCAVIGLIA, PETER JOSEPH (Inky)
B. Apr. 2, 1964, Pebble Beach, Calif.
BR TR 6'1" 225 lbs.

Year	Team	Games	BA	SA	AB	H	2B	3B	HR	HR%	R	RBI	BB	SO	SB	AB	H	PO	A	E	DP	TC/G	FA	G by Pos
1986	TEX A	153	.250	.463	540	135	21	2	30	5.6	82	88	55	**185**	3	4	0	157	6	14	1	1.2	.921	OF-114, DH-36
1987		139	.271	.497	509	138	26	4	27	5.3	85	80	48	168	9	3	0	216	8	13	0	1.7	.945	OF-132, DH-6
1988		116	.249	.467	418	104	19	3	22	5.3	59	54	39	153	6	0	0	172	12	2	1	1.6	.989	OF-93, DH-21
1989		133	.236	.453	453	107	27	4	21	4.6	48	81	32	136	5	5	2	213	7	6	2	1.7	.973	OF-125, DH-5
1990		153	.233	.420	529	123	27	0	24	4.5	59	85	45	146	3	13	2	290	12	8	2	2.1	.974	OF-145, DH-2
1991	DET A	97	.214	.353	337	72	12	1	11	3.3	38	38	36	92	1	3	0	106	4	3	2	1.2	.973	OF-54, DH-41
1992	HOU N	113	.266	.430	349	93	22	1	11	3.2	31	44	25	99	2	18	4	188	8	6	1	2.1	.970	OF-98
1993	PHI N	116	.274	.530	368	101	16	3	24	6.5	60	89	21	82	1	24	6	164	4	5	1	1.8	.971	OF-97
1994		80	.230	.439	244	56	10	1	13	5.3	28	32	16	71	1	20	7	90	2	2	0	1.5	.979	OF-63
1996	2 teams PHI N (99G –.234) BAL A (12G –.303)																							
"	total	111	.242	.464	302	73	9	2	18	6.0	37	50	30	89	2	29	3	100	5	3	1	1.3	.972	OF-78, DH-4
10 yrs.		1211	.247	.453	4049	1002	189	21	201	5.0	527	641	347	1221	33	119	24	1696	68	62	10	1.6	.966	OF-999, DH-115

DIVISIONAL PLAYOFF SERIES

Year	Team	Games	BA	SA	AB	H	2B	3B	HR	HR%	R	RBI	BB	SO	SB	AB	H	PO	A	E	DP	TC/G	FA	G by Pos
1996	BAL A	2	.200	.200	5	1	0	0	0	0.0	1	0	0	4	0	1	0	0	0	0	0	0.0	.000	OF-2

LEAGUE CHAMPIONSHIP SERIES

Year	Team	Games	BA	SA	AB	H	2B	3B	HR	HR%	R	RBI	BB	SO	SB	AB	H	PO	A	E	DP	TC/G	FA	G by Pos
1993	PHI N	3	.167	.417	12	2	0	0	1	8.3	2	1	0	3	0	0	0	8	0	0	0	2.7	1.000	OF-3
1996	BAL A	1	.500	.500	2	1	0	0	0	0.0	1	0	0	0	0	0	0	0	0	0	0	0.0	.000	DH-1
2 yrs.		4	.214	.429	14	3	0	0	1	7.1	3	1	0	3	0	0	0	8	0	0	0	2.0	1.000	OF-3, DH-1

Year	Team	Games	BA	SA	AB	H	2B	3B	HR	HR%	R	RBI	BB	SO	SB	AB	H	PO	A	E	DP	TC/G	FA	G by Pos

Pete Incaviglia *continued*

WORLD SERIES

| 1993 | PHI N | 4 | .125 | .125 | 8 | 1 | 0 | 0 | 0 | 0.0 | 0 | 1 | 0 | 4 | 0 | 1 | 0 | 7 | 0 | 0 | 0 | 1.8 | 1.000 | OF-4 |

Damian Jackson

JACKSON, DAMIAN JACQUES
B. Aug. 16, 1973, Los Angeles, Calif.

BR TR 5'10" 160 lbs.

| 1996 | CLE A | 5 | .300 | .500 | 10 | 3 | 2 | 0 | 0 | 0.0 | 2 | 1 | 1 | 4 | 0 | 1 | 1 | 3 | 13 | 0 | 4 | 3.2 | 1.000 | SS-5 |

John Jaha

JAHA, JOHN EMIL
B. May 27, 1966, Portland, Ore.

BR TR 6'1" 195 lbs.

1992	MIL A	47	.226	.308	133	30	3	0	2	1.5	17	10	12	30	10	3	2	286	22	0	22	6.6	1.000	1B-38, DH-8, OF-1
1993		153	.264	.416	515	136	21	0	19	3.7	78	70	51	109	13	4	0	1187	128	10	116	8.7	.992	1B-150, 2B-1, 3B-1
1994		84	.241	.412	291	70	14	0	12	4.1	45	39	32	75	3	1	0	660	47	8	60	8.5	.989	1B-73, DH-11
1995		88	.313	.579	316	99	20	2	20	6.3	59	65	36	66	2	1	1	648	62	2	86	8.2	.997	1B-81, DH-6
1996		148	.300	.543	543	163	28	1	34	6.3	108	118	85	118	3	3	0	675	59	6	84	5.0	.992	1B-85, DH-63
5 yrs.		520	.277	.474	1798	498	86	4	87	4.8	307	302	216	398	31	12	3	3456	318	26	368	7.3	.993	1B-427, DH-88, 3B-1, 2B-1, OF-1

Dion James

JAMES, DION
B. Nov. 9, 1962, Philadelphia, Pa.

BL TL 6'1" 170 lbs.

1983	MIL A	11	.100	.100	20	2	0	0	0	0.0	1	1	2	1	1	0	0	12	1	0	0	1.2	1.000	OF-9, DH-2
1984		128	.295	.377	387	114	19	5	1	0.3	52	30	32	41	10	17	3	252	7	3	1	2.2	.989	OF-118
1985		18	.224	.245	49	11	1	0	0	0.0	5	3	6	6	0	4	0	20	0	0	0	1.4	1.000	OF-11, DH-3
1987	ATL N	134	.312	.472	494	154	37	6	10	2.0	80	61	70	63	10	11	1	262	4	1	1	2.1	.996	OF-126
1988		132	.256	.350	386	99	17	5	3	0.8	46	30	58	59	9	15	1	222	5	3	0	1.9	.987	OF-120
1989	2 teams ATL N (63G –.259) CLE A (71G –.306)																							
"	total	134	.287	.366	415	119	18	0	5	1.2	41	40	49	49	2	28	5	211	8	3	5	1.9	.986	OF-83, DH-27, 1B-10
1990	CLE A	87	.274	.363	248	68	15	2	1	0.4	28	22	27	23	5	14	3	282	17	4	21	3.9	.987	1B-35, OF-33, DH-10
1992	NY A	67	.262	.379	145	38	8	0	3	2.1	24	17	22	15	1	17	2	62	1	0	0	1.2	1.000	OF-46, DH-5
1993		115	.332	.466	343	114	21	2	7	2.0	62	36	31	31	0	22	9	141	4	5	1	1.4	.967	OF-103, 1B-1, DH-1
1995		85	.287	.354	209	60	6	1	2	1.0	22	26	20	16	4	25	7	61	4	1	1	1.1	.985	OF-29, DH-27, 1B-6
1996		6	.167	.167	12	2	0	0	0	0.0	1	0	1	2	1	0	0	3	0	0	0	0.6	1.000	OF-4, DH-1
11 yrs.		917	.288	.392	2708	781	142	21	32	1.2	362	266	318	307	43	153	33	1528	51	20	30	2.0	.987	OF-682, DH-76, 1B-52

DIVISIONAL PLAYOFF SERIES

| 1995 | NY A | 4 | .083 | .083 | 12 | 1 | 0 | 0 | 0 | 0.0 | 0 | 0 | 1 | 1 | 0 | 0 | 0 | 6 | 0 | 0 | 0 | 1.5 | 1.000 | OF-4 |

Stan Javier

JAVIER, STANLEY JULIAN
Born Stanley Julian Javier (DeJavier).
Son of Julian Javier.
B. Jan. 9, 1964, San Francisco de Macoris, Dominican Republic

BB TR 6' 180 lbs.

1984	NY A	7	.143	.143	7	1	0	0	0	0.0	1	0	0	1	0	0	0	3	0	0	0	0.6	1.000	OF-5
1986	OAK A	59	.202	.272	114	23	8	0	0	0.0	13	8	16	27	8	0	0	118	1	0	1	2.2	1.000	OF-51, DH-2
1987		81	.185	.258	151	28	3	1	2	1.3	22	9	19	33	3	7	0	149	5	3	4	2.0	.981	OF-71, 1B-6, DH-1
1988		125	.257	.320	397	102	13	3	2	0.5	49	35	32	63	20	9	2	274	7	5	5	2.4	.983	OF-115, 1B-4, DH-2
1989		112	.248	.316	310	77	12	3	1	0.3	42	28	31	45	12	7	0	221	8	2	2	2.1	.991	OF-107, 2B-1, 1B-1
1990	2 teams OAK A (19G –.242) LA N (104G –.304)																							
"	total	123	.298	.395	309	92	9	6	3	1.0	60	27	40	50	15	31	8	223	2	0	1	2.2	1.000	OF-100, DH-2
1991	LA N	121	.205	.284	176	36	5	3	1	0.6	21	11	16	36	7	52	5	90	4	3	1	1.4	.969	OF-69, 1B-2
1992	2 teams LA N (56G –.190) PHI N (74G –.261)																							
"	total	130	.249	.314	334	83	17	1	1	0.3	42	29	37	54	18	30	7	229	7	3	1	2.4	.987	OF-101
1993	CAL A	92	.291	.405	237	69	10	4	3	1.3	33	28	27	33	12	27	7	167	4	4	2	2.2	.977	OF-64, 1B-12, 2B-2, DH-1
1994	OAK A	109	.272	.399	419	114	23	0	10	2.4	75	44	49	76	24	1	0	274	4	4	0	2.6	.986	OF-108, 3B-1, 1B-1
1995		130	.278	.387	442	123	20	2	8	1.8	81	56	49	63	36	11	3	332	3	0	1	2.7	1.000	OF-124, 3B-1
1996	SF N	71	.270	.383	274	74	25	0	2	0.7	44	22	25	51	14	0	0	180	2	3	0	2.6	.984	OF-71
12 yrs.		1160	.259	.351	3170	822	145	23	33	1.0	483	297	341	532	169	175	32	2260	47	27	18	2.3	.988	OF-986, 1B-26, DH-8, 2B-3, 3B-2

LEAGUE CHAMPIONSHIP SERIES

1988	OAK A	2	.500	.500	4	2	0	0	0	0.0	0	1	1	0	0	0	0	5	0	0	0	2.5	1.000	OF-2
1989		1	.000	.000	2	0	0	0	0	0.0	0	0	0	1	0	0	0	1	0	0	0	1.0	1.000	OF-1
2 yrs.		3	.333	.333	6	2	0	0	0	0.0	0	1	1	1	0	0	0	6	0	0	0	2.0	1.000	OF-3

WORLD SERIES

1988	OAK A	3	.500	.500	4	2	0	0	0	0.0	0	2	0	1	0	1	0	1	0	0	0	0.5	1.000	OF-2
1989		1	—	—	0	0	0	0	0	0.0	0	0	0	0	0	0	0	0	0	0	0	0.0	.000	OF-1
2 yrs.		4	.500	.500	4	2	0	0	0	0.0	0	2	0	1	0	1	0	1	0	0	0	0.3	1.000	OF-3

Gregg Jefferies

JEFFERIES, GREGORY SCOTT
B. Aug. 1, 1967, Burlingame, Calif.

BB TR 5'11" 175 lbs.

1987	NY N	6	.500	.667	6	3	1	0	0	0.0	0	2	0	0	0	6	3	0	0	0	0	0.0	—	
1988		29	.321	.596	109	35	8	2	6	5.5	19	17	8	10	5	1	0	33	46	2	9	2.7	.975	3B-20, 2B-10
1989		141	.258	.392	508	131	28	2	12	2.4	72	56	39	46	21	7	1	242	280	14	44	3.7	.974	2B-123, 3B-20
1990		153	.283	.434	604	171	40	3	15	2.5	96	68	46	40	11	4	1	242	341	16	54	3.9	.973	2B-118, 3B-34
1991		136	.272	.374	486	132	19	2	9	1.9	59	62	47	38	26	9	2	170	271	17	21	3.6	.963	2B-77, 3B-51
1992	KC A	152	.285	.404	604	172	36	3	10	1.7	66	75	43	29	19	3	0	96	304	26	22	2.9	.939	3B-146, DH-1, 2B-1
1993	STL N	142	.342	.485	544	186	24	3	16	2.9	89	83	62	32	46	1	1	1281	77	9	115	9.7	.993	1B-140, 2B-1
1994		103	.325	.489	397	129	27	1	12	3.0	52	55	45	26	12	3	2	890	52	7	91	9.3	.993	1B-102
1995	PHI N	114	.306	.448	480	147	31	2	11	2.3	69	56	35	26	9	1	0	578	36	3	53	5.4	.995	1B-59, OF-55
1996		104	.292	.401	404	118	17	3	7	1.7	59	51	36	21	20	1	1	521	39	1	38	5.4	.998	1B-53, OF-51
10 yrs.		1080	.296	.432	4142	1224	231	21	98	2.4	581	525	361	268	169	36	11	4053	1446	95	447	5.3	.983	1B-354, 2B-330, 3B-271, OF-106, DH-1

Year	Team	Games	BA	SA	AB	H	2B	3B	HR	HR%	R	RBI	BB	SO	SB	Pinch Hit AB	Pinch Hit H	PO	A	E	DP	TC/G	FA	G by Pos

Gregg Jefferies *continued*

LEAGUE CHAMPIONSHIP SERIES

Year	Team	Games	BA	SA	AB	H	2B	3B	HR	HR%	R	RBI	BB	SO	SB	AB	H	PO	A	E	DP	TC/G	FA	G by Pos
1988	NY N	7	.333	.407	27	9	2	0	0	0.0	2	1	4	0	0	0	0	5	8	1	0	2.0	.929	3B-7

Reggie Jefferson

JEFFERSON, REGINALD JIROD
B. Sept. 25, 1968, Tallahassee, Fla.

BB TL 6'4" 210 lbs.

Year	Team	Games	BA	SA	AB	H	2B	3B	HR	HR%	R	RBI	BB	SO	SB	AB	H	PO	A	E	DP	TC/G	FA	G by Pos
1991	2 teams	CIN N (5G –.143)		CLE A (26G –.198)																				
"	total	31	.194	.306	108	21	3	0	3	2.8	11	13	4	24	0	2	0	266	25	2	31	10.5	.993	1B-28
1992	CLE A	24	.337	.483	89	30	6	2	1	1.1	8	6	1	17	0	2	1	129	12	1	9	6.5	.993	1B-15, DH-7
1993		113	.249	.372	366	91	11	2	10	2.7	35	34	28	78	1	17	3	112	10	3	10	1.2	.976	DH-88, 1B-15
1994	SEA A	63	.327	.543	162	53	11	0	8	4.9	24	32	17	32	0	16	7	95	10	2	14	2.3	.981	DH-32, 1B-13, OF-2
1995	BOS A	46	.289	.479	121	35	8	0	5	4.1	21	26	9	24	0	8	3	28	4	0	4	0.8	1.000	DH-32, 1B-7, OF-2
1996		122	.347	.593	386	134	30	4	19	4.9	67	74	25	89	0	21	3	178	17	3	8	1.8	.985	DH-49, OF-45, 1B-16
6 yrs.		399	.295	.476	1232	364	69	8	46	3.7	166	185	84	264	1	66	17	808	78	11	76	2.6	.988	DH-208, 1B-94, OF-49

DIVISIONAL PLAYOFF SERIES

Year	Team	Games	BA	SA	AB	H	2B	3B	HR	HR%	R	RBI	BB	SO	SB	AB	H	PO	A	E	DP	TC/G	FA	G by Pos
1995	BOS A	1	.250	.250	4	1	0	0	0	0.0	1	0	0	1	0	0	0	0	0	0	0	0.0	.000	DH-1

Robin Jennings

JENNINGS, ROBIN CHRISTOPHER
B. Apr. 11, 1972, Singapore

BL TL 6'2" 205 lbs.

Year	Team	Games	BA	SA	AB	H	2B	3B	HR	HR%	R	RBI	BB	SO	SB	AB	H	PO	A	E	DP	TC/G	FA	G by Pos
1996	CHI N	31	.224	.310	58	13	5	0	0	0.0	7	4	3	9	1	20	3	19	2	0	0	1.9	1.000	OF-11

Marcus Jensen

JENSEN, MARCUS C.
B. Dec. 14, 1972, Oakland, Calif.

BB TR 6'4" 195 lbs.

Year	Team	Games	BA	SA	AB	H	2B	3B	HR	HR%	R	RBI	BB	SO	SB	AB	H	PO	A	E	DP	TC/G	FA	G by Pos
1996	SF N	9	.211	.263	19	4	1	0	0	0.0	4	4	8	7	0	2	0	37	5	2	1	6.3	.955	C-7

Derek Jeter

JETER, DEREK SANDERSON
B. June 26, 1974, Pequannock, N. J.

BR TR 6'3" 175 lbs.

Year	Team	Games	BA	SA	AB	H	2B	3B	HR	HR%	R	RBI	BB	SO	SB	AB	H	PO	A	E	DP	TC/G	FA	G by Pos
1995	NY A	15	.250	.375	48	12	4	1	0	0.0	5	7	3	11	0	0	0	17	34	2	6	3.5	.962	SS-15
1996		157	.314	.430	582	183	25	6	10	1.7	104	78	48	102	14	0	0	245	443	22	85	4.5	.969	SS-157
2 yrs.		172	.310	.425	630	195	29	7	10	1.6	109	85	51	113	14	0	0	262	477	24	91	4.4	.969	SS-172

DIVISIONAL PLAYOFF SERIES

Year	Team	Games	BA	SA	AB	H	2B	3B	HR	HR%	R	RBI	BB	SO	SB	AB	H	PO	A	E	DP	TC/G	FA	G by Pos
1996	NY A	4	.412	.471	17	7	1	0	0	0.0	2	1	0	2	0	0	0	8	10	2	2	5.0	.900	SS-4

LEAGUE CHAMPIONSHIP SERIES

Year	Team	Games	BA	SA	AB	H	2B	3B	HR	HR%	R	RBI	BB	SO	SB	AB	H	PO	A	E	DP	TC/G	FA	G by Pos
1996	NY A	5	.417	.625	24	10	0	1	1	4.2	5	1	0	5	2	0	0	6	13	0	0	3.8	1.000	SS-5

WORLD SERIES

Year	Team	Games	BA	SA	AB	H	2B	3B	HR	HR%	R	RBI	BB	SO	SB	AB	H	PO	A	E	DP	TC/G	FA	G by Pos
1996	NY A	6	.250	.250	20	5	0	0	0	0.0	5	1	4	6	1	0	0	14	22	2	5	6.3	.947	SS-6

Brian Johnson

JOHNSON, BRIAN DAVID
B. Jan. 8, 1968, Oakland, Calif.

BR TR 6'2" 210 lbs.

Year	Team	Games	BA	SA	AB	H	2B	3B	HR	HR%	R	RBI	BB	SO	SB	AB	H	PO	A	E	DP	TC/G	FA	G by Pos
1994	SD N	36	.247	.409	93	23	4	1	3	3.2	7	16	5	21	0	10	4	185	15	0	1	6.9	1.000	C-24, 1B-5
1995		68	.251	.338	207	52	9	0	3	1.4	20	29	11	39	0	13	5	403	31	4	2	7.7	.991	C-55, 1B-2
1996		82	.272	.432	243	66	13	1	8	3.3	18	35	4	36	0	15	5	457	21	5	4	7.1	.990	C-66, 1B-1, 3B-1
3 yrs.		186	.260	.392	543	141	26	2	14	2.6	45	80	20	96	0	38	14	1045	67	9	7	7.3	.992	C-145, 1B-8, 3B-1

DIVISIONAL PLAYOFF SERIES

Year	Team	Games	BA	SA	AB	H	2B	3B	HR	HR%	R	RBI	BB	SO	SB	AB	H	PO	A	E	DP	TC/G	FA	G by Pos
1996	SD N	2	.375	.500	8	3	1	0	0	0.0	2	0	0	1	0	0	0	15	3	0	2	9.0	1.000	C-2

Charles Johnson

JOHNSON, CHARLES EDWARD, JR.
B. July 20, 1971, Fort Pierce, Fla.

BR TR 6'2" 215 lbs.

Year	Team	Games	BA	SA	AB	H	2B	3B	HR	HR%	R	RBI	BB	SO	SB	AB	H	PO	A	E	DP	TC/G	FA	G by Pos
1994	FLA N	4	.455	.818	11	5	1	0	1	9.1	5	4	4	4	0	0	0	18	2	0	0	5.0	1.000	C-4
1995		97	.251	.410	315	79	15	1	11	3.5	40	39	46	71	0	0	0	641	63	6	3	7.3	.992	C-97
1996		120	.218	.358	386	84	13	1	13	3.4	34	37	40	91	1	2	1	751	70	4	11	6.9	.995	C-120
3 yrs.		221	.236	.388	712	168	29	2	25	3.5	79	80	87	166	1	2	1	1410	135	10	14	7.0	.994	C-221

Lance Johnson

JOHNSON, KENNETH LANCE
B. July 6, 1963, Cincinnati, Ohio

BL TL 5'10" 160 lbs.

Year	Team	Games	BA	SA	AB	H	2B	3B	HR	HR%	R	RBI	BB	SO	SB	AB	H	PO	A	E	DP	TC/G	FA	G by Pos
1987	STL N	33	.220	.288	59	13	2	1	0	0.0	4	7	4	6	6	8	2	27	0	2	0	1.2	.931	OF-25
1988	CHI A	33	.185	.234	124	23	4	1	0	0.0	11	6	6	11	6	3	0	63	1	2	0	2.1	.970	OF-31, DH-1
1989		50	.300	.367	180	54	8	2	0	0.0	28	16	17	24	16	3	1	113	0	2	0	2.5	.983	OF-45, DH-1
1990		151	.285	.357	541	154	18	9	1	0.2	76	51	33	45	36	17	4	353	5	10	3	2.5	.973	OF-148, DH-1
1991		160	.274	.342	588	161	14	13	0	0.0	72	49	26	58	26	4	2	425	11	2	3	2.8	.995	OF-158
1992		157	.279	.363	567	158	15	12	3	0.5	67	47	34	33	41	3	1	433	11	6	3	2.9	.987	OF-157
1993		147	.311	.396	540	168	18	14	0	0.0	75	47	36	33	35	2	0	427	7	9	1	3.0	.980	OF-146
1994		106	.277	.393	412	114	11	14	3	0.7	56	54	26	23	26	3	0	317	1	0	0	3.1	1.000	OF-103, DH-1
1995		142	.306	.425	607	186	18	12	10	1.6	98	57	32	31	40	5	2	335	8	3	2	2.5	.991	OF-140, DH-1
1996	NY N	160	.333	.479	682	227	31	21	9	1.3	117	69	33	40	50	3	2	390	9	12	3	2.6	.971	OF-157
10 yrs.		1139	.293	.389	4300	1258	139	99	26	0.6	604	403	247	304	282	51	14	2883	53	48	15	2.7	.984	OF-1110, DH-5

LEAGUE CHAMPIONSHIP SERIES

Year	Team	Games	BA	SA	AB	H	2B	3B	HR	HR%	R	RBI	BB	SO	SB	AB	H	PO	A	E	DP	TC/G	FA	G by Pos
1987	STL N	1	—		0	0	0	0	0	—	1	0	0	0	1	0	0	0	0	0	0	0.0	—	
1993	CHI A	6	.217	.478	23	5	1	1	1	4.3	2	6	2	1	1	0	0	15	0	0	0	2.5	1.000	OF-6
2 yrs.		7	.217	.478	23	5	1	1	1	4.3	3	6	2	1	2	0	0	15	0	0	0	2.5	1.000	OF-6

WORLD SERIES

Year	Team	Games	BA	SA	AB	H	2B	3B	HR	HR%	R	RBI	BB	SO	SB	AB	H	PO	A	E	DP	TC/G	FA	G by Pos
1987	STL N	1	—		0	0	0	0	0	—	0	0	0	0	1	0	0	0	0	0	0	0.0	—	

Year	Team	Games	BA	SA	AB	H	2B	3B	HR	HR%	R	RBI	BB	SO	SB	Pinch Hit AB	Pinch Hit H	PO	A	E	DP	TC/G	FA	G by Pos

Mark Johnson

JOHNSON, MARK PATRICK B. Oct. 17, 1967, Worcester, Mass.   BL TL 6'4" 230 lbs.

Year	Team	Games	BA	SA	AB	H	2B	3B	HR	HR%	R	RBI	BB	SO	SB	PH AB	PH H	PO	A	E	DP	TC/G	FA	G by Pos
1995	PIT N	79	.208	.421	221	46	6	1	13	5.9	32	28	37	66	5	12	2	527	34	8	53	8.1	.986	1B-70
1996		127	.274	.458	343	94	24	0	13	3.8	55	47	44	64	6	31	14	776	73	6	64	8.5	.993	1B-100, OF-1
2 yrs.		206	.248	.443	564	140	30	1	26	4.6	87	75	81	130	11	43	16	1303	107	14	117	8.3	.990	1B-170, OF-1

Andruw Jones

JONES, ANDRUW RUDOLF B. Apr. 23, 1977, Willemstad, Curacao   BR TR 6'1" 170 lbs.

Year	Team	Games	BA	SA	AB	H	2B	3B	HR	HR%	R	RBI	BB	SO	SB	PH AB	PH H	PO	A	E	DP	TC/G	FA	G by Pos
1996	ATL N	31	.217	.443	106	23	7	1	5	4.7	11	13	7	29	3	4	1	73	4	2	0	2.7	.975	OF-29
DIVISIONAL PLAYOFF SERIES																								
1996		3	—	—	0	0	0	0	0	0.0	0	0	1	0	1	0	0	2	0	0	0	0.7	1.000	OF-3
LEAGUE CHAMPIONSHIP SERIES																								
1996		5	.222	.556	9	2	0	0	1	11.1	3	3	3	2	0	2	0	5	0	0	0	1.0	1.000	OF-5
WORLD SERIES																								
1996		6	.400	.750	20	8	1	0	2	10.0	4	6	3	6	1	0	0	7	1	0	1	1.3	1.000	OF-6

Chipper Jones

JONES, LARRY WAYNE B. Apr. 24, 1972, Deland, Fla.   BB TR 6'3" 185 lbs.

Year	Team	Games	BA	SA	AB	H	2B	3B	HR	HR%	R	RBI	BB	SO	SB	PH AB	PH H	PO	A	E	DP	TC/G	FA	G by Pos
1993	ATL N	8	.667	1.000	3	2	1	0	0	0.0	2	0	1	0	0	1	0					0.7	1.000	SS-3
1995		140	.265	.450	524	139	22	3	23	4.4	87	86	73	99	8	1	0	102	259	25	19	2.7	.935	3B-123, OF-20
1996		157	.309	.530	598	185	32	5	30	5.0	114	110	87	88	14	1	0	105	287	17	36	2.6	.958	3B-118, SS-38, OF-1
3 yrs.		305	.290	.494	1125	326	55	8	53	4.7	203	196	161	188	22	4	1	208	547	42	55	2.6	.947	3B-241, SS-41, OF-21
DIVISIONAL PLAYOFF SERIES																								
1995	ATL N	4	.389	.833	18	7	2	0	2	11.1	4	4	2	2	0	0	0	3	4	0	0	1.8	1.000	3B-4
1996		3	.222	.556	9	2	0	0	1	11.1	2	2	3	4	1	0	0	1	3	0	0	1.3	1.000	3B-3
2 yrs.		7	.333	.741	27	9	2	0	3	11.1	6	6	5	6	1	0	0	4	7	0	0	1.6	1.000	3B-7
LEAGUE CHAMPIONSHIP SERIES																								
1995	ATL N	4	.438	.625	16	7	0	0	1	6.3	3	3	3	1	1	0	0	4	13	0	2	4.3	1.000	3B-4
1996		7	.440	.520	25	11	0	0	0	0.0	6	4	3	1	0	0	0	5	7	1	2	1.9	.923	3B-7
2 yrs.		11	.439	.561	41	18	0	0	1	2.4	9	7	6	2	1	0	0	9	20	1	4	2.7	.967	3B-11
WORLD SERIES																								
1995	ATL N	6	.286	.429	21	6	3	0	0	0.0	3	1	4	3	0	0	0	6	12	1	1	3.2	.947	3B-6
1996		6	.286	.429	21	6	3	0	0	0.0	3	3	4	2	1	0	0	4	7	0	1	1.6	1.000	3B-6, SS-1
2 yrs.		12	.286	.429	42	12	6	0	0	0.0	6	4	8	5	1	0	0	10	19	1	2	2.3	.967	3B-12, SS-1

Chris Jones

JONES, CHRISTOPHER CARLOS B. Dec. 16, 1965, Utica, N.Y.   BR TR 6'2" 200 lbs.

Year	Team	Games	BA	SA	AB	H	2B	3B	HR	HR%	R	RBI	BB	SO	SB	PH AB	PH H	PO	A	E	DP	TC/G	FA	G by Pos
1991	CIN N	52	.292	.416	89	26	1	2	2	2.2	14	6	2	31	2	26	8	27	1	0	0	1.1	1.000	OF-26
1992	HOU N	54	.190	.302	63	12	2	1	1	1.6	7	4	7	21	3	14	1	27	0	2	0	0.7	.931	OF-43
1993	CLR N	86	.273	.450	209	57	11	4	6	2.9	29	31	10	48	9	22	8	114	2	2	0	1.7	.983	OF-70
1994		21	.300	.400	40	12	2	1	0	0.0	6	2	2	14	0	9	1	16	0	1	0	1.2	.941	OF-14
1995	NY N	79	.280	.467	182	51	6	2	8	4.4	33	31	13	45	2	25	10	122	6	2	4	2.3	.985	OF-52, 1B-5
1996		89	.242	.369	149	36	7	0	4	2.7	22	18	12	42	1	22	7	83	1	3	1	1.2	.966	OF-66, 1B-5
6 yrs.		381	.265	.418	732	194	29	10	21	2.9	111	92	46	201	17	118	35	389	10	10	5	1.5	.976	OF-271, 1B-10

Dax Jones

JONES, DAX XENOS B. Aug. 4, 1970, Pittsburgh, Pa.   BR TR 6' 180 lbs.

Year	Team	Games	BA	SA	AB	H	2B	3B	HR	HR%	R	RBI	BB	SO	SB	PH AB	PH H	PO	A	E	DP	TC/G	FA	G by Pos
1996	SF N	34	.172	.293	58	10	0	2	1	1.7	7	7	8	12	2	5	0	46	1	0	0	1.4	1.000	OF-33

Terry Jones

JONES, TERRY LEE B. Feb. 15, 1971, Birmingham, Ala.   BB TR 5'10" 165 lbs.

Year	Team	Games	BA	SA	AB	H	2B	3B	HR	HR%	R	RBI	BB	SO	SB	PH AB	PH H	PO	A	E	DP	TC/G	FA	G by Pos
1996	CLR N	12	.300	.300	10	3	0	0	0	0.0	6	1	0	3	0	1	0	5	0	0	0	1.2	1.000	OF-4

Brian Jordan

JORDAN, BRIAN O'NEAL B. Mar. 29, 1967, Baltimore, Md.   BR TR 6'1" 205 lbs.

Year	Team	Games	BA	SA	AB	H	2B	3B	HR	HR%	R	RBI	BB	SO	SB	PH AB	PH H	PO	A	E	DP	TC/G	FA	G by Pos
1992	STL N	55	.207	.373	193	40	9	4	5	2.6	17	22	10	48	7	5	1	101	4	1	0	2.0	.991	OF-53
1993		67	.309	.543	223	69	10	6	10	4.5	33	44	12	35	6	2	0	140	4	4	0	2.3	.973	OF-65
1994		53	.258	.410	178	46	8	2	5	2.8	14	15	16	40	4	5	3	105	6	1	1	2.4	.991	OF-46, 1B-1
1995		131	.296	.488	490	145	20	4	22	4.5	83	81	22	79	24	6	3	268	4	1	2	2.2	.996	OF-126
1996		140	.310	.483	513	159	36	1	17	3.3	82	104	29	84	22	5	3	310	9	2	0	2.3	.994	OF-136, 1B-1
5 yrs.		446	.287	.472	1597	459	83	17	59	3.7	229	266	89	286	63	23	10	924	27	9	3	2.2	.991	OF-426, 1B-2
DIVISIONAL PLAYOFF SERIES																								
1996	STL N	3	.333	.583	12	4	0	0	1	8.3	4	3	1	3	1	0	0	5	0	0	0	1.7	1.000	OF-3
LEAGUE CHAMPIONSHIP SERIES																								
1996	STL N	7	.240	.480	25	6	1	1	1	4.0	3	2	1	0	0	0	0	13	0	0	1	1.9	1.000	OF-7

Kevin Jordan

JORDAN, KEVIN WAYNE B. Oct. 9, 1969, San Francisco, Calif.   BR TR 6'1" 185 lbs.

Year	Team	Games	BA	SA	AB	H	2B	3B	HR	HR%	R	RBI	BB	SO	SB	PH AB	PH H	PO	A	E	DP	TC/G	FA	G by Pos
1995	PHI N	24	.185	.315	54	10	1	0	2	3.7	6	6	2	9	0	10	1	29	35	1	8	6.5	.985	2B-9, 3B-1
1996		43	.282	.427	131	37	10	0	3	2.3	15	12	5	20	2	5	0	244	27	0	23	7.1	1.000	1B-30, 2B-7, 3B-1
2 yrs.		67	.254	.395	185	47	11	0	5	2.7	21	18	7	29	2	15	1	273	62	1	31	7.0	.997	1B-30, 2B-16, 3B-2

Year	Team	Games	BA	SA	AB	H	2B	3B	HR	HR%	R	RBI	BB	SO	SB	Pinch Hit AB	Pinch Hit H	PO	A	E	DP	TC/G	FA	G by Pos

Ricky Jordan
JORDAN, PAUL SCOTT
B. May 26, 1965, Richmond, Calif. — BR TR 6'5" 210 lbs.

Year	Team	Games	BA	SA	AB	H	2B	3B	HR	HR%	R	RBI	BB	SO	SB	PH AB	PH H	PO	A	E	DP	TC/G	FA	G by Pos
1988	PHI N	69	.308	.491	273	84	15	1	11	4.0	41	43	7	39	1	0	0	579	35	5	41	9.0	.992	1B-69
1989		144	.285	.407	523	149	22	3	12	2.3	63	75	23	62	4	10	4	1271	61	9	99	9.6	.993	1B-140
1990		92	.241	.352	324	78	21	0	5	1.5	32	44	13	39	2	8	2	743	37	4	65	9.3	.995	1B-84
1991		101	.272	.452	301	82	21	3	9	3.0	38	49	14	49	0	28	9	626	37	9	37	9.3	.987	1B-72
1992		94	.304	.417	276	84	19	0	4	1.4	33	34	5	44	3	28	8	427	27	2	34	7.0	.996	1B-54, OF-11
1993		90	.289	.421	159	46	4	1	5	3.1	21	18	8	32	0	53	16	201	4	2	20	6.3	.990	1B-33
1994		72	.282	.473	220	62	14	2	8	3.6	29	37	6	32	0	23	4	430	14	3	41	9.1	.993	1B-49
1996	SEA A	15	.250	.357	28	7	0	0	1	3.6	4	4	1	6	0	5	0	40	1	0	5	3.7	1.000	1B-9, DH-2
8 yrs.		677	.281	.424	2104	592	116	10	55	2.6	261	304	77	303	10	155	43	4317	216	34	342	8.7	.993	1B-510, OF-11, DH-2

LEAGUE CHAMPIONSHIP SERIES

| 1993 | PHI N | 2 | .000 | .000 | 1 | 0 | 0 | 0 | 0 | 0.0 | 0 | 0 | 1 | 0 | 0 | 1 | 0 | 0 | 0 | 0 | 0 | 0.0 | — | |

WORLD SERIES

| 1993 | PHI N | 3 | .200 | .200 | 10 | 2 | 0 | 0 | 0 | 0.0 | 0 | 0 | 0 | 2 | 0 | 1 | 0 | 0 | 0 | 0 | 0 | 0.0 | .000 | DH-2 |

Wally Joyner
JOYNER, WALLACE KEITH (Wally World)
B. June 16, 1962, Atlanta, Ga. — BL TL 6'2" 185 lbs.

Year	Team	Games	BA	SA	AB	H	2B	3B	HR	HR%	R	RBI	BB	SO	SB	PH AB	PH H	PO	A	E	DP	TC/G	FA	G by Pos
1986	CAL A	154	.290	.457	593	172	27	3	22	3.7	82	100	57	58	5	4	1	1222	139	15	128	9.1	.989	1B-152
1987		149	.285	.528	564	161	33	1	34	6.0	100	117	72	64	8	2	0	1276	92	10	133	9.2	.993	1B-149
1988		158	.295	.419	597	176	31	2	13	2.2	81	85	55	51	8	4	2	1369	143	8	148	9.7	.995	1B-156
1989		159	.282	.420	593	167	30	2	16	2.7	78	79	46	58	3	2	1	1487	99	4	146	10.0	.997	1B-159
1990		83	.268	.394	310	83	15	0	8	2.6	35	41	41	34	2	1	0	727	62	4	78	9.6	.995	1B-83
1991		143	.301	.488	551	166	34	3	21	3.8	79	96	52	66	2	2	0	1335	98	8	124	10.2	.994	1B-141
1992	KC A	149	.269	.386	572	154	36	2	9	1.6	66	66	55	50	11	1	0	1236	137	10	138	9.3	.993	1B-145, DH-4
1993		141	.292	.467	497	145	36	3	15	3.0	83	65	66	67	5	1	0	1116	145	7	116	9.1	.994	1B-140
1994		97	.311	.449	363	113	20	3	8	2.2	52	57	47	43	3	0	0	779	64	8	67	8.8	.991	1B-86, DH-11
1995		131	.310	.447	465	144	28	0	12	2.6	69	83	69	65	3	7	1	1111	118	3	119	9.6	.998	1B-126, DH-2
1996	SD N	121	.277	.404	433	120	29	1	8	1.8	59	65	69	71	5	2	0	1059	88	3	86	9.7	.997	1B-119
11 yrs.		1485	.289	.444	5538	1601	319	20	166	3.0	784	854	629	627	55	26	5	12717	1185	80	1283	9.5	.994	1B-1456, DH-17

DIVISIONAL PLAYOFF SERIES

| 1996 | SD N | 3 | .111 | .111 | 9 | 1 | 0 | 0 | 0 | 0.0 | 0 | 0 | 0 | 2 | 1 | 0 | 0 | 12 | 2 | 0 | 2 | 4.7 | 1.000 | 1B-3 |

LEAGUE CHAMPIONSHIP SERIES

| 1986 | CAL A | 3 | .455 | .909 | 11 | 5 | 2 | 0 | 1 | 9.1 | 3 | 2 | 2 | 0 | 0 | 0 | 0 | 26 | 1 | 0 | 2 | 9.0 | 1.000 | 1B-3 |

David Justice
JUSTICE, DAVID CHRISTOPHER
B. Apr. 14, 1966, Cincinnati, Ohio — BL TL 6'3" 195 lbs.

Year	Team	Games	BA	SA	AB	H	2B	3B	HR	HR%	R	RBI	BB	SO	SB	PH AB	PH H	PO	A	E	DP	TC/G	FA	G by Pos
1989	ATL N	16	.235	.353	51	12	3	0	1	2.0	7	3	9	22	2	0	0	24	0	0	0	1.5	1.000	OF-16
1990		127	.282	.535	439	124	23	2	28	6.4	76	78	64	92	11	5	2	604	42	14	44	5.1	.979	1B-69, OF-61
1991		109	.275	.503	396	109	25	1	21	5.3	67	87	65	81	8	3	0	204	9	7	0	2.1	.968	OF-106
1992		144	.256	.446	484	124	19	5	21	4.3	78	72	79	85	2	3	0	313	8	8	2	2.3	.976	OF-140
1993		157	.270	.515	585	158	15	4	40	6.8	90	120	78	90	3	0	0	323	9	5	2	2.1	.985	OF-157
1994		104	.313	.531	352	110	16	2	19	5.4	61	59	69	45	2	2	1	193	6	11	0	2.1	.948	OF-102
1995		120	.253	.479	411	104	17	2	24	5.8	73	78	73	68	4	0	0	233	8	4	0	2.0	.984	OF-120
1996		40	.321	.514	140	45	9	0	6	4.3	23	25	21	22	1	0	0	88	3	0	1	2.3	1.000	OF-40
8 yrs.		817	.275	.499	2858	786	127	16	160	5.6	475	522	452	492	33	13	3	1982	85	49	49	2.6	.977	OF-742, 1B-69

DIVISIONAL PLAYOFF SERIES

| 1995 | ATL N | 4 | .231 | .231 | 13 | 3 | 0 | 0 | 0 | 0.0 | 2 | 0 | 5 | 2 | 0 | 0 | 0 | 6 | 0 | 1 | 0 | 1.8 | .857 | OF-4 |

LEAGUE CHAMPIONSHIP SERIES

1991	ATL N	7	.200	.360	25	5	1	0	1	4.0	4	2	3	1	0	0	0	17	0	1	0	2.6	.944	OF-7
1992		7	.280	.560	25	7	1	0	2	8.0	5	6	6	2	0	0	0	19	3	0	0	3.1	1.000	OF-7
1993		6	.143	.190	21	3	1	0	0	0.0	2	4	3	3	0	0	0	14	0	1	0	2.5	.933	OF-7
1995		3	.273	.273	11	3	0	0	0	0.0	1	1	2	1	0	0	0	4	0	0	0	1.3	1.000	OF-3
4 yrs.		23	.220	.366	82	18	3	0	3	3.7	12	13	14 (6th)	13	0	0	0	54	3	2	0	2.6	.966	OF-23

WORLD SERIES

1991	ATL N	7	.259	.481	27	7	0	0	2	7.4	5	6	5	5	1	0	0	21	1	1	0	3.3	.957	OF-7
1992		6	.158	.316	19	3	0	0	1	5.3	4	3	6	5	1	0	0	15	0	1	0	2.7	.938	OF-6
1995		6	.250	.450	20	5	1	0	1	5.0	3	5	5	1	0	0	0	16	0	0	0	2.7	1.000	OF-6
3 yrs.		19	.227	.424	66	15	1	0	4	6.1	12	14	16	11	2	0	0	52	1	2	0	2.9	.964	OF-19

Ron Karkovice
KARKOVICE, RONALD JOSEPH
B. Aug. 8, 1963, Union, N. J. — BR TR 6'1" 210 lbs.

Year	Team	Games	BA	SA	AB	H	2B	3B	HR	HR%	R	RBI	BB	SO	SB	PH AB	PH H	PO	A	E	DP	TC/G	FA	G by Pos
1986	CHI A	37	.247	.443	97	24	7	0	4	4.1	13	13	9	37	1	0	0	227	19	1	4	6.7	.996	C-37
1987		39	.071	.141	85	6	0	0	2	2.4	7	7	7	40	3	0	0	147	20	3	3	4.6	.982	C-37
1988		46	.174	.287	115	20	4	0	3	2.6	10	9	7	30	4	0	0	190	24	1	4	4.7	.995	C-46
1989		71	.264	.385	182	48	9	2	3	1.6	21	24	10	56	0	0	0	299	47	5	6	5.0	.986	C-68, DH-2
1990		68	.246	.399	183	45	10	0	6	3.3	30	20	16	52	2	4	2	296	31	2	4	5.1	.994	C-64, DH-1
1991		75	.246	.413	167	41	13	0	5	3.0	25	22	15	42	0	4	0	309	28	4	4	4.9	.988	C-69, OF-1
1992		123	.237	.392	342	81	12	1	13	3.8	39	50	30	89	10	4	0	536	53	6	8	5.0	.990	C-119, OF-1
1993		128	.228	.424	403	92	17	1	20	5.0	60	54	29	126	2	2	0	769	63	5	4	6.6	.994	C-127
1994		77	.213	.425	207	44	9	1	11	5.3	33	29	36	68	0	6	0	417	19	3	1	5.8	.993	C-76
1995		113	.217	.387	323	70	14	1	13	4.0	44	51	39	84	2	4	1	629	42	6	1	6.0	.991	C-113
1996		111	.220	.366	355	78	22	0	10	2.8	44	38	24	93	0	0	0	680	45	5	6	6.6	.993	C-111
11 yrs.		888	.223	.386	2459	549	117	6	90	3.7	326	317	222	717	24	24	3	4499	391	41	47	5.7	.992	C-867, DH-3, OF-2

LEAGUE CHAMPIONSHIP SERIES

| 1993 | CHI A | 6 | .000 | .000 | 15 | 0 | 0 | 0 | 0 | 0.0 | 0 | 0 | 1 | 7 | 0 | 0 | 0 | 30 | 2 | 0 | 0 | 5.3 | 1.000 | C-6 |

Year	Team	Games	BA	SA	AB	H	2B	3B	HR	HR%	R	RBI	BB	SO	SB	Pinch Hit AB	Pinch Hit H	PO	A	E	DP	TC/G	FA	G by Pos

Eric Karros

KARROS, ERIC PETER
B. Nov. 4, 1967, Hackensack, N. J.
BR TR 6'4" 205 lbs.

Year	Team	Games	BA	SA	AB	H	2B	3B	HR	HR%	R	RBI	BB	SO	SB	AB	H	PO	A	E	DP	TC/G	FA	G by Pos
1991	LA N	14	.071	.143	14	1	1	0	0	0.0	0	1	6	0	4	1	33	2	0	5	3.5	1.000	1B-10
1992		149	.257	.426	545	140	30	1	20	3.7	63	88	37	103	2	7	4	1211	126	9	98	9.4	.993	1B-143
1993		158	.247	.409	619	153	27	2	23	3.7	74	80	34	82	0	1	0	1335	147	12	118	9.5	.992	1B-157
1994		111	.266	.426	406	108	21	1	14	3.4	51	46	29	53	2	2	0	896	116	9	79	9.4	.991	1B-109
1995		143	.298	.535	551	164	29	3	32	5.8	83	105	61	115	4	0	0	1234	109	7	100	9.4	.995	1B-143
1996		154	.260	.479	608	158	29	1	34	5.6	84	111	53	121	8	0	0	1314	118	15	131	9.4	.990	1B-154
6 yrs.		729	.264	.454	2743	724	137	8	123	4.5	355	431	215	480	16	14	5	6023	618	52	531	9.3	.992	1B-716
DIVISIONAL PLAYOFF SERIES																								
1995	LA N	3	.500	1.083	12	6	1	0	2	16.7	3	4	1	0	0	0	0	14	0	0	2	4.7	1.000	1B-3
1996		3	.000	.000	9	0	0	0	0	0.0	0	0	2	3	0	0	0	28	2	0	1	10.0	1.000	1B-3
2 yrs.		6	.286	.619	21	6	1	0	2	9.5	3	4	3	3	0	0	0	42	2	0	3	7.3	1.000	1B-6

Mike Kelly

KELLY, MICHAEL RAYMOND
B. June 2, 1970, Los Angeles, Calif.
BR TR 6'4" 195 lbs.

Year	Team	Games	BA	SA	AB	H	2B	3B	HR	HR%	R	RBI	BB	SO	SB	AB	H	PO	A	E	DP	TC/G	FA	G by Pos
1994	ATL N	30	.273	.506	77	21	10	1	2	2.6	14	9	2	17	0	6	0	25	0	1	0	1.0	.962	OF-25
1995		97	.190	.314	137	26	6	1	3	2.2	26	17	11	49	7	14	3	63	0	4	0	0.8	.940	OF-83
1996	CIN N	19	.184	.327	49	9	4	0	1	2.0	5	7	9	11	4	1	0	34	1	1	1	2.1	.972	OF-17
3 yrs.		146	.213	.373	263	56	20	2	6	2.3	45	33	22	77	11	21	3	122	1	6	1	1.0	.953	OF-125

Pat Kelly

KELLY, PATRICK FRANKLIN
B. Oct. 14, 1967, Philadelphia, Pa.
BR TR 6' 180 lbs.

Year	Team	Games	BA	SA	AB	H	2B	3B	HR	HR%	R	RBI	BB	SO	SB	AB	H	PO	A	E	DP	TC/G	FA	G by Pos
1991	NY A	96	.242	.339	298	72	12	4	3	1.0	35	23	15	52	12	0	0	78	204	18	29	3.0	.940	3B-80, 2B-19
1992		106	.226	.374	318	72	22	2	7	2.2	38	27	25	72	8	0	0	203	296	11	64	5.0	.978	2B-101, DH-1
1993		127	.273	.389	406	111	24	1	7	1.7	49	51	24	68	14	2	0	245	369	14	84	5.0	.978	2B-125
1994		93	.280	.399	286	80	21	2	3	1.0	35	41	19	51	6	1	0	182	257	10	69	4.8	.978	2B-93
1995		89	.237	.333	270	64	12	1	4	1.5	32	29	23	65	8	2	0	161	255	7	52	4.8	.983	2B-87, DH-1
1996		13	.143	.143	21	3	0	0	0	0.0	4	2	2	9	0	0	0	8	24	1	3	2.5	.970	2B-10, DH-3
6 yrs.		524	.251	.366	1599	402	91	10	24	1.5	193	173	108	317	48	5	0	877	1405	61	301	4.5	.974	2B-435, 3B-80, DH-5
DIVISIONAL PLAYOFF SERIES																								
1995	NY A	5	.000	.000	3	0	0	0	0	0.0	3	1	1	3	0	0	0	2	4	0	2	1.5	1.000	2B-4

Roberto Kelly

KELLY, ROBERTO CONRADO
Born Roberto Conrado Kelly (Gray).
B. Oct. 1, 1964, Panama City, Panama
BR TR 6'2" 180 lbs.

Year	Team	Games	BA	SA	AB	H	2B	3B	HR	HR%	R	RBI	BB	SO	SB	AB	H	PO	A	E	DP	TC/G	FA	G by Pos
1987	NY A	23	.269	.385	52	14	3	0	1	1.9	12	7	5	15	9	0	0	42	0	2	0	2.6	.955	OF-17
1988		38	.247	.364	77	19	4	1	1	1.3	9	7	3	15	5	1	1	70	1	1	0	2.4	.986	OF-30
1989		137	.302	.417	441	133	18	3	9	2.0	65	48	41	89	35	2	2	353	9	6	2	2.7	.984	OF-137
1990		162	.285	.418	641	183	32	4	15	2.3	85	61	42	148	42	4	1	420	5	5	0	2.7	.988	OF-160, DH-1
1991		126	.267	.444	486	130	22	2	20	4.1	68	69	45	77	32	2	1	268	8	4	1	2.2	.986	OF-125
1992		152	.272	.384	580	158	31	2	10	1.7	81	66	41	96	28	5	0	389	8	7	3	2.8	.983	OF-146
1993	CIN N	78	.319	.475	320	102	17	3	9	2.8	44	35	17	43	21	0	0	198	3	1	1	2.6	.995	OF-77
1994	2 teams CIN N (47G –.302)	ATL N (63G –.286)																						
"	total	110	.293	.422	434	127	23	3	9	2.1	73	45	35	71	19	0	0	247	5	3	0	2.3	.988	OF-110
1995	2 teams MON N (24G –.274)	LA N (112G –.279)																						
"	total	136	.278	.373	504	140	23	2	7	1.4	58	57	22	79	19	3	1	225	6	6	0	1.7	.974	OF-134
1996	MIN A	98	.323	.457	322	104	17	4	6	1.9	41	47	23	53	10	2	0	203	4	2	0	2.2	.990	OF-93, DH-2
10 yrs.		1060	.288	.417	3857	1110	190	24	87	2.3	536	442	265	686	220	19	6	2415	46	37	7	2.4	.985	OF-1029, DH-3
DIVISIONAL PLAYOFF SERIES																								
1995	LA N	3	.364	.364	11	4	0	0	0	0.0	0	0	1	0	0	0	0	8	0	1	0	3.0	.889	OF-3

Jason Kendall

KENDALL, JASON DANIEL
Son of Fred Kendall.
B. June 26, 1974, San Diego, Calif.
BR TR 6' 181 lbs.

Year	Team	Games	BA	SA	AB	H	2B	3B	HR	HR%	R	RBI	BB	SO	SB	AB	H	PO	A	E	DP	TC/G	FA	G by Pos
1996	PIT N	130	.300	.401	414	124	23	5	3	0.7	54	42	35	30	5	3	2	797	70	18	10	6.9	.885	C-129

Jeff Kent

KENT, JEFFREY FRANKLIN
B. Mar. 7, 1968, Bellflower, Calif.
BR TR 6'1" 185 lbs.

Year	Team	Games	BA	SA	AB	H	2B	3B	HR	HR%	R	RBI	BB	SO	SB	AB	H	PO	A	E	DP	TC/G	FA	G by Pos
1992	2 teams TOR A (65G –.240)	NY N (37G –.239)																						
"	total	102	.239	.430	305	73	21	2	11	3.6	52	50	27	76	2	3	1	124	205	14	23	3.3	.959	2B-51, 3B-50, 1B-3, SS-1
1993	NY N	140	.270	.446	496	134	24	0	21	4.2	65	80	30	88	4	1	0	261	341	22	73	4.4	.965	2B-127, 3B-12, SS-2
1994		107	.292	.475	415	121	24	5	14	3.4	53	68	23	84	1	0	0	221	338	14	76	5.4	.976	2B-107
1995		125	.278	.464	472	131	22	3	20	4.2	65	65	29	89	3	3	0	246	354	10	66	5.0	.984	2B-122
1995	2 teams NY N (89G –.290)	CLE A (39G –.265)																						
"	total	128	.284	.432	437	124	27	1	12	2.7	61	55	31	78	6	1	0	200	229	22	33	3.5	.951	3B-95, 1B-20, 2B-9, DH-5
5 yrs.		602	.274	.450	2125	583	118	11	78	3.7	296	318	140	415	16	8	1	1052	1467	82	271	4.3	.968	2B-416, 3B-157, 1B-23, DH-5, SS-3
DIVISIONAL PLAYOFF SERIES																								
1996	CLE A	4	.125	.250	8	1	1	0	0	0.0	2	0	0	0	0	0	0	3	3	0	0	1.5	1.000	3B-2, 2B-1, 1B-1

Brooks Kieschnick

KIESCHNICK, MICHAEL BROOKS
B. June 6, 1972, Robstown, Tex.
BL TR 6'4" 225 lbs.

Year	Team	Games	BA	SA	AB	H	2B	3B	HR	HR%	R	RBI	BB	SO	SB	AB	H	PO	A	E	DP	TC/G	FA	G by Pos
1996	CHI N	25	.345	.517	29	10	2	0	1	3.4	6	6	3	8	0	17	6	5	0	1	0	0.8	.833	OF-8

Year	Team	Games	BA	SA	AB	H	2B	3B	HR	HR%	R	RBI	BB	SO	SB	Pinch Hit AB	Pinch Hit H	PO	A	E	DP	TC/G	FA	G by Pos

Jeff King

KING, JEFFREY WAYNE
B. Dec. 26, 1964, Marion, Ind.
BR TR 6'1" 175 lbs.

Year	Team	Games	BA	SA	AB	H	2B	3B	HR	HR%	R	RBI	BB	SO	SB	PH AB	PH H	PO	A	E	DP	TC/G	FA	G by Pos
1989	PIT N	75	.195	.353	215	42	13	3	5	2.3	31	19	20	34	4	15	3	403	59	4	36	7.0	.991	1B-46, 3B-13, 2B-7, SS-1
1990		127	.245	.410	371	91	17	1	14	3.8	46	53	21	50	3	19	5	61	215	18	15	2.5	.939	3B-115, 1B-1
1991		33	.239	.376	109	26	1	1	4	3.7	16	18	14	15	3	0	0	15	62	2	0	2.4	.975	3B-33
1992		130	.231	.371	480	111	21	2	14	2.9	56	65	27	56	4	7	1	368	234	12	58	4.3	.980	3B-73, 1B-32, 2B-32, SS-6, OF-1
1993		158	.295	.406	611	180	35	3	9	1.5	82	98	59	54	8	1	0	108	362	18	30	3.0	.963	3B-156, SS-2, 2B-2
1994		94	.263	.375	339	89	23	0	5	1.5	36	42	30	38	3	1	0	61	198	13	26	3.0	.952	3B-91, 2B-1
1995		122	.265	.456	445	118	27	2	18	4.0	61	87	55	63	7	3	2	350	204	17	40	4.4	.970	3B-84, 1B-35, 2B-8, SS-2
1996		155	.271	.497	591	160	36	4	30	5.1	91	111	70	95	15	5	1	897	250	11	102	6.4	.991	1B-92, 2B-71, 3B-17
8 yrs.		894	.258	.417	3161	817	173	16	99	3.1	419	493	296	405	47	51	12	2263	1584	95	307	4.3	.976	3B-582, 1B-206, 2B-121, SS-11, OF-1

LEAGUE CHAMPIONSHIP SERIES

Year	Team	Games	BA	SA	AB	H	2B	3B	HR	HR%	R	RBI	BB	SO	SB	PH AB	PH H	PO	A	E	DP	TC/G	FA	G by Pos
1990	PIT N	5	.100	.100	10	1	0	0	0	0.0	0	0	1	5	0	2	0	1	4	0	0	1.3	1.000	3B-4
1992		7	.241	.379	29	7	4	0	0	0.0	4	2	0	1	0	0	0	11	19	1	5	4.4	.968	3B-7
2 yrs.		12	.205	.308	39	8	4	0	0	0.0	4	2	1	6	0	2	0	12	23	1	5	3.3	.972	3B-11

Mike Kingery

KINGERY, MICHAEL SCOTT
B. Mar. 29, 1961, St. James, Minn.
BL TL 6' 180 lbs.

Year	Team	Games	BA	SA	AB	H	2B	3B	HR	HR%	R	RBI	BB	SO	SB	PH AB	PH H	PO	A	E	DP	TC/G	FA	G by Pos
1986	KC A	62	.258	.388	209	54	8	5	3	1.4	25	14	12	30	7	5	2	102	6	3	2	1.9	.973	OF-59
1987	SEA A	120	.280	.449	354	99	25	4	9	2.5	38	52	27	43	7	9	3	226	15	2	3	2.1	.992	OF-114, DH-4
1988		57	.203	.276	123	25	6	0	1	0.8	21	9	19	23	3	5	0	102	6	2	1	2.0	.982	OF-44, 1B-10
1989		31	.224	.342	76	17	3	0	2	2.6	14	6	7	14	1	6	0	70	0	0	0	3.0	1.000	OF-23
1990	SF N	105	.295	.338	207	61	7	1	0	0.0	24	24	12	19	6	17	7	126	7	3	2	1.4	.978	OF-95
1991		91	.182	.236	110	20	2	2	0	0.0	13	8	15	21	1	44	11	60	2	1	2	1.4	.984	OF-38, 1B-6
1992	OAK A	12	.107	.107	28	3	0	0	0	0.0	3	1	1	3	0	3	0	14	0	0	0	1.4	1.000	OF-10
1994	CLR N	105	.349	.532	301	105	27	8	4	1.3	56	41	30	26	5	12	3	187	5	4	1	2.0	.980	OF-98, 1B-1
1995		119	.269	.411	350	94	18	4	8	2.3	66	37	45	40	13	15	4	205	5	5	0	1.9	.977	OF-108, 1B-5
1996	PIT N	117	.246	.337	276	68	12	5	3	1.1	32	27	23	29	2	40	10	133	2	2	0	1.7	.985	OF-83
10 yrs.		819	.268	.391	2034	546	108	26	30	1.5	292	219	191	248	45	156	40	1225	48	22	11	1.9	.983	OF-672, 1B-22, DH-4

DIVISIONAL PLAYOFF SERIES

Year	Team	Games	BA	SA	AB	H	2B	3B	HR	HR%	R	RBI	BB	SO	SB	PH AB	PH H	PO	A	E	DP	TC/G	FA	G by Pos
1995	CLR N	4	.200	.200	10	2	0	0	0	0.0	1	0	0	1	0	0	0	5	0	0	0	1.3	1.000	OF-4

Gene Kingsale

KINGSALE, EUGENE HUMPHREY
B. Aug. 20, 1976, Aruba
BB TR 6'3" 170 lbs.

Year	Team	Games	BA	SA	AB	H	2B	3B	HR	HR%	R	RBI	BB	SO	SB	PH AB	PH H	PO	A	E	DP	TC/G	FA	G by Pos
1996	BAL A	3	—	—	0	0	0	0	0	0.0	0	0	0	0	0	0	0	2	0	0	0	1.0	1.000	OF-2

Wayne Kirby

KIRBY, WAYNE LEONARD
B. Jan. 22, 1964, Williamsburg, Va.
BL TR 5'11" 185 lbs.

Year	Team	Games	BA	SA	AB	H	2B	3B	HR	HR%	R	RBI	BB	SO	SB	PH AB	PH H	PO	A	E	DP	TC/G	FA	G by Pos
1991	CLE A	21	.209	.256	43	9	2	0	0	0.0	4	5	2	6	1	1	0	40	1	0	0	2.0	1.000	OF-21
1992		21	.167	.389	18	3	1	0	1	5.6	9	1	3	2	0	9	2	3	0	0	0	0.5	1.000	DH-4, OF-2
1993		131	.269	.371	458	123	19	5	6	1.3	71	60	37	58	17	10	0	273	19	5	5	2.3	.983	OF-123, DH-5
1994		78	.293	.403	191	56	6	0	5	2.6	33	23	13	30	11	15	5	92	2	4	1	1.4	.959	OF-68, DH-2
1995		101	.207	.298	188	39	10	2	1	0.5	29	14	13	32	10	27	5	95	2	1	1	1.3	.990	OF-68, DH-7
1996	2 teams CLE A (27G –.250) LA N (65G –.271)																							
"	total	92	.270	.348	204	55	11	1	1	0.5	26	12	19	19	4	17	3	101	2	3	0	1.4	.972	OF-71, DH-3
6 yrs.		444	.259	.356	1102	285	49	8	14	1.3	172	115	87	147	43	79	15	604	26	13	7	1.7	.980	OF-353, DH-21

DIVISIONAL PLAYOFF SERIES

Year	Team	Games	BA	SA	AB	H	2B	3B	HR	HR%	R	RBI	BB	SO	SB	PH AB	PH H	PO	A	E	DP	TC/G	FA	G by Pos
1995	CLE A	3	1.000	1.000	1	1	0	0	0	0.0	0	0	0	0	0	0	0	0	0	0	0	0.0	.000	OF-2
1996	LA N	3	.125	.125	8	1	0	0	0	0.0	1	0	2	1	0	0	0	4	0	0	0	1.3	1.000	OF-3
2 yrs.		6	.222	.222	9	2	0	0	0	0.0	1	0	2	1	0	0	0	4	0	0	0	0.8	1.000	OF-5

LEAGUE CHAMPIONSHIP SERIES

Year	Team	Games	BA	SA	AB	H	2B	3B	HR	HR%	R	RBI	BB	SO	SB	PH AB	PH H	PO	A	E	DP	TC/G	FA	G by Pos
1995	CLE A	5	.200	.200	5	1	0	0	0	0.0	0	0	1	0	0	1	0	3	0	0	0	0.8	1.000	OF-4

WORLD SERIES

Year	Team	Games	BA	SA	AB	H	2B	3B	HR	HR%	R	RBI	BB	SO	SB	PH AB	PH H	PO	A	E	DP	TC/G	FA	G by Pos
1995	CLE A	3	.000	.000	1	0	0	0	0	0.0	0	0	0	0	0	1	0	1	0	0	0	1.0	1.000	OF-1

Ryan Klesko

KLESKO, RYAN ANTHONY
B. June 12, 1971, Westminster, Calif.
BL TL 6'3" 220 lbs.

Year	Team	Games	BA	SA	AB	H	2B	3B	HR	HR%	R	RBI	BB	SO	SB	PH AB	PH H	PO	A	E	DP	TC/G	FA	G by Pos
1992	ATL N	13	.000	.000	14	0	0	0	0	0.0	0	1	0	5	0	7	0	25	0	0	2	5.0	1.000	1B-5
1993		22	.353	.765	17	6	1	0	2	11.8	3	5	3	4	0	15	6	8	0	0	0	1.6	1.000	1B-3, OF-2
1994		92	.278	.563	245	68	13	3	17	6.9	42	47	26	48	1	14	3	89	3	7	1	1.2	.929	OF-74, 1B-6
1995		107	.310	.608	329	102	25	2	23	7.0	48	70	47	72	5	6	2	131	4	8	0	1.3	.944	OF-102, 1B-2
1996		153	.282	.530	528	149	21	4	34	6.4	90	93	68	129	6	6	0	203	8	5	3	1.5	.977	OF-144, 1B-2
5 yrs.		387	.287	.557	1133	325	60	9	76	6.7	183	216	144	258	12	48	11	456	15	20	6	1.4	.959	OF-322, 1B-20

DIVISIONAL PLAYOFF SERIES

Year	Team	Games	BA	SA	AB	H	2B	3B	HR	HR%	R	RBI	BB	SO	SB	PH AB	PH H	PO	A	E	DP	TC/G	FA	G by Pos
1995	ATL N	4	.467	.533	15	7	1	0	0	0.0	5	1	0	3	0	0	0	3	0	0	0	0.8	1.000	OF-4
1996		3	.125	.500	8	1	0	0	1	12.5	1	1	3	4	1	0	0	2	0	1	0	1.0	.667	OF-3
2 yrs.		7	.348	.522	23	8	1	0	1	4.3	6	2	3	7	1	0	0	5	0	1	0	0.9	.833	OF-7

LEAGUE CHAMPIONSHIP SERIES

Year	Team	Games	BA	SA	AB	H	2B	3B	HR	HR%	R	RBI	BB	SO	SB	PH AB	PH H	PO	A	E	DP	TC/G	FA	G by Pos
1995	ATL N	4	.000	.000	7	0	0	0	0	0.0	0	0	3	4	0	1	0	1	0	0	0	0.3	1.000	OF-3
1996		6	.250	.438	16	4	0	0	1	6.3	1	3	2	6	0	0	0	13	0	0	0	2.2	1.000	OF-6
2 yrs.		10	.174	.304	23	4	0	0	1	4.3	1	3	5	10	0	2	0	14	0	0	0	1.6	1.000	OF-9

WORLD SERIES

Year	Team	Games	BA	SA	AB	H	2B	3B	HR	HR%	R	RBI	BB	SO	SB	PH AB	PH H	PO	A	E	DP	TC/G	FA	G by Pos
1995	ATL N	6	.313	.875	16	5	0	0	3	18.8	4	4	3	4	0	0	0	1	0	0	0	0.2	1.000	OF-3, DH-3
1996		5	.100	.100	10	1	0	0	0	0.0	2	1	2	4	0	0	0	1	0	1	0	0.5	.500	OF-2, 1B-1, DH-1
2 yrs.		11	.231	.577	26	6	0	0	3	11.5	6	5	5	8	0	0	0	2	0	1	0	0.3	.667	OF-5, DH-4, 1B-1

Year	Team	Games	BA	SA	AB	H	2B	3B	HR	HR%	R	RBI	BB	SO	SB	Pinch Hit AB	Pinch Hit H	PO	A	E	DP	TC/G	FA	G by Pos

Chuck Knoblauch

KNOBLAUCH, EDWARD CHARLES
B. July 7, 1968, Houston, Tex.
BR TR 5'9" 175 lbs.

Year	Team	Games	BA	SA	AB	H	2B	3B	HR	HR%	R	RBI	BB	SO	SB	AB	H	PO	A	E	DP	TC/G	FA	G by Pos
1991	MIN A	151	.281	.350	565	159	24	6	1	0.2	78	50	59	40	25	3	2	249	460	18	94	4.8	.975	2B-148, SS-2
1992		155	.297	.358	600	178	19	6	2	0.3	104	56	88	60	34	1	0	306	415	6	104	4.7	.992	2B-154, SS-1, DH-1
1993		153	.277	.346	602	167	27	4	2	0.3	82	41	65	44	29	4	0	302	431	9	99	4.8	.988	2B-148, SS-6, OF-1
1994		109	.312	.461	445	139	45	3	5	1.1	85	51	41	56	35	0	0	190	285	3	60	4.3	.994	2B-109, SS-1
1995		136	.333	.487	538	179	34	8	11	2.0	107	63	78	95	46	0	0	254	400	10	85	4.8	.985	2B-136, SS-2
1996		153	.341	.517	578	197	35	14	13	2.2	140	72	98	74	45	0	0	274	389	8	94	4.4	.988	2B-151, DH-1
6 yrs.		857	.306	.417	3328	1019	184	41	34	1.0	596	333	429	369	214	8	2	1575	2380	54	536	4.7	.987	2B-846, SS-12, DH-2, OF-1

LEAGUE CHAMPIONSHIP SERIES

| 1991 | MIN A | 5 | .350 | .450 | 20 | 7 | 2 | 0 | 0 | 0.0 | 5 | 3 | 3 | 3 | 2 | 0 | 0 | 8 | 14 | 0 | 3 | 4.4 | 1.000 | 2B-5 |

WORLD SERIES

| 1991 | MIN A | 7 | .308 | .346 | 26 | 8 | 1 | 0 | 0 | 0.0 | 3 | 2 | 4 | 2 | 4 | 0 | 0 | 15 | 14 | 1 | 1 | 4.3 | .967 | 2B-7 |

Randy Knorr

KNORR, RANDY DUANE
B. Nov. 12, 1968, San Gabriel, Calif.
BR TR 6'2" 205 lbs.

Year	Team	Games	BA	SA	AB	H	2B	3B	HR	HR%	R	RBI	BB	SO	SB	AB	H	PO	A	E	DP	TC/G	FA	G by Pos
1991	TOR A	3	.000	.000	1	0	0	0	0	0.0	0	0	1	1	0	0	0	6	1	0	0	2.3	1.000	C-3
1992		8	.263	.421	19	5	0	0	1	5.3	1	2	1	5	0	0	0	33	3	0	0	4.0	1.000	C-8, DH-1
1993		39	.248	.436	101	25	3	2	4	4.0	11	20	9	29	0	1	0	168	20	0	4	4.8	1.000	C-39
1994		40	.242	.427	124	30	2	0	7	5.6	20	19	10	35	0	1	0	247	21	2	1	6.8	.993	C-40
1995		45	.212	.341	132	28	8	0	3	2.3	18	16	11	28	0	2	1	243	22	8	1	6.1	.971	C-45
1996	HOU N	37	.195	.287	87	17	5	0	1	1.1	7	7	5	18	0	4	1	204	14	0	1	6.6	1.000	C-33
6 yrs.		172	.226	.377	464	105	18	2	16	3.4	57	64	37	116	0	8	2	901	81	10	7	5.9	.990	C-168, DH-1

WORLD SERIES

| 1993 | TOR A | 1 | — | — | 0 | 0 | 0 | 0 | 0 | — | 0 | 0 | 0 | 0 | 0 | 0 | 0 | 3 | 0 | 0 | 0 | 3.0 | 1.000 | C-1 |

Chad Kreuter

KREUTER, CHADDEN MICHAEL
B. Aug. 26, 1964, Greenbrae, Calif.
BB TR 6'2" 190 lbs.

Year	Team	Games	BA	SA	AB	H	2B	3B	HR	HR%	R	RBI	BB	SO	SB	AB	H	PO	A	E	DP	TC/G	FA	G by Pos
1988	TEX A	16	.275	.412	51	14	2	1	1	2.0	3	5	7	13	0	0	0	93	8	1	0	6.4	.990	C-16
1989		87	.152	.266	158	24	3	0	5	3.2	16	9	27	40	0	1	0	453	26	4	4	5.7	.992	C-85
1990		22	.045	.091	22	1	1	0	0	0.0	2	2	8	9	0	0	0	39	4	1	0	2.1	.977	C-20, DH-1
1991		3	.000	.000	4	0	0	0	0	0.0	0	0	1	0	0	1	0	5	0	0	0	5.0	1.000	C-1
1992	DET A	67	.253	.332	190	48	9	0	2	1.1	22	16	20	38	0	3	2	271	22	5	6	4.7	.983	C-62, DH-1
1993		119	.286	.484	374	107	23	3	15	4.0	59	51	49	92	2	8	4	522	70	7	10	5.2	.988	C-112, DH-2, 1B-1
1994		65	.224	.288	170	38	8	0	1	0.6	17	19	28	36	0	1	1	280	22	4	1	4.6	.987	C-64, OF-1, 1B-1
1995	SEA A	26	.227	.333	75	17	5	0	1	1.3	12	8	5	22	0	5	4	151	12	4	1	7.3	.976	C-23
1996	CHI A	46	.219	.368	114	25	8	0	3	2.6	14	18	13	29	0	16	2	182	12	2	4	4.8	.990	C-38, 1B-2, DH-1
9 yrs.		451	.237	.367	1158	274	59	4	28	2.4	145	128	157	280	2	35	13	1996	176	28	26	5.1	.987	C-421, DH-5, 1B-4, OF-1

Tom Lampkin

LAMPKIN, THOMAS MICHAEL
B. Mar. 4, 1964, Cincinnati, Ohio
BL TR 5'11" 180 lbs.

Year	Team	Games	BA	SA	AB	H	2B	3B	HR	HR%	R	RBI	BB	SO	SB	AB	H	PO	A	E	DP	TC/G	FA	G by Pos
1988	CLE A	4	.000	.000	4	0	0	0	0	0.0	0	0	1	0	0	1	0	3	0	0	0	1.0	1.000	C-3
1990	SD N	26	.222	.302	63	14	0	1	1	1.6	4	4	4	9	0	6	1	91	10	3	1	5.2	.971	C-20
1991		38	.190	.276	58	11	3	1	0	0.0	4	3	3	9	0	24	5	49	5	0	0	4.9	1.000	C-11
1992		9	.235	.235	17	4	0	0	0	0.0	3	0	6	1	2	1	0	30	3	0	0	4.1	1.000	C-7, OF-1
1993	MIL A	73	.198	.321	162	32	8	0	4	2.5	22	25	20	26	7	13	2	242	24	6	2	4.3	.978	C-60, OF-3, DH-1
1995	SF N	65	.276	.342	76	21	2	0	1	1.3	8	9	9	8	2	39	8	62	5	0	0	2.9	1.000	C-17, OF-6
1996		66	.232	.379	177	41	8	0	6	3.4	26	29	20	22	1	16	2	342	25	3	4	7.0	.992	C-53
7 yrs.		281	.221	.330	557	123	21	2	12	2.2	67	70	63	75	12	100	18	819	72	12	7	5.0	.987	C-171, OF-10, DH-1

Ray Lankford

LANKFORD, RAYMOND LEWIS
B. June 5, 1967, Los Angeles, Calif.
BL TL 5'11" 180 lbs.

Year	Team	Games	BA	SA	AB	H	2B	3B	HR	HR%	R	RBI	BB	SO	SB	AB	H	PO	A	E	DP	TC/G	FA	G by Pos
1990	STL N	39	.286	.452	126	36	10	1	3	2.4	12	12	13	27	8	7	3	92	1	1	0	2.7	.989	OF-35
1991		151	.251	.392	566	142	23	15	9	1.6	83	69	41	114	44	5	1	367	7	6	2	2.6	.984	OF-149
1992		153	.293	.480	598	175	40	6	20	3.3	87	86	72	147	42	1	0	438	5	2	0	2.9	.996	OF-153
1993		127	.238	.346	407	97	17	3	7	1.7	64	45	81	111	14	8	1	312	6	7	0	2.7	.978	OF-121
1994		109	.267	.488	416	111	25	5	19	4.6	89	57	58	113	11	5	0	259	5	6	1	2.6	.978	OF-104
1995		132	.277	.513	483	134	35	2	25	5.2	81	82	63	110	24	3	1	300	7	3	1	2.4	.990	OF-129
1996		149	.275	.486	545	150	36	8	21	3.9	100	86	79	133	35	5	1	356	9	1	0	2.5	.997	OF-144
7 yrs.		860	.269	.453	3141	845	186	40	104	3.3	516	437	407	755	178	34	7	2124	40	26	4	2.6	.988	OF-835

DIVISIONAL PLAYOFF SERIES

| 1996 | STL N | 1 | .500 | .500 | 2 | 1 | 0 | 0 | 0 | 0.0 | 1 | 0 | 1 | 0 | 0 | 1 | 0 | 4 | 0 | 0 | 0 | 4.0 | 1.000 | OF-1 |

LEAGUE CHAMPIONSHIP SERIES

| 1996 | STL N | 5 | .000 | .000 | 13 | 0 | 0 | 0 | 0 | 0.0 | 1 | 1 | 1 | 4 | 0 | 2 | 0 | 7 | 0 | 0 | 0 | 2.3 | 1.000 | OF-3 |

Mike Lansing

LANSING, MICHAEL THOMAS (The Laser)
B. Apr. 3, 1968, Rawlins, Wyo.
BR TR 6' 175 lbs.

Year	Team	Games	BA	SA	AB	H	2B	3B	HR	HR%	R	RBI	BB	SO	SB	AB	H	PO	A	E	DP	TC/G	FA	G by Pos
1993	MON N	141	.287	.369	491	141	29	1	3	0.6	64	45	46	56	23	4	1	136	336	24	53	3.2	.952	3B-81, SS-51, 2B-25
1994		106	.266	.368	394	105	21	2	5	1.3	44	35	30	37	12	0	0	164	283	10	54	3.7	.978	2B-82, 3B-28, SS-12
1995		127	.255	.392	467	119	30	2	10	2.1	47	62	28	65	27	0	0	307	373	6	77	5.3	.991	2B-127, SS-2
1996		159	.285	.406	641	183	40	2	11	1.7	99	53	44	85	23	0	0	349	393	11	85	4.7	.985	2B-159, SS-2
4 yrs.		533	.275	.386	1993	548	120	7	29	1.5	254	195	148	243	85	4	1	956	1385	51	269	4.2	.979	2B-393, 3B-109, SS-67

Barry Larkin

LARKIN, BARRY LOUIS
B. Apr. 28, 1964, Cincinnati, Ohio
BR TR 6' 185 lbs.

Year	Team	Games	BA	SA	AB	H	2B	3B	HR	HR%	R	RBI	BB	SO	SB	Pinch Hit AB	Pinch Hit H	PO	A	E	DP	TC/G	FA	G by Pos
1986	CIN N	41	.283	.403	159	45	4	3	3	1.9	27	19	9	21	8	4	0	51	125	4	22	4.6	.978	SS-36, 2B-3
1987		125	.244	.371	439	107	16	2	12	2.7	64	43	36	52	21	4	1	168	358	19	72	4.6	.965	SS-119
1988		151	.296	.429	588	174	32	5	12	2.0	91	56	41	24	40	2	0	231	470	29	67	4.9	.960	SS-148
1989		97	.342	.446	325	111	14	4	4	1.2	47	36	20	23	10	10	4	142	267	10	31	5.1	.976	SS-82
1990		158	.301	.396	614	185	25	6	7	1.1	85	67	49	49	30	3	1	254	469	17	86	4.7	.977	SS-156
1991		123	.302	.506	464	140	27	4	20	4.3	88	69	55	64	24	2	0	226	372	15	65	5.2	.976	SS-119
1992		140	.304	.454	533	162	32	6	12	2.3	76	78	63	58	15	0	0	233	408	11	67	4.7	.983	SS-140
1993		100	.315	.445	384	121	20	3	8	2.1	57	51	51	33	14	0	0	159	281	16	56	4.6	.965	SS-99
1994		110	.279	.419	427	119	23	5	9	2.1	78	52	64	58	26	0	0	178	312	10	56	4.5	.980	SS-110
1995		131	.319	.492	496	158	29	6	15	3.0	98	66	61	49	51	0	0	192	342	11	71	4.2	.980	SS-131
1996		152	.298	.567	517	154	32	4	33	6.4	117	89	96	52	36	3	1	231	426	17	80	4.5	.975	SS-151
11 yrs.		1328	.298	.451	4946	1476	254	48	135	2.7	828	626	545	483	275	28	7	2065	3830	159	673	4.7	.974	SS-1291, 2B-3

DIVISIONAL PLAYOFF SERIES
Year	Team	Games	BA	SA	AB	H	2B	3B	HR	HR%	R	RBI	BB	SO	SB	PH AB	PH H	PO	A	E	DP	TC/G	FA	G by Pos
1995	CIN N	3	.385	.385	13	5	0	0	0	0.0	2	1	1	2	4	0	0	3	8	0	1	3.7	1.000	SS-3

LEAGUE CHAMPIONSHIP SERIES
Year	Team	Games	BA	SA	AB	H	2B	3B	HR	HR%	R	RBI	BB	SO	SB	PH AB	PH H	PO	A	E	DP	TC/G	FA	G by Pos
1990	CIN N	6	.261	.348	23	6	2	0	0	0.0	5	1	3	1	3	0	0	21	15	1	2	6.2	.973	SS-6
1995		4	.389	.611	18	7	2	1	0	0.0	1	0	1	1	1	0	0	10	15	1	2	6.5	.962	SS-4
2 yrs.		10	.317	.463	41	13	4	1	0	0.0	6	1	4	2	4	0	0	31	30	2	4	6.3	.968	SS-10

WORLD SERIES
Year	Team	Games	BA	SA	AB	H	2B	3B	HR	HR%	R	RBI	BB	SO	SB	PH AB	PH H	PO	A	E	DP	TC/G	FA	G by Pos
1990	CIN N	4	.353	.529	17	6	1	1	0	0.0	3	1	2	0	0	0	0	1	14	0	2	3.8	1.000	SS-4

Matt Lawton

LAWTON, MATTHEW
Brother of Marcus Lawton.
B. Nov. 3, 1971, Gulfport, Miss.
BL TR 5'10" 180 lbs.

Year	Team	Games	BA	SA	AB	H	2B	3B	HR	HR%	R	RBI	BB	SO	SB	PH AB	PH H	PO	A	E	DP	TC/G	FA	G by Pos
1995	MIN A	21	.317	.467	60	19	4	1	1	1.7	11	12	7	11	1	4	0	34	1	1	0	1.8	.972	OF-19, DH-1
1996		79	.258	.365	252	65	7	1	6	2.4	34	42	28	28	4	10	5	196	4	3	0	2.7	.985	OF-75, DH-1
2 yrs.		100	.269	.385	312	84	11	2	7	2.2	45	54	35	39	5	14	5	230	5	4	0	2.5	.983	OF-94, DH-2

Scott Leius

LEIUS, SCOTT THOMAS
B. Sept. 24, 1965, Yonkers, N.Y.
BR TR 6'3" 180 lbs.

Year	Team	Games	BA	SA	AB	H	2B	3B	HR	HR%	R	RBI	BB	SO	SB	PH AB	PH H	PO	A	E	DP	TC/G	FA	G by Pos
1990	MIN A	14	.240	.400	25	6	1	0	1	4.0	4	4	2	2	0	0	0	20	25	0	10	3.5	1.000	SS-12, 3B-1
1991		109	.286	.417	199	57	7	2	5	2.5	35	20	30	35	5	25	11	56	129	7	15	1.9	.964	3B-79, SS-19, OF-2
1992		129	.249	.318	409	102	18	2	2	0.5	50	35	34	61	6	3	2	63	261	15	13	2.5	.956	3B-125, SS-10
1993		10	.167	.167	18	3	0	0	0	0.0	4	2	2	4	0	0	0	10	26	2	7	4.2	.947	SS-9
1994		97	.246	.417	350	86	16	1	14	4.0	57	49	37	58	2	5	1	63	184	8	13	2.6	.969	3B-95, SS-2
1995		117	.247	.349	372	92	16	5	4	1.1	51	45	49	54	2	8	3	60	185	14	21	2.1	.946	3B-112, SS-7, DH-3
1996	CLE A	27	.140	.302	43	6	4	0	1	2.3	3	3	3	2	0	8	0	45	16	1	3	2.8	.984	3B-8, 1B-7, 2B-6, DH-1
7 yrs.		503	.249	.364	1416	352	62	10	27	1.9	204	158	156	222	15	49	17	317	826	47	82	2.4	.961	3B-420, SS-59, 1B-7, 2B-6, DH-4, OF-2

LEAGUE CHAMPIONSHIP SERIES
Year	Team	Games	BA	SA	AB	H	2B	3B	HR	HR%	R	RBI	BB	SO	SB	PH AB	PH H	PO	A	E	DP	TC/G	FA	G by Pos
1991	MIN A	3	.000	.000	4	0	0	0	0	0.0	0	0	1	1	0	1	0	1	4	0	1	1.7	1.000	3B-3

WORLD SERIES
Year	Team	Games	BA	SA	AB	H	2B	3B	HR	HR%	R	RBI	BB	SO	SB	PH AB	PH H	PO	A	E	DP	TC/G	FA	G by Pos
1991	MIN A	7	.357	.571	14	5	0	0	1	7.1	2	2	1	2	0	1	0	5	8	1	0	2.0	.929	3B-6, SS-1

Mark Lemke

LEMKE, MARK ALAN
B. Aug. 13, 1965, Utica, N.Y.
BB TR 5'10" 167 lbs.

Year	Team	Games	BA	SA	AB	H	2B	3B	HR	HR%	R	RBI	BB	SO	SB	PH AB	PH H	PO	A	E	DP	TC/G	FA	G by Pos
1988	ATL N	16	.224	.293	58	13	4	0	0	0.0	8	2	4	5	0	0	0	47	51	3	11	6.3	.970	2B-16
1989		14	.182	.364	55	10	2	1	2	3.6	4	10	5	7	0	1	1	25	40	0	7	4.6	1.000	2B-14
1990		102	.226	.280	239	54	13	0	0	0.0	22	21	21	22	0	15	2	90	193	4	29	3.2	.986	3B-45, 2B-44, SS-1
1991		136	.234	.312	269	63	11	2	2	0.7	36	23	29	27	1	27	9	162	215	10	40	3.1	.974	2B-110, 3B-15
1992		155	.227	.304	427	97	7	4	6	1.4	38	26	50	39	0	10	0	236	335	9	56	3.7	.984	2B-145, 3B-13
1993		151	.252	.341	493	124	19	2	7	1.4	52	49	65	50	1	1	0	329	442	14	100	5.2	.982	2B-150
1994		104	.294	.363	350	103	15	0	3	0.9	40	31	38	37	0	2	0	208	300	3	54	5.0	.994	2B-103
1995		116	.253	.356	399	101	16	5	5	1.3	42	38	44	40	2	1	0	205	305	5	61	4.5	.990	2B-115
1996		135	.255	.319	498	127	17	0	5	1.0	64	37	53	48	5	2	1	228	408	15	70	4.9	.977	2B-133
9 yrs.		929	.248	.328	2788	692	104	14	30	1.1	306	237	309	275	9	59	13	1530	2289	63	428	4.3	.984	2B-830, 3B-73, SS-1

DIVISIONAL PLAYOFF SERIES
Year	Team	Games	BA	SA	AB	H	2B	3B	HR	HR%	R	RBI	BB	SO	SB	PH AB	PH H	PO	A	E	DP	TC/G	FA	G by Pos
1995	ATL N	4	.211	.263	19	4	1	0	0	0.0	3	1	1	3	0	0	0	8	16	0	3	6.0	1.000	2B-4
1996		3	.167	.250	12	2	1	0	0	0.0	1	2	0	1	0	0	0	4	8	0	1	4.0	1.000	2B-3
2 yrs.		7	.194	.258	31	6	2	0	0	0.0	4	3	1	4	0	0	0	12	24	0	4	5.1	1.000	2B-7

LEAGUE CHAMPIONSHIP SERIES
Year	Team	Games	BA	SA	AB	H	2B	3B	HR	HR%	R	RBI	BB	SO	SB	PH AB	PH H	PO	A	E	DP	TC/G	FA	G by Pos
1991	ATL N	7	.200	.250	20	4	1	0	0	0.0	1	1	4	0	0	0	0	12	10	1	2	3.3	.957	2B-7
1992		7	.333	.381	21	7	1	0	0	0.0	2	2	5	3	0	0	0	11	16	0	3	3.4	1.000	2B-7, 3B-1
1993		6	.208	.292	24	5	2	0	0	0.0	2	4	1	6	0	0	0	6	19	2	1	4.5	.926	2B-6
1995		4	.167	.167	18	3	0	0	0	0.0	2	1	1	0	0	0	0	13	16	0	5	7.3	1.000	2B-4
1996		7	.444	.630	27	12	2	0	1	3.7	4	5	4	2	0	0	0	9	18	0	3	3.9	1.000	2B-7
5 yrs.		31	.282	.364	110	31	6	0	1	0.9	11	13	15	11	0	0	0	51	79	3	14	4.2	.977	2B-31, 3B-1
	3rd				5th		6th	7th					5th											

WORLD SERIES
Year	Team	Games	BA	SA	AB	H	2B	3B	HR	HR%	R	RBI	BB	SO	SB	PH AB	PH H	PO	A	E	DP	TC/G	FA	G by Pos
1991	ATL N	6	.417	.708	24	10	1	3	0	0.0	4	4	2	4	0	0	0	14	19	1	4	5.7	.971	2B-6
1992		6	.211	.211	19	4	0	0	0	0.0	0	2	1	3	0	0	0	19	12	0	5	5.2	1.000	2B-6
1995		6	.273	.273	22	6	0	0	0	0.0	1	0	3	2	0	0	0	10	24	1	2	5.8	.971	2B-6
1996		6	.231	.269	26	6	1	0	0	0.0	2	2	0	3	0	0	0	11	24	0	3	5.8	1.000	2B-6
4 yrs.		24	.286	.374	91	26	2	3	0	0.0	7	8	6	12	0	0	0	54	79	2	14	5.6	.985	2B-24
							4th																	

Year	Team	Games	BA	SA	AB	H	2B	3B	HR	HR%	R	RBI	BB	SO	SB	Pinch Hit AB	Pinch Hit H	PO	A	E	DP	TC/G	FA	G by Pos

Patrick Lennon
LENNON, PATRICK ORLANDO
B. Apr. 27, 1968, Whiteville, N. C. BR TR 6'2" 200 lbs.

Year	Team	Games	BA	SA	AB	H	2B	3B	HR	HR%	R	RBI	BB	SO	SB	PH AB	PH H	PO	A	E	DP	TC/G	FA	G by Pos
1991	SEA A	9	.125	.250	8	1	1	0	0	0.0	2	1	3	1	0	4	1	2	0	0	0	0.3	1.000	DH-5, OF-1
1992		1	.000	.000	2	0	0	0	0	0.0	0	0	0	0	0	0	0	5	0	0	1	5.0	1.000	1B-1
1996	KC A	14	.233	.333	30	7	3	0	0	0.0	5	1	7	10	0	6	0	18	0	1	0	1.6	.947	OF-11, DH-1
3 yrs.		24	.200	.300	40	8	4	0	0	0.0	7	2	10	11	0	10	1	25	0	1	1	1.4	.962	OF-12, DH-6, 1B-1

Brian Lesher
LESHER, BRIAN HERBERT
B. Mar. 5, 1971, Belgium BR TL 6'5" 205 lbs.

| 1996 | OAK A | 26 | .232 | .451 | 82 | 19 | 3 | 0 | 5 | 6.1 | 11 | 16 | 5 | 17 | 0 | 3 | 0 | 46 | 2 | 1 | 0 | 1.9 | .980 | OF-25, 1B-1 |

Jesse Levis
LEVIS, JESSE
B. Apr. 14, 1968, Philadelphia, Pa. BL TR 5'9" 180 lbs.

1992	CLE A	28	.279	.442	43	12	4	0	1	2.3	2	3	0	5	0	12	1	59	5	1	0	3.0	.985	C-21, DH-1
1993		31	.175	.206	63	11	2	0	0	0.0	7	4	2	10	0	8	1	109	7	1	3	4.0	.991	C-29
1994		1	1.000	1.000	1	1	0	0	0	0.0	0	0	0	0	0	1	1	0	0	0	0	0.0	—	
1995		12	.333	.444	18	6	2	0	0	0.0	1	3	1	0	0	1	0	33	5	0	0	3.2	1.000	C-12
1996	MIL A	104	.236	.283	233	55	6	1	1	0.4	27	21	38	15	0	36	11	372	27	1	4	4.2	.998	C-90, DH-6
5 yrs.		176	.237	.299	358	85	14	1	2	0.6	37	31	41	30	0	58	14	573	44	3	7	3.9	.995	C-152, DH-7

Darren Lewis
LEWIS, DARREN JOEL
B. Aug. 28, 1967, Berkeley, Calif. BR TR 6' 180 lbs.

1990	OAK A	25	.229	.229	35	8	0	0	0	0.0	4	1	7	4	2	4	0	33	0	0	0	1.3	1.000	OF-23, DH-2
1991	SF N	72	.248	.311	222	55	5	3	1	0.5	41	15	36	30	13	4	1	159	2	0	0	2.4	1.000	OF-68
1992		100	.231	.272	320	74	8	1	1	0.3	38	18	29	46	28	6	1	225	3	0	2	2.4	1.000	OF-94
1993		136	.253	.324	522	132	17	7	2	0.4	84	48	30	40	46	9	2	344	4	0	1	2.7	1.000	OF-131
1994		114	.257	.357	451	116	15	9	4	0.9	70	29	53	50	30	1	0	281	5	2	1	2.5	.993	OF-113
1995	2 teams	SF N (74G –.252)	CIN N (58G –.245)																					
"	total	132	.250	.297	472	118	13	3	1	0.2	66	24	34	57	32	9	1	321	5	2	0	2.4	.994	OF-130
1996	CHI A	141	.228	.312	337	77	12	2	4	1.2	55	53	45	40	21	0	0	287	0	3	0	2.1	.990	OF-138
7 yrs.		720	.246	.313	2359	580	70	25	13	0.6	358	188	234	267	172	33	5	1650	19	7	6	2.4	.996	OF-697, DH-2

DIVISIONAL PLAYOFF SERIES

| 1995 | CIN N | 3 | .000 | .000 | 3 | 0 | 0 | 0 | 0 | 0.0 | 0 | 0 | 0 | 1 | 0 | 1 | 0 | 3 | 0 | 0 | 0 | 1.0 | 1.000 | OF-3 |

LEAGUE CHAMPIONSHIP SERIES

| 1995 | CIN N | 2 | .000 | .000 | 1 | 0 | 0 | 0 | 0 | 0.0 | 0 | 0 | 0 | 0 | 0 | 0 | 0 | 2 | 0 | 0 | 0 | 1.0 | 1.000 | OF-2 |

Mark Lewis
LEWIS, MARK DAVID
B. Nov. 30, 1969, Hamilton, Ohio BR TR 6'1" 190 lbs.

1991	CLE A	84	.264	.318	314	83	15	1	0	0.0	29	30	15	45	2	2	2	129	231	9	47	4.3	.976	2B-50, SS-36
1992		122	.264	.351	413	109	21	0	5	1.2	44	30	25	69	4	0	0	184	336	26	71	4.5	.952	SS-121, 3B-1
1993		14	.250	.346	52	13	2	0	1	1.9	6	5	0	7	3	0	0	22	31	2	10	4.2	.964	SS-13
1994		20	.205	.315	73	15	5	0	1	1.4	6	8	2	13	1	0	0	17	40	6	4	3.2	.905	SS-13, 3B-6, 2B-1
1995	CIN N	81	.339	.480	171	58	13	1	3	1.8	25	30	21	33	0	17	4	19	108	4	4	1.7	.969	3B-72, SS-2, 2B-2
1996	DET A	145	.270	.396	545	147	30	3	11	2.0	69	55	42	109	6	0	0	265	412	9	94	4.7	.987	2B-144, DH-1
6 yrs.		466	.271	.372	1568	425	86	5	21	1.3	179	158	105	276	16	19	6	636	1158	56	230	4.0	.970	2B-197, SS-185, 3B-79, DH-1

DIVISIONAL PLAYOFF SERIES

| 1995 | CIN N | 2 | .500 | 2.000 | 2 | 1 | 0 | 0 | 1 | 50.0 | 2 | 5 | 1 | 0 | 0 | 2 | 1 | 0 | 0 | 1 | 0 | 0.5 | .000 | 3B-2 |

LEAGUE CHAMPIONSHIP SERIES

| 1995 | CIN N | 2 | .250 | .250 | 4 | 1 | 0 | 0 | 0 | 0.0 | 0 | 0 | 1 | 1 | 0 | 0 | 0 | 2 | 3 | 0 | 0 | 2.5 | 1.000 | 3B-2 |

Jim Leyritz
LEYRITZ, JAMES JOSEPH
B. Dec. 27, 1963, Lakewood, Ohio BR TR 6' 190 lbs.

1990	NY A	92	.257	.356	303	78	13	1	5	1.7	28	25	27	51	2	4	2	117	107	13	5	2.5	.945	3B-69, OF-14, C-11
1991		32	.182	.221	77	14	3	0	0	0.0	8	4	13	15	0	9	2	38	21	3	3	2.3	.952	3B-18, C-5, 1B-3, DH-1
1992		63	.257	.444	144	37	6	0	7	4.9	17	26	14	22	0	7	1	96	15	1	2	2.0	.991	DH-31, C-18, 1B-2, 3B-2, OF-2, 2B-1
1993		95	.309	.525	259	80	14	0	14	5.4	43	53	37	59	0	13	4	333	15	2	22	3.9	.994	1B-29, OF-28, DH-21, C-12
1994		75	.265	.518	249	66	12	0	17	6.8	47	58	35	61	0	7	1	282	15	0	6	4.1	1.000	C-37, DH-25, 1B-10
1995		77	.269	.394	264	71	12	0	7	2.7	37	37	37	73	1	3	0	418	23	3	12	5.6	.993	C-46, 1B-18, DH-15
1996		88	.264	.381	265	70	10	0	7	2.6	23	40	30	68	2	10	3	387	30	6	5	4.6	.986	C-55, 3B-13, DH-13, 1B-5, OF-3, 2B-2
7 yrs.		522	.266	.422	1561	416	70	1	57	3.7	203	243	193	349	5	56	13	1671	226	28	55	3.8	.985	C-184, DH-106, 3B-102, 1B-67, OF-47, 2B-3

DIVISIONAL PLAYOFF SERIES

1995	NY A	2	.143	.571	7	1	0	0	1	14.3	1	2	1	2	0	1	0	13	0	0	0	6.5	1.000	C-2
1996		2	.000	.000	3	0	0	0	0	0.0	0	1	0	1	0	1	0	4	0	0	0	2.0	1.000	C-1, DH-1
2 yrs.		4	.100	.400	10	1	0	0	1	10.0	1	3	0	2	0	2	0	17	0	0	0	4.3	1.000	C-3, DH-1

LEAGUE CHAMPIONSHIP SERIES

| 1996 | NY A | 3 | .250 | .625 | 8 | 2 | 0 | 0 | 1 | 12.5 | 1 | 2 | 1 | 4 | 0 | 1 | 0 | 11 | 2 | 0 | 0 | 4.3 | 1.000 | C-2, OF-1 |

WORLD SERIES

| 1996 | NY A | 4 | .375 | .750 | 8 | 3 | 0 | 0 | 1 | 12.5 | 1 | 3 | 3 | 2 | 1 | 1 | 0 | 15 | 0 | 0 | 0 | 5.0 | 1.000 | C-3 |

Mike Lieberthal
LIEBERTHAL, MICHAEL SCOTT
B. Jan. 18, 1972, Glendale, Calif. BR TR 6' 170 lbs.

1994	PHI N	24	.266	.367	79	21	3	1	1	1.3	6	5	3	5	0	2	0	122	5	4	0	6.0	.969	C-22
1995		16	.255	.298	47	12	2	0	0	0.0	1	4	5	5	0	2	0	95	10	1	1	7.6	.991	C-14
1996		50	.253	.428	166	42	8	0	7	4.2	21	23	10	30	0	8	1	285	19	3	4	7.1	.990	C-43
3 yrs.		90	.257	.390	292	75	13	1	8	2.7	28	32	18	40	0	12	1	502	34	8	5	6.9	.985	C-79

Year	Team	Games	BA	SA	AB	H	2B	3B	HR	HR%	R	RBI	BB	SO	SB	Pinch Hit AB	Pinch Hit H	PO	A	E	DP	TC/G	FA	G by Pos

Nelson Liriano — LIRIANO, NELSON ARTURO
Born Nelson Arturo Liriano (Bonilla).
B. June 3, 1964, Puerto Plata, Dominican Republic — BB TR 5'10" 165 lbs.

Year	Team	Games	BA	SA	AB	H	2B	3B	HR	HR%	R	RBI	BB	SO	SB	PH AB	PH H	PO	A	E	DP	TC/G	FA	G by Pos
1987	TOR A	37	.241	.342	158	38	6	2	2	1.3	29	10	16	22	13	1	1	83	107	1	28	5.2	.995	2B-37
1988		99	.264	.333	276	73	6	2	3	1.1	36	23	11	40	12	16	4	121	177	12	48	3.4	.961	2B-80, DH-11, 3B-1
1989		132	.263	.376	418	110	26	3	5	1.2	51	53	43	51	16	7	4	267	330	12	76	4.8	.980	2B-122, DH-5
1990	2 teams TOR A (50G –.212) MIN A (53G –.254)																							
"	total	103	.234	.327	355	83	12	9	1	0.3	46	28	38	44	8	5	2	176	260	11	53	4.4	.975	2B-99, DH-2, SS-1
1991	KC A	10	.409	.409	22	9	0	0	0	0.0	5	1	0	2	0	0	0	11	23	0	3	3.4	1.000	2B-10
1993	CLR N	48	.305	.424	151	46	6	3	2	1.3	28	15	18	22	6	3	2	65	103	6	20	3.3	.966	SS-35, 2B-16, 3B-1
1994		87	.255	.396	255	65	17	5	3	1.2	39	31	42	44	0	3	1	146	225	10	42	4.5	.974	2B-79, SS-3, 3B-2
1995	PIT N	107	.286	.398	259	74	12	1	5	1.9	29	38	24	34	2	37	9	130	137	5	31	3.7	.982	2B-67, 3B-5, SS-1
1996		112	.267	.392	217	58	14	2	3	1.4	23	30	14	22	2	65	17	58	98	3	16	3.2	.981	2B-36, 3B-9, SS-5
9 yrs.		735	.263	.370	2111	556	99	27	24	1.1	286	229	206	281	59	137	40	1057	1460	60	317	4.1	.977	2B-546, SS-45, DH-18, 3B-18

LEAGUE CHAMPIONSHIP SERIES

1989	TOR A	3	.429	.429	7	3	0	0	0	0.0	1	1	2	0	3	0	0	4	3	1	1	2.7	.875	2B-3

Pat Listach — LISTACH, PATRICK ALAN
B. Sept. 12, 1967, Natchitoches, La. — BR TR 5'9" 170 lbs.

Year	Team	Games	BA	SA	AB	H	2B	3B	HR	HR%	R	RBI	BB	SO	SB	PH AB	PH H	PO	A	E	DP	TC/G	FA	G by Pos
1992	MIL A	149	.290	.349	579	168	19	6	1	0.2	93	47	55	124	54	1	0	238	449	24	89	4.7	.966	SS-148, OF-1, 2B-1
1993		98	.244	.317	356	87	15	1	0	0.8	50	30	37	70	18	2	1	135	267	10	53	4.1	.976	SS-95, OF-6
1994		16	.296	.352	54	16	3	0	0	0.0	8	2	3	8	2	1	0	19	51	3	10	4.6	.959	SS-16
1995		101	.219	.254	334	73	8	2	0	0.0	35	25	25	61	13	3	1	169	273	6	73	4.1	.987	2B-59, SS-36, OF-11, 3B-2
1996		87	.240	.312	317	76	16	2	1	0.3	51	33	36	51	25	6	2	194	42	5	10	2.7	.979	OF-68, 2B-12, SS-7, DH-1
5 yrs.		451	.256	.316	1640	420	61	11	5	0.3	237	137	156	314	112	13	4	755	1082	48	235	4.1	.975	SS-302, OF-86, 2B-72, 3B-2, DH-1

Scott Livingstone — LIVINGSTONE, SCOTT LOUIS
B. July 15, 1965, Dallas, Tex. — BL TR 6' 190 lbs.

Year	Team	Games	BA	SA	AB	H	2B	3B	HR	HR%	R	RBI	BB	SO	SB	PH AB	PH H	PO	A	E	DP	TC/G	FA	G by Pos
1991	DET A	44	.291	.378	127	37	5	0	2	1.6	19	11	10	25	2	2	1	32	67	2	6	2.3	.980	3B-43
1992		117	.282	.376	354	100	21	0	4	1.1	43	46	21	36	1	13	3	67	189	10	15	2.4	.962	3B-112
1993		98	.293	.359	304	89	10	2	2	0.7	39	39	19	32	1	9	3	33	94	6	6	1.4	.955	3B-62, DH-32
1994	2 teams DET A (15G –.217) SD N (57G –.272)																							
"	total	72	.266	.369	203	54	13	1	2	1.0	11	11	7	26	2	9	3	26	81	6	7	1.8	.947	3B-51, 1B-6, DH-5
1995	SD N	99	.337	.490	196	66	15	0	5	2.6	26	32	15	22	2	43	14	301	33	3	26	5.6	.991	1B-43, 3B-13, 2B-4
1996		102	.297	.366	172	51	11	2	2	1.2	20	20	9	22	0	61	19	143	34	2	17	4.7	.989	1B-22, 3B-16
6 yrs.		532	.293	.386	1356	397	68	4	17	1.3	158	159	81	163	8	137	43	602	498	29	77	2.8	.974	3B-297, 1B-71, DH-37, 2B-4

DIVISIONAL PLAYOFF SERIES

1996	SD N	2	.500	.500	2	1	0	0	0	0.0	1	0	0	0	0	2	1	0	0	0	0	0.0	—	

Keith Lockhart — LOCKHART, KEITH VIRGIL
B. Nov. 10, 1964, Whittier, Calif. — BL TR 5'10" 170 lbs.

Year	Team	Games	BA	SA	AB	H	2B	3B	HR	HR%	R	RBI	BB	SO	SB	PH AB	PH H	PO	A	E	DP	TC/G	FA	G by Pos
1994	SD N	27	.209	.349	43	9	0	0	2	4.7	4	6	4	10	1	13	3	10	21	1	3	1.6	.969	3B-13, 2B-5, SS-1, OF-1
1995	KC A	94	.321	.478	274	88	19	3	6	2.2	41	33	14	21	8	21	6	112	178	8	44	3.2	.973	2B-61, 3B-17, DH-14
1996		138	.273	.411	433	118	33	3	7	1.6	49	55	30	40	11	20	8	138	282	13	59	3.1	.970	2B-84, 3B-55, DH-1
3 yrs.		259	.287	.432	750	215	52	6	15	2.0	94	94	48	71	20	54	17	260	481	22	106	3.0	.971	2B-150, 3B-85, DH-15, SS-1, OF-1

Kenny Lofton — LOFTON, KENNETH
B. May 31, 1967, East Chicago, Ind. — BL TL 6' 180 lbs.

Year	Team	Games	BA	SA	AB	H	2B	3B	HR	HR%	R	RBI	BB	SO	SB	PH AB	PH H	PO	A	E	DP	TC/G	FA	G by Pos
1991	HOU N	20	.203	.216	74	15	1	0	0	0.0	9	0	5	19	2	1	0	41	1	1	0	2.2	.977	OF-20
1992	CLE A	148	.285	.365	576	164	15	8	5	0.9	96	42	68	54	66	2	0	420	14	8	3	3.1	.982	OF-143
1993		148	.325	.408	569	185	28	8	1	0.2	116	42	81	83	70	2	0	402	11	9	3	2.9	.979	OF-146
1994		112	.349	.536	459	160	32	9	12	2.6	105	57	52	56	60	0	0	276	13	2	3	2.6	.993	OF-112
1995		118	.310	.453	481	149	22	13	7	1.5	93	53	40	49	54	1	0	248	11	8	2	2.3	.970	OF-114, DH-2
1996		154	.317	.446	662	210	35	4	14	2.1	132	67	61	82	75	0	0	375	13	10	3	2.6	.975	OF-153
6 yrs.		700	.313	.431	2821	883	133	42	39	1.4	551	261	307	343	327	6	0	1762	63	38	14	2.7	.980	OF-688, DH-2

DIVISIONAL PLAYOFF SERIES

1995	CLE A	3	.154	.154	13	2	0	0	0	0.0	1	0	1	3	0	0	0	9	0	2	0	3.7	.818	OF-3
1996		4	.167	.167	18	3	0	0	0	0.0	3	1	2	3	5	0	0	10	0	0	0	2.5	1.000	OF-4
2 yrs.		7	.161	.161	31	5	0	0	0	0.0	4	1	3	6	5	0	0	19	0	2	0	3.0	.905	OF-7

LEAGUE CHAMPIONSHIP SERIES

1995	CLE A	6	.458	.625	24	11	0	2 (4th)	0	0.0	4	3	4	6	5	0	0	15	0	0	0	2.5	1.000	OF-6

WORLD SERIES

1995	CLE A	6	.200	.240	25	5	1	0	0	0.0	6	0	3	1	6	0	0	12	0	0	0	2.0	1.000	OF-6

Javier Lopez — LOPEZ, JAVIER
Born Javier Lopez (Torres).
B. Nov. 5, 1970, Ponce, Puerto Rico — BR TR 6'3" 185 lbs.

Year	Team	Games	BA	SA	AB	H	2B	3B	HR	HR%	R	RBI	BB	SO	SB	PH AB	PH H	PO	A	E	DP	TC/G	FA	G by Pos
1992	ATL N	9	.375	.500	16	6	2	0	0	0.0	3	2	0	1	0	2	1	28	2	0	0	3.3	1.000	C-9
1993		8	.375	.750	16	6	1	1	1	6.3	1	2	0	2	0	2	0	37	2	1	0	5.7	.975	C-7
1994		80	.245	.419	277	68	9	0	13	4.7	27	35	17	61	0	6	1	560	35	3	0	8.0	.995	C-75
1995		100	.315	.498	333	105	11	4	14	4.2	37	51	14	57	0	11	6	625	50	8	2	7.3	.988	C-93
1996		138	.282	.466	489	138	19	1	23	4.7	56	69	28	84	1	6	1	993	81	6	9	8.0	.994	C-135
5 yrs.		335	.286	.469	1131	323	42	6	51	4.5	124	159	59	205	1	27	4	2243	170	18	11	7.6	.993	C-319

Year	Team	Games	BA	SA	AB	H	2B	3B	HR	HR%	R	RBI	BB	SO	SB	Pinch Hit AB	H	PO	A	E	DP	TC/G	FA	G by Pos

Javier Lopez *continued*

DIVISIONAL PLAYOFF SERIES

Year	Team	Games	BA	SA	AB	H	2B	3B	HR	HR%	R	RBI	BB	SO	SB	PH AB	PH H	PO	A	E	DP	TC/G	FA	G by Pos
1995	ATL N	3	.444	.444	9	4	0	0	0	0.0	0	3	0	3	0	0	0	22	3	0	1	8.3	1.000	C-3
1996		2	.286	.714	7	2	0	0	1	14.3	1	1	1	0	1	0	0	21	1	1	0	11.5	.957	C-2
2 yrs.		5	.375	.563	16	6	0	0	1	6.3	1	4	1	3	1	0	0	43	4	1	1	9.6	.979	C-5

LEAGUE CHAMPIONSHIP SERIES

Year	Team	Games	BA	SA	AB	H	2B	3B	HR	HR%	R	RBI	BB	SO	SB	PH AB	PH H	PO	A	E	DP	TC/G	FA	G by Pos
1992	ATL N	1	.000	.000	1	0	0	0	0	0.0	0	0	0	0	0	0	0	2	0	0	0	2.0	1.000	C-1
1995		3	.357	.643	14	5	1	0	1	7.1	2	3	0	1	0	0	0	28	2	0	0	10.0	1.000	C-3
1996		7	.542	1.000	24	13	5	0	2	8.3	8	6	3	1	1	0	0	48	3	0	0	7.3	1.000	C-7
3 yrs.		11	.462	.846	39	18	6	0	3	7.7	10	9	3	2	1	0	0	78	5	0	0	7.5	1.000	C-11
							7th																	

WORLD SERIES

Year	Team	Games	BA	SA	AB	H	2B	3B	HR	HR%	R	RBI	BB	SO	SB	PH AB	PH H	PO	A	E	DP	TC/G	FA	G by Pos
1995	ATL N	6	.176	.471	17	3	2	0	1	5.9	1	3	1	1	0	1	0	32	4	0	0	6.0	1.000	C-6
1996		6	.190	.190	21	4	0	0	0	0.0	3	1	3	4	0	0	0	41	4	0	0	7.5	1.000	C-6
2 yrs.		12	.184	.316	38	7	2	0	1	2.6	4	4	4	5	0	1	0	73	8	0	0	6.8	1.000	C-12

Luis Lopez

LOPEZ, LUIS MANUEL
Born Luis Manuel Lopez (Santos).
B. Sept. 4, 1970, Cidra, Puerto Rico

BB TR 5'11" 175 lbs.

Year	Team	Games	BA	SA	AB	H	2B	3B	HR	HR%	R	RBI	BB	SO	SB	PH AB	PH H	PO	A	E	DP	TC/G	FA	G by Pos
1993	SD N	17	.116	.140	43	5	1	0	0	0.0	1	1	0	8	0	1	1	23	34	1	5	3.9	.983	2B-15
1994		77	.277	.379	235	65	16	1	2	0.9	29	20	15	39	3	8	1	101	174	14	23	3.8	.952	SS-43, 2B-29, 3B-5
1996		63	.180	.245	139	25	3	0	2	1.4	10	11	9	35	0	11	3	57	100	4	18	2.7	.975	SS-35, 2B-22, 3B-2
3 yrs.		157	.228	.309	417	95	20	1	4	1.0	40	32	24	82	3	20	5	181	308	19	46	3.4	.963	SS-78, 2B-66, 3B-7

DIVISIONAL PLAYOFF SERIES

Year	Team	Games	BA	SA	AB	H	2B	3B	HR	HR%	R	RBI	BB	SO	SB	PH AB	PH H	PO	A	E	DP	TC/G	FA	G by Pos
1996	SD N	1	—	—	0	0	0	0	0	0.0	0	0	0	0	0	0	0	0	0	0	0	0.0		

Mark Loretta

LORETTA, MARK DAVID
B. Aug. 14, 1971, Santa Monica, Calif.

BR TR 6' 175 lbs.

Year	Team	Games	BA	SA	AB	H	2B	3B	HR	HR%	R	RBI	BB	SO	SB	PH AB	PH H	PO	A	E	DP	TC/G	FA	G by Pos
1995	MIL A	19	.260	.380	50	13	3	0	1	2.0	13	3	4	7	1	4	2	19	42	1	8	3.4	.984	SS-13, 2B-4, DH-1
1996		73	.279	.318	154	43	3	0	1	0.6	20	13	14	15	2	6	2	63	115	2	29	2.5	.989	2B-28, 3B-23, SS-21
2 yrs.		92	.275	.333	204	56	6	0	2	1.0	33	16	18	22	3	10	4	82	157	3	37	2.7	.988	SS-34, 2B-32, 3B-23, DH-1

Torey Lovullo

LOVULLO, SALVATORE ANTHONY
B. July 25, 1965, Santa Monica, Calif.

BB TR 6' 185 lbs.

Year	Team	Games	BA	SA	AB	H	2B	3B	HR	HR%	R	RBI	BB	SO	SB	PH AB	PH H	PO	A	E	DP	TC/G	FA	G by Pos
1988	DET A	12	.381	.667	21	8	1	1	1	4.8	2	2	1	2	0	0	0	12	19	0	2	2.6	1.000	2B-9, 3B-3
1989		29	.115	.172	87	10	2	0	1	1.1	8	4	14	20	0	4	0	134	24	1	15	5.5	.994	1B-18, 3B-11
1991	NY A	22	.176	.216	51	9	2	0	0	0.0	0	2	5	7	0	0	0	14	33	3	1	2.3	.940	3B-22
1993	CAL A	116	.251	.354	367	92	20	0	6	1.6	42	30	36	49	7	12	5	208	249	11	70	4.0	.976	2B-91, 3B-14, SS-9, OF-2, 1B-1
1994	SEA A	36	.222	.375	72	16	5	0	2	2.8	9	7	9	13	1	8	2	19	49	1	8	2.7	.986	2B-20, 3B-5, DH-1
1996	OAK A	65	.220	.378	82	18	4	0	3	3.7	15	9	11	17	1	9	1	134	21	1	24	2.6	.994	1B-42, 3B-11, DH-4, 2B-2, OF-1, SS-1
6 yrs.		280	.225	.335	680	153	34	1	13	1.9	76	54	76	108	9	33	8	521	395	17	120	3.5	.982	2B-122, 3B-66, 1B-61, SS-10, DH-5, OF-3

Rob Lukachyk

LUKACHYK, ROBERT JAMES
B. Jul. 24, 1968, Jersey City, N.J.

BL TR 6' 185 lbs.

Year	Team	Games	BA	SA	AB	H	2B	3B	HR	HR%	R	RBI	BB	SO	SB	PH AB	PH H	PO	A	E	DP	TC/G	FA	G by Pos
1996	MTL N	2	.000	.000	2	0	0	0	0	0.0	0	0	0	1	0	2	0	0	0	0	0	0.0	—	

Matt Luke

LUKE, MATTHEW CLIFFORD
B. Feb. 26, 1971, Long Beach, Calif.

BL TL 6'5" 220 lbs.

Year	Team	Games	BA	SA	AB	H	2B	3B	HR	HR%	R	RBI	BB	SO	SB	PH AB	PH H	PO	A	E	DP	TC/G	FA	G by Pos
1996	NY A	1	—	—	0	0	0	0	0	0.0	1	0	0	0	0	0	0	0	0	0	0	2.3	—	DH-1

John Mabry

MABRY, JOHN STEVEN
B. Oct. 17, 1970, Wilmington, Del.

BL TR 6'4" 195 lbs.

Year	Team	Games	BA	SA	AB	H	2B	3B	HR	HR%	R	RBI	BB	SO	SB	PH AB	PH H	PO	A	E	DP	TC/G	FA	G by Pos
1994	STL N	6	.304	.435	23	7	3	0	0	0.0	2	3	2	4	0	0	0	16	0	0	0	2.7	1.000	OF-6
1995		129	.307	.405	388	119	21	1	5	1.3	35	41	24	45	0	27	8	652	56	4	65	6.4	.994	1B-73, OF-39
1996		151	.297	.431	543	161	30	2	13	2.4	63	74	37	84	3	2	0	1184	75	8	107	7.9	.994	1B-146, OF-14
3 yrs.		286	.301	.420	954	287	54	3	18	1.9	100	118	63	133	3	29	8	1852	131	12	172	7.2	.994	1B-219, OF-59

DIVISIONAL PLAYOFF SERIES

Year	Team	Games	BA	SA	AB	H	2B	3B	HR	HR%	R	RBI	BB	SO	SB	PH AB	PH H	PO	A	E	DP	TC/G	FA	G by Pos
1996	STL N	3	.300	.500	10	3	0	0	0	0.0	1	1	1	1	0	0	0	20	1	0	0	7.0	1.000	1B-3

LEAGUE CHAMPIONSHIP SERIES

Year	Team	Games	BA	SA	AB	H	2B	3B	HR	HR%	R	RBI	BB	SO	SB	PH AB	PH H	PO	A	E	DP	TC/G	FA	G by Pos
1996	STL N	7	.261	.261	23	6	0	0	0	0.0	1	0	6	6	0	0	0	45	1	0	4	5.8	1.000	1B-6, OF-2

Mike Macfarlane

MACFARLANE, MICHAEL ANDREW (Mac)
B. Apr. 12, 1964, Stockton, Calif.

BR TR 6'1" 200 lbs.

Year	Team	Games	BA	SA	AB	H	2B	3B	HR	HR%	R	RBI	BB	SO	SB	PH AB	PH H	PO	A	E	DP	TC/G	FA	G by Pos
1987	KC A	8	.211	.263	19	4	1	0	0	0.0	0	3	2	2	0	0	0	29	2	0	0	3.9	1.000	C-8
1988		70	.265	.393	211	56	15	0	4	1.9	25	26	21	37	0	4	0	309	18	2	3	4.8	.994	C-68
1989		69	.223	.299	157	35	6	0	2	1.3	13	19	7	27	0	12	2	249	17	1	4	4.2	.996	C-59, DH-4
1990		124	.255	.380	400	102	24	4	6	1.5	37	58	25	69	1	13	3	660	23	6	9	5.9	.991	C-112, DH-5
1991		84	.277	.506	267	74	18	2	13	4.9	34	41	17	52	1	13	4	391	28	3	4	5.8	.993	C-69, DH-4
1992		129	.234	.445	402	94	28	3	17	4.2	51	48	30	89	1	16	4	527	43	4	7	4.9	.993	C-104, DH-13
1993		117	.273	.497	388	106	27	0	20	5.2	55	67	40	83	2	12	5	647	68	11	11	6.4	.985	C-114
1994		92	.255	.462	314	80	17	3	14	4.5	53	47	35	71	1	6	1	498	39	4	2	6.1	.993	C-81, DH-8

Year	Team	Games	BA	SA	AB	H	2B	3B	HR	HR%	R	RBI	BB	SO	SB	Pinch Hit AB	Pinch Hit H	PO	A	E	DP	TC/G	FA	G by Pos

Mike Macfarlane *continued*

1995	BOS A	115	.225	.404	364	82	18	1	15	4.1	45	51	38	78	2	3	0	618	49	5	3	5.9	.993	C-111, DH-3
1996	KC A	112	.274	.499	379	104	24	2	19	5.0	58	54	31	57	3	8	3	511	35	4	2	5.1	.993	C-99, DH-9
10 yrs.		920	.254	.440	2901	737	178	15	110	3.8	371	414	246	565	11	87	22	4439	322	40	45	5.5	.992	C-825, DH-46

DIVISIONAL PLAYOFF SERIES

| 1995 | BOS A | 3 | .333 | .333 | 9 | 3 | 0 | 0 | 0 | 0.0 | 0 | 1 | 0 | 3 | 0 | 0 | 0 | 18 | 0 | 2 | 0 | 6.7 | .900 | C-3 |

Robert Machado
MACHADO, ROBERT ALEXIS
B. June 3, 1973, Caracas, Venezuela — BR TR 6'1" 205 lbs.

| 1996 | CHI A | 4 | .667 | .833 | 6 | 4 | 1 | 0 | 0 | 0.0 | 1 | 2 | 0 | 0 | 0 | 0 | 0 | 6 | 0 | 0 | 0 | 1.5 | 1.000 | C-4 |

Dave Magadan
MAGADAN, DAVID JOSEPH
B. Sept. 30, 1962, Tampa, Fla. — BL TR 6'3" 190 lbs.

1986	NY N	10	.444	.444	18	8	0	0	0	0.0	3	3	3	1	0	1	1	48	5	0	5	5.9	1.000	1B-9
1987		85	.318	.443	192	61	13	1	3	1.6	21	24	22	22	0	30	6	88	92	4	9	2.9	.978	3B-50, 1B-13
1988		112	.277	.334	314	87	15	0	1	0.3	39	35	60	39	0	12	1	459	99	10	42	4.8	.982	1B-71, 3B-48
1989		127	.286	.393	374	107	22	3	4	1.1	47	41	49	37	1	23	5	587	89	7	54	5.9	.990	1B-87, 3B-28
1990		144	.328	.457	451	148	28	6	6	1.3	74	72	74	55	2	22	9	837	99	3	53	7.1	.997	1B-113, 3B-19
1991		124	.258	.342	418	108	23	0	4	1.0	58	51	83	50	1	4	3	1035	90	5	73	9.3	.996	1B-122
1992		99	.283	.346	321	91	9	1	3	0.9	33	28	56	44	1	5	0	54	136	11	11	2.1	.945	3B-93, 1B-2
1993	2 teams FLA N (66G –.286) SEA A (71G –.259)																							
"	total	137	.273	.356	455	124	23	0	5	1.1	49	50	80	63	2	10	3	380	194	12	50	4.3	.980	3B-90, 1B-43, DH-2
1994	FLA N	74	.275	.322	211	58	7	0	1	0.5	30	17	39	25	0	14	6	127	78	4	12	3.3	.981	3B-48, 1B-16
1995	HOU N	127	.313	.399	348	109	24	0	2	0.6	44	51	71	56	2	20	6	121	165	18	13	2.7	.941	3B-100, 1B-11
1996	CHI N	78	.254	.367	169	43	10	0	3	1.8	23	17	29	23	0	18	8	75	68	3	8	2.4	.979	3B-51, 1B-10
11 yrs.		1117	.289	.378	3271	944	174	11	32	1.0	421	389	566	415	9	159	48	3811	1115	77	330	4.9	.985	3B-527, 1B-497, DH-2

LEAGUE CHAMPIONSHIP SERIES

| 1988 | NY N | 3 | .000 | .000 | 3 | 0 | 0 | 0 | 0 | 0.0 | 0 | 0 | 2 | 0 | 0 | 2 | 0 | 0 | 0 | 0 | 0 | 0.0 | — | |

Wendell Magee
MAGEE, WENDELL ERROL
B. Aug. 3, 1973, Hattiesburg, Miss. — BR TR 6' 225 lbs.

| 1996 | PHI N | 38 | .204 | .296 | 142 | 29 | 7 | 0 | 2 | 1.4 | 9 | 14 | 9 | 33 | 0 | 1 | 0 | 88 | 2 | 2 | 2 | 2.5 | .978 | OF-37 |

Jose Malave
MALAVE, JOSE FRANCISCO
B. May 31, 1971, Cumana, Venezuela — BR TR 6'2" 212 lbs.

| 1996 | BOS A | 41 | .235 | .382 | 102 | 24 | 4 | 0 | 4 | 3.9 | 12 | 17 | 12 | 25 | 0 | 8 | 3 | 43 | 1 | 1 | 0 | 1.2 | .978 | OF-38 |

Kirt Manwaring
MANWARING, KIRT DEAN
B. July 15, 1965, Elmira, N.Y. — BR TR 5'11" 185 lbs.

1987	SF N	6	.143	.143	7	1	0	0	0	0.0	0	0	0	1	0	0	0	9	1	1	0	1.8	.909	C-6
1988		40	.250	.336	116	29	7	0	1	0.9	12	15	2	21	0	0	0	162	24	4	2	4.8	.979	C-40
1989		85	.210	.250	200	42	4	2	0	0.0	14	18	11	28	2	9	2	289	32	6	3	4.0	.982	C-81
1990		8	.154	.308	13	2	0	1	0	0.0	0	1	0	3	0	0	0	22	3	0	1	3.1	1.000	C-8
1991		67	.225	.275	178	40	9	0	0	0.0	16	19	9	22	1	1	1	315	28	4	7	5.2	.988	C-67
1992		109	.244	.335	349	85	10	5	4	1.1	24	26	29	42	2	2	1	564	68	4	12	5.9	.994	C-108
1993		130	.275	.350	432	119	15	1	5	1.2	48	49	41	76	1	0	0	739	70	2	12	6.2	.998	C-130
1994		97	.250	.320	316	79	17	1	1	0.3	30	29	25	50	1	0	0	540	53	4	4	6.2	.993	C-97
1995		118	.251	.332	379	95	15	2	4	1.1	21	36	27	72	1	1	0	607	55	7	5	5.7	.990	C-118
1996	2 teams SF N (49G –.234) HOU N (37G –.220)																							
"	total	86	.229	.282	227	52	9	0	1	0.4	14	18	19	40	0	0	0	438	45	3	7	5.7	.994	C-86
10 yrs.		746	.245	.317	2217	544	86	12	16	0.7	179	211	163	355	8	13	4	3685	379	35	53	5.5	.991	C-741

LEAGUE CHAMPIONSHIP SERIES

| 1989 | SF N | 3 | .000 | .000 | 2 | 0 | 0 | 0 | 0 | 0.0 | 0 | 0 | 0 | 0 | 0 | 1 | 0 | 5 | 0 | 0 | 0 | 1.7 | 1.000 | C-3 |

WORLD SERIES

| 1989 | SF N | 1 | 1.000 | 2.000 | 1 | 1 | 1 | 0 | 0 | 0.0 | 1 | 0 | 0 | 0 | 0 | 0 | 0 | 0 | 0 | 0 | 0 | 0.0 | .000 | C-1 |

Oreste Marrero
MARRERO, ORESTE VILATO
Born Oreste Vilato Marrero (Vazquez).
B. Oct. 31, 1969, Bayamon, Puerto Rico — BL TL 6' 195 lbs.

1993	MON N	32	.210	.333	81	17	5	1	1	1.2	10	4	14	16	1	0	0	194	15	2	21	6.6	.991	1B-32
1996	LA N	10	.375	.500	8	3	1	0	0	0.0	2	1	1	3	0	7	3	1	0	0	0	1.0	1.000	1B-1
2 yrs.		42	.225	.348	89	20	6	1	1	1.1	12	5	15	19	1	7	3	195	15	2	21	6.4	.991	1B-33

Al Martin
MARTIN, ALBERT LEE
B. Nov. 24, 1967, West Covina, Calif. — BL TL 6'2" 220 lbs.

1992	PIT N	12	.167	.333	12	2	0	0	0	0.0	1	0	0	5	0	6	1	6	0	0	0	0.9	1.000	OF-7
1993		143	.281	.481	480	135	26	8	18	3.8	85	64	42	122	16	14	5	268	6	7	0	2.1	.975	OF-136
1994		82	.286	.457	276	79	12	4	9	3.3	48	33	34	56	15	3	0	129	8	3	1	1.8	.979	OF-77
1995		124	.282	.442	439	124	25	3	13	3.0	70	41	44	92	20	12	2	205	8	5	2	1.8	.977	OF-121
1996		155	.300	.452	630	189	40	1	18	2.9	101	72	54	116	38	6	1	216	5	8	0	1.5	.965	OF-152
5 yrs.		516	.288	.457	1837	529	103	17	58	3.2	305	212	174	391	89	41	9	824	27	23	3	1.8	.974	OF-493

Year	Team	Games	BA	SA	AB	H	2B	3B	HR	HR%	R	RBI	BB	SO	SB	Pinch Hit AB	Pinch Hit H	PO	A	E	DP	TC/G	FA	G by Pos

Norberto Martin

MARTIN, NORBERTO ENRIQUE (Paco)
Born Norberto Enrique Martin (McDonald).
B. Dec. 10, 1966, San Pedro de Macoris, Dominican Republic
BR TR 5'10" 175 lbs.

Year	Team	Games	BA	SA	AB	H	2B	3B	HR	HR%	R	RBI	BB	SO	SB	AB	H	PO	A	E	DP	TC/G	FA	G by Pos
1993	CHI A	8	.357	.357	14	5	0	0	0	0.0	3	2	1	1	0	1	0	13	9	1	4	3.8	.957	2B-5, DH-1
1994		45	.275	.366	131	36	7	1	1	0.8	19	16	9	16	4	5	1	58	77	2	11	3.3	.985	2B-28, SS-6, 3B-5, OF-2, DH-1
1995		72	.269	.400	160	43	7	4	2	1.3	17	17	3	25	5	18	6	52	67	7	16	2.3	.944	2B-17, OF-12, DH-10, 3B-9, SS-7
1996		70	.350	.421	140	49	7	0	1	0.7	30	14	6	17	10	13	4	61	79	6	25	2.6	.959	SS-24, DH-19, 2B-10, 3B-3
4 yrs.		195	.299	.396	445	133	21	5	4	0.9	69	49	19	59	19	37	11	184	232	16	56	2.7	.963	2B-60, SS-37, DH-31, 3B-17, OF-14

Dave Martinez

MARTINEZ, DAVID
B. Sept. 26, 1964, New York, N.Y.
BL TL 5'10" 150 lbs.

Year	Team	Games	BA	SA	AB	H	2B	3B	HR	HR%	R	RBI	BB	SO	SB	AB	H	PO	A	E	DP	TC/G	FA	G by Pos
1986	CHI N	53	.139	.194	108	15	1	1	1	0.9	13	7	6	22	4	5	1	77	2	1	1	1.7	.988	OF-46
1987		142	.292	.418	459	134	18	8	8	1.7	70	36	57	96	16	11	3	283	10	6	1	2.2	.980	OF-139
1988	2 teams	CHI N (75G –.254)		MON N (63G –.257)																				
"	total	138	.255	.351	447	114	13	6	6	1.3	51	46	38	94	23	11	1	281	4	6	1	2.2	.979	OF-132
1989	MON N	126	.274	.382	361	99	16	7	3	0.8	41	27	27	57	23	11	3	199	7	7	1	1.8	.967	OF-118
1990		118	.279	.422	391	109	13	5	11	2.8	60	39	24	48	13	14	3	257	6	3	1	2.4	.989	OF-108, P-1
1991		124	.295	.419	396	117	18	5	7	1.8	47	42	20	54	16	11	4	213	10	4	0	2.0	.982	OF-111
1992	CIN N	135	.254	.354	393	100	20	5	3	0.8	47	31	42	54	12	12	0	382	18	6	23	3.1	.985	OF-111, 1B-21
1993	SF N	91	.241	.361	241	58	12	1	5	2.1	28	27	27	39	6	20	3	131	6	1	2	1.9	.993	OF-73
1994		97	.247	.362	235	58	9	3	4	1.7	23	27	21	22	3	25	8	255	18	3	17	3.3	.989	OF-58, 1B-25
1995	CHI A	118	.307	.436	303	93	16	4	5	1.7	49	37	32	41	8	16	6	392	25	3	38	3.8	.993	OF-59, 1B-48, DH-4, P-1
1996		146	.318	.468	440	140	20	8	10	2.3	85	53	52	52	15	16	4	367	16	6	9	2.7	.985	OF-121, 1B-23
11 yrs.		1288	.275	.394	3774	1037	156	53	63	1.7	514	372	346	579	139	152	36	2837	122	46	94	2.5	.985	OF-1077, 1B-117, DH-4, P-2

Edgar Martinez

MARTINEZ, EDGAR
B. Jan. 2, 1963, New York, N.Y.
BR TR 6' 175 lbs.

Year	Team	Games	BA	SA	AB	H	2B	3B	HR	HR%	R	RBI	BB	SO	SB	AB	H	PO	A	E	DP	TC/G	FA	G by Pos
1987	SEA A	13	.372	.581	43	16	5	2	0	0.0	6	5	2	5	0	1	0	13	19	0	1	2.5	1.000	3B-12, DH-1
1988		14	.281	.406	32	9	4	0	0	0.0	0	5	4	7	0	1	1	5	8	1	1	1.1	.929	3B-13
1989		65	.240	.304	171	41	5	0	2	1.2	20	20	17	26	2	8	1	40	72	6	9	1.9	.949	3B-61
1990		144	.302	.433	487	147	27	2	11	2.3	71	49	74	62	1	1	0	89	259	27	16	2.6	.928	3B-143, DH-2
1991		150	.307	.452	544	167	35	1	14	2.6	98	52	84	72	0	3	1	84	299	15	25	2.7	.962	3B-144, DH-2
1992		135	.343	.544	528	181	46	3	18	3.4	100	73	54	61	14	3	0	88	211	17	25	2.4	.946	3B-103, DH-28, 1B-2
1993		42	.237	.378	135	32	7	0	4	3.0	20	13	28	19	0	2	1	5	11	2	1	0.4	.889	DH-24, 3B-16
1994		89	.285	.482	326	93	23	1	13	4.0	47	51	53	42	6	0	0	44	127	9	8	2.0	.950	3B-65, DH-23
1995		145	.356	.628	511	182	52	0	29	5.7	121	113	116	87	4	0	0	30	4	2	0	0.2	.944	DH-138, 3B-4, 1B-3
1996		139	.327	.595	499	163	52	2	26	5.2	121	103	123	84	3	0	0	29	1	1	3	0.2	.968	DH-134, 1B-4, 3B-2
10 yrs.		936	.315	.507	3276	1031	256	11	117	3.6	604	484	555	465	30	19	4	427	1011	80	89	1.6	.947	3B-563, DH-352, 1B-9

DIVISIONAL PLAYOFF SERIES

Year	Team	Games	BA	SA	AB	H	2B	3B	HR	HR%	R	RBI	BB	SO	SB	AB	H	PO	A	E	DP	TC/G	FA	G by Pos
1995	SEA A	5	.571	1.000	21	12	3	0	2	9.5	6	10	6	2	0	0	0	0	0	0	0	0.0	.000	DH-5

LEAGUE CHAMPIONSHIP SERIES

Year	Team	Games	BA	SA	AB	H	2B	3B	HR	HR%	R	RBI	BB	SO	SB	AB	H	PO	A	E	DP	TC/G	FA	G by Pos
1995	SEA A	6	.087	.087	23	2	0	0	0	0.0	0	0	2	5	1	0	0	0	0	0	0	0.0	.000	DH-6

Manny Martinez

MARTINEZ, MANUEL
Born Manuel Martinez (DeJesus).
B. Oct. 3, 1970, San Pedro de Macoris, Dominican Republic
BR TR 6'2" 169 lbs.

Year	Team	Games	BA	SA	AB	H	2B	3B	HR	HR%	R	RBI	BB	SO	SB	AB	H	PO	A	E	DP	TC/G	FA	G by Pos
1996	SEA A	9	.235	.471	17	4	2	1	0	0.0	3	3	3	5	2	1	0	12	2	0	0	1.8	1.000	OF-8

Pablo Martinez

MARTINEZ, PABLO MADE
Born Pablo Made Martinez (Valera).
B. Jun. 29, 1969, Sabana Grande, Dominican Republic
BB TR 5'10" 155 lbs.

Year	Team	Games	BA	SA	AB	H	2B	3B	HR	HR%	R	RBI	BB	SO	SB	AB	H	PO	A	E	DP	TC/G	FA	G by Pos
1996	ATL N	4	.500	.500	2	1	0	0	0	0.0	1	0	0	0	0	0	0	0	2	0	1	2.0	1.000	SS-1

Sandy Martinez

MARTINEZ, ANGEL SANDY
Born Angel Sandy Martinez (Martinez).
B. Oct. 3, 1972, Villa Mella, Dominican Republic
BL TR 6'2" 200 lbs.

Year	Team	Games	BA	SA	AB	H	2B	3B	HR	HR%	R	RBI	BB	SO	SB	AB	H	PO	A	E	DP	TC/G	FA	G by Pos
1995	TOR A	62	.241	.335	191	46	12	0	2	1.0	12	25	7	45	0	3	0	329	28	5	5	5.9	.986	C-61
1996		76	.227	.332	229	52	9	3	3	1.3	17	18	16	58	0	3	1	413	33	3	9	6.0	.993	C-75
2 yrs.		138	.233	.333	420	98	21	3	5	1.2	29	43	23	103	0	6	1	742	61	8	14	6.0	.990	C-136

Tino Martinez

MARTINEZ, CONSTANTINO
B. Dec. 7, 1967, Tampa, Fla.
BL TR 6'2" 205 lbs.

Year	Team	Games	BA	SA	AB	H	2B	3B	HR	HR%	R	RBI	BB	SO	SB	AB	H	PO	A	E	DP	TC/G	FA	G by Pos
1990	SEA A	24	.221	.279	68	15	4	0	0	0.0	4	5	9	9	0	2	0	155	12	0	25	7.3	1.000	1B-23
1991		36	.205	.330	112	23	2	0	4	3.6	11	9	11	24	0	5	2	249	22	2	24	8.0	.993	1B-29, DH-5
1992		136	.257	.411	460	118	19	2	16	3.5	53	66	42	77	2	11	1	678	58	4	62	5.9	.995	1B-78, DH-47
1993		109	.265	.456	408	108	25	1	17	4.2	48	60	45	56	0	0	0	932	60	3	89	9.1	.997	1B-103, DH-6
1994		97	.261	.508	329	86	21	0	20	6.1	42	61	29	52	1	5	1	705	45	2	62	8.4	.997	1B-82, DH-8
1995		141	.293	.551	519	152	35	3	31	6.0	92	111	62	91	0	3	1	1043	103	8	86	8.2	.993	1B-139, DH-1
1996	NY A	155	.292	.466	595	174	28	0	25	4.2	82	117	68	85	2	1	0	1238	84	5	119	8.6	.996	1B-151, DH-3
7 yrs.		698	.271	.466	2491	676	134	6	113	4.5	332	429	266	394	5	27	5	5000	384	24	467	8.0	.996	1B-605, DH-70

Year	Team	Games	BA	SA	AB	H	2B	3B	HR	HR%	R	RBI	BB	SO	SB	Pinch Hit AB	H	PO	A	E	DP	TC/G	FA	G by Pos

Tino Martinez continued

DIVISIONAL PLAYOFF SERIES

Year	Team	Games	BA	SA	AB	H	2B	3B	HR	HR%	R	RBI	BB	SO	SB	AB	H	PO	A	E	DP	TC/G	FA	G by Pos
1995	SEA A	5	.409	.591	22	9	1	0	1	4.5	4	5	3	4	0	0	0	39	5	0	4	8.8	1.000	1B-5
1996	NY A	4	.267	.400	15	4	2	0	0	0.0	3	0	3	1	0	0	0	33	3	0	2	9.0	1.000	1B-4
2 yrs.		9	.351	.514	37	13	3	0	1	2.7	7	5	6	5	0	0	0	72	8	0	6	8.9	1.000	1B-9

LEAGUE CHAMPIONSHIP SERIES

Year	Team	Games	BA	SA	AB	H	2B	3B	HR	HR%	R	RBI	BB	SO	SB	AB	H	PO	A	E	DP	TC/G	FA	G by Pos
1995	SEA A	6	.136	.136	22	3	0	0	0	0.0	1	0	3	7	0	0	0	45	5	1	6	8.5	.980	1B-6
1996	NY A	5	.182	.227	22	4	1	0	0	0.0	3	0	0	2	0	0	0	49	2	0	1	10.2	1.000	1B-5
2 yrs.		11	.159	.182	44	7	1	0	0	0.0	4	0	3	9	0	0	0	94	7	1	7	9.3	.990	1B-11

WORLD SERIES

Year	Team	Games	BA	SA	AB	H	2B	3B	HR	HR%	R	RBI	BB	SO	SB	AB	H	PO	A	E	DP	TC/G	FA	G by Pos
1996	NY A	6	.091	.091	11	1	0	0	0	0.0	0	2	5	0	1	0	27	0	0	3	5.4	1.000	1B-5

John Marzano

MARZANO, JOHN ROBERT
B. Feb. 14, 1963, Philadelphia, Pa.

BR TR 5'11" 185 lbs.

Year	Team	Games	BA	SA	AB	H	2B	3B	HR	HR%	R	RBI	BB	SO	SB	AB	H	PO	A	E	DP	TC/G	FA	G by Pos
1987	BOS A	52	.244	.399	168	41	11	0	5	3.0	20	24	7	41	0	1	0	337	24	5	7	7.0	.986	C-52
1988		10	.138	.172	29	4	1	0	0	0.0	3	1	1	3	0	0	0	77	4	0	0	8.1	1.000	C-10
1989		7	.444	.778	18	8	3	0	1	5.6	5	3	0	2	0	1	1	29	4	0	0	4.7	1.000	C-7
1990		32	.241	.289	83	20	4	0	0	0.0	8	6	5	10	0	0	0	153	14	0	3	5.2	1.000	C-32
1991		49	.263	.333	114	30	8	0	0	0.0	10	9	1	16	0	1	1	174	20	3	0	4.1	.985	C-48
1992		19	.080	.160	50	4	2	1	0	0.0	4	1	2	12	0	1	0	81	9	3	1	4.9	.968	C-18, DH-1
1995	TEX A	2	.333	.333	6	2	0	0	0	0.0	1	0	0	0	0	0	0	7	1	0	0	4.0	1.000	C-2
1996	SEA A	41	.245	.302	106	26	6	0	0	0.0	8	6	7	15	0	2	1	194	10	3	1	5.3	.986	C-39
8 yrs.		212	.235	.331	574	135	35	1	6	1.0	59	50	23	99	0	6	3	1052	86	14	12	5.5	.988	C-208, DH-1

Damon Mashore

MASHORE, DAMON WAYNE
B. Oct. 31, 1969, Ponce, Puerto Rico

BR TR 5'11" 195 lbs.

Year	Team	Games	BA	SA	AB	H	2B	3B	HR	HR%	R	RBI	BB	SO	SB	AB	H	PO	A	E	DP	TC/G	FA	G by Pos
1996	OAK A	50	.267	.438	105	28	7	1	3	2.9	20	12	16	31	4	6	0	65	1	1	0	1.4	.985	OF-48

Mike Matheny

MATHENY, MICHAEL SCOTT
B. Sept. 22, 1970, Columbus, Ohio

BR TR 6'3" 205 lbs.

Year	Team	Games	BA	SA	AB	H	2B	3B	HR	HR%	R	RBI	BB	SO	SB	AB	H	PO	A	E	DP	TC/G	FA	G by Pos
1994	MIL A	28	.226	.340	53	12	3	0	1	1.9	3	2	3	13	0	2	0	81	8	1	1	3.3	.989	C-27
1995		80	.247	.313	166	41	9	1	0	0.0	13	21	12	28	2	1	0	261	18	4	2	3.5	.986	C-80
1996		106	.204	.342	313	64	15	2	8	2.6	31	46	14	80	3	2	1	476	40	8	5	5.0	.985	C-104, DH-1
3 yrs.		214	.220	.333	532	117	27	3	9	1.7	47	69	29	121	5	5	1	818	66	13	8	4.2	.986	C-211, DH-1

Derrick May

MAY, DERRICK BRANT
Son of Dave May.
B. July 14, 1968, Rochester, N. Y.

BL TR 6'4" 210 lbs.

Year	Team	Games	BA	SA	AB	H	2B	3B	HR	HR%	R	RBI	BB	SO	SB	AB	H	PO	A	E	DP	TC/G	FA	G by Pos
1990	CHI N	17	.246	.344	61	15	3	0	1	1.6	8	11	2	7	1	0	0	34	1	1	0	2.1	.972	OF-17
1991		15	.227	.455	22	5	2	0	1	4.5	4	3	2	1	0	7	1	11	1	0	0	1.7	1.000	OF-7
1992		124	.274	.373	351	96	11	0	8	2.3	33	45	14	40	5	21	6	153	3	5	1	1.5	.969	OF-108
1993		128	.295	.422	465	137	25	2	10	2.2	62	77	31	41	10	10	1	220	8	7	1	1.9	.970	OF-122
1994		100	.284	.420	345	98	19	2	8	2.3	43	51	30	34	3	11	1	154	4	1	0	1.7	.994	OF-92
1995	2 teams MIL A (32G –.248) HOU N (78G –.301)																							
"	total	110	.282	.436	319	90	18	2	9	2.8	44	50	24	42	1	23	9	141	1	4	0	1.7	.973	OF-87, 1B-1
1996	HOU N	109	.251	.378	259	65	12	3	5	1.9	24	33	30	33	2	30	9	125	5	4	0	1.9	.970	OF-71
7 yrs.		603	.278	.406	1822	506	90	9	42	2.3	218	270	133	198	26	102	27	838	23	22	1	1.7	.975	OF-504, 1B-1

Brent Mayne

MAYNE, BRENT DANEM
B. Apr. 19, 1968, Loma Linda, Calif.

BL TR 6'1" 195 lbs.

Year	Team	Games	BA	SA	AB	H	2B	3B	HR	HR%	R	RBI	BB	SO	SB	AB	H	PO	A	E	DP	TC/G	FA	G by Pos
1990	KC A	5	.231	.231	13	3	0	0	0	0.0	2	1	3	3	0	1	0	29	3	1	0	6.6	.970	C-5
1991		85	.251	.325	231	58	8	0	3	1.3	22	31	23	42	2	8	2	425	38	6	4	5.8	.987	C-80, DH-1
1992		82	.225	.272	213	48	10	0	0	0.0	16	18	11	26	0	14	4	281	33	3	2	4.5	.991	C-62, 3B-8, DH-1
1993		71	.254	.337	205	52	9	1	2	1.0	22	22	18	31	3	4	1	356	27	2	1	5.6	.995	C-68, DH-1
1994		46	.257	.347	144	37	5	1	2	1.4	19	20	14	27	1	4	0	246	13	1	1	5.8	.996	C-42, DH-3
1995		110	.251	.326	307	77	18	1	1	0.3	23	27	25	41	0	7	0	540	39	3	8	5.7	.995	C-103
1996	NY N	70	.263	.354	99	26	6	0	1	1.0	9	6	12	22	0	42	7	85	3	0	2	4.2	1.000	C-21
7 yrs.		469	.248	.322	1212	301	56	3	9	0.7	113	125	106	192	6	80	14	1962	156	16	18	5.4	.993	C-381, 3B-8, DH-6

David McCarty

McCARTY, DAVID ANDREW
B. Nov. 23, 1969, Houston, Tex.

BR TL 6'5" 210 lbs.

Year	Team	Games	BA	SA	AB	H	2B	3B	HR	HR%	R	RBI	BB	SO	SB	AB	H	PO	A	E	DP	TC/G	FA	G by Pos
1993	MIN A	98	.214	.286	350	75	15	2	2	0.6	36	21	19	80	2	5	1	412	38	8	25	4.4	.983	OF-67, 1B-36, DH-2
1994		44	.260	.374	131	34	8	2	1	0.8	21	12	7	32	2	3	0	244	27	5	19	6.0	.982	1B-32, OF-14
1995	2 teams MIN A (25G –.218) SF N (12G –.250)																							
"	total	37	.227	.307	75	17	4	1	0	0.0	11	6	6	22	1	9	4	149	10	2	13	5.6	.988	1B-20, OF-9
1996	SF N	91	.217	.337	175	38	3	0	6	3.4	16	24	18	43	2	30	5	291	17	3	30	4.4	.990	1B-51, OF-20
4 yrs.		270	.224	.316	731	164	30	5	9	1.2	84	63	50	177	7	47	10	1096	92	18	87	4.8	.985	1B-139, OF-110, DH-2

Quinton McCracken

McCRACKEN, QUINTON ANTOINE
B. Mar. 16, 1970, Wilmington, N. C.

BB TR 5'7" 170 lbs.

Year	Team	Games	BA	SA	AB	H	2B	3B	HR	HR%	R	RBI	BB	SO	SB	AB	H	PO	A	E	DP	TC/G	FA	G by Pos
1995	CLR N	3	.000	.000	1	0	0	0	0	0.0	0	0	0	1	0	1	0	0	0	0	0	0.0	.000	OF-1
1996		124	.290	.410	283	82	13	6	3	1.1	50	40	32	62	17	36	7	131	3	6	0	1.5	.957	OF-93
2 yrs.		127	.289	.408	284	82	13	6	3	1.1	50	40	32	63	17	37	7	131	3	6	0	1.5	.957	OF-94

Year	Team	Games	BA	SA	AB	H	2B	3B	HR	HR%	R	RBI	BB	SO	SB	Pinch Hit AB	Pinch Hit H	PO	A	E	DP	TC/G	FA	G by Pos

Willie McGee

McGEE, WILLIE DEAN
B. Nov. 2, 1958, San Francisco, Calif.
BB TR 6'1" 176 lbs.

Year	Team	Games	BA	SA	AB	H	2B	3B	HR	HR%	R	RBI	BB	SO	SB	PH AB	PH H	PO	A	E	DP	TC/G	FA	G by Pos
1982	STL N	123	.296	.391	422	125	12	8	4	0.9	43	56	12	58	24	15	6	245	3	11	0	2.2	.958	OF-117
1983		147	.286	.374	601	172	22	8	5	0.8	75	75	26	98	39	3	2	385	7	5	1	2.7	.987	OF-145
1984		145	.291	.394	571	166	19	11	6	1.1	82	50	29	80	43	5	0	374	10	6	4	2.8	.985	OF-141
1985		152	**.353**	.503	612	**216**	26	**18**	10	1.6	114	82	34	86	56	4	2	382	11	9	2	2.7	.978	OF-149
1986		124	.256	.370	497	127	22	7	7	1.4	65	48	37	82	19	2	0	325	9	3	0	2.8	.991	OF-121
1987		153	.285	.434	620	177	37	11	11	1.8	76	105	24	90	16	2	1	354	10	7	1	2.4	.981	OF-152, SS-1
1988		137	.292	.372	562	164	24	6	3	0.5	73	50	32	84	41	2	1	348	9	9	0	2.7	.975	OF-135
1989		58	.236	.352	199	47	10	2	3	1.5	23	17	10	34	8	10	2	118	2	3	0	2.6	.976	OF-47
1990	2 teams STL N (125G –.335) OAK A (29G –.274)																							
"	total	154	**.324**	.419	614	199	35	7	3	0.5	99	77	48	104	31	2	0	413	14	17	5	2.9	.962	OF-152, DH-1
1991	SF N	131	.312	.408	497	155	30	3	4	0.8	67	43	34	74	17	4	2	259	6	6	3	2.1	.978	OF-128
1992		138	.297	.354	474	141	20	2	1	0.2	56	36	29	88	13	21	11	231	11	6	2	2.1	.976	OF-119
1993		130	.301	.389	475	143	28	1	4	0.8	53	46	38	67	10	7	1	224	9	5	1	1.9	.979	OF-126
1994		45	.282	.397	156	44	3	0	5	3.2	19	23	15	24	3	4	0	79	2	1	0	2.0	.988	OF-42
1995	BOS A	67	.285	.400	200	57	11	3	2	1.0	32	15	9	41	5	14	4	101	7	3	1	1.7	.973	OF-64
1996	STL N	123	.307	.417	309	95	15	2	5	1.6	52	41	18	60	5	41	15	141	10	5	2	1.8	.968	OF-83, 1B-6
15 yrs.		1827	.298	.402	6809	2028	314	89	73	1.1	929	764	395	1070	330	136	47	3979	120	96	22	2.4	.977	OF-1721, 1B-6, DH-1, SS-1

DIVISIONAL PLAYOFF SERIES

Year	Team	Games	BA	SA	AB	H	2B	3B	HR	HR%	R	RBI	BB	SO	SB	PH AB	PH H	PO	A	E	DP	TC/G	FA	G by Pos
1995	BOS A	2	.250	.250	4	1	0	0	0	0.0	0	1	0	2	0	1	0	0	0	0	0	0.0	.000	OF-2
1996	STL N	3	.100	.100	10	1	0	0	0	0.0	1	1	1	3	0	0	0	9	0	1	0	3.3	.900	OF-3
2 yrs.		5	.143	.143	14	2	0	0	0	0.0	1	2	1	5	0	1	0	9	0	1	0	2.0	.900	OF-5

LEAGUE CHAMPIONSHIP SERIES

Year	Team	Games	BA	SA	AB	H	2B	3B	HR	HR%	R	RBI	BB	SO	SB	PH AB	PH H	PO	A	E	DP	TC/G	FA	G by Pos
1982	STL N	3	.308	.846	13	4	0	2	1	7.7	4	5	0	5	0	0	0	12	0	1	0	4.3	.923	OF-3
1985		6	.269	.308	26	7	1	0	0	0.0	6	3	3	6	2	0	0	17	0	0	0	2.8	1.000	OF-6
1987		7	.308	.423	26	8	1	1	0	0.0	2	2	0	5	0	0	0	16	0	0	0	2.3	1.000	OF-7
1990	OAK A	3	.222	.333	9	2	1	0	0	0.0	3	0	1	2	2	0	0	2	0	0	0	1.0	1.000	OF-2
1996	STL N	6	.333	.333	15	5	0	0	0	0.0	0	0	0	3	0	1	0	5	0	1	0	1.2	.833	OF-5
5 yrs.		25	.292	.427	89	26	3 (2nd)	3	1	1.1	15 (7th)	10	4	21 (5th)	4	1	0	52	0	2	0	2.3	.963	OF-23

WORLD SERIES

Year	Team	Games	BA	SA	AB	H	2B	3B	HR	HR%	R	RBI	BB	SO	SB	PH AB	PH H	PO	A	E	DP	TC/G	FA	G by Pos
1982	STL N	6	.240	.480	25	6	0	0	2	8.0	6	5	1	3	0	0	0	24	0	0	0	4.0	1.000	OF-6
1985		7	.259	.444	27	7	2	0	1	3.7	2	2	1	3	1	0	0	15	0	0	0	2.1	1.000	OF-7
1987		7	.370	.444	27	10	2	0	0	0.0	2	4	0	9	0	0	0	21	1	1	0	3.3	.957	OF-7
1990	OAK A	4	.200	.300	10	2	1	0	0	0.0	1	0	0	2	1	1	0	5	0	0	0	1.7	1.000	OF-3
4 yrs.		24	.281	.438	89	25	5	0	3	3.4	11	11	2	17	4	1	0	65	1	1	0	2.9	.985	OF-23

Fred McGriff

McGRIFF, FREDERICK STANLEY (Crime Dog)
B. Oct. 31, 1963, Tampa, Fla.
BL TL 6'3" 200 lbs.

Year	Team	Games	BA	SA	AB	H	2B	3B	HR	HR%	R	RBI	BB	SO	SB	PH AB	PH H	PO	A	E	DP	TC/G	FA	G by Pos
1986	TOR A	3	.200	.200	5	1	0	0	0	0.0	1	0	0	2	0	0	0	3	0	0	0	1.0	1.000	DH-2, 1B-1
1987		107	.247	.505	295	73	16	0	20	6.8	58	43	60	104	3	14	1	108	7	2	5	1.1	.983	DH-90, 1B-14
1988		154	.282	.552	536	151	35	4	34	6.3	100	82	79	149	6	5	2	1344	93	5	143	9.4	.997	1B-153
1989		161	.269	.525	551	148	27	3	**36**	6.5	98	92	119	132	7	1	0	1460	115	17	148	9.9	.989	1B-159, DH-2
1990		153	.300	.530	557	167	21	1	35	6.3	91	88	94	108	5	0	0	1246	126	6	119	9.0	.996	1B-147, DH-6
1991	SD N	153	.278	.494	528	147	19	1	31	5.9	84	106	105	135	4	0	0	1370	87	14	111	9.6	.990	1B-153
1992		152	.286	.556	531	152	30	4	**35**	6.6	79	104	96	108	8	1	0	1219	108	12	95	8.9	.991	1B-151
1993	2 teams SD N (83G –.275) ATL N (68G –.310)																							
"	total	151	.291	.549	557	162	29	2	37	6.6	111	101	76	106	5	2	1	1203	92	17	102	8.8	.987	1B-149
1994	ATL N	113	.318	.623	424	135	25	1	34	8.0	81	94	50	76	7	1	0	1004	66	7	73	9.6	.994	1B-112
1995		144	.280	.489	528	148	27	1	27	5.1	85	93	65	99	3	0	0	1286	93	5	104	9.6	.996	1B-144
1996		159	.295	.494	617	182	37	1	28	4.5	81	107	68	116	7	1	0	1415	121	12	118	9.8	.992	1B-158
11 yrs.		1450	.286	.530	5129	1466	266	18	317	6.2	869	910	812	1135	55	25	4	11658	908	97	1018	8.8	.992	1B-1341, DH-100

DIVISIONAL PLAYOFF SERIES

Year	Team	Games	BA	SA	AB	H	2B	3B	HR	HR%	R	RBI	BB	SO	SB	PH AB	PH H	PO	A	E	DP	TC/G	FA	G by Pos
1995	ATL N	4	.333	.667	18	6	0	0	2	11.1	4	6	2	3	0	0	0	39	2	0	5	10.3	1.000	1B-4
1996		3	.333	.778	9	3	1	0	1	11.1	1	3	2	1	0	0	0	25	3	0	1	9.3	1.000	1B-3
2 yrs.		7	.333	.704	27	9	1	0	3	11.1	5	9	4	4	0	0	0	64	5	0	6	9.9	1.000	1B-7

LEAGUE CHAMPIONSHIP SERIES

Year	Team	Games	BA	SA	AB	H	2B	3B	HR	HR%	R	RBI	BB	SO	SB	PH AB	PH H	PO	A	E	DP	TC/G	FA	G by Pos
1989	TOR A	5	.143	.143	21	3	0	0	0	0.0	1	3	0	4	0	0	0	35	2	1	3	7.6	.974	1B-5
1993	ATL N	6	.435	.652	23	10	2	0	1	4.3	6	4	4	7	0	0	0	50	3	0	1	8.8	1.000	1B-6
1995		4	.438	.688	16	7	4	0	0	0.0	5	0	3	0	0	0	0	42	4	0	8	11.5	1.000	1B-4
1996		7	.250	.536	28	7	0	1	2	7.1	6	7	3	5	0	0	0	55	2	1	5	8.3	.983	1B-7
4 yrs.		22	.307	.500	88	27 (10th)	6 (7th)	1	3	3.4	18	14	10	16 (2nd)	0 (9th)	0	0	182	11	2	17	8.9	.990	1B-22

WORLD SERIES

Year	Team	Games	BA	SA	AB	H	2B	3B	HR	HR%	R	RBI	BB	SO	SB	PH AB	PH H	PO	A	E	DP	TC/G	FA	G by Pos
1995	ATL N	6	.261	.609	23	6	2	0	2	8.7	5	3	3	7	1	0	0	68	2	1	2	11.8	.986	1B-6
1996		6	.300	.600	20	6	0	0	2	10.0	4	6	5	4	0	0	0	62	5	0	6	11.2	1.000	1B-6
2 yrs.		12	.279	.605	43	12	2	0	4	9.3	9	9	8	11	1	0	0	130	7	1	8	11.5	.993	1B-12

Mark McGwire

McGWIRE, MARK DAVID
B. Oct. 1, 1963, Pomona, Calif.
BR TR 6'5" 215 lbs.

Year	Team	Games	BA	SA	AB	H	2B	3B	HR	HR%	R	RBI	BB	SO	SB	PH AB	PH H	PO	A	E	DP	TC/G	FA	G by Pos
1986	OAK A	18	.189	.377	53	10	1	0	3	5.7	10	9	4	18	0	3	1	10	20	6	1	2.3	.833	3B-16
1987		151	.289	**.618**	557	161	28	4	**49**	8.8	97	118	71	131	1	2	1	1176	101	13	91	8.3	.990	1B-145, 3B-8, OF-3
1988		155	.260	.478	550	143	22	1	32	5.8	87	99	76	117	0	4	2	1228	88	9	118	8.5	.993	1B-154, OF-1
1989		143	.231	.467	490	113	17	0	33	6.7	74	95	83	94	1	1	0	1170	114	6	122	9.0	.995	1B-141, DH-2
1990		156	.235	.489	523	123	16	0	39	7.5	87	108	**110**	116	2	1	0	1329	95	5	126	9.2	.997	1B-154, DH-2
1991		154	.201	.383	483	97	22	0	22	4.6	62	75	93	116	2	4	1	1191	101	4	120	8.5	.997	1B-152
1992		139	.268	**.585**	467	125	22	0	42	9.0	87	104	90	105	0	1	0	1118	71	6	118	8.5	.995	1B-139, DH-1

Mark McGwire *continued*

Year	Team	Games	BA	SA	AB	H	2B	3B	HR	HR%	R	RBI	BB	SO	SB	PH AB	PH H	PO	A	E	DP	TC/G	FA	G by Pos
1993		27	.333	.726	84	28	6	0	9	10.7	16	24	21	19	0	1	0	197	14	0	20	8.4	1.000	1B-25
1994		47	.252	.474	135	34	3	0	9	6.7	26	25	37	40	0	2	0	311	17	4	25	7.4	.988	1B-40, DH-5
1995		104	.274	.685	317	87	13	0	39	**12.3**	75	90	88	77	1	1	0	775	63	12	64	8.4	.986	1B-91, DH-10
1996		130	.312	**.730**	423	132	21	0	**52**	12.3[1]	104	113	116	112	0	4	2	913	59	10	117	7.7	.990	1B-109, DH-18
11 yrs.		1224	.258	.544	4082	1053	171	5	329	8.1 2nd	725	860	789	945	7	24	7	9418	743	75	922	8.4	.993	1B-1150, DH-38, 3B-24, OF-4

LEAGUE CHAMPIONSHIP SERIES

Year	Team	Games	BA	SA	AB	H	2B	3B	HR	HR%	R	RBI	BB	SO	SB	PH AB	PH H	PO	A	E	DP	TC/G	FA	G by Pos
1988	OAK A	4	.333	.533	15	5	0	0	1	6.7	4	3	1	5	0	0	0	24	2	0	4	6.5	1.000	1B-4
1989		5	.389	.611	18	7	1	0	1	5.6	3	3	1	4	0	0	0	46	1	1	4	9.6	.979	1B-5
1990		4	.154	.154	13	2	0	0	0	0.0	2	2	3	3	0	0	0	40	0	0	3	10.0	1.000	1B-4
1992		6	.150	.300	20	3	0	0	1	5.0	1	3	5	4	0	0	0	46	2	1	3	8.2	.980	1B-6
4 yrs.		19	.258	.409	66	17	1	0	3	4.5	10	11	10	16	0	0	0	156	5	2	14	8.6	.988	1B-19

WORLD SERIES

Year	Team	Games	BA	SA	AB	H	2B	3B	HR	HR%	R	RBI	BB	SO	SB	PH AB	PH H	PO	A	E	DP	TC/G	FA	G by Pos
1988	OAK A	5	.059	.235	17	1	0	0	1	5.9	1	1	3	4	0	0	0	40	3	0	2	8.6	1.000	1B-5
1989		4	.294	.353	17	5	1	0	0	0.0	1	1	1	3	0	0	0	28	2	0	1	7.5	1.000	1B-4
1990		4	.214	.214	14	3	0	0	0	0.0	0	1	2	4	0	0	0	42	1	2	5	11.3	.956	1B-4
3 yrs.		13	.188	.271	48	9	1	0	1	2.1	2	2	6	11	0	0	0	110	6	2	8	9.1	.983	1B-13

Tim McIntosh

McINTOSH, TIMOTHY ALLEN
B. Mar. 21, 1965, Minneapolis, Minn.   BR TR 5'11" 195 lbs.

Year	Team	Games	BA	SA	AB	H	2B	3B	HR	HR%	R	RBI	BB	SO	SB	PH AB	PH H	PO	A	E	DP	TC/G	FA	G by Pos
1990	MIL A	5	.200	.800	5	1	0	0	1	20.0	1	1	0	2	0	1	0	6	1	1	0	2.0	.875	C-4
1991		7	.364	.727	11	4	1	0	1	9.1	2	1	0	4	0	1	0	1	0	0	0	0.1	1.000	OF-4, DH-2, 1B-1
1992		35	.182	.221	77	14	3	0	0	0.0	7	6	3	9	1	1	0	122	10	1	6	3.9	.992	C-14, OF-10, 1B-7, DH-3
1993	2 teams MIL A (1G –.000) MON N (20G –.095)																							
"	total	21	.095	.143	21	2	1	0	0	0.0	2	2	0	7	0	11	1	8	1	0	0	0.7	1.000	OF-7, C-6
1996	NY A	3	.000	.000	3	0	0	0	0	0.0	0	0	0	0	0	0	0	6	1	0	1	2.3	1.000	3B-1, 1B-1, C-1
5 yrs.		71	.179	.274	117	21	5	0	2	1.7	12	10	3	22	1	15	1	143	13	2	7	2.6	.987	C-25, OF-21, 1B-9, DH-5, 3B-1

Walt McKeel

McKEEL, WALTER THOMAS
B. Jan. 17, 1972, Wilson, N.C.   BR TR 6'2" 200 lbs.

Year	Team	Games	BA	SA	AB	H	2B	3B	HR	HR%	R	RBI	BB	SO	SB	PH AB	PH H	PO	A	E	DP	TC/G	FA	G by Pos
1996	BOS A	1	—	—	0	0	0	0	0	0	0	0	0	0	0	0	0	0	0	0	0	0.0	—	C-1

Mark McLemore

McLEMORE, MARK TREMELL
B. Oct. 4, 1964, San Diego, Calif.   BB TR 5'11" 175 lbs.

Year	Team	Games	BA	SA	AB	H	2B	3B	HR	HR%	R	RBI	BB	SO	SB	PH AB	PH H	PO	A	E	DP	TC/G	FA	G by Pos
1986	CAL A	5	.000	.000	4	0	0	0	0	0.0	0	0	1	2	0	0	0	3	10	0	1	6.5	1.000	2B-2
1987		138	.236	.300	433	102	13	3	3	0.7	61	41	48	72	25	1	0	293	363	17	98	4.8	.975	2B-132, SS-6, DH-3
1988		77	.240	.330	233	56	11	2	2	0.9	38	16	25	28	13	9	3	108	178	6	53	4.2	.979	2B-63, 3B-5, DH-1
1989		32	.243	.291	103	25	3	1	0	0.0	12	14	7	19	6	1	0	55	88	5	24	5.3	.966	2B-27, DH-1
1990	2 teams CAL A (20G –.146) CLE A (8G –.167)																							
"	total	28	.150	.183	60	9	2	0	0	0.0	6	2	4	15	1	2	0	37	39	4	10	3.2	.950	2B-11, SS-8, 3B-4, DH-2
1991	HOU N	21	.148	.164	61	9	1	0	0	0.0	6	2	6	13	0	2	0	25	54	2	8	4.3	.975	2B-19
1992	BAL A	101	.246	.294	228	56	7	2	0	0.0	40	27	21	26	11	11	4	126	186	7	47	3.7	.978	2B-70, DH-16
1993		148	.284	.368	581	165	27	5	4	0.7	81	72	64	92	21			335	80	6	23	2.7	.986	OF-124, 2B-25, 3B-4, DH-1
1994		104	.257	.321	343	88	11	1	3	0.9	44	29	51	50	20	4	0	220	270	9	53	4.8	.982	2B-96, OF-7, DH-1
1995	TEX A	129	.261	.358	467	122	20	5	5	1.1	73	41	59	71	21	3	1	246	184	4	40	3.1	.991	OF-73, 2B-66, DH-1
1996		147	.290	.379	517	150	23	4	5	1.0	84	46	87	69	27	0	0	312	471	12	114	5.4	.985	2B-147, OF-1
11 yrs.		930	.258	.334	3030	782	118	23	22	0.7	445	290	373	457	145	33	8	1760	1923	72	471	4.1	.981	2B-658, OF-205, DH-26, SS-14, 3B-13

DIVISIONAL PLAYOFF SERIES

Year	Team	Games	BA	SA	AB	H	2B	3B	HR	HR%	R	RBI	BB	SO	SB	PH AB	PH H	PO	A	E	DP	TC/G	FA	G by Pos
1996	TEX A	4	.133	.133	15	2	0	0	0	0.0	1	2	0	4	0	0	0	10	16	0	2	6.5	1.000	2B-4

Billy McMillon

McMILLON, WILLIAM EDWARD
B. Nov. 17, 1971, Otero, N.M.   BL TL 5'11" 172 lbs.

Year	Team	Games	BA	SA	AB	H	2B	3B	HR	HR%	R	RBI	BB	SO	SB	PH AB	PH H	PO	A	E	DP	TC/G	FA	G by Pos
1996	FLA N	28	.216	.216	51	11	0	0	0	0.0	4	4	5	14	0	13	0	17	0	0	0	1.1	1.000	OF-15

Brian McRae

McRAE, BRIAN WESLEY
Son of Hal McRae.
B. Aug. 27, 1967, Bradenton, Fla.   BB TR 6' 175 lbs.

Year	Team	Games	BA	SA	AB	H	2B	3B	HR	HR%	R	RBI	BB	SO	SB	PH AB	PH H	PO	A	E	DP	TC/G	FA	G by Pos
1990	KC A	46	.286	.405	168	48	8	3	2	1.2	21	23	9	29	4	1	1	120	1	0	0	2.7	1.000	OF-45
1991		152	.261	.372	629	164	28	9	8	1.3	86	64	24	99	20	2	1	405	2	3	0	2.7	.993	OF-150
1992		149	.223	.308	533	119	23	5	4	0.8	63	52	42	88	18	5	2	419	8	3	2	2.9	.993	OF-148, DH-1
1993		153	.282	.413	627	177	28	9	12	1.9	78	69	37	105	23	3	0	394	4	7	3	2.6	.983	OF-153
1994		114	.273	.383	436	119	22	6	4	0.9	71	40	54	67	28	1	0	252	2	3	0	2.3	.988	OF-110, DH-4
1995	CHI N	137	.288	.440	**580**	167	38	7	12	2.1	92	48	47	92	27	1	0	345	4	3	0	2.5	.991	OF-137
1996		157	.276	.425	624	172	32	5	17	2.7	111	66	73	84	37	4	1	343	2	5	1	2.3	.986	OF-155
7 yrs.		908	.269	.392	3597	966	179	44	59	1.6	522	362	286	564	157	17	5	2278	23	24	6	2.6	.990	OF-898, DH-5

Pat Meares

MEARES, PATRICK JAMES
B. Sept. 6, 1968, Salina, Kans.   BR TR 6' 185 lbs.

Year	Team	Games	BA	SA	AB	H	2B	3B	HR	HR%	R	RBI	BB	SO	SB	PH AB	PH H	PO	A	E	DP	TC/G	FA	G by Pos
1993	MIN A	111	.251	.309	346	87	14	3	0	0.0	33	33	7	52	4	1	0	165	304	19	70	4.4	.961	SS-111
1994		80	.266	.354	229	61	12	1	2	0.9	29	24	14	50	5	1	0	134	209	13	45	4.5	.963	SS-79
1995		116	.269	.431	390	105	19	4	12	3.1	57	49	15	68	10	3	1	186	317	18	67	4.5	.965	SS-114, OF-3
1996		152	.267	.391	517	138	26	7	8	1.5	66	67	17	90	9	3	2	257	344	22	85	4.1	.965	SS-150, OF-1
4 yrs.		459	.264	.377	1482	391	71	15	22	1.5	185	173	53	260	28	8	3	742	1174	72	267	4.3	.964	SS-454, OF-4

Miguel Mejia

MEJIA, MIGUEL
B. Mar. 25, 1975, San Pedro de Macoris, Dominican Republic
BR TR 6'1" 155 lbs.

Year	Team	Games	BA	SA	AB	H	2B	3B	HR	HR%	R	RBI	BB	SO	SB	PH AB	PH H	PO	A	E	DP	TC/G	FA	G by Pos
1996	STL N	45	.087	.087	23	2	0	0	0	0.0	10	0	0	10	6	10	1	15	0	1	0	0.7	933	

DIVISIONAL PLAYOFF SERIES

| 1996 | STL N | 1 | — | — | 0 | 0 | 0 | 0 | 0 | 0.0 | 0 | 0 | 0 | 0 | 0 | 0 | 0 | 0 | 0 | 0 | 0 | 0.0 | — | |

LEAGUE CHAMPIONSHIP SERIES

| 1996 | STL N | 3 | .000 | .000 | 1 | 0 | 0 | 0 | 0 | 0.0 | 1 | 0 | 0 | 1 | 0 | 0 | 0 | 2 | 0 | 0 | 0 | 1.0 | 1.000 | OF-2 |

Orlando Merced

MERCED, ORLANDO LUIS
Born Orlando Luis Merced (Villanueva).
B. Nov. 2, 1966, Hato Rey, Puerto Rico
BB TR 6' 180 lbs.

Year	Team	Games	BA	SA	AB	H	2B	3B	HR	HR%	R	RBI	BB	SO	SB	PH AB	PH H	PO	A	E	DP	TC/G	FA	G by Pos
1990	PIT N	25	.208	.250	24	5	1	0	0	0.0	3	0	1	9	0	24	5	0	0	0	0	0.0		OF-1, C-1
1991		120	.275	.399	411	113	17	2	10	2.4	83	50	64	81	8	17	6	916	60	12	64	8.8	.988	1B-105, OF-7
1992		134	.247	.385	405	100	28	5	6	1.5	50	60	52	63	5	25	10	906	75	5	74	7.5	.995	1B-114, OF-17
1993		137	.313	.443	447	140	26	4	8	1.8	68	70	77	64	3	15	9	485	31	10	27	3.5	.981	OF-109, 1B-42
1994		108	.272	.412	386	105	21	3	9	2.3	48	51	42	58	4	2	0	509	29	5	46	4.4	.991	OF-68, 1B-55
1995		132	.300	.468	487	146	29	4	15	3.1	75	83	52	74	7	9	2	375	23	6	24	2.8	.985	OF-107, 1B-35
1996		120	.287	.457	453	130	24	1	17	3.8	69	80	51	74	8	5	1	242	15	3	6	2.2	.988	OF-115, 1B-1
7 yrs.		776	.283	.428	2613	739	146	19	65	2.5	396	394	339	423	35	97	33	3433	233	41	241	4.8	.989	OF-424, 1B-352, C-1

LEAGUE CHAMPIONSHIP SERIES

1991	PIT N	3	.222	.556	9	2	0	0	1	11.1	1	1	0	1	0	0	0	13	0	1	0	7.0	.929	1B-2
1992		4	.100	.200	10	1	1	0	0	0.0	0	2	2	4	0	1	0	27	2	1	3	7.5	.967	1B-4
2 yrs.		7	.158	.368	19	3	1	0	1	5.3	1	3	2	5	0	1	0	40	2	2	3	7.3	.955	1B-6

Henry Mercedes

MERCEDES, HENRY FELIPE
Born Henry Felipe Mercedes (Perez).
B. July 23, 1969, Santo Domingo, Dominican Republic
BR TR 5'11" 185 lbs.

Year	Team	Games	BA	SA	AB	H	2B	3B	HR	HR%	R	RBI	BB	SO	SB	PH AB	PH H	PO	A	E	DP	TC/G	FA	G by Pos
1992	OAK A	9	.800	1.200	5	4	0	1	0	0.0	1	0	0	1	0	2	1	7	0	1	0	0.9	.875	C-9
1993		20	.213	.255	47	10	2	0	0	0.0	5	3	2	15	1	2	0	66	10	1	1	4.1	.987	C-18, DH-1
1995	KC A	23	.256	.302	43	11	2	0	0	0.0	7	9	8	13	0	1	0	62	8	1	1	3.2	.986	C-22
1996		4	.250	.250	4	1	0	0	0	0.0	1	0	0	1	0	0	0	2	0	0	0	0.5	1.000	C-4
4 yrs.		56	.263	.323	99	26	4	1	0	0.0	14	13	10	30	1	5	1	137	18	3	2	2.9	.981	C-53, DH-1

Matt Mieske

MIESKE, MATTHEW TODD
B. Feb. 13, 1968, Midland, Mich.
BR TR 6' 185 lbs.

Year	Team	Games	BA	SA	AB	H	2B	3B	HR	HR%	R	RBI	BB	SO	SB	PH AB	PH H	PO	A	E	DP	TC/G	FA	G by Pos
1993	MIL A	23	.241	.397	58	14	0	0	3	5.2	9	7	4	14	0	0	0	43	1	3	0	2.1	.936	OF-22
1994		84	.259	.432	259	67	13	1	10	3.9	39	38	21	62	3	0	0	155	7	4	1	2.0	.976	OF-80, DH-1
1995		117	.251	.442	267	67	13	1	12	4.5	42	48	27	45	2	11	2	177	7	4	0	1.7	.979	OF-108, DH-2
1996		127	.278	.471	374	104	24	3	14	3.7	46	64	26	76	1	9	1	249	7	1	1	2.0	.996	OF-122
4 yrs.		351	.263	.448	958	252	50	5	39	4.1	136	157	78	197	6	20	3	624	22	12	2	2.0	.982	OF-332, DH-3

Ralph Milliard

MILLIARD, RALPH GREGORY
B. Dec. 30, 1973, Willemstad, Curacao
BR TR 5'11" 170 lbs.

Year	Team	Games	BA	SA	AB	H	2B	3B	HR	HR%	R	RBI	BB	SO	SB	PH AB	PH H	PO	A	E	DP	TC/G	FA	G by Pos
1996	FLA N	24	.161	.194	62	10	2	0	0	0.0	7	1	14	16	2	0	0	42	65	5	14	4.7	.955	2B-24

Doug Mirabelli

MIRABELLI, DOUGLAS ANTHONY
B. Oct. 18, 1970, Kingman, Ariz.
BR TR 6'1" 205 lbs.

Year	Team	Games	BA	SA	AB	H	2B	3B	HR	HR%	R	RBI	BB	SO	SB	PH AB	PH H	PO	A	E	DP	TC/G	FA	G by Pos
1996	SF N	9	.222	.278	18	4	1	0	0	0.0	2	1	3	4	0	1	0	29	2	0	0	3.9	1.000	C-8

Keith Mitchell

MITCHELL, KEITH ALEXANDER
B. Aug. 6, 1969, San Diego, Calif.
BR TR 5'10" 180 lbs.

Year	Team	Games	BA	SA	AB	H	2B	3B	HR	HR%	R	RBI	BB	SO	SB	PH AB	PH H	PO	A	E	DP	TC/G	FA	G by Pos
1991	ATL N	48	.318	.409	66	21	0	0	2	3.0	11	5	8	12	3	10	2	31	1	0	0	1.0	.970	OF-34
1994	SEA A	46	.227	.359	128	29	2	0	5	3.9	21	15	18	22	0	6	1	49	0	1	0	1.1	.980	OF-39, DH-6
1996	CIN N	11	.267	.533	15	4	1	0	1	6.7	2	3	1	3	0	7	3	7	0	1	0	1.6	.875	OF-5
3 yrs.		105	.258	.388	209	54	3	0	8	3.8	34	23	27	37	3	23	6	87	1	3	0	1.1	.967	OF-78, DH-6

LEAGUE CHAMPIONSHIP SERIES

| 1991 | ATL N | 5 | .000 | .000 | 4 | 0 | 0 | 0 | 0 | 0.0 | 0 | 0 | 0 | 1 | 0 | 1 | 0 | 2 | 0 | 0 | 0 | 0.4 | 1.000 | OF-5 |

WORLD SERIES

| 1991 | ATL N | 3 | .000 | .000 | 2 | 0 | 0 | 0 | 0 | 0.0 | 0 | 0 | 0 | 1 | 0 | 0 | 0 | 0 | 0 | 0 | 0 | 0.0 | .000 | OF-3 |

Kevin Mitchell

MITCHELL, KEVIN DARNELL (Mitch, World)
B. Jan. 13, 1962, San Diego, Calif.
BR TR 5'10" 210 lbs.

Year	Team	Games	BA	SA	AB	H	2B	3B	HR	HR%	R	RBI	BB	SO	SB	PH AB	PH H	PO	A	E	DP	TC/G	FA	G by Pos
1984	NY N	7	.214	.214	14	3	0	0	0	0.0	0	1	0	3	0	4	1	1	4	1	2	1.2	.833	3B-5
1986		108	.277	.466	328	91	22	2	12	3.7	51	43	33	61	3	20	3	158	69	10	10	2.3	.958	OF-68, SS-24, 3B-7, 1B-2
1987	2 teams SD N (62G –.245) SF N (69G –.306)																							
"	total	131	.280	.474	464	130	20	2	22	4.7	68	70	48	88	9	9	2	76	240	15	19	2.6	.955	3B-119, OF-6, SS-1
1988	SF N	148	.251	.442	505	127	25	7	19	3.8	60	80	48	85	5	10	2	118	205	22	18	2.4	.936	3B-102, OF-40
1989		154	.291	.635	543	158	34	6	47	8.7	100	125	87	115	3	3	1	305	10	7	0	2.2	.978	OF-147, 3B-2
1990		140	.290	.544	524	152	24	2	35	6.7	90	93	58	87	4	2	1	295	9	9	3	2.3	.971	OF-138
1991		113	.256	.515	371	95	13	1	27	7.3	52	69	43	57	2	13	0	188	6	6	1	2.0	.970	OF-100, 1B-1
1992	SEA A	99	.286	.428	360	103	24	0	9	2.5	48	67	35	46	0	5	3	130	4	0	0	1.4	1.000	OF-69, DH-26

Year	Team	Games	BA	SA	AB	H	2B	3B	HR	HR%	R	RBI	BB	SO	SB	Pinch Hit AB	H	PO	A	E	DP	TC/G	FA	G by Pos

Kevin Mitchell *continued*

Year	Team	Games	BA	SA	AB	H	2B	3B	HR	HR%	R	RBI	BB	SO	SB	AB	H	PO	A	E	DP	TC/G	FA	G by Pos
1993	CIN N	93	.341	.601	323	110	21	3	19	5.9	56	64	25	48	1	3	0	149	7	7	2	1.9	.957	OF-87
1994		95	.326	.681	310	101	18	1	30	9.7	57	77	59	62	2	4	1	139	10	4	2	1.7	.974	OF-89, 1B-1
1996	2 teams BOS A		(27G –.304)		CIN N		(37G –.325)																	
"	total	64	.316	.505	206	65	15	0	8	3.9	27	39	37	30	0	6	0	101	2	4	4	1.8	.963	OF-52, DH-4, 1B-3
11 yrs.		1152	.287	.528	3948	1135	216	24	228	5.8	609	728	473	682	29	79	14	1660	566	85	61	2.1	.963	OF-796, 3B-235, DH-30, SS-25, 1B-7
LEAGUE CHAMPIONSHIP SERIES																								
1986	NY N	2	.250	.250	8	2	0	0	0	0.0	1	0	0	1	0	0	0	3	0	0	0	1.5	1.000	OF-2
1987	SF N	7	.267	.400	30	8	1	0	1	3.3	2	2	0	3	1	0	0	4	10	1	1	2.1	.933	3B-7
1989		5	.353	.706	17	6	0	0	2	11.8	5	7	3	3	0	0	0	15	1	1	1	3.4	.941	OF-5
3 yrs.		14	.291	.473	55	16	1	0	3	5.5	8	9	3	7	1	0	0	22	11	2	2	2.5	.943	3B-7, OF-7
WORLD SERIES																								
1986	NY N	5	.250	.250	8	2	0	0	0	0.0	1	0	0	3	0	2	1	0	0	0	0	0.7	1.000	OF-2, DH-1
1989	SF N	4	.294	.471	17	5	0	0	1	5.9	2	2	0	3	0	0	0	10	0	1	0	2.8	.909	OF-4
2 yrs.		9	.280	.400	25	7	0	0	1	4.0	3	2	0	6	0	2	1	10	0	1	0	1.9	.923	OF-6, DH-1

Izzy Molina

MOLINA, ISLAY
B. Jun. 3, 1971, New York, N. Y.

BR TR 6'1" 200 lbs.

Year	Team	Games	BA	SA	AB	H	2B	3B	HR	HR%	R	RBI	BB	SO	SB	AB	H	PO	A	E	DP	TC/G	FA	G by Pos
1996	OAK A	14	.200	.280	25	5	2	0	0	0.0	0	1	1	3	0	3	1	31	1	0	1	2.7	1.000	C-12, DH-1

Paul Molitor

MOLITOR, PAUL LEO
B. Aug. 22, 1956, St. Paul, Minn.

BR TR 6' 185 lbs.

Year	Team	Games	BA	SA	AB	H	2B	3B	HR	HR%	R	RBI	BB	SO	SB	AB	H	PO	A	E	DP	TC/G	FA	G by Pos
1978	MIL A	125	.273	.372	521	142	26	4	6	1.2	73	45	19	54	30	3	0	253	401	22	74	5.4	.967	2B-91, SS-31, DH-2, 3B-1
1979		140	.322	.469	584	188	27	16	9	1.5	88	62	48	48	33	2	0	309	440	16	84	5.5	.979	2B-122, SS-10, DH-8
1980		111	.304	.438	450	137	29	2	9	2.0	81	37	48	48	34	2	1	260	336	20	90	5.5	.968	2B-91, SS-12, DH-7, 3B-1
1981		64	.267	.335	251	67	11	0	2	0.8	45	19	25	29	10	1	0	119	4	3	1	2.0	.976	OF-46, DH-16
1982		160	.302	.450	666	201	26	8	19	2.9	136	71	69	93	41	0	0	134	350	32	48	3.2	.938	3B-150, DH-6, SS-4
1983		152	.270	.410	608	164	28	6	15	2.5	95	47	59	74	41	2	0	105	343	16	37	3.1	.966	3B-146, DH-2
1984		13	.217	.239	46	10	1	0	0	0.0	3	6	2	8	1	2	0	7	21	2	3	2.7	.933	3B-7, DH-4
1985		140	.297	.408	576	171	28	3	10	1.7	93	48	54	80	21	1	0	126	263	19	30	2.9	.953	3B-135, DH-4
1986		105	.281	.426	437	123	24	6	9	2.1	62	55	40	81	20	0	0	86	171	15	25	2.6	.945	3B-91, DH-10, OF-4
1987		118	.353	.566	465	164	41	5	16	3.4	114	75	69	67	45	1	0	60	113	5	24	1.5	.972	DH-58, 3B-41, 2B-19
1988		154	.312	.452	609	190	34	6	13	2.1	115	60	71	54	41	2	0	87	188	17	15	1.9	.942	3B-105, DH-49, 2B-1
1989		155	.315	.439	615	194	35	4	11	1.8	84	56	64	67	27	0	0	106	287	18	27	2.6	.956	3B-112, DH-28, 2B-16
1990		103	.285	.464	418	119	27	6	12	2.9	64	45	37	51	18	1	0	463	222	10	65	6.7	.986	2B-60, 1B-37, DH-4, 3B-2
1991		158	.325	.489	665	216	32	13	17	2.6	133	75	77	62	19	0	0	389	32	6	52	2.7	.986	DH-112, 1B-46
1992		158	.320	.461	609	195	36	7	12	2.0	89	89	73	66	31	2	0	461	26	2	44	3.1	.996	DH-108, 1B-48
1993	TOR A	160	.332	.509	636	211	37	5	22	3.5	121	111	77	71	22	0	0	178	14	3	16	1.2	.985	DH-137, 1B-23
1994		115	.341	.518	454	155	30	4	14	3.1	86	75	55	48	20	0	0	47	3	0	6	0.4	1.000	DH-110, 1B-5
1995		130	.270	.423	525	142	31	2	15	2.9	63	60	61	57	12	0	0	0	0	0	0	0.0	.000	DH-129
1996	MIN A	161	.341	.468	660	225	41	8	9	1.4	99	113	56	72	18	1	1	138	13	1	13	0.9	.993	DH-143, 1B-17
19 yrs.		2422	.308	.452	9795	3014	544	105	220	2.2	1644	1149	1004	1130	484	18	2	3328	3227	207	654	2.8	.969	DH-937, 3B-791, 2B-400, 1B-176, SS-57, OF-50
DIVISIONAL PLAYOFF SERIES																								
1981	MIL A	5	.250	.400	20	5	0	0	1	5.0	2	1	2	5	0	0	0	12	0	0	0	2.4	1.000	OF-5
LEAGUE CHAMPIONSHIP SERIES																								
1982	MIL A	5	.316	.684	19	6	1	0	2	10.5	4	5	2	3	1	0	0	4	11	2	2	3.4	.882	3B-5
1993	TOR A	6	.391	.696	23	9	2	1	1	4.3	7	5	3	3	0	0	0	0	0	0	0	0.0	.000	DH-6
2 yrs.		11	.357	.690	42	15	3	1	3	7.1	11	10	5	6	1	0	0	4	11	2	2	1.5	.882	DH-6, 3B-5
WORLD SERIES																								
1982	MIL A	7	.355	.355	31	11	0	0	0	0.0	5	2	2	4	1	0	0	4	9	0	1	1.9	1.000	3B-7
1993	TOR A	6	.500	1.000	24	12	2	2	2	8.3	10	8	3	0	1	0	0	7	3	0	2	1.7	1.000	DH-3, 3B-2, 1B-1
2 yrs.		13	.418	.636	55	23	2	2	2	3.6	15	10	5	4	2	0	0	11	12	0	3	1.8	1.000	3B-9, DH-3, 1B-1
			1st	7th																				

Raul Mondesi

MONDESI, RAUL RAMON
Born Raul Ramon Mondesi (Avelino).
B. Mar. 12, 1971, San Cristobal, Dominican Republic

BR TR 5'11" 202 lbs.

Year	Team	Games	BA	SA	AB	H	2B	3B	HR	HR%	R	RBI	BB	SO	SB	AB	H	PO	A	E	DP	TC/G	FA	G by Pos
1993	LA N	42	.291	.488	86	25	3	1	4	4.7	13	10	4	16	4	7	3	55	3	3	1	1.5	.951	OF-40
1994		112	.306	.516	434	133	27	8	16	3.7	63	56	16	78	11	0	0	206	16	8	1	2.1	.965	OF-112
1995		139	.285	.496	536	153	23	6	26	4.9	91	88	33	96	27	1	0	281	16	6	2	2.2	.980	OF-138
1996		157	.297	.495	634	188	40	7	24	3.8	98	88	32	122	14	0	0	338	11	12	3	2.3	.967	OF-157
4 yrs.		450	.295	.501	1690	499	93	22	70	4.1	265	242	85	312	56	8	3	880	46	29	7	2.1	.970	OF-447
DIVISIONAL PLAYOFF SERIES																								
1995	LA N	3	.222	.222	9	2	0	0	0	0.0	0	1	0	4	0	0	0	8	0	0	0	2.7	1.000	OF-3
1996		3	.182	.364	11	2	2	0	0	0.0	0	1	0	4	0	0	0	2	0	0	0	0.7	1.000	OF-3
2 yrs.		6	.200	.300	20	4	2	0	0	0.0	0	2	0	8	0	0	0	10	0	0	0	1.7	1.000	OF-6

Ray Montgomery

MONTGOMERY, RAYMOND JAMES
B. Aug. 8, 1969, Bronxville, N. Y.

BR TR 6'3" 195 lbs.

Year	Team	Games	BA	SA	AB	H	2B	3B	HR	HR%	R	RBI	BB	SO	SB	AB	H	PO	A	E	DP	TC/G	FA	G by Pos
1996	HOU N	12	.214	.500	14	3	1	0	1	7.1	4	4	1	5	0	4	1	6	0	0	0	1.0	1.000	OF-6

Kerwin Moore

MOORE, KERWIN LAMAR
B. Oct. 29, 1970, Detroit, Mich.

BB TR 6'1" 190 lbs.

Year	Team	Games	BA	SA	AB	H	2B	3B	HR	HR%	R	RBI	BB	SO	SB	AB	H	PO	A	E	DP	TC/G	FA	G by Pos
1996	OAK A	22	.063	.125	16	1	1	0	0	0.0	4	0	2	6	1	1	0	19	0	0	0	1.1	1.000	OF-18, DH-1

Year	Team	Games	BA	SA	AB	H	2B	3B	HR	HR%	R	RBI	BB	SO	SB	Pinch Hit AB	Pinch Hit H	PO	A	E	DP	TC/G	FA	G by Pos

Mickey Morandini

MORANDINI, MICHAEL ROBERT
B. Apr. 22, 1966, Kittanning, Pa.
BL TR 5'11" 170 lbs.

Year	Team	Games	BA	SA	AB	H	2B	3B	HR	HR%	R	RBI	BB	SO	SB	AB	H	PO	A	E	DP	TC/G	FA	G by Pos
1990	PHI N	25	.241	.329	79	19	4	6	1	1.3	9	3	6	19	3	1	0	37	61	1	10	4.0	.990	2B-25
1991		98	.249	.317	325	81	11	4	1	0.3	38	20	29	45	13	0	0	183	254	6	45	4.6	.986	2B-97
1992		127	.265	.344	422	112	8	8	3	0.7	47	30	25	64	8	6	3	239	336	6	65	4.6	.990	2B-124, SS-3
1993		120	.247	.355	425	105	19	9	3	0.7	57	33	34	73	13	11	3	208	288	5	48	4.5	.990	2B-111
1994		87	.292	.409	274	80	16	5	2	0.7	40	26	34	33	10	8	3	167	216	6	38	4.9	.985	2B-79
1995		127	.283	.417	494	140	34	7	6	1.2	65	49	42	80	9	9	1	268	336	7	73	5.0	.989	2B-122
1996		140	.250	.334	539	135	24	6	3	0.6	64	32	49	87	26	4	0	286	352	12	87	4.7	.982	2B-137
7 yrs.		724	.263	.361	2558	672	116	39	19	0.7	320	193	219	401	82	39	10	1388	1843	43	366	4.7	.987	2B-695, SS-3

LEAGUE CHAMPIONSHIP SERIES

Year	Team	Games	BA	SA	AB	H	2B	3B	HR	HR%	R	RBI	BB	SO	SB	AB	H	PO	A	E	DP	TC/G	FA	G by Pos
1993	PHI N	4	.250	.375	16	4	0	1	0	0.0	1	2	0	3	1	1	0	8	9	1	2	4.5	.944	2B-4

WORLD SERIES

Year	Team	Games	BA	SA	AB	H	2B	3B	HR	HR%	R	RBI	BB	SO	SB	AB	H	PO	A	E	DP	TC/G	FA	G by Pos
1993	PHI N	3	.200	.200	5	1	0	0	0	0.0	1	0	1	2	0	1	0	2	0	0	0	2.0	1.000	2B-1

Mike Mordecai

MORDECAI, MICHAEL HOWARD
B. Dec. 13, 1967, Birmingham, Ala.
BB TR 5'11" 175 lbs.

Year	Team	Games	BA	SA	AB	H	2B	3B	HR	HR%	R	RBI	BB	SO	SB	AB	H	PO	A	E	DP	TC/G	FA	G by Pos
1994	ATL N	4	.250	1.000	4	1	0	0	1	25.0	1	3	1	0	0	1	0	1	4	0	0	1.3	1.000	SS-4
1995		69	.280	.480	75	21	6	0	3	4.0	10	11	9	16	0	29	7	39	31	0	12	1.6	1.000	2B-21, 1B-9, SS-6, 3B-6, OF-1
1996		66	.241	.343	108	26	5	0	2	1.9	12	8	9	24	1	33	7	33	52	2	8	2.4	.977	2B-20, 3B-9, SS-6, 1B-2
3 yrs.		139	.257	.412	187	48	11	0	6	3.2	23	22	19	40	1	63	14	73	87	2	20	1.9	.988	2B-41, SS-16, 3B-15, 1B-11, OF-1

DIVISIONAL PLAYOFF SERIES

Year	Team	Games	BA	SA	AB	H	2B	3B	HR	HR%	R	RBI	BB	SO	SB	AB	H	PO	A	E	DP	TC/G	FA	G by Pos
1995	ATL N	2	.667	1.000	3	2	1	0	0	0.0	1	2	0	0	0	2	2	1	0	0	0	1.0	1.000	SS-1

LEAGUE CHAMPIONSHIP SERIES

Year	Team	Games	BA	SA	AB	H	2B	3B	HR	HR%	R	RBI	BB	SO	SB	AB	H	PO	A	E	DP	TC/G	FA	G by Pos
1995	ATL N	2	.000	.000	2	0	0	0	0	0.0	0	0	0	1	0	1	0	0	0	0	0	0.0	.000	SS-1
1996		4	.250	.250	4	1	0	0	0	0.0	1	0	0	1	0	2	0	1	1	0	1	0.7	1.000	2B-2, 3B-1
2 yrs.		6	.167	.167	6	1	0	0	0	0.0	1	0	0	2	0	3	0	1	1	0	1	0.5	1.000	2B-2, 3B-1, SS-1

WORLD SERIES

Year	Team	Games	BA	SA	AB	H	2B	3B	HR	HR%	R	RBI	BB	SO	SB	AB	H	PO	A	E	DP	TC/G	FA	G by Pos
1995	ATL N	3	.333	.333	3	1	0	0	0	0.0	0	0	0	0	0	1	0	0	6	0	0	2.0	1.000	SS-2, DH-1
1996		1	.000	.000	1	0	0	0	0	0.0	0	0	0	1	0	1	0	0	0	0	0	0.0	—	
2 yrs.		4	.250	.250	4	1	0	0	0	0.0	0	0	0	1	0	2	0	0	6	0	0	2.0	1.000	SS-2, DH-1

Russ Morman

MORMAN, RUSSELL LEE
B. Apr. 28, 1962, Independence, Mo.
BR TR 6'4" 215 lbs.

Year	Team	Games	BA	SA	AB	H	2B	3B	HR	HR%	R	RBI	BB	SO	SB	AB	H	PO	A	E	DP	TC/G	FA	G by Pos
1986	CHI A	49	.252	.358	159	40	5	0	4	2.5	18	17	16	36	1	1	0	342	26	4	31	7.9	.989	1B-47
1988		40	.240	.267	75	18	2	0	0	0.0	8	3	3	17	0	5	2	114	5	2	8	3.5	.983	1B-22, OF-10, DH-3
1989		37	.224	.259	58	13	2	0	0	0.0	5	8	6	16	1	2	2	157	13	2	21	4.8	.988	1B-35, DH-1
1990	KC A	12	.270	.568	37	10	4	2	1	2.7	5	3	3	3	0	1	0	27	4	0	1	2.6	1.000	OF-8, 1B-3, DH-1
1991		12	.261	.261	23	6	0	0	0	0.0	1	1	1	5	0	4	0	47	3	0	2	4.5	1.000	1B-8, OF-2, DH-1
1994	FLA N	13	.212	.364	33	7	0	1	1	3.0	2	2	2	9	0	4	0	66	9	1	9	9.5	.987	1B-8
1995		34	.278	.458	72	20	1	0	3	4.2	9	7	13	12	0	13	4	31	1	1	1	1.6	.970	OF-18, 1B-3
1996		6	.167	.333	6	1	1	0	0	0.0	0	0	1	2	0	5	1	2	0	0	1	1.0	1.000	1B-2
8 yrs.		203	.248	.359	463	115	16	4	9	1.9	48	41	35	100	2	35	9	786	61	10	74	5.0	.988	1B-128, OF-38, DH-6

Hal Morris

MORRIS, WILLIAM HAROLD
B. Apr. 9, 1965, Fort Rucker, Ala.
BL TL 6'3" 200 lbs.

Year	Team	Games	BA	SA	AB	H	2B	3B	HR	HR%	R	RBI	BB	SO	SB	AB	H	PO	A	E	DP	TC/G	FA	G by Pos
1988	NY A	15	.100	.100	20	2	0	0	0	0.0	1	0	0	9	0	10	2	7	0	0	0	1.4	1.000	OF-4, DH-1
1989		15	.278	.278	18	5	0	0	0	0.0	2	4	1	4	0	9	1	12	0	0	2	1.5	1.000	OF-5, 1B-2, DH-1
1990	CIN N	107	.340	.498	309	105	22	3	7	2.3	50	36	21	32	9	21	7	595	53	4	50	7.6	.994	1B-80, OF-6
1991		136	.318	.479	478	152	33	1	14	2.9	72	59	46	61	10	9	3	979	100	9	87	8.4	.992	1B-128, OF-1
1992		115	.271	.385	395	107	21	3	6	1.5	41	53	45	53	6	8	2	841	86	1	65	8.5	.999	1B-109
1993		101	.317	.420	379	120	18	0	7	1.8	48	49	34	51	2	4	0	746	75	5	61	8.4	.994	1B-98
1994		112	.335	.491	436	146	30	4	10	2.3	60	78	34	62	6	1	0	899	77	6	76	8.8	.994	1B-112
1995		101	.279	.451	359	100	25	2	11	3.1	53	51	29	58	1	5	1	755	72	5	79	8.4	.994	1B-99
1996		142	.313	.479	528	165	32	4	16	3.0	82	80	50	76	7	6	2	1128	92	8	102	8.6	.993	1B-140
9 yrs.		844	.309	.455	2922	902	181	17	71	2.4	409	410	260	406	41	73	18	5962	555	38	522	8.3	.994	1B-768, OF-16, DH-2

DIVISIONAL PLAYOFF SERIES

Year	Team	Games	BA	SA	AB	H	2B	3B	HR	HR%	R	RBI	BB	SO	SB	AB	H	PO	A	E	DP	TC/G	FA	G by Pos
1995	CIN N	3	.500	.600	10	5	1	0	0	0.0	5	2	3	1	1	0	0	22	2	0	1	8.0	1.000	1B-3

LEAGUE CHAMPIONSHIP SERIES

Year	Team	Games	BA	SA	AB	H	2B	3B	HR	HR%	R	RBI	BB	SO	SB	AB	H	PO	A	E	DP	TC/G	FA	G by Pos
1990	CIN N	5	.417	.500	12	5	1	0	0	0.0	3	1	1	0	0	1	1	20	2	0	2	5.5	1.000	1B-4
1995		4	.167	.250	12	2	1	0	0	0.0	0	1	1	1	1	1	0	27	3	0	2	7.5	1.000	1B-4
2 yrs.		9	.292	.375	24	7	2	0	0	0.0	3	2	2	1	1	2	1	47	5	0	4	6.5	1.000	1B-8

WORLD SERIES

Year	Team	Games	BA	SA	AB	H	2B	3B	HR	HR%	R	RBI	BB	SO	SB	AB	H	PO	A	E	DP	TC/G	FA	G by Pos
1990	CIN N	4	.071	.071	14	1	0	0	0	0.0	0	2	1	1	0	0	0	18	1	0	1	4.8	1.000	1B-2, DH-2

Julio Mosquera

MOSQUERA, JULIO ALBERTO
Born Julio Alberto Mosquera (Cervantes).
B. Jan. 29, 1972, Panama City, Panama
BR TR 6' 185 lbs.

Year	Team	Games	BA	SA	AB	H	2B	3B	HR	HR%	R	RBI	BB	SO	SB	AB	H	PO	A	E	DP	TC/G	FA	G by Pos
1996	TOR A	8	.227	.318	22	5	2	0	0	0.0	2	2	0	3	0	0	0	48	1	0	0	6.1	1.000	C-8

Chad Mottola

MOTTOLA CHARLES EDWARD
B. Oct. 15, 1971, Augusta, Ga.
BR TR 6'3" 220 lbs.

Year	Team	Games	BA	SA	AB	H	2B	3B	HR	HR%	R	RBI	BB	SO	SB	AB	H	PO	A	E	DP	TC/G	FA	G by Pos
1996	CIN N	35	.215	.367	79	17	3	0	3	3.8	10	6	6	16	2	4	0	42	2	0	0	1.4	1.000	OF-31

Year	Team	Games	BA	SA	AB	H	2B	3B	HR	HR%	R	RBI	BB	SO	SB	Pinch Hit AB	H	PO	A	E	DP	TC/G	FA	G by Pos

James Mouton

MOUTON, JAMES RALEIGH
B. Dec. 29, 1968, Denver, Colo.

BR TR 5'9" 175 lbs.

Year	Team	Games	BA	SA	AB	H	2B	3B	HR	HR%	R	RBI	BB	SO	SB	AB	H	PO	A	E	DP	TC/G	FA	G by Pos
1994	HOU N	99	.245	.300	310	76	11	0	2	0.6	43	16	27	69	24	3	2	163	5	3	2	1.8	.982	OF-96
1995		104	.262	.376	298	78	18	2	4	1.3	42	27	25	59	25	14	4	134	4	0	0	1.5	1.000	OF-94
1996		122	.263	.350	300	79	15	1	3	1.0	40	34	38	55	21	19	4	157	7	5	1	1.6	.970	OF-108
3 yrs.		325	.257	.341	908	233	44	3	9	1.0	125	77	90	183	70	36	10	454	16	8	3	1.6	.983	OF-298

Lyle Mouton

MOUTON, LYLE JOSEPH
B. May 13, 1969, Lafayette, La.

BR TR 6'4" 240 lbs.

Year	Team	Games	BA	SA	AB	H	2B	3B	HR	HR%	R	RBI	BB	SO	SB	AB	H	PO	A	E	DP	TC/G	FA	G by Pos
1995	CHI A	58	.302	.475	179	54	16	0	5	2.8	23	27	19	46	1	5	3	94	5	1	1	1.8	.990	OF-53, DH-2
1996		87	.294	.439	214	63	8	1	7	3.3	25	39	22	50	3	14	2	65	1	2	0	0.9	.971	OF-47, DH-28
2 yrs.		145	.298	.455	393	117	24	1	12	3.1	48	66	41	96	4	19	5	159	6	3	1	1.3	.982	OF-100, DH-30

Bill Mueller

MUELLER, WILLIAM RICHARD
B. Mar. 7, 1971, Maryland Heights, Mo.

BB TR 5'11" 175 lbs.

Year	Team	Games	BA	SA	AB	H	2B	3B	HR	HR%	R	RBI	BB	SO	SB	AB	H	PO	A	E	DP	TC/G	FA	G by Pos
1996	SF N	55	.330	.415	200	66	15	1	0	0.0	31	19	24	26	0	4	0	51	99	6	17	2.9	.962	3B-45, 2B-8

Sean Mulligan

MULLIGAN, SEAN PATRICK
B. Apr. 25, 1970, Lynwood, Calif.

BR TR 6'2" 210 lbs.

Year	Team	Games	BA	SA	AB	H	2B	3B	HR	HR%	R	RBI	BB	SO	SB	AB	H	PO	A	E	DP	TC/G	FA	G by Pos
1996	SD N	2	.000	.000	1	0	0	0	0	0.0	0	0	0	0	0	1	0	0	0	0	0	0.0	—	

Jose Munoz

MUNOZ, JOSE LUIS
B. Nov. 11, 1967, Chicago, Ill.

BB TR 5'11" 165 lbs.

Year	Team	Games	BA	SA	AB	H	2B	3B	HR	HR%	R	RBI	BB	SO	SB	AB	H	PO	A	E	DP	TC/G	FA	G by Pos
1996	CHI A	17	.259	.259	27	7	0	0	0	0.0	7	1	4	1	0	6	1	12	13	2	2	2.5	.926	2B-7, SS-2, DH-2, 3B-1, OF-1

Pedro Munoz

MUNOZ, PEDRO JAVIER
Born Pedro Javier Munoz (Gonzalez).
B. Sept. 19, 1968, Ponce, Puerto Rico

BR TR 5'11" 170 lbs.

Year	Team	Games	BA	SA	AB	H	2B	3B	HR	HR%	R	RBI	BB	SO	SB	AB	H	PO	A	E	DP	TC/G	FA	G by Pos
1990	MIN A	22	.271	.341	85	23	4	1	0	0.0	13	5	2	16	3	0	0	34	1	1	1	1.6	.972	OF-21, DH-1
1991		51	.283	.500	138	39	7	1	7	5.1	15	26	9	31	3	6	1	89	3	1	2	2.0	.989	OF-44, DH-2
1992		127	.270	.409	418	113	16	3	12	2.9	44	71	17	90	4	6	1	220	8	3	4	1.8	.987	OF-122, DH-3
1993		104	.233	.393	326	76	11	1	13	4.0	34	38	25	97	1	3	0	172	5	3	2	1.8	.983	OF-102
1994		75	.295	.508	244	72	15	2	11	4.5	35	36	19	67	0	7	1	110	1	4	0	1.6	.965	OF-58, DH-12
1995		104	.301	.489	376	113	17	0	18	4.8	45	58	19	86	0	5	2	29	4	5	1	0.4	.868	DH-77, OF-25, 1B-3
1996	OAK A	34	.256	.446	121	31	5	0	6	5.0	17	18	9	31	0	4	2	15	0	0	0	0.5	1.000	DH-18, OF-14
7 yrs.		517	.273	.444	1708	467	75	8	67	3.9	203	252	100	418	11	31	7	669	22	17	10	1.4	.976	OF-386, DH-113, 1B-3

Eddie Murray

MURRAY, EDDIE CLARENCE
Brother of Rich Murray.
B. Feb. 24, 1956, Los Angeles, Calif.

BB TR 6'2" 190 lbs.

Year	Team	Games	BA	SA	AB	H	2B	3B	HR	HR%	R	RBI	BB	SO	SB	AB	H	PO	A	E	DP	TC/G	FA	G by Pos
1977	BAL A	160	.283	.470	611	173	29	2	27	4.4	81	88	48	104	0	4	0	375	17	3	34	2.5	.992	DH-111, 1B-42, OF-3
1978		161	.285	.480	610	174	32	3	27	4.4	85	95	70	97	6	0	0	1507	112	6	144	10.1	.996	1B-157, 3B-3, DH-1
1979		159	.295	.475	606	179	30	2	25	4.1	90	99	72	78	10	0	0	1456	107	10	135	9.9	.994	1B-157, DH-2
1980		158	.300	.519	621	186	36	2	32	5.2	100	116	54	71	7	3	1	1369	77	9	158	9.4	.994	1B-154, DH-1
1981		99	.294	.534	378	111	21	2	**22**	5.8	57	**78**	40	43	2	0	0	899	91	1	98	10.0	.999	1B-99
1982		151	.316	.549	550	174	30	1	32	5.8	87	110	70	82	7	0	0	1269	97	4	106	9.1	.997	1B-149, DH-2
1983		156	.306	.538	582	178	30	3	33	5.7	115	111	86	90	5	2	0	1393	114	10	136	9.8	.993	1B-153, DH-2
1984		162	.306	.509	588	180	26	3	29	4.9	97	110	**107**	87	10	0	0	1538	143	13	152	10.5	.992	1B-159, DH-3
1985		156	.297	.523	583	173	37	1	31	5.3	111	124	84	68	5	0	0	1338	152	19	154	9.7	.987	1B-154, DH-2
1986		137	.305	.463	495	151	25	1	17	3.4	61	84	78	49	3	2	0	1045	88	13	100	8.5	.989	1B-119, DH-16
1987		160	.277	.477	618	171	28	3	30	4.9	89	91	73	80	1	0	0	1371	145	10	146	9.5	.993	1B-156, DH-4
1988		161	.284	.474	603	171	27	2	28	4.6	75	84	75	78	5	0	0	867	106	11	101	6.1	.989	1B-103, DH-58
1989	LA N	160	.247	.401	594	147	29	1	20	3.4	66	88	87	85	7	1	1	1316	137	6	122	9.1	.996	1B-159, 3B-2
1990		155	.330	.520	558	184	22	3	26	4.7	96	95	82	64	8	4	0	1180	113	10	88	8.7	.995	1B-150
1991		153	.260	.403	576	150	23	1	19	3.3	69	96	55	74	10	3	2	1327	128	7	96	9.7	.995	1B-149, 3B-1
1992	NY N	156	.261	.423	551	144	37	2	16	2.9	64	93	66	74	4	3	1	1283	96	12	109	9.0	.991	1B-154
1993		154	.285	.467	610	174	28	1	27	4.4	77	100	40	61	2	0	0	1319	111	18	118	9.4	.988	1B-154
1994	CLE A	108	.254	.425	433	110	21	1	17	3.9	57	76	31	53	8	0	0	241	14	3	25	2.4	.988	DH-82, 1B-26
1995		113	.323	.516	436	141	21	0	21	4.8	68	82	39	65	5	1	1	160	22	3	12	1.6	.984	DH-95, 1B-18
1996	2 teams CLE A (88G –.262) BAL A (64G –.257)																							
"	total	152	.260	.417	566	147	22	3	22	3.9	69	79	61	87	4	4	2	10	1	0	0	0.1	1.000	DH-149, 1B-1
20 yrs.		2971	.288	.478	11169	3218	553	35	501	4.5	1614	1899	1318	1490	109	27	8	21263	1871	168	2034	7.9	.993	1B-2413, DH-528, 3B-6, OF-3
			8th			5th						8th												

DIVISIONAL PLAYOFF SERIES

Year	Team	Games	BA	SA	AB	H	2B	3B	HR	HR%	R	RBI	BB	SO	SB	AB	H	PO	A	E	DP	TC/G	FA	G by Pos
1995	CLE A	3	.385	.769	13	5	0	1	1	7.7	3	3	2	1	0	0	0	0	0	0	0	0.0	.000	DH-3
1996	BAL A	4	.400	.467	15	6	1	0	0	0.0	1	1	3	4	1	0	0	0	0	0	0	0.0	.000	DH-4
2 yrs.		7	.393	.607	28	11	1	1	1	3.6	4	4	5	5	1	0	0	0	0	0	0	0.0		DH-7

LEAGUE CHAMPIONSHIP SERIES

Year	Team	Games	BA	SA	AB	H	2B	3B	HR	HR%	R	RBI	BB	SO	SB	AB	H	PO	A	E	DP	TC/G	FA	G by Pos
1979	BAL A	4	.417	.667	12	5	0	0	1	8.3	3	5	5	2	0	0	0	44	3	2	4	12.3	.959	1B-4
1983		4	.267	.467	15	4	0	0	1	6.7	5	3	3	3	1	0	0	36	2	1	2	9.8	.974	1B-4
1995	CLE A	6	.250	.417	24	6	1	0	1	4.2	2	3	2	3	0	0	0	0	0	0	0	0.0	.000	DH-6
1996	BAL A	5	.267	.467	15	4	0	0	1	6.7	1	2	2	2	0	1	0	0	0	0	0	0.0	.000	DH-5
4 yrs.		19	.288	.485	66	19	1	0	4	6.1	11	13	12	10	1	1	0	80	5	3	6	4.6	.966	DH-11, 1B-8
													10th											

Year	Team	Games	BA	SA	AB	H	2B	3B	HR	HR%	R	RBI	BB	SO	SB	Pinch Hit AB	Pinch Hit H	PO	A	E	DP	TC/G	FA	G by Pos

Eddie Murray *continued*

WORLD SERIES

Year	Team	Games	BA	SA	AB	H	2B	3B	HR	HR%	R	RBI	BB	SO	SB	AB	H	PO	A	E	DP	TC/G	FA	G by Pos
1979	BAL A	7	.154	.308	26	4	1	0	1	3.8	3	2	4	4	1	0	0	60	7	0	5	9.6	1.000	1B-7
1983		5	.250	.550	20	5	0	0	2	10.0	2	3	1	4	0	0	0	46	1	1	5	9.6	.979	1B-5
1995	CLE A	6	.105	.263	19	2	0	0	1	5.3	1	3	5	4	0	0	0	27	0	0	3	4.5	1.000	1B-3, DH-3
3 yrs.		18	.169	.369	65	11	1	0	4	6.2	6	8	10	12	1	0	0	133	8	1	13	7.9	.993	1B-15, DH-3

Glenn Murray

MURRAY, GLENN EVERETT
B. Nov. 23, 1970, Manning, S. C.

BR TR 6′2″ 225 lbs.

Year	Team	Games	BA	SA	AB	H	2B	3B	HR	HR%	R	RBI	BB	SO	SB	AB	H	PO	A	E	DP	TC/G	FA	G by Pos
1996	PHI N	38	.196	.289	97	19	3	0	2	2.1	8	6	7	36	1	13	2	52	1	0	0	2.0	1.000	OF-27

Greg Myers

MYERS, GREGORY RICHARD
B. Apr. 14, 1966, Riverside, Calif.

BL TR 6′1″ 200 lbs.

Year	Team	Games	BA	SA	AB	H	2B	3B	HR	HR%	R	RBI	BB	SO	SB	AB	H	PO	A	E	DP	TC/G	FA	G by Pos
1987	TOR A	7	.111	.111	9	1	0	0	0	0.0	1	0	0	3	0	0	0	24	1	0	0	3.6	1.000	C-7
1989		17	.114	.159	44	5	2	0	0	0.0	0	1	2	9	0	1	0	46	6	0	1	3.1	1.000	C-11, DH-6
1990		87	.236	.332	250	59	7	1	5	2.0	33	22	22	33	0	7	2	411	30	3	4	5.1	.993	C-87
1991		107	.262	.411	309	81	22	0	8	2.6	25	36	21	45	0	10	2	484	37	11	5	5.1	.979	C-104
1992	2 teams	TOR A	(22G −.230)		CAL A	(8G −.235)																		
"	total	30	.231	.359	78	18	7	0	1	1.3	4	13	5	11	0	4	1	125	16	1	1	5.3	.993	C-26, DH-1
1993	CAL A	108	.255	.362	290	74	10	0	7	2.4	27	40	17	47	3	25	8	369	44	6	5	4.2	.986	C-97, DH-2
1994		45	.246	.341	126	31	6	0	2	1.6	10	8	10	27	0	6	0	194	28	2	0	5.3	.991	C-41, DH-1
1995		85	.260	.418	273	71	12	2	9	3.3	35	38	17	49	0	12	0	340	21	4	5	4.7	.985	C-61, DH-16
1996	MIN A	97	.286	.426	329	94	22	3	6	1.8	37	47	19	52	0	16	6	488	26	8	5	5.8	.985	C-90
9 yrs.		583	.254	.379	1708	434	88	6	38	2.2	172	205	113	276	3	81	19	2481	209	35	26	5.0	.987	C-524, DH-26

Tim Naehring

NAEHRING, TIMOTHY JAMES
B. Feb. 1, 1967, Cincinnati, Ohio

BR TR 6′2″ 190 lbs.

Year	Team	Games	BA	SA	AB	H	2B	3B	HR	HR%	R	RBI	BB	SO	SB	AB	H	PO	A	E	DP	TC/G	FA	G by Pos
1990	BOS A	24	.271	.412	85	23	6	0	2	2.4	10	12	8	15	0	0	0	36	66	9	13	4.4	.919	SS-19, 3B-5, 2B-1
1991		20	.109	.127	55	6	1	0	0	0.0	1	3	6	15	0	1	0	17	53	3	9	3.7	.959	SS-17, 3B-2, 2B-1
1992		72	.231	.323	186	43	8	0	3	1.6	12	14	18	31	0	8	0	95	170	3	31	3.9	.989	SS-30, 2B-23, 3B-10, DH-4, OF-1
1993		39	.331	.433	127	42	10	0	1	0.8	14	17	10	26	1	6	2	45	44	2	15	2.4	.978	2B-15, DH-10, 3B-9, SS-4
1994		80	.276	.414	297	82	18	1	7	2.4	41	42	30	56	1	2	1	190	182	6	45	4.5	.984	2B-49, 3B-11, SS-9, 1B-8, DH-7
1995		126	.307	.448	433	133	27	2	10	2.3	61	57	77	66	0	2	1	86	244	16	22	2.8	.954	3B-124, DH-1
1996		116	.288	.444	430	124	16	0	17	4.0	77	65	49	63	2	2	0	81	206	11	17	2.5	.963	3B-116, 2B-1
7 yrs.		477	.281	.412	1613	453	86	3	40	2.5	216	210	198	272	4	21	4	550	965	50	152	3.3	.968	3B-277, 2B-90, SS-79, DH-22, 1B-8, OF-1

DIVISIONAL PLAYOFF SERIES

Year	Team	Games	BA	SA	AB	H	2B	3B	HR	HR%	R	RBI	BB	SO	SB	AB	H	PO	A	E	DP	TC/G	FA	G by Pos
1995	BOS A	3	.308	.538	13	4	0	0	1	7.7	2	1	0	1	0	0	0	5	5	0	0	3.3	1.000	3B-3

Bob Natal

NATAL, ROBERT MARCEL
B. Nov. 13, 1965, Long Beach, Calif.

BR TR 5′11″ 190 lbs.

Year	Team	Games	BA	SA	AB	H	2B	3B	HR	HR%	R	RBI	BB	SO	SB	AB	H	PO	A	E	DP	TC/G	FA	G by Pos
1992	MON N	5	.000	.000	6	0	0	0	0	0.0	0	0	1	1	0	1	0	10	0	1	0	2.8	.909	C-4
1993	FLA N	41	.214	.291	117	25	4	1	1	0.9	3	6	6	22	1	2	0	196	18	0	2	5.6	1.000	C-38
1994		10	.276	.345	29	8	2	0	0	0.0	2	2	5	5	1	2	0	50	9	1	0	7.5	.983	C-8
1995		16	.233	.465	43	10	2	1	2	4.7	2	6	1	9	0	3	0	80	3	1	1	6.5	.988	C-13
1996		44	.133	.167	90	12	1	1	0	0.0	4	2	15	31	0	1	0	187	14	5	1	4.8	.976	C-43
5 yrs.		116	.193	.277	285	55	9	3	3	1.1	11	16	28	68	2	9	0	523	44	8	4	5.4	.986	C-106

Phil Nevin

NEVIN, PHILLIP JOSEPH
B. Jan. 19, 1971, Fullerton, Calif.

BR TR 6′2″ 180 lbs.

Year	Team	Games	BA	SA	AB	H	2B	3B	HR	HR%	R	RBI	BB	SO	SB	AB	H	PO	A	E	DP	TC/G	FA	G by Pos
1995	2 teams	HOU N	(18G −.117)		DET A	(29G −.219)																		
"	total	47	.179	.256	156	28	4	1	2	1.3	13	13	18	40	1	4	0	60	34	5	3	2.2	.949	OF-27, 3B-17, DH-2
1996	DET A	38	.292	.533	120	35	5	0	8	6.7	15	19	8	39	1	3	0	45	51	5	6	2.7	.950	3B-24, OF-9, C-4, DH-1
2 yrs.		85	.228	.377	276	63	9	1	10	3.6	28	32	26	79	2	4	0	105	85	10	9	2.4	.950	3B-41, OF-36, C-4, DH-3

Marc Newfield

NEWFIELD, MARC ALEXANDER
B. Oct. 19, 1972, Sacramento, Calif.

BR TR 6′4″ 205 lbs.

Year	Team	Games	BA	SA	AB	H	2B	3B	HR	HR%	R	RBI	BB	SO	SB	AB	H	PO	A	E	DP	TC/G	FA	G by Pos
1993	SEA A	22	.227	.318	66	15	3	0	1	1.5	5	7	2	8	0	3	0	0	0	0	0	0.0		DH-15, OF-5
1994		12	.184	.289	38	7	1	0	1	2.6	3	4	2	4	0	2	0	2	0	0	0	0.2	1.000	DH-9, OF-3
1995	2 teams	SEA A	(24G −.188)		SD N	(21G −.309)																		
"	total	45	.236	.393	140	33	8	1	4	2.9	13	21	5	24	0	3	2	68	1	0	0	1.6	1.000	OF-43
1996	2 teams	SD N	(84G −.251)		MIL A	(49G −.307)																		
"	total	133	.278	.446	370	103	26	0	12	3.2	48	57	27	70	1	31	6	169	4	4	1	1.7	.977	OF-100, 1B-2
4 yrs.		212	.257	.410	614	158	38	1	18	2.9	69	89	36	106	1	39	8	239	5	4	1	1.4	.984	OF-151, DH-24, 1B-2

Warren Newson

NEWSON, WARREN DALE
B. July 3, 1964, Newnan, Ga.

BL TL 5′7″ 190 lbs.

Year	Team	Games	BA	SA	AB	H	2B	3B	HR	HR%	R	RBI	BB	SO	SB	AB	H	PO	A	E	DP	TC/G	FA	G by Pos
1991	CHI A	71	.295	.424	132	39	5	0	4	3.0	20	25	28	34	2	22	8	48	3	2	0	1.0	.962	OF-50, DH-3
1992		63	.221	.265	136	30	3	0	1	0.7	19	11	37	38	3	15	3	67	5	0	3	1.3	1.000	OF-50, DH-4
1993		26	.300	.450	40	12	0	0	2	5.0	9	6	9	12	0	11	5	5	0	0	0	0.3	1.000	DH-10, OF-5

Year	Team	Games	BA	SA	AB	H	2B	3B	HR	HR%	R	RBI	BB	SO	SB	Pinch Hit AB	H	PO	A	E	DP	TC/G	FA	G by Pos

Warren Newson continued

Year	Team	Games	BA	SA	AB	H	2B	3B	HR	HR%	R	RBI	BB	SO	SB	PH AB	PH H	PO	A	E	DP	TC/G	FA	G by Pos
1994		63	.255	.363	102	26	5	0	2	2.0	16	7	14	23	1	25	7	45	1	1	1	1.3	.979	OF-34, DH-3
1995	2 teams CHI A (51G −.235)				SEA A (33G −.292)																			
"	total	84	.261	.395	157	41	2	2	5	3.2	34	15	39	45	2	26	6	77	2	2	0	1.5	.975	OF-47, DH-7
1996	TEX A	91	.255	.451	235	60	14	1	10	4.3	34	31	37	82	3	17	3	122	5	1	2	1.7	.992	OF-66, DH-8
6 yrs.		398	.259	.393	802	208	29	3	24	3.0	132	95	164	234	11	116	32	364	16	6	6	1.3	.984	OF-252, DH-35
DIVISIONAL PLAYOFF SERIES																								
1995	SEA A	1	.000	.000	1	0	0	0	0	0.0	0	0	0	1	0	1	0	0	0	0	0	0.0	—	
1996	TEX A	2	.000	.000	1	0	0	0	0	0.0	0	0	1	0	0	1	0	0	0	0	0	0.0	—	
2 yrs.		3	.000	.000	2	0	0	0	0	0.0	0	0	1	1	0	2	0							
LEAGUE CHAMPIONSHIP SERIES																								
1993	CHI A	2	.200	.800	5	1	0	0	1	20.0	1	1	0	1	0	1	0	0	0	0	0	0.0	.000	DH-1

Melvin Nieves

NIEVES, MELVIN
Born Melvin Nieves (Ramos).
B. Dec. 28, 1971, San Juan, Puerto Rico

BB TR 6'2" 185 lbs.

Year	Team	Games	BA	SA	AB	H	2B	3B	HR	HR%	R	RBI	BB	SO	SB	PH AB	PH H	PO	A	E	DP	TC/G	FA	G by Pos
1992	ATL N	12	.211	.263	19	4	1	0	0	0.0	0	1	2	7	0	6	1	8	0	3	0	1.8	.727	OF-6
1993	SD N	19	.191	.319	47	9	0	0	2	4.3	4	3	3	21	0	6	0	27	0	2	0	1.9	.931	OF-15
1994		10	.263	.474	19	5	1	0	1	5.3	2	4	3	10	0	4	1	11	1	0	0	2.0	1.000	OF-6
1995		98	.205	.419	234	48	6	1	14	6.0	32	38	19	88	2	27	2	106	5	2	2	1.4	.982	OF-79, 1B-2
1996	DET A	120	.246	.485	431	106	23	4	24	5.6	71	60	44	158	1	4	1	207	9	13	2	2.0	.943	OF-105, DH-11
5 yrs.		259	.229	.448	750	172	31	5	41	5.5	109	106	71	284	3	47	5	359	15	20	4	1.8	.949	OF-211, DH-11, 1B-2

Dave Nilsson

NILSSON, DAVID WAYNE
B. Dec. 14, 1969, Brisbane, Australia

BL TR 6'3" 185 lbs.

Year	Team	Games	BA	SA	AB	H	2B	3B	HR	HR%	R	RBI	BB	SO	SB	PH AB	PH H	PO	A	E	DP	TC/G	FA	G by Pos
1992	MIL A	51	.232	.354	164	38	8	0	4	2.4	15	25	17	18	2	1	0	231	16	2	2	4.9	.992	C-46, 1B-3, DH-2
1993		100	.257	.375	296	76	10	2	7	2.4	35	40	37	36	3	4	1	457	33	9	6	5.0	.982	C-91, 1B-4, DH-4
1994		109	.275	.451	397	109	28	3	12	3.0	51	69	34	61	1	5	1	315	15	2	4	3.1	.994	C-60, DH-43, 1B-5
1995		81	.278	.468	263	73	12	1	12	4.6	41	53	24	41	2	14	2	117	7	2	1	1.6	.987	OF-58, 1B-7, C-2
1996		123	.331	.525	453	150	33	2	17	3.8	81	84	57	68	2	6	3	251	19	7	16	2.2	.975	OF-61, DH-40, 1B-24, C-2
5 yrs.		464	.284	.451	1573	446	91	8	52	3.3	223	271	169	224	10	30	7	1371	90	22	29	3.2	.985	C-201, OF-119, DH-103, 1B-43

Otis Nixon

NIXON, OTIS JUNIOR
Brother of Donell Nixon.
B. Jan. 9, 1959, Evergreen, N. C.

BB TR 6'2" 175 lbs.

Year	Team	Games	BA	SA	AB	H	2B	3B	HR	HR%	R	RBI	BB	SO	SB	PH AB	PH H	PO	A	E	DP	TC/G	FA	G by Pos
1983	NY A	13	.143	.143	14	2	0	0	0	0.0	2	0	1	5	2	0	0	14	0	1	0	1.8	.938	OF-9
1984	CLE A	49	.154	.154	91	14	0	0	0	0.0	16	1	8	11	12	0	0	81	3	0	0	1.8	1.000	OF-46
1985		104	.235	.315	162	38	4	0	3	1.9	34	9	8	27	20	2	0	129	5	4	1	1.5	.971	OF-80, DH-11
1986		105	.263	.326	95	25	4	1	0	0.0	33	8	13	12	23	3	1	90	3	3	0	1.0	.969	OF-95, DH-5
1987		19	.059	.059	17	1	0	0	0	0.0	2	1	3	4	2	0	0	21	0	0	0	1.2	1.000	OF-17
1988	MON N	90	.244	.288	271	66	8	2	0	0.0	47	15	28	42	46	11	6	176	2	1	1	2.2	.994	OF-82
1989		126	.217	.260	258	56	7	2	0	0.0	41	21	33	36	37	21	2	160	2	2	0	1.7	.988	OF-98
1990		119	.251	.307	231	58	6	2	1	0.4	46	20	28	33	50	28	6	149	6	1	1	1.8	.994	OF-88, SS-1
1991	ATL N	124	.297	.327	401	119	10	1	0	0.0	81	26	47	40	72	8	3	218	6	3	1	2.0	.987	OF-115
1992		120	.294	.346	456	134	14	2	2	0.4	79	22	39	54	41	9	4	333	6	3	1	3.1	.991	OF-111
1993		134	.269	.315	461	124	12	3	1	0.2	77	24	61	63	47	13	2	308	4	3	1	2.7	.990	OF-116
1994	BOS A	103	.274	.317	398	109	15	1	0	0.0	60	25	55	65	42	0	0	254	4	3	1	2.5	.989	OF-103
1995	TEX A	139	.295	.338	589	174	21	2	0	0.0	87	45	58	85	50	0	0	355	4	4	0	2.6	.989	OF-138
1996	TOR A	125	.286	.327	496	142	15	1	1	0.2	87	29	71	68	54	0	0	341	5	2	1	2.8	.994	OF-125
14 yrs.		1370	.270	.314	3940	1062	116	17	8	0.2	692	246	453	545	498	95	24	2629	51	30	8	2.2	.989	OF-1223, DH-16, SS-1
LEAGUE CHAMPIONSHIP SERIES																								
1992	ATL N	7	.286	.357	28	8	2	0	0	0.0	5	2	4	4	3	0	0	16	0	0	0	2.3	1.000	OF-7
1993		6	.348	.435	23	8	2	0	0	0.0	3	4	5	6	0	0	0	13	0	0	0	2.2	1.000	OF-6
2 yrs.		13	.314	.392	51	16	4	0	0	0.0	8	6	9	10	3	0	0	29	0	0	0	2.2	1.000	OF-13
WORLD SERIES																								
1992	ATL N	6	.296	.333	27	8	1	0	0	0.0	3	1	1	3	5	0	0	18	0	0	0	3.0	1.000	OF-6

Trot Nixon

NIXON, CHRISTOPHER TROTMAN
B. Apr. 11, 1974, Durham, N. C.

BL TL 6'1" 195 lbs.

Year	Team	Games	BA	SA	AB	H	2B	3B	HR	HR%	R	RBI	BB	SO	SB	PH AB	PH H	PO	A	E	DP	TC/G	FA	G by Pos
1996	BOS A	2	.500	.750	4	2	1	0	0	0.0	2	0	0	1	1	0	0	3	0	0	0	1.5	1.000	OF-2

Les Norman

NORMAN, LESLIE EUGENE
B. Feb. 25, 1969, Warren, Mich.

BR TR 6'1" 185 lbs.

Year	Team	Games	BA	SA	AB	H	2B	3B	HR	HR%	R	RBI	BB	SO	SB	PH AB	PH H	PO	A	E	DP	TC/G	FA	G by Pos
1995	KC A	24	.225	.275	40	9	0	1	0	0.0	6	4	6	6	0	5	1	23	1	1	0	1.1	.960	OF-17, DH-5
1996		54	.122	.122	49	6	0	0	0	0.0	9	0	6	14	1	8	0	44	1	0	0	1.0	1.000	OF-38, DH-7
2 yrs.		78	.169	.191	89	15	0	1	0	0.0	15	4	12	20	1	13	1	67	2	1	0	1.0	.986	OF-55, DH-12

Greg Norton

NORTON, GREGORY BLAKEMOOR
B. Jul. 6, 1972, San Leandro, Calif.

BB TR 6'1" 190 lbs.

Year	Team	Games	BA	SA	AB	H	2B	3B	HR	HR%	R	RBI	BB	SO	SB	PH AB	PH H	PO	A	E	DP	TC/G	FA	G by Pos
1996	CHI A	11	.217	.478	23	5	0	0	2	8.7	4	3	4	6	0	4	2	8	5	2	1	1.9	.867	SS-6, 3B-2, DH-1

Year	Team	Games	BA	SA	AB	H	2B	3B	HR	HR%	R	RBI	BB	SO	SB	AB	H	PO	A	E	DP	TC/G	FA	G by Pos

Jon Nunnally
NUNNALLY, JONATHAN KEITH
B. Nov. 9, 1971, Pelham, N. C. — BL TR 5'10" 190 lbs.

Year	Team	Games	BA	SA	AB	H	2B	3B	HR	HR%	R	RBI	BB	SO	SB	AB	H	PO	A	E	DP	TC/G	FA	G by Pos
1995	KC A	119	.244	.472	303	74	15	6	14	4.6	51	42	51	86	6	19	4	196	5	6	1	1.9	.971	OF-107, DH-4
1996		35	.211	.456	90	19	5	1	5	5.6	16	17	13	25	0	6	2	61	0	2	0	1.9	.968	OF-29, DH-4
2 yrs.		154	.237	.468	393	93	20	7	19	4.8	67	59	64	111	6	25	6	257	5	8	1	1.9	.970	OF-136, DH-8

Sherman Obando
OBANDO, SHERMAN OMAR
Born Sherman Omar Obando (Gainor).
B. Jan. 23, 1970, Bocas del Toro, Panama — BR TR 6'4" 215 lbs.

Year	Team	Games	BA	SA	AB	H	2B	3B	HR	HR%	R	RBI	BB	SO	SB	AB	H	PO	A	E	DP	TC/G	FA	G by Pos
1993	BAL A	31	.272	.391	92	25	2	0	3	3.3	8	15	4	26	0	3	0	13	0	1	0	0.5	.929	DH-21, OF-8
1995		16	.263	.289	38	10	1	0	0	0.0	0	3	2	12	1	6	2	12	0	1	0	0.9	.923	OF-7, DH-7
1996	MON N	89	.247	.433	178	44	9	0	8	4.5	30	22	22	48	2	41	9	74	2	3	0	1.7	.962	OF-47
3 yrs.		136	.256	.403	308	79	12	0	11	3.6	38	40	28	86	3	50	11	99	2	5	0	1.2	.953	OF-62, DH-28

Charlie O'Brien
O'BRIEN, CHARLES HUGH
B. May 1, 1960, Tulsa, Okla. — BR TR 6'2" 195 lbs.

Year	Team	Games	BA	SA	AB	H	2B	3B	HR	HR%	R	RBI	BB	SO	SB	AB	H	PO	A	E	DP	TC/G	FA	G by Pos
1985	OAK A	16	.273	.364	11	3	1	0	0	0.0	3	3	0	0	0	0	0	23	0	1	0	1.5	.958	C-16
1987	MIL A	10	.200	.343	35	7	3	1	0	0.0	2	0	4	4	0	0	0	78	11	0	0	8.9	1.000	C-10
1988		40	.220	.322	118	26	6	0	2	1.7	12	9	5	16	0	0	0	210	20	2	4	5.8	.991	C-40
1989		62	.234	.383	188	44	10	0	6	3.2	22	35	21	11	0	0	0	314	36	5	5	5.7	.986	C-62
1990	2 teams	MIL A (46G –.186)		NY N (28G –.162)																				
"	total	74	.178	.244	213	38	10	2	0	0.0	17	20	21	34	0	0	0	408	45	5	6	6.2	.989	C-74
1991	NY N	69	.185	.256	168	31	6	0	2	1.2	16	14	17	25	0	2	0	396	37	4	7	6.5	.991	C-67
1992		68	.212	.327	156	33	12	0	2	1.3	15	13	16	18	0	4	0	287	44	7	4	5.3	.979	C-64
1993		67	.255	.378	188	48	11	0	4	2.1	15	23	14	14	1	3	1	325	39	5	5	5.7	.986	C-65
1994	ATL N	51	.243	.474	152	37	11	0	8	5.3	24	28	15	24	0	3	1	308	26	3	1	7.0	.991	C-48
1995		67	.227	.399	198	45	9	0	9	4.5	18	23	29	40	0	4	1	447	23	4	5	7.4	.992	C-64
1996	TOR A	109	.238	.410	324	77	17	0	13	4.0	33	44	29	68	0	13	4	613	37	3	5	6.2	.995	C-105
11 yrs.		633	.222	.358	1751	389	94	3	46	2.6	177	210	174	257	1	29	7	3409	318	39	42	6.1	.990	C-615

DIVISIONAL PLAYOFF SERIES
| 1995 | ATL N | 2 | .200 | .200 | 5 | 1 | 0 | 0 | 0 | 0.0 | 0 | 0 | 1 | 1 | 0 | 0 | 0 | 8 | 1 | 0 | 0 | 4.5 | 1.000 | C-2 |

LEAGUE CHAMPIONSHIP SERIES
| 1995 | ATL N | 2 | .400 | 1.000 | 5 | 2 | 0 | 0 | 1 | 20.0 | 1 | 3 | 0 | 1 | 0 | 1 | 0 | 3 | 1 | 0 | 0 | 4.0 | 1.000 | C-1 |

WORLD SERIES
| 1995 | ATL N | 2 | .000 | .000 | 3 | 0 | 0 | 0 | 0 | 0.0 | 0 | 0 | 0 | 1 | 0 | 0 | 0 | 7 | 2 | 0 | 0 | 4.5 | 1.000 | C-2 |

Alex Ochoa
OCHOA, ALEX
B. Mar. 29, 1972, Miami Lakes, Fla. — BR TR 6' 175 lbs.

Year	Team	Games	BA	SA	AB	H	2B	3B	HR	HR%	R	RBI	BB	SO	SB	AB	H	PO	A	E	DP	TC/G	FA	G by Pos
1995	NY N	11	.297	.324	37	11	1	0	0	0.0	7	0	2	10	1	1	1	20	0	0	0	2.1	1.000	OF-10
1996		82	.294	.426	282	83	19	3	4	1.4	37	33	17	30	4	5	0	135	8	5	3	1.9	.966	OF-76
2 yrs.		93	.295	.414	319	94	20	3	4	1.3	44	33	19	40	5	6	1	155	9	5	3	2.0	.970	OF-86

Jose Offerman
OFFERMAN, JOSE ANTONIO
Born Jose Antonio Oferman (Dono).
B. Nov. 8, 1968, San Pedro de Macoris, Dominican Republic — BB TR 6' 150 lbs.

Year	Team	Games	BA	SA	AB	H	2B	3B	HR	HR%	R	RBI	BB	SO	SB	AB	H	PO	A	E	DP	TC/G	FA	G by Pos
1990	LA N	29	.155	.207	58	9	0	0	1	1.7	7	7	4	14	1	1	0	30	40	4	5	2.7	.946	SS-27
1991		52	.195	.212	113	22	2	0	0	0.0	10	3	25	32	3	2	0	50	121	10	17	3.6	.945	SS-50
1992		149	.260	.333	534	139	20	8	1	0.2	67	30	57	98	23	1	0	208	398	42	74	4.3	.935	SS-149
1993		158	.269	.331	590	159	21	6	1	0.2	77	62	71	75	30	1	0	250	454	37	95	4.7	.950	SS-158
1994		72	.210	.288	243	51	8	4	1	0.4	27	25	38	38	2	0	0	123	194	11	45	4.6	.966	SS-72
1995		119	.287	.375	429	123	14	6	4	0.9	69	33	69	67	2	3	0	166	312	35	56	4.5	.932	SS-115
1996	KC A	151	.303	.417	561	170	33	8	5	0.9	85	47	74	98	24	7	3	920	234	16	141	6.8	.986	1B-96, 2B-38, SS-37, OF-1
7 yrs.		730	.266	.346	2528	673	98	32	13	0.5	342	207	338	422	85	15	3	1747	1753	155	433	4.9	.958	SS-608, 1B-96, 2B-38, OF-1

DIVISIONAL PLAYOFF SERIES
| 1995 | LA N | 1 | — | — | 0 | 0 | 0 | 0 | 0 | — | 0 | 0 | 0 | 0 | 0 | 0 | 0 | 0 | 0 | 0 | 0 | 0.0 | — | |

Troy O'Leary
O'LEARY, TROY FRANKLIN
B. Aug. 4, 1969, Compton, Calif. — BL TL 6' 175 lbs.

Year	Team	Games	BA	SA	AB	H	2B	3B	HR	HR%	R	RBI	BB	SO	SB	AB	H	PO	A	E	DP	TC/G	FA	G by Pos
1993	MIL A	19	.293	.366	41	12	3	0	0	0.0	3	3	5	9	0	2	1	32	1	0	0	1.7	1.000	OF-19
1994		27	.273	.409	66	18	1	1	2	3.0	9	7	5	12	1	4	1	37	2	0	1	1.8	1.000	OF-21, DH-1
1995	BOS A	112	.308	.491	399	123	31	6	10	2.5	60	49	29	64	5	12	5	196	6	5	1	1.9	.976	OF-105, DH-3
1996		149	.260	.427	497	129	28	5	15	3.0	68	81	47	80	3	12	2	227	8	7	0	1.7	.971	OF-146
4 yrs.		307	.281	.449	1003	282	63	12	27	2.7	140	140	86	165	9	30	9	492	17	12	2	1.8	.977	OF-291, DH-4

John Olerud
OLERUD, JOHN GARRETT
B. Aug. 5, 1968, Seattle, Wash. — BL TL 6'5" 205 lbs.

Year	Team	Games	BA	SA	AB	H	2B	3B	HR	HR%	R	RBI	BB	SO	SB	AB	H	PO	A	E	DP	TC/G	FA	G by Pos
1989	TOR A	6	.375	.375	8	3	0	0	0	0.0	0	0	1	0	1	0	1	0	19	2	0	0	3.5	1.000	1B-5, DH-1
1990		111	.265	.430	358	95	15	1	14	3.9	43	48	57	75	0	7	1	133	10	2	10	1.3	.986	DH-90, 1B-18
1991		139	.256	.438	454	116	30	1	17	3.7	64	68	68	84	0	9	1	1120	78	5	77	8.8	.996	1B-135, DH-1
1992		138	.284	.450	458	130	28	0	16	3.5	68	66	70	61	1	10	4	1057	81	7	72	8.5	.994	1B-133, DH-1
1993		158	**.363**	.599	551	200	**54**	2	24	4.4	109	107	114	65	0	1	0	1160	97	10	107	8.1	.992	1B-137, DH-20

Year	Team	Games	BA	SA	AB	H	2B	3B	HR	HR%	R	RBI	BB	SO	SB	Pinch Hit AB	H	PO	A	E	DP	TC/G	FA	G by Pos

John Olerud continued

Year	Team	Games	BA	SA	AB	H	2B	3B	HR	HR%	R	RBI	BB	SO	SB	PH AB	PH H	PO	A	E	DP	TC/G	FA	G by Pos
1994		108	.297	.477	384	114	29	2	12	3.1	47	67	61	53	1	3	0	823	68	6	82	8.4	.993	1B-104, DH-3
1995		135	.291	.404	492	143	32	0	8	1.6	72	54	84	54	0	3	1	1098	90	4	102	9.0	.997	1B-133
1996		125	.274	.472	398	109	25	0	18	4.5	59	61	60	37	1	15	3	782	55	2	107	7.2	.998	1B-101, DH-15
8 yrs.		920	.293	.471	3103	910	213	6	109	3.5	464	471	514	430	3	49	10	6192	481	36	557	7.5	.995	1B-766, DH-131

LEAGUE CHAMPIONSHIP SERIES

Year	Team	Games	BA	SA	AB	H	2B	3B	HR	HR%	R	RBI	BB	SO	SB	PH AB	PH H	PO	A	E	DP	TC/G	FA	G by Pos
1991	TOR A	5	.158	.158	19	3	0	0	0	0.0	1	3	3	1	0	0	0	40	3	0	5	8.6	1.000	1B-5
1992		6	.348	.565	23	8	2	0	1	4.3	4	4	2	5	0	0	0	51	1	0	6	8.7	1.000	1B-6
1993		6	.348	.391	23	8	1	0	0	0.0	5	3	4	1	0	0	0	48	9	1	5	9.7	.983	1B-6
3 yrs.		17	.292	.385	65	19	3	0	1	1.5	10	10	9	7	0	0	0	139	13	1	16	9.0	.993	1B-17

WORLD SERIES

Year	Team	Games	BA	SA	AB	H	2B	3B	HR	HR%	R	RBI	BB	SO	SB	PH AB	PH H	PO	A	E	DP	TC/G	FA	G by Pos
1992	TOR A	4	.308	.308	13	4	0	0	0	0.0	2	0	0	4	0	0	0	25	3	0	2	7.0	1.000	1B-4
1993		5	.235	.471	17	4	1	0	1	5.9	5	2	4	1	0	0	0	36	0	0	3	7.2	1.000	1B-5
2 yrs.		9	.267	.400	30	8	1	0	1	3.3	7	2	4	5	0	0	0	61	3	0	5	7.1	1.000	1B-9

Joe Oliver

OLIVER, JOSEPH MELTON
B. July 24, 1965, Memphis, Tenn.

BR TR 6'3" 215 lbs.

Year	Team	Games	BA	SA	AB	H	2B	3B	HR	HR%	R	RBI	BB	SO	SB	PH AB	PH H	PO	A	E	DP	TC/G	FA	G by Pos
1989	CIN N	49	.272	.384	151	41	8	0	3	2.0	13	23	6	28	0	7	2	260	21	4	1	6.1	.986	C-47
1990		121	.231	.360	364	84	23	0	8	2.2	34	52	37	75	1	8	4	686	59	6	8	6.4	.992	C-118
1991		94	.216	.379	269	58	11	0	11	4.1	21	41	18	53	0	7	0	496	40	11	6	6.1	.980	C-90
1992		143	.270	.388	485	131	25	1	10	2.1	42	57	35	75	2	2	1	926	64	8	8	7.0	.992	C-141, 1B-1
1993		139	.239	.384	482	115	28	0	14	2.9	40	75	27	91	0	3	1	825	70	7	13	6.2	.992	C-133, 1B-12, OF-1
1994		6	.211	.368	19	4	0	0	1	5.3	1	5	2	3	0	0	0	48	2	1	0	8.5	.980	C-6
1995	MIL A	97	.273	.439	337	92	20	0	12	3.6	43	51	27	66	2	1	0	414	40	8	3	4.7	.983	C-91, DH-6, 1B-2
1996	CIN N	106	.242	.405	289	70	12	1	11	3.8	31	46	28	54	2	11	1	583	44	5	7	6.1	.992	C-97, OF-3, 1B-3
8 yrs.		755	.248	.391	2396	595	127	2	70	2.9	225	350	180	445	7	39	9	4238	340	50	46	6.2	.989	C-723, 1B-18, DH-6, OF-4

LEAGUE CHAMPIONSHIP SERIES

Year	Team	Games	BA	SA	AB	H	2B	3B	HR	HR%	R	RBI	BB	SO	SB	PH AB	PH H	PO	A	E	DP	TC/G	FA	G by Pos
1990	CIN N	5	.143	.143	14	2	0	0	0	0.0	1	0	1	2	0	0	0	27	1	0	0	5.6	1.000	C-5

WORLD SERIES

Year	Team	Games	BA	SA	AB	H	2B	3B	HR	HR%	R	RBI	BB	SO	SB	PH AB	PH H	PO	A	E	DP	TC/G	FA	G by Pos
1990	CIN N	4	.333	.500	18	6	3	0	0	0.0	2	2	0	1	0	0	0	27	1	3	0	7.8	.903	C-4

Paul O'Neill

O'NEILL, PAUL ANDREW
B. Feb. 25, 1963, Columbus, Ohio

BL TL 6'4" 200 lbs.

Year	Team	Games	BA	SA	AB	H	2B	3B	HR	HR%	R	RBI	BB	SO	SB	PH AB	PH H	PO	A	E	DP	TC/G	FA	G by Pos
1985	CIN N	5	.333	.417	12	4	1	0	0	0.0	1	1	0	2	0	3	1	3	1	0	0	2.0	1.000	OF-2
1986		3	.000	.000	2	0	0	0	0	0.0	0	1	1	1	0	2	0	0	0	0	0	0.0	—	
1987		84	.256	.487	160	41	14	1	7	4.4	24	28	18	29	2	37	11	90	2	4	2	2.1	.958	OF-42, 1B-2, P-1
1988		145	.252	.414	485	122	25	3	16	3.3	58	73	38	65	8	11	0	410	13	6	14	3.1	.986	OF-118, 1B-21
1989		117	.276	.446	428	118	24	2	15	3.5	49	74	46	64	20	3	3	223	7	4	1	2.0	.983	OF-115
1990		145	.270	.421	503	136	28	0	16	3.2	59	78	53	103	13	8	2	271	12	2	0	2.0	.993	OF-141
1991		152	.256	.481	532	136	36	0	28	5.3	71	91	73	107	12	4	1	301	13	2	2	2.1	.994	OF-150
1992		148	.246	.373	496	122	19	1	14	2.8	59	66	77	85	6	9	3	291	12	1	2	2.1	.997	OF-143
1993	NY A	141	.311	.504	498	155	34	1	20	4.0	71	75	44	69	2	12	1	230	7	2	1	1.7	.992	OF-138, DH-2
1994		103	.359	.603	368	132	25	1	21	5.7	68	83	72	56	5	9	4	203	7	1	0	2.0	.995	OF-99, DH-4
1995		127	.300	.526	460	138	30	4	22	4.8	82	96	71	76	1	5	2	218	3	3	0	1.8	.987	OF-121, DH-4
1996		150	.302	.474	546	165	35	1	19	3.5	89	91	102	76	0	2	0	294	7	0	3	2.0	1.000	OF-146, DH-3, 1B-1
12 yrs.		1320	.283	.468	4490	1269	271	14	178	4.0	631	756	595	733	69	105	28	2534	84	25	25	2.1	.991	OF-1215, 1B-24, DH-13, P-1

DIVISIONAL PLAYOFF SERIES

Year	Team	Games	BA	SA	AB	H	2B	3B	HR	HR%	R	RBI	BB	SO	SB	PH AB	PH H	PO	A	E	DP	TC/G	FA	G by Pos
1995	NY A	5	.333	.833	18	6	0	0	3	16.7	5	6	5	5	0	0	0	13	0	0	0	2.6	1.000	OF-5
1996		4	.133	.133	15	2	0	0	0	0.0	0	0	0	2	0	0	0	13	0	0	0	3.3	1.000	OF-4
2 yrs.		9	.242	.515	33	8	0	0	3	9.1	5	6	5	7	0	0	0	26	0	0	0	2.9	1.000	OF-9

LEAGUE CHAMPIONSHIP SERIES

Year	Team	Games	BA	SA	AB	H	2B	3B	HR	HR%	R	RBI	BB	SO	SB	PH AB	PH H	PO	A	E	DP	TC/G	FA	G by Pos
1990	CIN N	5	.471	.824	17	8	3	0	1	5.9	1	4	1	1	1	0	0	9	2	0	1	2.2	1.000	OF-5
1996	NY A	4	.273	.545	11	3	0	0	1	9.1	1	2	3	2	0	0	0	9	1	0	0	2.5	1.000	OF-4
2 yrs.		9	.393	.714	28	11	3	0	2	7.1	2	6	4	3	1	0	0	18	3	0	1	2.3	1.000	OF-9

WORLD SERIES

Year	Team	Games	BA	SA	AB	H	2B	3B	HR	HR%	R	RBI	BB	SO	SB	PH AB	PH H	PO	A	E	DP	TC/G	FA	G by Pos
1990	CIN N	4	.083	.083	12	1	0	0	0	0.0	2	1	5	2	0	0	0	11	0	0	0	2.8	1.000	OF-4
1996	NY A	5	.167	.333	12	2	2	0	0	0.0	1	0	3	2	1	0	0	12	0	0	0	3.0	1.000	OF-4
2 yrs.		9	.125	.208	24	3	2	0	0	0.0	3	1	8	4	1	0	0	23	0	0	0	2.9	1.000	OF-8

Rey Ordonez

ORDONEZ, REYNALDO
B. Jan. 11, 1972, Havana, Cuba

BR TR 5'9" 160 lbs.

Year	Team	Games	BA	SA	AB	H	2B	3B	HR	HR%	R	RBI	BB	SO	SB	PH AB	PH H	PO	A	E	DP	TC/G	FA	G by Pos
1996	NY N	151	.257	.303	502	129	12	4	1	0.2	51	30	22	53	1	2	0	230	452	27	103	4.7	.962	SS-150

Joe Orsulak

ORSULAK, JOSEPH MICHAEL
B. May 31, 1962, Glen Ridge, N. J.

BL TL 6'1" 185 lbs.

Year	Team	Games	BA	SA	AB	H	2B	3B	HR	HR%	R	RBI	BB	SO	SB	PH AB	PH H	PO	A	E	DP	TC/G	FA	G by Pos
1983	PIT N	7	.182	.182	11	2	0	0	0	0.0	0	1	0	2	0	3	0	2	0	0	0	1.0	1.000	OF-4
1984		32	.254	.328	67	17	1	2	0	0.0	12	3	1	7	3	6	1	41	1	0	0	1.7	1.000	OF-25
1985		121	.300	.365	397	119	14	6	0	0.0	54	21	26	27	24	8	4	229	10	6	1	2.1	.976	OF-115
1986		138	.249	.342	401	100	19	6	2	0.5	60	19	28	38	24	22	4	193	11	4	2	1.7	.981	OF-120
1988	BAL A	125	.288	.422	379	109	21	3	8	2.1	48	27	23	30	9	17	4	228	6	5	2	2.0	.979	OF-117
1989		123	.285	.421	390	111	22	5	7	1.8	59	55	41	35	5	15	6	250	10	4	2	2.3	.985	OF-109, DH-5
1990		124	.269	.397	413	111	14	3	11	2.7	49	57	46	48	6	14	3	267	5	3	2	2.4	.989	OF-109, DH-5
1991		143	.278	.358	486	135	22	1	5	1.0	57	43	28	45	6	14	3	273	22	1	4	2.2	.997	OF-132, DH-2

Joe Orsulak *continued*

Year	Team	Games	BA	SA	AB	H	2B	3B	HR	HR%	R	RBI	BB	SO	SB	Pinch Hit AB	H	PO	A	E	DP	TC/G	FA	G by Pos
1992		117	.289	.381	391	113	18	3	4	1.0	45	39	28	34	5	8	1	228	9	4	1	2.2	.983	OF-110, DH-1
1993	NY N	134	.284	.399	409	116	15	4	8	2.0	59	35	28	25	5	31	10	231	10	5	1	2.1	.980	OF-114, 1B-4
1994		96	.260	.353	292	76	3	0	8	2.7	39	42	16	21	4	13	2	148	9	3	3	1.7	.981	OF-90, 1B-6
1995		108	.283	.372	290	82	19	2	1	0.3	41	37	19	35	1	35	11	111	4	4	0	1.4	.966	OF-86, 1B-1
1996	FLA N	120	.221	.286	217	48	6	1	2	0.9	23	19	16	38	1	56	10	83	7	4	1	1.5	.957	OF-59, 1B-2
13 yrs.		1388	.275	.375	4143	1139	174	36	56	1.4	546	398	300	385	93	242	59	2284	106	43	19	2.0	.982	OF-1190, 1B-13, DH-13

Luis Ortiz

ORTIZ, LUIS ALBERTO
Born Luis Alberto Ortiz (Galarza).
B. May 25, 1970, Santo Domingo, Dominican Republic

BR TR 6' 190 lbs.

Year	Team	Games	BA	SA	AB	H	2B	3B	HR	HR%	R	RBI	BB	SO	SB	Pinch Hit AB	H	PO	A	E	DP	TC/G	FA	G by Pos
1993	BOS A	9	.250	.250	12	3	0	0	0	0.0	0	1	0	2	0	5	1	2	2	0	1	0.6	1.000	3B-5, DH-2
1994		7	.167	.278	18	3	2	0	0	0.0	3	6	1	5	0	1	0	0	0	0	0	0.0	.000	DH-6
1995	TEX A	41	.231	.343	108	25	5	2	1	0.9	10	18	6	18	0	10	1	9	43	8	2	1.6	.867	3B-35, DH-3
1996		3	.286	1.000	7	2	0	1	1	14.3	1	1	0	1	0	2	0	0	0	0	0	0.0	.000	DH-1
4 yrs.		60	.228	.359	145	33	7	3	2	1.4	14	26	7	26	0	18	2	11	45	8	3	1.2	.875	3B-40, DH-12

Keith Osik

OSIK, KEITH RICHARD
B. Oct. 22, 1968, Port Jefferson, N.Y.

BR TR 6' 185 lbs.

Year	Team	Games	BA	SA	AB	H	2B	3B	HR	HR%	R	RBI	BB	SO	SB	Pinch Hit AB	H	PO	A	E	DP	TC/G	FA	G by Pos
1996	PIT N	48	.293	.429	140	41	14	1	1	0.7	18	14	14	22	1	2	0	237	25	6	3	6.0	.978	C-41, 3B-2, OF-2

Ricky Otero

OTERO, RICARDO
Born Ricardo Otero (Figueroa).
B. Apr. 15, 1972, Vega Baja, Puerto Rico

BB TR 5'7" 150 lbs.

Year	Team	Games	BA	SA	AB	H	2B	3B	HR	HR%	R	RBI	BB	SO	SB	Pinch Hit AB	H	PO	A	E	DP	TC/G	FA	G by Pos
1995	NY N	35	.137	.176	51	7	2	0	0	0.0	5	1	3	10	2	11	3	31	1	0	0	1.4	1.000	OF-23
1996	PHI N	104	.273	.348	411	112	11	7	2	0.5	54	32	34	30	16	4	0	247	8	4	2	2.6	.985	OF-100
2 yrs.		139	.258	.329	462	119	13	7	2	0.4	59	33	37	40	18	15	3	278	9	4	2	2.4	.986	OF-123

Eric Owens

OWENS, ERIC BLAKE
B. Feb. 3, 1971, Danville, Va.

BR TR 6'1" 185 lbs.

Year	Team	Games	BA	SA	AB	H	2B	3B	HR	HR%	R	RBI	BB	SO	SB	Pinch Hit AB	H	PO	A	E	DP	TC/G	FA	G by Pos
1995	CIN N	2	1.000	1.000	2	2	0	0	0	0.0	0	1	0	0	0	1	1	0	0	0	0	0.0	.000	3B-2
1996		88	.200	.229	205	41	6	0	0	0.0	26	9	23	38	16	27	4	76	14	2	1	1.5	.978	OF-52, 2B-6, 3B-5
2 yrs.		90	.208	.237	207	43	6	0	0	0.0	26	10	23	38	16	28	5	76	14	2	1	1.4	.978	OF-52, 3B-7, 2B-6

Jayhawk Owens

OWENS, CLAUDE JAYHAWK
B. Feb. 10, 1969, Cincinnati, Ohio

BR TR 6'1" 213 lbs.

Year	Team	Games	BA	SA	AB	H	2B	3B	HR	HR%	R	RBI	BB	SO	SB	Pinch Hit AB	H	PO	A	E	DP	TC/G	FA	G by Pos
1993	CLR N	33	.209	.372	86	18	5	0	3	3.5	12	6	6	30	1	2	0	138	19	7	3	5.1	.957	C-32
1994		6	.250	.417	12	3	0	1	0	0.0	4	1	3	3	0	0	0	25	3	0	0	4.7	1.000	C-6
1995		18	.244	.556	45	11	2	0	4	8.9	7	12	2	15	0	2	1	79	6	1	2	5.4	.988	C-16
1996		73	.239	.367	180	43	9	1	4	2.2	31	17	27	56	4	7	1	312	27	9	3	5.1	.974	C-68
4 yrs.		130	.232	.396	323	75	16	2	11	3.4	54	36	38	104	5	11	2	554	55	17	8	5.1	.973	C-122

DIVISIONAL PLAYOFF SERIES

Year	Team	Games	BA	SA	AB	H	2B	3B	HR	HR%	R	RBI	BB	SO	SB	Pinch Hit AB	H	PO	A	E	DP	TC/G	FA	G by Pos
1995	CLR N	1	.000	.000	1	0	0	0	0	0.0	0	0	0	1	0	0	0	2	1	0	0	3.0	1.000	C-1

Tom Pagnozzi

PAGNOZZI, THOMAS ALAN
B. July 30, 1962, Tucson, Ariz.

BR TR 6' 190 lbs.

Year	Team	Games	BA	SA	AB	H	2B	3B	HR	HR%	R	RBI	BB	SO	SB	Pinch Hit AB	H	PO	A	E	DP	TC/G	FA	G by Pos
1987	STL N	27	.188	.333	48	9	1	0	2	4.2	8	9	4	13	1	7	2	61	5	0	2	2.5	1.000	C-25, 1B-1
1988		81	.282	.328	195	55	9	0	0	0.0	17	15	11	32	0	26	4	340	30	4	11	6.1	.989	1B-28, C-28, 3B-5
1989		52	.150	.175	80	12	2	0	0	0.0	3	3	6	19	0	15	2	100	9	2	1	2.7	.982	C-38, 1B-2, 3B-1
1990		69	.277	.373	220	61	15	0	2	0.9	20	23	14	37	1	4	2	345	39	4	4	6.0	.990	C-63, 1B-2
1991		140	.264	.351	459	121	24	5	2	0.4	38	57	36	63	9	0	0	682	81	7	9	5.4	.991	C-139, 1B-3
1992		139	.249	.359	485	121	26	3	7	1.4	33	44	28	64	2	3	0	688	53	1	10	5.4	.999	C-138
1993		92	.258	.373	330	85	15	1	7	2.1	31	41	19	30	1	1	0	421	44	4	4	5.1	.991	C-92
1994		70	.272	.416	243	66	12	1	7	2.9	21	40	21	39	0	0	0	370	41	1	3	5.8	.998	C-70, 1B-1
1995		62	.215	.315	219	47	14	1	2	0.9	17	15	11	31	0	1	0	336	38	2	1	6.2	.995	C-61
1996		119	.270	.423	407	110	23	0	13	3.2	48	55	24	78	4	2	2	717	48	8	6	6.6	.990	C-116, 1B-1
10 yrs.		851	.256	.363	2686	687	141	11	42	1.6	236	302	174	406	18	59	12	4060	388	33	51	5.5	.993	C-770, 1B-38, 3B-6

DIVISIONAL PLAYOFF SERIES

Year	Team	Games	BA	SA	AB	H	2B	3B	HR	HR%	R	RBI	BB	SO	SB	Pinch Hit AB	H	PO	A	E	DP	TC/G	FA	G by Pos
1996	STL N	3	.273	.273	11	3	0	0	0	0.0	0	2	1	3	0	0	0	28	0	0	0	9.3	1.000	C-3

LEAGUE CHAMPIONSHIP SERIES

Year	Team	Games	BA	SA	AB	H	2B	3B	HR	HR%	R	RBI	BB	SO	SB	Pinch Hit AB	H	PO	A	E	DP	TC/G	FA	G by Pos
1987	STL N	1	.000	.000	1	0	0	0	0	0.0	0	0	0	1	0	1	0	0	0	0	0	0.0	—	
1996		7	.158	.211	19	3	1	0	0	0.0	1	1	1	4	0	1	0	49	1	0	0	7.1	1.000	C-7
2 yrs.		8	.150	.200	20	3	1	0	0	0.0	1	1	1	4	0	1	0	49	1	0	0	7.1	1.000	C-7

WORLD SERIES

Year	Team	Games	BA	SA	AB	H	2B	3B	HR	HR%	R	RBI	BB	SO	SB	Pinch Hit AB	H	PO	A	E	DP	TC/G	FA	G by Pos
1987	STL N	2	.250	.250	4	1	0	0	0	0.0	0	0	0	0	0	1	0	0	0	0	0	0.0	.000	DH-1

Orlando Palmeiro

PALMEIRO, ORLANDO
B. Jan. 19, 1969, Hoboken, N.J.

BL TR 5'11" 155 lbs.

Year	Team	Games	BA	SA	AB	H	2B	3B	HR	HR%	R	RBI	BB	SO	SB	Pinch Hit AB	H	PO	A	E	DP	TC/G	FA	G by Pos
1995	CAL A	15	.350	.350	20	7	0	0	0	0.0	3	1	1	1	0	9	3	7	0	0	0	0.9	1.000	OF-7, DH-1
1996		50	.287	.379	87	25	6	1	0	0.0	6	6	8	13	0	17	4	34	0	0	0	1.0	1.000	OF-31, DH-4
2 yrs.		65	.299	.374	107	32	6	1	0	0.0	9	7	9	14	0	26	7	41	0	0	0	1.0	1.000	OF-38, DH-5

Year	Team	Games	BA	SA	AB	H	2B	3B	HR	HR%	R	RBI	BB	SO	SB	Pinch Hit AB	Pinch Hit H	PO	A	E	DP	TC/G	FA	G by Pos

Rafael Palmeiro

PALMEIRO, RAFAEL
Born Rafael Palmeiro (Corrales).
B. Sept. 24, 1964, Havana, Cuba
BL TL 6' 180 lbs.

Year	Team	Games	BA	SA	AB	H	2B	3B	HR	HR%	R	RBI	BB	SO	SB	PH AB	PH H	PO	A	E	DP	TC/G	FA	G by Pos
1986	CHI N	22	.247	.425	73	18	4	0	3	4.1	9	12	4	6	1	2	0	34	2	4	1	2.0	.900	OF-20
1987		84	.276	.543	221	61	15	1	14	6.3	32	30	20	26	2	27	5	176	9	1	16	3.0	.995	OF-45, 1B-18
1988		152	.307	.436	580	178	41	5	8	1.4	75	53	38	34	12	5	0	322	11	5	2	2.2	.985	OF-147, 1B-5
1989	TEX A	156	.275	.374	559	154	23	4	8	1.4	76	64	63	48	4	3	1	1167	119	12	106	8.5	.991	1B-147, DH-6
1990		154	.319	.468	598	**191**	35	6	14	2.3	72	89	40	59	3	4	0	1215	91	7	123	8.6	.995	1B-146, DH-6
1991		159	.322	.532	631	203	**49**	3	26	4.1	115	88	68	72	4	3	2	1305	96	12	119	8.9	.992	1B-157, DH-2
1992		159	.268	.434	608	163	27	4	22	3.6	84	85	72	83	2	3	0	1251	143	7	131	8.9	.995	1B-156, DH-2
1993		160	.295	.554	597	176	40	2	37	6.2	**124**	105	73	85	22	1	0	1388	147	5	133	9.6	.997	1B-160
1994	BAL A	111	.319	.550	436	139	32	0	23	5.3	82	76	54	63	7	0	0	958	67	4	86	9.3	.996	1B-111
1995		143	.310	.583	554	172	30	2	39	7.0	89	104	62	65	3	1	0	1178	123	4	120	9.2	.997	1B-142
1996		162	.289	.546	626	181	40	2	39	6.2	110	142	95	96	8	0	0	1383	116	8	157	9.3	.995	1B-159, DH-3
11 yrs.		1462	.298	.498	5483	1636	336	29	233	4.2	868	848	589	637	68	49	8	10377	924	69	994	7.9	.994	1B-1201, OF-212, DH-19

DIVISIONAL PLAYOFF SERIES

1996	BAL A	4	.176	.412	17	3	1	0	1	5.9	4	2	1	6	0	0	0	35	1	1	2	9.3	.973	1B-4

LEAGUE CHAMPIONSHIP SERIES

1996	BAL A	5	.235	.588	17	4	0	0	2	11.8	4	4	4	4	0	0	0	44	3	0	6	9.4	1.000	1B-5

Dean Palmer

PALMER, DEAN WILLIAM
B. Dec. 27, 1968, Tallahassee, Fla.
BR TR 6'1" 175 lbs.

Year	Team	Games	BA	SA	AB	H	2B	3B	HR	HR%	R	RBI	BB	SO	SB	PH AB	PH H	PO	A	E	DP	TC/G	FA	G by Pos
1989	TEX A	16	.105	.211	19	2	2	0	0	0.0	0	1	0	12	0	6	0	3	4	2	0	0.6	.778	3B-6, DH-6, SS-1, OF-1
1991		81	.187	.403	268	50	9	2	15	5.6	38	37	32	98	0	5	2	69	75	9	6	1.8	.941	3B-50, OF-29, DH-5
1992		152	.229	.420	541	124	25	0	26	4.8	74	72	62	**154**	10	4	2	124	254	22	24	2.7	.945	3B-150
1993		148	.245	.503	519	127	31	2	33	6.4	88	96	53	154	11	0	0	86	258	29	21	2.5	.922	3B-148, SS-1
1994		93	.246	.465	342	84	14	2	19	5.6	50	59	26	89	3	3	1	50	181	22	7	2.8	.913	3B-91
1995		36	.336	.613	119	40	6	0	9	7.6	30	24	21	21	1	1	0	19	73	5	7	2.7	.948	3B-36
1996		154	.280	.527	582	163	26	2	38	6.5	98	107	59	145	2	0	0	105	218	16	17	2.2	.953	3B-154, DH-1
7 yrs.		680	.247	.477	2390	590	113	8	140	5.9	378	396	253	673	27	19	5	456	1063	105	82	2.4	.935	3B-635, OF-30, DH-12, SS-2

DIVISIONAL PLAYOFF SERIES

1996	TEX A	4	.211	.421	19	4	1	0	1	5.3	3	2	0	5	0	0	0	3	10	1	0	3.5	.929	3B-4

Craig Paquette

PAQUETTE, CRAIG HAROLD
B. Mar. 28, 1969, Long Beach, Calif.
BR TR 6' 190 lbs.

Year	Team	Games	BA	SA	AB	H	2B	3B	HR	HR%	R	RBI	BB	SO	SB	PH AB	PH H	PO	A	E	DP	TC/G	FA	G by Pos
1993	OAK A	105	.219	.382	393	86	20	4	12	3.1	35	46	14	108	4	4	1	82	165	13	17	2.5	.950	3B-104, OF-1, DH-1
1994		14	.143	.184	49	7	2	0	0	0.0	0	0	0	14	1	1	0	14	22	0	3	2.6	1.000	3B-14
1995		105	.226	.417	283	64	13	1	13	4.6	42	49	12	88	5	8	3	72	91	8	18	1.6	.953	3B-75, OF-20, SS-8, 1B-3
1996	KC A	118	.259	.452	429	111	15	1	22	5.1	61	67	23	101	5	4	1	261	101	14	35	2.8	.963	3B-51, OF-47, 1B-19, SS-11, DH-6
4 yrs.		342	.232	.408	1154	268	50	6	47	4.1	138	162	49	311	15	17	5	429	379	35	73	2.3	.958	3B-244, OF-68, 1B-22, SS-19, DH-7

Mark Parent

PARENT, MARK ALAN
B. Sept. 16, 1961, Ashland, Ore.
BR TR 6'5" 215 lbs.

Year	Team	Games	BA	SA	AB	H	2B	3B	HR	HR%	R	RBI	BB	SO	SB	PH AB	PH H	PO	A	E	DP	TC/G	FA	G by Pos
1986	SD N	8	.143	.143	14	2	0	0	0	0.0	1	0	1	3	0	4	0	16	0	2	0	6.0	.889	C-3
1987		12	.080	.080	25	2	0	0	0	0.0	0	2	0	9	0	2	0	36	3	0	0	3.9	1.000	C-10
1988		41	.195	.373	118	23	3	0	6	5.1	9	15	6	23	0	3	1	203	15	3	3	6.1	.986	C-36
1989		52	.191	.369	141	27	4	0	7	5.0	12	21	8	34	1	9	2	246	17	0	2	6.3	1.000	C-41, 1B-1
1990		65	.222	.328	189	42	11	0	3	1.6	13	16	16	29	1	5	1	324	31	3	6	6.0	.992	C-60
1991	TEX A	3	.000	.000	1	0	0	0	0	0.0	0	0	0	1	0	0	0	5	0	0	0	1.7	1.000	C-3
1992	BAL A	17	.235	.441	34	8	1	0	2	5.9	4	4	3	7	0	1	0	73	7	1	1	5.1	.988	C-16
1993		22	.259	.519	54	14	2	0	4	7.4	7	12	3	14	0	2	1	83	5	1	0	4.0	.989	C-21, DH-1
1994	CHI N	44	.263	.394	99	26	4	0	3	3.0	8	16	13	24	0	4	2	184	21	5	1	5.7	.976	C-37
1995	2 teams	PIT N (69G –.232)		CHI N (12G –.250)																				
"	total	81	.234	.479	265	62	11	0	18	6.8	30	38	26	69	0	7	2	431	44	4	1	6.2	.992	C-77
1996	2 teams	DET A (38G –.240)		BAL A (18G –.182)																				
"	total	56	.226	.474	137	31	7	0	9	6.6	17	23	5	37	0	3	1	232	16	2	5	4.8	.992	C-51, 1B-1
11 yrs.		401	.220	.405	1077	237	43	0	52	4.8	101	147	81	250	2	40	10	1833	159	21	19	5.6	.990	C-355, 1B-2, DH-1

DIVISIONAL PLAYOFF SERIES

1996	BAL A	4	.200	.200	5	1	0	0	0	0.0	0	0	0	2	0	0	0	19	0	0	0	4.8	1.000	C-4

LEAGUE CHAMPIONSHIP SERIES

1996	BAL A	2	.167	.167	6	1	0	0	0	0.0	0	0	0	2	0	0	0	14	0	0	0	7.0	1.000	C-2

Rick Parker

PARKER, RICHARD ALAN
B. Mar. 20, 1963, Kansas City, Mo.
BR TR 6' 185 lbs.

Year	Team	Games	BA	SA	AB	H	2B	3B	HR	HR%	R	RBI	BB	SO	SB	PH AB	PH H	PO	A	E	DP	TC/G	FA	G by Pos
1990	SF N	54	.243	.346	107	26	5	0	2	1.9	19	14	10	15	6	19	4	45	3	2	0	1.3	.960	OF-35, 2B-2, SS-1, 3B-1
1991		13	.071	.071	14	1	0	0	0	0.0	0	0	1	5	0	8	0	5	0	0	0	1.3	1.000	OF-4
1993	HOU N	45	.333	.400	45	15	3	0	0	0.0	11	4	3	8	1	18	5	18	0	0	0	1.0	1.000	OF-16, 2B-1, SS-1
1994	NY N	8	.063	.063	16	1	0	0	0	0.0	1	0	0	2	0	1	0	14	1	0	0	2.5	1.000	OF-6
1995	LA N	27	.276	.276	29	8	0	0	0	0.0	3	4	2	4	1	4	0	20	1	0	1	0.8	1.000	OF-21, SS-2, 3B-2
1996		16	.286	.357	14	4	1	0	0	0.0	2	1	0	2	1	10	3	1	0	0	0	0.3	1.000	OF-4
6 yrs.		163	.244	.311	225	55	9	0	2	0.9	36	24	16	36	9	60	12	103	5	2	1	1.1	.982	OF-86, SS-4, 3B-3, 2B-3

Year	Team	Games	BA	SA	AB	H	2B	3B	HR	HR%	R	RBI	BB	SO	SB	Pinch Hit AB	H	PO	A	E	DP	TC/G	FA	G by Pos

Dan Peltier

PELTIER, DANIEL EDWARD
B. June 30, 1968, Clifton Park, N. Y.

BL TL 6' 1" 200 lbs.

Year	Team	Games	BA	SA	AB	H	2B	3B	HR	HR%	R	RBI	BB	SO	SB	PH AB	PH H	PO	A	E	DP	TC/G	FA	G by Pos
1992	TEX A	12	.167	.167	24	4	0	0	0	0.0	1	2	0	3	0	3	0	6	0	1	0	0.7	.857	OF-10
1993		65	.269	.344	160	43	7	1	1	0.6	23	17	20	27	0	8	0	80	4	4	2	1.5	.955	OF-55, 1B-5
1996	SF N	31	.254	.288	59	15	2	0	0	0.0	3	9	7	9	0	14	5	87	6	0	11	6.6	1.000	1B-13, OF-1
3 yrs.		108	.255	.313	243	62	9	1	1	0.4	27	28	27	39	0	25	5	173	10	5	13	2.2	.973	OF-66, 1B-18

Rudy Pemberton

PEMBERTON, RUDY HECTOR
Born Rudy Hector Pemberton (Perez).
B. Dec. 17, 1969, San Pedro de Macoris, Dominican Republic

BR TR 6' 1" 185 lbs.

Year	Team	Games	BA	SA	AB	H	2B	3B	HR	HR%	R	RBI	BB	SO	SB	PH AB	PH H	PO	A	E	DP	TC/G	FA	G by Pos
1995	DET A	12	.300	.467	30	9	3	1	0	0.0	3	3	1	5	0	1	0	15	0	0	0	1.4	1.000	OF-8, DH-3
1996	BOS A	13	.512	.780	41	21	8	0	1	2.4	11	10	2	4	3	2	1	9	0	0	0	0.7	1.000	OF-13
2 yrs.		25	.423	.648	71	30	11	1	1	1.4	14	13	3	9	3	3	1	24	0	0	0	1.0	1.000	OF-21, DH-3

Geronimo Pena

PENA, GERONIMO
Born Geronimo Pena (Martinez).
B. Mar. 29, 1967, Distrito Nacional, Dominican Republic

BB TR 6' 1" 170 lbs.

Year	Team	Games	BA	SA	AB	H	2B	3B	HR	HR%	R	RBI	BB	SO	SB	PH AB	PH H	PO	A	E	DP	TC/G	FA	G by Pos
1990	STL N	18	.244	.289	45	11	2	0	0	0.0	5	2	4	14	1	6	3	24	30	1	7	5.0	.982	2B-11
1991		104	.243	.400	185	45	8	3	5	2.7	38	17	18	45	15	11	3	101	146	6	28	2.9	.976	2B-83, OF-4
1992		62	.305	.478	203	62	12	1	7	3.4	31	31	24	37	13	3	2	125	184	5	40	5.5	.984	2B-57
1993		74	.256	.406	254	65	19	2	5	2.0	34	30	25	71	13	8	0	140	200	12	47	5.5	.966	2B-64
1994		83	.254	.479	213	54	13	1	11	5.2	33	34	24	54	9	17	2	119	170	3	42	4.9	.990	2B-59, 3B-1
1995		32	.267	.376	101	27	6	1	1	1.0	20	8	16	30	3	6	0	50	73	3	18	4.0	.976	2B-25
1996	CLE A	5	.111	.444	9	1	0	0	1	11.1	1	2	1	4	0	2	0	2	3	0	1	1.3	1.000	3B-3, 2B-1
7 yrs.		378	.262	.427	1010	265	60	8	30	3.0	162	124	112	255	54	53	10	561	806	30	183	4.5	.979	2B-300, 3B-4, OF-4

Tony Pena

PENA, ANTONIO FRANCESCO
Born Antonio Francesco Pena (Padilla).
Brother of Ramon Pena.
B. June 4, 1957, Monte Cristi, Dominican Republic

BR TR 6' 175 lbs.

Year	Team	Games	BA	SA	AB	H	2B	3B	HR	HR%	R	RBI	BB	SO	SB	PH AB	PH H	PO	A	E	DP	TC/G	FA	G by Pos
1980	PIT N	8	.429	.571	21	9	1	1	0	0.0	1	1	0	4	0	2	1	38	2	2	0	7.0	.952	C-6
1981		66	.300	.381	210	63	9	1	2	1.0	16	17	8	23	1	2	1	286	41	5	10	5.2	.985	C-64
1982		138	.296	.435	497	147	28	4	11	2.2	53	63	17	57	2	0	0	763	89	16	6	6.3	.982	C-137
1983		151	.301	.435	542	163	22	3	15	2.8	51	70	31	73	6	2	1	976	90	9	9	7.2	.992	C-149
1984		147	.286	.425	546	156	27	2	15	2.7	77	78	36	79	12	1	1	895	95	9	15	6.8	.991	C-146
1985		147	.249	.361	546	136	27	2	10	1.8	53	59	29	67	12	0	0	925	102	12	9	7.1	.988	C-146, 1B-1
1986		144	.288	.406	510	147	26	2	10	2.0	56	52	53	69	9	7	1	824	99	18	13	6.6	.981	C-139, 1B-4
1987	STL N	116	.214	.307	384	82	13	4	5	1.3	40	44	36	54	6	4	1	624	51	8	8	5.8	.988	C-112, 1B-4, OF-2
1988		149	.263	.372	505	133	23	1	10	2.0	55	51	33	60	6	8	1	796	72	6	9	6.0	.993	C-142, 1B-3
1989		141	.259	.337	424	110	17	2	4	0.9	36	37	35	33	5	7	1	675	70	2	13	5.5	.997	C-134, OF-1
1990	BOS A	143	.263	.348	491	129	19	1	7	1.4	62	56	43	71	8	5	2	866	74	5	13	6.6	.995	C-142, 1B-1
1991		141	.231	.321	464	107	23	2	5	1.1	45	48	37	53	8	1	0	864	60	5	15	6.6	.995	C-140
1992		133	.241	.305	410	99	21	1	1	0.2	39	38	24	61	3	1	1	786	57	6	12	6.4	.993	C-132
1993		126	.181	.257	304	55	11	0	4	1.3	20	19	25	46	1	0	0	698	53	4	6	6.0	.995	C-125
1994	CLE A	40	.295	.438	112	33	8	1	2	1.8	18	10	9	11	0	0	0	209	17	1	0	5.7	.996	C-40
1995		91	.262	.376	263	69	15	0	5	1.9	25	28	14	44	1	0	0	508	36	7	2	6.1	.987	C-91
1996		67	.195	.236	174	34	4	0	1	0.6	14	27	15	25	0	0	0	337	26	3	6	5.5	.992	C-67
17 yrs.		1948	.261	.366	6403	1672	294	27	107	1.7	661	698	445	830	80	40	11	11070	1034	118	146	6.3	.990	C-1912, 1B-13, OF-3

DIVISIONAL PLAYOFF SERIES

Year	Team	Games	BA	SA	AB	H	2B	3B	HR	HR%	R	RBI	BB	SO	SB	PH AB	PH H	PO	A	E	DP	TC/G	FA	G by Pos
1995	CLE A	2	.500	2.000	2	1	0	0	1	50.0	1	1	0	0	0	0	0	5	0	0	0	2.5	1.000	C-2
1996		1	—	—	0	0	0	0	0	—	0	0	0	0	0	0	0	1	0	0	0	1.0	1.000	C-1
2 yrs.		3	.500	2.000	2	1	0	0	1	50.0	1	1	0	0	0	0	0	6	0	0	0	2.0	1.000	C-3

LEAGUE CHAMPIONSHIP SERIES

Year	Team	Games	BA	SA	AB	H	2B	3B	HR	HR%	R	RBI	BB	SO	SB	PH AB	PH H	PO	A	E	DP	TC/G	FA	G by Pos
1987	STL N	7	.381	.476	21	8	1	0	0	0.0	5	0	3	4	1	0	0	55	5	0	0	8.6	1.000	C-7
1990	BOS A	4	.214	.214	14	3	0	0	0	0.0	0	0	0	0	0	0	0	22	4	1	1	6.8	.963	C-4
1995	CLE A	4	.333	.500	6	2	1	0	0	0.0	1	0	1	0	0	0	0	15	1	0	0	4.0	1.000	C-4
3 yrs.		15	.317	.390	41	13	1	1	0	0.0	6	0	4	4	1	0	0	92	10	1	1	6.9	.990	C-15

WORLD SERIES

Year	Team	Games	BA	SA	AB	H	2B	3B	HR	HR%	R	RBI	BB	SO	SB	PH AB	PH H	PO	A	E	DP	TC/G	FA	G by Pos
1987	STL N	7	.409	.455	22	9	1	0	0	0.0	2	4	3	2	1	0	0	32	1	1	0	4.9	.971	C-6, DH-1
1995	CLE A	2	.167	.167	6	1	0	0	0	0.0	0	0	0	2	0	0	0	7	1	0	0	4.0	1.000	C-2
2 yrs.		9	.357	.393	28	10	1	0	0	0.0	2	4	3	2	1	0	0	39	2	1	0	4.7	.976	C-8, DH-1

Terry Pendleton

PENDLETON, TERRY LEE
B. July 16, 1960, Los Angeles, Calif.

BB TR 5' 9" 180 lbs.

Year	Team	Games	BA	SA	AB	H	2B	3B	HR	HR%	R	RBI	BB	SO	SB	PH AB	PH H	PO	A	E	DP	TC/G	FA	G by Pos
1984	STL N	67	.324	.420	262	85	16	3	1	0.4	37	33	16	32	20	1	0	59	155	13	10	3.4	.943	3B-66
1985		149	.240	.306	559	134	16	3	5	0.9	56	69	37	75	17	2	1	129	361	18	26	3.4	.965	3B-149
1986		159	.239	.306	578	138	26	5	1	0.2	56	59	34	59	24	3	0	133	371	20	36	3.3	.962	3B-156, OF-1
1987		159	.286	.412	583	167	29	4	12	2.1	82	96	70	74	19	1	1	117	369	26	27	3.2	.949	3B-158
1988		110	.253	.361	391	99	20	2	6	1.5	44	53	21	51	3	11	4	75	239	12	13	3.2	.963	3B-101
1989		162	.264	.390	613	162	28	5	13	2.1	83	74	44	81	9	3	0	113	392	15	25	3.2	.971	3B-161
1990		121	.230	.324	447	103	20	2	6	1.3	46	58	30	58	7	5	3	91	248	19	18	3.1	.947	3B-117
1991	ATL N	153	.319	.517	586	187	34	8	22	3.8	94	86	43	70	10	4	1	108	349	24	31	3.3	.950	3B-148
1992		160	.311	.473	640	199	39	1	21	3.3	98	105	37	67	5	2	0	133	325	19	27	3.0	.960	3B-158
1993		161	.272	.408	633	172	33	1	17	2.7	81	84	36	97	5	2	0	128	319	19	32	2.9	.959	3B-161

Year	Team	Games	BA	SA	AB	H	2B	3B	HR	HR%	R	RBI	BB	SO	SB	Pinch Hit AB	H	PO	A	E	DP	TC/G	FA	G by Pos

Terry Pendleton *continued*

Year	Team	Games	BA	SA	AB	H	2B	3B	HR	HR%	R	RBI	BB	SO	SB	AB	H	PO	A	E	DP	TC/G	FA	G by Pos
1994		77	.252	.398	309	78	18	3	7	2.3	25	30	12	57	2	0	0	60	147	11	12	2.8	.950	3B-77
1995	FLA N	133	.290	.439	513	149	32	1	14	2.7	70	78	38	84	1	4	1	104	249	18	21	2.9	.951	3B-130
1996	2 teams	FLA N (111G –.251)			ATL N (42G –.204)																			
"	total	153	.238	.345	568	135	26	1	11	1.9	51	75	41	111	2	4	0	109	292	19	25	2.8	.955	3B-149
13 yrs.		1764	.271	.394	6682	1808	337	39	136	2.0	823	900	459	916	124	42	11	1359	3816	233	303	3.1	.957	3B-1731, OF-1

DIVISIONAL PLAYOFF SERIES

Year	Team	Games	BA	SA	AB	H	2B	3B	HR	HR%	R	RBI	BB	SO	SB	AB	H	PO	A	E	DP	TC/G	FA	G by Pos
1996	ATL N	1	.000	.000	1	0	0	0	0	0.0	0	0	0	1	0	1	0	0	0	0	0	0.0	—	

LEAGUE CHAMPIONSHIP SERIES

Year	Team	Games	BA	SA	AB	H	2B	3B	HR	HR%	R	RBI	BB	SO	SB	AB	H	PO	A	E	DP	TC/G	FA	G by Pos
1985	STL N	6	.208	.250	24	5	1	0	0	0.0	2	4	1	2	0	0	0	6	18	1	2	4.2	.960	3B-6
1987		6	.211	.316	19	4	0	1	0	0.0	3	1	0	6	0	0	0	3	11	0	1	2.3	1.000	3B-6
1991	ATL N	7	.167	.267	30	5	1	0	0	0.0	1	1	1	3	0	0	0	5	11	0	1	2.3	1.000	3B-7
1992		7	.233	.300	30	7	2	0	0	0.0	2	3	0	2	0	0	0	4	18	0	2	3.1	1.000	3B-7
1993		6	.346	.500	26	9	1	0	1	3.8	4	5	0	2	0	0	0	7	5	0	1	2.0	1.000	3B-6
1996		6	.000	.000	6	0	0	0	0	0.0	0	0	1	3	0	4	0	0	1	0	1	0.5	1.000	3B-2
6 yrs.		38	.222	.311	135	30	5	2	1	0.7	12	14	3	18	0	4	0	25	64	1	8	2.6	.989	3B-34
		2nd			2nd	7th		4th				9th		10th										

WORLD SERIES

Year	Team	Games	BA	SA	AB	H	2B	3B	HR	HR%	R	RBI	BB	SO	SB	AB	H	PO	A	E	DP	TC/G	FA	G by Pos
1985	STL N	7	.261	.391	23	6	1	1	0	0.0	3	3	3	2	0	0	0	6	14	1	3	3.0	.952	3B-7
1987		3	.429	.429	7	3	0	0	0	0.0	2	1	1	1	2	0	0	0	0	0	0	0.0	.000	DH-2
1991	ATL N	7	.367	.667	30	11	3	0	2	6.7	6	3	3	1	0	0	0	3	20	2	2	3.6	.920	3B-7
1992		6	.240	.320	25	6	2	0	0	0.0	2	2	1	5	0	0	0	4	19	0	1	3.8	1.000	3B-6
1996		4	.222	.333	9	2	1	0	0	0.0	1	0	1	1	0	1	0	0	2	0	0	0.7	1.000	DH-2, 3B-1
5 yrs.		27	.298	.457	94	28	7	1	2	2.1	14	9	9	10	2	1	0	13	55	3	6	2.8	.958	3B-21, DH-4

Shannon Penn

PENN, SHANNON DION
B. Sept. 11, 1969, Cincinnati, Ohio
BB TR 5'10" 163 lbs.

Year	Team	Games	BA	SA	AB	H	2B	3B	HR	HR%	R	RBI	BB	SO	SB	AB	H	PO	A	E	DP	TC/G	FA	G by Pos
1995	DET A	3	.333	.333	9	3	0	0	0	0.0	0	1	0	2	0	0	0	10	9	3	4	7.3	.864	2B-3
1996		6	.071	.071	14	1	0	0	0	0.0	0	1	0	3	0	1	0	0	0	0	0	0.0		DH-4, OF-1
2 yrs.		9	.174	.174	23	4	0	0	0	0.0	0	1	1	5	0	1	0	10	9	3	4	2.8	.864	DH-4, 2B-3, OF-1

Danny Perez

PEREZ, DANIEL
B. Feb. 26, 1971, El Paso, Tex.
BR TR 5'10" 188 lbs.

Year	Team	Games	BA	SA	AB	H	2B	3B	HR	HR%	R	RBI	BB	SO	SB	AB	H	PO	A	E	DP	TC/G	FA	G by Pos
1966	MIL A	4	.000	.000	4	0	0	0	0	0.0	0	0	0	0	0	0	0	5	0	0	0	1.7	1.000	OF-3, DH-1

Eddie Perez

PEREZ, EDUARDO
B. May 4, 1968, Ciudad Ojeda, Venezuela
BR TR 6'1" 175 lbs.

Year	Team	Games	BA	SA	AB	H	2B	3B	HR	HR%	R	RBI	BB	SO	SB	AB	H	PO	A	E	DP	TC/G	FA	G by Pos
1995	ATL N	7	.308	.615	13	4	1	0	1	7.7	1	4	0	2	0	1	0	34	2	0	3	6.0	1.000	C-5, 1B-1
1996		68	.256	.404	156	40	9	1	4	2.6	19	17	8	19	0	5	1	281	22	3	11	5.0	.990	C-54, 1B-7
2 yrs.		75	.260	.420	169	44	10	1	5	3.0	20	21	8	21	0	6	1	315	24	3	14	5.1	.991	C-59, 1B-8

DIVISIONAL PLAYOFF SERIES

Year	Team	Games	BA	SA	AB	H	2B	3B	HR	HR%	R	RBI	BB	SO	SB	AB	H	PO	A	E	DP	TC/G	FA	G by Pos
1996	ATL N	1	.333	.333	3	1	0	0	0	0.0	0	0	0	0	0	0	0	10	0	0	0	10.0	1.000	C-1

LEAGUE CHAMPIONSHIP SERIES

Year	Team	Games	BA	SA	AB	H	2B	3B	HR	HR%	R	RBI	BB	SO	SB	AB	H	PO	A	E	DP	TC/G	FA	G by Pos
1996	ATL N	4	.000	.000	1	0	0	0	0	0.0	0	0	1	0	0	0	0	7	0	0	1	1.8	1.000	C-3, 1B-1

WORLD SERIES

Year	Team	Games	BA	SA	AB	H	2B	3B	HR	HR%	R	RBI	BB	SO	SB	AB	H	PO	A	E	DP	TC/G	FA	G by Pos
1996	ATL N	2	.000	.000	1	0	0	0	0	0.0	0	0	0	0	0	0	0	2	0	0	0	1.0	1.000	C-2

Eduardo Perez

PEREZ, EDUARDO ATANACIO
Son of Tony Perez.
B. Sept. 11, 1969, Cincinnati, Ohio
BR TR 6'4" 215 lbs.

Year	Team	Games	BA	SA	AB	H	2B	3B	HR	HR%	R	RBI	BB	SO	SB	AB	H	PO	A	E	DP	TC/G	FA	G by Pos
1993	CAL A	52	.250	.372	180	45	6	2	4	2.2	16	30	9	39	5	4	0	24	101	5	7	2.7	.962	3B-45, DH-3
1994		38	.209	.380	129	27	7	0	5	3.9	10	16	12	29	3	1	0	305	15	1	29	8.4	.997	1B-38
1995		29	.169	.296	71	12	4	1	1	1.4	9	7	12	9	0	4	1	16	37	7	3	2.5	.883	3B-23, DH-1
1996	CIN N	18	.222	.472	36	8	0	0	3	8.3	8	5	5	9	0	7	1	59	11	0	6	6.4	1.000	1B-8, 3B-3
4 yrs.		137	.221	.370	416	92	17	3	13	3.1	43	58	38	86	8	16	2	404	164	13	45	4.8	.978	3B-71, 1B-46, DH-4

Neifi Perez

PEREZ, NEIFI NEFTALI
Born Neifi Neftali Perez (Diaz).
B. Feb. 2, 1975, Villa Mella, Dominican Republic
BB TR 6' 175 lbs.

Year	Team	Games	BA	SA	AB	H	2B	3B	HR	HR%	R	RBI	BB	SO	SB	AB	H	PO	A	E	DP	TC/G	FA	G by Pos
1996	CLR N	17	.156	.200	45	7	2	0	0	0.0	4	3	0	8	2	3	0	21	28	2	11	2.8	.961	SS-14, 2B-4

Robert Perez

PEREZ, ROBERT ALEXANDER
Born Robert Alexander Perez (Jimenez).
B. June 4, 1969, Bolivar, Venezuela
BR TR 6'3" 205 lbs.

Year	Team	Games	BA	SA	AB	H	2B	3B	HR	HR%	R	RBI	BB	SO	SB	AB	H	PO	A	E	DP	TC/G	FA	G by Pos
1994	TOR A	4	.125	.125	8	1	0	0	0	0.0	0	0	0	1	0	0	0	3	1	0	0	1.0	1.000	OF-4
1995		17	.188	.292	48	9	2	0	1	2.1	2	3	0	5	0	4	2	30	0	0	0	2.0	1.000	OF-15
1996		86	.327	.406	202	66	10	0	2	1.0	30	21	8	17	3	21	5	114	3	2	0	1.5	.983	OF-79, DH-2
3 yrs.		107	.295	.376	258	76	12	0	3	1.2	32	24	8	23	3	25	7	147	4	2	0	1.5	.987	OF-98, DH-2

Tomas Perez

PEREZ, TOMAS ORLANDO
B. Dec. 29, 1973, Barquisimeto, Venezuela
BB TR 5'11" 165 lbs.

Year	Team	Games	BA	SA	AB	H	2B	3B	HR	HR%	R	RBI	BB	SO	SB	AB	H	PO	A	E	DP	TC/G	FA	G by Pos
1995	TOR A	41	.245	.327	98	24	3	1	1	1.0	12	8	7	18	0	2	1	49	78	5	17	3.4	.962	SS-31, 2B-7, 3B-1
1996		91	.251	.332	295	74	13	4	1	0.3	24	19	25	29	1	0	0	151	250	15	68	4.6	.964	2B-75, 3B-11, SS-5
2 yrs.		132	.249	.331	393	98	16	5	2	0.5	36	27	32	47	1	2	1	200	328	20	85	4.2	.964	2B-82, SS-36, 3B-12

Year	Team	Games	BA	SA	AB	H	2B	3B	HR	HR%	R	RBI	BB	SO	SB	Pinch Hit AB	Pinch Hit H	PO	A	E	DP	TC/G	FA	G by Pos

Herbert Perry

PERRY, HERBERT EDWARD, JR.
B. Sept. 15, 1969, Live Oak, Fla.

BR TR 6'2" 210 lbs.

Year	Team	Games	BA	SA	AB	H	2B	3B	HR	HR%	R	RBI	BB	SO	SB	PH AB	PH H	PO	A	E	DP	TC/G	FA	G by Pos
1994	CLE A	4	.111	.111	9	1	0	0	0	0.0	1	1	3	1	0	0	0	25	5	1	1	7.8	.968	3B-2, 1B-2
1995		52	.315	.463	162	51	13	1	3	1.9	23	23	13	28	1	3	0	391	30	0	30	8.3	1.000	1B-45, DH-5, 3B-1
1996		7	.083	.167	12	1	1	0	0	0.0	1	0	1	2	1	2	0	29	2	0	3	5.2	1.000	1B-5, 3B-1
3 yrs.		63	.290	.426	183	53	14	1	3	1.6	25	24	17	31	2	5	0	445	37	1	34	7.9	.998	1B-52, DH-5, 3B-4

DIVISIONAL PLAYOFF SERIES

Year	Team	Games	BA	SA	AB	H	2B	3B	HR	HR%	R	RBI	BB	SO	SB	PH AB	PH H	PO	A	E	DP	TC/G	FA	G by Pos
1995	CLE A	1	.000	.000	1	0	0	0	0	0.0	0	0	0	0	0	1	0	0	0	0	0	0.0	—	

LEAGUE CHAMPIONSHIP SERIES

Year	Team	Games	BA	SA	AB	H	2B	3B	HR	HR%	R	RBI	BB	SO	SB	PH AB	PH H	PO	A	E	DP	TC/G	FA	G by Pos
1995	CLE A	3	.000	.000	8	0	0	0	0	0.0	0	0	1	3	0	0	0	30	0	0	2	10.0	1.000	1B-3

WORLD SERIES

Year	Team	Games	BA	SA	AB	H	2B	3B	HR	HR%	R	RBI	BB	SO	SB	PH AB	PH H	PO	A	E	DP	TC/G	FA	G by Pos
1995	CLE A	3	.000	.000	5	0	0	0	0	0.0	0	0	0	2	0	0	0	13	2	0	2	5.0	1.000	1B-3

Roberto Petagine

PETAGINE, ROBERTO ANTONIO
Born Roberto Antonio Petagine (Guerra).
B. June 7, 1971, Nueva Esparita, Venezuela

BL TL 6'1" 172 lbs.

Year	Team	Games	BA	SA	AB	H	2B	3B	HR	HR%	R	RBI	BB	SO	SB	PH AB	PH H	PO	A	E	DP	TC/G	FA	G by Pos
1994	HOU N	8	.000	.000	7	0	0	0	0	0.0	0	0	1	3	0	6	0	3	0	0	0	1.5	1.000	1B-2
1995	SD N	89	.234	.371	124	29	8	0	3	2.4	15	17	26	41	0	30	8	264	22	1	21	5.4	.997	1B-51, OF-2
1996	NY N	50	.232	.384	99	23	3	0	4	4.0	10	17	9	27	0	15	4	209	22	1	20	5.8	.996	1B-40
3 yrs.		147	.226	.365	230	52	11	0	7	3.0	25	34	36	71	0	51	12	476	44	2	41	5.5	.996	1B-93, OF-2

J. R. Phillips

PHILLIPS, CHARLES GENE
B. Apr. 29, 1970, West Covina, Calif.

BL TL 6'2" 205 lbs.

Year	Team	Games	BA	SA	AB	H	2B	3B	HR	HR%	R	RBI	BB	SO	SB	PH AB	PH H	PO	A	E	DP	TC/G	FA	G by Pos
1993	SF N	11	.313	.688	16	5	1	1	1	6.3	1	4	0	5	0	6	1	32	2	1	1	7.0	.971	1B-5
1994		15	.132	.211	38	5	0	0	1	2.6	1	3	1	13	1	5	0	79	10	1	7	9.0	.989	1B-10
1995		92	.195	.351	231	45	9	0	9	3.9	27	28	19	69	1	14	3	536	36	4	45	7.2	.993	1B-79, OF-1
1996	2 teams	SF N	(15G –.200)	PHI N	(35G –.152)																			
"	total	50	.163	.413	104	17	5	0	7	6.7	12	15	11	51	0	13	2	161	6	3	12	4.7	.982	1B-21, OF-15
4 yrs.		168	.185	.368	389	72	15	1	18	4.6	41	50	31	138	2	38	6	808	54	9	65	6.6	.990	1B-115, OF-16

Tony Phillips

PHILLIPS, KEITH ANTHONY
B. Apr. 25, 1959, Atlanta, Ga.

BB TR 5'9" 155 lbs.

Year	Team	Games	BA	SA	AB	H	2B	3B	HR	HR%	R	RBI	BB	SO	SB	PH AB	PH H	PO	A	E	DP	TC/G	FA	G by Pos
1982	OAK A	40	.210	.284	81	17	2	2	0	0.0	11	8	12	26	2	0	0	46	95	7	17	3.8	.953	SS-39
1983		148	.248	.320	412	102	12	3	4	1.0	54	35	48	70	16	1	1	218	383	30	85	3.7	.952	SS-101, 2B-63, 3B-4, DH-1
1984		154	.266	.359	451	120	24	3	4	0.9	62	37	42	86	10	2	0	255	391	28	90	3.7	.958	SS-91, 2B-90, OF-1
1985		42	.280	.453	161	45	12	2	4	2.5	23	17	13	34	3	1	0	54	103	3	13	2.9	.981	3B-31, 2B-24
1986		118	.256	.345	441	113	14	5	5	1.1	76	52	76	82	15	0	0	191	326	13	43	4.2	.975	2B-88, 3B-30, OF-4, DH-2, SS-1
1987		111	.240	.372	379	91	20	0	10	2.6	48	46	57	76	7	6	1	179	299	14	47	4.5	.972	2B-87, 3B-11, SS-9, OF-2
1988		79	.203	.307	212	43	8	4	2	0.9	32	17	36	50	0	5	1	84	80	10	18	1.7	.943	3B-32, OF-31, 2B-27, SS-10, 1B-3
1989		143	.262	.348	451	118	15	6	4	0.9	48	47	58	66	3	10	3	184	321	15	54	3.1	.971	2B-84, 3B-49, SS-17, OF-16, 1B-1
1990	DET A	152	.251	.351	573	144	23	5	8	1.4	97	55	99	85	19	1	0	180	368	23	62	3.3	.960	3B-104, 2B-47, SS-11, OF-8, DH-4
1991		146	.284	.438	564	160	28	4	17	3.0	87	72	79	95	10	6	2	269	237	8	51	3.0	.984	OF-56, 3B-46, 2B-36, DH-18, SS-13
1992		159	.276	.388	606	167	32	3	10	1.7	**114**	64	114	93	12	1	0	301	195	11	45	2.8	.978	OF-69, 2B-57, DH-34, 3B-20, SS-1
1993		151	.313	.398	566	177	27	0	7	1.2	113	57	**132**	102	16	3	2	321	165	13	34	3.0	.974	OF-108, 2B-51, DH-4, 3B-1
1994		114	.281	.468	438	123	19	3	19	4.3	91	61	95	105	13	1	1	254	42	6	7	2.5	.980	OF-104, 2B-12, DH-6
1995	CAL A	139	.261	.459	525	137	21	1	27	5.1	119	61	113	135	13	2	0	166	179	20	17	2.6	.945	3B-88, OF-48, DH-2
1996	CHI A	153	.277	.399	581	161	29	3	12	2.1	119	63	**125**	132	13	3	1	350	18	7	5	2.5	.981	OF-150, 2B-2, 1B-1
15 yrs.		1849	.267	.387	6441	1718	286	44	133	2.1	1094	692	1099	1237	152	42	12	3052	3202	208	588	3.2	.968	2B-668, OF-597, 3B-416, SS-293, DH-71, 1B-5

LEAGUE CHAMPIONSHIP SERIES

Year	Team	Games	BA	SA	AB	H	2B	3B	HR	HR%	R	RBI	BB	SO	SB	PH AB	PH H	PO	A	E	DP	TC/G	FA	G by Pos
1988	OAK A	2	.286	.429	7	2	1	0	0	0.0	0	0	1	3	0	0	0	10	0	0	1	3.3	1.000	OF-2, 2B-1
1989		5	.167	.222	18	3	0	0	0	0.0	1	1	2	4	2	0	0	4	14	0	2	3.0	1.000	3B-3, 2B-3
2 yrs.		7	.200	.280	25	5	2	0	0	0.0	1	1	3	7	2	0	0	14	14	0	3	3.1	1.000	2B-4, 3B-3, OF-2

WORLD SERIES

Year	Team	Games	BA	SA	AB	H	2B	3B	HR	HR%	R	RBI	BB	SO	SB	PH AB	PH H	PO	A	E	DP	TC/G	FA	G by Pos
1988	OAK A	2	.250	.250	4	1	0	0	0	0.0	1	0	1	2	0	0	0	3	5	0	1	4.0	1.000	2B-1, OF-1
1989		4	.235	.471	17	4	0	0	1	5.9	2	3	0	3	0	0	0	8	15	0	1	3.3	1.000	2B-4, 3B-2, OF-1
2 yrs.		6	.238	.429	21	5	0	0	1	4.8	3	3	1	5	0	0	0	11	20	0	2	3.4	1.000	2B-5, 3B-2, OF-2

Mike Piazza

PIAZZA, MICHAEL JOSEPH
B. Sept. 4, 1968, Norristown, Pa.

BR TR 6'3" 200 lbs.

Year	Team	Games	BA	SA	AB	H	2B	3B	HR	HR%	R	RBI	BB	SO	SB	PH AB	PH H	PO	A	E	DP	TC/G	FA	G by Pos
1992	LA N	21	.232	.319	69	16	3	0	1	1.4	5	7	4	12	0	5	2	94	7	1	1	6.4	.990	C-16
1993		149	.318	.561	547	174	24	2	35	6.4	81	112	46	86	3	5	0	901	98	11	11	6.9	.989	C-146, 1B-1
1994		107	.319	.541	405	129	18	0	24	5.9	64	92	33	65	1	8	3	640	38	10	3	6.6	.985	C-104
1995		112	.346	.606	434	150	17	0	32	**7.4**	82	93	39	80	1	2	1	805	51	9	5	7.7	.990	C-112
1996		148	.336	.563	547	184	16	0	36	6.6	87	105	81	93	0	3	1	1056	70	9	6	7.7	.992	C-147
5 yrs.		537	.326	.559	2002	653	78	2	128	6.4	319	409	203	336	5	23	7	3496	264	40	26	7.2	.989	C-525, 1B-1

DIVISIONAL PLAYOFF SERIES

Year	Team	Games	BA	SA	AB	H	2B	3B	HR	HR%	R	RBI	BB	SO	SB	PH AB	PH H	PO	A	E	DP	TC/G	FA	G by Pos
1995	LA N	3	.214	.500	14	3	1	0	1	7.1	1	1	0	2	0	0	0	31	0	0	0	10.3	1.000	C-3
1996		3	.300	.300	10	3	0	0	0	0.0	1	2	1	2	0	0	0	25	4	0	2	9.7	1.000	C-3
2 yrs.		6	.250	.417	24	6	1	0	1	4.2	2	3	1	4	0	0	0	56	4	0	2	10.0	1.000	C-6

Year	Team	Games	BA	SA	AB	H	2B	3B	HR	HR%	R	RBI	BB	SO	SB	Pinch Hit AB	H	PO	A	E	DP	TC/G	FA	G by Pos

Greg Pirkl

PIRKL, GREGORY DANIEL
B. Aug. 7, 1970, Long Beach, Calif.
BR TR 6'5" 225 lbs.

Year	Team	Games	BA	SA	AB	H	2B	3B	HR	HR%	R	RBI	BB	SO	SB	PH-AB	PH-H	PO	A	E	DP	TC/G	FA	G by Pos
1993	SEA A	7	.174	.304	23	4	0	0	1	4.3	1	4	0	4	0	0	0	42	5	0	8	6.7	1.000	1B-5, DH-2
1994		19	.264	.660	53	14	3	0	6	11.3	7	11	1	12	0	4	3	56	1	1	3	3.4	.983	DH-10, 1B-7
1995		10	.235	.235	17	4	0	0	0	0.0	2	0	1	7	0	5	0	32	3	0	1	5.0	1.000	1B-6, DH-1
1996	2 teams SEA A (7G –.190)				BOS A (2G –.000)																			
"	total	9	.174	.348	23	4	1	0	1	4.3	2	1	0	4	0	4	1	14	2	0	2	3.2	1.000	DH-3, 1B-2
	4 yrs.	45	.224	.466	116	26	4	0	8	6.9	12	16	2	27	0	13	4	144	11	1	14	4.3	.994	1B-20, DH-16

Phil Plantier

PLANTIER, PHILLIP ALAN
B. Jan. 27, 1969, Manchester, N. H.
BL TR 6' 175 lbs.

Year	Team	Games	BA	SA	AB	H	2B	3B	HR	HR%	R	RBI	BB	SO	SB	PH-AB	PH-H	PO	A	E	DP	TC/G	FA	G by Pos
1990	BOS A	14	.133	.200	15	2	1	0	0	0.0	1	3	4	6	0	6	1	0	0	0	0	0.0		DH-4, OF-1
1991		53	.331	.615	148	49	7	1	11	7.4	27	35	23	38	1	8	3	80	1	2	0	1.8	.976	OF-40, DH-5
1992		108	.246	.361	349	86	19	0	7	2.0	46	30	44	83	2	12	4	148	6	4	0	1.6	.975	OF-76, DH-23
1993	SD N	138	.240	.509	462	111	20	1	34	7.4	67	100	61	124	4	5	0	272	14	3	3	2.2	.990	OF-134
1994		96	.220	.440	341	75	21	0	18	5.3	44	41	36	91	3	6	0	159	5	2	0	1.8	.988	OF-91
1995	2 teams HOU N (22G –.250)				SD N (54G –.257)																			
"	total	76	.255	.407	216	55	6	0	9	4.2	33	34	28	48	1	12	2	89	5	4	1	1.7	.959	OF-59
1996	OAK A	73	.212	.346	231	49	8	1	7	3.0	29	31	28	56	2	3	0	137	8	4	2	2.2	.973	OF-68, DH-1
	7 yrs.	558	.242	.439	1762	427	82	3	86	4.9	247	274	224	446	13	52	10	885	39	19	6	1.9	.980	OF-469, DH-33

Luis Polonia

POLONIA, LUIS ANDREW
Born Luis Andrew Polonia (Almonte).
B. Oct. 12, 1964, Santiago City, Dominican Republic
BL TL 5'8" 155 lbs.
BB 1987

Year	Team	Games	BA	SA	AB	H	2B	3B	HR	HR%	R	RBI	BB	SO	SB	PH-AB	PH-H	PO	A	E	DP	TC/G	FA	G by Pos
1987	OAK A	125	.287	.398	435	125	16	10	4	0.9	78	49	32	64	29	8	3	235	2	5	1	2.0	.979	OF-104, DH-18
1988		84	.292	.378	288	84	11	4	2	0.7	51	27	21	40	24	9	2	155	3	2	1	2.1	.988	OF-76, DH-2
1989	2 teams OAK A (59G –.286)				NY A (66G –.313)																			
"	total	125	.300	.388	433	130	17	6	3	0.7	70	46	25	44	22	14	6	231	9	4	2	2.1	.984	OF-108, DH-9
1990	2 teams NY A (11G –.318)				CAL A (109G –.336)																			
"	total	120	.335	.412	403	135	7	9	2	0.5	52	35	25	43	21	19	6	142	3	3	2	1.5	.980	OF-85, DH-15
1991	CAL A	150	.296	.379	604	179	28	8	2	0.3	92	50	52	74	48	5	1	246	9	5	1	1.8	.981	OF-143, DH-4
1992		149	.286	.329	577	165	17	4	0	0.0	83	35	45	64	51	4	1	192	8	4	1	1.4	.980	OF-99, DH-47
1993		152	.271	.326	576	156	17	6	1	0.2	75	32	48	53	55	8	2	286	12	5	3	2.1	.983	OF-141, DH-3
1994	NY A	95	.311	.414	350	109	21	6	1	0.3	62	36	37	36	20	10	4	154	9	4	2	1.9	.976	OF-84, DH-2
1995	2 teams NY A (67G –.261)				ATL N (28G –.264)																			
"	total	95	.261	.357	291	76	16	3	2	0.7	43	17	28	38	13	24	9	143	5	0	1	1.9	1.000	OF-79
1996	2 teams BAL A (58G –.240)				ATL N (22G –.419)																			
"	total	80	.267	.325	206	55	4	1	2	1.0	28	16	11	23	9	26	8	60	2	2	0	1.1	.969	OF-41, DH-18
	10 yrs.	1175	.292	.370	4163	1214	154	57	19	0.5	634	343	324	479	292	127	42	1844	62	34	14	1.8	.982	OF-960, DH-118

DIVISIONAL PLAYOFF SERIES

Year	Team	Games	BA	SA	AB	H	2B	3B	HR	HR%	R	RBI	BB	SO	SB	PH-AB	PH-H	PO	A	E	DP	TC/G	FA	G by Pos
1995	ATL N	3	.333	.333	3	1	0	0	0	0.0	0	2	0	1	1	3	1	0	0	0	0	0.0		
1996		2	.000	.000	2	0	0	0	0	0.0	0	0	0	1	0	2	0	0	0	0	0	0.0	—	
	2 yrs.	5	.200	.200	5	1	0	0	0	0.0	0	2	0	2	1	5	1							

LEAGUE CHAMPIONSHIP SERIES

Year	Team	Games	BA	SA	AB	H	2B	3B	HR	HR%	R	RBI	BB	SO	SB	PH-AB	PH-H	PO	A	E	DP	TC/G	FA	G by Pos
1988	OAK A	3	.400	.400	5	2	0	0	0	0.0	0	0	1	2	0	0	0	2	0	0	0	2.0	1.000	OF-1
1995	ATL N	3	.500	.500	2	1	0	0	0	0.0	0	1	0	0	0	2	1	0	0	0	0	0.0	.000	OF-1
1996		3	.000	.000	3	0	0	0	0	0.0	0	0	0	0	0	3	0	0	0	0	0	0.0	—	
	3 yrs.	9	.300	.300	10	3	0	0	0	0.0	0	1	1	2	0	5	1	2	0	0	0	1.0	1.000	OF-2

WORLD SERIES

Year	Team	Games	BA	SA	AB	H	2B	3B	HR	HR%	R	RBI	BB	SO	SB	PH-AB	PH-H	PO	A	E	DP	TC/G	FA	G by Pos
1988	OAK A	3	.111	.111	9	1	0	0	0	0.0	1	0	0	2	0	2	0	2	0	0	0	1.0	1.000	OF-2
1995	ATL N	6	.286	.571	14	4	1	0	1	7.1	3	4	1	3	1	2	0	3	0	0	0	0.8	1.000	OF-4
1996		6	.000	.000	5	0	0	0	0	0.0	0	0	1	3	0	5	0	0	0	0	0	0.0	—	
	3 yrs.	15	.179	.321	28	5	1	0	1	3.6	4	4	2	8	1	9	0	5	0	0	0	0.8	1.000	OF-6

Jorge Posada

POSADA, JORGE RAFAEL
Born Jorge Rafael Posada (Villeta).
B. Aug. 17, 1971, Santurce, Puerto Rico
BB TR 6'2" 190 lbs.

Year	Team	Games	BA	SA	AB	H	2B	3B	HR	HR%	R	RBI	BB	SO	SB	PH-AB	PH-H	PO	A	E	DP	TC/G	FA	G by Pos
1995	NY A	1	—	—	0	0	0	0	0	—	0	0	0	0	0	0	0	1	0	0	0	1.0	1.000	C-1
1996		8	.071	.071	14	1	0	0	0	0.0	1	0	1	6	0	3	0	17	2	0	0	2.7	1.000	C-4, DH-3
	2 yrs.	9	.071	.071	14	1	0	0	0	0.0	1	0	1	6	0	3	0	18	2	0	0	2.5	1.000	C-5, DH-3

DIVISIONAL PLAYOFF SERIES

Year	Team	Games	BA	SA	AB	H	2B	3B	HR	HR%	R	RBI	BB	SO	SB	PH-AB	PH-H	PO	A	E	DP	TC/G	FA	G by Pos
1995	NY A	1	—	—	0	0	0	0	0	—	1	0	0	0	0	0	0	0	0	0	0	0.0	—	

Arquimedez Pozo

POZO, ARQUIMEDEZ
Born Arquimedez Pozo (Ortiz).
B. Aug. 24, 1973, Santo Domingo, Dominican Republic
BR TR 5'10" 160 lbs.

Year	Team	Games	BA	SA	AB	H	2B	3B	HR	HR%	R	RBI	BB	SO	SB	PH-AB	PH-H	PO	A	E	DP	TC/G	FA	G by Pos
1995	SEA A	1	.000	.000	1	0	0	0	0	0.0	0	0	0	0	0	1	0	0	1	0	0	1.0	1.000	2B-1
1996	BOS A	21	.172	.310	58	10	3	1	1	1.7	4	11	2	10	1	1	1	23	39	4	4	3.1	.939	2B-10, 3B-10, DH-1
	2 yrs.	22	.169	.305	59	10	3	1	1	1.7	4	11	2	10	1	2	1	23	40	4	4	3.0	.940	2B-11, 3B-10, DH-1

Curtis Pride

PRIDE, CURTIS JOHN
B. Dec. 17, 1968, Washington, D. C.
BL TR 6' 205 lbs.

Year	Team	Games	BA	SA	AB	H	2B	3B	HR	HR%	R	RBI	BB	SO	SB	PH-AB	PH-H	PO	A	E	DP	TC/G	FA	G by Pos
1993	MON N	10	.444	1.111	9	4	1	1	1	11.1	3	5	0	3	1	8	4	2	0	0	0	1.0	1.000	OF-2
1995		48	.175	.190	63	11	1	0	0	0.0	10	2	5	16	3	18	2	23	0	2	0	1.0	.920	OF-24
1996	DET A	95	.300	.513	267	80	17	5	10	3.7	52	31	31	63	11	20	3	89	0	3	0	1.2	.967	OF-48, DH-31
	3 yrs.	153	.280	.469	339	95	19	6	11	3.2	65	38	36	82	15	46	9	114	0	5	0	1.1	.958	OF-74, DH-31

Year	Team	Games	BA	SA	AB	H	2B	3B	HR	HR%	R	RBI	BB	SO	SB	Pinch Hit AB	Pinch Hit H	PO	A	E	DP	TC/G	FA	G by Pos

Tom Prince

PRINCE, THOMAS ALBERT
B. Aug. 13, 1964, Kankakee, Ill.   BR TR 5'11" 185 lbs.

Year	Team	Games	BA	SA	AB	H	2B	3B	HR	HR%	R	RBI	BB	SO	SB	AB	H	PO	A	E	DP	TC/G	FA	G by Pos
1987	PIT N	4	.222	.667	9	2	1	0	1	11.1	1	2	0	2	0	0	0	14	3	0	0	4.3	1.000	C-4
1988		29	.176	.203	74	13	2	0	0	0.0	3	6	4	15	0	2	0	108	8	2	1	4.2	.983	C-28
1989		21	.135	.212	52	7	4	0	0	0.0	1	5	6	12	1	0	0	85	11	4	1	4.8	.960	C-21
1990		4	.100	.100	10	1	0	0	0	0.0	1	0	1	2	0	1	0	16	1	0	0	5.7	1.000	C-3
1991		26	.265	.441	34	9	3	0	1	2.9	4	2	7	3	0	5	0	53	9	1	0	3.2	.984	C-19, 1B-1
1992		27	.091	.136	44	4	2	0	0	0.0	1	5	6	9	1	6	0	76	8	2	0	4.3	.977	C-19, 3B-1
1993		66	.196	.307	179	35	14	0	2	1.1	14	24	13	38	1	8	3	271	31	5	6	5.2	.984	C-59
1994	LA N	3	.333	.333	6	2	0	0	0	0.0	2	1	1	3	0	0	0	11	1	0	0	4.0	1.000	C-3
1995		18	.200	.375	40	8	2	1	1	2.5	3	4	4	10	1	2	0	71	8	1	1	4.7	.988	C-17
1996		40	.297	.438	64	19	6	0	1	1.6	6	11	6	15	0	5	2	161	11	1	2	4.9	.994	C-35
10 yrs.		238	.195	.301	512	100	34	1	6	1.2	36	60	48	109	3	29	5	866	91	16	11	4.6	.984	C-208, 3B-1, 1B-1

Harvey Pulliam

PULLIAM, HARVEY JEROME
B. Oct. 20, 1967, San Francisco, Calif.   BR TR 6' 210 lbs.

Year	Team	Games	BA	SA	AB	H	2B	3B	HR	HR%	R	RBI	BB	SO	SB	AB	H	PO	A	E	DP	TC/G	FA	G by Pos
1991	KC A	18	.273	.576	33	9	1	0	3	9.1	4	4	3	9	0	3	0	21	1	2	0	1.6	.917	OF-15
1992		4	.200	.400	5	1	1	0	0	0.0	2	0	1	3	0	0	0	3	0	0	0	1.0	1.000	DH-2, OF-1
1993		27	.258	.387	62	16	5	0	1	1.6	7	6	2	14	0	6	1	33	0	1	0	1.3	.971	OF-26
1995	CLR N	5	.400	1.200	5	2	1	0	1	20.0	1	3	0	2	0	4	2	0	0	0	0	0.0	.000	OF-1
1996		10	.133	.133	15	2	0	0	0	0.0	2	0	2	6	0	7	1	4	0	0	0	1.3	1.000	OF-3
5 yrs.		64	.250	.442	120	30	8	0	5	4.2	16	13	8	34	0	20	4	61	1	3	0	1.4	.954	OF-46, DH-2

Tom Quinlan

QUINLAN, THOMAS RAYMOND
B. Mar. 27, 1968, St. Paul, Minn.   BR TR 6'3" 200 lbs.

Year	Team	Games	BA	SA	AB	H	2B	3B	HR	HR%	R	RBI	BB	SO	SB	AB	H	PO	A	E	DP	TC/G	FA	G by Pos
1990	TOR A	1	.500	.500	2	1	0	0	0	0.0	0	0	0	0	0	0	0	0	1	0	0	1.0	1.000	3B-1
1992		13	.067	.133	15	1	1	0	0	0.0	2	2	2	9	0	1	0	4	6	1	0	0.8	.909	3B-13
1994	PHI N	24	.200	.343	35	7	2	0	1	2.9	6	3	3	13	0	4	0	9	19	1	1	1.5	.966	3B-20
1996	MIN A	4	.000	.000	6	0	0	0	0	0.0	0	0	0	3	0	0	0	0	2	1	0	0.8	.667	3B-4
4 yrs.		42	.155	.259	58	9	3	0	1	1.7	8	5	5	26	0	5	0	13	28	3	1	1.2	.932	3B-38

Brian Raabe

RAABE, BRIAN CHARLES
B. Nov. 5, 1967, New Ulm, Minn.   BR TR 5'9" 170 lbs.

Year	Team	Games	BA	SA	AB	H	2B	3B	HR	HR%	R	RBI	BB	SO	SB	AB	H	PO	A	E	DP	TC/G	FA	G by Pos
1995	MIN A	6	.214	.214	14	3	0	0	0	0.0	4	1	1	0	0	1	1	5	7	0	3	2.0	1.000	2B-4, 3B-2
1996		7	.222	.222	9	2	0	0	0	0.0	0	1	0	1	0	3	1	2	4	1	1	1.0	.857	3B-6, 2B-1
2 yrs.		13	.217	.217	23	5	0	0	0	0.0	4	2	1	1	0	4	2	7	11	1	4	1.5	.947	3B-8, 2B-5

Tim Raines

RAINES, TIMOTHY (Rock)
B. Sept. 16, 1959, Sanford, Fla.   BB TR 5'8" 160 lbs.

Year	Team	Games	BA	SA	AB	H	2B	3B	HR	HR%	R	RBI	BB	SO	SB	AB	H	PO	A	E	DP	TC/G	FA	G by Pos
1979	MON N	6	—	—	0	0	0	0	0	—	3	0	0	0	2	0	0	0	0	0	0	0.0	—	
1980		15	.050	.050	20	1	0	0	0	0.0	5	0	6	3	5	0	0	15	16	0	2	3.9	1.000	2B-7, OF-1
1981		88	.304	.438	313	95	13	7	5	1.6	61	37	45	31	71	0	0	162	8	4	0	2.1	.977	OF-81, 2B-1
1982		156	.277	.369	647	179	32	8	4	0.6	90	43	75	83	78	0	0	293	126	8	12	2.7	.981	OF-120, 2B-36
1983		156	.298	.429	615	183	32	8	11	1.8	133	71	97	70	90	1	1	314	23	4	3	2.1	.988	OF-154, 2B-7
1984		160	.309	.437	622	192	38	9	8	1.3	106	60	87	69	75	0	0	420	8	6	1	2.7	.986	OF-160, 2B-2
1985		150	.320	.475	575	184	30	13	11	1.9	115	41	81	60	70	7	0	284	8	2	4	2.0	.993	OF-145
1986		151	.334	.476	580	194	35	10	9	1.6	91	62	78	60	70	4	1	270	13	6	1	2.0	.979	OF-147
1987		139	.330	.526	530	175	34	8	18	3.4	123	68	90	52	50	0	0	297	9	4	1	2.2	.987	OF-139
1988		109	.270	.431	429	116	19	7	12	2.8	66	48	53	44	33	1	0	235	5	3	1	2.3	.988	OF-108
1989		145	.286	.418	517	148	29	6	9	1.7	76	60	93	48	41	4	3	253	7	1	0	1.9	.996	OF-139
1990		130	.287	.392	457	131	11	5	9	2.0	65	62	70	43	49	8	2	239	3	6	1	1.9	.976	OF-123
1991	CHI A	155	.268	.345	609	163	20	6	5	0.8	102	50	83	68	51	5	0	273	12	3	3	1.9	.990	OF-133, DH-19
1992		144	.294	.405	551	162	22	9	7	1.3	102	54	81	48	45	4	3	312	12	2	0	2.3	.994	OF-129, DH-14
1993		115	.306	.480	415	127	16	4	16	3.9	75	54	64	35	21	4	1	200	5	0	1	1.8	1.000	OF-112
1994		101	.266	.409	384	102	15	5	10	2.6	80	52	61	43	13	4	0	203	3	4	1	2.2	.981	OF-97
1995		133	.285	.422	502	143	25	4	12	2.4	81	67	70	52	13	9	1	193	7	4	1	1.6	.980	OF-108, DH-22
1996	NY A	59	.284	.468	201	57	10	0	9	4.5	45	33	34	29	10	7	0	78	3	1	0	1.5	.988	OF-51, DH-2
18 yrs.		2112	.295	.429	7967	2352	381	109	155	1.9	1419	862	1168	838	787 4th	60	12	4041	268	58	32	2.1	.987	OF-1947, DH-57, 2B-53

DIVISIONAL PLAYOFF SERIES

Year	Team	Games	BA	SA	AB	H	2B	3B	HR	HR%	R	RBI	BB	SO	SB	AB	H	PO	A	E	DP	TC/G	FA	G by Pos
1996	NY A	4	.250	.250	16	4	0	0	0	0.0	3	0	3	1	0	0	0	5	0	0	0	1.3	1.000	OF-4

LEAGUE CHAMPIONSHIP SERIES

Year	Team	Games	BA	SA	AB	H	2B	3B	HR	HR%	R	RBI	BB	SO	SB	AB	H	PO	A	E	DP	TC/G	FA	G by Pos
1981	MON N	5	.238	.333	21	5	2	0	0	0.0	1	1	0	3	1	0	0	9	0	0	0	1.8	1.000	OF-5
1993	CHI A	6	.444	.519	27	12	2	0	0	0.0	5	5	2	1	1	0	0	12	2	0	0	2.3	1.000	OF-6
1996	NY A	5	.267	.333	15	4	1	0	0	0.0	2	0	1	1	0	0	0	5	0	0	0	1.0	1.000	OF-5
3 yrs.		16	.333	.413	63	21	5	0	0	0.0	8	2	3	6	1	0	0	26	2	0	0	1.8	1.000	OF-16

WORLD SERIES

Year	Team	Games	BA	SA	AB	H	2B	3B	HR	HR%	R	RBI	BB	SO	SB	AB	H	PO	A	E	DP	TC/G	FA	G by Pos
1996	NY A	4	.214	.214	14	3	0	0	0	0.0	2	1	0	0	0	0	0	5	0	1	0	1.5	.833	OF-4

Manny Ramirez

RAMIREZ, MANUEL ARISTIDES
Born Manuel Aristides Ramirez (Onelcida).
B. May 30, 1972, Santo Domingo, Dominican Republic   BR TR 6' 190 lbs.

Year	Team	Games	BA	SA	AB	H	2B	3B	HR	HR%	R	RBI	BB	SO	SB	AB	H	PO	A	E	DP	TC/G	FA	G by Pos
1993	CLE A	22	.170	.302	53	9	1	0	2	3.8	5	5	2	8	0	4	1	3	0	0	0	0.1	1.000	DH-20, OF-1
1994		91	.269	.521	290	78	22	0	17	5.9	51	60	42	72	4	5	0	150	7	1	2	1.8	.994	OF-84, DH-5
1995		137	.308	.558	484	149	26	1	31	6.4	85	107	75	112	6	3	0	219	3	5	2	1.7	.978	OF-131, DH-3
1996		152	.309	.582	550	170	45	3	33	6.0	94	112	85	104	8	2	0	272	19	9	4	2.0	.970	OF-149, DH-3
4 yrs.		402	.295	.550	1377	406	94	4	83	6.0	235	284	204	296	18	14	1	644	29	15	8	1.7	.978	OF-365, DH-33

Year	Team	Games	BA	SA	AB	H	2B	3B	HR	HR%	R	RBI	BB	SO	SB	Pinch Hit AB	Pinch Hit H	PO	A	E	DP	TC/G	FA	G by Pos

Manny Ramirez *continued*

DIVISIONAL PLAYOFF SERIES

Year	Team	Games	BA	SA	AB	H	2B	3B	HR	HR%	R	RBI	BB	SO	SB	AB	H	PO	A	E	DP	TC/G	FA	G by Pos
1995	CLE A	3	.000	.000	12	0	0	0	0	0.0	1	0	1	2	0	0	0	3	0	0	0	1.0	1.000	OF-3
1996		4	.375	.875	16	6	2	0	2	12.5	4	2	1	4	0	0	0	8	2	0	0	2.5	1.000	OF-4
2 yrs.		7	.214	.500	28	6	2	0	2	7.1	5	2	2	6	0	0	0	11	2	0	0	1.9	1.000	OF-7

LEAGUE CHAMPIONSHIP SERIES

Year	Team	Games	BA	SA	AB	H	2B	3B	HR	HR%	R	RBI	BB	SO	SB	AB	H	PO	A	E	DP	TC/G	FA	G by Pos
1995	CLE A	6	.286	.571	21	6	0	0	2	9.5	2	2	2	5	0	0	0	9	0	0	0	1.5	1.000	OF-6

WORLD SERIES

Year	Team	Games	BA	SA	AB	H	2B	3B	HR	HR%	R	RBI	BB	SO	SB	AB	H	PO	A	E	DP	TC/G	FA	G by Pos
1995	CLE A	6	.222	.389	18	4	0	0	1	5.6	2	2	4	5	1	0	0	8	0	0	0	1.3	1.000	OF-6

Joe Randa

RANDA, JOSEPH GREGORY
B. Dec. 18, 1969, Milwaukee, Wis.

BR TR 5'11" 190 lbs.

Year	Team	Games	BA	SA	AB	H	2B	3B	HR	HR%	R	RBI	BB	SO	SB	AB	H	PO	A	E	DP	TC/G	FA	G by Pos
1995	KC A	34	.171	.243	70	12	2	0	1	1.4	6	5	6	17	0	5	0	15	44	3	4	1.9	.952	3B-22, 2B-9, DH-2
1996		110	.303	.433	337	102	24	1	6	1.8	36	47	26	47	13	10	3	80	160	10	17	2.2	.960	3B-92, 2B-15, 1B-7, DH-1
2 yrs.		144	.280	.400	407	114	26	1	7	1.7	42	52	32	64	13	15	3	95	204	13	21	2.1	.958	3B-114, 2B-24, 1B-7, DH-3

Jeff Reboulet

REBOULET, JEFFREY ALLEN
B. Apr. 30, 1967, Dayton, Ohio

BR TR 6' 167 lbs.

Year	Team	Games	BA	SA	AB	H	2B	3B	HR	HR%	R	RBI	BB	SO	SB	AB	H	PO	A	E	DP	TC/G	FA	G by Pos
1992	MIN A	73	.190	.277	137	26	7	1	1	0.7	15	16	23	26	3	2	0	71	163	5	31	3.0	.979	SS-36, 3B-22, 2B-13, OF-7, DH-1
1993		109	.258	.304	240	62	8	0	1	0.4	33	15	35	37	5	5	1	122	215	6	40	3.1	.983	SS-62, 3B-35, 2B-11, OF-3, DH-1
1994		74	.259	.376	189	49	11	1	3	1.6	28	23	18	23	0	3	2	150	131	7	29	3.7	.976	SS-42, 2B-14, 1B-10, 3B-6, OF-4, DH-1
1995		87	.292	.398	216	63	11	0	4	1.9	39	23	27	34	1	10	3	164	159	4	36	3.5	.988	SS-39, 3B-22, 1B-17, 2B-15, C-1
1996		107	.222	.261	234	52	9	0	0	0.0	20	23	25	34	4	10	2	139	114	2	29	2.2	.992	SS-37, 3B-36, 2B-22, 1B-13, OF-7, DH-3
5 yrs.		450	.248	.324	1016	252	46	2	9	0.9	135	100	128	154	13	30	8	646	782	24	165	3.0	.983	SS-216, 3B-121, 2B-75, 1B-40, OF-21, DH-6, C-1

Jeff Reed

REED, JEFFREY SCOTT
B. Nov. 12, 1962, Joliet, Ill.

BL TR 6'2" 190 lbs.

Year	Team	Games	BA	SA	AB	H	2B	3B	HR	HR%	R	RBI	BB	SO	SB	AB	H	PO	A	E	DP	TC/G	FA	G by Pos
1984	MIN A	18	.143	.286	21	3	3	0	0	0.0	3	1	2	6	0	0	0	41	2	1	1	2.4	.977	C-18
1985		7	.200	.200	10	2	0	0	0	0.0	2	0	0	3	0	1	0	9	3	0	0	1.7	1.000	C-7
1986		68	.236	.321	165	39	6	1	2	1.2	13	9	16	19	1	7	3	332	19	2	5	5.5	.994	C-64
1987	MON N	75	.213	.280	207	44	11	0	1	0.5	15	21	12	20	1	5	1	357	36	12	6	5.5	.970	C-74
1988	2 teams MON N	(43G –.220)	CIN N	(49G –.232)																				
"	total	92	.226	.287	265	60	9	2	1	0.4	20	16	28	41	1	6	1	468	38	3	3	5.8	.994	C-88
1989	CIN N	102	.223	.293	287	64	11	0	3	1.0	16	23	34	46	3	5	0	504	50	7	2	5.7	.988	C-99
1990		72	.251	.360	175	44	8	1	3	1.7	12	16	24	26	0	3	0	358	26	5	1	5.6	.987	C-70
1991		91	.267	.370	270	72	15	2	3	1.1	20	31	23	38	0	4	1	527	29	5	7	6.3	.991	C-89
1992		15	.160	.160	25	4	0	0	0	0.0	2	2	1	4	0	9	0	29	2	0	0	5.2	1.000	C-9
1993	SF N	66	.261	.437	119	31	3	0	6	5.0	10	12	16	22	0	33	6	180	14	0	4	5.2	1.000	C-37
1994		50	.175	.233	103	18	3	0	1	1.0	11	7	11	21	0	19	4	138	9	1	1	4.5	.993	C-33
1995		66	.265	.283	113	30	2	0	0	0.0	12	9	20	17	0	25	4	175	21	1	2	4.7	.995	C-42
1996	CLR N	116	.284	.419	341	97	20	1	8	2.3	34	37	43	65	2	8	1	546	50	11	2	5.5	.982	C-111
13 yrs.		838	.242	.332	2101	508	91	7	28	1.3	170	184	230	328	4	125	21	3664	299	48	34	5.4	.988	C-738

LEAGUE CHAMPIONSHIP SERIES

Year	Team	Games	BA	SA	AB	H	2B	3B	HR	HR%	R	RBI	BB	SO	SB	AB	H	PO	A	E	DP	TC/G	FA	G by Pos
1990	CIN N	4	.000	.000	7	0	0	0	0	0.0	0	0	0	2	0	0	0	24	1	0	0	6.3	1.000	C-4

Jody Reed

REED, JODY ERIC
B. July 26, 1962, Tampa, Fla.

BR TR 5'9" 170 lbs.

Year	Team	Games	BA	SA	AB	H	2B	3B	HR	HR%	R	RBI	BB	SO	SB	AB	H	PO	A	E	DP	TC/G	FA	G by Pos
1987	BOS A	9	.300	.400	30	9	1	1	0	0.0	4	8	4	0	1	0	0	11	26	0	9	4.1	1.000	SS-6, 2B-2, 3B-1
1988		109	.293	.376	338	99	23	1	1	0.3	60	28	45	21	1	0	0	147	282	11	57	4.0	.975	SS-94, 2B-11, 3B-4
1989		146	.288	.393	524	151	42	2	3	0.6	76	40	73	44	4	3	1	255	423	19	88	4.6	.973	SS-77, 2B-70, 3B-4, OF-1, DH-1
1990		155	.289	.390	598	173	**45**	0	5	0.8	70	51	75	65	4	1	0	278	478	16	103	4.5	.979	2B-119, SS-50, DH-1
1991		153	.283	.382	618	175	42	2	5	0.8	87	60	60	53	6	0	0	314	449	14	110	4.9	.982	2B-152, SS-6
1992		143	.247	.316	550	136	27	1	3	0.5	64	40	62	44	7	0	0	304	472	14	113	5.5	.982	2B-142, DH-1
1993	LA N	132	.276	.346	445	123	21	2	2	0.4	48	31	38	40	1	1	1	280	413	5	93	5.3	.993	2B-132
1994	MIL A	108	.271	.341	399	108	22	0	2	0.5	48	37	57	34	5	2	0	231	351	3	72	5.5	.995	2B-106
1995	SD N	131	.256	.328	445	114	18	1	4	0.9	58	40	59	38	6	0	0	305	366	4	78	5.0	.994	2B-130, SS-5
1996		146	.244	.297	495	121	20	0	2	0.4	45	49	59	53	2	3	0	274	412	9	87	4.8	.987	2B-145
10 yrs.		1232	.272	.354	4442	1209	261	10	27	0.6	560	384	532	392	37	10	2	2399	3672	95	793	4.9	.985	2B-1009, SS-238, 3B-9, DH-3, OF-1

DIVISIONAL PLAYOFF SERIES

Year	Team	Games	BA	SA	AB	H	2B	3B	HR	HR%	R	RBI	BB	SO	SB	AB	H	PO	A	E	DP	TC/G	FA	G by Pos
1996	SD N	3	.273	.364	11	3	1	0	0	0.0	0	2	0	1	0	0	0	6	6	0	2	4.0	1.000	2B-3

LEAGUE CHAMPIONSHIP SERIES

Year	Team	Games	BA	SA	AB	H	2B	3B	HR	HR%	R	RBI	BB	SO	SB	AB	H	PO	A	E	DP	TC/G	FA	G by Pos
1988	BOS A	4	.273	.364	11	3	1	0	0	0.0	0	0	2	1	0	0	0	3	10	0	2	3.3	1.000	SS-4
1990		4	.133	.133	15	2	0	0	0	0.0	0	1	0	4	0	0	0	11	11	0	4	3.1	1.000	2B-4, SS-3
2 yrs.		8	.192	.231	26	5	1	0	0	0.0	0	1	2	3	0	0	0	14	21	0	6	3.2	1.000	SS-7, 2B-4

Desi Relaford

RELAFORD, DESMOND LAMONT
B. Sept. 16, 1973, Valdosta, Ga.

BB TR 5'8" 155 lbs.

Year	Team	Games	BA	SA	AB	H	2B	3B	HR	HR%	R	RBI	BB	SO	SB	AB	H	PO	A	E	DP	TC/G	FA	G by Pos
1996	PHI N	15	.175	.225	40	7	2	0	0	0.0	2	1	3	9	1	5	0	21	26	2	6	3.8	.959	SS-9, 2B-4

Year	Team	Games	BA	SA	AB	H	2B	3B	HR	HR%	R	RBI	BB	SO	SB	Pinch Hit AB	Pinch Hit H	PO	A	E	DP	TC/G	FA	G by Pos

Edgar Renteria

RENTERIA, EDGAR ENRIQUE
B. Aug. 7, 1976, Barranquilla, Colombia
BR TR 6'1" 172 lbs.

Year	Team	Games	BA	SA	AB	H	2B	3B	HR	HR%	R	RBI	BB	SO	SB	AB	H	PO	A	E	DP	TC/G	FA	G by Pos
1996	FLA N	106	.309	.399	431	133	18	3	5	1.2	68	31	33	68	16	0	0	162	344	11	76	4.9	.979	SS-106

Billy Ripken

RIPKEN, WILLIAM OLIVER
Son of Cal Ripken. Brother of Cal Ripken.
B. Dec. 16, 1964, Havre de Grace, Md.
BR TR 6'1" 180 lbs.

Year	Team	Games	BA	SA	AB	H	2B	3B	HR	HR%	R	RBI	BB	SO	SB	AB	H	PO	A	E	DP	TC/G	FA	G by Pos
1987	BAL A	58	.308	.372	234	72	9	0	2	0.9	27	20	21	23	4	0	0	133	162	3	53	5.1	.990	2B-58
1988		150	.207	.258	512	106	18	1	2	0.4	52	34	33	63	8	0	0	310	440	12	110	5.0	.984	2B-149, 3B-2
1989		115	.239	.305	318	76	11	2	2	0.6	31	26	22	53	1	0	0	255	335	9	81	5.2	.985	2B-114, DH-1
1990		129	.291	.387	406	118	28	1	3	0.7	48	38	28	43	5	1	1	250	366	8	84	4.9	.987	2B-127
1991		104	.216	.261	287	62	11	1	0	0.0	24	14	15	31	0	0	0	201	284	7	75	4.8	.986	2B-103
1992		111	.230	.312	330	76	15	0	4	1.2	35	36	18	26	2	0	0	217	317	4	66	4.9	.993	2B-108, DH-2
1993	TEX A	50	.189	.220	132	25	4	0	0	0.0	12	11	11	19	0	0	0	80	123	2	28	3.9	.990	2B-34, SS-18, 3B-1
1994		32	.309	.370	81	25	5	0	0	0.0	9	6	3	11	2	4	1	29	50	2	10	2.5	.975	3B-18, 2B-12, 1B-1
1995	CLE A	8	.412	.765	17	7	0	0	2	11.8	4	3	0	3	0	0	0	7	6	0	1	1.6	1.000	2B-7, 3B-1
1996	BAL A	57	.230	.333	135	31	8	0	2	1.5	19	12	9	18	0	7	2	40	95	3	17	2.5	.978	2B-30, 3B-25, 1B-1
10 yrs.		814	.244	.313	2452	598	109	5	17	0.7	261	200	160	290	22	12	4	1522	2178	50	525	4.6	.987	2B-742, 3B-47, SS-20, DH-3, 1B-2

Cal Ripken

RIPKEN, CALVIN EDWIN, JR.
Brother of Billy Ripken. Son of Cal Ripken.
B. Aug. 24, 1960, Havre de Grace, Md.
BR TR 6'4" 200 lbs.

Year	Team	Games	BA	SA	AB	H	2B	3B	HR	HR%	R	RBI	BB	SO	SB	AB	H	PO	A	E	DP	TC/G	FA	G by Pos
1981	BAL A	23	.128	.128	39	5	0	0	0	0.0	1	0	1	8	0	4	0	13	30	3	6	2.6	.935	SS-12, 3B-6
1982		160	.264	.475	598	158	32	5	28	4.7	90	93	46	95	3	0	0	221	440	19	64	4.1	.972	SS-94, 3B-71
1983		162	.318	.517	663	211	47	2	27	4.1	121	102	58	97	0	0	0	272	534	25	113	5.1	.970	SS-162
1984		162	.304	.510	641	195	37	7	27	4.2	103	86	71	89	2	0	0	297	583	26	122	5.6	.971	SS-162
1985		161	.282	.469	642	181	32	5	26	4.0	116	110	67	68	2	0	0	286	474	26	123	4.9	.967	SS-161
1986		162	.282	.461	627	177	35	1	25	4.0	98	81	70	60	4	0	0	240	482	13	105	4.5	.982	SS-162
1987		162	.252	.436	624	157	28	3	27	4.3	97	98	81	77	3	0	0	240	480	20	103	4.6	.973	SS-162
1988		161	.264	.431	575	152	25	1	23	4.0	87	81	102	69	2	0	0	284	480	21	119	4.9	.973	SS-162
1989		162	.257	.401	646	166	30	0	21	3.3	80	93	57	72	3	0	0	276	531	8	119	5.0	.990	SS-162
1990		161	.250	.415	600	150	28	4	21	3.5	78	84	82	66	3	0	0	242	435	3	94	4.2	.996	SS-161
1991		162	.323	.566	650	210	46	5	34	5.2	99	114	53	46	6	0	0	267	528	11	114	5.0	.986	SS-162
1992		162	.251	.366	637	160	29	1	14	2.2	73	72	64	50	4	0	0	287	445	12	119	4.6	.984	SS-162
1993		162	.257	.420	641	165	26	3	24	3.7	87	90	65	58	1	0	0	226	495	17	101	4.6	.977	SS-162
1994		112	.315	.459	444	140	19	3	13	2.9	71	75	32	41	1	0	0	130	321	7	70	4.1	.985	SS-112
1995		144	.262	.422	550	144	33	2	17	3.1	71	88	52	59	0	0	0	205	409	7	99	4.3	.989	SS-144
1996		163	.278	.466	640	178	40	1	26	4.1	94	102	59	78	1	0	0	234	482	14	110	4.5	.981	SS-158, 3B-6
16 yrs.		2381	.277	.454	9217	2549	487	43	353	3.8	1366	1369	960	1033	35	4	0	3720	7149	232	1581	4.7	.979	SS-2299, 3B-83

DIVISIONAL PLAYOFF SERIES

Year	Team	Games	BA	SA	AB	H	2B	3B	HR	HR%	R	RBI	BB	SO	SB	AB	H	PO	A	E	DP	TC/G	FA	G by Pos
1996	BAL A	4	.444	.611	18	8	3	0	0	0.0	2	2	0	3	0	0	0	7	15	0	1	5.5	1.000	SS-4

LEAGUE CHAMPIONSHIP SERIES

Year	Team	Games	BA	SA	AB	H	2B	3B	HR	HR%	R	RBI	BB	SO	SB	AB	H	PO	A	E	DP	TC/G	FA	G by Pos
1983	BAL A	4	.400	.533	15	6	2	0	0	0.0	5	1	2	3	0	0	0	7	11	0	2	4.5	1.000	SS-4
1996		5	.250	.300	20	5	1	0	0	0.0	1	0	1	4	0	0	0	4	14	1	5	3.8	.947	SS-5
2 yrs.		9	.314	.400	35	11	3	0	0	0.0	6	1	3	7	0	0	0	11	25	1	7	4.1	.973	SS-9

WORLD SERIES

Year	Team	Games	BA	SA	AB	H	2B	3B	HR	HR%	R	RBI	BB	SO	SB	AB	H	PO	A	E	DP	TC/G	FA	G by Pos
1983	BAL A	5	.167	.167	18	3	0	0	0	0.0	2	1	3	4	0	0	0	6	14	0	3	4.0	1.000	SS-5

Ruben Rivera

RIVERA, RUBEN
Born Ruben Rivera (Moreno).
B. Nov. 14, 1973, Chorrera, Panama
BR TR 6'3" 200 lbs.

Year	Team	Games	BA	SA	AB	H	2B	3B	HR	HR%	R	RBI	BB	SO	SB	AB	H	PO	A	E	DP	TC/G	FA	G by Pos
1995	NY A	5	.000	.000	1	0	0	0	0	0.0	0	0	0	1	0	0	0	2	0	0	0	0.5	1.000	OF-4
1996		46	.284	.443	88	25	6	1	2	2.3	17	16	13	26	6	2	1	78	2	0	0	1.8	1.000	OF-45
2 yrs.		51	.281	.438	89	25	6	1	2	2.2	17	16	13	27	6	2	1	80	2	0	0	1.7	1.000	OF-49

DIVISIONAL PLAYOFF SERIES

Year	Team	Games	BA	SA	AB	H	2B	3B	HR	HR%	R	RBI	BB	SO	SB	AB	H	PO	A	E	DP	TC/G	FA	G by Pos
1996	NY A	2	.000	.000	1	0	0	0	0	0.0	0	0	0	1	0	1	0	0	0	0	0	0.0	.000	OF-2

Kevin Roberson

ROBERSON, KEVIN LYNN
B. Jan. 29, 1968, Decatur, Ill.
BB TR 6'4" 210 lbs.

Year	Team	Games	BA	SA	AB	H	2B	3B	HR	HR%	R	RBI	BB	SO	SB	AB	H	PO	A	E	DP	TC/G	FA	G by Pos
1993	CHI N	62	.189	.372	180	34	4	1	9	5.0	23	27	12	48	0	14	2	77	2	3	0	1.6	.963	OF-51
1994		44	.218	.509	55	12	4	0	4	7.3	8	9	2	14	0	35	9	7	1	2	0	1.1	.800	OF-9
1995		32	.184	.526	38	7	1	0	4	10.5	5	6	6	14	0	20	4	8	0	0	0	0.7	1.000	OF-11
1996	NY N	27	.222	.500	36	8	1	0	3	8.3	8	9	7	17	0	12	3	12	0	0	0	1.2	1.000	OF-10
4 yrs.		165	.197	.430	309	61	10	1	20	6.5	44	51	27	93	0	81	18	104	3	5	0	1.4	.955	OF-81

Bip Roberts

ROBERTS, LEON JOSEPH
B. Oct. 27, 1963, Berkeley, Calif.
BB TR 5'7" 150 lbs.

Year	Team	Games	BA	SA	AB	H	2B	3B	HR	HR%	R	RBI	BB	SO	SB	AB	H	PO	A	E	DP	TC/G	FA	G by Pos
1986	SD N	101	.253	.303	241	61	5	2	1	0.4	34	12	14	29	14	3	1	166	172	10	33	4.0	.971	2B-87
1988		5	.333	.333	9	3	0	0	0	0.0	1	0	1	2	0	2	0	2	3	1	1	2.0	.833	3B-2, 2B-1
1989		117	.301	.422	329	99	15	8	3	0.9	81	25	49	45	21	17	6	134	113	9	17	2.2	.965	OF-54, 3B-37, SS-14, 2B-9
1990		149	.309	.433	556	172	36	3	9	1.6	104	44	55	65	46	5	0	227	160	13	22	2.5	.967	OF-75, 3B-56, SS-18, 2B-8
1991		117	.281	.347	424	119	13	3	3	0.7	66	32	37	71	26	7	1	239	185	10	35	3.8	.977	2B-68, OF-46
1992	CIN N	147	.323	.432	532	172	34	6	4	0.8	92	45	62	54	44	12	4	209	152	7	13	2.3	.981	OF-79, 2B-42, 3B-36
1993		83	.240	.295	292	70	13	0	1	0.3	46	18	38	46	26	3	0	152	176	6	31	4.2	.982	2B-64, OF-11, 3B-3, SS-1
1994	SD N	105	.320	.397	403	129	15	5	2	0.5	52	31	39	57	21	2	2	177	221	9	41	3.7	.978	2B-90, OF-20

Year	Team	Games	BA	SA	AB	H	2B	3B	HR	HR%	R	RBI	BB	SO	SB	Pinch Hit AB	H	PO	A	E	DP	TC/G	FA	G by Pos

Bip Roberts *continued*

Year	Team	Games	BA	SA	AB	H	2B	3B	HR	HR%	R	RBI	BB	SO	SB	AB	H	PO	A	E	DP	TC/G	FA	G by Pos
1995		73	.304	.372	296	90	14	0	2	0.7	40	25	17	36	20	2	1	133	88	4	15	2.7	.982	OF-50, 2B-25, SS-7
1996	KC A	90	.283	.357	339	96	21	2	0	0.0	39	52	25	38	12	9	3	115	189	4	42	3.4	.987	2B-63, DH-16, OF-11
10 yrs.		987	.296	.383	3421	1011	166	29	25	0.7	555	284	337	443	230	62	18	1554	1459	73	250	3.1	.976	2B-457, OF-346, 3B-134, SS-40, DH-16

Mike Robertson

ROBERTSON, MICHAEL FRANCIS
B. Oct. 9, 1970, Norwich, Conn.

BL TL 6' 180 lbs.

Year	Team	Games	BA	SA	AB	H	2B	3B	HR	HR%	R	RBI	BB	SO	SB	AB	H	PO	A	E	DP	TC/G	FA	G by Pos
1996	CHI A	6	.143	.286	7	1	1	0	1	0.0	0	0	0	1	0	2	0	12	1	0	2	6.5	1.000	1B-2, DH-1

Alex Rodriguez

RODRIGUEZ, ALEXANDER EMMANUEL
B. July 27, 1975, New York, N. Y.

BR TR 6'3" 190 lbs.

Year	Team	Games	BA	SA	AB	H	2B	3B	HR	HR%	R	RBI	BB	SO	SB	AB	H	PO	A	E	DP	TC/G	FA	G by Pos
1994	SEA A	17	.204	.204	54	11	0	0	0	0.0	4	2	3	20	3	0	0	20	45	6	9	4.2	.915	SS-17
1995		48	.232	.408	142	33	6	2	5	3.5	15	19	6	42	4	0	0	55	106	8	14	3.6	.953	SS-46, DH-1
1996		146	.358	.631	601	215	54	1	36	6.0	141	123	59	104	15	1	0	239	403	15	92	4.5	.977	SS-146
3 yrs.		211	.325	.562	797	259	60	3	41	5.1	160	144	68	166	22	1	0	314	554	29	115	4.3	.968	SS-209, DH-1

DIVISIONAL PLAYOFF SERIES

Year	Team	Games	BA	SA	AB	H	2B	3B	HR	HR%	R	RBI	BB	SO	SB	AB	H	PO	A	E	DP	TC/G	FA	G by Pos
1995	SEA A	1	.000	.000	1	0	0	0	0	0.0	1	0	0	0	0	0	0	0	0	0	0	0.0	.000	SS-1

LEAGUE CHAMPIONSHIP SERIES

Year	Team	Games	BA	SA	AB	H	2B	3B	HR	HR%	R	RBI	BB	SO	SB	AB	H	PO	A	E	DP	TC/G	FA	G by Pos
1995	SEA A	1	.000	.000	1	0	0	0	0	0.0	0	0	0	1	0	1	0	0	0	0	0	0.0	—	

Henry Rodriguez

RODRIGUEZ, HENRY ANDERSON
Born Henry Anderson Rodriguez (Lorenzo).
B. Nov. 8, 1967, Santo Domingo, Dominican Republic

BL TL 6'1" 180 lbs.

Year	Team	Games	BA	SA	AB	H	2B	3B	HR	HR%	R	RBI	BB	SO	SB	AB	H	PO	A	E	DP	TC/G	FA	G by Pos
1992	LA N	53	.219	.329	146	32	7	0	3	2.1	11	14	8	30	0	5	0	68	8	3	2	1.6	.962	OF-48, 1B-1
1993		76	.222	.415	176	39	10	0	8	4.5	20	23	11	39	1	15	4	127	9	1	2	2.2	.993	OF-48, 1B-13
1994		104	.268	.405	306	82	14	2	8	2.6	33	49	17	58	0	15	4	198	9	2	3	2.0	.990	OF-86, 1B-17
1995	2 teams	LA N (21G –.263)		MON N (24G –.207)																				
"	total	45	.239	.326	138	33	4	1	2	1.4	13	15	11	28	0	8	0	126	7	1	8	3.4	.993	OF-28, 1B-11
1996	MON N	145	.276	.562	532	147	42	1	36	6.8	81	103	37	160	2	7	3	528	33	11	27	4.1	.981	OF-90, 1B-51
5 yrs.		423	.257	.454	1298	333	77	4	57	4.4	158	204	84	315	3	50	11	1047	66	18	42	2.9	.984	OF-300, 1B-93

Ivan Rodriguez

RODRIGUEZ, IVAN (Pudge)
Born Ivan Rodriguez (Torres).
B. Nov. 27, 1971, Manati, Puerto Rico

BR TR 5'9" 165 lbs.

Year	Team	Games	BA	SA	AB	H	2B	3B	HR	HR%	R	RBI	BB	SO	SB	AB	H	PO	A	E	DP	TC/G	FA	G by Pos
1991	TEX A	88	.264	.354	280	74	16	0	3	1.1	24	27	5	42	0	2	0	517	62	10	6	6.7	.983	C-88
1992		123	.260	.360	420	109	16	1	8	1.9	39	37	24	73	0	9	1	763	85	15	10	7.3	.983	C-116, DH-2
1993		137	.273	.412	473	129	28	4	10	2.1	56	66	29	70	8	5	3	801	76	8	6	6.6	.991	C-134, DH-1
1994		99	.298	.488	363	108	19	1	16	4.4	56	57	31	42	6	1	0	600	44	5	2	6.6	.992	C-99
1995		130	.303	.449	492	149	32	2	12	2.4	56	67	16	48	0	6	4	707	67	8	3	6.1	.990	C-127, DH-1
1996		153	.300	.473	639	192	47	3	19	3.0	116	86	38	55	5	4	2	850	80	10	11	6.1	.989	C-147, DH-6
6 yrs.		730	.285	.429	2667	761	158	11	68	2.5	347	340	143	330	19	27	10	4238	414	56	38	6.5	.988	C-711, DH-10

DIVISIONAL PLAYOFF SERIES

Year	Team	Games	BA	SA	AB	H	2B	3B	HR	HR%	R	RBI	BB	SO	SB	AB	H	PO	A	E	DP	TC/G	FA	G by Pos
1996	TEX A	4	.375	.438	16	6	1	0	0	0.0	1	2	2	3	0	0	0	21	3	0	1	6.0	1.000	C-4

Tony Rodriguez

RODRIGUEZ, LUIS ANTONIO
B. Aug. 15, 1970, Rio Piedras, Puerto Rico

BR TR 5'11" 165 lbs.

Year	Team	Games	BA	SA	AB	H	2B	3B	HR	HR%	R	RBI	BB	SO	SB	AB	H	PO	A	E	DP	TC/G	FA	G by Pos
1996	BOS A	27	.239	.299	67	16	1	0	1	1.5	7	9	4	8	0	0	0	31	64	3	1	3.8	.969	SS-21, 3B-5

Scott Rolen

ROLEN, SCOTT BRUCE
B. Apr. 4, 1975, Evansville, Ind.

BR TR 6'4" 210 lbs.

Year	Team	Games	BA	SA	AB	H	2B	3B	HR	HR%	R	RBI	BB	SO	SB	AB	H	PO	A	E	DP	TC/G	FA	G by Pos
1996	PHI N	37	.254	.400	130	33	7	0	4	3.1	10	18	13	27	0	0	0	29	54	4	4	2.4	.954	3B-37

Chris Sabo

SABO, CHRISTOPHER ANDREW (Spuds)
B. Jan. 19, 1962, Detroit, Mich.

BR TR 5'11" 185 lbs.

Year	Team	Games	BA	SA	AB	H	2B	3B	HR	HR%	R	RBI	BB	SO	SB	AB	H	PO	A	E	DP	TC/G	FA	G by Pos
1988	CIN N	137	.271	.414	538	146	40	2	11	2.0	74	44	29	52	46	2	0	75	318	14	31	3.0	.966	3B-135, SS-2
1989		82	.260	.395	304	79	21	1	6	2.0	40	29	25	33	14	5	0	36	145	11	12	2.5	.943	3B-76
1990		148	.270	.476	567	153	38	2	25	4.4	95	71	61	58	25	1	0	70	273	12	17	2.4	.966	3B-146
1991		153	.301	.505	582	175	35	3	26	4.5	91	88	44	79	19	2	1	86	255	12	24	2.3	.966	3B-151
1992		96	.244	.422	344	84	19	3	12	3.5	42	43	30	54	4	2	0	60	159	9	13	2.5	.961	3B-93
1993		148	.259	.440	552	143	33	2	21	3.8	86	82	43	105	6	0	0	79	242	11	16	2.2	.967	3B-148
1994	BAL A	68	.256	.465	258	66	15	3	11	4.3	41	42	20	38	1	2	0	52	49	4	5	1.5	.962	3B-37, OF-22, DH-10
1995	2 teams	CHI A (20G –.254)		STL N (5G –.154)																				
"	total	25	.238	.345	84	20	6	0	1	1.2	10	11	4	14	3	4	1	21	4	2	2	1.4	.926	DH-15, 1B-3, 3B-2
1996	CIN N	54	.256	.440	125	32	7	1	3	2.4	15	16	18	27	2	14	4	27	71	4	6	2.4	.961	3B-43
9 yrs.		911	.268	.445	3354	898	214	17	116	3.5	494	426	274	460	120	32	6	506	1516	79	126	2.4	.962	3B-831, DH-25, OF-22, 1B-3, SS-2

LEAGUE CHAMPIONSHIP SERIES

Year	Team	Games	BA	SA	AB	H	2B	3B	HR	HR%	R	RBI	BB	SO	SB	AB	H	PO	A	E	DP	TC/G	FA	G by Pos
1990	CIN N	6	.227	.364	22	5	0	0	1	4.5	1	3	1	4	0	0	0	7	7	0	1	2.3	1.000	3B-6

WORLD SERIES

Year	Team	Games	BA	SA	AB	H	2B	3B	HR	HR%	R	RBI	BB	SO	SB	AB	H	PO	A	E	DP	TC/G	FA	G by Pos
1990	CIN N	4	.563	1.000	16	9	1	0	2	12.5	2	5	2	2	0	0	0	3	14	0	0	4.3	1.000	3B-4

Year	Team	Games	BA	SA	AB	H	2B	3B	HR	HR%	R	RBI	BB	SO	SB	Pinch Hit AB	Pinch Hit H	PO	A	E	DP	TC/G	FA	G by Pos

Tim Salmon
SALMON, TIMOTHY JAMES
B. Aug. 24, 1968, Long Beach, Calif. BR TR 6'3" 200 lbs.

Year	Team	Games	BA	SA	AB	H	2B	3B	HR	HR%	R	RBI	BB	SO	SB	AB	H	PO	A	E	DP	TC/G	FA	G by Pos
1992	CAL A	23	.177	.266	79	14	1	0	2	2.5	8	6	11	23	1	0	0	40	1	2	1	2.0	.953	OF-21
1993		142	.283	.536	515	146	35	1	31	6.0	93	95	82	135	5	0	0	335	12	7	2	2.5	.980	OF-140, DH-1
1994		100	.287	.531	373	107	18	2	23	6.2	67	70	54	102	1	1	1	219	9	8	1	2.4	.966	OF-99
1995		143	.330	.594	537	177	34	3	34	6.3	111	105	91	111	5	0	0	319	7	4	0	2.3	.988	OF-142, DH-1
1996		156	.286	.501	581	166	27	4	30	5.2	90	98	93	125	4	1	0	299	13	8	0	2.1	.975	OF-153, DH-3
5 yrs.		564	.293	.530	2085	610	115	10	120	5.8	369	374	331	496	16	2	1	1212	42	29	4	2.3	.977	OF-555, DH-5

Juan Samuel
SAMUEL, JUAN MILTON (Sammy)
Born Juan Milton Romero (Samuel).
B. Dec. 9, 1960, San Pedro de Macoris, Dominican Republic BR TR 5'11" 170 lbs.

Year	Team	Games	BA	SA	AB	H	2B	3B	HR	HR%	R	RBI	BB	SO	SB	AB	H	PO	A	E	DP	TC/G	FA	G by Pos
1983	PHI N	18	.277	.446	65	18	1	2	2	3.1	14	5	4	16	3	0	0	44	54	9	9	5.9	.916	2B-18
1984		160	.272	.442	**701**	191	36	**19**	15	2.1	105	69	28	**168**	72	2	1	388	438	33	77	5.4	.962	2B-160
1985		161	.264	.436	**663**	175	31	13	19	2.9	101	74	33	**141**	53	1	0	389	463	15	88	5.5	.983	2B-159
1986		145	.266	.448	591	157	36	12	16	2.7	90	78	26	**142**	42	2	2	290	440	25	83	5.3	.967	2B-143
1987		160	.272	.502	**655**	178	37	**15**	28	4.3	113	100	60	**162**	35	0	0	374	434	18	99	5.2	.978	2B-160
1988		157	.243	.380	629	153	32	9	12	1.9	68	67	39	151	33	1	1	351	387	16	92	4.8	.979	2B-152, OF-3, 3B-1
1989	2 teams PHI N (51G –.246) NY N (86G –.228)																							
"	total	137	.235	.335	532	125	16	2	11	2.1	69	48	42	120	42	2	1	339	6	4	3	2.6	.989	OF-134
1990	LA N	143	.242	.382	492	119	24	3	13	2.6	62	52	51	126	38	6	1	273	262	16	47	4.0	.971	2B-108, OF-31
1991		153	.271	.389	594	161	22	6	12	2.0	74	58	49	133	23	2	1	300	442	17	73	5.0	.978	2B-152
1992	2 teams LA N (47G –.262) KC A (29G –.284)																							
"	total	76	.272	.344	224	61	8	4	0	0.0	22	23	14	49	8	15	4	121	106	11	22	3.6	.954	2B-48, OF-19
1993	CIN N	103	.230	.345	261	60	10	4	4	1.5	31	26	23	53	9	18	3	151	172	10	33	4.0	.970	2B-70, 1B-6, 3B-4, OF-3
1994	DET A	59	.309	.559	136	42	7	3	5	3.7	32	21	10	26	5	5	2	82	28	1	4	2.4	.991	OF-27, DH-10, 2B-8, 1B-2
1995	2 teams DET A (76G –.281) KC A (15G –.176)																							
"	total	91	.263	.498	205	54	10	1	12	5.9	31	39	29	49	6	29	7	300	35	9	29	4.2	.974	1B-38, DH-23, OF-14, 2B-6
1996	TOR A	69	.255	.457	188	48	8	3	8	4.3	34	26	15	65	9	18	12	117	3	2	7	1.9	.984	OF-24, DH-24, 1B-17
14 yrs.		1632	.260	.419	5936	1542	280	98	157	2.6	846	686	423	1401	378	101	25	3519	3270	186	666	4.5	.973	2B-1184, OF-255, 1B-63, DH-57, 3B-5

LEAGUE CHAMPIONSHIP SERIES

| 1983 | PHI N | 1 | — | — | 0 | 0 | 0 | 0 | 0 | — | 0 | 0 | 0 | 0 | 0 | 0 | 0 | 0 | 0 | 0 | 0 | 0.0 | — | |

WORLD SERIES

| 1983 | PHI N | 3 | .000 | .000 | 1 | 0 | 0 | 0 | 0 | 0.0 | 0 | 0 | 0 | 0 | 0 | 1 | 0 | 0 | 0 | 0 | 0 | 0.0 | — | |

Rey Sanchez
SANCHEZ, REY FRANCISCO
Born Rey Francisco Sanchez (Guadalupe).
B. Oct. 5, 1967, Rio Piedras, Puerto Rico BR TR 5'10" 180 lbs.

Year	Team	Games	BA	SA	AB	H	2B	3B	HR	HR%	R	RBI	BB	SO	SB	AB	H	PO	A	E	DP	TC/G	FA	G by Pos
1991	CHI N	13	.261	.261	23	6	0	0	0	0.0	2	4	2	4	0	0	0	11	25	0	1	3.0	1.000	SS-10, 2B-2
1992		74	.251	.341	255	64	14	3	1	0.4	24	19	10	17	2	3	1	148	202	9	52	5.0	.975	SS-68, 2B-4
1993		105	.282	.326	344	97	11	2	0	0.0	35	28	15	22	1	10	4	158	316	15	60	5.0	.969	SS-98
1994		96	.285	.337	291	83	13	1	0	0.0	26	24	20	29	2	7	1	152	275	9	52	4.5	.979	2B-50, SS-30, 3B-17
1995		114	.278	.360	428	119	22	2	3	0.7	57	27	14	48	6	1	0	195	351	7	59	4.8	.987	2B-111, SS-4
1996		95	.211	.253	289	61	9	0	1	0.3	28	12	22	42	7	1	0	152	309	11	55	5.1	.977	SS-92
6 yrs.		497	.264	.325	1630	430	69	8	5	0.3	171	112	85	161	18	22	6	816	1478	51	279	4.8	.978	SS-302, 2B-167, 3B-17

Ryne Sandberg
SANDBERG, RYNE DEE (Ryno)
B. Sept. 18, 1959, Spokane, Wash. BR TR 6'1" 175 lbs.

Year	Team	Games	BA	SA	AB	H	2B	3B	HR	HR%	R	RBI	BB	SO	SB	AB	H	PO	A	E	DP	TC/G	FA	G by Pos
1981	PHI N	13	.167	.167	6	1	0	0	0	0.0	2	0	0	1	0	0	0	7	7	0	1	2.3	1.000	SS-5, 2B-1
1982	CHI N	156	.271	.372	635	172	33	5	7	1.1	103	54	36	90	32	1	0	136	373	12	28	3.3	.977	3B-133, 2B-24
1983		158	.261	.351	633	165	25	4	8	1.3	94	48	51	79	37	4	2	330	571	13	126	5.8	.986	2B-157, SS-1
1984		156	.314	.520	636	200	36	**19**	19	3.0	**114**	84	52	101	32	0	0	314	550	6	102	5.4	.993	2B-156
1985		153	.305	.504	609	186	31	6	26	4.3	113	83	57	97	54	1	0	353	501	12	99	5.6	.986	2B-153, SS-1
1986		154	.284	.411	627	178	28	5	14	2.2	68	76	46	79	34	1	1	309	492	5	86	5.3	.994	2B-153
1987		132	.294	.442	523	154	25	2	16	3.1	81	59	59	79	21	2	1	294	375	10	84	5.2	.985	2B-131
1988		155	.264	.419	618	163	23	8	19	3.1	77	69	54	91	25	2	0	291	522	11	79	5.4	.987	2B-153
1989		157	.290	.497	606	176	25	5	30	5.0	**104**	76	59	85	15	2	0	294	466	6	87	4.9	.992	2B-155
1990		155	.306	.559	615	188	30	3	**40**	6.5	**116**	100	50	84	25	2	0	278	469	8	81	4.9	.989	2B-154
1991		158	.291	.485	585	170	32	2	26	4.4	104	100	87	89	22	3	1	267	515	4	66	5.0	.995	2B-157
1992		158	.304	.510	612	186	32	8	26	4.2	100	87	68	73	17	1	0	283	539	8	94	5.3	.990	2B-157
1993		117	.309	.412	456	141	20	0	9	2.0	67	45	37	62	9	3	1	209	347	7	76	4.9	.988	2B-115
1994		57	.238	.390	223	53	9	5	5	2.2	36	24	23	40	2	0	0	96	202	4	35	5.3	.987	2B-57
1996		150	.244	.444	554	135	28	4	25	4.5	85	92	54	116	12	5	2	228	421	6	81	4.5	.991	2B-146
15 yrs.		2029	.286	.454	7938	2268	377	76	270	3.4	1264	997	733	1166	337	27	8	3689	6350	112	1118	5.1	.989	2B-1869, 3B-133, SS-7

LEAGUE CHAMPIONSHIP SERIES

1984	CHI N	5	.368	.474	19	7	2	0	0	0.0	3	2	3	2	3	0	0	12	18	1	6	6.2	.968	2B-5
1989		5	.400	.800	20	8	3	1	1	5.0	6	4	3	4	0	0	0	7	11	0	1	3.6	1.000	2B-5
2 yrs.		10	.385	.641	39	15	5	1	1	2.6	9	6	6	6	3	0	0	19	29	1	7	4.9	.980	2B-10

Reggie Sanders
SANDERS, REGINALD LAVERNE
B. Dec. 1, 1967, Florence, S.C. BR TR 6' 180 lbs.

Year	Team	Games	BA	SA	AB	H	2B	3B	HR	HR%	R	RBI	BB	SO	SB	AB	H	PO	A	E	DP	TC/G	FA	G by Pos
1991	CIN N	9	.200	.275	40	8	1	1	2	2.5	6	6	0	9	1	0	0	22	0	0	0	2.4	1.000	OF-9
1992		116	.270	.462	385	104	26	6	12	3.1	62	36	48	98	16	11	3	262	11	6	4	2.5	.978	OF-110
1993		138	.274	.444	496	136	16	4	20	4.0	90	83	51	118	27	1	0	312	3	8	0	2.4	.975	OF-137

Year	Team	Games	BA	SA	AB	H	2B	3B	HR	HR%	R	RBI	BB	SO	SB	Pinch Hit AB	Pinch Hit H	PO	A	E	DP	TC/G	FA	G by Pos

Reggie Sanders continued

Year	Team	Games	BA	SA	AB	H	2B	3B	HR	HR%	R	RBI	BB	SO	SB	PH AB	PH H	PO	A	E	DP	TC/G	FA	G by Pos
1994		107	.263	.480	400	105	20	8	17	4.3	66	62	41	114	21	3	0	217	12	6	2	2.3	.974	OF-104
1995		133	.306	.579	484	148	36	6	28	5.8	91	99	69	122	36	3	0	268	12	5	2	2.2	.982	OF-130
1996		81	.251	.463	287	72	17	1	14	4.9	49	33	44	86	24	0	0	160	7	2	1	2.1	.988	OF-80
6 yrs.		584	.274	.485	2092	573	115	25	92	4.4	364	316	253	547	125	18	3	1241	45	27	9	2.3	.979	OF-570

DIVISIONAL PLAYOFF SERIES

| 1995 | CIN N | 3 | .154 | .462 | 13 | 2 | 1 | 0 | 1 | 7.7 | 3 | 2 | 1 | 9 | 2 | 0 | 0 | 7 | 0 | 1 | 0 | 2.7 | .875 | OF-3 |

LEAGUE CHAMPIONSHIP SERIES

| 1995 | CIN N | 4 | .125 | .125 | 16 | 2 | 0 | 0 | 0 | 0.0 | 0 | 0 | 2 | 10 | 0 | 0 | 0 | 7 | 0 | 1 | 0 | 2.0 | .875 | OF-4 |

F. P. Santangelo

SANTANGELO, FRANK-PAUL
B. Oct. 24, 1967, Livonia, Mich.

BB TR 5'10" 165 lbs.

Year	Team	Games	BA	SA	AB	H	2B	3B	HR	HR%	R	RBI	BB	SO	SB	PH AB	PH H	PO	A	E	DP	TC/G	FA	G by Pos
1995	MON N	35	.296	.398	98	29	5	1	1	1.0	11	9	12	9	1	9	3	47	0	1	0	1.6	.979	OF-25, 2B-5
1996		152	.277	.407	393	109	20	5	7	1.8	54	56	49	61	5	13	3	250	45	6	5	2.0	.980	OF-124, 3B-23, 2B-5, SS-1
2 yrs.		187	.281	.405	491	138	25	6	8	1.6	65	65	61	70	6	22	6	297	45	7	5	1.9	.980	OF-149, 3B-23, 2B-10, SS-1

Benito Santiago

SANTIAGO, BENITO
Born Benito Santiago (Rivera).
B. Mar. 9, 1965, Ponce, Puerto Rico

BR TR 6'1" 180 lbs.

Year	Team	Games	BA	SA	AB	H	2B	3B	HR	HR%	R	RBI	BB	SO	SB	PH AB	PH H	PO	A	E	DP	TC/G	FA	G by Pos
1986	SD N	17	.290	.468	62	18	2	0	3	4.8	10	6	2	12	0	0	0	80	7	5	2	5.4	.946	C-17
1987		146	.300	.467	546	164	33	2	18	3.3	64	79	16	112	21	0	0	817	80	22	12	6.3	.976	C-146
1988		139	.248	.362	492	122	22	2	10	2.0	49	46	24	82	15	7	2	725	75	12	11	6.0	.985	C-136
1989		129	.236	.387	462	109	16	3	16	3.5	50	62	26	89	11	4	0	685	81	20	10	6.2	.975	C-127
1990		100	.270	.419	344	93	8	5	11	3.2	42	53	27	55	5	4	1	538	51	12	6	6.1	.980	C-98
1991		152	.267	.403	580	155	22	3	17	2.9	60	87	23	114	8	2	2	830	100	14	14	6.2	.985	C-151, OF-1
1992		106	.251	.383	386	97	21	0	10	2.6	37	42	21	52	2	4	1	584	53	12	6	6.3	.982	C-103
1993	FLA N	139	.230	.380	469	108	19	6	13	2.8	49	50	37	88	10	5	1	740	64	11	4	5.9	.987	C-136, OF-1
1994		101	.273	.424	337	92	14	2	11	3.3	35	41	25	57	1	8	2	511	64	5	3	6.0	.991	C-97
1995	CIN N	81	.286	.485	266	76	20	0	11	4.1	40	44	24	48	2	7	3	481	33	2	6	6.2	.996	C-75, 1B-8
1996	PHI N	136	.264	.503	481	127	21	2	30	6.2	71	85	49	104	2	10	5	833	67	11	14	7.1	.988	C-114, 1B-14
11 yrs.		1246	.262	.420	4425	1161	198	25	150	3.4	507	595	274	813	77	49	17	6824	675	126	88	6.2	.983	C-1200, 1B-22, OF-2

DIVISIONAL PLAYOFF SERIES

| 1995 | CIN N | 3 | .333 | .667 | 9 | 3 | 0 | 0 | 1 | 11.1 | 2 | 3 | 3 | 3 | 0 | 0 | 0 | 20 | 0 | 0 | 0 | 6.7 | 1.000 | C-3 |

LEAGUE CHAMPIONSHIP SERIES

| 1995 | CIN N | 4 | .231 | .231 | 13 | 3 | 0 | 0 | 0 | 0.0 | 0 | 0 | 2 | 3 | 0 | 0 | 0 | 23 | 1 | 0 | 1 | 6.0 | 1.000 | C-4 |

Steve Scarsone

SCARSONE, STEVEN WAYNE
B. Apr. 11, 1966, Anaheim, Calif.

BR TR 6'2" 170 lbs.

Year	Team	Games	BA	SA	AB	H	2B	3B	HR	HR%	R	RBI	BB	SO	SB	PH AB	PH H	PO	A	E	DP	TC/G	FA	G by Pos
1992	2 teams	PHI N (7G –.154)		BAL A (11G –.176)																				
"	total	18	.167	.167	30	5	0	0	0	3	0.0	2	12	0	5	1	9	11	2	5	2.0	.909	2B-8, 3B-2, SS-1
1993	SF N	44	.252	.398	103	26	9	0	2	1.9	16	15	4	32	0	10	3	53	44	1	11	2.9	.990	2B-20, 3B-8, 1B-6
1994		52	.272	.408	103	28	8	0	2	1.9	21	13	10	20	0	15	4	66	80	2	23	4.0	.986	2B-22, 3B-8, 1B-6, SS-1
1995		80	.266	.476	233	62	10	3	11	4.7	33	29	18	82	3	8	3	135	112	11	31	3.5	.957	3B-50, 2B-13, 1B-11
1996		105	.219	.322	283	62	12	1	5	1.8	28	23	25	91	2	18	4	168	178	11	49	4.0	.969	2B-74, 3B-14, 1B-1, SS-1
5 yrs.		299	.243	.386	752	183	39	4	20	2.7	101	80	59	237	5	56	15	431	425	27	119	3.6	.969	2B-137, 3B-82, 1B-24, SS-3

Gene Schall

SCHALL, EUGENE DAVID
B. June 5, 1970, Abington, Pa.

BR TR 6'3" 190 lbs.

Year	Team	Games	BA	SA	AB	H	2B	3B	HR	HR%	R	RBI	BB	SO	SB	PH AB	PH H	PO	A	E	DP	TC/G	FA	G by Pos
1995	PHI N	24	.231	.262	65	15	2	0	0	0.0	2	5	6	16	0	5	2	114	10	2	8	7.0	.984	1B-14, OF-4
1996		28	.273	.470	66	18	5	1	2	3.0	7	10	12	15	0	8	5	135	8	2	16	7.6	.986	1B-19
2 yrs.		52	.252	.366	131	33	7	1	2	1.5	9	15	18	31	0	13	7	249	18	4	24	7.3	.985	1B-33, OF-4

Dick Schofield

SCHOFIELD, RICHARD CRAIG
Son of Dick Schofield.
B. Nov. 21, 1962, Springfield, Ill.

BR TR 5'10" 175 lbs.

Year	Team	Games	BA	SA	AB	H	2B	3B	HR	HR%	R	RBI	BB	SO	SB	PH AB	PH H	PO	A	E	DP	TC/G	FA	G by Pos
1983	CAL A	21	.204	.407	54	11	2	0	3	5.6	4	4	6	8	0	0	0	24	67	7	10	4.7	.929	SS-21
1984		140	.193	.263	400	77	10	3	4	1.0	39	21	33	79	4	0	0	218	420	12	95	4.6	.982	SS-140
1985		147	.219	.331	438	96	19	3	8	1.8	50	41	35	70	11	0	0	261	397	25	108	4.6	.963	SS-147
1986		139	.249	.397	458	114	17	6	13	2.8	67	57	48	55	23	0	0	246	389	18	103	4.8	.972	SS-137
1987		134	.251	.355	479	120	17	3	9	1.9	52	46	37	63	19	0	0	205	351	9	76	4.2	.984	SS-131, 2B-2, DH-1
1988		155	.239	.317	527	126	11	6	6	1.1	61	34	40	57	20	0	0	278	492	13	125	5.1	.983	SS-155
1989		91	.228	.318	302	69	11	2	4	1.3	42	26	28	47	9	1	1	118	276	7	56	4.5	.983	SS-90
1990		99	.255	.297	310	79	8	1	1	0.3	41	18	52	61	3	0	0	170	318	17	77	5.1	.966	SS-99
1991		134	.225	.260	427	96	9	3	0	0.0	44	31	50	69	8	3	0	186	398	15	83	4.5	.975	SS-133
1992	2 teams	CAL A (1G –.333)		NY N (142G –.205)																				
"	total	143	.206	.286	423	87	18	2	4	0.9	52	36	61	82	11	0	0	208	392	7	78	4.3	.988	SS-142
1993	TOR A	36	.191	.236	110	21	1	2	0	0.0	11	5	16	25	3	0	0	61	106	4	23	4.8	.977	SS-36
1994		95	.255	.342	325	83	14	1	4	1.2	38	32	34	62	7	0	0	150	235	11	58	4.2	.972	SS-95
1995	2 teams	LA N (9G –.100)		CAL A (12G –.250)																				
"	total	21	.200	.200	30	6	0	0	0	0.0	1	2	5	5	0	6	1	11	32	0	5	2.7	1.000	SS-15, 3B-1
1996	CAL A	13	.250	.250	16	4	0	0	0	0.0	3	0	1	1	1	0	0	9	10	1	2	2.0	.950	SS-7, 2B-2, 3B-1
14 yrs.		1368	.230	.316	4299	989	137	32	56	1.3	505	353	446	684	119	11	2	2145	3883	146	899	4.6	.976	SS-1348, 2B-4, 3B-2, DH-1

Year	Team	Games	BA	SA	AB	H	2B	3B	HR	HR%	R	RBI	BB	SO	SB	Pinch Hit AB	Pinch Hit H	PO	A	E	DP	TC/G	FA	G by Pos

Dick Schofield *continued*

LEAGUE CHAMPIONSHIP SERIES

Year	Team	Games	BA	SA	AB	H	2B	3B	HR	HR%	R	RBI	BB	SO	SB	Pinch Hit AB	Pinch Hit H	PO	A	E	DP	TC/G	FA	G by Pos
1986	CAL A	7	.300	.433	30	9	1	0	1	3.3	4	2	1	5	1	0	0	12	23	2	3	5.3	.946	SS-7

Rick Schu

SCHU, RICHARD SPENCER
B. Jan. 26, 1962, Philadelphia, Pa.
BR TR 6' 170 lbs.

Year	Team	Games	BA	SA	AB	H	2B	3B	HR	HR%	R	RBI	BB	SO	SB	Pinch Hit AB	Pinch Hit H	PO	A	E	DP	TC/G	FA	G by Pos
1984	PHI N	17	.276	.621	29	8	2	1	2	6.9	12	5	6	6	0	2	0	7	13	1	3	1.4	.952	3B-15
1985		112	.252	.373	416	105	21	4	7	1.7	54	24	38	78	8	1	0	86	191	20	19	2.7	.933	3B-111
1986		92	.274	.447	208	57	10	1	8	3.8	32	25	18	44	2	29	7	42	94	13	6	2.6	.913	3B-58
1987		92	.235	.403	196	46	6	3	7	3.6	24	23	20	36	0	24	2	193	71	10	11	3.8	.964	3B-45, 1B-28
1988	BAL A	89	.256	.363	270	69	9	4	4	1.5	22	20	21	49	6	5	1	94	110	11	8	2.5	.949	3B-72, DH-9, 1B-4
1989	**2 teams**	BAL A (1G –.000)		DET A (98G –.214)																				
"	**total**	99	.214	.335	266	57	11	0	7	2.6	25	21	24	37	1	10	2	59	126	12	14	1.9	.939	3B-83, DH-9, 2B-6, SS-3, 1B-3
1990	CAL A	61	.268	.433	157	42	8	0	6	3.8	19	14	11	25	0	11	2	104	81	11	16	3.4	.944	3B-38, 1B-15, OF-4, 2B-1
1991	PHI N	17	.091	.091	22	2	0	0	0	0.0	1	2	1	7	0	13	1	15	1	1	0	4.3	.941	3B-3, 1B-1
1996	MON N	1	.000	.000	4	0	0	0	0	0.0	0	0	0	0	0	0	0	0	2	1	0	3.0	.667	3B-1
9 yrs.		580	.246	.384	1568	386	67	13	41	2.6	189	134	139	282	17	95	15	600	689	80	77	2.7	.942	3B-426, 1B-51, DH-18, 2B-7, OF-4, SS-3

Kevin Sefcik

SEFCIK, KEVIN JOHN
B. Feb. 10, 1971, Tinley Park, Ill.
BR TR 5'11" 175 lbs.

Year	Team	Games	BA	SA	AB	H	2B	3B	HR	HR%	R	RBI	BB	SO	SB	Pinch Hit AB	Pinch Hit H	PO	A	E	DP	TC/G	FA	G by Pos
1995	PHI N	5	.000	.000	4	0	0	0	0	0.0	1	0	0	2	0	2	0	0	1	0	1	0.5	1.000	3B-2
1996		44	.284	.379	116	33	5	3	0	0.0	10	9	9	16	3	4	2	31	83	7	12	2.9	.942	SS-21, 3B-20, 2B-1
2 yrs.		49	.275	.367	120	33	5	3	0	0.0	11	9	9	18	3	6	2	31	84	7	13	2.8	.943	3B-22, SS-21, 2B-1

David Segui

SEGUI, DAVID VINCENT
Son of Diego Segui.
B. June 19, 1966, Kansas City, Kans.
BB TL 6'1" 170 lbs.

Year	Team	Games	BA	SA	AB	H	2B	3B	HR	HR%	R	RBI	BB	SO	SB	Pinch Hit AB	Pinch Hit H	PO	A	E	DP	TC/G	FA	G by Pos
1990	BAL A	40	.244	.350	123	30	7	0	2	1.6	14	15	11	15	0	0	0	283	26	3	24	7.8	.990	1B-36, DH-4
1991		86	.278	.340	212	59	7	0	2	0.9	15	22	12	19	1	24	6	264	23	3	22	3.7	.990	1B-42, OF-33, DH-4
1992		115	.233	.296	189	44	9	0	1	0.5	21	17	20	23	1	11	4	406	35	1	42	3.9	.998	1B-95, OF-18
1993		146	.273	.400	450	123	27	0	10	2.2	54	60	58	53	2	2	0	1152	98	5	122	8.7	.996	1B-144, DH-1
1994	NY N	92	.241	.387	336	81	17	1	10	3.0	46	43	33	43	0	1	0	696	52	5	65	7.6	.993	1B-78, OF-21
1995	**2 teams**	NY N (33G –.329)		MON N (97G –.305)																				
"	**total**	130	.309	.461	456	141	25	4	12	2.6	68	68	40	47	2	9	4	898	73	3	71	7.9	.997	1B-104, OF-20
1996	MON N	115	.286	.442	416	119	30	1	11	2.6	69	58	60	54	4	1	0	943	89	7	79	9.1	.993	1B-114
7 yrs.		724	.274	.401	2182	597	122	6	48	2.2	287	283	234	254	10	48	14	4642	396	27	425	7.1	.995	1B-613, OF-92, DH-9

Kevin Seitzer

SEITZER, KEVIN LEE
B. Mar. 26, 1962, Springfield, Ill.
BR TR 5'11" 180 lbs.

Year	Team	Games	BA	SA	AB	H	2B	3B	HR	HR%	R	RBI	BB	SO	SB	Pinch Hit AB	Pinch Hit H	PO	A	E	DP	TC/G	FA	G by Pos
1986	KC A	28	.323	.448	96	31	4	1	2	2.1	16	11	19	14	0	1	1	224	19	3	17	8.2	.988	1B-22, OF-5, 3B-3
1987		161	.323	.470	641	207	33	8	15	2.3	105	83	80	85	12	0	0	290	315	24	51	3.7	.962	3B-141, 1B-25, OF-3
1988		149	.304	.406	559	170	32	5	5	0.9	90	60	72	64	10	1	0	93	297	26	33	2.8	.938	3B-147, OF-1, DH-1
1989		160	.281	.337	597	168	17	2	4	0.7	78	48	102	76	17	0	0	118	277	20	30	2.4	.952	3B-159, SS-6, OF-3, 1B-2
1990		158	.275	.370	622	171	31	5	6	1.0	91	38	67	66	7	5	3	118	281	19	36	2.6	.955	3B-152, 2B-10
1991		85	.265	.350	234	62	11	3	1	0.4	28	25	29	21	4	20	11	45	127	11	8	2.6	.940	3B-68, DH-3
1992	MIL N	148	.270	.367	540	146	35	1	5	0.9	74	71	57	44	13	0	0	102	277	12	18	2.6	.969	3B-146, 2B-2, 1B-1
1993	**2 teams**	OAK A (73G –.255)		MIL A (47G –.290)																				
"	**total**	120	.269	.396	417	112	16	2	11	2.6	45	57	44	48	7	13	2	276	151	12	43	3.5	.973	3B-79, 1B-31, DH-6, OF-4, 2B-3, SS-1, P-1
1994	MIL A	80	.314	.453	309	97	24	2	5	1.6	44	49	30	38	2	1	1	329	104	11	51	5.4	.975	3B-43, 1B-35, DH-4
1995		132	.311	.421	492	153	33	3	5	1.0	56	69	64	57	2	2	1	340	179	10	55	3.8	.981	3B-88, 1B-36, DH-14
1996	**2 teams**	MIL A (132G –.316)		CLE A (22G –.386)																				
"	**total**	154	.326	.466	573	187	35	3	13	2.3	85	78	87	79	6	3	2	529	75	5	59	3.9	.992	DH-73, 1B-70, 3B-12
11 yrs.		1375	.296	.406	5080	1504	271	35	72	1.4	712	589	651	592	80	46	21	2464	2102	153	401	3.4	.968	3B-1038, 1B-222, DH-101, OF-16, 2B-15, SS-7, P-1

DIVISIONAL PLAYOFF SERIES

Year	Team	Games	BA	SA	AB	H	2B	3B	HR	HR%	R	RBI	BB	SO	SB	Pinch Hit AB	Pinch Hit H	PO	A	E	DP	TC/G	FA	G by Pos
1996	CLE A	4	.294	.353	17	5	1	0	0	0.0	1	4	2	4	1	0	0	7	1	1	1	2.3	.889	DH-3, 1B-1

Bill Selby

SELBY, WILLIAM FRANK
B. Jun. 11, 1970, Monroeville, Ala.
BL TR 5'9" 190 lbs.

Year	Team	Games	BA	SA	AB	H	2B	3B	HR	HR%	R	RBI	BB	SO	SB	Pinch Hit AB	Pinch Hit H	PO	A	E	DP	TC/G	FA	G by Pos
1996	BOS A	40	.274	.411	95	26	4	0	3	3.2	12	6	9	11	1	10	4	30	43	4	5	2.3	.948	2B-14, 3B-14, OF-6, DH-1

Scott Servais

SERVAIS, SCOTT DANIEL
B. June 14, 1967, La Crosse, Wis.
BR TR 6'2" 195 lbs.

Year	Team	Games	BA	SA	AB	H	2B	3B	HR	HR%	R	RBI	BB	SO	SB	Pinch Hit AB	Pinch Hit H	PO	A	E	DP	TC/G	FA	G by Pos
1991	HOU N	16	.162	.243	37	6	3	0	0	0.0	0	6	4	8	0	2	0	77	4	0	0	5.9	.988	C-14
1992		77	.239	.283	205	49	9	0	0	0.0	12	15	11	25	0	7	1	386	27	2	5	5.7	.995	C-73
1993		85	.244	.415	258	63	11	0	11	4.3	24	32	22	45	0	5	0	493	40	2	9	6.5	.996	C-82
1994		78	.195	.371	251	49	15	1	9	3.6	27	41	10	44	0	0	0	481	29	2	1	6.6	.996	C-78
1995	**2 teams**	HOU N (28G –.225)		CHI N (52G –.286)																				
"	**total**	80	.265	.496	264	70	22	0	13	4.9	38	47	32	52	2	2	0	526	48	12	4	7.3	.980	C-80
1996	CHI N	129	.265	.384	445	118	20	0	11	2.5	42	63	30	75	0	3	0	798	72	11	11	6.8	.988	C-128, 1B-1
6 yrs.		465	.243	.390	1460	355	80	1	44	3.0	143	204	109	249	2	19	1	2761	220	30	30	6.6	.990	C-455, 1B-1

Year	Team	Games	BA	SA	AB	H	2B	3B	HR	HR%	R	RBI	BB	SO	SB	Pinch Hit AB	Pinch Hit H	PO	A	E	DP	TC/G	FA	G by Pos

Danny Sheaffer
SHEAFFER, DANNY TODD
B. Aug. 2, 1961, Jacksonville, Fla.
BR TR 6' 185 lbs.

Year	Team	Games	BA	SA	AB	H	2B	3B	HR	HR%	R	RBI	BB	SO	SB	PH AB	PH H	PO	A	E	DP	TC/G	FA	G by Pos
1987	BOS A	25	.121	.182	66	8	1	0	1	1.5	5	5	0	14	0	1	1	121	5	3	1	5.2	.977	C-25
1989	CLE A	7	.063	.063	16	1	0	0	0	0.0	1	0	2	2	0	1	0	4	0	0	0	0.7	1.000	DH-3, 3B-2, OF-1
1993	CLR N	82	.278	.384	216	60	9	1	4	1.9	26	32	8	15	2	7	2	337	32	2	6	4.9	.995	C-65, 1B-7, OF-2, 3B-1
1994		44	.218	.282	110	24	4	0	1	0.9	11	12	10	11	0	11	3	181	17	1	3	6.0	.995	C-30, 1B-2, OF-1
1995	STL N	76	.231	.361	208	48	10	1	5	2.4	24	30	23	38	0	6	1	391	44	3	7	6.2	.993	C-67, 1B-3, 3B-1
1996		79	.227	.333	198	45	9	3	2	1.0	10	20	9	25	3	19	4	277	42	6	4	4.5	.982	C-47, 3B-17, 1B-6, OF-3
6 yrs.		313	.229	.329	814	186	33	5	13	1.6	77	99	52	105	5	45	11	1311	140	15	21	5.2	.990	C-234, 3B-21, 1B-18, OF-7, DH-3

LEAGUE CHAMPIONSHIP SERIES

Year	Team	Games	BA	SA	AB	H	2B	3B	HR	HR%	R	RBI	BB	SO	SB	PH AB	PH H	PO	A	E	DP	TC/G	FA	G by Pos
1996	STL N	2	.000	.000	3	0	0	0	0	0.0	0	0	0	1	0	1	0	3	0	0	0	1.5	1.000	C-2

Andy Sheets
SHEETS, ANDREW MARK
B. Nov. 19, 1971, Baton Rouge, La.
BR TR 6'2" 180 lbs.

Year	Team	Games	BA	SA	AB	H	2B	3B	HR	HR%	R	RBI	BB	SO	SB	PH AB	PH H	PO	A	E	DP	TC/G	FA	G by Pos
1996	SEA A	47	.191	.264	110	21	8	0	1	0.9	18	9	10	41	2	3	0	40	77	5	18	2.4	.959	3B-25, 2B-18, SS-7

Gary Sheffield
SHEFFIELD, GARY ANTONIAN
B. Nov. 18, 1968, Tampa, Fla.
BR TR 5'11" 190 lbs.

Year	Team	Games	BA	SA	AB	H	2B	3B	HR	HR%	R	RBI	BB	SO	SB	PH AB	PH H	PO	A	E	DP	TC/G	FA	G by Pos
1988	MIL A	24	.237	.400	80	19	1	0	4	5.0	12	12	7	7	3	0	0	39	48	3	9	3.8	.967	SS-24
1989		95	.247	.337	368	91	18	0	5	1.4	34	32	27	33	10	0	0	100	238	16	44	3.7	.955	SS-70, 3B-21, DH-4
1990		125	.294	.421	487	143	30	1	10	2.1	67	67	44	41	25	0	0	98	254	25	16	3.0	.934	3B-125
1991		50	.194	.320	175	34	12	2	2	1.1	25	22	19	15	5	0	0	29	65	8	7	2.1	.922	3B-43, DH-5
1992	SD N	146	.330	.580	557	184	34	3	33	5.9	87	100	48	40	5	2	1	99	299	16	25	2.9	.961	3B-144
1993	2 teams		SD N (68G –.295)		FLA N (72G –.292)																			
"	total	140	.294	.476	494	145	20	5	20	4.0	67	73	47	64	17	4	1	79	225	34	15	2.5	.899	3B-133
1994	FLA N	87	.276	.584	322	89	16	1	27	8.4	61	78	51	50	12	1	1	153	7	5	2	1.9	.970	OF-87
1995		63	.324	.587	213	69	8	0	16	7.5	46	46	55	45	19	0	0	108	5	7	1	2.0	.942	OF-61
1996		161	.314	.624	519	163	33	1	42	8.1	118	120	142	66	16	1	0	238	7	6	0	1.6	.976	OF-161
9 yrs.		891	.291	.501	3215	937	172	13	159	4.9	517	550	440	361	112	8	3	943	1148	120	119	2.5	.946	3B-466, OF-309, SS-94, DH-9

Craig Shipley
SHIPLEY, CRAIG BARRY
B. Jan. 7, 1963, Parramatta, Australia
BR TR 6'1" 175 lbs.

Year	Team	Games	BA	SA	AB	H	2B	3B	HR	HR%	R	RBI	BB	SO	SB	PH AB	PH H	PO	A	E	DP	TC/G	FA	G by Pos
1986	LA N	12	.111	.148	27	3	1	0	0	0.0	3	4	2	5	0	0	0	16	18	3	4	3.1	.919	SS-10, 3B-1, 2B-1
1987		26	.257	.286	35	9	1	0	0	0.0	3	2	0	6	0	2	0	15	28	3	2	1.9	.935	SS-18, 3B-6
1989	NY N	4	.143	.143	7	1	0	0	0	0.0	3	0	0	1	0	0	0	0	4	0	0	0.8	1.000	SS-3, 3B-2
1991	SD N	37	.275	.341	91	25	3	0	1	1.1	6	6	2	14	0	4	0	39	70	7	14	3.5	.940	SS-19, 2B-14
1992		52	.248	.305	105	26	6	0	0	0.0	7	7	2	21	1	14	6	52	74	1	18	3.0	.992	SS-23, 2B-11, 3B-8
1993		105	.235	.326	230	54	14	0	4	1.7	25	22	10	31	12	28	6	84	121	7	15	2.3	.967	SS-38, 3B-37, 2B-12, OF-5
1994		81	.333	.475	240	80	14	4	4	1.7	32	30	9	28	6	13	6	65	108	9	12	2.2	.951	3B-53, SS-14, 2B-13, OF-2, 1B-1
1995	HOU N	92	.263	.345	232	61	8	1	3	1.3	23	24	8	28	6	25	9	44	114	3	7	2.0	.981	3B-65, SS-11, 2B-5, 1B-1
1996	SD N	33	.315	.402	92	29	5	0	1	1.1	13	7	2	15	7	5	1	35	64	1	7	3.2	.990	2B-17, SS-7, 3B-4, OF-3
9 yrs.		442	.272	.363	1059	288	47	5	13	1.2	115	102	35	149	32	91	28	350	601	34	79	2.4	.965	3B-176, SS-143, 2B-73, OF-10, 1B-2

Terry Shumpert
SHUMPERT, TERRANCE DARNELL
B. Aug. 16, 1966, Paducah, Ky.
BR TR 5'11" 190 lbs.

Year	Team	Games	BA	SA	AB	H	2B	3B	HR	HR%	R	RBI	BB	SO	SB	PH AB	PH H	PO	A	E	DP	TC/G	FA	G by Pos
1990	KC A	32	.275	.363	91	25	6	1	0	0.0	7	8	2	17	3	0	0	56	74	3	15	4.4	.977	2B-27, DH-3
1991		144	.217	.322	369	80	16	4	5	1.4	45	34	30	75	17	0	0	249	368	16	81	4.4	.975	2B-144
1992		36	.149	.255	94	14	5	1	1	1.1	6	11	3	17	2	0	0	50	77	4	17	3.7	.969	2B-33, SS-1, DH-1
1993		8	.100	.100	10	1	0	0	0	0.0	0	0	2	1	1	0	0	11	11	0	3	2.8	1.000	2B-8
1994		64	.240	.426	183	44	6	2	8	4.4	28	24	13	39	18	1	0	69	129	8	16	3.2	.961	2B-38, 3B-24, DH-2, SS-1
1995	BOS A	21	.234	.298	47	11	3	0	0	0.0	6	3	4	13	3	2	0	21	35	2	7	3.4	.966	2B-8, 3B-5, SS-3, DH-1
1996	CHI N	27	.226	.452	31	7	1	0	2	6.5	5	6	2	11	0	13	1	11	9	1	2	1.4	.952	3B-10, 2B-4, SS-1
7 yrs.		332	.221	.343	825	182	37	8	16	1.9	97	86	56	174	44	16	1	467	703	34	141	3.8	.972	2B-262, 3B-39, DH-7, SS-6

Joe Siddall
SIDDALL, JOSEPH TODD
B. Oct. 25, 1967, Windsor, Ont., Canada.
BL TR 6'1" 200 lbs.

Year	Team	Games	BA	SA	AB	H	2B	3B	HR	HR%	R	RBI	BB	SO	SB	PH AB	PH H	PO	A	E	DP	TC/G	FA	G by Pos
1993	MON N	19	.100	.150	20	2	1	0	0	0.0	0	1	1	5	0	3	0	33	5	0	0	2.2	1.000	C-15, OF-1, 1B-1
1995		7	.300	.300	10	3	0	0	0	0.0	4	1	3	3	0	1	0	14	1	2	0	2.4	.882	C-7
1996	FLA N	18	.149	.170	47	7	1	0	0	0.0	0	3	2	8	0	1	0	78	8	2	1	4.9	.977	C-18
3 yrs.		44	.156	.182	77	12	2	0	0	0.0	4	5	6	16	0	4	0	125	14	4	1	3.4	.972	C-40, OF-1, 1B-1

Ruben Sierra
SIERRA, RUBEN ANGEL
Born Ruben Angel Sierra (Garcia).
B. Oct. 6, 1965, Rio Piedras, Puerto Rico
BB TR 6'1" 175 lbs.

Year	Team	Games	BA	SA	AB	H	2B	3B	HR	HR%	R	RBI	BB	SO	SB	PH AB	PH H	PO	A	E	DP	TC/G	FA	G by Pos
1986	TEX A	113	.264	.476	382	101	13	10	16	4.2	50	55	22	65	7	6	1	200	9	6	1	1.9	.972	OF-107, DH-3
1987		158	.263	.470	643	169	35	4	30	4.7	97	109	39	114	16	2	0	272	17	11	6	1.9	.963	OF-157
1988		156	.254	.424	615	156	32	2	23	3.7	77	91	44	91	18	3	1	310	11	7	3	2.1	.979	OF-153, DH-1
1989		162	.306	.543	634	194	35	14	29	4.6	101	119	43	82	8	0	0	313	13	9	2	2.1	.973	OF-162
1990		159	.280	.424	608	170	37	2	16	2.6	70	96	49	86	9	2	1	283	7	10	1	1.9	.967	OF-151, DH-7
1991		161	.307	.502	661	203	44	5	25	3.8	110	116	56	91	16	1	1	305	15	7	3	2.0	.979	OF-161
1992	2 teams		TEX A (124G –.278)		OAK A (27G –.277)																			
"	total	151	.278	.443	601	167	34	7	17	2.8	83	87	45	68	14	3	1	283	6	7	0	2.0	.976	OF-144, DH-6
1993	OAK A	158	.233	.390	630	147	23	5	22	3.5	77	101	52	97	25	3	0	291	9	7	3	1.9	.977	OF-133, DH-25

Year	Team	Games	BA	SA	AB	H	2B	3B	HR	HR%	R	RBI	BB	SO	SB	Pinch Hit AB	H	PO	A	E	DP	TC/G	FA	G by Pos

Ruben Sierra *continued*

Year	Team	Games	BA	SA	AB	H	2B	3B	HR	HR%	R	RBI	BB	SO	SB	PH AB	H	PO	A	E	DP	TC/G	FA	G by Pos
1993	OAK A	158	.233	.390	630	147	23	5	22	3.5	77	101	52	97	25	2	0	291	9	7	3	1.9	.977	OF-133, DH-25
1994		110	.268	.484	426	114	21	1	23	5.4	71	92	23	64	8	3	2	155	8	9	2	1.6	.948	OF-98, DH-10
1995	2 teams OAK A	(70G –.265)			NY A	(56G –.260)																		
"	total	126	.263	.449	479	126	32	0	19	4.0	73	86	46	76	5	5	2	107	2	5	0	0.9	.956	OF-72, DH-53
1996	2 teams NY A	(96G –.258)		DET A	(46G –.222)																		
"	total	142	.247	.375	518	128	26	2	12	2.3	61	72	60	83	4	9	3	108	6	6	2	0.9	.950	DH-81, OF-56
11 yrs.		1596	.270	.453	6197	1675	332	52	232	3.7	870	1024	479	917	130	36	12	2627	101	84	23	1.8	.970	OF-1394, DH-186

DIVISIONAL PLAYOFF SERIES

| 1995 | NY A | 5 | .174 | .522 | 23 | 4 | 2 | 0 | 2 | 8.7 | 2 | 5 | 2 | 7 | 0 | 0 | 0 | 0 | 0 | 0 | 0 | 0.0 | .000 | DH-5 |

LEAGUE CHAMPIONSHIP SERIES

| 1992 | OAK A | 6 | .333 | .625 | 24 | 8 | 2 | 1 | 1 | 4.2 | 4 | 7 | 2 | 1 | 1 | 0 | 0 | 12 | 0 | 0 | 0 | 2.0 | 1.000 | OF-6 |

Dave Silvestri

SILVESTRI, DAVID JOSEPH
B. Sept. 29, 1967, St. Louis, Mo.   BR TR 6' 180 lbs.

Year	Team	Games	BA	SA	AB	H	2B	3B	HR	HR%	R	RBI	BB	SO	SB	PH AB	H	PO	A	E	DP	TC/G	FA	G by Pos
1992	NY A	7	.308	.615	13	4	0	2	0	0.0	3	1	0	3	0	1	0	4	12	2	3	3.0	.889	SS-6
1993		7	.286	.476	21	6	1	0	1	4.8	4	4	5	3	0	0	0	9	20	3	4	4.6	.906	SS-4, 3B-3
1994		12	.111	.389	18	2	0	1	1	5.6	3	2	4	9	0	1	0	14	16	1	3	2.6	.968	2B-9, 3B-2, SS-1
1995	2 teams NY A	(17G –.095)		MON N	(39G –.264)																		
"	total	56	.226	.387	93	21	6	0	3	3.2	16	11	13	36	2	15	6	62	48	1	8	2.6	.991	2B-10, SS-10, 1B-8, 3B-8, DH-4, OF-3
1996	MON N	86	.204	.247	162	33	4	0	1	0.6	16	17	34	41	2	19	5	23	91	10	5	2.0	.919	3B-47, SS-10, OF-2, 1B-1, 2B-1
5 yrs.		168	.215	.329	307	66	11	3	6	2.0	42	35	56	92	4	36	11	112	187	17	23	2.4	.946	3B-60, SS-31, 2B-20, 1B-9, OF-5, DH-4

Mike Simms

SIMMS, MICHAEL HOWARD
B. Jan. 12, 1967, Orange, Calif.   BR TR 6'4" 185 lbs.

Year	Team	Games	BA	SA	AB	H	2B	3B	HR	HR%	R	RBI	BB	SO	SB	PH AB	H	PO	A	E	DP	TC/G	FA	G by Pos
1990	HOU N	12	.308	.615	13	4	1	0	1	7.7	3	3	0	4	0	5	0	20	1	0	2	3.5	1.000	1B-6
1991		49	.203	.317	123	25	5	0	3	2.4	18	16	18	38	1	8	1	44	4	6	0	1.3	.889	OF-41
1992		15	.250	.417	24	6	1	0	1	4.2	1	3	2	9	0	6	1	10	2	0	0	1.2	1.000	OF-9, 1B-1
1994		6	.083	.167	12	1	1	0	0	0.0	1	0	0	5	1	2	0	6	0	1	0	2.3	.857	OF-3
1995		50	.256	.512	121	31	4	0	9	7.4	14	24	13	28	1	11	2	221	18	1	19	6.5	.996	1B-25, OF-12
1996		49	.176	.279	68	12	2	1	1	1.5	6	8	4	16	1	33	7	24	1	0	0	1.5	1.000	OF-12, 1B-5
6 yrs.		181	.219	.388	361	79	14	1	15	4.2	43	53	37	100	4	65	11	325	26	8	21	3.1	.978	OF-77, 1B-37

Duane Singleton

SINGLETON, DUANE EARL
B. Aug. 6, 1972, Staten Island, N. Y.   BL TR 6'1" 170 lbs.

Year	Team	Games	BA	SA	AB	H	2B	3B	HR	HR%	R	RBI	BB	SO	SB	PH AB	H	PO	A	E	DP	TC/G	FA	G by Pos
1994	MIL A	2	—	—	0	0	0	0	0		0	0	0	0	0	0	0	1	0	0	0	0.5	1.000	OF-2
1995		13	.065	.065	31	2	0	0	0	0.0	0	0	1	10	1	0	0	22	1	0	0	2.1	1.000	OF-11
1996	DET A	18	.161	.179	56	9	1	0	0	0.0	5	3	4	15	0	3	0	29	3	0	1	2.1	1.000	OF-15
3 yrs.		33	.126	.138	87	11	1	0	0	0.0	5	3	5	25	1	3	0	52	4	0	1	2.0	1.000	OF-28

Don Slaught

SLAUGHT, DONALD MARTIN (Sluggo)
B. Sept. 11, 1958, Long Beach, Calif.   BR TR 6'1" 190 lbs.

Year	Team	Games	BA	SA	AB	H	2B	3B	HR	HR%	R	RBI	BB	SO	SB	PH AB	H	PO	A	E	DP	TC/G	FA	G by Pos
1982	KC A	43	.278	.409	115	32	6	0	3	2.6	14	8	9	12	0	0	0	156	7	1	1	3.8	.994	C-43
1983		83	.312	.388	276	86	13	4	0	0.0	21	28	11	27	3	5	2	299	18	12	7	4.1	.964	C-79, DH-1
1984		124	.264	.379	409	108	27	4	4	1.0	48	42	20	55	0	5	2	547	44	11	8	4.9	.982	C-123, DH-1
1985	TEX A	102	.280	.423	343	96	17	4	8	2.3	34	35	20	41	5	1	0	550	33	6	4	5.8	.990	C-102
1986		95	.264	.449	314	83	17	1	13	4.1	39	46	16	59	3	3	3	533	40	4	1	6.2	.993	C-91, DH-2
1987		95	.224	.405	237	53	15	2	8	3.4	25	16	24	51	0	22	5	429	39	7	5	5.3	.985	C-85, DH-5
1988	NY A	97	.283	.450	322	91	25	1	9	2.8	33	43	24	54	1	6	2	496	24	11	4	5.6	.979	C-94, DH-1
1989		117	.251	.371	350	88	21	3	5	1.4	34	38	30	57	1	12	3	493	44	5	8	5.0	.991	C-105, DH-3
1990	PIT N	84	.300	.457	230	69	18	3	4	1.7	27	29	27	27	0	16	5	345	36	8	4	5.0	.979	C-78
1991		77	.295	.395	220	65	17	1	1	0.5	19	29	21	32	1	13	5	338	31	5	4	5.3	.987	C-69, 3B-1
1992		87	.345	.482	255	88	17	3	4	1.6	26	37	17	23	2	14	4	365	35	5	4	5.1	.988	C-79
1993		116	.300	.440	377	113	19	2	10	2.7	34	55	29	56	2	13	6	539	51	4	10	5.7	.993	C-105
1994		76	.287	.342	240	69	7	0	2	0.8	21	21	34	31	0	2	0	425	36	3	4	6.3	.994	C-74
1995		35	.304	.357	112	34	6	0	0	0.0	13	13	9	8	0	4	2	220	9	1	2	7.0	.996	C-33
1996	2 teams CAL A	(62G –.324)		CHI A	(14G –.250)																		
"	total	76	.313	.428	243	76	10	0	6	2.5	25	36	15	22	0	10	4	408	27	4	1	6.0	.991	C-71, DH-2
15 yrs.		1307	.285	.414	4043	1151	235	28	77	1.9	413	476	306	555	18	126	40	6143	474	87	67	5.4	.987	C-1231, DH-15, 3B-1

LEAGUE CHAMPIONSHIP SERIES

1984	KC A	3	.364	.364	11	4	0	0	0	0.0	0	0	0	0	0	0	0	17	0	3	0	6.7	.850	C-3
1990	PIT N	4	.091	.182	11	1	1	0	0	0.0	0	1	2	3	0	0	0	22	1	1	0	6.0	.958	C-4
1991		6	.235	.235	17	4	0	0	0	0.0	0	1	1	4	0	1	1	30	5	0	1	5.8	1.000	C-6
1992		5	.333	.667	12	4	1	0	1	8.3	5	5	6	3	0	0	0	17	1	0	0	3.6	1.000	C-5
4 yrs.		18	.255	.353	51	13	2	0	1	2.0	5	7	9	10	0	2	1	86	7	4	1	5.4	.959	C-18

Dwight Smith

SMITH, JOHN DWIGHT
B. Nov. 8, 1963, Tallahassee, Fla.   BL TR 5'11" 175 lbs.

Year	Team	Games	BA	SA	AB	H	2B	3B	HR	HR%	R	RBI	BB	SO	SB	PH AB	H	PO	A	E	DP	TC/G	FA	G by Pos
1989	CHI N	109	.324	.493	343	111	19	6	9	2.6	52	52	31	51	9	15	8	188	7	5	3	2.0	.975	OF-102
1990		117	.262	.376	290	76	15	0	6	2.1	34	27	28	46	11	34	8	139	4	2	2	1.8	.986	OF-81
1991		90	.228	.347	167	38	7	2	3	1.8	16	21	11	32	2	45	11	73	3	3	1	1.9	.962	OF-42
1992		109	.276	.392	217	60	10	3	3	1.4	28	24	13	40	9	49	14	93	2	2	0	1.5	.979	OF-63
1993		111	.300	.494	310	93	17	5	11	3.5	51	35	25	51	8	24	9	163	5	8	2	2.0	.955	OF-89
1994	2 teams CAL A	(45G –.262)		BAL A	(28G –.311)																		
"	total	73	.281	.459	196	55	7	2	8	4.1	31	30	12	37	2	19	5	81	2	7	1	1.6	.922	OF-53, DH-5

Year	Team	Games	BA	SA	AB	H	2B	3B	HR	HR%	R	RBI	BB	SO	SB	Pinch Hit AB	H	PO	A	E	DP	TC/G	FA	G by Pos

Dwight Smith *continued*

Year	Team	Games	BA	SA	AB	H	2B	3B	HR	HR%	R	RBI	BB	SO	SB	AB	H	PO	A	E	DP	TC/G	FA	G by Pos
1995	ATL N	103	.252	.412	131	33	8	2	3	2.3	16	21	13	35	0	69	16	24	0	2	0	1.0	.923	OF-25
1996		101	.203	.294	153	31	5	0	3	2.0	16	16	17	42	1	**69**	16	49	1	2	0	1.8	.962	OF-29
8 yrs.		813	.275	.422	1807	497	88	20	46	2.5	244	226	150	334	42	324	87	810	24	31	9	1.8	.964	OF-484, DH-5

DIVISIONAL PLAYOFF SERIES

| 1995 | ATL N | 4 | .667 | 1.000 | 3 | 2 | 1 | 0 | 0 | 0.0 | 0 | 1 | 0 | 0 | 0 | 3 | 2 | 0 | 0 | 0 | 0 | 0.0 | — | |

LEAGUE CHAMPIONSHIP SERIES

1989	CHI N	4	.200	.267	15	3	1	0	0	0.0	2	0	2	2	1	0	0	10	0	0	0	2.5	1.000	OF-4
1995	ATL N	2	.000	.000	2	0	0	0	0	0.0	0	0	0	0	0	2	0	0	0	0	0	0.0	—	
2 yrs.		6	.176	.235	17	3	1	0	0	0.0	2	0	2	2	1	2	0	10	0	0	0	2.5	1.000	OF-4

WORLD SERIES

| 1995 | ATL N | 3 | .500 | .500 | 2 | 1 | 0 | 0 | 0 | 0.0 | 0 | 0 | 0 | 1 | 0 | 2 | 1 | 0 | 0 | 0 | 0 | 0.0 | — | |

Mark Smith

SMITH, MARK EDWARD
B. May 7, 1970, Pasadena, Calif.
BR TR 6'3" 205 lbs.

1994	BAL A	3	.143	.143	7	1	0	0	0	0.0	0	2	0	2	0	0	0	8	0	0	0	2.7	1.000	OF-3
1995		37	.231	.365	104	24	5	0	3	2.9	11	15	12	22	3	4	1	60	2	0	0	1.8	1.000	OF-32, DH-3
1996		27	.244	.423	78	19	2	0	4	5.1	9	10	3	20	0	6	1	50	0	1	0	2.0	.980	OF-20, DH-6
3 yrs.		67	.233	.381	189	44	7	0	7	3.7	20	27	15	44	3	10	2	118	2	1	0	1.9	.992	OF-55, DH-9

Ozzie Smith

SMITH, OSBORNE EARL (The Wizard)
B. Dec. 26, 1954, Mobile, Ala.
BB TR 5'11" 150 lbs.

1978	SD N	159	.258	.312	590	152	17	6	1	0.2	69	46	47	43	40	1	0	264	548	25	98	5.3	.970	SS-159
1979		156	.211	.262	587	124	18	6	0	0.0	77	27	37	37	28	0	0	256	555	20	86	5.4	.974	SS-155
1980		158	.230	.276	609	140	18	5	0	0.0	67	35	71	49	57	0	0	288	621	24	113	5.9	.974	SS-158
1981		110	.222	.256	**450**	100	11	2	0	0.0	53	21	41	37	22	0	0	220	422	16	72	6.0	.976	SS-110
1982	STL N	140	.248	.314	488	121	24	1	2	0.4	58	43	68	32	25	1	0	279	535	13	101	5.9	.984	SS-139
1983		159	.243	.335	552	134	30	6	3	0.5	69	50	64	36	34	2	0	304	519	21	100	5.3	.975	SS-158
1984		124	.257	.337	412	106	20	5	1	0.2	53	44	56	17	35	0	0	233	437	12	94	5.5	.982	SS-124
1985		158	.276	.361	537	148	22	3	6	1.1	70	54	65	27	31	0	0	264	549	14	111	5.2	.983	SS-158
1986		153	.280	.333	514	144	19	4	0	0.0	67	54	79	27	31	8	2	229	453	15	96	4.8	.978	SS-144
1987		158	.303	.383	600	182	40	4	0	0.0	104	75	89	36	43	2	1	245	516	10	111	4.9	.987	SS-158
1988		153	.270	.336	575	155	27	1	3	0.5	80	51	74	43	57	2	0	234	519	22	79	5.2	.972	SS-150
1989		155	.273	.361	593	162	30	8	2	0.3	82	50	55	37	29	2	1	209	483	17	73	4.6	.976	SS-153
1990		143	.254	.305	512	130	21	1	1	0.2	61	50	61	33	32	2	0	212	378	12	66	4.3	.980	SS-140
1991		150	.285	.367	550	157	30	3	3	0.5	96	50	83	36	35	0	0	244	387	8	79	4.3	.987	SS-150
1992		132	.295	.342	518	153	20	2	0	0.0	73	31	59	34	43	0	0	232	420	10	82	5.0	.985	SS-132
1993		141	.288	.356	545	157	22	6	1	0.2	75	53	43	18	21	5	0	251	451	19	98	5.4	.974	SS-134
1994		98	.262	.349	381	100	18	3	3	0.8	51	30	38	26	6	2	0	136	292	8	65	4.5	.982	SS-96
1995		44	.199	.244	156	31	5	1	0	0.0	16	11	17	12	4	3	0	60	128	7	27	4.8	.964	SS-41
1996		82	.282	.370	227	64	10	2	2	0.9	36	18	25	9	7	28	7	90	162	8	36	5.0	.969	SS-52
19 yrs.		2573	.262	.328	9396	2460	402	69	28	0.3	1257	793	1072	589	580	58	11	4250	8375	281	1587	5.1	.978	SS-2511

DIVISIONAL PLAYOFF SERIES

| 1996 | STL N | 2 | .333 | .333 | 3 | 1 | 0 | 0 | 0 | 0.0 | 1 | 0 | 2 | 0 | 0 | 1 | 0 | 2 | 1 | 0 | 0 | 3.0 | 1.000 | SS-1 |

LEAGUE CHAMPIONSHIP SERIES

1982	STL N	3	.556	.556	9	5	0	0	0	0.0	0	3	3	0	1	0	0	4	11	0	1	5.0	1.000	SS-3
1985		6	.435	.696	23	10	1	1	1	4.3	4	3	3	1	1	0	0	6	16	0	2	3.7	1.000	SS-6
1987		7	.200	.280	25	5	0	1	0	0.0	2	1	3	4	0	0	0	10	19	1	4	4.3	.967	SS-7
1996		3	.000	.000	9	0	0	0	0	0.0	0	0	0	1	0	1	0	7	2	0	1	4.5	1.000	SS-2
4 yrs.		19	.303	.424	66	20	1	2 (4th)	1	1.5	6	7	9	6	2	1	0	27	48	1	8	4.2	.987	SS-18

WORLD SERIES

1982	STL N	7	.208	.208	24	5	0	0	0	0.0	3	1	3	0	1	0	0	22	17	0	5	5.6	1.000	SS-7
1985		7	.087	.087	23	2	0	0	0	0.0	1	0	4	0	1	0	0	10	16	1	5	3.9	.963	SS-7
1987		7	.214	.214	28	6	0	0	0	0.0	3	2	2	3	2	0	0	7	19	0	1	3.7	1.000	SS-7
3 yrs.		21	.173	.173	75	13	0	0	0	0.0	7	3	9	3	4	0	0	39	52	1	11	4.4	.989	SS-21

Chris Snopek

SNOPEK, CHRISTOPHER CHARLES
B. Sept. 20, 1970, Cynthiana, Ky.
BR TR 6'1" 180 lbs.

1995	CHI A	22	.324	.426	68	22	4	0	1	1.5	12	7	9	12	1	1	1	25	31	2	5	2.5	.966	3B-17, SS-6
1996		46	.260	.510	104	27	6	1	6	5.8	18	18	6	16	0	6	0	25	65	5	10	2.3	.947	3B-27, SS-12, DH-3
2 yrs.		68	.285	.477	172	49	10	1	7	4.1	30	25	15	28	1	7	1	50	96	7	15	2.4	.954	3B-44, SS-18, DH-3

J. T. Snow

SNOW, JACK THOMAS
B. Feb. 26, 1968, Long Beach, Calif.
BB TL 6'2" 200 lbs.

1992	NY A	7	.143	.214	14	2	1	0	0	0.0	1	2	5	5	0	0	0	43	2	0	7	7.5	1.000	1B-6
1993	CAL A	129	.241	.408	419	101	18	2	16	3.8	60	57	55	88	3	2	0	1010	81	6	103	8.5	.995	1B-129
1994		61	.220	.345	223	49	4	0	8	3.6	22	30	19	48	0	0	0	489	37	2	56	8.7	.996	1B-61
1995		143	.289	.465	544	157	22	1	24	4.4	80	102	52	91	2	0	0	1161	56	4	106	8.5	.997	1B-143
1996		155	.257	.384	575	148	20	1	17	3.0	69	67	56	96	1	3	2	1274	105	10	136	9.0	.993	1B-154
5 yrs.		495	.257	.408	1775	457	65	4	65	3.7	232	258	187	328	6	5	2	3977	281	22	408	8.7	.995	1B-493

Luis Sojo

SOJO, LUIS BELTRAN
Born Luis Beltran Sojo (Sojo).
B. Jan. 3, 1966, Caracas, Venezuela
BR TR 5'11" 172 lbs.

1990	TOR A	33	.225	.300	80	18	3	0	1	1.3	14	9	5	5	1	4	0	34	31	5	7	2.2	.929	2B-15, OF-5, SS-5, 3B-4, DH-3
1991	CAL A	113	.258	.327	364	94	14	1	3	0.8	38	20	14	26	4	0	0	233	335	11	78	5.2	.981	2B-107, SS-2, OF-1, 3B-1, DH-1
1992		106	.272	.378	368	100	12	3	7	1.9	37	43	14	24	7	4	1	196	293	9	73	4.5	.982	2B-96, 3B-9, SS-5

Year	Team	Games	BA	SA	AB	H	2B	3B	HR	HR%	R	RBI	BB	SO	SB	Pinch Hit AB	Pinch Hit H	PO	A	E	DP	TC/G	FA	G by Pos

Luis Sojo *continued*

Year	Team	Games	BA	SA	AB	H	2B	3B	HR	HR%	R	RBI	BB	SO	SB	AB	H	PO	A	E	DP	TC/G	FA	G by Pos
1993	TOR A	19	.170	.213	47	8	2	0	0	0.0	5	6	4	2	0	1	0	24	35	2	8	3.2	.967	2B-8, SS-8, 3B-3
1994	SEA A	63	.277	.423	213	59	9	2	6	2.8	32	22	8	25	2	2	1	97	186	7	36	4.3	.976	2B-40, SS-24, DH-2, 3B-1
1995		102	.289	.416	339	98	18	2	7	2.1	50	39	23	19	4	3	1	141	220	9	38	3.5	.976	SS-80, 2B-19, OF-6
1996	2 teams SEA A (77G –.211) NY A (18G –.275)																							
"	total	95	.220	.272	287	63	10	1	1	0.3	23	21	11	17	2	10	0	112	196	8	42	3.2	.975	2B-41, 3B-34, SS-23
7 yrs.		531	.259	.354	1698	440	68	9	25	1.5	199	160	79	118	20	24	3	837	1296	51	282	4.0	.977	2B-326, SS-147, 3B-52, OF-12, DH-6
DIVISIONAL PLAYOFF SERIES																								
1995	SEA A	5	.250	.250	20	5	0	0	0	0.0	0	3	0	3	0	0	0	9	15	1	3	5.0	.960	SS-5
1996	NY A	2	—	—	0	0	0	0	0	—	0	0	0	0	0	0	0	1	1	0	0	1.0	1.000	2B-2
2 yrs.		7	.250	.250	20	5	0	0	0	0.0	0	3	0	3	0	0	0	10	16	1	3	3.9	.963	SS-5, 2B-2
LEAGUE CHAMPIONSHIP SERIES																								
1995	SEA A	6	.250	.350	20	5	2	0	0	0.0	0	1	0	2	0	0	0	9	18	1	7	4.7	.964	SS-6
1996	NY A	3	.200	.200	5	1	0	0	0	0.0	0	0	0	1	0	0	0	4	4	0	0	2.7	1.000	2B-3
2 yrs.		9	.240	.320	25	6	2	0	0	0.0	0	1	0	3	0	0	0	13	22	1	7	4.0	.972	SS-6, 2B-3
WORLD SERIES																								
1996	NY A	5	.600	.800	5	3	1	0	0	0.0	0	1	0	0	0	2	1	5	2	0	0	2.3	1.000	2B-3

Paul Sorrento

SORRENTO, PAUL ANTHONY
B. Nov. 17, 1965, Somerville, Mass.
BL TR 6'2" 195 lbs.

Year	Team	Games	BA	SA	AB	H	2B	3B	HR	HR%	R	RBI	BB	SO	SB	AB	H	PO	A	E	DP	TC/G	FA	G by Pos
1989	MIN A	14	.238	.238	21	5	0	0	0	0.0	2	1	5	4	0	3	0	13	0	0	1	1.3	1.000	1B-5, DH-5
1990		41	.207	.380	121	25	4	1	5	4.1	11	13	12	31	1	6	2	118	7	1	14	3.3	.992	DH-23, 1B-15
1991		26	.255	.553	47	12	2	0	4	8.5	6	13	4	11	0	12	3	70	7	0	7	5.1	1.000	1B-13, DH-2
1992	CLE A	140	.269	.443	458	123	24	1	18	3.9	52	60	51	89	0	14	2	996	78	8	108	8.2	.993	1B-121, DH-11
1993		148	.257	.434	463	119	26	1	18	3.9	75	65	58	121	3	13	3	1015	86	6	107	7.5	.995	1B-144, OF-3, DH-1
1994		95	.280	.453	322	90	14	0	14	4.3	43	62	34	68	0	8	2	798	58	4	79	9.1	.995	1B-86, DH-8
1995		104	.235	.511	323	76	14	0	25	7.7	50	79	51	71	1	9	1	816	57	7	87	8.6	.992	1B-91, DH-11
1996	SEA A	143	.289	.507	471	136	32	1	23	4.9	67	93	57	103	0	14	3	955	80	11	112	7.6	.989	1B-138
8 yrs.		711	.263	.463	2226	586	116	4	107	4.8	306	386	272	498	5	79	16	4781	373	37	515	7.7	.993	1B-613, DH-61, OF-3
DIVISIONAL PLAYOFF SERIES																								
1995	CLE A	3	.300	.300	10	3	0	0	0	0.0	2	1	2	3	0	0	0	27	5	2	0	11.3	.941	1B-3
LEAGUE CHAMPIONSHIP SERIES																								
1991	MIN A	1	.000	.000	1	0	0	0	0	0.0	0	0	0	1	0	1	0	0	0	0	0	0.0	—	1B-1
1995	CLE A	4	.154	.231	13	2	1	0	0	0.0	2	0	2	3	0	0	0	34	1	2	1	9.3	.946	1B-4
2 yrs.		5	.143	.214	14	2	1	0	0	0.0	2	0	2	4	0	1	0	34	1	2	1	9.3	.946	1B-4
WORLD SERIES																								
1991	MIN A	3	.000	.000	2	0	0	0	0	0.0	0	0	1	2	0	2	0	1	1	0	1	2.0	1.000	1B-1
1995	CLE A	6	.182	.273	11	2	1	0	0	0.0	0	0	0	4	0	3	1	19	2	1	2	7.3	.955	1B-3
2 yrs.		9	.154	.231	13	2	1	0	0	0.0	0	0	1	6	0	5	1	20	3	1	3	6.0	.958	1B-4

Sammy Sosa

SOSA, SAMUEL
Born Samuel Sosa (Peralta).
B. Nov. 12, 1968, San Pedro de Macoris, Dominican Republic
BR TR 6' 165 lbs.

Year	Team	Games	BA	SA	AB	H	2B	3B	HR	HR%	R	RBI	BB	SO	SB	AB	H	PO	A	E	DP	TC/G	FA	G by Pos
1989	2 teams TEX A (25G –.238) CHI A (33G –.273)																							
"	total	58	.257	.366	183	47	8	0	4	2.2	27	13	11	47	7	4	0	94	2	4	0	1.7	.960	OF-52, DH-6
1990	CHI A	153	.233	.404	532	124	26	10	15	2.8	72	70	33	150	32	0	0	315	14	13	1	2.3	.962	OF-152
1991		116	.203	.335	316	64	10	1	10	3.2	39	33	14	98	13	7	2	214	6	6	0	2.0	.973	OF-111, DH-2
1992	CHI N	67	.260	.393	262	68	7	2	8	3.1	41	25	19	63	15	0	0	145	4	6	1	2.3	.961	OF-67
1993		159	.261	.485	598	156	25	5	33	5.5	92	93	38	135	36	2	1	344	17	9	4	2.3	.976	OF-158
1994		105	.300	.545	426	128	17	6	25	5.9	59	70	25	92	22	0	0	248	5	7	0	2.5	.973	OF-105
1995		144	.268	.500	564	151	17	3	36	6.4	89	119	58	134	34	1	0	320	13	13	2	2.4	.962	OF-143
1996		124	.273	.564	498	136	21	2	40	8.0	84	100	34	134	18	0	0	255	15	10	1	2.3	.964	OF-124
8 yrs.		926	.259	.466	3379	874	131	29	171	5.1	503	523	232	853	177	14	3	1935	76	68	9	2.3	.967	OF-912, DH-8

Tim Spehr

SPEHR, TIMOTHY JOSEPH
B. July 2, 1966, Excelsior Springs, Mo.
BR TR 6'2" 205 lbs.

Year	Team	Games	BA	SA	AB	H	2B	3B	HR	HR%	R	RBI	BB	SO	SB	AB	H	PO	A	E	DP	TC/G	FA	G by Pos
1991	KC A	37	.189	.378	74	14	5	0	3	4.1	7	14	9	18	1	1	0	190	19	3	3	5.7	.986	C-37
1993	MON N	53	.230	.368	87	20	6	0	2	2.3	14	10	6	20	2	3	0	166	22	9	3	4.0	.954	C-49
1994		52	.250	.389	36	9	3	1	0	0.0	8	5	4	11	2	2	1	104	6	0	1	2.3	1.000	C-46, OF-2
1995		41	.257	.486	35	9	5	0	1	2.9	4	3	6	7	0	2	1	92	12	1	0	2.8	.990	C-38
1996		63	.091	.182	44	4	1	0	1	2.3	4	3	3	15	1	4	1	121	7	2	0	2.2	.985	C-58, OF-1
5 yrs.		246	.203	.359	276	56	20	1	7	2.5	37	35	28	71	6	12	3	673	66	15	7	3.3	.980	C-228, OF-3

Bill Spiers

SPIERS, WILLIAM JAMES
B. June 5, 1966, Orangeburg, S. C.
BL TR 6'2" 190 lbs.

Year	Team	Games	BA	SA	AB	H	2B	3B	HR	HR%	R	RBI	BB	SO	SB	AB	H	PO	A	E	DP	TC/G	FA	G by Pos
1989	MIL A	114	.255	.333	345	88	9	3	4	1.2	44	33	21	63	10	4	3	164	295	21	62	4.3	.956	SS-89, 3B-12, DH-4, 2B-4, 1B-2
1990		112	.242	.317	363	88	15	3	2	0.6	44	36	16	45	11	2	1	159	326	12	72	4.5	.976	SS-111
1991		133	.283	.401	414	117	13	6	8	1.9	71	54	34	55	14	1	0	201	345	17	93	4.3	.970	SS-128, OF-1
1992		12	.313	.438	16	5	2	0	0	0.0	2	2	1	4	1	1	0	6	6	0	0	1.1	1.000	SS-5, 2B-4, DH-1, 3B-1
1993		113	.238	.303	340	81	8	4	2	0.6	43	36	29	51	9	3	1	213	231	13	55	3.9	.972	2B-104, OF-7, SS-4, DH-1

Year	Team	Games	BA	SA	AB	H	2B	3B	HR	HR%	R	RBI	BB	SO	SB	Pinch Hit AB	Pinch Hit H	PO	A	E	DP	TC/G	FA	G by Pos

Bill Spiers *continued*

Year	Team	Games	BA	SA	AB	H	2B	3B	HR	HR%	R	RBI	BB	SO	SB	PH AB	PH H	PO	A	E	DP	TC/G	FA	G by Pos
1994		73	.252	.308	214	54	10	1	0	0.0	27	17	19	42	7	10	0	70	128	8	26	2.7	.961	3B-35, SS-35, DH-3, OF-2, 1B-1
1995	NY N	63	.208	.264	72	15	2	1	0	0.0	5	11	12	15	0	40	9	13	30	7	3	2.9	.860	3B-11, 2B-6
1996	HOU N	122	.252	.390	218	55	10	1	6	2.8	27	26	20	34	7	33	6	44	107	5	13	1.7	.968	3B-76, 2B-7, SS-5, 1B-4, OF-2
8 yrs.		742	.254	.341	1982	503	69	19	22	1.1	263	215	152	309	59	94	20	870	1468	83	324	3.6	.966	SS-377, 3B-135, 2B-125, OF-12, DH-11, 1B-7

Scott Spiezio

SPIEZIO, SCOTT EDWARD
Son of Ed Spiezio.
B. Sept. 21, 1972, Joliet, Ill.

BB TR 6'2" 195 lbs.

Year	Team	Games	BA	SA	AB	H	2B	3B	HR	HR%	R	RBI	BB	SO	SB	PH AB	PH H	PO	A	E	DP	TC/G	FA	G by Pos
1996	OAK A	9	.310	.586	29	9	2	0	2	6.9	6	8	4	4	0	0	0	6	5	2	0	2.6	.846	3B-5, DH-4

Ed Sprague

SPRAGUE, EDWARD NELSON, JR.
Son of Ed Sprague.
B. July 25, 1967, Castro Valley, Calif.

BR TR 6'2" 215 lbs.

Year	Team	Games	BA	SA	AB	H	2B	3B	HR	HR%	R	RBI	BB	SO	SB	PH AB	PH H	PO	A	E	DP	TC/G	FA	G by Pos
1991	TOR A	61	.275	.394	160	44	7	0	4	2.5	17	20	19	43	0	1	1	167	72	14	14	4.1	.945	3B-35, 1B-2, C-2, DH-2
1992		22	.234	.340	47	11	2	0	1	2.1	6	7	3	7	0	3	2	82	5	1	1	4.0	.989	C-15, 1B-4, DH-2, 3B-1
1993		150	.260	.386	546	142	31	1	12	2.2	50	73	32	85	1	0	0	127	232	17	21	2.5	.955	3B-150
1994		109	.240	.373	405	97	19	1	11	2.7	38	44	23	95	1	0	0	118	147	14	20	2.5	.950	3B-107, 1B-3
1995		144	.244	.407	521	127	27	2	18	3.5	77	74	58	96	0	0	0	167	234	17	23	2.8	.959	3B-139, 1B-7, DH-2
1996		159	.247	.496	591	146	35	2	36	6.1	88	101	60	146	0	1	0	108	217	15	30	2.2	.956	3B-148, DH-10
6 yrs.		645	.250	.417	2270	567	121	6	82	3.6	276	319	195	472	2	5	3	769	907	78	109	2.7	.956	3B-580, 1B-36, C-17, DH-16

LEAGUE CHAMPIONSHIP SERIES

Year	Team	Games	BA	SA	AB	H	2B	3B	HR	HR%	R	RBI	BB	SO	SB	PH AB	PH H	PO	A	E	DP	TC/G	FA	G by Pos
1992	TOR A	2	.500	.500	2	1	0	0	0	0.0	0	0	0	1	0	2	1	0	0	0	0	0.0	—	
1993		6	.286	.381	21	6	0	1	0	0.0	0	4	2	4	0	0	0	5	9	0	1	2.3	1.000	3B-6
2 yrs.		8	.304	.391	23	7	0	1	0	0.0	0	4	2	5	0	2	1	5	9	0	1	2.3	1.000	3B-6

WORLD SERIES

Year	Team	Games	BA	SA	AB	H	2B	3B	HR	HR%	R	RBI	BB	SO	SB	PH AB	PH H	PO	A	E	DP	TC/G	FA	G by Pos
1992	TOR A	3	.500	2.000	2	1	0	0	1	50.0	1	2	1	0	0	2	1	0	0	0	0	0.0	.000	1B-1
1993		5	.067	.067	15	1	0	0	0	0.0	0	2	1	6	0	1	0	4	9	2	1	3.0	.867	3B-4, 1B-1
2 yrs.		8	.118	.294	17	2	0	0	1	5.9	1	4	2	6	0	3	1	4	9	2	1	2.5	.867	3B-4, 1B-2

Scott Stahoviak

STAHOVIAK, SCOTT EDMUND
B. Mar. 6, 1970, Waukegan, Ill.

BL TR 6'5" 210 lbs.

Year	Team	Games	BA	SA	AB	H	2B	3B	HR	HR%	R	RBI	BB	SO	SB	PH AB	PH H	PO	A	E	DP	TC/G	FA	G by Pos
1993	MIN A	20	.193	.263	57	11	4	0	0	0.0	1	1	3	22	0	5	0	9	38	4	1	2.7	.922	3B-19
1995		94	.266	.373	263	70	19	0	3	1.1	28	23	30	61	5	10	2	503	91	5	49	6.5	.992	1B-69, 3B-22, DH-1
1996		130	.284	.469	405	115	30	3	13	3.2	72	61	59	114	3	12	4	800	90	5	78	7.3	.994	1B-114, DH-9
3 yrs.		244	.270	.418	725	196	53	3	16	2.2	101	85	92	197	8	27	6	1312	219	14	128	6.6	.991	1B-183, 3B-41, DH-10

Matt Stairs

STAIRS, MATTHEW WADE
B. Feb. 27, 1968, Fredericton, N. B., Canada.

BL TR 5'9" 175 lbs.

Year	Team	Games	BA	SA	AB	H	2B	3B	HR	HR%	R	RBI	BB	SO	SB	PH AB	PH H	PO	A	E	DP	TC/G	FA	G by Pos
1992	MON N	13	.167	.233	30	5	2	0	0	0.0	2	5	7	7	0	3	1	14	0	1	0	1.5	.933	OF-10
1993		6	.375	.500	8	3	1	0	0	0.0	1	2	0	1	0	5	2	1	0	0	0	1.0	1.000	OF-1
1995	BOS A	39	.261	.398	88	23	7	1	1	1.1	8	17	4	14	0	16	4	19	2	2	0	0.9	.913	OF-23, DH-2
1996	OAK A	61	.277	.547	137	38	5	1	10	7.3	21	23	19	23	1	17	8	64	11	1	4	1.5	.987	OF-44, DH-5, 1B-1
4 yrs.		119	.262	.460	263	69	15	2	11	4.2	32	47	30	45	1	41	15	98	13	4	4	1.3	.965	OF-78, DH-7, 1B-1

DIVISIONAL PLAYOFF SERIES

Year	Team	Games	BA	SA	AB	H	2B	3B	HR	HR%	R	RBI	BB	SO	SB	PH AB	PH H	PO	A	E	DP	TC/G	FA	G by Pos
1995	BOS A	1	.000	.000	1	0	0	0	0	0.0	0	0	0	1	0	1	0	0	0	0	0	0.0	—	

Andy Stankiewicz

STANKIEWICZ, ANDREW NEAL
B. Aug. 10, 1964, Inglewood, Calif.

BR TR 5'9" 165 lbs.

Year	Team	Games	BA	SA	AB	H	2B	3B	HR	HR%	R	RBI	BB	SO	SB	PH AB	PH H	PO	A	E	DP	TC/G	FA	G by Pos
1992	NY A	116	.268	.347	400	107	22	2	2	0.5	52	25	38	42	9	3	0	185	346	12	74	4.7	.978	SS-81, 2B-34, DH-1
1993		16	.000	.000	9	0	0	0	0	0.0	5	0	1	1	0	0	0	7	15	0	4	1.8	1.000	2B-6, 3B-4, SS-1, DH-1
1994	HOU N	37	.259	.370	54	14	3	0	1	1.9	10	5	12	12	1	8	3	12	45	0	7	2.4	1.000	SS-17, 2B-6, 3B-1
1995		43	.115	.135	52	6	1	0	0	0.0	6	7	12	19	4	12	3	20	59	1	6	3.5	.988	SS-14, 2B-6, 3B-3
1996	MON N	64	.286	.377	77	22	5	1	0	0.0	12	9	6	12	1	29	9	16	43	3	6	1.9	.952	2B-19, SS-13, 3B-1
5 yrs.		276	.252	.329	592	149	31	3	3	0.5	85	46	69	86	15	52	15	240	508	16	97	3.7	.979	SS-126, 2B-71, 3B-9, DH-2

Mike Stanley

STANLEY, ROBERT MICHAEL
B. June 25, 1963, Fort Lauderdale, Fla.

BR TR 6'1" 185 lbs.

Year	Team	Games	BA	SA	AB	H	2B	3B	HR	HR%	R	RBI	BB	SO	SB	PH AB	PH H	PO	A	E	DP	TC/G	FA	G by Pos
1986	TEX A	15	.333	.533	30	10	3	0	1	3.3	4	1	3	7	1	5	2	14	8	1	2	1.5	.957	3B-7, C-4, DH-3, OF-1
1987		78	.273	.403	216	59	8	1	6	2.8	34	37	31	48	3	6	4	389	26	7	7	5.7	.983	C-61, 1B-12, OF-1
1988		94	.229	.297	249	57	8	0	3	1.2	21	27	37	62	0	15	3	342	17	4	4	5.0	.989	C-64, 1B-7, 3B-2
1989		67	.246	.311	122	30	3	1	1	0.8	9	11	12	29	1	23	6	117	8	3	3	2.3	.977	C-25, DH-21, 1B-7, 3B-3
1990		103	.249	.333	189	47	8	1	2	1.1	21	19	30	25	1	27	7	261	25	4	2	3.2	.986	C-63, DH-14, 3B-8, 1B-6
1991		95	.249	.381	181	45	13	1	3	1.7	25	25	34	44	1	27	6	288	20	6	7	3.8	.981	C-58, 1B-12, 3B-6, DH-6, OF-1
1992	NY A	68	.249	.428	173	43	7	0	8	4.6	24	27	33	45	0	5	1	287	30	6	5	5.0	.981	C-55, DH-6, 1B-4
1993		130	.305	.534	423	129	17	1	26	6.1	70	84	57	85	1	11	3	652	46	3	5	5.7	.996	C-122, DH-2
1994		82	.300	.545	290	87	20	0	17	5.9	54	57	39	56	0	1	0	444	33	5	3	5.8	.990	C-72, 1B-7, DH-4
1995		118	.268	.481	399	107	29	1	18	4.5	63	83	57	106	1	2	0	651	35	5	3	5.9	.993	C-107, DH-10
1996	BOS A	121	.270	.506	397	107	20	1	24	6.0	73	69	69	62	2	11	3	654	19	10	2	5.9	.985	C-105, DH-10
11 yrs.		971	.270	.449	2669	721	136	7	109	4.1	398	440	402	569	10	133	35	4099	267	54	38	4.9	.988	C-736, DH-76, 1B-55, 3B-26, OF-3

Year	Team	Games	BA	SA	AB	H	2B	3B	HR	HR%	R	RBI	BB	SO	SB	Pinch Hit AB	H	PO	A	E	DP	TC/G	FA	G by Pos

Mike Stanley *continued*

DIVISIONAL PLAYOFF SERIES

Year	Team	Games	BA	SA	AB	H	2B	3B	HR	HR%	R	RBI	BB	SO	SB	AB	H	PO	A	E	DP	TC/G	FA	G by Pos
1995	NY A	4	.313	.500	16	5	0	0	1	6.3	2	3	2	1	0	0	0	30	0	1	0	7.8	.968	C-4

Terry Steinbach

STEINBACH, TERRY LEE   BR TR 6'1" 195 lbs.
B. Mar. 2, 1962, New Ulm, Minn.

Year	Team	Games	BA	SA	AB	H	2B	3B	HR	HR%	R	RBI	BB	SO	SB	AB	H	PO	A	E	DP	TC/G	FA	G by Pos
1986	OAK A	6	.333	.733	15	5	0	0	2	13.3	3	4	1	0	0	2	1	21	4	1	1	5.2	.962	C-5
1987		122	.284	.463	391	111	16	3	16	4.1	66	56	32	66	1	7	4	642	44	10	6	5.9	.986	C-107, 3B-10, 1B-1
1988		104	.265	.402	351	93	19	1	9	2.6	42	51	33	47	3	4	2	536	58	9	10	5.5	.985	C-84, 3B-9, 1B-8, DH-7, OF-1
1989		130	.273	.352	454	124	13	1	7	1.5	37	42	30	66	1	8	2	612	47	11	14	5.0	.984	C-103, OF-14, 1B-10, DH-4, 3B-3
1990		114	.251	.372	379	95	15	2	9	2.4	32	57	19	66	0	14	4	401	31	5	1	3.9	.989	C-83, DH-25, 1B-3
1991		129	.274	.386	456	125	31	1	6	1.3	50	67	22	70	2	7	4	639	53	15	11	5.5	.979	C-117, 1B-9, DH-2
1992		128	.279	.411	438	122	20	1	12	2.7	48	53	45	58	2	5	0	598	72	10	10	5.2	.985	C-124, 1B-5, DH-2
1993		104	.285	.416	389	111	19	1	10	2.6	47	43	25	65	3	4	1	524	47	7	18	5.4	.988	C-86, 1B-15, DH-6
1994		103	.285	.442	369	105	21	2	11	3.0	51	57	26	62	2	0	0	592	60	1	7	6.3	.998	C-93, DH-6, 1B-5
1995		114	.278	.458	406	113	26	1	15	3.7	43	65	25	74	1	3	1	686	57	6	6	6.6	.992	C-111, 1B-2
1996		145	.272	.529	514	140	25	1	35	6.8	79	100	49	115	0	10	5	733	45	7	7	5.5	.991	C-137, DH-4, 1B-1
11 yrs.		1199	.275	.426	4162	1144	205	14	132	3.2	498	595	307	689	15	64	24	5984	518	82	91	5.5	.988	C-1050, 1B-59, DH-56, 3B-22, OF-15

LEAGUE CHAMPIONSHIP SERIES

Year	Team	Games	BA	SA	AB	H	2B	3B	HR	HR%	R	RBI	BB	SO	SB	AB	H	PO	A	E	DP	TC/G	FA	G by Pos
1988	OAK A	2	.250	.250	4	1	0	0	0	0.0	0	0	2	0	0	0	0	12	0	0	0	6.0	1.000	C-2
1989		4	.200	.200	15	3	0	0	0	0.0	0	1	1	5	0	0	0	17	0	0	0	4.3	1.000	C-3, DH-1
1990		3	.455	.455	11	5	0	0	0	0.0	2	1	1	2	0	0	0	11	0	0	0	3.7	1.000	C-3
1992		6	.292	.417	24	7	0	0	1	4.2	1	5	2	7	0	0	0	30	7	0	0	6.2	1.000	C-6
4 yrs.		15	.296	.352	54	16	0	0	1	1.9	3	7	6	14	0	0	0	70	7	0	0	5.1	1.000	C-14, DH-1

WORLD SERIES

Year	Team	Games	BA	SA	AB	H	2B	3B	HR	HR%	R	RBI	BB	SO	SB	AB	H	PO	A	E	DP	TC/G	FA	G by Pos
1988	OAK A	3	.364	.455	11	4	1	0	0	0.0	0	0	0	0	0	0	0	11	3	0	0	4.7	1.000	C-2, DH-1
1989		4	.250	.563	16	4	0	1	1	6.3	3	7	2	1	0	0	0	27	2	0	0	7.3	1.000	C-4
1990		3	.125	.125	8	1	0	0	0	0.0	0	0	0	3	0	0	0	8	1	0	0	3.0	1.000	C-3
3 yrs.		10	.257	.429	35	9	1	1	1	2.9	3	7	2	4	0	0	0	46	6	0	0	5.2	1.000	C-9, DH-1

Lee Stevens

STEVENS, DeWAIN LEE   BL TL 6'4" 205 lbs.
B. July 10, 1967, Kansas City, Mo.

Year	Team	Games	BA	SA	AB	H	2B	3B	HR	HR%	R	RBI	BB	SO	SB	AB	H	PO	A	E	DP	TC/G	FA	G by Pos
1990	CAL A	67	.214	.339	248	53	10	0	7	2.8	28	32	22	75	1	3	0	597	36	4	62	9.5	.994	1B-67
1991		18	.293	.414	58	17	7	0	0	0.0	8	9	6	12	1	0	0	100	6	1	5	5.3	.991	1B-11, OF-9
1992		106	.221	.349	312	69	19	0	7	2.2	25	37	29	64	1	12	3	764	49	4	88	8.8	.995	1B-91, DH-2
1996	TEX A	27	.231	.449	78	18	2	3	3	3.8	6	12	6	22	0	5	0	157	14	1	21	7.5	.994	1B-18, OF-5
4 yrs.		218	.226	.362	696	157	38	3	17	2.4	67	90	63	173	3	20	3	1618	105	10	176	8.5	.994	1B-187, OF-14, DH-2

Todd Steverson

STEVERSON, TODD ANTHONY   BR TR 6'2" 194 lbs.
B. Nov. 15, 1971, Los Angeles, Calif.

Year	Team	Games	BA	SA	AB	H	2B	3B	HR	HR%	R	RBI	BB	SO	SB	AB	H	PO	A	E	DP	TC/G	FA	G by Pos
1995	DET A	30	.262	.405	42	11	0	0	2	4.8	11	6	6	10	2	3	1	22	1	0	0	0.8	1.000	OF-27, DH-1
1996	SD N	1	.000	.000	1	0	0	0	0	0.0	0	0	0	1	0	1	0	0	0	0	0	0.0	—	
2 yrs.		31	.256	.395	43	11	0	0	2	4.7	11	6	6	11	2	4	1	22	1	0	0	0.8	1.000	OF-27, DH-1

Shannon Stewart

STEWART, SHANNON HAROLD   BR TR 6' 175 lbs.
B. Feb. 25, 1974, Cincinnati, Ohio

Year	Team	Games	BA	SA	AB	H	2B	3B	HR	HR%	R	RBI	BB	SO	SB	AB	H	PO	A	E	DP	TC/G	FA	G by Pos
1995	TOR A	12	.211	.211	38	8	0	0	0	0.0	2	1	5	5	2	0	0	20	1	1	0	1.8	.955	OF-12
1996		7	.176	.235	17	3	1	0	0	0.0	2	2	1	4	1	0	0	4	0	1	0	0.8	.800	OF-6
2 yrs.		19	.200	.218	55	11	1	0	0	0.0	4	3	6	9	3	0	0	24	1	2	0	1.5	.926	OF-18

Kurt Stillwell

STILLWELL, KURT ANDREW   BB TR 5'11" 165 lbs.
Son of Ron Stillwell.
B. June 4, 1965, Glendale, Calif.

Year	Team	Games	BA	SA	AB	H	2B	3B	HR	HR%	R	RBI	BB	SO	SB	AB	H	PO	A	E	DP	TC/G	FA	G by Pos
1986	CIN N	104	.229	.258	279	64	6	1	0	0.0	31	26	30	47	6	20	6	107	205	16	40	4.1	.951	SS-80
1987		131	.258	.375	395	102	20	7	4	1.0	54	33	32	50	4	29	8	144	247	23	38	3.8	.944	SS-51, 2B-37, 3B-20
1988	KC A	128	.251	.399	459	115	28	5	10	2.2	63	53	47	76	6	4	0	170	349	13	60	4.3	.976	SS-124
1989		130	.261	.380	463	121	20	7	7	1.5	52	54	42	64	9	4	1	179	334	16	65	4.1	.970	SS-130
1990		144	.249	.352	506	126	35	4	3	0.6	60	51	39	60	0	9	2	181	350	24	79	3.9	.957	SS-141
1991		122	.265	.361	385	102	17	1	6	1.6	44	51	33	56	3	18	2	163	263	18	66	3.8	.959	SS-118
1992	SD N	114	.227	.298	379	86	15	3	2	0.5	35	24	26	58	4	5	1	250	266	16	66	4.8	.970	2B-111
1993	2 teams		SD N	(57G –.215)		CAL A	(22G –.262)																	
"	total	79	.231	.302	182	42	6	2	1	0.5	11	14	15	33	6	28	7	93	114	14	21	3.8	.937	SS-37, 2B-18, 3B-3
1996	TEX A	46	.273	.364	77	21	4	0	1	1.3	12	4	10	11	2	11	1	30	39	3	5	1.9	.958	2B-21, SS-9, 3B-6, 1B-1, DH-1
9 yrs.		998	.249	.349	3125	779	151	30	34	1.1	362	310	274	455	38	128	28	1317	2167	143	440	4.0	.961	SS-690, 2B-187, 3B-29, 1B-1, DH-1

Kelly Stinnett

STINNETT, KELLY LEE   BR TR 5'11" 195 lbs.
B. Feb. 14, 1970, Lawton, Okla.

Year	Team	Games	BA	SA	AB	H	2B	3B	HR	HR%	R	RBI	BB	SO	SB	AB	H	PO	A	E	DP	TC/G	FA	G by Pos
1994	NY N	47	.253	.360	150	38	6	2	2	1.3	20	14	11	28	2	4	0	211	20	5	2	5.4	.979	C-44
1995		77	.219	.332	196	43	8	1	4	2.0	23	18	29	65	2	9	1	380	22	7	1	6.1	.983	C-67
1996	MIL A	14	.077	.077	26	2	0	0	0	0.0	1	0	2	11	0	1	0	46	2	2	1	3.3	.960	C-14, DH-1
3 yrs.		138	.223	.325	372	83	14	3	6	1.6	44	32	42	104	4	14	1	637	44	14	4	5.5	.980	C-125, DH-1

Year	Team	Games	BA	SA	AB	H	2B	3B	HR	HR%	R	RBI	BB	SO	SB	Pinch Hit AB	H	PO	A	E	DP	TC/G	FA	G by Pos

Kevin Stocker

STOCKER, KEVIN DOUGLAS
B. Feb. 13, 1970, Spokane, Wash. — BB TR 6'1" 175 lbs.

Year	Team	Games	BA	SA	AB	H	2B	3B	HR	HR%	R	RBI	BB	SO	SB	Pinch Hit AB	H	PO	A	E	DP	TC/G	FA	G by Pos
1993	PHI N	70	.324	.417	259	84	12	3	2	0.8	46	31	30	43	5	0	0	118	202	14	44	4.8	.958	SS-70
1994		82	.273	.351	271	74	11	2	2	0.7	38	28	44	41	2	0	0	118	253	16	46	4.7	.959	SS-82
1995		125	.218	.274	412	90	14	3	1	0.2	42	32	43	75	6	0	0	148	383	17	71	4.4	.969	SS-125
1996		119	.254	.378	394	100	22	6	5	1.3	46	41	43	89	6	3	2	165	352	13	79	4.5	.975	SS-119
4 yrs.		396	.260	.348	1336	348	59	14	10	0.7	172	132	160	248	19	3	2	549	1190	60	240	4.5	.967	SS-396

LEAGUE CHAMPIONSHIP SERIES

| 1993 | PHI N | 6 | .182 | .227 | 22 | 4 | 1 | 0 | 0 | 0.0 | 0 | 1 | 2 | 5 | 0 | 0 | 0 | 9 | 14 | 1 | 1 | 4.0 | .958 | SS-6 |

WORLD SERIES

| 1993 | PHI N | 6 | .211 | .263 | 19 | 4 | 1 | 0 | 0 | 0.0 | 1 | 1 | 5 | 5 | 0 | 0 | 0 | 8 | 13 | 0 | 4 | 3.5 | 1.000 | SS-6 |

Doug Strange

STRANGE, JOSEPH DOUGLAS
B. Apr. 13, 1964, Greenville, S. C. — BB TR 6'2" 170 lbs.

Year	Team	Games	BA	SA	AB	H	2B	3B	HR	HR%	R	RBI	BB	SO	SB	Pinch Hit AB	H	PO	A	E	DP	TC/G	FA	G by Pos
1989	DET A	64	.214	.260	196	42	4	1	1	0.5	16	14	17	36	3	3	0	53	118	19	17	2.6	.900	3B-54, SS-9, 2B-9, DH-1
1991	CHI N	3	.444	.556	9	4	1	0	0	0.0	0	1	0	1	1	0	0	1	3	1	0	1.7	.800	3B-3
1992		52	.160	.202	94	15	1	0	1	1.1	7	5	10	15	1	10	1	24	51	6	4	1.8	.926	3B-33, 2B-12
1993	TEX A	145	.256	.360	484	124	29	0	7	1.4	58	60	43	69	6	12	4	276	374	13	83	4.6	.980	2B-135, 3B-9, SS-1
1994		73	.212	.341	226	48	12	1	5	2.2	26	26	15	38	1	6	1	88	174	11	39	4.0	.960	2B-53, 3B-13, OF-3
1995	SEA A	74	.271	.394	155	42	9	2	2	1.3	19	21	10	25	0	32	10	39	70	5	2	2.2	.956	3B-41, 2B-5, OF-4, DH-1
1996		88	.235	.333	183	43	7	1	3	1.6	19	23	14	31	1	42	10	26	39	2	4	1.0	.970	3B-39, OF-11, DH-10, 2B-3, 1B-3
7 yrs.		499	.236	.333	1347	318	63	5	19	1.4	145	150	109	215	13	105	26	507	829	57	149	3.1	.959	2B-217, 3B-192, OF-18, DH-12, SS-10, 1B-3

DIVISIONAL PLAYOFF SERIES

| 1995 | SEA A | 2 | .000 | .000 | 4 | 0 | 0 | 0 | 0 | 0.0 | 0 | 1 | 1 | 1 | 0 | 1 | 0 | 0 | 0 | 0 | 0 | 0.0 | .000 | 3B-2 |

LEAGUE CHAMPIONSHIP SERIES

| 1995 | SEA A | 4 | .000 | .000 | 4 | 0 | 0 | 0 | 0 | 0.0 | 0 | 0 | 0 | 2 | 0 | 2 | 0 | 2 | 3 | 0 | 0 | 2.5 | 1.000 | 3B-2 |

Darryl Strawberry

STRAWBERRY, DARRYL EUGENE (The Straw Man)
B. Mar. 12, 1962, Los Angeles, Calif. — BL TL 6'6" 190 lbs.

Year	Team	Games	BA	SA	AB	H	2B	3B	HR	HR%	R	RBI	BB	SO	SB	Pinch Hit AB	H	PO	A	E	DP	TC/G	FA	G by Pos
1983	NY N	122	.257	.512	420	108	15	7	26	6.2	63	74	47	128	19	4	0	232	8	4	0	2.1	.984	OF-117
1984		147	.251	.467	522	131	27	4	26	5.0	75	97	75	131	27	4	2	276	11	6	3	2.0	.980	OF-146
1985		111	.277	.557	393	109	15	4	29	7.4	78	79	73	96	26	2	0	211	5	2	2	2.0	.991	OF-110
1986		136	.259	.507	475	123	27	5	27	5.7	76	93	72	141	28	8	0	226	10	6	3	1.8	.975	OF-131
1987		154	.284	.583	532	151	32	5	39	7.3	108	104	97	122	36	3	1	272	6	8	3	1.9	.972	OF-151
1988		153	.269	**.545**	543	146	27	3	**39**	7.2	101	101	85	127	29	2	0	297	4	9	3	2.1	.971	OF-150
1989		134	.225	.466	476	107	26	1	29	6.1	69	77	61	105	11	6	1	272	4	8	2	2.2	.972	OF-131
1990		152	.277	.518	542	150	18	1	37	6.8	92	108	70	110	15	5	0	268	10	3	4	1.9	.989	OF-149
1991	LA N	139	.265	.491	505	134	22	4	28	5.5	86	99	75	125	10	3	1	209	11	5	2	1.7	.978	OF-136
1992		43	.237	.385	156	37	8	0	5	3.2	20	25	19	34	3	2	1	67	2	1	0	1.7	.986	OF-42
1993		32	.140	.310	100	14	2	0	5	5.0	12	12	16	19	1	3	1	37	1	4	0	1.4	.905	OF-29
1994	SF N	29	.239	.424	92	22	3	1	4	4.3	13	17	19	22	0	0	0	61	1	2	1	2.4	.969	OF-27
1995	NY A	32	.276	.448	87	24	4	1	3	3.4	15	13	10	22	0	5	1	18	2	2	1	0.8	.909	DH-15, OF-11
1996		63	.262	.490	202	53	13	0	11	5.4	35	36	31	55	6	6	1	45	1	0	0	0.8	1.000	OF-34, DH-26
14 yrs.		1447	.259	.504	5045	1309	239	36	308	6.1	843	935	750	1237	211	53	9	2491	76	60	24	1.9	.977	OF-1364, DH-41

DIVISIONAL PLAYOFF SERIES

1995	NY A	2	.000	.000	2	0	0	0	0	0.0	0	0	0	1	0	2	0	0	0	0	0	0.0	—	
1996		2	.000	.000	5	0	0	0	0	0.0	0	0	0	2	0	1	0	11	0	0	0	2.2	1.000	OF-5
2 yrs.		4	.000	.000	7	0	0	0	0	0.0	0	0	0	3	0	3	0	11	0	0	0	0.0		DH-2

LEAGUE CHAMPIONSHIP SERIES

1986	NY N	6	.227	.545	22	5	1	0	2	9.1	4	5	3	12	1	0	0	9	0	0	0	1.5	1.000	OF-6
1988		7	.300	.467	30	9	2	0	1	3.3	5	6	2	5	0	0	0	11	0	0	0	1.6	1.000	OF-7
1996	NY A	4	.417	1.167	12	5	0	0	3	25.0	4	5	2	2	0	0	0	5	0	0	0	1.3	1.000	OF-4
3 yrs.		17	.297	.625 5th	64	19	3	0	6	9.4 3rd 1st	13	16	7	19 7th	1	0	0	25	0	0	0	1.5	1.000	OF-17

WORLD SERIES

1986	NY N	7	.208	.375	24	5	1	0	1	4.2	4	1	4	6	3	0	0	19	0	0	0	2.7	1.000	OF-7
1996	NY A	5	.188	.188	16	3	0	0	0	0.0	0	1	4	6	0	0	0	11	0	0	0	2.2	1.000	
2 yrs.		12	.200	.300	40	8	1	0	1	2.5	4	2	8	12	3	0	0	30	0	0	0	2.5	1.000	OF-12

Chris Stynes

STYNES, CHRISTOPHER DESMOND
B. Jan. 19, 1973, Queens, N. Y. — BR TR 5'9" 175 lbs.

Year	Team	Games	BA	SA	AB	H	2B	3B	HR	HR%	R	RBI	BB	SO	SB	Pinch Hit AB	H	PO	A	E	DP	TC/G	FA	G by Pos
1995	KC A	22	.171	.200	35	6	1	0	0	0.0	7	2	4	3	0	3	1	22	35	1	12	3.2	.983	2B-17, DH-1
1996		36	.293	.359	92	27	6	0	0	0.0	8	6	2	5	5	6	1	38	8	3	2	1.7	.939	OF-19, 2B-5, DH-3, 3B-2
2 yrs.		58	.260	.315	127	33	7	0	0	0.0	15	8	6	8	5	9	2	60	43	4	14	2.3	.963	2B-22, OF-19, DH-4, 3B-2

B. J. Surhoff

SURHOFF, WILLIAM JAMES
Brother of Rich Surhoff.
B. Aug. 4, 1964, Bronx, N. Y. — BL TR 6'1" 185 lbs.

Year	Team	Games	BA	SA	AB	H	2B	3B	HR	HR%	R	RBI	BB	SO	SB	Pinch Hit AB	H	PO	A	E	DP	TC/G	FA	G by Pos
1987	MIL A	115	.299	.423	395	118	22	3	7	1.8	50	68	36	30	11	10	3	648	56	11	12	6.6	.985	C-98, 3B-10, 1B-1
1988		139	.245	.318	493	121	21	0	5	1.0	47	38	31	49	21	9	2	550	94	8	3	4.6	.988	C-106, 3B-31, 1B-2, SS-1, OF-1
1989		126	.248	.339	436	108	17	4	5	1.1	42	55	25	29	14	5	0	530	58	10	7	4.8	.983	C-106, DH-12, 3B-6
1990		135	.276	.376	474	131	21	4	6	1.3	55	59	41	37	18	8	2	619	62	12	11	5.1	.983	C-125, 3B-11
1991		143	.289	.372	505	146	19	4	5	1.0	57	68	26	33	5	10	2	665	71	4	11	5.2	.995	C-127, DH-6, 3B-5, OF-2, 2B-1

98

Year	Team	Games	BA	SA	AB	H	2B	3B	HR	HR%	R	RBI	BB	SO	SB	Pinch Hit AB	Pinch Hit H	PO	A	E	DP	TC/G	FA	G by Pos

B. J. Surhoff continued

Year	Team	Games	BA	SA	AB	H	2B	3B	HR	HR%	R	RBI	BB	SO	SB	AB	H	PO	A	E	DP	TC/G	FA	G by Pos
1992		139	.252	.321	480	121	19	1	4	0.8	63	62	46	41	14	4	1	699	74	6	25	5.4	.992	C-109, 1B-17, DH-9, OF-7, 3B-3
1993		148	.274	.391	552	151	38	3	7	1.3	66	79	36	47	12	5	2	175	220	18	21	2.6	.956	3B-121, OF-24, 1B-8, C-3, DH-1
1994		40	.261	.485	134	35	11	2	5	3.7	20	22	16	14	0	1	0	121	29	4	12	3.7	.974	3B-18, C-12, 1B-8, OF-3, DH-1
1995		117	.320	.492	415	133	26	3	13	3.1	72	73	37	43	7	3	0	529	44	5	45	4.3	.991	OF-60, 1B-55, C-18, DH-3
1996	BAL A	143	.292	.482	537	157	27	6	21	3.9	74	82	47	79	0	3	0	137	177	15	22	2.3	.954	3B-106, OF-27, DH-10, 1B-2
10 yrs.		1245	.276	.393	4421	1221	221	30	78	1.8	546	606	341	402	102	58	12	4673	885	93	169	4.4	.984	C-704, 3B-311, OF-124, 1B-93, DH-42, 2B-1, SS-1

DIVISIONAL PLAYOFF SERIES
Year	Team	Games	BA	SA	AB	H	2B	3B	HR	HR%	R	RBI	BB	SO	SB	AB	H	PO	A	E	DP	TC/G	FA	G by Pos
1996	BAL A	4	.385	1.077	13	5	0	0	3	23.1	3	5	0	1	0	1	1	6	0	0	0	2.0	1.000	OF-3

LEAGUE CHAMPIONSHIP SERIES
Year	Team	Games	BA	SA	AB	H	2B	3B	HR	HR%	R	RBI	BB	SO	SB	AB	H	PO	A	E	DP	TC/G	FA	G by Pos
1996	BAL A	5	.267	.267	15	4	0	0	0	0.0	0	2	1	2	0	1	1	11	1	0	0	2.4	1.000	OF-5

Dale Sveum
SVEUM, DALE CURTIS
B. Nov. 23, 1963, Richmond, Calif.
BB TR 6' 2" 185 lbs.

Year	Team	Games	BA	SA	AB	H	2B	3B	HR	HR%	R	RBI	BB	SO	SB	AB	H	PO	A	E	DP	TC/G	FA	G by Pos
1986	MIL A	91	.246	.366	317	78	13	2	7	2.2	35	35	32	63	4	2	0	92	179	30	19	3.3	.900	3B-65, SS-13, 2B-13
1987		153	.252	.454	535	135	27	3	25	4.7	86	95	40	133	2	1	1	242	396	33	89	4.3	.956	SS-142, 2B-13
1988		129	.242	.347	467	113	14	4	9	1.9	41	51	21	122	1	0	0	209	375	27	94	4.7	.956	SS-127, 2B-1, DH-1
1990		48	.197	.282	117	23	7	0	1	0.9	15	12	12	30	0	6	0	59	63	6	10	2.7	.953	3B-22, 2B-16, SS-5, 1B-5
1991		90	.241	.365	266	64	19	1	4	1.5	33	43	32	78	2	6	0	85	189	10	33	3.0	.965	SS-51, 3B-38, DH-3, 2B-2
1992	2 teams	PHI N (54G –.178)			CHI A (40G –.219)																			
"	total	94	.197	.297	249	49	13	0	4	1.6	28	28	28	68	1	19	1	121	198	16	38	4.0	.952	SS-71, 3B-7, 1B-6
1993	OAK A	30	.177	.304	79	14	2	1	2	2.5	12	6	16	21	0	7	3	128	17	3	13	5.1	.980	1B-14, 3B-7, 2B-4, DH-2, SS-1, OF-1
1994	SEA A	10	.185	.296	27	5	0	0	1	3.7	3	2	2	10	0	4	0	2	8	1	0	1.6	.909	DH-4, 3B-3
1996	PIT N	12	.353	.588	34	12	5	0	1	2.9	9	5	6	6	0	2	0	4	17	2	1	2.3	.913	3B-10
9 yrs.		657	.236	.372	2091	493	100	11	54	2.6	262	277	189	531	10	47	5	942	1442	118	297	3.9	.953	SS-410, 3B-152, 2B-49, 1B-25, DH-10, OF-1

Mark Sweeney
SWEENEY, MARK PATRICK
B. Oct. 26, 1969, Framingham, Mass.
BL TL 6' 1" 195 lbs.

Year	Team	Games	BA	SA	AB	H	2B	3B	HR	HR%	R	RBI	BB	SO	SB	AB	H	PO	A	E	DP	TC/G	FA	G by Pos
1995	STL N	37	.273	.377	77	21	2	0	2	2.6	5	13	10	15	1	15	8	153	11	2	20	8.3	.988	1B-19, OF-1
1996		98	.265	.371	170	45	9	0	3	1.8	32	22	33	29	3	37	9	126	3	3	7	2.3	.977	OF-43, 1B-15
2 yrs.		135	.267	.372	247	66	11	0	5	2.0	37	35	43	44	4	52	17	279	14	5	27	3.8	.983	OF-44, 1B-34

DIVISIONAL PLAYOFF SERIES
Year	Team	Games	BA	SA	AB	H	2B	3B	HR	HR%	R	RBI	BB	SO	SB	AB	H	PO	A	E	DP	TC/G	FA	G by Pos
1996	STL N	1	1.000	1.000	1	1	0	0	0	0.0	0	0	0	0	0	1	1	0	0	0	0	0.0	—	

LEAGUE CHAMPIONSHIP SERIES
Year	Team	Games	BA	SA	AB	H	2B	3B	HR	HR%	R	RBI	BB	SO	SB	AB	H	PO	A	E	DP	TC/G	FA	G by Pos
1996	STL N	5	.000	.000	4	0	0	0	0	0.0	0	1	0	2	0	2	0	2	0	0	0	1.0	1.000	OF-2

Mike Sweeney
SWEENEY, MICHAEL JOHN
B. July 22, 1973, Orange, Calif.
BR TR 6' 1" 195 lbs.

Year	Team	Games	BA	SA	AB	H	2B	3B	HR	HR%	R	RBI	BB	SO	SB	AB	H	PO	A	E	DP	TC/G	FA	G by Pos
1995	KC A	4	.250	.250	4	1	0	0	0	0.0	0	0	0	0	0	3	1	7	0	1	0	2.0	.875	C-4
1996		50	.279	.412	165	46	10	0	4	2.4	23	24	18	21	1	2	1	158	7	1	3	3.5	.994	C-26, DH-22
2 yrs.		54	.278	.408	169	47	10	0	4	2.4	24	24	18	21	1	5	2	165	7	2	3	3.3	.989	C-30, DH-22

Tony Tarasco
TARASCO, ANTONIO GIACINTO
B. Dec. 9, 1970, New York, N.Y.
BL TR 6' 185 lbs.

Year	Team	Games	BA	SA	AB	H	2B	3B	HR	HR%	R	RBI	BB	SO	SB	AB	H	PO	A	E	DP	TC/G	FA	G by Pos
1993	ATL N	24	.229	.286	35	8	0	0	0	0.0	6	2	0	5	0	13	4	11	0	0	0	0.9	1.000	OF-12
1994		87	.273	.432	132	36	6	0	5	3.8	16	19	9	17	5	46	10	42	1	0	0	0.9	1.000	OF-46
1995	MON N	126	.249	.404	438	109	18	4	14	3.2	64	40	51	78	24	8	2	229	7	5	2	2.1	.979	OF-117
1996	BAL A	31	.238	.310	84	20	3	0	1	1.2	14	9	7	15	5	6	1	50	1	0	0	1.8	1.000	OF-23, DH-5
4 yrs.		268	.251	.392	689	173	29	4	20	2.9	100	70	67	115	34	73	17	332	9	5	2	1.7	.986	OF-198, DH-5

LEAGUE CHAMPIONSHIP SERIES
Year	Team	Games	BA	SA	AB	H	2B	3B	HR	HR%	R	RBI	BB	SO	SB	AB	H	PO	A	E	DP	TC/G	FA	G by Pos
1993	ATL N	2	.000	.000	1	0	0	0	0	0.0	0	0	0	1	0	0	0	0	0	0	0	0.0	.000	OF-2
1996	BAL A	2	.000	.000	1	0	0	0	0	0.0	0	0	0	1	0	0	0	2	0	0	0	1.0	1.000	OF-2
2 yrs.		4	.000	.000	2	0	0	0	0	0.0	0	0	0	2	0	0	0	2	0	0	0	0.5	1.000	OF-4

Danny Tartabull
TARTABULL, DANILO
Born Danilo Tartabull (Mora).
Son of Jose Tartabull.
B. Oct. 30, 1962, San Juan, Puerto Rico
BR TR 6' 1" 185 lbs.

Year	Team	Games	BA	SA	AB	H	2B	3B	HR	HR%	R	RBI	BB	SO	SB	AB	H	PO	A	E	DP	TC/G	FA	G by Pos
1984	SEA A	10	.300	.650	20	6	1	0	2	10.0	3	7	2	3	0	1	0	8	21	2	5	3.4	.935	SS-8, 2B-1
1985		19	.328	.525	61	20	7	1	1	1.6	8	7	8	14	1	3	1	28	43	4	11	3.8	.947	SS-16, 3B-4
1986		137	.270	.489	511	138	25	6	25	4.9	76	96	61	157	4	2	1	233	111	18	28	2.7	.950	OF-101, 2B-31, DH-3, 3B-1
1987	KC A	158	.309	.541	582	180	27	3	34	5.8	95	101	79	136	9	3	0	228	11	6	1	1.6	.976	OF-149, DH-6
1988		146	.274	.515	507	139	38	3	26	5.1	80	102	76	119	8	4	1	227	8	9	1	1.7	.963	OF-130, DH-13
1989		133	.268	.440	441	118	22	0	18	4.1	54	62	69	123	4	4	1	108	3	2	0	0.9	.982	OF-71, DH-55
1990		88	.268	.473	313	84	19	0	15	4.8	41	60	36	93	1	4	1	81	1	3	0	1.0	.965	OF-52, DH-32
1991		132	.316	.593	484	153	35	3	31	6.4	78	100	65	121	6	1	0	190	4	7	0	1.5	.965	OF-124, DH-6
1992	NY A	123	.266	.489	421	112	19	0	25	5.9	72	85	103	115	2	3	1	142	3	3	1	1.2	.980	OF-69, DH-53
1993		138	.250	.503	513	128	33	2	31	6.0	87	102	92	156	0	0	0	88	3	2	2	0.7	.978	DH-88, OF-50

Year	Team	Games	BA	SA	AB	H	2B	3B	HR	HR%	R	RBI	BB	SO	SB	Pinch Hit AB	Pinch Hit H	PO	A	E	DP	TC/G	FA	G by Pos

Danny Tartabull *continued*

Year	Team	Games	BA	SA	AB	H	2B	3B	HR	HR%	R	RBI	BB	SO	SB	AB	H	PO	A	E	DP	TC/G	FA	G by Pos
1994		104	.256	.464	399	102	24	1	19	4.8	68	67	66	111	1	3	1	43	1	0	0	0.4	1.000	DH-78, OF-26
1995	2 teams NY A (59G –.224) OAK A (24G –.261)																							
"	total	83	.236	.379	280	66	16	0	8	2.9	34	35	43	82	0	6	3	28	1	0	1	0.4	1.000	DH-61, OF-19
1996	CHI A	132	.254	.487	472	120	23	3	27	5.7	58	101	64	128	1	4	0	253	4	7	1	2.0	.973	OF-122, DH-10
13 yrs.		1403	.273	.497	5004	1366	289	22	262	5.2	754	925	764	1358	37	38	9	1657	214	63	51	1.4	.967	OF-913, DH-405, 2B-32, SS-24, 3B-5

Jim Tatum

TATUM, JAMES RAY
B. Oct. 9, 1967, San Diego, Calif.

BR TR 6'2" 200 lbs.

Year	Team	Games	BA	SA	AB	H	2B	3B	HR	HR%	R	RBI	BB	SO	SB	AB	H	PO	A	E	DP	TC/G	FA	G by Pos
1992	MIL A	5	.125	.125	8	1	0	0	0	0.0	0	1	2	0	0	0	0	6	0	0	0	1.6	1.000	3B-5
1993	CLR N	92	.204	.286	98	20	5	0	1	1.0	7	12	5	27	0	67	17	45	5	2	7	2.5	.962	1B-12, 3B-6, OF-3
1995		34	.235	.324	34	8	1	1	0	0.0	4	4	1	7	0	30	7	4	0	0	0	1.3	1.000	OF-2, C-1
1996	2 teams BOS A (2G –.125) SD N (5G –.000)																							
"	total	7	.091	.091	11	1	0	0	0	0.0	1	0	0	3	0	3	0	3	2	0	0	1.7	1.000	3B-3
4 yrs.		138	.199	.272	151	30	6	1	1	0.7	12	16	7	39	0	100	24	58	9	2	7	2.2	.971	3B-14, 1B-12, OF-5, C-1

Eddie Taubensee

TAUBENSEE, EDWARD KENNETH
B. Oct. 31, 1968, Beeville, Tex.

BL TR 6'4" 205 lbs.

Year	Team	Games	BA	SA	AB	H	2B	3B	HR	HR%	R	RBI	BB	SO	SB	AB	H	PO	A	E	DP	TC/G	FA	G by Pos
1991	CLE A	26	.242	.303	66	16	2	1	0	0.0	5	8	5	16	0	2	0	89	6	2	1	3.9	.979	C-25
1992	HOU N	104	.222	.323	297	66	15	0	5	1.7	23	28	31	78	2	4	0	557	66	5	6	6.1	.992	C-103
1993		94	.250	.389	288	72	11	1	9	3.1	26	42	21	44	1	7	2	551	41	5	5	6.6	.992	C-90
1994	2 teams HOU N (5G –.100) CIN N (61G –.294)																							
"	total	66	.283	.476	187	53	8	2	8	4.3	29	21	15	31	2	4	0	380	19	4	1	6.1	.990	C-66
1995	CIN N	80	.284	.491	218	62	14	2	9	4.1	32	44	22	52	2	14	6	338	22	6	2	5.4	.984	C-65, 1B-3
1996		108	.291	.462	327	95	20	0	12	3.7	46	48	26	64	3	20	3	538	42	11	7	6.3	.981	C-94
6 yrs.		478	.263	.416	1383	364	70	6	43	3.1	161	191	120	285	10	51	11	2453	196	33	22	6.0	.988	C-443, 1B-3

LEAGUE CHAMPIONSHIP SERIES

Year	Team	Games	BA	SA	AB	H	2B	3B	HR	HR%	R	RBI	BB	SO	SB	AB	H	PO	A	E	DP	TC/G	FA	G by Pos
1995	CIN N	2	.500	.500	2	1	0	0	0	0.0	0	0	0	1	0	1	0	0	0	0	0	0.0	.000	C-1

Jesus Tavarez

TAVAREZ, JESUS RAFAEL
Born Jesus Rafael Tavarez (Alcantras).
B. Mar. 26, 1971, Santo Domingo, Dominican Republic

BB TR 6' 170 lbs.

Year	Team	Games	BA	SA	AB	H	2B	3B	HR	HR%	R	RBI	BB	SO	SB	AB	H	PO	A	E	DP	TC/G	FA	G by Pos
1994	FLA N	17	.179	.179	39	7	0	0	0	0.0	4	4	1	5	1	6	2	28	1	0	0	2.6	1.000	OF-11
1995		63	.289	.374	190	55	6	2	1	0.5	31	13	16	27	7	2	0	119	1	0	1	2.0	1.000	OF-61
1996		98	.219	.246	114	25	3	0	0	0.0	14	6	7	18	5	30	9	57	0	0	0	0.9	1.000	OF-65
3 yrs.		178	.254	.309	343	87	9	2	2	0.6	49	23	24	50	13	38	11	204	2	0	1	1.5	1.000	OF-137

Mickey Tettleton

TETTLETON, MICKEY LEE
B. Sept. 16, 1960, Oklahoma City, Okla.

BB TR 6'2" 190 lbs.

Year	Team	Games	BA	SA	AB	H	2B	3B	HR	HR%	R	RBI	BB	SO	SB	AB	H	PO	A	E	DP	TC/G	FA	G by Pos
1984	OAK A	33	.263	.355	76	20	2	1	1	1.3	10	5	11	21	0	3	0	112	10	1	1	3.8	.992	C-32
1985		78	.251	.351	211	53	12	0	3	1.4	23	15	28	59	2	3	1	344	24	4	9	4.8	.989	C-76, DH-1
1986		90	.204	.389	211	43	9	0	10	4.7	26	35	39	51	7	2	0	463	32	8	6	5.7	.984	C-89
1987		82	.194	.322	211	41	3	0	8	3.8	19	26	30	65	1	2	0	435	29	6	1	5.7	.987	C-80, 1B-1, DH-1
1988	BAL A	86	.261	.424	283	74	11	1	11	3.9	31	37	28	70	0	9	0	361	31	3	1	4.9	.992	C-80
1989		117	.258	.509	411	106	21	2	26	6.3	72	65	73	117	3	3	1	297	42	2	1	2.9	.994	C-75, DH-43
1990		135	.223	.381	444	99	21	2	15	3.4	68	51	106	160	2	2	1	458	39	5	4	3.7	.990	C-90, DH-40, 1B-5, OF-1
1991	DET A	154	.263	.491	501	132	17	2	31	6.2	85	89	101	131	3	13	4	562	55	6	2	4.1	.990	C-125, DH-24, OF-3, 1B-1
1992		157	.238	.469	525	125	25	0	32	6.1	82	83	122	137	0	4	1	481	47	7	11	3.4	.986	C-113, DH-40, 1B-3, OF-2
1993		152	.245	.492	522	128	25	4	32	6.1	79	110	109	139	3	4	1	724	47	6	43	4.5	.992	1B-59, C-56, OF-55, DH-4
1994		107	.248	.463	339	84	18	2	17	5.0	57	51	97	98	0	2	1	367	30	5	7	3.4	.988	C-53, 1B-24, DH-22, OF-18
1995	TEX A	134	.238	.510	429	102	19	1	32	7.5	76	78	107	110	0	2	0	185	10	3	8	1.5	.985	OF-63, DH-58, 1B-9, C-3
1996		143	.246	.450	491	121	26	1	24	4.9	78	83	95	137	2	4	0	161	11	4	14	1.3	.977	DH-115, 1B-23
13 yrs.		1468	.242	.450	4654	1128	209	16	242	5.2	706	728	946	1295	23	53	10	4950	407	55	108	3.6	.990	C-872, DH-348, OF-142, 1B-125

DIVISIONAL PLAYOFF SERIES

Year	Team	Games	BA	SA	AB	H	2B	3B	HR	HR%	R	RBI	BB	SO	SB	AB	H	PO	A	E	DP	TC/G	FA	G by Pos
1996	TEX A	4	.083	.083	12	1	0	0	0	0.0	1	1	5	7	0	0	0	0	0	0	0	0.0	.000	DH-4

Frank Thomas

THOMAS, FRANK EDWARD (The Big Hurt)
B. May 27, 1968, Columbus, Ga.

BR TR 6'5" 240 lbs.

Year	Team	Games	BA	SA	AB	H	2B	3B	HR	HR%	R	RBI	BB	SO	SB	AB	H	PO	A	E	DP	TC/G	FA	G by Pos
1990	CHI A	60	.330	.529	191	63	11	3	7	3.7	39	31	44	54	0	1	1	428	26	5	53	7.8	.989	1B-51, DH-8
1991		158	.318	.553	559	178	31	2	32	5.7	104	109	138	112	1	1	1	459	27	2	43	3.1	.996	DH-101, 1B-56
1992		160	.323	.536	573	185	46	2	24	4.2	108	115	122	88	6	1	0	1428	92	13	112	9.6	.992	1B-158, DH-2
1993		153	.317	.607	549	174	36	0	41	7.5	106	128	112	54	4	0	0	1222	83	15	128	8.6	.989	1B-150, DH-4
1994		113	.353	.729	399	141	34	1	38	9.5	106	101	109	61	2	1	0	735	45	7	74	7.0	.991	1B-99, DH-13
1995		145	.308	.606	493	152	27	0	40	8.1	102	111	136	74	3	3	0	743	35	7	66	5.5	.991	1B-91, DH-53
1996		141	.349	.626	527	184	26	0	40	7.6	110	134	109	70	1	2	1	1097	84	9	111	8.6	.992	1B-139
7 yrs.		930	.327	.599	3291	1077	211	8	222	6.7	675	729	770	513	17	9	3	6112	392	58	587	7.1	.991	1B-744, DH-181

LEAGUE CHAMPIONSHIP SERIES

Year	Team	Games	BA	SA	AB	H	2B	3B	HR	HR%	R	RBI	BB	SO	SB	AB	H	PO	A	E	DP	TC/G	FA	G by Pos
1993	CHI A	6	.353	.529	17	6	0	0	1	5.9	2	3	10	5	0	0	0	24	3	0	3	4.5	1.000	1B-4, DH-2

Jim Thome

THOME, JAMES HOWARD
B. Aug. 27, 1970, Peoria, Ill.

BL TR 6'3" 190 lbs.

Year	Team	Games	BA	SA	AB	H	2B	3B	HR	HR%	R	RBI	BB	SO	SB	AB	H	PO	A	E	DP	TC/G	FA	G by Pos
1991	CLE A	27	.255	.367	98	25	4	2	1	1.0	7	9	5	16	1	0	0	12	60	8	6	3.0	.900	3B-27
1992		40	.205	.299	117	24	3	1	2	1.7	8	12	10	34	2	1	0	21	61	11	3	2.3	.882	3B-40

Year	Team	Games	BA	SA	AB	H	2B	3B	HR	HR%	R	RBI	BB	SO	SB	Pinch Hit AB	Pinch Hit H	PO	A	E	DP	TC/G	FA	G by Pos

Jim Thome *continued*

Year	Team	Games	BA	SA	AB	H	2B	3B	HR	HR%	R	RBI	BB	SO	SB	AB	H	PO	A	E	DP	TC/G	FA	G by Pos
1993		47	.266	.474	154	41	11	0	7	4.5	28	22	29	36	2	2	0	29	86	6	10	2.6	.950	3B-47
1994		98	.268	.523	321	86	20	1	20	6.2	58	52	46	84	3	7	2	62	173	15	12	2.7	.940	3B-94
1995		137	.314	.558	452	142	29	3	25	5.5	92	73	97	113	4	5	0	75	214	16	19	2.3	.948	3B-134, DH-1
1996		151	.311	.612	505	157	28	5	38	7.5	122	116	123	141	2	4	2	86	261	17	24	2.4	.953	3B-150, DH-1
6 yrs.		500	.288	.530	1647	475	95	12	93	5.6	315	284	310	424	14	19	4	285	855	73	74	2.5	.940	3B-492, DH-2

DIVISIONAL PLAYOFF SERIES

Year	Team	Games	BA	SA	AB	H	2B	3B	HR	HR%	R	RBI	BB	SO	SB	AB	H	PO	A	E	DP	TC/G	FA	G by Pos
1995	CLE A	3	.154	.385	13	2	0	0	1	7.7	1	3	1	6	0	0	0	6	6	0	1	4.0	1.000	3B-3
1996		4	.300	.300	10	3	0	0	0	0.0	1	0	1	5	0	0	0	1	1	0	0	0.5	1.000	3B-4
2 yrs.		7	.217	.348	23	5	0	0	1	4.3	2	3	2	11	0	0	0	7	7	0	1	2.0	1.000	3B-7

LEAGUE CHAMPIONSHIP SERIES

Year	Team	Games	BA	SA	AB	H	2B	3B	HR	HR%	R	RBI	BB	SO	SB	AB	H	PO	A	E	DP	TC/G	FA	G by Pos
1995	CLE A	5	.267	.667	15	4	0	0	2	13.3	2	5	2	3	0	0	0	1	5	1	0	1.4	.857	3B-5

WORLD SERIES

Year	Team	Games	BA	SA	AB	H	2B	3B	HR	HR%	R	RBI	BB	SO	SB	AB	H	PO	A	E	DP	TC/G	FA	G by Pos
1995	CLE A	6	.211	.421	19	4	1	0	1	5.3	1	2	2	5	0	1	1	3	5	1	0	1.5	.889	3B-6

Jason Thompson

THOMPSON, JASON MICHAEL
B. Jun. 13, 1971, Orlando, Fla.

BL TL 6'4" 200 lbs.

Year	Team	Games	BA	SA	AB	H	2B	3B	HR	HR%	R	RBI	BB	SO	SB	AB	H	PO	A	E	DP	TC/G	FA	G by Pos
1996	SD N	13	.224	.429	49	11	4	0	2	4.1	4	6	1	14	0	0	0	94	13	4	6	8.5	.964	OF-52, DH-3

Milt Thompson

THOMPSON, MILTON BERNARD
B. Jan. 5, 1959, Washington, D. C.

BL TR 5'11" 170 lbs.

Year	Team	Games	BA	SA	AB	H	2B	3B	HR	HR%	R	RBI	BB	SO	SB	AB	H	PO	A	E	DP	TC/G	FA	G by Pos
1984	ATL N	25	.303	.374	99	30	1	0	2	2.0	16	4	11	11	14	2	2	37	6	2	1	1.8	.956	OF-25
1985		73	.302	.363	182	55	7	4	0	0.0	17	6	7	36	9	30	13	78	2	3	0	1.7	.964	OF-49
1986	PHI N	96	.251	.341	299	75	7	1	6	2.0	38	23	26	62	19	10	1	212	1	2	1	2.4	.991	OF-89
1987		150	.302	.425	527	159	26	9	7	1.3	86	43	42	87	46	15	5	354	4	4	1	2.5	.989	OF-146
1988		122	.288	.357	378	109	16	2	2	0.5	53	33	39	59	17	16	4	278	5	5	1	2.6	.983	OF-112
1989	STL N	155	.290	.393	545	158	28	8	4	0.7	60	68	39	91	27	10	1	348	5	8	1	2.5	.978	OF-147
1990		135	.218	.328	418	91	14	7	6	1.4	42	30	39	60	25	21	4	232	4	7	0	2.1	.971	OF-116
1991		115	.307	.442	326	100	16	5	6	1.8	55	34	32	53	16	28	10	207	8	2	1	2.4	.991	OF-91
1992		109	.293	.404	208	61	9	4	4	1.9	31	17	16	39	18	58	16	74	1	1	1	1.7	.974	OF-45
1993	PHI N	129	.262	.350	340	89	14	2	4	1.2	42	44	40	57	9	25	8	162	6	1	1	1.6	.994	OF-106
1994	2 teams PHI N (87G –.273) HOU N (9G –.286)																							
"	total	96	.274	.353	241	66	7	0	4	1.7	34	33	24	30	9	13	2	126	2	0	1	1.5	1.000	OF-85
1995	HOU N	92	.220	.333	132	29	9	0	2	1.5	14	19	14	37	4	54	13	45	2	1	1	1.4	.979	OF-34
1996	2 teams LA N (48G –.118) CLR N (14G –.067)																							
"	total	62	.106	.136	66	7	2	0	0	0.0	3	3	7	13	1	37	4	15	0	0	0	0.8	1.000	OF-18
13 yrs.		1359	.274	.372	3761	1029	156	37	47	1.2	491	357	336	635	214	319	81	2168	46	37	10	2.1	.984	OF-1063

LEAGUE CHAMPIONSHIP SERIES

Year	Team	Games	BA	SA	AB	H	2B	3B	HR	HR%	R	RBI	BB	SO	SB	AB	H	PO	A	E	DP	TC/G	FA	G by Pos
1993	PHI N	6	.231	.308	13	3	1	0	0	0.0	2	0	1	2	0	1	0	8	0	1	0	1.8	.889	OF-5

WORLD SERIES

Year	Team	Games	BA	SA	AB	H	2B	3B	HR	HR%	R	RBI	BB	SO	SB	AB	H	PO	A	E	DP	TC/G	FA	G by Pos
1993	PHI N	6	.313	.688	16	5	1	1	1	6.3	3	6	1	2	0	0	0	10	0	1	0	1.8	.909	OF-6

Robby Thompson

THOMPSON, ROBERT RANDALL
B. May 10, 1962, West Palm Beach, Fla.

BR TR 5'11" 165 lbs.

Year	Team	Games	BA	SA	AB	H	2B	3B	HR	HR%	R	RBI	BB	SO	SB	AB	H	PO	A	E	DP	TC/G	FA	G by Pos
1986	SF N	149	.271	.370	549	149	27	3	7	1.3	73	47	42	112	12	1	0	255	451	17	97	4.8	.976	2B-149, SS-1
1987		132	.262	.419	420	110	26	5	10	2.4	62	44	40	91	16	4	2	246	341	17	99	4.8	.972	2B-126
1988		138	.264	.384	477	126	24	6	7	1.5	66	48	40	111	14	5	1	255	365	14	88	4.7	.978	2B-134
1989		148	.241	.400	547	132	26	11	13	2.4	91	50	51	133	12	0	0	307	425	8	88	5.0	.989	2B-148
1990		144	.245	.392	498	122	22	3	15	3.0	67	56	34	96	14	3	1	287	441	8	94	5.2	.989	2B-142
1991		144	.262	.447	492	129	24	5	19	3.9	74	48	63	95	14	0	0	320	402	11	98	5.1	.985	2B-144
1992		128	.260	.415	443	115	25	1	14	3.2	54	49	43	75	5	8	1	296	382	15	101	5.8	.978	2B-120
1993		128	.312	.496	494	154	30	2	19	3.8	85	65	45	97	10	2	1	273	384	8	95	5.2	.988	2B-128
1994		35	.209	.349	129	27	8	2	2	1.6	13	7	15	32	3	0	0	67	121	2	24	5.4	.989	2B-35
1995		95	.223	.339	336	75	15	0	8	2.4	51	23	42	76	1	4	1	181	238	3	49	4.6	.993	2B-91
1996		63	.211	.335	227	48	11	1	5	2.2	35	21	24	69	2	2	0	124	155	7	39	4.6	.976	2B-62
11 yrs.		1304	.257	.403	4612	1187	238	39	119	2.6	671	458	439	987	103	29	7	2611	3705	110	872	5.0	.983	2B-1279, SS-1

LEAGUE CHAMPIONSHIP SERIES

Year	Team	Games	BA	SA	AB	H	2B	3B	HR	HR%	R	RBI	BB	SO	SB	AB	H	PO	A	E	DP	TC/G	FA	G by Pos
1987	SF N	7	.100	.350	20	2	0	1	1	5.0	4	2	5	7	2	1	0	11	19	1	6	5.2	.968	2B-6
1989		5	.278	.611	18	5	0	0	2	11.1	5	3	3	2	0	0	0	10	13	0	4	4.6	1.000	2B-5
2 yrs.		12	.184	.474	38	7	0	1	3	7.9	9	5	8	9	2	1	0	21	32	1	10	4.9	.981	2B-11

WORLD SERIES

Year	Team	Games	BA	SA	AB	H	2B	3B	HR	HR%	R	RBI	BB	SO	SB	AB	H	PO	A	E	DP	TC/G	FA	G by Pos
1989	SF N	4	.091	.091	11	1	0	0	0	0.0	0	2	0	4	0	1	1	4	10	0	2	3.5	1.000	2B-4

Ryan Thompson

THOMPSON, RYAN ORLANDO
B. Nov. 4, 1967, Chestertown, Md.

BR TR 6'3" 200 lbs.

Year	Team	Games	BA	SA	AB	H	2B	3B	HR	HR%	R	RBI	BB	SO	SB	AB	H	PO	A	E	DP	TC/G	FA	G by Pos
1992	NY N	30	.222	.389	108	24	7	1	3	2.8	15	10	8	24	2	1	0	77	2	1	0	2.8	.988	OF-29
1993		80	.250	.444	288	72	19	2	11	3.8	34	26	19	81	2	1	1	228	4	3	0	3.1	.987	OF-76
1994		98	.225	.434	334	75	14	1	18	5.4	39	59	28	94	1	0	0	274	5	3	1	2.9	.989	OF-98
1995		75	.251	.378	267	67	13	0	7	2.6	39	31	19	77	3	1	1	193	4	3	3	2.7	.985	OF-74
1996	CLE A	8	.318	.455	22	7	0	0	1	4.5	2	5	1	6	0	2	1	5	0	0	0	0.6	1.000	OF-8
5 yrs.		291	.240	.418	1019	245	53	4	40	3.9	129	131	75	282	8	5	4	777	15	10	4	2.8	.988	OF-285

Year	Team	Games	BA	SA	AB	H	2B	3B	HR	HR%	R	RBI	BB	SO	SB	Pinch Hit AB	Pinch Hit H	PO	A	E	DP	TC/G	FA	G by Pos

Ozzie Timmons
TIMMONS, OSBORNE LLEWELLYN
B. Sept. 18, 1970, Tampa, Fla.
BR TR 6'2" 205 lbs.

Year	Team	Games	BA	SA	AB	H	2B	3B	HR	HR%	R	RBI	BB	SO	SB	PH AB	PH H	PO	A	E	DP	TC/G	FA	G by Pos
1995	CHI N	77	.263	.474	171	45	10	1	8	4.7	30	28	13	32	3	26	5	63	1	2	1	1.2	.970	OF-55
1996		65	.200	.379	140	28	4	0	7	5.0	18	16	15	30	1	25	4	65	1	0	0	1.4	1.000	OF-47
2 yrs.		142	.235	.431	311	73	14	1	15	4.8	48	44	28	62	4	51	9	128	2	2	1	1.3	.985	OF-102

Lee Tinsley
TINSLEY, LEE OWEN
B. Mar. 4, 1969, Shelbyville, Ky.
BB TR 5'11" 190 lbs.

Year	Team	Games	BA	SA	AB	H	2B	3B	HR	HR%	R	RBI	BB	SO	SB	PH AB	PH H	PO	A	E	DP	TC/G	FA	G by Pos
1993	SEA A	11	.158	.368	19	3	1	0	1	5.3	2	2	2	9	0	5	1	9	0	1	0	1.3	.900	OF-6, DH-2
1994	BOS A	78	.222	.292	144	32	4	0	2	1.4	27	14	19	36	13	4	0	114	1	1	1	1.7	.991	OF-60, DH-9
1995		100	.284	.402	341	97	17	1	7	2.1	61	41	39	74	18	4	2	227	4	5	1	2.4	.979	OF-97
1996	2 teams	PHI N (31G –.135)		BOS A (92G –.245)																				
""	total	123	.221	.291	244	54	6	1	3	1.2	29	16	17	78	8	12	1	156	8	2	1	1.6	.988	OF-105
4 yrs.		312	.249	.344	748	186	28	2	13	1.7	119	73	77	197	39	25	4	506	13	9	3	1.9	.983	OF-268, DH-11
DIVISIONAL PLAYOFF SERIES																								
1995	BOS A	1	.000	.000	5	0	0	0	0	0.0	0	0	1	2	0	0	0	1	0	0	0	1.0	1.000	OF-1

Andy Tomberlin
TOMBERLIN, ANDY LEE
B. Nov. 7, 1966, Monroe, N. C.
BL TL 5'11" 160 lbs.

Year	Team	Games	BA	SA	AB	H	2B	3B	HR	HR%	R	RBI	BB	SO	SB	PH AB	PH H	PO	A	E	DP	TC/G	FA	G by Pos
1993	PIT N	27	.286	.405	42	12	0	1	1	2.4	9	2	14	0	18	4	9	1	0	0	1.4	1.000	OF-7
1994	BOS A	17	.194	.333	36	7	0	1	1	2.8	1	1	6	12	1	4	1	12	2	0	1	0.8	1.000	OF-11, DH-5, P-1
1995	OAK A	46	.212	.353	85	18	0	0	4	4.7	15	10	5	22	4	6	2	45	1	1	0	1.1	.979	OF-42, DH-1
1996	NY N	63	.258	.455	66	17	4	0	3	4.5	12	10	9	27	0	42	9	8	1	0	0	0.5	1.000	OF-17, 1B-1
4 yrs.		153	.236	.389	229	54	4	2	9	3.9	32	26	22	75	5	70	16	74	5	1	1	0.9	.988	OF-77, DH-6, 1B-1, P-1

Alan Trammell
TRAMMELL, ALAN STUART
B. Feb. 21, 1958, Garden Grove, Calif.
BR TR 6' 165 lbs.

Year	Team	Games	BA	SA	AB	H	2B	3B	HR	HR%	R	RBI	BB	SO	SB	PH AB	PH H	PO	A	E	DP	TC/G	FA	G by Pos
1977	DET A	19	.186	.186	43	8	0	0	0	0.0	6	0	4	12	0	0	0	15	34	2	5	2.7	.961	SS-19
1978		139	.268	.339	448	120	14	6	2	0.4	49	34	45	56	3	0	0	239	421	14	95	4.8	.979	SS-139
1979		142	.276	.357	460	127	11	4	6	1.3	68	50	43	55	17	0	0	245	388	26	99	4.6	.961	SS-142
1980		146	.300	.404	560	168	21	5	9	1.6	107	65	69	63	12	2	0	225	412	13	89	4.5	.983	SS-144
1981		105	.258	.327	392	101	15	3	2	0.5	52	31	49	31	10	1	1	181	347	9	65	5.1	.983	SS-105
1982		157	.258	.395	489	126	34	3	9	1.8	66	57	52	47	19	0	0	259	459	16	97	4.7	.978	SS-157
1983		142	.319	.471	505	161	31	2	14	2.8	83	66	57	64	30	0	0	236	367	13	71	4.4	.979	SS-140
1984		139	.314	.468	555	174	34	5	14	2.5	85	69	60	63	19	3	1	180	314	10	71	3.7	.980	SS-114, DH-22
1985		149	.258	.380	605	156	21	7	13	2.1	79	57	50	71	14	0	0	225	400	15	89	4.3	.977	SS-149
1986		151	.277	.469	574	159	33	7	21	3.7	107	75	59	57	25	1	0	238	445	22	99	4.7	.969	SS-149, DH-2
1987		151	.343	.551	597	205	34	3	28	4.7	109	105	60	47	21	3	0	222	421	19	94	4.4	.971	SS-149
1988		128	.311	.464	466	145	24	1	15	3.2	73	69	46	46	7	2	2	195	355	11	67	4.5	.980	SS-125
1989		121	.243	.334	449	109	20	3	5	1.1	54	43	45	45	10	2	1	188	396	9	71	5.0	.985	SS-117, DH-2
1990		146	.304	.449	559	170	37	1	14	2.5	71	89	68	55	12	2	0	232	409	14	102	4.5	.979	SS-142, DH-3
1991		101	.248	.373	375	93	20	0	9	2.4	57	55	37	39	11	4	1	131	296	9	60	4.4	.979	SS-92, DH-6
1992		29	.275	.392	102	28	7	1	1	1.0	11	11	15	4	2	0	0	46	80	3	16	4.8	.977	SS-27
1993		112	.329	.496	401	132	25	3	12	3.0	72	60	38	38	12	11	2	113	238	9	31	3.2	.975	SS-63, 3B-35, OF-8, DH-6
1994		76	.267	.414	292	78	17	1	8	2.7	38	28	16	35	3	6	1	117	180	10	43	4.1	.967	SS-63, DH-11
1995		74	.269	.350	223	60	12	0	2	0.9	28	23	27	19	3	11	4	86	158	5	34	3.8	.980	SS-60, DH-6
1996		66	.233	.259	193	45	2	0	1	0.5	16	16	10	27	6	7	1	75	144	6	22	3.6	.973	SS-43, 2B-11, 3B-8, OF-1
20 yrs.		2293	.285	.415	8288	2365	412	55	185	2.2	1231	1003	850	874	236	55	14	3448	6264	235	1320	4.4	.976	SS-2139, DH-58, 3B-43, 2B-11, OF-9
LEAGUE CHAMPIONSHIP SERIES																								
1984	DET A	3	.364	.818	11	4	0	1	1	9.1	2	3	3	1	0	0	0	1	8	0	0	3.0	1.000	SS-3
1987		5	.200	.250	20	4	1	0	0	0.0	3	2	1	2	0	0	0	6	9	1	1	3.2	.938	SS-5
2 yrs.		8	.258	.452	31	8	1	1	1	3.2	5	5	4	3	0	0	0	7	17	1	1	3.1	.960	SS-8
WORLD SERIES																								
1984	DET A	5	.450	.800	20	9	1	0	2	10.0	5	6	2	2	1	0	0	8	9	1	0	3.6	.944	SS-5

Michael Tucker
TUCKER, MICHAEL ANTHONY
B. June 25, 1971, South Boston, Va.
BL TR 6'2" 185 lbs.

Year	Team	Games	BA	SA	AB	H	2B	3B	HR	HR%	R	RBI	BB	SO	SB	PH AB	PH H	PO	A	E	DP	TC/G	FA	G by Pos
1995	KC A	62	.260	.384	177	46	10	0	4	2.3	23	17	18	51	2	6	0	67	3	1	0	1.2	.986	OF-36, DH-22
1996		108	.260	.442	339	88	18	4	12	3.5	55	53	40	69	10	10	4	235	8	2	7	2.2	.992	OF-98, 1B-9, DH-4
2 yrs.		170	.260	.422	516	134	28	4	16	3.1	78	70	58	120	12	16	4	302	11	3	7	1.9	.991	OF-134, DH-26, 1B-9

Chris Turner
TURNER, CHRISTOPHER WAN
B. Mar. 23, 1969, Bowling Green, Ky.
BR TR 6'2" 190 lbs.

Year	Team	Games	BA	SA	AB	H	2B	3B	HR	HR%	R	RBI	BB	SO	SB	PH AB	PH H	PO	A	E	DP	TC/G	FA	G by Pos
1993	CAL A	25	.280	.387	75	21	5	0	1	1.3	9	13	9	16	1	0	0	116	14	1	0	5.2	.992	C-25
1994		58	.242	.322	149	36	7	1	1	0.7	23	12	10	29	3	2	0	268	29	1	0	5.2	.997	C-57
1995		5	.100	.100	10	1	0	0	0	0.0	0	1	0	3	0	1	0	17	2	0	0	4.8	1.000	C-4
1996		4	.333	.333	3	1	0	0	0	0.0	1	1	1	0	0	0	0	3	2	0	0	1.3	1.000	C-3, OF-1
4 yrs.		92	.249	.333	237	59	12	1	2	0.8	33	27	20	48	4	3	0	404	47	2	0	5.0	.996	C-89, OF-1

Tim Unroe
UNROE, TIMOTHY BRIAN
B. Oct. 7, 1970, Round Lake Beach, Ill.
BR TR 6'3" 200 lbs.

Year	Team	Games	BA	SA	AB	H	2B	3B	HR	HR%	R	RBI	BB	SO	SB	PH AB	PH H	PO	A	E	DP	TC/G	FA	G by Pos
1995	MIL A	2	.250	.250	4	1	0	0	0	0.0	0	0	0	0	0	0	0	11	0	0	3	5.5	1.000	1B-2
1996		14	.188	.188	16	3	0	0	0	0.0	5	0	4	5	0	0	0	41	10	1	4	3.3	.981	1B-11, 3B-3, OF-1, DH-1
2 yrs.		16	.200	.200	20	4	0	0	0	0.0	5	0	4	5	0	0	0	52	10	1	7	3.5	.984	1B-13, 3B-3, OF-1, DH-1

Year	Team	Games	BA	SA	AB	H	2B	3B	HR	HR%	R	RBI	BB	SO	SB	Pinch Hit AB	Pinch Hit H	PO	A	E	DP	TC/G	FA	G by Pos

Pedro Valdes

VALDES, PEDRO JOSE
Born Pedro Jose Valdes (Manzo).
B. Jun. 29, 1973, Fajardo, Puerto Rico

BL TL 6'1" 180 lbs.

Year	Team	Games	BA	SA	AB	H	2B	3B	HR	HR%	R	RBI	BB	SO	SB	PH AB	PH H	PO	A	E	DP	TC/G	FA	G by Pos
1996	CHI N	9	.125	.250	8	1	1	0	0	0.0	2	1	1	5	0	6	1	1	0	0	0	0.5	1.000	OF-2

Omar Vizquel

VIZQUEL, OMAR ENRIQUE
Born Omar Enrique Vizquel (Gonzalez).
B. May 15, 1967, Caracas, Venezuela

BB TR 5'9" 155 lbs.

Year	Team	Games	BA	SA	AB	H	2B	3B	HR	HR%	R	RBI	BB	SO	SB	PH AB	PH H	PO	A	E	DP	TC/G	FA	G by Pos
1989	SEA A	143	.220	.261	387	85	7	3	1	0.3	45	20	28	40	1	2	0	208	388	18	102	4.3	.971	SS-143
1990		81	.247	.298	255	63	3	2	2	0.8	19	18	18	22	4	0	0	103	239	7	48	4.3	.980	SS-81
1991		142	.230	.293	426	98	16	4	1	0.2	42	41	45	37	7	8	0	224	422	13	105	4.7	.980	SS-138, 2B-1
1992		136	.294	.352	483	142	20	4	0	0.0	49	21	32	38	15	5	0	223	403	7	92	4.7	.989	SS-136
1993		158	.255	.298	560	143	14	2	2	0.4	68	31	50	71	12	1	1	245	475	15	108	4.7	.980	SS-155, DH-2
1994	CLE A	69	.273	.325	286	78	10	1	1	0.3	39	33	23	23	13	1	1	114	204	6	53	4.7	.981	SS-69
1995		136	.266	.351	542	144	28	0	6	1.1	87	56	59	59	29	1	0	211	407	9	85	4.6	.986	SS-136
1996		151	.297	.417	542	161	36	1	9	1.7	98	64	56	42	35	2	1	227	446	20	92	4.6	.971	SS-150
8 yrs.		1016	.263	.330	3481	914	134	17	22	0.6	447	284	311	332	116	20	3	1555	2984	95	685	4.6	.979	SS-1008, DH-2, 2B-1

DIVISIONAL PLAYOFF SERIES

Year	Team	Games	BA	SA	AB	H	2B	3B	HR	HR%	R	RBI	BB	SO	SB	PH AB	PH H	PO	A	E	DP	TC/G	FA	G by Pos
1995	CLE A	3	.167	.250	12	2	1	0	0	0.0	2	4	2	2	1	0	0	4	11	0	0	5.0	1.000	SS-3
1996		4	.429	.500	14	6	1	0	0	0.0	4	2	3	4	0	0	0	6	10	0	2	4.0	1.000	SS-4
2 yrs.		7	.308	.385	26	8	2	0	0	0.0	6	6	5	6	1	0	0	10	21	0	2	4.4	1.000	SS-7

LEAGUE CHAMPIONSHIP SERIES

Year	Team	Games	BA	SA	AB	H	2B	3B	HR	HR%	R	RBI	BB	SO	SB	PH AB	PH H	PO	A	E	DP	TC/G	FA	G by Pos
1995	CLE A	6	.087	.130	23	2	1	0	0	0.0	2	2	5	2	3	0	0	9	21	0	3	5.0	1.000	SS-6

WORLD SERIES

Year	Team	Games	BA	SA	AB	H	2B	3B	HR	HR%	R	RBI	BB	SO	SB	PH AB	PH H	PO	A	E	DP	TC/G	FA	G by Pos
1995	CLE A	6	.174	.261	23	4	0	1	0	0.0	3	1	3	5	1	0	0	12	22	0	7	5.7	1.000	SS-6

Jack Voigt

VOIGT, JOHN DAVID
B. May 17, 1966, Sarasota, Fla.

BR TR 6'1" 170 lbs.

Year	Team	Games	BA	SA	AB	H	2B	3B	HR	HR%	R	RBI	BB	SO	SB	PH AB	PH H	PO	A	E	DP	TC/G	FA	G by Pos
1992	BAL A	1	—	—	0	0	0	0	0		0	0	0	0	0	0	0	0	0	0	0	0.0	—	
1993		64	.296	.500	152	45	11	1	6	3.9	32	23	25	33	1	10	2	101	6	1	3	1.8	.991	OF-43, DH-8, 1B-5, 3B-3
1994		59	.241	.340	141	34	5	0	3	2.1	15	20	18	25	0	3	1	114	5	2	2	2.0	.983	OF-54, 1B-6, DH-2
1995	2 teams	BAL A (3G –1.000)			TEX A (33G –.161)																			OF-25, 1B-6, DH-2
"	total	36	.175	.317	63	11	3	0	2	3.2	9	8	10	14	0	3	1	56	3	1	3	1.8	.983	OF-25, 1B-6, DH-2
1996	TEX A	5	.111	.111	9	1	0	0	0	0.0	1	0	0	2	0	2	0	5	1	0	0	1.5	1.000	OF-3, 3B-1
5 yrs.		165	.249	.397	365	91	19	1	11	3.0	57	51	53	74	1	18	4	276	15	4	8	1.9	.986	OF-125, 1B-17, DH-12, 3B-4

Matt Walbeck

WALBECK, MATTHEW LOVICK
B. Oct. 2, 1969, Sacramento, Calif.

BB TR 5'11" 195 lbs.

Year	Team	Games	BA	SA	AB	H	2B	3B	HR	HR%	R	RBI	BB	SO	SB	PH AB	PH H	PO	A	E	DP	TC/G	FA	G by Pos
1993	CHI N	11	.200	.367	30	6	2	0	1	3.3	2	6	1	6	0	3	1	49	2	0	0	4.6	1.000	C-11
1994	MIN A	97	.204	.284	338	69	12	0	5	1.5	31	35	17	37	1	3	0	496	45	4	0	5.7	.993	C-95, DH-1
1995		115	.257	.316	393	101	18	1	1	0.3	40	44	25	71	3	3	0	604	35	6	3	5.7	.991	C-113
1996		63	.223	.298	215	48	10	0	2	0.9	25	24	9	34	3	5	1	326	18	2	2	5.7	.994	C-61
4 yrs.		286	.230	.302	976	224	42	1	9	0.9	98	109	52	148	7	14	2	1475	100	12	5	5.6	.992	C-280, DH-1

Larry Walker

WALKER, LARRY KENNETH ROBERT
B. Dec. 1, 1966, Maple Ridge, B. C., Canada.

BL TR 6'2" 185 lbs.

Year	Team	Games	BA	SA	AB	H	2B	3B	HR	HR%	R	RBI	BB	SO	SB	PH AB	PH H	PO	A	E	DP	TC/G	FA	G by Pos
1989	MON N	20	.170	.170	47	8	0	0	0	0.0	4	4	5	13	1	7	0	19	2	0	1	1.4	1.000	OF-15
1990		133	.241	.434	419	101	18	3	19	4.5	59	51	49	112	21	11	1	249	12	4	5	2.1	.985	OF-124
1991		137	.290	.458	487	141	30	2	16	3.3	59	64	42	102	14	2	1	536	36	6	30	4.1	.990	OF-102, 1B-39
1992		143	.301	.506	528	159	31	4	23	4.4	85	93	41	97	18	3	1	269	16	2	2	2.1	.993	OF-139
1993		138	.265	.469	490	130	24	5	22	4.5	85	86	80	76	29	2	0	316	16	4	6	2.5	.988	OF-132, 1B-4
1994		103	.322	.587	395	127	44	2	19	4.8	76	86	47	74	15	1	0	423	29	9	21	4.5	.980	OF-68, 1B-35
1995	CLR N	131	.306	.607	494	151	31	5	36	7.3	96	101	49	72	16	1	1	225	13	3	0	1.9	.988	OF-129
1996		83	.276	.570	272	75	18	4	18	6.6	58	58	20	58	18	0	0	152	4	1	0	1.9	.994	OF-83
8 yrs.		888	.285	.510	3132	892	196	25	153	4.9	522	543	333	604	132	27	4	2189	128	31	63	2.7	.987	OF-792, 1B-78

DIVISIONAL PLAYOFF SERIES

Year	Team	Games	BA	SA	AB	H	2B	3B	HR	HR%	R	RBI	BB	SO	SB	PH AB	PH H	PO	A	E	DP	TC/G	FA	G by Pos
1995	CLR N	4	.214	.429	14	3	0	0	1	7.1	3	3	3	4	1	0	0	3	0	0	0	0.8	1.000	OF-4

Todd Walker

WALKER, TODD ARTHUR
B. May 25, 1973, Bakersfield, Calif.

BL TR 6' 180 lbs.

Year	Team	Games	BA	SA	AB	H	2B	3B	HR	HR%	R	RBI	BB	SO	SB	PH AB	PH H	PO	A	E	DP	TC/G	FA	G by Pos
1996	MIN A	25	.256	.329	82	21	6	0	0	0.0	8	6	4	13	2	2	0	16	39	2	4	2.3	.964	3B-20, 2B-4, DH-1

Tim Wallach

WALLACH, TIMOTHY CHARLES
B. Sept. 14, 1957, Huntington Park, Calif.

BR TR 6'3" 220 lbs.

Year	Team	Games	BA	SA	AB	H	2B	3B	HR	HR%	R	RBI	BB	SO	SB	PH AB	PH H	PO	A	E	DP	TC/G	FA	G by Pos
1980	MON N	5	.182	.455	11	2	0	0	1	9.1	1	2	1	5	0	2	0	12	0	0	0	3.0	1.000	OF-3, 1B-1
1981		71	.236	.344	212	50	9	1	4	1.9	19	13	15	37	0	6	1	207	31	1	9	3.6	.996	OF-35, 1B-16, 3B-15
1982		158	.268	.471	596	160	31	3	28	4.7	89	97	36	81	6	3	1	132	287	23	23	2.8	.948	3B-156, OF-2, 1B-1
1983		156	.269	.434	581	156	33	3	19	3.3	54	70	55	97	0	0	0	151	265	19	25	2.8	.956	3B-156
1984		160	.246	.395	582	143	25	4	18	3.1	55	72	50	101	3	0	0	162	332	21	29	3.2	.959	3B-160, SS-1
1985		155	.260	.450	569	148	36	3	22	3.9	70	81	38	79	9	2	0	148	383	18	34	3.6	.967	3B-154
1986		134	.233	.396	480	112	22	1	18	3.8	50	71	44	72	8	1	0	94	270	16	26	2.9	.958	3B-132
1987		153	.298	.514	593	177	42	4	26	4.4	89	123	37	98	9	0	0	128	292	21	21	2.9	.952	3B-150, P-1
1988		159	.257	.389	592	152	32	5	12	2.0	52	69	38	88	2	1	1	124	329	18	32	3.1	.962	3B-153, 2B-1
1989		154	.277	.419	573	159	42	0	13	2.3	76	77	58	81	3	1	1	113	302	18	20	2.8	.958	3B-153, P-1

Year	Team	Games	BA	SA	AB	H	2B	3B	HR	HR%	R	RBI	BB	SO	SB	Pinch Hit AB	H	PO	A	E	DP	TC/G	FA	G by Pos

Tim Wallach continued

Year	Team	Games	BA	SA	AB	H	2B	3B	HR	HR%	R	RBI	BB	SO	SB	AB	H	PO	A	E	DP	TC/G	FA	G by Pos
1990		161	.296	.471	626	185	37	5	21	3.4	69	98	42	80	6	0	0	128	309	21	23	2.8	.954	3B-161
1991		151	.225	.334	577	130	22	1	13	2.3	60	73	50	100	2	0	0	107	310	14	27	2.9	.968	3B-149
1992		150	.223	.331	537	120	29	1	9	1.7	53	59	50	90	2	3	0	689	244	15	59	6.1	.984	3B-85, 1B-71
1993	LA N	133	.222	.342	477	106	19	1	12	2.5	42	62	32	70	0	5	0	121	229	15	15	2.8	.959	3B-130, 1B-1
1994		113	.280	.502	414	116	21	1	23	5.6	68	78	46	80	0	1	0	81	174	11	9	2.4	.959	3B-113
1995		97	.266	.428	327	87	22	2	9	2.8	24	38	27	69	0	1	0	61	156	5	9	2.3	.977	3B-96, 1B-1
1996	2 teams CAL A	(57G –.237)		LA N	(45G –.228)																			
"	total	102	.233	.369	352	82	10	1	12	3.4	37	42	30	79	1	6	1	85	149	11	9	2.4	.955	3B-91, DH-8, 1B-3
17 yrs.		2212	.257	.416	8099	2085	432	36	260	3.2	908	1125	649	1307	51	42	6	2543	4062	247	370	3.1	.964	3B-2054, 1B-94, OF-40, DH-8, P-2, 2B-1, SS-1

DIVISIONAL PLAYOFF SERIES

Year	Team	Games	BA	SA	AB	H	2B	3B	HR	HR%	R	RBI	BB	SO	SB	AB	H	PO	A	E	DP	TC/G	FA	G by Pos
1981	MON N	4	.250	.500	4	1	1	0	0	0.0	1	0	4	0	0	0	0	4	0	0	0	1.3	1.000	OF-3
1995	LA N	3	.083	.083	12	1	0	0	0	0.0	0	0	1	3	0	0	0	1	2	0	0	1.0	1.000	3B-3
1996		3	.000	.000	11	0	0	0	0	0.0	0	0	0	1	0	0	0	2	8	1	1	3.7	.909	3B-3
3 yrs.		10	.074	.111	27	2	1	0	0	0.0	1	0	5	4	0	0	0	7	10	1	1	2.0	.944	3B-6, OF-3

LEAGUE CHAMPIONSHIP SERIES

Year	Team	Games	BA	SA	AB	H	2B	3B	HR	HR%	R	RBI	BB	SO	SB	AB	H	PO	A	E	DP	TC/G	FA	G by Pos
1981	MON N	1	.000	.000	1	0	0	0	0	0.0	0	0	0	0	0	1	0	0	0	0	0	0.0	—	

Jerome Walton

WALTON, JEROME O'TERRELL
B. July 8, 1965, Newnan, Ga.

BR TR 6'1" 175 lbs.

Year	Team	Games	BA	SA	AB	H	2B	3B	HR	HR%	R	RBI	BB	SO	SB	AB	H	PO	A	E	DP	TC/G	FA	G by Pos
1989	CHI N	116	.293	.385	475	139	23	3	5	1.1	64	46	27	77	24	0	0	289	2	3	1	2.6	.990	OF-115
1990		101	.263	.329	392	103	16	2	2	0.5	63	21	50	70	14	0	0	247	3	6	0	2.6	.977	OF-98
1991		123	.219	.330	270	59	13	1	5	1.9	42	17	19	55	7	25	5	170	2	3	1	1.7	.983	OF-101
1992		30	.127	.164	55	7	0	1	0	0.0	7	1	9	13	1	5	0	34	0	2	0	1.5	.944	OF-24
1993	CAL A	5	.000	.000	2	0	0	0	0	0.0	2	0	1	2	1	0	0	2	0	0	0	0.5	1.000	DH-3, OF-1
1994	CIN N	46	.309	.412	68	21	4	0	1	1.5	9	10	4	12	1	15	2	58	1	1	2	1.8	.983	OF-26, 1B-7
1995		102	.290	.525	162	47	12	1	8	4.9	32	22	17	25	10	17	3	110	2	2	0	1.2	.982	OF-89, 1B-3
1996	ATL N	37	.340	.511	47	16	5	0	1	2.1	9	4	5	10	0	9	4	34	0	0	0	1.2	1.000	OF-28
8 yrs.		560	.266	.372	1471	392	73	8	22	1.5	229	120	132	264	58	71	14	944	10	17	4	2.0	.982	OF-482, 1B-10, DH-3

DIVISIONAL PLAYOFF SERIES

Year	Team	Games	BA	SA	AB	H	2B	3B	HR	HR%	R	RBI	BB	SO	SB	AB	H	PO	A	E	DP	TC/G	FA	G by Pos
1995	CIN N	3	.000	.000	3	0	0	0	0	0.0	0	0	0	0	0	0	0	3	0	0	0	1.0	1.000	OF-3

LEAGUE CHAMPIONSHIP SERIES

Year	Team	Games	BA	SA	AB	H	2B	3B	HR	HR%	R	RBI	BB	SO	SB	AB	H	PO	A	E	DP	TC/G	FA	G by Pos
1989	CHI N	5	.364	.364	22	8	0	0	0	0.0	4	2	2	2	0	0	0	11	0	0	0	2.2	1.000	OF-5
1995	CIN N	2	.000	.000	7	0	0	0	0	0.0	0	0	0	2	0	0	0	6	0	0	0	3.0	1.000	OF-2
2 yrs.		7	.276	.276	29	8	0	0	0	0.0	4	2	2	4	0	0	0	17	0	0	0	2.4	1.000	OF-7

Turner Ward

WARD, TURNER MAX
B. Apr. 11, 1965, Orlando, Fla.

BB TR 6'2" 200 lbs.

Year	Team	Games	BA	SA	AB	H	2B	3B	HR	HR%	R	RBI	BB	SO	SB	AB	H	PO	A	E	DP	TC/G	FA	G by Pos
1990	CLE A	14	.348	.500	46	16	2	1	1	2.2	10	10	3	8	3	0	0	20	2	1	0	1.6	.957	OF-13, DH-1
1991	2 teams CLE A	(40G –.230)		TOR A	(8G –.308)																			
"	total	48	.239	.301	113	27	7	0	0	0.0	12	7	11	18	0	3	1	70	1	0	0	1.6	1.000	OF-44
1992	TOR A	18	.345	.552	29	10	3	0	1	3.4	7	3	4	4	0	4	0	18	1	0	0	1.6	1.000	OF-12
1993		72	.192	.311	167	32	4	2	4	2.4	20	28	23	26	3	7	2	97	2	1	0	1.5	.990	OF-65, 1B-1
1994	MIL A	102	.232	.357	367	85	15	2	9	2.5	55	45	52	68	6	1	0	260	9	4	1	2.7	.985	OF-99, 3B-1
1995		44	.264	.395	129	34	3	1	4	3.1	19	16	14	21	6	4	1	81	5	1	1	2.1	.989	OF-40, DH-1
1996		43	.179	.328	67	12	2	1	2	3.0	7	10	13	17	3	10	2	54	1	0	0	1.7	1.000	OF-32, DH-1
7 yrs.		341	.235	.358	918	216	36	7	21	2.3	130	119	120	162	21	29	6	600	21	7	2	2.0	.989	OF-305, DH-3, 3B-1, 1B-1

Lenny Webster

WEBSTER, LEONARD IRELL
B. Feb. 10, 1965, New Orleans, La.

BR TR 5'9" 185 lbs.

Year	Team	Games	BA	SA	AB	H	2B	3B	HR	HR%	R	RBI	BB	SO	SB	AB	H	PO	A	E	DP	TC/G	FA	G by Pos
1989	MIN A	14	.300	.400	20	6	2	0	0	0.0	3	1	3	2	0	1	1	32	0	0	0	2.3	1.000	C-14
1990		2	.333	.500	6	2	1	0	0	0.0	1	0	1	1	0	0	0	9	0	0	1	4.5	1.000	C-2
1991		18	.294	.588	34	10	1	0	3	8.8	7	8	6	10	0	2	0	61	10	1	1	4.2	.986	C-17
1992		53	.280	.407	118	33	10	1	1	0.8	10	13	9	11	0	6	5	190	11	1	3	4.0	.995	C-49, DH-1
1993		49	.198	.245	106	21	2	0	1	0.9	14	8	11	8	1	3	0	177	13	0	1	4.1	1.000	C-45, DH-1
1994	MON N	57	.273	.448	143	39	10	0	5	3.5	13	23	16	24	0	13	1	237	19	1	0	5.6	.996	C-46
1995	PHI N	49	.267	.407	150	40	9	0	4	2.7	18	14	16	27	0	6	0	275	17	3	1	6.9	.990	C-43
1996	MON N	78	.230	.322	174	40	10	0	2	1.1	18	17	25	21	0	15	0	390	25	1	3	6.6	.998	C-63
8 yrs.		320	.254	.381	751	191	45	1	16	2.1	84	84	87	104	1	46	7	1371	95	7	9	5.2	.995	C-279, DH-2

John Wehner

WEHNER, JOHN PAUL
B. June 29, 1967, Pittsburgh, Pa.

BR TR 6'3" 205 lbs.

Year	Team	Games	BA	SA	AB	H	2B	3B	HR	HR%	R	RBI	BB	SO	SB	AB	H	PO	A	E	DP	TC/G	FA	G by Pos
1991	PIT N	37	.340	.406	106	36	7	0	0	0.0	15	7	7	17	3	3	2	23	65	6	9	2.6	.936	3B-36
1992		55	.179	.228	123	22	6	0	0	0.0	11	4	12	22	3	12	5	96	64	4	17	3.2	.976	3B-34, 1B-13, 2B-5
1993		29	.143	.143	35	5	0	0	0	0.0	3	0	6	10	0	9	0	17	8	0	3	1.3	1.000	OF-13, 3B-3, 2B-3
1994		2	.250	.500	4	1	1	0	0	0.0	1	3	0	1	0	1	1	0	2	0	0	2.0	1.000	3B-1
1995		52	.308	.364	107	33	0	3	0	0.0	13	5	10	17	3	14	2	35	29	0	2	1.5	1.000	OF-23, 3B-19, SS-1, C-1
1996		86	.259	.381	139	36	9	1	2	1.4	19	13	8	22	1	26	9	60	43	2	6	1.6	.981	OF-29, 3B-24, 2B-12, C-1
6 yrs.		261	.259	.331	514	133	23	4	2	0.4	62	32	43	89	10	65	19	231	211	12	37	2.1	.974	3B-117, OF-65, 2B-20, 1B-13, C-2, SS-1

LEAGUE CHAMPIONSHIP SERIES

Year	Team	Games	BA	SA	AB	H	2B	3B	HR	HR%	R	RBI	BB	SO	SB	AB	H	PO	A	E	DP	TC/G	FA	G by Pos
1992	PIT N	2	.000	.000	2	0	0	0	0	0.0	0	0	0	2	0	2	0	0	0	0	0	0.0	—	

Walt Weiss

WEISS, WALTER WILLIAM
B. Nov. 28, 1963, Tuxedo, N.Y.

BB TR 6' 175 lbs.

Year	Team	Games	BA	SA	AB	H	2B	3B	HR	HR%	R	RBI	BB	SO	SB	AB	H	PO	A	E	DP	TC/G	FA	G by Pos
1987	OAK A	16	.462	.615	26	12	4	0	0	0.0	3	1	2	2	1	0	0	8	30	1	4	3.5	.974	SS-11
1988		147	.250	.321	452	113	17	3	3	0.7	44	39	35	56	4	1	0	254	431	15	83	4.8	.979	SS-147

Year	Team	Games	BA	SA	AB	H	2B	3B	HR	HR%	R	RBI	BB	SO	SB	Pinch Hit AB	Pinch Hit H	PO	A	E	DP	TC/G	FA	G by Pos

Walt Weiss *continued*

Year	Team	Games	BA	SA	AB	H	2B	3B	HR	HR%	R	RBI	BB	SO	SB	PH AB	PH H	PO	A	E	DP	TC/G	FA	G by Pos
1989		84	.233	.318	236	55	11	0	3	1.3	30	21	21	39	6	0	0	106	195	15	44	3.8	.953	SS-84
1990		138	.265	.321	445	118	17	1	2	0.4	50	35	46	53	9	3	1	194	373	12	77	4.2	.979	SS-137
1991		40	.226	.286	133	30	6	1	0	0.0	15	13	12	14	6	1	1	64	99	5	21	4.2	.970	SS-40
1992		103	.212	.241	316	67	5	2	0	0.0	36	21	43	39	6	1	0	144	270	19	57	4.2	.956	SS-103
1993	FLA N	158	.266	.308	500	133	14	2	1	0.2	50	39	79	73	7	6	0	229	406	15	80	4.2	.977	SS-153
1994	CLR N	110	.251	.303	423	106	11	4	1	0.2	58	32	56	58	12	2	0	157	318	13	68	4.4	.973	SS-110
1995		137	.260	.321	427	111	17	3	1	0.2	65	25	98	57	15	1	0	202	407	16	98	4.6	.974	SS-136
1996		155	.282	.375	517	146	20	2	8	1.5	89	48	80	78	10	2	1	220	449	30	89	4.5	.957	SS-155
10 yrs.		1088	.256	.318	3475	891	122	18	19	0.5	440	274	472	469	76	18	3	1578	2978	141	621	4.4	.970	SS-1076
DIVISIONAL PLAYOFF SERIES																								
1995	CLR N	4	.167	.167	12	2	0	0	0	0.0	1	0	3	3	1	0	0	6	12	0	4	4.5	1.000	SS-4
LEAGUE CHAMPIONSHIP SERIES																								
1988	OAK A	4	.333	.467	15	5	2	0	0	0.0	2	2	0	0	0	0	0	7	10	0	3	4.3	1.000	SS-4
1989		4	.111	.222	9	1	1	0	0	0.0	2	0	1	1	1	0	0	5	9	0	2	3.5	1.000	SS-4
1990		2	.000	.000	7	0	0	0	0	0.0	2	0	2	2	0	0	0	2	7	1	1	5.0	.900	SS-2
1992		3	.167	.167	6	1	0	0	0	0.0	1	0	2	1	2	0	0	5	6	0	1	3.7	1.000	SS-3
4 yrs.		13	.189	.270	37	7	3	0	0	0.0	7	2	5	8	3	0	0	19	32	1	7	4.0	.981	SS-13
WORLD SERIES																								
1988	OAK A	5	.063	.063	16	1	0	0	0	0.0	1	0	0	2	1	0	0	5	11	1	1	3.4	.941	SS-5
1989		4	.133	.333	15	2	0	0	1	6.7	3	1	2	2	0	0	0	7	8	0	1	3.8	1.000	SS-4
2 yrs.		9	.097	.194	31	3	0	0	1	3.2	4	1	2	4	1	0	0	12	19	1	2	3.6	.969	SS-9

Devon White

WHITE, DEVON MARKES
B. Dec. 29, 1962, Kingston, Jamaica   BB TR 6'1" 170 lbs.

Year	Team	Games	BA	SA	AB	H	2B	3B	HR	HR%	R	RBI	BB	SO	SB	PH AB	PH H	PO	A	E	DP	TC/G	FA	G by Pos
1985	CAL A	21	.143	.143	7	1	0	0	0	0.0	7	0	1	3	3	0	0	10	1	0	0	0.7	1.000	OF-16
1986		28	.235	.353	51	12	1	1	1	2.0	8	3	6	8	6	0	0	49	0	2	0	1.8	.961	OF-28
1987		159	.263	.443	639	168	33	5	24	3.8	103	87	39	135	32	0	0	424	16	9	3	2.8	.980	OF-159
1988		122	.259	.389	455	118	22	2	11	2.4	76	51	23	84	17	5	2	364	7	9	2	3.3	.976	OF-116
1989		156	.245	.371	636	156	18	13	12	1.9	86	56	31	129	44	1	0	430	10	5	3	2.9	.989	OF-154, DH-1
1990		125	.217	.343	443	96	17	3	11	2.5	57	44	44	116	21	3	0	302	11	9	4	2.6	.972	OF-122
1991	TOR A	156	.282	.455	642	181	40	10	17	2.6	110	60	55	135	33	0	0	439	8	1	2	2.9	.998	OF-156
1992		153	.248	.390	641	159	26	7	17	2.7	98	60	47	133	37	0	0	443	8	7	2	3.0	.985	OF-152, DH-1
1993		146	.273	.438	598	163	42	6	15	2.5	116	52	57	127	34	0	0	399	6	3	2	2.8	.993	OF-145
1994		100	.270	.457	403	109	24	6	13	3.2	67	49	21	80	11	1	1	267	3	6	1	2.8	.978	OF-98
1995		101	.283	.431	427	121	23	5	10	2.3	61	53	29	97	11	1	0	260	7	3	0	2.7	.989	OF-100
1996	FLA N	146	.274	.455	552	151	37	6	17	3.1	77	84	38	99	22	8	3	296	5	4	1	2.2	.987	OF-139
12 yrs.		1413	.261	.417	5494	1435	283	64	148	2.7	866	599	391	1146	271	19	6	3683	82	58	20	2.8	.985	OF-1385, DH-2
LEAGUE CHAMPIONSHIP SERIES																								
1986	CAL A	3	.500	.500	2	1	0	0	0	0.0	2	0	0	1	0	0	0	2	0	0	0	0.7	1.000	OF-3
1991	TOR A	5	.364	.409	22	8	1	0	0	0.0	5	0	2	3	3	0	0	16	0	0	0	3.2	1.000	OF-5
1992		6	.348	.435	23	8	2	0	0	0.0	2	2	5	6	0	0	0	16	0	1	0	2.8	.941	OF-6
1993		6	.444	.667	27	12	1	1	1	3.7	3	2	1	5	0	0	0	15	0	0	0	2.5	1.000	OF-6
4 yrs.		20	.392 2nd	.514	74	29 8th	4	1	1	1.4	12	4	8	15	3	0	0	49	0	1	0	2.5	.980	OF-20
WORLD SERIES																								
1992	TOR A	6	.231	.269	26	6	1	0	0	0.0	2	2	0	6	1	0	0	22	1	0	1	3.8	1.000	OF-6
1993		6	.292	.708	24	7	3	2	1	4.2	8	7	4	7	1	0	0	16	0	0	0	2.7	1.000	OF-6
2 yrs.		12	.260	.480	50	13	4	2	1	2.0	10	9	4	13	2	0	0	38	1	0	1	3.3	1.000	OF-12

Rondell White

WHITE, RONDELL BERNARD
B. Feb. 23, 1972, Milledgeville, Ga.   BR TR 6'1" 193 lbs.

Year	Team	Games	BA	SA	AB	H	2B	3B	HR	HR%	R	RBI	BB	SO	SB	PH AB	PH H	PO	A	E	DP	TC/G	FA	G by Pos
1993	MON N	23	.260	.411	73	19	3	1	2	2.7	9	15	7	16	1	1	0	33	0	0	0	1.6	1.000	OF-21
1994		40	.278	.464	97	27	10	1	2	2.1	16	13	9	18	1	10	0	34	1	2	0	1.3	.946	OF-29
1995		130	.295	.464	474	140	33	4	13	2.7	87	57	41	87	25	9	2	268	5	4	2	2.3	.986	OF-119
1996		88	.293	.428	334	98	19	4	6	1.8	35	41	22	53	14	3	0	185	5	2	0	2.2	.990	OF-86
4 yrs.		281	.290	.448	978	284	65	10	23	2.4	147	126	79	174	41	23	2	520	11	8	2	2.1	.985	OF-255

Mark Whiten

WHITEN, MARK ANTHONY
B. Nov. 25, 1966, Pensacola, Fla.   BB TR 6'3" 210 lbs.

Year	Team	Games	BA	SA	AB	H	2B	3B	HR	HR%	R	RBI	BB	SO	SB	PH AB	PH H	PO	A	E	DP	TC/G	FA	G by Pos
1990	TOR A	33	.273	.375	88	24	1	1	2	2.3	12	7	7	14	2	3	0	60	3	0	0	2.0	1.000	OF-30, DH-2
1991	2 teams	TOR A (46G –.221)		CLE A (70G –.256)																				
"	total	116	.243	.388	407	99	18	7	9	2.2	46	45	30	85	4	5	0	256	13	7	2	2.5	.975	OF-109, DH-3
1992	CLE A	148	.254	.360	508	129	19	4	9	1.8	73	43	72	102	16	1	1	321	14	7	1	2.3	.980	OF-144, DH-2
1993	STL N	152	.253	.423	562	142	13	4	25	4.4	81	99	58	110	15	6	2	329	9	10	1	2.4	.971	OF-148
1994		92	.293	.485	334	98	18	2	14	4.2	57	53	37	75	10	2	1	234	9	9	0	2.8	.964	OF-90
1995	2 teams	BOS A (32G –.185)		PHI N (60G –.269)																				
"	total	92	.241	.400	320	77	13	1	12	3.8	51	47	39	86	8	7	2	157	8	4	1	1.9	.976	OF-86, DH-1
1996	3 teams	PHI N (60G –.236)		ATL N (36G –.256)		SEA A (40G –.300)																		
"	total	136	.262	.476	412	108	20	1	22	5.3	76	71	70	127	17	18	5	228	11	12	1	2.1	.952	OF-119
7 yrs.		769	.257	.417	2631	677	102	20	93	3.5	396	365	313	599	72	42	11	1585	67	49	6	2.3	.971	OF-726, DH-8

Chris Widger

WIDGER, CHRISTOPHER JON
B. May 21, 1971, Wilmington, Del.   BR TR 6'3" 195 lbs.

Year	Team	Games	BA	SA	AB	H	2B	3B	HR	HR%	R	RBI	BB	SO	SB	PH AB	PH H	PO	A	E	DP	TC/G	FA	G by Pos
1995	SEA A	23	.200	.267	45	9	0	0	1	2.2	2	2	3	11	0	3	0	64	1	0	0	2.8	1.000	C-19, OF-3, DH-1
1996		8	.182	.182	11	2	0	0	0	0.0	1	0	0	5	0	1	0	18	1	2	0	3.0	.905	C-7
2 yrs.		31	.196	.250	56	11	0	0	1	1.8	3	2	3	16	0	4	0	82	2	2	0	2.9	.977	C-26, OF-3, DH-1

Year	Team	Games	BA	SA	AB	H	2B	3B	HR	HR%	R	RBI	BB	SO	SB	Pinch Hit AB	Pinch Hit H	PO	A	E	DP	TC/G	FA	G by Pos

Chris Widger *continued*

DIVISIONAL PLAYOFF SERIES

Year	Team	Games	BA	SA	AB	H	2B	3B	HR	HR%	R	RBI	BB	SO	SB	AB	H	PO	A	E	DP	TC/G	FA	G by Pos
1995	SEA A	2	.000	.000	3	0	0	0	0	0.0	0	0	0	3	0	0	0	14	0	0	0	7.0	1.000	C-2

LEAGUE CHAMPIONSHIP SERIES

Year	Team	Games	BA	SA	AB	H	2B	3B	HR	HR%	R	RBI	BB	SO	SB	AB	H	PO	A	E	DP	TC/G	FA	G by Pos
1995	SEA A	3	.000	.000	1	0	0	0	0	0.0	0	0	0	1	0	0	0	7	0	0	0	2.3	1.000	C-3

Rick Wilkins

WILKINS, RICHARD DAVID
B. June 4, 1967, Jacksonville, Fla.

BL TR 6'2" 210 lbs.

Year	Team	Games	BA	SA	AB	H	2B	3B	HR	HR%	R	RBI	BB	SO	SB	AB	H	PO	A	E	DP	TC/G	FA	G by Pos
1991	CHI N	86	.222	.355	203	45	9	0	6	3.0	21	22	19	56	3	5	2	373	42	3	6	5.1	.993	C-82
1992		83	.270	.414	244	66	9	1	8	3.3	20	22	28	53	0	15	5	408	47	3	5	6.3	.993	C-73
1993		136	.303	.561	446	135	23	1	30	6.7	78	73	50	99	2	9	4	717	89	3	6	6.1	.996	C-133
1994		100	.227	.387	313	71	25	2	7	2.2	44	39	40	86	4	9	0	550	51	4	1	6.2	.993	C-95, 1B-2
1995	2 teams CHI N (50G –.191) HOU N (15G –.250)																							
"	total	65	.203	.322	202	41	3	0	7	3.5	30	19	46	61	0	3	0	381	34	4	2	6.5	.990	C-62, 1B-2
1996	2 teams HOU N (84G –.213) SF N (52G –.293)																							
"	total	136	.243	.399	411	100	18	2	14	3.4	53	59	67	121	0	13	3	790	73	8	10	6.6	.991	C-124, 1B-7
6 yrs.		606	.252	.425	1819	458	87	6	72	4.0	246	234	250	476	9	54	14	3219	336	25	33	6.2	.993	C-569, 1B-11

Bernie Williams

WILLIAMS, BERNABE
Born Bernabe Williams (Figueroa).
B. Sept. 13, 1968, San Juan, Puerto Rico

BB TR 6'2" 180 lbs.

Year	Team	Games	BA	SA	AB	H	2B	3B	HR	HR%	R	RBI	BB	SO	SB	AB	H	PO	A	E	DP	TC/G	FA	G by Pos
1991	NY A	85	.237	.350	320	76	19	4	3	0.9	43	34	48	57	10	0	0	230	3	5	0	2.8	.979	OF-85
1992		62	.280	.406	261	73	14	2	5	1.9	39	26	29	36	7	0	0	187	5	1	2	3.1	.995	OF-62
1993		139	.268	.400	567	152	31	4	12	2.1	67	68	53	106	9	0	0	366	5	4	0	2.7	.989	OF-139
1994		108	.289	.453	408	118	29	1	12	2.9	80	57	61	54	16	3	1	277	7	3	1	2.7	.990	OF-107
1995		144	.307	.487	563	173	29	9	18	3.2	93	82	75	98	8	0	0	431	1	8	0	3.1	.982	OF-144
1996		143	.305	.535	551	168	26	7	29	5.3	108	102	82	72	17	1	0	334	10	5	3	2.5	.986	OF-140, DH-2
6 yrs.		681	.285	.449	2670	760	148	27	79	3.0	430	369	348	423	67	4	1	1825	31	26	6	2.8	.986	OF-677, DH-2

DIVISIONAL PLAYOFF SERIES

Year	Team	Games	BA	SA	AB	H	2B	3B	HR	HR%	R	RBI	BB	SO	SB	AB	H	PO	A	E	DP	TC/G	FA	G by Pos
1995	NY A	5	.429	.810	21	9	2	0	2	9.5	8	5	7	1	1	0	0	13	0	0	0	2.6	1.000	OF-5
1996		4	.467	1.067	15	7	0	0	3	20.0	5	5	2	1	1	0	0	10	0	0	0	2.5	1.000	OF-4
2 yrs.		9	.444	.917	36	16	2	0	5	13.9	13	10	9	4	2	0	0	23	0	0	0	2.6	1.000	OF-9

LEAGUE CHAMPIONSHIP SERIES

Year	Team	Games	BA	SA	AB	H	2B	3B	HR	HR%	R	RBI	BB	SO	SB	AB	H	PO	A	E	DP	TC/G	FA	G by Pos
1996	NY A	5	.474	.947	19	9	3	0	2	10.5	6	6	5	4	1	0	0	20	0	0	0	4.0	1.000	OF-5

WORLD SERIES

Year	Team	Games	BA	SA	AB	H	2B	3B	HR	HR%	R	RBI	BB	SO	SB	AB	H	PO	A	E	DP	TC/G	FA	G by Pos
1996	NY A	6	.167	.292	24	4	0	0	1	4.2	3	4	3	6	1	0	0	15	0	0	0	2.5	1.000	OF-6

Eddie Williams

WILLIAMS, EDWARD LAQUAN
B. Nov. 1, 1964, Shreveport, La.

BR TR 6' 175 lbs.

Year	Team	Games	BA	SA	AB	H	2B	3B	HR	HR%	R	RBI	BB	SO	SB	AB	H	PO	A	E	DP	TC/G	FA	G by Pos
1986	CLE A	5	.143	.143	7	1	0	0	0	0.0	2	1	0	3	0	2	0	0	0	0	0	0.0	.000	OF-4
1987		22	.172	.281	64	11	4	0	1	1.6	9	4	9	19	0	0	0	17	37	1	6	2.5	.982	3B-22
1988		10	.190	.190	21	4	0	0	0	0.0	3	1	0	3	0	0	0	3	18	0	0	2.1	1.000	3B-10
1989	CHI A	66	.274	.358	201	55	8	0	3	1.5	25	10	18	31	1	1	0	37	123	16	21	2.7	.909	3B-65
1990	SD N	14	.286	.571	42	12	3	0	3	7.1	5	4	5	6	0	2	0	5	21	3	2	2.2	.897	3B-13
1994		49	.331	.594	175	58	11	1	11	6.3	32	42	15	26	0	2	0	382	29	5	28	8.9	.988	1B-46, 3B-1
1995		97	.260	.426	296	77	11	1	12	4.1	35	47	23	47	0	16	2	571	48	7	53	7.7	.989	1B-81
1996	DET A	77	.200	.307	215	43	5	0	6	2.8	22	26	18	50	0	15	1	25	2	0	7	0.4	1.000	DH-52, 1B-7, 3B-3, OF-2
8 yrs.		340	.256	.406	1021	261	42	2	36	3.5	133	135	88	185	1	38	3	1040	278	32	117	4.4	.976	1B-134, 3B-114, DH-52, OF-6

George Williams

WILLIAMS, GEORGE ERIK
B. Apr. 22, 1969, La Crosse, Wis.

BB TR 5'10" 190 lbs.

Year	Team	Games	BA	SA	AB	H	2B	3B	HR	HR%	R	RBI	BB	SO	SB	AB	H	PO	A	E	DP	TC/G	FA	G by Pos
1995	OAK A	29	.291	.494	79	23	5	1	3	3.8	13	14	11	21	0	7	3	58	7	3	0	3.0	.956	C-13, DH-10
1996		56	.152	.258	132	20	5	0	3	2.3	17	10	28	32	0	5	0	154	12	3	1	3.1	.982	C-43, DH-11
2 yrs.		85	.204	.346	211	43	10	1	6	2.8	30	24	39	53	0	12	3	212	19	6	1	3.1	.975	C-56, DH-21

Gerald Williams

WILLIAMS, GERALD FLOYD
B. Aug. 10, 1966, New Orleans, La.

BR TR 6'2" 190 lbs.

Year	Team	Games	BA	SA	AB	H	2B	3B	HR	HR%	R	RBI	BB	SO	SB	AB	H	PO	A	E	DP	TC/G	FA	G by Pos
1992	NY A	15	.296	.704	27	8	2	0	3	11.1	7	6	0	3	2	0	0	20	1	2	0	1.9	.913	OF-12
1993		42	.149	.269	67	10	2	3	0	0.0	11	6	1	14	2	4	1	41	2	2	0	1.2	.956	OF-37
1994		57	.291	.523	86	25	8	0	4	4.7	19	13	4	17	1	6	1	43	2	2	0	1.0	.957	OF-43, DH-2
1995		100	.247	.467	182	45	18	2	6	3.3	33	28	22	34	4	13	2	138	6	1	0	1.6	.993	OF-92, DH-1
1996	2 teams NY A (99G –.270) MIL A (26G –.207)																							
"	total	125	.252	.382	325	82	19	4	5	1.5	43	34	19	57	10	7	1	205	4	4	2	1.8	.981	OF-119, DH-2
5 yrs.		339	.247	.424	687	170	49	9	18	2.6	113	87	46	125	19	30	5	447	15	11	2	1.5	.977	OF-303, DH-5

DIVISIONAL PLAYOFF SERIES

Year	Team	Games	BA	SA	AB	H	2B	3B	HR	HR%	R	RBI	BB	SO	SB	AB	H	PO	A	E	DP	TC/G	FA	G by Pos
1995	NY A	5	.000	.000	5	0	0	0	0	0.0	1	0	2	3	0	0	0	7	1	0	0	1.6	1.000	OF-5

Keith Williams

WILLIAMS, DAVID KEITH
B. Apr. 21, 1972, Bedford, Pa.

BR TR 6' 190 lbs.

Year	Team	Games	BA	SA	AB	H	2B	3B	HR	HR%	R	RBI	BB	SO	SB	AB	H	PO	A	E	DP	TC/G	FA	G by Pos
1996	SF N	9	.250	.250	20	5	0	0	0	0.0	0	0	0	6	0	5	2	8	0	0	0	2.0	1.000	OF-4

Year	Team	Games	BA	SA	AB	H	2B	3B	HR	HR%	R	RBI	BB	SO	SB	Pinch Hit AB	Pinch Hit H	PO	A	E	DP	TC/G	FA	G by Pos

Matt Williams — WILLIAMS, MATTHEW DERRICK · B. Nov. 28, 1965, Bishop, Calif. · BR TR 6'2" 205 lbs.

Year	Team	Games	BA	SA	AB	H	2B	3B	HR	HR%	R	RBI	BB	SO	SB	PH AB	PH H	PO	A	E	DP	TC/G	FA	G by Pos
1987	SF N	84	.188	.339	245	46	9	2	8	3.3	28	21	16	68	4	3	2	110	234	9	52	4.1	.975	SS-70, 3B-17
1988		52	.205	.410	156	32	6	1	8	5.1	17	19	8	41	0	2	0	48	108	7	9	2.9	.957	3B-43, SS-14
1989		84	.202	.455	292	59	18	1	18	6.2	31	50	14	72	1	3	0	90	168	10	15	2.6	.963	3B-73, SS-30
1990		159	.277	.488	617	171	27	2	33	5.3	87	122	33	138	7	1	1	140	306	19	33	2.9	.959	3B-159
1991		157	.268	.499	589	158	24	5	34	5.8	72	98	33	128	5	3	0	134	295	16	32	2.8	.964	3B-155, SS-4
1992		146	.227	.384	529	120	13	5	20	3.8	58	66	39	109	7	5	1	105	289	23	33	2.9	.945	3B-144
1993		145	.294	.561	579	170	33	4	38	6.6	105	110	27	80	1	1	0	117	266	12	34	2.7	.970	3B-144
1994		112	.267	.607	445	119	16	3	43	9.7	74	96	33	87	1	2	0	79	234	12	21	3.0	.963	3B-110
1995		76	.336	.647	283	95	17	1	23	8.1	53	65	30	58	2	2	0	49	178	10	10	3.2	.958	3B-74
1996		105	.302	.510	404	122	16	1	22	5.4	69	85	39	91	1	2	0	164	188	14	28	3.5	.962	3B-92, 1B-13, SS-1
10 yrs.		1120	.264	.498	4139	1092	179	25	247	6.0	594	732	272	872	29	24	4	1036	2266	132	267	3.0	.962	3B-1011, SS-119, 1B-13

LEAGUE CHAMPIONSHIP SERIES
| 1989 | SF N | 5 | .300 | .650 | 20 | 6 | 1 | 0 | 2 | 10.0 | 2 | 9 | 0 | 2 | 0 | 0 | 0 | 5 | 12 | 0 | 2 | 2.8 | 1.000 | 3B-5, SS-1 |

WORLD SERIES
| 1989 | SF N | 4 | .125 | .313 | 16 | 2 | 0 | 0 | 1 | 6.3 | 1 | 1 | 0 | 6 | 0 | 0 | 0 | 4 | 12 | 0 | 2 | 2.3 | 1.000 | SS-4, 3B-3 |

Dan Wilson — WILSON, DANIEL ALLEN · B. Mar. 25, 1969, Arlington Heights, Ill. · BR TR 6'3" 190 lbs.

Year	Team	Games	BA	SA	AB	H	2B	3B	HR	HR%	R	RBI	BB	SO	SB	PH AB	PH H	PO	A	E	DP	TC/G	FA	G by Pos
1992	CIN N	12	.360	.400	25	9	1	0	0	0.0	2	3	3	8	0	4	0	42	4	0	0	5.1	1.000	C-9
1993		36	.224	.263	76	17	3	0	0	0.0	6	8	9	16	0	3	1	146	9	1	2	4.5	.994	C-35
1994	SEA A	91	.216	.312	282	61	14	2	3	1.1	24	27	10	57	1	0	0	602	41	9	2	7.2	.986	C-91
1995		119	.278	.416	399	111	22	3	9	2.3	40	51	33	63	2	1	1	897	51	5	2	8.0	.995	C-119
1996		138	.285	.444	491	140	24	0	18	3.7	51	83	32	88	1	3	1	835	57	4	5	6.6	.996	C-135
5 yrs.		396	.266	.394	1273	338	64	5	30	2.4	123	172	87	232	4	11	5	2522	162	19	11	6.9	.993	C-389

DIVISIONAL PLAYOFF SERIES
| 1995 | SEA A | 5 | .118 | .118 | 17 | 2 | 0 | 0 | 0 | 0.0 | 0 | 1 | 2 | 6 | 0 | 0 | 0 | 34 | 1 | 0 | 1 | 7.0 | 1.000 | C-5 |

LEAGUE CHAMPIONSHIP SERIES
| 1995 | SEA A | 6 | .000 | .000 | 16 | 0 | 0 | 0 | 0 | 0.0 | 0 | 0 | 0 | 4 | 0 | 0 | 0 | 35 | 3 | 1 | 0 | 6.5 | .974 | C-6 |

Desi Wilson — WILSON, DESI BERNARD · B. May 9, 1969, Glen Cove, N. Y. · BL TL 6'7" 230 lbs.

| 1996 | SF N | 41 | .271 | .339 | 118 | 32 | 2 | 0 | 2 | 1.7 | 10 | 12 | 12 | 27 | 0 | 9 | 1 | 6 | 6 | 3 | 2 | 7.5 | .800 | 2B-2 |

Nigel Wilson — WILSON, NIGEL EDWARD · B. Jan. 12, 1970, Oshawa, Ont., Canada. · BL TL 6'1" 185 lbs.

Year	Team	Games	BA	SA	AB	H	2B	3B	HR	HR%	R	RBI	BB	SO	SB	PH AB	PH H	PO	A	E	DP	TC/G	FA	G by Pos
1993	FLA N	7	.000	.000	16	0	0	0	0	0.0	0	0	0	11	0	4	0	4	0	0	0	1.3	1.000	OF-3
1995	CIN N	5	.000	.000	7	0	0	0	0	0.0	0	0	0	4	0	3	0	2	0	0	0	1.0	1.000	OF-2
1996	CLE A	10	.250	.750	12	3	0	0	2	16.7	2	5	1	6	0	8	2	0	0	0	0	0.0		DH-3, OF-1
3 yrs.		22	.086	.257	35	3	0	0	2	5.7	2	5	1	21	0	15	2	6	0	0	0	0.7	1.000	OF-6, DH-3

DIVISIONAL PLAYOFF SERIES
| 1996 | CLE A | 1 | .000 | .000 | 1 | 0 | 0 | 0 | 0 | 0.0 | 0 | 0 | 0 | 0 | 0 | 1 | 0 | 236 | 18 | 4 | 20 | 7.8 | .984 | 1B-33 |

Craig Worthington — WORTHINGTON, CRAIG RICHARD · B. Apr. 17, 1965, Los Angeles, Calif. · BR TR 6' 160 lbs.

Year	Team	Games	BA	SA	AB	H	2B	3B	HR	HR%	R	RBI	BB	SO	SB	PH AB	PH H	PO	A	E	DP	TC/G	FA	G by Pos
1988	BAL A	26	.185	.284	81	15	2	0	2	2.5	5	4	9	24	1	0	0	20	53	3	4	2.9	.961	3B-26
1989		145	.247	.384	497	123	23	0	15	3.0	57	70	61	114	1	0	0	113	277	20	22	2.8	.951	3B-145
1990		133	.226	.322	425	96	17	0	8	1.9	46	44	63	96	1	0	0	90	218	18	28	2.5	.945	3B-131, DH-2
1991		31	.225	.373	102	23	3	0	4	3.9	11	12	12	14	0	1	0	26	51	2	3	2.6	.975	3B-30
1992	CLE A	9	.167	.167	24	4	0	0	0	0.0	0	2	2	4	0	0	0	6	18	4	2	3.1	.857	3B-9
1995	2 teams	CIN N (10G –.278)					TEX A (26G –.221)																	
"	total	36	.233	.395	86	20	5	0	3	3.5	5	8	9	9	4	2	0	39	39	1	6	2.5	.987	3B-28, 1B-4
1996	TEX A	13	.158	.316	19	3	0	0	1	5.3	2	4	6	3	0	1	0	18	13	1	2	2.5	.969	3B-7, 1B-6
7 yrs.		393	.230	.351	1234	284	50	0	33	2.7	126	144	162	264	3	6	2	312	669	49	67	2.7	.952	3B-376, 1B-10, DH-2

Dmitri Young — YOUNG, DMITRI DELL · B. Oct. 11, 1973, Vicksburg, Miss. · BB TR 6'2" 215 lbs.

| 1996 | STL N | 16 | .241 | .241 | 29 | 7 | 0 | 0 | 0 | 0.0 | 3 | 2 | 4 | 5 | 0 | 7 | 4 | 39 | 1 | 1 | 5 | 4.1 | .976 | 1B-10 |

LEAGUE CHAMPIONSHIP SERIES
| 1996 | STL N | 4 | .286 | .571 | 7 | 2 | 0 | 1 | 0 | 0.0 | 1 | 2 | 0 | 2 | 0 | 3 | 2 | 11 | 1 | 0 | 0 | 6.0 | 1.000 | 1B-2 |

Eric Young — YOUNG, ERIC ORLANDO · B. Nov. 26, 1966, Jacksonville, Fla. · BR TR 5'9" 180 lbs.

Year	Team	Games	BA	SA	AB	H	2B	3B	HR	HR%	R	RBI	BB	SO	SB	PH AB	PH H	PO	A	E	DP	TC/G	FA	G by Pos
1992	LA N	49	.258	.288	132	34	1	0	1	0.8	9	11	8	9	6	0	0	85	114	9	19	4.8	.957	2B-43
1993	CLR N	144	.269	.353	490	132	16	8	3	0.6	82	42	42	41	42	14	5	254	230	18	44	3.8	.964	2B-79, OF-52
1994		90	.272	.430	228	62	13	1	7	3.1	37	30	38	17	18	21	3	97	4	2	0	1.7	.981	OF-60, 2B-1
1995		120	.317	.473	366	116	21	9	6	1.6	68	36	49	29	35	19	4	179	230	11	54	4.4	.974	2B-77, OF-19
1996		141	.324	.421	568	184	23	4	8	1.4	113	74	47	31	53	1	0	340	429	12	108	5.6	.985	2B-139
5 yrs.		544	.296	.404	1784	528	74	22	25	1.4	309	193	205	127	154	55	12	955	1007	52	225	4.3	.974	2B-339, OF-131

Year	Team	Games	BA	SA	AB	H	2B	3B	HR	HR%	R	RBI	BB	SO	SB	Pinch Hit AB	Pinch Hit H	PO	A	E	DP	TC/G	FA	G by Pos

Eric Young *continued*

DIVISIONAL PLAYOFF SERIES

Year	Team	Games	BA	SA	AB	H	2B	3B	HR	HR%	R	RBI	BB	SO	SB	AB	H	PO	A	E	DP	TC/G	FA	G by Pos
1995	CLR N	4	.438	.688	16	7	1	0	1	6.3	3	2	2	2	1	0	0	8	13	3	3	6.0	.875	2B-4

Ernie Young

YOUNG, ERNEST WESLEY
B. July 8, 1969, Chicago, Ill.

BR TR 6'1" 190 lbs.

Year	Team	Games	BA	SA	AB	H	2B	3B	HR	HR%	R	RBI	BB	SO	SB	AB	H	PO	A	E	DP	TC/G	FA	G by Pos
1994	OAK A	11	.067	.100	30	2	1	0	0	0.0	3	1	8	0	2	0	22	1	1	0	2.2	.958	OF-10, DH-1
1995		26	.200	.380	50	10	3	0	2	4.0	9	5	8	12	0	2	0	35	0	2	0	1.5	.946	OF-24
1996		141	.242	.424	462	112	19	4	19	4.1	72	64	52	118	7	5	2	352	8	1	4	2.6	.997	OF-140
3 yrs.		178	.229	.402	542	124	23	4	21	3.9	83	72	61	138	7	9	2	409	9	4	4	2.4	.991	OF-174, DH-1

Kevin Young

YOUNG, KEVIN STACEY
B. June 16, 1969, Alpena, Mich.

BR TR 6'3" 210 lbs.

Year	Team	Games	BA	SA	AB	H	2B	3B	HR	HR%	R	RBI	BB	SO	SB	AB	H	PO	A	E	DP	TC/G	FA	G by Pos
1992	PIT N	10	.571	.571	7	4	0	0	0	0.0	2	4	2	0	1	1	0	3	1	1	0	0.6	.800	3B-7, 1B-1
1993		141	.236	.343	449	106	24	3	6	1.3	38	47	36	82	2	6	2	1122	112	3	108	8.8	.998	1B-135, 3B-6
1994		59	.205	.320	122	25	7	2	1	0.8	15	11	8	34	0	10	0	178	45	3	21	4.1	.987	1B-37, 3B-17, OF-1
1995		56	.232	.381	181	42	9	0	6	3.3	13	22	8	53	1	3	0	58	110	12	9	3.3	.933	3B-48, 1B-6
1996	KC A	55	.242	.470	132	32	6	0	8	6.1	20	23	11	32	3	10	2	200	18	1	25	4.1	.995	1B-27, OF-17, 3B-7, DH-2
5 yrs.		321	.235	.368	891	209	46	5	21	2.4	88	107	65	201	7	30	4	1561	286	20	163	6.0	.989	1B-206, 3B-85, OF-18, DH-2

Greg Zaun

ZAUN, GREGORY OWEN
B. Apr. 4, 1971, Glendale, Calif.

BB TR 5'10" 170 lbs.

Year	Team	Games	BA	SA	AB	H	2B	3B	HR	HR%	R	RBI	BB	SO	SB	AB	H	PO	A	E	DP	TC/G	FA	G by Pos
1995	BAL A	40	.260	.394	104	27	5	0	3	2.9	18	14	16	14	1	2	1	216	13	3	2	5.9	.987	C-39
1996	2 teams BAL A (50G –.231) FLA N (10G –.290)																							
"	total	60	.245	.367	139	34	9	1	2	1.4	20	15	14	20	1	1	0	275	15	3	3	5.0	.990	C-59
2 yrs.		100	.251	.379	243	61	14	1	5	2.1	38	29	30	34	2	3	1	491	28	6	5	5.4	.989	C-98

Todd Zeile

ZEILE, TODD EDWARD
B. Sept. 9, 1965, Van Nuys, Calif.

BR TR 6'1" 190 lbs.

Year	Team	Games	BA	SA	AB	H	2B	3B	HR	HR%	R	RBI	BB	SO	SB	AB	H	PO	A	E	DP	TC/G	FA	G by Pos
1989	STL N	28	.256	.354	82	21	3	1	1	1.2	7	8	9	14	0	5	0	125	10	4	1	6.0	.971	C-23
1990		144	.244	.398	495	121	25	3	15	3.0	62	57	67	77	2	3	0	648	106	15	12	5.5	.980	C-105, 3B-24, 1B-11, OF-1
1991		155	.280	.412	565	158	36	3	11	1.9	76	81	62	94	17	0	0	124	290	25	18	2.9	.943	3B-154
1992		126	.257	.364	439	113	18	4	7	1.6	51	48	68	70	7	3	0	80	235	13	19	2.6	.960	3B-124
1993		157	.277	.433	571	158	36	1	17	3.0	82	103	70	76	5	3	1	83	310	33	26	2.8	.923	3B-153
1994		113	.267	.470	415	111	25	1	19	4.6	62	75	52	56	1	2	0	66	224	12	24	2.7	.960	3B-112
1995	2 teams STL N (34G –.291) CHI N (79G –.227)																							
"	total	113	.246	.397	426	105	22	0	14	3.3	50	52	34	76	1	2	0	361	163	19	44	4.8	.965	3B-75, 1B-35, OF-2
1996	2 teams PHI N (134G –.268) BAL A (29G –.239)																							
"	total	163	.263	.436	617	162	32	0	25	4.1	78	99	82	104	1	0	0	319	250	17	52	3.6	.971	3B-135, 1B-28
8 yrs.		999	.263	.415	3610	949	197	13	109	3.0	468	523	444	567	34	18	1	1806	1588	138	196	3.6	.961	3B-777, C-128, 1B-74, OF-3

DIVISIONAL PLAYOFF SERIES

Year	Team	Games	BA	SA	AB	H	2B	3B	HR	HR%	R	RBI	BB	SO	SB	AB	H	PO	A	E	DP	TC/G	FA	G by Pos
1996	BAL A	4	.263	.316	19	5	1	0	0	0.0	2	0	2	5	0	0	0	4	9	2	0	3.8	.867	3B-4

LEAGUE CHAMPIONSHIP SERIES

Year	Team	Games	BA	SA	AB	H	2B	3B	HR	HR%	R	RBI	BB	SO	SB	AB	H	PO	A	E	DP	TC/G	FA	G by Pos
1996	BAL A	5	.364	.773	22	8	0	0	3	13.6	3	5	2	1	0	0	0	3	7	1	2	2.2	.909	3B-5

Jon Zuber

ZUBER, JON EDWARD
B. Dec. 10, 1969, Encino, Calif.

BL TL 6'1" 190 lbs.

Year	Team	Games	BA	SA	AB	H	2B	3B	HR	HR%	R	RBI	BB	SO	SB	AB	H	PO	A	E	DP	TC/G	FA	G by Pos
1996	PHI N	30	.253	.330	91	23	4	0	1	1.1	7	10	6	11	1	10	1	146	11	2	10	7.2	.987	1B-22

Pitcher Register

The Pitcher Register is an alphabetical listing of every man who pitched in the major leagues in 1996.

As in the Player Register, boldfaced print indicates a league leader for the season. A superscript "1" means that the figure is the all-time single season record (since 1893, when the mound was fixed at a distance of 60 feet, 6 inches), and figures underneath a player's career, League Championship Series, and World Series career totals provide his rank in the top ten all-time.

Partial innings pitched are indicated by adding ".1" or ".2" to the figure in the IP column; "55.2" means that he had pitched fifty-five and two-third innings. Meaningless averages are indicated with a dash; these include the winning percentage of a pitcher with an 0-0 record, or the batting average of a pitcher with no at-bats. When the infinity symbol "•" is shown for a pitcher's earned run average, it means that he allowed at least one run in that season without retiring a batter.

An asterisk (*) shown in the lifetime batting totals means that that pitcher's complete batting record is included in the Player Register.

Year	Team	W	L	PCT	ERA	G	GS	CG	IP	H	BB	SO	ShO	Relief Pitching W	Relief Pitching L	Relief Pitching SV	Batting AB	Batting H	Batting HR	BA	PO	A	E	DP	TC/G	FA

Jim Abbott
ABBOTT, JAMES ANTHONY B. Sept. 19, 1967, Flint, Mich. BL TL 6'3" 200 lbs.

Year	Team	W	L	PCT	ERA	G	GS	CG	IP	H	BB	SO	ShO	RW	RL	SV	AB	H	HR	BA	PO	A	E	DP	TC/G	FA
1989	CAL A	12	12	.500	3.92	29	29	4	181.1	190	74	115	2	0	0	0	0	0	0	—	6	26	3	1	1.2	.914
1990		10	14	.417	4.51	33	33	4	211.2	246	72	105	1	0	0	0	0	0	0	—	8	36	1	4	1.4	.978
1991		18	11	.621	2.89	34	34	5	243	222	73	158	1	0	0	0	0	0	0	—	19	46	2	3	2.0	.970
1992		7	15	.318	2.77	29	29	7	211	208	68	130	0	0	0	0	0	0	0	—	11	35	0	1	1.6	1.000
1993	NY A	11	14	.440	4.37	32	32	4	214	221	73	95	1	0	0	0	0	0	0	—	4	42	1	3	1.5	.979
1994		9	8	.529	4.55	24	24	0	160.1	167	64	90	0	0	0	0	0	0	0	—	8	23	1	1	1.3	.969
1995	2 teams	CHI A	(17G 6-4)		CAL A	(13G 5-4)																				
"	total	11	8	.579	3.70	30	30	4	197	209	64	86	1	0	0	0	0	0	0	—	8	30	0	0	1.3	1.000
1996	CAL A	2	18	.100	7.48	27	23	1	142	171	78	58	0	0	0	0	0	0	0	—	3	27	0	1	1.1	1.000
	8 yrs.	80	100	.444	4.11	238	234	31	1560.1	1634	566	837	6	0	0	0	0	0	0		67	265	8	14	1.4	.976

Kyle Abbott
ABBOTT, LAWRENCE KYLE B. Feb. 18, 1968, Newburyport, Mass. BL TL 6'4" 200 lbs.

Year	Team	W	L	PCT	ERA	G	GS	CG	IP	H	BB	SO	ShO	RW	RL	SV	AB	H	HR	BA	PO	A	E	DP	TC/G	FA
1991	CAL A	1	2	.333	4.58	5	3	0	19.2	22	13	12	0	0	0	0	0	0	0	—	0	5	0	0	1.0	1.000
1992	PHI N	1	14	.067	5.13	31	19	0	133.1	147	45	88	0	0	0	0	29	2	0	.069	3	15	0	0	0.6	1.000
1995		2	0	1.000	3.81	18	0	0	28.1	28	16	21	0	2	0	0	2	1	0	.500	3	4	1	0	0.4	.875
1996	CAL A	0	1	.000	20.25	3	0	0	4	10	5	3	0	0	1	0	0	0	0	—	0	1	0	0	0.3	1.000
	4 yrs.	4	17	.190	5.20	57	22	0	185.1	207	79	124	0	2	1	0	31	3	0	.097	6	25	1	0	0.6	.969

Mark Acre
ACRE, MARK ROBERT B. Sept. 16, 1968, Concord, Calif. BR TR 6'8" 235 lbs.

Year	Team	W	L	PCT	ERA	G	GS	CG	IP	H	BB	SO	ShO	RW	RL	SV	AB	H	HR	BA	PO	A	E	DP	TC/G	FA
1994	OAK A	5	1	.833	3.41	34	0	0	34.1	24	23	21	0	5	0	0	0	0	0	—	0	3	1	0	0.1	.750
1995		1	2	.333	5.71	43	0	0	52	52	28	47	0	1	2	0	0	0	0	—	3	3	0	0	0.1	1.000
1996		1	3	.250	6.12	22	0	0	25	38	9	18	0	1	3	2	0	0	0	—	1	2	0	0	0.1	1.000
	3 yrs.	7	6	.538	5.09	99	0	0	111.1	114	60	86	0	7	6	2	0	0	0		4	8	1	0	0.1	.923

Terry Adams
ADAMS, TERRY WAYNE B. Mar. 6, 1973, Mobile, Ala. BR TR 6'3" 180 lbs.

Year	Team	W	L	PCT	ERA	G	GS	CG	IP	H	BB	SO	ShO	RW	RL	SV	AB	H	HR	BA	PO	A	E	DP	TC/G	FA
1995	CHI N	1	1	.500	6.50	18	0	0	18	22	10	15	0	1	1	1	0	0	0	.000	2	1	0	0	0.2	1.000
1996		3	6	.333	2.94	69	0	0	101	84	49	78	0	3	6	4	6	0	0	.000	8	11	0	1	0.3	1.000
	2 yrs.	4	7	.364	3.48	87	0	0	119	106	59	93	0	4	7	5	6	0	0	.000	10	12	0	1	0.3	1.000

Willie Adams
ADAMS, WILLIAM EDWARD B. Oct. 8, 1972, Gallup, N. M. BR TR 6'7" 215 lbs.

Year	Team	W	L	PCT	ERA	G	GS	CG	IP	H	BB	SO	ShO	RW	RL	SV	AB	H	HR	BA	PO	A	E	DP	TC/G	FA
1996	OAK A	1	3	.250	6.12	12	12	1	76.1	76	23	68	1	0	0	0	0	0	0	—	5	6	0	0	0.9	1.000

Joel Adamson
ADAMSON, JOEL LEE B. July 2, 1971, Lakewood, Calif. BL TL 6'4" 185 lbs.

Year	Team	W	L	PCT	ERA	G	GS	CG	IP	H	BB	SO	ShO	RW	RL	SV	AB	H	HR	BA	PO	A	E	DP	TC/G	FA
1996	FLA N	0	0	—	7.36	9	0	0	11	18	7	7	0	0	0	0	0	0	0	—	3	2	0	0	0.6	1.000

Rick Aguilera
AGUILERA, RICHARD WARREN (Aggie) B. Dec. 31, 1961, San Gabriel, Calif. BR TR 6'4" 195 lbs.

Year	Team	W	L	PCT	ERA	G	GS	CG	IP	H	BB	SO	ShO	RW	RL	SV	AB	H	HR	BA	PO	A	E	DP	TC/G	FA
1985	NY N	10	7	.588	3.24	21	19	2	122.1	118	37	74	0	1	0	0	36	10	0	.278	8	16	0	1	1.1	1.000
1986		10	7	.588	3.88	28	20	2	141.2	145	36	104	0	1	1	0	51	8	2	.157	13	26	0	1	1.4	1.000
1987		11	3	.786	3.60	18	17	1	115	124	33	77	0	0	0	0	40	9	1	.225	7	29	2	1	2.1	.947
1988		0	4	.000	6.93	11	3	0	24.2	29	10	16	0	0	2	0	4	1	0	.250	3	5	0	0	0.7	1.000
1989	2 teams	NY N	(36G 6-6)		MIN A	(11G 3-5)																				
"	total	9	11	.450	2.79	47	11	3	145	130	38	137	0	6	6	7	7	0	0	.000	6	21	1	2	0.6	.964
1990	MIN A	5	3	.625	2.76	56	0	0	65.1	55	19	61	0	5	3	32	0	0	0	—	2	5	0	0	0.1	1.000
1991		4	5	.444	2.35	63	0	0	69	44	30	61	0	4	5	42	0	0	0	—	7	5	0	0	0.2	1.000
1992		2	6	.250	2.84	64	0	0	66.2	60	17	52	0	2	6	41	0	0	0	—	2	5	0	0	0.1	1.000
1993		4	3	.571	3.11	65	0	0	72.1	60	14	59	0	4	3	34	0	0	0	—	12	8	0	0	0.3	1.000
1994		1	4	.200	3.63	44	0	0	44.2	57	10	46	0	1	4	23	0	0	0	—	4	9	0	0	0.3	1.000
1995	2 teams	MIN A	(22G 1-1)		BOS A	(30G 2-2)																				
"	total	3	3	.500	2.60	52	0	0	55.1	46	13	52	0	3	3	32	0	0	0	—	2	8	0	0	0.2	1.000
1996	MIN A	8	6	.571	5.42	19	19	2	111.1	124	27	83	0	0	0	0	0	0	0	—	13	5	2	0	1.1	.900
	12 yrs.	67	62	.519	3.48	488	89	10	1033.1	992	284	822	0	27	33	211	138	28	3	.203	79	141	5	5	0.5	.978

DIVISIONAL PLAYOFF SERIES

Year	Team	W	L	PCT	ERA	G	GS	CG	IP	H	BB	SO	ShO	RW	RL	SV	AB	H	HR	BA	PO	A	E	DP	TC/G	FA
1995	BOS A	0	0	—	13.50	1	0	0	0.2	3	0	1	0	0	0	0	0	0	0	—	0	0	0	0	0.0	.000

LEAGUE CHAMPIONSHIP SERIES

Year	Team	W	L	PCT	ERA	G	GS	CG	IP	H	BB	SO	ShO	RW	RL	SV	AB	H	HR	BA	PO	A	E	DP	TC/G	FA
1986	NY N	0	0	—	0.00	2	0	0	5	2	2	2	0	0	0	0	0	0	0	—	1	1	0	0	1.0	1.000
1988		0	0	—	1.29	3	0	0	7	3	2	4	0	0	0	0	1	0	0	.000	0	1	0	0	0.3	1.000
1991	MIN A	0	0	—	0.00	3	0	0	3.1	1	0	3	0	0	0	3	0	0	0	—	0	0	0	0	0.0	.000
	3 yrs.	0	0		0.59	8	0	0	15.1	6	4	9	0	0	0	3 (6th)	1	0	0	.000	1	2	0	0	0.4	1.000

WORLD SERIES

Year	Team	W	L	PCT	ERA	G	GS	CG	IP	H	BB	SO	ShO	RW	RL	SV	AB	H	HR	BA	PO	A	E	DP	TC/G	FA
1986	NY N	1	0	1.000	12.00	2	0	0	3	8	1	4	0	1	0	0	0	0	0	—	0	0	0	0	0.0	.000
1991	MIN A	1	1	.500	1.80	4	0	0	5	6	1	3	0	1	1	2	0	0	0	.000	0	0	0	0	0.0	.000
	2 yrs.	2	1	.667	5.63	6	0	0	8	14	2	7	0	2	1	2	1	0	0	.000	0	0	0	0	0.0	.000

PITCHER REGISTER

Year	Team	W	L	PCT	ERA	G	GS	CG	IP	H	BB	SO	ShO	Relief Pitching W	L	SV	Batting AB	H	HR	BA	PO	A	E	DP	TC/G	FA

Jose Alberro
ALBERRO, JOSE EDGARDO
B. June 29, 1969, San Juan, Puerto Rico — BR TR 6'2" 190 lbs.

1995	TEX A	0	0	—	7.40	12	0	0	20.2	26	12	10	0	0	0	0	0	0	0	—	2	4	0	0	0.5	1.000
1996		0	1	.000	5.79	5	1	0	9.1	14	7	2	0	0	0	0	0	0	0	—	1	2	0	0	0.6	1.000
2 yrs.		0	1	.000	6.90	17	1	0	30	40	19	12	0	0	0	0	0	0	0		3	6	0	0	0.5	1.000

Scott Aldred
ALDRED, SCOTT PHILLIP
B. June 12, 1968, Flint, Mich. — BL TL 6'4" 195 lbs.

1990	DET A	1	2	.333	3.77	4	3	0	14.1	13	10	7	0	0	0	0	0	0	0	—	0	2	0	0	0.5	1.000
1991		2	4	.333	5.18	11	11	1	57.1	58	30	35	0	0	0	0	0	0	0	—	3	8	0	0	1.0	1.000
1992		3	8	.273	6.78	16	13	0	65	80	33	34	0	1	1	0	0	0	0	—	5	10	0	1	0.9	1.000
1993	2 teams	CLR N	(5G 0-0)		MON N	(3G 1-0)																				
"	total	1	0	1.000	9.00	8	0	0	12	19	10	9	0	1	0	0	0	0	0	—	0	2	0	0	0.3	1.000
1996	2 teams	DET A	(11G 0-4)		MIN A	(25G 6-5)																				
"	total	6	9	.400	6.21	36	25	0	165.1	194	68	111	0	0	0	0	0	0	0	—	5	16	3	2	0.7	.875
5 yrs.		13	23	.361	6.13	75	52	1	314	364	151	196	0	2	1	0	0	0	0		13	38	3	3	0.7	.944

Mike Aldrete
ALDRETE, MICHAEL PETER
B. Jan. 29, 1961, Carmel, Calif. — BL TL 5'11" 180 lbs.

| 1996 | NY A | 0 | 0 | — | 0.00 | 1 | 0 | 0 | 1 | 1 | 0 | 0 | 0 | 0 | 0 | 0 | * | | | | 0 | 0 | 0 | 0 | 0.0 | — |

Manny Alexander
ALEXANDER, MANUEL
Born Manuel DeJesus (Alexander).
B. Mar. 20, 1971, San Pedro de Macoris, Domincan Republic — BR TR 5'10" 150 lbs.

| 1996 | BAL A | 0 | 0 | — | 67.50 | 1 | 0 | 0 | 0.2 | 1 | 4 | 0 | 0 | 0 | 0 | 0 | * | 0 | 0 | — | 0 | 0 | 0 | 0 | 0.0 | — |

Garvin Alston
ALSTON, GARVIN JAMES
B. Dec. 8, 1971, Mt. Vernon, N.Y. — BR TR 6'2" 185 lbs.

| 1996 | CLR N | 1 | 0 | 1.000 | 9.00 | 6 | 0 | 0 | 6 | 9 | 3 | 5 | 0 | 0 | 0 | 0 | 1 | 0 | 0 | .000 | 0 | 1 | 0 | 0 | 0.2 | 1.000 |

Tavo Alvarez
ALVAREZ, CESAR OCTAVIO
B. Nov. 25, 1971, Ciudad Obregon, Mexico — BR TR 6'3" 245 lbs.

1995	MON N	1	5	.167	6.75	8	8	0	37.1	46	14	17	0	0	0	0	12	0	0	.000	3	4	1	1	1.0	.875
1996		2	1	.667	3.00	11	5	0	21	19	12	9	0	1	0	0	4	2	0	.500	2	3	0	1	0.5	1.000
2 yrs.		3	6	.333	5.40	19	13	0	58.1	65	26	26	0	1	0	0	16	2	0	.125	5	7	1	2	0.7	.923

Wilson Alvarez
ALVAREZ, WILSON EDUARDO
Born Wilson Eduardo Alvarez (Funemayor).
B. Mar. 24, 1970, Maracaibo, Venezuela — BL TL 6'1" 175 lbs.

1989	TEX A	0	1	.000	∞	1	1	0		3	2	0	0	0	0	0	0	0	0	—	0	0	0	0	0.0	.000
1991	CHI A	3	2	.600	3.51	10	9	2	56.1	47	29	32	1	0	0	0	0	0	0	—	1	7	0	1	0.8	1.000
1992		5	3	.625	5.20	34	9	0	100.1	103	65	66	0	2	2	1	0	0	0	—	4	14	2	1	0.6	.900
1993		15	8	.652	2.95	31	31	1	207.2	168	122	155	1	0	0	0	0	0	0	—	5	28	1	2	1.1	.971
1994		12	8	.600	3.45	24	24	2	161.2	147	62	108	1	0	0	0	0	0	0	—	6	13	0	1	0.8	1.000
1995		8	11	.421	4.32	29	29	3	175	171	93	118	0	0	0	0	0	0	0	—	7	31	0	1	1.3	1.000
1996		15	10	.600	4.22	35	35	0	217.1	216	97	181	0	0	0	0	0	0	0	—	11	29	0	4	1.1	1.000
7 yrs.		58	43	.574	3.91	164	138	8	918.1	855	470	660	3	2	2	1	0	0	0		34	122	3	10	1.0	.981

LEAGUE CHAMPIONSHIP SERIES

| 1993 | CHI A | 1 | 0 | 1.000 | 1.00 | 1 | 1 | 1 | 9 | 7 | 2 | 6 | 0 | 0 | 0 | 0 | 0 | 0 | 0 | — | 0 | 2 | 0 | 1 | 2.0 | 1.000 |

Brian Anderson
ANDERSON, BRIAN JAMES
B. Apr. 26, 1972, Portsmouth, Va. — BL TL 6'1" 190 lbs.

1993	CAL A	0	0	—	3.97	4	1	0	11.1	11	2	4	0	0	0	0	0	0	0	—	0	1	0	0	0.3	1.000
1994		7	5	.583	5.22	18	18	0	101.2	120	27	47	0	0	0	0	0	0	0	—	6	10	1	0	0.9	.941
1995		6	8	.429	5.87	18	17	1	99.2	110	30	45	0	0	0	0	0	0	0	—	4	16	2	1	1.2	.909
1996	CLE A	3	1	.750	4.91	10	9	0	51.1	58	14	21	0	0	0	0	0	0	0	—	3	13	2	1	1.8	.889
4 yrs.		16	14	.533	5.35	50	45	1	264	299	73	117	0	0	0	0	0	0	0		13	40	5	2	1.2	.914

Luis Andujar
ANDUJAR, LUIS
Born Luis Andujar (Sanchez).
B. Nov. 22, 1972, Bani, Dominican Republic — BR TR 6'2" 175 lbs.

1995	CHI A	2	1	.667	3.26	5	5	0	30.1	26	14	9	0	0	0	0	0	0	0	—	1	1	0	0	0.4	1.000
1996	2 teams	CHI A	(5G 0-2)		TOR A	(3G 1-1)																				
"	total	1	3	.250	6.99	8	7	0	37.1	46	16	11	0	0	0	0	0	0	0	—	1	2	0	0	0.4	1.000
2 yrs.		3	4	.429	5.32	13	12	0	67.2	72	30	20	0	0	0	0	0	0	0		2	3	0	0	0.4	1.000

Kevin Appier
APPIER, ROBERT KEVIN
B. Dec. 6, 1967, Lancaster, Calif. — BR TR 6'2" 180 lbs.

1989	KC A	1	4	.200	9.14	6	5	0	21.2	34	12	10	0	0	0	0	0	0	0	—	1	0	0	0	0.2	1.000
1990		12	8	.600	2.76	32	24	3	185.2	179	54	127	3	0	0	0	0	0	0	—	15	21	3	3	1.2	.923
1991		13	10	.565	3.42	34	31	6	207.2	205	61	158	3	0	1	0	0	0	0	—	20	26	2	0	1.4	.958
1992		15	8	.652	2.46	30	30	3	208.1	167	68	150	3	0	0	0	0	0	0	—	19	21	1	4	1.4	.976
1993		18	8	.692	2.56	34	34	5	238.2	183	81	186	1	0	0	0	0	0	0	—	26	14	1	4	1.2	.976

Year	Team	W	L	PCT	ERA	G	GS	CG	IP	H	BB	SO	ShO	Relief Pitching W	L	SV	Batting AB	H	HR	BA	PO	A	E	DP	TC/G	FA

Kevin Appier *continued*

Year	Team	W	L	PCT	ERA	G	GS	CG	IP	H	BB	SO	ShO	W	L	SV	AB	H	HR	BA	PO	A	E	DP	TC/G	FA
1995		15	10	.600	3.89	31	31	4	201.1	163	80	185	1	0	0	0	0	0	0	—	16	20	0	3	1.2	1.000
1996		14	11	.560	3.62	32	32	5	211.1	192	75	207	1	0	0	0	0	0	0	—	19	16	0	2	1.1	1.000
8 yrs.		95	65	.594	3.28	222	210	27	1429.2	1260	494	1168	9	0	1	0	0	0	0		123	131	7	17	1.2	.973

Andy Ashby

ASHBY, ANDREW JASON
B. July 11, 1967, Kansas City, Mo.
BR TR 6'5" 180 lbs.

Year	Team	W	L	PCT	ERA	G	GS	CG	IP	H	BB	SO	ShO	W	L	SV	AB	H	HR	BA	PO	A	E	DP	TC/G	FA
1991	PHI N	1	5	.167	6.00	8	8	0	42	41	19	26	0	0	0	0	12	1	0	.083	7	4	0	1	1.4	1.000
1992		1	3	.250	7.54	10	8	0	37	42	21	24	0	0	0	0	11	1	0	.091	1	6	0	0	0.7	1.000
1993	2 teams	CLR N	(20G 0–4)			SD N	(12G 3–6)																			
"	total	3	10	.231	6.80	32	21	0	123	168	56	77	0	0	0	1	36	5	0	.139	15	19	0	1	1.1	1.000
1994	SD N	6	11	.353	3.40	24	24	4	164.1	145	43	121	0	0	0	0	49	8	0	.163	14	22	0	0	1.5	1.000
1995		12	10	.545	2.94	31	31	2	192.2	180	62	150	2	0	0	0	49	8	0	.163	6	21	1	0	0.9	.964
1996		9	5	.643	3.23	24	24	1	150.2	147	34	85	0	0	0	0	45	11	0	.244	10	29	2	3	1.7	.951
6 yrs.		32	44	.421	4.20	129	116	7	709.2	723	235	483	2	0	0	1	202	34	0	.168	53	101	3	5	1.2	.981

DIVISIONAL PLAYOFF SERIES

Year	Team	W	L	PCT	ERA	G	GS	CG	IP	H	BB	SO	ShO	W	L	SV	AB	H	HR	BA	PO	A	E	DP	TC/G	FA
1996	SD N	0	0	—	6.75	1	1	0	5.1	7	1	5	0	0	0	0	1	0	0	.000	0	0	0	0	0.0	.000

Paul Assenmacher

ASSENMACHER, PAUL ANDRE
B. Dec. 10, 1960, Detroit, Mich.
BL TL 6'3" 195 lbs.

Year	Team	W	L	PCT	ERA	G	GS	CG	IP	H	BB	SO	ShO	W	L	SV	AB	H	HR	BA	PO	A	E	DP	TC/G	FA
1986	ATL N	7	3	.700	2.50	61	0	0	68.1	61	26	56	0	7	3	7	6	0	0	.000	5	15	0	1	0.3	1.000
1987		1	1	.500	5.10	52	0	0	54.2	58	24	39	0	1	1	2	4	0	0	.000	2	3	0	0	0.1	1.000
1988		8	7	.533	3.06	64	0	0	79.1	72	32	71	0	8	7	5	3	1	0	.333	6	11	0	2	0.3	1.000
1989	2 teams	ATL N	(49G 1–3)			CHI N	(14G 2–1)																			
"	total	3	4	.429	3.99	63	0	0	76.2	74	28	79	0	3	4	0	5	0	0	.000	3	13	0	0	0.3	1.000
1990	CHI N	7	2	.778	2.80	74	1	0	103	90	36	95	0	7	2	10	8	0	0	.000	1	18	0	0	0.3	1.000
1991		7	8	.467	3.24	75	0	0	102.2	85	31	117	0	7	8	15	4	1	0	.250	4	10	1	0	0.2	.933
1992		4	4	.500	4.10	70	0	0	68	72	26	67	0	4	4	8	4	0	0	.000	3	6	0	1	0.1	1.000
1993	2 teams	CHI N	(46G 2–1)			NY A	(26G 2–2)																			
"	total	4	3	.571	3.38	72	0	0	56	54	22	45	0	4	3	0	2	1	0	.500	1	4	1	2	0.1	.833
1994	CHI A	1	2	.333	3.55	44	0	0	33	26	13	29	0	1	2	1	0	0	0	—	2	5	0	2	0.2	1.000
1995	CLE A	6	2	.750	2.82	47	0	0	38.1	32	12	40	0	6	2	0	0	0	0	—	0	5	0	1	0.1	1.000
1996		4	2	.667	3.09	63	0	0	46.2	46	14	44	0	4	2	1	0	0	0	—	0	4	0	1	0.1	1.000
11 yrs.		52	38	.578	3.38	685	1	0	726.2	670	264	682	0	52	38	49	36	3	0	.083	27	94	2	10	0.2	.984

DIVISIONAL PLAYOFF SERIES

Year	Team	W	L	PCT	ERA	G	GS	CG	IP	H	BB	SO	ShO	W	L	SV	AB	H	HR	BA	PO	A	E	DP	TC/G	FA
1995	CLE A	0	0	—	0.00	3	0	0	1.2	0	0	3	0	0	0	0	0	0	0	—	0	0	0	0	0.0	.000
1996		1	0	1.000	0.00	3	0	0	1.2	0	1	2	0	1	0	0	0	0	0	—	0	1	0	0	0.0	—
2 yrs.		1	0	1.000	0.00	6	0	0	3.1	0	1	5	0	1	0	0					0	1	0	0	0.2	1.000

LEAGUE CHAMPIONSHIP SERIES

Year	Team	W	L	PCT	ERA	G	GS	CG	IP	H	BB	SO	ShO	W	L	SV	AB	H	HR	BA	PO	A	E	DP	TC/G	FA
1989	CHI N	0	0	—	13.50	2	0	0	0.2	3	0	1	0	0	0	0	0	0	0	—	0	0	0	0	0.0	.000
1995	CLE A	0	0	—	0.00	3	0	0	1.1	0	1	2	0	0	0	0	0	0	0	—	0	0	0	0	0.0	.000
2 yrs.		0	0		4.50	5	0	0	2	3	1	2	0	0	0	0					0	0	0	0	0.0	

WORLD SERIES

Year	Team	W	L	PCT	ERA	G	GS	CG	IP	H	BB	SO	ShO	W	L	SV	AB	H	HR	BA	PO	A	E	DP	TC/G	FA
1995	CLE A	0	0	—	6.75	4	0	0	1.1	1	3	3	0	0	0	0	0	0	0	—	0	0	0	0	0.0	.000

Pedro Astacio

ASTACIO, PEDRO JULIO
Born Pedro Julio Astacio (Pura).
B. Nov. 28, 1969, Hato Mayor, Dominican Republic
BR TR 6'2" 174 lbs.

Year	Team	W	L	PCT	ERA	G	GS	CG	IP	H	BB	SO	ShO	W	L	SV	AB	H	HR	BA	PO	A	E	DP	TC/G	FA
1992	LA N	5	5	.500	1.98	11	11	4	82	80	20	43	4	0	0	0	24	3	0	.125	4	13	2	1	1.7	.895
1993		14	9	.609	3.57	31	31	3	186.1	165	68	122	2	0	0	0	62	10	0	.161	23	17	2	1	1.4	.952
1994		6	8	.429	4.29	23	23	3	149	142	47	108	1	0	0	0	47	3	0	.064	19	13	0	0	1.4	1.000
1995		7	8	.467	4.24	48	11	1	104	103	29	80	1	6	2	0	24	3	0	.125	11	11	0	0	0.5	1.000
1996		9	8	.529	3.44	35	32	0	211.2	207	67	130	0	0	0	0	68	6	0	.088	23	31	3	2	1.6	.947
5 yrs.		41	38	.519	3.60	148	108	11	733	697	231	483	8	6	2	0	225	25	0	.111	80	85	7	4	1.2	.959

DIVISIONAL PLAYOFF SERIES

Year	Team	W	L	PCT	ERA	G	GS	CG	IP	H	BB	SO	ShO	W	L	SV	AB	H	HR	BA	PO	A	E	DP	TC/G	FA
1995	LA N	0	0	—	0.00	3	0	0	3.1	1	0	5	0	0	0	0	0	0	0	—	0	2	0	0	0.7	1.000
1996		0	0	—	0.00	1	0	0	1.2	0	0	1	0	0	0	0	0	0	0	—	0	1	0	0	1.0	1.000
2 yrs.		0	0		0.00	4	0	0	5	1	0	6	0	0	0	0					0	3	0	0	0.8	1.000

Derek Aucoin

AUCOIN, DEREK ALFRED
B. Mar. 27, 1970, Lachine, Que., Canada
BR TR 6'7" 235 lbs.

Year	Team	W	L	PCT	ERA	G	GS	CG	IP	H	BB	SO	ShO	W	L	SV	AB	H	HR	BA	PO	A	E	DP	TC/G	FA
1996	MON N	0	1	.000	3.38	2	0	0	2.2	3	1	1	0	0	1	0	0	0	0	—	1	1	0	0	2.0	1.000

Steve Avery

AVERY, STEVEN THOMAS
B. Apr. 14, 1970, Trenton, Mich.
BL TL 6'4" 180 lbs.

Year	Team	W	L	PCT	ERA	G	GS	CG	IP	H	BB	SO	ShO	W	L	SV	AB	H	HR	BA	PO	A	E	DP	TC/G	FA
1990	ATL N	3	11	.214	5.64	21	20	1	99	121	45	75	1	0	0	0	30	4	0	.133	4	22	2	0	1.3	.929
1991		18	8	.692	3.38	35	35	3	210.1	189	65	137	1	0	0	0	79	17	0	.215	9	31	1	2	1.2	.976
1992		11	11	.500	3.20	35	35	2	233.2	216	71	129	2	0	0	0	76	13	0	.171	16	36	3	1	1.6	.945
1993		18	6	.750	2.94	35	35	3	223.1	216	43	125	1	0	0	0	75	12	0	.160	4	47	0	2	1.5	1.000
1994		8	3	.727	4.04	24	24	1	151.2	127	55	122	0	0	0	0	49	5	0	.102	4	26	1	0	1.3	.968
1995		7	13	.350	4.67	29	29	3	173.1	165	52	141	1	0	0	0	53	11	2	.208	3	37	2	2	1.4	.952
1996		7	10	.412	4.47	24	23	1	131	146	40	86	0	0	0	0	46	11	2	.239	8	26	2	0	1.5	.944
7 yrs.		72	62	.537	3.83	203	201	14	1222.1	1180	371	815	6	0	0	0	408	73	4	.179	48	225	11	7	1.4	.961

Year	Team	W	L	PCT	ERA	G	GS	CG	IP	H	BB	SO	ShO	Relief Pitching W	L	SV	Batting AB	H	HR	BA	PO	A	E	DP	TC/G	FA

Steve Avery *continued*

Year	Team	W	L	PCT	ERA	G	GS	CG	IP	H	BB	SO	ShO	W	L	SV	AB	H	HR	BA	PO	A	E	DP	TC/G	FA
1995	ATL N	0	0	—	13.50	1	0	0	0.2	1	0	1	0	0	0	0	0	0	0	—	0	0	0	0	0.0	.000

LEAGUE CHAMPIONSHIP SERIES

Year	Team	W	L	PCT	ERA	G	GS	CG	IP	H	BB	SO	ShO	W	L	SV	AB	H	HR	BA	PO	A	E	DP	TC/G	FA
1991	ATL N	2	0	1.000	0.00	2	2	0	16.1	9	4	17	0	0	0	0	7	1	0	.143	1	2	0	0	1.5	1.000
1992		1	1	.500	9.00	3	2	0	8	13	2	3	0	0	0	0	2	0	0	.000	0	0	0	0	0.0	.000
1993		0	0	—	2.77	2	2	0	13	9	6	10	0	0	0	0	4	2	0	.500	0	2	0	0	1.0	1.000
1995		1	0	1.000	0.00	2	1	0	6	2	4	6	0	0	0	0	2	1	0	.500	0	2	0	0	1.0	1.000
1996		0	0	—	0.00	2	0	0	2	2	1	1	0	0	0	0	0	0	0	—	0	0	0	0	0.0	.000
	5 yrs.	4	1	.800	2.38	11	7	0	45.1	35	17	37	0	0	0	0	15	4	0	.267	1	6	0	0	0.6	1.000
		4th	8th			10th					9th	6th														

WORLD SERIES

Year	Team	W	L	PCT	ERA	G	GS	CG	IP	H	BB	SO	ShO	W	L	SV	AB	H	HR	BA	PO	A	E	DP	TC/G	FA
1991	ATL N	0	0	—	3.46	2	2	0	13	10	1	8	0	0	0	0	3	0	0	.000	1	0	0	0	0.5	1.000
1992		0	1	.000	3.75	2	2	0	12	11	3	11	0	0	0	0	1	0	0	.000	0	2	0	0	1.0	1.000
1995		1	0	1.000	1.50	1	1	0	6	3	5	3	0	0	0	0	0	0	0	—	0	0	0	0	0.0	.000
1996		0	1	.000	13.50	1	0	0	0.2	1	3	0	0	0	1	0	0	0	0	—	0	0	0	0	0.0	.000
	4 yrs.	1	2	.333	3.41	6	5	0	31.2	25	12	22	0	0	1	0	4	0	0	.000	1	2	0	0	0.5	1.000

Bobby Ayala

AYALA, ROBERT JOSEPH
B. July 8, 1969, Ventura, Calif.

BR TR 6'2" 190 lbs.

Year	Team	W	L	PCT	ERA	G	GS	CG	IP	H	BB	SO	ShO	W	L	SV	AB	H	HR	BA	PO	A	E	DP	TC/G	FA
1992	CIN N	2	1	.667	4.34	5	5	0	29	33	13	23	0	0	0	0	9	0	0	.000	3	8	0	1	2.2	1.000
1993		7	10	.412	5.60	43	9	0	98	106	45	65	0	5	4	3	21	2	0	.095	12	10	6	1	0.7	.786
1994	SEA A	4	3	.571	2.86	46	0	0	56.2	42	26	76	0	4	3	18	0	0	0	—	2	5	2	0	0.2	.778
1995		6	5	.545	4.44	63	0	0	71	73	30	77	0	6	5	19	0	0	0	—	7	6	1	0	0.2	.929
1996		6	3	.667	5.88	50	0	0	67.1	65	25	61	0	6	3	3	0	0	0	—	5	9	0	1	0.3	1.000
	5 yrs.	25	22	.532	4.81	207	14	0	322	319	139	302	0	21	15	43	30	2	0	.067	29	38	9	3	0.4	.882

DIVISIONAL PLAYOFF SERIES

Year	Team	W	L	PCT	ERA	G	GS	CG	IP	H	BB	SO	ShO	W	L	SV	AB	H	HR	BA	PO	A	E	DP	TC/G	FA
1995	SEA A	0	0	—	54.00	2	0	0	0.2	6	1	0	0	0	0	0	0	0	0	—	0	0	0	0	0.0	.000

LEAGUE CHAMPIONSHIP SERIES

Year	Team	W	L	PCT	ERA	G	GS	CG	IP	H	BB	SO	ShO	W	L	SV	AB	H	HR	BA	PO	A	E	DP	TC/G	FA
1995	SEA A	0	0	—	2.45	2	0	0	3.2	3	3	3	0	0	0	0	0	0	0	—	0	1	0	0	0.5	1.000

Cory Bailey

BAILEY, PHILLIP CORY
B. Jan. 24, 1971, Herrin, Ill.

BR TR 6' 195 lbs.

Year	Team	W	L	PCT	ERA	G	GS	CG	IP	H	BB	SO	ShO	W	L	SV	AB	H	HR	BA	PO	A	E	DP	TC/G	FA
1993	BOS A	0	1	.000	3.45	11	0	0	15.2	12	12	11	0	0	1	0	0	0	0	—	0	5	0	1	0.5	1.000
1994		0	1	.000	12.46	5	0	0	4.1	10	3	4	0	0	1	0	0	0	0	—	0	0	0	0	0.0	.000
1995	STL N	0	0	—	7.36	3	0	0	3.2	2	2	5	0	0	0	0	0	0	0	—	0	1	0	0	0.3	1.000
1996		5	2	.714	3.00	51	0	0	57	57	30	38	0	5	2	0	1	0	0	.000	6	5	0	0	0.2	1.000
	4 yrs.	5	4	.556	3.79	70	0	0	80.2	81	47	58	0	5	4	0	1	0	0	.000	6	11	0	0	0.2	1.000

Roger Bailey

BAILEY, CHARLES ROGER
B. Oct. 3, 1970, Chattahoochee, Fla.

BR TR 6'1" 180 lbs.

Year	Team	W	L	PCT	ERA	G	GS	CG	IP	H	BB	SO	ShO	W	L	SV	AB	H	HR	BA	PO	A	E	DP	TC/G	FA
1995	CLR N	7	6	.538	4.98	39	6	0	81.1	88	39	33	0	3	5	0	16	2	0	.125	3	14	2	2	0.5	.895
1996		2	3	.400	6.24	24	11	0	83.2	94	52	45	0	0	0	1	19	5	1	.263	11	26	1	2	1.6	.974
	2 yrs.	9	9	.500	5.62	63	17	0	165	182	91	78	0	3	5	1	35	7	1	.200	14	40	3	4	0.9	.947

James Baldwin

BALDWIN, JAMES J.
B. July 15, 1971, Southern Pines, N. C.

BR TR 6'3" 210 lbs.

Year	Team	W	L	PCT	ERA	G	GS	CG	IP	H	BB	SO	ShO	W	L	SV	AB	H	HR	BA	PO	A	E	DP	TC/G	FA
1995	CHI A	0	1	.000	12.89	6	4	0	14.2	32	9	10	0	0	0	0	0	0	0	—	0	3	1	0	0.7	.750
1996		11	6	.647	4.42	28	28	0	169	168	57	127	0	0	0	0	0	0	0	—	12	16	3	1	1.1	.903
	2 yrs.	11	7	.611	5.10	34	32	0	183.2	200	66	137	0	0	0	0					12	19	4	1	1.0	.886

Brian Barber

BARBER, BRIAN SCOTT
B. Mar. 4, 1973, Hamilton, Ohio

BR TR 6'1" 175 lbs.

Year	Team	W	L	PCT	ERA	G	GS	CG	IP	H	BB	SO	ShO	W	L	SV	AB	H	HR	BA	PO	A	E	DP	TC/G	FA
1995	STL N	2	1	.667	5.22	9	4	0	29.1	31	16	27	0	0	0	0	8	1	0	.125	1	1	0	0	0.2	1.000
1996		0	0	—	15.00	1	1	0	3	4	6	1	0	0	0	0	0	0	0	—	0	0	0	0	0.0	.000
	2 yrs.	2	1	.667	6.12	10	5	0	32.1	35	22	28	0	0	0	0	8	1	0	.125	1	1	0	0	0.2	1.000

Shawn Barton

BARTON, SHAWN EDWARD
B. May 14, 1963, Los Angeles, Calif.

BR TL 6'3" 195 lbs.

Year	Team	W	L	PCT	ERA	G	GS	CG	IP	H	BB	SO	ShO	W	L	SV	AB	H	HR	BA	PO	A	E	DP	TC/G	FA
1992	SEA A	0	1	.000	2.92	14	0	0	12.1	10	7	4	0	0	1	0	0	0	0	—	2	3	1	0	0.4	.833
1995	SF N	4	1	.800	4.26	52	0	0	44.1	37	19	22	0	4	1	1	0	0	0	—	4	8	0	2	0.2	1.000
1996		0	0	—	9.72	7	0	0	8.1	19	1	3	0	0	0	0	0	0	0	—	1	2	0	0	0.4	1.000
	3 yrs.	4	2	.667	4.71	73	0	0	65	66	27	29	0	4	2	1	0	0	0	—	7	13	1	2	0.3	.952

Richard Batchelor

BATCHELOR, RICH ANTHONY
B. Apr. 8, 1967, Florence, S. C.

BR TR 6'1" 195 lbs.

Year	Team	W	L	PCT	ERA	G	GS	CG	IP	H	BB	SO	ShO	W	L	SV	AB	H	HR	BA	PO	A	E	DP	TC/G	FA
1993	STL N	0	0	—	8.10	9	0	0	10	14	3	4	0	0	0	0	1	0	0	.000	1	1	0	0	0.2	1.000
1996		2	0	1.000	1.20	11	0	0	15	9	1	11	0	2	0	0	1	0	0	.000	0	1	0	0	0.1	1.000
	2 yrs.	2	0	1.000	3.96	20	0	0	25	23	4	15	0	2	0	0	2	0	0	.000	1	2	0	0	0.2	1.000

Year	Team	W	L	PCT	ERA	G	GS	CG	IP	H	BB	SO	ShO	Relief Pitching W	L	SV	Batting AB	H	HR	BA	PO	A	E	DP	TC/G	FA

Miguel Batista

BATISTA, MIGUEL JEREZ
Born Miguel Jerez Batista (Decartes).
B. Feb. 19, 1971, Santo Domingo, Dominican Republic
BR TR 6' 160 lbs.

Year	Team	W	L	PCT	ERA	G	GS	CG	IP	H	BB	SO	ShO	W	L	SV	AB	H	HR	BA	PO	A	E	DP	TC/G	FA
1992	PIT N	0	0	—	9.00	1	0	0	2	4	3	1	0	0	0	0	0	0	0	—	0	0	0	0	0.0	.000
1996	FLA N	0	0	—	5.56	9	0	0	11.1	9	7	6	0	0	0	0	0	0	0	—	0	1	0	0	0.1	1.000
2 yrs.		0	0		6.07	10	0	0	13.1	13	10	7	0	0	0	0	0	0	0		0	1	0	0	0.1	1.000

Jose Bautista

BAUTISTA, JOSE JOAQUIN
Born Jose Joaquin Bautista (Arias).
B. July 25, 1964, Bani, Dominican Republic
BR TR 6'1" 177 lbs.

Year	Team	W	L	PCT	ERA	G	GS	CG	IP	H	BB	SO	ShO	W	L	SV	AB	H	HR	BA	PO	A	E	DP	TC/G	FA
1988	BAL A	6	15	.286	4.30	33	25	3	171.2	171	45	76	0	0	1	0	0	0	0	—	27	11	1	3	1.2	.974
1989		3	4	.429	5.31	15	10	0	78	84	15	30	0	0	0	0	0	0	0	—	3	10	1	0	0.9	.929
1990		1	0	1.000	4.05	22	0	0	26.2	28	7	15	0	1	0	0	0	0	0	—	1	2	0	0	0.1	1.000
1991		0	1	.000	16.88	5	0	0	5.1	13	5	3	0	0	1	0	0	0	0	—	0	1	0	0	0.2	1.000
1993	CHI N	10	3	.769	2.82	58	7	1	111.2	105	27	63	0	6	1	2	21	4	0	.190	14	18	2	2	0.6	.941
1994		4	5	.444	3.89	58	0	0	69.1	75	17	45	0	4	5	1	2	0	0	.000	5	9	0	0	0.2	1.000
1995	SF N	3	8	.273	6.44	52	6	0	100.2	120	26	45	0	2	5	0	18	0	0	.000	5	11	1	0	0.3	.941
1996		3	4	.429	3.36	37	1	0	69.2	66	15	28	0	3	3	0	9	1	0	.111	4	13	0	0	0.5	1.000
8 yrs.		30	40	.429	4.45	280	49	4	633	662	157	305	0	16	16	3	50	5	0	.100	59	75	5	5	0.5	.964

Rod Beck

BECK, RODNEY ROY
B. Aug. 3, 1968, Burbank, Calif.
BR TR 6'1" 215 lbs.

Year	Team	W	L	PCT	ERA	G	GS	CG	IP	H	BB	SO	ShO	W	L	SV	AB	H	HR	BA	PO	A	E	DP	TC/G	FA
1991	SF N	1	1	.500	3.78	31	0	0	52.1	53	13	38	0	1	1	1	2	1	0	.500	1	10	0	0	0.4	1.000
1992		3	3	.500	1.76	65	0	0	92	62	15	87	0	3	3	17	2	1	0	.500	2	13	1	0	0.2	.938
1993		3	1	.750	2.16	76	0	0	79.1	57	13	86	0	3	1	48	4	0	0	.000	0	8	1	1	0.1	.889
1994		2	4	.333	2.77	48	0	0	48.2	49	13	39	0	2	4	28	3	0	0	.000	4	4	0	0	0.2	1.000
1995		5	6	.455	4.45	60	0	0	58.2	60	21	42	0	5	6	33	3	1	0	.333	6	7	0	0	0.2	1.000
1996		0	9	.000	3.34	63	0	0	62	56	10	48	0	0	9	35	3	1	0	.333	2	6	0	1	0.1	1.000
6 yrs.		14	24	.368	2.89	343	0	0	393	337	85	340	0	14	24	162	17	4	0	.235	15	48	2	2	0.2	.969

Robbie Beckett

BECKETT, ROBERT JOSEPH
B. Jul. 1, 1972, Austin, Tex.
BR TL 6'5" 240 lbs.

Year	Team	W	L	PCT	ERA	G	GS	CG	IP	H	BB	SO	ShO	W	L	SV	AB	H	HR	BA	PO	A	E	DP	TC/G	FA
1996	CLR N	0	0	—	13.50	5	0	0	5.1	6	9	6	0	0	0	0	0	0	0	—	0	0	0	0	0.0	

Matt Beech

BEECH, LUCAS MATTHEW
B. Jan. 20, 1972, Oakland, Calif.
BL TL 6'2" 190 lbs.

Year	Team	W	L	PCT	ERA	G	GS	CG	IP	H	BB	SO	ShO	W	L	SV	AB	H	HR	BA	PO	A	E	DP	TC/G	FA
1996	PHI N	1	4	.200	6.97	8	8	0	41.1	49	11	33	0	0	0	0	14	1	0	.071	1	4	0	1	0.6	1.000

Tim Belcher

BELCHER, TIMOTHY WAYNE
B. Oct. 19, 1961, Mount Gilead, Ohio
BR TR 6'3" 210 lbs.

Year	Team	W	L	PCT	ERA	G	GS	CG	IP	H	BB	SO	ShO	W	L	SV	AB	H	HR	BA	PO	A	E	DP	TC/G	FA
1987	LA N	4	2	.667	2.38	6	5	0	34	30	7	23	0	1	0	0	10	2	0	.200	1	5	0	0	1.0	1.000
1988		12	6	.667	2.91	36	27	4	179.2	143	51	152	1	1	0	4	56	4	1	.071	14	19	0	2	0.9	1.000
1989		15	12	.556	2.82	39	30	10	230	182	80	200	8	1	2	1	70	7	0	.100	21	18	3	3	1.1	.929
1990		9	9	.500	4.00	24	24	5	153	136	48	102	2	0	0	0	43	7	0	.163	11	11	0	1	0.9	1.000
1991		10	9	.526	2.62	33	33	2	209.1	189	75	156	1	0	0	0	67	8	0	.119	11	20	2	2	1.0	.939
1992	CIN N	15	14	.517	3.91	35	34	2	227.2	201	80	149	1	0	1	0	76	8	1	.105	23	27	1	2	1.5	.980
1993	2 teams	CIN N	(22G 9–6)		CHI A	(12G 3–5)																				
"	total	12	11	.522	4.44	34	33	5	208.2	198	74	135	3	0	0	0	50	10	0	.200	19	17	2	2	1.1	.947
1994	DET A	7	15	.318	5.89	25	25	3	162	192	78	76	0	0	0	0	0	0	0	—	19	25	4	4	1.9	.917
1995	SEA A	10	12	.455	4.52	28	28	1	179.1	188	88	96	0	0	0	0	0	0	0	—	22	16	1	5	1.4	.974
1996	KC A	15	11	.577	3.92	35	35	4	238.2	262	68	113	0	0	0	0	0	0	0	—	18	32	2	4	1.5	.962
10 yrs.		109	101	.519	3.80	295	274	36	1822.1	1721	649	1202	17	3	3	5	372	46	2	.124	159	190	15	25	1.2	.959

DIVISIONAL PLAYOFF SERIES

Year	Team	W	L	PCT	ERA	G	GS	CG	IP	H	BB	SO	ShO	W	L	SV	AB	H	HR	BA	PO	A	E	DP	TC/G	FA
1995	SEA A	0	1	.000	6.23	2	0	0	4.1	4	5	0	0	0	1	0	0	0	0	—	0	1	0	0	0.5	1.000

LEAGUE CHAMPIONSHIP SERIES

Year	Team	W	L	PCT	ERA	G	GS	CG	IP	H	BB	SO	ShO	W	L	SV	AB	H	HR	BA	PO	A	E	DP	TC/G	FA
1988	LA N	2	0	1.000	4.11	2	2	0	15.1	12	4	16	0	0	0	0	8	1	0	.125	1	0	0	0	0.5	1.000
1993	CHI A	1	0	1.000	2.45	1	0	0	3.2	3	3	1	0	1	0	0	0	0	0	—	1	1	0	0	2.0	1.000
1995	SEA A	0	1	.000	6.35	1	1	0	5.2	9	2	1	0	0	0	0	0	0	0	—	1	0	0	0	1.0	1.000
3 yrs.		3	1	.750	4.38	4	3	0	24.2	24	9	18	0	1	0	0	8	1	0	.125	3	1	0	0	1.0	1.000

WORLD SERIES

Year	Team	W	L	PCT	ERA	G	GS	CG	IP	H	BB	SO	ShO	W	L	SV	AB	H	HR	BA	PO	A	E	DP	TC/G	FA
1988	LA N	1	0	1.000	6.23	2	2	0	8.2	10	6	10	0	0	0	0	0	0	0	—	0	0	0	0	0.0	.000

Stan Belinda

BELINDA, STANLEY PETER
B. Aug. 6, 1966, Huntingdon, Pa.
BR TR 6'3" 185 lbs.

Year	Team	W	L	PCT	ERA	G	GS	CG	IP	H	BB	SO	ShO	W	L	SV	AB	H	HR	BA	PO	A	E	DP	TC/G	FA
1989	PIT N	0	1	.000	6.10	8	0	0	10.1	13	2	10	0	0	1	0	0	0	0	—	0	0	0	0	0.0	.000
1990		3	4	.429	3.55	55	0	0	58.1	48	29	55	0	3	4	8	5	0	0	.000	2	4	0	0	0.1	1.000
1991		7	5	.583	3.45	60	0	0	78.1	50	35	71	0	7	5	16	7	0	0	.000	5	5	0	1	0.2	1.000
1992		6	4	.600	3.15	59	0	0	71.1	58	29	57	0	6	4	18	3	2	0	.667	4	4	0	0	0.1	1.000
1993	2 teams	PIT N	(40G 3–1)		KC A	(23G 1–1)																				
"	total	4	2	.667	3.88	63	0	0	69.2	65	17	55	0	4	2	19	1	0	0	.000	4	5	0	1	0.1	1.000
1994	KC A	2	2	.500	5.14	37	0	0	49	47	24	37	0	2	2	1	0	0	0	—	0	4	0	0	0.1	1.000
1995	BOS A	8	1	.889	3.10	63	0	0	69.2	51	28	57	0	8	1	10	0	0	0	—	3	5	0	0	0.1	1.000
1996		2	1	.667	6.59	31	0	0	28.2	31	20	18	0	2	1	2	0	0	0	—	3	3	0	0	0.2	1.000
8 yrs.		32	20	.615	3.89	376	0	0	435.1	363	184	360	0	32	20	74	16	2	0	.125	21	30	0	3	0.1	1.000

Stan Belinda continued

Year	Team	W	L	PCT	ERA	G	GS	CG	IP	H	BB	SO	ShO	Relief W	Relief L	SV	AB	H	HR	BA	PO	A	E	DP	TC/G	FA
1995	BOS A	0	0	—	0.00	1	0	0	0.1	0	0	0	0	0	0	0	0	0	0	—	0	0	0	0	0.0	.000

LEAGUE CHAMPIONSHIP SERIES

Year	Team	W	L	PCT	ERA	G	GS	CG	IP	H	BB	SO	ShO	Relief W	Relief L	SV	AB	H	HR	BA	PO	A	E	DP	TC/G	FA
1990	PIT N	0	0	—	2.45	3	0	0	3.2	3	0	4	0	0	0	0	0	0	0	—	0	0	0	0	0.0	.000
1991		1	0	1.000	0.00	3	0	0	5	0	3	4	0	1	0	0	0	0	0	—	0	2	0	0	0.7	1.000
1992		0	0	—	0.00	2	0	0	1.2	2	1	2	0	0	0	0	0	0	0		0	0	0	0	0.0	.000
3 yrs.		1	0	1.000	0.87	8	0	0	10.1	5	4	10	0	0	0	0	0	0	0		0	2	0	0	0.3	1.000

Alan Benes

BENES, ALAN PAUL
Brother of Andy Benes.
B. Jan. 21, 1972, Evansville, Ind.

BR TR 6'5" 215 lbs.

Year	Team	W	L	PCT	ERA	G	GS	CG	IP	H	BB	SO	ShO	Relief W	Relief L	SV	AB	H	HR	BA	PO	A	E	DP	TC/G	FA
1995	STL N	1	2	.333	8.44	3	3	0	16	24	4	20	0	0	0	0	6	0	0	.000	1	0	0	0	0.3	1.000
1996		13	10	.565	4.90	34	32	3	191	192	87	131	1	1	1	0	61	9	0	.148	8	19	3	3	0.9	.900
2 yrs.		14	12	.538	5.17	37	35	3	207	216	91	151	1	1	1	0	67	9	0	.134	9	19	3	3	0.8	.903

LEAGUE CHAMPIONSHIP SERIES

Year	Team	W	L	PCT	ERA	G	GS	CG	IP	H	BB	SO	ShO	Relief W	Relief L	SV	AB	H	HR	BA	PO	A	E	DP	TC/G	FA
1996	STL N	0	1	.000	2.84	2	1	0	6.1	3	2	5	0	0	0	0	1	0	0	.000	0	1	0	0	0.5	1.000

Andy Benes

BENES, ANDREW CHARLES
Brother of Alan Benes.
B. Aug. 20, 1967, Evansville, Ind.

BR TR 6'6" 235 lbs.

Year	Team	W	L	PCT	ERA	G	GS	CG	IP	H	BB	SO	ShO	Relief W	Relief L	SV	AB	H	HR	BA	PO	A	E	DP	TC/G	FA
1989	SD N	6	3	.667	3.51	10	10	0	66.2	51	31	66	0	0	0	0	24	6	1	.250	4	8	0	1	1.2	1.000
1990		10	11	.476	3.60	32	31	2	192.1	177	69	140	0	0	0	0	60	6	0	.100	15	9	1	1	0.8	.960
1991		15	11	.577	3.03	33	33	4	223	194	59	167	1	0	0	0	62	2	1	.032	8	29	0	3	1.1	1.000
1992		13	14	.481	3.35	34	34	2	231.1	230	61	169	2	0	0	0	67	10	1	.149	14	34	1	1	1.4	.980
1993		15	15	.500	3.78	34	34	4	230.2	200	86	179	2	0	0	0	72	9	1	.125	17	14	1	2	0.9	.969
1994		6	14	.300	3.86	25	25	2	172.1	155	51	189	2	0	0	0	49	8	0	.163	21	19	0	2	1.6	1.000
1995 2 teams	SD N (19G 4–7) SEA A (12G 7–2)																									
" total		11	9	.550	4.76	31	31	1	181.2	193	78	171	1	0	0	0	40	6	0	.150	8	15	1	1	0.8	.958
1996	STL N	18	10	.643	3.83	36	34	3	230.1	215	77	160	1	0	0	1	73	11	0	.151	8	24	2	1	0.9	.941
8 yrs.		94	87	.519	3.70	235	232	18	1528.1	1415	512	1241	9	0	0	1	447	58	4	.130	95	152	6	12	1.1	.976

DIVISIONAL PLAYOFF SERIES

Year	Team	W	L	PCT	ERA	G	GS	CG	IP	H	BB	SO	ShO	Relief W	Relief L	SV	AB	H	HR	BA	PO	A	E	DP	TC/G	FA
1995	SEA A	0	0	—	5.40	2	2	0	11.2	10	9	8	0	0	0	0	0	0	0	—	1	0	0	0	0.5	1.000
1996	STL N	0	0	—	5.14	1	1	0	7	6	1	9	0	0	0	0	0	0	0	—	0	0	0	0	0.0	—
2 yrs.		0	0	—	5.30	3	3	0	18.2	16	10	17	0	0	0	0	2	1	0	.500	2	0	0	0	0.7	1.000

LEAGUE CHAMPIONSHIP SERIES

Year	Team	W	L	PCT	ERA	G	GS	CG	IP	H	BB	SO	ShO	Relief W	Relief L	SV	AB	H	HR	BA	PO	A	E	DP	TC/G	FA
1995	SEA A	0	1	.000	23.14	1	1	0	2.1	6	2	3	0	0	0	0	0	0	0	—	0	0	0	0	0.0	.000
1996	STL N	0	0	—	5.28	3	2	0	15.1	19	3	9	0	0	0	0	4	1	0	.250	1	4	0	0	1.7	1.000
2 yrs.		0	1	.000	7.64	4	3	0	17.2	25	5	12	0	0	0	0	4	1	0	.250	1	4	0	0	1.3	1.000

Armando Benitez

BENITEZ, ARMANDO GERMAN
B. Nov. 3, 1972, Ramon Santana, Dominican Republic

BR TR 6'4" 180 lbs.

Year	Team	W	L	PCT	ERA	G	GS	CG	IP	H	BB	SO	ShO	Relief W	Relief L	SV	AB	H	HR	BA	PO	A	E	DP	TC/G	FA
1994	BAL A	0	0	—	0.90	3	0	0	10	8	4	14	0	0	0	0	0	0	0	—	0	1	0	0	0.3	1.000
1995		1	5	.167	5.66	44	0	0	47.2	37	37	56	0	1	5	2	0	0	0	—	1	0	1	1	0.0	.500
1996		1	0	1.000	3.77	18	0	0	14.1	7	6	20	0	1	0	4	0	0	0	—	1	1	1	0	0.2	.667
3 yrs.		2	5	.286	4.63	65	0	0	72	52	47	90	0	2	5	6	0	0	0		2	2	2	1	0.1	.667

DIVISIONAL PLAYOFF SERIES

Year	Team	W	L	PCT	ERA	G	GS	CG	IP	H	BB	SO	ShO	Relief W	Relief L	SV	AB	H	HR	BA	PO	A	E	DP	TC/G	FA
1996	BAL A	2	0	1.000	2.25	3	0	0	4	1	2	6	0	2	0	0	0	0	0	—	0	2	0	0	0.7	1.000

LEAGUE CHAMPIONSHIP SERIES

Year	Team	W	L	PCT	ERA	G	GS	CG	IP	H	BB	SO	ShO	Relief W	Relief L	SV	AB	H	HR	BA	PO	A	E	DP	TC/G	FA
1996	BAL A	0	0	—	7.71	3	0	0	2.1	3	3	2	0	0	0	1	0	0	0	—	0	0	0	0	0.0	.000

Erik Bennett

BENNETT, ERIK HANS
B. Sept. 13, 1968, Yreka, Calif.

BR TR 6'2" 205 lbs.

Year	Team	W	L	PCT	ERA	G	GS	CG	IP	H	BB	SO	ShO	Relief W	Relief L	SV	AB	H	HR	BA	PO	A	E	DP	TC/G	FA
1995	CAL A	0	0	—	0.00	1	0	0	0	0	0	0	0	0	0	0	0	0	0	—	0	0	0	0	0.0	.000
1996	MIN A	2	0	1.000	7.90	24	0	0	27.1	33	16	13	0	2	0	1	0	0	0	—	2	5	0	0	0.3	1.000
2 yrs.		2	0	1.000	7.81	25	0	0	27.2	33	16	13	0	2	0	1					2	5	0	0	0.3	1.000

Jason Bere

BERE, JASON PHILLIP
B. May 26, 1971, Cambridge, Mass.

BR TR 6'3" 185 lbs.

Year	Team	W	L	PCT	ERA	G	GS	CG	IP	H	BB	SO	ShO	Relief W	Relief L	SV	AB	H	HR	BA	PO	A	E	DP	TC/G	FA
1993	CHI A	12	5	.706	3.47	24	24	1	142.2	109	81	129	0	0	0	0	0	0	0	—	11	14	2	1	1.1	.926
1994		12	2	.857	3.81	24	24	0	141.2	119	80	127	0	0	0	0	0	0	0	—	9	12	2	1	1.0	.913
1995		8	15	.348	7.19	27	27	1	137.2	151	106	110	0	0	0	0	0	0	0	—	10	19	0	1	1.1	1.000
1996		0	1	.000	10.26	5	5	0	16.2	26	18	19	0	0	0	0	0	0	0	—	1	3	1	0	1.0	.800
4 yrs.		32	23	.582	5.01	80	80	2	438.2	405	285	385	0	0	0	0	0	0	0		31	48	5	3	1.0	.940

LEAGUE CHAMPIONSHIP SERIES

Year	Team	W	L	PCT	ERA	G	GS	CG	IP	H	BB	SO	ShO	Relief W	Relief L	SV	AB	H	HR	BA	PO	A	E	DP	TC/G	FA
1993	CHI A	0	0	—	11.57	1	1	0	2.1	5	2	3	0	0	0	0	0	0	0	—	0	0	0	0	0.0	.000

Sean Bergman

BERGMAN, SEAN FREDERICK
B. Apr. 11, 1970, Joliet, Ill.

BR TR 6'4" 205 lbs.

Year	Team	W	L	PCT	ERA	G	GS	CG	IP	H	BB	SO	ShO	Relief W	Relief L	SV	AB	H	HR	BA	PO	A	E	DP	TC/G	FA
1993	DET A	1	4	.200	5.67	9	6	1	39.2	47	23	19	0	1	0	0	0	0	0	—	3	6	0	1	1.0	1.000
1994		2	1	.667	5.60	3	3	0	17.2	22	7	12	0	0	0	0	0	0	0	—	2	1	0	0	1.0	1.000
1995		7	10	.412	5.12	28	28	1	135.1	169	67	86	0	0	0	0	0	0	0	—	9	15	3	0	1.0	.889
1996	SD N	6	8	.429	4.37	41	14	1	113.1	119	33	85	0	3	1	0	30	3	1	.100	11	19	0	0	0.7	1.000
4 yrs.		16	23	.410	4.94	81	51	2	306	357	130	202	1	4	1	0	30	3	1	.100	25	41	3	1	0.9	.957

Year	Team	W	L	PCT	ERA	G	GS	CG	IP	H	BB	SO	ShO	Relief Pitching W	L	SV	Batting AB	H	HR	BA	PO	A	E	DP	TC/G	FA

Mike Bertotti

BERTOTTI, MICHAEL DAVID
B. Jan. 18, 1970, Jersey City, N. J.
BL TL 6'1" 185 lbs.

Year	Team	W	L	PCT	ERA	G	GS	CG	IP	H	BB	SO	ShO	W	L	SV	AB	H	HR	BA	PO	A	E	DP	TC/G	FA
1995	CHI A	1	1	.500	12.56	4	4	0	14.1	23	11	15	0	0	0	0	0	0	0	—	0	0	0	0	0.0	.000
1996		2	0	1.000	5.14	15	2	0	28	28	20	19	0	1	0	0	0	0	0	—	0	6	0	0	0.4	1.000
	2 yrs.	3	1	.750	7.65	19	6	0	42.1	51	31	34	0	1	0	0	0	0	0	—	0	6	0	0	0.3	1.000

Andres Berumen

BERUMEN, ANDRES
B. Apr. 5, 1971, Tijuana, Mexico
BR TR 6'2" 210 lbs.

Year	Team	W	L	PCT	ERA	G	GS	CG	IP	H	BB	SO	ShO	W	L	SV	AB	H	HR	BA	PO	A	E	DP	TC/G	FA
1995	SD N	2	3	.400	5.68	37	0	0	44.1	37	36	42	0	2	3	1	1	0	0	.000	4	1	1	0	0.2	.833
1996		0	0	—	5.40	3	0	0	3.1	3	2	4	0	0	0	0	0	0	0	—	0	0	0	0	0.0	.000
	2 yrs.	2	3	.400	5.66	40	0	0	47.2	40	38	46	0	2	3	1	1	0	0	.000	4	1	1	0	0.2	.833

Lou Bevil

BEVIL, LOUIS EUGENE
Born Louis Eugene Bevilacqua.
B. Nov. 27, 1922, Nelson, Ill. D. Feb. 1, 1973, Dixon, Ill.
BB TR 5'11½" 190 lbs.

Year	Team	W	L	PCT	ERA	G	GS	CG	IP	H	BB	SO	ShO	W	L	SV	AB	H	HR	BA	PO	A	E	DP	TC/G	FA
1942	WAS A	0	1	.000	6.52	4	1	0	9.2	9	11	2	0	0	0	0	3	0	0	.000	0	1	0	0	0.3	1.000

Mike Bielecki

BIELECKI, MICHAEL JOSEPH
B. July 31, 1959, Baltimore, Md.
BR TR 6'3" 195 lbs.

Year	Team	W	L	PCT	ERA	G	GS	CG	IP	H	BB	SO	ShO	W	L	SV	AB	H	HR	BA	PO	A	E	DP	TC/G	FA
1984	PIT N	0	0	—	0.00	4	0	0	4.1	4	4	1	0	0	0	0	0	0	0	—	0	1	0	0	0.3	1.000
1985		2	3	.400	4.53	12	7	0	45.2	45	31	22	0	0	0	0	10	0	0	.000	5	11	0	1	1.3	1.000
1986		6	11	.353	4.66	31	27	0	148.2	149	83	83	0	0	0	0	48	3	0	.063	17	16	1	1	1.1	.971
1987		2	3	.400	4.73	8	8	2	45.2	43	12	25	0	0	0	0	16	1	0	.063	6	5	1	0	1.5	.917
1988	CHI N	2	2	.500	3.35	19	5	0	48.1	55	16	33	0	1	0	0	10	1	0	.100	4	5	0	0	0.5	1.000
1989		18	7	.720	3.14	33	33	4	212.1	187	81	147	3	0	0	0	70	3	0	.043	18	21	1	0	1.2	.975
1990		8	11	.421	4.93	36	29	0	168	188	70	103	0	0	0	1	43	7	0	.163	17	33	3	2	1.5	.943
1991	2 teams	CHI N	(39G 13–11)		ATL N	(2G 0–0)																				
"	total	13	11	.542	4.46	41	25	0	173.2	171	56	75	0	3	3	0	46	3	0	.065	22	24	0	3	1.1	1.000
1992	ATL N	2	4	.333	2.57	19	14	1	80.2	77	27	62	1	0	0	0	24	3	0	.125	5	14	0	0	1.0	1.000
1993	CLE A	4	5	.444	5.90	13	13	0	68.2	90	23	38	0	0	0	0	0	0	0	—	5	11	0	1	1.2	1.000
1994	ATL N	2	0	1.000	4.00	19	1	0	27	28	12	18	0	2	0	0	3	0	0	.000	3	4	0	1	0.4	1.000
1995	CAL A	4	6	.400	5.97	22	11	0	75.1	80	31	45	0	0	0	0	0	0	0	—	6	7	2	0	0.7	.867
1996	ATL N	4	3	.571	2.63	40	5	0	75.1	63	33	71	0	3	2	2	10	1	0	.100	3	14	0	0	0.4	1.000
	13 yrs.	67	66	.504	4.19	297	178	7	1173.2	1180	475	723	4	10	5	3	280	22	0	.079	111	166	8	8	1.0	.972

DIVISIONAL PLAYOFF SERIES

Year	Team	W	L	PCT	ERA	G	GS	CG	IP	H	BB	SO	ShO	W	L	SV	AB	H	HR	BA	PO	A	E	DP	TC/G	FA
1996	ATL N	0	0	—	0.00	1	0	0	0.2	0	1	1	0	0	0	0	0	0	0	—	0	0	0	0	0.0	.000

LEAGUE CHAMPIONSHIP SERIES

Year	Team	W	L	PCT	ERA	G	GS	CG	IP	H	BB	SO	ShO	W	L	SV	AB	H	HR	BA	PO	A	E	DP	TC/G	FA
1989	CHI N	0	1	.000	3.65	2	2	0	12.1	7	6	11	0	0	0	0	5	1	0	.200	1	2	0	0	1.5	1.000
1996	ATL N	0	0	—	0.00	3	0	0	3	0	1	5	0	0	0	0	0	0	0	—	0	0	0	0	0.0	.000
	2 yrs.	0	1	.000	2.93	5	2	0	15.1	7	7	16	0	0	0	0	5	1	0	.200	1	2	0	0	0.6	1.000

WORLD SERIES

Year	Team	W	L	PCT	ERA	G	GS	CG	IP	H	BB	SO	ShO	W	L	SV	AB	H	HR	BA	PO	A	E	DP	TC/G	FA
1996	ATL N	0	0	—	0.00	2	0	0	3	0	3	6	0	0	0	0	1	0	0	.000	1	0	0	0	0.5	1.000

Willie Blair

BLAIR, WILLIAM ALLEN
B. Dec. 18, 1965, Paintsville, Ky.
BR TR 6'1" 185 lbs.

Year	Team	W	L	PCT	ERA	G	GS	CG	IP	H	BB	SO	ShO	W	L	SV	AB	H	HR	BA	PO	A	E	DP	TC/G	FA
1990	TOR A	3	5	.375	4.06	27	6	0	68.2	66	28	43	0	3	2	0	0	0	0	—	3	6	0	0	0.3	1.000
1991	CLE A	2	3	.400	6.75	11	5	0	36	58	10	13	0	1	0	0	0	0	0	—	2	5	0	1	0.6	1.000
1992	HOU N	5	7	.417	4.00	29	8	0	78.2	74	25	48	0	4	2	0	17	1	0	.059	4	7	2	0	0.4	.846
1993	CLR N	6	10	.375	4.75	46	18	1	146	184	42	84	0	2	0	0	36	4	0	.111	9	16	0	0	0.5	1.000
1994		0	5	.000	5.79	47	1	0	77.2	98	39	68	0	0	4	3	6	0	0	.000	3	7	1	0	0.2	.909
1995	SD N	7	5	.583	4.34	40	12	0	114	112	45	83	0	3	1	0	24	0	0	.000	6	13	2	1	0.5	.905
1996		2	6	.250	4.60	60	0	0	88	80	29	67	0	2	6	1	3	0	0	.000	6	6	2	0	0.2	.857
	7 yrs.	25	41	.379	4.73	260	50	1	609	672	218	406	0	14	16	4	86	5	0	.058	33	60	7	2	0.4	.930

DIVISIONAL PLAYOFF SERIES

Year	Team	W	L	PCT	ERA	G	GS	CG	IP	H	BB	SO	ShO	W	L	SV	AB	H	HR	BA	PO	A	E	DP	TC/G	FA
1996	SD N	0	0	—	0.00	1	0	0	2	1	2	3	0	0	0	0	0	0	0	—	0	0	0	0	0.0	.000

Ron Blazier

BLAZIER, RONALD PATRICK
B. Jul. 30, 1971, Altoona, Pa.
BR TR 6'6" 215 lbs.

Year	Team	W	L	PCT	ERA	G	GS	CG	IP	H	BB	SO	ShO	W	L	SV	AB	H	HR	BA	PO	A	E	DP	TC/G	FA
1996	PHI N	3	1	.750	5.87	27	0	0	38.1	49	10	25	0	3	1	0	1	1	0	1.000	2	3	0	0	0.2	1.000

Jaime Bluma

BLUMA, JAMES ANDREW
B. May 18, 1972, Beaufort, S. C.
BR TR 5'11" 195 lbs.

Year	Team	W	L	PCT	ERA	G	GS	CG	IP	H	BB	SO	ShO	W	L	SV	AB	H	HR	BA	PO	A	E	DP	TC/G	FA
1996	KC A	0	0	—	3.60	17	0	0	20	18	4	14	0	0	0	0	0	0	0	—	1	6	0	1	0.4	1.000

Doug Bochtler

BOCHTLER, DOUGLAS EUGENE
B. July 5, 1970, West Palm Beach, Fla.
BR TR 6'3" 205 lbs.

Year	Team	W	L	PCT	ERA	G	GS	CG	IP	H	BB	SO	ShO	W	L	SV	AB	H	HR	BA	PO	A	E	DP	TC/G	FA
1995	SD N	4	4	.500	3.57	34	0	0	45.1	38	19	45	0	4	4	1	2	0	0	.000	1	7	0	1	0.2	1.000
1996		2	4	.333	3.02	63	0	0	65.2	45	39	68	0	2	4	3	0	0	0	—	2	3	0	0	0.1	1.000
	2 yrs.	6	8	.429	3.24	97	0	0	111	83	58	113	0	6	8	4	2	0	0	.000	3	10	0	1	0.1	1.000

DIVISIONAL PLAYOFF SERIES

Year	Team	W	L	PCT	ERA	G	GS	CG	IP	H	BB	SO	ShO	W	L	SV	AB	H	HR	BA	PO	A	E	DP	TC/G	FA
1996	SD N	0	1	.000	27.00	1	0	0	0.1	0	2	0	0	0	1	0	0	0	0	—	0	0	0	0	0.0	.000

Year	Team	W	L	PCT	ERA	G	GS	CG	IP	H	BB	SO	ShO	W	L	SV	AB	H	HR	BA	PO	A	E	DP	TC/G	FA
														Relief Pitching			Batting									

Brian Boehringer
BOEHRINGER, BRIAN EDWARD
B. Jan. 8, 1969, St. Louis, Mo. BB TR 6'2" 180 lbs.

Year	Team	W	L	PCT	ERA	G	GS	CG	IP	H	BB	SO	ShO	W	L	SV	AB	H	HR	BA	PO	A	E	DP	TC/G	FA
1995	NY A	0	3	.000	13.75	7	3	0	17.2	24	22	10	0	0	0	0	0	0	0	—	1	0	0	0	0.1	1.000
1996		2	4	.333	5.44	15	3	0	46.1	46	21	37	0	2	2	0	0	0	0		2	4	0	0	0.4	1.000
2 yrs.		2	7	.222	7.73	22	6	0	64	70	43	47	0	2	2	0					3	4	0	0	0.3	1.000

DIVISIONAL PLAYOFF SERIES
| 1996 | NY A | 1 | 0 | 1.000 | 6.75 | 2 | 0 | 0 | 1.1 | 3 | 2 | 0 | 0 | 1 | 0 | 0 | 0 | 0 | 0 | — | 0 | 0 | 0 | 0 | 0.0 | .000 |

WORLD SERIES
| 1996 | NY A | 0 | 0 | — | 5.40 | 2 | 0 | 0 | 5 | 5 | 0 | 5 | 0 | 0 | 0 | 0 | 0 | 0 | 0 | — | 0 | 0 | 0 | 0 | 0.0 | .000 |

Joe Boever
BOEVER, JOSEPH MARTIN
B. Oct. 4, 1960, Kirkwood, Mo. BR TR 6'1" 200 lbs.

Year	Team	W	L	PCT	ERA	G	GS	CG	IP	H	BB	SO	ShO	W	L	SV	AB	H	HR	BA	PO	A	E	DP	TC/G	FA
1985	STL N	0	0	—	4.41	13	0	0	16.1	17	4	20	0	0	0	0	0	0	0	0.0	0	0	0	0	0.0	.000
1986		0	1	.000	1.66	11	0	0	21.2	19	11	8	0	0	1	0	2	1	0	.500	1	2	0	0	0.3	1.000
1987	ATL N	1	0	1.000	7.36	14	0	0	18.1	29	12	18	0	1	0	0	0	0	0	—	0	2	0	0	0.1	1.000
1988		0	2	.000	1.77	16	0	0	20.1	12	1	7	0	0	2	1	0	0	0	—	2	3	0	1	0.3	1.000
1989		4	11	.267	3.94	66	0	0	82.1	78	34	68	0	4	11	21	1	0	0	.000	7	15	0	0	0.3	1.000
1990	2 teams	ATL N	(33G 1-3)		PHI N	(34G 2-3)																				
"	total	3	6	.333	3.36	67	0	0	88.1	77	51	75	0	3	6	14	3	0	0	.000	6	7	2	1	0.2	.867
1991	PHI N	3	5	.375	3.84	68	0	0	98.1	90	54	89	0	3	5	0	3	1	0	.333	1	10	0	0	0.2	1.000
1992	HOU N	3	6	.333	2.51	81	0	0	111.1	103	45	67	0	3	6	2	7	0	0	.000	4	19	2	2	0.3	.920
1993	2 teams	OAK A	(42G 4-2)		DET A	(19G 2-1)																				
"	total	6	3	.667	3.61	61	0	0	102.1	101	44	63	0	6	3	3	0	0	0		9	12	1	1	0.4	.955
1994	DET A	9	2	.818	3.98	46	0	0	81.1	80	37	49	0	9	2	3	0	0	0		10	13	1	1	0.5	.958
1995		5	7	.417	6.39	60	0	0	98.2	128	44	71	0	5	7	3	0	0	0	—	4	10	1	0	0.3	.933
1996	PIT N	0	2	.000	5.40	13	0	0	15	17	6	6	0	0	2	1	2	0	0	.000	2	1	0	0	0.2	1.000
12 yrs.		34	45	.430	3.93	516	0	0	754.1	751	343	541	0	34	45	49	17	2	0	.118	46	94	7	6	0.3	.952

Brian Bohanon
BOHANON, BRIAN EDWARD
B. Aug. 1, 1968, Denton, Tex. BL TL 6'2" 210 lbs.

Year	Team	W	L	PCT	ERA	G	GS	CG	IP	H	BB	SO	ShO	W	L	SV	AB	H	HR	BA	PO	A	E	DP	TC/G	FA
1990	TEX A	0	3	.000	6.62	11	6	0	34	40	18	15	0	0	0	0	0	0	0	—	1	10	0	2	1.0	1.000
1991		4	3	.571	4.84	11	11	1	61.1	66	23	34	0	0	0	0	0	0	0	—	3	6	0	1	0.8	1.000
1992		1	1	.500	6.31	18	7	0	45.2	57	25	29	0	0	0	0	0	0	0	—	5	3	1	0	0.5	.889
1993		4	4	.500	4.76	36	8	0	92.2	107	46	45	0	3	1	0	0	0	0	—	5	18	0	3	0.6	1.000
1994		2	2	.500	7.23	11	5	0	37.1	51	8	26	0	0	0	0	0	0	0	—	3	6	0	0	0.8	1.000
1995	DET A	1	1	.500	5.54	52	10	0	105.2	121	41	63	0	1	0	1	0	0	0	—	7	13	0	0	0.4	1.000
1996	TOR A	0	1	.000	7.77	20	0	0	22	27	19	17	0	0	1	1	0	0	0	—	2	2	0	0	0.2	1.000
7 yrs.		12	15	.444	5.71	159	47	1	398.2	469	180	229	0	4	2	2	0	0	0		26	58	1	6	0.5	.988

Ricky Bones
BONES, RICARDO
B. Apr. 7, 1969, Salinas, Puerto Rico BR TR 5'10" 175 lbs.

Year	Team	W	L	PCT	ERA	G	GS	CG	IP	H	BB	SO	ShO	W	L	SV	AB	H	HR	BA	PO	A	E	DP	TC/G	FA
1991	SD N	4	6	.400	4.83	11	11	0	54	57	18	31	0	0	0	0	13	1	0	.077	1	2	0	0	0.3	1.000
1992	MIL A	9	10	.474	4.57	31	28	0	163.1	169	48	65	0	0	0	0	0	0	0	—	17	13	2	1	1.0	.938
1993		11	11	.500	4.86	32	31	3	203.2	222	63	63	0	0	0	0	0	0	0	—	26	22	1	2	1.5	.980
1994		10	9	.526	3.43	24	24	4	170.2	166	45	57	1	0	0	0	0	0	0	—	8	14	1	2	1.0	.957
1995		10	12	.455	4.63	32	31	3	200.1	218	83	77	0	0	0	0	0	0	0	—	19	32	0	7	1.6	1.000
1996	2 teams	MIL A	(32G 7-14)		NY A	(4G 0-0)																				
"	total	7	14	.333	6.22	36	24	0	152	184	68	63	0	0	1	0	0	0	0	—	11	15	1	4	0.8	.963
6 yrs.		51	62	.451	4.72	166	149	10	944	1016	325	356	1	0	1	0	13	1	0	.077	82	98	5	16	1.1	.973

Pedro Borbon
BORBON, PEDRO FELIX
Born Pedro Felix Borbon (Marte).
Son of Pedro Borbon.
B. Nov. 15, 1967, Mao, Dominican Republic BR TL 6'1" 205 lbs.

Year	Team	W	L	PCT	ERA	G	GS	CG	IP	H	BB	SO	ShO	W	L	SV	AB	H	HR	BA	PO	A	E	DP	TC/G	FA
1992	ATL N	0	1	.000	6.75	2	0	0	1.1	2	1	1	0	0	1	0	0	0	0	—	0	0	0	0	0.0	.000
1993		0	0	—	21.60	3	0	0	1.2	3	3	2	0	0	0	0	0	0	0	—	0	0	0	0	0.0	.000
1995		2	2	.500	3.09	41	0	0	32	29	17	33	0	2	2	2	1	0	0	.000	1	6	0	1	0.2	1.000
1996		3	0	1.000	2.75	43	0	0	36	26	7	31	0	3	0	1	1	1	0	1.000	4	5	1	1	0.2	.900
4 yrs.		5	3	.625	3.42	89	0	0	71	60	28	67	0	5	3	3	2	1	0	.500	5	11	1	2	0.2	.941

DIVISIONAL PLAYOFF SERIES
| 1995 | ATL N | 0 | 0 | — | 0.00 | 1 | 0 | 0 | 1 | 1 | 0 | 3 | 0 | 0 | 0 | 0 | 0 | 0 | 0 | — | 0 | 0 | 0 | 0 | 0.0 | .000 |

WORLD SERIES
| 1995 | ATL N | 0 | 0 | — | 0.00 | 1 | 0 | 0 | 1 | 0 | 1 | 2 | 0 | 0 | 0 | 1 | 0 | 0 | 0 | — | 0 | 0 | 0 | 0 | 0.0 | .000 |

Toby Borland
BORLAND, TOBY SHAWN
B. May 29, 1969, Ruston, La. BR TR 6'6" 186 lbs.

Year	Team	W	L	PCT	ERA	G	GS	CG	IP	H	BB	SO	ShO	W	L	SV	AB	H	HR	BA	PO	A	E	DP	TC/G	FA
1994	PHI N	1	0	1.000	2.36	24	0	0	34.1	31	14	26	0	1	0	1	3	0	0	.000	5	1	0	0	0.3	1.000
1995		1	3	.250	3.77	50	0	0	74	81	37	59	0	1	3	6	5	1	0	.200	2	10	2	0	0.3	.857
1996		7	3	.700	4.07	69	0	0	90.2	83	43	76	0	7	3	0	4	0	0		4	7	0	1	0.2	1.000
3 yrs.		9	6	.600	3.66	143	0	0	199	195	94	161	0	9	6	7	12	1	0	.083	11	18	2	1	0.2	.935

Joe Borowski

BOROWSKI, JOSEPH THOMAS
B. May 4, 1971, Bayonne, N.J.   BR TR 6'2" 225 lbs.

Year	Team	W	L	PCT	ERA	G	GS	CG	IP	H	BB	SO	ShO	Relief Pitching W	L	SV	Batting AB	H	HR	BA	PO	A	E	DP	TC/G	FA
1995	BAL A	0	0	—	1.23	6	0	0	7.1	5	4	3	0	0	0	0	0	0	0		1	2	0	0	0.5	1.000
1996	ATL N	2	4	.333	4.85	22	0	0	26	33	13	15	0	2	4	0	2	0	0	.000	0	12	0	1	0.5	1.000
2 yrs.		2	4	.333	4.05	28	0	0	33.1	38	17	18	0	2	4	0	2	0	0	.000	1	14	0	1	0.5	1.000

Chris Bosio

BOSIO, CHRISTOPHER LOUIS
B. Apr. 3, 1963, Carmichael, Calif.   BR TR 6'3" 220 lbs.

Year	Team	W	L	PCT	ERA	G	GS	CG	IP	H	BB	SO	ShO	Relief Pitching W	L	SV	Batting AB	H	HR	BA	PO	A	E	DP	TC/G	FA
1986	MIL A	0	4	.000	7.01	10	4	0	34.2	41	13	29	0	0	1	0	0	0	0	—	4	5	1	1	1.0	.900
1987		11	8	.579	5.24	46	19	2	170	187	50	150	1	3	1	2	0	0	0	—	14	24	4	5	0.9	.905
1988		7	15	.318	3.36	38	22	9	182	190	38	84	1	1	3	6	0	0	0	—	22	33	3	7	1.5	.948
1989		15	10	.600	2.95	33	33	8	234.2	225	48	173	2	0	0	0	0	0	0	—	16	35	2	2	1.6	.962
1990		4	9	.308	4.00	20	20	4	132.2	131	38	76	1	0	0	0	0	0	0	—	12	24	1	2	1.9	.973
1991		14	10	.583	3.25	32	32	5	204.2	187	58	117	1	0	0	0	0	0	0	—	20	21	2	4	1.3	.953
1992		16	6	.727	3.62	33	33	4	231.1	223	44	120	0	0	0	0	0	0	0	—	20	26	0	5	1.4	1.000
1993	SEA A	9	9	.500	3.45	29	24	3	164.1	138	59	119	1	1	0	1	0	0	0	—	13	21	1	2	1.2	.971
1994		4	10	.286	4.32	19	19	4	125	137	40	67	0	0	0	0	0	0	0	—	11	24	0	3	1.8	1.000
1995		10	8	.556	4.92	31	31	0	170	211	69	85	0	0	0	0	0	0	0	—	12	23	1	3	1.2	.972
1996		4	4	.500	5.93	18	9	0	60.2	72	24	39	0	1	1	0	0	0	0	—	3	10	0	1	0.7	1.000
11 yrs.		94	93	.503	3.96	309	246	39	1710	1742	481	1059	9	6	6	9	0	0	0		147	246	15	35	1.3	.963

DIVISIONAL PLAYOFF SERIES

Year	Team	W	L	PCT	ERA	G	GS	CG	IP	H	BB	SO	ShO	Relief Pitching W	L	SV	Batting AB	H	HR	BA	PO	A	E	DP	TC/G	FA
1995	SEA A	0	0	—	10.57	2	2	0	7.2	10	4	2	0	0	0	0	0	0	0	—	1	0	0	0	0.5	1.000

LEAGUE CHAMPIONSHIP SERIES

Year	Team	W	L	PCT	ERA	G	GS	CG	IP	H	BB	SO	ShO	Relief Pitching W	L	SV	Batting AB	H	HR	BA	PO	A	E	DP	TC/G	FA
1995	SEA A	0	1	.000	3.38	1	1	0	5.1	7	2	3	0	0	0	0	0	0	0	—	0	2	0	0	2.0	1.000

Shawn Boskie

BOSKIE, SHAWN KEALOHA
B. May 28, 1967, Hawthorne, Nev.   BR TR 6'3" 205 lbs.

Year	Team	W	L	PCT	ERA	G	GS	CG	IP	H	BB	SO	ShO	Relief Pitching W	L	SV	Batting AB	H	HR	BA	PO	A	E	DP	TC/G	FA
1990	CHI N	5	6	.455	3.69	15	15	1	97.2	99	31	49	0	0	0	0	36	8	0	.222	12	12	0	2	1.6	1.000
1991		4	9	.308	5.23	28	20	0	129	150	52	62	0	1	0	0	41	7	1	.171	14	21	2	0	1.3	.946
1992		5	11	.313	5.01	23	18	0	91.2	96	36	39	0	2	1	0	27	5	0	.185	8	21	1	2	1.3	.967
1993		5	3	.625	3.43	39	2	0	65.2	63	21	39	0	4	2	0	11	3	0	.273	3	5	1	0	0.2	.889
1994	3 teams	CHI N (2G 0-0)						PHI N (18G 4-6)					SEA A (2G 0-1)													
"	total	4	7	.364	5.06	22	15	1	90.2	92	30	61	0	0	0	0	26	3	0	.115	8	13	1	2	1.0	.955
1995	CAL A	7	7	.500	5.64	20	20	1	111.2	127	25	51	0	0	0	0	0	0	0	—	4	19	0	1	1.1	1.000
1996		12	11	.522	5.32	37	28	1	189.1	226	67	133	0	3	1	0	0	0	0	—	7	29	1	1	1.0	.973
7 yrs.		42	54	.438	4.92	184	118	4	775.2	853	262	434	0	10	4	0	141	26	1	.184	56	120	6	8	1.0	.967

Ricky Bottalico

BOTTALICO, RICKY PAUL
B. Aug. 26, 1969, New Britain, Conn.   BL TR 6'1" 200 lbs.

Year	Team	W	L	PCT	ERA	G	GS	CG	IP	H	BB	SO	ShO	Relief Pitching W	L	SV	Batting AB	H	HR	BA	PO	A	E	DP	TC/G	FA
1994	PHI N	0	0	—	0.00	3	0	0	3	3	1	3	0	0	0	0	0	0	0	—	0	0	0	0	0.0	.000
1995		5	3	.625	2.46	62	0	0	87.2	56	42	87	0	5	3	1	5	0	0	.000	6	7	0	1	0.2	1.000
1996		4	5	.444	3.19	61	0	0	67.2	47	23	74	0	4	5	34	3	1	0	.333	1	5	0	1	0.1	1.000
3 yrs.		9	8	.529	2.73	126	0	0	158.1	100	66	164	0	9	8	35	8	1	0	.125	7	12	0	2	0.2	1.000

Kent Bottenfield

BOTTENFIELD, KENT DENNIS
B. Nov. 14, 1968, Portland, Ore.   BB TR 6'3" 225 lbs.

Year	Team	W	L	PCT	ERA	G	GS	CG	IP	H	BB	SO	ShO	Relief Pitching W	L	SV	Batting AB	H	HR	BA	PO	A	E	DP	TC/G	FA
1992	MON N	1	2	.333	2.23	10	4	0	32.1	26	11	14	0	0	1	1	8	3	0	.375	2	2	0	0	0.4	1.000
1993	2 teams	MON N (23G 2-5)						CLR N (14G 3-5)																		
"	total	5	10	.333	5.07	37	25	1	159.2	179	71	63	0	0	0	0	50	11	0	.220	9	32	2	5	1.2	.953
1994	2 teams	CLR N (15G 3-1)						SF N (1G 0-0)																		
"	total	3	1	.750	6.15	16	6	0	26.1	33	10	15	0	3	0	0	1	0	0	.000	1	2	1	0	0.3	.750
1996	CHI N	3	5	.375	2.63	48	0	0	61.2	59	19	33	0	3	5	1	2	1	0	.500	6	12	0	2	0.4	1.000
4 yrs.		12	18	.400	4.31	111	30	1	280	297	111	125	0	6	7	3	61	15	0	.246	18	48	3	7	0.6	.957

Steve Bourgeois

BOURGEOIS, STEVEN JAMES
B. Aug. 4, 1972, Lutcher, La.   BR TR 6'1" 220 lbs.

Year	Team	W	L	PCT	ERA	G	GS	CG	IP	H	BB	SO	ShO	Relief Pitching W	L	SV	Batting AB	H	HR	BA	PO	A	E	DP	TC/G	FA
1996	SF N	1	3	.250	6.30	15	5	0	40	60	21	17	0	1	0	0	11	3	0	.273	4	8	0	0	0.8	1.000

Marshall Boze

BOZE, MARSHALL WAYNE
B. May 23, 1971, San Manuel, Ariz.   BR TR 6'1" 214 lbs.

Year	Team	W	L	PCT	ERA	G	GS	CG	IP	H	BB	SO	ShO	Relief Pitching W	L	SV	Batting AB	H	HR	BA	PO	A	E	DP	TC/G	FA
1996	MIL A	0	2	.000	7.79	25	0	0	32.1	47	25	19	0	0	2	1	0	0	0	—	8	4	0	0	0.5	1.000

Mark Brandenburg

BRANDENBURG, MARK CLAY
B. July 14, 1970, Houston, Tex.   BR TR 6' 180 lbs.

Year	Team	W	L	PCT	ERA	G	GS	CG	IP	H	BB	SO	ShO	Relief Pitching W	L	SV	Batting AB	H	HR	BA	PO	A	E	DP	TC/G	FA
1995	TEX A	0	1	.000	5.93	11	0	0	27.1	36	7	21	0	0	1	0	0	0	0	—	1	2	0	0	0.3	1.000
1996	2 teams	TEX A (26G 1-3)						BOS A (29G 4-2)																		
"	total	5	5	.500	3.43	55	0	0	76	76	33	66	0	5	5	0	0	0	0	—	2	7	0	0	0.2	1.000
2 yrs.		5	6	.455	4.09	66	0	0	103.1	112	40	87	0	5	6	0					3	9	0	0	0.2	1.000

Jeff Brantley

BRANTLEY, JEFFREY HOKE
B. Sept. 5, 1963, Florence, Ala.   BR TR 5'11" 180 lbs.

Year	Team	W	L	PCT	ERA	G	GS	CG	IP	H	BB	SO	ShO	Relief Pitching W	L	SV	Batting AB	H	HR	BA	PO	A	E	DP	TC/G	FA
1988	SF N	0	1	.000	5.66	9	1	0	20.2	22	6	11	0	0	0	1	2	1	0	.500	0	7	0	0	0.8	1.000
1989		7	1	.875	4.07	59	1	0	97.1	101	37	69	0	7	0	0	12	1	0	.083	3	16	0	0	0.3	1.000

Year	Team	W	L	PCT	ERA	G	GS	CG	IP	H	BB	SO	ShO	Relief Pitching W	L	SV	Batting AB	H	HR	BA	PO	A	E	DP	TC/G	FA

Jeff Brantley *continued*

Year	Team	W	L	PCT	ERA	G	GS	CG	IP	H	BB	SO	ShO	W	L	SV	AB	H	HR	BA	PO	A	E	DP	TC/G	FA
1991		5	2	.714	2.45	67	0	0	95.1	78	52	81	0	5	2	15	3	0	0	.000	4	9	0	1	0.2	1.000
1992		7	7	.500	2.95	56	4	0	91.2	67	45	86	0	4	7	7	9	1	0	.111	4	9	0	0	0.2	1.000
1993		5	6	.455	4.28	53	12	0	113.2	112	46	76	0	2	1	0	28	3	0	.107	6	9	2	0	0.3	.882
1994	CIN N	6	6	.500	2.48	50	0	0	65.1	46	28	63	0	6	6	15	3	0	0	.000	2	10	0	1	0.2	1.000
1995		3	2	.600	2.82	56	0	0	70.1	53	20	62	0	3	2	28	3	0	0	.000	7	4	0	1	0.2	1.000
1996		1	2	.333	2.41	66	0	0	71	54	28	76	0	1	2	**44**	1	0	0	.000	7	4	0	0	0.2	1.000
9 yrs.		39	30	.565	3.05	471	18	0	712	610	295	585	0	33	23	129	68	8	0	.118	39	79	3	4	0.3	.975

DIVISIONAL PLAYOFF SERIES

Year	Team	W	L	PCT	ERA	G	GS	CG	IP	H	BB	SO	ShO	W	L	SV	AB	H	HR	BA	PO	A	E	DP	TC/G	FA
1995	CIN N	0	0	—	6.00	3	0	0	3	5	0	2	0	0	0	1	0	0	0	—	0	0	0	0	0.0	.000

LEAGUE CHAMPIONSHIP SERIES

Year	Team	W	L	PCT	ERA	G	GS	CG	IP	H	BB	SO	ShO	W	L	SV	AB	H	HR	BA	PO	A	E	DP	TC/G	FA
1989	SF N	0	0	—	0.00	3	0	0	5	1	2	3	0	0	0	0	0	0	0	—	0	0	0	0	0.0	.000
1995	CIN N	0	0	—	0.00	2	0	0	2.2	0	2	1	0	0	0	0	0	0	0	—	2	0	0	0	1.0	1.000
2 yrs.		0	0		0.00	5	0	0	7.2	1	4	4	0	0	0	0	0	0	0		2	0	0	0	0.4	1.000

WORLD SERIES

Year	Team	W	L	PCT	ERA	G	GS	CG	IP	H	BB	SO	ShO	W	L	SV	AB	H	HR	BA	PO	A	E	DP	TC/G	FA
1989	SF N	0	0	—	4.15	3	0	0	4.1	5	3	1	0	0	0	0	0	0	0	—	1	0	0	0	0.3	1.000

Billy Brewer

BREWER, WILLIAM ROBERT
B. Apr. 15, 1968, Fort Worth, Tex.   BL TL 6'1" 175 lbs.

Year	Team	W	L	PCT	ERA	G	GS	CG	IP	H	BB	SO	ShO	W	L	SV	AB	H	HR	BA	PO	A	E	DP	TC/G	FA
1993	KC A	2	2	.500	3.46	46	0	0	39	31	20	28	0	2	2	0	0	0	0	—	1	4	2	0	0.2	.714
1994		4	1	.800	2.56	50	0	0	38.2	28	16	25	0	4	1	3	0	0	0	—	2	6	1	0	0.2	.889
1995		2	4	.333	5.56	48	0	0	45.1	54	20	31	0	2	4	0	0	0	0	—	3	4	0	1	0.1	1.000
1996	NY A	1	0	1.000	9.53	4	0	0	5.2	7	8	8	0	1	0	0	0	0	0	—	0	1	0	0	0.3	1.000
4 yrs.		9	7	.563	4.20	148	0	0	128.2	120	64	92	0	9	7	3	0	0	0		6	15	3	1	0.2	.875

John Briscoe

BRISCOE, JOHN ERIC
B. Sept. 22, 1967, La Grange, Ill.   BR TR 6'3" 185 lbs.

Year	Team	W	L	PCT	ERA	G	GS	CG	IP	H	BB	SO	ShO	W	L	SV	AB	H	HR	BA	PO	A	E	DP	TC/G	FA
1991	OAK A	0	0	—	7.07	11	0	0	14	12	10	9	0	0	0	0	0	0	0	—	0	1	0	0	0.1	1.000
1992		0	1	.000	6.43	7	2	0	7	12	9	4	0	0	0	0	0	0	0	—	0	1	1	0	1.0	.500
1993		1	0	1.000	8.03	17	0	0	24.2	26	26	24	0	1	0	0	0	0	0	—	1	4	0	0	0.3	1.000
1994		4	2	.667	4.01	37	0	0	49.1	31	39	45	0	4	2	1	0	0	0	—	2	2	0	1	0.1	1.000
1995		0	1	.000	8.35	16	0	0	18.1	25	21	19	0	0	1	0	0	0	0	—	2	2	0	1	0.3	1.000
1996		0	1	.000	3.76	17	0	0	26.1	18	24	14	0	0	1	1	0	0	0	—	1	2	0	1	0.2	1.000
6 yrs.		5	5	.500	5.67	100	2	0	139.2	124	129	115	0	5	4	2	0	0	0		6	12	1	3	0.2	.947

Doug Brocail

BROCAIL, DOUGLAS KEITH
B. May 16, 1967, Clearfield, Pa.   BL TR 6'5" 220 lbs.

Year	Team	W	L	PCT	ERA	G	GS	CG	IP	H	BB	SO	ShO	W	L	SV	AB	H	HR	BA	PO	A	E	DP	TC/G	FA
1992	SD N	0	0	—	6.43	3	3	0	14	17	5	15	0	0	0	0	5	1	0	.200	1	1	1	0	1.0	.667
1993		4	13	.235	4.56	24	24	0	128.1	143	42	70	0	0	0	0	33	6	0	.182	8	20	2	1	1.3	.933
1994		0	0	—	5.82	12	0	0	17	21	5	11	0	0	0	0	2	0	0	.000	1	2	1	0	0.3	.750
1995	HOU N	6	4	.600	4.19	37	7	0	77.1	87	22	39	0	4	2	1	16	4	0	.250	11	9	0	0	0.6	1.000
1996		1	5	.167	4.58	23	4	0	53	58	23	34	0	1	2	0	11	0	0	.000	6	5	0	0	0.5	1.000
5 yrs.		11	22	.333	4.63	98	38	0	289.2	326	97	169	0	5	4	1	67	11	0	.164	27	37	4	1	0.7	.941

Scott Brow

BROW, SCOTT JOHN
B. Mar. 17, 1969, Butte, Mont.   BR TR 6'3" 200 lbs.

Year	Team	W	L	PCT	ERA	G	GS	CG	IP	H	BB	SO	ShO	W	L	SV	AB	H	HR	BA	PO	A	E	DP	TC/G	FA
1993	TOR A	1	1	.500	6.00	6	3	0	18	19	10	7	0	0	0	0	0	0	0	—	3	8	0	1	1.8	1.000
1994		0	3	.000	5.90	18	0	0	29	34	19	15	0	0	3	2	0	0	0	—	1	4	0	1	0.3	1.000
1996		1	0	1.000	5.59	18	1	0	38.2	45	25	23	0	1	0	0	0	0	0	—	3	4	0	0	0.4	1.000
3 yrs.		2	4	.333	5.78	42	4	0	85.2	98	54	45	0	1	3	2	0	0	0		7	16	0	2	0.5	1.000

Kevin Brown

BROWN, JAMES KEVIN
B. Mar. 14, 1965, Milledgeville, Ga.   BR TR 6'4" 195 lbs.

Year	Team	W	L	PCT	ERA	G	GS	CG	IP	H	BB	SO	ShO	W	L	SV	AB	H	HR	BA	PO	A	E	DP	TC/G	FA
1986	TEX A	1	0	1.000	3.60	1	1	0	5	6	0	4	0	0	0	0	0	0	0	—	0	1	0	0	1.0	1.000
1988		1	1	.500	4.24	4	4	1	23.1	33	8	12	0	0	0	0	0	0	0	—	1	2	0	0	0.8	1.000
1989		12	9	.571	3.35	28	28	7	191	167	70	104	0	0	0	0	0	0	0	—	15	41	2	6	2.1	.966
1990		12	10	.545	3.60	26	26	6	180	175	60	88	2	0	0	0	1	0	0	.000	15	24	3	0	1.6	.929
1991		9	12	.429	4.40	33	33	0	210.2	233	90	96	0	0	0	0	0	0	0	—	18	32	2	3	1.6	.962
1992		21	11	.656	3.32	35	35	11	265.2	262	76	173	1	0	0	0	0	0	0	—	37	36	8	4	2.3	.901
1993		15	12	.556	3.59	34	34	12	233	228	74	142	3	0	0	0	0	0	0	—	28	42	3	2	2.1	.959
1994		7	9	.438	4.82	26	25	3	170	218	50	123	0	0	1	0	0	0	0	—	20	29	4	2	2.0	.925
1995	BAL A	10	9	.526	3.60	26	26	3	172.1	155	48	117	0	0	0	0	0	0	0	—	41	41	2	3	3.2	.976
1996	FLA N	17	11	.607	1.89	32	32	5	233	187	33	159	3	0	0	0	75	9	0	.120	29	54	1	4	2.6	.988
10 yrs.		105	84	.556	3.52	245	244	48	1684	1664	509	1018	10	0	1	0	76	9	0	.118	204	302	25	24	2.2	.953

Jim Bruske

BRUSKE, JAMES SCOTT
B. Oct. 7, 1964, East St. Louis, Ill.   BR TR 6'1" 185 lbs.

Year	Team	W	L	PCT	ERA	G	GS	CG	IP	H	BB	SO	ShO	W	L	SV	AB	H	HR	BA	PO	A	E	DP	TC/G	FA
1995	LA N	0	0	—	4.50	9	0	0	10	12	4	5	0	0	0	1	0	0	0	—	1	0	0	0	0.1	1.000
1996		0	0	—	5.68	11	0	0	12.2	17	3	12	0	0	0	0	0	0	0	—	0	2	0	0	0.2	1.000
2 yrs.		0	0		5.16	20	0	0	22.2	29	7	17	0	0	0	1	0	0	0		1	2	0	0	0.2	1.000

Year	Team	W	L	PCT	ERA	G	GS	CG	IP	H	BB	SO	ShO	Relief Pitching W	L	SV	Batting AB	H	HR	BA	PO	A	E	DP	TC/G	FA

Jim Bullinger

BULLINGER, JAMES ERIC
B. Aug. 21, 1965, New Orleans, La.   BR TR 6' 2" 185 lbs.

Year	Team	W	L	PCT	ERA	G	GS	CG	IP	H	BB	SO	ShO	W	L	SV	AB	H	HR	BA	PO	A	E	DP	TC/G	FA
1992	CHI N	2	8	.200	4.66	39	9	1	85	72	54	36	0	1	2	7	20	5	1	.250	17	17	0	2	0.9	1.000
1993		1	0	1.000	4.32	15	0	0	16.2	18	9	10	0	1	0	1	1	0	0	.000	1	1	0	0	0.1	1.000
1994		6	2	.750	3.60	33	10	1	100	87	34	72	0	2	0	2	22	3	0	.136	6	11	0	0	0.5	1.000
1995		12	8	.600	4.14	24	24	1	150	152	65	93	1	0	0	0	47	6	0	.128	20	20	0	2	1.7	1.000
1996		6	10	.375	6.54	37	20	1	129.1	144	68	90	1	1	1	1	32	8	2	.250	15	20	0	0	0.9	1.000
5 yrs.		27	28	.491	4.77	148	63	4	481	473	230	301	2	5	3	11	122	22	3	.180	59	69	0	4	0.9	1.000

Dave Burba

BURBA, DAVID ALLEN
B. July 7, 1966, Dayton, Ohio   BR TR 6' 4" 220 lbs.

Year	Team	W	L	PCT	ERA	G	GS	CG	IP	H	BB	SO	ShO	W	L	SV	AB	H	HR	BA	PO	A	E	DP	TC/G	FA
1990	SEA A	0	0	—	4.50	6	0	0	8	8	2	4	0	0	0	0	0	0	0	—	1	2	1	0	0.7	.750
1991		2	2	.500	3.68	22	2	0	36.2	34	14	16	0	1	1	1	0	0	0	—	2	4	0	0	0.3	1.000
1992	SF N	2	7	.222	4.97	23	11	0	70.2	80	31	47	0	1	1	0	15	1	0	.067	3	8	0	0	0.5	1.000
1993		10	3	.769	4.25	54	5	0	95.1	95	37	88	0	7	2	0	17	5	0	.294	7	12	1	0	0.4	.950
1994		3	6	.333	4.38	57	0	0	74	59	45	84	0	3	6	0	3	0	0	.000	3	5	0	1	0.1	1.000
1995	2 teams	SF N	(37G 4-2)		CIN N	(15G 6-2)																				
"	total	10	4	.714	3.97	52	9	1	106.2	90	51	96	1	6	2	0	15	1	0	.067	10	7	0	0	0.3	1.000
1996	CIN N	11	13	.458	3.83	34	33	0	195	179	97	148	0	0	0	0	67	7	2	.104	15	14	2	2	0.9	.935
7 yrs.		38	35	.521	4.13	248	60	1	586.1	545	277	483	1	18	12	1	117	14	2	.120	41	52	4	3	0.4	.959

DIVISIONAL PLAYOFF SERIES

Year	Team	W	L	PCT	ERA	G	GS	CG	IP	H	BB	SO	ShO	W	L	SV	AB	H	HR	BA	PO	A	E	DP	TC/G	FA
1995	CIN N	1	0	1.000	0.00	1	0	0	1	2	1	0	0	1	0	0	0	0	0	—	0	0	0	0	0.0	.000

LEAGUE CHAMPIONSHIP SERIES

Year	Team	W	L	PCT	ERA	G	GS	CG	IP	H	BB	SO	ShO	W	L	SV	AB	H	HR	BA	PO	A	E	DP	TC/G	FA
1995	CIN N	0	0	—	0.00	2	0	0	3.2	3	4	0	0	0	0	0	0	0	0	—	0	0	0	0	0.0	.000

John Burke

BURKE, JOHN C.
B. Feb. 9, 1970, Durango, Colo.   BB TR 6' 4" 220 lbs.

Year	Team	W	L	PCT	ERA	G	GS	CG	IP	H	BB	SO	ShO	W	L	SV	AB	H	HR	BA	PO	A	E	DP	TC/G	FA
1996	CLR N	2	1	.667	7.47	11	0	0	15.2	21	7	19	0	2	1	0	2	1	0	.500	2	1	0	0	0.3	1.000

John Burkett

BURKETT, JOHN DAVID
B. Nov. 28, 1964, New Brighton, Pa.   BR TR 6' 2" 175 lbs.

Year	Team	W	L	PCT	ERA	G	GS	CG	IP	H	BB	SO	ShO	W	L	SV	AB	H	HR	BA	PO	A	E	DP	TC/G	FA
1987	SF N	0	0	—	4.50	3	0	0	6	7	3	5	0	0	0	0	1	0	0	.000	0	1	0	1	0.3	1.000
1990		14	7	.667	3.79	33	32	2	204	201	61	118	0	0	0	1	63	3	0	.048	11	25	4	1	1.1	.973
1991		12	11	.522	4.18	36	34	3	206.2	223	60	131	0	0	0	0	55	5	0	.091	13	25	1	2	1.1	.974
1992		13	9	.591	3.84	32	32	3	189.2	194	45	107	1	0	0	0	55	1	0	.018	11	18	1	0	0.9	.967
1993		22	7	.759	3.65	34	34	2	231.2	224	40	145	1	0	0	0	76	9	0	.118	21	36	0	2	1.7	1.000
1994		6	8	.429	3.62	25	25	0	159.1	176	36	85	0	0	0	0	51	3	0	.059	14	23	0	0	1.5	1.000
1995	FLA N	14	14	.500	4.30	30	30	4	188.1	208	57	126	0	0	0	0	66	7	0	.106	17	26	0	0	1.4	1.000
1996	2 teams	FLA N	(24G 6-10)		TEX A	(10G 5-2)																				
"	total	11	12	.478	4.24	34	34	2	222.2	229	58	155	1	0	0	0	52	9	0	.173	19	25	1	1	1.3	.978
8 yrs.		92	68	.575	3.96	227	221	16	1408.1	1462	360	872	4	0	0	1	419	37	0	.088	106	179	4	11	1.3	.986

DIVISIONAL PLAYOFF SERIES

Year	Team	W	L	PCT	ERA	G	GS	CG	IP	H	BB	SO	ShO	W	L	SV	AB	H	HR	BA	PO	A	E	DP	TC/G	FA
1996	TEX A	1	0	1.000	2.00	1	1	1	9	10	1	7	0	0	0	0	0	0	0	—	1	0	0	0	1.0	1.000

Terry Burrows

BURROWS, TERRY DALE
B. Nov. 28, 1968, Lake Charles, La.   BL TL 6' 1" 185 lbs.

Year	Team	W	L	PCT	ERA	G	GS	CG	IP	H	BB	SO	ShO	W	L	SV	AB	H	HR	BA	PO	A	E	DP	TC/G	FA
1994	TEX A	0	0	—	9.00	1	0	0	1	1	1	1	0	0	0	0	0	0	0	—	0	0	0	0	0.0	.000
1995		2	2	.500	6.45	28	3	0	44.2	60	19	22	0	2	2	1	0	0	0	—	3	4	0	0	0.3	1.000
1996	MIL A	2	0	1.000	2.84	8	0	0	12.2	12	10	5	0	2	0	0	0	0	0	—	2	1	0	0	0.4	1.000
3 yrs.		4	2	.667	5.71	37	3	0	58.1	73	30	27	0	4	2	1	0	0	0	—	5	5	0	0	0.3	1.000

Steve Busby

BUSBY, STEVEN LEE
B. Sept. 29, 1949, Burbank, Calif.   BR TR 6' 2" 205 lbs.

Year	Team	W	L	PCT	ERA	G	GS	CG	IP	H	BB	SO	ShO	W	L	SV	AB	H	HR	BA	PO	A	E	DP	TC/G	FA
1972	KC A	3	1	.750	1.58	5	5	3	40	28	8	31	0	0	0	0	15	3	0	.200	1	4	1	0	1.2	.833
1973		16	15	.516	4.24	37	37	7	238	246	105	174	1	0	0	0	0	0	0	—	10	47	6	3	1.7	.905
1974		22	14	.611	3.39	38	38	20	292.1	284	92	198	3	0	0	0	0	0	0	—	24	53	8	2	2.2	.906
1975		18	12	.600	3.08	34	34	18	260.1	233	81	160	3	0	0	0	0	0	0	—	22	52	3	2	2.3	.961
1976		3	3	.500	4.38	13	13	1	72	58	49	29	0	0	0	0	0	0	0	—	10	9	3	0	1.7	.864
1978		1	0	1.000	7.59	7	5	0	21.1	24	15	10	0	0	0	0	0	0	0	—	0	5	1	0	0.9	.833
1979		6	6	.500	3.64	22	12	4	94	71	64	45	0	1	2	0	0	0	0	—	4	24	0	1	1.3	1.000
1980		1	3	.250	6.21	11	6	0	42	59	19	12	0	0	0	0	0	0	0	—	5	4	1	0	0.9	.900
8 yrs.		70	54	.565	3.72	167	150	53	1060	1003	433	659	7	1	2	0	15	3	0	.200	76	198	23	8	1.8	.923

Paul Byrd

BYRD, PAUL GREGORY
B. Dec. 3, 1970, Louisville, Ky.   BR TR 6' 1" 185 lbs.

Year	Team	W	L	PCT	ERA	G	GS	CG	IP	H	BB	SO	ShO	W	L	SV	AB	H	HR	BA	PO	A	E	DP	TC/G	FA
1995	NY N	2	0	1.000	2.05	17	0	0	22	18	7	26	0	2	0	0	1	1	0	1.000	1	3	1	0	0.3	.800
1996		1	2	.333	4.24	38	0	0	46.2	48	21	31	0	1	2	0	2	0	0	.000	4	6	0	0	0.3	1.000
2 yrs.		3	2	.600	3.54	55	0	0	68.2	66	28	57	0	3	2	0	3	1	0	.333	5	9	1	0	0.3	.933

Mike Campbell

CAMPBELL, MICHAEL THOMAS
B. Feb. 17, 1964, Seattle, Wash.   BR TR 6' 3" 210 lbs.

Year	Team	W	L	PCT	ERA	G	GS	CG	IP	H	BB	SO	ShO	W	L	SV	AB	H	HR	BA	PO	A	E	DP	TC/G	FA
1987	SEA A	1	4	.200	4.74	9	9	1	49.1	41	25	35	0	0	0	0	0	0	0	—	6	5	0	0	1.2	1.000
1988		6	10	.375	5.89	20	20	1	114.2	128	43	63	0	0	0	0	0	0	0	—	7	13	3	1	1.1	.870
1989		1	2	.333	7.29	5	5	0	21	28	10	6	0	0	0	0	0	0	0	—	2	1	0	0	0.6	1.000

Year	Team	W	L	PCT	ERA	G	GS	CG	IP	H	BB	SO	ShO	W	L	SV	AB	H	HR	BA	PO	A	E	DP	TC/G	FA

Mike Campbell *continued*

1994	SD N	1	1	.500	12.96	3	2	0	8.1	13	5	10	0	1	0	0	3	1	0	.333	0	0	0	0	0.0	.000
1996	CHI N	3	1	.750	4.46	13	5	0	36.1	29	10	19	0	1	1	0	11	4	0	.364	2	1	0	0	0.2	1.000
	6 yrs.	12	19	.387	5.86	51	41	3	233.1	242	95	135	0	2	2	0	14	5	0	.357	17	20	3	1	0.8	.925

Tom Candiotti

CANDIOTTI, THOMAS CAESAR
B. Aug. 31, 1957, Walnut Creek, Calif.   BR TR 6'3" 205 lbs.

1983	MIL A	4	4	.500	3.23	10	8	2	55.2	62	16	21	1	0	0	0	0	0	0	—	4	5	0	1	0.9	1.000
1984		2	2	.500	5.29	8	6	0	32.1	38	10	23	0	0	0	0	0	0	0	—	3	1	0	0	0.5	1.000
1986	CLE A	16	12	.571	3.57	36	34	17	252.1	234	106	167	3	0	0	0	0	0	0	—	27	41	3	7	2.0	.958
1987		7	18	.280	4.78	32	32	7	201.2	193	93	111	2	0	0	0	0	0	0	—	17	29	1	1	1.5	.979
1988		14	8	.636	3.28	31	31	11	216.2	225	53	137	1	0	0	0	0	0	0	—	17	36	1	2	1.7	.981
1989		13	10	.565	3.10	31	31	4	206	188	55	124	0	0	0	0	0	0	0	—	28	41	3	1	2.3	.986
1990		15	11	.577	3.65	31	29	3	202	207	55	128	1	0	0	0	0	0	0	—	22	37	2	1	2.0	.967
1991	2 teams			CLE A	(15G 7-6)		TOR A	(19G 6-7)																		
"	total	13	13	.500	2.65	34	34	6	238	202	73	167	0	0	0	0	0	0	0	—	19	28	1	1	1.4	.979
1992	LA N	11	15	.423	3.00	32	30	6	203.2	177	63	152	2	1	0	0	56	6	0	.107	16	32	1	3	1.5	.980
1993		8	10	.444	3.12	33	32	2	213.2	192	71	155	0	0	0	0	60	8	0	.133	10	30	3	3	1.3	.930
1994		7	7	.500	4.12	23	22	5	153	149	54	102	0	0	0	0	50	7	0	.140	14	22	0	1	1.6	1.000
1995		7	14	.333	3.50	30	30	1	190.1	187	58	141	1	0	0	0	55	6	0	.109	15	24	1	0	1.3	.975
1996		9	11	.450	4.49	28	27	1	152.1	172	43	79	0	0	0	0	45	4	0	.089	13	36	1	4	1.8	.980
	13 yrs.	126	135	.483	3.53	359	346	65	2317.2	2226	750	1507	11	1	0	0	266	31	0	.117	205	362	15	25	1.6	.974

DIVISIONAL PLAYOFF SERIES

| 1996 | LA N | 0 | 0 | — | 0.00 | 1 | 0 | 0 | 2 | 0 | 0 | 1 | 0 | 0 | 0 | 0 | 0 | 0 | 0 | — | 0 | 0 | 0 | 0 | 0.0 | .000 |

LEAGUE CHAMPIONSHIP SERIES

| 1991 | TOR A | 0 | 1 | .000 | 8.22 | 2 | 2 | 0 | 7.2 | 17 | 2 | 5 | 0 | 0 | 0 | 0 | 0 | 0 | 0 | — | 0 | 2 | 0 | 1 | 1.0 | 1.000 |

Dan Carlson

CARLSON, DANIEL STEVEN
B. Jan. 26, 1970, Portland, Ore.   BR TR 6'1" 180 lbs.

| 1996 | SF N | 1 | 0 | 1.000 | 2.70 | 5 | 0 | 0 | 10 | 13 | 2 | 4 | 0 | 1 | 0 | 0 | 1 | 0 | 0 | .000 | 1 | 1 | 0 | 0 | 0.4 | 1.000 |

Rafael Carmona

CARMONA, RAFAEL
B. Oct. 2, 1972, Rio Piedras, Puerto Rico   BL TR 6'2" 185 lbs.

1995	SEA A	2	4	.333	5.66	15	3	0	47.2	55	34	28	0	2	2	1	0	0	0	—	9	5	1	1	1.0	.933
1996		8	3	.727	4.28	53	1	0	90.1	95	55	62	0	8	2	1	0	0	0	—	2	14	1	0	0.3	.941
	2 yrs.	10	7	.588	4.76	68	4	0	138	150	89	90	0	10	4	2					11	19	2	1	0.5	.938

Cris Carpenter

CARPENTER, CRIS HOWELL
B. Apr. 5, 1965, St. Augustine, Fla.   BR TR 6'1" 195 lbs.

1988	STL N	2	3	.400	4.72	8	8	1	47.2	56	9	24	0	0	0	0	14	2	0	.143	6	4	0	1	1.3	1.000
1989		4	4	.500	3.18	36	5	0	68	70	26	35	0	3	2	0	9	4	0	.444	3	10	0	1	0.4	1.000
1990		0	0	—	4.50	4	0	0	8	5	2	6	0	0	0	0	1	0	0	.000	0	0	1	0	0.3	.000
1991		10	4	.714	4.23	59	0	0	66	53	20	47	0	10	4	0	3	1	0	.333	4	8	0	0	0.2	1.000
1992		5	4	.556	2.97	73	0	0	88	69	27	46	0	5	4	1	3	1	0	.333	7	10	0	1	0.2	1.000
1993	2 teams			FLA N	(29G 0-1)		TEX A	(27G 4-1)																		
"	total	4	2	.667	3.50	56	0	0	69.1	64	25	53	0	4	2	1	0	0	0	—	3	12	0	1	0.3	1.000
1994	TEX A	2	5	.286	5.03	47	0	0	59	69	20	39	0	2	5	5	0	0	0	—	2	8	1	1	0.2	.909
1996	MIL A	0	0	—	7.56	8	0	0	8.1	12	2	2	0	0	0	0	0	0	0	—	0	0	0	0	0.0	.000
	8 yrs.	27	22	.551	3.91	291	13	1	414.1	398	131	252	0	24	17	7	30	8	0	.267	25	52	2	5	0.3	.975

Giovanni Carrara

CARRARA, GIOVANNI
Born Giovanni Carrara (Jimenez).
B. Mar. 4, 1968, Edo Anzoategui, Venezuela   BR TR 6'2" 225 lbs.

1995	TOR A	2	4	.333	7.21	12	7	1	48.2	64	25	27	0	1	0	0	0	0	0	—	1	3	0	0	0.3	1.000
1996	2 teams			TOR A	(11G 0-1)		CIN N	(8G 1-0)																		
"	total	1	1	.500	8.05	19	5	0	38	54	25	23	0	0	0	0	7	0	0	.000	2	4	0	0	0.3	1.000
	2 yrs.	3	5	.375	7.58	31	12	1	86.2	118	50	50	0	1	1	0	7	0	0	.000	3	7	0	0	0.3	1.000

Hector Carrasco

CARRASCO, HECTOR
Born Hector Carrasco (Pacheco).
B. Oct. 22, 1969, San Pedro de Macoris, Dominican Republic   BR TR 6'2" 175 lbs.

1994	CIN N	5	6	.455	2.24	45	0	0	56.1	42	30	41	0	5	6	6	6	0	0	.000	3	7	1	0	0.2	.909
1995		2	7	.222	4.12	64	0	0	87.1	86	46	64	0	2	7	5	7	0	0	.000	4	9	2	1	0.2	.867
1996		4	3	.571	3.75	56	0	0	74.1	58	45	59	0	4	3	0	5	1	0	.200	3	12	2	1	0.3	.882
	3 yrs.	11	16	.407	3.51	165	0	0	218	186	121	164	0	11	16	11	18	1	0	.056	10	28	5	2	0.3	.884

LEAGUE CHAMPIONSHIP SERIES

| 1995 | CIN N | 0 | 0 | — | 0.00 | 1 | 0 | 0 | 1.1 | 1 | 0 | 3 | 0 | 0 | 0 | 0 | 0 | 0 | 0 | — | 0 | 0 | 0 | 0 | 0.0 | .000 |

Larry Casian

CASIAN, LAWRENCE PAUL
B. Oct. 28, 1965, Lynwood, Calif.   BR TL 6'1" 170 lbs.

| 1990 | MIN A | 2 | 1 | .667 | 3.22 | 5 | 3 | 0 | 22.1 | 26 | 4 | 11 | 0 | 0 | 0 | 0 | 0 | 0 | 0 | — | 0 | 3 | 0 | 1 | 0.6 | 1.000 |
| 1991 | | 0 | 0 | — | 7.36 | 15 | 0 | 0 | 18.1 | 28 | 7 | 6 | 0 | 0 | 0 | 0 | 0 | 0 | 0 | — | 3 | 4 | 0 | 0 | 0.5 | 1.000 |

Year	Team	W	L	PCT	ERA	G	GS	CG	IP	H	BB	SO	ShO	Relief Pitching W	L	SV	Batting AB	H	HR	BA	PO	A	E	DP	TC/G	FA

Larry Casian *continued*

Year	Team	W	L	PCT	ERA	G	GS	CG	IP	H	BB	SO	ShO	W	L	SV	AB	H	HR	BA	PO	A	E	DP	TC/G	FA
1993		5	3	.625	3.02	54	0	0	56.2	59	14	31	0	5	3	1	0	0	0	—	4	4	0	0	0.1	1.000
1994	2 teams	MIN A	(33G 1-3)	CLE A	(7G 0-2)																					
"	total	1	5	.167	7.35	40	0	0	49	73	16	20	0	1	5	1	0	0	0		2	14	0	0	0.4	1.000
1995	CHI N	1	0	1.000	1.93	42	0	0	23.1	23	15	11	0	1	0	0	2	0	0	.000	2	4	0	0	0.1	1.000
1996		1	1	.500	1.88	35	0	0	24	14	11	15	0	1	1	0	0	0	0	—	2	5	1	1	0.2	.875
7 yrs.		11	10	.524	4.22	197	3	0	200.1	230	68	96	0	10	9	2	2	0	0	.000	14	35	1	3	0.3	.980

Frank Castillo

CASTILLO, FRANK ANTHONY
B. Apr. 1, 1969, El Paso, Tex.

BR TR 6'1" 180 lbs.

Year	Team	W	L	PCT	ERA	G	GS	CG	IP	H	BB	SO	ShO	W	L	SV	AB	H	HR	BA	PO	A	E	DP	TC/G	FA
1991	CHI N	6	7	.462	4.35	18	18	4	111.2	107	33	73	0	0	0	0	35	5	0	.143	6	16	0	0	1.2	1.000
1992		10	11	.476	3.46	33	33	0	205.1	179	63	135	0	0	0	0	65	6	0	.092	10	28	1	2	1.2	.974
1993		5	8	.385	4.84	29	25	2	141.1	162	39	84	0	0	0	0	43	7	0	.163	7	34	1	1	1.4	.976
1994		2	1	.667	4.30	4	4	1	23	25	5	19	0	0	0	0	9	0	0	.000	1	3	2	0	1.5	.667
1995		11	10	.524	3.21	29	29	2	188	179	52	135	2	0	0	0	59	6	0	.102	11	24	2	0	1.3	.946
1996		7	16	.304	5.28	33	33	1	182.1	209	46	139	1	0	0	0	57	5	0	.088	18	23	3	2	1.3	.932
6 yrs.		41	53	.436	4.16	146	142	10	851.2	861	238	585	3	0	0	0	268	29	0	.108	53	128	9	5	1.3	.953

Tony Castillo

CASTILLO, ANTONIO JOSE
Born Antonio Jose Castillo (Jimenez).
B. Mar. 1, 1963, Quibor, Venezuela

BL TL 5'10" 177 lbs.

Year	Team	W	L	PCT	ERA	G	GS	CG	IP	H	BB	SO	ShO	W	L	SV	AB	H	HR	BA	PO	A	E	DP	TC/G	FA
1988	TOR A	1	0	1.000	3.00	14	0	0	15	10	2	14	0	1	0	0	0	0	0	—	0	3	0	0	0.2	1.000
1989	2 teams	TOR A	(17G 1-1)	ATL N	(12G 0-1)																					
"	total	1	2	.333	5.67	29	0	0	27	31	14	15	0	1	2	1	1	0	0	.000	2	3	0	0	0.2	1.000
1990	ATL N	5	1	.833	4.23	52	3	0	76.2	93	20	64	0	3	1	1	7	1	0	.143	5	13	0	1	0.3	1.000
1991	2 teams	ATL N	(7G 1-1)	NY N	(10G 1-0)																					
"	total	2	1	.667	3.34	17	0	0	32.1	40	11	18	0	1	1	0	4	0	0	.000	3	6	0	1	0.5	1.000
1993	TOR A	3	2	.600	3.38	51	0	0	50.2	44	22	28	0	3	2	0	0	0	0	—	3	9	1	1	0.3	.923
1994		5	2	.714	2.51	41	0	0	68	66	28	43	0	5	2	1	0	0	0	—	4	16	1	0	0.5	.952
1995		1	5	.167	3.22	55	0	0	72.2	64	24	38	0	1	5	13	0	0	0	—	3	10	0	1	0.2	1.000
1996	2 teams	TOR A	(40G 2-3)	CHI A	(15G 3-1)																					
"	total	5	4	.556	3.60	55	0	0	95	95	24	57	0	5	4	2	0	0	0	—	9	15	0	1	0.4	1.000
8 yrs.		23	17	.575	3.54	314	6	0	437.1	443	145	277	0	20	17	18	12	1	0	.083	29	75	2	3	0.3	.981

LEAGUE CHAMPIONSHIP SERIES

Year	Team	W	L	PCT	ERA	G	GS	CG	IP	H	BB	SO	ShO	W	L	SV	AB	H	HR	BA	PO	A	E	DP	TC/G	FA
1993	TOR A	0	0	—	0.00	2	0	0	2	0	1	1	0	0	0	0	0	0	0	—	0	1	0	0	0.5	1.000

WORLD SERIES

Year	Team	W	L	PCT	ERA	G	GS	CG	IP	H	BB	SO	ShO	W	L	SV	AB	H	HR	BA	PO	A	E	DP	TC/G	FA
1993	TOR A	1	0	1.000	8.10	2	0	0	3.1	6	3	1	0	1	0	0	1	0	0	.000	0	0	0	0	0.0	.000

Norm Charlton

CHARLTON, NORMAN WOOD
B. Jan. 6, 1963, Fort Polk, La.

BB TL 6'3" 195 lbs.

Year	Team	W	L	PCT	ERA	G	GS	CG	IP	H	BB	SO	ShO	W	L	SV	AB	H	HR	BA	PO	A	E	DP	TC/G	FA
1988	CIN N	4	5	.444	3.96	10	10	0	61.1	60	20	39	0	0	0	0	15	0	0	.000	1	9	0	0	1.0	1.000
1989		8	3	.727	2.93	69	0	0	95.1	67	40	98	0	8	3	0	5	0	0	.000	3	13	3	0	0.3	.842
1990		12	9	.571	2.74	56	16	1	154.1	131	70	117	1	6	4	2	37	5	0	.135	6	23	1	3	0.5	.967
1991		3	5	.375	2.91	39	11	0	108.1	92	34	77	0	0	0	1	23	1	0	.043	4	20	1	1	0.6	.960
1992		4	2	.667	2.99	64	0	0	81.1	79	26	90	0	4	2	26	5	1	0	.200	2	8	3	1	0.2	.786
1993	SEA A	1	3	.250	2.34	34	0	0	34.2	22	17	48	0	1	3	18	0	0	0	—	0	2	0	1	0.1	1.000
1995	2 teams	PHI N	(25G 2-5)	SEA A	(30G 2-1)																					
"	total	4	6	.400	3.36	55	0	0	69.2	46	31	70	0	4	6	14	1	1	0	1.000	2	6	0	0	0.1	1.000
1996	SEA A	4	7	.364	4.04	70	0	0	75.2	68	38	73	0	4	7	20	0	0	0	—	4	9	1	1	0.2	.929
8 yrs.		40	40	.500	3.12	397	37	1	680.2	565	276	612	1	27	25	81	86	8	0	.093	23	90	9	7	0.3	.926

DIVISIONAL PLAYOFF SERIES

Year	Team	W	L	PCT	ERA	G	GS	CG	IP	H	BB	SO	ShO	W	L	SV	AB	H	HR	BA	PO	A	E	DP	TC/G	FA
1995	SEA A	1	0	1.000	2.45	4	0	0	7.1	4	3	9	0	1	0	1	0	0	0	—	0	0	0	0	0.0	.000

LEAGUE CHAMPIONSHIP SERIES

Year	Team	W	L	PCT	ERA	G	GS	CG	IP	H	BB	SO	ShO	W	L	SV	AB	H	HR	BA	PO	A	E	DP	TC/G	FA
1990	CIN N	1	1	.500	1.80	4	0	0	5	4	3	3	0	1	1	0	0	0	0	—	1	0	0	1	0.3	1.000
1995	SEA A	1	0	1.000	0.00	3	0	0	6	1	1	5	0	1	0	1	0	0	0	—	0	0	0	0	0.0	.000
2 yrs.		2	1	.667	0.82	7	0	0	11	5	4	8	0	2	1	1	0	0	0	—	1	0	0	1	0.1	1.000

WORLD SERIES

Year	Team	W	L	PCT	ERA	G	GS	CG	IP	H	BB	SO	ShO	W	L	SV	AB	H	HR	BA	PO	A	E	DP	TC/G	FA
1990	CIN N	0	0	—	0.00	1	0	0	1	0	1	1	0	0	0	0	0	0	0	—	0	0	0	0	0.0	.000

Bobby Chouinard

CHOUINARD, ROBERT WILLIAM
B. May 1, 1972, Manila, Philippines

BR TR 6'1" 188 lbs.

Year	Team	W	L	PCT	ERA	G	GS	CG	IP	H	BB	SO	ShO	W	L	SV	AB	H	HR	BA	PO	A	E	DP	TC/G	FA
1996	OAK A	4	2	.667	6.10	13	11	0	59	75	32	32	0	0	0	0	0	0	0	—	3	13	0	2	1.2	1.000

Clay Christiansen

CHRISTIANSEN, CLAY C.
B. June 28, 1958, Wichita, Kans.

BR TR 6'5" 215 lbs.

Year	Team	W	L	PCT	ERA	G	GS	CG	IP	H	BB	SO	ShO	W	L	SV	AB	H	HR	BA	PO	A	E	DP	TC/G	FA
1984	NY A	2	4	.333	6.05	24	1	0	38.2	50	12	27	0	2	3	2	0	0	0	—	5	3	1	0	0.4	.889

Jason Christiansen

CHRISTIANSEN, JASON SAMUEL
B. Sept. 21, 1969, Omaha, Neb.

BR TL 6'5" 230 lbs.

Year	Team	W	L	PCT	ERA	G	GS	CG	IP	H	BB	SO	ShO	W	L	SV	AB	H	HR	BA	PO	A	E	DP	TC/G	FA
1995	PIT N	1	3	.250	4.15	63	0	0	56.1	49	34	53	0	1	3	0	1	0	0	.000	2	8	2	0	0.2	.833
1996		3	3	.500	6.70	33	0	0	44.1	56	19	38	0	3	3	0	4	0	0	.000	0	7	0	0	0.2	1.000
2 yrs.		4	6	.400	5.27	96	0	0	100.2	105	53	91	0	4	6	0	5	0	0	.000	2	15	2	0	0.2	.895

Year	Team	W	L	PCT	ERA	G	GS	CG	IP	H	BB	SO	ShO	Relief Pitching W	L	SV	Batting AB	H	HR	BA	PO	A	E	DP	TC/G	FA

Mike Christopher
CHRISTOPHER, MICHAEL WAYNE
B. Nov. 3, 1963, Petersburg, Va.
BR TR 6'5" 205 lbs.

Year	Team	W	L	PCT	ERA	G	GS	CG	IP	H	BB	SO	ShO	W	L	SV	AB	H	HR	BA	PO	A	E	DP	TC/G	FA
1991	LA N	0	0	—	0.00	3	0	0	4	2	3	2	0	0	0	0	0	0	0	—	0	1	0	0	0.3	1.000
1992	CLE A	0	0	—	3.00	10	0	0	18	17	10	13	0	0	0	0	0	0	0	—	1	2	0	0	0.3	1.000
1993		0	0	—	3.86	9	0	0	11.2	14	2	8	0	0	0	0	0	0	0	—	0	1	0	0	0.1	1.000
1995	DET A	4	0	1.000	3.82	36	0	0	61.1	71	14	34	0	4	0	1	0	0	0	—	4	8	0	0	0.3	1.000
1996		1	1	.500	9.30	13	0	0	30	47	11	19	0	1	1	0	0	0	0		1	3	0	0	0.3	1.000
	5 yrs.	5	1	.833	4.90	71	0	0	125	151	40	76	0	5	1	1	0	0	0		6	15	0	0	0.3	1.000

Mark Clark
CLARK, MARK WILLARD
B. May 12, 1968, Bath, Ill.
BR TR 6'5" 225 lbs.

Year	Team	W	L	PCT	ERA	G	GS	CG	IP	H	BB	SO	ShO	W	L	SV	AB	H	HR	BA	PO	A	E	DP	TC/G	FA
1991	STL N	1	1	.500	4.03	7	2	0	22.1	17	11	13	0	1	1	0	7	0	0	.000	2	1	0	0	0.4	1.000
1992		3	10	.231	4.45	20	20	1	113.1	117	36	44	1	0	0	0	36	5	0	.139	2	13	1	0	0.8	.938
1993	CLE A	7	5	.583	4.28	26	15	1	109.1	119	25	57	0	0	0	0	0	0	0	—	4	10	2	0	0.6	.875
1994		11	3	.786	3.82	20	20	4	127.1	133	40	60	1	0	0	0	0	0	0	—	5	23	0	3	1.4	1.000
1995		9	7	.563	5.27	22	21	2	124.2	143	42	68	0	1	0	0	0	0	0	—	8	15	0	3	1.0	1.000
1996	NY N	14	11	.560	3.43	32	32	2	212.1	217	48	142	0	0	0	0	69	3	0	.043	9	24	0	1	1.0	1.000
	6 yrs.	45	37	.549	4.14	127	110	10	709.1	746	202	384	2	2	1	0	112	8	0	.071	30	86	3	7	0.9	.975

Terry Clark
CLARK, TERRY LEE
B. Oct. 18, 1960, Los Angeles, Calif.
BR TR 6'2" 190 lbs.

Year	Team	W	L	PCT	ERA	G	GS	CG	IP	H	BB	SO	ShO	W	L	SV	AB	H	HR	BA	PO	A	E	DP	TC/G	FA
1988	CAL A	6	6	.500	5.07	15	15	2	94	120	31	39	1	0	0	0	0	0	0	—	8	13	0	0	1.4	1.000
1989		0	2	.000	4.91	4	2	0	11	13	3	7	0	0	0	0	0	0	0	—	0	2	0	0	0.5	1.000
1990	HOU N	0	0	—	13.50	1	1	0	4	9	3	2	0	0	0	0	2	1	0	.500	0	0	0	0	0.0	.000
1995	2 teams	ATL N	(3G 0–0)		BAL A		(38G 2–5)																			
"	total	2	5	.286	3.59	41	0	0	42.2	43	20	20	0	2	5	1	0	0	0	—	2	3	1	1	0.1	.833
1996	2 teams	KC A	(12G 1–1)		HOU N		(5G 0–2)																			
"	total	1	3	.250	8.75	17	0	0	23.2	44	9	17	0	1	3	0	0	0	0	—	3	4	0	1	0.4	1.000
	5 yrs.	9	16	.360	5.39	78	18	2	175.1	229	66	85	1	3	8	1	2	1	0	.500	13	22	1	2	0.5	.972

Roger Clemens
CLEMENS, WILLIAM ROGER (Rocket Man)
B. Aug. 4, 1962, Dayton, Ohio
BR TR 6'4" 205 lbs.

Year	Team	W	L	PCT	ERA	G	GS	CG	IP	H	BB	SO	ShO	W	L	SV	AB	H	HR	BA	PO	A	E	DP	TC/G	FA
1984	BOS A	9	4	.692	4.32	21	20	5	133.1	146	29	126	1	0	0	0	0	0	0	—	11	14	0	0	1.2	1.000
1985		7	5	.583	3.29	15	15	3	98.1	83	37	74	1	0	0	0	0	0	0	—	12	9	0	1	1.4	1.000
1986		24	4	.857	2.48	33	33	10	254	179	67	238	1	0	0	0	0	0	0	—	27	21	4	0	1.6	.923
1987		20	9	.690	2.97	36	36	18	281.2	248	83	256	7	0	0	0	0	0	0	—	15	25	0	1	1.1	1.000
1988		18	12	.600	2.93	35	35	14	264	217	62	291	8	0	0	0	0	0	0	—	17	17	1	1	1.0	.971
1989		17	11	.607	3.13	35	35	8	253.1	215	93	230	3	0	0	0	0	0	0	—	17	27	0	1	1.3	1.000
1990		21	6	.778	1.93	31	31	7	228.1	193	54	209	4	0	0	0	0	0	0	—	23	26	2	1	1.6	.961
1991		18	10	.643	2.62	35	35	13	271.1	219	65	241	4	0	0	0	0	0	0	—	31	30	1	1	1.8	.984
1992		18	11	.621	2.41	32	32	11	246.2	203	62	208	5	0	0	0	0	0	0	—	19	25	1	0	1.4	.978
1993		11	14	.440	4.46	29	29	2	191.2	175	67	160	1	0	0	0	0	0	0	—	11	20	1	1	1.1	.969
1994		9	7	.563	2.85	24	24	3	170.2	124	71	168	1	0	0	0	0	0	0	—	8	19	2	2	1.2	.931
1995		10	5	.667	4.18	23	23	0	140	141	60	132	0	0	0	0	0	0	0	—	13	19	1	1	1.4	.970
1996		10	13	.435	3.63	34	34	6	242.2	216	106	257	2	0	0	0	1	1	0	1.000	10	22	2	2	1.0	.941
	13 yrs.	192	111	.634	3.06	383	382	100	2776	2359	856	2590	38	0	0	0	1	1	0	1.000	214	274	15	12	1.3	.970

DIVISIONAL PLAYOFF SERIES

Year	Team	W	L	PCT	ERA	G	GS	CG	IP	H	BB	SO	ShO	W	L	SV	AB	H	HR	BA	PO	A	E	DP	TC/G	FA
1995	BOS A	0	0	—	3.86	1	1	0	7	5	1	5	0	0	0	0	0	0	0	—	0	0	0	0	0.0	.000

LEAGUE CHAMPIONSHIP SERIES

Year	Team	W	L	PCT	ERA	G	GS	CG	IP	H	BB	SO	ShO	W	L	SV	AB	H	HR	BA	PO	A	E	DP	TC/G	FA
1986	BOS A	1	1	.500	4.37	3	3	0	22.2	22	7	17	0	0	0	0	0	0	0	—	1	2	0	0	1.0	1.000
1988		0	0	—	3.86	1	1	0	7	6	0	8	0	0	0	0	0	0	0	—	0	0	1	0	1.0	1.000
1990		0	1	.000	3.52	2	2	0	7.2	7	5	4	0	0	0	0	0	0	0	—	0	1	0	0	0.5	1.000
	3 yrs.	1	2	.333	4.10	6	6	0	37.1	35	12	29	0	0	0	0	0	0	0		1	3	1	0	0.8	.800

WORLD SERIES

Year	Team	W	L	PCT	ERA	G	GS	CG	IP	H	BB	SO	ShO	W	L	SV	AB	H	HR	BA	PO	A	E	DP	TC/G	FA
1986	BOS A	0	0	—	3.18	2	2	0	11.1	9	6	11	0	0	0	0	4	0	0	.000	1	2	0	0	1.5	1.000

Brad Clontz
CLONTZ, JOHN BRADLEY
B. Apr. 25, 1971, Stuart, Va.
BR TR 6'1" 180 lbs.

Year	Team	W	L	PCT	ERA	G	GS	CG	IP	H	BB	SO	ShO	W	L	SV	AB	H	HR	BA	PO	A	E	DP	TC/G	FA
1995	ATL N	8	1	.889	3.65	59	0	0	69	71	22	55	0	8	1	4	2	0	0	.000	7	8	0	1	0.3	1.000
1996		6	3	.667	5.69	81	0	0	80.2	78	33	49	0	6	3	1	2	0	0	.000	1	18	1	1	0.2	.950
	2 yrs.	14	4	.778	4.75	140	0	0	149.2	149	55	104	0	14	4	5	4	0	0	.000	8	26	1	2	0.3	.971

DIVISIONAL PLAYOFF SERIES

Year	Team	W	L	PCT	ERA	G	GS	CG	IP	H	BB	SO	ShO	W	L	SV	AB	H	HR	BA	PO	A	E	DP	TC/G	FA
1995	ATL N	0	0	—	0.00	1	0	0	1.1	0	0	2	0	0	0	0	0	0	0	—	0	1	0	0	1.0	1.000

LEAGUE CHAMPIONSHIP SERIES

Year	Team	W	L	PCT	ERA	G	GS	CG	IP	H	BB	SO	ShO	W	L	SV	AB	H	HR	BA	PO	A	E	DP	TC/G	FA
1995	ATL N	0	0	—	0.00	1	0	0	0.1	1	0	0	0	0	0	0	0	0	0	—	0	0	0	0	0.0	.000
1996		0	0	—	0.00	1	0	0	0.2	0	1	2	0	0	0	0	0	0	0	—	0	0	0	0	0.0	.000
	2 yrs.	0	0		0.00	2	0	0	1	1	1	2	0	0	0	0	0	0	0		0	0	0	0	0.0	

WORLD SERIES

Year	Team	W	L	PCT	ERA	G	GS	CG	IP	H	BB	SO	ShO	W	L	SV	AB	H	HR	BA	PO	A	E	DP	TC/G	FA
1995	ATL N	0	0	—	2.70	2	0	0	3.1	2	0	2	0	0	0	0	0	0	0	—	0	0	0	0	0.0	.000
1996		0	0	—	0.00	3	0	0	1.2	1	1	2	0	0	0	0	0	0	0	—	0	0	0	0	0.0	.000
	2 yrs.	0	0		1.80	5	0	0	5	3	1	4	0	0	0	0	0	0	0		0	0	0	0	0.0	

Year	Team	W	L	PCT	ERA	G	GS	CG	IP	H	BB	SO	ShO	W	L	SV	AB	H	HR	BA	PO	A	E	DP	TC/G	FA

David Cone — CONE, DAVID BRIAN — B. Jan. 2, 1963, Kansas City, Mo. — BL TR 6'1" 180 lbs.

Year	Team	W	L	PCT	ERA	G	GS	CG	IP	H	BB	SO	ShO	W	L	SV	AB	H	HR	BA	PO	A	E	DP	TC/G	FA
1986	KC A	0	0	—	5.56	11	0	0	22.2	29	13	21	0	0	0	0	0	0	0	—	4	0	0	0	0.4	1.000
1987	NY N	5	6	.455	3.71	21	13	1	99.1	87	44	68	0	1	1	1	31	2	0	.065	12	10	1	0	1.1	.957
1988		20	3	.870	2.22	35	28	8	231.1	178	80	213	4	2	0	0	80	12	0	.150	17	23	1	0	1.2	.976
1989		14	8	.636	3.52	34	33	7	219.2	183	74	190	2	0	0	0	77	18	0	.234	21	14	1	0	1.1	.972
1990		14	10	.583	3.23	31	30	6	211.2	177	65	233	2	0	0	0	70	14	0	.200	17	20	3	1	1.3	.925
1991		14	14	.500	3.29	34	34	5	232.2	204	73	241	2	0	0	0	72	9	0	.125	18	26	4	2	1.4	.917
1992	2 teams	NY N	(27G 13-7)		TOR A	(8G 4-3)																				
"	total	17	10	.630	2.81	35	34	7	249.2	201	111	261	5	0	0	0	65	6	0	.092	18	22	2	1	1.2	.952
1993	KC A	11	14	.440	3.33	34	34	6	254	205	114	191	1	0	0	0	0	0	0	—	24	24	1	3	1.4	.980
1994		16	5	.762	2.94	23	23	4	171.2	130	54	132	3	0	0	0	0	0	0	—	20	18	3	3	1.8	.927
1995	2 teams	TOR A	(17G 9-6)		NY A	(13G 9-2)																				
"	total	18	8	.692	3.57	30	30	6	229.1	195	88	191	2	0	0	0	0	0	0	—	12	27	3	2	1.4	.929
1996	NY A	7	2	.778	2.88	11	11	1	72	50	34	71	0	0	0	0	0	0	0	—	7	4	1	1	1.1	.917
	11 yrs.	136	80	.630	3.16	299	270	51	1994	1639	750	1812	21	3	1	1	395	61	0	.154	170	188	20	13	1.3	.947

DIVISIONAL PLAYOFF SERIES

Year	Team	W	L	PCT	ERA	G	GS	CG	IP	H	BB	SO	ShO	W	L	SV	AB	H	HR	BA	PO	A	E	DP	TC/G	FA
1995	NY A	1	0	1.000	4.60	2	2	0	15.2	15	9	14	0	0	0	0	0	0	0	—	1	0	0	0	0.5	1.000
1996		0	1	.000	9.00	1	1	0	6	8	2	8	0	0	0	0	2	0	0	.000	1	0	0	0	1.0	1.000
	2 yrs.	1	1	.500	5.82	3	3	0	21.2	23	11	22	0	0	0	0					2	0	0	0	0.7	1.000

LEAGUE CHAMPIONSHIP SERIES

Year	Team	W	L	PCT	ERA	G	GS	CG	IP	H	BB	SO	ShO	W	L	SV	AB	H	HR	BA	PO	A	E	DP	TC/G	FA
1988	NY N	1	1	.500	4.50	3	2	1	12	10	5	9	0	0	0	0	4	0	0	.000	1	0	0	0	0.3	1.000
1992	TOR A	1	1	.500	3.00	2	2	0	12	11	5	9	0	0	0	0	0	1	0	—	0	1	1	0	1.0	.500
1996	NY A	0	0	—	3.00	1	1	0	6	5	5	5	0	0	0	0	0	0	0	—	0	0	0	0	1.0	1.000
	3 yrs.	2	2	.500	3.60	6	5	1	30	26	15	23	0	0	0	0	4	0	0	.000	1	2	1	0	0.7	.750

WORLD SERIES

Year	Team	W	L	PCT	ERA	G	GS	CG	IP	H	BB	SO	ShO	W	L	SV	AB	H	HR	BA	PO	A	E	DP	TC/G	FA
1992	TOR A	0	0	—	3.48	2	2	0	10.1	9	8	8	0	0	0	0	4	2	0	.500	0	0	0	0	0.0	.000
1996	NY A	1	0	1.000	1.50	1	1	0	6	4	4	3	0	0	0	0	2	0	0	.000	2	1	0	0	3.0	1.000
	2 yrs.	1	0	1.000	2.76	3	3	0	16.1	13	12	11	0	0	0	0	6	2	0	.333	2	1	0	0	1.0	1.000

Dennis Cook — COOK, DENNIS BRYAN — B. Oct. 4, 1962, LaMarque, Tex. — BL TL 6'3" 185 lbs.

Year	Team	W	L	PCT	ERA	G	GS	CG	IP	H	BB	SO	ShO	W	L	SV	AB	H	HR	BA	PO	A	E	DP	TC/G	FA
1988	SF N	2	1	.667	2.86	4	4	1	22	9	11	13	1	0	0	0	4	0	0	.000	0	1	0	0	0.3	1.000
1989	2 teams	SF N	(2G 1-0)		PHI N	(21G 6-8)																				
"	total	7	8	.467	3.72	23	18	2	121	110	38	67	1	1	0	0	42	9	0	.214	4	16	3	0	1.0	.870
1990	2 teams	PHI N	(42G 8-3)		LA N	(5G 1-1)																				
"	total	9	4	.692	3.92	47	16	2	156	155	56	64	1	3	1	1	49	15	1	.306	10	22	0	1	0.7	1.000
1991	LA N	1	0	1.000	0.51	20	1	0	17.2	12	7	8	0	0	0	0	1	0	0	.000	0	4	0	0	0.2	1.000
1992	CLE A	5	7	.417	3.82	32	25	1	158	156	50	96	0	0	1	0	0	0	0	—	3	15	1	2	0.6	.947
1993		5	5	.500	5.67	25	6	0	54	62	16	34	0	4	2	0	0	0	0	—	2	6	2	1	0.4	.800
1994	CHI A	3	1	.750	3.55	38	0	0	33	29	14	26	0	3	1	0	0	0	0	—	2	2	0	0	0.1	1.000
1995	2 teams	CLE A	(11G 0-0)		TEX A	(35G 0-2)																				
"	total	0	2	.000	4.53	46	1	0	57.2	63	26	53	0	0	2	2	0	0	0	—	0	6	0	0	0.1	1.000
1996	TEX A	5	2	.714	4.09	60	0	0	70.1	53	35	64	0	5	2	0	0	0	0	—	4	5	0	0	0.2	1.000
	9 yrs.	37	30	.552	3.93	295	71	6	689.2	649	253	425	3	16	8	3	96	24	1	.250	25	77	6	4	0.4	.944

DIVISIONAL PLAYOFF SERIES

Year	Team	W	L	PCT	ERA	G	GS	CG	IP	H	BB	SO	ShO	W	L	SV	AB	H	HR	BA	PO	A	E	DP	TC/G	FA
1996	TEX A	0	0	—	0.00	2	0	0	1.1	0	1	0	0	0	0	0	0	0	0	—	0	0	0	0	0.0	.000

Steve Cooke — COOKE, STEVEN MONTAGUE — B. Jan. 14, 1970, Lihue, Hawaii — BR TL 6'6" 220 lbs.

Year	Team	W	L	PCT	ERA	G	GS	CG	IP	H	BB	SO	ShO	W	L	SV	AB	H	HR	BA	PO	A	E	DP	TC/G	FA
1992	PIT N	2	0	1.000	3.52	11	0	0	23	22	4	10	0	2	0	1	3	1	0	.333	3	0	0	0	0.3	1.000
1993		10	10	.500	3.89	32	32	3	210.2	207	59	132	1	0	0	0	71	11	0	.155	7	23	3	0	1.0	.909
1994		4	11	.267	5.02	25	23	2	134.1	157	46	74	0	1	0	0	42	8	0	.190	3	16	1	1	0.8	.950
1996		0	0	—	7.56	3	0	0	8.1	11	5	7	0	0	0	0	1	0	0	.000	0	0	0	0	0.0	.000
	4 yrs.	16	21	.432	4.35	71	55	5	376.1	397	114	223	1	3	0	1	117	20	0	.171	10	42	4	1	0.8	.929

Rocky Coppinger — COPPINGER, JOHN THOMAS — B. Mar. 19, 1974, El Paso, Tex. — BR TR 6'5" 245 lbs.

Year	Team	W	L	PCT	ERA	G	GS	CG	IP	H	BB	SO	ShO	W	L	SV	AB	H	HR	BA	PO	A	E	DP	TC/G	FA
1996	BAL A	10	6	.625	5.18	23	22	0	125	126	60	104	0	1	0	0	0	0	0	—	6	8	0	1	0.6	1.000

LEAGUE CHAMPIONSHIP SERIES

Year	Team	W	L	PCT	ERA	G	GS	CG	IP	H	BB	SO	ShO	W	L	SV	AB	H	HR	BA	PO	A	E	DP	TC/G	FA
1996	BAL A	0	1	.000	8.44	1	1	0	5.1	6	1	3	0	0	0	0	0	0	0	—	1	1	0	0	1.0	1.000

Archie Corbin — CORBIN, ARCHIE RAY — B. Dec. 30, 1967, Beaumont, Tex. — BR TR 6'4" 190 lbs.

Year	Team	W	L	PCT	ERA	G	GS	CG	IP	H	BB	SO	ShO	W	L	SV	AB	H	HR	BA	PO	A	E	DP	TC/G	FA
1991	KC A	0	0	—	3.86	2	0	0	2.1	3	2	1	0	0	0	0	0	0	0	—	0	0	0	0	0.0	.000
1996	BAL A	2	0	1.000	2.30	18	0	0	27.1	22	22	20	0	2	0	0	0	0	0	—	0	1	0	0	0.1	1.000
	2 yrs.	2	0	1.000	2.43	20	0	0	29.2	25	24	21	0	2	0	0	0	0	0	—	0	1	0	0	0.1	1.000

Francisco Cordova — CORDOVA, FRANCISCO — B. Apr. 26, 1972, Vercruz, Mexico — BR TR 5'1" 165 lbs.

Year	Team	W	L	PCT	ERA	G	GS	CG	IP	H	BB	SO	ShO	W	L	SV	AB	H	HR	BA	PO	A	E	DP	TC/G	FA
1996	PIT N	4	7	.364	4.09	59	6	0	99	103	20	95	0	2	7	12	16	2	0	.125	6	16	2	1	0.4	.917

Year	Team	W	L	PCT	ERA	G	GS	CG	IP	H	BB	SO	ShO	W	L	SV	AB	H	HR	BA	PO	A	E	DP	TC/G	FA

Rheal Cormier

CORMIER, RHEAL PAUL
B. Apr. 23, 1967, Moncton, N. B., Canada.

BL TL 5'10" 185 lbs.

Year	Team	W	L	PCT	ERA	G	GS	CG	IP	H	BB	SO	ShO	W	L	SV	AB	H	HR	BA	PO	A	E	DP	TC/G	FA
1991	STL N	4	5	.444	4.12	11	10	2	67.2	74	8	38	0	0	0	0	21	5	0	.238	3	8	0	0	1.0	1.000
1992		10	10	.500	3.68	31	30	3	186	194	33	117	0	0	0	0	59	6	0	.102	9	34	0	2	1.4	1.000
1993		7	6	.538	4.33	38	21	1	145.1	163	27	75	0	1	1	0	47	11	0	.234	8	27	3	2	1.0	.921
1994		3	2	.600	5.45	7	7	0	39.2	40	7	26	0	0	0	0	14	4	0	.286	1	3	1	0	0.7	.800
1995	BOS A	7	5	.583	4.07	48	12	0	115	131	31	69	0	3	2	0	0	0	0	—	7	21	2	3	0.6	.933
1996	MON N	7	10	.412	4.17	33	27	1	159.2	165	41	100	1	0	0	0	43	8	0	.186	15	35	2	1	1.6	.962
6 yrs.		38	38	.500	4.13	168	107	7	713.1	767	147	425	1	4	3	0	184	34	0	.185	43	128	8	8	1.1	.955

DIVISIONAL PLAYOFF SERIES

Year	Team	W	L	PCT	ERA	G	GS	CG	IP	H	BB	SO	ShO	W	L	SV	AB	H	HR	BA	PO	A	E	DP	TC/G	FA
1995	BOS A	0	0	—	13.50	2	0	0	0.2	2	1	2	0	0	0	0	0	0	0	—	0	0	0	0	0.0	.000

Jim Corsi

CORSI, JAMES BERNARD
B. Sept. 9, 1961, Newton, Mass.

BR TR 6'1" 210 lbs.

Year	Team	W	L	PCT	ERA	G	GS	CG	IP	H	BB	SO	ShO	W	L	SV	AB	H	HR	BA	PO	A	E	DP	TC/G	FA
1988	OAK A	0	1	.000	3.80	11	1	0	21.1	20	6	10	0	0	1	0	0	0	0	—	0	3	1	0	0.4	.750
1989		1	2	.333	1.88	22	0	0	38.1	26	10	21	0	1	2	0	0	0	0	—	3	5	0	0	0.4	1.000
1991	HOU N	0	5	.000	3.71	47	0	0	77.2	76	23	53	0	0	5	0	1	0	0	.000	6	15	1	1	0.5	.955
1992	OAK A	4	2	.667	1.43	32	0	0	44	44	18	19	0	4	2	0	0	0	0	—	6	10	0	0	0.5	1.000
1993	FLA N	0	2	.000	6.64	15	0	0	20.1	28	10	7	0	0	2	0	0	0	0	—	1	4	0	0	0.3	1.000
1995	OAK A	2	4	.333	2.20	38	0	0	45	31	26	26	0	2	4	2	0	0	0	—	3	9	0	1	0.3	1.000
1996		6	0	1.000	4.03	57	0	0	73.2	71	34	43	0	6	0	3	0	0	0	—	6	17	0	2	0.4	1.000
7 yrs.		13	16	.448	3.23	222	1	0	320.1	296	127	179	0	13	16	5	1	0	0	.000	25	63	2	4	0.4	.978

LEAGUE CHAMPIONSHIP SERIES

Year	Team	W	L	PCT	ERA	G	GS	CG	IP	H	BB	SO	ShO	W	L	SV	AB	H	HR	BA	PO	A	E	DP	TC/G	FA
1992	OAK A	0	0	—	0.00	3	0	0	2	2	3	0	0	0	0	0	0	0	0	—	0	0	0	0	0.0	.000

Tim Crabtree

CRABTREE, TIMOTHY LYLE
B. Oct. 13, 1969, Jackson, Mich.

BR TR 6'4" 205 lbs.

Year	Team	W	L	PCT	ERA	G	GS	CG	IP	H	BB	SO	ShO	W	L	SV	AB	H	HR	BA	PO	A	E	DP	TC/G	FA
1995	TOR A	0	2	.000	3.09	31	0	0	32	30	13	21	0	0	2	0	0	0	0	—	2	8	0	1	0.3	1.000
1996		5	3	.625	2.54	53	0	0	67.1	59	22	57	0	5	3	1	0	0	0	—	4	10	1	1	0.3	.933
2 yrs.		5	5	.500	2.72	84	0	0	99.1	89	35	78	0	5	5	1					6	18	1	2	0.3	.960

Carlos Crawford

CRAWFORD, CARLOS LAMONTE
B. Oct. 4, 1971, Charlotte, N. C.

BR TR 6'1" 190 lbs.

Year	Team	W	L	PCT	ERA	G	GS	CG	IP	H	BB	SO	ShO	W	L	SV	AB	H	HR	BA	PO	A	E	DP	TC/G	FA
1996	PHI N	0	1	.000	4.91	1	1	0	3.2	7	2	4	0	0	0	0	1	0	0	.000	1	0	1	0	1.0	.000

Doug Creek

CREEK, PAUL DOUGLAS
B. Mar. 1, 1969, Winchester, Va.

BL TL 5'10" 205 lbs.

Year	Team	W	L	PCT	ERA	G	GS	CG	IP	H	BB	SO	ShO	W	L	SV	AB	H	HR	BA	PO	A	E	DP	TC/G	FA
1995	STL N	0	0	—	0.00	6	0	0	6.2	2	3	10	0	0	0	0	0	0	0	—	0	0	0	0	0.0	.000
1996	SF N	0	2	.000	6.52	63	0	0	48.1	45	32	38	0	0	2	0	1	0	0	.000	3	2	0	1	0.1	1.000
2 yrs.		0	2	.000	5.73	69	0	0	55	47	35	48	0	0	2	0	1	0	0	.000	3	2	0	1	0.1	1.000

John Cummings

CUMMINGS, JOHN RUSSELL
B. May 10, 1969, Torrance, Calif.

BL TL 6'3" 200 lbs.

Year	Team	W	L	PCT	ERA	G	GS	CG	IP	H	BB	SO	ShO	W	L	SV	AB	H	HR	BA	PO	A	E	DP	TC/G	FA
1993	SEA A	0	6	.000	6.02	10	8	1	46.1	59	16	19	0	0	0	0	0	0	0	—	3	6	2	0	1.1	.818
1994		2	4	.333	5.63	17	8	0	64	66	37	33	0	1	0	0	0	0	0	—	2	5	0	0	0.4	1.000
1995	2 teams	SEA A	(4G 0-0)			LA N	(35G 3-1)																			
"	total	3	1	.750	4.06	39	0	0	44.1	46	17	25	0	3	1	0	3	0	0	.000	4	5	0	2	0.2	1.000
1996	2 teams	LA N	(4G 0-1)			DET A	(21G 3-3)																			
"	total	3	4	.429	5.35	25	0	0	37	48	22	29	0	3	4	0	0	0	0	—	1	5	0	0	0.2	1.000
4 yrs.		8	15	.348	5.31	91	16	1	191.2	219	92	106	0	7	5	0	3	0	0	.000	10	21	2	2	0.4	.939

DIVISIONAL PLAYOFF SERIES

Year	Team	W	L	PCT	ERA	G	GS	CG	IP	H	BB	SO	ShO	W	L	SV	AB	H	HR	BA	PO	A	E	DP	TC/G	FA
1995	LA N	0	0	—	20.25	2	0	0	1.1	3	2	3	0	0	0	0	0	0	0	—	0	0	0	0	0.0	.000

Omar Daal

DAAL, OMAR JESUS
Born Omar Jesus Daal (Cordero).
B. Mar. 1, 1972, Maracaibo, Venezuela

BL TL 6'3" 160 lbs.

Year	Team	W	L	PCT	ERA	G	GS	CG	IP	H	BB	SO	ShO	W	L	SV	AB	H	HR	BA	PO	A	E	DP	TC/G	FA
1993	LA N	2	3	.400	5.09	47	0	0	35.1	36	21	19	0	2	3	0	0	0	0	—	5	6	0	0	0.2	1.000
1994		0	0	—	3.29	24	0	0	13.2	12	5	9	0	0	0	0	0	0	0	—	1	2	1	0	0.2	.750
1995		4	0	1.000	7.20	28	0	0	20	29	15	11	0	4	0	0	0	0	0	—	0	2	0	0	0.1	1.000
1996	MON N	4	5	.444	4.02	64	6	0	87.1	74	37	82	0	2	2	0	11	0	0	.000	4	16	1	0	0.3	.952
4 yrs.		10	8	.556	4.61	163	6	0	156.1	151	78	121	0	8	5	0	11	0	0	.000	10	26	2	0	0.2	.947

Jeff D'Amico

D'AMICO, JEFFREY CHARLES
B. Dec. 27, 1975, St. Petersburg, Fla.

BR TR 6'7" 250 lbs.

Year	Team	W	L	PCT	ERA	G	GS	CG	IP	H	BB	SO	ShO	W	L	SV	AB	H	HR	BA	PO	A	E	DP	TC/G	FA
1996	MIL A	6	6	.500	5.44	17	17	0	86	88	31	53	0	0	0	0	0	0	0	—	10	6	0	0	0.9	1.000

Danny Darwin

DARWIN, DANIEL WAYNE
Brother of Jeff Darwin.
B. Oct. 25, 1955, Bonham, Tex.

BR TR 6'3" 185 lbs.

Year	Team	W	L	PCT	ERA	G	GS	CG	IP	H	BB	SO	ShO	W	L	SV	AB	H	HR	BA	PO	A	E	DP	TC/G	FA
1978	TEX A	1	0	1.000	4.15	3	1	0	8.2	11	1	8	0	0	0	0	0	0	0	—	0	0	0	0	0.0	.000
1979		4	4	.500	4.04	20	6	1	78	50	30	58	0	1	3	0	0	0	0	—	2	6	0	0	0.4	1.000
1980		13	4	.765	2.62	53	2	0	110	98	50	104	0	12	3	8	0	0	0	—	7	11	0	1	0.3	1.000

Year	Team	W	L	PCT	ERA	G	GS	CG	IP	H	BB	SO	ShO	W	L	SV	AB	H	HR	BA	PO	A	E	DP	TC/G	FA
														Relief Pitching			**Batting**									

Danny Darwin *continued*

Year	Team	W	L	PCT	ERA	G	GS	CG	IP	H	BB	SO	ShO	W	L	SV	AB	H	HR	BA	PO	A	E	DP	TC/G	FA
1982		10	8	.556	3.44	56	1	0	89	95	37	61	0	10	7	7	0	0	0	—	5	19	0	0	0.4	1.000
1983		8	13	.381	3.49	28	26	9	183	175	62	92	2	0	0	0	0	0	0	—	20	18	3	1	1.5	.927
1984		8	12	.400	3.94	35	32	5	223.2	249	54	123	1	0	0	0	0	0	0	—	13	21	3	2	1.1	.919
1985	MIL A	8	18	.308	3.80	39	29	11	217.2	212	65	125	1	1	2	2	0	0	0	—	15	16	2	1	0.8	.939
1986	2 teams	MIL A	(27G 6-8)		HOU N	(12G 5-2)																				
"	total	11	10	.524	3.17	39	22	6	184.2	170	44	120	1	3	1	0	16	1	0	.063	10	27	3	2	1.0	.925
1987	HOU N	9	10	.474	3.59	33	30	3	195.2	184	69	134	1	0	0	0	66	12	0	.182	10	22	2	0	1.0	.941
1988		8	13	.381	3.84	44	20	3	192	189	48	129	0	4	3	3	56	4	1	.071	14	37	1	2	1.2	.981
1989		11	4	.733	2.36	68	0	0	122	92	33	104	0	11	4	7	17	2	0	.118	2	12	2	2	0.2	.875
1990		11	4	.733	**2.21**	48	17	3	162.2	136	31	109	0	2	1	2	38	5	0	.132	11	15	1	1	0.6	.963
1991	BOS A	3	6	.333	5.16	12	12	0	68	71	15	42	0	0	0	0	0	0	0	—	6	9	0	0	1.3	1.000
1992		9	9	.500	3.96	51	15	2	161.1	159	53	124	0	5	4	3	0	0	0	—	9	13	1	2	0.5	.957
1993		15	11	.577	3.26	34	34	2	229.1	196	49	130	1	0	0	0	0	0	0	—	14	31	2	2	1.4	.957
1994		7	5	.583	6.30	13	13	0	75.2	101	24	54	0	0	0	0	0	0	0	—	5	8	0	0	1.0	1.000
1995	2 teams	TOR A	(13G 1-8)		TEX A	(7G 2-2)																				
"	total	3	10	.231	7.45	20	15	1	99	131	31	58	0	0	0	0	0	0	0	—	3	7	2	1	0.6	.833
1996	2 teams	PIT N	(19G 7-9)		HOU N	(15G 3-2)																				
"	total	10	11	.476	3.77	34	25	0	164.2	160	27	96	0	2	0	0	49	9	1	.184	12	25	1	3	1.1	.974
	19 yrs.	158	161	.495	3.71	652	322	52	2711	2594	780	1769	9	51	28	32	242	33	2	.136	166	313	25	23	0.8	.950

Jeff Darwin

DARWIN, JEFFREY SCOTT
Brother of Danny Darwin.
B. July 6, 1969, Sherman, Tex.

BR TR 6'3" 180 lbs.

Year	Team	W	L	PCT	ERA	G	GS	CG	IP	H	BB	SO	ShO	W	L	SV	AB	H	HR	BA	PO	A	E	DP	TC/G	FA
1994	SEA A	0	0	—	13.50	2	0	0	4	7	3	1	0	0	0	0	0	0	0	—	0	0	0	0	0.0	.000
1996	CHI A	0	1	.000	2.93	22	0	0	30.2	26	9	15	0	0	1	0	0	0	0	—	3	2	0	0	0.2	1.000
	2 yrs.	0	1	.000	4.15	24	0	0	34.2	33	12	16	0	0	1	0	0	0	0	—	3	2	0	0	0.2	1.000

Tim Davis

DAVIS, TIMOTHY HOWARD
B. July 14, 1970, Marianna, Fla.

BL TL 5'11" 165 lbs.

Year	Team	W	L	PCT	ERA	G	GS	CG	IP	H	BB	SO	ShO	W	L	SV	AB	H	HR	BA	PO	A	E	DP	TC/G	FA
1994	SEA A	2	2	.500	4.01	42	1	0	49.1	57	25	28	0	1	2	2	0	0	0	—	2	8	0	0	0.2	1.000
1995		2	1	.667	6.38	5	5	0	24	30	18	19	0	0	0	0	0	0	0	—	1	7	0	0	1.6	1.000
1996		2	2	.500	4.01	40	0	0	42.2	43	17	34	0	2	2	0	0	0	0	—	3	5	1	1	0.2	.889
	3 yrs.	6	5	.545	4.50	87	6	0	116	130	60	81	0	3	4	2	0	0	0	—	6	20	1	1	0.3	.963

Scott Davison

DAVISON, SCOTTY RAY
B. Oct. 16, 1970, Inglewood, Calif.

BR TR 6' 190 lbs.

Year	Team	W	L	PCT	ERA	G	GS	CG	IP	H	BB	SO	ShO	W	L	SV	AB	H	HR	BA	PO	A	E	DP	TC/G	FA
1995	SEA A	0	0	—	6.23	3	0	0	4.1	7	1	3	0	0	0	0	0	0	0	—	0	1	0	0	0.3	1.000
1996		0	0	—	9.00	5	0	0	9	11	3	9	0	0	0	0	0	0	0	—	3	0	0	0	0.6	1.000
	2 yrs.	0	0		8.10	8	0	0	13.1	18	4	12	0	0	0	0					3	1	0	0	0.5	1.000

Rich DeLucia

DeLUCIA, RICHARD ANTHONY
B. Oct. 7, 1964, Reading, Pa.

BR TR 6' 185 lbs.

Year	Team	W	L	PCT	ERA	G	GS	CG	IP	H	BB	SO	ShO	W	L	SV	AB	H	HR	BA	PO	A	E	DP	TC/G	FA
1990	SEA A	1	2	.333	2.00	5	5	1	36	30	9	20	0	0	0	0	0	0	0	—	3	2	1	0	1.2	.833
1991		12	13	.480	5.09	32	31	0	182	176	78	98	0	1	0	0	0	0	0	—	8	19	0	1	0.8	1.000
1992		3	6	.333	5.49	30	11	0	83.2	100	35	66	0	0	0	1	0	0	0	—	8	6	1	0	0.5	.933
1993		3	6	.333	4.64	30	1	0	42.2	46	23	48	0	3	5	0	0	0	0	—	2	7	0	0	0.3	1.000
1994	CIN N	0	0	—	4.22	8	0	0	10.2	9	5	15	0	0	0	0	0	0	0	—	1	0	0	0	0.1	1.000
1995	STL N	8	7	.533	3.39	56	0	0	82.1	63	36	76	0	8	6	0	10	2	0	.200	3	14	2	1	0.3	.895
1996	SF N	3	6	.333	5.84	56	0	0	61.2	62	31	55	0	3	6	0	4	1	0	.250	4	12	0	2	0.3	1.000
	7 yrs.	30	40	.429	4.69	217	49	1	499	486	217	378	0	15	17	1	14	3	0	.214	29	60	4	4	0.4	.957

Elmer Dessens

DESSENS, ELMER
B. Jan. 13, 1972, Hermosillo, Mexico

BR TR 6' 190 lbs.

Year	Team	W	L	PCT	ERA	G	GS	CG	IP	H	BB	SO	ShO	W	L	SV	AB	H	HR	BA	PO	A	E	DP	TC/G	FA
1996	PIT N	0	2	.000	8.28	15	3	0	25	40	4	13	0	0	0	0	5	2	0	.400	1	2	0	0	0.2	1.000

Mark Dewey

DEWEY, MARK ALAN
B. Jan. 3, 1965, Grand Rapids, Mich.

BR TR 6' 185 lbs.

Year	Team	W	L	PCT	ERA	G	GS	CG	IP	H	BB	SO	ShO	W	L	SV	AB	H	HR	BA	PO	A	E	DP	TC/G	FA
1990	SF N	1	1	.500	2.78	14	0	0	22.2	22	5	11	0	1	1	0	1	0	0	.000	2	2	0	1	0.3	1.000
1992	NY N	1	0	1.000	4.32	20	0	0	33.1	37	10	24	0	1	0	0	1	0	0	.000	3	5	0	0	0.4	1.000
1993	PIT N	1	2	.333	2.36	21	0	0	26.2	14	10	14	0	1	2	7	0	0	0	—	2	6	0	0	0.4	1.000
1994		2	1	.667	3.68	45	0	0	51.1	61	19	30	0	2	1	1	1	1	0	1.000	4	4	1	1	0.2	.889
1995	SF N	1	0	1.000	3.13	27	0	0	31.2	30	17	32	0	1	0	0	1	0	0	.000	1	3	1	1	0.2	.800
1996		6	3	.667	4.21	78	0	0	83.1	79	41	57	0	6	3	0	7	0	0	.000	8	17	0	2	0.3	1.000
	6 yrs.	12	7	.632	3.65	205	0	0	249	243	102	168	0	12	7	8	11	1	0	.091	20	37	2	5	0.3	.966

Jason Dickson

DICKSON, JASON ROYCE
B. Mar. 30, 1973, London, Ont., Canada

BL TR 6' 190 lbs.

Year	Team	W	L	PCT	ERA	G	GS	CG	IP	H	BB	SO	ShO	W	L	SV	AB	H	HR	BA	PO	A	E	DP	TC/G	FA
1996	CAL A	1	4	.200	4.57	7	7	0	43.1	52	18	20	0	0	0	0	0	0	0	—	3	5	1	0	1.3	.889

Year	Team	W	L	PCT	ERA	G	GS	CG	IP	H	BB	SO	ShO	Relief Pitching W	L	SV	Batting AB	H	HR	BA	PO	A	E	DP	TC/G	FA

Jerry DiPoto

DiPOTO, GERALD PETER III
B. May 24, 1968, Jersey City, N. J. — BR TR 6'2" 203 lbs.

Year	Team	W	L	PCT	ERA	G	GS	CG	IP	H	BB	SO	ShO	W	L	SV	AB	H	HR	BA	PO	A	E	DP	TC/G	FA
1993	CLE A	4	4	.500	2.40	46	0	0	56.1	57	30	41	0	4	4	11	0	0	0	—	4	10	2	1	0.3	.875
1994		0	0	—	8.04	7	0	0	15.2	26	10	9	0	0	0	0	0	0	0	—	0	1	0	0	0.1	1.000
1995	NY N	4	6	.400	3.78	58	0	0	78.2	77	29	49	0	4	6	2	5	0	0	.000	4	16	3	1	0.4	.870
1996		7	2	.778	4.19	57	0	0	77.1	91	45	52	0	7	2	0	1	0	0	.000	6	11	0	1	0.3	1.000
4 yrs.		15	12	.556	3.87	168	0	0	228	251	114	151	0	15	12	13	6	0	0	.000	14	38	5	3	0.3	.912

Glenn Dishman

DISHMAN, GLENELG EDWARD
B. Nov. 5, 1970, Baltimore, Md. — BR TL 6'1" 195 lbs.

Year	Team	W	L	PCT	ERA	G	GS	CG	IP	H	BB	SO	ShO	W	L	SV	AB	H	HR	BA	PO	A	E	DP	TC/G	FA
1995	SD N	4	8	.333	5.01	19	16	0	97	104	34	43	0	0	0	0	30	6	0	.200	4	13	0	1	0.9	1.000
1996	2 teams	SD N	(3G 0-0)			PHI N	(4G 0-0)																			
" total		0	0		7.71	7	1	0	9.1	12	3	3	0	0	0	0	0	0	0	—	1	0	0	0	0.1	1.000
2 yrs.		4	8	.333	5.25	26	17	0	106.1	116	37	46	0	0	0	0	30	6	0	.200	5	13	0	1	0.7	1.000

John Doherty

DOHERTY, JOHN HAROLD
B. June 11, 1967, Bronx, N. Y. — BR TR 6'4" 190 lbs.

Year	Team	W	L	PCT	ERA	G	GS	CG	IP	H	BB	SO	ShO	W	L	SV	AB	H	HR	BA	PO	A	E	DP	TC/G	FA
1992	DET A	7	4	.636	3.88	47	11	0	116	131	25	37	0	2	2	3	0	0	0	—	10	19	1	4	0.6	.967
1993		14	11	.560	4.44	32	31	3	184.2	205	48	63	2	0	0	0	0	0	0	—	14	20	5	1	1.2	.872
1994		6	7	.462	6.48	18	17	2	101.1	139	26	28	0	0	0	0	0	0	0	—	6	25	0	4	1.7	1.000
1995		5	9	.357	5.10	48	2	0	113	130	37	46	0	5	7	6	0	0	0	—	12	17	0	1	0.6	1.000
1996	BOS A	0	0	—	5.68	3	0	0	6.1	8	4	3	0	0	0	0	0	0	0	—	1	4	0	0	1.7	1.000
5 yrs.		32	31	.508	4.87	148	61	5	521.1	613	140	177	2	7	9	9	0	0	0	—	43	85	6	10	0.9	.955

Jim Dougherty

DOUGHERTY, JAMES E.
B. Mar. 8, 1968, Brentwood, N. Y. — BR TR 6' 210 lbs.

Year	Team	W	L	PCT	ERA	G	GS	CG	IP	H	BB	SO	ShO	W	L	SV	AB	H	HR	BA	PO	A	E	DP	TC/G	FA
1995	HOU N	8	4	.667	4.92	56	0	0	67.2	76	25	49	0	8	4	0	8	1	0	.125	4	14	0	4	0.3	1.000
1996		0	2	.000	9.00	12	0	0	13	14	11	6	0	0	2	0	0	0	0	—	1	3	0	0	0.3	1.000
2 yrs.		8	6	.571	5.58	68	0	0	80.2	90	36	55	0	8	6	0	8	1	0	.125	5	17	0	4	0.3	1.000

Doug Drabek

DRABEK, DOUGLAS DEAN
B. July 25, 1962, Victoria, Tex. — BR TR 6'1" 185 lbs.

Year	Team	W	L	PCT	ERA	G	GS	CG	IP	H	BB	SO	ShO	W	L	SV	AB	H	HR	BA	PO	A	E	DP	TC/G	FA
1986	NY A	7	8	.467	4.10	27	21	0	131.2	126	50	76	0	0	0	0	0	0	0	—	5	13	0	0	0.7	1.000
1987	PIT N	11	12	.478	3.88	29	28	1	176.1	165	46	120	1	0	0	0	59	7	0	.119	24	23	2	0	1.7	.959
1988		15	7	.682	3.08	33	32	3	219.1	194	50	127	1	0	0	0	76	13	0	.171	29	21	6	6	1.7	.893
1989		14	12	.538	2.80	35	34	8	244.1	215	69	123	5	1	0	0	77	8	0	.104	24	34	2	0	1.7	.967
1990		22	6	.786	2.76	33	33	9	231.1	190	56	131	3	0	0	0	84	18	1	.214	25	36	1	1	1.9	.984
1991		15	14	.517	3.07	35	35	5	234.2	245	62	142	2	0	0	0	84	15	0	.179	27	41	5	1	2.1	.932
1992		15	11	.577	2.77	34	34	10	256.2	218	54	177	4	0	0	0	89	14	0	.157	29	36	3	4	2.0	.956
1993	HOU N	9	18	.333	3.79	34	34	7	237.2	242	60	157	2	0	0	0	71	6	1	.085	19	32	0	2	1.5	1.000
1994		12	6	.667	2.84	23	23	6	164.2	132	45	121	2	0	0	0	58	14	0	.241	21	28	3	2	2.3	.942
1995		10	9	.526	4.77	31	31	2	185	205	54	143	1	0	0	0	60	14	0	.233	24	20	2	3	1.5	.957
1996		7	9	.438	4.57	30	30	1	175.1	208	60	137	0	0	0	0	56	10	0	.179	17	23	3	0	1.4	.930
11 yrs.		137	112	.550	3.41	344	335	52	2257	2140	606	1454	21	1	0	0	714	119	2	.167	244	307	27	19	1.7	.953

LEAGUE CHAMPIONSHIP SERIES

Year	Team	W	L	PCT	ERA	G	GS	CG	IP	H	BB	SO	ShO	W	L	SV	AB	H	HR	BA	PO	A	E	DP	TC/G	FA
1990	PIT N	1	1	.500	1.65	2	2	1	16.1	12	3	13	0	0	0	0	6	1	0	.167	1	6	1	0	4.0	.875
1991		1	1	.500	0.60	2	2	1	15	10	5	10	0	0	0	0	5	1	0	.200	3	0	0	0	1.5	1.000
1992		0	3	.000	3.71	3	3	0	17	18	6	10	0	0	0	0	6	0	0	.000	0	0	0	0	0.0	.000
3 yrs.		2	5	.286	2.05	7	7	2	48.1	40	14	33	0	0	0	0	17	2	0	.118	4	6	1	0	1.6	.909
				2nd			5th	4th			8th								9th							

Darren Dreifort

DREIFORT, DARREN JAMES
B. May 18, 1972, Wichita, Kans. — BR TR 6'2" 205 lbs.

Year	Team	W	L	PCT	ERA	G	GS	CG	IP	H	BB	SO	ShO	W	L	SV	AB	H	HR	BA	PO	A	E	DP	TC/G	FA
1994	LA N	0	5	.000	6.21	27	0	0	29	45	15	22	0	0	5	6	1	1	0	1.000	2	8	2	0	0.4	.833
1996		1	4	.200	4.94	19	0	0	23.2	23	12	24	0	1	4	0	3	0	0	.000	3	6	0	0	0.5	1.000
2 yrs.		1	9	.100	5.64	46	0	0	52.2	68	27	46	0	1	9	6	4	1	0	.250	5	14	2	0	0.5	.905

DIVISIONAL PLAYOFF SERIES

Year	Team	W	L	PCT	ERA	G	GS	CG	IP	H	BB	SO	ShO	W	L	SV	AB	H	HR	BA	PO	A	E	DP	TC/G	FA
1996	LA N	0	0	—	0.00	1	0	0	0.2	0	0	0	0	0	0	0	0	0	0	—	1	1	0	1	2.0	1.000

Mike Dyer

DYER, MICHAEL LAWRENCE
B. Sept. 8, 1966, Upland, Calif. — BR TR 6'3" 195 lbs.

Year	Team	W	L	PCT	ERA	G	GS	CG	IP	H	BB	SO	ShO	W	L	SV	AB	H	HR	BA	PO	A	E	DP	TC/G	FA
1989	MIN A	4	7	.364	4.82	16	12	1	71	74	37	37	0	0	1	0	0	0	0	—	6	3	0	1	0.6	1.000
1994	PIT N	1	1	.500	5.87	14	0	0	15.1	15	12	13	0	1	1	4	1	0	0	—	0	1	0	0	0.1	1.000
1995		4	5	.444	4.34	55	0	0	74.2	81	30	53	0	4	5	0	7	4	0	.571	3	13	0	2	0.3	1.000
1996	MON N	5	5	.500	4.40	70	1	0	75.2	79	34	51	0	5	4	2	7	0	0	.000	7	13	0	2	0.3	1.000
4 yrs.		14	18	.438	4.60	155	13	1	236.2	249	113	154	0	10	11	6	15	4	0	.267	16	30	0	5	0.3	1.000

Dennis Eckersley

ECKERSLEY, DENNIS LEE (The Eck)
B. Oct. 3, 1954, Oakland, Calif. — BR TR 6'2" 190 lbs.

Year	Team	W	L	PCT	ERA	G	GS	CG	IP	H	BB	SO	ShO	W	L	SV	AB	H	HR	BA	PO	A	E	DP	TC/G	FA
1975	CLE A	13	7	.650	2.60	34	24	6	186.2	147	90	152	2	1	0	0	0	0	0	—	7	12	1	0	0.6	.950
1976		13	12	.520	3.44	36	30	9	199	155	78	200	3	1	0	1	0	0	0	—	9	20	1	1	0.8	.967
1977		14	13	.519	3.53	33	33	12	247	214	54	191	3	0	0	0	0	0	0	—	6	22	2	1	0.9	.933
1979		17	10	.630	2.99	33	33	17	247	234	59	150	2	0	0	0	0	0	0	—	12	42	6	3	1.8	.900
1980		12	14	.462	4.27	30	30	8	198	188	44	121	0	0	0	0	0	0	0	—	10	24	3	0	1.2	.919
1981		9	8	.529	4.27	23	23	8	154	160	35	79	2	0	0	0	0	0	0	—	12	19	1	1	1.4	.969

Year	Team	W	L	PCT	ERA	G	GS	CG	IP	H	BB	SO	ShO	Relief Pitching W	L	SV	Batting AB	H	HR	BA	PO	A	E	DP	TC/G	FA

Dennis Eckersley *continued*

Year	Team	W	L	PCT	ERA	G	GS	CG	IP	H	BB	SO	ShO	W	L	SV	AB	H	HR	BA	PO	A	E	DP	TC/G	FA
1982		13	13	.500	3.73	33	33	11	224.1	228	43	127	3	0	0	0	0	0	0	—	21	21	1	2	1.3	.977
1983		9	13	.409	5.61	28	28	2	176.1	223	39	77	0	0	0	0	0	0	0	—	19	18	1	0	1.4	.974
1984	2 teams	BOS A	(9G 4–4)		CHI N	(24G 10–8)																				
"	total	14	12	.538	3.60	33	33	4	225	223	49	114	0	0	0	0	55	6	0	.109	27	38	5	3	2.1	.929
1985	CHI N	11	7	.611	3.08	25	25	6	169.1	145	19	117	2	0	0	0	56	7	1	.125	10	26	3	1	1.6	.923
1986		6	11	.353	4.57	33	32	1	201	226	43	137	0	0	0	0	69	11	2	.159	16	28	3	3	1.4	.936
1987	OAK A	6	8	.429	3.03	54	2	0	115.2	99	17	113	0	6	6	16	0	0	0	—	4	13	1	0	0.3	.944
1988		4	2	.667	2.35	60	0	0	72.2	52	11	70	0	4	2	45	0	0	0	—	7	3	0	0	0.2	1.000
1989		4	0	1.000	1.56	51	0	0	57.2	32	3	55	0	4	0	33	0	0	0	—	4	4	0	1	0.2	1.000
1990		4	2	.667	0.61	63	0	0	73.1	41	4	73	0	4	2	48	0	0	0	—	3	1	0	0	0.1	1.000
1991		5	4	.556	2.96	67	0	0	76	60	9	87	0	5	4	43	0	0	0	—	6	9	0	0	0.2	1.000
1992		7	1	.875	1.91	69	0	0	80	62	11	93	0	7	1	51	0	0	0	—	3	10	0	1	0.2	1.000
1993		2	4	.333	4.16	64	0	0	67	67	13	80	0	2	4	36	0	0	0	—	0	5	0	0	0.1	1.000
1994		5	4	.556	4.26	45	0	0	44.1	49	13	47	0	5	4	19	0	0	0	—	2	1	0	0	0.1	1.000
1995		4	6	.400	4.83	52	0	0	50.1	53	11	40	0	4	6	29	0	0	0	—	3	5	1	2	0.2	.889
1996	STL N	0	6	.000	3.30	63	0	0	60	65	6	49	0	0	6	30	1	0	0	.000	3	6	1	0	0.2	.900
22 yrs.		192	165	.538	3.48	964 6th	361	100	3193	2981	722	2334	20	43	35	353 3rd	181	24	3	.133	203	356	30	20	0.6	.949

DIVISIONAL PLAYOFF SERIES
Year	Team	W	L	PCT	ERA	G	GS	CG	IP	H	BB	SO	ShO	W	L	SV	AB	H	HR	BA	PO	A	E	DP	TC/G	FA
1996	STL N	0	0	—	0.00	3	0	0	3.2	3	0	2	0	0	0	3	0	0	0	—	0	1	0	0	0.3	1.000

LEAGUE CHAMPIONSHIP SERIES
Year	Team	W	L	PCT	ERA	G	GS	CG	IP	H	BB	SO	ShO	W	L	SV	AB	H	HR	BA	PO	A	E	DP	TC/G	FA
1984	CHI N	0	1	.000	8.44	1	1	0	5.1	9	0	0	0	0	0	0	2	0	0	.000	0	0	0	0	0.0	.000
1988	OAK A	0	0	—	0.00	4	0	0	6	1	2	5	0	0	0	4	0	0	0	—	2	0	0	0	0.5	.000
1989		0	0	—	1.59	4	0	0	5.2	4	0	2	0	0	0	3	0	0	0	—	0	1	0	0	0.3	1.000
1990		0	0	—	0.00	3	0	0	3.1	2	0	3	0	0	0	2	0	0	0	—	0	0	0	0	0.0	.000
1992		0	0	—	6.00	3	0	0	3	8	0	2	0	0	0	1	0	0	0	—	0	0	0	0	0.0	.000
1996	STL N	1	0	1.000	0.00	3	0	0	3.1	2	0	4	0	1	0	1	0	0	0	—	0	1	0	0	0.3	1.000
6 yrs.		1	1	.500	2.70	18 2nd	1	0	26.2	26	2	16	0	1	0	11 1st	2	0	0	.000	2	2	0	0	0.2	1.000

WORLD SERIES
Year	Team	W	L	PCT	ERA	G	GS	CG	IP	H	BB	SO	ShO	W	L	SV	AB	H	HR	BA	PO	A	E	DP	TC/G	FA
1988	OAK A	0	1	.000	10.80	2	0	0	1.2	2	1	2	0	0	1	0	0	0	0	—	0	0	0	0	0.0	.000
1989		0	0	—	0.00	2	0	0	1.2	0	0	0	0	0	0	1	0	0	0	—	1	0	0	0	0.5	.000
1990		0	1	.000	6.75	2	0	0	1.1	3	0	1	0	0	1	0	0	0	0	—	0	0	0	0	0.0	.000
3 yrs.		0	2	.000	5.79	6	0	0	4.2	5	1	3	0	0	2	1	0	0	0	—	1	0	0	0	0.1	1.000

Ken Edenfield
EDENFIELD, KENNETH EDWARD
B. Mar. 18, 1967, Jessup, Ga.

BR TR 6′1″ 165 lbs.

Year	Team	W	L	PCT	ERA	G	GS	CG	IP	H	BB	SO	ShO	W	L	SV	AB	H	HR	BA	PO	A	E	DP	TC/G	FA
1995	CAL A	0	0	—	4.26	7	0	0	12.2	15	5	6	0	0	0	0	0	0	0	—	0	2	0	0	0.3	1.000
1996		0	0	—	10.38	2	0	0	4.1	10	2	4	0	0	0	0	0	0	0	—	1	0	0	0	0.5	1.000
2 yrs.		0	0	—	5.82	9	0	0	17	25	7	10	0	0	0	0					1	2	0	0	0.3	1.000

Mark Eichhorn
EICHHORN, MARK ANTHONY
B. Nov. 21, 1960, San Jose, Calif.

BR TR 6′4″ 200 lbs.

Year	Team	W	L	PCT	ERA	G	GS	CG	IP	H	BB	SO	ShO	W	L	SV	AB	H	HR	BA	PO	A	E	DP	TC/G	FA
1982	TOR A	0	3	.000	5.45	7	7	0	38	40	14	16	0	0	0	0	0	0	0	—	1	3	0	0	0.6	1.000
1986		14	6	.700	1.72	69	0	0	157	105	45	166	0	14	6	10	0	0	0	—	16	21	0	1	0.5	1.000
1987		10	6	.625	3.17	89	0	0	127.2	110	52	96	0	10	6	4	0	0	0	—	2	30	1	2	0.4	.970
1988		0	3	.000	4.18	37	0	0	66.2	79	27	28	0	0	3	1	0	0	0	—	5	13	0	1	0.5	1.000
1989	ATL N	5	5	.500	4.35	45	0	0	68.1	70	19	49	0	5	5	0	2	0	0	.000	9	17	0	1	0.6	1.000
1990	CAL A	2	5	.286	3.08	60	0	0	84.2	98	23	69	0	2	5	13	0	0	0	—	7	16	0	0	0.4	1.000
1991		3	3	.500	1.98	70	0	0	81.2	63	13	49	0	3	3	1	0	0	0	—	4	18	0	2	0.3	1.000
1992	2 teams	CAL A	(42G 2–4)		TOR A	(23G 2–0)																				
"	total	4	4	.500	3.08	65	0	0	87.2	86	25	61	0	4	4	2	0	0	0	—	5	19	1	0	0.4	.960
1993	TOR A	3	1	.750	2.72	54	0	0	72.2	76	22	47	0	3	1	0	0	0	0	—	7	18	0	1	0.5	1.000
1994	BAL A	6	5	.545	2.15	43	0	0	71	62	19	35	0	6	5	1	0	0	0	—	3	19	0	1	0.5	1.000
1996	CAL A	1	2	.333	5.04	24	0	0	30.1	36	11	24	0	1	2	0	0	0	0	—	2	6	0	0	0.3	1.000
11 yrs.		48	43	.527	3.00	563	7	0	885.2	825	270	640	0	48	40	32	2	0	0	.000	61	180	2	9	0.4	.992

LEAGUE CHAMPIONSHIP SERIES
Year	Team	W	L	PCT	ERA	G	GS	CG	IP	H	BB	SO	ShO	W	L	SV	AB	H	HR	BA	PO	A	E	DP	TC/G	FA
1992	TOR A	0	0	—	0.00	1	0	0	1	0	0	0	0	0	0	0	0	0	0	—	0	0	0	0	0.0	.000
1993		0	0	—	0.00	1	0	0	2	1	1	1	0	0	0	0	0	0	0	—	0	0	0	0	0.0	.000
2 yrs.		0	0		0.00	2	0	0	3	1	1	1	0	0	0	0	0	0	0		0	0	0	0	0.0	

WORLD SERIES
Year	Team	W	L	PCT	ERA	G	GS	CG	IP	H	BB	SO	ShO	W	L	SV	AB	H	HR	BA	PO	A	E	DP	TC/G	FA
1992	TOR A	0	0	—	0.00	1	0	0	1	0	0	1	0	0	0	0	0	0	0	—	0	0	0	0	0.0	.000
1993		0	0	—	0.00	1	0	0	0.1	1	1	0	0	0	0	0	0	0	0	—	0	0	0	0	0.0	.000
2 yrs.		0	0		0.00	2	0	0	1.1	1	1	1	0	0	0	0	0	0	0		0	0	0	0	0.0	

Joey Eischen
EISCHEN, JOSEPH RAYMOND
B. May 25, 1970, West Covina, Calif.

BL TL 6′1″ 190 lbs.

Year	Team	W	L	PCT	ERA	G	GS	CG	IP	H	BB	SO	ShO	W	L	SV	AB	H	HR	BA	PO	A	E	DP	TC/G	FA
1994	MON N	0	0	—	54.00	1	0	0	0.2	4	0	1	0	0	0	0	0	0	0	—	0	0	0	0	0.0	.000
1995	LA N	0	0	—	3.10	17	0	0	20.1	19	11	15	0	0	0	0	1	0	0	.000	3	1	0	0	0.2	1.000
1996	2 teams	LA N	(28G 0–1)		DET A	(24G 1–1)																				
"	total	1	2	.333	4.21	52	0	0	68.1	75	34	51	0	1	2	0	6	0	0	.000	0	11	0	2	0.2	1.000
3 yrs.		1	2	.333	4.33	70	0	0	89.1	98	45	67	0	1	2	0	7	0	0	.000	3	12	0	2	0.2	1.000

Year	Team	W	L	PCT	ERA	G	GS	CG	IP	H	BB	SO	ShO	Relief Pitching W	L	SV	Batting AB	H	HR	BA	PO	A	E	DP	TC/G	FA

Cal Eldred

ELDRED, CALVIN JOHN
B. Nov. 24, 1967, Cedar Rapids, Iowa
BR TR 6'4" 215 lbs.

Year	Team	W	L	PCT	ERA	G	GS	CG	IP	H	BB	SO	ShO	W	L	SV	AB	H	HR	BA	PO	A	E	DP	TC/G	FA
1991	MIL A	2	0	1.000	4.50	3	3	0	16	20	6	10	0	0	0	0	0	0	0	—	2	1	0	0	1.0	1.000
1992		11	2	.846	1.79	14	14	2	100.1	76	23	62	1	0	0	0	0	0	0	—	4	12	1	0	1.2	.941
1993		16	16	.500	4.01	36	36	8	258	232	91	180	1	0	0	0	0	0	0	—	26	27	2	4	1.5	.964
1994		11	11	.500	4.68	25	25	6	179	158	84	98	0	0	0	0	0	0	0	—	20	23	0	2	1.7	1.000
1995		1	1	.500	3.42	4	4	0	23.2	24	10	18	0	0	0	0	0	0	0	—	2	2	1	0	1.3	.800
1996		4	4	.500	4.46	15	15	0	84.2	82	38	50	0	0	0	0	0	0	0	—	4	10	0	0	0.9	1.000
6 yrs.		45	34	.570	3.90	97	97	16	661.2	592	252	418	2	0	0	0	0	0	0		58	75	4	6	1.4	.971

Robert Ellis

ELLIS, ROBERT RANDOLPH
B. Dec. 15, 1970, Baton Rouge, La.
BR TR 6'5" 220 lbs.

Year	Team	W	L	PCT	ERA	G	GS	CG	IP	H	BB	SO	ShO	W	L	SV	AB	H	HR	BA	PO	A	E	DP	TC/G	FA
1996	CAL A	0	0	—	0.00	3	0	0	5	0	4	5	0	0	0	0	0	0	0	—	0	0	0	0	0.0	—

Alan Embree

EMBREE, ALAN DUANE
B. Jan. 23, 1970, Vancouver, Wash.
BL TL 6'2" 185 lbs.

Year	Team	W	L	PCT	ERA	G	GS	CG	IP	H	BB	SO	ShO	W	L	SV	AB	H	HR	BA	PO	A	E	DP	TC/G	FA
1992	CLE A	0	2	.000	7.00	4	4	0	18	19	8	12	0	0	0	0	0	0	0	—	1	0	1	0	0.5	.500
1995		3	2	.600	5.11	23	0	0	24.2	23	16	23	0	3	2	1	0	0	0	—	0	3	0	0	0.1	1.000
1996		1	1	.500	6.39	24	0	0	31	30	21	33	0	1	1	0	0	0	0	—	1	2	0	0	0.1	1.000
3 yrs.		4	5	.444	6.11	51	4	0	73.2	72	45	68	0	4	3	1	0	0	0		2	5	1	0	0.2	.875

DIVISIONAL PLAYOFF SERIES

Year	Team	W	L	PCT	ERA	G	GS	CG	IP	H	BB	SO	ShO	W	L	SV	AB	H	HR	BA	PO	A	E	DP	TC/G	FA
1996	CLE A	0	0	—	9.00	3	0	0	1	0	0	1	0	0	0	0	0	0	0	—	0	0	0	0	0.0	.000

LEAGUE CHAMPIONSHIP SERIES

Year	Team	W	L	PCT	ERA	G	GS	CG	IP	H	BB	SO	ShO	W	L	SV	AB	H	HR	BA	PO	A	E	DP	TC/G	FA
1995	CLE A	0	0	—	0.00	1	0	0	0.1	0	0	0	0	0	0	0	0	0	0	—	0	0	0	0	0.0	.000

WORLD SERIES

Year	Team	W	L	PCT	ERA	G	GS	CG	IP	H	BB	SO	ShO	W	L	SV	AB	H	HR	BA	PO	A	E	DP	TC/G	FA
1995	CLE A	0	0	—	2.70	4	0	0	3.1	0	0	0	0	0	0	0	0	0	0	—	0	1	0	0	0.3	1.000

John Ericks

ERICKS, JOHN EDWARD III
B. Sept. 16, 1967, Tinley Park, Ill.
BR TR 6'7" 220 lbs.

Year	Team	W	L	PCT	ERA	G	GS	CG	IP	H	BB	SO	ShO	W	L	SV	AB	H	HR	BA	PO	A	E	DP	TC/G	FA
1995	PIT N	3	9	.250	4.58	19	18	1	106	108	50	80	0	0	0	0	31	3	0	.097	7	10	3	0	1.1	.850
1996		4	5	.444	5.79	28	4	0	46.2	56	19	46	0	4	2	8	5	0	0	.000	1	2	0	0	0.1	1.000
2 yrs.		7	14	.333	4.95	47	22	1	152.2	164	69	126	0	4	2	8	36	3	0	.083	8	12	3	0	0.5	.870

Scott Erickson

ERICKSON, SCOTT GAVIN
B. Feb. 2, 1968, Long Beach, Calif.
BR TR 6'4" 220 lbs.

Year	Team	W	L	PCT	ERA	G	GS	CG	IP	H	BB	SO	ShO	W	L	SV	AB	H	HR	BA	PO	A	E	DP	TC/G	FA
1990	MIN A	8	4	.667	2.87	19	17	1	113	108	51	53	0	0	0	0	0	0	0	—	10	13	0	0	1.2	1.000
1991		20	8	.714	3.18	32	32	5	204	189	71	108	3	0	0	0	0	0	0	—	19	31	1	3	1.6	.980
1992		13	12	.520	3.40	32	32	5	212	197	83	101	3	0	0	0	0	0	0	—	18	34	1	3	1.7	.981
1993		8	19	.296	5.19	34	34	1	218.2	266	71	116	0	0	0	0	0	0	0	—	18	34	3	3	1.6	.945
1994		8	11	.421	5.44	23	23	2	144	173	59	104	1	0	0	0	0	0	0	—	9	23	4	4	1.6	.889
1995	2 teams	MIN A	(15G 4–6)			BAL A	(17G 9–4)																			
"	total	13	10	.565	4.81	32	31	7	196.1	213	67	106	2	0	0	0	0	0	0	—	26	40	1	2	2.1	.985
1996	BAL A	13	12	.520	5.02	34	34	6	222.1	262	66	100	0	0	0	0	0	0	0	—	30	43	2	6	2.2	.973
7 yrs.		83	76	.522	4.33	206	203	27	1310.1	1408	468	688	9	0	0	0	0	0	0		130	218	12	21	1.7	.967

DIVISIONAL PLAYOFF SERIES

Year	Team	W	L	PCT	ERA	G	GS	CG	IP	H	BB	SO	ShO	W	L	SV	AB	H	HR	BA	PO	A	E	DP	TC/G	FA
1996	BAL A	0	0	—	4.05	1	1	0	6.2	6	2	6	0	0	0	0	0	0	0	—	1	3	0	1	4.0	1.000

LEAGUE CHAMPIONSHIP SERIES

Year	Team	W	L	PCT	ERA	G	GS	CG	IP	H	BB	SO	ShO	W	L	SV	AB	H	HR	BA	PO	A	E	DP	TC/G	FA
1991	MIN A	0	0	—	4.50	1	1	0	4	3	5	2	0	0	0	0	0	0	0	—	1	1	0	0	2.0	1.000
1996	MIN A	0	1	.000	2.38	2	2	0	11.1	14	4	8	0	0	0	0	0	0	0	—	0	2	0	0	1.0	1.000
2 yrs.		0	1	.000	2.93	3	3	0	15.1	17	9	10	0	0	0	0	0	0	0		1	3	0	0	1.3	1.000

WORLD SERIES

Year	Team	W	L	PCT	ERA	G	GS	CG	IP	H	BB	SO	ShO	W	L	SV	AB	H	HR	BA	PO	A	E	DP	TC/G	FA
1991	MIN A	0	0	—	5.06	2	2	0	10.2	10	4	5	0	0	0	0	1	0	0	.000	1	0	0	0	0.5	1.000

Vaughn Eshelman

ESHELMAN, VAUGHN MICHAEL
B. May 22, 1969, Philadelphia, Pa.
BL TL 6'3" 205 lbs.

Year	Team	W	L	PCT	ERA	G	GS	CG	IP	H	BB	SO	ShO	W	L	SV	AB	H	HR	BA	PO	A	E	DP	TC/G	FA
1995	BOS A	6	3	.667	4.85	23	14	0	81.2	86	36	41	0	1	0	0	0	0	0	—	6	8	1	1	0.7	.933
1996		6	3	.667	7.08	39	10	0	87.2	112	58	59	0	2	1	0	0	0	0	—	5	16	3	0	0.6	.875
2 yrs.		12	6	.667	6.01	62	24	0	169.1	198	94	100	0	3	1	0					11	24	4	1	0.6	.897

Shawn Estes

ESTES, AARON SHAWN
B. Feb. 18, 1973, San Bernardino, Calif.
BB TL 6'2" 185 lbs.

Year	Team	W	L	PCT	ERA	G	GS	CG	IP	H	BB	SO	ShO	W	L	SV	AB	H	HR	BA	PO	A	E	DP	TC/G	FA
1995	SF N	0	3	.000	6.75	3	3	0	17.1	16	5	14	0	0	0	0	5	0	0	.000	0	1	0	0	0.3	1.000
1996		3	5	.375	3.60	11	11	0	70	63	39	60	0	0	0	0	19	3	0	.158	2	11	0	0	1.2	1.000
2 yrs.		3	8	.273	4.23	14	14	0	87.1	79	44	74	0	0	0	0	24	3	0	.125	2	12	0	0	1.0	1.000

Michael Farmer

FARMER, MICHAEL ANTHONY
Brother of Howard Farmer.
B. Jul. 3, 1968, Gary, Ind.
BB TL 6'1" 193 lbs.

Year	Team	W	L	PCT	ERA	G	GS	CG	IP	H	BB	SO	ShO	W	L	SV	AB	H	HR	BA	PO	A	E	DP	TC/G	FA
1996	CLR N	0	1	.000	7.71	7	4	0	28	32	13	16	0	0	1	0	10	4	0	.400	1	3	0	0	0.6	1.000

Year	Team	W	L	PCT	ERA	G	GS	CG	IP	H	BB	SO	ShO	Relief Pitching W	L	SV	Batting AB	H	HR	BA	PO	A	E	DP	TC/G	FA

John Farrell

FARRELL, JOHN EDWARD
B. Aug. 4, 1962, Monmouth Beach, N. J.   BR TR 6'4"   210 lbs.

Year	Team	W	L	PCT	ERA	G	GS	CG	IP	H	BB	SO	ShO	W	L	SV	AB	H	HR	BA	PO	A	E	DP	TC/G	FA
1987	CLE A	5	1	.833	3.39	10	9	1	69	68	22	28	0	1	0	0	0	0	0	—	8	7	2	1	1.7	.882
1988		14	10	.583	4.24	31	30	4	210.1	216	67	92	0	0	0	0	0	0	0	—	21	23	0	2	1.4	1.000
1989		9	14	.391	3.63	31	31	7	208	196	71	132	2	0	0	0	0	0	0	—	18	20	2	1	1.3	.950
1990		4	5	.444	4.28	17	17	1	96.2	108	33	44	0	0	0	0	0	0	0	—	8	12	2	1	1.3	.909
1993	CAL A	3	12	.200	7.35	21	17	0	90.2	110	44	45	0	0	1	0	0	0	0	—	5	11	0	0	0.8	1.000
1994		1	2	.333	9.00	3	3	0	13	16	8	10	0	0	0	0	0	0	0	—	1	6	1	1	2.7	.875
1995	CLE A	0	0	—	3.86	1	0	0	4.2	7	0	4	0	0	0	0	0	0	0	—	1	0	1	1	2.0	.500
1996	DET A	0	2	.000	14.21	2	2	0	6.1	11	5	0	0	0	0	0	0	0	0	—	1	0	0	0	0.5	1.000
8 yrs.		36	46	.439	4.56	116	109	13	698.2	732	250	355	2	1	1	0	0	0	0		63	79	8	7	1.3	.947

Jeff Fassero

FASSERO, JEFFREY JOSEPH
B. Jan. 5, 1963, Springfield, Ill.   BL TL 6'1"   180 lbs.

Year	Team	W	L	PCT	ERA	G	GS	CG	IP	H	BB	SO	ShO	W	L	SV	AB	H	HR	BA	PO	A	E	DP	TC/G	FA
1991	MON N	2	5	.286	2.44	51	0	0	55.1	39	17	42	0	2	5	8	3	0	0	.000	3	11	1	1	0.3	.933
1992		8	7	.533	2.84	70	0	0	85.2	81	34	63	0	8	7	1	7	1	0	.143	1	15	0	0	0.2	1.000
1993		12	5	.706	2.29	56	15	1	149.2	119	54	140	0	5	1	1	32	2	0	.063	5	22	3	0	0.5	.900
1994		8	6	.571	2.99	21	21	0	138.2	119	40	119	0	0	0	0	44	3	0	.068	9	33	0	1	2.0	1.000
1995		13	14	.481	4.33	30	30	1	189	207	74	164	0	0	0	0	57	4	0	.070	7	35	4	1	1.5	.913
1996		15	11	.577	3.30	34	34	5	231.2	217	55	222	1	0	0	0	64	6	0	.094	12	41	1	2	1.6	.981
6 yrs.		58	48	.547	3.20	262	100	8	850	782	274	750	1	15	13	10	207	16	0	.077	37	157	9	5	0.8	.956

Alex Fernandez

FERNANDEZ, ALEXANDER
B. Aug. 13, 1969, Miami, Fla.   BR TR 6'2"   200 lbs.

Year	Team	W	L	PCT	ERA	G	GS	CG	IP	H	BB	SO	ShO	W	L	SV	AB	H	HR	BA	PO	A	E	DP	TC/G	FA
1990	CHI A	5	5	.500	3.80	13	13	3	87.2	89	34	61	0	0	0	0	0	0	0	—	3	12	2	0	1.3	.882
1991		9	13	.409	4.51	34	32	2	191.2	186	88	145	0	0	0	0	0	0	0	—	7	31	3	2	1.2	.927
1992		8	11	.421	4.27	29	29	4	187.2	199	50	95	2	0	0	0	0	0	0	—	10	33	2	5	1.6	.956
1993		18	9	.667	3.13	34	34	3	247.1	221	67	169	1	0	0	0	0	0	0	—	18	38	0	2	1.6	1.000
1994		11	7	.611	3.86	24	24	4	170.1	163	50	122	3	0	0	0	0	0	0	—	16	39	1	4	2.3	.982
1995		12	8	.600	3.80	30	30	5	203.2	200	65	159	2	0	0	0	0	0	0	—	11	26	3	5	1.3	.925
1996		16	10	.615	3.45	35	35	6	258	248	72	200	1	0	0	0	0	0	0	—	27	43	2	7	2.1	.972
7 yrs.		79	63	.556	3.78	199	197	27	1346.1	1306	426	951	9	0	0	0	0	0	0		92	222	13	25	1.6	.960

LEAGUE CHAMPIONSHIP SERIES

Year	Team	W	L	PCT	ERA	G	GS	CG	IP	H	BB	SO	ShO	W	L	SV	AB	H	HR	BA	PO	A	E	DP	TC/G	FA
1993	CHI A	0	2	.000	1.80	2	2	0	15	15	6	10	0	0	0	0	0	0	0	—	2	1	0	1	1.5	1.000

Sid Fernandez

FERNANDEZ, CHARLES SIDNEY (El Sid)
B. Oct. 12, 1962, Honolulu, Hawaii   BL TL 6'1"   220 lbs.

Year	Team	W	L	PCT	ERA	G	GS	CG	IP	H	BB	SO	ShO	W	L	SV	AB	H	HR	BA	PO	A	E	DP	TC/G	FA
1983	LA N	0	1	.000	6.00	2	1	0	6	7	7	9	0	0	0	0	1	1	0	1.000	1	1	0	0	1.0	1.000
1984	NY N	6	6	.500	3.50	15	15	0	90	74	34	62	0	0	0	0	28	5	0	.179	0	6	0	0	0.4	1.000
1985		9	9	.500	2.80	26	26	3	170.1	108	80	180	0	0	0	0	52	11	0	.212	1	23	0	0	0.9	1.000
1986		16	6	.727	3.52	32	31	2	204.1	161	91	200	1	0	0	1	68	11	0	.162	3	18	1	1	0.7	.955
1987		12	8	.600	3.81	28	27	3	156	130	67	134	0	0	0	0	43	7	0	.163	4	14	0	0	0.6	.941
1988		12	10	.545	3.03	31	31	1	187	127	70	189	1	0	0	0	56	14	0	.250	2	13	0	0	0.5	1.000
1989		14	5	.737	2.83	35	32	6	219.1	157	75	198	2	0	0	0	71	15	1	.211	4	13	0	2	0.5	1.000
1990		9	14	.391	3.46	30	30	2	179.1	130	67	181	1	0	0	0	58	11	0	.190	1	16	2	0	0.6	.895
1991		1	3	.250	2.86	8	8	0	44	36	9	31	0	0	0	0	13	2	0	.154	1	11	0	0	1.5	1.000
1992		14	11	.560	2.73	32	32	5	214.2	162	67	193	2	0	0	0	74	15	0	.203	4	21	1	1	0.8	.962
1993		5	6	.455	2.93	18	18	1	119.2	82	36	81	1	0	0	0	32	3	0	.094	2	10	0	1	0.7	1.000
1994	BAL A	6	6	.500	5.15	19	19	2	115.1	109	46	95	0	0	0	0	0	0	0	—	1	9	0	0	0.5	1.000
1995	2 teams	BAL A	(8G 0-4)		PHI N	(11G 6-1)																				
"	total	6	5	.545	4.56	19	18	0	92.2	84	38	110	0	0	0	0	23	1	0	.043	0	3	1	0	0.2	.750
1996	PHI N	3	6	.333	3.43	11	11	0	63	50	26	77	0	0	0	0	19	2	0	.105	1	3	0	0	0.4	1.000
14 yrs.		113	96	.541	3.36	306	299	25	1861.2	1417	713	1740	9	0	0	1	538	98	1	.182	25	159	6	5	0.6	.968

LEAGUE CHAMPIONSHIP SERIES

Year	Team	W	L	PCT	ERA	G	GS	CG	IP	H	BB	SO	ShO	W	L	SV	AB	H	HR	BA	PO	A	E	DP	TC/G	FA
1986	NY N	0	1	.000	4.50	1	1	0	6	3	1	5	0	0	0	0	1	0	0	.000	0	0	0	0	0.0	.000
1988		0	1	.000	13.50	1	1	0	4	7	1	4	0	0	0	0	1	0	0	.000	0	0	0	0	0.0	.000
2 yrs.		0	2	.000	8.10	2	2	0	10	10	2	10	0	0	0	0	2	0	0	.000	0	0	0	0	0.0	

WORLD SERIES

Year	Team	W	L	PCT	ERA	G	GS	CG	IP	H	BB	SO	ShO	W	L	SV	AB	H	HR	BA	PO	A	E	DP	TC/G	FA
1986	NY N	0	0	—	1.35	3	0	0	6.2	6	1	10	0	0	0	0	0	0	0	—	0	0	0	0	0.0	.000

Osvaldo Fernandez

FERNANDEZ, OSVALDO
B. Nov. 4, 1968, Holguin, Cuba   BR TR 6'2"   190 lbs.

Year	Team	W	L	PCT	ERA	G	GS	CG	IP	H	BB	SO	ShO	W	L	SV	AB	H	HR	BA	PO	A	E	DP	TC/G	FA
1996	SF N	7	13	.350	4.61	30	28	2	171.2	193	57	106	0	0	1	0	57	5	0	.088	10	31	2	1	1.4	953

Mike Fetters

FETTERS, MICHAEL LEE
B. Dec. 19, 1964, Van Nuys, Calif.   BR TR 6'4"   200 lbs.

Year	Team	W	L	PCT	ERA	G	GS	CG	IP	H	BB	SO	ShO	W	L	SV	AB	H	HR	BA	PO	A	E	DP	TC/G	FA
1989	CAL A	0	0	—	8.10	1	0	0	3.1	5	1	4	0	0	0	0	0	0	0	—	0	1	0	0	1.0	1.000
1990		1	1	.500	4.12	26	2	0	67.2	77	20	35	0	1	1	1	0	0	0	—	9	11	1	0	0.8	.952
1991		2	5	.286	4.84	19	4	0	44.2	53	28	24	0	2	1	0	0	0	0	—	2	4	1	0	0.4	.857
1992	MIL A	5	1	.833	1.87	50	0	0	62.2	38	24	43	0	5	1	2	0	0	0	—	3	11	0	1	0.3	1.000
1993		3	3	.500	3.34	45	0	0	59.1	59	22	23	0	3	3	0	0	0	0	—	5	7	1	4	0.3	.923

Year	Team	W	L	PCT	ERA	G	GS	CG	IP	H	BB	SO	ShO	Relief Pitching W	L	SV	Batting AB	H	HR	BA	PO	A	E	DP	TC/G	FA

Mike Fetters *continued*

Year	Team	W	L	PCT	ERA	G	GS	CG	IP	H	BB	SO	ShO	W	L	SV	AB	H	HR	BA	PO	A	E	DP	TC/G	FA
1994		1	4	.200	2.54	42	0	0	46	41	27	31	0	1	4	17	0	0	0	—	3	5	1	1	0.2	.889
1995		0	3	.000	3.38	40	0	0	34.2	40	20	33	0	0	3	22	0	0	0	—	2	1	1	0	0.1	.750
1996		3	3	.500	3.38	61	0	0	61.1	65	26	53	0	3	3	32	0	0	0	—	7	5	0	0	0.2	1.000
8 yrs.		15	20	.429	3.37	284	6	0	379.2	378	168	246	0	15	16	74	0	0	0		31	45	5	6	0.3	.938

Chuck Finley

FINLEY, CHARLES EDWARD
B. Nov. 26, 1962, Monroe, La.

BL TL 6'6" 220 lbs.

Year	Team	W	L	PCT	ERA	G	GS	CG	IP	H	BB	SO	ShO	W	L	SV	AB	H	HR	BA	PO	A	E	DP	TC/G	FA
1986	CAL A	3	1	.750	3.30	25	0	0	46.1	40	23	37	0	3	1	0	0	0	0	—	8	8	0	1	0.6	1.000
1987		2	7	.222	4.67	35	3	0	90.2	102	43	63	0	2	6	0	0	0	0	—	6	11	1	1	0.5	.944
1988		9	15	.375	4.17	31	31	2	194.1	191	82	111	0	0	0	0	0	0	0	—	5	24	1	1	1.0	.967
1989		16	9	.640	2.57	29	29	9	199.2	171	82	156	1	0	0	0	0	0	0	—	4	16	2	0	0.8	.909
1990		18	9	.667	2.40	32	32	7	236	210	81	177	2	0	0	0	0	0	0	—	14	21	5	2	1.3	.875
1991		18	9	.667	3.80	34	34	4	227.1	205	101	171	2	0	0	0	0	0	0	—	11	16	2	3	0.9	.931
1992		7	12	.368	3.96	31	31	4	204.1	212	98	124	1	0	0	0	0	0	0	—	3	17	3	1	0.7	.870
1993		16	14	.533	3.15	35	35	13	251.1	243	82	187	2	0	0	0	0	0	0	—	10	26	5	0	1.2	.878
1994		10	10	.500	4.32	25	25	7	183.1	178	71	148	2	0	0	0	0	0	0	—	9	17	4	1	1.2	.867
1995		15	12	.556	4.21	32	32	2	203	192	93	195	1	0	0	0	0	0	0	—	4	18	4	4	0.8	.846
1996		15	16	.484	4.16	35	35	4	238	241	94	215	1	0	0	0	0	0	0	—	9	28	3	4	1.1	.925
11 yrs.		129	114	.531	3.65	344	287	52	2074.1	1985	850	1584	12	5	7	0	0	0	0		83	202	30	18	0.9	.905

LEAGUE CHAMPIONSHIP SERIES

Year	Team	W	L	PCT	ERA	G	GS	CG	IP	H	BB	SO	ShO	W	L	SV	AB	H	HR	BA	PO	A	E	DP	TC/G	FA
1986	CAL A	0	0	—	0.00	3	0	0	2	1	0	1	0	0	0	0	0	0	0	—	0	0	0	0	0.0	.000

Huck Flener

FLENER, GREGORY ALAN
B. Feb. 25, 1969, Austin, Tex.

BB TL 5'11" 175 lbs.

Year	Team	W	L	PCT	ERA	G	GS	CG	IP	H	BB	SO	ShO	W	L	SV	AB	H	HR	BA	PO	A	E	DP	TC/G	FA
1993	TOR A	0	0	—	4.05	6	0	0	6.2	7	4	2	0	0	0	0	0	0	0	—	2	2	0	0	0.7	1.000
1996		3	2	.600	4.58	15	11	0	70.2	68	33	44	0	1	1	0	0	0	0	—	6	12	2	1	1.3	.900
2 yrs.		3	2	.600	4.54	21	11	0	77.1	75	37	46	0	1	1	0	0	0	0		8	14	2	1	1.1	.917

Paul Fletcher

FLETCHER, EDWARD PAUL
B. Jan. 14, 1967, Gallipolis, Ohio

BR TR 6'1" 190 lbs.

Year	Team	W	L	PCT	ERA	G	GS	CG	IP	H	BB	SO	ShO	W	L	SV	AB	H	HR	BA	PO	A	E	DP	TC/G	FA
1993	PHI N	0	0	—	0.00	1	0	0	0.1	0	0	0	0	0	0	0	0	0	0	—	0	0	0	0	0.0	.000
1995		1	0	1.000	5.40	10	0	0	13.1	15	9	10	0	1	0	0	0	0	0	—	0	1	0	0	0.1	1.000
1996	OAK A	0	0	—	20.25	1	0	0	1.1	6	1	0	0	0	0	0	0	0	0	—	0	0	1	0	1.0	.000
3 yrs.		1	0	1.000	6.60	12	0	0	15	21	10	10	0	1	0	0	0	0	0		0	1	1	0	0.2	.500

Bryce Florie

FLORIE, BRYCE BETTENCOURT
B. May 21, 1970, Charleston, S. C.

BR TR 6' 185 lbs.

Year	Team	W	L	PCT	ERA	G	GS	CG	IP	H	BB	SO	ShO	W	L	SV	AB	H	HR	BA	PO	A	E	DP	TC/G	FA
1994	SD N	0	0	—	0.96	9	0	0	9.1	8	3	8	0	0	0	0	0	0	0	—	2	3	0	0	0.6	1.000
1995		2	2	.500	3.01	47	0	0	68.2	49	38	68	0	2	2	1	2	0	0	.000	4	10	1	0	0.3	.933
1996	2 teams	SD N	(39G 2–2)		MIL A		(15G 0–1)																			
"	total	2	3	.400	4.74	54	0	0	68.1	65	40	63	0	2	3	0	3	0	0	.000	7	9	2	0	0.3	.889
3 yrs.		4	5	.444	3.69	110	0	0	146.1	122	81	139	0	4	5	1	5	0	0	.000	13	22	3	0	0.3	.921

Tony Fossas

FOSSAS, EMILIO ANTONIO
Born Emilio Antonio Fossas (Morejon).
B. Sept. 23, 1957, Havana, Cuba

BL TL 6' 195 lbs.

Year	Team	W	L	PCT	ERA	G	GS	CG	IP	H	BB	SO	ShO	W	L	SV	AB	H	HR	BA	PO	A	E	DP	TC/G	FA
1988	TEX A	0	0	—	4.76	5	0	0	5.2	11	2	0	0	0	0	0	0	0	0	—	1	1	0	1	0.4	1.000
1989	MIL A	2	2	.500	3.54	51	0	0	61	57	22	42	0	2	2	1	0	0	0	—	1	12	2	0	0.3	.867
1990		2	3	.400	6.44	32	0	0	29.1	44	10	24	0	2	3	0	0	0	0	—	1	4	3	0	0.3	.625
1991	BOS A	3	2	.600	3.47	64	0	0	57	49	28	29	0	3	2	1	0	0	0	—	6	12	2	2	0.3	.900
1992		1	2	.333	2.43	60	0	0	29.2	31	14	19	0	1	2	2	0	0	0	—	2	6	0	0	0.1	1.000
1993		1	1	.500	5.17	71	0	0	40	38	15	39	0	1	1	0	0	0	0	—	0	7	1	0	0.1	.875
1994		2	0	1.000	4.76	44	0	0	34	35	15	31	0	2	0	1	0	0	0	—	0	5	2	0	0.2	.714
1995	STL N	3	0	1.000	1.47	58	0	0	36.2	28	10	40	0	3	0	0	0	0	0	—	1	3	1	0	0.1	.800
1996		0	4	.000	2.68	65	0	0	47	43	21	36	0	0	4	2	1	0	0	.000	2	6	0	0	0.2	1.000
9 yrs.		14	14	.500	3.68	450	0	0	340.1	336	137	260	0	14	14	7	1	0	0	.000	15	57	11	3	0.2	.867

LEAGUE CHAMPIONSHIP SERIES

Year	Team	W	L	PCT	ERA	G	GS	CG	IP	H	BB	SO	ShO	W	L	SV	AB	H	HR	BA	PO	A	E	DP	TC/G	FA
1996	STL N	0	0	—	2.08	5	0	0	4.1	1	3	1	0	0	0	0	0	0	0	—	0	0	0	0	0.0	.000

Kevin Foster

FOSTER, KEVIN CHRISTOPHER
B. Jan. 13, 1969, Evanston, Ill.

BR TR 6'1" 160 lbs.

Year	Team	W	L	PCT	ERA	G	GS	CG	IP	H	BB	SO	ShO	W	L	SV	AB	H	HR	BA	PO	A	E	DP	TC/G	FA
1993	PHI N	0	1	.000	14.85	2	1	0	6.2	13	7	6	0	0	0	0	2	0	0	.000	1	0	0	0	0.5	1.000
1994	CHI N	3	4	.429	2.89	13	13	0	81	70	35	75	0	0	0	0	27	2	0	.074	4	5	0	0	0.7	1.000
1995		12	11	.522	4.51	30	28	0	167.2	149	65	146	0	0	0	0	60	15	1	.250	7	14	0	0	0.7	1.000
1996		7	6	.538	6.21	17	16	1	87	98	35	53	0	0	0	0	27	8	0	.296	6	16	1	0	1.4	.957
4 yrs.		22	22	.500	4.76	62	58	1	342.1	330	142	280	0	0	0	0	116	25	1	.216	18	35	1	0	0.9	.981

John Franco

FRANCO, JOHN ANTHONY
B. Sept. 17, 1960, Brooklyn, N. Y.

BL TL 5'10" 175 lbs.

Year	Team	W	L	PCT	ERA	G	GS	CG	IP	H	BB	SO	ShO	W	L	SV	AB	H	HR	BA	PO	A	E	DP	TC/G	FA
1984	CIN N	6	2	.750	2.61	54	0	0	79.1	74	36	55	0	6	2	4	3	0	0	.000	5	15	0	0	0.4	1.000
1985		12	3	.800	2.18	67	0	0	99	83	40	61	0	12	3	12	6	2	0	.333	9	21	1	1	0.5	.968
1986		6	6	.500	2.94	74	0	0	101	90	44	84	0	6	6	29	4	0	0	.000	6	22	4	2	0.4	.875

Year	Team	W	L	PCT	ERA	G	GS	CG	IP	H	BB	SO	ShO	Relief Pitching			Batting			BA	PO	A	E	DP	TC/G	FA
														W	L	SV	AB	H	HR							

John Franco *continued*

Year	Team	W	L	PCT	ERA	G	GS	CG	IP	H	BB	SO	ShO	W	L	SV	AB	H	HR	BA	PO	A	E	DP	TC/G	FA
1987		8	5	.615	2.52	68	0	0	82	76	27	61	0	8	5	32	2	0	0	.000	4	7	0	0	0.2	1.000
1988		6	6	.500	1.57	70	0	0	86	60	27	46	0	6	6	**39**	1	0	0	.000	3	18	1	1	0.3	.955
1989		4	8	.333	3.12	60	0	0	80.2	77	36	60	0	4	8	32	3	1	0	.333	2	19	1	1	0.4	.955
1990	NY N	5	3	.625	2.53	55	0	0	67.2	66	21	56	0	5	3	**33**	5	0	0	.000	4	13	1	0	0.3	.944
1991		5	9	.357	2.93	52	0	0	55.1	61	18	45	0	5	**9**	30	1	0	0	.000	3	10	1	1	0.3	.929
1992		6	2	.750	1.64	31	0	0	33	24	11	20	0	6	2	15	1	0	0	.000	2	12	0	2	0.5	1.000
1993		4	3	.571	5.20	35	0	0	36.1	46	19	29	0	4	3	10	1	0	0	.000	3	9	0	0	0.3	1.000
1994		1	4	.200	2.70	47	0	0	50	47	19	42	0	1	4	**30**	3	0	0	.000	4	7	0	1	0.2	1.000
1995		5	3	.625	2.44	48	0	0	51.2	48	17	41	0	5	3	29	0	0	0	—	2	9	0	1	0.2	1.000
1996		4	3	.571	1.83	51	0	0	54	54	21	48	0	4	3	28	1	0	0	.000	1	8	0	1	0.2	1.000
13 yrs.		72	57	.558	2.57	712	0	0	876	806	336	648	0	72	57	323 5th	31	3	0	.097	48	170	9	10	0.3	.960

Marvin Freeman

FREEMAN, MARVIN (Starvin' Marvin)   BR TR   6'7"   200 lbs.
B. Apr. 10, 1963, Chicago, Ill.

Year	Team	W	L	PCT	ERA	G	GS	CG	IP	H	BB	SO	ShO	W	L	SV	AB	H	HR	BA	PO	A	E	DP	TC/G	FA
1986	PHI N	2	0	1.000	2.25	3	3	0	16	6	10	8	0	0	0	0	6	0	0	.000	0	1	0	0	0.3	1.000
1988		2	3	.400	6.10	11	11	0	51.2	55	43	37	0	0	0	0	14	3	0	.214	2	9	0	0	1.0	1.000
1989		0	0	—	6.00	1	1	0	3	2	5	0	0	0	0	0	2	0	0	.000	0	0	0	0	0.0	.000
1990	2 teams	PHI N	(16G 0-2)		ATL N	(9G 1-0)																				
"	total	1	2	.333	4.31	25	3	0	48	41	17	38	0	1	1	1	7	0	0	.000	1	6	1	1	0.3	.875
1991	ATL N	1	0	1.000	3.00	34	0	0	48	37	13	34	0	1	0	1	7	0	0	.000	3	4	0	0	0.2	1.000
1992		7	5	.583	3.22	58	0	0	64.1	61	29	41	0	7	5	3	4	2	0	.500	4	5	2	0	0.2	.818
1993		2	0	1.000	6.08	21	0	0	23.2	24	10	25	0	2	0	0	1	0	0	—	1	0	0	0	0.0	1.000
1994	CLR N	10	2	.833	2.80	19	18	0	112.2	113	23	67	0	1	0	0	36	4	1	.111	8	20	0	0	1.5	1.000
1995		3	7	.300	5.89	22	18	0	94.2	122	41	61	0	0	0	0	23	2	1	.087	9	11	3	0	1.0	.870
1996	2 teams	CLR N	(26G 7-9)		CHI A	(1G 0-0)																				
"	total	7	9	.438	6.15	27	24	0	131.2	155	58	72	0	0	1	0	41	5	0	.122	3	26	2	2	1.1	.935
10 yrs.		35	28	.556	4.64	221	78	0	593.2	616	249	383	0	12	7	5	140	16	2	.114	31	82	8	3	0.5	.934

LEAGUE CHAMPIONSHIP SERIES

Year	Team	W	L	PCT	ERA	G	GS	CG	IP	H	BB	SO	ShO	W	L	SV	AB	H	HR	BA	PO	A	E	DP	TC/G	FA
1992	ATL N	0	0	—	14.73	3	0	0	3.2	8	2	1	0	0	0	0	0	0	0	—	0	2	0	0	0.7	1.000

Steve Frey

FREY, STEVEN FRANCIS   BR TL   5'9"   170 lbs.
B. July 29, 1963, Meadowbrook, Pa.

Year	Team	W	L	PCT	ERA	G	GS	CG	IP	H	BB	SO	ShO	W	L	SV	AB	H	HR	BA	PO	A	E	DP	TC/G	FA
1989	MON N	3	2	.600	5.48	20	0	0	21.1	29	11	15	0	3	2	0	0	0	0	—	1	2	0	0	0.2	1.000
1990		8	2	.800	2.10	51	0	0	55.2	44	29	29	0	8	2	9	1	0	0	.000	4	7	1	0	0.2	.917
1991		0	1	.000	4.99	31	0	0	39.2	43	23	21	0	0	1	1	2	0	0	.000	1	4	0	0	0.2	1.000
1992	CAL A	4	2	.667	3.57	51	0	0	45.1	39	22	24	0	4	2	4	0	0	0	—	4	5	0	1	0.2	1.000
1993		2	3	.400	2.98	55	0	0	48.1	41	26	22	0	2	3	13	0	0	0	—	2	6	0	1	0.1	1.000
1994	SF N	1	0	1.000	4.94	44	0	0	31	37	15	20	0	1	0	0	0	0	0	—	2	4	0	0	0.1	1.000
1995	3 teams	SF N	(9G 0-1)		SEA A	(13G 0-3)		PHI N	(9G 0-0)																	
"	total	0	4	.000	3.18	31	0	0	28.1	26	10	14	0	0	4	1	1	0	0	.000	1	6	1	0	0.3	.875
1996	PHI N	0	1	.000	4.72	31	0	0	34.1	38	18	12	0	0	1	0	0	0	0	—	1	8	0	1	0.3	1.000
8 yrs.		18	15	.545	3.76	314	0	0	304	297	154	157	0	18	15	28	4	0	0	.000	16	42	2	2	0.2	.967

Todd Frohwirth

FROHWIRTH, TODD GERARD   BR TR   6'4"   190 lbs.
B. Sept. 28, 1962, Milwaukee, Wis.

Year	Team	W	L	PCT	ERA	G	GS	CG	IP	H	BB	SO	ShO	W	L	SV	AB	H	HR	BA	PO	A	E	DP	TC/G	FA
1987	PHI N	1	0	1.000	0.00	10	0	0	11	12	2	9	0	1	0	0	1	0	0	.000	1	1	0	1	0.2	1.000
1988		1	2	.333	8.25	12	0	0	12	16	11	11	0	1	2	0	0	0	0	—	0	5	0	0	0.4	1.000
1989		1	0	1.000	3.59	45	0	0	62.2	56	18	39	0	1	0	0	0	0	0	.000	5	8	0	0	0.3	1.000
1990		0	1	.000	18.00	5	0	0	1	3	6	1	0	0	1	0	0	0	0	—	0	1	1	0	0.4	.500
1991	BAL A	7	3	.700	1.87	51	0	0	96.1	64	29	77	0	7	3	3	0	0	0	—	14	24	3	3	0.8	.927
1992		4	3	.571	2.46	65	0	0	106	97	41	58	0	4	3	4	0	0	0	—	8	24	1	4	0.5	.970
1993		6	7	.462	3.83	70	0	0	96.1	91	44	50	0	6	7	3	0	0	0	—	8	21	1	3	0.4	.967
1994	BOS A	0	3	.000	10.80	22	0	0	26.2	40	17	13	0	0	3	1	0	0	0	—	1	8	1	0	0.5	.900
1996	CAL A	0	0	—	11.12	4	0	0	5.2	10	4	1	0	0	0	0	0	0	0	—	0	0	0	0	0.0	.000
9 yrs.		20	19	.513	3.60	284	0	0	417.2	389	172	259	0	20	19	11	2	0	0	.000	37	92	7	11	0.5	.949

Mike Fyhrie

FYHRIE, MICHAEL EDWIN   BR TR   6'2"   190 lbs.
B. Dec. 9, 1969, Long Beach, Calif.

Year	Team	W	L	PCT	ERA	G	GS	CG	IP	H	BB	SO	ShO	W	L	SV	AB	H	HR	BA	PO	A	E	DP	TC/G	FA
1996	NY N	0	1	.000	15.43	2	0	0	2.1	4	3	0	0	0	1	0	0	0	0	—	0	1	0	0	0.5	1.000

Rich Garces

GARCES, RICHARD ARON   BR TR   6'   187 lbs.
Born Richard Aron Garces (Mendoza).
B. May 18, 1971, Maracay, Venezuela

Year	Team	W	L	PCT	ERA	G	GS	CG	IP	H	BB	SO	ShO	W	L	SV	AB	H	HR	BA	PO	A	E	DP	TC/G	FA
1990	MIN A	0	0	—	1.59	5	0	0	5.2	4	4	1	0	0	0	2	0	0	0	—	0	1	0	0	0.2	1.000
1993		0	0	—	0.00	3	0	0	4	4	2	3	0	0	0	0	0	0	0	—	0	0	0	0	0.0	.000
1995	2 teams	CHI N	(7G 0-0)		FLA N	(11G 0-2)																				
"	total	0	2	.000	4.44	18	0	0	24.1	25	11	22	0	0	2	0	1	0	0	.000	2	1	0	0	0.2	1.000
1996	BOS A	3	2	.600	4.91	37	0	0	44	42	33	55	0	3	2	0	0	0	0	—	1	8	1	2	0.3	.900
4 yrs.		3	4	.429	4.27	63	0	0	78	75	50	81	0	3	4	2	1	0	0	.000	3	10	1	2	0.2	.929

Year	Team	W	L	PCT	ERA	G	GS	CG	IP	H	BB	SO	ShO	W	L	SV	AB	H	HR	BA	PO	A	E	DP	TC/G	FA
														Relief Pitching			Batting									

Ramon Garcia

GARCIA, RAMON ANTONIO
Born Ramon Antonio Garcia (Fortunato).
B. Feb. 9, 1969, Guanare, Venezuela

BR TR 6'2" 200 lbs.

Year	Team	W	L	PCT	ERA	G	GS	CG	IP	H	BB	SO	ShO	W	L	SV	AB	H	HR	BA	PO	A	E	DP	TC/G	FA
1991	CHI A	4	4	.500	5.40	16	15	0	78.1	79	31	40	0	0	0	0	0	0	0	—	9	12	1	2	1.4	.955
1996	MIL A	4	4	.500	6.66	37	2	0	75.2	84	21	40	0	3	3	4	0	0	0	—	6	10	0	2	0.4	1.000
2 yrs.		8	8	.500	6.02	53	17	0	154	163	52	80	0	3	3	4	0	0	0		15	22	1	4	0.7	.974

Bill Gardner

GARDNER, WILLIAM A.
B. Sept. 1868, Baltimore, Mass.   Deceased.

Year	Team	W	L	PCT	ERA	G	GS	CG	IP	H	BB	SO	ShO	W	L	SV	AB	H	HR	BA	PO	A	E	DP	TC/G	FA
1887	BAL AA	0	1	.000	11.08	3	2	1	13	23	10	3	0	0	0	0	11	3	0	.273	2	2	1	1	1.0	.800

Mark Gardner

GARDNER, MARK ALLAN
B. Mar. 1, 1962, Los Angeles, Calif.

BR TR 6'1" 190 lbs.

Year	Team	W	L	PCT	ERA	G	GS	CG	IP	H	BB	SO	ShO	W	L	SV	AB	H	HR	BA	PO	A	E	DP	TC/G	FA
1989	MON N	0	3	.000	5.13	7	4	0	26.1	26	11	21	0	0	0	0	6	1	0	.167	1	3	0	0	0.6	1.000
1990		7	9	.438	3.42	27	26	3	152.2	129	61	135	3	0	1	0	44	5	0	.114	9	25	0	4	1.3	1.000
1991		9	11	.450	3.85	27	27	0	168.1	139	75	107	0	0	0	0	55	5	0	.091	12	15	1	1	1.0	.964
1992		12	10	.545	4.36	33	30	0	179.2	179	60	132	0	1	0	0	50	7	0	.140	14	22	2	0	1.2	.947
1993	KC A	4	6	.400	6.19	17	16	0	91.2	92	36	54	0	0	0	0	0	0	0	—	6	5	1	1	0.7	.917
1994	FLA N	4	4	.500	4.87	20	14	0	92.1	97	30	57	0	0	0	0	25	1	0	.040	8	8	0	0	0.8	1.000
1995		5	5	.500	4.49	39	11	1	102.1	109	43	87	1	1	1	1	21	4	0	.190	3	10	2	1	0.4	.867
1996	SF N	12	7	.632	4.42	30	28	4	179.1	200	57	145	1	0	0	0	68	11	0	.162	10	14	0	1	0.8	1.000
8 yrs.		53	55	.491	4.39	200	156	8	992.2	971	373	738	5	2	2	1	269	34	0	.126	63	102	6	8	0.9	.965

Paul Gibson

GIBSON, PAUL MARSHALL
B. Jan. 4, 1960, Southampton, N. Y.

BR TL 6' 165 lbs.

Year	Team	W	L	PCT	ERA	G	GS	CG	IP	H	BB	SO	ShO	W	L	SV	AB	H	HR	BA	PO	A	E	DP	TC/G	FA
1988	DET A	4	2	.667	2.93	40	1	0	92	83	34	50	0	3	2	0	0	0	0	—	7	11	0	2	0.4	1.000
1989		4	8	.333	4.64	45	13	0	132	129	57	77	0	3	3	0	0	0	0	—	6	20	2	0	0.6	.929
1990		5	4	.556	3.05	61	0	0	97.1	99	44	56	0	5	4	3	0	0	0	—	9	11	0	1	0.3	1.000
1991		5	7	.417	4.59	68	0	0	96	112	48	52	0	5	7	8	0	0	0	—	6	13	0	1	0.3	1.000
1992	NY N	0	1	.000	5.23	43	1	0	62	70	25	49	0	0	1	0	6	0	0	.000	2	6	0	0	0.2	1.000
1993	2 teams																									
"	NY N (8G 1-1)				NY A	(20G 2-0)																				
"	total	3	1	.750	3.48	28	0	0	44	45	11	37	0	3	1	0	0	0	0	—	3	5	0	1	0.3	1.000
1994	NY A	1	1	.500	4.97	30	0	0	29	26	17	21	0	1	1	0	0	0	0	—	2	4	0	0	0.2	1.000
1996		0	0	—	6.23	4	0	0	4.1	6	0	3	0	0	0	0	0	0	0	—	1	0	0	0	0.3	1.000
8 yrs.		22	24	.478	4.07	319	15	0	556.2	570	236	345	0	20	19	11	6	0	0	.000	36	70	2	4	0.3	.981

Brian Givens

GIVENS, BRIAN ALLEN
B. Nov. 6, 1965, Lompoc, Calif.

BR TL 6'6" 220 lbs.

Year	Team	W	L	PCT	ERA	G	GS	CG	IP	H	BB	SO	ShO	W	L	SV	AB	H	HR	BA	PO	A	E	DP	TC/G	FA
1995	MIL A	5	7	.417	4.95	19	19	0	107.1	116	54	73	0	0	0	0	0	0	0	—	4	10	2	2	0.8	.875
1996		1	3	.250	12.86	4	4	0	14	32	7	10	0	0	0	0	0	0	0	—	1	0	1	0	0.5	.500
2 yrs.		6	10	.375	5.86	23	23	0	121.1	148	61	83	0	0	0	0					5	10	3	2	0.8	.833

Tom Glavine

GLAVINE, THOMAS MICHAEL
B. Mar. 25, 1966, Concord, Mass.

BL TL 6' 175 lbs.

Year	Team	W	L	PCT	ERA	G	GS	CG	IP	H	BB	SO	ShO	W	L	SV	AB	H	HR	BA	PO	A	E	DP	TC/G	FA
1987	ATL N	2	4	.333	5.54	9	9	0	50.1	55	33	20	0	0	0	0	16	2	0	.125	1	13	1	0	1.7	.933
1988		7	17	.292	4.56	34	34	1	195.1	201	63	84	0	0	0	0	60	11	0	.183	12	41	4	3	1.7	.930
1989		14	8	.636	3.68	29	29	6	186	172	40	90	4	0	0	0	67	10	0	.149	7	37	4	4	1.7	.917
1990		10	12	.455	4.28	33	33	1	214.1	232	78	129	0	0	0	0	62	7	0	.113	19	33	1	1	1.6	.981
1991		20	11	.645	2.55	34	34	9	246.2	201	69	192	1	0	0	0	74	17	0	.230	16	45	0	4	1.8	1.000
1992		20	8	.714	2.76	33	33	7	225	197	70	129	5	0	0	0	77	19	0	.247	18	31	0	2	1.5	1.000
1993		22	6	.786	3.20	36	36	4	239.1	236	90	120	2	0	0	0	81	14	0	.173	17	36	2	4	1.5	.964
1994		13	9	.591	3.97	25	25	2	165.1	173	70	140	0	0	0	0	56	10	0	.179	11	33	1	1	1.8	.978
1995		16	7	.696	3.08	29	29	3	198.2	182	66	127	1	0	0	0	63	14	1	.222	14	42	1	6	2.0	.982
1996		15	10	.600	2.98	36	36	1	235.1	222	85	181	0	0	0	0	76	22	0	.289	14	50	1	1	1.8	.985
10 yrs.		139	92	.602	3.45	298	298	34	1956.1	1871	664	1212	13	0	0	0	632	126	1	.199	129	361	15	26	1.7	.970

DIVISIONAL PLAYOFF SERIES

Year	Team	W	L	PCT	ERA	G	GS	CG	IP	H	BB	SO	ShO	W	L	SV	AB	H	HR	BA	PO	A	E	DP	TC/G	FA
1995	ATL N	0	0	—	2.57	1	1	0	7	5	1	3	0	0	0	0	3	1	0	.333	1	1	0	0	2.0	1.000
1996		1	0	1.000	1.35	1	1	0	6.2	5	3	7	0	0	0	0	2	1	0	.500	0	1	0	0	1.0	1.000
2 yrs.		1	0	1.000	1.98	2	2	0	13.2	10	4	10	0	0	0	0	5	2	0	.400	1	2	0	0	1.5	1.000

LEAGUE CHAMPIONSHIP SERIES

Year	Team	W	L	PCT	ERA	G	GS	CG	IP	H	BB	SO	ShO	W	L	SV	AB	H	HR	BA	PO	A	E	DP	TC/G	FA
1991	ATL N	0	2	.000	3.21	2	2	0	14	12	6	11	0	0	0	0	4	1	0	.250	1	3	0	0	2.0	1.000
1992		0	2	.000	12.27	2	2	0	7.1	13	3	2	0	0	0	0	2	0	0	.000	1	2	0	0	1.5	1.000
1993		1	0	1.000	2.57	1	1	0	7	6	0	5	0	0	0	0	3	0	0	.000	0	3	0	0	3.0	1.000
1995		0	0	—	1.29	1	1	0	7	7	2	5	0	0	0	0	1	0	0	.000	0	1	0	1	1.0	1.000
1996		1	1	.500	2.08	2	2	0	13	10	0	9	0	0	0	0	6	1	0	.167	0	3	0	1	1.5	1.000
5 yrs.		2 (2nd)	5	.286	3.91	8	8	0	48.1 (8th)	48	11	32 (10th)	0	0	0	0	16	2	0	.125	2	12	0	2	1.8	1.000

WORLD SERIES

Year	Team	W	L	PCT	ERA	G	GS	CG	IP	H	BB	SO	ShO	W	L	SV	AB	H	HR	BA	PO	A	E	DP	TC/G	FA
1991	ATL N	1	1	.500	2.70	2	2	1	13.1	8	7	8	0	0	0	0	2	0	0	.000	0	3	0	1	1.5	1.000
1992		1	1	.500	1.59	2	2	2	17	10	4	8	0	0	0	0	2	0	0	.000	0	2	0	0	1.0	1.000
1995		2	0	1.000	1.29	2	2	0	14	4	6	11	0	0	0	0	4	0	0	.000	1	3	0	0	2.0	1.000
1996		0	1	.000	1.29	1	1	0	7	4	3	8	0	0	0	0	2	0	0	.000	0	2	0	0	2.0	1.000
4 yrs.		4	3	.571	1.75	7	7	3	51.1	26	20	35	0	0	0	0	9	0	0	.000	1	10	0	1	1.6	1.000

Year	Team	W	L	PCT	ERA	G	GS	CG	IP	H	BB	SO	ShO	Relief Pitching W	L	SV	Batting AB	H	HR	BA	PO	A	E	DP	TC/G	FA

Greg Gohr

GOHR, GREGORY JAMES
B. Oct. 29, 1967, Santa Clara, Calif.   BR TR   6'3"   205 lbs.

Year	Team	W	L	PCT	ERA	G	GS	CG	IP	H	BB	SO	ShO	W	L	SV	AB	H	HR	BA	PO	A	E	DP	TC/G	FA
1993	DET A	0	0	—	5.96	16	0	0	22.2	26	14	23	0	0	0	0	0	0	0	—	1	1	0	1	0.1	1.000
1994		2	2	.500	4.50	8	6	0	34	36	21	21	0	1	0	0	0	0	0	—	2	1	0	0	0.4	1.000
1995		1	0	1.000	0.87	10	0	0	10.1	9	3	12	0	1	0	0	0	0	0	—	0	1	0	0	0.1	1.000
1996	**2 teams** DET A (17G 4-8) CAL A (15G 1-1)																									
"	total	5	9	.357	7.24	32	16	0	115.2	163	44	75	0	1	1	1	0	0	0	—	7	10	1	0	0.6	.944
4 yrs.		8	11	.421	6.21	66	22	0	182.2	234	82	131	0	3	1	1	0	0	0		10	13	1	1	0.4	.958

Dwight Gooden

GOODEN, DWIGHT EUGENE (Doc)
B. Nov. 16, 1964, Tampa, Fla.   BR TR   6'2"   190 lbs.

Year	Team	W	L	PCT	ERA	G	GS	CG	IP	H	BB	SO	ShO	W	L	SV	AB	H	HR	BA	PO	A	E	DP	TC/G	FA
1984	NY N	17	9	.654	2.60	31	31	7	218	161	73	**276**	3	0	0	0	70	14	0	.200	21	22	2	0	1.5	.956
1985		24	4	.857	**1.53**	35	35	16	**276.2**	198	69	268	8	0	0	0	93	21	1	.226	25	38	2	6	1.9	.969
1986		17	6	.739	2.84	33	33	12	250	197	80	200	2	0	0	0	81	7	0	.086	36	36	2	5	2.2	.973
1987		15	7	**.682**	3.21	25	25	7	179.2	162	53	148	3	0	0	0	64	14	0	.219	15	23	3	3	1.6	.925
1988		18	9	.667	3.19	34	34	10	248.1	242	57	175	3	0	0	0	90	16	1	.178	27	56	5	3	2.6	.943
1989		9	4	.692	2.89	19	17	0	118.1	93	47	101	0	0	0	1	40	8	0	.200	8	16	3	0	1.4	.889
1990		19	7	.731	3.83	34	34	2	232.2	229	70	223	1	0	0	0	75	14	1	.187	15	35	4	5	1.6	.926
1991		13	7	.650	3.60	27	27	3	190	185	56	150	1	0	0	0	63	15	1	.238	15	28	2	3	1.7	.956
1992		10	13	.435	3.67	31	31	3	206	197	70	145	0	0	0	0	72	19	1	.264	9	40	6	1	1.8	.891
1993		12	15	.444	3.45	29	29	7	208.2	188	61	149	0	0	0	0	70	14	2	.200	19	24	2	1	1.6	.956
1994		3	4	.429	6.31	7	7	0	41.1	46	15	40	0	0	0	0	12	2	0	.167	1	11	1	1	1.9	.923
1996	NY A	11	7	.611	5.01	29	29	1	170.2	169	88	126	1	0	0	0	0	0	0	—	9	26	1	1	1.2	.972
12 yrs.		168	92	.646	3.24	334	332	68	2340.1	2067	739	2001	24	0	0	1	730	144	7	.197	200	354	33	29	1.8	.944

LEAGUE CHAMPIONSHIP SERIES

Year	Team	W	L	PCT	ERA	G	GS	CG	IP	H	BB	SO	ShO	W	L	SV	AB	H	HR	BA	PO	A	E	DP	TC/G	FA
1986	NY N	0	1	.000	1.06	2	2	0	17	16	5	9	0	0	0	0	5	0	0	.000	3	2	0	0	2.5	1.000
1988		0	0	—	2.95	3	2	0	18.1	10	8	20	0	0	0	0	5	1	0	.200	1	3	0	0	1.3	1.000
2 yrs.		0	1	.000	2.04 10th	5	4	0	35.1	26	13	29	0	0	0	0	10	1	0	.100	4	5	0	0	1.8	1.000

WORLD SERIES

Year	Team	W	L	PCT	ERA	G	GS	CG	IP	H	BB	SO	ShO	W	L	SV	AB	H	HR	BA	PO	A	E	DP	TC/G	FA
1986	NY N	0	2	.000	8.00	2	2	0	9	17	4	9	0	0	0	0	2	1	0	.500	1	2	0	0	1.5	1.000

Tom Gordon

GORDON, THOMAS (Flash)
B. Nov. 18, 1967, Sebring, Fla.   BR TR   5'9"   160 lbs.

Year	Team	W	L	PCT	ERA	G	GS	CG	IP	H	BB	SO	ShO	W	L	SV	AB	H	HR	BA	PO	A	E	DP	TC/G	FA
1988	KC A	0	2	.000	5.17	5	2	0	15.2	16	7	18	0	0	0	0	0	0	0	—	2	2	0	0	0.8	1.000
1989		17	9	.654	3.64	49	16	1	163	122	86	153	1	10	2	1	0	0	0	—	15	26	0	7	1.0	1.000
1990		12	11	.522	3.73	32	32	6	195.1	192	99	175	1	0	0	0	0	0	0	—	17	24	1	1	1.3	.976
1991		9	14	.391	3.87	45	14	1	158	129	87	167	0	4	7	1	0	0	0	—	12	17	2	1	0.7	.935
1992		6	10	.375	4.59	40	11	0	117.2	116	55	98	0	6	5	0	0	0	0	—	11	14	1	1	0.6	.962
1993		12	6	.667	3.58	48	14	2	155.2	125	77	143	0	4	2	1	0	0	0	—	18	21	2	1	0.9	.951
1994		11	7	.611	4.35	24	24	0	155.1	136	87	126	0	0	0	0	0	0	0	—	12	25	2	3	1.6	.949
1995		12	12	.500	4.43	31	31	2	189	204	89	119	0	0	0	0	0	0	0	—	25	26	2	3	1.7	.962
1996	BOS A	12	9	.571	5.59	34	34	4	215.2	249	105	171	1	0	0	0	0	0	0	—	14	30	3	3	1.4	.936
9 yrs.		91	80	.532	4.27	308	178	16	1365.1	1289	692	1170	3	24	16	3	0	0	0		126	185	13	20	1.0	.960

Mike Grace

GRACE, MICHAEL JAMES
B. June 20, 1970, Joliet, Ill.   BR TR   6'4"   210 lbs.

Year	Team	W	L	PCT	ERA	G	GS	CG	IP	H	BB	SO	ShO	W	L	SV	AB	H	HR	BA	PO	A	E	DP	TC/G	FA
1995	PHI N	1	1	.500	3.18	2	2	0	11.1	10	4	7	0	0	0	0	2	0	0	.000	1	2	0	0	1.5	1.000
1996		7	2	.778	3.49	12	12	1	80	72	16	49	1	0	0	0	29	4	0	.138	6	17	0	0	1.9	1.000
2 yrs.		8	3	.727	3.45	14	14	1	91.1	82	20	56	1	0	0	0	31	4	0	.129	7	19	0	0	1.9	1.000

Jeff Granger

GRANGER, JEFFREY ADAM
B. Dec. 16, 1971, San Pedro, Calif.   BR TL   6'4"   200 lbs.

Year	Team	W	L	PCT	ERA	G	GS	CG	IP	H	BB	SO	ShO	W	L	SV	AB	H	HR	BA	PO	A	E	DP	TC/G	FA
1993	KC A	0	0	—	27.00	1	0	0	1	3	2	1	0	0	0	0	0	0	0	—	0	0	0	0	0.0	.000
1994		0	1	.000	6.75	2	2	0	9.1	13	6	3	0	0	0	0	0	0	0	—	0	2	0	0	1.0	1.000
1996		0	0	—	6.61	15	0	0	16.1	21	10	11	0	0	0	0	0	0	0	—	3	1	0	0	0.3	1.000
3 yrs.		0	1	.000	7.43	18	2	0	26.2	37	18	15	0	0	0	0	0	0	0		3	3	0	0	0.3	1.000

Danny Graves

GRAVES, DANIEL PETER
B. Aug. 7, 1973, Saigon, South Vietnam   BR TR   5'11"   200 lbs.

Year	Team	W	L	PCT	ERA	G	GS	CG	IP	H	BB	SO	ShO	W	L	SV	AB	H	HR	BA	PO	A	E	DP	TC/G	FA
1996	CLE A	2	0	1.000	4.55	15	0	0	29.2	29	10	22	0	2	0	0	*			—	2	2	0	0	0.3	1.000

Jason Grimsley

GRIMSLEY, JASON ALAN
B. Aug. 7, 1967, Cleveland, Tex.   BR TR   6'3"   180 lbs.

Year	Team	W	L	PCT	ERA	G	GS	CG	IP	H	BB	SO	ShO	W	L	SV	AB	H	HR	BA	PO	A	E	DP	TC/G	FA
1989	PHI N	1	3	.250	5.89	4	4	0	18.1	19	19	7	0	0	0	0	5	0	0	.000	1	4	1	1	1.5	.833
1990		3	2	.600	3.30	11	11	0	57.1	47	43	41	0	0	0	0	16	3	0	.188	13	8	1	2	2.0	.955
1991		1	7	.125	4.87	12	12	0	61	54	41	42	0	0	0	0	17	1	0	.059	2	14	1	3	1.4	.941
1993	CLE A	3	4	.429	5.31	10	6	0	42.1	52	20	27	0	1	2	0	0	0	0	—	4	4	0	0	0.8	1.000
1994		5	2	.714	4.57	14	13	1	82.2	91	34	59	0	0	0	0	0	0	0	—	6	9	0	1	1.1	1.000
1995		0	0	—	6.09	15	2	0	34	37	32	25	0	0	0	1	0	0	0	—	0	8	0	1	0.5	1.000
1996	CAL A	5	7	.417	6.84	35	20	2	130.1	150	74	82	1	0	0	0	0	0	0	—	23	18	2	2	1.2	.953
7 yrs.		18	25	.419	5.39	101	68	3	426	450	263	283	1	1	2	1	38	4	0	.105	49	65	5	10	1.2	.958

Year	Team	W	L	PCT	ERA	G	GS	CG	IP	H	BB	SO	ShO	W	L	SV	AB	H	HR	BA	PO	A	E	DP	TC/G	FA
														Relief Pitching			Batting									

Buddy Groom

GROOM, WEDSEL GARY
B. July 10, 1965, Dallas, Tex.   BL TL 6'2" 200 lbs.

Year	Team	W	L	PCT	ERA	G	GS	CG	IP	H	BB	SO	ShO	W	L	SV	AB	H	HR	BA	PO	A	E	DP	TC/G	FA
1992	DET A	0	5	.000	5.82	12	7	0	38.2	48	22	15	0	0	0	1	0	0	0	—	0	6	0	0	0.5	1.000
1993		0	2	.000	6.14	19	3	0	36.2	48	13	15	0	0	1	0	0	0	0	—	1	7	1	0	0.5	.889
1994		0	1	.000	3.94	40	0	0	32	31	13	27	0	0	1	1	0	0	0	—	0	0	0	0	0.0	.000
1995	2 teams		DET A	(23G 1–3)		FLA N	(14G 1–2)																				
"	total	2	5	.286	7.44	37	4	0	55.2	81	32	35	0	1	4	1	0	0	0	—	2	6	1	0	0.2	.889
1996	OAK A	5	0	1.000	3.84	72	1	0	77.1	85	34	57	0	5	0	2	0	0	0	—	2	6	1	0	0.1	.889
5 yrs.		7	13	.350	5.36	180	15	0	240.1	293	114	149	0	6	6	5	0	0	0		5	25	3	0	0.2	.909

Kevin Gross

GROSS, KEVIN FRANK
B. June 8, 1961, Downey, Calif.   BR TR 6'5" 200 lbs.

Year	Team	W	L	PCT	ERA	G	GS	CG	IP	H	BB	SO	ShO	W	L	SV	AB	H	HR	BA	PO	A	E	DP	TC/G	FA
1983	PHI N	4	6	.400	3.56	17	17	1	96	100	35	66	1	0	0	0	33	3	0	.091	11	13	0	0	1.4	1.000
1984		8	5	.615	4.12	44	14	1	129	140	44	84	0	4	0	1	30	2	0	.067	9	22	3	3	0.8	.939
1985		15	13	.536	3.41	38	31	6	205.2	194	81	151	2	1	2	0	65	9	1	.138	18	34	3	0	1.4	.945
1986		12	12	.500	4.02	37	36	7	241.2	240	94	154	2	0	0	0	80	15	1	.188	25	28	2	2	1.5	.964
1987		9	16	.360	4.35	34	33	3	200.2	205	87	110	1	1	0	0	63	12	1	.190	13	23	3	1	1.1	.923
1988		12	14	.462	3.69	33	33	5	231.2	209	**89**	162	1	0	0	0	75	13	0	.173	13	34	2	2	1.5	.959
1989	MON N	11	12	.478	4.38	31	31	4	201.1	188	88	158	3	0	0	0	64	9	0	.141	15	25	2	1	1.4	.952
1990		9	12	.429	4.57	31	26	2	163.1	171	65	111	0	1	0	0	50	10	1	.200	6	13	1	0	0.6	.950
1991	LA N	10	11	.476	3.58	46	10	0	115.2	123	50	95	0	6	6	3	25	7	0	.280	9	14	1	0	0.5	.958
1992		8	13	.381	3.17	34	30	4	204.2	182	77	158	3	0	0	0	63	6	0	.095	11	25	1	2	1.1	.973
1993		13	13	.500	4.14	33	32	3	202.1	224	74	150	0	0	1	0	64	13	1	.203	11	40	0	1	1.5	1.000
1994		9	7	.563	3.60	25	23	1	157.1	162	43	124	0	0	0	1	47	7	1	.149	14	29	1	1	1.8	.977
1995	TEX A	9	15	.375	5.54	31	30	4	183.2	200	89	106	0	0	0	0	0	0	0	—	15	20	2	5	1.2	.946
1996		11	8	.579	5.22	28	19	1	129.1	151	50	78	0	2	1	0	0	0	0	—	11	19	2	1	1.1	.938
14 yrs.		140	157	.471	4.09	462	365	42	2462.1	2489	966	1707	14	15	10	5	659	106	6	.161	181	339	22	19	1.2	.959

Ken Grundt

GRUNDT, KENNETH ALLAN
B. Aug. 26, 1969, Melrose Park, Ill.   BL TL 6'4" 195 lbs.

Year	Team	W	L	PCT	ERA	G	GS	CG	IP	H	BB	SO	ShO	W	L	SV	AB	H	HR	BA	PO	A	E	DP	TC/G	FA
1996	BOS A	0	0	—	27.00	1	0	0	0.1	1	0	0	0	0	0	1	0	0	0	—	0	0	0	0	0.0	—

Eddie Guardado

GUARDADO, EDWARD ADRIAN
B. Oct. 2, 1970, Stockton, Calif.   BR TL 6' 195 lbs.

Year	Team	W	L	PCT	ERA	G	GS	CG	IP	H	BB	SO	ShO	W	L	SV	AB	H	HR	BA	PO	A	E	DP	TC/G	FA
1993	MIN A	3	8	.273	6.18	19	16	0	94.2	123	36	46	0	0	0	0	0	0	0	—	6	9	0	1	0.8	1.000
1994		0	2	.000	8.47	4	4	0	17	26	4	8	0	0	0	0	0	0	0	—	0	0	0	0	0.0	.000
1995		4	9	.308	5.12	51	5	0	91.1	99	45	71	0	4	4	2	0	0	0	—	4	8	1	0	0.3	.923
1996		6	5	.545	5.25	83	0	0	73.2	61	33	74	0	6	5	4	0	0	0	—	0	9	0	1	0.1	1.000
4 yrs.		13	24	.351	5.73	157	25	0	276.2	309	118	199	0	10	9	6	0	0	0		10	26	1	2	0.2	.973

Mark Gubicza

GUBICZA, MARK STEVEN
B. Aug. 14, 1962, Philadelphia, Pa.   BR TR 6'6" 215 lbs.

Year	Team	W	L	PCT	ERA	G	GS	CG	IP	H	BB	SO	ShO	W	L	SV	AB	H	HR	BA	PO	A	E	DP	TC/G	FA
1984	KC A	10	14	.417	4.05	29	29	4	189	172	75	111	2	0	0	0	0	0	0	—	19	31	2	1	1.8	.962
1985		14	10	.583	4.06	29	28	0	177.1	160	77	99	0	1	0	0	0	0	0	—	23	26	0	4	1.7	1.000
1986		12	6	.667	3.64	35	24	3	180.2	155	84	118	2	1	1	0	0	0	0	—	17	32	0	3	1.4	1.000
1987		13	18	.419	3.98	35	35	10	241.2	231	120	166	2	0	0	0	0	0	0	—	32	40	2	7	2.1	.973
1988		20	8	.714	2.70	35	35	8	269.2	237	83	183	4	0	0	0	0	0	0	—	29	44	1	3	2.1	.986
1989		15	11	.577	3.04	36	**36**	8	255	252	63	173	2	0	0	0	0	0	0	—	18	49	5	0	2.0	.931
1990		4	7	.364	4.50	16	16	2	94	101	38	71	0	0	0	0	0	0	0	—	9	10	1	3	1.3	.950
1991		9	12	.429	5.68	26	26	0	133	168	42	89	0	0	0	0	0	0	0	—	8	29	3	5	1.5	.925
1992		7	6	.538	3.72	18	18	2	111.1	110	36	81	1	0	0	0	0	0	0	—	10	12	0	2	1.2	1.000
1993		5	8	.385	4.66	49	6	0	104.1	128	43	80	0	5	4	2	0	0	0	—	11	7	1	0	0.4	.947
1994		7	9	.438	4.50	22	22	0	130	158	26	59	0	0	0	0	0	0	0	—	17	20	3	1	1.8	.925
1995		12	14	.462	3.75	33	33	3	213.1	222	62	81	2	0	0	0	0	0	0	—	28	36	0	2	1.9	1.000
1996		4	12	.250	5.13	19	19	2	119.1	132	34	55	1	0	0	0	0	0	0	—	15	16	1	1	1.7	.969
13 yrs.		132	135	.494	3.91	382	327	42	2218.2	2226	783	1366	16	7	5	2	0	0	0		236	352	19	32	1.6	.969

LEAGUE CHAMPIONSHIP SERIES

Year	Team	W	L	PCT	ERA	G	GS	CG	IP	H	BB	SO	ShO	W	L	SV	AB	H	HR	BA	PO	A	E	DP	TC/G	FA
1985	KC A	1	0	1.000	3.24	2	1	0	8.1	4	4	4	0	0	0	0	0	0	0	—	0	1	0	0	0.5	1.000

Lee Guetterman

GUETTERMAN, ARTHUR LEE
B. Nov. 22, 1958, Chattanooga, Tenn.   BL TL 6'8" 225 lbs.

Year	Team	W	L	PCT	ERA	G	GS	CG	IP	H	BB	SO	ShO	W	L	SV	AB	H	HR	BA	PO	A	E	DP	TC/G	FA
1984	SEA A	0	0	—	4.15	3	0	0	4.1	9	2	2	0	0	0	0	0	0	0	—	0	1	0	1	0.3	1.000
1986		0	4	.000	7.34	41	4	1	76	108	30	38	0	0	2	0	0	0	0	—	5	12	2	1	0.5	.895
1987		11	4	.733	3.81	25	17	2	113.1	117	35	42	1	1	0	0	0	0	0	—	7	22	0	3	1.2	1.000
1988	NY A	1	2	.333	4.65	20	2	0	40.2	49	14	15	0	1	0	0	0	0	0	—	2	5	0	0	0.3	1.000
1989		5	5	.500	2.45	70	0	0	103	98	26	51	0	5	5	13	0	0	0	—	6	24	3	4	0.5	.909
1990		11	7	.611	3.39	64	0	0	93	80	26	48	0	11	7	2	0	0	0	—	6	19	2	1	0.4	.926
1991		3	4	.429	3.68	64	0	0	88	91	25	35	0	3	4	6	0	0	0	—	9	13	3	1	0.4	.880
1992	2 teams		NY A	(15G 1–1)		NY N	(43G 3–4)																				
"	total	4	5	.444	7.09	58	0	0	66	92	27	20	0	4	5	2	2	0	0	.000	4	8	0	1	0.2	1.000

Year	Team	W	L	PCT	ERA	G	GS	CG	IP	H	BB	SO	ShO	W	L	SV	AB	H	HR	BA	PO	A	E	DP	TC/G	FA
														Relief Pitching			**Batting**									

Lee Guetterman *continued*

Year	Team	W	L	PCT	ERA	G	GS	CG	IP	H	BB	SO	ShO	W	L	SV	AB	H	HR	BA	PO	A	E	DP	TC/G	FA
1993	STL N	3	3	.500	2.93	40	0	0	46	41	16	19	0	3	3	1	2	1	0	.500	1	4	2	0	0.2	.714
1995	SEA A	0	0	—	6.88	23	0	0	17	21	11	11	0	0	0	1	0	0	0	—	2	5	0	1	0.3	1.000
1996		0	2	.000	4.09	17	0	0	11	11	10	6	0	0	2	0	0	0	0	—	2	3	0	0	0.3	1.000
11 yrs.		38	36	.514	4.33	425	23	3	658.1	717	222	287	1	28	28	25	4	1	0	.250	44	116	12	13	0.4	.930

Eric Gunderson

GUNDERSON, ERIC ANDREW
B. Mar. 29, 1966, Portland, Ore.   BR TL 6' 175 lbs.

Year	Team	W	L	PCT	ERA	G	GS	CG	IP	H	BB	SO	ShO	W	L	SV	AB	H	HR	BA	PO	A	E	DP	TC/G	FA
1990	SF N	1	2	.333	5.49	7	4	0	19.2	24	11	14	0	0	0	0	6	0	0	.000	0	4	0	0	0.6	1.000
1991		0	0	—	5.40	2	0	0	3.1	6	1	2	0	0	0	1	0	0	0	—	0	1	0	0	0.5	1.000
1992	SEA A	2	1	.667	8.68	9	0	0	9.1	12	5	2	0	2	1	0	0	0	0	—	1	2	0	0	0.3	1.000
1994	NY N	0	0	—	0.00	14	0	0	9	5	4	4	0	0	0	0	0	0	0	—	0	1	0	0	0.1	1.000
1995	2 teams			NY N		(30G 1–1)		BOS A		(19G 2–1)																
"	total	3	2	.600	4.17	49	0	0	36.2	38	17	28	0	3	2	0	0	0	0	—	3	8	0	0	0.2	1.000
1996	BOS A	0	1	.000	8.31	28	0	0	17.1	21	8	7	0	0	1	0	0	0	0	—	0	0	0	0	0.0	.000
6 yrs.		6	6	.500	5.29	109	4	0	95.1	106	46	57	0	5	4	1	6	0	0	.000	4	16	0	0	0.2	1.000

Mark Guthrie

GUTHRIE, MARK ANDREW
B. Sept. 22, 1965, Buffalo, N. Y.   BB TR 6'4" 192 lbs.

Year	Team	W	L	PCT	ERA	G	GS	CG	IP	H	BB	SO	ShO	W	L	SV	AB	H	HR	BA	PO	A	E	DP	TC/G	FA
1989	MIN A	2	4	.333	4.55	13	8	0	57.1	66	21	38	0	0	0	0	0	0	0	—	2	8	0	0	0.8	1.000
1990		7	9	.438	3.79	24	21	3	144.2	154	39	101	1	1	0	0	0	0	0	—	5	23	1	0	1.2	.966
1991		7	5	.583	4.32	41	12	0	98	116	41	72	0	2	1	2	0	0	0	—	5	10	1	0	0.4	.938
1992		2	3	.400	2.88	54	0	0	75	59	23	76	0	2	3	5	0	0	0	—	4	6	1	0	0.2	.909
1993		2	1	.667	4.71	22	0	0	21	20	16	15	0	2	1	0	0	0	0	—	0	5	0	0	0.2	1.000
1994		4	2	.667	6.14	50	2	0	51.1	65	18	38	0	4	1	1	0	0	0	—	3	8	0	0	0.2	1.000
1995	2 teams			MIN A		(36G 5–3)		LA N		(24G 0–2)																
"	total	5	5	.500	4.21	60	0	0	62	66	25	67	0	5	5	1	0	0	0	.000	0	5	2	0	0.1	.714
1996	LA N	2	3	.400	2.22	66	0	0	73	65	22	56	0	2	3	1	3	0	0	.000	1	11	1	1	0.2	.923
8 yrs.		31	32	.492	3.93	330	43	3	582.1	611	205	463	1	18	14	9	4	0	0	.000	20	76	6	1	0.3	.941

DIVISIONAL PLAYOFF SERIES

Year	Team	W	L	PCT	ERA	G	GS	CG	IP	H	BB	SO	ShO	W	L	SV	AB	H	HR	BA	PO	A	E	DP	TC/G	FA
1995	LA N	0	0	—	6.75	3	0	0	1.1	2	1	1	0	0	0	0	0	0	0	—	0	0	0	0	0.0	.000
1996		0	0	—	0.00	1	0	0	0.1	0	1	1	0	0	0	0	0	0	0	—	0	0	0	0	0.0	.000
2 yrs.		0	0	—	5.40	4	0	0	1.2	2	2	2	0	0	0	0	0	0	0	—	0	0	0	0	0.0	

LEAGUE CHAMPIONSHIP SERIES

Year	Team	W	L	PCT	ERA	G	GS	CG	IP	H	BB	SO	ShO	W	L	SV	AB	H	HR	BA	PO	A	E	DP	TC/G	FA
1991	MIN A	1	0	1.000	0.00	2	0	0	2.2	0	0	0	0	1	0	0	0	0	0	—	0	1	0	0	0.5	1.000

WORLD SERIES

Year	Team	W	L	PCT	ERA	G	GS	CG	IP	H	BB	SO	ShO	W	L	SV	AB	H	HR	BA	PO	A	E	DP	TC/G	FA
1991	MIN A	0	1	.000	2.25	4	0	0	4	3	4	3	0	0	1	0	0	0	0	—	0	1	0	0	0.3	1.000

Juan Guzman

GUZMAN, JUAN ANDRES
Born Juan Andres Guzman (Correa).
B. Oct. 28, 1966, Santo Domingo, Dominican Republic   BR TR 5'11" 190 lbs.

Year	Team	W	L	PCT	ERA	G	GS	CG	IP	H	BB	SO	ShO	W	L	SV	AB	H	HR	BA	PO	A	E	DP	TC/G	FA
1991	TOR A	10	3	.769	2.99	23	23	0	138.2	98	66	123	0	0	0	0	0	0	0	—	5	9	3	1	0.7	.824
1992		16	5	.762	2.64	28	28	1	180.2	135	72	165	0	0	0	0	0	0	0	—	12	11	0	0	0.8	1.000
1993		14	3	.824	3.99	33	33	2	221	211	110	194	1	0	0	0	0	0	0	—	11	16	1	0	0.8	.964
1994		12	11	.522	5.68	25	25	2	147.1	165	76	124	0	0	0	0	0	0	0	—	5	12	2	1	0.8	.895
1995		4	14	.222	6.32	24	24	3	135.1	151	73	94	0	0	0	0	0	0	0	—	7	12	2	0	0.9	.905
1996		11	8	.579	2.93	27	27	4	187.2	158	53	165	1	0	0	0	0	0	0	—	9	22	3	2	1.3	.912
6 yrs.		67	44	.604	3.97	160	160	13	1010.2	918	450	865	2	0	0	0	0	0	0	—	49	82	11	4	0.9	.923

LEAGUE CHAMPIONSHIP SERIES

Year	Team	W	L	PCT	ERA	G	GS	CG	IP	H	BB	SO	ShO	W	L	SV	AB	H	HR	BA	PO	A	E	DP	TC/G	FA
1991	TOR A	1	0	1.000	3.18	1	1	0	5.2	4	4	2	0	0	0	0	0	0	0	—	0	0	0	0	0.0	.000
1992		2	0	1.000	2.08	2	2	0	13	12	5	11	0	0	0	0	0	0	0	—	0	0	0	0	0.0	.000
1993		2	0	1.000	2.08	2	2	0	13	8	9	9	0	0	0	0	0	0	0	—	0	4	0	0	2.0	1.000
3 yrs.		5	0	1.000	2.27	5	5	0	31.2	24	18	22	0	0	0	0	0	0	0	—	0	4	0	0	0.8	1.000
		3rd	1st									7th														

WORLD SERIES

Year	Team	W	L	PCT	ERA	G	GS	CG	IP	H	BB	SO	ShO	W	L	SV	AB	H	HR	BA	PO	A	E	DP	TC/G	FA
1992	TOR A	0	0	—	1.13	1	1	0	8	8	1	7	0	0	0	0	0	0	0	—	2	0	0	0	2.0	1.000
1993		0	1	.000	3.75	2	2	0	12	10	8	12	0	0	0	0	2	0	0	.000	0	1	0	0	0.5	1.000
2 yrs.		0	1	.000	2.70	3	3	0	20	18	9	19	0	0	0	0	2	0	0	.000	2	1	0	0	1.0	1.000

John Habyan

HABYAN, JOHN GABRIEL
B. Jan. 29, 1964, Bay Shore, N. Y.   BR TR 6'1" 195 lbs.

Year	Team	W	L	PCT	ERA	G	GS	CG	IP	H	BB	SO	ShO	W	L	SV	AB	H	HR	BA	PO	A	E	DP	TC/G	FA
1985	BAL A	1	0	1.000	0.00	2	0	0	2.2	3	0	2	0	1	0	0	0	0	0	—	1	0	0	0	0.5	1.000
1986		1	3	.250	4.44	6	5	0	26.1	24	18	14	0	0	0	0	0	0	0	—	1	3	0	0	0.7	1.000
1987		6	7	.462	4.80	27	13	0	116.1	110	40	64	0	4	0	1	0	0	0	—	15	17	0	2	1.2	1.000
1988		1	0	1.000	4.30	7	0	0	14.2	22	4	4	0	1	0	0	0	0	0	—	5	1	0	0	0.9	1.000
1990	NY A	0	0	—	2.08	6	0	0	8.2	10	4	2	0	0	0	0	0	0	0	—	2	0	0	0	0.3	1.000
1991		4	2	.667	2.30	66	0	0	90	73	20	70	0	4	2	2	0	0	0	—	6	12	0	0	0.3	1.000
1992		5	6	.455	3.84	56	0	0	72.2	84	21	44	0	5	6	7	0	0	0	—	3	15	0	1	0.3	1.000
1993	2 teams			NY A		(36G 2–1)		KC A		(12G 0–0)																
"	total	2	1	.667	4.15	48	0	0	56.1	59	20	39	0	2	1	1	0	0	0		5	7	0	0	0.3	1.000

PITCHER REGISTER

Year	Team	W	L	PCT	ERA	G	GS	CG	IP	H	BB	SO	ShO	W	L	SV	AB	H	HR	BA	PO	A	E	DP	TC/G	FA
John Habyan *continued*																										
1994	STL N	1	0	1.000	3.23	52	0	0	47.1	50	20	46	0	1	0	1	0	0	0	—	4	8	1	0	0.3	.923
1995	2 teams	STL N	(31G 3-2)		CAL A	(28G 1-2)																				
"	total	4	4	.500	3.44	59	0	0	73.1	68	27	60	0	4	4	0	2	0	0	.000	4	8	0	0	0.2	1.000
1996	CLR N	1	1	.500	7.13	19	0	0	24	34	14	25	0	1	1	0	3	0	0	.000	1	2	0	0	0.2	1.000
11 yrs.		26	24	.520	3.85	348	18	0	532.1	537	186	372	0	23	14	12	5	0	0	.000	47	73	1	3	0.3	.992

Darren Hall
HALL, MICHAEL DARREN B. July 14, 1964, Marysville, Ohio — BR TR 6'3" 205 lbs.

Year	Team	W	L	PCT	ERA	G	GS	CG	IP	H	BB	SO	ShO	W	L	SV	AB	H	HR	BA	PO	A	E	DP	TC/G	FA
1994	TOR A	2	3	.400	3.41	30	0	0	31.2	26	14	28	0	2	3	17	0	0	0	—	2	6	0	2	0.3	1.000
1995		0	2	.000	4.41	17	0	0	16.1	21	9	11	0	0	2	3	0	0	0	—	2	1	0	0	0.2	1.000
1996	LA N	0	2	.000	6.00	9	0	0	12	13	5	12	0	0	2	0	0	0	0		0	0	0	0	0.0	.000
3 yrs.		2	7	.222	4.20	56	0	0	60	60	28	51	0	2	7	20	0	0	0		4	7	0	2	0.2	1.000

Joey Hamilton
HAMILTON, JOHNS JOSEPH B. Sept. 9, 1970, Statesboro, Ga. — BR TR 6'4" 220 lbs.

Year	Team	W	L	PCT	ERA	G	GS	CG	IP	H	BB	SO	ShO	W	L	SV	AB	H	HR	BA	PO	A	E	DP	TC/G	FA
1994	SD N	9	6	.600	2.98	16	16	1	108.2	98	29	61	1	0	0	0	40	0	0	.000	7	16	1	3	1.5	.958
1995		6	9	.400	3.08	31	30	2	204.1	189	56	123	2	0	0	0	65	7	0	.108	12	30	6	1	1.5	.875
1996		15	9	.625	4.17	34	33	3	211.2	206	83	184	1	0	0	0	68	11	1	.162	17	26	1	2	1.3	.977
3 yrs.		30	24	.556	3.50	81	79	6	524.2	493	168	368	4	0	0	0	173	18	1	.104	36	72	8	6	1.4	.931
DIVISIONAL PLAYOFF SERIES																										
1996	SD N	0	1	.000	4.50	1	1	0	6	5	0	6	0	0	0	0	2	0	0	.000	1	0	0	0	1.0	1.000

Chris Hammond
HAMMOND, CHRISTOPHER ANDREW B. Jan. 21, 1966, Atlanta, Ga. — BL TL 6'1" 190 lbs.

Year	Team	W	L	PCT	ERA	G	GS	CG	IP	H	BB	SO	ShO	W	L	SV	AB	H	HR	BA	PO	A	E	DP	TC/G	FA
1990	CIN N	0	2	.000	6.35	3	3	0	11.1	13	12	4	0	0	0	0	3	0	0	.000	0	3	2	0	1.7	.600
1991		7	7	.500	4.06	20	18	0	99.2	92	48	50	0	0	0	0	34	12	0	.353	6	18	2	1	1.3	.923
1992		7	10	.412	4.21	28	26	0	147.1	149	55	79	0	0	0	1	44	6	1	.136	9	22	2	1	1.2	.939
1993	FLA N	11	12	.478	4.66	32	32	1	191	207	66	108	0	0	0	0	63	12	2	.190	8	32	4	1	1.4	.909
1994		4	4	.500	3.07	13	13	1	73.1	79	23	40	1	0	0	0	22	3	0	.136	1	6	1	0	0.6	.875
1995		9	6	.600	3.80	25	24	3	161	157	47	126	2	0	0	0	48	13	1	.271	8	21	1	2	1.2	.967
1996		5	8	.385	6.56	38	9	0	81	104	27	50	0	3	2	0	15	1	0	.067	6	13	2	1	0.6	.905
7 yrs.		43	49	.467	4.39	159	125	5	764.2	801	278	457	3	3	2	0	229	47	4	.205	38	115	14	6	1.1	.916

Mike Hampton
HAMPTON, MICHAEL WILLIAM B. Sept. 9, 1972, Brooksville, Fla. — BR TL 5'10" 185 lbs.

Year	Team	W	L	PCT	ERA	G	GS	CG	IP	H	BB	SO	ShO	W	L	SV	AB	H	HR	BA	PO	A	E	DP	TC/G	FA
1993	SEA A	1	3	.250	9.53	13	3	0	17	28	17	8	0	1	0	1	0	0	0	—	0	2	1	0	0.2	.667
1994	HOU N	2	1	.667	3.70	44	0	0	41.1	46	16	24	0	2	1	0	1	0	0	.000	6	11	0	2	0.4	1.000
1995		9	8	.529	3.35	24	24	0	150.2	141	49	115	0	0	0	0	48	7	0	.146	10	24	3	2	1.5	.919
1996		10	10	.500	3.59	27	27	2	160.1	175	49	101	1	0	0	0	42	10	0	.238	13	32	2	3	1.7	.957
4 yrs.		22	22	.500	3.78	108	54	2	369.1	390	131	248	1	3	1	1	91	17	0	.187	29	69	6	7	1.0	.942

Lee Hancock
HANCOCK, LELAND DAVID B. June 27, 1967, North Hollywood, Calif. — BL TL 6'4" 215 lbs.

Year	Team	W	L	PCT	ERA	G	GS	CG	IP	H	BB	SO	ShO	W	L	SV	AB	H	HR	BA	PO	A	E	DP	TC/G	FA
1995	PIT N	0	0	—	1.93	11	0	0	14	10	2	6	0	0	0	0	0	0	0	—	1	1	0	1	0.2	1.000
1996		0	0		6.38	13	0	0	18.1	21	10	13	0	0	0	0	0	0	0	—	3	7	1	2	0.8	.909
2 yrs.		0	0		4.45	24	0	0	32.1	31	12	19	0	0	0	0	0	0	0		4	8	1	3	0.5	.923

Ryan Hancock
HANCOCK, RYAN LEE B. Nov. 11, 1971, Santa Clara, Calif. — BR TR 6'2" 215 lbs.

Year	Team	W	L	PCT	ERA	G	GS	CG	IP	H	BB	SO	ShO	W	L	SV	AB	H	HR	BA	PO	A	E	DP	TC/G	FA
1996	CAL A	4	1	.800	7.48	11	4	0	27.2	34	17	19	0	2	0	0	1	1	0	1.000	2	3	0	1	0.5	1.000

Chris Haney
HANEY, CHRISTOPHER DEANE Son of Larry Haney. B. Nov. 16, 1968, Baltimore, Md. — BL TL 6'3" 185 lbs.

Year	Team	W	L	PCT	ERA	G	GS	CG	IP	H	BB	SO	ShO	W	L	SV	AB	H	HR	BA	PO	A	E	DP	TC/G	FA
1991	MON N	3	7	.300	4.04	16	16	0	84.2	94	43	51	0	0	0	0	27	2	0	.074	6	18	2	1	1.6	.923
1992	2 teams	MON N	(9G 2-3)		KC A	(7G 2-3)																				
"	total	4	6	.400	4.61	16	13	2	80	75	26	54	2	0	0	0	9	2	0	.222	2	6	0	0	0.5	1.000
1993	KC A	9	9	.500	6.02	23	23	1	124	141	53	65	1	0	0	0	0	0	0	—	7	19	0	1	1.1	1.000
1994		2	2	.500	7.31	6	6	0	28.1	36	11	18	0	0	0	0	0	0	0	—	3	5	0	2	1.3	1.000
1995		3	4	.429	3.65	16	13	1	81.1	78	33	31	0	0	0	0	1	15	0	—	1	15	0	1	1.0	1.000
1996		10	14	.417	4.70	35	35	4	228	267	51	115	0	0	0	0	0	0	0	—	9	27	0	1	1.0	1.000
6 yrs.		31	42	.425	4.84	112	106	8	626.1	691	217	334	4	0	0	0	36	4	0	.111	28	90	2	4	1.1	.983

Greg Hansell
HANSELL, GREGORY MICHAEL B. Mar. 12, 1971, Bellflower, Calif. — BR TR 6'5" 213 lbs.

Year	Team	W	L	PCT	ERA	G	GS	CG	IP	H	BB	SO	ShO	W	L	SV	AB	H	HR	BA	PO	A	E	DP	TC/G	FA
1995	LA N	0	1	.000	7.45	20	0	0	19.1	29	6	13	0	0	1	0	0	0	0	—	2	1	0	0	0.2	1.000
1996	MIN A	3	0	1.000	5.69	50	0	0	74.1	83	31	46	0	3	0	3	0	0	0	—	8	4	0	0	0.2	1.000
2 yrs.		3	1	.750	6.05	70	0	0	93.2	112	37	59	0	3	1	3	0	0	0		10	5	0	0	0.2	1.000

138

Year	Team	W	L	PCT	ERA	G	GS	CG	IP	H	BB	SO	ShO	Relief Pitching W	L	SV	Batting AB	H	HR	BA	PO	A	E	DP	TC/G	FA

Erik Hanson

HANSON, ERIK BRIAN
B. May 18, 1965, Kinnelon, N. J.

BR TR 6'6" 210 lbs.

Year	Team	W	L	PCT	ERA	G	GS	CG	IP	H	BB	SO	ShO	W	L	SV	AB	H	HR	BA	PO	A	E	DP	TC/G	FA
1988	SEA A	2	3	.400	3.24	6	6	0	41.2	35	12	36	0	0	0	0	0	0	0	—	0	4	0	1	0.7	1.000
1989		9	5	.643	3.18	17	17	1	113.1	103	32	75	0	0	0	0	0	0	0	—	8	16	0	0	1.4	1.000
1990		18	9	.667	3.24	33	33	5	236	205	68	211	1	0	0	0	0	0	0	—	30	20	4	0	1.6	.926
1991		8	8	.500	3.81	27	27	2	174.2	182	56	143	1	0	0	0	0	0	0	—	14	16	1	0	1.1	.968
1992		8	17	.320	4.82	31	30	6	186.2	209	57	112	1	1	0	0	0	0	0	—	14	23	1	2	1.2	.974
1993		11	12	.478	3.47	31	30	7	215	215	60	163	0	0	1	0	0	0	0	—	25	25	3	3	1.7	.943
1994	CIN N	5	5	.500	4.11	22	21	0	122.2	137	23	101	0	0	0	0	39	6	0	.154	11	16	0	0	1.2	1.000
1995	BOS A	15	5	.750	4.24	29	29	1	186.2	187	59	139	1	0	0	0	0	0	0	—	17	21	2	1	1.4	.950
1996	TOR A	13	17	.433	5.41	35	35	4	214.2	243	102	156	1	0	0	0	0	0	0	—	8	16	3	3	0.8	.889
9 yrs.		89	81	.524	4.04	231	228	26	1491.1	1516	469	1136	5	1	1	0	39	6	0	.154	127	157	14	10	1.3	.953
DIVISIONAL PLAYOFF SERIES																										
1995	BOS A	0	1	.000	4.50	1	1	1	8	4	4	5	0	0	0	0	0	0	0	—	1	3	0	0	4.0	1.000

Tim Harikkala

HARIKKALA, TIMOTHY ALLAN
B. July 15, 1971, West Palm Beach, Fla.

BR TR 6'2" 185 lbs.

Year	Team	W	L	PCT	ERA	G	GS	CG	IP	H	BB	SO	ShO	W	L	SV	AB	H	HR	BA	PO	A	E	DP	TC/G	FA
1995	SEA A	0	0	—	16.20	1	0	0	3.1	7	1	1	0	0	0	0	0	0	0	—	0	0	0	0	0.0	.000
1996		0	1	.000	12.46	1	1	0	4.1	4	2	1	0	0	0	0	0	0	0	—	0	2	0	0	2.0	1.000
2 yrs.		0	1	.000	14.09	2	1	0	7.2	11	3	2	0	0	0	0					0	2	0	0	1.0	1.000

Pete Harnisch

HARNISCH, PETER THOMAS
B. Sept. 23, 1966, Commack, N. Y.

BB TR 6'1" 195 lbs.

Year	Team	W	L	PCT	ERA	G	GS	CG	IP	H	BB	SO	ShO	W	L	SV	AB	H	HR	BA	PO	A	E	DP	TC/G	FA
1988	BAL A	0	2	.000	5.54	2	2	0	13	13	9	10	0	0	0	0	0	0	0	—	2	2	0	0	2.0	1.000
1989		5	9	.357	4.62	18	17	2	103.1	97	64	70	0	0	0	0	0	0	0	—	7	9	0	2	0.9	1.000
1990		11	11	.500	4.34	31	31	3	188.2	189	86	122	0	0	0	0	0	0	0	—	12	14	1	0	0.9	.963
1991	HOU N	12	9	.571	2.70	33	33	4	216.2	169	83	172	2	0	0	0	62	6	0	.097	7	18	1	0	0.8	.962
1992		9	10	.474	3.70	34	34	0	206.2	182	64	164	0	0	0	0	67	11	0	.164	16	15	2	1	1.0	.939
1993		16	9	.640	2.98	33	33	5	217.2	171	79	185	4	0	0	0	67	7	0	.104	3	15	2	0	0.6	.900
1994		8	5	.615	5.40	17	17	1	95	100	39	62	0	0	0	0	35	6	0	.171	11	8	0	1	1.1	1.000
1995	NY N	2	8	.200	3.68	18	18	0	110	111	24	82	0	0	0	0	33	3	0	.091	9	12	2	1	1.3	.913
1996		8	12	.400	4.21	31	31	2	194.2	195	61	114	1	0	0	0	55	5	0	.091	10	16	3	1	1.0	.897
9 yrs.		71	75	.486	3.79	217	216	17	1345.2	1227	509	981	7	0	0	0	319	38	0	.119	77	109	11	5	0.9	.944

Pep Harris

HARRIS, HERNANDO PETROCELLI
B. Sept. 23, 1972, Lancaster, S. C.

BR TR 6'2" 185 lbs.

Year	Team	W	L	PCT	ERA	G	GS	CG	IP	H	BB	SO	ShO	W	L	SV	AB	H	HR	BA	PO	A	E	DP	TC/G	FA
1996	CAL A	2	0	1.000	3.90	11	3	0	32.1	31	17	20	0	1	0	0	0	0	0	—	1	6	0	1	0.6	1.000

Reggie Harris

HARRIS, REGINALD ALLEN
B. Aug. 12, 1968, Waynesboro, Va.

BR TR 6'1" 180 lbs.

Year	Team	W	L	PCT	ERA	G	GS	CG	IP	H	BB	SO	ShO	W	L	SV	AB	H	HR	BA	PO	A	E	DP	TC/G	FA
1990	OAK A	1	0	1.000	3.48	16	1	0	41.1	25	21	31	0	1	0	0	0	0	0	—	2	3	0	1	0.3	1.000
1991		0	0	—	12.00	2	0	0	3	5	3	2	0	0	0	0	0	0	0	—	0	0	0	0	0.0	.000
1996	BOS A	0	0	—	12.46	4	0	0	4.1	7	5	4	0	0	0	0	0	0	0	—	0	0	0	0	0.0	.000
3 yrs.		1	0	1.000	4.81	22	1	0	48.2	37	29	37	0	1	0	0	0	0	0	—	2	3	0	1	0.2	1.000

Dean Hartgraves

HARTGRAVES, DEAN CHARLES
B. Aug. 12, 1966, Bakersfield, Calif.

BR TL 6' 185 lbs.

Year	Team	W	L	PCT	ERA	G	GS	CG	IP	H	BB	SO	ShO	W	L	SV	AB	H	HR	BA	PO	A	E	DP	TC/G	FA
1995	HOU N	2	0	1.000	3.22	40	0	0	36.1	30	16	24	0	2	0	0	2	0	0	.000	3	5	0	0	0.2	1.000
1996	2 teams		HOU N	(19G 0–0)		ATL N	(20G 1–0)																			
"	total	1	0	1.000	4.78	39	0	0	37.2	34	23	30	0	1	0	0	1	0	0	.000	3	5	0	0	0.2	1.000
2 yrs.		3	0	1.000	4.01	79	0	0	74	64	39	54	0	3	0	0	3	0	0	.000	6	10	0	0	0.2	1.000

Ryan Hawblitzel

HAWBLITZEL, RYAN WADE
B. Apr. 30, 1971, W. Palm Beach, Fla.

BR TR 6'2" 170 lbs.

Year	Team	W	L	PCT	ERA	G	GS	CG	IP	H	BB	SO	ShO	W	L	SV	AB	H	HR	BA	PO	A	E	DP	TC/G	FA
1996	CLR N	0	1	.000	6.00	8	0	0	15	18	6	7	0	0	1	0	1	0	0	.000	2	2	0	0	0.5	1.000

LaTroy Hawkins

HAWKINS, LaTROY
B. Dec. 21, 1972, Gary, Ind.

BR TR 6'5" 195 lbs.

Year	Team	W	L	PCT	ERA	G	GS	CG	IP	H	BB	SO	ShO	W	L	SV	AB	H	HR	BA	PO	A	E	DP	TC/G	FA
1995	MIN A	2	3	.400	8.67	6	6	1	27	39	12	9	0	0	0	0	0	0	0	—	3	3	0	1	1.0	1.000
1996		1	1	.500	8.20	7	6	0	26.1	42	9	24	0	0	0	0	0	0	0	—	3	4	0	1	1.0	1.000
2 yrs.		3	4	.429	8.44	13	12	1	53.1	81	21	33	0	0	0	0					6	7	0	2	1.0	1.000

Jimmy Haynes

HAYNES, JIMMY WAYNE
B. Sept. 5, 1972, La Grange, Ga.

BR TR 6'4" 185 lbs.

Year	Team	W	L	PCT	ERA	G	GS	CG	IP	H	BB	SO	ShO	W	L	SV	AB	H	HR	BA	PO	A	E	DP	TC/G	FA
1995	BAL A	2	1	.667	2.25	4	3	0	24	11	12	22	0	0	0	0	0	0	0	—	0	3	0	0	0.8	1.000
1996		3	6	.333	8.29	26	11	0	89	122	58	65	0	2	0	1	0	0	0	—	6	12	1	1	0.7	.947
2 yrs.		5	7	.417	7.01	30	14	0	113	133	70	87	0	2	0	1					6	15	1	1	0.7	.955

Bronson Heflin

HEFLIN, BRONSON WAYNE
B. Aug. 29, 1971, Clarksville, Tenn.

BR TR 6'3" 195 lbs.

Year	Team	W	L	PCT	ERA	G	GS	CG	IP	H	BB	SO	ShO	W	L	SV	AB	H	HR	BA	PO	A	E	DP	TC/G	FA
1996	PHI N	0	0	—	6.75	3	0	0	6.2	11	3	4	0	0	0	0	0	0	0	—	0	0	0	0	0.0	—

PITCHER REGISTER

Year	Team	W	L	PCT	ERA	G	GS	CG	IP	H	BB	SO	ShO	W	L	SV	AB	H	HR	BA	PO	A	E	DP	TC/G	FA

Rick Helling
HELLING, RICKY ALLEN B. Dec. 15, 1970, Devils Lake, N. D. — BR TR 6'3" 215 lbs.

Year	Team	W	L	PCT	ERA	G	GS	CG	IP	H	BB	SO	ShO	W	L	SV	AB	H	HR	BA	PO	A	E	DP	TC/G	FA
1994	TEX A	3	2	.600	5.88	9	9	1	52	62	18	25	1	0	0	0	0	0	0	—	2	3	0	0	0.6	1.000
1995		0	2	.000	6.57	3	3	0	12.1	17	8	5	0	0	0	0	0	0	0	—	0	1	0	0	0.3	1.000
1996	2 teams			TEX A (6G 1–2)				FLA N (5G 2–1)																		
"	total	3	3	.500	4.31	11	6	0	48	37	16	42	0	0	1	0	9	1	0	.111	2	3	0	0	0.5	1.000
	3 yrs.	6	7	.462	5.29	23	18	1	112.1	116	42	72	1	0	1	0	9	1	0	.111	4	7	0	0	0.5	1.000

Mike Henneman
HENNEMAN, MICHAEL ALAN B. Dec. 11, 1961, St. Charles, Mo. — BR TR 6'4" 205 lbs.

Year	Team	W	L	PCT	ERA	G	GS	CG	IP	H	BB	SO	ShO	W	L	SV	AB	H	HR	BA	PO	A	E	DP	TC/G	FA
1987	DET A	11	3	.786	2.98	55	0	0	96.2	86	30	75	0	11	3	7	1	0	0	.000	8	11	0	2	0.3	1.000
1988		9	6	.600	1.87	65	0	0	91.1	72	24	58	0	9	6	22	0	0	0	—	4	8	1	0	0.2	.923
1989		11	4	.733	3.70	60	0	0	90	84	51	69	0	11	4	8	0	0	0	—	5	12	0	2	0.3	1.000
1990		8	6	.571	3.05	69	0	0	94.1	90	33	50	0	8	6	22	0	0	0	—	7	16	3	2	0.4	.885
1991		10	2	.833	2.88	60	0	0	84.1	81	34	61	0	10	2	21	0	0	0	—	6	10	2	1	0.3	.889
1992		2	6	.250	3.96	60	0	0	77.1	75	20	58	0	2	6	24	0	0	0	—	9	9	1	1	0.3	.947
1993		5	3	.625	2.64	63	0	0	71.2	69	32	58	0	5	3	24	0	0	0	—	6	5	1	0	0.2	.917
1994		1	3	.250	5.19	30	0	0	34.2	43	17	27	0	1	3	8	0	0	0	—	6	4	0	0	0.3	1.000
1995	2 teams			DET A (29G 0–1)				HOU N (21G 0–1)																		
"	total	0	2	.000	2.15	50	0	0	50.1	45	13	43	0	0	2	26	0	0	0	—	3	2	0	0	0.1	1.000
1996	TEX A	0	7	.000	5.79	49	0	0	42	41	17	34	0	0	7	31	0	0	0	—	1	6	1	0	0.2	.875
	10 yrs.	57	42	.576	3.21	561	0	0	732.2	686	271	533	0	57	42	193	1	0	0	.000	55	83	9	8	0.3	.939
DIVISIONAL PLAYOFF SERIES																										
1996	TEX A	0	0	—	0.00	3	0	0	1	1	1	1	0	0	0	0	0	0	0	—	0	0	0	0	0.0	.000
LEAGUE CHAMPIONSHIP SERIES																										
1987	DET A	1	0	1.000	10.80	3	0	0	5	6	6	3	0	0	0	0	0	0	0	—	0	2	0	0	0.7	1.000

Doug Henry
HENRY, RICHARD DOUGLAS B. Dec. 10, 1963, Sacramento, Calif. — BR TR 6'4" 185 lbs.

Year	Team	W	L	PCT	ERA	G	GS	CG	IP	H	BB	SO	ShO	W	L	SV	AB	H	HR	BA	PO	A	E	DP	TC/G	FA
1991	MIL A	2	1	.667	1.00	32	0	0	36	16	14	28	0	2	1	15	0	0	0	—	4	1	0	0	0.2	1.000
1992		1	4	.200	4.02	68	0	0	65	64	24	52	0	1	4	29	0	0	0	—	10	4	0	2	0.2	1.000
1993		4	4	.500	5.56	54	0	0	55	67	25	38	0	4	4	17	0	0	0	—	5	7	0	0	0.2	1.000
1994		2	3	.400	4.60	25	0	0	31.1	32	23	20	0	2	3	0	1	0	0	.000	2	3	0	0	0.2	1.000
1995	NY N	3	6	.333	2.96	51	0	0	67	48	25	62	0	3	6	4	1	1	0	1.000	4	9	1	0	0.3	.929
1996		2	8	.200	4.68	58	0	0	75	82	36	58	0	2	8	9	5	0	0	.000	4	7	2	0	0.2	.846
	6 yrs.	14	26	.350	3.94	288	0	0	329.1	309	147	258	0	14	26	74	7	1	0	.143	29	31	3	2	0.2	.952

Pat Hentgen
HENTGEN, PATRICK GEORGE B. Nov. 13, 1968, Detroit, Mich. — BR TR 6'2" 210 lbs.

Year	Team	W	L	PCT	ERA	G	GS	CG	IP	H	BB	SO	ShO	W	L	SV	AB	H	HR	BA	PO	A	E	DP	TC/G	FA
1991	TOR A	0	0	—	2.45	3	1	0	7.1	5	3	3	0	0	0	0	0	0	0	—	0	2	0	1	0.7	1.000
1992		5	2	.714	5.36	28	2	0	50.1	49	32	39	0	5	1	0	0	0	0	—	0	4	0	1	0.1	1.000
1993		19	9	.679	3.87	34	32	3	216.1	215	74	122	0	0	1	0	0	0	0	—	12	22	1	1	1.0	.971
1994		13	8	.619	3.40	24	24	6	174.2	158	59	147	3	0	0	0	0	0	0	—	12	21	0	2	1.4	1.000
1995		10	14	.417	5.11	30	30	2	200.2	236	90	135	0	0	0	0	0	0	0	—	12	18	2	2	1.1	.938
1996		20	10	.667	3.22	35	35	10	265.2	238	94	177	3	0	0	0	0	0	0	—	11	31	1	7	1.2	.977
	6 yrs.	67	43	.609	3.93	154	124	21	915	901	352	623	6	5	2	0	0	0	0	—	47	98	4	14	1.0	.973
LEAGUE CHAMPIONSHIP SERIES																										
1993	TOR A	0	1	.000	18.00	1	1	0	3	9	1	4	0	0	0	0	0	0	0	—	1	0	0	0	1.0	1.000
WORLD SERIES																										
1993	TOR A	1	0	1.000	1.50	1	1	0	6	5	3	6	0	0	0	0	3	0	0	.000	0	0	0	0	0.0	.000

Felix Heredia
HEREDIA, FELIX Born Felix Heredia (Perez). B. Jun. 18, 1976, Barahona, Domincan Republic — BL TL 6' 160 lbs.

Year	Team	W	L	PCT	ERA	G	GS	CG	IP	H	BB	SO	ShO	W	L	SV	AB	H	HR	BA	PO	A	E	DP	TC/G	FA
1996	FLA N	1	1	.500	4.32	21	0	0	16.2	21	10	10	0	1	1	0	0	0	0	—	0	0	0	0	0.0	—

Gil Heredia
HEREDIA, GILBERT B. Oct. 26, 1965, Nogales, Ariz. — BR TR 6'1" 190 lbs.

Year	Team	W	L	PCT	ERA	G	GS	CG	IP	H	BB	SO	ShO	W	L	SV	AB	H	HR	BA	PO	A	E	DP	TC/G	FA
1991	SF N	0	2	.000	3.82	7	4	0	33	27	7	13	0	0	0	0	7	3	0	.429	2	2	0	0	0.6	1.000
1992	2 teams			SF N (13G 2–3)				MON N (7G 0–0)																		
"	total	2	3	.400	4.23	20	5	0	44.2	44	20	22	0	2	0	0	9	1	0	.111	0	5	0	0	0.3	1.000
1993	MON N	4	2	.667	3.92	20	9	1	57.1	66	14	40	0	0	0	2	13	2	0	.154	4	11	0	1	0.8	1.000
1994		6	3	.667	3.46	39	3	0	75.1	85	13	62	0	4	3	0	16	5	0	.313	5	12	1	0	0.5	.944
1995		5	6	.455	4.31	40	18	0	119	137	21	74	0	1	0	1	33	6	0	.182	9	21	0	0	0.8	1.000
1996	TEX A	2	5	.286	5.89	44	0	0	73.1	91	14	43	0	2	5	1	0	0	0	—	7	7	0	0	0.3	1.000
	6 yrs.	19	21	.475	4.34	170	39	1	402.2	450	89	254	0	9	8	4	78	17	0	.218	27	58	1	1	0.5	.988

Dustin Hermanson
HERMANSON, DUSTIN MICHAEL B. Dec. 21, 1972, Springfield, Ohio — BR TR 6'3" 195 lbs.

Year	Team	W	L	PCT	ERA	G	GS	CG	IP	H	BB	SO	ShO	W	L	SV	AB	H	HR	BA	PO	A	E	DP	TC/G	FA
1995	SD N	3	1	.750	6.82	26	0	0	31.2	35	22	19	0	3	1	0	0	0	0	—	4	4	0	2	0.3	1.000
1996		1	0	1.000	8.56	8	0	0	13.2	18	4	11	0	1	0	0	0	0	0	—	2	2	1	2	0.6	.800
	2 yrs.	4	1	.800	7.35	34	0	0	45.1	53	26	30	0	4	1	0	0	0	0	—	6	6	1	4	0.4	.923

Year	Team	W	L	PCT	ERA	G	GS	CG	IP	H	BB	SO	ShO	Relief Pitching W	L	SV	Batting AB	H	HR	BA	PO	A	E	DP	TC/G	FA

Livan Hernandez

HERNANDEZ, EISLER LIVAN
B. Feb. 20, 1975, Villa Clara, Cuba — BR TR 6'2" 220 lbs.

Year	Team	W	L	PCT	ERA	G	GS	CG	IP	H	BB	SO	ShO	W	L	SV	AB	H	HR	BA	PO	A	E	DP	TC/G	FA
1996	FLA N	0	0	—	0.00	1	0	0	3	3	2	2	0	0	0	0	1	1	0	1.000	0	0	0	0	0.0	—

Roberto Hernandez

HERNANDEZ, ROBERTO MANUEL
Born Roberto Manuel Hernandez (Rodriguez).
B. Nov. 11, 1964, Santurce, Puerto Rico — BR TR 6'4" 220 lbs.

Year	Team	W	L	PCT	ERA	G	GS	CG	IP	H	BB	SO	ShO	W	L	SV	AB	H	HR	BA	PO	A	E	DP	TC/G	FA
1991	CHI A	1	0	1.000	7.80	9	3	0	15	18	7	6	0	0	0	0	0	0	0	—	0	2	0	0	0.2	1.000
1992		7	3	.700	1.65	43	0	0	71	45	20	68	0	7	3	12	0	0	0	—	7	4	1	1	0.3	.917
1993		3	4	.429	2.29	70	0	0	78.2	66	20	71	0	3	4	38	0	0	0	—	2	11	1	1	0.3	.929
1994		4	4	.500	4.91	45	0	0	47.2	44	19	50	0	4	4	14	0	0	0	—	0	2	1	0	0.1	.667
1995		3	7	.300	3.92	60	0	0	59.2	63	28	84	0	3	7	32	0	0	0	—	2	5	1	0	0.1	.875
1996		6	5	.545	1.91	72	0	0	84.2	65	38	85	0	6	5	38	0	0	0	—	3	6	1	0	0.1	.900
6 yrs.		24	23	.511	2.93	299	3	0	356.2	301	132	364	0	23	23	134	0	0	0	—	14	30	5	2	0.2	.898

LEAGUE CHAMPIONSHIP SERIES

Year	Team	W	L	PCT	ERA	G	GS	CG	IP	H	BB	SO	ShO	W	L	SV	AB	H	HR	BA	PO	A	E	DP	TC/G	FA
1993	CHI A	0	0	—	0.00	4	0	0	4	4	0	1	0	0	0	1	0	0	0	—	0	0	0	0	0.0	.000

Xavier Hernandez

HERNANDEZ, FRANCIS XAVIER
B. Aug. 16, 1965, Port Arthur, Tex. — BL TR 6'2" 185 lbs.

Year	Team	W	L	PCT	ERA	G	GS	CG	IP	H	BB	SO	ShO	W	L	SV	AB	H	HR	BA	PO	A	E	DP	TC/G	FA
1989	TOR A	1	0	1.000	4.76	7	0	0	22.2	25	8	7	0	1	0	0	0	0	0	—	1	2	1	0	0.6	.750
1990	HOU N	2	1	.667	4.62	34	1	0	62.1	60	24	24	0	2	0	0	3	1	0	.333	3	5	0	0	0.2	1.000
1991		2	7	.222	4.71	32	6	0	63	66	32	55	0	2	3	3	10	0	0	.000	6	9	0	0	0.5	1.000
1992		9	1	.900	2.11	77	0	0	111	81	42	96	0	9	1	7	9	0	0	.000	9	7	1	0	0.2	.941
1993		4	5	.444	2.61	72	0	0	96.2	75	28	101	0	4	5	9	5	0	0	.000	1	8	0	0	0.1	1.000
1994	NY A	4	4	.500	5.85	31	0	0	40	48	21	37	0	4	4	6	0	0	0	—	2	8	0	3	0.3	1.000
1995	CIN N	7	2	.778	4.60	59	0	0	90	95	31	84	0	7	2	3	8	0	0	.000	10	7	0	0	0.3	1.000
1996	2 teams	CIN N	(3G 0-0)		HOU N	(58G 5-5)																				
"	total	5	5	.500	4.62	61	0	0	78	77	28	81	0	5	5	6	2	0	0	.000	2	9	0	0	0.2	1.000
8 yrs.		34	25	.576	3.88	373	7	0	563.2	527	214	485	0	34	19	34	37	1	0	.027	34	55	2	3	0.2	.978

LEAGUE CHAMPIONSHIP SERIES

Year	Team	W	L	PCT	ERA	G	GS	CG	IP	H	BB	SO	ShO	W	L	SV	AB	H	HR	BA	PO	A	E	DP	TC/G	FA
1995	CIN N	0	0	—	27.00	1	0	0	2	3	0	0	0	0	0	0	0	0	0	—	0	0	0	0	0.0	.000

Orel Hershiser

HERSHISER, OREL LEONARD QUINTON IV (Bulldog)
B. Sept. 16, 1958, Buffalo, N.Y. — BR TR 6'3" 190 lbs.

Year	Team	W	L	PCT	ERA	G	GS	CG	IP	H	BB	SO	ShO	W	L	SV	AB	H	HR	BA	PO	A	E	DP	TC/G	FA
1983	LA N	0	0	—	3.38	8	0	0	8	7	6	5	0	0	0	1	0	0	0	—	0	2	0	1	0.3	1.000
1984		11	8	.579	2.66	45	20	8	189.2	160	50	150	4	2	2	2	50	10	0	.200	17	28	5	2	1.1	.900
1985		19	3	.864	2.03	36	34	9	239.2	179	68	157	5	1	0	0	76	15	0	.197	20	45	7	4	2.0	.903
1986		14	14	.500	3.85	35	35	8	231.1	213	86	153	1	0	0	0	71	17	0	.239	22	36	3	6	1.7	.951
1987		16	16	.500	3.06	37	35	10	264.2	247	74	190	1	0	1	1	90	19	0	.211	37	34	5	6	2.1	.934
1988		23	8	.742	2.26	35	34	15	267	208	73	178	8	0	0	1	85	11	0	.129	32	60	6	6	2.8	.939
1989		15	15	.500	2.31	35	33	8	256.2	226	77	178	4	0	0	0	77	14	0	.182	24	51	4	2	2.3	.949
1990		1	1	.500	4.26	4	4	0	25.1	26	4	16	0	0	0	0	7	0	0	.000	1	3	0	0	1.0	1.000
1991		7	2	.778	3.46	21	21	0	112	112	32	73	0	0	0	0	31	8	0	.258	12	18	1	1	1.5	.968
1992		10	15	.400	3.67	33	33	1	210.2	209	69	130	0	0	0	0	68	15	0	.221	28	41	3	2	2.2	.958
1993		12	14	.462	3.59	33	33	5	215.2	201	72	141	1	0	0	0	73	26	0	.356	20	43	3	1	1.9	.955
1994		6	6	.500	3.79	21	21	1	135.1	146	42	72	0	0	0	0	44	9	0	.205	22	24	2	3	2.3	.958
1995	CLE A	16	6	.727	3.87	26	26	1	167.1	151	51	111	1	0	0	0	0	0	0	—	16	31	2	1	1.9	.959
1996		15	9	.625	4.24	33	33	1	206	238	58	125	0	0	0	0	0	0	0	—	20	47	2	3	2.1	.971
14 yrs.		165	117	.585	3.16	402	362	67	2529.1	2323	762	1679	25	3	3	5	672	144	0	.214	271	463	43	38	1.9	.945

DIVISIONAL PLAYOFF SERIES

Year	Team	W	L	PCT	ERA	G	GS	CG	IP	H	BB	SO	ShO	W	L	SV	AB	H	HR	BA	PO	A	E	DP	TC/G	FA
1995	CLE A	1	0	1.000	0.00	1	1	0	7.1	3	2	7	0	0	0	0	0	0	0	—	0	0	0	0	0.0	.000
1996		0	0	—	5.40	1	1	0	5	7	3	3	0	0	0	0	0	0	0	—	1	1	0	1	2.0	1.000
2 yrs.		1	0	1.000	2.19	2	2	0	12.1	10	5	10	0	0	0	0					1	1	0	1	1.0	1.000

LEAGUE CHAMPIONSHIP SERIES

Year	Team	W	L	PCT	ERA	G	GS	CG	IP	H	BB	SO	ShO	W	L	SV	AB	H	HR	BA	PO	A	E	DP	TC/G	FA
1985	LA N	1	0	1.000	3.52	2	2	1	15.1	17	6	5	0	0	0	0	7	2	0	.286	2	2	0	0	2.0	1.000
1988		1	0	1.000	1.09	4	3	1	24.2	18	7	15	1	0	0	0	9	0	0	.000	3	3	0	0	1.5	1.000
1995	CLE A	2	0	1.000	1.29	2	2	0	14	9	3	15	0	0	0	1	0	0	0	—	0	4	0	0	2.0	1.000
3 yrs.		4	0	1.000	1.83	8	7	2	54	44	16	35	1	0	0	1	16	2	0	.125	5	9	0	1	1.8	1.000
		4th	1st		4th		5th	4th	5th			8th	1st													

WORLD SERIES

Year	Team	W	L	PCT	ERA	G	GS	CG	IP	H	BB	SO	ShO	W	L	SV	AB	H	HR	BA	PO	A	E	DP	TC/G	FA
1988	LA N	2	0	1.000	1.00	2	2	2	18	7	6	17	1	0	0	0	3	3	0	1.000	1	1	0	0	1.0	1.000
1995	CLE A	1	1	.500	2.57	2	2	0	14	8	4	13	0	0	0	0	2	0	0	.000	1	7	1	0	4.5	.889
2 yrs.		3	1	.750	1.69	4	4	2	32	15	10	30	1	0	0	0	5	3	0	.600	2	8	1	0	2.8	.909

Ken Hill

HILL, KENNETH WADE (Thrill)
B. Dec. 14, 1965, Lynn, Mass. — BR TR 6'4" 200 lbs.

Year	Team	W	L	PCT	ERA	G	GS	CG	IP	H	BB	SO	ShO	W	L	SV	AB	H	HR	BA	PO	A	E	DP	TC/G	FA
1988	STL N	0	1	.000	5.14	4	1	0	14	16	6	6	0	0	0	0	3	0	0	.000	0	3	0	0	0.8	1.000
1989		7	15	.318	3.80	33	33	2	196.2	186	99	112	1	0	0	0	59	9	0	.153	12	31	1	1	1.3	.977
1990		5	6	.455	5.49	17	14	1	78.2	79	33	58	0	0	0	0	19	4	0	.211	7	10	1	1	1.1	.944
1991		11	10	.524	3.57	30	30	0	181.1	147	67	121	0	0	0	0	50	5	0	.100	15	26	2	1	1.4	.953
1992	MON N	16	9	.640	2.68	33	33	3	218	187	75	150	3	0	0	0	62	11	1	.177	21	36	4	3	1.8	.934
1993		9	7	.563	3.23	28	28	2	183.2	163	74	90	0	0	0	0	52	6	0	.115	24	38	1	2	2.3	.984
1994		16	5	.762	3.32	23	23	2	154.2	145	44	85	1	0	0	0	48	7	0	.146	15	33	2	2	2.2	.960

Year	Team	W	L	PCT	ERA	G	GS	CG	IP	H	BB	SO	ShO	W	L	SV	AB	H	HR	BA	PO	A	E	DP	TC/G	FA

Ken Hill *continued*

Year	Team	W	L	PCT	ERA	G	GS	CG	IP	H	BB	SO	ShO	W	L	SV	AB	H	HR	BA	PO	A	E	DP	TC/G	FA
1995	2 teams	STL N	(18G 6–7)		CLE A	(12G 4–1)																				
"	total	10	8	.556	4.62	30	29	1	185	202	77	98	0	0	0	0	31	6	0	.194	23	35	1	2	2.0	.983
1996	TEX A	16	10	.615	3.63	35	35	7	250.2	250	95	170	3	0	0	0	0	0	0	—	22	37	1	5	1.7	.983
9 yrs.		90	71	.559	3.66	233	226	18	1462.2	1375	570	890	8	0	0	0	324	48	1	.148	139	249	13	17	1.7	.968

DIVISIONAL PLAYOFF SERIES

Year	Team	W	L	PCT	ERA	G	GS	CG	IP	H	BB	SO	ShO	W	L	SV	AB	H	HR	BA	PO	A	E	DP	TC/G	FA
1995	CLE A	1	0	1.000	0.00	1	0	0	1.1	1	0	2	0	1	0	0	0	0	0	—	0	2	0	0	2.0	1.000
1996	TEX A	0	0	—	4.50	1	1	0	6	5	3	1	0	0	0	0	0	0	0	—	0	0	0	0	0.0	—
2 yrs.		1	0	1.000	3.68	2	1	0	7.1	6	3	3	0	1	0	0					1	4	0	0	2.5	1.000

LEAGUE CHAMPIONSHIP SERIES

Year	Team	W	L	PCT	ERA	G	GS	CG	IP	H	BB	SO	ShO	W	L	SV	AB	H	HR	BA	PO	A	E	DP	TC/G	FA
1995	CLE A	1	0	1.000	0.00	1	1	0	7	5	3	6	0	0	0	0	0	0	0	—	1	1	0	0	2.0	1.000

WORLD SERIES

Year	Team	W	L	PCT	ERA	G	GS	CG	IP	H	BB	SO	ShO	W	L	SV	AB	H	HR	BA	PO	A	E	DP	TC/G	FA
1995	CLE A	0	1	.000	4.26	2	1	0	6.1	7	4	1	0	0	0	0	0	0	0	—	1	2	0	0	1.5	1.000

Sterling Hitchcock

HITCHCOCK, STERLING ALEX
B. Apr. 29, 1971, Fayetteville, N. C.

BL TL 6′1″ 200 lbs.

Year	Team	W	L	PCT	ERA	G	GS	CG	IP	H	BB	SO	ShO	W	L	SV	AB	H	HR	BA	PO	A	E	DP	TC/G	FA
1992	NY A	0	2	.000	8.31	3	3	0	13	23	6	6	0	0	0	0	0	0	0	—	0	2	0	0	0.7	1.000
1993		1	2	.333	4.65	6	6	0	31	32	14	26	0	0	0	0	0	0	0	—	1	3	0	1	0.7	1.000
1994		4	1	.800	4.20	23	5	1	49.1	48	29	37	0	1	1	2	0	0	0	—	1	7	2	0	0.4	.800
1995		11	10	.524	4.70	27	27	4	168.1	155	68	121	1	0	0	0	0	0	0	—	4	12	0	1	0.6	1.000
1996	SEA A	13	9	.591	5.35	35	35	0	196.2	245	73	132	0	0	0	0	0	0	0	—	6	23	3	2	0.9	.906
5 yrs.		29	24	.547	5.03	94	76	5	458.1	503	190	322	1	1	1	2	0	0	0		12	47	5	4	0.7	.922

DIVISIONAL PLAYOFF SERIES

Year	Team	W	L	PCT	ERA	G	GS	CG	IP	H	BB	SO	ShO	W	L	SV	AB	H	HR	BA	PO	A	E	DP	TC/G	FA
1995	NY A	0	0	—	5.40	2	0	0	1.2	2	2	1	0	0	0	0	0	0	0	—	0	1	0	0	0.5	1.000

Trevor Hoffman

HOFFMAN, TREVOR WILLIAM
Brother of Glenn Hoffman.
B. Oct. 13, 1967, Bellflower, Calif.

BR TR 6′1″ 200 lbs.

Year	Team	W	L	PCT	ERA	G	GS	CG	IP	H	BB	SO	ShO	W	L	SV	AB	H	HR	BA	PO	A	E	DP	TC/G	FA
1993	2 teams	FLA N	(28G 2–2)		SD N	(39G 2–4)																				
"	total	4	6	.400	3.90	67	0	0	90	80	39	79	0	4	6	5	7	1	0	.143	6	11	0	0	0.3	1.000
1994	SD N	4	4	.500	2.57	47	0	0	56	39	20	68	0	4	4	20	3	0	0	.000	4	5	0	1	0.2	1.000
1995		7	4	.636	3.88	55	0	0	53.1	48	14	52	0	7	4	31	2	1	0	.500	5	1	0	0	0.1	1.000
1996		9	5	.643	2.25	70	0	0	88	50	31	111	0	9	5	42	8	0	0	.000	8	6	0	0	0.2	1.000
4 yrs.		24	19	.558	3.13	239	0	0	287.1	217	104	310	0	24	19	98	20	2	0	.100	23	23	0	1	0.2	1.000

DIVISIONAL PLAYOFF SERIES

Year	Team	W	L	PCT	ERA	G	GS	CG	IP	H	BB	SO	ShO	W	L	SV	AB	H	HR	BA	PO	A	E	DP	TC/G	FA
1996	SD N	0	1	.000	10.80	2	0	0	1.2	3	1	2	0	0	0	0	0	0	0	—	0	1	0	0	0.5	1.000

Darren Holmes

HOLMES, DARREN LEE
B. Apr. 25, 1966, Asheville, N. C.

BR TR 6′ 199 lbs.

Year	Team	W	L	PCT	ERA	G	GS	CG	IP	H	BB	SO	ShO	W	L	SV	AB	H	HR	BA	PO	A	E	DP	TC/G	FA
1990	LA N	0	1	.000	5.19	14	0	0	17.1	15	11	19	0	0	1	0	0	0	0	—	1	1	0	0	0.1	1.000
1991	MIL A	1	4	.200	4.72	40	0	0	76.1	90	27	59	0	1	4	3	0	0	0	—	4	14	1	0	0.5	.947
1992		4	4	.500	2.55	41	0	0	42.1	35	11	31	0	4	4	6	0	0	0	—	5	4	1	1	0.2	.900
1993	CLR N	3	3	.500	4.05	62	0	0	66.2	56	20	60	0	3	3	25	0	0	0	—	7	6	1	1	0.2	.929
1994		0	3	.000	6.35	29	0	0	28.1	35	24	33	0	0	3	3	1	0	0	.000	2	3	1	0	0.2	.833
1995		6	1	.857	3.24	68	0	0	66.2	59	28	61	0	6	1	14	1	0	0	.000	6	13	1	0	0.3	.950
1996		5	4	.556	3.97	62	0	0	77	78	28	73	0	5	4	1	2	0	0	.000	1	10	3	0	0.2	.786
7 yrs.		19	20	.487	4.08	316	0	0	374.2	368	149	336	0	19	20	52	4	0	0	.000	26	51	8	2	0.3	.906

DIVISIONAL PLAYOFF SERIES

Year	Team	W	L	PCT	ERA	G	GS	CG	IP	H	BB	SO	ShO	W	L	SV	AB	H	HR	BA	PO	A	E	DP	TC/G	FA
1995	CLR N	1	0	1.000	0.00	3	0	0	1.2	6	0	2	0	1	0	0	0	0	0	—	0	0	0	0	0.0	.000

Chris Holt

HOLT, CHRISTOPHER MICHAEL
B. Sept. 18, 1971, Dallas, Tex.

BR TR 6′4″ 205 lbs.

Year	Team	W	L	PCT	ERA	G	GS	CG	IP	H	BB	SO	ShO	W	L	SV	AB	H	HR	BA	PO	A	E	DP	TC/G	FA
1996	HOU N	0	1	.000	5.79	4	0	0	4.2	5	3	0	0	0	1	0	1	0	0	.000	0	2	0	0	0.5	1.000

Mike Holtz

HOLTZ, MICHAEL JAMES
B. Oct. 10, 1972, Arlington, Va.

BL TL 5′9″ 172 lbs.

Year	Team	W	L	PCT	ERA	G	GS	CG	IP	H	BB	SO	ShO	W	L	SV	AB	H	HR	BA	PO	A	E	DP	TC/G	FA
1996	CAL A	3	3	.500	2.45	30	0	0	29.1	21	19	31	0	3	3	0	0	0	0	—	2	4	0	0	0.2	1.000

Mark Holzemer

HOLZEMER, MARK HAROLD
B. Aug. 20, 1969, Littleton, Colo.

BL TL 6′ 165 lbs.

Year	Team	W	L	PCT	ERA	G	GS	CG	IP	H	BB	SO	ShO	W	L	SV	AB	H	HR	BA	PO	A	E	DP	TC/G	FA
1993	CAL A	0	3	.000	8.87	5	4	0	23.1	34	13	10	0	0	0	0	0	0	0	—	0	5	0	0	1.0	1.000
1995		0	1	.000	5.40	12	0	0	8.1	11	7	5	0	0	1	0	0	0	0	—	1	3	0	0	0.3	1.000
1996		1	0	1.000	8.76	25	0	0	24.2	35	8	20	0	1	0	0	0	0	0	—	4	5	1	0	0.4	.900
3 yrs.		1	4	.200	8.31	42	4	0	56.1	80	28	35	0	1	1	0	0	0	0		5	13	1	0	0.5	.947

Rick Honeycutt

HONEYCUTT, FREDERICK WAYNE
B. June 29, 1952, Chattanooga, Tenn.

BL TL 6′1″ 185 lbs.

Year	Team	W	L	PCT	ERA	G	GS	CG	IP	H	BB	SO	ShO	W	L	SV	AB	H	HR	BA	PO	A	E	DP	TC/G	FA
1977	SEA A	0	1	.000	4.34	10	3	0	29	26	11	17	0	0	0	0	0	0	0	—	0	2	0	0	0.2	1.000
1978		5	11	.313	4.89	26	24	4	134.1	150	49	50	1	0	0	0	0	0	0	—	9	28	2	1	1.5	.949
1979		11	12	.478	4.04	33	28	8	194	201	67	83	1	1	3	0	0	0	0	—	6	28	5	2	1.2	.872
1980		10	17	.370	3.95	30	30	9	203	221	60	79	1	0	0	0	0	0	0	—	9	32	2	1	1.4	.953
1981	TEX A	11	6	.647	3.30	20	20	8	128	120	17	40	2	0	0	0	0	0	0	—	3	30	3	1	1.8	.917

Rick Honeycutt *continued*

Year	Team	W	L	PCT	ERA	G	GS	CG	IP	H	BB	SO	ShO	Relief Pitching			Batting			BA	PO	A	E	DP	TC/G	FA
														W	L	SV	AB	H	HR							
1982		5	17	.227	5.27	30	26	4	164	201	54	64	1	0	0	0	0	0	0	—	3	35	2	0	1.3	.950
1983	2 teams	TEX A (25G 14-8)			LA N (9G 2-3)																					
"	total	16	11	.593	3.03	34	32	6	213.2	214	50	74	2	0	0	0	12	1	0	.083	13	55	1	5	2.0	.986
1984	LA N	10	9	.526	2.84	29	28	6	183.2	180	51	75	2	0	0	0	56	8	0	.143	10	42	3	2	1.9	.945
1985		8	12	.400	3.42	31	25	1	142	141	49	67	0	0	1	1	38	5	0	.132	9	37	2	1	1.5	.958
1986		11	9	.550	3.32	32	28	0	171	164	45	100	0	1	0	0	43	3	0	.070	9	35	1	2	1.4	.978
1987	2 teams	LA N (27G 2-12)			OAK A (7G 1-4)																					
"	total	3	16	.158	4.72	34	24	1	139.1	158	54	102	1	0	1	0	30	7	0	.233	5	20	2	0	0.8	.926
1988	OAK A	3	2	.600	3.50	55	0	0	79.2	74	25	47	0	3	2	7	0	0	0	—	3	18	2	3	0.4	.913
1989		2	2	.500	2.35	64	0	0	76.2	56	26	52	0	2	2	12	0	0	0	—	4	16	1	1	0.3	.952
1990		2	2	.500	2.70	63	0	0	63.1	46	22	38	0	2	2	7	2	0	0	.000	0	15	1	0	0.3	.938
1991		2	4	.333	3.58	43	0	0	37.2	37	20	26	0	2	4	0	0	0	0	—	4	4	0	1	0.2	1.000
1992		1	4	.200	3.69	54	0	0	39	41	10	32	0	1	4	3	0	0	0	—	3	2	1	0	0.1	.833
1993		1	4	.200	2.81	52	0	0	41.2	30	20	21	0	1	4	1	0	0	0	—	2	5	1	1	0.2	.875
1994	TEX A	1	2	.333	7.20	42	0	0	25	37	9	18	0	1	2	1	0	0	0	—	2	7	1	0	0.2	.900
1995	2 teams	OAK A (49G 5-1)			NY A (3G 0-0)																					
"	total	5	1	.833	2.96	52	0	0	45.2	39	10	21	0	5	1	2	0	0	0	—	3	5	1	0	0.2	.889
1996	STL N	2	1	.667	2.85	61	0	0	47.1	42	7	30	0	2	1	4	1	0	0	.000	2	12	1	0	0.2	.933
20 yrs.		109	143	.433	3.71	795	268	47	2158	2178	656	1036	11	21	27	38	182	24	0	.132	99	428	32	21	0.7	.943

DIVISIONAL PLAYOFF SERIES

Year	Team	W	L	PCT	ERA	G	GS	CG	IP	H	BB	SO	ShO	W	L	SV	AB	H	HR	BA	PO	A	E	DP	TC/G	FA
1996	STL N	1	0	1.000	3.38	3	0	0	2.2	3	1	2	0	1	0	0	1	0	0	.000	0	1	0	0	0.3	1.000

LEAGUE CHAMPIONSHIP SERIES

Year	Team	W	L	PCT	ERA	G	GS	CG	IP	H	BB	SO	ShO	W	L	SV	AB	H	HR	BA	PO	A	E	DP	TC/G	FA
1983	LA N	0	0	—	21.60	2	0	0	1.2	4	0	2	0	0	0	0	0	0	0	—	1	0	0	0	0.5	1.000
1985		0	0	—	13.50	2	0	0	1.1	4	2	1	0	0	0	0	0	0	0	—	0	1	0	0	0.5	1.000
1988	OAK A	1	0	1.000	0.00	3	0	0	2	0	2	0	0	1	0	0	0	0	0	—	0	0	0	0	0.0	.000
1989		0	0	—	32.40	3	0	0	1.2	6	5	1	0	0	0	0	0	0	0	—	0	0	0	0	0.0	.000
1990		0	0	—	0.00	3	0	0	1.2	0	0	0	0	0	0	1	0	0	0	—	0	1	0	0	0.3	1.000
1992		0	0	—	0.00	2	0	0	2	0	0	1	0	0	0	0	0	0	0	—	0	0	0	0	0.0	.000
1996	STL N	0	0	—	9.00	5	0	0	4	5	3	3	0	0	0	0	0	0	0	—	0	0	0	0	0.0	.000
7 yrs.		1	0	1.000	10.05	20 (1st)	0	0	14.1	19	12	8	0	1	0	0	0	0	0	—	1	2	0	0	0.2	1.000

WORLD SERIES

Year	Team	W	L	PCT	ERA	G	GS	CG	IP	H	BB	SO	ShO	W	L	SV	AB	H	HR	BA	PO	A	E	DP	TC/G	FA
1988	OAK A	1	0	1.000	0.00	3	0	0	3.1	1	0	5	0	1	0	0	0	0	0	—	0	0	0	0	0.0	.000
1989		0	0	—	6.75	3	0	0	2.2	4	0	2	0	0	0	0	0	0	0	—	0	0	0	0	0.0	.000
1990		0	0	—	0.00	1	0	0	1.2	2	1	0	0	0	0	0	0	0	0	—	0	0	0	0	0.0	—
3 yrs.		1	0	1.000	2.35	7	0	0	7.2	6	1	7	0	1	0	0	0	0	0	—	0	0	0	0	0.0	

Chris Hook

HOOK, CHRISTOPHER WAYNE
B. Aug. 4, 1968, San Diego, Calif.

BR TR 6'5" 230 lbs.

Year	Team	W	L	PCT	ERA	G	GS	CG	IP	H	BB	SO	ShO	W	L	SV	AB	H	HR	BA	PO	A	E	DP	TC/G	FA
1995	SF N	5	1	.833	5.50	45	0	0	52.1	55	29	40	0	5	1	0	3	0	0	.000	5	4	0	1	0.2	1.000
1996		0	1	.000	7.42	10	0	0	13.1	16	14	4	0	0	1	0	2	1	0	.500	3	3	0	0	0.6	1.000
2 yrs.		5	2	.714	5.89	55	0	0	65.2	71	43	44	0	5	2	0	5	1	0	.200	8	7	0	1	0.3	1.000

John Hope

HOPE, JOHN ALAN
B. Dec. 21, 1970, Ft. Lauderdale, Fla.

BR TR 6'3" 195 lbs.

Year	Team	W	L	PCT	ERA	G	GS	CG	IP	H	BB	SO	ShO	W	L	SV	AB	H	HR	BA	PO	A	E	DP	TC/G	FA
1993	PIT N	0	2	.000	4.03	7	7	0	38	47	8	8	0	0	0	0	13	1	0	.077	1	10	1	0	1.7	.917
1994		0	0	—	5.79	9	0	0	14	18	4	6	0	0	0	0	3	1	0	.333	1	3	0	0	0.4	1.000
1995		0	0	—	30.86	3	0	0	2.1	8	4	2	0	0	0	0	0	0	0	—	0	0	0	0	0.0	.000
1996		1	3	.250	6.98	5	4	0	19.1	17	11	13	0	0	0	0	5	1	0	.200	2	5	2	0	1.8	.778
4 yrs.		1	5	.167	5.99	24	11	0	73.2	90	27	29	0	0	0	0	21	3	0	.143	4	18	3	0	1.0	.880

Steve Howe

HOWE, STEVEN ROY
B. Mar. 10, 1958, Pontiac, Mich.

BL TL 6'1" 180 lbs.

Year	Team	W	L	PCT	ERA	G	GS	CG	IP	H	BB	SO	ShO	W	L	SV	AB	H	HR	BA	PO	A	E	DP	TC/G	FA
1980	LA N	7	9	.438	2.65	59	0	0	85	83	22	39	0	7	9	17	11	1	0	.091	3	20	1	0	0.4	.958
1981		5	3	.625	2.50	41	0	0	54	51	18	32	0	5	3	8	1	0	0	.000	1	5	0	0	0.1	1.000
1982		7	5	.583	2.08	66	0	0	99.1	87	17	49	0	7	5	13	7	0	0	.000	2	17	1	0	0.3	.950
1983		4	7	.364	1.44	46	0	0	68.2	55	12	52	0	4	7	18	8	1	0	.125	4	15	0	0	0.4	1.000
1985	2 teams	LA N (19G 1-1)			MIN A (13G 2-3)																					
"	total	3	4	.429	5.49	32	0	0	41	58	12	21	0	3	4	3	0	0	0	—	3	7	1	0	0.3	.909
1987	TEX A	3	3	.500	4.31	24	0	0	31.1	33	8	19	0	3	3	1	0	0	0	—	4	4	0	0	0.3	1.000
1991	NY A	3	1	.750	1.68	37	0	0	48.1	39	7	34	0	3	1	3	0	0	0	—	5	6	3	1	0.4	.786
1992		3	0	1.000	2.45	20	0	0	22	9	3	12	0	3	0	6	0	0	0	—	2	7	1	0	0.5	.900
1993		3	5	.375	4.97	51	0	0	50.2	58	10	19	0	3	5	4	0	0	0	—	2	13	1	0	0.3	.938
1994		3	0	1.000	1.80	40	0	0	40	28	7	18	0	3	0	15	0	0	0	—	2	4	0	0	0.2	1.000
1995		6	3	.667	4.96	56	0	0	49	66	17	28	0	6	3	2	0	0	0	—	3	11	0	1	0.3	1.000
1996		0	1	.000	6.35	25	0	0	17	19	6	5	0	0	1	1	0	0	0	—	0	5	1	1	0.2	.833
12 yrs.		47	41	.534	3.03	497	0	0	606.1	586	139	328	0	47	41	91	27	2	0	.074	31	114	9	3	0.3	.942

DIVISIONAL PLAYOFF SERIES

Year	Team	W	L	PCT	ERA	G	GS	CG	IP	H	BB	SO	ShO	W	L	SV	AB	H	HR	BA	PO	A	E	DP	TC/G	FA
1981	LA N	0	0	—	0.00	2	0	0	2	1	0	2	0	0	0	0	0	0	0	—	0	0	0	0	0.0	.000
1995	NY A	0	0	—	18.00	2	0	0	1	4	0	0	0	0	0	0	0	0	0	—	0	0	0	0	0.0	—
2 yrs.		0	0	—	6.00	4	0	0	3	5	0	2	0	0	0	0	0	0	0	—	0	0	0	0	0.0	

LEAGUE CHAMPIONSHIP SERIES

Year	Team	W	L	PCT	ERA	G	GS	CG	IP	H	BB	SO	ShO	W	L	SV	AB	H	HR	BA	PO	A	E	DP	TC/G	FA
1981	LA N	0	0	—	0.00	2	0	0	2	1	0	2	0	0	0	0	0	0	0	—	0	0	0	0	0.0	.000

Year	Team	W	L	PCT	ERA	G	GS	CG	IP	H	BB	SO	ShO	Relief Pitching W	L	SV	Batting AB	H	HR	BA	PO	A	E	DP	TC/G	FA

Steve Howe *continued*

WORLD SERIES
Year	Team	W	L	PCT	ERA	G	GS	CG	IP	H	BB	SO	ShO	RP W	L	SV	AB	H	HR	BA	PO	A	E	DP	TC/G	FA
1981	LA N	1	0	1.000	3.86	3	0	0	7	7	1	4	0	1	0	1	2	0	0	.000	0	1	1	0	0.7	.500

John Hudek

HUDEK, JOHN RAYMOND
B. Aug. 8, 1966, Tampa, Fla.   BB TR 6'1" 200 lbs.

Year	Team	W	L	PCT	ERA	G	GS	CG	IP	H	BB	SO	ShO	RP W	L	SV	AB	H	HR	BA	PO	A	E	DP	TC/G	FA
1994	HOU N	0	2	.000	2.97	42	0	0	39.1	24	18	39	0	0	2	16	0	0	0	—	4	3	0	0	0.2	1.000
1995		2	2	.500	5.40	19	0	0	20	19	5	29	0	2	2	7	1	1	0	1.000	1	5	0	0	0.3	1.000
1996		2	0	1.000	2.81	15	0	0	16	12	5	14	0	2	0	2	0	0	0	—	1	5	0	0	0.4	1.000
3 yrs.		4	4	.500	3.58	76	0	0	75.1	55	28	82	0	4	4	25	1	1	0	1.000	6	13	0	0	0.3	1.000

Joe Hudson

HUDSON, JOSEPH PAUL
B. Sept. 29, 1970, Philadelphia, Pa.   BR TR 6'1" 173 lbs.

Year	Team	W	L	PCT	ERA	G	GS	CG	IP	H	BB	SO	ShO	RP W	L	SV	AB	H	HR	BA	PO	A	E	DP	TC/G	FA
1995	BOS A	0	1	.000	4.11	39	0	0	46	53	23	29	0	0	1	1	0	0	0	—	1	6	0	1	0.2	1.000
1996		3	5	.375	5.40	36	0	0	45	57	32	19	0	3	5	1	0	0	0	—	1	9	2	1	0.3	.833
2 yrs.		3	6	.333	4.75	75	0	0	91	110	55	48	0	3	6	2	0	0	0	—	2	15	2	2	0.3	.895

DIVISIONAL PLAYOFF SERIES
Year	Team	W	L	PCT	ERA	G	GS	CG	IP	H	BB	SO	ShO	RP W	L	SV	AB	H	HR	BA	PO	A	E	DP	TC/G	FA
1995	BOS A	0	0	—	0.00	1	0	0	1	2	1	0	0	0	0	0	0	0	0	—	0	0	0	0	0.0	.000

Rick Huisman

HUISMAN, RICHARD ALLEN
B. May 17, 1969, Oak Park, Ill.   BR TR 6'3" 200 lbs.

Year	Team	W	L	PCT	ERA	G	GS	CG	IP	H	BB	SO	ShO	RP W	L	SV	AB	H	HR	BA	PO	A	E	DP	TC/G	FA
1995	KC A	0	0	—	7.45	7	0	0	9.2	14	1	12	0	0	0	0	0	0	0	—	0	1	0	0	0.1	1.000
1996		2	1	.667	4.60	22	0	0	29.1	25	18	23	0	2	1	1	0	0	0	—	0	5	0	0	0.2	1.000
2 yrs.		2	1	.667	5.31	29	0	0	39	39	19	35	0	2	1	1	0	0	0	—	0	6	0	0	0.2	1.000

Rich Hunter

HUNTER, RICHARD THOMAS
B. Sept 25, 1974, Pasadena, Calif.   BR TR 6'1" 185 lbs.

Year	Team	W	L	PCT	ERA	G	GS	CG	IP	H	BB	SO	ShO	RP W	L	SV	AB	H	HR	BA	PO	A	E	DP	TC/G	FA
1996	PHI N	3	7	.300	6.49	14	14	0	69.1	84	33	32	0	0	0	0	18	3	0	.167	5	13	1	0	1.4	.947

Bill Hurst

HURST, WILLIAM HANSEL
B. Apr. 28, 1970, Miami Beach, Fla.   BR TR 6'7" 220 lbs.

Year	Team	W	L	PCT	ERA	G	GS	CG	IP	H	BB	SO	ShO	RP W	L	SV	AB	H	HR	BA	PO	A	E	DP	TC/G	FA
1996	FLA N	0	0	—	0.00	2	0	0	2	3	1	1	0	0	0	0	0	0	0	—	0	0	0	0	0.0	—

Edwin Hurtado

HURTADO, EDWIN AMILGAR
B. Feb. 1, 1970, Barquisimeto, Venezuela   BR TR 6'3" 215 lbs.

Year	Team	W	L	PCT	ERA	G	GS	CG	IP	H	BB	SO	ShO	RP W	L	SV	AB	H	HR	BA	PO	A	E	DP	TC/G	FA
1995	TOR A	5	2	.714	5.45	14	10	1	77.2	81	40	33	0	1	0	0	0	0	0	—	6	8	0	3	1.0	1.000
1996	SEA A	2	5	.286	7.74	16	4	0	47.2	61	30	36	0	2	2	2	0	0	0	—	3	9	0	1	0.8	1.000
2 yrs.		7	7	.500	6.32	30	14	1	125.1	142	70	69	0	3	2	2					9	17	0	4	0.9	1.000

Mark Hutton

HUTTON, MARK STEVEN
B. Feb. 6, 1970, South Adelaide, Australia   BR TR 6'6" 240 lbs.

Year	Team	W	L	PCT	ERA	G	GS	CG	IP	H	BB	SO	ShO	RP W	L	SV	AB	H	HR	BA	PO	A	E	DP	TC/G	FA
1993	NY A	1	1	.500	5.73	7	4	0	22	24	17	12	0	0	0	0	0	0	0	—	1	2	1	0	0.6	.750
1994		0	0	—	4.91	2	2	0	3.2	4	0	1	0	0	0	0	0	0	0	—	0	0	0	0	0.0	.000
1996	2 teams	NY A	(12G 0–2)		FLA N	(13G 5–1)																				
"	total	5	3	.625	4.15	25	11	0	86.2	79	36	56	0	1	0	0	19	6	1	.316	6	4	2	0	0.5	.833
3 yrs.		6	4	.600	4.49	34	15	0	112.1	107	53	69	0	1	0	0	19	6	1	.316	7	6	3	0	0.5	.813

Jason Isringhausen

ISRINGHAUSEN, JASON DERIK (Izzy)
B. Sept. 7, 1972, Brighton, Ill.   BR TR 6'3" 195 lbs.

Year	Team	W	L	PCT	ERA	G	GS	CG	IP	H	BB	SO	ShO	RP W	L	SV	AB	H	HR	BA	PO	A	E	DP	TC/G	FA
1995	NY N	9	2	.818	2.81	14	14	0	93	88	31	55	0	0	0	0	27	4	0	.148	8	11	2	1	1.5	.905
1996		6	14	.300	4.77	27	27	2	171.2	190	73	114	1	0	0	0	51	13	2	.255	13	28	5	1	1.7	.891
2 yrs.		15	16	.484	4.08	41	41	3	264.2	278	104	169	1	0	0	0	78	17	2	.218	21	39	7	2	1.6	.896

Danny Jackson

JACKSON, DANNY LYNN
B. Jan. 5, 1962, San Antonio, Tex.   BR TL 6' 205 lbs.

Year	Team	W	L	PCT	ERA	G	GS	CG	IP	H	BB	SO	ShO	RP W	L	SV	AB	H	HR	BA	PO	A	E	DP	TC/G	FA
1983	KC A	1	1	.500	5.21	4	3	0	19	26	6	9	0	1	0	0	0	0	0	—	2	3	0	0	1.3	1.000
1984		2	6	.250	4.26	15	11	1	76	84	35	40	0	1	0	0	0	0	0	—	6	7	1	2	0.9	.929
1985		14	12	.538	3.42	32	32	4	208	209	76	114	3	0	0	0	0	0	0	—	8	27	3	2	1.2	.921
1986		11	12	.478	3.20	32	27	4	185.2	177	79	115	1	0	0	1	0	0	0	—	14	21	2	1	1.2	.946
1987		9	18	.333	4.02	36	34	11	224	219	109	152	1	0	0	0	0	0	0	—	13	23	2	1	1.1	.947
1988	CIN N	23	8	.742	2.73	35	35	15	260.2	206	71	161	6	0	0	0	90	13	0	.144	10	52	3	2	1.9	.954
1989		6	11	.353	5.60	20	20	1	115.2	122	57	70	0	0	0	0	36	8	0	.222	5	15	0	0	1.0	1.000
1990		6	6	.500	3.61	22	21	0	117.1	119	40	76	0	0	0	0	37	2	0	.054	4	13	1	0	0.8	.944
1991	CHI N	1	5	.167	6.75	17	14	0	70.2	89	48	31	0	0	0	0	23	2	0	.087	4	7	1	0	0.7	.917
1992	2 teams	CHI N	(19G 4–9)		PIT N	(15G 4–4)																				
"	total	8	13	.381	3.84	34	34	0	201.1	211	77	97	0	0	0	0	60	5	0	.083	9	33	8	2	1.5	.840
1993	PHI N	12	11	.522	3.77	32	32	2	210.1	214	80	120	1	0	0	0	65	5	0	.077	7	26	4	3	1.2	.892
1994		14	6	.700	3.26	25	25	4	179.1	183	46	129	1	0	0	0	57	9	0	.158	12	30	0	3	1.7	1.000
1995	STL N	2	12	.143	5.90	19	19	2	100.2	120	48	52	1	0	0	0	31	5	0	.161	7	12	3	1	1.2	.864
1996		1	1	.500	4.46	13	4	0	36.1	33	16	27	0	0	0	0	9	3	0	.333	0	7	0	0	0.6	1.000
14 yrs.		110	122	.474	3.89	336	311	44	2005	2012	788	1193	15	2	0	1	408	52	0	.127	102	276	28	18	1.2	.931

Year	Team	W	L	PCT	ERA	G	GS	CG	IP	H	BB	SO	ShO	Relief Pitching W	L	SV	Batting AB	H	HR	BA	PO	A	E	DP	TC/G	FA

Danny Jackson *continued*

LEAGUE CHAMPIONSHIP SERIES

Year	Team	W	L	PCT	ERA	G	GS	CG	IP	H	BB	SO	ShO	W	L	SV	AB	H	HR	BA	PO	A	E	DP	TC/G	FA
1985	KC A	1	0	1.000	0.00	2	1	1	10	10	1	7	1	0	0	0	0	0	0	—	0	0	0	0	0.0	.000
1990	CIN N	1	0	1.000	2.38	2	2	0	11.1	8	7	8	0	0	0	0	3	0	0	.000	0	2	0	0	1.0	1.000
1992	PIT N	0	1	.000	21.60	1	1	0	1.2	4	2	0	0	0	0	0	0	0	0	—	0	0	0	0	0.0	.000
1993	PHI N	1	0	1.000	1.17	1	1	0	7.2	9	2	6	0	0	0	0	4	1	0	.250	0	0	0	0	0.0	.000
1996	STL N	0	0	—	9.00	1	0	0	3	7	3	3	0	0	0	0	1	0	0	.000	0	0	0	0	0.0	.000
5 yrs.		3	1	.750	2.94	7	5	1	33.2	38	15	24	1 / 1st	0	0	0	8	1	0	.125	0	2	0	0	0.3	1.000

WORLD SERIES

Year	Team	W	L	PCT	ERA	G	GS	CG	IP	H	BB	SO	ShO	W	L	SV	AB	H	HR	BA	PO	A	E	DP	TC/G	FA
1985	KC A	1	1	.500	1.69	2	2	1	16	9	5	12	0	0	0	0	6	0	0	.000	0	4	1	0	2.5	.800
1990	CIN N	0	0	—	10.13	1	1	0	2.2	6	2	0	0	0	0	0	1	0	0	.000	0	1	1	0	2.0	.500
1993	PHI N	0	1	.000	7.20	1	1	0	5	6	1	1	0	0	0	0	1	0	0	.000	0	0	0	0	0.0	.000
3 yrs.		1	2	.333	3.80	4	4	1	23.2	21	8	13	0	0	0	0	8	0	0	.000	0	5	2	0	1.8	.714

Mike Jackson

JACKSON, MICHAEL RAY — BR TR 6'1" 185 lbs.
B. Dec. 22, 1964, Houston, Tex.

Year	Team	W	L	PCT	ERA	G	GS	CG	IP	H	BB	SO	ShO	W	L	SV	AB	H	HR	BA	PO	A	E	DP	TC/G	FA
1986	PHI N	0	0	—	3.38	9	0	0	13.1	12	4	3	0	0	0	0	0	0	0	—	2	0	0	0	0.2	1.000
1987		3	10	.231	4.20	55	7	0	109.1	88	56	93	0	2	6	1	17	2	0	.118	5	12	1	0	0.3	.944
1988	SEA A	6	5	.545	2.63	62	0	0	99.1	74	43	76	0	6	5	4	0	0	0	—	4	11	0	0	0.2	1.000
1989		4	6	.400	3.17	65	0	0	99.1	81	54	94	0	4	6	7	0	0	0	—	3	11	2	0	0.2	.875
1990		5	7	.417	4.54	63	0	0	77.1	64	44	69	0	5	7	3	0	0	0	—	5	12	0	3	0.3	1.000
1991		7	7	.500	3.25	72	0	0	88.2	64	34	74	0	7	7	14	0	0	0	—	2	8	1	1	0.2	.909
1992	SF N	6	6	.500	3.73	67	0	0	82	76	33	80	0	6	6	2	2	0	0	.000	6	9	1	0	0.2	.938
1993		6	6	.500	3.03	81	0	0	77.1	58	24	70	0	6	6	1	3	2	0	.667	3	13	1	0	0.2	.941
1994		3	2	.600	1.49	36	0	0	42.1	23	11	51	0	3	2	4	1	0	0	.000	0	7	0	1	0.2	1.000
1995	CIN N	6	1	.857	2.39	40	0	0	49	38	19	41	0	6	1	2	4	1	0	.250	2	3	0	0	0.1	1.000
1996	SEA A	1	1	.500	3.63	73	0	0	72	61	24	70	0	1	1	6	0	0	0	—	1	16	1	0	0.2	.944
11 yrs.		47	51	.480	3.33	623	7	0	810	639	346	721	0	46	47	44	27	5	0	.185	33	102	7	5	0.2	.951

DIVISIONAL PLAYOFF SERIES

Year	Team	W	L	PCT	ERA	G	GS	CG	IP	H	BB	SO	ShO	W	L	SV	AB	H	HR	BA	PO	A	E	DP	TC/G	FA
1995	CIN N	0	0	—	0.00	3	0	0	3.2	4	0	1	0	0	0	0	1	1	0	1.000	1	1	0	0	0.7	1.000

LEAGUE CHAMPIONSHIP SERIES

Year	Team	W	L	PCT	ERA	G	GS	CG	IP	H	BB	SO	ShO	W	L	SV	AB	H	HR	BA	PO	A	E	DP	TC/G	FA
1995	CIN N	0	1	.000	23.14	3	0	0	2.1	5	4	1	0	0	1	0	0	0	0	—	0	1	0	0	0.3	1.000

Jason Jacome

JACOME, JASON JAMES — BL TL 6'1" 155 lbs.
B. Nov. 24, 1970, Tulsa, Okla.

Year	Team	W	L	PCT	ERA	G	GS	CG	IP	H	BB	SO	ShO	W	L	SV	AB	H	HR	BA	PO	A	E	DP	TC/G	FA
1994	NY N	4	3	.571	2.67	8	8	1	54	54	17	30	1	0	0	0	16	1	0	.063	4	9	0	2	1.6	1.000
1995	2 teams	NY N	(5G 0–4)		KC A	(15G 4–6)																				
"	total	4	10	.286	6.34	20	19	1	105	134	36	50	0	0	0	0	7	0	0	.000	6	24	2	2	1.6	.938
1996	KC A	0	4	.000	4.72	49	2	0	47.2	67	22	32	0	0	3	1	0	0	0	—	2	14	0	3	0.3	1.000
3 yrs.		8	17	.320	5.01	77	29	2	206.2	255	75	112	1	0	3	1	23	1	0	.043	12	47	2	7	0.8	.967

Mike James

JAMES, MICHAEL ELMO — BR TR 6'4" 216 lbs.
B. Aug. 15, 1967, Fort Walton Beach, Fla.

Year	Team	W	L	PCT	ERA	G	GS	CG	IP	H	BB	SO	ShO	W	L	SV	AB	H	HR	BA	PO	A	E	DP	TC/G	FA
1995	CAL A	3	0	1.000	3.88	46	0	0	55.2	49	26	36	0	3	0	1	0	0	0	—	2	8	0	0	0.2	1.000
1996		5	5	.500	2.67	69	0	0	81	62	42	65	0	5	5	1	0	0	0	—	5	12	0	2	0.3	1.000
2 yrs.		8	5	.615	3.16	115	0	0	136.2	111	68	101	0	8	5	2	0	0	0	—	7	20	0	2	0.2	1.000

Marty Janzen

JANZEN, MARTIN THOMAS — BR TR 6'3" 197 lbs.
B. May 31, 1973, Homestead, Fla.

Year	Team	W	L	PCT	ERA	G	GS	CG	IP	H	BB	SO	ShO	W	L	SV	AB	H	HR	BA	PO	A	E	DP	TC/G	FA
1996	TOR A	4	6	.400	7.33	15	11	0	73.2	95	38	47	0	2	0	0	0	0	0	—	5	6	2	1	0.9	.846

Kevin Jarvis

JARVIS, KEVIN THOMAS — BL TR 6'2" 200 lbs.
B. Aug. 1, 1969, Lexington, Ky.

Year	Team	W	L	PCT	ERA	G	GS	CG	IP	H	BB	SO	ShO	W	L	SV	AB	H	HR	BA	PO	A	E	DP	TC/G	FA
1994	CIN N	1	1	.500	7.13	6	3	0	17.2	22	5	10	0	0	1	0	4	1	0	.250	2	3	1	0	1.0	.833
1995		3	4	.429	5.70	19	11	1	79	91	32	33	1	0	0	0	21	3	0	.143	8	12	2	1	1.2	.909
1996		8	9	.471	5.98	24	20	2	120.1	152	43	63	0	0	1	0	36	6	0	.167	13	12	3	2	1.2	.893
3 yrs.		12	14	.462	5.97	49	34	3	217	265	80	106	2	0	2	0	61	10	0	.164	23	27	6	3	1.1	.893

Doug Johns

JOHNS, DOUGLAS ALAN — BR TL 6'2" 185 lbs.
B. Dec. 19, 1967, South Bend, Ind.

Year	Team	W	L	PCT	ERA	G	GS	CG	IP	H	BB	SO	ShO	W	L	SV	AB	H	HR	BA	PO	A	E	DP	TC/G	FA
1995	OAK A	5	3	.625	4.61	11	9	1	54.2	44	26	25	1	0	0	0	0	0	0	—	6	10	1	0	1.5	.941
1996		6	12	.333	5.98	40	23	1	158	187	69	71	0	0	1	1	0	0	0	—	17	29	2	7	1.2	.958
2 yrs.		11	15	.423	5.63	51	32	2	212.2	231	95	96	1	0	1	1	0	0	0	—	23	39	3	7	1.3	.954

Dane Johnson

JOHNSON, DANE EDWARD — BR TR 6'5" 205 lbs.
B. Feb. 10, 1963, Coral Gables, Fla.

Year	Team	W	L	PCT	ERA	G	GS	CG	IP	H	BB	SO	ShO	W	L	SV	AB	H	HR	BA	PO	A	E	DP	TC/G	FA
1994	CHI A	2	1	.667	6.57	15	0	0	12.1	16	11	7	0	2	1	0	0	0	0	—	0	1	0	0	0.1	1.000
1996	TOR A	0	0	—	3.00	10	0	0	9	5	5	7	0	0	0	0	0	0	0	—	2	1	0	0	0.3	1.000
2 yrs.		2	1	.667	5.06	25	0	0	21.1	21	16	14	0	2	1	0	0	0	0	—	2	2	0	0	0.2	1.000

Year	Team	W	L	PCT	ERA	G	GS	CG	IP	H	BB	SO	ShO	W	L	SV	AB	H	HR	BA	PO	A	E	DP	TC/G	FA
														Relief Pitching			Batting									

Randy Johnson

JOHNSON, RANDALL DAVID (Big Unit)
B. Sept. 10, 1963, Walnut Creek, Calif. — BR TL 6'10" 225 lbs.

Year	Team	W	L	PCT	ERA	G	GS	CG	IP	H	BB	SO	ShO	W	L	SV	AB	H	HR	BA	PO	A	E	DP	TC/G	FA
1988	MON N	3	0	1.000	2.42	4	4	1	26	23	7	25	0	0	0	0	9	1	0	.111	0	0	1	0	0.3	.000
1989	2 teams			MON N	(7G 0–4)			SEA A	(22G 7–9)																	
"	total	7	13	.350	4.82	29	28	2	160.2	147	96	130	0	0	0	0	7	1	0	.143	8	26	7	1	1.4	.829
1990	SEA A	14	11	.560	3.65	33	33	5	219.2	174	120	194	2	0	0	0	0	0	0	—	6	24	5	2	1.1	.857
1991		13	10	.565	3.98	33	33	2	201.1	151	152	228	1	0	0	0	0	0	0	—	0	23	5	3	0.8	.821
1992		12	14	.462	3.77	31	31	6	210.1	154	144	241	2	0	0	0	0	0	0	—	5	20	3	0	0.9	.893
1993		19	8	.704	3.24	35	34	10	255.1	185	99	308	3	0	0	1	0	0	0	—	10	29	0	2	1.1	1.000
1994		13	6	.684	3.19	23	23	9	172	132	72	204	4	0	0	0	0	0	0	—	12	27	0	0	1.7	1.000
1995		18	2	.900	2.48	30	30	6	214.1	159	65	294	3	0	0	0	0	0	0	—	7	24	1	0	1.1	.969
1996		5	0	1.000	3.67	14	8	0	61.1	48	25	85	0	0	0	1	0	0	0	—	1	8	1	0	0.7	.900
	9 yrs.	104	64	.619	3.53	232	224	41	1521	1173	780	1709	15	0	0	2	16	2	0	.125	49	181	23	8	1.1	.909

DIVISIONAL PLAYOFF SERIES

Year	Team	W	L	PCT	ERA	G	GS	CG	IP	H	BB	SO	ShO	W	L	SV	AB	H	HR	BA	PO	A	E	DP	TC/G	FA
1995	SEA A	2	0	1.000	2.70	2	1	0	10	5	6	16	0	0	0	0	0	0	0	—	0	0	0	0	0.0	.000

LEAGUE CHAMPIONSHIP SERIES

Year	Team	W	L	PCT	ERA	G	GS	CG	IP	H	BB	SO	ShO	W	L	SV	AB	H	HR	BA	PO	A	E	DP	TC/G	FA
1995	SEA A	0	1	.000	2.35	2	2	0	15.1	12	2	13	0	0	0	0	0	0	0	—	1	1	0	0	1.0	1.000

John Johnstone

JOHNSTONE, JOHN WILLIAM
B. Nov. 25, 1968, Liverpool, N. Y. — BR TR 6'3" 195 lbs.

Year	Team	W	L	PCT	ERA	G	GS	CG	IP	H	BB	SO	ShO	W	L	SV	AB	H	HR	BA	PO	A	E	DP	TC/G	FA
1993	FLA N	0	2	.000	5.91	7	0	0	10.2	16	7	5	0	0	2	0	0	0	0	—	1	1	0	0	0.3	1.000
1994		1	2	.333	5.91	17	0	0	21.1	23	16	23	0	1	2	0	0	0	0	—	0	3	0	0	0.2	1.000
1995		0	0	—	3.86	4	0	0	4.2	7	2	3	0	0	0	0	0	0	0	—	1	0	0	0	0.3	1.000
1996	HOU N	1	0	1.000	5.54	9	0	0	13	17	5	5	0	1	0	0	0	0	0	—	1	1	0	0	0.2	1.000
	4 yrs.	2	4	.333	5.62	37	0	0	49.2	63	30	36	0	2	4	0	0	0	0	—	3	5	0	0	0.2	1.000

Bobby Jones

JONES, ROBERT JOSEPH
B. Feb. 10, 1970, Fresno, Calif. — BR TR 6'4" 210 lbs.

Year	Team	W	L	PCT	ERA	G	GS	CG	IP	H	BB	SO	ShO	W	L	SV	AB	H	HR	BA	PO	A	E	DP	TC/G	FA
1993	NY N	2	4	.333	3.65	9	9	0	61.2	61	22	35	0	0	0	0	20	1	0	.050	5	8	0	0	1.4	1.000
1994		12	7	.632	3.15	24	24	1	160	157	56	80	1	0	0	0	46	5	0	.109	11	33	0	3	1.8	1.000
1995		10	10	.500	4.19	30	30	3	195.2	209	53	127	1	0	0	0	56	9	0	.161	11	30	6	1	1.6	.872
1996		12	8	.600	4.42	31	31	3	195.2	219	46	116	1	0	0	0	60	7	0	.117	11	31	1	3	1.4	.977
	4 yrs.	36	29	.554	3.93	94	94	7	613	646	177	358	3	0	0	0	182	22	0	.121	38	102	7	7	1.6	.952

Doug Jones

JONES, DOUGLAS REID
B. June 24, 1957, Covina, Calif. — BR TR 6'3" 195 lbs.

Year	Team	W	L	PCT	ERA	G	GS	CG	IP	H	BB	SO	ShO	W	L	SV	AB	H	HR	BA	PO	A	E	DP	TC/G	FA
1982	MIL A	0	0	—	10.13	4	0	0	2.2	5	1	1	0	0	0	0	0	0	0	—	1	0	0	0	0.3	1.000
1986	CLE A	1	0	1.000	2.50	11	0	0	18	18	6	12	0	1	0	1	0	0	0	—	1	4	0	1	0.5	1.000
1987		6	5	.545	3.15	49	0	0	91.1	101	24	87	0	6	5	8	0	0	0	—	8	13	5	3	0.5	.808
1988		3	4	.429	2.27	51	0	0	83.1	69	16	72	0	3	4	37	0	0	0	—	7	11	2	0	0.4	.900
1989		7	10	.412	2.34	59	0	0	80.2	76	13	65	0	7	10	32	0	0	0	—	3	14	0	1	0.3	1.000
1990		5	5	.500	2.56	66	0	0	84.1	66	22	55	0	5	5	43	0	0	0	—	0	9	2	0	0.2	.818
1991		4	8	.333	5.54	36	4	0	63.1	87	17	48	0	1	7	7	0	0	0	—	7	10	0	1	0.5	1.000
1992	HOU N	11	8	.579	1.85	80	0	0	111.2	96	17	93	0	11	8	36	4	0	0	.000	5	12	2	0	0.2	.895
1993		4	10	.286	4.54	71	0	0	85.1	102	21	66	0	4	10	26	0	0	0	—	2	12	1	0	0.2	.933
1994	PHI N	2	4	.333	2.17	47	0	0	54	55	6	38	0	2	4	27	1	1	0	1.000	2	10	2	0	0.3	.857
1995	BAL A	0	4	.000	5.01	52	0	0	46.2	55	16	42	0	0	4	22	0	0	0	—	4	6	1	3	0.2	.909
1996	2 teams			CHI N	(28G 2–2)			MIL A	(24G 5–0)																	
"	total	7	2	.778	4.22	52	0	0	64	72	20	60	0	7	2	3	0	0	0	—	1	6	0	1	0.1	1.000
	12 yrs.	50	60	.455	3.21	578	4	0	785.1	802	179	639	0	47	59	242	5	1	0	.200	41	107	15	10	0.3	.908

Ricardo Jordan

JORDAN, RICARDO
B. June 27, 1970, Boynton Beach, Fla. — BL TL 6' 175 lbs.

Year	Team	W	L	PCT	ERA	G	GS	CG	IP	H	BB	SO	ShO	W	L	SV	AB	H	HR	BA	PO	A	E	DP	TC/G	FA
1995	TOR A	1	0	1.000	6.60	15	0	0	15	18	13	10	0	1	0	1	0	0	0	—	1	2	0	0	0.2	1.000
1996	PHI N	2	2	.500	1.80	26	0	0	25	18	12	17	0	2	2	0	1	0	0	.000	0	3	0	0	0.1	1.000
	2 yrs.	3	2	.600	3.60	41	0	0	40	36	25	27	0	3	2	1	1	0	0	.000	1	5	0	0	0.1	1.000

Stacy Jones

JONES, JOSEPH STACY
B. May 26, 1967, Gadsden, Ala. — BR TR 6'6" 225 lbs.

Year	Team	W	L	PCT	ERA	G	GS	CG	IP	H	BB	SO	ShO	W	L	SV	AB	H	HR	BA	PO	A	E	DP	TC/G	FA
1991	BAL A	0	0	—	4.09	4	1	0	11	11	5	10	0	0	0	0	0	0	0	—	2	1	0	0	0.8	1.000
1996	CHI A	0	0	—	0.00	2	0	0	2	0	1	1	0	0	0	0	0	0	0	—	0	0	0	0	0.0	.000
	2 yrs.	0	0		3.46	6	1	0	13	11	6	11	0	0	0	0	0	0	0	—	2	1	0	0	0.5	1.000

Todd Jones

JONES, TODD BARTON GIVIN
B. Apr. 24, 1968, Marietta, Ga. — BL TR 6'3" 200 lbs.

Year	Team	W	L	PCT	ERA	G	GS	CG	IP	H	BB	SO	ShO	W	L	SV	AB	H	HR	BA	PO	A	E	DP	TC/G	FA
1993	HOU N	1	2	.333	3.13	27	0	0	37.1	28	15	25	0	1	2	2	0	0	0	—	4	2	0	0	0.2	1.000
1994		5	2	.714	2.72	48	0	0	72.2	52	26	63	0	5	2	5	5	2	0	.400	4	3	0	0	0.1	1.000
1995		6	5	.545	3.07	68	0	0	99.2	89	52	96	0	6	5	15	5	1	0	.200	3	11	1	1	0.2	.933
1996		6	3	.667	4.40	51	0	0	57.1	61	32	44	0	6	3	17	1	0	0	.000	4	6	0	0	0.2	1.000
	4 yrs.	18	12	.600	3.27	194	0	0	267	230	125	228	0	18	12	39	11	3	0	.273	15	22	1	1	0.2	.974

Year	Team	W	L	PCT	ERA	G	GS	CG	IP	H	BB	SO	ShO	W	L	SV	AB	H	HR	BA	PO	A	E	DP	TC/G	FA
														Relief Pitching			Batting									

Ricardo Jordan

JORDAN, RICARDO
B. June 27, 1970, Boynton Beach, Fla. BL TL 6' 175 lbs.

Year	Team	W	L	PCT	ERA	G	GS	CG	IP	H	BB	SO	ShO	W	L	SV	AB	H	HR	BA	PO	A	E	DP	TC/G	FA
1995	TOR A	1	0	1.000	6.60	15	0	0	15	18	13	10	0	1	0	1	0	0	0	—	1	2	0	0	0.2	1.000
1996	PHI N	2	2	.500	1.80	26	0	0	25	18	12	17	0	2	2	0	1	0	0	.000	0	3	0	0	0.1	1.000
	2 yrs.	3	2	.600	3.60	41	0	0	40	36	25	27	0	3	2	1	1	0	0	.000	1	5	0	0	0.1	1.000

Jeff Juden

JUDEN, JEFFREY DANIEL
B. Jan. 19, 1971, Salem, Mass. BR TR 6'7" 245 lbs.

Year	Team	W	L	PCT	ERA	G	GS	CG	IP	H	BB	SO	ShO	W	L	SV	AB	H	HR	BA	PO	A	E	DP	TC/G	FA
1991	HOU N	0	2	.000	6.00	4	3	0	18	19	7	11	0	0	0	0	5	0	0	.000	0	2	3	0	1.3	.400
1993		0	1	.000	5.40	2	0	0	5	4	4	7	0	0	1	0	0	0	0	—	0	0	0	0	0.0	.000
1994	PHI N	1	4	.200	6.18	6	5	0	27.2	29	12	22	0	0	0	0	9	1	0	.111	1	3	1	0	0.8	.800
1995		2	4	.333	4.02	13	10	1	62.2	53	31	47	0	0	0	0	18	1	1	.056	3	8	0	0	0.8	1.000
1996	2 teams	SF N	(36G 4-0)		MON N	(22G 1-0)																				
"	total	5	0	1.000	3.27	58	0	0	74.1	61	34	61	0	5	0	0	3	0	0	.000	1	7	1	2	0.2	.889
	5 yrs.	8	11	.421	4.27	83	18	1	187.2	166	88	148	0	5	1	0	35	2	1	.057	5	20	5	2	0.4	.833

Scott Kamieniecki

KAMIENIECKI, SCOTT ANDREW
B. Apr. 19, 1964, Mt. Clemens, Mich. BR TR 6' 195 lbs.

Year	Team	W	L	PCT	ERA	G	GS	CG	IP	H	BB	SO	ShO	W	L	SV	AB	H	HR	BA	PO	A	E	DP	TC/G	FA
1991	NY A	4	4	.500	3.90	9	9	0	55.1	54	22	34	0	0	0	0	0	0	0	—	5	9	0	0	1.6	1.000
1992		6	14	.300	4.36	28	28	4	188	193	74	88	0	0	0	0	0	0	0	—	15	19	0	3	1.2	1.000
1993		10	7	.588	4.08	30	20	2	154.1	163	59	72	0	0	1	1	0	0	0	—	17	23	0	0	1.3	1.000
1994		8	6	.571	3.76	22	16	1	117.1	115	59	71	0	1	0	0	0	0	0	—	8	17	1	1	1.2	.962
1995		7	6	.538	4.01	17	16	1	89.2	83	49	43	0	0	0	0	0	0	0	—	3	10	0	2	0.8	1.000
1996		1	2	.333	11.12	7	5	0	22.2	36	19	15	0	0	0	0	0	0	0	—	0	4	0	0	0.6	1.000
	6 yrs.	36	39	.480	4.33	113	94	8	627.1	644	282	323	0	1	1	1	0	0	0		48	82	1	6	1.2	.992

DIVISIONAL PLAYOFF SERIES

Year	Team	W	L	PCT	ERA	G	GS	CG	IP	H	BB	SO	ShO	W	L	SV	AB	H	HR	BA	PO	A	E	DP	TC/G	FA
1995	NY A	0	0	—	7.20	1	1	0	5	9	4	4	0	0	0	0	0	0	0	—	0	0	0	0	0.0	.000

Matt Karchner

KARCHNER, MATTHEW DEAN
B. June 28, 1967, Berwick, Pa. BR TR 6'4" 245 lbs.

Year	Team	W	L	PCT	ERA	G	GS	CG	IP	H	BB	SO	ShO	W	L	SV	AB	H	HR	BA	PO	A	E	DP	TC/G	FA
1995	CHI A	4	2	.667	1.69	31	0	0	32	33	12	24	0	4	0	0	0	0	0	—	6	3	0	2	0.3	1.000
1996		7	4	.636	5.76	50	0	0	59.1	61	41	46	0	7	4	1	0	0	0	—	4	3	2	1	0.2	.778
	2 yrs.	11	6	.647	4.34	81	0	0	91.1	94	53	70	0	11	6	1					10	6	2	3	0.2	.889

Scott Karl

KARL, RANDALL SCOTT
B. Aug. 9, 1971, Fontana, Calif. BL TL 6'2" 195 lbs.

Year	Team	W	L	PCT	ERA	G	GS	CG	IP	H	BB	SO	ShO	W	L	SV	AB	H	HR	BA	PO	A	E	DP	TC/G	FA
1995	MIL A	6	7	.462	4.14	25	18	1	124	141	50	59	0	0	0	0	0	0	0	—	5	21	3	3	1.2	.897
1996		13	9	.591	4.86	32	32	3	207.1	220	72	121	1	0	0	0	0	0	0	—	13	27	3	2	1.3	.930
	2 yrs.	19	16	.543	4.59	57	50	4	331.1	361	122	180	1	0	0	0					18	48	6	5	1.3	.917

Greg Keagle

KEAGLE, GREGORY CHARLES
B. June 28, 1971, Corning, N.Y. BR TR 6'1" 185 lbs.

Year	Team	W	L	PCT	ERA	G	GS	CG	IP	H	BB	SO	ShO	W	L	SV	AB	H	HR	BA	PO	A	E	DP	TC/G	FA
1996	DET A	3	6	.333	7.39	26	6	0	87.2	104	68	70	0	3	1	0	0	0	0	—	7	8	0	1	0.6	1.000

Jimmy Key

KEY, JAMES EDWARD
B. Apr. 22, 1961, Huntsville, Ala. BR TL 6'1" 180 lbs.

Year	Team	W	L	PCT	ERA	G	GS	CG	IP	H	BB	SO	ShO	W	L	SV	AB	H	HR	BA	PO	A	E	DP	TC/G	FA
1984	TOR A	4	5	.444	4.65	63	0	0	62	70	32	44	0	4	5	10	0	0	0	—	9	11	1	0	0.3	.952
1985		14	6	.700	3.00	35	32	3	212.2	188	50	85	0	1	0	0	0	0	0	—	15	52	3	3	1.9	.957
1986		14	11	.560	3.57	36	35	4	232	222	74	141	2	0	0	0	0	0	0	—	18	42	0	4	1.7	1.000
1987		17	8	.680	2.76	36	36	8	261	210	66	161	1	0	0	0	0	0	0	—	17	44	3	5	1.8	.953
1988		12	5	.706	3.29	21	21	2	131.1	127	30	65	2	0	0	0	0	0	0	—	5	19	0	1	1.1	1.000
1989		13	14	.481	3.88	33	33	5	216	226	27	118	1	0	0	0	0	0	0	—	11	44	2	2	1.7	.965
1990		13	7	.650	4.25	27	27	0	154.2	169	22	88	0	0	0	0	0	0	0	—	8	22	1	3	1.1	.968
1991		16	12	.571	3.05	33	33	2	209.1	207	44	125	2	0	0	0	0	0	0	—	22	37	2	3	1.8	.967
1992		13	13	.500	3.53	33	33	4	216.2	205	59	117	2	0	0	0	0	0	0	—	18	27	1	4	1.4	.978
1993	NY A	18	6	.750	3.00	34	34	4	236.2	219	43	173	2	0	0	0	0	0	0	—	14	33	4	1	1.5	.922
1994		17	4	.810	3.27	25	25	1	168	177	52	97	0	0	0	0	0	0	0	—	6	40	2	3	1.9	.958
1995		1	2	.333	5.64	5	5	0	30.1	40	6	14	0	0	0	0	0	0	0	—	4	3	0	2	1.4	1.000
1996		12	11	.522	4.68	30	30	0	169.1	171	58	116	0	0	0	0	0	0	0	—	9	30	1	1	1.3	.975
	13 yrs.	164	104	.612	3.49	411	344	33	2300	2231	563	1344	12	5	5	10	0	0	0		156	404	20	30	1.4	.966

DIVISIONAL PLAYOFF SERIES

Year	Team	W	L	PCT	ERA	G	GS	CG	IP	H	BB	SO	ShO	W	L	SV	AB	H	HR	BA	PO	A	E	DP	TC/G	FA
1996	NY A	0	0	—	3.60	1	1	0	5	5	1	3	0	0	0	0	0	0	0	—	0	0	0	0	0.0	.000

LEAGUE CHAMPIONSHIP SERIES

Year	Team	W	L	PCT	ERA	G	GS	CG	IP	H	BB	SO	ShO	W	L	SV	AB	H	HR	BA	PO	A	E	DP	TC/G	FA
1985	TOR A	0	1	.000	5.19	2	2	0	8.2	15	2	5	0	0	0	0	0	0	0	—	0	3	0	0	1.5	1.000
1989		1	0	1.000	4.50	1	1	0	6	7	2	2	0	0	0	0	0	0	0	—	0	0	0	0	0.0	.000
1991		0	0	—	3.00	1	1	0	6	5	1	1	0	0	0	0	0	0	0	—	3	0	0	1	3.0	1.000
1992		0	0	—	0.00	1	0	0	3	2	1	1	0	0	0	0	0	0	0	—	0	0	0	0	0.0	.000
1996	NY A	1	0	1.000	2.25	1	1	0	8	3	1	5	0	0	0	0	0	0	0	—	1	0	0	0	1.0	1.000
	5 yrs.	2	1	.667	3.41	6	5	0	31.2	32	8	14	0	0	0	0	0	0	0	—	1	6	0	1	1.2	1.000

WORLD SERIES

Year	Team	W	L	PCT	ERA	G	GS	CG	IP	H	BB	SO	ShO	W	L	SV	AB	H	HR	BA	PO	A	E	DP	TC/G	FA
1992	TOR A	2	0	1.000	1.00	2	1	0	9	6	0	6	0	1	0	0	1	0	0	.000	2	4	0	0	3.0	1.000
1996	NY A	1	1	.500	3.97	2	2	0	11.1	15	5	1	0	0	0	0	0	0	0	—	0	3	0	1	1.5	1.000
	2 yrs.	3	1	.750	2.66	4	3	0	20.1	21	5	7	0	1	0	0	1	0	0	.000	2	7	0	1	2.3	1.000

Year	Team	W	L	PCT	ERA	G	GS	CG	IP	H	BB	SO	ShO	Relief Pitching W	L	SV	Batting AB	H	HR	BA	PO	A	E	DP	TC/G	FA

Brian Keyser
KEYSER, BRIAN LEE
B. Oct. 31, 1966, Castro Valley, Calif. BR TR 6'1" 180 lbs.

Year	Team	W	L	PCT	ERA	G	GS	CG	IP	H	BB	SO	ShO	W	L	SV	AB	H	HR	BA	PO	A	E	DP	TC/G	FA
1995	CHI A	5	6	.455	4.97	23	10	0	92.1	114	27	48	0	3	1	0	0	0	0	—	9	17	1	1	1.2	.963
1996		1	2	.333	4.98	28	0	0	59.2	78	28	19	0	1	2	1	0	0	0	—	6	16	1	3	0.8	.957
	2 yrs.	6	8	.429	4.97	51	10	0	152	192	55	67	0	4	3	1					15	33	2	4	1.0	.960

Mark Kiefer
KIEFER, MARK ANDREW
Brother of Steve Kiefer.
B. Nov. 13, 1968, Orange, Calif. BR TR 6'4" 175 lbs.

Year	Team	W	L	PCT	ERA	G	GS	CG	IP	H	BB	SO	ShO	W	L	SV	AB	H	HR	BA	PO	A	E	DP	TC/G	FA
1993	MIL A	0	0	—	0.00	6	0	0	9.1	3	5	7	0	0	0	1	0	0	0	—	1	1	0	0	0.3	1.000
1994		1	0	1.000	8.44	7	0	0	10.2	15	8	8	0	1	0	0	0	0	0	—	0	1	0	0	0.1	1.000
1995		4	1	.800	3.44	24	0	0	49.2	37	27	41	0	4	1	0	0	0	0	—	0	3	0	1	0.1	1.000
1996		0	0	—	8.10	7	0	0	10	15	5	5	0	0	0	0	0	0	0	—	0	0	0	0	0.0	.000
	4 yrs.	5	1	.833	4.29	44	0	0	79.2	70	45	61	0	5	1	1	0	0	0		1	5	0	1	0.1	1.000

Darryl Kile
KILE, DARRYL ANDREW
B. Dec. 2, 1968, Garden Grove, Calif. BR TR 6'5" 185 lbs.

Year	Team	W	L	PCT	ERA	G	GS	CG	IP	H	BB	SO	ShO	W	L	SV	AB	H	HR	BA	PO	A	E	DP	TC/G	FA
1991	HOU N	7	11	.389	3.69	37	22	0	153.2	144	84	100	0	0	2	0	38	0	0	.000	7	17	3	1	0.7	.889
1992		5	10	.333	3.95	22	22	2	125.1	124	63	90	0	0	0	0	32	5	0	.156	2	12	5	0	0.9	.737
1993		15	8	.652	3.51	32	26	4	171.2	152	69	141	2	1	0	0	53	5	1	.094	9	15	3	0	0.8	.889
1994		9	6	.600	4.57	24	24	0	147.2	153	82	105	0	0	0	0	47	7	0	.149	9	19	1	0	1.2	.966
1995		4	12	.250	4.96	25	21	0	127	114	73	113	0	0	0	0	36	4	0	.111	11	25	3	2	1.6	.923
1996		12	11	.522	4.19	35	33	4	219	233	97	219	0	0	0	0	73	10	0	.137	12	28	3	6	1.2	.930
	6 yrs.	52	58	.473	4.12	175	148	10	944.1	920	468	768	2	1	2	0	279	31	1	.111	50	116	18	9	1.1	.902

Scott Klingenbeck
KLINGENBECK, SCOTT EDWARD
B. Feb. 3, 1971, Cincinnati, Ohio BR TR 6'2" 205 lbs.

Year	Team	W	L	PCT	ERA	G	GS	CG	IP	H	BB	SO	ShO	W	L	SV	AB	H	HR	BA	PO	A	E	DP	TC/G	FA
1994	BAL A	1	0	1.000	3.86	1	1	0	7	6	4	5	0	0	0	0	0	0	0	—	1	0	0	0	1.0	1.000
1995	2 teams	BAL A	(6G 2-2)		MIN A	(18G 0-2)																				
"	total	2	4	.333	7.12	24	9	0	79.2	101	42	42	0	0	0	0	0	0	0	—	8	10	1	0	0.8	.947
1996	MIN A	1	1	.500	7.85	10	3	0	28.2	42	10	15	0	0	0	0	0	0	0	—	6	3	0	0	0.9	1.000
	3 yrs.	4	5	.444	7.10	35	13	0	115.1	149	56	62	0	0	0	0	0	0	0		15	13	1	0	0.8	.966

Joe Klink
KLINK, JOSEPH CHARLES
B. Feb. 3, 1962, Johnstown, Pa. BL TL 5'11" 170 lbs.

Year	Team	W	L	PCT	ERA	G	GS	CG	IP	H	BB	SO	ShO	W	L	SV	AB	H	HR	BA	PO	A	E	DP	TC/G	FA
1987	MIN A	0	1	.000	6.65	12	0	0	23	37	11	17	0	0	1	0	0	0	0	—	0	2	0	1	0.2	1.000
1990	OAK A	0	0	—	2.04	40	0	0	39.2	34	18	19	0	0	0	1	0	0	0	—	1	1	0	0	0.1	1.000
1991		10	3	.769	4.35	62	0	0	62	60	21	34	0	10	3	2	0	0	0	—	4	8	0	1	0.2	1.000
1993	FLA N	0	2	.000	5.02	59	0	0	37.2	37	24	22	0	0	2	0	2	0	0	.000	3	2	0	1	0.1	1.000
1996	SEA A	0	0	—	3.86	3	0	0	2.1	3	1	2	0	0	0	0	0	0	0	—	0	0	0	0	0.0	.000
	5 yrs.	10	6	.625	4.26	176	0	0	164.2	171	75	94	0	10	6	3	2	0	0	.000	8	13	0	2	0.1	1.000

WORLD SERIES

Year	Team	W	L	PCT	ERA	G	GS	CG	IP	H	BB	SO	ShO	W	L	SV	AB	H	HR	BA	PO	A	E	DP	TC/G	FA
1990	OAK A	0	0	—	0.00	1	0	0	0	1	0	1	0	0	0	0	0	0	0	—	0	0	0	0	0.0	.000

Brent Knackert
KNACKERT, BRENT BRADLEY
B. Aug. 1, 1969, Los Angeles, Calif. BR TR 6'3" 185 lbs.

Year	Team	W	L	PCT	ERA	G	GS	CG	IP	H	BB	SO	ShO	W	L	SV	AB	H	HR	BA	PO	A	E	DP	TC/G	FA
1990	SEA A	1	1	.500	6.51	24	2	0	37.1	50	21	28	0	1	1	0	0	0	0	—	4	4	2	0	0.4	.800
1996	BOS A	0	1	.000	9.00	8	0	0	10	16	7	5	0	0	1	0	0	0	0	—	0	4	0	1	0.5	1.000
	2 yrs.	1	2	.333	7.04	32	2	0	47.1	66	28	33	0	1	2	0	0	0	0		4	8	2	1	0.4	.857

Rick Krivda
KRIVDA, RICK MICHAEL
B. Jan. 19, 1970, McKeesport, Pa. BR TL 6'1" 180 lbs.

Year	Team	W	L	PCT	ERA	G	GS	CG	IP	H	BB	SO	ShO	W	L	SV	AB	H	HR	BA	PO	A	E	DP	TC/G	FA
1995	BAL A	2	7	.222	4.54	13	13	1	75.1	76	25	53	0	0	0	0	0	0	0	—	0	7	1	0	0.6	.875
1996		3	5	.375	4.96	22	11	0	81.2	89	39	54	0	1	1	0	0	0	0	—	1	10	0	0	0.5	1.000
	2 yrs.	5	12	.294	4.76	35	24	1	157	165	64	107	0	1	1	0					1	17	1	0	0.5	.947

Kerry Lacy
LACY, KERRY ARDEEN
B. Aug 7, 1972, Chattanooga, Tenn. BR TR 6'2" 195 lbs.

Year	Team	W	L	PCT	ERA	G	GS	CG	IP	H	BB	SO	ShO	W	L	SV	AB	H	HR	BA	PO	A	E	DP	TC/G	FA
1996	BOS A	2	0	1.000	3.38	11	0	0	10.2	15	8	9	0	2	0	0	0	0	0	—	1	1	1	1	0.2	.666

Mark Langston
LANGSTON, MARK EDWARD
B. Aug. 20, 1960, San Diego, Calif. BR TL 6'2" 175 lbs.

Year	Team	W	L	PCT	ERA	G	GS	CG	IP	H	BB	SO	ShO	W	L	SV	AB	H	HR	BA	PO	A	E	DP	TC/G	FA
1984	SEA A	17	10	.630	3.40	35	33	5	225	188	118	204	2	1	0	0	0	0	0	—	15	30	2	2	1.3	.957
1985		7	14	.333	5.47	24	24	2	126.2	122	91	72	0	0	0	0	0	0	0	—	9	26	2	4	1.5	.946
1986		12	14	.462	4.85	37	36	9	239.1	234	123	245	0	0	0	0	0	0	0	—	7	27	6	3	1.1	.850
1987		19	13	.594	3.84	35	35	14	272	242	114	262	3	0	0	0	0	0	0	—	8	41	2	3	1.5	.961
1988		15	11	.577	3.34	35	35	9	261.1	222	110	235	3	0	0	0	0	0	0	—	11	45	4	6	1.7	.933
1989	2 teams	SEA A	(10G 4-5)		MON N	(24G 12-9)																				
"	total	16	14	.533	2.74	34	34	8	250	198	112	235	5	0	0	0	64	11	0	.172	15	28	2	2	1.3	.956
1990	CAL A	10	17	.370	4.40	33	33	5	223	215	104	195	1	0	0	0	0	0	0	—	7	42	3	0	1.6	.942
1991		19	8	.704	3.00	34	34	7	246.1	190	96	183	0	0	0	0	0	0	0	—	15	34	3	1	1.5	.942
1992		13	14	.481	3.66	32	32	9	229	206	74	174	2	0	0	0	2	0	0	.000	7	41	3	1	1.5	.941
1993		16	11	.593	3.20	35	35	7	256.1	220	85	196	0	0	0	0	0	0	0	—	10	47	2	4	1.7	.966

Year	Team	W	L	PCT	ERA	G	GS	CG	IP	H	BB	SO	ShO	W	L	SV	AB	H	HR	BA	PO	A	E	DP	TC/G	FA

Mark Langston *continued*

Year	Team	W	L	PCT	ERA	G	GS	CG	IP	H	BB	SO	ShO	W	L	SV	AB	H	HR	BA	PO	A	E	DP	TC/G	FA
1994		7	8	.467	4.68	18	18	2	119.1	121	54	109	1	0	0	0	0	0	0	—	3	27	2	1	1.8	.938
1995		15	7	.682	4.63	31	31	2	200.1	212	64	142	1	0	0	0	0	0	0	—	2	43	3	2	1.5	.938
1996		6	5	.545	4.82	18	18	2	123.1	116	45	83	0	0	0	0	0	0	0	—	7	27	1	2	1.9	.971
13 yrs.		172	146	.541	3.85	401	398	81	2772	2486	1190	2335	18	1	0	0	66	11	0	.167	116	458	35	32	1.5	.943

Andy Larkin

LARKIN, ANDREW DANE
B. June 27, 1974, Chelan, Wash.

BR TR 6'4" 175 lbs.

Year	Team	W	L	PCT	ERA	G	GS	CG	IP	H	BB	SO	ShO	W	L	SV	AB	H	HR	BA	PO	A	E	DP	TC/G	FA
1996	FLA N	0	0	—	1.80	1	1	0	5	3	4	2	0	0	0	0	2	0	0	.000	1	0	0	0	1.0	1.000

Phil Leftwich

LEFTWICH, PHILLIP DALE
B. May 19, 1969, Lynchburg, Va.

BR TR 6'5" 205 lbs.

Year	Team	W	L	PCT	ERA	G	GS	CG	IP	H	BB	SO	ShO	W	L	SV	AB	H	HR	BA	PO	A	E	DP	TC/G	FA
1993	CAL A	4	6	.400	3.79	12	12	1	80.2	81	27	31	0	0	0	0	0	0	0	—	5	11	1	2	1.4	.941
1994		5	10	.333	5.68	20	20	1	114	127	42	67	0	0	0	0	0	0	0	—	9	15	3	0	1.4	.889
1996		0	1	.000	7.36	2	2	0	7.1	12	3	4	0	0	0	0	0	0	0	—	0	1	0	0	0.5	1.000
3 yrs.		9	17	.346	4.99	34	34	2	202	220	72	102	0	0	0	0	0	0	0	—	14	27	4	2	1.3	.911

Dave Leiper

LEIPER, DAVID PAUL
B. June 18, 1962, Whittier, Calif.

BL TL 6'1" 160 lbs.

Year	Team	W	L	PCT	ERA	G	GS	CG	IP	H	BB	SO	ShO	W	L	SV	AB	H	HR	BA	PO	A	E	DP	TC/G	FA
1984	OAK A	1	0	1.000	9.00	8	0	0	7	12	5	3	0	1	0	0	0	0	0	—	1	2	0	0	0.4	1.000
1986		2	2	.500	4.83	33	0	0	31.2	28	18	15	0	2	2	1	0	0	0	—	0	6	0	0	0.2	1.000
1987	2 teams	OAK A	(45G 2-1)			SD N	(12G 1-0)																			
"	total	3	1	.750	3.95	57	0	0	68.1	65	23	43	0	3	1	2	0	0	0	—	5	14	2	1	0.4	.905
1988	SD N	3	0	1.000	2.17	35	0	0	54	45	14	33	0	3	0	1	2	1	0	.500	3	9	0	1	0.3	1.000
1989		0	1	.000	5.02	22	0	0	28.2	40	20	7	0	0	1	0	1	0	0	.000	4	7	1	0	0.5	.917
1994	OAK A	0	0	—	1.93	26	0	0	18.2	13	6	14	0	0	0	1	0	0	0	—	0	1	0	1	0.0	1.000
1995	2 teams	OAK A	(24G 1-1)			MON N	(26G 0-2)																			
"	total	1	3	.250	3.22	50	0	0	44.2	39	19	22	0	1	3	2	1	0	0	.000	1	8	0	0	0.2	1.000
1996	2 teams	PHI N	(26G 2-0)			MON N	(7G 0-1)																			
"	total	2	1	.667	7.20	33	0	0	25	40	9	13	0	2	1	0	0	0	0	—	0	6	1	0	0.2	.857
8 yrs.		12	8	.600	3.98	264	0	0	278	282	114	150	0	12	8	7	4	1	0	.250	14	53	4	3	0.3	.944

Al Leiter

LEITER, ALOIS TERRY
Brother of Mark Leiter.
B. Oct. 23, 1965, Toms River, N. J.

BL TL 6'2" 200 lbs.

Year	Team	W	L	PCT	ERA	G	GS	CG	IP	H	BB	SO	ShO	W	L	SV	AB	H	HR	BA	PO	A	E	DP	TC/G	FA
1987	NY A	2	2	.500	6.35	4	4	0	22.2	24	15	28	0	0	0	0	0	0	0	—	0	2	0	0	0.5	1.000
1988		4	4	.500	3.92	14	14	0	57.1	49	33	60	0	0	0	0	0	0	0	—	0	11	1	0	0.9	.917
1989	2 teams	NY A	(4G 1-2)			TOR A	(1G 0-0)																			
"	total	1	2	.333	5.67	5	5	0	33.1	32	23	26	0	0	0	0	0	0	0	—	1	2	0	0	0.6	1.000
1990	TOR A	0	0	—	0.00	4	0	0	6.1	1	2	5	0	0	0	0	0	0	0	—	1	1	0	0	0.5	1.000
1991		0	0	—	27.00	3	0	0	1.2	3	5	1	0	0	0	0	0	0	0	—	0	1	0	0	0.3	1.000
1992		0	0	—	9.00	1	0	0	1	1	2	0	0	0	0	0	0	0	0	—	0	0	0	0	0.0	.000
1993		9	6	.600	4.11	34	12	1	105	93	56	66	1	3	1	2	0	0	0	—	4	12	1	0	0.5	.941
1994		6	7	.462	5.08	20	20	1	111.2	125	65	100	0	0	0	0	0	0	0	—	3	13	0	1	0.8	1.000
1995		11	11	.500	3.64	28	28	2	183	162	108	153	1	0	0	0	0	0	0	—	7	15	0	2	0.8	1.000
1996	FLA N	16	12	.571	2.93	33	33	2	215.1	153	**119**	200	1	0	0	0	70	7	0	.100	8	22	2	3	1.0	.938
10 yrs.		49	44	.527	3.94	146	116	6	737.1	643	428	639	3	3	1	2	70	7	0	.100	24	79	4	6	0.7	.963

LEAGUE CHAMPIONSHIP SERIES

| 1993 | TOR A | 0 | 0 | — | 3.38 | 2 | 0 | 0 | 2.2 | 4 | 2 | 2 | 0 | 0 | 0 | 0 | 0 | 0 | 0 | — | 0 | 0 | 0 | 0 | 0.0 | .000 |

WORLD SERIES

| 1993 | TOR A | 1 | 0 | 1.000 | 7.71 | 3 | 0 | 0 | 7 | 12 | 2 | 5 | 0 | 1 | 0 | 0 | 1 | 1 | 0 | 1.000 | 0 | 0 | 0 | 0 | 0.0 | .000 |

Mark Leiter

LEITER, MARK EDWARD
Brother of Al Leiter.
B. Apr. 13, 1963, Joliet, Ill.

BR TR 6'3" 200 lbs.

Year	Team	W	L	PCT	ERA	G	GS	CG	IP	H	BB	SO	ShO	W	L	SV	AB	H	HR	BA	PO	A	E	DP	TC/G	FA
1990	NY A	1	1	.500	6.84	8	3	0	26.1	33	9	21	0	0	0	0	0	0	0	—	0	8	0	1	1.0	1.000
1991	DET A	9	7	.563	4.21	38	15	1	134.2	125	50	103	0	2	1	1	0	0	0	—	3	17	1	1	0.6	.952
1992		8	5	.615	4.18	35	14	1	112	116	43	75	0	3	2	0	0	0	0	—	8	15	1	0	0.7	.958
1993		6	6	.500	4.72	27	13	1	106.2	111	44	70	0	1	2	0	0	0	0	—	5	11	2	1	0.7	.889
1994	CAL A	4	7	.364	4.72	40	7	0	95.1	99	35	71	0	2	4	2	0	0	0	—	5	16	1	0	0.6	.955
1995	SF N	10	12	.455	3.82	30	29	7	195.2	185	55	129	1	0	1	0	61	6	0	.098	7	19	4	4	1.0	.867
1996	2 teams	SF N	(23G 4-10)			MON N	(12G 4-2)																			
"	total	8	12	.400	4.92	35	34	2	205	219	69	164	0	0	0	0	67	8	0	.119	8	25	2	1	1.0	.943
7 yrs.		46	50	.479	4.48	213	115	12	875.2	888	305	633	1	8	11	3	128	14	0	.109	36	111	11	8	0.7	.930

Curtis Leskanic

LESKANIC, CURTIS JOHN
B. Apr. 2, 1968, Homestead, Pa.

BR TR 6' 180 lbs.

Year	Team	W	L	PCT	ERA	G	GS	CG	IP	H	BB	SO	ShO	W	L	SV	AB	H	HR	BA	PO	A	E	DP	TC/G	FA
1993	CLR N	1	5	.167	5.37	18	8	0	57	59	27	30	0	0	0	0	13	2	0	.154	5	5	1	2	0.6	.909
1994		1	1	.500	5.64	8	3	0	22.1	27	10	17	0	0	0	0	6	1	0	.167	1	2	0	0	0.4	1.000
1995		6	3	.667	3.40	76	0	0	98	83	33	107	0	6	3	10	7	1	0	.143	9	17	0	1	0.3	1.000
1996		7	5	.583	6.23	70	0	0	73.2	82	38	76	0	7	5	6	3	1	0	.333	4	7	1	0	0.2	.917
4 yrs.		15	14	.517	4.88	172	11	0	251	251	108	230	0	13	9	16	29	5	0	.172	19	31	2	3	0.3	.962

Year	Team	W	L	PCT	ERA	G	GS	CG	IP	H	BB	SO	ShO	W	L	SV	AB	H	HR	BA	PO	A	E	DP	TC/G	FA

Curtis Leskanic continued

DIVISIONAL PLAYOFF SERIES

1995	CLR N	0	1	.000	6.00	3	0	0	3	3	0	4	0	0	1	0	0	0	0	—	0	0	0	0	0.0	.000

Al Levine

LEVINE, ALAN BRIAN
B. May 22, 1968, Park Ridge, Ill.

BL TR 6'3" 180 lbs.

| 1996 | CHI A | 0 | 1 | .000 | 5.40 | 16 | 0 | 0 | 18.1 | 22 | 7 | 12 | 0 | 0 | 1 | 0 | 0 | 0 | 0 | — | 0 | 6 | 0 | 1 | 0.4 | 1.000 |

Richie Lewis

LEWIS, RICHIE TODD
B. Jan. 25, 1966, Muncie, Ind.

BR TR 5'10" 175 lbs.

1992	BAL A	1	1	.500	10.80	2	2	0	6.2	13	7	4	0	0	0	0	0	0	0	—	1	1	0	0	1.0	1.000
1993	FLA N	6	3	.667	3.26	57	0	0	77.1	68	43	65	0	6	3	0	2	1	0	.500	3	13	1	1	0.3	.941
1994		1	4	.200	5.67	45	0	0	54	62	38	45	0	1	4	0	5	0	0	.000	6	5	2	1	0.3	.846
1995		0	1	.000	3.75	21	1	0	36	30	15	32	0	0	1	0	1	0	0	.000	8	2	2	0	0.6	.833
1996	DET A	4	6	.400	4.18	72	0	0	90.1	78	65	78	0	4	6	2	1	0	0	.000	4	6	0	1	0.1	1.000
5 yrs.		12	15	.444	4.32	197	3	0	264.1	251	168	224	0	11	14	2	9	1	0	.111	22	27	5	3	0.3	.907

Jon Lieber

LIEBER, JONATHAN RAY
B. Apr. 2, 1970, Council Bluffs, Iowa

BL TR 6'3" 220 lbs.

1994	PIT N	6	7	.462	3.73	17	17	1	108.2	116	25	71	0	0	0	0	39	4	0	.103	10	8	2	1	1.2	.900
1995		4	7	.364	6.32	21	12	0	72.2	103	14	45	0	1	0	0	21	1	0	.048	2	16	1	0	0.9	.947
1996		9	5	.643	3.99	51	15	0	142	156	28	94	0	2	3	1	36	7	0	.194	17	25	0	0	0.8	1.000
3 yrs.		19	19	.500	4.43	89	44	1	323.1	375	67	210	0	3	3	1	96	12	0	.125	29	49	3	1	0.9	.963

Derek Lilliquist

LILLIQUIST, DEREK JANSEN
B. Feb. 20, 1966, Winter Park, Fla.

BL TL 6' 200 lbs.

1989	ATL N	8	10	.444	3.97	32	30	0	165.2	202	34	79	0	0	0	0	63	12	0	.190	9	20	2	1	1.0	.935
1990	2 teams	ATL N	(12G 2-8)		SD	N	(16G 3-3)																			
"	total	5	11	.313	5.31	28	18	1	122	136	42	63	1	0	0	0	43	11	2	.256	4	7	0	0	0.4	1.000
1991	SD N	0	2	.000	8.79	6	2	0	14.1	25	4	7	0	0	0	0	2	0	0	.000	1	4	0	0	0.8	1.000
1992	CLE A	5	3	.625	1.75	71	0	0	61.2	39	18	47	0	5	3	6	0	0	0	—	3	9	0	0	0.2	1.000
1993		4	4	.500	2.25	56	2	0	64	64	19	40	0	4	4	10	0	0	0	—	1	9	1	0	0.2	.909
1994		1	3	.250	4.91	36	0	0	29.1	34	8	15	0	1	3	1	0	0	0	—	0	2	0	0	0.1	1.000
1995	BOS A	2	1	.667	6.26	28	0	0	23	27	9	9	0	2	1	0	0	0	0	—	2	2	0	0	0.1	1.000
1996	CIN N	0	0	—	7.36	5	0	0	3.2	5	0	1	0	0	0	0	0	0	0	—	1	2	0	0	0.6	1.000
8 yrs.		25	34	.424	4.13	262	52	1	483.2	532	134	261	1	12	12	17	108	23	2	.213	21	55	3	1	0.3	.962

Jose Lima

LIMA, JOSE DESIDERIO RODRIGUEZ
B. Sept. 20, 1972, Santiago, Dominican Republic

BR TR 6'2" 170 lbs.

1994	DET A	0	1	.000	13.50	3	1	0	6.2	11	3	7	0	0	0	0	0	0	0	—	1	0	0	0	0.3	1.000
1995		3	9	.250	6.11	15	15	0	73.2	85	18	37	0	0	0	0	0	0	0	—	5	2	0	0	0.5	1.000
1996		5	6	.455	5.70	39	4	0	72.2	87	22	59	0	5	2	3	0	0	0	—	11	17	0	1	0.7	1.000
3 yrs.		8	16	.333	6.24	57	20	0	153	183	43	103	0	5	2	3	0	0	0		17	19	0	1	0.6	1.000

Graeme Lloyd

LLOYD, GRAEME JOHN
B. Apr. 9, 1967, Geelong, Australia

BL TL 6'8" 225 lbs.

1993	MIL A	3	4	.429	2.83	55	0	0	63.2	64	13	31	0	3	4	0	0	0	0	—	4	12	1	1	0.3	.941
1994		2	3	.400	5.17	43	0	0	47	49	15	31	0	2	3	3	0	0	0	—	6	2	0	1	0.2	1.000
1995		0	5	.000	4.50	33	0	0	32	28	8	13	0	0	5	4	0	0	0	—	2	7	0	0	0.3	1.000
1996	2 teams	MIL A	(52G 2-4)		NY	A	(13G 0-2)																			
"	total	2	6	.250	4.29	65	0	0	56.2	61	22	30	0	2	6	0	0	0	0	—	2	7	0	1	0.1	1.000
4 yrs.		7	18	.280	4.06	196	0	0	199.1	202	58	105	0	7	18	7	0	0	0		14	28	1	3	0.2	.977

DIVISIONAL PLAYOFF SERIES

| 1996 | NY A | 0 | 0 | — | 0.00 | 2 | 0 | 0 | 1 | 1 | 0 | 0 | 0 | 0 | 0 | 0 | 0 | 0 | 0 | — | 1 | 0 | 0 | 0 | 0.5 | 1.000 |

LEAGUE CHAMPIONSHIP SERIES

| 1996 | NY A | 0 | 0 | — | 0.00 | 2 | 0 | 0 | 1.2 | 0 | 0 | 1 | 0 | 0 | 0 | 0 | 0 | 0 | 0 | — | 0 | 0 | 0 | 0 | 0.0 | .000 |

WORLD SERIES

| 1996 | NY A | 1 | 0 | 1.000 | 0.00 | 4 | 0 | 0 | 2.2 | 0 | 0 | 4 | 0 | 1 | 0 | 0 | 1 | 0 | 0 | .000 | 0 | 0 | 0 | 0 | 0.0 | .000 |

Esteban Loaiza

LOAIZA, ESTEBAN ANTONIO VEYNA
B. Dec. 31, 1971, Tijuana, Mexico

BR TR 6'4" 190 lbs.

1995	PIT N	8	9	.471	5.16	32	31	1	172.2	205	55	85	0	0	0	0	52	10	0	.192	13	26	0	3	1.2	1.000
1996		2	3	.400	4.96	10	10	1	52.2	65	19	32	1	0	0	0	17	2	0	.118	6	12	1	0	1.9	.947
2 yrs.		10	12	.455	5.11	42	41	2	225.1	270	74	117	1	0	0	0	69	12	0	.174	19	38	1	3	1.4	.983

Rich Loiselle

LOISELLE, RICHARD FRANK
B. Jan. 12, 1972, Meenah, Wisc.

BR TR 6'5" 225 lbs.

| 1996 | PIT N | 1 | 0 | 1.000 | 3.05 | 5 | 3 | 0 | 20.2 | 22 | 8 | 9 | 0 | 0 | 0 | 0 | 8 | 2 | 0 | .250 | 2 | 5 | 0 | 0 | 1.4 | 1.000 |

Year	Team	W	L	PCT	ERA	G	GS	CG	IP	H	BB	SO	ShO	Relief Pitching W	L	SV	Batting AB	H	HR	BA	PO	A	E	DP	TC/G	FA

Kevin Lomon
LOMON, KEVIN DALE
B. Nov. 20, 1971, Fort Smith, Ark.
BR TR 6'1" 195 lbs.

Year	Team	W	L	PCT	ERA	G	GS	CG	IP	H	BB	SO	ShO	W	L	SV	AB	H	HR	BA	PO	A	E	DP	TC/G	FA
1995	NY N	0	1	.000	6.75	6	0	0	9.1	17	5	6	0	0	1	0	0	0	0	—	1	0	1	0	0.3	.500
1996	ATL N	0	0	—	4.91	6	0	0	7.1	7	3	1	0	0	0	0	0	0	0	—	2	2	0	2	0.7	1.000
	2 yrs.	0	1	.000	5.94	12	0	0	16.2	24	8	7	0	0	1	0	0	0	0		3	2	1	2	0.5	.833

Albie Lopez
LOPEZ, ALBERT ANTHONY
B. Aug. 18, 1971, Mesa, Ariz.
BR TR 6'1" 205 lbs.

Year	Team	W	L	PCT	ERA	G	GS	CG	IP	H	BB	SO	ShO	W	L	SV	AB	H	HR	BA	PO	A	E	DP	TC/G	FA
1993	CLE A	3	1	.750	5.98	9	9	0	49.2	49	32	25	0	0	0	0	0	0	0	—	5	6	2	0	1.4	.846
1994		1	2	.333	4.24	4	4	1	17	20	6	18	1	0	0	0	0	0	0	—	2	0	1	0	0.8	.667
1995		0	0	—	3.13	6	2	0	23	17	7	22	0	0	0	0	0	0	0	—	1	2	0	0	0.5	1.000
1996		5	4	.556	6.39	13	10	0	62	80	22	45	0	1	1	0	0	0	0	—	1	9	2	0	0.9	.833
	4 yrs.	9	7	.563	5.52	32	25	1	151.2	166	67	110	1	1	1	0	0	0	0		9	17	5	0	1.0	.839

Eric Ludwick
LUDWICK, ERIC DAVID
B. Dec. 14, 1971, Whiteman AFB, Mo.
BR TR 6'5" 210 lbs.

Year	Team	W	L	PCT	ERA	G	GS	CG	IP	H	BB	SO	ShO	W	L	SV	AB	H	HR	BA	PO	A	E	DP	TC/G	FA
1996	STL N	0	1	.000	9.00	6	1	0	10	11	3	12	0	0	0	0	2	0	0	.000	1	1	1	0	0.5	.667

Curt Lyons
LYONS, CURT RUSSELL
B. Oct. 17, 1974, Greencastle, Ind.
BR TR 6'5" 230 lbs.

Year	Team	W	L	PCT	ERA	G	GS	CG	IP	H	BB	SO	ShO	W	L	SV	AB	H	HR	BA	PO	A	E	DP	TC/G	FA
1996	CIN N	2	0	1.000	4.50	3	3	0	16	17	7	14	0	0	0	0	5	0	0	.000	0	2	0	0	0.7	1.000

Bob MacDonald
MacDONALD, ROBERT JOSEPH
B. Apr. 27, 1965, East Orange, N. J.
BL TL 6'3" 200 lbs.

Year	Team	W	L	PCT	ERA	G	GS	CG	IP	H	BB	SO	ShO	W	L	SV	AB	H	HR	BA	PO	A	E	DP	TC/G	FA
1990	TOR A	0	0	—	0.00	4	0	0	2.1	0	2	0	0	0	0	0	0	0	0	—	0	0	0	0	0.0	.000
1991		3	3	.500	2.85	45	0	0	53.2	51	25	24	0	3	3	0	0	0	0	—	4	5	0	0	0.2	1.000
1992		1	0	1.000	4.37	27	0	0	47.1	50	16	26	0	1	0	0	0	0	0	—	2	2	0	0	0.1	1.000
1993	DET A	3	3	.500	5.35	68	0	0	65.2	67	33	39	0	3	3	3	0	0	0	—	3	13	1	0	0.3	.941
1995	NY A	1	1	.500	4.86	33	0	0	46.1	50	22	41	0	1	1	0	0	0	0	—	2	4	0	0	0.2	1.000
1996	NY N	0	2	.000	4.26	20	0	0	19	16	9	12	0	0	2	0	0	0	0	—	1	2	0	0	0.2	1.000
	6 yrs.	8	9	.471	4.34	197	0	0	234.1	234	107	142	0	8	9	3	0	0	0		12	26	1	0	0.2	.974

LEAGUE CHAMPIONSHIP SERIES

Year	Team	W	L	PCT	ERA	G	GS	CG	IP	H	BB	SO	ShO	W	L	SV	AB	H	HR	BA	PO	A	E	DP	TC/G	FA
1991	TOR A	0	0	—	9.00	1	0	0	1	1	1	0	0	0	0	0	0	0	0	—	0	0	0	0	0.0	.000

Greg Maddux
MADDUX, GREGORY ALAN
Brother of Mike Maddux.
B. Apr. 14, 1966, San Angelo, Tex.
BR TR 6' 170 lbs.

Year	Team	W	L	PCT	ERA	G	GS	CG	IP	H	BB	SO	ShO	W	L	SV	AB	H	HR	BA	PO	A	E	DP	TC/G	FA
1986	CHI N	2	4	.333	5.52	6	5	1	31	44	11	20	0	0	1	0	12	4	0	.333	1	6	1	0	1.3	.875
1987		6	14	.300	5.61	30	27	1	155.2	181	74	101	1	0	0	0	42	5	0	.119	16	50	4	7	2.3	.943
1988		18	8	.692	3.18	34	34	9	249	230	81	140	3	0	0	0	96	19	0	.198	28	45	3	3	2.2	.961
1989		19	12	.613	2.95	35	35	7	238.1	222	82	135	1	0	0	0	81	17	0	.210	35	41	3	4	2.3	.962
1990		15	15	.500	3.46	35	35	8	237	242	71	144	2	0	0	0	83	12	0	.145	39	55	0	6	2.7	1.000
1991		15	11	.577	3.35	37	37	7	263	232	66	198	2	0	0	0	88	18	1	.205	39	50	2	5	2.5	.978
1992		20	11	.645	2.18	35	35	9	268	201	70	199	4	0	0	0	88	15	1	.170	30	64	3	1	2.8	.969
1993	ATL N	20	10	.667	2.36	36	36	8	267	228	52	197	1	0	0	0	91	15	0	.165	39	59	7	5	2.9	.933
1994		16	6	.727	1.56	25	25	10	202	150	31	156	3	0	0	0	63	14	0	.222	20	37	4	4	2.4	.934
1995		19	2	.905	1.63	28	28	10	209.2	147	23	181	3	0	0	0	72	11	0	.153	18	53	0	4	2.5	1.000
1996		15	11	.577	2.72	35	35	5	245	225	28	172	1	0	0	0	68	10	0	.147	35	69	1	6	3.1	.990
	11 yrs.	165	104	.613	2.86	336	332	75	2365.2	2102	589	1643	21	0	1	0	784	140	2	.179	300	529	28	45	2.6	.967

DIVISIONAL PLAYOFF SERIES

Year	Team	W	L	PCT	ERA	G	GS	CG	IP	H	BB	SO	ShO	W	L	SV	AB	H	HR	BA	PO	A	E	DP	TC/G	FA
1995	ATL N	1	0	1.000	4.50	2	2	0	14	19	2	7	0	0	0	0	6	1	0	.167	1	4	0	1	2.5	1.000
1996		1	0	1.000	0.00	1	1	0	7	3	0	7	0	0	0	0	2	0	0	.000	2	2	0	0	4.0	1.000
	2 yrs.	2	0	1.000	3.00	3	3	0	21	22	2	14	0	0	0	0	8	1	0	.125	3	6	0	1	3.0	1.000

LEAGUE CHAMPIONSHIP SERIES

Year	Team	W	L	PCT	ERA	G	GS	CG	IP	H	BB	SO	ShO	W	L	SV	AB	H	HR	BA	PO	A	E	DP	TC/G	FA
1989	CHI N	0	1	.000	13.50	2	2	0	7.1	13	4	5	0	0	0	0	3	0	0	.000	0	1	0	0	0.5	.000
1993	ATL N	1	1	.500	4.97	2	2	0	12.2	11	7	11	0	0	0	0	4	1	0	.250	3	5	1	0	4.5	.889
1995		1	0	1.000	1.13	1	1	0	8	7	2	4	0	0	0	0	3	0	0	.000	1	1	0	0	2.0	1.000
1996		1	1	.500	2.51	2	2	0	14.1	15	2	10	0	0	0	0	4	0	0	.000	1	4	0	0	2.5	1.000
	4 yrs.	3	3	.500 6th	4.89	7	7	0	42.1	46	15	30	0	0	0	0	14	1	0	.071	5	10	2	0	2.4	.882

WORLD SERIES

Year	Team	W	L	PCT	ERA	G	GS	CG	IP	H	BB	SO	ShO	W	L	SV	AB	H	HR	BA	PO	A	E	DP	TC/G	FA
1995	ATL N	1	1	.500	2.25	2	2	1	16	9	3	8	0	0	0	0	3	0	0	.000	2	4	0	0	3.0	1.000
1996		1	1	.500	1.72	2	2	0	15.2	14	1	5	0	0	0	0	0	0	0	—	2	7	0	0	4.5	1.000
	2 yrs.	2	2	.500	1.99	4	4	1	31.2	23	4	13	0	0	0	0	3	0	0	.000	4	11	0	0	3.8	1.000

Mike Maddux
MADDUX, MICHAEL AUSLEY
Brother of Greg Maddux.
B. Aug. 27, 1961, Dayton, Ohio
BL TR 6'2" 180 lbs.

Year	Team	W	L	PCT	ERA	G	GS	CG	IP	H	BB	SO	ShO	W	L	SV	AB	H	HR	BA	PO	A	E	DP	TC/G	FA
1986	PHI N	3	7	.300	5.42	16	16	0	78	88	34	44	0	0	0	0	22	1	0	.045	5	10	2	0	1.1	.882
1987		2	0	1.000	2.65	7	2	0	17	17	5	15	0	1	0	0	3	0	0	.000	1	1	1	0	0.4	.667
1988		4	3	.571	3.76	25	11	0	88.2	91	34	59	0	2	0	0	23	3	0	.130	8	18	4	1	1.2	.867
1989		1	3	.250	5.15	16	4	2	43.2	52	14	26	1	0	1	1	10	0	0	.000	7	12	0	1	1.2	1.000
1990	LA N	0	1	.000	6.53	11	2	0	20.2	24	4	11	0	0	0	0	2	0	0	.000	0	2	0	0	0.2	1.000

Year	Team	W	L	PCT	ERA	G	GS	CG	IP	H	BB	SO	ShO	W	L	SV	AB	H	HR	BA	PO	A	E	DP	TC/G	FA
														Relief Pitching			**Batting**									

Mike Maddux *continued*

Year	Team	W	L	PCT	ERA	G	GS	CG	IP	H	BB	SO	ShO	W	L	SV	AB	H	HR	BA	PO	A	E	DP	TC/G	FA
1991	SD N	7	2	.778	2.46	64	1	0	98.2	78	27	57	0	6	2	5	13	1	0	.077	9	18	1	1	0.4	.964
1992		2	2	.500	2.37	50	1	0	79.2	71	24	60	0	2	1	5	9	1	0	.111	9	18	1	1	0.6	.964
1993	NY N	3	8	.273	3.60	58	0	0	75	67	27	57	0	3	8	5	3	0	0	.000	6	16	1	1	0.4	.957
1994		2	1	.667	5.11	27	0	0	44	45	13	32	0	2	1	2	3	0	0	.000	2	11	1	2	0.5	.929
1995	2 teams	PIT N	(8G 1-0)		**BOS A**	(36G 4-1)																				
"	total	5	1	.833	4.10	44	4	0	98.2	100	18	69	0	3	1	1	0	0	0	—	9	12	1	1	0.5	.955
1996	BOS A	3	2	.600	4.48	23	7	0	64.1	76	27	32	0	0	1	0	0	0	0	—	7	12	0	1	0.8	1.000
	11 yrs.	32	30	.516	3.93	341	48	2	708.1	709	227	462	1	19	15	19	88	6	0	.068	63	130	12	10	0.6	.941

DIVISIONAL PLAYOFF SERIES

Year	Team	W	L	PCT	ERA	G	GS	CG	IP	H	BB	SO	ShO	W	L	SV	AB	H	HR	BA	PO	A	E	DP	TC/G	FA
1995	BOS A	0	0	—	0.00	2	0	0	3	2	1	1	0	0	0	0	0	0	0	—	1	2	0	0	1.5	1.000

Calvin Maduro

MADURO, CALVIN GREGORY
B. Sept 5, 1974, Santa Cruz, Aruba — BR TR 6' 175 lbs.

Year	Team	W	L	PCT	ERA	G	GS	CG	IP	H	BB	SO	ShO	W	L	SV	AB	H	HR	BA	PO	A	E	DP	TC/G	FA
1996	PHI N	0	1	.000	3.52	4	2	0	15.1	13	3	11	0	0	0	0	4	0	0	.000	0	1	0	0	0.3	1.000

Mike Magnante

MAGNANTE, MICHAEL ANTHONY
B. Sept 5, 1965, Glendale, Calif. — BL TL 6'1" 180 lbs.

Year	Team	W	L	PCT	ERA	G	GS	CG	IP	H	BB	SO	ShO	W	L	SV	AB	H	HR	BA	PO	A	E	DP	TC/G	FA
1991	KC A	0	1	.000	2.45	38	0	0	55	55	23	42	0	0	1	0	0	0	0	—	3	6	1	1	0.3	.900
1992		4	9	.308	4.94	44	12	0	89.1	115	35	31	0	1	4	0	0	0	0	—	9	20	0	3	0.7	1.000
1993		1	2	.333	4.08	7	6	0	35.1	37	11	16	0	0	0	0	0	0	0	—	4	6	0	1	1.4	1.000
1994		2	3	.400	4.60	36	1	0	47	55	16	21	0	2	2	0	0	0	0	—	4	7	1	1	0.3	.917
1995		1	1	.500	4.23	28	0	0	44.2	45	16	28	0	1	1	0	0	0	0	—	8	9	2	2	0.7	.895
1996		2	2	.500	5.67	38	0	0	54	58	24	32	0	2	2	0	0	0	0	—	4	15	0	2	0.5	1.000
	6 yrs.	10	18	.357	4.40	191	19	0	325.1	365	125	170	0	6	10	0	0	0	0		32	63	4	10	0.5	.960

Joe Magrane

MAGRANE, JOSEPH DAVID
B. July 2, 1964, Des Moines, Iowa — BR TL 6'6" 225 lbs.

Year	Team	W	L	PCT	ERA	G	GS	CG	IP	H	BB	SO	ShO	W	L	SV	AB	H	HR	BA	PO	A	E	DP	TC/G	FA
1987	STL N	9	7	.563	3.54	27	26	4	170.1	157	60	101	2	0	0	0	52	7	1	.135	10	26	3	3	1.4	.923
1988		5	9	.357	**2.18**	24	24	4	165.1	133	51	100	3	0	0	0	48	8	1	.167	16	37	5	0	2.4	.914
1989		18	9	.667	2.91	34	33	9	234.2	219	72	127	3	0	0	0	80	11	1	.138	11	31	2	1	1.3	.955
1990		10	17	.370	3.59	31	31	3	203.1	204	59	100	2	0	0	0	55	7	0	.127	8	38	1	1	1.5	.979
1992		1	2	.333	4.02	5	5	0	31.1	34	15	20	0	0	0	0	10	2	1	.200	1	5	0	1	1.2	1.000
1993	2 teams	STL N	(22G 8-10)		**CAL A**	(8G 3-2)																				
"	total	11	12	.478	4.66	30	28	0	164	175	58	62	0	0	1	0	35	4	0	.114	12	36	2	3	1.7	.960
1994	CAL A	2	6	.250	7.30	20	11	1	74	89	51	33	0	0	0	0	0	0	0	—	2	10	0	1	0.6	1.000
1996	CHI A	1	5	.167	6.88	19	8	0	53.2	70	25	21	0	1	0	0	0	0	0	—	2	8	2	0	0.6	.833
	8 yrs.	57	67	.460	3.81	190	166	21	1096.2	1081	391	564	10	1	2	0	280	39	4	.139	62	191	15	9	1.4	.944

LEAGUE CHAMPIONSHIP SERIES

Year	Team	W	L	PCT	ERA	G	GS	CG	IP	H	BB	SO	ShO	W	L	SV	AB	H	HR	BA	PO	A	E	DP	TC/G	FA
1987	STL N	0	0	—	9.00	1	1	0	4	4	2	3	0	0	0	0	1	0	0	.000	0	1	0	0	1.0	1.000

WORLD SERIES

Year	Team	W	L	PCT	ERA	G	GS	CG	IP	H	BB	SO	ShO	W	L	SV	AB	H	HR	BA	PO	A	E	DP	TC/G	FA
1987	STL N	0	1	.000	8.59	2	2	0	7.1	9	5	5	0	0	0	0	0	0	0	—	1	0	0	0	1.0	1.000

Pat Mahomes

MAHOMES, PATRICK LAVON
B. Aug. 9, 1970, Bryan, Tex. — BR TR 6'1" 175 lbs.

Year	Team	W	L	PCT	ERA	G	GS	CG	IP	H	BB	SO	ShO	W	L	SV	AB	H	HR	BA	PO	A	E	DP	TC/G	FA
1992	MIN A	3	4	.429	5.04	14	13	0	69.2	73	37	44	0	0	0	0	0	0	0	—	5	4	0	0	0.6	1.000
1993		1	5	.167	7.71	12	5	0	37.1	47	16	23	0	1	0	0	0	0	0	—	4	4	0	1	0.7	1.000
1994		9	5	.643	4.72	21	21	0	120	121	62	53	0	0	0	0	0	0	0	—	11	12	1	2	1.1	.958
1995		4	10	.286	6.37	47	7	0	94.2	100	47	67	0	4	6	3	0	0	0	—	11	9	0	3	0.4	1.000
1996	2 teams	MIN A	(20G 1-4)		**BOS A**	(11G 2-0)																				
"	total	3	4	.429	6.91	31	5	0	57.1	72	33	36	0	3	1	2	0	0	0	—	4	8	0	0	0.4	1.000
	5 yrs.	20	28	.417	5.82	125	51	0	379	413	195	223	0	8	7	5	0	0	0		35	37	1	6	0.6	.986

Matt Mantei

MANTEI, MATTHEW BRUCE
B. July 7, 1973, Tampa, Fla. — BR TR 6'1" 181 lbs.

Year	Team	W	L	PCT	ERA	G	GS	CG	IP	H	BB	SO	ShO	W	L	SV	AB	H	HR	BA	PO	A	E	DP	TC/G	FA
1995	FLA N	0	1	.000	4.72	12	0	0	13.1	12	13	15	0	0	1	0	0	0	0	—	1	2	0	2	0.3	1.000
1996		1	0	1.000	6.38	14	0	0	18.1	13	21	25	0	1	0	0	1	0	0	.000	3	4	0	0	0.5	1.000
	2 yrs.	1	1	.500	5.68	26	0	0	31.2	25	34	40	0	1	1	0	1	0	0	.000	4	6	0	2	0.4	1.000

Barry Manuel

MANUEL, BARRY PAUL
B. Aug. 12, 1965, Mamou, La. — BR TR 5'11" 175 lbs.

Year	Team	W	L	PCT	ERA	G	GS	CG	IP	H	BB	SO	ShO	W	L	SV	AB	H	HR	BA	PO	A	E	DP	TC/G	FA
1991	TEX A	1	0	1.000	1.13	8	0	0	16	7	6	5	0	1	0	0	0	0	0	—	0	6	0	1	0.8	1.000
1992		1	0	1.000	4.76	3	0	0	5.2	6	1	9	0	1	0	0	0	0	0	—	0	0	0	0	0.0	.000
1996	MON N	4	1	.800	3.24	53	0	0	86	70	26	62	0	4	1	0	7	0	0	.000	1	11	0	1	0.2	1.000
	3 yrs.	6	1	.857	3.01	64	0	0	107.2	83	33	76	0	6	1	0	7	0	0	.000	1	17	0	1	0.3	1.000

Dennis Martinez

MARTINEZ, JOSE DENNIS (El Presidente)
Born Jose Dennis Martinez (Emilia).
B. May 14, 1955, Granada, Nicaragua — BR TR 6'1" 175 lbs.

Year	Team	W	L	PCT	ERA	G	GS	CG	IP	H	BB	SO	ShO	W	L	SV	AB	H	HR	BA	PO	A	E	DP	TC/G	FA
1976	BAL A	1	2	.333	2.57	4	2	1	28	23	8	18	0	1	0	0	0	0	0	—	3	4	0	0	1.8	1.000
1977		14	7	.667	4.10	42	13	5	167	157	64	107	0	8	4	4	0	0	0	—	9	26	1	2	0.9	.972

Year	Team	W	L	PCT	ERA	G	GS	CG	IP	H	BB	SO	ShO	W	L	SV	AB	H	HR	BA	PO	A	E	DP	TC/G	FA
														Relief Pitching			Batting									

Dennis Martinez continued

Year	Team	W	L	PCT	ERA	G	GS	CG	IP	H	BB	SO	ShO	W	L	SV	AB	H	HR	BA	PO	A	E	DP	TC/G	FA
1978		16	11	.593	3.52	40	38	15	276.1	257	93	142	2	0	0	0	0	0	0	—	27	51	1	6	2.0	.987
1979		15	16	.484	3.67	40	39	18	292	279	78	132	3	0	0	0	0	0	0	—	26	59	5	3	2.3	.944
1980		6	4	.600	3.96	25	12	2	100	103	44	42	0	0	1	1	0	0	0	—	5	16	0	1	0.8	1.000
1981		14	5	.737	3.32	25	24	9	179	173	62	88	2	0	0	0	0	0	0	—	20	44	2	4	2.6	.970
1982		16	12	.571	4.21	40	39	10	252	262	87	111	2	0	0	0	0	0	0	—	13	38	1	2	1.3	.981
1983		7	16	.304	5.53	32	25	4	153	209	45	71	0	1	0	0	0	0	0	—	16	42	1	0	1.8	.983
1984		6	9	.400	5.02	34	20	2	141.2	145	37	77	0	1	2	0	0	0	0	—	17	19	2	4	1.1	.947
1985		13	11	.542	5.15	33	31	3	180	203	63	68	1	1	0	0	0	0	0	—	17	26	1	0	1.3	.977
1986	2 teams	BAL A		(4G 0-0)			MON N		(19G 3-6)																	
"	total	3	6	.333	4.73	23	15	1	104.2	114	30	65	1	0	0	0	30	3	0	.100	4	25	1	0	1.3	.967
1987	MON N	11	4	.733	3.30	22	22	2	144.2	133	40	84	1	0	0	0	46	3	0	.065	10	23	1	3	1.5	.971
1988		15	13	.536	2.72	34	34	9	235.1	215	55	120	2	0	0	0	78	15	0	.192	19	39	6	3	1.9	.906
1989		16	7	.696	3.18	34	33	5	232	227	49	142	2	0	1	0	72	9	0	.125	11	50	2	6	1.9	.968
1990		10	11	.476	2.95	32	32	7	226	191	49	156	2	0	0	0	68	7	0	.103	16	35	1	2	1.6	.981
1991		14	11	.560	2.39	31	31	9	222	187	62	123	5	0	0	0	72	11	0	.153	21	48	4	5	2.4	.945
1992		16	11	.593	2.47	32	32	6	226.1	172	60	147	0	0	0	0	74	14	0	.189	20	45	4	3	2.2	.942
1993		15	9	.625	3.85	35	34	2	224.2	211	64	138	0	0	0	1	69	11	0	.159	17	46	1	1	1.8	.984
1994	CLE A	11	6	.647	3.52	24	24	7	176.2	166	44	92	3	0	0	0	0	0	0	—	11	33	0	2	1.8	1.000
1995		12	5	.706	3.08	28	28	3	187	174	46	99	2	0	0	0	0	0	0	—	15	46	4	3	2.3	.938
1996		9	6	.600	4.50	20	20	1	112	122	37	48	1	0	0	0	0	0	0	—	11	25	1	1	1.9	.973
21 yrs.		240	182	.569	3.63	630	548	121	3860.1	3723	1117	2070	29	12	8	6	509	73	0	.143	308	740	39	51	1.7	.964

DIVISIONAL PLAYOFF SERIES

Year	Team	W	L	PCT	ERA	G	GS	CG	IP	H	BB	SO	ShO	W	L	SV	AB	H	HR	BA	PO	A	E	DP	TC/G	FA
1995	CLE A	0	0	—	3.00	1	1	0	6	5	0	2	0	0	0	0	0	0	0	—	0	1	0	0	1.0	1.000

LEAGUE CHAMPIONSHIP SERIES

Year	Team	W	L	PCT	ERA	G	GS	CG	IP	H	BB	SO	ShO	W	L	SV	AB	H	HR	BA	PO	A	E	DP	TC/G	FA
1979	BAL A	0	0	—	3.24	1	1	0	8.1	8	0	4	0	0	0	0	0	0	0	—	2	0	0	0	2.0	1.000
1995	CLE A	1	1	.500	2.02	2	2	0	13.1	10	3	7	0	0	0	0	0	0	0	—	1	1	0	0	1.0	1.000
2 yrs.		1	1	.500	2.49	3	3	0	21.2	18	3	11	0	0	0	0	0	0	0		3	1	0	0	1.3	1.000

WORLD SERIES

Year	Team	W	L	PCT	ERA	G	GS	CG	IP	H	BB	SO	ShO	W	L	SV	AB	H	HR	BA	PO	A	E	DP	TC/G	FA
1979	BAL A	0	0	—	18.00	2	1	0	2	6	0	0	0	0	0	0	0	0	0	—	0	1	0	0	0.5	1.000
1995	CLE A	0	1	.000	3.48	2	2	0	10.1	12	8	5	0	0	0	0	3	0	0	.000	0	3	1	0	2.0	.750
2 yrs.		0	1	.000	5.84	4	3	0	12.1	18	8	5	0	0	0	0	3	0	0	.000	0	4	1	1	1.3	.800

Pedro Martinez

MARTINEZ, PEDRO
Born Pedro Martinez (Aquino).
B. Nov. 29, 1968, Villa Mella, Dominican Republic

BL TL 6' 2" 155 lbs.

Year	Team	W	L	PCT	ERA	G	GS	CG	IP	H	BB	SO	ShO	W	L	SV	AB	H	HR	BA	PO	A	E	DP	TC/G	FA
1993	SD N	3	1	.750	2.43	32	0	0	37	23	13	32	0	3	1	0	4	0	0	.000	2	4	1	0	0.2	.857
1994		3	2	.600	2.90	48	1	0	68.1	52	49	52	0	3	2	3	5	0	0	.000	5	17	4	1	0.5	.846
1995	HOU N	0	0	—	7.40	25	0	0	20.2	29	16	17	0	0	0	0	0	0	0	—	3	2	0	0	0.2	1.000
1996	2 teams	NY N		(5G 0-0)			CIN N		(4G 0-0)																	
"	total	0	0		6.30	9	0	0	10	13	8	9	0	0	0	0	0	0	0	—	0	1	0	0	0.1	1.000
4 yrs.		6	3	.667	3.71	114	1	0	136	117	86	110	0	6	3	3	9	0	0	.000	10	24	5	1	0.3	.872

Pedro Martinez

MARTINEZ, PEDRO
Born Pedro Jaime (Martinez).
Brother of Ramon Martinez.
B. July 25, 1971, Manoguayabo, Dominican Republic

BR TR 5'11" 150 lbs.

Year	Team	W	L	PCT	ERA	G	GS	CG	IP	H	BB	SO	ShO	W	L	SV	AB	H	HR	BA	PO	A	E	DP	TC/G	FA
1992	LA N	0	1	.000	2.25	2	1	0	8	6	1	8	0	0	0	0	2	0	0	.000	0	0	0	0	0.0	.000
1993		10	5	.667	2.61	65	2	0	107	76	57	119	0	10	3	2	4	0	0	.000	4	4	0	1	0.1	1.000
1994	MON N	11	5	.688	3.42	24	23	1	144.2	115	45	142	1	0	0	1	44	4	0	.091	9	15	4	0	1.2	.857
1995		14	10	.583	3.51	30	30	2	194.2	158	66	174	2	0	0	0	63	7	0	.111	13	23	2	0	1.3	.947
1996		13	10	.565	3.70	33	33	4	216.2	189	70	222	1	0	0	0	64	6	0	.094	11	17	3	1	0.9	.903
5 yrs.		48	31	.608	3.39	154	89	7	671	544	239	665	4	10	3	3	177	17	0	.096	37	59	9	2	0.7	.914

Ramon Martinez

MARTINEZ, RAMON
Born Ramon Jaime (Martinez).
Brother of Pedro Martinez.
B. Mar. 22, 1968, Santo Domingo, Dominican Republic

BR TR 6' 4" 165 lbs.

Year	Team	W	L	PCT	ERA	G	GS	CG	IP	H	BB	SO	ShO	W	L	SV	AB	H	HR	BA	PO	A	E	DP	TC/G	FA
1988	LA N	1	3	.250	3.79	9	6	0	35.2	27	22	23	0	0	0	0	7	0	0	.000	1	5	0	0	0.7	1.000
1989		6	4	.600	3.19	15	15	2	98.2	79	41	89	2	0	0	0	37	6	0	.162	11	14	0	1	1.7	1.000
1990		20	6	.769	2.92	33	33	12	234.1	191	67	223	3	0	0	0	80	10	0	.125	16	27	1	0	1.3	.977
1991		17	13	.567	3.27	33	33	6	220.1	190	69	150	4	0	0	0	79	9	1	.117	22	21	2	0	1.4	.956
1992		8	11	.421	4.00	25	25	1	150.2	141	69	101	1	0	0	0	50	6	0	.120	10	18	2	1	1.2	.933
1993		10	12	.455	3.44	32	32	4	211.2	202	104	127	3	0	0	0	70	9	0	.129	28	31	0	4	1.8	1.000
1994		12	7	.632	3.97	24	24	4	170	160	56	119	3	0	0	0	66	18	0	.273	21	17	3	0	1.7	.927
1995		17	7	.708	3.66	30	30	4	206.1	176	81	138	2	0	0	0	64	11	0	.172	16	27	3	2	1.5	.935
1996		15	6	.714	3.42	28	27	2	168.2	153	86	134	2	0	1	0	59	7	0	.119	6	28	2	1	1.3	.944
9 yrs.		106	69	.606	3.47	229	225	35	1496.1	1319	595	1104	20	0	1	0	510	76	1	.149	131	188	13	9	1.4	.961

DIVISIONAL PLAYOFF SERIES

Year	Team	W	L	PCT	ERA	G	GS	CG	IP	H	BB	SO	ShO	W	L	SV	AB	H	HR	BA	PO	A	E	DP	TC/G	FA
1995	LA N	0	1	.000	14.54	1	1	0	4.1	10	2	3	0	0	0	0	1	0	0	.000	0	1	0	0	1.0	1.000
1996		0	0	—	1.13	1	1	0	8	3	3	6	0	0	0	0	3	0	0	.000	0	0	0	0	0.0	.000
2 yrs.		0	1	.000	5.84	2	2	0	12.1	13	5	9	0	0	0	0	4	0	0	.000	0	1	0	0	0.5	1.000

Year	Team	W	L	PCT	ERA	G	GS	CG	IP	H	BB	SO	ShO	Relief Pitching W	L	SV	Batting AB	H	HR	BA	PO	A	E	DP	TC/G	FA

T. J. Mathews

MATHEWS, TIMOTHY JAY
Son of Nelson Mathews.
B. Jan. 9, 1970, Belleville, Ill.
BR TR 6' 2" 200 lbs.

Year	Team	W	L	PCT	ERA	G	GS	CG	IP	H	BB	SO	ShO	W	L	SV	AB	H	HR	BA	PO	A	E	DP	TC/G	FA
1995	STL N	1	1	.500	1.52	23	0	0	29.2	21	11	28	0	1	1	2	2	0	0	.000	4	5	1	1	0.4	.900
1996		2	6	.250	3.01	67	0	0	83.2	62	32	80	0	2	6	6	4	0	0	.000	0	6	2	0	0.1	.750
2 yrs.		3	7	.300	2.62	90	0	0	113.1	83	43	108	0	3	7	8	6	0	0	.000	4	11	3	1	0.2	.833

DIVISIONAL PLAYOFF SERIES
| 1996 | STL N | 1 | 0 | 1.000 | 0.00 | 1 | 0 | 0 | 1 | 1 | 0 | 2 | 0 | 1 | 0 | 0 | 0 | 0 | 0 | — | 0 | 0 | 0 | 0 | 0.0 | .000 |

LEAGUE CHAMPIONSHIP SERIES
| 1996 | STL N | 0 | 0 | — | 0.00 | 2 | 0 | 0 | 0.2 | 2 | 1 | 2 | 0 | 0 | 0 | 0 | 0 | 0 | 0 | — | 0 | 0 | 0 | 0 | 0.0 | .000 |

Terry Mathews

MATHEWS, TERRY ALAN
B. Oct. 5, 1964, Alexandria, Va.
BL TR 6' 2" 200 lbs.

Year	Team	W	L	PCT	ERA	G	GS	CG	IP	H	BB	SO	ShO	W	L	SV	AB	H	HR	BA	PO	A	E	DP	TC/G	FA
1991	TEX A	4	0	1.000	3.61	34	2	0	57.1	54	18	51	0	4	0	1	0	0	0	—	8	5	0	0	0.4	1.000
1992		2	4	.333	5.95	40	0	0	42.1	48	31	26	0	2	4	0	0	0	0	—	5	4	0	1	0.2	1.000
1994	FLA N	2	1	.667	3.35	24	2	0	43	45	9	21	0	1	0	0	6	3	0	.500	5	6	0	1	0.5	1.000
1995		4	4	.500	3.38	57	0	0	82.2	70	27	72	0	4	4	3	13	6	0	.462	6	9	0	0	0.3	1.000
1996	2 teams FLA N (57G 2-4) BAL A (14G 2-2)																									
"	total	4	6	.400	4.52	71	0	0	73.2	79	34	62	0	4	6	4	4	0	0	.000	10	6	1	2	0.2	.941
5 yrs.		16	15	.516	4.06	226	4	0	299	296	119	232	0	15	14	8	23	9	0	.391	34	30	1	4	0.3	.985

DIVISIONAL PLAYOFF SERIES
| 1996 | BAL A | 0 | 0 | — | 0.00 | 3 | 0 | 0 | 2.2 | 3 | 1 | 2 | 0 | 0 | 0 | 0 | 0 | 0 | 0 | — | 0 | 1 | 0 | 0 | 0.3 | 1.000 |

LEAGUE CHAMPIONSHIP SERIES
| 1996 | BAL A | 0 | 0 | — | 0.00 | 3 | 0 | 0 | 2.1 | 0 | 2 | 3 | 0 | 0 | 0 | 0 | 0 | 0 | 0 | — | 0 | 0 | 0 | 0 | 0.0 | 1.000 |

Brian Maxcy

MAXCY, DAVID BRIAN
B. May 4, 1971, Amory, Miss.
BR TR 6' 1" 170 lbs.

Year	Team	W	L	PCT	ERA	G	GS	CG	IP	H	BB	SO	ShO	W	L	SV	AB	H	HR	BA	PO	A	E	DP	TC/G	FA
1995	DET A	4	5	.444	6.88	41	0	0	52.1	61	31	20	0	4	5	0	0	0	0	—	6	14	2	1	0.5	.909
1996		0	0	—	13.50	2	0	0	3.1	8	2	1	0	0	0	0	0	0	0	—	1	1	0	0	1.0	1.000
2 yrs.		4	5	.444	7.28	43	0	0	55.2	69	33	21	0	4	5	0					7	15	2	1	0.6	.917

Darrell May

MAY, DARRELL KEVIN
B. June 13, 1972, San Bernardino, Calif.
BL TL 6' 2" 170 lbs.

Year	Team	W	L	PCT	ERA	G	GS	CG	IP	H	BB	SO	ShO	W	L	SV	AB	H	HR	BA	PO	A	E	DP	TC/G	FA
1995	ATL N	0	0	—	11.25	2	0	0	4	10	1	0	0	0	0	0	0	0	0	—	0	1	0	0	0.5	1.000
1996	2 teams PIT N (5G 0-1) CAL A (5G 0-0)																									
"	total	0	1	.000	9.53	10	2	0	11.1	18	6	6	0	0	0	0	3	1	0	.333	0	2	0	0	0.2	1.000
2 yrs.		0	1	.000	9.98	12	2	0	15.1	28	6	7	0	0	0	0	3	1	0	.333	0	3	0	0	0.3	1.000

Greg McCarthy

McCARTHY, GREGORY O'NEILL
B. Oct. 30, 1968, Norwalk, Conn.
BL TL 6' 2" 195 lbs.

Year	Team	W	L	PCT	ERA	G	GS	CG	IP	H	BB	SO	ShO	W	L	SV	AB	H	HR	BA	PO	A	E	DP	TC/G	FA
1996	SEA A	0	0	—	1.86	10	0	0	9.2	8	4	7	0	0	0	0	0	0	0	—	0	3	0	1	0.3	1.000

Kirk McCaskill

McCASKILL, KIRK EDWARD
B. Apr. 9, 1961, Kapuskasing, Ont., Canada.
BR TR 6' 1" 185 lbs.

Year	Team	W	L	PCT	ERA	G	GS	CG	IP	H	BB	SO	ShO	W	L	SV	AB	H	HR	BA	PO	A	E	DP	TC/G	FA
1985	CAL A	12	12	.500	4.70	30	29	6	189.2	189	64	102	1	0	0	0	0	0	0	—	11	27	3	1	1.4	.927
1986		17	10	.630	3.36	34	33	10	246.1	207	92	202	2	0	0	0	0	0	0	—	24	26	1	0	1.5	.980
1987		4	6	.400	5.67	14	13	1	74.2	84	34	56	1	0	0	0	0	0	0	—	8	12	1	1	1.5	.952
1988		8	6	.571	4.31	23	23	4	146.1	155	61	98	2	0	0	0	0	0	0	—	12	18	3	2	1.4	.909
1989		15	10	.600	2.93	32	32	6	212	202	59	107	4	0	0	0	0	0	0	—	16	42	3	5	1.9	.951
1990		12	11	.522	3.25	29	29	2	174.1	161	72	78	1	0	0	0	0	0	0	—	19	29	3	4	1.8	.941
1991		10	19	.345	4.26	30	30	1	177.2	193	66	71	0	0	0	0	0	0	0	—	17	25	1	4	1.4	.977
1992	CHI A	12	13	.480	4.18	34	34	0	209	193	95	109	0	0	0	0	0	0	0	—	24	31	2	0	1.7	.965
1993		4	8	.333	5.23	30	14	0	113.2	144	36	65	0	0	1	2	0	0	0	—	7	23	2	4	1.1	.938
1994		1	4	.200	3.42	40	0	0	52.2	51	22	37	0	1	4	3	0	0	0	—	4	8	0	0	0.3	1.000
1995		6	4	.600	4.89	55	1	0	81	97	33	50	0	6	4	2	0	0	0	—	5	13	2	0	0.4	.900
1996		5	5	.500	6.97	29	4	0	51.2	72	31	28	0	4	4	0	0	0	0	—	3	12	0	1	0.5	1.000
12 yrs.		106	108	.495	4.12	380	242	30	1729	1748	665	1003	11	11	13	7	0	0	0	—	150	266	21	20	1.1	.952

LEAGUE CHAMPIONSHIP SERIES
1986	CAL A	0	2	.000	7.71	2	2	0	9.1	16	5	7	0	0	0	0	0	0	0	—	0	0	0	0	0.0	.000
1993	CHI A	0	0	—	0.00	3	0	0	3.2	3	1	3	0	0	0	0	0	0	0	—	0	2	0	0	0.7	1.000
2 yrs.		0	2	.000	5.54	5	2	0	13	19	6	10	0	0	0	0	0	0	0	—	0	2	0	0	0.4	1.000

Jeff McCurry

McCURRY, JEFFREY DEE
B. Jan. 21, 1970, Tokyo, Japan
BR TR 6' 7" 210 lbs.

Year	Team	W	L	PCT	ERA	G	GS	CG	IP	H	BB	SO	ShO	W	L	SV	AB	H	HR	BA	PO	A	E	DP	TC/G	FA
1995	PIT N	1	4	.200	5.02	55	0	0	61	82	30	27	0	1	4	1	3	0	0	.000	1	12	0	0	0.2	1.000
1996	DET A	0	0	—	24.30	2	0	0	3.1	9	2	0	0	0	0	0	0	0	0	—	0	4	0	0	2.0	1.000
2 yrs.		1	4	.200	6.02	57	0	0	64.1	91	32	27	0	1	4	1	3	0	0	.000	1	16	0	0	0.3	1.000

Ben McDonald

McDONALD, LARRY BENARD (Big Ben)
B. Nov. 24, 1967, Baton Rouge, La.
BR TR 6' 7" 212 lbs.

Year	Team	W	L	PCT	ERA	G	GS	CG	IP	H	BB	SO	ShO	W	L	SV	AB	H	HR	BA	PO	A	E	DP	TC/G	FA
1989	BAL A	1	0	1.000	8.59	6	0	0	7.1	8	4	3	0	1	0	0	0	0	0	—	0	2	0	0	0.3	1.000
1990		8	5	.615	2.43	21	15	3	118.2	88	35	65	2	0	0	0	0	0	0	—	15	14	1	1	1.4	.967
1991		6	8	.429	4.84	21	21	1	126.1	126	43	85	0	0	0	0	0	0	0	—	12	8	0	1	1.0	1.000

Year	Team	W	L	PCT	ERA	G	GS	CG	IP	H	BB	SO	ShO	W	L	SV	AB	H	HR	BA	PO	A	E	DP	TC/G	FA

Ben McDonald *continued*

Year	Team	W	L	PCT	ERA	G	GS	CG	IP	H	BB	SO	ShO	W	L	SV	AB	H	HR	BA	PO	A	E	DP	TC/G	FA
1992		13	13	.500	4.24	35	35	4	227	213	74	158	2	0	0	0	0	0	0	—	22	29	0	2	1.5	1.000
1993		13	14	.481	3.39	34	34	7	220.1	185	86	171	1	0	0	0	0	0	0	—	15	42	2	2	1.7	.966
1994		14	7	.667	4.06	24	24	5	157.1	151	54	94	1	0	0	0	0	0	0	—	7	25	0	1	1.3	1.000
1995		3	6	.333	4.16	14	13	1	80	67	38	62	0	0	0	0	0	0	0	—	5	13	1	0	1.4	.947
1996	MIL A	12	10	.545	3.90	35	35	2	221.1	228	67	146	0	0	0	0	0	0	0	—	13	30	6	3	1.4	.878
8 yrs.		70	63	.526	3.89	190	177	23	1158.1	1066	401	784	6	1	0	0	0	0	0		89	163	10	10	1.4	.962

Jack McDowell

McDOWELL, JACK BURNS (Black Jack)
B. Jan. 16, 1966, Van Nuys, Calif.   BR TR 6'5" 180 lbs.

Year	Team	W	L	PCT	ERA	G	GS	CG	IP	H	BB	SO	ShO	W	L	SV	AB	H	HR	BA	PO	A	E	DP	TC/G	FA
1987	CHI A	3	0	1.000	1.93	4	4	0	28	16	6	15	0	0	0	0	0	0	0	—	1	6	0	0	1.8	1.000
1988		5	10	.333	3.97	26	26	1	158.2	147	68	84	0	0	0	0	0	0	0	—	12	16	5	1	1.3	.848
1990		14	9	.609	3.82	33	33	4	205	189	77	165	0	0	0	0	0	0	0	—	17	20	1	3	1.2	.974
1991		17	10	.630	3.41	35	35	15	253.2	212	82	191	3	0	0	0	0	0	0	—	19	32	0	1	1.5	1.000
1992		20	10	.667	3.18	34	34	13	260.2	247	75	178	1	0	0	0	0	0	0	—	16	27	2	3	1.3	.956
1993		22	10	.688	3.37	34	34	10	256.2	261	69	158	4	0	0	0	0	0	0	—	23	43	3	2	2.0	.957
1994		10	9	.526	3.73	25	25	6	181	186	42	127	2	0	0	0	0	0	0	—	8	24	0	0	1.3	1.000
1995	NY A	15	10	.600	3.93	30	30	8	217.2	211	78	157	2	0	0	0	0	0	0	—	18	23	1	1	1.4	.976
1996	CLE A	13	9	.591	5.11	30	30	5	192	214	67	141	1	0	0	0	0	0	0	—	20	26	1	0	1.6	.979
9 yrs.		119	77	.607	3.73	251	251	62	1753.1	1683	564	1216	13	0	0	0	0	0	0		134	217	13	11	1.5	.964

DIVISIONAL PLAYOFF SERIES

Year	Team	W	L	PCT	ERA	G	GS	CG	IP	H	BB	SO	ShO	W	L	SV	AB	H	HR	BA	PO	A	E	DP	TC/G	FA
1995	NY A	0	2	.000	9.00	2	1	0	7	8	4	6	0	0	1	0	0	0	0	—	0	0	0	0	0.0	.000
1996	CLE A	0	0	—	6.35	1	1	0	5.2	6	1	5	0	0	0	0	0	0	0		0	0	0	0	0.0	—
2 yrs.		0	2	.000	7.82	3	2	0	12.2	14	5	11	0	0	1	0					1	2	0	0	1.0	1.000

LEAGUE CHAMPIONSHIP SERIES

Year	Team	W	L	PCT	ERA	G	GS	CG	IP	H	BB	SO	ShO	W	L	SV	AB	H	HR	BA	PO	A	E	DP	TC/G	FA
1993	CHI A	0	2	.000	10.00	2	2	0	9	18	5	5	0	0	0	0	0	0	0	—	0	1	1	0	1.0	.500

Roger McDowell

McDOWELL, ROGER ALAN
B. Dec. 21, 1960, Cincinnati, Ohio   BR TR 6'1" 175 lbs.

Year	Team	W	L	PCT	ERA	G	GS	CG	IP	H	BB	SO	ShO	W	L	SV	AB	H	HR	BA	PO	A	E	DP	TC/G	FA
1985	NY N	6	5	.545	2.83	62	2	0	127.1	108	37	70	0	6	4	17	19	3	0	.158	17	27	4	2	0.8	.917
1986		14	9	.609	3.02	75	0	0	128	107	42	65	0	14	9	22	18	5	0	.278	17	30	0	0	0.6	1.000
1987		7	5	.583	4.16	56	0	0	88.2	95	28	32	0	7	5	25	13	3	0	.231	10	17	0	1	0.5	1.000
1988		5	5	.500	2.63	62	0	0	89	80	31	46	0	5	5	16	9	3	0	.333	11	19	1	0	0.5	.968
1989	2 teams			NY N (25G 1-5)		PHI N	(44G 3-3)																				
"	total	4	8	.333	1.96	69	0	0	92	79	38	47	0	4	8	23	3	1	0	.333	17	25	3	3	0.7	.933
1990	PHI N	6	8	.429	3.86	72	0	0	86.1	92	35	39	0	6	8	22	2	0	0	.000	1	23	5	2	0.4	.828
1991	2 teams			PHI N (38G 3-6)		LA N	(33G 6-3)																				
"	total	9	9	.500	2.93	71	0	0	101.1	100	48	50	0	9	9	10	3	0	0	.000	8	25	3	3	0.5	.917
1992	LA N	6	10	.375	4.09	65	0	0	83.2	103	42	50	0	6	10	14	3	0	0	.000	8	21	3	2	0.5	.906
1993		5	3	.625	2.25	54	0	0	68	76	30	27	0	5	3	2	2	1	0	.500	11	24	3	3	0.7	.921
1994		0	3	.000	5.23	32	0	0	41.1	50	22	29	0	0	3	0	1	0	0	.000	2	7	0	0	0.3	1.000
1995	TEX A	7	4	.636	4.02	64	0	0	85	86	34	49	0	7	4	4	0	0	0	—	8	20	1	3	0.5	.966
1996	BAL A	1	1	.500	4.25	41	0	0	59.1	69	23	20	0	1	1	4	0	0	0	—	8	14	1	2	0.6	.957
12 yrs.		70	70	.500	3.30	723	2	0	1050	1045	410	524	0	70	69	159	72	16	0	.222	118	252	24	23	0.5	.939

LEAGUE CHAMPIONSHIP SERIES

Year	Team	W	L	PCT	ERA	G	GS	CG	IP	H	BB	SO	ShO	W	L	SV	AB	H	HR	BA	PO	A	E	DP	TC/G	FA
1986	NY N	0	0	—	0.00	2	0	0	7	1	0	3	0	0	0	0	1	0	0	.000	3	1	0	0	2.0	1.000
1988		0	1	.000	4.50	4	0	0	6	6	2	5	0	0	1	0	0	0	0	—	0	3	1	0	1.0	.750
2 yrs.		0	1	.000	2.08	6	0	0	13	7	2	8	0	0	1	0	1	0	0	.000	3	4	1	0	1.3	.875

WORLD SERIES

Year	Team	W	L	PCT	ERA	G	GS	CG	IP	H	BB	SO	ShO	W	L	SV	AB	H	HR	BA	PO	A	E	DP	TC/G	FA
1986	NY N	1	0	1.000	4.91	5	0	0	7.1	10	6	2	0	1	0	0	0	0	0	—	1	4	0	0	1.0	1.000

Chuck McElroy

McELROY, CHARLES DWAYNE
B. Oct. 1, 1967, Port Arthur, Tex.   BL TL 6' 160 lbs.

Year	Team	W	L	PCT	ERA	G	GS	CG	IP	H	BB	SO	ShO	W	L	SV	AB	H	HR	BA	PO	A	E	DP	TC/G	FA
1989	PHI N	0	0	—	1.74	11	0	0	10.1	12	4	8	0	0	0	0	0	0	0	—	1	0	0	0	0.1	1.000
1990		0	1	.000	7.71	16	0	0	14	24	10	16	0	0	1	0	0	0	0	—	1	0	1	0	0.1	.500
1991	CHI N	6	2	.750	1.95	71	0	0	101.1	73	57	92	0	6	2	3	10	3	0	.300	8	14	0	1	0.3	1.000
1992		4	7	.364	3.55	72	0	0	83.2	73	51	83	0	4	7	6	6	4	0	.667	3	8	1	2	0.2	.917
1993		2	2	.500	4.56	49	0	0	47.1	51	25	31	0	2	2	0	6	0	0	.000	3	5	0	1	0.2	1.000
1994	CIN N	1	2	.333	2.34	52	0	0	57.2	52	15	38	0	1	2	5	6	1	0	.167	1	5	0	0	0.1	1.000
1995		3	4	.429	6.02	44	0	0	40.1	46	15	27	0	3	4	0	3	0	0	.000	2	4	1	0	0.1	1.000
1996	2 teams			CIN N (12G 2-0)		CAL A	(40G 5-1)																				
"	total	7	1	.875	3.86	52	0	0	49	45	23	45	0	7	1	0	2	0	0	.000	3	12	1	1	0.3	.938
8 yrs.		23	19	.548	3.48	367	0	0	403.2	376	200	340	0	23	19	14	33	8	0	.242	22	48	3	6	0.2	.959

Greg McMichael

McMICHAEL, GREGORY WINSTON
B. Dec. 1, 1966, Knoxville, Tenn.   BR TR 6'3" 215 lbs.

Year	Team	W	L	PCT	ERA	G	GS	CG	IP	H	BB	SO	ShO	W	L	SV	AB	H	HR	BA	PO	A	E	DP	TC/G	FA
1993	ATL N	2	3	.400	2.06	74	0	0	91.2	68	29	89	0	2	3	19	4	0	0	.000	7	18	1	2	0.4	.962
1994		4	6	.400	3.84	51	0	0	58.2	66	19	47	0	4	6	21	1	0	0	.000	2	6	2	0	0.2	.800
1995		7	2	.778	2.79	67	0	0	80.2	64	32	74	0	7	2	2	6	0	0	.000	4	6	1	0	0.2	.909
1996		5	3	.625	3.22	73	0	0	86.2	84	27	78	0	5	3	2	0	0	0		4	17	1	1	0.3	.955
4 yrs.		18	14	.563	2.89	265	0	0	317.2	282	107	288	0	18	14	44	11	0	0	.000	17	47	5	3	0.3	.928

Year	Team	W	L	PCT	ERA	G	GS	CG	IP	H	BB	SO	ShO	Relief Pitching W	L	SV	Batting AB	H	HR	BA	PO	A	E	DP	TC/G	FA

Greg McMichael *continued*

DIVISIONAL PLAYOFF SERIES

Year	Team	W	L	PCT	ERA	G	GS	CG	IP	H	BB	SO	ShO	W	L	SV	AB	H	HR	BA	PO	A	E	DP	TC/G	FA
1995	ATL N	0	0	—	6.75	2	0	0	1.1	1	2	1	0	0	0	0	0	0	0	—	0	0	0	0	0.0	.000
1996		0	0	—	6.75	2	0	0	1.1	1	1	3	0	0	0	0	0	0	0	—	0	0	0	0	0.0	.000
2 yrs.		0	0		6.75	4	0	0	2.2	2	3	4	0	0	0	0	0	0	0		0	0	0	0	0.0	

LEAGUE CHAMPIONSHIP SERIES

Year	Team	W	L	PCT	ERA	G	GS	CG	IP	H	BB	SO	ShO	W	L	SV	AB	H	HR	BA	PO	A	E	DP	TC/G	FA
1993	ATL N	0	1	.000	6.75	4	0	0	4	7	2	1	0	0	1	0	0	0	0	—	0	1	0	0	0.3	1.000
1995		1	0	1.000	0.00	3	0	0	2.2	0	1	2	0	1	0	1	0	0	0	—	0	0	0	0	0.0	.000
1996		0	1	.000	9.00	3	0	0	2	4	1	3	0	0	1	0	0	0	0	—	0	0	0	0	0.0	.000
3 yrs.		1	2	.333	5.19	10	0	0	8.2	11	4	6	0	1	2	1	0	0	0		0	1	0	0	0.2	1.000

WORLD SERIES

Year	Team	W	L	PCT	ERA	G	GS	CG	IP	H	BB	SO	ShO	W	L	SV	AB	H	HR	BA	PO	A	E	DP	TC/G	FA
1995	ATL N	0	0	—	2.70	3	0	0	3.1	3	2	2	0	0	0	0	0	0	0	—	0	1	0	0	0.3	1.000
1996		0	0	—	27.00	2	0	0	1	5	0	1	0	0	0	0	0	0	0	—	0	0	0	0	0.0	.000
2 yrs.		0	0		8.31	5	0	0	4.1	8	2	3	0	0	0	0	0	0	0		0	1	0	0	0.2	1.000

Rusty Meacham

MEACHAM, RUSSELL LOREN
B. Jan. 27, 1968, Stuart, Fla.

BR TR 6'3" 155 lbs.

Year	Team	W	L	PCT	ERA	G	GS	CG	IP	H	BB	SO	ShO	W	L	SV	AB	H	HR	BA	PO	A	E	DP	TC/G	FA
1991	DET A	2	1	.667	5.20	10	4	0	27.2	35	11	14	0	0	0	0	0	0	0	—	4	4	0	0	0.8	1.000
1992	KC A	10	4	.714	2.74	64	0	0	101.2	88	21	64	0	10	4	2	0	0	0	—	13	18	1	1	0.5	.969
1993		2	2	.500	5.57	15	0	0	21	31	5	13	0	2	2	0	0	0	0	—	2	4	0	1	0.4	1.000
1994		3	3	.500	3.73	36	0	0	50.2	51	12	36	0	3	3	4	0	0	0	—	1	9	0	1	0.3	1.000
1995		4	3	.571	4.98	49	0	0	59.2	72	19	30	0	4	3	2	0	0	0	—	5	9	1	2	0.3	.933
1996	SEA A	1	1	.500	5.74	15	5	0	42.1	57	13	25	0	0	0	1	0	0	0	—	3	3	1	1	0.5	.857
6 yrs.		22	14	.611	4.19	189	9	0	303	334	81	182	0	19	12	9	0	0	0		28	47	3	6	0.4	.962

Jim Mecir

MECIR, JAMES JASON
B. May 16, 1970, Bayside, N.Y.

BB TR 6'1" 195 lbs.

Year	Team	W	L	PCT	ERA	G	GS	CG	IP	H	BB	SO	ShO	W	L	SV	AB	H	HR	BA	PO	A	E	DP	TC/G	FA
1995	SEA A	0	0	—	0.00	2	0	0	4.2	5	2	3	0	0	0	0	0	0	0	—	0	0	0	0	0.0	.000
1996	NY A	1	1	.500	5.13	26	0	0	40.1	42	23	38	0	1	1	0	0	0	0	—	1	13	0	0	0.5	1.000
2 yrs.		1	1	.500	4.60	28	0	0	45	47	25	41	0	1	1	0					1	13	0	0	0.5	1.000

Ramiro Mendoza

MENDOZA, RAMIRO
B. June 15, 1972, Los Santos, Panama

BR TR 6'2" 154 lbs.

Year	Team	W	L	PCT	ERA	G	GS	CG	IP	H	BB	SO	ShO	W	L	SV	AB	H	HR	BA	PO	A	E	DP	TC/G	FA
1996	NY A	4	5	.445	6.79	12	11	0	53	80	10	34	0	1	0	0	0	0	0	—	2	11	0	0	1.1	1.000

Paul Menhart

MENHART, PAUL GERARD
B. Mar. 25, 1969, St. Louis, Mo.

BR TR 6'2" 190 lbs.

Year	Team	W	L	PCT	ERA	G	GS	CG	IP	H	BB	SO	ShO	W	L	SV	AB	H	HR	BA	PO	A	E	DP	TC/G	FA
1995	TOR A	1	4	.200	4.92	21	9	1	78.2	72	47	50	0	1	1	0	0	0	0	—	2	11	1	1	0.7	.929
1996	SEA A	2	2	.500	7.29	11	6	0	42	55	25	18	0	0	1	0	0	0	0	—	5	7	1	2	1.2	.923
2 yrs.		3	6	.333	5.74	32	15	1	120.2	127	72	68	0	1	2	0					7	18	2	3	0.8	.926

Jose Mercedes

MERCEDES, JOSE MIGUEL
Born Jose Miguel Mercedes (Santana).
B. Mar. 5, 1971, El Seibo, Dominican Republic

BR TR 6'1" 180 lbs.

Year	Team	W	L	PCT	ERA	G	GS	CG	IP	H	BB	SO	ShO	W	L	SV	AB	H	HR	BA	PO	A	E	DP	TC/G	FA
1994	MIL A	2	0	1.000	2.32	19	0	0	31	22	16	11	0	2	0	0	0	0	0	—	1	3	1	0	0.3	.800
1995		0	1	.000	9.82	5	0	0	7.1	12	8	6	0	0	1	0	0	0	0	—	0	0	0	0	0.0	.000
1996		0	2	.000	9.18	11	0	0	16.2	20	5	6	0	0	2	0	0	0	0	—	0	2	0	0	0.2	1.000
3 yrs.		2	3	.400	5.40	35	0	0	55	54	29	23	0	2	3	0	0	0	0		1	5	1	0	0.2	.857

Kent Mercker

MERCKER, KENT FRANKLIN
B. Feb. 1, 1968, Dublin, Ohio

BL TL 6'1" 175 lbs.

Year	Team	W	L	PCT	ERA	G	GS	CG	IP	H	BB	SO	ShO	W	L	SV	AB	H	HR	BA	PO	A	E	DP	TC/G	FA
1989	ATL N	0	0	—	12.46	2	1	0	4.1	8	6	4	0	0	0	0	1	0	0	.000	0	0	0	0	0.0	.000
1990		4	7	.364	3.17	36	0	0	48.1	43	24	39	0	4	7	7	3	0	0	.000	2	1	1	0	0.1	.750
1991		5	3	.625	2.58	50	4	0	73.1	56	35	62	0	4	3	6	10	1	0	.100	2	7	1	1	0.2	.900
1992		3	2	.600	3.42	53	0	0	68.1	51	35	49	0	3	2	6	5	0	0	.000	1	2	0	0	0.1	1.000
1993		3	1	.750	2.86	43	6	0	66	52	36	59	0	2	0	0	13	0	0	.000	1	4	1	0	0.1	.833
1994		9	4	.692	3.45	20	17	2	112.1	90	45	111	1	0	0	0	37	2	0	.054	4	15	0	1	0.9	1.000
1995		7	8	.467	4.15	29	26	0	143	140	61	102	0	0	0	0	48	5	0	.104	5	23	1	2	1.0	.966
1996	2 teams	BAL A	(14G 3–6)		CLE A	(10G 1–0)																				
"	total	4	6	.400	6.98	24	12	0	69.2	83	38	29	0	0	0	0	0	0	0	—	8	4	0	0	0.5	.923
8 yrs.		35	31	.530	3.91	257	66	2	585.1	523	280	455	1	14	13	19	117	8	0	.068	23	56	5	4	0.3	.940

DIVISIONAL PLAYOFF SERIES

Year	Team	W	L	PCT	ERA	G	GS	CG	IP	H	BB	SO	ShO	W	L	SV	AB	H	HR	BA	PO	A	E	DP	TC/G	FA
1995	ATL N	0	0	—	0.00	1	0	0	0.1	0	0	0	0	0	0	0	0	0	0	—	0	0	0	0	0.0	.000

LEAGUE CHAMPIONSHIP SERIES

Year	Team	W	L	PCT	ERA	G	GS	CG	IP	H	BB	SO	ShO	W	L	SV	AB	H	HR	BA	PO	A	E	DP	TC/G	FA
1991	ATL N	0	1	.000	13.50	1	0	0	0.2	0	2	0	0	0	1	0	0	0	0	—	0	0	0	0	0.0	.000
1992		0	0	—	0.00	2	0	0	3	1	1	1	0	0	0	0	0	0	0	—	0	0	0	0	0.0	.000
1993		0	0	—	1.80	5	0	0	5	3	2	4	0	0	0	0	0	0	0	—	0	0	0	0	0.0	.000
3 yrs.		0	1	.000	2.08	8	0	0	8.2	4	5	5	0	0	1	0	0	0	0		0	0	0	0	0.0	

WORLD SERIES

Year	Team	W	L	PCT	ERA	G	GS	CG	IP	H	BB	SO	ShO	W	L	SV	AB	H	HR	BA	PO	A	E	DP	TC/G	FA
1991	ATL N	0	0	—	0.00	2	0	0	1	0	0	1	0	0	0	0	0	0	0	—	0	0	0	0	0.0	.000
1995		0	0	—	4.50	1	0	0	2	1	2	2	0	0	0	0	0	0	0	—	0	0	0	0	0.0	.000
2 yrs.		0	0		3.00	3	0	0	3	1	2	3	0	0	0	0	0	0	0		0	0	0	0	0.0	

Year	Team	W	L	PCT	ERA	G	GS	CG	IP	H	BB	SO	ShO	Relief Pitching W	L	SV	Batting AB	H	HR	BA	PO	A	E	DP	TC/G	FA

Jose Mesa

MESA, JOSE RAMON
Born Jose Ramon Nova (Mesa).
B. May 22, 1966, Pueblo Viejo, Dominican Republic
BR TR 6'3" 170 lbs.

Year	Team	W	L	PCT	ERA	G	GS	CG	IP	H	BB	SO	ShO	W	L	SV	AB	H	HR	BA	PO	A	E	DP	TC/G	FA
1987	BAL A	1	3	.250	6.03	6	5	0	31.1	38	15	17	0	0	0	0	0	0	0	—	1	1	0	0	0.3	1.000
1990		3	2	.600	3.86	7	7	0	46.2	37	27	24	0	0	0	0	0	0	0	—	3	5	1	1	1.3	.889
1991		6	11	.353	5.97	23	23	2	123.2	151	62	64	1	0	0	0	0	0	0	—	17	17	0	0	1.5	1.000
1992	2 teams	BAL A	(13G 3-8)		CLE A	(15G 4-4)																				
"	total	7	12	.368	4.59	28	27	1	160.2	169	70	62	1	0	0	0	0	0	0	—	12	21	2	0	1.3	.943
1993	CLE A	10	12	.455	4.92	34	33	3	208.2	232	62	118	0	0	0	0	0	0	0	—	15	29	3	0	1.4	.936
1994		7	5	.583	3.82	51	0	0	73	71	26	63	0	7	5	2	0	0	0	—	3	11	2	0	0.3	.875
1995		3	0	1.000	1.13	62	0	0	64	49	17	58	0	3	0	**46**	0	0	0	—	6	10	1	0	0.3	.941
1996		2	7	.222	3.73	69	0	0	72.1	69	28	64	0	2	7	39	0	0	0	—	5	3	1	1	0.1	.889
	8 yrs.	39	52	.429	4.48	280	95	6	780.1	816	307	470	2	12	12	87	0	0	0		62	97	10	2	0.6	.941
DIVISIONAL PLAYOFF SERIES																										
1995	CLE A	0	0	—	0.00	2	0	0	2	0	2	0	0	0	0	0	0	0	0	—	0	0	0	0	0.0	.000
1996		0	1	.000	3.86	2	0	0	4.2	8	0	7	0	0	1	0	0	0	0	—	0	0	0	0	0.0	—
	2 yrs.	0	1	.000	2.70	4	0	0	6.2	8	2	7	0	0	1	0	0	0	0		0	0	0	0	0.0	
LEAGUE CHAMPIONSHIP SERIES																										
1995	CLE A	0	0	—	2.25	4	0	0	4	3	1	1	0	0	0	1	0	0	0	—	1	2	0	1	0.8	1.000
WORLD SERIES																										
1995	CLE A	1	0	1.000	4.50	2	0	0	4	5	1	4	0	1	0	1	0	0	0	—	0	0	0	0	0.0	.000

Dan Miceli

MICELI, DANIEL
B. Sept. 9, 1970, Newark, N. J.
BR TR 6'1" 185 lbs.

Year	Team	W	L	PCT	ERA	G	GS	CG	IP	H	BB	SO	ShO	W	L	SV	AB	H	HR	BA	PO	A	E	DP	TC/G	FA
1993	PIT N	0	0	—	5.06	9	0	0	5.1	6	3	4	0	0	0	0	0	0	0	—	0	0	0	0	0.0	.000
1994		2	1	.667	5.93	28	0	0	27.1	28	11	27	0	2	1	2	3	0	0	.000	1	5	0	0	0.2	1.000
1995		4	4	.500	4.66	58	0	0	58	61	28	56	0	4	4	21	1	0	0	.000	2	5	0	0	0.1	1.000
1996		2	10	.167	5.78	44	9	0	85.2	99	45	66	0	1	5	1	13	0	0	.000	6	3	3	0	0.3	.750
	4 yrs.	8	15	.348	5.41	139	9	0	176.1	194	87	153	0	7	10	24	17	0	0	.000	9	13	3	0	0.2	.880

Bob Milacki

MILACKI, ROBERT
B. July 28, 1964, Trenton, N. J.
BR TR 6'4" 220 lbs.

Year	Team	W	L	PCT	ERA	G	GS	CG	IP	H	BB	SO	ShO	W	L	SV	AB	H	HR	BA	PO	A	E	DP	TC/G	FA
1988	BAL A	2	0	1.000	0.72	3	3	1	25	9	9	18	1	0	0	0	0	0	0	—	4	3	0	1	2.3	1.000
1989		14	12	.538	3.74	37	**36**	3	243	233	88	113	2	0	0	0	0	0	0	—	27	28	2	5	1.5	.965
1990		5	8	.385	4.46	27	24	1	135.1	143	61	60	1	0	0	0	0	0	0	—	21	16	1	2	1.4	.974
1991		10	9	.526	4.01	31	26	3	184	175	53	108	1	1	0	0	0	0	0	—	23	24	2	4	1.6	.959
1992		6	8	.429	5.84	23	20	0	115.2	140	44	51	0	0	0	1	0	0	0	—	14	10	0	0	1.1	1.000
1993	CLE A	1	1	.500	3.38	5	2	0	16	19	11	7	0	1	0	0	0	0	0	—	0	3	0	0	0.6	1.000
1994	KC A	0	5	.000	6.14	10	10	0	55.2	68	20	17	0	0	0	0	0	0	0	—	8	13	1	0	2.2	.955
1996	SEA A	1	4	.200	6.86	7	4	0	21	30	15	13	0	0	1	0	0	0	0	—	3	1	0	1	0.6	1.000
	8 yrs.	39	47	.453	4.38	143	125	8	795.2	817	301	387	5	2	1	1	0	0	0		100	98	6	13	1.4	.971

Mike Milchen

MILCHEN, MICHAEL WAYNE
B. Feb. 28, 1968, Knoxville, Tenn.
BL TL 6'3" 180 lbs.

Year	Team	W	L	PCT	ERA	G	GS	CG	IP	H	BB	SO	ShO	W	L	SV	AB	H	HR	BA	PO	A	E	DP	TC/G	FA
1996	2 teams	BAL A	(13G 1-0)		MIN A	(26G 2-1)																				
"	total	3	1	.750	7.44	39	0	0	32.2	44	17	29	0	3	1	0	0	0	0	—	3	5	0	0	0.2	1.000

Kurt Miller

MILLER, KURT EVERETT
B. Aug. 24, 1972, Tucson, Ariz.
BR TR 6'5" 205 lbs.

Year	Team	W	L	PCT	ERA	G	GS	CG	IP	H	BB	SO	ShO	W	L	SV	AB	H	HR	BA	PO	A	E	DP	TC/G	FA
1994	FLA N	1	3	.250	8.10	4	4	0	20	26	7	11	0	0	0	0	6	1	0	.167	3	4	0	2	1.8	1.000
1996		1	3	.250	6.80	26	5	0	46.1	57	33	30	0	0	2	0	8	3	0	.375	2	8	1	1	0.4	.909
	2 yrs.	2	6	.250	7.19	30	9	0	66.1	83	40	41	0	0	2	0	14	4	0	.286	5	12	1	3	0.6	.944

Travis Miller

MILLER, TRAVIS EUGENE
B. Nov. 2, 1972, Dayton, Ohio
BR TL 6'3" 205 lbs.

Year	Team	W	L	PCT	ERA	G	GS	CG	IP	H	BB	SO	ShO	W	L	SV	AB	H	HR	BA	PO	A	E	DP	TC/G	FA
1996	MIN A	1	2	.333	9.23	7	7	0	26.1	45	9	15	0	0	0	0	0	0	0	—	0	2	0	0	0.3	1.000

Trever Miller

MILLER, TREVER DOUGLAS
B. May 29, 1973, Louisville, Ky.
BR TL 6'3" 175 lbs.

Year	Team	W	L	PCT	ERA	G	GS	CG	IP	H	BB	SO	ShO	W	L	SV	AB	H	HR	BA	PO	A	E	DP	TC/G	FA
1996	DET A	0	4	.000	9.18	5	4	0	16.2	28	9	8	0	0	1	0	0	0	0	—	1	4	0	0	1.0	1.000

Alan Mills

MILLS, ALAN BERNARD
B. Oct. 18, 1966, Lakeland, Fla.
BR TR 6'1" 190 lbs.

Year	Team	W	L	PCT	ERA	G	GS	CG	IP	H	BB	SO	ShO	W	L	SV	AB	H	HR	BA	PO	A	E	DP	TC/G	FA
1990	NY A	1	5	.167	4.10	36	0	0	41.2	48	33	24	0	1	5	0	0	0	0	—	3	10	2	0	0.4	.867
1991		1	1	.500	4.41	6	2	0	16.1	18	8	11	0	1	0	0	0	0	0	—	0	5	0	0	0.8	1.000
1992	BAL A	10	4	.714	2.61	35	3	0	103.1	78	54	60	0	9	3	2	0	0	0	—	9	17	0	2	0.7	1.000
1993		5	4	.556	3.23	45	0	0	100.1	80	51	68	0	5	4	4	0	0	0	—	7	11	3	2	0.5	.857
1994		3	3	.500	5.16	47	0	0	45.1	43	24	44	0	3	3	2	0	0	0	—	3	2	0	0	0.1	1.000
1995		3	0	1.000	7.43	21	0	0	23	30	18	16	0	3	0	0	0	0	0	—	0	0	0	0	0.0	1.000
1996		3	2	.600	4.28	49	0	0	54.2	40	35	50	0	3	2	3	0	0	0	—	4	7	0	2	0.2	1.000
	7 yrs.	26	19	.578	3.84	239	5	0	384.2	335	223	273	0	25	17	11	0	0	0		26	53	5	6	0.4	.940
LEAGUE CHAMPIONSHIP SERIES																										
1996	BAL A	0	0	—	3.86	3	0	0	2.1	3	1	3	0	0	0	0	0	0	0	—	0	0	0	0	0.0	.000

Year	Team	W	L	PCT	ERA	G	GS	CG	IP	H	BB	SO	ShO	W	L	SV	AB	H	HR	BA	PO	A	E	DP	TC/G	FA

Michael Mimbs
MIMBS, MICHAEL RANDALL
B. Feb. 13, 1969, Macon, Ga.　　　　　　　　　BL TL 6'2" 182 lbs.

Year	Team	W	L	PCT	ERA	G	GS	CG	IP	H	BB	SO	ShO	W	L	SV	AB	H	HR	BA	PO	A	E	DP	TC/G	FA
1995	PHI N	9	7	.563	4.15	35	19	2	136.2	127	75	93	1	2	0	1	35	5	0	.143	6	22	1	4	0.8	.966
1996		3	9	.250	5.53	21	17	0	99.1	116	41	56	0	0	0	0	33	4	0	.121	3	14	1	0	0.9	.944
2 yrs.		12	16	.429	4.73	56	36	2	236	243	116	149	1	2	0	1	68	9	0	.132	9	36	2	4	0.8	.957

Nate Minchey
MINCHEY, NATHAN DEREK
B. Aug. 31, 1969, Austin, Tex.　　　　　　　　BR TR 6'8" 225 lbs.

Year	Team	W	L	PCT	ERA	G	GS	CG	IP	H	BB	SO	ShO	W	L	SV	AB	H	HR	BA	PO	A	E	DP	TC/G	FA
1993	BOS A	1	2	.333	3.55	5	5	1	33	35	8	18	0	0	0	0	0	0	0	—	1	3	1	0	1.0	.800
1994		2	3	.400	8.61	6	5	0	23	44	14	15	0	0	0	0	0	0	0	—	0	4	0	0	0.7	1.000
1996		0	2	.000	15.00	2	2	0	6	16	5	4	0	0	0	0	0	0	0	—	0	1	0	0	0.5	1.000
3 yrs.		3	7	.300	6.53	13	12	1	62	95	27	37	0	0	0	0	0	0	0		1	8	1	0	0.8	.900

Blas Minor
MINOR, BLAS
B. Mar. 20, 1966, Merced, Calif.　　　　　　　BR TR 6'3" 195 lbs.

Year	Team	W	L	PCT	ERA	G	GS	CG	IP	H	BB	SO	ShO	W	L	SV	AB	H	HR	BA	PO	A	E	DP	TC/G	FA
1992	PIT N	0	0	—	4.50	1	0	0	2	3	0	0	0	0	0	0	0	0	0	—	0	1	1	1	2.0	.500
1993		8	6	.571	4.10	65	0	0	94.1	94	26	84	0	8	6	2	10	2	0	.200	8	15	0	0	0.4	1.000
1994		0	1	.000	8.05	17	0	0	19	27	9	17	0	0	1	0	0	0	0	—	1	2	0	0	0.2	1.000
1995	NY N	4	2	.667	3.66	35	0	0	46.2	44	13	43	0	4	2	1	2	0	0	.000	3	7	0	0	0.3	1.000
1996	2 teams	NY N	(17G 0-0)		SEA A	(11G 0-1)																				
"	total	0	1	.000	4.24	28	0	0	51	50	17	34	0	0	1	0	1	0	0	.000	1	7	0	1	0.3	1.000
5 yrs.		12	10	.545	4.39	146	0	0	213	218	65	178	0	12	10	4	13	2	0	.154	13	32	1	2	0.3	.978

Angel Miranda
MIRANDA, ANGEL LUIS
Born Angel Luis Miranda (Andujar).
B. Nov. 9, 1969, Arecibo, Puerto Rico　　　　BL TL 6'1" 160 lbs.

Year	Team	W	L	PCT	ERA	G	GS	CG	IP	H	BB	SO	ShO	W	L	SV	AB	H	HR	BA	PO	A	E	DP	TC/G	FA
1993	MIL A	4	5	.444	3.30	22	17	2	120	100	52	88	0	0	0	0	0	0	0	—	4	13	2	1	0.9	.895
1994		2	5	.286	5.28	8	8	1	46	39	27	24	0	0	0	0	0	0	0	—	1	3	0	1	0.5	1.000
1995		4	5	.444	5.23	30	10	0	74	83	49	45	0	2	2	1	0	0	0	—	5	9	0	1	0.5	1.000
1996		7	6	.538	4.94	46	12	0	109.1	116	69	78	0	4	1	1	0	0	0	—	3	14	2	0	0.4	.895
4 yrs.		17	21	.447	4.48	106	47	3	349.1	338	197	235	0	6	3	2	0	0	0		13	39	4	2	0.5	.929

Larry Mitchell
MITCHELL, LARRY PAUL
B. Oct. 16, 1971, Flint, Mich.　　　　　　　　BR TR 6'1" 220 lbs.

Year	Team	W	L	PCT	ERA	G	GS	CG	IP	H	BB	SO	ShO	W	L	SV	AB	H	HR	BA	PO	A	E	DP	TC/G	FA
1996	PHI N	0	0	—	4.50	7	0	0	12	14	5	7	0	0	0	0	2	0	0	.000	1	0	1	0	0.3	.500

Dave Mlicki
MLICKI, DAVID JOHN
B. June 8, 1968, Cleveland, Ohio　　　　　　　BR TR 6'4" 185 lbs.

Year	Team	W	L	PCT	ERA	G	GS	CG	IP	H	BB	SO	ShO	W	L	SV	AB	H	HR	BA	PO	A	E	DP	TC/G	FA
1992	CLE A	0	2	.000	4.98	4	4	0	21.2	23	16	16	0	0	0	0	0	0	0	—	6	3	0	1	2.3	1.000
1993		0	0	—	3.38	3	3	0	13.1	11	6	7	0	0	0	0	0	0	0	—	1	1	0	0	0.7	1.000
1995	NY N	9	7	.563	4.26	29	25	0	160.2	160	54	123	0	1	0	0	39	2	0	.051	10	15	1	3	0.9	.962
1996		6	7	.462	3.30	51	2	0	90	95	33	83	0	6	5	1	10	1	0	.100	3	6	2	2	0.2	.818
4 yrs.		15	16	.484	3.97	87	34	0	285.2	289	109	229	0	7	5	1	49	3	0	.061	20	25	3	6	0.6	.938

Brian Moehler
MOEHLER, BRIAN MERRITT
B. Dec. 3, 1971, Rockingham, N. C.　　　　　BR TR 6'3" 195 lbs.

Year	Team	W	L	PCT	ERA	G	GS	CG	IP	H	BB	SO	ShO	W	L	SV	AB	H	HR	BA	PO	A	E	DP	TC/G	FA
1996	DET A	0	1	.000	4.35	2	2	0	10.1	11	8	2	0	0	0	0	0	0	0	—	0	1	1	0	1.0	.500

Mike Mohler
MOHLER, MICHAEL ROSS
B. July 26, 1968, Dayton, Ohio　　　　　　　　BR TL 6'2" 195 lbs.

Year	Team	W	L	PCT	ERA	G	GS	CG	IP	H	BB	SO	ShO	W	L	SV	AB	H	HR	BA	PO	A	E	DP	TC/G	FA
1993	OAK A	1	6	.143	5.60	42	9	0	64.1	57	44	42	0	1	1	0	0	0	0	—	2	9	1	2	0.3	.917
1994		0	1	.000	7.71	1	1	0	2.1	2	2	4	0	0	0	0	0	0	0	—	0	0	0	0	0.0	.000
1995		1	1	.500	3.04	28	0	0	23.2	16	18	15	0	1	1	1	0	0	0	—	2	2	0	0	0.1	1.000
1996		6	3	.667	3.67	72	0	0	81	79	41	64	0	6	3	7	0	0	0	—	6	13	1	3	0.3	.950
4 yrs.		8	11	.421	4.36	143	10	0	171.1	154	105	125	0	8	5	8	0	0	0		10	24	2	5	0.3	.944

Rich Monteleone
MONTELEONE, RICHARD
B. Mar. 22, 1963, Tampa, Fla.　　　　　　　　BR TR 6'2" 205 lbs.

Year	Team	W	L	PCT	ERA	G	GS	CG	IP	H	BB	SO	ShO	W	L	SV	AB	H	HR	BA	PO	A	E	DP	TC/G	FA
1987	SEA A	0	0	—	6.43	3	0	0	7	10	4	2	0	0	0	0	0	0	0	—	0	3	0	0	1.0	1.000
1988	CAL A	0	0	—	0.00	3	0	0	4.1	4	1	3	0	0	0	0	0	0	0	—	0	1	0	0	0.3	1.000
1989		2	2	.500	3.18	24	0	0	39.2	39	13	27	0	2	2	0	0	0	0	—	1	9	1	1	0.5	.909
1990	NY A	0	1	.000	6.14	5	0	0	7.1	8	2	8	0	0	1	0	0	0	0	—	1	1	0	0	0.4	1.000
1991		3	1	.750	3.64	26	0	0	47	42	19	34	0	3	1	0	0	0	0	—	1	10	1	1	0.5	.917
1992		7	3	.700	3.30	47	0	0	92.2	82	27	62	0	7	3	0	0	0	0	—	6	7	0	1	0.3	1.000
1993		7	4	.636	4.94	42	0	0	85.2	85	35	50	0	7	4	0	0	0	0	—	9	11	1	0	0.5	.952
1994	SF N	4	3	.571	3.18	39	0	0	45.1	43	13	16	0	4	3	0	3	0	0	.000	2	3	0	0	0.1	1.000
1995	CAL A	1	0	1.000	2.00	9	0	0	9	8	4	5	0	1	0	0	0	0	0	—	0	1	0	1	0.1	1.000
1996		0	3	.000	5.87	12	0	0	15.1	23	2	5	0	0	3	0	0	0	0	—	1	0	0	0	0.1	1.000
10 yrs.		24	17	.585	3.87	210	0	0	353.1	344	119	212	0	24	17	0	3	0	0	.000	21	46	3	3	0.3	.957

Jeff Montgomery
MONTGOMERY, JEFFREY THOMAS
B. Jan. 7, 1962, Wellston, Ohio　　　　　　　BR TR 5'11" 170 lbs.

Year	Team	W	L	PCT	ERA	G	GS	CG	IP	H	BB	SO	ShO	W	L	SV	AB	H	HR	BA	PO	A	E	DP	TC/G	FA
1987	CIN N	2	2	.500	6.52	14	1	0	19.1	25	9	13	0	2	1	0	2	0	0	.000	1	3	0	0	1.0	1.000
1988	KC A	7	2	.778	3.45	45	0	0	62.2	54	30	47	0	7	2	1	0	0	0	—	3	10	1	0	0.3	.929

Year	Team	W	L	PCT	ERA	G	GS	CG	IP	H	BB	SO	ShO	Relief Pitching W	L	SV	Batting AB	H	HR	BA	PO	A	E	DP	TC/G	FA

Jeff Montgomery continued

Year	Team	W	L	PCT	ERA	G	GS	CG	IP	H	BB	SO	ShO	W	L	SV	AB	H	HR	BA	PO	A	E	DP	TC/G	FA
1989		7	3	.700	1.37	63	0	0	92	66	25	94	0	7	3	18	0	0	0	—	11	6	2	1	0.3	.895
1990		6	5	.545	2.39	73	0	0	94.1	81	34	94	0	6	5	24	0	0	0	—	3	13	0	0	0.2	1.000
1991		4	4	.500	2.90	67	0	0	90	83	28	77	0	4	4	33	0	0	0	—	10	8	0	0	0.3	1.000
1992		1	6	.143	2.18	65	0	0	82.2	61	27	69	0	1	6	39	0	0	0	—	12	13	1	2	0.4	.962
1993		7	5	.583	2.27	69	0	0	87.1	65	23	66	0	7	5	**45**	0	0	0	—	6	13	0	0	0.3	1.000
1994		2	3	.400	4.03	42	0	0	44.2	48	15	50	0	2	3	27	0	0	0	—	2	2	1	0	0.1	.800
1995		2	3	.400	3.43	54	0	0	65.2	60	25	49	0	2	3	31	0	0	0	—	13	4	1	1	0.3	.944
1996		4	6	.400	4.26	48	0	0	63.1	59	19	45	0	4	6	24	0	0	0	—	6	13	0	1	0.4	1.000
10 yrs.		42	39	.519	2.86	540	1	0	702	602	235	604	0	42	38	242	2	0	0	.000	67	85	6	5	0.3	.962

Steve Montgomery

MONTGOMERY, STEVEN LEWIS
B. Dec. 25, 1970, Westminster, Calif.

BR TR 6'4" 210 lbs.

Year	Team	W	L	PCT	ERA	G	GS	CG	IP	H	BB	SO	ShO	W	L	SV	AB	H	HR	BA	PO	A	E	DP	TC/G	FA
1996	OAK A	1	0	1.000	9.22	8	0	0	13.2	18	13	8	0	1	0	0	0	0	0	—	0	0	0	0	0.0	—

Marcus Moore

MOORE, MARCUS BRAYMONT
B. Nov. 2, 1970, Oakland, Calif.

BB TR 6'5" 195 lbs.

Year	Team	W	L	PCT	ERA	G	GS	CG	IP	H	BB	SO	ShO	W	L	SV	AB	H	HR	BA	PO	A	E	DP	TC/G	FA
1993	CLR N	3	1	.750	6.84	27	0	0	26.1	30	20	13	0	3	1	0	1	0	0	.000	0	1	2	0	0.1	.333
1994		1	1	.500	6.15	29	0	0	33.2	33	21	33	0	1	1	0	1	0	0	.000	2	3	0	0	0.2	1.000
1996	CIN N	3	3	.500	5.81	23	0	0	26.1	26	22	27	0	3	3	2	3	1	0	.333	0	1	0	0	0.0	1.000
3 yrs.		7	5	.583	6.25	79	0	0	86.1	89	63	73	0	7	5	2	5	1	0	.200	2	5	2	0	0.1	.778

Ramon Morel

MOREL, RAMON RAFAEL
B. Aug. 15, 1974, Villa Gonzalez, Dominican Republic

BR TR 6'2" 175 lbs.

Year	Team	W	L	PCT	ERA	G	GS	CG	IP	H	BB	SO	ShO	W	L	SV	AB	H	HR	BA	PO	A	E	DP	TC/G	FA
1995	PIT N	0	1	.000	2.84	5	0	0	6.1	6	2	3	0	0	1	0	0	0	0	—	1	2	0	0	0.6	1.000
1996		2	1	.667	5.36	29	0	0	42	57	19	22	0	2	1	0	4	0	0	.000	4	3	0	0	0.2	1.000
2 yrs.		2	2	.500	5.03	34	0	0	48.1	63	21	25	0	2	2	0	4	0	0	.000	5	5	0	0	0.3	1.000

Mike Morgan

MORGAN, MICHAEL THOMAS
B. Oct. 8, 1959, Tulare, Calif.

BR TR 6'3" 195 lbs.

Year	Team	W	L	PCT	ERA	G	GS	CG	IP	H	BB	SO	ShO	W	L	SV	AB	H	HR	BA	PO	A	E	DP	TC/G	FA
1978	OAK A	0	3	.000	7.30	3	3	1	12.1	19	8	0	0	0	0	0	0	0	0	—	1	4	0	1	1.7	1.000
1979		2	10	.167	5.96	13	13	2	77	102	50	17	0	0	0	0	0	0	0	—	9	15	1	0	1.9	.960
1982	NY A	7	11	.389	4.37	30	23	2	150.1	167	67	71	0	2	1	0	0	0	0	—	4	26	0	1	1.0	1.000
1983	TOR A	0	3	.000	5.16	16	4	0	45.1	48	21	22	0	0	1	0	0	0	0	—	2	10	1	0	0.8	.923
1985	SEA A	1	1	.500	12.00	2	2	0	6	11	5	2	0	0	0	0	0	0	0	—	0	1	0	0	0.5	1.000
1986		11	**17**	.393	4.53	37	33	9	216.1	243	86	116	1	0	0	1	0	0	0	—	14	27	2	5	1.2	.953
1987		12	17	.414	4.65	34	31	8	207	245	53	85	2	0	0	0	0	0	0	—	18	35	2	5	1.6	.964
1988	BAL A	1	6	.143	5.43	22	10	0	71.1	70	23	29	0	1	0	1	0	0	0	—	9	9	0	1	0.8	1.000
1989	LA N	8	11	.421	2.53	40	19	0	152.2	130	33	72	0	2	0	0	36	3	0	.083	20	41	2	2	1.6	.968
1990		11	15	.423	3.75	33	33	6	211	216	60	106	4	0	0	0	71	8	0	.113	25	39	1	3	2.0	.985
1991		14	10	.583	2.78	34	33	5	236.1	197	61	140	1	0	0	0	76	7	0	.092	25	41	2	3	2.0	.971
1992	CHI N	16	8	.667	2.55	34	34	6	240	203	79	123	1	0	0	0	74	8	0	.108	19	45	3	3	2.0	.955
1993		10	15	.400	4.03	32	32	1	207.2	206	74	111	0	0	0	0	66	4	0	.061	11	33	1	3	1.4	.978
1994		2	10	.167	6.69	15	15	1	80.2	111	35	57	0	0	0	0	24	3	0	.125	3	8	3	0	0.9	.786
1995	2 teams	CHI N	(4G 2–1)	STL N	(17G 5–6)																					
"	total	7	7	.500	3.56	21	21	1	131.1	133	34	61	0	0	0	0	38	2	0	.053	13	27	1	2	2.0	.976
1996	2 teams	STL N	(18G 4–8)	CIN N	(5G 2–3)																					
"	total	6	11	.353	4.63	23	23	0	130.1	146	47	74	0	0	0	0	40	2	0	.050	4	16	1	1	0.9	.952
16 yrs.		108	155	.411	4.02	389	329	44	2175.2	2247	736	1086	10	5	2	3	425	37	0	.087	177	377	20	32	1.5	.965

Alvin Morman

MORMAN, ALVIN
B. Jan. 6, 1969, Rockingham, N. C.

BL TL 6'3" 210 lbs.

Year	Team	W	L	PCT	ERA	G	GS	CG	IP	H	BB	SO	ShO	W	L	SV	AB	H	HR	BA	PO	A	E	DP	TC/G	FA
1996	HOU N	4	1	.800	4.93	53	0	0	42	43	24	31	0	4	1	0	0	0	0	—	2	8	1	0	0.2	.909

Jamie Moyer

MOYER, JAMIE
B. Nov. 11, 1962, Sellersville, Pa.

BL TL 6' 170 lbs.

Year	Team	W	L	PCT	ERA	G	GS	CG	IP	H	BB	SO	ShO	W	L	SV	AB	H	HR	BA	PO	A	E	DP	TC/G	FA
1986	CHI N	7	4	.636	5.05	16	16	1	87.1	107	42	45	1	0	0	0	22	2	0	.091	2	22	0	1	1.5	1.000
1987		12	15	.444	5.10	35	33	1	201	210	97	147	1	0	1	0	61	14	0	.230	15	37	4	3	1.6	.929
1988		9	15	.375	3.48	34	30	3	202	212	55	121	1	1	0	0	60	5	0	.083	11	45	1	3	1.7	.982
1989	TEX A	4	9	.308	4.86	15	15	1	76	84	33	44	0	0	0	0	0	0	0	—	5	14	0	2	1.3	1.000
1990		2	6	.250	4.66	33	10	1	102.1	115	39	58	0	1	0	0	0	0	0	—	6	14	0	0	0.6	1.000
1991	STL N	0	5	.000	5.74	8	7	0	31.1	38	16	20	0	0	0	0	8	0	0	.000	0	5	0	0	0.6	1.000
1993	BAL A	12	9	.571	3.43	25	25	3	152	154	38	90	1	0	0	0	0	0	0	—	14	25	1	1	1.6	.975
1994		5	7	.417	4.77	23	23	0	149	158	38	87	0	0	0	0	0	0	0	—	12	17	0	1	1.3	1.000
1995		8	6	.571	5.21	27	18	0	115.2	117	30	65	0	0	0	0	0	0	0	—	8	20	0	4	1.0	1.000
1996	2 teams	BOS A	(23G 7–1)	SEA A	(11G 6–2)																					
"	total	13	3	.813	3.98	34	21	0	160.2	177	46	79	0	0	0	0	0	0	0	—	6	25	3	2	1.0	.912
10 yrs.		72	79	.477	4.44	250	198	10	1277.1	1372	434	756	3	5	2	0	151	21	0	.139	79	224	9	18	1.2	.971

Terry Mulholland

MULHOLLAND, TERENCE JOHN
B. Mar. 9, 1963, Uniontown, Pa.

BR TL 6'3" 200 lbs.

Year	Team	W	L	PCT	ERA	G	GS	CG	IP	H	BB	SO	ShO	W	L	SV	AB	H	HR	BA	PO	A	E	DP	TC/G	FA
1986	SF N	1	7	.125	4.94	15	10	0	54.2	51	35	27	0	0	0	0	19	1	0	.053	1	9	3	0	0.9	.769
1988		2	1	.667	3.72	9	6	2	46	50	7	18	1	0	0	0	14	0	0	.000	7	7	0	0	1.6	1.000

Year	Team	W	L	PCT	ERA	G	GS	CG	IP	H	BB	SO	ShO	W	L	SV	AB	H	HR	BA	PO	A	E	DP	TC/G	FA

Relief Pitching spans W L SV; **Batting** spans AB H HR.

Terry Mulholland *continued*

Year	Team	W	L	PCT	ERA	G	GS	CG	IP	H	BB	SO	ShO	W	L	SV	AB	H	HR	BA	PO	A	E	DP	TC/G	FA
1989	2 teams	SF N	(5G 0–0)		PHI N	(20G 4–7)																				
"	total	4	7	.364	4.92	25	18	2	115.1	137	36	66	1	0	0	0	36	2	0	.056	2	25	4	1	1.2	.871
1990	PHI N	9	10	.474	3.34	33	26	6	180.2	172	42	75	1	0	0	0	62	6	0	.097	8	17	3	0	0.8	.893
1991		16	13	.552	3.61	34	34	8	232	231	49	142	3	0	0	0	80	7	0	.087	12	28	5	2	1.3	.889
1992		13	11	.542	3.81	32	32	12	229	227	46	125	2	0	0	0	83	8	0	.096	6	47	3	0	1.8	.946
1993		12	9	.571	3.25	29	28	7	191	177	40	116	2	0	0	0	62	4	0	.065	5	27	2	1	1.2	.941
1994	NY A	6	7	.462	6.49	24	19	2	120.2	150	37	72	0	0	0	0	0	0	0	—	4	15	1	0	0.8	.950
1995	SF N	5	13	.278	5.80	29	24	2	149	190	38	65	0	0	0	0	49	5	1	.102	5	23	3	2	1.1	.903
1996	2 teams	PHI N	(21G 8–7)		SEA A	(12G 5–4)																				
"	total	13	11	.542	4.66	33	33	3	202.2	232	49	86	0	0	0	0	45	8	1	.178	6	26	6	2	1.2	.842
	10 yrs.	81	89	.476	4.30	263	230	44	1521	1617	379	792	10	0	0	0	450	41	2	.091	56	224	30	8	1.2	.903

LEAGUE CHAMPIONSHIP SERIES

| 1993 | PHI N | 0 | 1 | .000 | 7.20 | 1 | 1 | 0 | 5 | 9 | 1 | 2 | 0 | 0 | 0 | 0 | 2 | 0 | 0 | .000 | 0 | 2 | 0 | 0 | 2.0 | 1.000 |

WORLD SERIES

| 1993 | PHI N | 1 | 0 | 1.000 | 6.75 | 2 | 2 | 0 | 10.2 | 14 | 3 | 5 | 0 | 0 | 0 | 0 | 0 | 0 | 0 | — | 1 | 1 | 0 | 0 | 1.0 | 1.000 |

Bobby Munoz

MUNOZ, ROBERTO
Born Roberto Munoz (Sbert).
B. Mar. 3, 1968, Rio Piedras, Puerto Rico

BR TR 6'7" 237 lbs.

Year	Team	W	L	PCT	ERA	G	GS	CG	IP	H	BB	SO	ShO	W	L	SV	AB	H	HR	BA	PO	A	E	DP	TC/G	FA
1993	NY A	3	3	.500	5.32	38	0	0	45.2	48	26	33	0	3	3	0	0	0	0	—	1	6	0	1	0.2	1.000
1994	PHI N	7	5	.583	2.67	21	14	1	104.1	101	35	59	0	0	0	1	34	7	1	.206	8	18	1	1	1.3	.963
1995		0	2	.000	5.74	3	3	0	15.2	15	9	6	0	0	0	0	5	0	0	.000	0	3	1	0	1.3	.750
1996		0	3	.000	7.82	6	6	0	25.1	42	7	8	0	0	0	0	7	1	0	.143	0	1	0	0	0.5	1.000
	4 yrs.	10	13	.435	4.24	68	23	1	191	206	77	106	0	3	3	1	46	8	1	.174	9	30	2	2	0.6	.951

Mike Munoz

MUNOZ, MICHAEL ANTHONY
B. July 12, 1965, Baldwin Park, Calif.

BL TL 6'2" 190 lbs.

Year	Team	W	L	PCT	ERA	G	GS	CG	IP	H	BB	SO	ShO	W	L	SV	AB	H	HR	BA	PO	A	E	DP	TC/G	FA
1989	LA N	0	0	—	16.88	3	0	0	2.2	5	2	3	0	0	0	0	0	0	0	—	1	1	0	0	0.7	1.000
1990		0	0	.000	3.18	8	0	0	5.2	6	3	2	0	0	1	0	0	0	0	.000	0	0	0	0	0.0	.000
1991	DET A	0	0	—	9.64	6	0	0	9.1	14	5	3	0	0	0	0	0	0	0	—	0	3	0	0	0.5	1.000
1992		1	2	.333	3.00	65	0	0	48	44	25	23	0	1	2	2	0	0	0	—	8	12	0	0	0.3	1.000
1993	2 teams	DET A	(8G 0–1)		CLR N	(21G 2–1)																				
"	total	2	2	.500	4.71	29	0	0	21	25	15	17	0	2	2	0	0	0	0	—	1	5	0	0	0.2	1.000
1994	CLR N	4	2	.667	3.74	57	0	0	45.2	37	31	32	0	4	2	1	0	0	0	—	6	12	1	0	0.3	.947
1995		2	4	.333	7.42	64	0	0	43.2	54	27	37	0	2	4	2	2	1	0	.500	5	7	0	0	0.2	1.000
1996		2	2	.500	6.65	54	0	0	44.2	55	16	45	0	2	2	0	1	0	0	.000	5	11	1	1	0.3	.941
	8 yrs.	11	13	.458	5.38	286	0	0	220.2	240	124	162	0	11	13	5	4	1	0	.250	26	51	2	3	0.3	.975

DIVISIONAL PLAYOFF SERIES

| 1995 | CLR N | 0 | 0 | .000 | 13.50 | 4 | 0 | 0 | 1.1 | 4 | 1 | 1 | 0 | 0 | 0 | 0 | 0 | 0 | 0 | — | 0 | 0 | 0 | 0 | 0.0 | .000 |

Mike Mussina

MUSSINA, MICHAEL COLE
B. Dec. 8, 1968, Williamsport, Pa.

BR TR 6'2" 185 lbs.

Year	Team	W	L	PCT	ERA	G	GS	CG	IP	H	BB	SO	ShO	W	L	SV	AB	H	HR	BA	PO	A	E	DP	TC/G	FA
1991	BAL A	4	5	.444	2.87	12	12	3	87.2	77	21	52	0	0	0	0	0	0	0	.	4	11	0	1	1.3	1.000
1992		18	5	.783	2.54	32	32	8	241	212	48	130	4	0	0	0	0	0	0	—	13	31	1	0	1.4	.978
1993		14	6	.700	4.46	25	25	3	167.2	163	44	117	2	0	0	0	0	0	0	—	12	19	0	1	1.2	1.000
1994		16	5	.762	3.06	24	24	3	176.1	163	42	99	0	0	0	0	0	0	0	—	14	28	1	1	1.8	.977
1995		19	9	.679	3.29	32	32	7	221.2	187	50	158	4	0	0	0	0	0	0	—	13	26	2	3	1.3	.951
1996		19	11	.633	4.81	36	36	4	243.1	264	69	204	1	0	0	0	0	0	0	—	14	34	0	0	1.3	1.000
	6 yrs.	90	41	.687	3.56	161	161	27	1137.2	1066	274	760	11	0	0	0	0	0	0		70	149	4	9	1.4	.982

DIVISIONAL PLAYOFF SERIES

| 1996 | BAL A | 0 | 0 | — | 4.50 | 1 | 1 | 0 | 6 | 7 | 2 | 6 | 0 | 0 | 0 | 0 | 0 | 0 | 0 | — | 0 | 0 | 0 | 0 | 0.0 | .000 |

LEAGUE CHAMPIONSHIP SERIES

| 1996 | BAL A | 0 | 1 | .000 | 5.87 | 1 | 1 | 0 | 7.2 | 8 | 2 | 6 | 0 | 0 | 0 | 0 | 0 | 0 | 0 | — | 0 | 0 | 0 | 0 | 0.0 | .000 |

Jimmy Myers

MYERS, JAMES XAVIER
B. Apr. 28, 1969, Oklahoma City, Okla.

BR TR 6'1" 190 lbs.

Year	Team	W	L	PCT	ERA	G	GS	CG	IP	H	BB	SO	ShO	W	L	SV	AB	H	HR	BA	PO	A	E	DP	TC/G	FA
1996	BAL A	0	0	—	7.07	11	0	0	14	18	3	6	0	0	0	0	0	0	0	—	1	2	1	0	0.4	.750

Mike Myers

MYERS, MICHAEL STANLEY
B. June 26, 1969, Cook County, Ill.

BL TL 6'3" 197 lbs.

Year	Team	W	L	PCT	ERA	G	GS	CG	IP	H	BB	SO	ShO	W	L	SV	AB	H	HR	BA	PO	A	E	DP	TC/G	FA
1995	2 teams	FLA N	(2G 0–0)		DET A	(11G 1–0)																				
"	total	1	0	1.000	7.56	13	0	0	8.1	11	7	4	0	1	0	0	0	0	0	—	1	1	0	0	0.2	1.000
1996	DET A	1	5	.167	5.01	83	0	0	64.2	70	34	69	0	1	5	6	0	0	0	—	2	15	1	2	0.2	.944
	2 yrs.	2	5	.286	5.30	96	0	0	73	81	41	73	0	2	5	6	0	0	0	—	3	16	1	2	0.2	.950

Randy Myers

MYERS, RANDALL KIRK
B. Sept. 19, 1962, Vancouver, Wash.

BL TL 6'1" 190 lbs.

Year	Team	W	L	PCT	ERA	G	GS	CG	IP	H	BB	SO	ShO	W	L	SV	AB	H	HR	BA	PO	A	E	DP	TC/G	FA
1985	NY N	0	0	—	0.00	1	0	0	2	0	1	2	0	0	0	0	0	0	0	—	0	1	0	0	1.0	1.000
1986		0	0	—	4.22	10	0	0	10.2	11	9	13	0	0	0	0	0	0	0	—	0	2	0	0	0.2	1.000
1987		3	6	.333	3.96	54	0	0	75	61	30	92	0	3	6	6	7	2	0	.286	5	9	1	0	0.3	.933

Year	Team	W	L	PCT	ERA	G	GS	CG	IP	H	BB	SO	ShO	Relief Pitching W	L	SV	Batting AB	H	HR	BA	PO	A	E	DP	TC/G	FA

Randy Myers *continued*

Year	Team	W	L	PCT	ERA	G	GS	CG	IP	H	BB	SO	ShO	W	L	SV	AB	H	HR	BA	PO	A	E	DP	TC/G	FA
1988		7	3	.700	1.72	55	0	0	68	45	17	69	0	7	3	26	4	1	0	.250	4	3	0	1	0.1	1.000
1989		7	4	.636	2.35	65	0	0	84.1	62	40	88	0	7	4	24	5	0	0	.000	3	11	0	0	0.2	1.000
1990	CIN N	4	6	.400	2.08	66	0	0	86.2	59	38	98	0	4	6	31	4	1	0	.250	1	12	0	0	0.2	1.000
1991		6	13	.316	3.55	58	12	1	132	116	80	108	0	4	7	6	29	5	0	.172	6	12	2	0	0.3	.900
1992	SD N	3	6	.333	4.29	66	0	0	79.2	84	34	66	0	3	6	38	7	1	0	.143	2	12	0	0	0.2	1.000
1993	CHI N	2	4	.333	3.11	73	0	0	75.1	65	26	86	0	2	4	**53**	2	1	0	.500	1	7	0	0	0.1	1.000
1994		1	5	.167	3.79	38	0	0	40.1	40	16	32	0	1	5	21	1	0	0	.000	0	3	1	0	0.1	.750
1995		1	2	.333	3.88	57	0	0	55.2	49	28	59	0	1	2	**38**	0	0	0	—	2	9	0	0	0.2	1.000
1996	BAL A	4	4	.500	3.53	62	0	0	58.2	60	29	74	0	4	4	31	0	0	0	—	2	4	1	1	0.1	.857
12 yrs.		38	53	.418	3.20	605	12	1	768.1	652	348	787	0	36	47	274 **9th**	59	11	0	.186	26	85	5	2	0.2	.957

DIVISIONAL PLAYOFF SERIES
| 1996 | BAL A | 0 | 0 | — | 0.00 | 3 | 0 | 0 | 3 | 0 | 0 | 3 | 0 | 0 | 0 | 0 | 0 | 0 | 0 | — | 0 | 0 | 0 | 0 | 0.0 | .000 |

LEAGUE CHAMPIONSHIP SERIES
1988	NY N	2	0	1.000	0.00	3	0	0	4.2	1	2	0	0	2	0	0	0	0	0	—	0	1	0	0	0.3	1.000
1990	CIN N	0	0	—	0.00	4	0	0	5.2	3	3	7	0	0	0	3	0	0	0	—	0	0	0	0	0.0	.000
1996	BAL A	0	1	.000	2.25	3	0	0	4	4	3	2	0	0	1	0	0	0	0	—	0	0	0	0	0.0	.000
3 yrs.		2	1	.667	0.63	10	0	0	14.1	7	8	9	0	2	1	3 **6th**	0	0	0	—	0	1	0	0	0.1	1.000

WORLD SERIES
| 1990 | CIN N | 0 | 0 | — | 0.00 | 3 | 0 | 0 | 3 | 2 | 0 | 3 | 0 | 0 | 0 | 1 | 0 | 0 | 0 | — | 0 | 0 | 0 | 0 | 0.0 | .000 |

Rodney Myers

MYERS, RODNEY LUTHER
B. June 26, 1969, Rockford, Ill.

BR TR 6'1" 200 lbs.

| 1996 | CHI N | 2 | 1 | .667 | 4.68 | 45 | 0 | 0 | 67.1 | 61 | 38 | 50 | 0 | 2 | 1 | 0 | 5 | 0 | 0 | .000 | 9 | 4 | 1 | 0 | 0.3 | .929 |

Charles Nagy

NAGY, CHARLES HARRISON
B. May 5, 1967, Bridgeport, Conn.

BL TR 6'3" 200 lbs.

1990	CLE A	2	4	.333	5.91	9	8	0	45.2	58	21	26	0	0	0	0	0	0	0	—	3	8	1	2	1.3	.917
1991		10	15	.400	4.13	33	33	6	211.1	228	66	109	1	0	0	0	0	0	0	—	17	20	2	4	1.2	.949
1992		17	10	.630	2.96	33	33	10	252	245	57	169	3	0	0	0	0	0	0	—	22	43	1	3	2.0	.985
1993		2	6	.250	6.29	9	9	1	48.2	66	13	30	0	0	0	0	0	0	0	—	8	14	1	2	2.6	.957
1994		10	8	.556	3.45	23	23	3	169.1	175	48	108	0	0	0	0	0	0	0	—	9	26	2	1	1.6	.946
1995		16	6	.727	4.55	29	29	2	178	194	61	139	1	0	0	0	0	0	0	—	19	34	1	4	1.9	.981
1996		17	5	.773	3.41	32	32	5	222	217	61	167	0	0	0	0	0	0	0	—	29	37	0	3	2.1	1.000
7 yrs.		74	54	.578	3.86	168	167	27	1127	1183	327	748	5	0	0	0	0	0	0		107	182	8	19	1.8	.973

DIVISIONAL PLAYOFF SERIES
1995	CLE A	1	0	1.000	1.29	1	1	0	7	4	5	6	0	0	0	0	0	0	0	—	2	1	0	0	3.0	1.000
1996		0	1	.000	7.15	2	2	0	11.1	15	5	13	0	0	0	0	0	0	0	—	0	0	0	0	0.0	—
2 yrs.		1	1	.500	4.91	3	3	0	18.1	19	10	19	0	0	0	0					2	5	0	0	2.3	1.000

LEAGUE CHAMPIONSHIP SERIES
| 1995 | CLE A | 0 | 0 | — | 1.13 | 1 | 1 | 0 | 8 | 5 | 0 | 6 | 0 | 0 | 0 | 0 | 0 | 0 | 0 | — | 0 | 1 | 0 | 0 | 1.0 | 1.000 |

WORLD SERIES
| 1995 | CLE A | 0 | 0 | — | 6.43 | 1 | 1 | 0 | 7 | 8 | 1 | 4 | 0 | 0 | 0 | 0 | 0 | 0 | 0 | — | 1 | 1 | 0 | 0 | 2.0 | 1.000 |

Dan Naulty

NAULTY, DANIEL DONOVAN
B. Jan. 6, 1970, Los Angeles, Calif.

BR TR 6'6" 211 lbs.

| 1996 | MIN A | 3 | 2 | .600 | 3.79 | 49 | 0 | 0 | 57 | 43 | 35 | 56 | 0 | 3 | 2 | 4 | 0 | 0 | 0 | — | 7 | 5 | 0 | 1 | 0.2 | 1.000 |

Jaime Navarro

NAVARRO, JAIME
Born Jaime Navarro (Cintron).
Son of Julio Navarro.
B. Mar. 27, 1967, Bayamon, Puerto Rico

BR TR 6'4" 210 lbs.

1989	MIL A	7	8	.467	3.12	19	17	1	109.2	119	32	56	0	1	0	0	0	0	0	—	6	16	2	0	1.3	.917
1990		8	7	.533	4.46	32	22	3	149.1	176	41	75	0	0	0	1	0	0	0	—	10	19	1	2	0.9	.967
1991		15	12	.556	3.92	34	34	10	234	237	73	114	2	0	0	0	0	0	0	—	16	28	3	3	1.4	.936
1992		17	11	.607	3.33	34	34	5	246	224	64	100	3	0	0	0	0	0	0	—	17	18	4	1	1.1	.897
1993		11	12	.478	5.33	35	34	5	214.1	254	73	114	1	0	0	0	0	0	0	—	14	21	2	2	1.1	.946
1994		4	9	.308	6.62	29	10	0	89.2	115	35	65	0	2	3	0	0	0	0	—	4	7	0	1	0.4	1.000
1995	CHI N	14	6	.700	3.28	29	29	1	200.1	194	56	128	1	0	0	0	65	12	0	.185	14	13	1	1	1.0	.964
1996		15	12	.556	3.92	35	35	4	236.2	**244**	72	158	1	0	0	0	77	10	0	.130	8	25	5	1	1.1	.868
8 yrs.		91	77	.542	4.10	247	215	29	1480	1563	446	810	8	3	3	1	142	22	0	.155	89	147	18	11	1.0	.929

Denny Neagle

NEAGLE, DENNIS EDWARD
B. Sept. 13, 1968, Gambrills, Md.

BL TL 6'4" 200 lbs.

1991	MIN A	0	1	.000	4.05	7	3	0	20	28	7	14	0	0	0	0	0	0	0	—	0	1	0	0	0.1	1.000
1992	PIT N	4	6	.400	4.48	55	6	0	86.1	81	43	77	0	3	3	2	11	0	0	.000	2	11	0	0	0.2	1.000
1993		3	5	.375	5.31	50	7	0	81.1	82	37	73	0	1	2	1	14	0	0	.000	1	5	0	0	0.1	1.000

Year	Team	W	L	PCT	ERA	G	GS	CG	IP	H	BB	SO	ShO	W	L	SV	AB	H	HR	BA	PO	A	E	DP	TC/G	FA

Denny Neagle *continued*

Year	Team	W	L	PCT	ERA	G	GS	CG	IP	H	BB	SO	ShO	W	L	SV	AB	H	HR	BA	PO	A	E	DP	TC/G	FA
1994		9	10	.474	5.12	24	24	2	137	135	49	122	0	0	0	0	42	8	1	.190	3	21	1	2	1.0	.960
1995		13	8	.619	3.43	31	31	5	209.2	221	45	150	1	0	0	0	74	9	1	.122	13	32	1	5	1.5	.978
1996	2 teams	PIT N	(27G 14–6)		ATL N	(6G 2–3)																				
"	total	16	9	.640	3.50	33	33	2	221.1	226	48	149	0	0	0	0	69	12	0	.174	5	30	1	4	1.1	.972
6 yrs.		45	39	.536	4.10	200	104	9	755.2	773	229	585	1	4	5	3	210	29	2	.138	24	100	3	11	0.6	.976
LEAGUE CHAMPIONSHIP SERIES
1992	PIT N	0	0	—	27.00	2	0	0	1.2	4	3	0	0	0	0	0	0	0	0	—	0	0	0	0	0.0	.000
1996	ATL N	0	0	—	2.35	2	1	0	7.2	2	3	8	0	0	0	0	2	1	0	.500	0	1	0	0	0.5	1.000
2 yrs.		0	0	—	6.75	4	1	0	9.1	6	6	8	0	0	0	0	2	1	0	.500	0	1	0	0	0.3	1.000
WORLD SERIES
1996	ATL N	0	0	—	3.00	2	1	0	6	5	4	3	0	0	0	0	1	0	0	.000	0	1	0	0	0.5	1.000

Jeff Nelson
NELSON, JEFFREY ALLAN
B. Nov. 17, 1966, Baltimore, Md. — BR TR 6'8" 225 lbs.

Year	Team	W	L	PCT	ERA	G	GS	CG	IP	H	BB	SO	ShO	W	L	SV	AB	H	HR	BA	PO	A	E	DP	TC/G	FA
1992	SEA A	1	7	.125	3.44	66	0	0	81	71	44	46	0	1	7	6	0	0	0	—	3	12	2	2	0.3	.882
1993		5	3	.625	4.35	71	0	0	60	57	34	61	0	5	3	1	0	0	0	—	3	12	0	2	0.2	1.000
1994		0	0	—	2.76	28	0	0	42.1	35	20	44	0	0	0	0	0	0	0	—	1	5	2	1	0.3	.750
1995		7	3	.700	2.17	62	0	0	78.2	58	27	96	0	7	3	2	0	0	0	—	2	10	1	1	0.2	.923
1996	NY A	4	4	.500	4.36	73	0	0	74.1	75	36	91	0	4	4	2	0	0	0	—	4	15	1	1	0.3	.950
5 yrs.		17	17	.500	3.43	300	0	0	336.1	296	161	338	0	17	17	11	0	0	0		13	54	6	7	0.2	.918
DIVISIONAL PLAYOFF SERIES
1995	SEA A	0	1	.000	3.18	3	0	0	5.2	7	3	7	0	0	1	0	0	0	0	—	0	1	0	0	0.3	1.000
1996	NY A	1	0	1.000	0.00	2	0	0	3.2	2	2	5	0	1	0	0	0	0	0	—	0	1	0	0	0.5	1.000
2 yrs.		1	1	.500	1.93	5	0	0	9.1	9	5	12	0	1	1	0	0	0	0		0	2	0	0	0.4	1.000
LEAGUE CHAMPIONSHIP SERIES
1995	SEA A	0	0	—	0.00	3	0	0	3	3	5	3	0	0	0	0	0	0	0	—	0	3	0	1	1.0	1.000
1996	NY A	0	1	.000	11.57	2	0	0	2.1	5	0	2	0	0	1	0	0	0	0	—	0	0	0	0	0.0	.000
2 yrs.		0	1	.000	5.06	5	0	0	5.1	8	5	5	0	0	1	0	0	0	0		0	3	0	1	0.6	1.000
WORLD SERIES
1996	NY A	0	0	—	0.00	3	0	0	4.1	1	1	5	0	0	0	0	0	0	0	—	2	0	0	0	0.7	1.000

Robb Nen
NEN, ROBERT ALLEN
Son of Dick Nen.
B. Nov. 28, 1969, San Pedro, Calif. — BR TR 6'4" 200 lbs.

Year	Team	W	L	PCT	ERA	G	GS	CG	IP	H	BB	SO	ShO	W	L	SV	AB	H	HR	BA	PO	A	E	DP	TC/G	FA
1993	2 teams	TEX A	(9G 1–1)		FLA N	(15G 1–0)																				
"	total	2	1	.667	6.75	24	4	0	56	63	46	39	0	0	0	0	4	0	0	.000	6	6	0	2	0.5	1.000
1994	FLA N	5	5	.500	2.95	44	0	0	58	46	17	60	0	5	5	15	3	0	0	.000	3	6	1	1	0.2	.900
1995		0	7	.000	3.29	62	0	0	65.2	62	23	68	0	0	7	23	0	0	0	—	3	9	0	1	0.2	1.000
1996		5	1	.833	1.95	75	0	0	83	67	21	92	0	5	1	35	2	0	0	.000	3	9	0	1	0.2	1.000
4 yrs.		12	14	.462	3.53	205	4	0	262.2	238	107	259	0	10	13	73	9	0	0	.000	15	30	1	5	0.2	.978

Dave Nied
NIED, DAVID GLEN
B. Dec. 22, 1968, Dallas, Tex. — BR TR 6'2" 175 lbs.

Year	Team	W	L	PCT	ERA	G	GS	CG	IP	H	BB	SO	ShO	W	L	SV	AB	H	HR	BA	PO	A	E	DP	TC/G	FA
1992	ATL N	3	0	1.000	1.17	6	2	0	23	10	5	19	0	2	0	0	7	2	0	.286	0	0	0	0	0.3	1.000
1993	CLR N	5	9	.357	5.17	16	16	1	87	99	42	46	0	0	0	0	23	4	0	.174	4	16	0	0	1.3	1.000
1994		9	7	.563	4.80	22	22	2	122	137	47	74	1	0	0	0	40	4	0	.100	4	12	0	2	0.7	1.000
1995		0	0	—	20.77	2	0	0	4.1	11	3	3	0	0	0	0	0	0	0	—	0	0	0	0	0.0	.000
1996		0	2	.000	13.50	6	1	0	5.1	5	8	4	0	0	1	0	1	0	0	.000	0	2	0	0	0.3	1.000
5 yrs.		17	18	.486	5.06	52	41	3	241.2	262	105	146	1	2	1	0	71	10	0	.141	8	30	0	2	0.7	1.000

C. J. Nitkowski
NITKOWSKI, CHRISTOPHER JOHN
B. Mar. 9, 1973, Suffern, N. Y. — BL TL 6'2" 185 lbs.

Year	Team	W	L	PCT	ERA	G	GS	CG	IP	H	BB	SO	ShO	W	L	SV	AB	H	HR	BA	PO	A	E	DP	TC/G	FA
1995	2 teams	CIN N	(9G 1–3)		DET A	(11G 1–4)																				
"	total	2	7	.222	6.66	20	18	0	71.2	94	35	31	0	0	0	0	10	2	0	.200	5	8	2	0	0.8	.867
1996	DET A	2	3	.400	8.08	11	8	0	45.2	62	38	36	0	0	0	0	0	0	0	—	2	5	0	0	0.6	1.000
2 yrs.		4	10	.286	7.21	31	26	0	117.1	156	73	67	0	0	0	0	10	2	0	.200	7	13	2	0	0.7	.909

Hideo Nomo
NOMO, HIDEO (The Tornado)
B. Aug. 31, 1968, Osaka, Japan — BR TR 6'2" 210 lbs.

Year	Team	W	L	PCT	ERA	G	GS	CG	IP	H	BB	SO	ShO	W	L	SV	AB	H	HR	BA	PO	A	E	DP	TC/G	FA
1995	LA N	13	6	.684	2.54	28	28	4	191.1	124	78	236	3	0	0	0	66	6	0	.091	6	12	3	2	0.8	.857
1996		16	11	.593	3.19	33	33	3	228.1	180	85	234	2	0	0	0	75	10	0	.133	12	20	1	0	1.0	.970
2 yrs.		29	17	.630	2.90	61	61	7	419.2	304	163	470	5	0	0	0	141	16	0	.113	18	32	4	2	0.9	.926
DIVISIONAL PLAYOFF SERIES
1995	LA N	0	1	.000	9.00	1	1	0	5	7	2	6	0	0	0	0	2	0	0	.000	0	0	0	0	0.0	.000
1996		0	1	.000	12.27	1	1	0	3.2	5	5	3	0	0	0	0	1	0	0	.000	1	0	0	0	1.0	1.000
2 yrs.		0	2	.000	10.38	2	2	0	8.2	12	7	9	0	0	0	0	3	0	0	.000	1	0	0	0	0.5	1.000

Chad Ogea
OGEA, CHAD WAYNE
B. Nov. 9, 1970, Lake Charles, La. — BR TR 6'2" 200 lbs.

Year	Team	W	L	PCT	ERA	G	GS	CG	IP	H	BB	SO	ShO	W	L	SV	AB	H	HR	BA	PO	A	E	DP	TC/G	FA
1994	CLE A	0	1	.000	6.06	4	1	0	16.1	21	10	11	0	0	0	0	0	0	0	—	0	2	0	0	0.5	1.000
1995		8	3	.727	3.05	20	14	1	106.1	95	29	57	0	0	0	0	0	0	0	—	3	14	0	1	0.9	1.000
1996		10	6	.625	4.79	29	21	1	146.2	151	42	101	1	3	0	0	0	0	0	—	4	16	2	1	0.8	.909
3 yrs.		18	10	.643	4.18	53	36	2	269.1	267	81	169	1	3	0	0	0	0	0		7	32	2	2	0.8	.951

Year	Team	W	L	PCT	ERA	G	GS	CG	IP	H	BB	SO	ShO	Relief Pitching W	L	SV	Batting AB	H	HR	BA	PO	A	E	DP	TC/G	FA

Chad Ogea *continued*

DIVISIONAL PLAYOFF SERIES

Year	Team	W	L	PCT	ERA	G	GS	CG	IP	H	BB	SO	ShO	W	L	SV	AB	H	HR	BA	PO	A	E	DP	TC/G	FA
1996	CLE A	0	0	—	0.00	1	0	0	0.1	0	1	0	0	0	0	0	0	0	0	—	0	0	0	0	0.0	.000

LEAGUE CHAMPIONSHIP SERIES

Year	Team	W	L	PCT	ERA	G	GS	CG	IP	H	BB	SO	ShO	W	L	SV	AB	H	HR	BA	PO	A	E	DP	TC/G	FA
1995	CLE A	0	0	—	0.00	1	0	0	0.2	1	0	2	0	0	0	0	0	0	0	—	0	0	0	0	0.0	.000

Omar Olivares

OLIVARES, OMAR
Born Omar Olivares (Palqu).
Son of Ed Olivares.
B. July 6, 1967, Mayaguez, Puerto Rico

BR TR 6' 1" 185 lbs.

Year	Team	W	L	PCT	ERA	G	GS	CG	IP	H	BB	SO	ShO	W	L	SV	AB	H	HR	BA	PO	A	E	DP	TC/G	FA
1990	STL N	1	1	.500	2.92	9	6	0	49.1	45	17	20	0	0	0	0	17	3	0	.176	7	8	0	0	1.7	1.000
1991		11	7	.611	3.71	28	24	0	167.1	148	61	91	0	0	0	1	53	12	0	.226	16	30	2	5	1.7	.958
1992		9	9	.500	3.84	32	30	1	197	189	63	124	0	0	0	0	68	16	1	.235	15	40	0	4	1.7	1.000
1993		5	3	.625	4.17	58	9	0	118.2	134	54	63	0	3	0	1	26	7	0	.269	9	36	4	3	0.8	.918
1994		3	4	.429	5.74	14	12	1	73.2	84	37	26	0	0	0	0	28	6	1	.214	7	14	1	1	1.6	.955
1995	2 teams	CLR N	(11G 1-3)		PHI N	(5G 0-1)																				
"	total	1	4	.200	6.91	16	6	0	41.2	55	23	22	0	0	2	0	9	2	1	.222	4	8	0	1	0.8	1.000
1996	DET A	7	11	.389	4.89	25	25	4	160	169	75	81	0	0	0	0	0	0	0	—	12	22	1	2	1.4	.971
7 yrs.		37	39	.487	4.35	182	112	6	807.2	824	330	427	0	3	2	3	201	46	4	.229	70	158	8	16	1.3	.966

Darren Oliver

OLIVER, DARREN CHRISTOPHER
Son of Bob Oliver.
B. Oct. 6, 1970, Kansas City, Mo.

BR TL 6' 170 lbs.

Year	Team	W	L	PCT	ERA	G	GS	CG	IP	H	BB	SO	ShO	W	L	SV	AB	H	HR	BA	PO	A	E	DP	TC/G	FA
1993	TEX A	0	0	—	2.70	2	0	0	3.1	2	1	4	0	0	0	0	0	0	0	—	0	1	1	0	1.0	.500
1994		4	0	1.000	3.42	43	0	0	50	40	35	50	0	4	0	2	0	0	0	—	5	14	0	3	0.4	1.000
1995		4	2	.667	4.22	17	7	0	49	47	32	39	0	1	0	0	0	0	0	—	4	8	0	1	0.7	1.000
1996		14	6	.700	4.66	30	30	1	173.2	190	76	112	1	0	0	0	0	0	0	—	4	23	1	3	0.9	.964
4 yrs.		22	8	.733	4.34	92	37	1	276	279	144	205	1	5	0	2	0	0	0		13	46	2	7	0.7	.967

DIVISIONAL PLAYOFF SERIES

Year	Team	W	L	PCT	ERA	G	GS	CG	IP	H	BB	SO	ShO	W	L	SV	AB	H	HR	BA	PO	A	E	DP	TC/G	FA
1996	TEX A	0	1	.000	3.38	1	1	0	8	6	2	3	0	0	0	0	0	0	0	—	0	3	0	2	3.0	1.000

Gregg Olson

OLSON, GREGGORY WILLIAM
B. Oct. 11, 1966, Scribner, Neb.

BR TR 6' 4" 210 lbs.

Year	Team	W	L	PCT	ERA	G	GS	CG	IP	H	BB	SO	ShO	W	L	SV	AB	H	HR	BA	PO	A	E	DP	TC/G	FA
1988	BAL A	1	1	.500	3.27	10	0	0	11	10	10	9	0	1	1	0	0	0	0	—	1	2	0	0	0.3	1.000
1989		5	2	.714	1.69	64	0	0	85	57	46	90	0	5	2	27	0	0	0	—	5	12	1	0	0.3	.944
1990		6	5	.545	2.42	64	0	0	74.1	57	31	74	0	6	5	37	0	0	0	—	4	4	0	1	0.1	1.000
1991		4	6	.400	3.18	72	0	0	73.2	74	29	72	0	4	6	31	0	0	0	—	6	11	3	0	0.3	.850
1992		1	5	.167	2.05	60	0	0	61.1	46	24	58	0	1	5	36	0	0	0	—	5	9	0	2	0.2	1.000
1993		0	2	.000	1.60	50	0	0	45	37	18	44	0	0	2	29	1	0	0	.000	2	7	0	0	0.2	1.000
1994	ATL N	0	2	.000	9.20	16	0	0	14.2	19	13	10	0	0	2	1	1	0	0	.000	0	0	0	0	0.0	.000
1995	2 teams	CLE A	(3G 0-0)		KC A	(20G 3-3)																				
"	total	3	3	.500	4.09	23	0	0	33	28	19	21	0	3	3	3	0	0	0	—	1	5	0	1	0.3	1.000
1996	2 teams	DET A	(43G 3-0)		HOU N	(9G 1-0)																				
"	total	4	0	1.000	4.99	52	0	0	52.1	55	35	37	0	4	0	8	0	0	0	—	6	3	0	0	0.2	1.000
9 yrs.		24	26	.480	2.94	411	0	0	450.1	383	225	415	0	24	26	172	2	0	0	.000	30	53	4	4	0.2	.954

Mike Oquist

OQUIST, MICHAEL LEE
B. May 30, 1968, La Junta, Colo.

BR TR 6' 2" 170 lbs.

Year	Team	W	L	PCT	ERA	G	GS	CG	IP	H	BB	SO	ShO	W	L	SV	AB	H	HR	BA	PO	A	E	DP	TC/G	FA
1993	BAL A	0	0	—	3.86	5	0	0	11.2	12	4	8	0	0	0	0	0	0	0	—	1	0	0	0	0.2	1.000
1994		3	3	.500	6.17	15	9	0	58.1	75	30	39	0	2	0	0	0	0	0	—	6	7	0	0	0.9	1.000
1995		2	1	.667	4.17	27	0	0	54	51	41	27	0	2	1	0	0	0	0	—	1	8	0	0	0.3	1.000
1996	SD N	0	0	—	2.35	8	0	0	7.2	6	4	4	0	0	0	0	0	0	0	—	0	1	0	0	0.1	1.000
4 yrs.		5	4	.556	4.92	55	9	0	131.2	144	79	78	0	4	1	0	0	0	0		8	16	0	0	0.4	1.000

Jesse Orosco

OROSCO, JESSE RUSSELL
B. Apr. 21, 1957, Santa Barbara, Calif.

BR TL 6' 2" 174 lbs.

Year	Team	W	L	PCT	ERA	G	GS	CG	IP	H	BB	SO	ShO	W	L	SV	AB	H	HR	BA	PO	A	E	DP	TC/G	FA
1979	NY N	1	2	.333	4.89	18	2	0	35	33	22	22	0	1	2	0	6	0	0	.000	2	9	0	1	0.6	1.000
1981		0	1	.000	1.59	8	0	0	17	13	6	18	0	0	1	1	2	0	0	.000	1	2	0	0	0.4	1.000
1982		4	10	.286	2.72	54	2	0	109.1	92	40	89	0	4	8	4	14	2	0	.143	4	16	0	1	0.4	1.000
1983		13	7	.650	1.47	62	0	0	110	76	38	84	0	13	7	17	12	4	0	.333	2	19	0	0	0.4	1.000
1984		10	6	.625	2.59	60	0	0	87	58	34	85	0	10	6	31	4	1	0	.250	2	11	1	1	0.2	.929
1985		8	6	.571	2.73	54	0	0	79	66	34	68	0	8	6	17	7	3	0	.429	3	8	1	2	0.2	.917
1986		8	6	.571	2.33	58	0	0	81	64	35	62	0	8	6	21	3	0	0	.000	5	8	0	0	0.2	1.000
1987		3	9	.250	4.44	58	0	0	77	78	31	78	0	3	9	16	8	0	0	.000	4	9	0	1	0.2	1.000
1988	LA N	3	2	.600	2.72	55	0	0	53	41	30	43	0	3	2	9	2	0	0	.000	1	3	0	0	0.1	1.000
1989	CLE A	3	4	.429	2.08	69	0	0	78	54	26	79	0	3	4	3	0	0	0	—	6	13	0	1	0.3	1.000
1990		5	4	.556	3.90	55	0	0	64.2	58	38	55	0	5	4	2	0	0	0	—	1	14	1	1	0.3	.938
1991		2	0	1.000	3.74	47	0	0	45.2	52	15	36	0	2	0	0	0	0	0	—	3	3	0	0	0.1	1.000
1992	MIL A	3	1	.750	3.23	59	0	0	39	33	13	40	0	3	1	1	0	0	0	—	2	3	0	0	0.1	1.000
1993		3	5	.375	3.18	57	0	0	56.2	47	17	67	0	3	5	8	1	0	0	.000	1	19	0	0	0.4	1.000
1994		3	1	.750	5.08	40	0	0	39	32	26	36	0	3	1	0	0	0	0	—	3	3	0	1	0.2	1.000

Year	Team	W	L	PCT	ERA	G	GS	CG	IP	H	BB	SO	ShO	W	L	SV	AB	H	HR	BA	PO	A	E	DP	TC/G	FA
														Relief Pitching			**Batting**									

Jesse Orosco *continued*

Year	Team	W	L	PCT	ERA	G	GS	CG	IP	H	BB	SO	ShO	W	L	SV	AB	H	HR	BA	PO	A	E	DP	TC/G	FA
1995	BAL A	2	4	.333	3.26	65	0	0	49.2	28	27	58	0	2	4	3	0	0	0	—	3	8	0	0	0.2	1.000
1996		3	1	.750	3.40	66	0	0	55.2	42	28	52	0	3	1	0	0	0	0	—	2	8	0	0	0.2	1.000
17 yrs.		74	69	.517	2.98	885	4	0	1076.2	867	460	972	0	74	67	133	59	10	0	.169	48	163	3	10	0.2	.986

DIVISIONAL PLAYOFF SERIES

| 1996 | BAL A | 0 | 1 | .000 | 36.00 | 4 | 0 | 0 | 1 | 2 | 3 | 2 | 0 | 0 | 1 | 0 | 0 | 0 | 0 | — | 0 | 0 | 0 | 0 | 0.0 | .000 |

LEAGUE CHAMPIONSHIP SERIES

1986	NY N	3	0	1.000	3.38	4	0	0	8	5	2	10	0	3	0	0	0	0	0	—	1	1	0	0	0.5	1.000
1988	LA N	0	0	—	7.71	4	0	0	2.1	4	3	0	0	0	0	0	0	0	0	—	1	0	0	0	0.3	1.000
1996	BAL A	0	0	—	4.50	4	0	0	2	2	1	2	0	0	0	0	0	0	0	—	0	1	0	0	0.3	1.000
3 yrs.		3	0	1.000	4.38	12	0	0	12.1	11	6	12	0	3	0	0	0	0	0	—	2	2	0	0	0.3	1.000
						8th																				

WORLD SERIES

| 1986 | NY N | 0 | 0 | — | 0.00 | 4 | 0 | 0 | 5.2 | 2 | 0 | 6 | 0 | 0 | 0 | 0 | 1 | 1 | 0 | 1.000 | 0 | 0 | 0 | 0 | 0.0 | .000 |

Donovan Osborne

OSBORNE, DONOVAN ALAN
B. June 21, 1969, Roseville, Calif.

BB TL 6' 2" 195 lbs.

Year	Team	W	L	PCT	ERA	G	GS	CG	IP	H	BB	SO	ShO	W	L	SV	AB	H	HR	BA	PO	A	E	DP	TC/G	FA
1992	STL N	11	9	.550	3.77	34	29	0	179	193	38	104	0	1	1	0	58	7	0	.121	6	18	2	2	0.8	.923
1993		10	7	.588	3.76	26	26	1	155.2	153	47	83	0	0	0	0	49	10	0	.204	8	24	0	1	1.2	1.000
1995		4	6	.400	3.81	19	19	0	113.1	112	34	82	0	0	0	0	31	5	0	.161	3	16	0	0	1.0	1.000
1996		13	9	.591	3.53	30	30	2	198.2	191	57	134	1	0	0	0	59	13	1	.220	6	23	1	0	1.0	.967
4 yrs.		38	31	.551	3.70	109	104	3	646.2	649	176	403	1	1	1	0	197	35	1	.178	23	81	3	3	1.0	.972

DIVISIONAL PLAYOFF SERIES

| 1996 | STL N | 0 | 0 | — | 9.00 | 1 | 1 | 0 | 4 | 7 | 0 | 5 | 0 | 0 | 0 | 0 | 1 | 0 | 0 | .000 | 0 | 1 | 0 | 0 | 1.000 |

LEAGUE CHAMPIONSHIP SERIES

| 1996 | STL N | 1 | 1 | .500 | 9.39 | 2 | 2 | 0 | 7.2 | 12 | 4 | 6 | 0 | 0 | 0 | 0 | 3 | 0 | 0 | .000 | 0 | 1 | 0 | 0 | 0.5 | 1.000 |

Al Osuna

OSUNA, ALFONSO
B. Aug. 10, 1965, Inglewood, Calif.

BR TL 6' 3" 200 lbs.

Year	Team	W	L	PCT	ERA	G	GS	CG	IP	H	BB	SO	ShO	W	L	SV	AB	H	HR	BA	PO	A	E	DP	TC/G	FA
1990	HOU N	2	0	1.000	4.76	12	0	0	11.1	10	6	6	0	2	0	0	0	0	0	—	1	1	0	0	0.2	1.000
1991		7	6	.538	3.42	71	0	0	81.2	59	46	68	0	7	6	12	2	0	0	.000	4	10	1	2	0.2	.933
1992		6	3	.667	4.23	66	0	0	61.2	52	38	37	0	6	3	0	0	0	0	—	2	11	0	0	0.2	1.000
1993		1	1	.500	3.20	44	0	0	25.1	17	13	21	0	1	1	2	0	0	0	—	0	2	1	0	0.1	.667
1994	LA N	2	0	1.000	6.23	15	0	0	8.2	13	4	7	0	2	0	0	0	0	0	—	0	0	0	0	0.0	.000
1996	SD N	0	0	—	2.25	10	0	0	4	5	2	4	0	0	0	0	1	0	0	.000	1	1	0	0	0.2	1.000
6 yrs.		18	10	.643	3.83	218	0	0	192.2	156	109	143	0	18	10	14	3	0	0	.000	8	25	2	2	0.2	.943

Antonio Osuna

OSUNA, ANTONIO PEDRO
B. Apr. 12, 1973, Sinaloa, Mexico

BR TR 5'11" 160 lbs.

Year	Team	W	L	PCT	ERA	G	GS	CG	IP	H	BB	SO	ShO	W	L	SV	AB	H	HR	BA	PO	A	E	DP	TC/G	FA
1995	LA N	2	4	.333	4.43	39	0	0	44.2	39	20	46	0	2	4	0	2	0	0	.000	0	7	0	1	0.2	1.000
1996		9	6	.600	3.00	73	0	0	84	65	32	85	0	9	6	4	1	0	0	.000	3	11	0	1	0.2	1.000
2 yrs.		11	10	.524	3.50	112	0	0	128.2	104	52	131	0	11	10	4	3	0	0	.000	3	18	0	3	0.2	1.000

DIVISIONAL PLAYOFF SERIES

1995	LA N	0	1	.000	2.70	3	0	0	3.1	3	1	3	0	0	1	0	0	0	0	—	0	0	1	0	0.3	.000
1996		0	1	.000	4.50	2	0	0	2	3	1	4	0	0	1	0	0	0	0	—	0	0	0	0	0.0	.000
2 yrs.		0	2	.000	3.38	5	0	0	5.1	6	2	7	0	0	2	0	0	0	0	—	0	0	1	0	0.2	.000

Alex Pacheco

PACHECO, ALEXANDER MELCHOR
Born Alexander Melchor Pacheco (Lara).
B. July 19, 1973, Caracas, Venezuela

BR TR 6' 3" 200 lbs.

Year	Team	W	L	PCT	ERA	G	GS	CG	IP	H	BB	SO	ShO	W	L	SV	AB	H	HR	BA	PO	A	E	DP	TC/G	FA
1996	MON N	0	0	—	11.12	5	0	0	5.2	8	1	7	0	0	0	0	0	0	0	—	0	0	0	0	0.0	—

Lance Painter

PAINTER, LANCE TELFORD
B. July 21, 1967, Bedford, England

BL TL 6' 1" 195 lbs.

Year	Team	W	L	PCT	ERA	G	GS	CG	IP	H	BB	SO	ShO	W	L	SV	AB	H	HR	BA	PO	A	E	DP	TC/G	FA
1993	CLR N	2	2	.500	6.00	10	6	1	39	52	9	16	0	0	0	0	10	3	0	.300	1	9	0	0	1.0	1.000
1994		4	6	.400	6.11	15	14	0	73.2	91	26	41	0	0	0	0	21	3	0	.143	5	11	0	0	1.1	1.000
1995		3	0	1.000	4.37	33	1	0	45.1	55	10	36	0	2	0	1	9	1	0	.111	3	6	0	0	0.3	1.000
1996		4	2	.667	5.86	34	1	0	50.2	56	25	48	0	4	1	1	15	2	0	.133	2	7	3	0	0.4	.750
4 yrs.		13	10	.565	5.65	92	22	1	208.2	254	70	141	0	6	1	1	55	9	0	.164	11	33	3	0	0.5	.936

DIVISIONAL PLAYOFF SERIES

| 1995 | CLR N | 0 | 0 | — | 5.40 | 1 | 1 | 0 | 5 | 5 | 2 | 4 | 0 | 0 | 0 | 0 | 2 | 0 | 0 | .000 | 0 | 0 | 0 | 0 | 0.0 | .000 |

Donn Pall

PALL, DONN STEVEN
B. Jan. 11, 1962, Chicago, Ill.

BR TR 6' 2" 185 lbs.

Year	Team	W	L	PCT	ERA	G	GS	CG	IP	H	BB	SO	ShO	W	L	SV	AB	H	HR	BA	PO	A	E	DP	TC/G	FA
1988	CHI A	0	2	.000	3.45	17	0	0	28.2	39	8	16	0	0	2	0	0	0	0	—	4	6	0	1	0.6	1.000
1989		4	5	.444	3.31	53	0	0	87	90	19	58	0	4	5	6	0	0	0	—	5	7	2	0	0.3	.857
1990		3	5	.375	3.32	56	0	0	76	63	24	39	0	3	5	2	0	0	0	—	1	11	0	2	0.2	1.000
1991		7	2	.778	2.41	51	0	0	71	59	20	40	0	7	2	0	0	0	0	—	4	8	1	0	0.3	.923
1992		5	2	.714	4.93	39	0	0	73	79	27	27	0	5	2	1	0	0	0	—	5	6	1	2	0.3	.917
1993	2 teams					CHI A	(39G 2–3)		PHI N	(8G 1–0)																
"	total	3	3	.500	3.07	47	0	0	76.1	77	14	40	0	3	3	1	0	0	0	—	5	13	1	0	0.4	.947

Year	Team	W	L	PCT	ERA	G	GS	CG	IP	H	BB	SO	ShO	Relief Pitching W	L	SV	Batting AB	H	HR	BA	PO	A	E	DP	TC/G	FA

Donn Pall *continued*

Year	Team	W	L	PCT	ERA	G	GS	CG	IP	H	BB	SO	ShO	W	L	SV	AB	H	HR	BA	PO	A	E	DP	TC/G	FA
1994	2 teams	NY A	(26G 1-2)	CHI N	(2G 0-0)																				
"	total	1	2	.333	3.69	28	0	0	39	51	10	23	0	1	2	0	0	0	0		4	4	0	0	0.3	1.000
1996	FLA N	1	1	.500	5.79	12	0	0	18.2	16	9	9	0	1	1	0	2	0	0	.000	1	1	0	0	0.2	1.000
	8 yrs.	24	22	.522	3.53	303	0	0	469.2	474	131	252	0	24	22	10	2	0	0	.000	29	56	5	5	0.3	.944

Jose Paniagua

PANIAGUA, JOSE LUIS
Born Jose Luis Paniagua (Sanchez).
B. Aug. 20, 1973, San Jose De Ocoa, Dominican Republic

BR TR 6'2" 185 lbs.

Year	Team	W	L	PCT	ERA	G	GS	CG	IP	H	BB	SO	ShO	W	L	SV	AB	H	HR	BA	PO	A	E	DP	TC/G	FA
1996	MON N	2	4	.333	3.53	13	11	0	51	55	23	27	0	0	0	0	11	0	0	.000	3	10	0	0	1.0	1.000

Chan Ho Park

PARK, CHAN HO
B. June 3, 1973, Kongju, South Korea

BR TR 6'2" 185 lbs.

Year	Team	W	L	PCT	ERA	G	GS	CG	IP	H	BB	SO	ShO	W	L	SV	AB	H	HR	BA	PO	A	E	DP	TC/G	FA
1994	LA N	0	0	—	11.25	2	0	0	4	5	5	6	0	0	0	0	0	0	0		0	0	0	0	0.0	.000
1995		0	0	—	4.50	2	1	0	4	2	2	7	0	0	0	0	1	0	0	.000	0	0	0	0	0.0	.000
1996		5	5	.500	3.64	48	10	0	108.2	82	71	119	0	2	2	0	19	1	0	.053	10	21	1	3	0.7	.969
	3 yrs.	5	5	.500	3.93	52	11	0	116.2	89	78	132	0	2	2	0	20	1	0	.050	10	21	1	3	0.6	.969

Jose Parra

PARRA, JOSE MIGUEL
B. Nov. 28, 1972, Jacaqua Santiago, Dominican Republic

BR TR 5'11" 160 lbs.

Year	Team	W	L	PCT	ERA	G	GS	CG	IP	H	BB	SO	ShO	W	L	SV	AB	H	HR	BA	PO	A	E	DP	TC/G	FA
1995	2 teams	LA N	(8G 0-0)	MIN A	(12G 1-5)																				
"	total	1	5	.167	7.13	20	12	0	72	93	28	36	0	0	0	0	0	0	0	—	4	9	2	1	0.8	.867
1996	MIN A	5	5	.500	6.04	27	5	0	70	88	27	50	0	4	2	0	0	0	0	—	7	7	0	2	0.5	1.000
	2 yrs.	6	10	.375	6.59	47	17	0	142	181	55	86	0	4	2	0	0	0	0		11	16	2	3	0.6	.931

Jeff Parrett

PARRETT, JEFFREY DALE
B. Aug. 26, 1961, Indianapolis, Ind.

BR TR 6'4" 185 lbs.

Year	Team	W	L	PCT	ERA	G	GS	CG	IP	H	BB	SO	ShO	W	L	SV	AB	H	HR	BA	PO	A	E	DP	TC/G	FA
1986	MON N	0	1	.000	4.87	12	0	0	20.1	19	13	21	0	0	1	0	2	1	0	.500	1	2	0	1	0.3	1.000
1987		7	6	.538	4.21	45	0	0	62	53	30	56	0	7	6	6	5	0	0	.000	3	9	2	1	0.3	.857
1988		12	4	.750	2.65	61	0	0	91.2	66	45	62	0	12	4	6	0	0	0	—	7	9	1	0	0.3	.941
1989	PHI N	12	6	.667	2.98	72	0	0	105.2	90	44	98	0	12	6	6	5	0	0	.000	2	9	0	0	0.2	1.000
1990	2 teams	PHI N	(47G 4-9)	ATL N	(20G 1-1)																				
"	total	5	10	.333	4.64	67	5	0	108.2	119	55	86	0	4	7	2	11	1	0	.091	1	18	4	1	0.3	.826
1991	ATL N	1	2	.333	6.33	18	0	0	21.1	31	12	14	0	1	2	1	0	0	0	—	3	5	1	1	0.5	.889
1992	OAK A	9	1	.900	3.02	66	0	0	98.1	81	42	78	0	9	1	0	0	0	0	—	5	7	1	2	0.2	.923
1993	CLR N	3	3	.500	5.38	40	6	0	73.2	78	45	66	0	1	2	1	11	1	0	.091	3	9	1	0	0.3	.923
1995	STL N	4	7	.364	3.64	59	0	0	76.2	71	28	71	0	4	7	0	2	1	0	.500	7	6	2	0	0.3	.867
1996	2 teams	STL N	(33G 2-2)	PHI N	(18G 1-1)																				
"	total	3	3	.500	3.39	51	0	0	66.1	64	31	64	0	3	3	0	2	0	0	.000	3	9	0	1	0.2	1.000
	10 yrs.	56	43	.566	3.80	491	11	0	724.2	672	345	616	0	53	39	22	38	4	0	.105	35	83	12	7	0.3	.908

LEAGUE CHAMPIONSHIP SERIES

Year	Team	W	L	PCT	ERA	G	GS	CG	IP	H	BB	SO	ShO	W	L	SV	AB	H	HR	BA	PO	A	E	DP	TC/G	FA
1992	OAK A	0	0	—	11.57	3	0	0	2.1	6	0	1	0	0	0	0	0	0	0	—	0	1	0	0	0.3	1.000

Steve Parris

PARRIS, STEVEN MICHAEL
B. Dec. 17, 1967, Joliet, Ill.

BR TR 6' 190 lbs.

Year	Team	W	L	PCT	ERA	G	GS	CG	IP	H	BB	SO	ShO	W	L	SV	AB	H	HR	BA	PO	A	E	DP	TC/G	FA
1995	PIT N	6	6	.500	5.38	15	15	1	82	89	33	61	1	0	0	0	28	7	0	.250	4	10	0	0	0.9	1.000
1996		0	3	.000	7.18	8	4	0	26.1	35	11	27	0	0	0	0	6	1	0	.167	2	4	1	1	0.9	.857
	2 yrs.	6	9	.400	5.82	23	19	1	108.1	124	44	88	1	0	0	0	34	8	0	.235	6	14	1	1	0.9	.952

Bob Patterson

PATTERSON, ROBERT CHANDLER
B. May 16, 1959, Jacksonville, Fla.

BR TR 6'2" 185 lbs.

Year	Team	W	L	PCT	ERA	G	GS	CG	IP	H	BB	SO	ShO	W	L	SV	AB	H	HR	BA	PO	A	E	DP	TC/G	FA
1985	SD N	0	0	—	24.75	3	0	0	4	13	3	1	0	0	0	0	0	0	0	—	0	0	0	0	0.0	.000
1986	PIT N	2	3	.400	4.95	11	5	0	36.1	49	5	20	0	1	2	0	8	1	0	.125	1	9	0	1	0.9	1.000
1987		1	4	.200	6.70	15	7	0	43	49	22	27	0	0	0	0	12	1	0	.083	0	7	0	0	0.5	1.000
1989		4	3	.571	4.05	12	3	0	26.2	23	8	20	0	3	1	1	3	0	0	.000	1	2	0	0	0.3	1.000
1990		8	5	.615	2.95	55	5	0	94.2	88	21	70	0	6	3	5	19	1	0	.053	9	10	0	0	0.3	1.000
1991		4	3	.571	4.11	54	1	0	65.2	67	15	57	0	4	3	2	4	1	0	.250	4	9	0	1	0.2	1.000
1992		6	3	.667	2.92	60	0	0	64.2	59	23	43	0	6	3	9	6	2	0	.333	3	7	0	1	0.2	1.000
1993	TEX A	2	4	.333	4.78	52	0	0	52.2	59	11	46	0	2	4	1	0	0	0	—	3	7	0	0	0.2	1.000
1994	CAL A	2	3	.400	4.07	47	0	0	42	35	15	30	0	2	3	1	0	0	0	—	2	1	0	0	0.1	1.000
1995		5	2	.714	3.04	62	0	0	53.1	48	13	41	0	5	2	0	0	0	0	—	0	5	0	0	0.1	1.000
1996	CHI N	3	3	.500	3.13	79	0	0	54.2	46	22	53	0	3	3	8	3	1	0	.333	1	3	0	0	0.1	1.000
	11 yrs.	37	33	.529	4.03	450	21	0	537.2	536	158	408	0	32	24	27	55	7	0	.127	24	60	0	3	0.2	1.000

LEAGUE CHAMPIONSHIP SERIES

Year	Team	W	L	PCT	ERA	G	GS	CG	IP	H	BB	SO	ShO	W	L	SV	AB	H	HR	BA	PO	A	E	DP	TC/G	FA
1990	PIT N	0	0	—	0.00	2	0	0	1	1	2	0	0	0	0	0	0	0	0	—	0	1	0	0	0.5	1.000
1991		0	0	—	0.00	1	0	0	2	1	0	3	0	0	0	0	0	0	0	—	0	0	0	0	0.0	.000
1992		0	0	—	5.40	2	0	0	1.2	3	1	1	0	0	0	0	0	0	0	—	0	0	0	0	0.0	.000
	3 yrs.	0	0		1.93	5	0	0	4.2	5	3	4	0	0	0	1	0	0	0		0	1	0	0	0.2	1.000

Danny Patterson

PATTERSON, DANNY SHANE
B. Feb 17, 1971, San Gabriel, Calif.

BR TR 6' 175 lbs.

Year	Team	W	L	PCT	ERA	G	GS	CG	IP	H	BB	SO	ShO	W	L	SV	AB	H	HR	BA	PO	A	E	DP	TC/G	FA
1996	TEX A	0	0	—	0.00	7	0	0	8.2	10	3	5	0	0	0	0	0	0	0	—	0	2	0	0	0.3	1.000

Year	Team	W	L	PCT	ERA	G	GS	CG	IP	H	BB	SO	ShO	W	L	SV	AB	H	HR	BA	PO	A	E	DP	TC/G	FA
														Relief Pitching			Batting									

Danny Patterson *continued*

DIVISIONAL PLAYOFF SERIES

Year	Team	W	L	PCT	ERA	G	GS	CG	IP	H	BB	SO	ShO	W	L	SV	AB	H	HR	BA	PO	A	E	DP	TC/G	FA
1996	TEX A	0	0	—	0.00	1	0	0	0.1	1	0	0	0	0	0	0	0	0	0	—	0	0	0	0	0.0	—

Dave Pavlas

PAVLAS, DAVID LEE
B. Aug. 12, 1962, Frankfurt, Germany — BR TR 6'7" 180 lbs.

Year	Team	W	L	PCT	ERA	G	GS	CG	IP	H	BB	SO	ShO	W	L	SV	AB	H	HR	BA	PO	A	E	DP	TC/G	FA
1990	CHI N	2	0	1.000	2.11	13	0	0	21.1	23	6	12	0	2	0	0	1	0	0	.000	1	2	0	0	0.2	1.000
1991		0	0	—	18.00	1	0	0	1	3	0	0	0	0	0	0	0	0	0	—	0	0	0	0	0.0	.000
1995	NY A	0	0	—	3.18	4	0	0	5.2	8	0	3	0	0	0	0	0	0	0	—	0	0	0	0	0.0	.000
1996		0	0	—	2.35	16	0	0	23	23	7	18	0	0	0	1	0	0	0	—	2	3	0	0	0.3	1.000
4 yrs.		2	0	1.000	2.65	34	0	0	51	57	13	33	0	2	0	1	1	0	0	.000	3	5	0	0	0.2	1.000

Roger Pavlik

PAVLIK, ROGER ALLEN
B. Oct. 4, 1967, Houston, Tex. — BR TR 6'3" 220 lbs.

Year	Team	W	L	PCT	ERA	G	GS	CG	IP	H	BB	SO	ShO	W	L	SV	AB	H	HR	BA	PO	A	E	DP	TC/G	FA
1992	TEX A	4	4	.500	4.21	13	12	1	62	66	34	45	0	0	0	0	0	0	0	—	6	3	1	0	0.8	.900
1993		12	6	.667	3.41	26	26	2	166.1	151	80	131	0	0	0	0	0	0	0	—	10	27	3	2	1.5	.925
1994		2	5	.286	7.69	11	11	0	50.1	61	30	31	0	0	0	0	0	0	0	—	2	8	0	1	0.9	1.000
1995		10	10	.500	4.37	31	31	2	191.2	174	90	149	1	0	0	0	0	0	0	—	20	32	1	4	1.7	.981
1996		15	8	.652	5.19	34	34	7	201	216	81	127	0	0	0	0	0	0	0	—	9	14	2	1	0.7	.920
5 yrs.		43	33	.566	4.61	115	114	12	671.1	668	315	483	1	0	0	0	0	0	0		47	84	7	8	1.2	.949

DIVISIONAL PLAYOFF SERIES

Year	Team	W	L	PCT	ERA	G	GS	CG	IP	H	BB	SO	ShO	W	L	SV	AB	H	HR	BA	PO	A	E	DP	TC/G	FA
1996	TEX A	0	1	.000	6.75	1	0	0	2.2	4	0	1	0	0	1	0	0	0	0	—	1	0	0	0	1.0	1.000

Alejandro Pena

PENA, ALEJANDRO
Born Alejandro Pena (Vasquez).
B. June 25, 1959, Cambiaso, Dominican Republic — BR TR 6'1" 200 lbs.

Year	Team	W	L	PCT	ERA	G	GS	CG	IP	H	BB	SO	ShO	W	L	SV	AB	H	HR	BA	PO	A	E	DP	TC/G	FA
1981	LA N	1	1	.500	2.88	14	0	0	25	18	11	14	0	1	1	2	6	0	0	.000	1	5	1	0	0.5	.857
1982		0	2	.000	4.79	29	0	0	35.2	37	21	20	0	0	2	0	0	0	0	—	3	11	2	1	0.6	.875
1983		12	9	.571	2.75	34	26	4	177	152	51	120	3	2	1	1	60	6	1	.100	13	32	4	4	1.4	.918
1984		12	6	.667	2.48	28	28	8	199.1	186	46	135	4	0	0	0	66	8	0	.121	17	21	4	1	1.5	.905
1985		0	1	.000	8.31	2	1	0	4.1	7	3	2	0	0	1	0	1	0	0	.000	0	1	1	0	1.0	.500
1986		1	2	.333	4.89	24	10	0	70	74	30	46	0	0	1	1	17	3	0	.176	1	8	0	0	0.4	1.000
1987		2	7	.222	3.50	37	7	0	87.1	82	37	76	0	2	1	11	13	1	0	.077	4	1	1	0	0.2	.833
1988		6	7	.462	1.91	60	0	0	94.1	75	27	83	0	6	7	12	6	0	0	.000	9	10	2	1	0.3	.905
1989		4	3	.571	2.13	53	0	0	76	62	18	75	0	4	3	5	1	1	0	1.000	1	5	1	0	0.1	.857
1990	NY N	3	3	.500	3.20	52	0	0	76	71	22	76	0	3	3	5	6	1	0	.167	2	4	0	0	0.1	1.000
1991	2 teams				NY N	(44G	6-1)		ATL N		(15G	2-0)														
"	total	8	1	.889	2.40	59	0	0	82.1	74	22	62	0	8	1	15	1	0	0	.000	6	9	1	1	0.3	.938
1992	ATL N	1	6	.143	4.07	41	0	0	42	40	13	34	0	1	6	15	2	0	0	.000	2	1	0	0	0.1	1.000
1994	PIT N	3	2	.600	5.02	22	0	0	28.2	22	10	27	0	3	2	7	1	0	0	.000	1	1	1	0	0.1	.667
1995	3 teams				BOS A	(17G	1-1)		FLA N		(13G	2-0)		ATL N		(14G	0-0)								
"	total	3	1	.750	4.72	44	0	0	55.1	55	19	64	0	3	1	0	1	0	0	.000	2	3	0	0	0.1	1.000
1996	FLA N	0	1	.000	4.50	4	0	0	4	4	1	5	0	0	1	0	0	0	0	—	0	0	0	0	0.0	.000
15 yrs.		56	52	.519	3.11	503	72	12	1057.1	959	331	839	7	33	32	74	181	20	1	.110	62	112	18	8	0.4	.906

DIVISIONAL PLAYOFF SERIES

Year	Team	W	L	PCT	ERA	G	GS	CG	IP	H	BB	SO	ShO	W	L	SV	AB	H	HR	BA	PO	A	E	DP	TC/G	FA
1995	ATL N	2	0	1.000	0.00	3	0	0	3	3	1	2	0	2	0	0	0	0	0	—	0	0	0	0	0.0	.000

LEAGUE CHAMPIONSHIP SERIES

Year	Team	W	L	PCT	ERA	G	GS	CG	IP	H	BB	SO	ShO	W	L	SV	AB	H	HR	BA	PO	A	E	DP	TC/G	FA
1981	LA N	0	0	—	0.00	2	0	0	2.1	1	0	0	0	0	0	0	0	0	0	—	0	0	0	0	0.0	.000
1983		0	0	—	6.75	1	0	0	2.2	4	1	3	0	0	0	0	1	1	0	1.000	0	0	0	0	0.0	.000
1988		1	1	.500	4.15	3	0	0	4.1	1	5	1	0	1	1	1	0	0	0	—	0	0	0	0	0.0	.000
1991	ATL N	0	0	—	0.00	4	0	0	4.1	1	0	4	0	0	0	3	0	0	0	—	1	2	0	0	0.8	1.000
1995		0	0	—	0.00	3	0	0	3	2	1	4	0	0	0	0	0	0	0	—	0	0	0	0	0.0	.000
5 yrs.		1	1	.500	2.16	13 (5th)	0	0	16.2	9	7	12	0	1	1	4 (3rd)	1	1	0	1.000	1	2	0	0	0.2	1.000

WORLD SERIES

Year	Team	W	L	PCT	ERA	G	GS	CG	IP	H	BB	SO	ShO	W	L	SV	AB	H	HR	BA	PO	A	E	DP	TC/G	FA
1988	LA N	1	0	1.000	0.00	2	0	0	5	2	1	7	0	1	0	0	0	0	0	—	0	0	0	0	0.0	.000
1991	ATL N	0	1	.000	3.38	3	0	0	5.1	6	3	7	0	0	1	0	0	0	0	—	0	0	0	0	0.0	.000
1995		0	1	.000	9.00	2	0	0	1	3	2	0	0	0	1	0	0	0	0	—	0	0	0	0	0.0	.000
3 yrs.		1	2	.333	2.38	7	0	0	11.1	11	6	14	0	1	2	0	0	0	0		0	0	0	0	0.0	

Brad Pennington

PENNINGTON, BRAD LEE
B. Apr. 14, 1969, Salem, Ind. — BL TL 6'5" 205 lbs.

Year	Team	W	L	PCT	ERA	G	GS	CG	IP	H	BB	SO	ShO	W	L	SV	AB	H	HR	BA	PO	A	E	DP	TC/G	FA
1993	BAL A	3	2	.600	6.55	34	0	0	33	34	25	39	0	3	2	4	0	0	0	—	1	2	0	0	0.1	1.000
1994		0	1	.000	12.00	8	0	0	6	9	8	7	0	0	1	0	0	0	0	—	0	0	1	0	0.1	.000
1995	2 teams				BAL A	(8G	0-1)		CIN N		(6G	0-0)														
"	total	0	1	.000	6.61	14	0	0	16.1	12	22	17	0	0	1	0	2	0	0	.000	1	0	1	0	0.1	.500
1996	2 teams				BOS A	(14G	0-2)		CAL A		(8G	0-0)														
"	total	0	2	.000	6.20	22	0	0	20.1	11	31	20	0	0	2	0	0	0	0	—	0	2	0	0	0.1	1.000
4 yrs.		3	6	.333	6.90	78	0	0	75.2	66	86	83	0	3	6	4	2	0	0	.000	2	4	2	0	0.1	.750

Troy Percival

PERCIVAL, TROY EUGENE
B. Aug. 9, 1969, Fontana, Calif. — BR TR 6'3" 200 lbs.

Year	Team	W	L	PCT	ERA	G	GS	CG	IP	H	BB	SO	ShO	W	L	SV	AB	H	HR	BA	PO	A	E	DP	TC/G	FA
1995	CAL A	3	2	.600	1.95	62	0	0	74	37	26	94	0	3	2	3	0	0	0	—	2	4	0	0	0.1	1.000
1996		0	2	.000	2.31	62	0	0	74	38	31	100	1	0	2	36	0	0	0	.000	4	1	1	0	0.1	.833
2 yrs.		3	4	.429	2.13	124	0	0	148	75	57	194	0	3	4	39	1	0	0	.000	6	5	1	0	0.1	.917

Year	Team	W	L	PCT	ERA	G	GS	CG	IP	H	BB	SO	ShO	Relief Pitching W	L	SV	Batting AB	H	HR	BA	PO	A	E	DP	TC/G	FA

Mike Perez

PEREZ, MICHAEL IRVIN
Born Michael Irvin Perez (Ortega).
B. Oct. 19, 1964, Yauco, Puerto Rico
BR TR 6' 185 lbs.

Year	Team	W	L	PCT	ERA	G	GS	CG	IP	H	BB	SO	ShO	W	L	SV	AB	H	HR	BA	PO	A	E	DP	TC/G	FA
1990	STL N	1	0	1.000	3.95	13	0	0	13.2	12	3	5	0	1	0	1	1	0	0	.000	3	2	0	0	0.4	1.000
1991		0	2	.000	5.82	14	0	0	17	19	7	7	0	0	2	0	0	0	0	—	0	2	0	0	0.1	1.000
1992		9	3	.750	1.84	77	0	0	93	70	32	46	0	9	3	0	4	0	0	.000	9	15	0	2	0.3	1.000
1993		7	2	.778	2.48	65	0	0	72.2	65	20	58	0	7	2	7	1	0	0	.000	2	12	0	2	0.2	1.000
1994		2	3	.400	8.71	36	0	0	31	52	10	20	0	2	3	12	0	0	0	—	1	4	2	1	0.2	.714
1995	CHI N	2	6	.250	3.66	68	0	0	71.1	72	27	49	0	2	6	2	4	0	0	.000	5	8	1	1	0.2	.929
1996		1	0	1.000	4.67	24	0	0	27	29	13	22	0	1	0	0	1	0	0	.000	1	3	0	0	0.2	1.000
7 yrs.		22	16	.579	3.56	297	0	0	325.2	319	112	207	0	22	16	22	11	0	0	.000	21	46	3	6	0.2	.957

Yorkis Perez

PEREZ, YORKIS MIGUEL
Born Yorkis Miguel Perez (Vargas).
B. Sept. 30, 1967, Bajos de Haina, Dominican Republic
BL TL 6' 180 lbs.

Year	Team	W	L	PCT	ERA	G	GS	CG	IP	H	BB	SO	ShO	W	L	SV	AB	H	HR	BA	PO	A	E	DP	TC/G	FA
1991	CHI N	1	0	1.000	2.08	3	0	0	4.1	2	2	3	0	1	0	0	0	0	0	—	0	1	0	0	0.3	1.000
1994	FLA N	3	0	1.000	3.54	44	0	0	40.2	33	14	41	0	3	0	0	2	0	0	.000	5	1	0	0	0.1	1.000
1995		2	6	.250	5.21	69	0	0	46.2	35	28	47	0	2	6	1	2	0	0	.000	1	4	0	0	0.1	1.000
1996		3	4	.429	5.29	64	0	0	47.2	51	31	47	0	3	4	0	1	0	0	.000	2	9	2	0	0.2	.846
4 yrs.		9	10	.474	4.65	180	0	0	139.1	121	75	138	0	9	10	1	5	0	0	.000	8	15	2	0	0.1	.920

Robert Person

PERSON, ROBERT ALAN
B. Oct. 6, 1969, Lowell, Mass.
BR TR 6' 180 lbs.

Year	Team	W	L	PCT	ERA	G	GS	CG	IP	H	BB	SO	ShO	W	L	SV	AB	H	HR	BA	PO	A	E	DP	TC/G	FA
1995	NY N	1	0	1.000	0.75	3	1	0	12	5	2	10	0	0	0	0	3	2	0	.667	0	0	0	0	0.0	.000
1996		4	5	.444	4.52	27	13	0	89.2	86	35	76	0	0	1	0	21	3	0	.143	2	8	4	0	0.5	.714
2 yrs.		5	5	.500	4.07	30	14	0	101.2	91	37	86	0	0	1	0	24	5	0	.208	2	8	4	0	0.5	.714

Chris Peters

PETERS, CHRISTOPHER MICHAEL
B. Jan. 28, 1972, Ft. Thomas, Ky.
BL TL 6'1" 162 lbs.

Year	Team	W	L	PCT	ERA	G	GS	CG	IP	H	BB	SO	ShO	W	L	SV	AB	H	HR	BA	PO	A	E	DP	TC/G	FA
1996	PIT N	2	4	.333	5.63	16	10	0	64	72	25	28	0	1	0	0	19	4	0	.211	3	8	1	3	0.8	.917

Mark Petkovsek

PETKOVSEK, MARK JOSEPH
B. Nov. 18, 1965, Beaumont, Tex.
BR TR 6' 185 lbs.

Year	Team	W	L	PCT	ERA	G	GS	CG	IP	H	BB	SO	ShO	W	L	SV	AB	H	HR	BA	PO	A	E	DP	TC/G	FA
1991	TEX A	0	1	.000	14.46	4	1	0	9.1	21	4	6	0	0	0	0	0	0	0	—	1	0	0	0	0.3	1.000
1993	PIT N	3	0	1.000	6.96	26	0	0	32.1	43	9	14	0	3	0	0	0	0	0	—	0	10	0	0	0.4	1.000
1995	STL N	6	6	.500	4.00	26	21	1	137.1	136	35	71	1	1	0	0	37	3	0	.081	8	17	0	1	1.0	1.000
1996		11	2	.846	3.55	48	6	0	88.2	83	35	45	0	8	2	0	16	3	0	.188	6	14	2	3	0.5	.909
4 yrs.		20	9	.690	4.57	104	28	1	267.2	283	83	136	1	12	2	0	53	6	0	.113	15	41	2	4	0.6	.966

DIVISIONAL PLAYOFF SERIES

Year	Team	W	L	PCT	ERA	G	GS	CG	IP	H	BB	SO	ShO	W	L	SV	AB	H	HR	BA	PO	A	E	DP	TC/G	FA
1996	STL N	0	0	—	0.00	1	0	0	2	0	0	1	0	0	0	0	0	0	0	—	0	0	0	0	0.0	.000

LEAGUE CHAMPIONSHIP SERIES

Year	Team	W	L	PCT	ERA	G	GS	CG	IP	H	BB	SO	ShO	W	L	SV	AB	H	HR	BA	PO	A	E	DP	TC/G	FA
1996	STL N	0	1	.000	7.36	6	0	0	7.1	11	3	7	0	0	1	0	0	0	0	—	1	2	0	1	0.7	.750

Andy Pettitte

PETTITTE, ANDREW EUGENE
B. June 15, 1972, Baton Rouge, La.
BL TL 6'5" 235 lbs.

Year	Team	W	L	PCT	ERA	G	GS	CG	IP	H	BB	SO	ShO	W	L	SV	AB	H	HR	BA	PO	A	E	DP	TC/G	FA
1995	NY A	12	9	.571	4.17	31	26	3	175	183	63	114	0	0	0	0				—	5	26	1	0	1.0	.969
1996		21	8	.724	3.87	35	34	2	221	229	72	162	0	1	0	0				—	6	38	3	3	1.3	.936
2 yrs.		33	17	.660	4.00	66	60	5	396	412	135	276	0	1	0	0					11	64	4	3	1.2	.949

DIVISIONAL PLAYOFF SERIES

Year	Team	W	L	PCT	ERA	G	GS	CG	IP	H	BB	SO	ShO	W	L	SV	AB	H	HR	BA	PO	A	E	DP	TC/G	FA
1995	NY A	0	0	—	5.14	1	1	0	7	9	3	3	0	0	0	0				—	0	3	0	0	3.0	1.000
1996		0	0	—	5.68	1	1	0	6.1	4	6	3	0	0	0	0	4	0	0	.000	0	2	0	1	2.0	1.000
2 yrs.		0	0		5.40	2	2	0	13.1	13	9	3	0	0	0	0					0	5	0	1	2.5	1.000

LEAGUE CHAMPIONSHIP SERIES

Year	Team	W	L	PCT	ERA	G	GS	CG	IP	H	BB	SO	ShO	W	L	SV	AB	H	HR	BA	PO	A	E	DP	TC/G	FA
1996	NY A	1	0	1.000	3.60	2	2	0	15	10	5	7	0	0	0	0					2	0	0	0	1.0	1.000

WORLD SERIES

Year	Team	W	L	PCT	ERA	G	GS	CG	IP	H	BB	SO	ShO	W	L	SV	AB	H	HR	BA	PO	A	E	DP	TC/G	FA
1996	NY A	1	1	.500	5.91	2	2	0	10.2	11	4	5	0	0	0	0	4	0	0	.000	0	5	0	1	2.5	1.000

Hipolito Pichardo

PICHARDO, HIPOLITO ANTONIO
Born Hipolito Antonio Pichardo (Balbina).
B. Aug. 22, 1969, Esperanza, Dominican Republic
BR TR 6'1" 160 lbs.

Year	Team	W	L	PCT	ERA	G	GS	CG	IP	H	BB	SO	ShO	W	L	SV	AB	H	HR	BA	PO	A	E	DP	TC/G	FA
1992	KC A	9	6	.600	3.95	31	24	1	143.2	148	49	59	1	0	1	0	0	0	0	—	19	16	2	2	1.2	.946
1993		7	8	.467	4.04	30	25	2	165	183	53	70	0	0	1	0	0	0	0	—	20	27	0	1	1.6	1.000
1994		5	3	.625	4.92	45	0	0	67.2	82	24	36	0	5	3	3	0	0	0	—	4	16	5	2	0.6	.800
1995		8	4	.667	4.36	44	0	0	64	66	30	43	0	8	4	1	2	0	0	.000	2	12	0	1	0.3	1.000
1996		3	5	.375	5.43	57	0	0	68	74	26	43	0	3	5	3	0	0	0	—	7	13	1	2	0.4	.952
5 yrs.		32	26	.552	4.36	207	49	3	508.1	553	182	251	1	16	14	7	2	0	0	.000	52	84	8	8	0.7	.944

Dan Plesac

PLESAC, DANIEL THOMAS
B. Feb. 4, 1962, Gary, Ind.
BL TL 6'5" 205 lbs.

Year	Team	W	L	PCT	ERA	G	GS	CG	IP	H	BB	SO	ShO	W	L	SV	AB	H	HR	BA	PO	A	E	DP	TC/G	FA
1986	MIL A	10	7	.588	2.97	51	0	0	91	81	29	75	0	10	7	14	0	0	0	—	1	11	0	0	0.2	1.000
1987		5	6	.455	2.61	57	0	0	79.1	63	23	89	0	5	6	23	0	0	0	—	0	12	2	1	0.2	.857
1988		1	2	.333	2.41	50	0	0	52.1	46	12	52	0	1	2	30	0	0	0	—	0	11	0	0	0.1	1.000

Year	Team	W	L	PCT	ERA	G	GS	CG	IP	H	BB	SO	ShO	Relief Pitching W	L	SV	Batting AB	H	HR	BA	PO	A	E	DP	TC/G	FA

Dan Plesac *continued*

Year	Team	W	L	PCT	ERA	G	GS	CG	IP	H	BB	SO	ShO	W	L	SV	AB	H	HR	BA	PO	A	E	DP	TC/G	FA
1989		3	4	.429	2.35	52	0	0	61.1	47	17	52	0	3	4	33	0	0	0	—	2	8	0	0	0.2	1.000
1990		3	7	.300	4.43	66	0	0	69	67	31	65	0	3	7	24	0	0	0	—	1	7	0	1	0.1	1.000
1991		2	7	.222	4.29	45	10	0	92.1	92	39	61	0	0	4	8	0	0	0	—	2	5	0	0	0.2	1.000
1992		5	4	.556	2.96	44	4	0	79	64	35	54	0	4	3	1	0	0	0	—	1	8	0	1	0.2	1.000
1993	CHI N	2	1	.667	4.74	57	0	0	62.2	74	21	47	0	2	1	0	1	0	0	.000	0	9	1	2	0.2	.900
1994		2	3	.400	4.61	54	0	0	54.2	61	13	53	0	2	3	1	4	0	0	.000	0	3	0	0	0.1	1.000
1995	PIT N	4	4	.500	3.58	58	0	0	60.1	53	27	57	0	4	4	3	4	1	0	.250	1	8	0	1	0.2	1.000
1996		6	5	.545	4.09	73	0	0	70.1	67	24	76	0	6	5	11	5	0	0	.000	0	1	0	0	0.0	1.000
11 yrs.		43	50	.462	3.54	607	14	0	772.1	715	271	681	0	40	46	148	14	1	0	.071	8	78	3	6	0.1	.966

Eric Plunk

PLUNK, ERIC VAUGHN
B. Sept. 3, 1963, Wilmington, Calif.

BR TR 6' 5" 210 lbs.

Year	Team	W	L	PCT	ERA	G	GS	CG	IP	H	BB	SO	ShO	W	L	SV	AB	H	HR	BA	PO	A	E	DP	TC/G	FA
1986	OAK A	4	7	.364	5.31	26	15	0	120.1	91	102	98	0	0	1	0	0	0	0	—	3	6	1	0	0.4	.900
1987		4	6	.400	4.74	32	11	0	95	91	62	90	0	3	2	2	0	0	0	—	1	9	0	0	0.3	1.000
1988		7	2	.778	3.00	49	0	0	78	62	39	79	0	7	2	5	0	0	0	—	2	5	1	0	0.2	.875
1989	2 teams	OAK A	(23G 1–1)		NY A	(27G 7–5)																				
"	total	8	6	.571	3.28	50	7	0	104.1	82	64	85	0	4	3	1	0	0	0	—	2	7	1	0	0.2	.900
1990	NY A	6	3	.667	2.72	47	0	0	72.2	58	43	67	0	6	3	0	0	0	0	—	3	18	2	2	0.5	.913
1991		2	5	.286	4.76	43	8	0	111.2	128	62	103	0	2	2	0	0	0	0	—	4	7	2	0	0.3	.846
1992	CLE A	9	6	.600	3.64	58	0	0	71.2	61	38	50	0	9	6	4	0	0	0	—	7	7	1	0	0.3	.933
1993		4	5	.444	2.79	70	0	0	71	61	30	77	0	4	5	15	0	0	0	—	5	2	1	0	0.1	.875
1994		7	2	.778	2.54	41	0	0	71	61	37	73	0	7	2	3	0	0	0	—	8	3	0	0	0.3	1.000
1995		6	2	.750	2.67	56	0	0	64	48	27	71	0	6	2	2	0	0	0	—	2	7	0	1	0.2	1.000
1996		3	2	.600	2.43	56	0	0	77.2	56	34	85	0	3	2	2	0	0	0	—	4	7	0	0	0.2	1.000
11 yrs.		60	46	.566	3.62	528	41	0	937.1	799	538	878	0	51	30	34	0	0	0		41	78	9	3	0.2	.930
DIVISIONAL PLAYOFF SERIES																										
1995	CLE A	0	0	—	0.00	1	0	0	1.1	1	1	1	0	0	0	0	0	0	0	—	0	1	0	0	1.0	1.000
1996		0	1	.000	6.75	3	0	0	4	1	2	6	0	0	1	0	0	0	0	—	0	0	0	0	0.0	—
2 yrs.		0	1	.000	5.06	4	0	0	5.1	2	3	7	0	0	1	0	0	0	0		0	1	0	0	0.3	1.000
LEAGUE CHAMPIONSHIP SERIES																										
1988	OAK A	0	0	—	0.00	1	0	0	0.1	1	0	1	0	0	0	0	0	0	0	—	0	0	0	0	0.0	.000
1995	CLE A	0	0	—	9.00	3	0	0	2	1	3	2	0	0	0	0	0	0	0	—	0	0	0	0	0.0	.000
2 yrs.		0	0	—	7.71	4	0	0	2.1	2	3	3	0	0	0	0	0	0	0		0	0	0	0	0.0	
WORLD SERIES																										
1988	OAK A	0	0	—	0.00	2	0	0	1.2	0	0	3	0	0	0	0	0	0	0	—	0	0	0	0	0.0	.000

Dale Polley

POLLEY, EZRA DALE
B. Aug. 9, 1965, Georgetown, Ky.

BR TL 6' 165 lbs.

Year	Team	W	L	PCT	ERA	G	GS	CG	IP	H	BB	SO	ShO	W	L	SV	AB	H	HR	BA	PO	A	E	DP	TC/G	FA
1996	NY A	1	3	.250	7.89	32	0	0	21.2	23	11	14	0	1	3	0	0	0	0	—	0	4	1	0	0.2	.800

Jim Poole

POOLE, JAMES RICHARD
B. Apr. 28, 1966, Rochester, N.Y.

BL TL 6' 2" 190 lbs.

Year	Team	W	L	PCT	ERA	G	GS	CG	IP	H	BB	SO	ShO	W	L	SV	AB	H	HR	BA	PO	A	E	DP	TC/G	FA
1990	LA N	0	0	—	4.22	16	0	0	10.2	7	8	6	0	0	0	0	0	0	0	—	0	1	0	0	0.1	1.000
1991	2 teams	TEX A	(5G 0–0)		BAL A	(24G 3–2)																				
"	total	3	2	.600	2.36	29	0	0	42	29	12	38	0	3	2	1	0	0	0	—	2	6	1	0	0.3	.889
1992	BAL A	0	0	—	0.00	3	0	0	3.1	3	1	3	0	0	0	0	0	0	0	—	0	2	0	0	0.3	1.000
1993		2	1	.667	2.15	55	0	0	50.1	30	21	29	0	2	1	2	0	0	0	—	4	7	1	0	0.2	.917
1994		1	0	1.000	6.64	38	0	0	20.1	32	11	18	0	1	0	0	0	0	0	—	3	4	0	0	0.2	1.000
1995	CLE A	3	3	.500	3.75	42	0	0	50.1	40	17	41	0	3	3	0	0	0	0	—	2	9	1	0	0.3	.917
1996	2 teams	CLE A	(32G 4–0)		SF N	(35G 2–1)																				
"	total	6	1	.857	2.86	67	0	0	50.1	44	27	38	0	6	1	0	2	0	0	.000	4	11	1	1	0.2	.938
7 yrs.		15	7	.682	3.17	253	0	0	227.1	185	97	173	0	15	7	3	2	0	0	.000	15	40	4	1	0.2	.932
DIVISIONAL PLAYOFF SERIES																										
1995	CLE A	0	0	—	5.40	1	0	0	1.2	2	1	2	0	0	0	0	0	0	0	—	0	1	0	0	1.0	1.000
LEAGUE CHAMPIONSHIP SERIES																										
1995	CLE A	0	0	—	0.00	1	0	0	1	0	0	2	0	0	0	0	0	0	0	—	0	0	0	0	0.0	.000
WORLD SERIES																										
1995	CLE A	0	1	.000	3.86	2	0	0	2.1	1	0	1	0	0	1	0	1	0	0	.000	0	0	0	0	0.0	.000

Mark Portugal

PORTUGAL, MARK STEVEN
B. Oct. 30, 1962, Los Angeles, Calif.

BR TR 6' 170 lbs.

Year	Team	W	L	PCT	ERA	G	GS	CG	IP	H	BB	SO	ShO	W	L	SV	AB	H	HR	BA	PO	A	E	DP	TC/G	FA
1985	MIN A	1	3	.250	5.55	6	4	0	24.1	24	14	12	0	0	0	0	0	0	0	—	4	7	1	1	2.0	.917
1986		6	10	.375	4.31	27	15	3	112.2	112	50	67	0	0	4	1	0	0	0	—	5	14	1	3	0.7	.950
1987		1	3	.250	7.77	13	7	0	44	58	24	28	0	0	1	0	0	0	0	—	1	6	0	2	0.5	1.000
1988		3	3	.500	4.53	26	0	0	57.2	60	17	31	0	3	3	3	0	0	0	—	2	1	1	0	0.2	.750
1989	HOU N	7	1	.875	2.75	20	15	2	108	91	37	86	1	0	0	0	34	7	1	.206	11	15	2	0	1.4	.929
1990		11	10	.524	3.62	32	32	1	196.2	187	67	136	0	0	0	0	66	9	0	.136	23	19	1	2	1.3	.977
1991		10	12	.455	4.49	32	27	1	168.1	163	59	120	0	0	2	0	46	9	0	.196	16	17	3	1	1.1	.917
1992		6	3	.667	2.66	18	16	1	101.1	76	41	62	1	0	0	0	28	3	0	.107	16	13	3	1	1.8	.906
1993		18	4	**.818**	2.77	33	33	1	208	194	77	131	1	0	0	0	65	15	0	.231	21	28	2	2	1.5	.961
1994	SF N	10	8	.556	3.93	21	21	1	137.1	135	45	87	0	0	0	0	48	17	0	.354	10	12	1	1	1.1	.957

Year	Team	W	L	PCT	ERA	G	GS	CG	IP	H	BB	SO	ShO	Relief Pitching W	L	SV	Batting AB	H	HR	BA	PO	A	E	DP	TC/G	FA

Mark Portugal *continued*

Year	Team	W	L	PCT	ERA	G	GS	CG	IP	H	BB	SO	ShO	W	L	SV	AB	H	HR	BA	PO	A	E	DP	TC/G	FA
1995	2 teams	SF N	(17G 5-5)				CIN N		(14G 6-5)																	
"	total	11	10	.524	4.01	31	31	1	181.2	185	56	96	0	0	0	0	58	8	0	.138	9	21	1	2	1.0	.968
1996	CIN N	8	9	.471	3.98	27	26	1	156	146	42	93	1	0	0	0	48	8	0	.167	11	16	2	1	1.1	.931
12 yrs.		92	76	.548	3.83	286	227	12	1496	1431	529	949	4	6	10	5	393	76	2	.193	129	169	18	16	1.1	.943

LEAGUE CHAMPIONSHIP SERIES

1995	CIN N	0	1	.000	36.00	1	0	0	1	3	1	0	0	0	1	0	0	0	0	—	0	0	0	0	0.0	.000

Mike Potts

POTTS, MICHAEL LARRY
B. Sept. 5, 1970, Langdale, Ala. BL TL 5'9" 170 lbs.

Year	Team	W	L	PCT	ERA	G	GS	CG	IP	H	BB	SO	ShO	W	L	SV	AB	H	HR	BA	PO	A	E	DP	TC/G	FA
1996	MIL A	1	2	.33	7.15	24	0	0	45.1	58	30	21	0	1	2	1	0	0	0	—	3	2	0	0	0.2	1.000

Jay Powell

POWELL, JAMES WILLARD
B. Jan. 9, 1972, Meridian, Miss. BR TR 6'4" 220 lbs.

Year	Team	W	L	PCT	ERA	G	GS	CG	IP	H	BB	SO	ShO	W	L	SV	AB	H	HR	BA	PO	A	E	DP	TC/G	FA
1995	FLA N	0	0	—	1.08	9	0	0	8.1	7	6	4	0	0	0	0	0	0	0	—	1	3	0	0	0.4	1.000
1996		4	3	.571	4.54	67	0	0	71.1	71	36	52	0	4	3	2	5	0	0	.000	5	6	0	0	0.2	1.000
2 yrs.		4	3	.571	4.18	76	0	0	79.2	78	42	56	0	4	3	2	5	0	0	.000	6	9	0	0	0.2	1.000

Ariel Prieto

PRIETO, ARIEL
B. Oct. 22, 1969, Havana, Cuba BR TR 6'3" 220 lbs.

Year	Team	W	L	PCT	ERA	G	GS	CG	IP	H	BB	SO	ShO	W	L	SV	AB	H	HR	BA	PO	A	E	DP	TC/G	FA
1995	OAK A	2	6	.250	4.97	14	9	1	58	57	32	37	0	0	0	0	0	0	0	—	0	8	1	0	0.6	.889
1996		6	7	.462	4.15	21	21	2	125.2	130	54	75	0	0	0	0	0	0	0	—	10	17	0	0	1.3	1.000
2 yrs.		8	13	.381	4.41	35	30	3	183.2	187	86	112	0	0	0	0					10	25	1	0	1.0	.972

Tim Pugh

PUGH, TIMOTHY DEAN
B. Jan. 26, 1967, Lake Tahoe, Calif. BR TR 6'6" 225 lbs.

Year	Team	W	L	PCT	ERA	G	GS	CG	IP	H	BB	SO	ShO	W	L	SV	AB	H	HR	BA	PO	A	E	DP	TC/G	FA
1992	CIN N	4	2	.667	2.58	7	7	0	45.1	47	13	18	0	0	0	0	13	1	0	.077	2	6	0	0	1.1	1.000
1993		10	15	.400	5.26	31	27	3	164.1	200	59	94	1	0	1	0	54	12	0	.222	9	23	1	1	1.1	.970
1994		3	3	.500	6.04	10	9	1	47.2	60	26	24	0	0	0	0	14	5	0	.357	5	7	1	0	1.3	.923
1995		6	5	.545	3.84	28	12	0	98.1	100	32	38	0	1	1	0	28	4	0	.143	10	9	1	0	0.7	.950
1996	2 teams	CIN N	(10G 1-1)				KC A		(19G 0-1)																	
"	total	1	2	.333	7.27	29	1	0	52	66	23	36	0	1	2	0	0	0	0	—	5	10	0	0	0.5	1.000
5 yrs.		24	27	.471	4.97	105	56	4	407.2	473	153	210	1	2	4	0	109	22	0	.202	31	55	3	1	0.8	.966

Paul Quantrill

QUANTRILL, PAUL JOHN
B. Nov. 3, 1968, London, Ont., Canada. BL TR 6'1" 175 lbs.

Year	Team	W	L	PCT	ERA	G	GS	CG	IP	H	BB	SO	ShO	W	L	SV	AB	H	HR	BA	PO	A	E	DP	TC/G	FA
1992	BOS A	2	3	.400	2.19	27	0	0	49.1	55	15	24	0	2	3	1	0	0	0	—	4	6	2	0	0.4	.833
1993		6	12	.333	3.91	49	14	1	138	151	44	66	1	4	5	1	0	0	0	—	4	18	1	3	0.5	.957
1994	2 teams	BOS A	(17G 1-1)				PHI N		(18G 2-2)																	
"	total	3	3	.500	4.92	35	1	0	53	64	15	28	0	3	2	1	3	0	0	.000	2	8	1	0	0.3	.909
1995	PHI N	11	12	.478	4.67	33	29	0	179.1	212	44	103	0	1	0	0	57	6	0	.105	9	32	1	2	1.3	.976
1996	TOR A	5	14	.263	5.43	38	20	0	134.1	172	51	86	0	1	4	0	0	0	0	—	4	23	0	1	0.7	1.000
5 yrs.		27	44	.380	4.47	182	64	1	554	654	169	307	1	11	14	3	60	6	0	.100	23	87	5	7	0.6	.957

Rafael Quirico

QUIRICO, RAFAEL OCTAVIO
Born Rafael Octavio Quirico (Dottin).
B. Sept. 7, 1969, Santo Domingo, Dominican Republic BL TL 6'3" 170 lbs.

Year	Team	W	L	PCT	ERA	G	GS	CG	IP	H	BB	SO	ShO	W	L	SV	AB	H	HR	BA	PO	A	E	DP	TC/G	FA
1996	PHI N	0	1	.000	37.80	1	1	0	1.2	4	5	1	0	0	0	0	0	0	0	—	1	0	0	0	1.0	1.000

Scott Radinsky

RADINSKY, SCOTT DAVID
B. Mar. 3, 1968, Glendale, Calif. BL TL 6'3" 190 lbs.

Year	Team	W	L	PCT	ERA	G	GS	CG	IP	H	BB	SO	ShO	W	L	SV	AB	H	HR	BA	PO	A	E	DP	TC/G	FA
1990	CHI A	6	1	.857	4.82	62	0	0	52.1	47	36	46	0	6	1	4	0	0	0	—	7	4	0	0	0.2	1.000
1991		5	5	.500	2.02	67	0	0	71.1	53	23	49	0	5	5	8	0	0	0	—	6	11	0	0	0.3	1.000
1992		3	7	.300	2.73	68	0	0	59.1	54	34	48	0	3	7	15	0	0	0	—	2	9	0	1	0.2	1.000
1993		8	2	.800	4.28	73	0	0	54.2	61	19	44	0	8	2	4	0	0	0	—	1	9	2	0	0.2	.833
1995		2	1	.667	5.45	46	0	0	38	46	17	14	0	2	1	1	0	0	0	—	3	5	0	1	0.2	1.000
1996	LA N	5	1	.833	2.41	58	0	0	52.1	52	17	48	0	5	1	1	1	0	0	.000	3	8	0	0	0.2	1.000
6 yrs.		29	17	.630	3.43	374	0	0	328	313	146	249	0	29	17	33	1	0	0	.000	22	46	2	2	0.2	.971

DIVISIONAL PLAYOFF SERIES

1996	LA N	0	0	—	0.00	1	0	0	1.1	1	1	2	0	0	0	0	0	0	0	—	0	0	0	0	0.0	.000

LEAGUE CHAMPIONSHIP SERIES

1993	CHI A	0	0	—	10.80	4	0	0	1.2	3	1	1	0	0	0	0	0	0	0	—	0	0	0	1	0.3	.000

Brad Radke

RADKE, BRAD WILLIAM
B. Oct. 27, 1972, Eau Claire, Wis. BR TR 6'2" 180 lbs.

Year	Team	W	L	PCT	ERA	G	GS	CG	IP	H	BB	SO	ShO	W	L	SV	AB	H	HR	BA	PO	A	E	DP	TC/G	FA
1995	MIN A	11	14	.440	5.32	29	28	2	181	195	47	75	1	0	0	0	0	0	0	—	17	20	0	1	1.3	1.000
1996		11	16	.407	4.46	35	35	3	232	231	57	148	0	0	0	0	0	0	0	—	22	15	0	0	1.1	1.000
2 yrs.		22	30	.423	4.84	64	63	5	413	426	104	223	1	0	0	0					39	35	0	1	1.2	1.000

Year	Team		W	L	PCT	ERA	G	GS	CG	IP	H	BB	SO	ShO	Relief Pitching W	L	SV	Batting AB	H	HR	BA	PO	A	E	DP	TC/G	FA

Pat Rapp
RAPP, PATRICK LELAND
B. July 13, 1967, Jennings, La.
BR TR 6' 3" 195 lbs.

Year	Team		W	L	PCT	ERA	G	GS	CG	IP	H	BB	SO	ShO	W	L	SV	AB	H	HR	BA	PO	A	E	DP	TC/G	FA
1992	SF	N	0	2	.000	7.20	3	2	0	10	8	6	3	0	0	0	0	2	0	0	.000	2	2	0	0	1.3	1.000
1993	FLA	N	4	6	.400	4.02	16	16	1	94	101	39	57	0	0	0	0	31	6	0	.194	5	15	1	0	1.3	.952
1994			7	8	.467	3.85	24	23	2	133.1	132	69	75	1	0	0	0	41	5	0	.122	8	15	0	1	1.0	1.000
1995			14	7	.667	3.44	28	28	3	167.1	158	76	102	2	0	0	0	56	6	0	.107	13	20	1	1	1.2	.971
1996			8	16	.333	5.10	30	29	0	162.1	184	91	86	0	0	1	0	58	7	0	.121	11	24	2	3	1.2	.946
5 yrs.			33	39	.458	4.17	101	98	6	567	583	281	323	3	0	1	0	188	24	0	.128	39	76	4	5	1.2	.966

Steve Reed
REED, STEVEN VINCENT
B. Mar. 11, 1966, Los Angeles, Calif.
BR TR 6' 2" 200 lbs.

Year	Team		W	L	PCT	ERA	G	GS	CG	IP	H	BB	SO	ShO	W	L	SV	AB	H	HR	BA	PO	A	E	DP	TC/G	FA
1992	SF	N	1	0	1.000	2.30	18	0	0	15.2	13	3	11	0	1	0	0	0	0	0	—	3	4	0	0	0.4	1.000
1993	CLR	N	9	5	.643	4.48	64	0	0	84.1	80	30	51	0	9	5	3	9	0	0	.000	3	14	1	1	0.3	.944
1994			3	2	.600	3.94	61	0	0	64	79	26	51	0	3	2	3	2	0	0	.000	0	5	0	0	0.1	1.000
1995			5	2	.714	2.14	71	0	0	84	61	21	79	0	5	2	3	3	1	0	.333	4	16	1	1	0.3	.952
1996			4	3	.571	3.96	70	0	0	75	66	19	51	0	4	3	0	3	1	0	.333	3	8	0	1	0.2	1.000
5 yrs.			22	12	.647	3.54	284	0	0	323	299	99	243	0	22	12	9	17	2	0	.118	13	47	2	3	0.2	.968
DIVISIONAL PLAYOFF SERIES																											
1995	CLR	N	0	0	—	0.00	3	0	0	2.2	2	1	3	0	0	0	0	0	0	0	—	0	1	0	0	0.3	1.000

Bryan Rekar
REKAR, BRYAN ROBERT
B. June 3, 1972, Oaklawn, Ill.
BR TR 6' 3" 205 lbs.

Year	Team		W	L	PCT	ERA	G	GS	CG	IP	H	BB	SO	ShO	W	L	SV	AB	H	HR	BA	PO	A	E	DP	TC/G	FA
1995	CLR	N	4	6	.400	4.98	15	14	1	85	95	24	60	0	0	0	0	26	1	0	.038	9	16	1	0	1.7	.962
1996			2	4	.333	8.95	14	11	0	58.1	87	26	25	0	0	1	0	15	4	0	.267	2	9	1	1	0.9	.917
2 yrs.			6	10	.375	6.59	29	25	1	143.1	182	50	85	0	0	1	0	41	5	0	.122	11	25	2	1	1.3	.947

Mike Remlinger
REMLINGER, MICHAEL JOHN
B. Mar. 23, 1966, Middletown, N.Y.
BL TL 6' 195 lbs.

Year	Team		W	L	PCT	ERA	G	GS	CG	IP	H	BB	SO	ShO	W	L	SV	AB	H	HR	BA	PO	A	E	DP	TC/G	FA
1991	SF	N	2	1	.667	4.37	8	6	1	35	36	20	19	0	0	0	0	7	0	0	.000	1	6	1	0	1.0	.875
1994	NY	N	1	5	.167	4.61	10	9	0	54.2	55	35	33	0	0	0	0	16	0	0	.000	1	4	0	0	0.5	1.000
1995	2 teams	NY N	(5G 0-1)		CIN N		(2G 0-0)																				
"	total		0	1	.000	6.75	7	0	0	6.2	9	5	7	0	0	0	0	1	0	0	.000	0	0	0	0	0.0	
1996	CIN	N	0	1	.000	5.60	19	4	0	27.1	24	19	19	0	0	0	0	7	1	0	.143	3	5	0	0	0.4	1.000
4 yrs.			3	8	.273	4.88	44	19	1	123.2	124	79	78	1	0	0	0	31	1	0	.032	5	15	1	0	0.5	.952

Alberto Reyes
REYES, RAFAEL ALBERTO
B. Apr. 10, 1971, San Cristobal, Dominican Republic
BR TR 6' 1" 193 lbs.

Year	Team		W	L	PCT	ERA	G	GS	CG	IP	H	BB	SO	ShO	W	L	SV	AB	H	HR	BA	PO	A	E	DP	TC/G	FA
1995	MIL	A	1	1	.500	2.43	27	0	0	33.1	19	18	29	0	1	1	1	0	0	0	—	0	6	0	1	0.2	1.000
1996			1	0	1.000	7.94	5	0	0	5.2	8	2	2	0	1	0	0	0	0	0	—	0	0	0	0	0.0	.000
2 yrs.			2	1	.667	3.23	32	0	0	39	27	20	31	0	2	1	1	0	0	0	—	0	6	0	1	0.2	1.000

Carlos Reyes
REYES, CARLOS ALBERTO, JR.
B. Apr. 4, 1969, Miami, Fla.
BR TR 6' 1" 190 lbs.

Year	Team		W	L	PCT	ERA	G	GS	CG	IP	H	BB	SO	ShO	W	L	SV	AB	H	HR	BA	PO	A	E	DP	TC/G	FA
1994	OAK	A	0	3	.000	4.15	27	9	0	78	71	44	57	0	0	1	1	0	0	0	—	3	7	0	1	0.4	1.000
1995			4	6	.400	5.09	40	1	0	69	71	28	48	0	4	5	0	0	0	0	—	3	13	0	0	0.4	1.000
1996			7	10	.412	4.78	46	10	0	122.1	134	61	78	0	4	3	0	0	0	0	—	7	10	2	2	0.4	.895
3 yrs.			11	19	.367	4.68	113	20	0	269.1	276	133	183	0	8	9	1	0	0	0	—	13	30	2	3	0.4	.956

Shane Reynolds
REYNOLDS, RICHARD SHANE
B. Mar. 26, 1968, Bastrop, La.
BR TR 6' 3" 210 lbs.

Year	Team		W	L	PCT	ERA	G	GS	CG	IP	H	BB	SO	ShO	W	L	SV	AB	H	HR	BA	PO	A	E	DP	TC/G	FA
1992	HOU	N	1	3	.250	7.11	8	5	0	25.1	42	6	10	0	0	0	0	4	2	0	.500	0	7	1	0	1.0	.875
1993			0	0	—	0.82	5	1	0	11	11	6	10	0	0	0	0	2	1	0	.500	1	0	0	0	0.2	1.000
1994			8	5	.615	3.05	33	14	1	124	128	21	110	1	3	1	0	33	3	0	.091	10	16	0	0	0.8	1.000
1995			10	11	.476	3.47	30	30	3	189.1	196	37	175	2	0	0	0	63	8	0	.127	13	38	1	0	1.7	.981
1996			16	10	.615	3.65	35	35	4	239	227	44	204	1	0	0	0	76	14	2	.184	19	26	0	2	1.3	1.000
5 yrs.			35	29	.547	3.56	111	85	8	588.2	604	114	509	4	3	1	0	178	28	2	.157	42	88	2	2	1.2	.985

Armando Reynoso
REYNOSO, ARMANDO MARTIN
Born Armando Martin Reynoso (Gutierrez).
B. May 1, 1966, San Luis Potosi, Mexico
BR TR 6' 186 lbs.

Year	Team		W	L	PCT	ERA	G	GS	CG	IP	H	BB	SO	ShO	W	L	SV	AB	H	HR	BA	PO	A	E	DP	TC/G	FA
1991	ATL	N	2	1	.667	6.17	6	5	0	23.1	26	10	10	0	0	0	0	7	0	0	.000	3	12	0	0	2.5	1.000
1992			1	0	1.000	4.70	3	1	0	7.2	11	2	2	0	0	0	1	2	0	0	.000	0	2	0	1	0.7	1.000
1993	CLR	N	12	11	.522	4.00	30	30	4	189	206	63	117	0	0	0	0	63	8	2	.127	16	35	6	5	1.9	.895
1994			3	4	.429	4.82	9	9	1	52.1	54	22	25	0	0	0	0	17	3	0	.176	1	20	0	0	2.3	1.000
1995			7	7	.500	5.32	20	18	0	93	116	36	40	0	0	0	0	30	4	0	.133	7	29	2	2	1.9	.947
1996			8	9	.471	4.96	30	30	0	168.2	195	49	88	0	0	0	0	52	9	0	.173	12	37	3	3	1.7	.942
6 yrs.			33	32	.508	4.72	98	93	5	534	608	182	282	0	0	0	1	171	24	2	.140	39	135	11	11	1.9	.941
DIVISIONAL PLAYOFF SERIES																											
1995	CLR	N	0	0	—	0.00	1	0	0	1	2	0	0	0	0	0	0	0	0	0	—	0	0	0	0	0.0	.000

Arthur Rhodes
RHODES, ARTHUR LEE
B. Oct. 24, 1969, Waco, Tex.
BL TL 6' 2" 190 lbs.

Year	Team		W	L	PCT	ERA	G	GS	CG	IP	H	BB	SO	ShO	W	L	SV	AB	H	HR	BA	PO	A	E	DP	TC/G	FA
1991	BAL	A	0	3	.000	8.00	8	8	0	36	47	23	23	0	0	0	0	0	0	0	—	0	1	0	0	0.1	1.000
1992			7	5	.583	3.63	15	15	2	94.1	87	38	77	1	0	0	0	0	0	0	—	1	13	0	2	0.9	1.000

Year	Team	W	L	PCT	ERA	G	GS	CG	IP	H	BB	SO	ShO	Relief Pitching W	L	SV	Batting AB	H	HR	BA	PO	A	E	DP	TC/G	FA

Arthur Rhodes *continued*

1993		5	6	.455	6.51	17	17	0	85.2	91	49	49	0	0	0	0	0	0	0	—	2	9	1	0	0.7	.917
1994		3	5	.375	5.81	10	10	3	52.2	51	30	47	2	0	0	0	0	0	0	—	0	2	1	0	0.3	.667
1995		2	5	.286	6.21	19	9	0	75.1	68	48	77	0	0	2	0	0	0	0	—	3	7	2	0	0.6	.833
1996		9	1	.900	4.08	28	2	0	53	48	23	62	0	8	1	0	0	0	0	—	1	2	0	0	0.1	1.000
6 yrs.		26	25	.510	5.49	97	61	5	397	392	211	335	3	8	3	1	0	0	0	—	7	34	4	2	0.5	.911

DIVISIONAL PLAYOFF SERIES
| 1996 | BAL A | 0 | 0 | — | 9.00 | 2 | 0 | 0 | 1 | 1 | 1 | 1 | 0 | 0 | 0 | 0 | 0 | 0 | 0 | — | 0 | 0 | 0 | 0 | 0.0 | .000 |

LEAGUE CHAMPIONSHIP SERIES
| 1996 | BAL A | 0 | 0 | — | 0.00 | 3 | 0 | 0 | 2 | 2 | 0 | 2 | 0 | 0 | 0 | 0 | 0 | 0 | 0 | — | 0 | 0 | 0 | 0 | 0.0 | .000 |

Bill Risley — RISLEY, WILLIAM CHARLES — B. May 29, 1967, Chicago, Ill. — BR TR 6' 2" 215 lbs.

1992	MON N	1	0	1.000	1.80	1	1	0	5	4	1	2	0	0	0	0	2	0	0	.000	0	1	0	0	1.0	1.000
1993		0	0	—	6.00	2	0	0	3	2	2	2	0	0	0	0	0	0	0	—	1	0	0	0	0.5	1.000
1994	SEA A	9	6	.600	3.44	37	0	0	52.1	31	19	61	0	9	6	0	0	0	0	—	5	2	1	1	0.2	.875
1995		2	1	.667	3.13	45	0	0	60.1	55	18	65	0	2	1	1	0	0	0	—	2	3	0	0	0.1	1.000
1996	TOR A	0	1	.000	3.89	25	0	0	41.2	33	25	29	0	0	1	0	0	0	0	—	1	3	0	1	0.2	1.000
5 yrs.		12	8	.600	3.44	110	1	0	162.1	125	65	159	0	11	8	1	2	0	0	.000	9	9	1	2	0.2	.947

DIVISIONAL PLAYOFF SERIES
| 1995 | SEA A | 0 | 0 | — | 6.00 | 4 | 0 | 0 | 3 | 2 | 1 | 0 | 0 | 0 | 0 | 1 | 0 | 0 | 0 | — | 0 | 0 | 0 | 0 | 0.0 | .000 |

LEAGUE CHAMPIONSHIP SERIES
| 1995 | SEA A | 0 | 0 | — | 0.00 | 3 | 0 | 0 | 2.2 | 2 | 1 | 2 | 0 | 0 | 0 | 0 | 0 | 0 | 0 | — | 0 | 0 | 0 | 1 | 0.0 | .000 |

Kevin Ritz — RITZ, KEVIN D. — B. June 8, 1965, Eatontown, N.J. — BR TR 6' 4" 195 lbs.

1989	DET A	4	6	.400	4.38	12	12	1	74	75	44	56	0	0	0	0	0	0	0	—	4	10	0	0	1.2	1.000
1990		0	4	.000	11.05	4	4	0	7.1	14	14	3	0	0	0	0	0	0	0	—	2	4	1	0	1.8	.857
1991		0	3	.000	11.74	11	5	0	15.1	17	22	9	0	0	0	0	0	0	0	—	1	4	1	0	0.5	.833
1992		2	5	.286	5.60	23	11	0	80.1	88	44	57	0	0	0	0	0	0	0	—	6	10	0	1	0.6	1.000
1994	CLR N	5	6	.455	5.62	15	15	0	73.2	88	35	53	0	0	0	0	20	0	0	.000	6	13	0	3	1.3	1.000
1995		11	11	.500	4.21	31	28	0	173.1	171	65	120	0	0	0	2	48	9	0	.188	10	39	0	1	1.6	1.000
1996		17	11	.607	5.28	35	35	2	213	236	105	105	0	0	0	1	65	15	1	.231	18	49	0	3	2.0	1.000
7 yrs.		39	46	.459	5.19	131	110	3	637	689	329	403	0	0	0	2	133	24	1	.180	45	129	2	8	1.4	.989

DIVISIONAL PLAYOFF SERIES
| 1995 | CLR N | 0 | 0 | — | 7.71 | 2 | 1 | 0 | 7 | 12 | 3 | 5 | 0 | 0 | 0 | 0 | 2 | 0 | 0 | .000 | 0 | 1 | 1 | 0 | 1.0 | .500 |

Mariano Rivera — RIVERA, MARIANO — B. Nov. 29, 1969, Panama City, Panama — BR TR 6' 4" 168 lbs.

1995	NY A	5	3	.625	5.51	19	10	0	67	71	30	51	0	2	0	0	0	0	0	—	2	14	0	1	0.8	1.000
1996		8	3	.727	2.09	61	0	0	107.2	73	34	130	0	8	3	5	0	0	0	—	4	13	0	0	0.3	1.000
2 yrs.		13	6	.684	3.40	80	10	0	174.2	144	64	181	0	10	3	5					6	27	0	1	0.4	1.000

DIVISIONAL PLAYOFF SERIES
1995	NY A	1	0	1.000	0.00	3	0	0	5.1	3	1	8	0	1	0	0	0	0	0	—	0	0	0	0	0.0	.000
1996		0	0	—	0.00	2	0	0	4.2	1	1	1	0	0	0	0	1	0	0	.000	0	0	0	0	0.0	.000
2 yrs.		1	0	1.000	0.00	5	0	0	10	3	2	9	0	1	0	0					0	0	0	0		

LEAGUE CHAMPIONSHIP SERIES
| 1996 | NY A | 1 | 0 | 1.000 | 0.00 | 2 | 0 | 0 | 4 | 6 | 1 | 5 | 0 | 1 | 0 | 0 | 0 | 0 | 0 | — | 0 | 0 | 0 | 0 | 0.0 | .000 |

WORLD SERIES
| 1996 | NY A | 0 | 0 | — | 1.59 | 4 | 0 | 0 | 5.2 | 4 | 3 | 4 | 0 | 0 | 0 | 0 | 1 | 0 | 0 | .000 | 0 | 2 | 0 | 0 | 0.5 | 1.000 |

Joe Roa — ROA, JOSEPH RODGER — B. Oct. 11, 1971, Southfield, Mich. — BR TR 6' 1" 195 lbs.

1995	CLE A	0	1	.000	6.00	1	1	0	6	9	2	0	0	0	0	0	0	0	0	—	2	0	0	0	4.0	1.000
1996		0	0	—	10.80	1	0	0	1.2	4	3	0	0	0	0	0	0	0	0	—	0	0	0	0	0.0	.000
2 yrs.		0	1	.000	7.04	2	1	0	7.2	13	5	0	0	0	0	0					2	2	0	0	2.0	1.000

Rich Robertson — ROBERTSON, RICHARD WAYNE — B. Sept. 15, 1968, Nacogdoches, Tex. — BL TL 6' 4" 175 lbs.

1993	PIT N	0	1	.000	6.00	9	0	0	9	15	4	5	0	0	1	0	0	0	0	—	0	0	0	0	0.0	.000
1994		0	0	—	6.89	8	0	0	15.2	20	10	8	0	0	0	0	4	1	0	.250	0	2	0	0	0.3	1.000
1995	MIN A	2	0	1.000	3.83	25	4	1	51.2	48	31	38	0	0	0	0	0	0	0	—	3	4	1	0	0.3	.875
1996		7	17	.292	5.12	36	31	5	186.1	197	116	114	3	1	1	0	0	0	0	—	15	31	1	5	1.3	.979
4 yrs.		9	18	.333	5.00	78	35	6	262.2	280	161	165	3	1	2	0	4	1	0	.250	18	37	2	5	0.7	.965

Kenny Robinson — ROBINSON, KENNETH NEAL, JR. — B. Nov. 3, 1969, Barberton, Ohio — BR TR 5' 9" 175 lbs.

1995	TOR A	1	2	.333	3.69	21	0	0	39	25	22	31	0	1	2	0	0	0	0	—	2	1	0	0	0.1	1.000
1996	KC A	1	0	1.000	6.00	5	0	0	6	9	3	5	0	1	0	0	0	0	0	—	1	0	0	0	0.3	1.000
2 yrs.		2	2	.500	4.00	26	0	0	45	34	25	36	0	2	2	0					3	1	0	0	0.2	1.000

Year	Team	W	L	PCT	ERA	G	GS	CG	IP	H	BB	SO	ShO	Relief Pitching W	L	SV	Batting AB	H	HR	BA	PO	A	E	DP	TC/G	FA

Frank Rodriguez

RODRIGUEZ, FRANCISCO
B. Dec. 11, 1972, Brooklyn, N. Y.   BR TR 6'   193 lbs.

Year	Team	W	L	PCT	ERA	G	GS	CG	IP	H	BB	SO	ShO	W	L	SV	AB	H	HR	BA	PO	A	E	DP	TC/G	FA
1995	2 teams	BOS A	(9G 0-2)			MIN A	(16G 5-6)																				
"	total	5	8	.385	6.13	25	18	0	105.2	114	57	59	0	0	1	0	0	0	0	—	12	23	0	3	1.4	1.000
1996	MIN A	13	14	.481	5.05	38	33	3	206.2	218	78	110	0	1	0	2	0	0	0	—	24	30	2	4	1.5	.964
2 yrs.		18	22	.450	5.42	63	51	3	312.1	332	135	169	0	1	1	2					36	53	2	7	1.4	.978

Nerio Rodriguez

RODRIGUEZ, NERIO
B. Mar. 22, 1973, San Pedro de Macoris, Dominican Republic   BR TR 6'1"   195 lbs.

Year	Team	W	L	PCT	ERA	G	GS	CG	IP	H	BB	SO	ShO	W	L	SV	AB	H	HR	BA	PO	A	E	DP	TC/G	FA
1996	BAL A	0	1	.000	4.32	8	1	0	16.2	18	7	12	0	0	0	0	0	0	0	—	1	0	0	0	0.1	1.000

Kenny Rogers

ROGERS, KENNETH SCOTT
B. Nov. 10, 1964, Savannah, Ga.   BL TL 6'1"   200 lbs.

Year	Team	W	L	PCT	ERA	G	GS	CG	IP	H	BB	SO	ShO	W	L	SV	AB	H	HR	BA	PO	A	E	DP	TC/G	FA
1989	TEX A	3	4	.429	2.93	73	0	0	73.2	60	42	63	0	3	4	2	0	0	0	—	1	22	0	0	0.3	1.000
1990		10	6	.625	3.13	69	3	0	97.2	93	42	74	0	9	4	15	0	0	0	—	5	22	2	1	0.4	.931
1991		10	10	.500	5.42	63	9	0	109.2	121	61	73	0	6	6	5	0	0	0	—	5	15	3	1	0.4	.870
1992		3	6	.333	3.09	81	0	0	78.2	80	26	70	0	3	6	6	0	0	0	—	4	17	2	0	0.3	.913
1993		16	10	.615	4.10	35	33	5	208.1	210	71	140	0	0	0	0	0	0	0	—	18	46	4	4	1.9	.941
1994		11	8	.579	4.46	24	24	6	167.1	169	52	120	0	0	0	0	0	0	0	—	9	33	4	4	1.9	.913
1995		17	7	.708	3.38	31	31	3	208	192	76	140	1	0	0	0	0	0	0	—	10	35	2	2	1.5	.957
1996	NY A	12	8	.600	4.68	30	30	2	179	179	83	92	0	0	0	0	0	0	0	—	15	34	2	1	1.7	.961
8 yrs.		82	59	.582	4.01	406	130	16	1122.1	1104	453	772	4	21	20	28	0	0	0		67	224	19	13	0.8	.939

DIVISIONAL PLAYOFF SERIES

Year	Team	W	L	PCT	ERA	G	GS	CG	IP	H	BB	SO	ShO	W	L	SV	AB	H	HR	BA	PO	A	E	DP	TC/G	FA
1996	NY A	0	0	—	9.00	2	1	0	2	5	2	1	0	0	0	0	0	0	0	—	0	0	0	0	0.0	.000

LEAGUE CHAMPIONSHIP SERIES

Year	Team	W	L	PCT	ERA	G	GS	CG	IP	H	BB	SO	ShO	W	L	SV	AB	H	HR	BA	PO	A	E	DP	TC/G	FA
1996	NY A	0	0	—	12.00	1	1	0	3	5	2	3	0	0	0	0	0	0	0	—	0	0	0	0	0.0	.000

WORLD SERIES

Year	Team	W	L	PCT	ERA	G	GS	CG	IP	H	BB	SO	ShO	W	L	SV	AB	H	HR	BA	PO	A	E	DP	TC/G	FA
1996	NY A	0	0	—	22.50	2	1	0	2	5	2	0	0	0	0	0	1	1	0	1.000	0	0	0	0	0.0	.000

Mel Rojas

ROJAS, MELQUIADES
Born Melquiades Rojas (Medrano).
B. Dec. 10, 1966, Haina, Dominican Republic   BR TR 5'11"   175 lbs.

Year	Team	W	L	PCT	ERA	G	GS	CG	IP	H	BB	SO	ShO	W	L	SV	AB	H	HR	BA	PO	A	E	DP	TC/G	FA
1990	MON N	3	1	.750	3.60	23	0	0	40	34	24	26	0	3	1	1	3	0	0	.000	2	4	1	0	0.3	.857
1991		3	3	.500	3.75	37	0	0	48	42	13	37	0	3	3	6	4	0	0	.000	2	5	0	0	0.2	1.000
1992		7	1	.875	1.43	68	0	0	100.2	71	34	70	0	7	1	10	15	1	0	.067	9	12	2	1	0.3	.913
1993		5	8	.385	2.95	66	0	0	88.1	80	30	48	0	5	8	10	12	1	0	.083	7	9	0	1	0.2	1.000
1994		3	2	.600	3.32	58	0	0	84	71	21	84	0	3	2	16	10	2	0	.200	8	10	0	1	0.3	1.000
1995		1	4	.200	4.12	59	0	0	67.2	69	29	61	0	1	4	30	6	0	0	.000	4	7	0	1	0.2	1.000
1996		7	4	.636	3.22	74	0	0	81	56	28	92	0	7	4	36	8	3	0	.375	4	13	1	0	0.2	.944
7 yrs.		29	23	.558	3.04	385	0	0	509.2	423	179	418	0	29	23	109	58	7	0	.121	36	60	4	4	0.3	.960

Jose Rosado

ROSADO, JOSE ANTONIA
B. Nov 9, 1974, Jersey City, N. J.   BL TL 6'   175 lbs.

Year	Team	W	L	PCT	ERA	G	GS	CG	IP	H	BB	SO	ShO	W	L	SV	AB	H	HR	BA	PO	A	E	DP	TC/G	FA
1996	KC A	8	6	.571	3.21	16	16	2	106.2	101	26	64	1	0	0	0	0	0	0	—	3	15	1	1	1.2	.947

Matt Ruebel

RUEBEL, MATTHEW ALEXANDER
B. Oct. 16, 1969, Cincinnati, Ohio   BL TL 6'2"   180 lbs.

Year	Team	W	L	PCT	ERA	G	GS	CG	IP	H	BB	SO	ShO	W	L	SV	AB	H	HR	BA	PO	A	E	DP	TC/G	FA
1996	PIT N	1	1	.500	4.60	26	7	0	58.2	64	25	22	0	0	0	1	13	3	0	.231	7	9	1	0	0.7	.941

Kirk Rueter

RUETER, KIRK WESLEY
B. Dec. 1, 1970, Hoyleton, Ill.   BL TL 6'3"   190 lbs.

Year	Team	W	L	PCT	ERA	G	GS	CG	IP	H	BB	SO	ShO	W	L	SV	AB	H	HR	BA	PO	A	E	DP	TC/G	FA
1993	MON N	8	0	1.000	2.73	14	14	1	85.2	85	18	31	0	0	0	0	26	2	0	.077	7	19	1	4	1.9	.963
1994		7	3	.700	5.17	20	20	0	92.1	106	23	50	0	0	0	0	34	4	0	.118	4	17	1	0	1.1	.955
1995		5	3	.625	3.23	9	9	1	47.1	38	9	28	0	0	0	0	16	0	0	.000	8	9	0	1	1.9	1.000
1996	2 teams	MON N	(16G 5-6)			SF N	(4G 1-2)																				
"	total	6	8	.429	3.97	20	19	0	102	109	27	46	0	0	0	0	32	4	0	.125	8	24	0	2	1.6	1.000
4 yrs.		26	14	.650	3.88	63	62	2	327.1	338	77	155	1	0	0	0	108	10	0	.093	27	69	2	7	1.6	.980

Scott Ruffcorn

RUFFCORN, SCOTT PATRICK
B. Dec. 29, 1969, New Braunfels, Tex.   BR TR 6'4"   215 lbs.

Year	Team	W	L	PCT	ERA	G	GS	CG	IP	H	BB	SO	ShO	W	L	SV	AB	H	HR	BA	PO	A	E	DP	TC/G	FA
1993	CHI A	0	2	.000	8.10	3	2	0	10	9	10	2	0	0	0	0	0	0	0	—	0	0	3	0	1.0	.000
1994		0	2	.000	12.79	2	2	0	6.1	15	5	3	0	0	0	0	0	0	0	—	0	0	0	0	0.0	.000
1995		0	0	—	7.88	4	0	0	8	10	13	5	0	0	0	0	0	0	0	—	1	2	0	0	0.8	1.000
1996		0	1	.000	11.37	3	1	0	6.1	10	6	3	0	0	0	0	0	0	0	—	1	0	0	0	0.3	1.000
4 yrs.		0	5	.000	9.68	12	5	0	30.2	44	34	13	0	0	0	0	0	0	0		2	2	3	0	0.6	.571

Bruce Ruffin

RUFFIN, BRUCE WAYNE
B. Oct. 4, 1963, Lubbock, Tex.   BB TL 6'2"   205 lbs.
BR 1986–1987

Year	Team	W	L	PCT	ERA	G	GS	CG	IP	H	BB	SO	ShO	W	L	SV	AB	H	HR	BA	PO	A	E	DP	TC/G	FA
1986	PHI N	9	4	.692	2.46	21	21	6	146.1	138	44	70	0	0	0	0	55	4	0	.073	8	20	1	0	1.4	.966
1987		11	14	.440	4.35	35	35	3	204.2	236	73	93	1	0	0	0	73	4	0	.055	7	32	2	3	1.2	.951
1988		6	10	.375	4.43	55	15	3	144.1	151	80	82	0	2	4	3	33	4	0	.121	11	25	2	0	0.7	.947
1989		6	10	.375	4.44	24	23	1	125.2	152	62	70	0	0	0	0	34	6	0	.176	3	34	4	0	1.7	.902
1990		6	13	.316	5.38	32	25	2	149	178	62	79	1	0	0	0	44	3	0	.068	5	23	0	2	0.9	1.000

Year	Team	W	L	PCT	ERA	G	GS	CG	IP	H	BB	SO	ShO	W	L	SV	AB	H	HR	BA	PO	A	E	DP	TC/G	FA
														Relief Pitching			**Batting**									

Bruce Ruffin *continued*

Year	Team	W	L	PCT	ERA	G	GS	CG	IP	H	BB	SO	ShO	W	L	SV	AB	H	HR	BA	PO	A	E	DP	TC/G	FA
1991		4	7	.364	3.78	31	15	1	119	125	38	85	1	1	0	0	24	0	0	.000	8	15	2	1	0.8	.920
1992	MIL A	1	6	.143	6.67	25	6	1	58	66	41	45	0	1	2	0	0	0	0	—	4	5	0	0	0.4	1.000
1993	CLR N	6	5	.545	3.87	59	12	0	139.2	145	69	126	0	3	1	2	25	2	0	.080	7	16	1	3	0.4	.958
1994		4	5	.444	4.04	56	0	0	55.2	55	30	65	0	4	5	16	4	1	0	.250	2	10	0	0	0.2	1.000
1995		0	1	.000	2.12	37	0	0	34	26	19	23	0	0	1	11	2	0	0	.000	0	8	0	0	0.2	1.000
1996		7	5	.583	4.00	71	0	0	69.2	55	29	74	0	7	5	24	1	0	0	.000	2	9	0	0	0.2	1.000
11 yrs.		60	80	.429	4.17	446	152	17	1246	1327	547	812	3	18	18	56	295	24	0	.081	57	197	12	11	0.6	.955

DIVISIONAL PLAYOFF SERIES
Year	Team	W	L	PCT	ERA	G	GS	CG	IP	H	BB	SO	ShO	W	L	SV	AB	H	HR	BA	PO	A	E	DP	TC/G	FA
1995	CLR N	0	0	—	2.70	4	0	0	3.1	3	2	2	0	0	0	0	0	0	0	—	0	0	0	0	0.0	.000

Johnny Ruffin

RUFFIN, JOHNNY RENANDO
B. July 29, 1971, Butler, Ala.

BR TR 6'3" 172 lbs.

Year	Team	W	L	PCT	ERA	G	GS	CG	IP	H	BB	SO	ShO	W	L	SV	AB	H	HR	BA	PO	A	E	DP	TC/G	FA
1993	CIN N	2	1	.667	3.58	21	0	0	37.2	36	11	30	0	2	1	2	3	1	0	.333	4	5	0	0	0.4	1.000
1994		7	2	.778	3.09	51	0	0	70	57	27	44	0	7	2	1	8	0	0	.000	10	2	0	0	0.2	1.000
1995		0	0	—	1.35	10	0	0	13.1	4	11	11	0	0	0	0	2	0	0	.000	2	1	0	1	0.3	1.000
1996		1	3	.250	5.49	49	0	0	62.1	71	37	69	0	1	3	0	4	2	0	.500	4	5	1	1	0.2	.900
4 yrs.		10	6	.625	3.88	131	0	0	183.1	168	86	154	0	10	6	3	17	3	0	.176	20	13	1	2	0.3	.971

Jeff Russell

RUSSELL, JEFFREY LEE
B. Sept. 2, 1961, Cincinnati, Ohio

BR TR 6'4" 200 lbs.

Year	Team	W	L	PCT	ERA	G	GS	CG	IP	H	BB	SO	ShO	W	L	SV	AB	H	HR	BA	PO	A	E	DP	TC/G	FA
1983	CIN N	4	5	.444	3.03	10	10	2	68.1	58	22	40	0	0	0	0	21	3	1	.143	2	10	1	0	1.3	.923
1984		6	18	.250	4.26	33	30	4	181.2	186	65	101	2	0	0	0	57	8	0	.140	7	34	2	4	1.3	.953
1985	TEX A	3	6	.333	7.55	13	13	0	62	85	27	44	0	0	0	0	0	0	0	—	6	10	1	1	1.2	1.000
1986		5	2	.714	3.40	37	0	0	82	74	31	54	0	5	2	2	0	0	0	—	6	17	0	3	0.6	1.000
1987		5	4	.556	4.44	52	2	0	97.1	109	52	56	0	5	3	3	0	0	0	—	11	17	0	2	0.5	1.000
1988		10	9	.526	3.82	34	24	5	188.2	183	66	88	0	1	0	0	1	0	0	.000	12	37	5	3	1.6	.907
1989		6	4	.600	1.98	71	0	0	72.2	45	24	77	0	6	4	**38**	0	0	0	—	6	14	0	3	0.3	1.000
1990		1	5	.167	4.26	27	0	0	25.1	23	16	16	0	1	5	10	0	0	0	—	1	5	1	0	0.3	.857
1991		6	4	.600	3.29	68	0	0	79.1	71	26	52	0	6	4	30	0	0	0	—	6	18	1	1	0.4	.960
1992	2 teams	TEX A	(51G 2-3)		OAK A			(8G 2-0)																		
"	total	4	3	.571	1.63	59	0	0	66.1	55	25	48	0	4	3	30	0	0	0	—	8	8	0	0	0.3	1.000
1993	BOS A	1	4	.200	2.70	51	0	0	46.2	39	14	45	0	1	4	33	0	0	0	—	2	10	0	0	0.2	1.000
1994	2 teams	BOS A	(29G 0-5)		CLE A			(13G 1-1)																		
"	total	1	6	.143	5.09	42	0	0	40.2	43	16	28	0	1	6	17	0	0	0	—	1	2	0	0	0.1	1.000
1995	TEX A	1	0	1.000	3.03	37	0	0	32.2	36	9	21	0	1	0	20	0	0	0	—	2	2	0	0	0.1	1.000
1996		3	3	.500	3.38	55	0	0	56	58	22	23	0	3	3	3	0	0	0	—	1	8	0	0	0.2	1.000
14 yrs.		56	73	.434	3.75	589	79	11	1099.2	1065	415	693	2	34	34	186	79	11	1	.139	71	192	10	17	0.5	.963

DIVISIONAL PLAYOFF SERIES
Year	Team	W	L	PCT	ERA	G	GS	CG	IP	H	BB	SO	ShO	W	L	SV	AB	H	HR	BA	PO	A	E	DP	TC/G	FA
1996	TEX A	0	0	—	3.00	2	0	0	3	3	0	1	0	0	0	0	0	0	0	—	0	0	0	0	0.0	.000

LEAGUE CHAMPIONSHIP SERIES
Year	Team	W	L	PCT	ERA	G	GS	CG	IP	H	BB	SO	ShO	W	L	SV	AB	H	HR	BA	PO	A	E	DP	TC/G	FA
1992	OAK A	1	0	1.000	9.00	3	0	0	2	2	4	0	0	1	0	0	0	0	0	—	0	0	0	0	0.0	.000

Ken Ryan

RYAN, KENNETH FREDERICK
B. Oct. 24, 1968, Pawtucket, R. I.

BR TR 6'3" 200 lbs.

Year	Team	W	L	PCT	ERA	G	GS	CG	IP	H	BB	SO	ShO	W	L	SV	AB	H	HR	BA	PO	A	E	DP	TC/G	FA
1992	BOS A	0	0	—	6.43	7	0	0	7	4	5	5	0	0	0	1	0	0	0	—	1	2	0	0	0.4	1.000
1993		7	2	.778	3.60	47	0	0	50	43	29	49	0	7	2	1	0	0	0	—	3	7	1	0	0.2	.909
1994		2	3	.400	2.44	42	0	0	48	46	17	32	0	2	3	13	0	0	0	—	2	4	0	0	0.1	1.000
1995		0	4	.000	4.96	28	0	0	32.2	34	24	34	0	0	4	7	0	0	0	—	1	1	1	1	0.1	.667
1996	PHI N	3	5	.375	2.43	62	0	0	89	71	45	70	0	3	5	8	7	1	0	.143	8	11	0	3	0.3	1.000
5 yrs.		12	14	.462	3.18	186	0	0	226.2	198	120	190	0	12	14	30	7	1	0	.143	15	25	2	4	0.2	.952

Brian Sackinsky

SACKINSKY, BRIAN WALTER
B. June 22, 1971, Pittsburgh, Pa.

BR TR 6'4" 220 lbs.

Year	Team	W	L	PCT	ERA	G	GS	CG	IP	H	BB	SO	ShO	W	L	SV	AB	H	HR	BA	PO	A	E	DP	TC/G	FA
1996	BAL A	0	0	—	3.86	3	0	0	4.2	6	3	2	0	0	0	0	0	0	0	—	0	0	0	0	1.0	—

A. J. Sager

SAGER, ANTHONY JOSEPH
B. Mar. 3, 1965, Columbus, Ohio

BR TR 6'4" 220 lbs.

Year	Team	W	L	PCT	ERA	G	GS	CG	IP	H	BB	SO	ShO	W	L	SV	AB	H	HR	BA	PO	A	E	DP	TC/G	FA
1994	SD N	1	4	.200	5.98	22	3	0	46.2	62	16	26	0	1	3	0	10	1	0	.100	6	15	0	1	1.0	1.000
1995	CLR N	0	0	—	7.36	10	0	0	14.2	19	7	10	0	0	0	0	3	0	0	.000	1	5	0	1	0.6	1.000
1996	DET A	4	5	.444	5.01	22	9	0	79	91	29	52	0	1	3	0	0	0	0	—	5	9	1	1	0.7	.933
3 yrs.		5	9	.357	5.58	54	12	0	140.1	172	52	88	0	2	6	0	13	1	0	.077	12	29	1	3	0.8	.976

Roger Salkeld

SALKELD, ROGER WILLIAM
B. Mar. 6, 1971, Burbank, Calif.

BR TR 6'5" 215 lbs.

Year	Team	W	L	PCT	ERA	G	GS	CG	IP	H	BB	SO	ShO	W	L	SV	AB	H	HR	BA	PO	A	E	DP	TC/G	FA
1993	SEA A	0	0	—	2.51	3	2	0	14.1	13	4	13	0	0	0	0	0	0	0	—	0	2	0	0	0.7	1.000
1994		2	5	.286	7.17	13	13	0	59	76	45	46	0	0	0	0	0	0	0	—	1	3	0	0	0.3	1.000
1996	CIN N	8	5	.615	5.20	29	19	1	116	114	54	82	1	2	0	0	32	1	0	.031	7	16	1	0	0.8	.958
3 yrs.		10	10	.500	5.61	45	34	1	189.1	203	103	141	1	2	0	0	32	1	0	.031	8	21	1	0	0.7	.967

Year	Team	W	L	PCT	ERA	G	GS	CG	IP	H	BB	SO	ShO	W	L	SV	AB	H	HR	BA	PO	A	E	DP	TC/G	FA

Scott Sanders

SANDERS, SCOTT GERALD
B. Mar. 25, 1969, Hannibal, Mo. — BR TR 6'4" 210 lbs.

Year	Team	W	L	PCT	ERA	G	GS	CG	IP	H	BB	SO	ShO	W	L	SV	AB	H	HR	BA	PO	A	E	DP	TC/G	FA
1993	SD N	3	3	.500	4.13	9	9	0	52.1	54	23	37	0	0	0	0	16	1	0	.063	3	2	0	0	0.6	1.000
1994		4	8	.333	4.78	23	20	0	111	103	48	109	0	0	0	1	32	4	0	.125	9	15	0	0	1.0	1.000
1995		5	5	.500	4.30	17	15	1	90	79	31	88	0	0	0	0	27	8	0	.296	6	3	0	0	0.5	1.000
1996		9	5	.643	3.38	46	16	0	144	117	48	157	0	1	2	0	36	7	0	.194	15	10	2	0	0.6	.926
4 yrs.		21	21	.500	4.08	95	60	1	397.1	353	150	391	0	1	2	1	111	20	0	.180	33	30	2	0	0.7	.969

DIVISIONAL PLAYOFF SERIES

| 1996 | SD N | 0 | 0 | — | 8.31 | 1 | 1 | 0 | 4.1 | 3 | 4 | 4 | 0 | 0 | 0 | 0 | 1 | 0 | 0 | .000 | 0 | 1 | 0 | 0 | 1.0 | 1.000 |

Scott Sanderson

SANDERSON, SCOTT DOUGLAS
B. July 22, 1956, Dearborn, Mich. — BR TR 6'5" 195 lbs.

Year	Team	W	L	PCT	ERA	G	GS	CG	IP	H	BB	SO	ShO	W	L	SV	AB	H	HR	BA	PO	A	E	DP	TC/G	FA
1978	MON N	4	2	.667	2.51	10	9	1	61	52	21	50	1	0	0	0	19	2	0	.105	2	6	1	0	0.9	.889
1979		9	8	.529	3.43	34	24	5	168	148	54	138	3	1	1	1	50	8	0	.160	9	13	1	1	0.7	.957
1980		16	11	.593	3.11	33	33	7	211	206	56	125	3	0	0	0	64	5	0	.078	14	21	1	0	1.1	.972
1981		9	7	.563	2.96	22	22	4	137	122	31	77	1	0	0	0	35	4	0	.114	6	14	0	0	0.9	1.000
1982		12	12	.500	3.46	32	32	7	224	212	58	158	0	0	0	0	57	8	1	.140	13	16	1	1	0.9	.967
1983		6	7	.462	4.65	18	16	0	81.1	98	20	55	0	0	0	1	28	4	0	.143	4	6	2	0	0.7	.833
1984	CHI N	8	5	.615	3.14	24	23	3	140.2	140	24	76	0	0	0	0	42	5	0	.119	11	24	1	0	1.5	.972
1985		5	6	.455	3.12	19	19	2	121	100	27	80	0	0	0	0	31	2	0	.065	11	21	0	2	1.7	1.000
1986		9	11	.450	4.19	37	28	1	169.2	165	37	124	1	2	0	1	51	3	0	.059	11	20	2	3	0.9	.939
1987		8	9	.471	4.29	32	22	0	144.2	156	50	106	0	1	2	2	40	3	1	.075	10	14	2	3	0.8	.923
1988		1	2	.333	5.28	11	0	0	15.1	13	3	6	0	1	2	0	0	0	0	—	1	0	0	0	0.1	1.000
1989		11	9	.550	3.94	37	23	2	146.1	155	31	86	0	1	2	0	43	2	0	.047	10	12	0	1	0.6	1.000
1990	OAK A	17	11	.607	3.88	34	34	2	206.1	205	66	128	1	0	0	0	0	0	0	—	11	18	2	2	0.9	.935
1991	NY A	16	10	.615	3.81	34	34	2	208	200	29	130	2	0	0	0	0	0	0	—	15	13	1	0	0.9	.966
1992		12	11	.522	4.93	33	33	2	193.1	220	64	104	1	0	0	0	0	0	0	—	4	18	1	1	0.7	.917
1993	2 teams CAL A (21G 7-11)	SF N (11G 4-2)																								
"	total	11	13	.458	4.21	32	29	4	184	201	34	102	1	0	0	0	14	0	0	.000	13	23	2	1	1.2	.947
1994	CHI A	8	4	.667	5.09	18	14	1	92	110	12	36	0	0	1	0	0	0	0	—	4	18	0	1	1.2	1.000
1995	CAL A	1	3	.250	4.12	7	7	0	39.1	48	4	23	0	0	0	0	0	0	0	—	3	4	0	1	1.0	1.000
1996		0	2	.000	7.50	5	4	0	18	39	4	7	0	0	0	0	0	0	0	—	2	3	0	0	1.0	1.000
19 yrs.		163	143	.533	3.84	472	407	43	2561	2590	625	1611	14	6	8	5	474	46	2	.097	153	265	18	17	0.9	.959

DIVISIONAL PLAYOFF SERIES

| 1981 | MON N | 0 | 0 | — | 6.75 | 1 | 1 | 0 | 2.2 | 4 | 2 | 2 | 0 | 0 | 0 | 0 | 1 | 0 | 0 | .000 | 0 | 0 | 0 | 0 | 0.0 | .000 |

LEAGUE CHAMPIONSHIP SERIES

1984	CHI N	0	0	—	5.79	1	1	0	4.2	6	1	2	0	0	0	0	2	0	0	.000	0	1	0	0	1.0	1.000
1989		0	0	—	0.00	1	0	0	2	2	0	1	0	0	0	0	0	0	0	—	0	0	0	0	0.0	.000
2 yrs.		0	0	—	4.05	2	1	0	6.2	8	1	3	0	0	0	0	2	0	0	.000	0	1	0	0	0.5	1.000

WORLD SERIES

| 1990 | OAK A | 0 | 0 | — | 10.80 | 2 | 0 | 0 | 1.2 | 4 | 1 | 0 | 0 | 0 | 0 | 0 | 0 | 0 | 0 | — | 0 | 0 | 0 | 0 | 0.0 | .000 |

Rich Sauveur

SAUVEUR, RICHARD DANIEL
B. Nov. 23, 1963, Arlington, Va. — BL TL 6'4" 163 lbs.

Year	Team	W	L	PCT	ERA	G	GS	CG	IP	H	BB	SO	ShO	W	L	SV	AB	H	HR	BA	PO	A	E	DP	TC/G	FA
1986	PIT N	0	0	—	6.00	3	3	0	12	17	6	6	0	0	0	0	3	1	0	.333	1	5	0	1	2.0	1.000
1988	MON N	0	0	—	6.00	4	0	0	3	3	2	3	0	0	0	0	0	0	0	—	0	1	0	0	0.3	1.000
1991	NY N	0	0	—	10.80	6	0	0	3.1	7	2	4	0	0	0	0	0	0	0	—	0	2	0	0	0.3	1.000
1992	KC A	0	1	.000	4.40	8	0	0	14.1	15	8	7	0	0	0	0	0	0	0	—	0	1	0	0	0.1	1.000
1996	CHI A	0	0	—	15.00	3	0	0	3	3	5	1	0	0	0	0	0	0	0	—	0	1	0	1	0.3	1.000
5 yrs.		0	1	.000	6.56	24	3	0	35.2	45	23	21	0	0	1	0	3	1	0	.333	1	10	0	2	0.5	1.000

Bob Scanlan

SCANLAN, ROBERT GUY
B. Aug. 9, 1966, Los Angeles, Calif. — BR TR 6'7" 215 lbs.

Year	Team	W	L	PCT	ERA	G	GS	CG	IP	H	BB	SO	ShO	W	L	SV	AB	H	HR	BA	PO	A	E	DP	TC/G	FA
1991	CHI N	7	8	.467	3.89	40	13	0	111	114	40	44	0	5	4	1	24	1	0	.042	9	16	2	0	0.7	.926
1992		3	6	.333	2.89	69	0	0	87.1	76	30	42	0	3	6	14	4	0	0	.000	5	22	2	0	0.4	.931
1993		4	5	.444	4.54	70	0	0	75.1	79	28	44	0	4	5	0	2	1	0	.500	3	6	0	0	0.1	1.000
1994	MIL A	2	6	.250	4.11	30	12	0	103	117	28	65	0	0	3	2	0	0	0	—	8	12	1	0	0.7	.952
1995		4	7	.364	6.59	17	14	0	83.1	101	44	29	0	1	0	0	0	0	0	—	6	14	2	1	1.3	.909
1996	2 teams DET A (8G 0-0)	KC A (9G 0-1)																								
"	total	0	1	.000	6.85	17	0	0	22.1	29	12	6	0	0	1	0	0	0	0	—	1	4	4	0	0.5	.556
6 yrs.		20	33	.377	4.46	243	39	0	482.1	516	182	230	0	13	19	17	30	2	0	.067	32	74	11	2	0.5	.906

Curt Schilling

SCHILLING, CURTIS MONTAGUE
B. Nov. 14, 1966, Anchorage, Alaska — BR TR 6'5" 205 lbs.

Year	Team	W	L	PCT	ERA	G	GS	CG	IP	H	BB	SO	ShO	W	L	SV	AB	H	HR	BA	PO	A	E	DP	TC/G	FA
1988	BAL A	0	3	.000	9.82	4	4	0	14.2	22	10	4	0	0	0	0	0	0	0	—	0	0	1	0	0.3	.000
1989		0	1	.000	6.23	5	1	0	8.2	10	3	6	0	0	0	0	0	0	0	—	1	0	0	0	0.3	1.000
1990		1	2	.333	2.54	35	0	0	46	38	19	32	0	1	2	3	0	0	0	—	1	4	0	0	0.2	1.000
1991	HOU N	3	5	.375	3.81	56	0	0	75.2	79	39	71	0	3	5	8	3	1	0	.333	6	4	1	0	0.2	.909
1992	PHI N	14	11	.560	2.35	42	26	10	226.1	165	59	147	4	2	2	2	64	10	0	.156	14	21	3	1	0.9	.921
1993		16	7	.696	4.02	34	34	7	235.1	234	57	186	2	0	0	0	75	11	0	.147	6	36	0	1	1.2	1.000
1994		2	8	.200	4.48	13	13	1	82.1	87	28	58	0	0	0	0	28	3	0	.107	2	11	0	0	1.1	.929
1995		7	5	.583	3.57	17	17	1	116	96	26	114	0	0	0	0	40	7	0	.175	2	8	1	1	0.6	.909
1996		9	10	.474	3.19	26	26	8	183.1	149	50	182	0	0	0	0	63	11	0	.175	10	8	1	0	0.7	.947
9 yrs.		52	52	.500	3.49	232	121	27	988.1	880	291	800	8	6	9	13	273	43	0	.158	42	92	8	3	0.6	.944

LEAGUE CHAMPIONSHIP SERIES

| 1993 | PHI N | 0 | 0 | — | 1.69 | 2 | 2 | 0 | 16 | 11 | 5 | 19 | 0 | 0 | 0 | 0 | 5 | 0 | 0 | .000 | 0 | 0 | 0 | 0 | 0.0 | .000 |

Year	Team		W	L	PCT	ERA	G	GS	CG	IP	H	BB	SO	ShO	W	L	SV	AB	H	HR	BA	PO	A	E	DP	TC/G	FA
															Relief Pitching			**Batting**									

Curt Schilling *continued*

Year	Team		W	L	PCT	ERA	G	GS	CG	IP	H	BB	SO	ShO	W	L	SV	AB	H	HR	BA	PO	A	E	DP	TC/G	FA
WORLD SERIES 1993	PHI	N	1	1	.500	3.52	2	2	1	15.1	13	5	9	1	0	0	0	2	1	0	.500	0	3	0	0	1.5	1.000

Jason Schmidt

SCHMIDT, JASON DAVID
B. Jan. 29, 1973, Kelson, Wash.
BR TR 6'5" 185 lbs.

Year	Team		W	L	PCT	ERA	G	GS	CG	IP	H	BB	SO	ShO	W	L	SV	AB	H	HR	BA	PO	A	E	DP	TC/G	FA
1995	ATL	N	2	2	.500	5.76	9	2	0	25	27	18	19	0	1	1	0	5	1	0	.200	3	3	0	1	0.7	1.000
1996 2 teams	ATL N (13G 3-4)	PIT N (6G 2-2)																									
" total			5	6	.455	5.70	19	17	1	96.1	108	53	74	0	0	0	0	31	1	0	.032	5	9	1	0	0.8	.933
2 yrs.			7	8	.467	5.71	28	19	1	121.1	135	71	93	0	1	1	0	36	2	0	.056	8	12	1	1	0.8	.952

Jeff Schmidt

SCHMIDT, JEFFREY THOMAS
B. Feb. 21, 1971, Northfield, Minn.
BR TR 6'5" 205 lbs.

Year	Team		W	L	PCT	ERA	G	GS	CG	IP	H	BB	SO	ShO	W	L	SV	AB	H	HR	BA	PO	A	E	DP	TC/G	FA
1996	CAL	A	2	0	1.000	7.88	9	0	0	8	13	8	2	0	2	0	0	0	0	0	—	0	0	0	0	0.0	—

Pete Schourek

SCHOUREK, PETER ALAN
B. May 10, 1969, Austin, Tex.
BL TL 6'5" 195 lbs.

Year	Team		W	L	PCT	ERA	G	GS	CG	IP	H	BB	SO	ShO	W	L	SV	AB	H	HR	BA	PO	A	E	DP	TC/G	FA
1991	NY	N	5	4	.556	4.27	35	8	1	86.1	82	43	67	1	2	1	2	22	3	0	.136	6	14	0	1	0.6	1.000
1992			6	8	.429	3.64	22	21	0	136	137	44	60	0	1	0	0	42	2	0	.048	7	13	0	1	0.9	1.000
1993			5	12	.294	5.96	41	18	0	128.1	168	45	72	0	0	1	0	32	7	0	.219	5	17	0	2	0.5	1.000
1994	CIN	N	7	2	.778	4.09	22	10	0	81.1	90	29	69	0	3	0	0	23	4	1	.174	1	13	0	2	0.6	1.000
1995			18	7	.720	3.22	29	29	2	190.1	158	45	160	0	0	0	0	59	13	0	.220	7	29	1	2	1.3	.973
1996			4	5	.444	6.01	12	12	0	67.1	79	24	54	0	0	0	0	19	5	0	.263	2	10	0	0	1.0	1.000
6 yrs.			45	38	.542	4.32	161	98	3	689.2	714	230	482	1	6	2	2	197	34	1	.173	28	96	1	8	0.8	.992
DIVISIONAL PLAYOFF SERIES 1995	CIN	N	1	0	1.000	2.57	1	1	0	7	5	3	5	0	0	0	0	2	0	0	.000	0	2	0	1	2.0	1.000
LEAGUE CHAMPIONSHIP SERIES 1995	CIN	N	0	1	.000	1.26	2	2	0	14.1	14	3	13	0	0	0	0	5	0	0	.000	1	3	0	1	2.0	1.000

Carl Schutz

SCHUTZ, CARL JAMES
B. Aug. 22, 1971, Hammond, La.
BL TL 5'11" 208 lbs.

Year	Team		W	L	PCT	ERA	G	GS	CG	IP	H	BB	SO	ShO	W	L	SV	AB	H	HR	BA	PO	A	E	DP	TC/G	FA
1996	ATL	N	0	0	—	2.70	3	0	0	3.1	3	2	5	0	0	0	0	0	0	0	—	0	0	0	0	0.0	—

Tim Scott

SCOTT, TIMOTHY DALE
B. Nov. 16, 1966, Hanford, Calif.
BR TR 6'2" 185 lbs.

Year	Team		W	L	PCT	ERA	G	GS	CG	IP	H	BB	SO	ShO	W	L	SV	AB	H	HR	BA	PO	A	E	DP	TC/G	FA
1991	SD	N	0	0	—	9.00	2	0	0	1	0	1	0	0	0	0	0	0	0	0	—	0	0	0	0	0.0	.000
1992			4	1	.800	5.26	34	0	0	37.2	39	21	30	0	4	1	0	0	0	0	—	0	4	0	0	0.1	1.000
1993 2 teams	SD N (24G 2-0)	MON N (32G 5-2)																									
" total			7	2	.778	3.01	56	0	0	71.2	69	34	65	0	7	1	0	4	0	0	.000	3	8	1	1	0.2	.917
1994	MON	N	5	2	.714	2.70	40	0	0	53.1	51	18	37	0	5	2	1	2	0	0	.000	2	0	0	0	0.1	1.000
1995			2	0	1.000	3.98	62	0	0	63.1	52	23	57	0	2	0	2	4	1	0	.250	3	4	0	1	0.1	1.000
1996 2 teams	MON N (45G 3-5)	SF N (20G 2-2)																									
" total			5	7	.417	4.64	65	0	0	66	65	30	47	0	5	7	1	5	0	0	.000	5	7	0	1	0.2	1.000
6 yrs.			23	12	.657	3.84	259	0	0	293	278	126	237	0	23	12	5	15	1	0	.067	13	23	1	3	0.1	.973

Aaron Sele

SELE, AARON HELMER
B. June 25, 1970, Golden Valley, Minn.
BR TR 6'5" 205 lbs.

Year	Team		W	L	PCT	ERA	G	GS	CG	IP	H	BB	SO	ShO	W	L	SV	AB	H	HR	BA	PO	A	E	DP	TC/G	FA
1993	BOS	A	7	2	.778	2.74	18	18	0	111.2	100	48	93	0	0	0	0	0	0	0	—	3	9	5	1	0.9	.706
1994			8	7	.533	3.83	22	22	2	143.1	140	60	105	0	0	0	0	0	0	0	—	6	14	0	0	0.9	1.000
1995			3	1	.750	3.06	6	6	0	32.1	32	14	21	0	0	0	0	0	0	0	—	2	5	3	0	1.7	.700
1996			7	11	.389	5.32	29	29	1	157.1	192	67	137	0	0	0	0	0	0	0	—	8	18	1	1	1.0	.963
4 yrs.			25	21	.543	4.03	75	75	3	444.2	464	189	356	0	0	0	0	0	0	0	—	19	46	9	2	1.0	.878

Dan Serafini

SERAFINI, DANIEL JOSEPH
B. Jan. 25, 1974, San Francisco, Calif.
BB TL 6'1" 180 lbs.

Year	Team		W	L	PCT	ERA	G	GS	CG	IP	H	BB	SO	ShO	W	L	SV	AB	H	HR	BA	PO	A	E	DP	TC/G	FA
1996	MIN	A	0	1	.000	10.38	1	1	0	4.1	7	2	1	0	0	0	0	0	0	0	—	0	0	0	0	0.0	—

Scott Service

SERVICE, DAVID SCOTT
B. Feb. 26, 1967, Cincinnati, Ohio
BR TR 6'6" 225 lbs.

Year	Team		W	L	PCT	ERA	G	GS	CG	IP	H	BB	SO	ShO	W	L	SV	AB	H	HR	BA	PO	A	E	DP	TC/G	FA
1988	PHI	N	0	0	—	1.69	5	0	0	5.1	7	1	6	0	0	0	0	0	0	0	—	0	0	0	0	0.0	.000
1992	MON	N	0	0	—	14.14	5	0	0	7	15	5	11	0	0	0	0	2	0	0	.000	0	0	0	0	0.0	.000
1993 2 teams	CLR N (3G 0-0)	CIN N (26G 2-2)																									
" total			2	2	.500	4.30	29	0	0	46	44	16	43	0	2	2	2	7	1	0	.143	6	5	0	0	0.4	1.000
1994	CIN	N	1	2	.333	7.36	6	0	0	7.1	8	3	5	0	1	2	0	0	0	0	—	0	3	0	0	0.5	1.000
1995	SF	N	3	1	.750	3.19	28	0	0	31	18	20	30	0	3	1	0	1	0	0	.000	2	2	0	0	0.1	1.000
1996	CIN	N	1	0	1.000	3.94	34	0	0	48	51	18	46	0	1	0	0	5	0	0	.000	1	9	0	0	0.3	1.000
6 yrs.			7	5	.583	4.48	107	1	0	144.2	143	63	141	0	7	5	2	15	1	0	.067	9	19	0	0	0.3	1.000

Jeff Shaw

SHAW, JEFFREY LEE
B. July 7, 1966, Washington Court House, Ohio
BR TR 6'2" 185 lbs.

Year	Team		W	L	PCT	ERA	G	GS	CG	IP	H	BB	SO	ShO	W	L	SV	AB	H	HR	BA	PO	A	E	DP	TC/G	FA
1990	CLE	A	3	4	.429	6.66	12	9	0	48.2	73	20	25	0	0	0	0	0	0	0	—	4	7	0	0	0.9	1.000
1991			0	5	.000	3.36	29	1	0	72.1	72	27	31	0	0	4	1	0	0	0	—	4	11	2	2	0.6	.882

Year	Team	W	L	PCT	ERA	G	GS	CG	IP	H	BB	SO	ShO	Relief Pitching W	L	SV	Batting AB	H	HR	BA	PO	A	E	DP	TC/G	FA

Jeff Shaw *continued*

Year	Team	W	L	PCT	ERA	G	GS	CG	IP	H	BB	SO	ShO	RP W	L	SV	AB	H	HR	BA	PO	A	E	DP	TC/G	FA
1992		0	1	.000	8.22	2	1	0	7.2	7	4	3	0	0	0	0	0	0	0	—	0	2	1	0	1.5	.667
1993	MON N	2	7	.222	4.14	55	8	0	95.2	91	32	50	0	1	3	0	15	1	0	.067	8	16	0	1	0.4	1.000
1994		5	2	.714	3.88	46	0	0	67.1	67	15	47	0	5	2	1	7	2	0	.286	8	12	0	0	0.4	1.000
1995	2 teams				MON N (50G 1-6)				CHI A (9G 0-0)																	
"	total	1	6	.143	4.88	59	0	0	72	70	27	51	0	1	6	3	6	0	0	.000	7	13	0	1	0.3	1.000
1996	CIN N	8	6	.571	2.49	78	0	0	104.2	99	29	69	0	8	6	4	5	0	0	.000	13	14	1	3	0.4	.964
7 yrs.		19	31	.380	4.05	281	19	0	468.1	479	154	276	0	15	21	9	33	3	0	.091	44	75	4	7	0.4	.967

Keith Shepherd

SHEPHERD, KEITH WAYNE
B. Jan. 21, 1968, Wabash, Ind.   BR TR 6'2" 205 lbs.

Year	Team	W	L	PCT	ERA	G	GS	CG	IP	H	BB	SO	ShO	RP W	L	SV	AB	H	HR	BA	PO	A	E	DP	TC/G	FA
1992	PHI N	1	1	.500	3.27	12	0	0	22	19	6	10	0	1	1	2	0	0	0	—	0	5	0	0	0.4	1.000
1993	CLR N	1	3	.250	6.98	14	1	0	19.1	26	4	7	0	1	3	1	2	0	0	.000	3	2	2	0	0.5	.714
1995	BOS A	0	0	—	36.00	2	0	0	1	4	2	0	0	0	0	0	0	0	0	—	0	1	0	0	0.5	1.000
1996	BAL A	0	1	.000	8.71	13	0	0	20.2	31	18	17	0	0	1	0	0	0	0	—	1	2	0	0	0.2	1.000
4 yrs.		2	5	.286	6.71	41	1	0	63	80	30	34	0	2	5	3	2	0	0	.000	4	10	2	0	0.4	.875

Paul Shuey

SHUEY, PAUL KENNETH
B. Sept. 16, 1970, Lima, Ohio   BR TR 6'3" 215 lbs.

Year	Team	W	L	PCT	ERA	G	GS	CG	IP	H	BB	SO	ShO	RP W	L	SV	AB	H	HR	BA	PO	A	E	DP	TC/G	FA
1994	CLE A	0	1	.000	8.49	14	0	0	11.2	14	12	16	0	0	1	5	0	0	0	—	0	0	0	0	0.0	.000
1995		0	2	.000	4.26	7	0	0	6.1	5	5	5	0	0	2	0	0	0	0	—	0	2	0	0	0.3	1.000
1996		5	2	.714	2.85	42	0	0	53.2	45	26	44	0	5	2	4	0	0	0	—	3	5	0	1	0.2	1.000
3 yrs.		5	5	.500	3.89	63	0	0	71.2	64	43	65	0	5	5	9	0	0	0	—	3	7	0	1	0.2	1.000
DIVISIONAL PLAYOFF SERIES																										
1996	CLE A	0	0	—	9.00	3	0	0	2	5	2	2	0	0	0	0	0	0	0	—	0	0	0	0	0.0	.000

Jose Silva

SILVA, JOSE LEONEL
B. Dec. 19, 1973, Tijuana, Mexico   BR TR 6'5" 210 lbs.

Year	Team	W	L	PCT	ERA	G	GS	CG	IP	H	BB	SO	ShO	RP W	L	SV	AB	H	HR	BA	PO	A	E	DP	TC/G	FA
1996	TOR A	0	0	—	13.50	2	0	0	2	5	0	0	0	0	0	0	0	0	0	—	0	1	0	0	0.5	1.000

Bill Simas

SIMAS, WILLIAM ANTHONY
B. Nov. 28, 1971, Hanford, Calif.   BL TR 6'3" 200 lbs.

Year	Team	W	L	PCT	ERA	G	GS	CG	IP	H	BB	SO	ShO	RP W	L	SV	AB	H	HR	BA	PO	A	E	DP	TC/G	FA
1995	CHI A	1	1	.500	2.57	14	0	0	14	15	10	16	0	1	1	0	0	0	0	—	0	0	0	0	0.0	.000
1996		2	8	.200	4.58	64	0	0	72.2	75	39	65	0	2	8	2	0	0	0	—	9	5	1	1	0.2	.933
2 yrs.		3	9	.250	4.26	78	0	0	86.2	90	49	81	0	3	9	2					9	5	1	1	0.2	.933

Mike Sirotka

SIROTKA, MICHAEL ROBERT
B. May 13, 1971, Houston, Tex.   BL TL 6'1" 190 lbs.

Year	Team	W	L	PCT	ERA	G	GS	CG	IP	H	BB	SO	ShO	RP W	L	SV	AB	H	HR	BA	PO	A	E	DP	TC/G	FA
1995	CHI A	1	2	.333	4.19	6	6	0	34.1	39	17	19	0	0	0	0	0	0	0	—	1	5	0	0	1.0	1.000
1996		1	2	.333	7.18	15	4	0	26.1	34	12	11	0	0	0	0	0	0	0	—	0	3	1	0	0.3	.750
2 yrs.		2	4	.333	5.49	21	10	0	60.2	73	29	30	0	0	0	0					1	8	1	0	0.5	.900

Heathcliff Slocumb

SLOCUMB, HEATH
B. June 7, 1966, Jamaica, N. Y.   BR TR 6'3" 180 lbs.

Year	Team	W	L	PCT	ERA	G	GS	CG	IP	H	BB	SO	ShO	RP W	L	SV	AB	H	HR	BA	PO	A	E	DP	TC/G	FA
1991	CHI N	2	1	.667	3.45	52	0	0	62.2	53	30	34	0	2	1	1	1	0	0	.000	5	10	1	0	0.3	.938
1992		0	3	.000	6.50	30	0	0	36	52	21	27	0	0	3	1	4	0	0	.000	3	4	2	0	0.3	.778
1993	2 teams				CHI N (10G 1-0)				CLE A (20G 3-1)																	
"	total	4	1	.800	4.03	30	0	0	38	35	20	22	0	4	1	0	1	0	0	.000	3	4	0	2	0.2	1.000
1994	PHI N	5	1	.833	2.86	52	0	0	72.1	75	28	58	0	5	1	0	4	1	0	.250	2	13	3	1	0.3	.833
1995		5	6	.455	2.89	61	0	0	65.1	64	35	63	0	5	6	32	1	0	0	.000	4	17	1	3	0.4	.955
1996	BOS A	5	5	.500	3.02	75	0	0	83.1	68	55	88	0	5	5	31	0	0	0	—	8	12	0	4	0.3	1.000
6 yrs.		21	17	.553	3.50	300	0	0	357.2	347	189	292	0	21	17	65	11	1	0	.091	25	60	7	10	0.3	.924

Mark Small

SLUSARSKI, JOSEPH ANDREW
B. Dec. 19, 1966, Indianapolis, Ind.   BR TR 6'4" 195 lbs.

Year	Team	W	L	PCT	ERA	G	GS	CG	IP	H	BB	SO	ShO	RP W	L	SV	AB	H	HR	BA	PO	A	E	DP	TC/G	FA
1991	OAK A	5	7	.417	5.27	20	19	1	109.1	121	52	60	0	0	0	0	0	0	0	—	7	10	1	0	0.9	.944

Aaron Small

SMALL, AARON JAMES
B. Nov. 23, 1971, Oxnard, Calif.   BR TR 6'5" 200 lbs.

Year	Team	W	L	PCT	ERA	G	GS	CG	IP	H	BB	SO	ShO	RP W	L	SV	AB	H	HR	BA	PO	A	E	DP	TC/G	FA
1994	TOR A	0	0	—	9.00	1	0	0	2	5	2	0	0	0	0	0	0	0	0	—	0	1	0	0	1.0	1.000
1995	FLA N	1	0	1.000	1.42	7	0	0	6.1	7	6	5	0	1	0	0	0	0	0	—	0	1	0	0	0.1	1.000
1996	OAK A	1	3	.250	8.16	12	3	0	28.2	37	22	17	0	0	1	0	0	0	0	—	3	4	0	1	0.6	1.000
3 yrs.		2	3	.400	7.05	20	3	0	37	49	30	22	0	1	1	0	0	0	0	—	3	6	0	1	0.4	1.000

John Smiley

SMILEY, JOHN PATRICK
B. Mar. 17, 1965, Phoenixville, Pa.   BL TL 6'4" 180 lbs.

Year	Team	W	L	PCT	ERA	G	GS	CG	IP	H	BB	SO	ShO	RP W	L	SV	AB	H	HR	BA	PO	A	E	DP	TC/G	FA
1986	PIT N	1	0	1.000	3.86	12	0	0	11.2	4	4	9	0	0	0	0	0	0	0	—	1	2	0	0	0.3	1.000
1987		5	5	.500	5.76	63	0	0	75	69	50	58	0	5	5	4	7	1	0	.143	7	9	0	2	0.3	1.000
1988		13	11	.542	3.25	34	32	5	205	185	46	129	1	0	0	0	63	5	0	.079	14	27	0	3	1.2	1.000
1989		12	8	.600	2.81	28	28	8	205.1	174	49	123	1	0	0	0	65	9	0	.138	7	23	4	2	1.2	.882
1990		9	10	.474	4.64	26	25	8	149.1	161	36	86	1	0	0	0	49	6	0	.122	8	24	2	1	1.3	.941

John Smiley *continued*

Year	Team	W	L	PCT	ERA	G	GS	CG	IP	H	BB	SO	ShO	Relief Pitching W	L	SV	Batting AB	H	HR	BA	PO	A	E	DP	TC/G	FA
1991		20	8	.714	3.08	33	32	2	207.2	194	44	129	1	1	0	0	70	7	0	.100	5	34	1	0	1.2	.975
1992	MIN A	16	9	.640	3.21	34	34	5	241	205	65	163	2	0	0	0	0	0	0	—	4	35	0	2	1.1	1.000
1993	CIN N	3	9	.250	5.62	18	18	2	105.2	117	31	60	0	0	0	0	32	8	0	.250	7	16	0	0	1.3	1.000
1994		11	10	.524	3.86	24	24	1	158.2	169	37	112	1	0	0	0	55	11	0	.200	8	19	2	1	1.2	.931
1995		12	5	.706	3.46	28	27	1	176.2	173	39	124	0	0	0	0	55	9	2	.164	3	27	0	3	1.1	1.000
1996		13	14	.481	3.64	35	34	2	217.1	207	54	171	2	0	0	0	68	13	0	.191	6	29	2	1	1.1	.946
11 yrs.		115	89	.564	3.67	335	254	28	1753.1	1658	455	1164	8	7	5	4	464	69	2	.149	70	245	11	15	1.0	.966

DIVISIONAL PLAYOFF SERIES

Year	Team	W	L	PCT	ERA	G	GS	CG	IP	H	BB	SO	ShO	W	L	SV	AB	H	HR	BA	PO	A	E	DP	TC/G	FA
1995	CIN N	0	0	—	3.00	1	1	0	6	9	0	1	0	0	0	0	2	0	0	.000	0	1	0	0	1.0	1.000

LEAGUE CHAMPIONSHIP SERIES

Year	Team	W	L	PCT	ERA	G	GS	CG	IP	H	BB	SO	ShO	W	L	SV	AB	H	HR	BA	PO	A	E	DP	TC/G	FA
1990	PIT N	0	0	—	0.00	1	0	0	2	2	0	0	0	0	0	0	0	0	0	—	0	0	0	0	0.0	.000
1991		0	2	.000	23.63	2	2	0	2.2	8	1	3	0	0	0	0	0	0	0	—	0	1	0	0	0.5	1.000
1995	CIN N	0	0	—	3.60	1	1	0	5	5	0	1	0	0	0	0	1	0	0	.000	1	1	0	0	2.0	1.000
3 yrs.		0	2	.000	8.38	4	3	0	9.2	15	1	4	0	0	0	0	1	0	0	.000	1	2	0	0	0.8	1.000

Lee Smith

SMITH, LEE ARTHUR, JR.
B. Dec. 4, 1957, Jamestown, La.
BR TR 6'5" 220 lbs.

Year	Team	W	L	PCT	ERA	G	GS	CG	IP	H	BB	SO	ShO	Relief Pitching W	L	SV	Batting AB	H	HR	BA	PO	A	E	DP	TC/G	FA
1980	CHI N	2	0	1.000	2.86	18	1	0	22	21	14	17	0	2	0	0	0	0	0	—	0	3	0	0	0.2	1.000
1981		3	6	.333	3.49	40	1	0	67	57	31	50	0	3	5	1	9	0	0	.000	3	9	0	0	0.3	1.000
1982		2	5	.286	2.69	72	5	0	117	105	37	99	0	2	1	17	16	1	1	.063	9	10	1	2	0.3	.950
1983		4	10	.286	1.65	66	0	0	103.1	70	41	91	0	4	10	29	9	1	0	.111	8	9	0	0	0.3	1.000
1984		9	7	.563	3.65	69	0	0	101	98	35	86	0	9	7	33	13	1	0	.077	6	13	0	2	0.3	1.000
1985		7	4	.636	3.04	65	0	0	97.2	87	32	112	0	7	4	33	6	0	0	.000	3	9	0	1	0.2	1.000
1986		9	9	.500	3.09	66	0	0	90.1	69	42	93	0	9	9	31	5	0	0	.000	1	12	0	1	0.2	1.000
1987		4	10	.286	3.12	62	0	0	83.2	84	32	96	0	4	10	36	2	0	0	.000	3	8	0	0	0.2	1.000
1988	BOS A	4	5	.444	2.80	64	0	0	83.2	72	37	96	0	4	5	29	0	0	0	—	5	4	1	0	0.2	.900
1989		6	1	.857	3.57	64	0	0	70.2	53	33	96	0	6	1	25	0	0	0	—	1	1	0	0	0.0	1.000
1990	2 teams	BOS A (11G 2-1)				STL N (53G 3-4)																				
"	total	5	5	.500	2.06	64	0	0	83	71	29	87	0	5	5	31	2	0	0	.000	2	3	0	0	0.1	1.000
1991	STL N	6	3	.667	2.34	67	0	0	73	70	13	67	0	6	3	47	0	0	0	—	3	6	0	0	0.1	1.000
1992		4	9	.308	3.12	70	0	0	75	62	26	60	0	4	9	43	0	0	0	—	1	7	1	1	0.1	.889
1993	2 teams	STL N (55G 2-4)				NY A (8G 0-0)																				
"	total	2	4	.333	3.88	63	0	0	58	53	14	60	0	2	4	46	0	0	0	.000	2	0	0	0	0.0	1.000
1994	BAL A	1	4	.200	3.29	41	0	0	38.1	34	11	42	0	1	4	33	0	0	0	—	2	2	1	0	0.1	.800
1995	CAL A	0	5	.000	3.47	52	0	0	49.1	42	25	43	0	0	5	37	0	0	0	—	1	4	0	0	0.1	1.000
1996	2 teams	CAL A (11G 0-0)				CIN N (43G 3-4)																				
"	total	3	4	.429	3.74	54	0	0	55.1	57	26	41	0	3	4	2	0	0	0	—	3	5	0	0	0.1	1.000
17 yrs.		71	91	.438	2.98 4th	997	6	0	1268.1	1105	478	1236	0	71	86	473 1st	64	3	1	.047	51	107	4	9	0.2	.975

LEAGUE CHAMPIONSHIP SERIES

Year	Team	W	L	PCT	ERA	G	GS	CG	IP	H	BB	SO	ShO	W	L	SV	AB	H	HR	BA	PO	A	E	DP	TC/G	FA
1984	CHI N	0	1	.000	9.00	2	0	0	2	3	0	3	0	0	1	1	0	0	0	—	0	0	0	0	0.0	.000
1988	BOS A	0	1	.000	8.10	2	0	0	3.1	6	1	4	0	0	1	0	0	0	0	—	0	0	0	0	0.0	.000
2 yrs.		0	2	.000	8.44	4	0	0	5.1	9	1	7	0	0	2	1	0	0	0	—	0	0	0	0	0.0	

Zane Smith

SMITH, ZANE WILLIAM
B. Dec. 28, 1960, Madison, Wis.
BL TL 6'2" 195 lbs.

Year	Team	W	L	PCT	ERA	G	GS	CG	IP	H	BB	SO	ShO	Relief Pitching W	L	SV	Batting AB	H	HR	BA	PO	A	E	DP	TC/G	FA
1984	ATL N	1	0	1.000	2.25	3	3	0	20	16	13	16	0	0	0	0	9	5	0	.556	2	3	1	1	2.0	.833
1985		9	10	.474	3.80	42	18	2	147	135	80	85	2	3	4	0	37	6	0	.162	7	35	3	2	1.1	.933
1986		8	16	.333	4.05	38	32	3	204.2	209	105	139	1	1	0	1	59	5	0	.085	7	45	1	4	1.4	.981
1987		15	10	.600	4.09	36	36	9	242	245	91	130	3	0	0	0	76	10	0	.132	15	43	0	4	1.6	1.000
1988		5	10	.333	4.30	23	22	3	140.1	159	44	59	0	0	0	0	42	7	0	.167	16	33	1	6	2.2	.980
1989	2 teams	ATL N (17G 1-12)				MON N (31G 0-1)																				
"	total	1	13	.071	3.49	48	17	0	147	141	52	93	0	0	1	2	32	6	0	.188	7	39	3	0	1.0	.939
1990	2 teams	MON N (22G 6-7)				PIT N (11G 6-2)																				
"	total	12	9	.571	2.55	33	31	4	215.1	196	50	130	2	0	0	0	68	11	0	.162	10	35	3	5	1.5	.938
1991	PIT N	16	10	.615	3.20	35	35	6	228	234	29	120	3	0	0	0	71	13	0	.183	12	39	3	5	1.5	.944
1992		8	8	.500	3.06	23	22	4	141	138	19	56	3	0	0	0	49	6	0	.122	6	29	0	2	1.5	1.000
1993		3	7	.300	4.55	14	14	1	83	97	22	32	0	0	0	0	25	2	0	.080	8	8	0	2	1.1	1.000
1994		10	8	.556	3.27	25	24	2	157	162	34	57	0	0	0	0	57	12	0	.211	8	40	0	1	1.9	1.000
1995	BOS A	8	8	.500	5.61	24	21	0	110.2	144	23	47	0	0	0	0	0	0	0	—	5	18	1	1	1.0	.958
1996	PIT N	4	6	.400	5.08	16	16	1	83.1	104	21	47	1	0	0	0	26	4	0	.154	1	13	1	1	0.9	.933
13 yrs.		100	115	.465	3.74	360	291	35	1919.1	1980	583	1011	16	4	5	3	551	87	0	.158	104	380	17	34	1.4	.966

DIVISIONAL PLAYOFF SERIES

Year	Team	W	L	PCT	ERA	G	GS	CG	IP	H	BB	SO	ShO	W	L	SV	AB	H	HR	BA	PO	A	E	DP	TC/G	FA
1995	BOS A	0	1	.000	6.75	1	0	0	1.1	1	0	0	0	0	0	0	0	0	0	—	0	0	0	0	0.0	.000

LEAGUE CHAMPIONSHIP SERIES

Year	Team	W	L	PCT	ERA	G	GS	CG	IP	H	BB	SO	ShO	W	L	SV	AB	H	HR	BA	PO	A	E	DP	TC/G	FA
1990	PIT N	0	2	.000	6.00	2	1	0	9	14	1	8	0	0	0	0	3	0	0	.000	0	1	0	0	0.5	1.000
1991		1	1	.500	0.61	2	2	0	14.2	15	3	10	0	0	0	0	5	0	0	.000	3	0	0	0	1.5	1.000
2 yrs.		1	3	.250 6th	2.66	4	3	0	23.2	29	4	18	0	0	1	0	8	0	0	.000	3	1	0	0	1.0	1.000

John Smoltz

SMOLTZ, JOHN ANDREW
B. May 15, 1967, Detroit, Mich.
BR TR 6'3" 210 lbs.

Year	Team	W	L	PCT	ERA	G	GS	CG	IP	H	BB	SO	ShO	W	L	SV	AB	H	HR	BA	PO	A	E	DP	TC/G	FA
1988	ATL N	2	7	.222	5.48	12	12	0	64	74	33	37	0	0	0	0	17	2	0	.118	4	6	0	1	0.8	1.000
1989		12	11	.522	2.94	29	29	5	208	160	72	168	0	0	0	0	62	7	1	.113	23	32	7	2	2.1	.887
1990		14	11	.560	3.85	34	34	6	231.1	206	90	170	2	0	0	0	74	12	0	.162	26	27	3	4	1.6	.946

Year	Team	W	L	PCT	ERA	G	GS	CG	IP	H	BB	SO	ShO	W	L	SV	AB	H	HR	BA	PO	A	E	DP	TC/G	FA

John Smoltz *continued*

Year	Team	W	L	PCT	ERA	G	GS	CG	IP	H	BB	SO	ShO	W	L	SV	AB	H	HR	BA	PO	A	E	DP	TC/G	FA
1991		14	13	.519	3.80	36	36	5	229.2	206	77	148	0	0	0	0	65	7	0	.108	15	34	1	1	1.4	.980
1992		15	12	.556	2.85	35	35	9	246.2	206	80	215	3	0	0	0	75	12	1	.160	23	26	1	3	1.4	.980
1993		15	11	.577	3.62	35	35	3	243.2	208	100	208	1	0	0	0	71	13	0	.183	29	23	0	1	1.5	1.000
1994		6	10	.375	4.14	21	21	1	134.2	120	48	113	0	0	0	0	37	6	1	.162	10	18	1	1	1.4	.966
1995		12	7	.632	3.18	29	29	2	192.2	166	72	193	1	0	0	0	56	6	0	.107	12	18	2	0	1.1	.938
1996		**24**	8	**.750**	2.94	35	35	6	253.2	199	55	**276**	2	0	0	0	78	17	1	.218	27	26	1	2	1.5	.981
9 yrs.		114	90	.559	3.45	266	266	37	1804.1	1545	627	1528	9	0	0	0	535	82	4	.153	169	210	16	15	1.5	.959

DIVISIONAL PLAYOFF SERIES

Year	Team	W	L	PCT	ERA	G	GS	CG	IP	H	BB	SO	ShO	W	L	SV	AB	H	HR	BA	PO	A	E	DP	TC/G	FA
1995	ATL N	0	0	—	7.94	1	1	0	5.2	5	1	6	0	0	0	0	2	0	0	.000	1	1	0	0	2.0	1.000
1996		1	0	1.000	1.00	1	1	0	9	4	2	7	0	0	0	0	2	0	0	.000	2	1	0	0	3.0	1.000
2 yrs.		1	0	1.000	3.68	2	2	0	14.2	9	3	13	0	0	0	0	4	0	0	.000	3	2	0	0	2.5	1.000

LEAGUE CHAMPIONSHIP SERIES

Year	Team	W	L	PCT	ERA	G	GS	CG	IP	H	BB	SO	ShO	W	L	SV	AB	H	HR	BA	PO	A	E	DP	TC/G	FA
1991	ATL N	2	0	1.000	1.76	2	2	1	15.1	14	3	15	1	0	0	0	5	1	0	.200	3	0	0	0	1.5	1.000
1992		2	0	1.000	2.66	3	3	0	20.1	14	10	19	0	0	0	0	7	2	0	.286	0	1	0	0	0.3	1.000
1993		0	1	.000	0.00	1	1	0	6.1	8	5	10	0	0	0	0	1	0	0	.000	0	0	0	0	0.0	1.000
1995		0	0	—	2.57	1	1	0	7	7	2	7	0	0	0	0	3	1	0	.333	0	1	1	0	2.0	.500
1996		2	0	1.000	1.20	2	2	0	15	12	3	12	0	0	0	0	7	2	0	.286	0	1	0	0	0.5	1.000
5 yrs.		6	1	.857	1.83	9	9	1	64	55	23	58	1	0	0	0	23	6	0	.261	3	3	1	0	0.8	.857
		2nd	7th		3rd		3rd		3rd		3rd	1st	1st													

WORLD SERIES

Year	Team	W	L	PCT	ERA	G	GS	CG	IP	H	BB	SO	ShO	W	L	SV	AB	H	HR	BA	PO	A	E	DP	TC/G	FA
1991	ATL N	0	0	—	1.26	2	2	0	14.1	13	1	11	0	0	0	0	2	0	0	.000	0	1	0	0	1.5	1.000
1992		1	0	1.000	2.70	2	2	0	13.1	13	7	12	0	0	0	0	3	0	0	.000	1	2	0	0	1.5	1.000
1995		0	0	—	15.43	1	1	0	2.1	6	2	4	0	0	0	0	0	0	0	—	0	0	0	0	0.0	.000
1996		1	1	.500	0.64	2	2	0	14	6	8	14	0	0	0	0	2	1	0	.500	0	1	0	0	0.5	1.000
4 yrs.		2	1	.667	2.25	7	7	0	44	38	18	41	0	0	0	0	7	1	0	.143	3	4	0	0	1.0	1.000

Steve Soderstrom

STEPHEN ANDREW SODERSTROM
B. Apr. 3, 1972, Turlock, Calif.

BR TR 6'3" 215 lbs.

Year	Team	W	L	PCT	ERA	G	GS	CG	IP	H	BB	SO	ShO	W	L	SV	AB	H	HR	BA	PO	A	E	DP	TC/G	FA
1996	SF N	2	0	1.000	5.27	3	3	0	13.2	16	6	9	0	0	0	0	5	0	0	.000	0	1	0	0	0.3	1.000

Clint Sodowsky

SODOWSKY, CLINT REA
B. July 13, 1972, Ponca City, Okla.

BL TR 6'3" 180 lbs.

Year	Team	W	L	PCT	ERA	G	GS	CG	IP	H	BB	SO	ShO	W	L	SV	AB	H	HR	BA	PO	A	E	DP	TC/G	FA
1995	DET A	2	2	.500	5.01	6	6	0	23.1	24	18	14	0	0	0	0	0	0	0	—	2	1	0	0	0.5	1.000
1996		1	3	.250	11.84	7	7	0	24.1	40	20	9	0	0	0	0	0	0	0	—	3	2	0	0	0.7	1.000
2 yrs.		3	5	.375	8.50	13	13	0	47.2	64	38	23	0	0	0	0					5	3	0	0	0.6	1.000

Steve Sparks

SPARKS, STEVEN WILLIAM
B. July 2, 1965, Tulsa, Okla.

BR TR 6' 187 lbs.

Year	Team	W	L	PCT	ERA	G	GS	CG	IP	H	BB	SO	ShO	W	L	SV	AB	H	HR	BA	PO	A	E	DP	TC/G	FA
1995	MIL A	9	11	.450	4.63	33	27	3	202	210	86	96	0	0	0	0	0	0	0	—	25	43	2	5	2.1	.971
1996		4	7	.364	6.60	20	13	1	88.2	103	52	21	0	0	0	0	0	0	0	—	9	23	1	1	1.6	.970
2 yrs.		13	18	.419	5.23	53	40	4	290.2	313	138	117	0	0	0	0	0	0	0		34	66	3	6	1.9	.971

Paul Spoljaric

SPOLJARIC, PAUL NIKOLA
B. Sept. 24, 1970, Kelowna, B. C., Canada.

BR TL 6'3" 205 lbs.

Year	Team	W	L	PCT	ERA	G	GS	CG	IP	H	BB	SO	ShO	W	L	SV	AB	H	HR	BA	PO	A	E	DP	TC/G	FA
1994	TOR A	0	1	.000	38.57	2	1	0	2.1	5	9	2	0	0	0	0	0	0	0	—	0	2	1	0	1.5	.667
1996		2	2	.500	3.08	28	1	0	38	30	19	38	0	2	2	1	0	0	0	—	1	5	0	3	0.2	1.000
2 yrs.		2	3	.400	5.13	30	1	0	40.1	35	28	40	0	2	2	1	0	0	0		1	7	1	3	0.3	.889

Jerry Spradlin

SPRADLIN, JERRY CARL
B. June 14, 1967, Fullerton, Calif.

BB TR 6'7" 230 lbs.

Year	Team	W	L	PCT	ERA	G	GS	CG	IP	H	BB	SO	ShO	W	L	SV	AB	H	HR	BA	PO	A	E	DP	TC/G	FA
1993	CIN N	2	1	.667	3.49	37	0	0	49	44	9	24	0	2	1	2	2	0	0	.000	2	1	0	0	0.1	1.000
1994		0	0	—	10.13	6	0	0	8	12	2	4	0	0	0	0	0	0	0	—	1	1	0	0	0.3	1.000
1996		0	0	—	0.00	1	0	0	0.1	0	0	0	0	0	0	0	0	0	0	—	0	0	0	0	0.0	.000
3 yrs.		2	1	.667	4.40	44	0	0	57.1	56	11	28	0	2	1	2	2	0	0	.000	3	3	0	0	0.1	1.000

Dennis Springer

SPRINGER, DENNIS LEROY
B. Feb. 12, 1965, Fresno, Calif.

BR TR 5'10" 185 lbs.

Year	Team	W	L	PCT	ERA	G	GS	CG	IP	H	BB	SO	ShO	W	L	SV	AB	H	HR	BA	PO	A	E	DP	TC/G	FA
1995	PHI N	0	3	.000	4.84	4	4	0	22.1	21	9	15	0	0	0	0	8	1	0	.125	2	1	1	0	1.0	.750
1996	CAL A	5	6	.455	5.51	20	15	2	94.2	91	43	64	1	0	0	0	0	0	0	—	5	7	1	0	0.6	.923
2 yrs.		5	9	.357	5.38	24	19	2	117	112	52	79	1	0	0	0	8	1	0	.125	7	8	2	0	0.7	.882

Russ Springer

SPRINGER, RUSSELL PAUL
B. Nov. 7, 1968, Alexandria, La.

BR TR 6'4" 195 lbs.

Year	Team	W	L	PCT	ERA	G	GS	CG	IP	H	BB	SO	ShO	W	L	SV	AB	H	HR	BA	PO	A	E	DP	TC/G	FA
1992	NY A	0	0	—	6.19	14	0	0	16	18	10	12	0	0	0	0	0	0	0	—	0	1	0	0	0.1	1.000
1993	CAL A	1	6	.143	7.20	14	9	1	60	73	32	31	0	0	0	0	0	0	0	—	3	2	0	0	0.4	1.000
1994		2	2	.500	5.52	18	5	0	45.2	53	14	28	0	1	0	2	0	0	0	—	2	3	0	1	0.3	1.000
1995	2 teams	CAL A	(19G 1-2)	PHI N	(14G 0-0)																					
"	total	1	2	.333	5.29	33	6	0	78.1	82	35	70	0	0	0	1	1	0	0	.000	3	10	0	2	0.4	1.000
1996	PHI N	3	10	.231	4.66	51	7	0	96.2	106	38	94	0	1	6	0	17	1	0	.059	3	10	2	0	0.3	.867
5 yrs.		7	20	.259	5.55	130	27	1	296.2	332	129	235	0	2	6	3	18	1	0	.056	11	26	2	3	0.3	.949

Year	Team	W	L	PCT	ERA	G	GS	CG	IP	H	BB	SO	ShO	Relief Pitching W	L	SV	Batting AB	H	HR	BA	PO	A	E	DP	TC/G	FA

Mike Stanton

STANTON, WILLIAM MICHAEL
B. June 2, 1967, Houston, Tex.

BL TL 6'1" 190 lbs.

Year	Team	W	L	PCT	ERA	G	GS	CG	IP	H	BB	SO	ShO	W	L	SV	AB	H	HR	BA	PO	A	E	DP	TC/G	FA
1989	ATL N	0	1	.000	1.50	20	0	0	24	17	8	27	0	0	1	7	0	0	0	—	1	2	1	0	0.2	.750
1990		0	3	.000	18.00	7	0	0	7	16	4	7	0	0	3	2	0	0	0	—	0	2	0	0	0.3	1.000
1991		5	5	.500	2.88	74	0	0	78	62	21	54	0	5	5	7	6	3	0	.500	6	16	0	0	0.3	1.000
1992		5	4	.556	4.10	65	0	0	63.2	59	20	44	0	5	4	8	2	1	0	.500	3	10	0	2	0.2	1.000
1993		4	6	.400	4.67	63	0	0	52	51	29	43	0	4	6	27	0	0	0	—	1	9	1	1	0.2	.909
1994		3	1	.750	3.55	49	0	0	45.2	41	26	35	0	3	1	3	3	2	0	.667	2	10	0	0	0.2	1.000
1995	2 teams	ATL N	(26G 1–1)					BOS A	(22G 1–0)																	
"	total	2	1	.667	4.24	48	0	0	40.1	48	14	23	0	2	1	1	0	0	0	—	1	9	4	0	0.3	.714
1996	2 teams	BOS A	(59G 4–3)					TEX A	(22G 0–1)																	
"	total	4	4	.500	3.66	81	0	0	78.2	78	27	60	0	4	4	1	0	0	0	—	2	7	0	0	0.1	1.000
8 yrs.		23	25	.479	3.88	407	0	0	389.1	372	149	293	0	23	25	56	11	6	0	.545	16	65	6	4	0.2	.931

DIVISIONAL PLAYOFF SERIES

Year	Team	W	L	PCT	ERA	G	GS	CG	IP	H	BB	SO	ShO	W	L	SV	AB	H	HR	BA	PO	A	E	DP	TC/G	FA
1995	BOS A	0	0	—	0.00	1	0	0	2.1	1	0	4	0	0	0	0	0	0	0	—	0	1	0	0	1.0	1.000
1996	TEX A	0	1	.000	2.70	3	0	0	3.1	2	3	3	0	0	1	0	0	0	0	—	0	0	0	0	0.0	—
2 yrs.		0	1	.000	1.59	4	0	0	5.2	3	3	7	0	0	1	0					0	2	0	0	0.5	1.000

LEAGUE CHAMPIONSHIP SERIES

Year	Team	W	L	PCT	ERA	G	GS	CG	IP	H	BB	SO	ShO	W	L	SV	AB	H	HR	BA	PO	A	E	DP	TC/G	FA
1991	ATL N	0	0	—	2.45	3	0	0	3.2	4	3	3	0	0	0	0	0	0	0	—	0	2	0	0	0.7	1.000
1992		0	0	—	0.00	5	0	0	4.1	2	2	5	0	0	0	0	1	1	0	1.000	0	1	0	0	0.2	1.000
1993		0	0	—	0.00	1	0	0	1	1	1	0	0	0	0	0	0	0	0	—	0	0	0	0	0.0	.000
3 yrs.		0	0		1.00	9	0	0	9	7	6	8	0	0	0	0	1	1	0	1.000	0	3	0	0	0.3	1.000

WORLD SERIES

Year	Team	W	L	PCT	ERA	G	GS	CG	IP	H	BB	SO	ShO	W	L	SV	AB	H	HR	BA	PO	A	E	DP	TC/G	FA
1991	ATL N	1	0	1.000	0.00	5	0	0	7.1	5	2	7	0	1	0	0	0	0	0	—	0	0	0	0	0.0	.000
1992		0	0	—	0.00	4	0	0	5	3	2	1	0	0	0	1	0	0	0	—	0	0	0	0	0.0	.000
2 yrs.		1	0	1.000	0.00	9	0	0	12.1	8	4	8	0	1	0	1	0	0	0		0	0	0	0	0.0	

Garrett Stephenson

STEPHENSON, GARRETT CHARLES
B. Jan 2, 1972, Takoma Park, Md.

BR TR 6'4" 195 lbs.

Year	Team	W	L	PCT	ERA	G	GS	CG	IP	H	BB	SO	ShO	W	L	SV	AB	H	HR	BA	PO	A	E	DP	TC/G	FA
1996	BAL A	0	1	.000	12.79	3	0	0	6.1	13	3	3	0	0	1	0	0	0	0	—	0	1	0	0	0.3	1.000

Dave Stevens

STEVENS, DAVID JAMES
B. Mar. 4, 1970, Fullerton, Calif.

BR TR 6'3" 210 lbs.

Year	Team	W	L	PCT	ERA	G	GS	CG	IP	H	BB	SO	ShO	W	L	SV	AB	H	HR	BA	PO	A	E	DP	TC/G	FA
1994	MIN A	5	2	.714	6.80	24	0	0	45	55	23	24	0	5	2	0	0	0	0	—	2	5	0	0	0.3	1.000
1995		5	4	.556	5.07	56	0	0	65.2	74	32	47	0	5	4	10	0	0	0	—	9	7	1	1	0.3	.941
1996		3	3	.500	4.66	49	0	0	58	58	25	29	0	3	3	11	0	0	0	—	7	6	0	0	0.3	1.000
3 yrs.		13	9	.591	5.39	129	0	0	168.2	187	80	100	0	13	9	21	0	0	0		18	18	1	1	0.3	.973

Todd Stottlemyre

STOTTLEMYRE, TODD VERNON
Brother of Mel Stottlemyre.   Son of Mel Stottlemyre.
B. May 20, 1965, Sunnyside, Wash.

BL TR 6'3" 195 lbs.

Year	Team	W	L	PCT	ERA	G	GS	CG	IP	H	BB	SO	ShO	W	L	SV	AB	H	HR	BA	PO	A	E	DP	TC/G	FA
1988	TOR A	4	8	.333	5.69	28	16	0	98	109	46	67	0	2	1	0	0	0	0	—	7	11	0	0	0.6	1.000
1989		7	7	.500	3.88	27	18	0	127.2	137	44	63	0	0	1	0	0	0	0	—	7	16	5	1	1.0	.821
1990		13	17	.433	4.34	33	33	4	203	214	69	115	0	0	0	0	0	0	0	—	17	30	1	5	1.5	.979
1991		15	8	.652	3.78	34	34	1	219	194	75	116	0	0	0	0	0	0	0	—	30	21	2	2	1.6	.962
1992		12	11	.522	4.50	28	27	6	174	175	63	98	2	1	0	0	0	0	0	—	15	17	1	2	1.2	.970
1993		11	12	.478	4.84	30	28	1	176.2	204	69	98	1	0	0	0	0	0	0	—	11	19	1	2	1.0	.968
1994		7	7	.500	4.22	26	19	3	140.2	149	48	105	1	2	0	1	0	0	0	—	10	12	0	0	0.8	1.000
1995	OAK A	14	7	.667	4.55	31	31	2	209.2	228	80	205	0	0	0	0	1	0	0	.000	16	18	2	1	1.2	.944
1996	STL N	14	11	.560	3.87	34	33	5	223.1	191	93	194	2	0	0	0	66	15	0	.227	8	38	2	2	1.4	.958
9 yrs.		97	88	.524	4.33	271	239	22	1572	1601	587	1061	6	5	2	1	67	15	0	.224	121	182	14	15	1.2	.956

DIVISIONAL PLAYOFF SERIES

Year	Team	W	L	PCT	ERA	G	GS	CG	IP	H	BB	SO	ShO	W	L	SV	AB	H	HR	BA	PO	A	E	DP	TC/G	FA
1996	STL N	1	0	1.000	1.35	1	1	0	6.2	5	2	7	0	0	0	0	2	0	0	.000	0	0	0	0	0.0	.000

LEAGUE CHAMPIONSHIP SERIES

Year	Team	W	L	PCT	ERA	G	GS	CG	IP	H	BB	SO	ShO	W	L	SV	AB	H	HR	BA	PO	A	E	DP	TC/G	FA
1989	TOR A	0	1	.000	7.20	1	1	0	5	7	2	3	0	0	0	0	0	0	0	—	0	0	0	0	0.0	.000
1991		0	1	.000	9.82	1	1	0	3.2	7	1	3	0	0	0	0	0	0	0	—	1	0	0	0	1.0	1.000
1992		0	0	—	2.45	1	0	0	3.2	3	0	1	0	0	0	0	0	0	0	—	0	0	0	0	0.0	.000
1993		0	1	.000	7.50	1	1	0	6	6	4	4	0	0	0	0	0	0	0	—	2	0	0	0	2.0	1.000
1996	STL N	1	1	.500	12.38	3	2	0	8	15	3	11	0	0	0	0	2	0	0	.000	0	0	0	0	0.0	.000
5 yrs.		1	4	.200	8.54	7	5	0	26.1	38	10	22	0	0	0	0	2	0	0	.000	3	0	0	0	0.4	1.000
			4th																							

WORLD SERIES

Year	Team	W	L	PCT	ERA	G	GS	CG	IP	H	BB	SO	ShO	W	L	SV	AB	H	HR	BA	PO	A	E	DP	TC/G	FA
1992	TOR A	0	0	—	0.00	4	0	0	3.2	4	0	4	0	0	0	0	0	0	0	—	0	0	0	0	0.0	.000
1993		0	0	—	27.00	1	1	0	2	3	4	1	0	0	0	0	0	0	0	—	0	0	0	0	0.0	.000
2 yrs.		0	0	—	9.53	5	1	0	5.2	7	4	5	0	0	0	0	0	0	0		0	0	0	0	0.0	

Tanyon Sturtze

STURTZE, TANYON JAMES
B. Oct. 12, 1970, Worcester, Mass.

BR TR 6'5" 190 lbs.

Year	Team	W	L	PCT	ERA	G	GS	CG	IP	H	BB	SO	ShO	W	L	SV	AB	H	HR	BA	PO	A	E	DP	TC/G	FA
1995	CHI N	0	0	—	9.00	2	0	0	2	2	1	0	0	0	0	0	0	0	0	—	0	0	0	0	0.0	.000
1996		1	0	1.000	9.00	6	0	0	11	16	5	7	0	1	0	0	1	0	0	.000	0	2	0	1	0.3	1.000
2 yrs.		1	0	1.000	9.00	8	0	0	13	18	6	7	0	1	0	0	1	0	0	.000	0	2	0	1	0.3	1.000

Year	Team	W	L	PCT	ERA	G	GS	CG	IP	H	BB	SO	ShO	Relief Pitching W	L	SV	Batting AB	H	HR	BA	PO	A	E	DP	TC/G	FA

Scott Sullivan

SULLIVAN, WILLIAM SCOTT
B. Mar. 13, 1971, Tuscaloosa, Ala. BR TR 6'3" 210 lbs.

Year	Team	W	L	PCT	ERA	G	GS	CG	IP	H	BB	SO	ShO	W	L	SV	AB	H	HR	BA	PO	A	E	DP	TC/G	FA
1995	CIN N	0	0	—	4.91	3	0	0	3.2	4	2	2	0	0	0	0	1	0	0	.000	0	1	0	0	0.3	1.000
1996		0	0	—	2.25	7	0	0	8	7	5	3	0	0	0	0	1	0	0	.000	0	2	0	0	0.3	1.000
	2 yrs.	0	0		3.09	10	0	0	11.2	11	7	5	0	0	0	0	2	0	0	.000	0	3	0	0	0.3	1.000

Jeff Suppan

SUPPAN, JEFFREY SCOT
B. Jan. 2, 1975, Oklahoma City, Okla. BR TR 6'1" 200 lbs.

Year	Team	W	L	PCT	ERA	G	GS	CG	IP	H	BB	SO	ShO	W	L	SV	AB	H	HR	BA	PO	A	E	DP	TC/G	FA
1995	BOS A	1	2	.333	5.96	8	3	0	22.2	29	5	19	0	1	0	0	0	0	0	—	2	2	0	0	0.5	1.000
1996		1	1	.500	7.54	8	4	0	22.2	29	13	13	0	0	0	0	0	0	0	—	0	2	0	0	0.3	1.000
	2 yrs.	2	3	.400	6.75	16	7	0	45.1	58	18	32	0	1	0	0					2	4	0	0	0.4	1.000

Mac Suzuki

SUZUKI, MAKOTO
B. May 31, 1975, Kobe, Japan BR TR 6'3" 195 lbs.

Year	Team	W	L	PCT	ERA	G	GS	CG	IP	H	BB	SO	ShO	W	L	SV	AB	H	HR	BA	PO	A	E	DP	TC/G	FA
1996	SEA A	0	0	—	20.25	1	0	0	1.1	2	2	1	0	0	0	0	0	0	0	—	0	0	0	0	0.0	—

Dave Swartzbaugh

SWARTZBAUGH, DAVID THEODORE
B. Feb. 11, 1968, Middletown, Ohio BR TR 6'2" 195 lbs.

Year	Team	W	L	PCT	ERA	G	GS	CG	IP	H	BB	SO	ShO	W	L	SV	AB	H	HR	BA	PO	A	E	DP	TC/G	FA
1995	CHI N	0	0	—	0.00	7	0	0	7.1	5	3	5	0	0	0	0	0	0	0	—	0	0	0	0	0.0	.000
1996		0	2	.000	6.38	6	5	0	24	26	14	13	0	0	0	0	6	0	0	.000	1	6	0	0	1.2	1.000
	2 yrs.	0	2	.000	4.88	13	5	0	31.1	31	17	18	0	0	0	0	6	0	0	.000	1	6	0	0	0.5	1.000

Bill Swift

SWIFT, WILLIAM CHARLES
B. Oct. 27, 1961, Portland, Me. BR TR 6' 170 lbs.

Year	Team	W	L	PCT	ERA	G	GS	CG	IP	H	BB	SO	ShO	W	L	SV	AB	H	HR	BA	PO	A	E	DP	TC/G	FA
1985	SEA A	6	10	.375	4.77	23	21	0	120.2	131	48	55	0	1	0	0	0	0	0	—	10	18	1	1	1.3	.966
1986		2	9	.182	5.46	29	17	1	115.1	148	55	55	0	0	0	0	0	0	0	—	13	21	1	1	1.2	.971
1988		8	12	.400	4.59	38	24	6	174.2	199	65	47	1	3	1	0	0	0	0	—	19	33	4	3	1.5	.929
1989		7	3	.700	4.43	37	16	0	130	140	38	45	0	2	0	1	0	0	0	—	18	39	2	5	1.6	.966
1990		6	4	.600	2.39	55	8	0	128	135	21	42	0	3	2	6	0	0	0	—	10	21	2	1	0.6	.939
1991		1	2	.333	1.99	71	0	0	90.1	74	26	48	0	1	2	17	0	0	0	—	6	25	3	4	0.5	.912
1992	SF N	10	4	.714	2.08	30	22	3	164.2	144	43	77	2	1	1	1	51	8	0	.157	18	33	1	3	1.7	.981
1993		21	8	.724	2.82	34	34	1	232.2	195	55	157	1	0	0	0	80	21	0	.263	17	44	6	3	2.0	.910
1994		8	7	.533	3.38	17	17	0	109.1	109	31	62	0	0	0	0	32	6	0	.188	8	12	2	1	1.3	.909
1995	CLR N	9	3	.750	4.94	19	19	0	105.2	122	43	68	0	0	0	0	36	7	1	.194	9	27	1	2	1.9	.973
1996		1	1	.500	5.40	7	3	0	18.1	23	5	5	0	0	0	2	6	2	0	.333	2	4	0	0	0.9	1.000
	11 yrs.	79	63	.556	3.64	360	181	11	1389.2	1420	430	661	4	11	6	27	205	44	1	.215	130	277	23	24	1.2	.947

DIVISIONAL PLAYOFF SERIES

Year	Team	W	L	PCT	ERA	G	GS	CG	IP	H	BB	SO	ShO	W	L	SV	AB	H	HR	BA	PO	A	E	DP	TC/G	FA
1995	CLR N	0	0	—	6.00	1	1	0	6	7	2	3	0	0	0	0	3	0	0	.000	0	0	0	0	0.0	.000

Greg Swindell

SWINDELL, FOREST GREGORY
B. Jan. 2, 1965, Fort Worth, Tex. BR TL 6'2" 225 lbs.

Year	Team	W	L	PCT	ERA	G	GS	CG	IP	H	BB	SO	ShO	W	L	SV	AB	H	HR	BA	PO	A	E	DP	TC/G	FA
1986	CLE A	5	2	.714	4.23	9	9	1	61.2	57	15	46	0	0	0	0	0	0	0	—	2	12	0	1	1.6	1.000
1987		3	8	.273	5.10	16	15	4	102.1	112	37	97	1	0	0	0	0	0	0	—	0	13	1	1	0.9	.929
1988		18	14	.563	3.20	33	33	12	242	234	45	180	4	0	0	0	0	0	0	—	8	29	1	0	1.2	.974
1989		13	6	.684	3.37	28	28	5	184.1	170	51	129	2	0	0	0	0	0	0	—	7	25	0	1	1.1	1.000
1990		12	9	.571	4.40	34	34	3	214.2	245	47	135	0	0	0	0	0	0	0	—	8	20	1	1	0.9	.966
1991		9	16	.360	3.48	33	33	7	238	241	31	169	0	0	0	0	0	0	0	—	7	30	1	2	1.2	.974
1992	CIN N	12	8	.600	2.70	31	30	5	213.2	210	41	138	3	0	0	0	80	10	0	.125	6	33	1	2	1.3	.975
1993	HOU N	12	13	.480	4.16	31	30	1	190.1	215	40	124	1	0	0	0	60	11	0	.183	2	32	1	0	1.1	.971
1994		8	9	.471	4.37	24	24	1	148.1	175	26	74	0	0	0	0	44	11	0	.250	6	13	1	0	0.8	.950
1995		10	9	.526	4.47	33	26	1	153	180	39	96	1	2	0	0	50	12	0	.240	9	31	1	3	1.2	.976
1996	2 teams	HOU N	(8G 0-3)	CLE A	(13G 1-1)																					
"	total	1	4	.200	7.14	21	6	0	51.2	66	19	36	0	1	2	0	6	2	0	.333	3	9	1	1	0.6	.923
	11 yrs.	103	98	.512	3.90	293	268	40	1800	1905	391	1224	12	3	2	0	240	46	0	.192	58	247	9	12	1.1	.971

Jeff Tabaka

TABAKA, JEFFREY JON
B. Jan. 17, 1964, Barberton, Ohio BR TL 6'2" 195 lbs.

Year	Team	W	L	PCT	ERA	G	GS	CG	IP	H	BB	SO	ShO	W	L	SV	AB	H	HR	BA	PO	A	E	DP	TC/G	FA
1994	2 teams	PIT N	(5G 0-0)	SD N	(34G 3-1)																					
"	total	3	1	.750	5.27	39	0	0	41	32	27	32	0	3	1	1	1	0	0	1.000	3	4	1	0	0.2	.875
1995	2 teams	SD N	(10G 0-0)	HOU N	(24G 1-0)																					
"	total	1	0	1.000	3.23	34	0	0	30.2	27	17	25	0	1	0	0	1	0	0	.000	1	3	0	0	0.1	1.000
1996	HOU N	0	2	.000	6.64	18	0	0	20.1	28	14	18	0	0	2	1	1	0	0	.000	1	0	0	0	0.1	1.000
	3 yrs.	4	3	.571	4.89	91	0	0	92	87	58	75	0	4	3	2	3	0	0	.333	5	7	1	0	0.1	.923

Kevin Tapani

TAPANI, KEVIN RAY
B. Feb. 18, 1964, Des Moines, Iowa BR TR 6' 180 lbs.

Year	Team	W	L	PCT	ERA	G	GS	CG	IP	H	BB	SO	ShO	W	L	SV	AB	H	HR	BA	PO	A	E	DP	TC/G	FA
1989	2 teams	NY N	(3G 0-0)	MIN A	(5G 2-2)																					
"	total	2	2	.500	3.83	8	5	0	40	39	12	23	0	0	0	0	2	0	0	.000	4	4	0	1	1.0	1.000
1990	MIN A	12	8	.600	4.07	28	28	1	159.1	164	29	101	1	0	0	0	0	0	0	—	14	20	1	1	1.3	.971
1991		16	9	.640	2.99	34	34	4	244	225	40	135	1	0	0	0	0	0	0	—	26	26	1	2	1.6	.981
1992		16	11	.593	3.97	34	34	4	220	226	48	138	1	0	0	0	0	0	0	—	17	26	2	0	1.3	.956
1993		12	15	.444	4.43	36	35	3	225.2	243	57	150	1	0	0	0	0	0	0	—	17	32	0	2	1.4	1.000

Year	Team	W	L	PCT	ERA	G	GS	CG	IP	H	BB	SO	ShO	Relief Pitching W	L	SV	Batting AB	H	HR	BA	PO	A	E	DP	TC/G	FA

Kevin Tapani *continued*

Year	Team	W	L	PCT	ERA	G	GS	CG	IP	H	BB	SO	ShO	W	L	SV	AB	H	HR	BA	PO	A	E	DP	TC/G	FA
1994		11	7	.611	4.62	24	24	4	156	181	39	91	1	0	0	0	0	0	0	—	11	27	1	2	1.6	.974
1995	2 teams	MIN A	(20G 6–11)		LA N	(13G 4–2)																				
"	total	10	13	.435	4.96	33	31	3	190.2	227	48	131	1	0	0	0	17	3	0	.176	20	21	1	1	1.3	.976
1996	CHI A	13	10	.565	4.59	34	34	1	225.1	236	76	150	0	0	0	0	0	0	0	—	15	26	1	4	1.2	.976
	8 yrs.	92	75	.551	4.18	231	225	20	1461	1541	349	919	6	0	0	0	19	3	0	.158	124	182	7	13	1.4	.978
DIVISIONAL PLAYOFF SERIES																										
1995	LA N	0	0	—	81.00	2	0	0	0.1	0	4	1	0	0	0	0	0	0	0	—	0	0	0	0	0.0	.000
LEAGUE CHAMPIONSHIP SERIES																										
1991	MIN A	0	1	.000	7.84	2	2	0	10.1	16	3	9	0	0	0	0	0	0	0	—	3	0	0	0	1.5	1.000
WORLD SERIES																										
1991	MIN A	1	1	.500	4.50	2	2	0	12	13	2	7	0	0	0	0	1	0	0	.000	0	2	0	0	1.0	1.000

Julian Tavarez

TAVAREZ, JULIAN   BR TR 6'2" 165 lbs.
Born Julian Tavarez (Carmen).
B. May 22, 1973, Santiago, Dominican Republic.

Year	Team	W	L	PCT	ERA	G	GS	CG	IP	H	BB	SO	ShO	W	L	SV	AB	H	HR	BA	PO	A	E	DP	TC/G	FA
1993	CLE A	2	2	.500	6.57	8	7	0	37	53	13	19	0	0	0	0	0	0	0	—	2	3	0	2	0.6	1.000
1994		0	1	.000	21.60	1	1	0	1.2	6	1	0	0	0	0	0	0	0	0	—	0	0	0	0	0.0	.000
1995		10	2	.833	2.44	57	0	0	85	76	21	68	0	10	2	0	0	0	0	—	7	11	2	1	0.4	.900
1996		4	7	.364	5.36	51	4	0	80.2	101	22	46	0	3	5	0	0	0	0	—	6	8	0	0	0.3	1.000
	4 yrs.	16	12	.571	4.49	117	12	0	204.1	236	57	133	0	13	7	0	0	0	0	—	15	22	2	3	0.3	.949
DIVISIONAL PLAYOFF SERIES																										
1995	CLE A	0	0	—	6.75	3	0	0	2.2	5	0	5	0	0	0	0	0	0	0	—	0	0	0	0	0.0	—
1996		0	0	—	0.00	2	0	0	1.1	1	2	1	0	0	0	0	0	0	0	—	0	0	0	0	0.0	—
	2 yrs.	0	0		4.50	5	0	0	4	6	2	4	0	0	0	0					0	0	0	0	0.0	
LEAGUE CHAMPIONSHIP SERIES																										
1995	CLE A	0	1	.000	2.70	4	0	0	3.1	3	1	2	0	0	0	0	0	0	0	—	0	1	0	0	0.3	1.000
WORLD SERIES																										
1995	CLE A	0	0	—	0.00	5	0	0	4.1	3	2	1	0	0	0	0	0	0	0	—	0	2	0	0	0.4	1.000

Bill Taylor

TAYLOR, WILLIAM HOWELL   BR TR 6'8" 200 lbs.
B. Oct. 16, 1961, Monticello, Fla.

Year	Team	W	L	PCT	ERA	G	GS	CG	IP	H	BB	SO	ShO	W	L	SV	AB	H	HR	BA	PO	A	E	DP	TC/G	FA
1994	OAK A	1	3	.250	3.50	41	0	0	46.1	38	18	48	0	1	3	1	0	0	0	—	2	3	0	0	0.1	1.000
1996		6	3	.667	4.33	55	0	0	60.1	52	25	67	0	6	3	17	0	0	0	—	4	9	0	0	0.2	1.000
	2 yrs.	7	6	.538	3.97	96	0	0	106.2	90	43	115	0	7	6	18	0	0	0		6	12	0	0	0.2	1.000

Amaury Telemaco

TELEMACO, AMAURY   BR TR 6'4" 220 lbs.
Born Amaury Telemaco (Regalado)
B. Jan. 19, 1974, Higuey, Dominican Republic

Year	Team	W	L	PCT	ERA	G	GS	CG	IP	H	BB	SO	ShO	W	L	SV	AB	H	HR	BA	PO	A	E	DP	TC/G	FA
1996	CHI N	5	7	.417	5.46	25	17	0	97.1	108	31	64	0	0	0	0	29	3	0	.103	9	9	1	0	0.8	.947

Dave Telgheder

TELGHEDER, DAVID WILLIAM   BR TR 6'3" 212 lbs.
B. Nov. 11, 1966, Middletown, N. Y.

Year	Team	W	L	PCT	ERA	G	GS	CG	IP	H	BB	SO	ShO	W	L	SV	AB	H	HR	BA	PO	A	E	DP	TC/G	FA
1993	NY N	6	2	.750	4.76	24	7	0	75.2	82	21	35	0	1	0	0	15	1	0	.067	4	9	0	0	0.5	1.000
1994		0	1	.000	7.20	6	0	0	10	11	8	4	0	0	1	0	0	0	0	—	0	0	1	0	0.2	.000
1995		1	2	.333	5.61	7	4	0	25.2	34	7	16	0	0	0	0	6	2	0	.333	2	6	0	0	1.1	1.000
1996	OAK A	4	7	.364	4.65	16	14	1	79.1	92	26	43	1	0	0	0	0	0	0	—	3	14	0	1	1.1	1.000
	4 yrs.	11	12	.478	4.96	53	25	1	190.2	219	62	98	1	1	1	0	21	3	0	.143	9	29	1	1	0.7	.974

Bob Tewksbury

TEWKSBURY, ROBERT ALAN   BR TR 6'4" 200 lbs.
B. Nov. 30, 1960, Concord, N. H.

Year	Team	W	L	PCT	ERA	G	GS	CG	IP	H	BB	SO	ShO	W	L	SV	AB	H	HR	BA	PO	A	E	DP	TC/G	FA
1986	NY A	9	5	.643	3.31	23	20	2	130.1	144	31	49	0	0	0	0	0	0	0	—	7	29	1	2	1.6	.973
1987	2 teams	NY A	(8G 1–4)		CHI N	(7G 0–4)																				
"	total	1	8	.111	6.66	15	9	0	51.1	79	20	22	0	0	1	0	5	0	0	.000	3	6	1	1	0.7	.900
1988	CHI N	0	0	—	8.10	1	1	0	3.1	6	2	1	0	0	0	0	2	0	0	.000	0	1	0	0	1.0	1.000
1989	STL N	1	0	1.000	3.30	7	4	1	30	25	10	17	1	0	0	0	9	1	0	.111	1	3	0	0	0.6	1.000
1990		10	9	.526	3.47	28	20	3	145.1	151	15	50	2	0	0	1	41	7	0	.171	6	20	1	2	1.0	.963
1991		11	12	.478	3.25	30	30	3	191	206	38	75	0	0	0	0	58	9	0	.155	9	34	2	2	1.5	.956
1992		16	5	**.762**	2.16	33	32	5	233	217	20	91	0	1	0	0	70	6	0	.086	14	42	1	2	1.7	.982
1993		17	10	.630	3.83	32	32	2	213.2	**258**	20	97	0	0	0	0	69	14	0	.203	19	46	0	2	2.0	1.000
1994		12	10	.545	5.32	24	24	4	155.2	**190**	22	79	1	0	0	0	54	10	0	.185	12	31	1	1	1.8	.977
1995	TEX A	8	7	.533	4.58	21	21	4	129.2	169	20	53	1	0	0	0	1	0	0	.000	12	24	1	3	1.8	.973
1996	SD N	10	10	.500	4.31	36	33	1	206.2	224	43	126	0	0	0	0	65	2	0	.031	21	48	0	3	1.9	1.000
	11 yrs.	95	76	.556	3.80	250	226	25	1490	1669	241	660	5	1	1	1	374	49	0	.131	104	284	8	18	1.6	.980

Tom Thobe

THOBE, THOMAS NEAL   BL TL 6'6" 195 lbs.
Brother of J. J. Thobe.
B. Sept. 3, 1969, Covington, Ky.

Year	Team	W	L	PCT	ERA	G	GS	CG	IP	H	BB	SO	ShO	W	L	SV	AB	H	HR	BA	PO	A	E	DP	TC/G	FA
1995	ATL N	0	0	—	10.80	3	0	0	3.1	7	0	2	0	0	0	0	0	0	0	—	0	0	0	0	0.0	.000
1996		0	1	.000	1.50	4	0	0	6	5	0	1	0	0	1	0	1	0	0	.000	0	0	2	0	0.5	.000
	2 yrs.	0	1	.000	4.82	7	0	0	9.1	12	0	3	0	0	1	0	1	0	0	.000	0	0	2	0	0.3	.000

Year	Team	W	L	PCT	ERA	G	GS	CG	IP	H	BB	SO	ShO	W	L	SV	AB	H	HR	BA	PO	A	E	DP	TC/G	FA
														Relief Pitching			**Batting**									

Larry Thomas
THOMAS, LARRY WAYNE
B. Oct. 25, 1969, Miami, Fla.
BR TL 6'1" 195 lbs.

Year	Team	W	L	PCT	ERA	G	GS	CG	IP	H	BB	SO	ShO	W	L	SV	AB	H	HR	BA	PO	A	E	DP	TC/G	FA
1995	CHI A	0	0	—	1.32	17	0	0	13.2	8	6	12	0	0	0	0	0	0	0	—	2	0	0	0	0.1	1.000
1996		2	3	.400	3.23	57	0	0	30.2	32	14	20	0	2	3	0	0	0	0	—	2	4	0	1	0.1	1.000
2 yrs.		2	3	.400	2.64	74	0	0	44.1	40	20	32	0	2	3	0	0	0	0		4	4	0	1	0.1	1.000

Justin Thompson
THOMPSON, JUSTIN WILLARD
B. Mar. 8, 1973, San Antonio, Tex.
BL TL 6'4" 215 lbs.

Year	Team	W	L	PCT	ERA	G	GS	CG	IP	H	BB	SO	ShO	W	L	SV	AB	H	HR	BA	PO	A	E	DP	TC/G	FA
1996	DET A	1	6	.143	4.58	11	11	0	59	62	31	44	0	0	0	0	0	0	0	—	2	13	0	1	1.4	1.000

Mark Thompson
THOMPSON, MARK RADFORD
B. Apr. 7, 1971, Russellville, Ky.
BR TR 6'2" 205 lbs.

Year	Team	W	L	PCT	ERA	G	GS	CG	IP	H	BB	SO	ShO	W	L	SV	AB	H	HR	BA	PO	A	E	DP	TC/G	FA
1994	CLR N	1	1	.500	9.00	2	2	0	9	16	8	5	0	0	0	0	4	0	0	.000	1	0	0	0	0.5	1.000
1995		2	3	.400	6.53	21	5	0	51	73	22	30	0	1	1	0	13	5	0	.385	3	10	0	1	0.6	1.000
1996		9	11	.450	5.30	34	28	3	169.2	189	74	99	1	0	0	0	58	8	0	.138	14	21	5	2	1.2	.875
3 yrs.		12	15	.444	5.72	57	35	3	229.2	278	104	134	1	1	1	0	75	13	0	.173	18	31	5	3	0.9	.907

DIVISIONAL PLAYOFF SERIES

Year	Team	W	L	PCT	ERA	G	GS	CG	IP	H	BB	SO	ShO	W	L	SV	AB	H	HR	BA	PO	A	E	DP	TC/G	FA
1995	CLR N	0	0	—	0.00	1	0	0	1	0	0	1	0	0	0	0	0	0	0	—	1	0	0	0	1.0	1.000

Mike Timlin
TIMLIN, MICHAEL AUGUST
B. Mar. 10, 1966, Midland, Tex.
BR TR 6'4" 205 lbs.

Year	Team	W	L	PCT	ERA	G	GS	CG	IP	H	BB	SO	ShO	W	L	SV	AB	H	HR	BA	PO	A	E	DP	TC/G	FA
1991	TOR A	11	6	.647	3.16	63	3	0	108.1	94	50	85	0	10	5	3	0	0	0	—	9	17	2	0	0.4	.929
1992		0	2	.000	4.12	26	0	0	43.2	45	20	35	0	0	2	1	0	0	0	—	2	5	0	1	0.3	1.000
1993		4	2	.667	4.69	54	0	0	55.2	63	27	49	0	4	2	1	0	0	0	—	7	10	1	1	0.3	.944
1994		0	1	.000	5.17	34	0	0	40	41	20	38	0	0	1	2	0	0	0	—	5	5	0	0	0.3	1.000
1995		4	3	.571	2.14	31	0	0	42	38	17	36	0	4	3	5	0	0	0	—	1	9	0	1	0.3	1.000
1996		1	6	.143	3.65	59	0	0	56.2	47	18	52	0	1	6	31	0	0	0	—	4	6	0	0	0.2	1.000
6 yrs.		20	20	.500	3.72	267	3	0	346.1	328	152	295	0	19	19	43	0	0	0		28	52	3	3	0.3	.964

LEAGUE CHAMPIONSHIP SERIES

Year	Team	W	L	PCT	ERA	G	GS	CG	IP	H	BB	SO	ShO	W	L	SV	AB	H	HR	BA	PO	A	E	DP	TC/G	FA
1991	TOR A	0	1	.000	3.18	4	0	0	5.2	5	2	5	0	0	1	0	0	0	0	—	0	2	1	0	0.8	.667
1992		0	0	—	6.75	2	0	0	1.1	4	0	1	0	0	0	0	0	0	0	—	0	0	0	0	0.0	1.000
1993		0	0	—	3.86	1	0	0	2.1	3	0	2	0	0	0	0	0	0	0	—	1	1	0	0	2.0	1.000
3 yrs.		0	1	.000	3.86	7	0	0	9.1	12	2	8	0	0	1	0	0	0	0		1	3	1	0	0.7	.800

WORLD SERIES

Year	Team	W	L	PCT	ERA	G	GS	CG	IP	H	BB	SO	ShO	W	L	SV	AB	H	HR	BA	PO	A	E	DP	TC/G	FA
1992	TOR A	0	0	—	0.00	2	0	0	1.1	0	0	0	0	0	0	1	0	0	0	—	0	1	0	0	0.5	1.000
1993		0	0	—	0.00	2	0	0	2.1	2	0	4	0	0	0	0	0	0	0	—	0	0	0	0	0.0	.000
2 yrs.		0	0		0.00	4	0	0	3.2	2	0	4	0	0	0	0	0	0	0		0	1	0	0	0.3	1.000

Salomon Torres
TORRES, SALOMON
Born Salomon Torres (Ramirez).
B. Mar. 11, 1972, San Pedro de Macoris, Dominican Republic
BR TR 5'11" 150 lbs.

Year	Team	W	L	PCT	ERA	G	GS	CG	IP	H	BB	SO	ShO	W	L	SV	AB	H	HR	BA	PO	A	E	DP	TC/G	FA
1993	SF N	3	5	.375	4.03	8	8	0	44.2	37	27	23	0	0	0	0	13	3	0	.231	4	9	0	0	1.6	1.000
1994		2	8	.200	5.44	16	14	1	84.1	95	34	42	0	0	0	0	26	4	0	.154	4	7	1	0	0.8	.917
1995	2 teams	SF N	(4G 0–1)			SEA A		(16G 3–8)																		
"	total	3	9	.250	6.30	20	14	1	80	100	49	47	0	0	1	0	1	0	0	.000	9	16	0	2	1.3	1.000
1996	SEA A	3	3	.500	4.59	10	7	1	49	44	23	36	1	0	0	0	0	0	0	—	6	1	0	0	0.7	1.000
4 yrs.		11	25	.306	5.30	54	43	3	258	276	133	148	1	0	1	0	40	7	0	.175	23	33	1	2	1.1	.982

Steve Trachsel
TRACHSEL, STEPHEN CHRISTOPHER
B. Oct. 31, 1970, Oxnard, Calif.
BR TR 6'3" 185 lbs.

Year	Team	W	L	PCT	ERA	G	GS	CG	IP	H	BB	SO	ShO	W	L	SV	AB	H	HR	BA	PO	A	E	DP	TC/G	FA
1993	CHI N	0	2	.000	4.58	3	3	0	19.2	16	3	14	0	0	0	0	6	1	0	.167	1	5	0	0	2.0	1.000
1994		9	7	.563	3.21	22	22	1	146	133	54	108	0	0	0	0	43	8	0	.186	10	33	2	0	2.0	.956
1995		7	13	.350	5.15	30	29	4	160.2	174	76	117	0	0	0	0	49	13	0	.265	7	13	1	0	0.7	.952
1996		13	9	.591	3.03	31	31	3	205	181	62	132	2	0	0	0	66	7	1	.106	16	29	1	0	1.5	.978
4 yrs.		29	31	.483	3.78	86	85	6	531.1	504	195	371	2	0	0	0	164	29	1	.177	34	80	4	0	1.4	.966

Rick Trlicek
TRLICEK, RICHARD ALAN
B. Apr. 26, 1969, Houston, Tex.
BR TR 6'3" 200 lbs.

Year	Team	W	L	PCT	ERA	G	GS	CG	IP	H	BB	SO	ShO	W	L	SV	AB	H	HR	BA	PO	A	E	DP	TC/G	FA
1992	TOR A	0	0	—	10.80	2	0	0	1.2	2	2	1	0	0	0	0	0	0	0	—	0	0	0	0	0.0	.000
1993	LA N	1	2	.333	4.08	41	0	0	64	59	21	41	0	1	2	1	4	1	0	.250	7	12	0	2	0.5	1.000
1994	BOS A	1	1	.500	8.06	12	0	0	22.1	32	16	7	0	1	0	0	0	0	0	—	4	1	0	0	0.4	1.000
1996	NY N	0	1	.000	3.38	5	0	0	5.1	3	3	3	0	0	1	0	0	0	0	—	0	2	0	0	0.4	1.000
4 yrs.		2	4	.333	5.11	60	1	0	93.1	96	42	52	0	2	3	1	4	1	0	.250	11	15	0	2	0.4	1.000

Mike Trombley
TROMBLEY, MICHAEL SCOTT
B. Apr. 14, 1967, Springfield, Mass.
BR TR 6'2" 200 lbs.

Year	Team	W	L	PCT	ERA	G	GS	CG	IP	H	BB	SO	ShO	W	L	SV	AB	H	HR	BA	PO	A	E	DP	TC/G	FA
1992	MIN A	3	2	.600	3.30	10	7	0	46.1	43	17	38	0	0	0	0	0	0	0	—	1	6	0	0	0.7	1.000
1993		6	6	.500	4.88	44	10	0	114.1	131	41	85	0	3	1	2	0	0	0	—	6	19	0	2	0.6	1.000
1994		2	0	1.000	6.33	24	0	0	48.1	56	18	32	0	2	0	0	0	0	0	—	5	3	1	0	0.4	.889

Year	Team	W	L	PCT	ERA	G	GS	CG	IP	H	BB	SO	ShO	W	L	SV	AB	H	HR	BA	PO	A	E	DP	TC/G	FA

Mike Trombley *continued*

Year	Team	W	L	PCT	ERA	G	GS	CG	IP	H	BB	SO	ShO	W	L	SV	AB	H	HR	BA	PO	A	E	DP	TC/G	FA
1995		4	8	.333	5.62	20	18	0	97.2	107	42	68	0	0	0	0	0	0	0	—	9	10	1	2	1.0	.950
1996		5	1	.833	3.01	43	0	0	68.2	61	25	57	0	5	1	6	0	0	0	—	6	6	0	0	0.3	1.000
5 yrs.		20	17	.541	4.72	141	35	0	375.1	398	143	280	0	10	2	8	0	0	0		27	44	2	4	0.5	.973

Tom Urbani

URBANI, THOMAS JAMES
B. Jan. 21, 1968, Santa Cruz, Calif.
BL TL 6'1" 190 lbs.

Year	Team	W	L	PCT	ERA	G	GS	CG	IP	H	BB	SO	ShO	W	L	SV	AB	H	HR	BA	PO	A	E	DP	TC/G	FA
1993	STL N	1	3	.250	4.65	18	9	0	62	73	26	33	0	0	1	0	16	3	0	.188	2	12	1	1	0.8	.933
1994		3	7	.300	5.15	20	10	0	80.1	98	21	43	0	0	2	0	24	6	0	.250	0	15	0	1	0.8	1.000
1995		3	5	.375	3.70	24	13	0	82.2	99	21	52	0	1	0	0	19	6	1	.316	4	19	0	0	1.0	1.000
1996	2 teams	STL N	(3G 1–0)			DET A	(16G 2–2)																			
"	total	3	2	.600	8.15	19	4	0	35.1	46	18	21	0	2	1	0	6	1	0	.167	0	4	0	0	0.2	1.000
4 yrs.		10	17	.370	4.98	81	36	0	260.1	316	86	149	0	3	4	0	65	16	1	.246	6	50	1	2	0.7	.982

Ugueth Urbina

URBINA, UGUETH URTAIN
Born Ugueth Urtain Urbina (Villarreal).
B. Feb. 15, 1974, Caracas, Venezuela
BR TR 6'2" 185 lbs.

Year	Team	W	L	PCT	ERA	G	GS	CG	IP	H	BB	SO	ShO	W	L	SV	AB	H	HR	BA	PO	A	E	DP	TC/G	FA
1995	MON N	2	2	.500	6.17	7	4	0	23.1	26	14	15	0	1	0	0	6	2	0	.333	5	4	0	0	1.3	1.000
1996		10	5	.667	3.71	33	17	0	114	102	44	108	0	3	0	0	29	3	0	.103	6	10	1	2	0.5	.941
2 yrs.		12	7	.632	4.13	40	21	0	137.1	128	58	123	0	4	0	0	35	5	0	.143	11	14	1	2	0.6	.962

Ismael Valdes

VALDES, ISMAEL
Born Ismael Valdes (Alvarez).
B. Aug. 21, 1973, Victoria, Mexico
BR TR 6'3" 185 lbs.

Year	Team	W	L	PCT	ERA	G	GS	CG	IP	H	BB	SO	ShO	W	L	SV	AB	H	HR	BA	PO	A	E	DP	TC/G	FA
1994	LA N	3	1	.750	3.18	21	1	0	28.1	21	10	28	0	3	1	0	2	0	0	.000	1	8	0	0	0.4	1.000
1995		13	11	.542	3.05	33	27	6	197.2	168	51	150	2	0	0	1	62	6	0	.097	16	31	1	0	1.5	.979
1996		15	7	.682	3.32	33	33	0	225	219	54	173	0	0	0	0	70	10	0	.143	19	27	1	3	1.4	.979
3 yrs.		31	19	.620	3.19	87	61	6	451	408	115	351	2	3	1	1	134	16	0	.119	36	66	2	3	1.2	.981

DIVISIONAL PLAYOFF SERIES

Year	Team	W	L	PCT	ERA	G	GS	CG	IP	H	BB	SO	ShO	W	L	SV	AB	H	HR	BA	PO	A	E	DP	TC/G	FA
1995	LA N	0	0	—	0.00	1	1	0	7	3	1	6	0	0	0	0	3	0	0	.000	0	0	0	0	0.0	.000
1996		0	1	.000	4.26	1	1	0	6.1	5	0	5	0	0	0	0	2	0	0	.000	1	2	0	0	3.0	1.000
2 yrs.		0	1	.000	2.03	2	2	0	13.1	8	1	11	0	0	0	0	5	0	0	.000	1	2	0	0	1.5	1.000

Marc Valdes

VALDES, MARC CHRISTOPHER
B. Dec. 20, 1971, Dayton, Ohio
BR TR 6' 170 lbs.

Year	Team	W	L	PCT	ERA	G	GS	CG	IP	H	BB	SO	ShO	W	L	SV	AB	H	HR	BA	PO	A	E	DP	TC/G	FA
1995	FLA N	0	0	—	14.14	3	3	0	7	17	9	2	0	0	0	0	2	0	0	.000	0	0	0	0	0.0	.000
1996		1	3	.250	4.81	11	8	0	48.2	63	23	13	0	0	0	0	14	0	0	.000	6	3	0	0	0.8	1.000
2 yrs.		1	3	.250	5.98	14	11	0	55.2	80	32	15	0	0	0	0	16	0	0	.000	6	3	0	0	0.6	1.000

Fernando Valenzuela

VALENZUELA, FERNANDO (El Toro)
Born Fernando Valenzuela (Anguamea).
B. Nov. 1, 1960, Navajoa, Mexico
BL TL 5'11" 180 lbs.

Year	Team	W	L	PCT	ERA	G	GS	CG	IP	H	BB	SO	ShO	W	L	SV	AB	H	HR	BA	PO	A	E	DP	TC/G	FA
1980	LA N	2	0	1.000	0.00	10	0	0	18	8	5	16	0	2	0	1	1	0	0	.000	0	3	0	1	0.3	1.000
1981		13	7	.650	2.48	25	25	11	192	140	61	180	8	0	0	0	64	16	0	.250	12	33	3	2	1.9	.938
1982		19	13	.594	2.87	37	37	18	285	247	83	199	4	0	0	0	95	16	1	.168	20	64	2	4	2.3	.977
1983		15	10	.600	3.75	35	35	9	257	245	99	189	4	0	0	0	91	17	1	.187	20	54	2	5	2.2	.974
1984		12	17	.414	3.03	34	34	12	261	218	106	240	2	0	0	0	79	15	3	.190	21	48	2	4	2.1	.972
1985		17	10	.630	2.45	35	35	14	272.1	211	101	208	5	0	0	0	97	21	1	.216	18	45	0	0	1.8	1.000
1986		21	11	.656	3.14	34	34	20	269.1	226	85	242	3	0	0	0	109	24	0	.220	29	47	1	2	2.3	.987
1987		14	14	.500	3.98	34	34	12	251	254	124	190	1	0	0	0	92	13	1	.141	15	53	4	2	2.1	.944
1988		5	8	.385	4.24	23	22	3	142.1	142	76	64	0	0	0	1	44	8	0	.182	6	38	1	2	2.0	.978
1989		10	13	.435	3.43	31	31	3	196.2	185	98	116	0	0	0	0	66	12	0	.182	20	35	5	4	1.9	.917
1990		13	13	.500	4.59	33	33	5	204	223	77	115	2	0	0	0	69	21	1	.304	5	31	3	2	1.2	.923
1991	CAL A	0	2	.000	12.15	2	2	0	6.2	14	3	5	0	0	0	0	0	0	0	—	0	1	0	0	0.5	1.000
1993	BAL A	8	10	.444	4.94	32	31	5	178.2	179	79	78	2	0	0	0	0	0	0	—	11	37	4	1	1.6	.923
1994	PHI N	1	2	.333	3.00	8	7	0	45	42	7	19	0	0	0	0	12	3	0	.250	2	8	0	0	1.3	1.000
1995	SD N	8	3	.727	4.98	29	15	0	90.1	101	34	57	0	2	0	0	32	8	2	.250	7	27	0	2	1.2	1.000
1996		13	8	.619	3.62	33	31	0	171.2	177	67	95	0	0	0	0	63	9	0	.143	11	38	1	1	1.5	.980
16 yrs.		171	141	.548	3.50	435	406	112	2841	2612	1105	2013	31	4	0	2	914	183	10	.200	197	562	28	32	1.8	.964

DIVISIONAL PLAYOFF SERIES

Year	Team	W	L	PCT	ERA	G	GS	CG	IP	H	BB	SO	ShO	W	L	SV	AB	H	HR	BA	PO	A	E	DP	TC/G	FA
1981	LA N	1	0	1.000	1.06	2	2	1	17	10	3	10	0	0	0	0	4	0	0	.000	0	0	0	0	0.0	.000
1996	SD N	0	0	—	0.00	1	0	0	0.2	0	2	0	0	0	0	0	0	0	0	—	0	1	0	0	1.0	1.000
2 yrs.		1	0	1.000	1.02	3	2	1	17.2	10	5	10	0	0	0	0	4	0	0	.000	0	1	0	0	0.3	1.000

LEAGUE CHAMPIONSHIP SERIES

Year	Team	W	L	PCT	ERA	G	GS	CG	IP	H	BB	SO	ShO	W	L	SV	AB	H	HR	BA	PO	A	E	DP	TC/G	FA
1981	LA N	1	1	.500	2.45	2	2	1	14.2	9	5	10	0	0	0	0	5	0	0	.000	0	0	0	0	1.0	1.000
1983		1	0	1.000	1.13	1	1	0	8	7	4	5	0	0	0	0	3	0	0	.000	1	0	0	0	1.0	1.000
1985		1	0	1.000	1.88	2	2	0	14.1	11	10	13	0	0	0	0	5	1	0	.200	1	3	1	0	2.5	.800
3 yrs.		3	1	.750	1.95 6th	5	5	0	37	28	19	28 4th	0	0	0	0	13	1	0	.077	2	5	1	0	1.6	.875

WORLD SERIES

Year	Team	W	L	PCT	ERA	G	GS	CG	IP	H	BB	SO	ShO	W	L	SV	AB	H	HR	BA	PO	A	E	DP	TC/G	FA
1981	LA N	1	0	1.000	4.00	1	1	1	9	9	7	6	0	0	0	0	3	0	0	.000	0	1	0	0	1.0	1.000

183

Year	Team	W	L	PCT	ERA	G	GS	CG	IP	H	BB	SO	ShO	Relief Pitching W	L	SV	Batting AB	H	HR	BA	PO	A	E	DP	TC/G	FA

Julio Valera

VALERA, JULIO ENRIQUE
Born Julio Enrique Valera (Torres).
B. Oct. 13, 1968, Aguadilla, Puerto Rico

BR TR 6′2″ 185 lbs.

Year	Team	W	L	PCT	ERA	G	GS	CG	IP	H	BB	SO	ShO	W	L	SV	AB	H	HR	BA	PO	A	E	DP	TC/G	FA
1990	NY N	1	1	.500	6.92	3	3	0	13	20	7	4	0	0	0	0	5	1	0	.200	1	0	1	0	0.7	.500
1991		0	0	—	0.00	2	0	0	2	1	4	3	0	0	0	0	0	0	0	—	0	0	0	0	0.0	.000
1992	CAL A	8	11	.421	3.73	30	28	4	188	188	64	113	2	1	0	0	0	0	0	—	10	13	1	0	0.8	.958
1993		3	6	.333	6.62	19	5	0	53	77	15	28	0	1	3	4	0	0	0	—	4	5	1	1	0.5	.900
1996	KC A	3	2	.600	6.46	31	2	0	61.1	75	27	31	0	3	1	1	0	0	0	—	5	7	1	1	0.4	.923
5 yrs.		15	20	.429	4.85	85	38	4	317.1	361	117	179	2	5	4	5	5	1	0	.200	20	25	4	2	0.6	.918

Tim VanEgmond

VanEGMOND, TIMOTHY LAYNE
B. May 31, 1969, Shreveport, La.

BR TR 6′2″ 185 lbs.

Year	Team	W	L	PCT	ERA	G	GS	CG	IP	H	BB	SO	ShO	W	L	SV	AB	H	HR	BA	PO	A	E	DP	TC/G	FA
1994	BOS A	2	3	.400	6.34	7	7	1	38.1	38	21	22	0	0	0	0	0	0	0	—	0	2	0	0	0.3	1.000
1995		0	1	.000	9.45	4	1	0	6.2	9	6	5	0	0	0	0	0	0	0	—	1	1	0	0	0.5	1.000
1996	MIL A	3	5	.375	5.27	12	9	0	54.2	58	23	33	0	0	0	0	0	0	0	—	6	7	0	1	1.1	1.000
3 yrs.		5	9	.357	5.96	23	17	1	99.2	105	50	60	0	0	0	0	0	0	0	—	7	10	0	1	0.7	1.000

William VanLandingham

VanLANDINGHAM, WILLIAM JOSEPH
B. July 16, 1970, Columbia, Tenn.

BR TR 6′2″ 210 lbs.

Year	Team	W	L	PCT	ERA	G	GS	CG	IP	H	BB	SO	ShO	W	L	SV	AB	H	HR	BA	PO	A	E	DP	TC/G	FA
1994	SF N	8	2	.800	3.54	16	14	0	84	70	43	56	0	0	0	0	31	2	0	.065	4	9	0	0	0.8	1.000
1995		6	3	.667	3.67	18	18	1	122.2	124	40	95	0	0	0	0	46	7	1	.152	7	19	1	2	1.5	.963
1996		9	14	.391	5.40	32	32	0	181.2	196	78	97	0	0	0	0	61	8	0	.131	14	15	2	0	1.0	.935
3 yrs.		23	19	.548	4.45	66	64	1	388.1	390	161	248	0	0	0	0	138	17	1	.123	25	43	3	2	1.1	.958

Todd Van Poppel

VAN POPPEL, TODD MATTHEW
B. Dec. 9, 1971, Hinsdale, Ill.

BR TR 6′5″ 210 lbs.

Year	Team	W	L	PCT	ERA	G	GS	CG	IP	H	BB	SO	ShO	W	L	SV	AB	H	HR	BA	PO	A	E	DP	TC/G	FA
1991	OAK A	0	0	—	9.64	1	1	0	4.2	7	2	6	0	0	0	0	0	1	0	—	0	1	0	0	1.0	1.000
1993		6	6	.500	5.04	16	16	0	84	76	62	47	0	0	0	0	0	0	0	—	6	4	0	1	0.6	1.000
1994		7	10	.412	6.09	23	23	0	116.2	108	89	83	0	0	0	0	0	0	0	—	1	11	0	1	0.5	1.000
1995		4	8	.333	4.88	36	14	1	138.1	125	56	122	0	1	2	0	0	0	0	—	4	11	1	0	0.4	.938
1996	2 teams		OAK A	(28G 1–5)		DET A		(9G 2–4)																		
"	total	3	9	.250	9.06	37	15	1	99.1	139	62	53	1	1	2	1	0	0	0	—	3	10	1	1	0.4	.929
5 yrs.		20	33	.377	6.22	113	69	2	443	455	271	311	1	2	4	1	0	0	0		14	37	2	3	0.5	.962

Ben VanRyn

VANRYN, BENJAMIN ASHLEY
B. Aug. 9, 1971, Fort Wayne, Ind.

BL TL 6′5″ 185 lbs.

Year	Team	W	L	PCT	ERA	G	GS	CG	IP	H	BB	SO	ShO	W	L	SV	AB	H	HR	BA	PO	A	E	DP	TC/G	FA
1996	CAL A	0	0	—	0.00	1	0	0	1.0	1	1	0	0	0	0	0	0	0	0	—	0	1	0	0	1.0	1.000

Dario Veras

VERAS, DARIO ANTONIO
B. Mar. 13, 1973, Santiago, Dominican Republic

BR TR 6′2″ 165 lbs.

Year	Team	W	L	PCT	ERA	G	GS	CG	IP	H	BB	SO	ShO	W	L	SV	AB	H	HR	BA	PO	A	E	DP	TC/G	FA
1996	SD N	3	1	.750	2.79	23	0	0	29	24	10	23	0	3	1	0	0	0	0	—	0	6	0	0	0.3	1.000

DIVISIONAL PLAYOFF SERIES

Year	Team	W	L	PCT	ERA	G	GS	CG	IP	H	BB	SO	ShO	W	L	SV	AB	H	HR	BA	PO	A	E	DP	TC/G	FA
1996	SD N	0	0	—	0.00	2	0	0	1	1	0	1	0	0	0	0	0	0	0	—	0	1	0	0	0.5	1.000

David Veres

VERES, DAVID SCOTT
B. Oct. 19, 1966, Montgomery, Ala.

BR TR 6′2″ 195 lbs.

Year	Team	W	L	PCT	ERA	G	GS	CG	IP	H	BB	SO	ShO	W	L	SV	AB	H	HR	BA	PO	A	E	DP	TC/G	FA
1994	HOU N	3	3	.500	2.41	32	0	0	41	39	7	28	0	3	3	1	2	1	0	.500	5	2	0	0	0.2	1.000
1995		5	1	.833	2.26	72	0	0	103.1	89	30	94	0	5	1	1	5	0	0	.000	6	11	1	0	0.3	.944
1996	MON N	6	3	.667	4.17	68	0	0	77.2	85	32	81	0	6	3	4	8	3	0	.375	3	9	2	0	0.2	.857
3 yrs.		14	7	.667	2.96	172	0	0	222	213	69	203	0	14	7	6	15	4	0	.267	14	22	3	0	0.2	.923

Randy Veres

VERES, RANDOLPH RUHLAND
B. Nov. 25, 1965, San Francisco, Calif.

BR TR 6′3″ 190 lbs.

Year	Team	W	L	PCT	ERA	G	GS	CG	IP	H	BB	SO	ShO	W	L	SV	AB	H	HR	BA	PO	A	E	DP	TC/G	FA
1989	MIL A	0	1	.000	4.32	3	1	0	8.1	9	4	8	0	0	0	0	0	0	0	—	0	1	0	0	0.3	1.000
1990		0	3	.000	3.67	26	0	0	41.2	38	16	16	0	0	3	1	0	0	0	—	2	10	0	2	0.5	1.000
1994	CHI N	1	1	.500	5.59	10	0	0	9.2	12	2	5	0	1	1	0	1	0	0	.000	0	2	0	0	0.2	1.000
1995	FLA N	4	4	.500	3.88	47	0	0	48.2	46	22	31	0	4	4	1	3	0	0	.000	2	3	1	0	0.1	.833
1996	DET A	0	4	.000	8.31	25	0	0	30.1	38	23	28	0	0	4	0	0	0	0	—	0	0	0	0	0.0	.000
5 yrs.		5	13	.278	4.93	111	1	0	138.2	143	67	88	0	5	12	2	4	0	0	.000	4	16	1	2	0.2	.952

Ron Villone

VILLONE, RONALD THOMAS, JR.
B. Jan. 16, 1970, Englewood, N. J.

BL TL 6′3″ 230 lbs.

Year	Team	W	L	PCT	ERA	G	GS	CG	IP	H	BB	SO	ShO	W	L	SV	AB	H	HR	BA	PO	A	E	DP	TC/G	FA
1995	2 teams		SEA A	(19G 0–2)		SD N		(19G 2–1)																		
"	total	2	3	.400	5.80	38	0	0	45	44	34	63	0	2	3	1	0	0	0	.000	0	4	1	0	0.1	.800
1996	2 teams		SD N	(21G 1–1)		MIL A		(23G 0–0)																		
"	total	1	1	.500	3.14	44	0	0	43	31	25	38	0	1	1	2	0	0	0	—	3	4	2	0	0.2	.778
2 yrs.		3	4	.429	4.50	82	0	0	88	75	59	101	0	3	4	3	1	0	0	.000	3	8	3	0	0.2	.786

Year	Team	W	L	PCT	ERA	G	GS	CG	IP	H	BB	SO	ShO	Relief Pitching W	L	SV	Batting AB	H	HR	BA	PO	A	E	DP	TC/G	FA

Frank Viola

VIOLA, FRANK JOHN, JR. (Sweet Music)
B. Apr. 19, 1960, Hempstead, N. Y.   BL TL 6'4" 195 lbs.

Year	Team	W	L	PCT	ERA	G	GS	CG	IP	H	BB	SO	ShO	W	L	SV	AB	H	HR	BA	PO	A	E	DP	TC/G	FA
1982	MIN A	4	10	.286	5.21	22	22	3	126	152	38	84	1	0	0	0	0	0	0	—	1	15	2	0	0.8	.889
1983		7	15	.318	5.49	35	34	4	210	242	92	127	0	0	0	0	0	0	0	—	7	23	1	2	0.9	.968
1984		18	12	.600	3.21	35	35	10	257.2	225	73	149	4	0	0	0	0	0	0	—	6	26	1	1	0.9	.970
1985		18	14	.563	4.09	36	36	9	250.2	262	68	135	0	0	0	0	0	0	0	—	6	33	5	0	1.2	.886
1986		16	13	.552	4.51	37	37	7	245.2	257	83	191	1	0	0	0	0	0	0	—	8	21	3	1	0.9	.906
1987		17	10	.630	2.90	36	36	7	251.2	230	66	197	1	0	0	0	0	0	0	—	6	34	3	1	1.2	.930
1988		**24**	7	**.774**	2.64	35	35	7	255.1	236	54	193	2	0	0	0	0	0	0	—	5	30	2	1	1.1	.946
1989	2 teams	MIN A	(24G 8-12)		NY	N	(12G 5-5)																			
"	total	13	17	.433	3.66	36	36	9	261	246	74	211	2	0	0	0	23	3	0	.130	10	35	4	3	1.4	.918
1990	NY N	20	12	.625	2.67	35	**35**	7	**249.2**	227	60	182	3	0	0	0	85	13	0	.153	11	34	1	1	1.3	.978
1991		13	15	.464	3.97	35	35	3	231.1	**259**	54	132	0	0	0	0	71	9	0	.127	6	34	4	1	1.3	.909
1992	BOS A	13	12	.520	3.44	35	35	6	238	214	89	121	1	0	0	0	0	0	0	—	6	47	2	6	1.6	.964
1993		11	8	.579	3.14	29	29	2	183.2	180	72	91	1	0	0	0	0	0	0	—	10	31	4	1	1.6	.911
1994		1	1	.500	4.65	6	6	0	31	34	17	9	0	0	0	0	0	0	0	—	0	4	0	1	0.7	1.000
1995	CIN N	0	1	.000	6.28	3	3	0	14.1	20	3	4	0	0	0	0	6	1	0	.167	0	2	0	0	0.7	1.000
1996	TOR A	1	3	.250	7.71	6	6	0	30.1	43	21	18	0	0	0	0	0	0	0	—	2	2	0	0	0.7	1.000
15 yrs.		176	150	.540	3.73	421	420	74	2836.1	2827	864	1844	16	0	0	0	185	26	0	.141	84	371	32	19	1.2	.934

LEAGUE CHAMPIONSHIP SERIES

1987	MIN A	1	0	1.000	5.25	2	2	0	12	14	5	9	0	0	0	0	0	0	0	—	0	1	0	0	0.5	1.000

WORLD SERIES

1987	MIN A	2	1	.667	3.72	3	3	0	19.1	17	3	16	0	0	0	0	1	0	0	.000	1	5	0	0	2.0	1.000

Ed Vosberg

VOSBERG, EDWARD JOHN
B. Sept. 28, 1961, Tucson, Ariz.   BL TL 6'1" 190 lbs.

Year	Team	W	L	PCT	ERA	G	GS	CG	IP	H	BB	SO	ShO	W	L	SV	AB	H	HR	BA	PO	A	E	DP	TC/G	FA
1986	SD N	0	1	.000	6.59	5	3	0	13.2	17	9	8	0	0	0	0	2	0	0	.000	0	1	1	0	0.4	.500
1990	SF N	1	1	.500	5.55	18	0	0	24.1	21	12	12	0	1	1	0	0	0	0	—	1	5	0	0	0.3	1.000
1994	OAK A	0	2	.000	3.95	16	0	0	13.2	16	5	12	0	0	2	0	0	0	0	—	2	5	0	1	0.4	1.000
1995	TEX A	5	5	.500	3.00	44	0	0	36	32	16	36	0	5	5	4	0	0	0	—	0	1	1	0	0.0	.500
1996		1	1	.500	3.27	52	0	0	44	51	21	32	0	1	1	8	0	0	0	—	1	11	0	0	0.2	1.000
5 yrs.		7	10	.412	4.03	135	3	0	131.2	137	63	100	0	7	9	12	2	0	0	.000	4	23	2	1	0.2	.931

DIVISIONAL PLAYOFF SERIES

1996	TEX A	0	0	—	0.00	1	0	0		1	0	0	0	0	0	0	0	0	0	—	0	0	0	0	0.0	.000

Terrell Wade

WADE, HAWATHA TERRELL
B. Jan. 25, 1973, Rembert, S. C.   BL TL 6'3" 205 lbs.

Year	Team	W	L	PCT	ERA	G	GS	CG	IP	H	BB	SO	ShO	W	L	SV	AB	H	HR	BA	PO	A	E	DP	TC/G	FA
1995	ATL N	0	1	.000	4.50	3	0	0	4	3	4	3	0	0	1	0	0	0	0	—	0	0	0	0	0.0	.000
1996		5	0	1.000	2.97	44	8	0	69.2	57	47	79	0	2	0	1	13	2	0	.154	2	9	1	1	0.3	.917
2 yrs.		5	1	.833	3.05	47	8	0	73.2	60	51	82	0	2	1	1	13	2	0	.154	2	9	1	1	0.3	.917

LEAGUE CHAMPIONSHIP SERIES

1996	ATL N	0	0	—	0.00	1	0	0	0.1	0	0	1	0	0	0	0	0	0	0	—	0	0	0	0	0.0	.000

WORLD SERIES

1996	ATL N	0	0	—	0.00	2	0	0	0.2	0	2	0	0	0	0	0	0	0	0	—	0	0	0	0	0.0	.000

Billy Wagner

WAGNER, WILLIAM EDWARD
B. July 25, 1971, Tannersville, Va.   BL TL 5'10" 180 lbs.

Year	Team	W	L	PCT	ERA	G	GS	CG	IP	H	BB	SO	ShO	W	L	SV	AB	H	HR	BA	PO	A	E	DP	TC/G	FA
1995	HOU N	0	0	—	0.00	1	0	0	0.1	0	0	0	0	0	0	0	0	0	0	—	0	0	0	0	0.0	.000
1996		2	2	.500	2.44	37	0	0	51.2	28	30	67	0	2	2	9	5	0	0	.000	2	3	0	0	0.1	1.000
2 yrs.		2	2	.500	2.42	38	0	0	52	28	30	67	0	2	2	9	5	0	0	.000	2	3	0	0	0.1	1.000

Matt Wagner

WAGNER, MATTHEW WILLIAM
B. Apr. 4, 1972, Cedar Falls, Iowa   BR TR 6'5" 215 lbs.

Year	Team	W	L	PCT	ERA	G	GS	CG	IP	H	BB	SO	ShO	W	L	SV	AB	H	HR	BA	PO	A	E	DP	TC/G	FA
1996	SEA A	3	5	.375	6.86	15	14	0	80	91	38	41	0	0	0	0	0	0	0	—	4	8	1	1	0.9	.923

Paul Wagner

WAGNER, PAUL ALAN
B. Nov. 14, 1967, Milwaukee, Wis.   BR TR 6'3" 205 lbs.

Year	Team	W	L	PCT	ERA	G	GS	CG	IP	H	BB	SO	ShO	W	L	SV	AB	H	HR	BA	PO	A	E	DP	TC/G	FA
1992	PIT N	2	0	1.000	0.69	6	1	0	13	9	5	5	0	2	0	0	3	1	0	.333	2	2	0	0	0.7	1.000
1993		8	8	.500	4.27	44	17	1	141.1	143	42	114	1	2	3	2	42	8	0	.190	9	13	0	3	0.5	1.000
1994		7	8	.467	4.59	29	17	1	119.2	136	50	86	0	2	0	0	37	6	0	.162	14	22	0	3	1.2	1.000
1995		5	**16**	.238	4.80	33	25	3	165	174	72	120	1	1	2	1	42	9	0	.214	12	24	0	1	1.1	1.000
1996		4	8	.333	5.40	16	15	1	81.2	86	39	81	0	0	0	0	25	1	0	.040	10	14	0	1	1.5	1.000
5 yrs.		26	40	.394	4.60	128	75	6	520.2	548	208	406	2	7	5	3	149	25	0	.168	47	75	0	8	1.0	1.000

Dave Wainhouse

WAINHOUSE, DAVID PAUL
B. Nov. 7, 1967, Toronto, Ont., Canada.   BL TR 6'2" 190 lbs.

Year	Team	W	L	PCT	ERA	G	GS	CG	IP	H	BB	SO	ShO	W	L	SV	AB	H	HR	BA	PO	A	E	DP	TC/G	FA
1991	MON N	0	1	.000	6.75	2	0	0	2.2	2	4	1	0	0	1	0	0	0	0	—	0	0	0	0	0.0	.000
1993	SEA A	0	0	—	27.00	3	0	0	2.1	7	5	2	0	0	0	0	0	0	0	—	0	0	0	0	0.0	.000
1996	PIT N	1	0	1.000	5.70	17	0	0	23.2	22	10	16	0	1	0	0	1	0	0	.000	3	7	1	1	0.6	.909
3 yrs.		1	1	.500	7.53	22	0	0	28.2	31	19	19	0	1	1	0	1	0	0	.000	3	7	1	1	0.5	.909

Year	Team	W	L	PCT	ERA	G	GS	CG	IP	H	BB	SO	ShO	Relief Pitching W	L	SV	Batting AB	H	HR	BA	PO	A	E	DP	TC/G	FA

Tim Wakefield
WAKEFIELD, TIMOTHY STEPHEN
B. Aug. 2, 1966, Melbourne, Fla.
BR TR 6' 2" 195 lbs.

Year	Team	W	L	PCT	ERA	G	GS	CG	IP	H	BB	SO	ShO	W	L	SV	AB	H	HR	BA	PO	A	E	DP	TC/G	FA
1992	PIT N	8	1	.889	2.15	13	13	4	92	76	35	51	1	0	0	0	28	2	0	.071	6	19	0	1	1.9	1.000
1993		6	11	.353	5.61	24	20	3	128.1	145	75	59	2	1	0	0	43	7	1	.163	8	15	4	2	1.1	.852
1995	BOS A	16	8	.667	2.95	27	27	6	195.1	163	68	119	1	0	0	0	0	0	0	—	15	19	2	4	1.3	.944
1996		14	13	.519	5.14	32	32	6	211.2	238	90	140	0	0	0	0	0	0	0	—	13	18	2	4	1.0	.939
4 yrs.		44	33	.571	4.12	96	92	19	627.1	622	268	369	4	1	0	0	71	9	1	.127	42	71	8	11	1.3	.934

DIVISIONAL PLAYOFF SERIES
| 1995 | BOS A | 0 | 1 | .000 | 11.81 | 1 | 1 | 0 | 5.1 | 5 | 5 | 4 | 0 | 0 | 0 | 0 | 0 | 0 | 0 | — | 0 | 0 | 0 | 0 | 0.0 | .000 |

LEAGUE CHAMPIONSHIP SERIES
| 1992 | PIT N | 2 | 0 | 1.000 | 3.00 | 2 | 2 | 2 (4th) | 18 | 14 | 5 | 7 | 0 | 0 | 0 | 0 | 6 | 0 | 0 | .000 | 3 | 2 | 0 | 0 | 2.5 | 1.000 |

Mike Walker
WALKER, MICHAEL CHARLES
B. Oct. 4, 1966, Chicago, Ill.
BR TR 6' 1" 175 lbs.

Year	Team	W	L	PCT	ERA	G	GS	CG	IP	H	BB	SO	ShO	W	L	SV	AB	H	HR	BA	PO	A	E	DP	TC/G	FA
1988	CLE A	0	1	.000	7.27	3	1	0	8.2	8	10	7	0	0	0	0	0	0	0	—	0	3	0	0	1.0	1.000
1990		2	6	.250	4.88	18	11	0	75.2	82	42	34	0	1	0	0	0	0	0	—	4	9	0	1	0.7	1.000
1991		0	1	.000	2.08	5	0	0	4.1	6	2	2	0	0	1	0	0	0	0	—	1	1	0	0	0.4	1.000
1995	CHI N	1	3	.250	3.22	42	0	0	44.2	45	24	20	0	1	3	1	3	0	0	.000	4	7	1	0	0.3	.917
1996	DET A	0	0	—	8.46	20	0	0	27.2	40	17	13	0	0	0	1	0	0	0	—	2	1	0	0	0.2	1.000
5 yrs.		3	11	.214	5.09	88	12	0	161	181	95	76	0	2	4	2	3	0	0	.000	11	21	1	1	0.4	.970

Pete Walker
WALKER, PETER BRIAN
B. Apr. 8, 1969, Beverly, Mass.
BR TR 6' 2" 195 lbs.

Year	Team	W	L	PCT	ERA	G	GS	CG	IP	H	BB	SO	ShO	W	L	SV	AB	H	HR	BA	PO	A	E	DP	TC/G	FA
1995	NY N	1	0	1.000	4.58	13	0	0	17.2	24	5	5	0	1	0	0	0	0	0	—	1	2	0	0	0.2	1.000
1996	SD N	0	0	—	0.00	1	0	0	0.2	0	3	1	0	0	0	0	0	0	0	—	0	0	0	0	0.0	.000
2 yrs.		1	0	1.000	4.42	14	0	0	18.1	24	8	6	0	1	0	0	0	0	0	—	1	2	0	0	0.2	1.000

Donne Wall
WALL, DONNELL LEE
B. July 11, 1967, Potosi, Mo.
BR TR 6' 1" 180 lbs.

Year	Team	W	L	PCT	ERA	G	GS	CG	IP	H	BB	SO	ShO	W	L	SV	AB	H	HR	BA	PO	A	E	DP	TC/G	FA
1995	HOU N	3	1	.750	5.55	6	5	0	24.1	33	5	16	0	0	0	0	5	0	0	.000	4	2	1	0	1.2	.857
1996		9	8	.529	4.56	26	23	2	150	170	34	99	1	0	0	0	44	9	0	.205	17	18	2	0	1.4	.946
2 yrs.		12	9	.571	4.70	32	28	2	174.1	203	39	115	1	0	0	0	49	9	0	.184	21	20	3	0	1.4	.932

Derek Wallace
WALLACE, DEREK ROBERT
B. Sept. 1, 1971, Van Nuys, Calif.
BR TR 6' 3" 200 lbs.

Year	Team	W	L	PCT	ERA	G	GS	CG	IP	H	BB	SO	ShO	W	L	SV	AB	H	HR	BA	PO	A	E	DP	TC/G	FA
1996	NY N	2	3	.400	4.01	19	0	0	24.2	29	14	15	0	2	3	3	0	0	0	—	3	2	0	0	0.3	1.000

Jeff Ware
WARE, JEFFREY ALLAN
B. Nov. 11, 1970, Norfolk, Va.
BR TR 6' 3" 190 lbs.

Year	Team	W	L	PCT	ERA	G	GS	CG	IP	H	BB	SO	ShO	W	L	SV	AB	H	HR	BA	PO	A	E	DP	TC/G	FA
1995	TOR A	2	1	.667	5.47	5	5	0	26.1	28	21	18	0	0	0	0	0	0	0	—	2	4	0	1	1.2	1.000
1996		1	5	.167	9.09	13	4	0	32.2	35	31	11	0	1	1	0	0	0	0	—	3	5	0	1	0.6	1.000
2 yrs.		3	6	.333	7.47	18	9	0	59	63	52	29	0	1	1	0					5	9	0	2	0.8	1.000

John Wasdin
WASDIN, JOHN TRUMAN
B. Aug. 5, 1972, Fort Belvoir, Va.
BR TR 6' 2" 190 lbs.

Year	Team	W	L	PCT	ERA	G	GS	CG	IP	H	BB	SO	ShO	W	L	SV	AB	H	HR	BA	PO	A	E	DP	TC/G	FA
1995	OAK A	1	1	.500	4.67	5	2	0	17.1	14	3	6	0	0	0	0	0	0	0	—	1	0	0	0	0.2	1.000
1996		8	7	.533	5.96	25	21	1	131.1	145	50	75	0	0	0	0	0	0	0	—	9	12	1	1	0.9	.955
2 yrs.		9	8	.529	5.81	30	23	1	148.2	159	53	81	0	0	0	0					10	12	1	1	0.8	.957

Allen Watson
WATSON, ALLEN KENNETH
B. Nov. 18, 1970, Jamaica, N. Y.
BL TL 6' 3" 195 lbs.

Year	Team	W	L	PCT	ERA	G	GS	CG	IP	H	BB	SO	ShO	W	L	SV	AB	H	HR	BA	PO	A	E	DP	TC/G	FA
1993	STL N	6	7	.462	4.60	16	15	0	86	90	28	49	0	0	1	0	26	6	0	.231	3	10	1	1	0.9	.929
1994		6	5	.545	5.52	22	22	0	115.2	130	53	74	0	0	0	0	38	6	0	.158	4	14	1	0	0.9	.947
1995		7	9	.438	4.96	21	19	0	114.1	126	41	49	0	0	0	0	36	15	0	.417	7	20	0	1	1.3	1.000
1996	SF N	8	12	.400	4.61	29	29	2	185.2	189	69	128	0	0	0	0	65	15	0	.231	6	21	1	2	1.0	.964
4 yrs.		27	33	.450	4.90	88	85	2	501.2	535	191	300	0	0	1	0	165	42	0	.255	20	65	3	3	1.0	.966

Dave Weathers
WEATHERS, JOHN DAVID
B. Sept. 25, 1969, Lawrenceburg, Tenn.
BR TR 6' 3" 205 lbs.

Year	Team	W	L	PCT	ERA	G	GS	CG	IP	H	BB	SO	ShO	W	L	SV	AB	H	HR	BA	PO	A	E	DP	TC/G	FA
1991	TOR A	1	0	1.000	4.91	15	0	0	14.2	15	17	13	0	1	0	0	0	0	0	—	0	1	0	0	0.1	1.000
1992		0	0	—	8.10	2	0	0	3.1	5	2	3	0	0	0	0	0	0	0	—	0	0	0	0	0.0	.000
1993	FLA N	2	3	.400	5.12	14	6	0	45.2	57	13	34	0	0	0	0	10	1	0	.100	5	3	0	0	0.6	1.000
1994		8	12	.400	5.27	24	24	0	135	166	59	72	0	0	0	0	44	3	0	.068	2	21	1	0	1.0	.958
1995		4	5	.444	5.98	28	15	0	90.1	104	52	60	0	1	1	0	26	4	0	.154	3	12	2	0	0.6	.882
1996 2 teams	FLA N (31G 2-2)	NY A	(11G 0-2)																							
" total		2	4	.333	5.48	42	12	0	88.2	108	42	53	0	0	1	0	19	3	1	.158	5	12	0	1	0.4	1.000
6 yrs.		17	24	.415	5.48	125	57	0	377.2	455	185	235	0	2	2	0	99	11	1	.111	15	49	3	1	0.5	.955

DIVISIONAL PLAYOFF SERIES
| 1996 | NY A | 1 | 0 | 1.000 | 0.00 | 2 | 0 | 0 | 5 | 1 | 0 | 5 | 0 | 1 | 0 | 0 | 0 | 0 | 0 | — | 0 | 1 | 0 | 0 | 0.5 | 1.000 |

LEAGUE CHAMPIONSHIP SERIES
| 1996 | NY A | 1 | 0 | 1.000 | 0.00 | 2 | 0 | 0 | 3 | 3 | 1 | 3 | 0 | 1 | 0 | 0 | 0 | 0 | 0 | — | 0 | 0 | 0 | 0 | 0.0 | .000 |

WORLD SERIES
| 1996 | NY A | 0 | 0 | — | 3.00 | 3 | 0 | 0 | 3 | 2 | 3 | 3 | 0 | 0 | 0 | 0 | 0 | 0 | 0 | — | 0 | 0 | 0 | 0 | 0.0 | .000 |

Year	Team	W	L	PCT	ERA	G	GS	CG	IP	H	BB	SO	ShO	Relief Pitching W	L	SV	Batting AB	H	HR	BA	PO	A	E	DP	TC/G	FA

Bob Wells

WELLS, ROBERT LEE — B. Nov. 1, 1966, Yakima, Wash. — BR TR 6' 180 lbs.

Year	Team	W	L	PCT	ERA	G	GS	CG	IP	H	BB	SO	ShO	W	L	SV	AB	H	HR	BA	PO	A	E	DP	TC/G	FA
1994	2 teams PHI N (6G 1-0) SEA A (1G 1-0)																									
"	total	2	0	1.000	2.00	7	0	0	9	8	4	6	0	2	0	0	0	0	0		0	0	0	0	0.0	
1995	SEA A	4	3	.571	5.75	30	4	0	76.2	88	39	38	0	4	1	0	0	0	0	—	7	8	0	0	0.5	1.000
1996		12	7	.632	5.30	36	16	1	130.2	141	46	94	1	5	1	0	0	0	0	—	8	12	2	1	0.6	.909
	3 yrs.	18	10	.643	5.33	73	20	1	216.1	237	89	138	1	11	2	0	0	0	0		15	20	2	1	0.5	.946

DIVISIONAL PLAYOFF SERIES

| 1995 | SEA A | 0 | 0 | — | 9.00 | 1 | 0 | 0 | 1 | 2 | 1 | 0 | 0 | 0 | 0 | 0 | 0 | 0 | 0 | — | 0 | 0 | 0 | 0 | 0.0 | .000 |

LEAGUE CHAMPIONSHIP SERIES

| 1995 | SEA A | 0 | 0 | — | 3.00 | 1 | 0 | 0 | 3 | 2 | 2 | 2 | 0 | 0 | 0 | 0 | 0 | 0 | 0 | — | 0 | 1 | 0 | 0 | 1.0 | 1.000 |

David Wells

WELLS, DAVID LEE — B. May 20, 1963, Torrance, Calif. — BL TL 6'3" 187 lbs.

Year	Team	W	L	PCT	ERA	G	GS	CG	IP	H	BB	SO	ShO	W	L	SV	AB	H	HR	BA	PO	A	E	DP	TC/G	FA
1987	TOR A	4	3	.571	3.99	18	2	0	29.1	37	12	32	0	4	1	1	0	0	0	—	2	4	0	1	0.3	1.000
1988		3	5	.375	4.62	41	0	0	64.1	65	31	56	0	3	5	4	0	0	0	—	5	5	0	1	0.2	1.000
1989		7	4	.636	2.40	54	0	0	86.1	66	28	78	0	7	4	2	0	0	0	—	9	11	1	0	0.4	.952
1990		11	6	.647	3.14	43	25	0	189	165	45	115	0	1	1	3	0	0	0	—	7	32	0	1	0.9	1.000
1991		15	10	.600	3.72	40	28	2	198.1	188	49	106	0	1	0	1	0	0	0	—	5	35	2	1	1.0	.952
1992		7	9	.438	5.40	41	14	0	120	138	36	62	0	1	2	2	0	0	0	—	9	14	1	0	0.6	.958
1993	DET A	11	9	.550	4.19	32	30	0	187	183	42	139	0	0	0	0	0	0	0	—	10	22	1	0	1.0	.970
1994		5	7	.417	3.96	16	16	5	111.1	113	24	71	1	0	0	0	0	0	0	—	6	11	0	0	1.1	1.000
1995	2 teams DET A (18G 10-3) CIN N (11G 6-5)																									
"	total	16	8	.667	3.24	29	29	6	203	194	53	133	0	0	0	0	28	4	0	.143	15	22	2	2	1.3	.949
1996	BAL A	11	14	.440	5.14	34	34	3	224.1	247	51	130	0	0	0	0	0	0	0	—	15	39	1	4	1.6	.982
	10 yrs.	90	75	.545	3.99	348	178	16	1413	1396	371	922	1	17	13	13	28	4	0	.143	83	195	8	11	0.8	.972

DIVISIONAL PLAYOFF SERIES

1995	CIN N	1	0	1.000	0.00	1	1	0	6.1	6	1	8	0	0	0	0	3	1	0	.333	1	1	0	0	2.0	1.000
1996	BAL A	1	0	1.000	4.61	2	2	0	13.2	15	4	6	0	0	0	0	0	0	0	—	0	0	0	0	0.0	—
	2 yrs.	2	0	1.000	3.15	3	3	0	20	21	5	14	0	0	0	0	3	1	0	.333	1	4	0	0	1.7	1.000

LEAGUE CHAMPIONSHIP SERIES

1989	TOR A	0	0	—	0.00	1	0	0	1	0	2	1	0	0	0	0	0	0	0	—	0	0	0	0	0.0	.000
1991		0	0	—	2.35	4	0	0	7.2	6	2	9	0	0	0	0	0	0	0	—	1	1	0	0	0.5	1.000
1995	CIN N	0	1	.000	4.50	1	1	0	6	8	2	3	0	0	0	0	2	1	0	.500	0	0	0	0	0.0	.000
1996	BAL A	1	0	1.000	4.05	1	1	0	6.2	8	3	6	0	0	0	0	0	0	0	—	1	0	0	0	1.0	1.000
	4 yrs.	1	1	.500	3.38	7	2	0	21.1	22	9	19	0	0	0	0	2	1	0	.500	2	1	0	0	0.4	1.000

WORLD SERIES

| 1992 | TOR A | 0 | 0 | — | 0.00 | 4 | 0 | 0 | 4.1 | 1 | 2 | 3 | 0 | 0 | 0 | 0 | 0 | 0 | 0 | — | 0 | 0 | 0 | 0 | 0.0 | .000 |

Turk Wendell

WENDELL, STEVEN JOHN — B. May 19, 1967, Pittsfield, Mass. — BB TR 6'2" 185 lbs.

Year	Team	W	L	PCT	ERA	G	GS	CG	IP	H	BB	SO	ShO	W	L	SV	AB	H	HR	BA	PO	A	E	DP	TC/G	FA
1993	CHI N	1	2	.333	4.37	7	4	0	22.2	24	8	15	0	0	0	0	7	1	0	.143	7	1	0	0	1.1	1.000
1994		0	1	.000	11.93	6	2	0	14.1	22	10	9	0	0	0	0	2	0	0	.000	1	3	0	0	0.7	1.000
1995		3	1	.750	4.92	43	0	0	60.1	71	24	50	0	3	1	0	7	0	0	.000	9	12	1	2	0.5	.955
1996		4	5	.444	2.84	70	0	0	79.1	58	44	75	0	4	5	18	2	1	0	.500	9	9	0	1	0.3	1.000
	4 yrs.	8	9	.471	4.48	126	6	0	176.2	175	86	149	0	7	6	18	18	2	0	.111	26	25	1	3	0.4	.981

Don Wengert

WENGERT, DONALD PAUL — B. Nov. 6, 1969, Sioux City, Iowa — BR TR 6'2" 205 lbs.

Year	Team	W	L	PCT	ERA	G	GS	CG	IP	H	BB	SO	ShO	W	L	SV	AB	H	HR	BA	PO	A	E	DP	TC/G	FA
1995	OAK A	1	1	.500	3.34	19	0	0	29.2	30	12	16	0	1	1	0	0	0	0	—	3	1	0	0	0.2	1.000
1996		7	11	.389	5.58	36	25	1	161.1	200	60	75	1	0	1	0	0	0	0	—	19	8	0	0	0.8	1.000
	2 yrs.	8	12	.400	5.23	55	25	1	191	230	72	91	1	1	2	0					22	9	0	0	0.6	1.000

David West

WEST, DAVID LEE — B. Sept. 1, 1964, Memphis, Tenn. — BL TL 6'6" 205 lbs.

Year	Team	W	L	PCT	ERA	G	GS	CG	IP	H	BB	SO	ShO	W	L	SV	AB	H	HR	BA	PO	A	E	DP	TC/G	FA
1988	NY N	1	0	1.000	3.00	2	1	0	6	6	3	3	0	0	0	0	2	2	0	1.000	1	0	0	0	0.5	1.000
1989	2 teams NY N (11G 0-2) MIN A (10G 3-2)																									
"	total	3	4	.429	6.79	21	7	0	63.2	73	33	50	0	0	0	0	5	1	0	.200	2	2	1	0	0.2	.800
1990	MIN A	7	9	.438	5.10	29	27	2	146.1	142	78	92	0	0	0	0	0	0	0	—	3	16	2	2	0.7	.905
1991		4	4	.500	4.54	15	12	0	71.1	66	28	52	0	0	0	0	0	0	0	—	1	11	1	1	0.9	.923
1992		1	3	.250	6.99	9	3	0	28.1	32	20	19	0	1	0	0	0	0	0	—	0	5	2	0	0.8	.714
1993	PHI N	6	4	.600	2.92	76	0	0	86.1	60	51	87	0	6	4	3	5	2	0	.400	2	4	2	1	0.1	.750
1994		4	10	.286	3.55	31	14	0	99	74	61	83	0	0	4	0	28	2	0	.071	3	6	0	1	0.3	1.000
1995		3	2	.600	3.79	8	8	0	38	34	19	25	0	0	0	0	8	1	1	.125	1	3	1	0	0.6	.800
1996		2	2	.500	4.76	7	6	0	28.1	31	11	22	0	0	0	0	7	2	0	.286	0	3	0	0	0.4	1.000
	9 yrs.	31	38	.449	4.58	198	78	2	567.1	518	304	433	0	7	8	3	55	10	1	.182	13	50	9	5	0.4	.875

LEAGUE CHAMPIONSHIP SERIES

1991	MIN A	1	0	1.000	0.00	2	0	0	5.2	1	4	4	0	1	0	0	0	0	0	—	0	0	0	0	0.0	.000
1993	PHI N	0	0	—	13.50	3	0	0	2.2	5	2	5	0	0	0	0	0	0	0	—	0	1	0	0	0.3	1.000
	2 yrs.	1	0	1.000	4.32	5	0	0	8.1	6	6	9	0	1	0	0	0	0	0	—	0	1	0	0	0.2	1.000

WORLD SERIES

1991	MIN A	0	0	—	∞	2	0	0	0	2	4	0	0	0	0	0	0	0	0	—	0	0	0	0	0.0	.000
1993	PHI N	0	0	—	27.00	3	0	0	1	5	1	0	0	0	0	0	0	0	0	—	0	0	0	0	0.0	.000
	2 yrs.	0	0		63.00	5	0	0	1	7	5	0	0	0	0	0	0	0	0		0	0	0	0	0.0	

Year	Team	W	L	PCT	ERA	G	GS	CG	IP	H	BB	SO	ShO	Relief Pitching W	L	SV	Batting AB	H	HR	BA	PO	A	E	DP	TC/G	FA

John Wetteland — WETTELAND, JOHN KARL
B. Aug. 21, 1966, San Mateo, Calif. BR TR 6'2" 195 lbs.

Year	Team	W	L	PCT	ERA	G	GS	CG	IP	H	BB	SO	ShO	RP W	L	SV	AB	H	HR	BA	PO	A	E	DP	TC/G	FA
1989	LA N	5	8	.385	3.77	31	12	0	102.2	81	34	96	0	3	2	1	21	3	0	.143	5	8	2	0	0.5	.867
1990		2	4	.333	4.81	22	5	0	43	44	17	36	0	2	1	0	7	1	1	.143	1	3	1	0	0.2	.800
1991		1	0	1.000	0.00	6	0	0	9	5	3	9	0	1	0	0	0	0	0	—	1	2	1	0	0.7	.750
1992	MON N	4	4	.500	2.92	67	0	0	83.1	64	36	99	0	4	4	37	5	1	0	.200	7	6	1	0	0.2	.929
1993		9	3	.750	1.37	70	0	0	85.1	58	28	113	0	9	3	43	4	0	0	.000	1	5	3	0	0.1	.667
1994		4	6	.400	2.83	52	0	0	63.2	46	21	68	0	4	6	25	4	1	0	.250	3	4	1	0	0.2	.875
1995	NY A	1	5	.167	2.93	60	0	0	61.1	40	14	66	0	1	5	31	0	0	0	—	2	3	1	1	0.1	.833
1996		2	3	.400	2.83	62	0	0	63.2	54	21	69	0	2	3	43	0	0	0	—	0	7	0	1	0.1	1.000
8 yrs.		28	33	.459	2.92	370	17	0	512	392	174	556	0	26	24	180	41	6	1	.146	20	38	10	2	0.2	.853

DIVISIONAL PLAYOFF SERIES

1995	NY A	0	1	.000	14.54	3	0	0	4.1	8	2	5	0	0	1	0	0	0	0	—	1	0	0	0	0.3	1.000
1996		0	0	—	0.00	3	0	0	4	2	4	4	0	0	0	0	0	0	0	—	1	2	0	0	1.0	1.000
2 yrs.		0	1	.000	7.56	6	0	0	8.1	10	6	9	0	0	1	2					2	2	0	0	0.7	1.000

LEAGUE CHAMPIONSHIP SERIES

1996	NY A	0	0	—	4.50	4	0	0	4	2	1	5	0	0	0	1	0	0	0	—	0	0	0	0	0.0	.000

WORLD SERIES

1996	NY A	0	0	—	2.08	5	0	0	4.1	4	1	6	0	0	0	4 (2nd)	0	0	0	—	0	0	0	0	0.0	.000

Wally Whitehurst — WHITEHURST, WALTER RICHARD
B. Apr. 11, 1964, Shreveport, La. BR TR 6'3" 180 lbs.

Year	Team	W	L	PCT	ERA	G	GS	CG	IP	H	BB	SO	ShO	RP W	L	SV	AB	H	HR	BA	PO	A	E	DP	TC/G	FA
1989	NY N	0	1	.000	4.50	9	1	0	14	17	5	9	0	0	0	0	1	0	0	.000	1	1	0	0	0.2	1.000
1990		1	0	1.000	3.29	38	0	0	65.2	63	9	46	0	1	0	0	8	2	0	.250	4	9	0	1	0.3	1.000
1991		7	12	.368	4.18	36	20	0	133.1	142	25	87	0	2	1	1	33	6	0	.182	11	24	2	2	1.0	.946
1992		3	9	.250	3.62	44	11	0	97	99	33	70	0	2	4	0	22	4	0	.182	6	17	1	1	0.5	.958
1993	SD N	4	7	.364	3.83	21	19	0	105.2	109	30	57	0	0	0	0	24	2	0	.083	3	18	2	2	1.1	.913
1994		4	7	.364	4.92	13	13	0	64	84	26	43	0	0	0	0	19	2	0	.105	4	10	1	0	1.2	.933
1996	NY A	1	1	.500	6.75	2	2	0	8	11	2	1	0	0	0	0	0	0	0	—	1	1	0	0	1.0	1.000
7 yrs.		20	37	.351	4.02	163	66	0	487.2	525	130	313	0	5	5	3	107	16	0	.150	30	80	6	6	0.7	.948

Matt Whiteside — WHITESIDE, MATTHEW CHRISTOPHER
B. Aug. 8, 1967, Charleston, Mo. BR TR 6' 185 lbs.

Year	Team	W	L	PCT	ERA	G	GS	CG	IP	H	BB	SO	ShO	RP W	L	SV	AB	H	HR	BA	PO	A	E	DP	TC/G	FA
1992	TEX A	1	1	.500	1.93	20	0	0	28	26	11	13	0	1	1	4	0	0	0		3	2	1	0	0.3	.833
1993		2	1	.667	4.32	60	0	0	73	78	23	39	0	2	1	1	0	0	0	—	5	7	2	3	0.2	.857
1994		2	2	.500	5.02	47	0	0	61	68	28	37	0	2	2	1	0	0	0	—	4	6	1	0	0.2	.909
1995		5	4	.556	4.08	40	0	0	53	48	19	46	0	5	4	3	0	0	0	—	4	0	0	0	0.1	1.000
1996		0	1	.000	6.68	14	0	0	32.1	43	11	15	0	0	1	0	0	0	0	—	1	4	0	0	0.4	1.000
5 yrs.		10	9	.526	4.48	181	0	0	247.1	263	92	150	0	10	9	9	0	0	0		13	23	4	3	0.2	.900

Kevin Wickander — WICKANDER, KEVIN DEAN
B. Jan. 4, 1965, Fort Dodge, Iowa BL TL 6'2" 202 lbs.

Year	Team	W	L	PCT	ERA	G	GS	CG	IP	H	BB	SO	ShO	RP W	L	SV	AB	H	HR	BA	PO	A	E	DP	TC/G	FA
1989	CLE A	0	0	—	3.38	2	0	0	2.2	6	2	2	0	0	0	0	0	0	0		0	0	0	0	0.0	.000
1990		0	1	.000	3.65	10	0	0	12.1	14	4	10	0	0	1	0	0	0	0	—	0	1	0	0	0.1	1.000
1992		2	0	1.000	3.07	44	0	0	41	39	28	38	0	2	0	1	0	0	0	—	0	5	0	1	0.1	1.000
1993	2 teams	CLE A (11G 0-0)								CIN N (33G 1-0)																
"	total	1	0		6.09	44	0	0	34	47	22	23	0	1	0	0	0	0	0	.000	0	3	0	0	0.1	1.000
1995	2 teams	DET A (21G 0-0)								MIL A (8G 0-0)																
"	total	0	0	—	1.93	29	0	0	23.1	19	12	11	0	0	0	1	0	0	0	—	1	4	0	0	0.2	1.000
1996	MIL A	2	0	1.000	4.97	21	0	0	25.1	26	17	19	0	2	0	0	0	0	0	—	1	4	0	0	0.2	1.000
6 yrs.		5	1	.833	4.02	150	0	0	138.2	151	85	101	0	5	1	2	2	0	0	.000	2	17	0	1	0.1	1.000

Bob Wickman — WICKMAN, ROBERT JOE
B. Feb. 6, 1969, Green Bay, Wis. BR TR 6'1" 207 lbs.

Year	Team	W	L	PCT	ERA	G	GS	CG	IP	H	BB	SO	ShO	RP W	L	SV	AB	H	HR	BA	PO	A	E	DP	TC/G	FA
1992	NY A	6	1	.857	4.11	8	8	0	50.1	51	20	21	0	0	0	0	0	0	0	—	4	6	0	3	1.3	1.000
1993		14	4	.778	4.63	41	19	1	140	156	69	70	1	6	0	4	0	0	0	—	7	19	2	1	0.7	.929
1994		5	4	.556	3.09	53	0	0	70	54	27	56	0	5	4	6	0	0	0	—	3	7	0	0	0.2	1.000
1995		2	4	.333	4.05	63	1	0	80	77	33	51	0	2	3	1	0	0	0	—	4	14	1	1	0.3	.947
1996	2 teams	NY A (58G 4-1)								MIL A (12G 3-0)																
"	total	7	1	.875	4.42	70	0	0	95.2	106	44	75	0	7	1	0	0	0	0	—	6	24	0	3	0.4	1.000
5 yrs.		34	14	.708	4.17	235	28	1	436	444	193	273	1	20	8	11	0	0	0		24	70	3	8	0.4	.969

DIVISIONAL PLAYOFF SERIES

1995	NY A	0	0	—	0.00	3	0	0	3	5	0	3	0	0	0	0	0	0	0	—	0	1	0	0	0.3	1.000

Marc Wilkins — WILKINS, MARC ALLEN
B. Oct. 21, 1970, Mansfield, Ohio BR TR 5'11" 205 lbs.

Year	Team	W	L	PCT	ERA	G	GS	CG	IP	H	BB	SO	ShO	RP W	L	SV	AB	H	HR	BA	PO	A	E	DP	TC/G	FA
1996	PIT N	4	3	.571	3.84	47	2	0	75	75	36	62	0	3	3	1	9	2	0	.222	2	10	0	3	0.3	1.000

Brian Williams — WILLIAMS, BRIAN O'NEAL
B. Feb. 15, 1969, Lancaster, S.C. BR TR 6'3" 205 lbs.

Year	Team	W	L	PCT	ERA	G	GS	CG	IP	H	BB	SO	ShO	RP W	L	SV	AB	H	HR	BA	PO	A	E	DP	TC/G	FA
1991	HOU N	0	1	.000	3.75	2	2	0	12	11	4	4	0	0	0	0	3	0	0	.000	1	2	0	0	1.5	1.000
1992		7	6	.538	3.92	16	16	0	96.1	92	42	54	0	0	0	0	30	4	0	.133	8	15	2	0	1.6	.920

Year	Team	W	L	PCT	ERA	G	GS	CG	IP	H	BB	SO	ShO	Relief Pitching W	L	SV	Batting AB	H	HR	BA	PO	A	E	DP	TC/G	FA

Brian Williams *continued*

Year	Team	W	L	PCT	ERA	G	GS	CG	IP	H	BB	SO	ShO	W	L	SV	AB	H	HR	BA	PO	A	E	DP	TC/G	FA
1993		4	4	.500	4.83	42	5	0	82	76	38	56	0	1	3	3	10	2	0	.200	7	20	1	0	0.7	.964
1994		6	5	.545	5.74	20	13	0	78.1	112	41	49	0	1	0	0	23	6	0	.261	8	9	4	0	1.0	.810
1995	SD N	3	10	.231	6.00	44	6	0	72	79	38	75	0	1	8	0	14	1	0	.071	6	9	0	0	0.3	1.000
1996	DET A	3	10	.231	6.77	40	17	2	121	145	85	72	1	0	1	2	0	0	0	—	6	17	2	3	0.6	.920
6 yrs.		23	36	.390	5.46	164	59	2	461.2	515	248	310	1	3	12	5	80	13	0	.162	36	72	9	3	0.7	.923

Mike Williams

WILLIAMS, MICHAEL DARREN
B. July 29, 1968, Radford, Va.
BR TR 6'2" 190 lbs.

Year	Team	W	L	PCT	ERA	G	GS	CG	IP	H	BB	SO	ShO	W	L	SV	AB	H	HR	BA	PO	A	E	DP	TC/G	FA
1992	PHI N	1	1	.500	5.34	5	5	1	28.2	29	7	5	0	0	0	0	10	4	0	.400	0	5	0	0	1.0	1.000
1993		1	3	.250	5.29	17	4	0	51	50	22	33	0	1	2	0	12	1	0	.083	2	6	0	1	0.5	1.000
1994		2	4	.333	5.01	12	8	0	50.1	61	20	29	0	0	0	0	12	2	0	.167	3	7	0	3	0.8	1.000
1995		3	3	.500	3.29	33	8	0	87.2	78	29	57	0	1	1	0	16	2	0	.125	4	19	1	0	0.7	.958
1996		6	14	.300	5.44	32	29	0	167	188	67	103	0	0	0	0	51	8	0	.157	19	32	1	4	1.6	.981
5 yrs.		13	25	.342	4.87	99	54	1	384.2	406	145	227	0	2	3	0	101	17	0	.168	28	69	2	8	1.0	.980

Shad Williams

WILLIAMS, SHAD CLAYTON
B. Mar. 10, 1971, Fresno, Calif.
BR TR 6'0" 185 lbs.

Year	Team	W	L	PCT	ERA	G	GS	CG	IP	H	BB	SO	ShO	W	L	SV	AB	H	HR	BA	PO	A	E	DP	TC/G	FA
1996	CAL A	01	2	.000	8.89	13	2	0	28.1	42	21	26	0	0	0	0	0	0	0	—	1	0	0	0	0.1	1.000

Woody Williams

WILLIAMS, GREGORY SCOTT
B. Aug. 19, 1966, Houston, Tex.
BR TR 6' 180 lbs.

Year	Team	W	L	PCT	ERA	G	GS	CG	IP	H	BB	SO	ShO	W	L	SV	AB	H	HR	BA	PO	A	E	DP	TC/G	FA
1993	TOR A	3	1	.750	4.38	30	0	0	37	40	22	24	0	3	1	0	0	0	0	—	5	6	0	1	0.4	1.000
1994		1	3	.250	3.64	38	0	0	59.1	44	33	56	0	1	3	0	0	0	0	—	2	6	1	2	0.2	.889
1995		1	2	.333	3.69	23	3	0	53.2	44	28	41	0	0	2	0	0	0	0	—	6	6	0	0	0.5	1.000
1996		4	5	.444	4.73	12	10	1	59	64	21	43	0	0	0	0	0	0	0	—	7	4	0	2	0.9	1.000
4 yrs.		9	11	.450	4.09	103	13	1	209	192	104	164	0	4	6	0	0	0	0		20	22	1	5	0.4	.977

Paul Wilson

WILSON, PAUL ANTHONY
B. Mar. 28, 1973, Orlando, Fla.
BR TR 6'5" 235 lbs.

Year	Team	W	L	PCT	ERA	G	GS	CG	IP	H	BB	SO	ShO	W	L	SV	AB	H	HR	BA	PO	A	E	DP	TC/G	FA
1996	NY N	5	12	.294	5.38	26	26	1	149	157	71	109	0	0	0	0	50	4	1	.080	11	11	2	2	0.9	.917

Jay Witasick

WITASICK, GERALD ALFONSE
B. Aug. 28, 1972, Baltimore, Md.
BR TR 6'4" 205 lbs.

Year	Team	W	L	PCT	ERA	G	GS	CG	IP	H	BB	SO	ShO	W	L	SV	AB	H	HR	BA	PO	A	E	DP	TC/G	FA
1996	OAK A	1	1	.500	6.23	12	0	0	13	12	5	12	0	1	1	0	0	0	0	—	0	0	0	0	0.0	—

Bobby Witt

WITT, ROBERT ANDREW
B. May 11, 1964, Arlington, Va.
BR TR 6'2" 190 lbs.

Year	Team	W	L	PCT	ERA	G	GS	CG	IP	H	BB	SO	ShO	W	L	SV	AB	H	HR	BA	PO	A	E	DP	TC/G	FA
1986	TEX A	11	9	.550	5.48	31	31	0	157.2	130	143	174	0	0	0	0	0	0	0	—	8	20	3	1	1.0	.903
1987		8	10	.444	4.91	26	25	1	143	114	140	160	0	0	0	0	1	0	0	.000	8	17	0	1	1.0	1.000
1988		8	10	.444	3.92	22	22	13	174.1	134	101	148	2	0	0	0	0	0	0	—	15	15	4	2	1.5	.882
1989		12	13	.480	5.14	31	31	5	194.1	182	114	166	1	0	0	0	0	0	0	—	13	22	1	1	1.2	.972
1990		17	10	.630	3.36	33	32	7	222	197	110	221	1	0	0	0	0	0	0	—	18	18	5	2	1.2	.878
1991		3	7	.300	6.09	17	16	1	88.2	84	74	82	1	0	0	0	0	0	0	—	7	6	2	1	0.9	.867
1992 2 teams	TEX A (25G 9-13)	OAK A	(6G 1-1)																							
total		10	14	.417	4.29	31	31	0	193	183	114	125	0	0	0	0	0	0	0	—	14	20	1	2	1.1	.971
1993	OAK A	14	13	.519	4.21	35	33	5	220	226	91	131	1	0	0	0	0	0	0	—	12	39	3	5	1.5	.944
1994		8	10	.444	5.04	24	24	5	135.2	151	70	111	3	0	0	0	0	0	0	—	7	13	4	2	1.0	.833
1995 2 teams	FLA N (19G 2-7)	TEX A	(10G 3-4)																							
total		5	11	.313	4.13	29	29	2	172	185	68	141	0	0	0	0	32	2	0	.063	8	20	0	0	1.0	1.000
1996	TEX A	16	12	.571	5.41	33	32	2	199.2	235	96	157	0	1	0	0	0	0	0	—	10	28	1	3	1.2	.974
11 yrs.		112	119	.485	4.61	312	306	41	1900.1	1821	1121	1616	9	1	0	0	33	2	0	.061	120	218	24	20	1.2	.934

DIVISIONAL PLAYOFF SERIES

Year	Team	W	L	PCT	ERA	G	GS	CG	IP	H	BB	SO	ShO	W	L	SV	AB	H	HR	BA	PO	A	E	DP	TC/G	FA
1996	TEX A	0	0	—	8.10	1	1	0	3.1	4	2	3	0	0	0	0	0	0	0	—	0	0	0	0	0.0	.000

LEAGUE CHAMPIONSHIP SERIES

Year	Team	W	L	PCT	ERA	G	GS	CG	IP	H	BB	SO	ShO	W	L	SV	AB	H	HR	BA	PO	A	E	DP	TC/G	FA
1992	OAK A	0	0	—	18.00	1	0	0	1	2	1	1	0	0	0	0	0	0	0	—	0	0	0	0	0.0	.000

Mark Wohlers

WOHLERS, MARK EDWARD
B. Jan. 23, 1970, Holyoke, Mass.
BR TR 6'4" 207 lbs.

Year	Team	W	L	PCT	ERA	G	GS	CG	IP	H	BB	SO	ShO	W	L	SV	AB	H	HR	BA	PO	A	E	DP	TC/G	FA
1991	ATL N	3	1	.750	3.20	17	0	0	19.2	17	13	13	0	3	1	2	1	0	0	.000	0	3	0	1	0.2	1.000
1992		1	2	.333	2.55	32	0	0	35.1	28	14	17	0	1	2	4	2	0	0	.000	2	7	0	0	0.3	1.000
1993		6	2	.750	4.50	46	0	0	48	37	22	45	0	6	2	0	0	0	0	—	6	6	0	1	0.3	1.000
1994		7	2	.778	4.59	51	0	0	51	51	33	58	0	7	2	1	1	1	0	1.000	3	7	1	0	0.2	.909
1995		7	3	.700	2.09	65	0	0	64.2	51	24	90	0	7	3	25	3	0	0	.000	4	3	0	0	0.1	1.000
1996		2	4	.333	3.03	77	0	0	77.1	71	21	100	0	2	4	39	3	0	0	.000	4	3	3	0	0.1	.700
6 yrs.		26	14	.650	3.28	288	0	0	296	255	127	323	0	26	14	71	10	1	0	.100	19	29	4	2	0.2	.923

DIVISIONAL PLAYOFF SERIES

Year	Team	W	L	PCT	ERA	G	GS	CG	IP	H	BB	SO	ShO	W	L	SV	AB	H	HR	BA	PO	A	E	DP	TC/G	FA
1995	ATL N	0	1	.000	6.75	3	0	0	2.2	6	1	4	0	0	1	2	0	0	0	—	0	0	0	0	0.0	.000
1996		0	0	—	0.00	3	0	0	3.1	1	1	4	0	0	0	3	0	0	0	—	0	0	0	0	0.0	.000
2 yrs.		0	1	.000	3.00	6	0	0	6	7	2	8	0	0	1	5	0	0	0		0	0	0	0	0.0	

Year	Team	W	L	PCT	ERA	G	GS	CG	IP	H	BB	SO	ShO	Relief Pitching W	L	SV	Batting AB	H	HR	BA	PO	A	E	DP	TC/G	FA

Mark Wohlers *continued*

LEAGUE CHAMPIONSHIP SERIES

Year	Team	W	L	PCT	ERA	G	GS	CG	IP	H	BB	SO	ShO	W	L	SV	AB	H	HR	BA	PO	A	E	DP	TC/G	FA
1991	ATL N	0	0	—	0.00	3	0	0	1.2	3	1	1	0	0	0	0	0	0	0	—	0	0	0	0	0.0	.000
1992		0	0	—	0.00	3	0	0	3	2	1	2	0	0	0	0	0	0	0	—	1	0	0	0	0.3	1.000
1993		0	1	.000	3.38	4	0	0	5.1	2	3	10	0	0	1	0	0	0	0	—	0	0	0	0	0.0	.000
1995		1	0	1.000	1.80	4	0	0	5	2	0	8	0	1	0	0	0	0	0	—	1	0	0	0	0.3	1.000
1996		0	0	—	0.00	3	0	0	3	0	0	4	0	0	0	2	1	0	0	.000	0	0	0	0	0.0	.000
5 yrs.		1	1	.500	1.50	17 3rd	0	0	18	9	5	25	0	1	1	2	1	0	0	.000	2	0	0	0	0.1	1.000

WORLD SERIES

Year	Team	W	L	PCT	ERA	G	GS	CG	IP	H	BB	SO	ShO	W	L	SV	AB	H	HR	BA	PO	A	E	DP	TC/G	FA
1991	ATL N	0	0	—	0.00	3	0	0	1.2	2	2	1	0	0	0	0	0	0	0	—	0	0	0	0	0.0	.000
1992		0	0	—	0.00	2	0	0	0.2	0	1	0	0	0	0	0	0	0	0	—	0	0	0	0	0.0	.000
1995		0	0	—	1.80	4	0	0	5	4	3	3	0	0	0	2	0	0	0	—	0	0	0	0	0.0	.000
1996		0	0	—	6.23	4	0	0	4.1	7	2	4	0	0	0	0	0	0	0	—	0	1	0	0	0.3	1.000
4 yrs.		0	0		3.09	13 6th	0	0	11.2	13	8	8	0	0	0	2	0	0	0		0	1	0	0	0.1	1.000

Steve Wojciechowski

WOJCIECHOWSKI, STEVEN JOSEPH
B. July 29, 1970, Blue Island, Ill.

BL TL 6'2" 185 lbs.

Year	Team	W	L	PCT	ERA	G	GS	CG	IP	H	BB	SO	ShO	W	L	SV	AB	H	HR	BA	PO	A	E	DP	TC/G	FA
1995	OAK A	2	3	.400	5.18	14	7	0	48.2	51	28	13	0	0	0	0	0	0	0	—	1	8	0	0	0.6	1.000
1996		5	5	.500	5.65	16	15	0	79.2	97	28	30	0	0	0	0	0	0	0	—	1	10	0	0	0.6	1.000
2 yrs.		7	8	.467	5.47	30	22	0	128.1	148	56	43	0	0	0	0	0	0	0		2	18	0	0	0.6	1.000

Bob Wolcott

WOLCOTT, ROBERT WILLIAM
B. Sept. 8, 1973, Huntington Beach, Calif.

BR TR 6' 190 lbs.

Year	Team	W	L	PCT	ERA	G	GS	CG	IP	H	BB	SO	ShO	W	L	SV	AB	H	HR	BA	PO	A	E	DP	TC/G	FA
1995	SEA A	3	2	.600	4.42	7	6	0	36.2	43	14	19	0	0	0	0	0	0	0	—	4	0	0	0	0.6	1.000
1996		7	10	.412	5.73	30	28	1	149.1	179	54	78	0	0	0	0	0	0	0	—	10	19	0	3	1.0	1.000
2 yrs.		10	12	.455	5.47	37	34	1	186	222	68	97	0	0	0	0					14	19	0	3	0.9	1.000

LEAGUE CHAMPIONSHIP SERIES

Year	Team	W	L	PCT	ERA	G	GS	CG	IP	H	BB	SO	ShO	W	L	SV	AB	H	HR	BA	PO	A	E	DP	TC/G	FA
1995	SEA A	1	0	1.000	2.57	1	1	0	7	8	5	2	0	0	0	0	0	0	0	—	1	1	0	0	2.0	1.000

Brad Woodall

WOODALL, DAVID BRADLEY
B. June 25, 1969, Atlanta, Ga.

BB TL 6' 175 lbs.

Year	Team	W	L	PCT	ERA	G	GS	CG	IP	H	BB	SO	ShO	W	L	SV	AB	H	HR	BA	PO	A	E	DP	TC/G	FA
1994	ATL N	0	1	.000	4.50	1	1	0	6	5	2	2	0	0	0	0	2	1	0	.500	0	3	0	1	3.0	1.000
1995		1	1	.500	6.10	9	0	0	10.1	13	8	5	0	1	1	0	1	1	0	1.000	0	2	0	1	0.2	1.000
1996		2	2	.500	7.32	8	3	0	19.2	28	4	20	0	2	0	0	5	1	0	.200	0	2	0	0	0.3	1.000
3 yrs.		3	4	.429	6.50	18	4	0	36	46	14	27	0	3	1	0	8	3	0	.375	0	7	0	2	0.4	1.000

Tim Worrell

WORRELL, TIMOTHY HOWARD
Brother of Todd Worrell.
B. July 5, 1967, Pasadena, Calif.

BR TR 6'4" 210 lbs.

Year	Team	W	L	PCT	ERA	G	GS	CG	IP	H	BB	SO	ShO	W	L	SV	AB	H	HR	BA	PO	A	E	DP	TC/G	FA
1993	SD N	2	7	.222	4.92	21	16	0	100.2	104	43	52	0	0	0	0	31	1	0	.032	6	11	1	0	0.9	.944
1994		0	1	.000	3.68	3	3	0	14.2	9	5	14	0	0	0	0	2	1	0	.500	4	2	0	0	2.0	1.000
1995		1	0	1.000	4.72	9	0	0	13.1	16	6	13	0	1	0	0	1	0	0	.000	0	2	0	0	0.2	1.000
1996		9	7	.563	3.05	50	11	0	121	109	39	99	0	6	1	1	20	3	0	.150	8	9	2	0	0.4	.895
4 yrs.		12	15	.444	3.93	83	30	0	249.2	238	93	178	0	7	1	1	54	5	0	.093	18	24	3	0	0.5	.933

DIVISIONAL PLAYOFF SERIES

Year	Team	W	L	PCT	ERA	G	GS	CG	IP	H	BB	SO	ShO	W	L	SV	AB	H	HR	BA	PO	A	E	DP	TC/G	FA
1996	SD N	0	0	—	2.45	2	0	0	3.2	4	1	2	0	0	0	0	0	0	0	—	0	1	0	0	0.5	1.000

Todd Worrell

WORRELL, SCOTT ROLAND
Brother of Tim Worrell.
B. Sept. 28, 1959, Arcadia, Calif.

BR TR 6'5" 215 lbs.

Year	Team	W	L	PCT	ERA	G	GS	CG	IP	H	BB	SO	ShO	W	L	SV	AB	H	HR	BA	PO	A	E	DP	TC/G	FA
1985	STL N	3	0	1.000	2.91	17	0	0	21.2	17	7	17	0	3	0	5	1	0	0	.000	3	0	0	0	0.2	1.000
1986		9	10	.474	2.08	74	0	0	103.2	86	41	73	0	9	10	36	7	1	0	.143	5	8	2	0	0.2	.867
1987		8	6	.571	2.66	75	0	0	94.2	86	34	92	0	8	6	33	10	1	0	.100	0	17	0	0	0.2	1.000
1988		5	9	.357	3.00	68	0	0	90	69	34	78	0	5	9	32	6	0	0	.000	3	10	0	4	0.2	1.000
1989		3	5	.375	2.96	47	0	0	51.2	42	26	41	0	3	5	20	1	0	0	.000	0	11	0	1	0.2	1.000
1992	LA N	5	3	.625	2.11	67	0	0	64	45	25	64	0	5	3	3	0	0	0	—	2	2	0	0	0.1	1.000
1993		1	1	.500	6.05	35	0	0	38.2	46	11	31	0	1	1	5	0	0	0	—	1	4	0	0	0.1	1.000
1994		6	5	.545	4.29	38	0	0	42	37	12	44	0	6	5	11	0	0	0	—	3	3	0	0	0.2	1.000
1995		4	1	.800	2.02	59	0	0	62.1	50	19	61	0	4	1	32	2	0	0	.000	6	11	0	2	0.3	1.000
1996		4	6	.400	3.03	72	0	0	65.1	70	15	66	0	4	6	44	0	0	0	—	3	6	1	0	0.1	.900
10 yrs.		48	46	.511	2.88	552	0	0	634	548	224	567	0	48	46	221	27	2	0	.074	26	72	3	7	0.2	.970

DIVISIONAL PLAYOFF SERIES

Year	Team	W	L	PCT	ERA	G	GS	CG	IP	H	BB	SO	ShO	W	L	SV	AB	H	HR	BA	PO	A	E	DP	TC/G	FA
1996	LA N	0	0	—	0.00	1	0	0	1	0	1	1	0	0	0	0	0	0	0	—	0	0	0	0	0.0	.000

LEAGUE CHAMPIONSHIP SERIES

Year	Team	W	L	PCT	ERA	G	GS	CG	IP	H	BB	SO	ShO	W	L	SV	AB	H	HR	BA	PO	A	E	DP	TC/G	FA
1985	STL N	1	0	1.000	1.42	4	0	0	6.1	4	2	3	0	1	0	0	0	0	0	—	0	1	0	0	0.3	1.000
1987		0	0	—	2.08	3	0	0	4.1	4	1	6	0	0	0	1	1	0	0	.000	0	0	0	0	0.0	
2 yrs.		1	0	1.000	1.69	7	0	0	10.2	8	3	9	0	1	0	1	1	0	0	.000	0	1	0	0	0.1	1.000

WORLD SERIES

Year	Team	W	L	PCT	ERA	G	GS	CG	IP	H	BB	SO	ShO	W	L	SV	AB	H	HR	BA	PO	A	E	DP	TC/G	FA
1985	STL N	0	1	.000	3.86	3	0	0	4.2	4	2	6	0	0	1	1	1	0	0	.000	0	1	0	0	0.3	1.000
1987		0	0	—	1.29	4	0	0	7	6	4	3	0	0	0	2	0	0	0	—	0	0	0	0	0.0	.000
2 yrs.		0	1	.000	2.31	7	0	0	11.2	10	6	9	0	0	1	3 5th	1	0	0	.000	0	1	0	0	0.1	1.000

Year	Team	W	L	PCT	ERA	G	GS	CG	IP	H	BB	SO	ShO	Relief Pitching W	L	SV	Batting AB	H	HR	BA	PO	A	E	DP	TC/G	FA

Jamey Wright

WRIGHT, JAMEY ALAN
B. Dec. 24, 1974, Oklahoma City, Okla.

BR TR 6'6" 205 lbs.

| 1996 | CLR N | 4 | 4 | .500. | 4.93 | 16 | 15 | 0 | 91.1 | 105 | 41 | 45 | 0 | 0 | 0 | 0 | 26 | 2 | 0 | .077 | 9 | 20 | 2 | 1 | 1.9 | .935 |

Esteban Yan

ESTEBAN LUIS YAN
B. June 22, 1974, Campina Del Seibo, Dominican Republic

BR TR 6'4" 230 lbs.

| 1996 | BAL A | 0 | 0 | — | 5.79 | 4 | 0 | 0 | 9.1 | 13 | 3 | 7 | 0 | 3 | 3 | 0 | 0 | 0 | 0 | — | 0 | 0 | 0 | 0 | 0.0 | — |

Anthony Young

YOUNG, ANTHONY WAYNE
B. Jan. 19, 1966, Houston, Tex.

BR TR 6'2" 200 lbs.

1991	NY N	2	5	.286	3.10	10	8	0	49.1	48	12	20	0	0	0	0	14	2	0	.143	4	4	1	0	0.9	.889
1992		2	14	.125	4.17	52	13	1	121	134	31	64	0	1	7	15	27	3	0	.111	13	15	2	1	0.6	.933
1993		1	16	.059	3.77	39	10	1	100.1	103	42	62	0	1	8	3	14	2	0	.143	9	14	3	1	0.7	.885
1994	CHI N	4	6	.400	3.92	20	19	0	114.2	103	46	65	0	0	0	0	34	6	0	.176	13	18	1	1	1.6	.969
1995		3	4	.429	3.70	32	1	0	41.1	47	14	15	0	3	3	2	3	2	0	.667	5	3	2	1	0.3	.800
1996	HOU N	3	3	.500	4.59	28	0	0	33.1	36	22	19	0	3	3	0	2	0	0	.000	1	5	0	1	0.2	1.000
6 yrs.		15	48	.238	3.89	181	51	2	460	471	167	245	0	8	21	20	94	15	0	.160	45	59	9	5	0.6	.920

Manager Register

The Manager Register is an alphabetical listing of every man who managed in the major leagues in 1996. Most of the information is self-explanatory. Column headings include G for games managed, W for wins, L for losses, T for ties, N for no-decision games, PCT for winning percentage, and Standing.

The figures in the Standing column show where the team stood at the end of the season and when there was a managerial change. There are only four possible cases:

Only Manager for the Team That Year. Indicated by a single boldfaced figure that appears in the extreme left-hand column and shows the final standing of the team.

Manager Started Season, but Did Not Finish. Indicated by two figures: the first is boldfaced and shows the standing of the team when this manager left; the second shows the final standing of the team. (See Tony La Russa, Chicago, 1986.)

Manager Finished Season, but Did Not Start. Indicated by two figures: the first shows the standing of the team when this manager started; the second is boldfaced and shows the final standing of the team. (See Tony La Russa, Oakland, 1986.)

Manager Did Not Start or Finish Season. Indicated by three figures: the first shows the standing of the team when this manager started; the second is boldfaced and shows the standing of the team when this manager left; the third shows the final standing of the team.

The managers' records for the 1981 split season are given separately for each half. "(1st)" or "(2nd)" appears to the right of the standings to indicate which half.

	G	W	L	T	N	PCT	Standing		

Felipe Alou

ALOU, FELIPE
Born Felipe Rojas (Alou).
Brother of Jesus Alou.
Brother of Matty Alou.
Father of Moises Alou.
B. May 12, 1935, Haina, Dominican Republic.

		G	W	L	T	N	PCT	Standing	
1992	MON N	125	70	55	0	0	.560	4	2
1993		163	94	68	1	0	.580	2	
1994		114	74	40	0	0	.649	1	
1995		144	66	78	0	0	.458	5	
1996		162	88	74	0	0	.543	2	
5 yrs.		708	392	315	1	0	.554		

Dusty Baker

BAKER, JOHNNIE B., JR.
B. June 15, 1949, Riverside, Calif.

		G	W	L	T	N	PCT	Standing
1993	SF N	162	103	59	0	0	.636	2
1994		115	55	60	0	0	.478	2
1995		144	67	77	0	0	.465	4
1996		162	68	94	0	0	.420	4
4 yrs.		583	293	290	0	0	.503	

Don Baylor

BAYLOR, DON EDWARD
B. June 28, 1949, Austin, Tex.

		G	W	L	T	N	PCT	Standing
1993	CLR N	162	67	95	0	0	.414	6
1994		117	53	64	0	0	.453	3
1995		144	77	67	0	0	.535	2
1996		162	83	79	0	0	.512	3
4 yrs.		585	280	305	0	0	.479	

DIVISIONAL PLAYOFF SERIES

		G	W	L	T	N	PCT
1995	CLR N	4	1	3	0	0	.250

Buddy Bell

BELL, DAVID GUS
Father of David Bell.
Son of Gus Bell.
B. Aug 27, 1951, Pittsburgh, Pa.

		G	W	L	T	N	PCT	Standing
1996	DET A	162	53	109	0	0	.327	5

Terry Bevington

BEVINGTON, TERRY PAUL
B. July 7, 1956, Akron, Ohio

		G	W	L	T	N	PCT	Standing	
1995	CHI A	113	57	56	0	0	.504	4	3
1996		162	85	77	0	0	.525	2	
2 yrs.		275	142	133	0	0	.516		

Bruce Bochy

BOCHY, BRUCE DOUGLAS
B. Apr. 16, 1955, Landes De Bussac, France

		G	W	L	T	N	PCT	Standing
1995	SD N	144	70	74	0	0	.486	3
1996		162	91	71	0	0	.562	1
2 yrs.		306	161	145	0	0	.526	

John Boles

BOLES, JOHN
B. Aug 19, 1948, Chicago, Ill.

		G	W	L	T	N	PCT	Standing	
1996	FLA N	75	40	35	0	0	.533	3	3

Bob Boone

BOONE, ROBERT RAYMOND
Son of Ray Boone.
Father of Bret Boone.
B. Nov. 19, 1947, San Diego, Calif.

		G	W	L	T	N	PCT	Standing
1995	KC A	144	70	74	0	0	.486	2
1996		161	75	86	0	0	.466	5
2 yrs.		305	145	160	0	0	.475	

Terry Collins

COLLINS, TERRY LEE
B. May 27, 1949, Midland, Mich.

		G	W	L	T	N	PCT	Standing
1994	HOU N	115	66	49	0	0	.574	2
1995		144	76	68	0	0	.528	2

Terry Collins *continued*

		G	W	L	T	N	PCT	Standing
1996		162	82	80	0	0	.506	2
3 yrs.		421	224	197	0	0	.532	

Bobby Cox

COX, ROBERT JOE
B. May 21, 1941, Tulsa, Okla.

		G	W	L	T	N	PCT	Standing		
1978	ATL N	162	69	93	0	0	.426	6		
1979		160	66	94	0	0	.412	6		
1980		161	81	80	0	0	.503	4		
1981		55	25	29	1	0	.463	4		(1st)
1981		52	25	27	0	0	.481	5		(2nd)
1982	TOR A	162	78	84	0	0	.481	6		
1983		162	89	73	0	0	.549	4		
1984		163	89	73	1	0	.549	2		
1985		161	99	62	0	0	.615	1		
1990	ATL N	97	40	57	0	0	.412	6	6	
1991		162	94	68	0	0	.580	1		
1992		162	98	64	0	0	.605	1		
1993		162	104	58	0	0	.642	1		
1994		114	68	46	0	0	.596	2		
1995		144	90	54	0	0	.625	1		
1996		162	96	66	0	0	.593	1		
15 yrs.		2241	1211	1028	2	0	.540			

DIVISIONAL PLAYOFF SERIES

		G	W	L	T	N	PCT
1995	ATL N	4	3	1	0	0	.750
1996		3	3	0	0	0	1.000
2 yrs.		7	6	1	0	0	.857

LEAGUE CHAMPIONSHIP SERIES

		G	W	L	T	N	PCT
1985	TOR A	7	3	4	0	0	.429
1991	ATL N	7	4	3	0	0	.571
1992		7	4	3	0	0	.571
1993		6	2	4	0	0	.333
1995		4	4	0	0	0	1.000
1996		7	4	3	0	0	.571
6 yrs.		38	21	17	0	0	.553
		1st	**2nd**	**1st**			**5th**

WORLD SERIES

		G	W	L	T	N	PCT
1991	ATL N	7	3	4	0	0	.429
1992		6	2	4	0	0	.333
1995		6	4	2	0	0	.667
1996		6	2	4	0	0	.333
4 yrs.		25	11	14	0	0	.440

Jim Fregosi

FREGOSI, JAMES LOUIS
B. Apr. 4, 1942, San Francisco, Calif.

		G	W	L	T	N	PCT	Standing		
1978	CAL A	117	62	55	0	0	.530	3	2	
1979		162	88	74	0	0	.543	1		
1980		160	65	95	0	0	.406	6		
1981		48	22	25	0	1	.468	4	4	(1st)
1986	CHI A	96	45	51	0	0	.469	5	5	
1987		162	77	85	0	0	.475	5		
1988		161	71	90	0	0	.441	5		
1991	PHI N	149	74	75	0	0	.497	6	3	
1992		162	70	92	0	0	.432	6		
1993		162	97	65	0	0	.599	1		
1994		115	54	61	0	0	.470	4		
1995		144	69	75	0	0	.479	2		
1996		162	67	95	0	0	.414	5		
13 yrs.		1800	861	938	0	1	.478			

LEAGUE CHAMPIONSHIP SERIES

		G	W	L	T	N	PCT
1979	CAL A	4	1	3	0	0	.250
1993	PHI N	6	4	2	0	0	.667
2 yrs.		10	5	5	0	0	.500

WORLD SERIES

		G	W	L	T	N	PCT
1993	PHI N	6	2	4	0	0	.333

Phil Garner

GARNER, PHILIP MASON (Scrap Iron)
B. Apr. 30, 1949, Jefferson City, Tenn.

		G	W	L	T	N	PCT	Standing
1992	MIL A	162	92	70	0	0	.568	2
1993		162	69	93	0	0	.426	7
1994		115	53	62	0	0	.461	5
1995		144	65	79	0	0	.451	4

Phil Garner *continued*

		G	W	L	T	N	PCT	Standing
1996		162	80	82	0	0	.494	3
5 yrs.		745	359	386	0	0	.482	

Cito Gaston

GASTON, CLARENCE EDWIN
B. Mar. 17, 1944, San Antonio, Tex.

		G	W	L	T	N	PCT	Standing	
1989	TOR A	126	77	49	0	0	.611	6	1
1990		162	86	76	0	0	.531	2	
1991		120	66	54	0	0	.550	1	1
1991		9	6	3	0	0	.667	1	1
1992		162	96	66	0	0	.593	1	
1993		162	95	67	0	0	.586	1	
1994		115	55	60	0	0	.478	3	
1995		144	56	88	0	0	.389	5	
1996		162	74	88	0	0	.457	4	
8 yrs.		1162	611	551	0	0	.526		

LEAGUE CHAMPIONSHIP SERIES

		G	W	L	T	N	PCT
1989	TOR A	5	1	4	0	0	.200
1991		5	1	4	0	0	.200
1992		6	4	2	0	0	.667
1993		6	4	2	0	0	.667
4 yrs.		22	10	12	0	0	.455
		6th	**7th**	**5th**			**10th**

WORLD SERIES

		G	W	L	T	N	PCT
1992	TOR A	6	4	2	0	0	.667
1993		6	4	2	0	0	.667
2 yrs.		12	8	4	0	0	.667

Dallas Green

GREEN, GEORGE DALLAS
B. Aug. 4, 1934, Newport, Del.

		G	W	L	T	N	PCT	Standing		
1979	PHI N	30	19	11	0	0	.633	5	4	
1980		162	91	71	0	0	.562	1		
1981		56	34	21	1	0	.618	1		(1st)
1981		53	25	27	1	0	.481	3		(2nd)
1989	NY A	121	56	65	0	0	.463	6	5	
1993	NY N	124	46	78	0	0	.371	7	7	
1994		113	55	58	0	0	.487	3		
1995		144	69	75	0	0	.479	2		
1996		131	59	72	0	0	.450	4	4	
8 yrs.		934	454	478	2	0	.486			

DIVISIONAL PLAYOFF SERIES

		G	W	L	T	N	PCT
1981	**PHI N**	**5**	**2**	**3**	**0**	**0**	**.400**

LEAGUE CHAMPIONSHIP SERIES

		G	W	L	T	N	PCT
1980	PHI N	5	3	2	0	0	.600

WORLD SERIES

		G	W	L	T	N	PCT
1980	PHI N	6	4	2	0	0	.667

Mike Hargrove

HARGROVE, DUDLEY MICHAEL
(The Human Rain Delay)
B. Oct. 26, 1949, Perryton, Tex.

		G	W	L	T	N	PCT	Standing	
1991	CLE A	85	32	53	0	0	.376	7	7
1992		162	76	86	0	0	.469	4	
1993		162	76	86	0	0	.469	6	
1994		113	66	47	0	0	.584	2	
1995		144	100	44	0	0	.694	1	
1996		161	99	62	0	0	.615	1	
6 yrs.		827	449	378	0	0	.543		

DIVISIONAL PLAYOFF SERIES

		G	W	L	T	N	PCT
1995	CLE A	3	3	0	0	0	1.000

LEAGUE CHAMPIONSHIP SERIES

		G	W	L	T	N	PCT
1995	CLE A	6	4	2	0	0	.667

WORLD SERIES

		G	W	L	T	N	PCT
1995	CLE A	6	2	4	0	0	.333

Art Howe

HOWE, ARTHUR HENRY, JR.
B. Dec. 15, 1946, Pittsburgh, Pa.

		G	W	L	T	N	PCT	Standing
1989	HOU N	162	86	76	0	0	.531	3
1990		162	75	87	0	0	.463	4
1991		162	65	97	0	0	.401	6
1992		162	81	81	0	0	.500	4
1993		162	85	77	0	0	.525	3

Art Howe continued

Year	Tm	Lg	G	W	L	T	N	PCT	Standing
1996	OAK	A	162	78	84	0	0	.481	3
6 yrs.			972	470	502	0	0	.484	

Davey Johnson

JOHNSON, DAVID ALLEN
B. Jan. 30, 1943, Orlando, Fla.

Year	Tm	Lg	G	W	L	T	N	PCT	Standing
1984	NY	N	162	90	72	0	0	.556	2
1985			162	98	64	0	0	.605	2
1986			162	108	54	0	0	.667	1
1987			162	92	70	0	0	.568	2
1988			160	100	60	0	0	.625	1
1989			162	87	75	0	0	.537	2
1990			42	20	22	0	0	.476	2
1993	CIN	N	118	53	65	0	0	.449	5 5
1994			115	66	48	1	0	.579	1
1995			144	85	59	0	0	.590	1
1996	BAL	A	162	88	74	0	0	.543	2
11 yrs.			1551	887	663	1	0	.572	

DIVISIONAL PLAYOFF SERIES

Year	Tm	Lg	G	W	L	T	N	PCT	Standing
1995	CIN	N	3	3	0	0	0	1.000	
1996	BAL	A	4	3	1	0	0	.750	
2 yrs.			7	6	1	0	0	.857	

LEAGUE CHAMPIONSHIP SERIES

Year	Tm	Lg	G	W	L	T	N	PCT	Standing
1986	NY	N	6	4	2	0	0	.667	
1988			7	3	4	0	0	.429	
1995	CIN	N	4	0	4	0	0	.000	
1996	BAL	A	5	1	4	0	0	.200	
4 yrs.			22	8	14	0	0	.364	
									7th

WORLD SERIES

Year	Tm	Lg	G	W	L	T	N	PCT	Standing
1986	NY	N	7	4	3	0	0	.571	

Tom Kelly

KELLY, JAY THOMAS
B. Aug. 15, 1950, Graceville, Minn.

Year	Tm	Lg	G	W	L	T	N	PCT	Standing
1986	MIN	A	23	12	11	0	0	.522	7 6
1987			162	85	77	0	0	.525	1
1988			162	91	71	0	0	.562	2
1989			162	80	82	0	0	.494	5
1990			162	74	88	0	0	.457	7
1991			162	95	67	0	0	.586	1
1992			162	90	72	0	0	.556	2
1993			162	71	91	0	0	.438	5
1994			113	53	60	0	0	.469	4
1995			144	56	88	0	0	.389	5
1996			162	78	84	0	0	.481	4
11 yrs.			1576	785	791	0	0	.498	

LEAGUE CHAMPIONSHIP SERIES

Year	Tm	Lg	G	W	L	T	N	PCT	Standing
1987	MIN	A	5	4	1	0	0	.800	
1991			5	4	1	0	0	.800	
2 yrs.			10	8	2	0	0	.800	
									9th

WORLD SERIES

Year	Tm	Lg	G	W	L	T	N	PCT	Standing
1987	MIN	A	7	4	3	0	0	.571	
1991			7	4	3	0	0	.571	
2 yrs.			14	8	6	0	0	.571	

Kevin Kennedy

KENNEDY, KEVIN CURTIS
B. May 26, 1954, Los Angeles, Calif.

Year	Tm	Lg	G	W	L	T	N	PCT	Standing
1993	TEX	A	162	86	76	0	0	.531	2
1994			114	52	62	0	0	.456	1
1995	BOS	A	144	86	58	0	0	.597	1
1996			162	85	77	0	0	.525	3
4 yrs.			582	309	273	0	0	.531	

DIVISIONAL PLAYOFF SERIES

Year	Tm	Lg	G	W	L	T	N	PCT	Standing
1995	BOS	A	3	0	3	0	0	.000	

Ray Knight

KNIGHT, CHARLES RAY
B. Dec. 28, 1952, Albany, Ga.

Year	Tm	Lg	G	W	L	T	N	PCT	Standing
1996	CIN	N	162	81	81	0	0	.500	3

Marcel Lachemann

LACHEMANN, MARCEL ERNEST
Brother of Rene Lachemann.
B. June 13, 1941, Los Angeles, Calif.

Year	Tm	Lg	G	W	L	T	N	PCT	Standing
1994	CAL	A	74	30	44	0	0	.405	2 4
1995			145	78	67	0	0	.538	2
1996			111	52	59	0	0	.468	4 4
3 yrs.			330	160	170	0	0	.485	

Rene Lachemann

LACHEMANN, RENE GEORGE
Brother of Marcel Lachemann.
B. May 4, 1945, Los Angeles, Calif.

Year	Tm	Lg	G	W	L	T	N	PCT	Standing	
1981	SEA	A	33	15	18	0	0	.455	7 6	(1st)
1981			52	23	29	0	0	.442	5	(2nd)
1982			162	76	86	0	0	.469	4	
1983			73	26	47	0	0	.356	7 7	
1984	MIL	A	161	67	94	0	0	.416	7	
1993	FLA	N	162	64	98	0	0	.395	6	
1994			115	51	64	0	0	.443	5	
1995			143	67	76	0	0	.469	4	
1996			86	39	47	0	0	.453	3 3	
8 yrs.			987	428	559	0	0	.429		

Tony La Russa

La RUSSA, ANTHONY
B. Oct. 4, 1944, Tampa, Fla.

Year	Tm	Lg	G	W	L	T	N	PCT	Standing	
1979	CHI	A	54	27	27	0	0	.500	5 5	
1980			162	70	90	2	0	.438	5	
1981			53	31	22	0	0	.585	3	(1st)
1981			53	23	30	0	0	.434	6	(2nd)
1982			162	87	75	0	0	.537	3	
1983			162	99	63	0	0	.611	1	
1984			162	74	88	0	0	.457	5	
1985			163	85	77	1	0	.525	3	
1986			64	26	38	0	0	.406	6 5	
1986	OAK	A	79	45	34	0	0	.570	7 3	
1987			162	81	81	0	0	.500	3	
1988			162	104	58	0	0	.642	1	
1989			162	99	63	0	0	.611	1	
1990			162	103	59	0	0	.636	1	
1991			162	84	78	0	0	.519	4	
1992			162	96	66	0	0	.593	1	
1993			162	68	94	0	0	.420	7	
1994			114	51	63	0	0	.447	2	
1995			144	67	77	0	0	.465	4	
1996	STL	N	162	88	74	0	0	.543	1	
18 yrs.			2668	1408	1257	3	0	.528		

DIVISIONAL PLAYOFF SERIES

Year	Tm	Lg	G	W	L	T	N	PCT	Standing
1996	STL	N	3	3	0	0	0	1.000	

LEAGUE CHAMPIONSHIP SERIES

Year	Tm	Lg	G	W	L	T	N	PCT	Standing
1983	CHI	A	4	1	3	0	0	.250	
1988	OAK	A	4	4	0	0	0	1.000	
1989			5	4	1	0	0	.800	
1990			4	4	0	0	0	1.000	
1992			6	2	4	0	0	.333	
1996	STL	N	7	3	4	0	0	1.000	
6 yrs.			30	18	12	0	0	.600	
				5th	5th				3rd

WORLD SERIES

Year	Tm	Lg	G	W	L	T	N	PCT	Standing
1988	OAK	A	5	1	4	0	0	.200	
1989			4	4	0	0	0	1.000	
1990			4	0	4	0	0	.000	
3 yrs.			13	5	8	0	0	.385	

Tom Lasorda

LASORDA, THOMAS CHARLES
B. Sept. 22, 1927, Norristown, Pa.

Year	Tm	Lg	G	W	L	T	N	PCT	Standing	
1976	LA	N	4	2	2	0	0	.500	2 2	
1977			162	98	64	0	0	.605	1	
1978			162	95	67	0	0	.586	1	
1979			162	79	83	0	0	.488	3	
1980			163	92	71	0	0	.564	2	
1981			57	36	21	0	0	.632	1	(1st)
1981			53	27	26	0	0	.509	4	(2nd)
1982			162	88	74	0	0	.543	2	

Tom Lasorda continued

Year	Tm	Lg	G	W	L	T	N	PCT	Standing	
1983			163	91	71	1	0	.562	1	
1984			162	79	83	0	0	.488	4	
1985			162	95	67	0	0	.586	1	
1986			162	73	89	0	0	.451	5	
1987			162	73	89	0	0	.451	4	
1988			162	94	67	1	0	.584	1	
1989			160	77	83	0	0	.481	4	
1990			162	86	76	0	0	.531	2	
1991			162	93	69	0	0	.574	2	
1992			162	63	99	0	0	.389	6	
1993			162	81	81	0	0	.500	4	
1994			114	58	56	0	0	.509	1	
1995			144	78	66	0	0	.542	1	
1996			76	41	35	0	0	.539	1 2	
21 yrs.			3040	1599	1439	2	0	.526		

DIVISIONAL PLAYOFF SERIES

Year	Tm	Lg	G	W	L	T	N	PCT	Standing
1981	LA	N	5	3	2	0	0	.600	
1995			3	0	3	0	0	.000	
2 yrs.			8	3	5	0	0	.375	

LEAGUE CHAMPIONSHIP SERIES

Year	Tm	Lg	G	W	L	T	N	PCT	Standing
1977	LA	N	4	3	1	0	0	.750	
1978			4	3	1	0	0	.750	
1981			5	3	2	0	0	.600	
1983			4	1	3	0	0	.250	
1985			6	2	4	0	0	.333	
1988			7	4	3	0	0	.571	
6 yrs.			30	16	14	0	0	.533	
				2nd 3rd	1st				6th

WORLD SERIES

Year	Tm	Lg	G	W	L	T	N	PCT	Standing
1977	LA	N	6	2	4	0	0	.333	
1978			6	2	4	0	0	.333	
1981			6	4	2	0	0	.667	
1988			5	4	1	0	0	.800	
4 yrs.			23	12	11	0	0	.522	
				10th	8th				8th

Jim Leyland

LEYLAND, JAMES RICHARD
B. Dec. 15, 1944, Toledo, Ohio

Year	Tm	Lg	G	W	L	T	N	PCT	Standing
1986	PIT	N	162	64	98	0	0	.395	6
1987			162	80	82	0	0	.494	4
1988			160	85	75	0	0	.531	2
1989			164	74	88	2	0	.457	5
1990			162	95	67	0	0	.586	1
1991			162	98	64	0	0	.605	1
1992			162	96	66	0	0	.593	1
1993			162	75	87	0	0	.463	5
1994			114	53	61	0	0	.465	3
1995			143	58	85	0	0	.406	5
1996			162	73	89	0	0	.451	5
11 yrs.			1715	851	862	2	0	.496	

LEAGUE CHAMPIONSHIP SERIES

Year	Tm	Lg	G	W	L	T	N	PCT	Standing
1990	PIT	N	6	2	4	0	0	.333	
1991			7	3	4	0	0	.429	
1992			7	3	4	0	0	.429	
3 yrs.			20	8	12	0	0	.400	
				9th 9th	5th				

John McNamara

McNAMARA, JOHN FRANCIS
B. June 4, 1932, Sacramento, Calif.

Year	Tm	Lg	G	W	L	T	N	PCT	Standing	
1969	OAK	A	13	8	5	0	0	.615	2 2	
1970			162	89	73	0	0	.549	2	
1974	SD	N	162	60	102	0	0	.370	6	
1975			162	71	91	0	0	.438	4	
1976			162	73	89	0	0	.451	5	
1977			48	20	28	0	0	.417	5 5	
1979	CIN	N	161	90	71	0	0	.559	1	
1980			163	89	73	1	0	.549	3	
1981			56	35	21	0	0	.625	2	(1st)
1981			52	31	21	0	0	.596	2	(2nd)
1982			92	34	58	0	0	.370	6 6	
1983	CAL	A	162	70	92	0	0	.432	5	
1984			162	81	81	0	0	.500	2	

John McNamara *continued*

Year	Tm	Lg	G	W	L	T	N	PCT	Standing	
1985	BOS	A	163	81	81	1	0	.500	5	
1986			161	95	66	0	0	.590	1	
1987			162	78	84	0	0	.481	5	
1988			85	43	42	0	0	.506	4	1
1990	CLE	A	162	77	85	0	0	.475	4	
1991			77	25	52	0	0	.325	7	7
1996	CAL	A	50	18	32	0	0	.360	4	4
19 yrs.			2417	1168	1247	2	0	.483		

LEAGUE CHAMPIONSHIP SERIES

Year	Tm	Lg	G	W	L	T	N	PCT
1979	CIN	N	3	0	3	0	0	.000
1986	BOS	A	7	4	3	0	0	.571
2 yrs.			10	4	6	0	0	.400

WORLD SERIES

Year	Tm	Lg	G	W	L	T	N	PCT
1986	BOS	A	7	3	4	0	0	.429

Johnny Oates

OATES, JOHNNY LANE
B. Jan. 21, 1946, Sylva, N. C.

Year	Tm	Lg	G	W	L	T	N	PCT	Standing	
1991	BAL	A	125	54	71	0	0	.432	7	6
1992			162	89	73	0	0	.549	3	
1993			162	85	77	0	0	.525	3	
1994			112	63	49	0	0	.563	2	
1995	TEX	A	144	74	70	0	0	.514	3	
1996			162	90	72	0	0	.556	1	
6 yrs.			867	455	412	0	0	.525		

Lou Piniella

PINIELLA, LOUIS VICTOR (Sweet Lou)
B. Aug. 28, 1943, Tampa, Fla.

Year	Tm	Lg	G	W	L	T	N	PCT	Standing	
1986	NY	A	162	90	72	0	0	.556	2	
1987			162	89	73	0	0	.549	4	
1988			93	45	48	0	0	.484	2	5
1990	CIN	N	162	91	71	0	0	.562	1	
1991			162	74	88	0	0	.457	5	
1992			162	90	72	0	0	.556	2	
1993	SEA	A	162	82	80	0	0	.506	4	
1994			112	49	63	0	0	.438	3	
1995			145	79	66	0	0	.545	1	
1996			161	85	76	0	0	.528	2	
9 yrs.			1483	774	709	0	0	.522		

DIVISIONAL PLAYOFF SERIES

Year	Tm	Lg	G	W	L	T	N	PCT
1995	SEA	A	5	3	2	0	0	.600

LEAGUE CHAMPIONSHIP SERIES

Year	Tm	Lg	G	W	L	T	N	PCT
1990	CIN	N	6	4	2	0	0	.667
1995	SEA	A	6	2	4	0	0	.333
2 yrs.			12	6	6	0	0	.500

8th

WORLD SERIES

Year	Tm	Lg	G	W	L	T	N	PCT
1990	CIN	N	4	4	0	0	0	1.000

Jim Riggleman

RIGGLEMAN, JAMES DAVID
B. Nov. 9, 1952, Ft. Dix, N. J.

Year	Tm	Lg	G	W	L	T	N	PCT	Standing	
1992	SD	N	12	4	8	0	0	.333	3	3
1993			162	61	101	0	0	.377	7	
1994			117	47	70	0	0	.402	4	
1995	CHI	N	144	73	71	0	0	.507	3	
1996			162	76	86	0	0	.469	4	
5 yrs.			597	261	336	0	0	.437		

Cookie Rojas

ROJAS, OCTAVIO VICTOR
Born Octavio Victor Rojas (Rivas).
B. Mar. 6, 1939, Havana, Cuba.

Year	Tm	Lg	G	W	L	T	N	PCT	Standing		
1988	CAL	A	154	75	79	0	0	.487	4	4	
1996	FLA	N	1	1	0	0	0	1.000	3	3	3
5 yrs.			597	261	336	0	0	.437			

Bill Russell

RUSSELL, WILLIAM ELLIS
B. Oct. 21, 1948, Pittsburg, Kans.

Year	Tm	Lg	G	W	L	T	N	PCT	Standing	
1996	LA	N	86	49	37	0	0	.570	1	2

Joe Torre

TORRE, JOSEPH PAUL
Brother of Frank Torre.
B. July 18, 1940, Brooklyn, N. Y.

Year	Tm	Lg	G	W	L	T	N	PCT	Standing		
1977	NY	N	117	49	68	0	0	.419	6	6	
1978			162	66	96	0	0	.407	6		
1979			163	63	99	1	0	.389	6		
1980			162	67	95	0	0	.414	5		
1981			52	17	34	1	0	.333	5		(1st)
1981			53	24	28	1	0	.462	4		(2nd)
1982	ATL	N	162	89	73	0	0	.549	1		
1983			162	88	74	0	0	.543	2		
1984			162	80	82	0	0	.494	2		
1990	STL	N	58	24	34	0	0	.414	6	6	
1991			162	84	78	0	0	.519	2		
1992			162	83	79	0	0	.512	3		
1993			162	87	75	0	0	.537	3		
1994			115	53	61	1	0	.465	3		
1995			47	20	27	0	0	.426	4	4	
1996	NY	A	162	92	70	0	0	.568	1		
15 yrs.			2063	986	1073	4	0	.478			

DIVISIONAL PLAYOFF SERIES

Year	Tm	Lg	G	W	L	T	N	PCT
1996	NY	A	4	3	1	0	0	.750

LEAGUE CHAMPIONSHIP SERIES

Year	Tm	Lg	G	W	L	T	N	PCT
1982	ATL	N	3	0	3	0	0	.000
1996	NY	A	5	4	1	0	0	.800
2 yrs.			8	4	4	0	0	.500

WORLD SERIES

Year	Tm	Lg	G	W	L	T	N	PCT
1996	NY	A	6	4	2	0	0	.667

Bobby Valentine

VALENTINE, ROBERT JOHN
B. May 13, 1950, Stamford, Conn.

Year	Tm	Lg	G	W	L	T	N	PCT	Standing	
1985	TEX	A	129	53	76	0	0	.411	7	7
1986			162	87	75	0	0	.537	2	
1987			162	75	87	0	0	.463	6	
1988			161	70	91	0	0	.435	6	
1989			162	83	79	0	0	.512	4	
1990			162	83	79	0	0	.512	3	
1991			162	85	77	0	0	.525	3	
1992			86	45	41	0	0	.523	3	4
1996	NY	N	31	12	19	0	0	.387	4	4
9 yrs.			1217	593	624	0	0	.487		

World Series and Championship Playoffs

This section provides details of the National and American League Division Series, Championship Series, and World Series of 1996. Facts are provided about the individual games, including line scores and highlights.

Pitchers are listed in order of appearance. In parentheses following each pitcher's name is the number of innings he worked. "Doe (2.1)" indicates that Doe worked two and one-third innings; "(2.0)" means that he faced at least one batter in his third inning of work, but did not retire anyone. The winning and losing pitchers are listed in boldfaced print; a pitcher who is credited with a save has a bold "SV" after his innings pitched.

Home runs are listed in the order they were hit.

1996 NATIONAL LEAGUE DIVISIONAL PLAYOFFS

LINE SCORES	PITCHERS (innings pitched)	HOME RUNS (men on)	HIGHLIGHTS

Atlanta (East) defeats Los Angeles (Wild Card) 3 games to 0

GAME 1 - OCTOBER 2

ATL E 000 100 000 1   2 4 1   **Smoltz** (9), Wohlers (1) **SV**   Lopez

LA *   000 010 000 0   1 5 0   Martinez (8), Radinsky (0.1), **Osuna** (1.2)

Lopez led off the tenth inning with a home run to make a winner of Smoltz, who allowed 4 hits and struck out 7. Dodger starter Ramon Martinez was equally sharp in his eight innings, giving up 3 hits and striking out 6 before giving way to Radinsky and Osuna, who allowed Lopez's homer.

GAME 2 - OCTOBER 3

ATL E 010 000 200   3 5 2   **Maddux** (7), McMichael (1), Wohlers (1) **SV**   Klesko, McGriff, Dye

LA *   100 100 000   2 3 0   Valdes (6.1), Astacio (1.2), Worrell (1)

Maddux and two relievers held Dodgers to three hits, while Braves reached Valdes for solo homers by Klesko, McGriff, and Dye, the latter two coming in the decisive seventh inning.

GAME 3 - OCTOBER 5

LA *   000 000 110   2 6 1   **Nomo** (3.2), Guthrie (0.1), Candiotti (2), Radinsky (1), Osuna (0.1), Dreifort (0.2)

ATL E 100 400 00x   5 7 0   **Glavine** (6.2), McMichael (0.1), Bielecki (0.2), Wohlers (1.1) **SV**   C. Jones (1 on)

Chipper Jones smacked a two-run homer and scored twice to back Glavine's strong pitching effort as the Braves completed a series sweep of the Dodgers.

Team totals

		W	AB	H	2B	3B	HR	R	RBI	BA	BB	SO	ERA
ATL	E	3	89	16	3	0	5	10	10	.180	12	24	0.96
LA	*	0	95	14	7	0	0	5	5	.147	7	29	3.33

Individual Batting

ATLANTA (EAST)

	AB	H	2B	3B	HR	R	RBI	BA
M. Lemke, 2b	12	2	1	0	0	1	2	.167
M. Grissom, of	12	1	0	0	0	2	0	.083
J. Dye, of	11	2	0	0	1	1	1	.182
F. McGriff, 1b	9	3	1	0	1	1	3	.333
C. Jones, 3b	9	2	0	0	1	2	2	.222
J. Blauser, ss	9	1	0	0	0	0	0	.111
R. Klesko, of	8	1	0	0	1	1	1	.125
J. Lopez, c	7	2	0	0	1	1	1	.286
E. Perez, c	3	1	0	0	0	0	0	.333
T. Glavine, p	2	1	1	0	0	1	0	.500
G. Maddux, p	2	0	0	0	0	0	0	.000
L. Polonia	2	0	0	0	0	0	0	.000
J. Smoltz, p	2	0	0	0	0	0	0	.000
T. Pendleton	1	0	0	0	0	0	0	.000
R. Belliard, ss	0	0	0	0	0	0	0	—
A. Jones, of	0	0	0	0	0	0	0	—

Errors: M. Grissom, R. Klesko, J. Lopez

Stolen Bases: J. Dye, M. Grissom, C. Jones, R. Klesko, J. Lopez

LOS ANGELES (Wild Card)

	AB	H	2B	3B	HR	R	RBI	BA
T. Hollandsworth, of	12	4	3	0	0	1	1	.333
G. Gagne, ss	11	3	1	0	0	2	0	.273
R. Mondesi, of	11	2	2	0	0	0	1	.182
T. Wallach, 3b	11	0	0	0	0	0	0	.000
M. Piazza, c	10	3	0	0	0	1	2	.300
E. Karros, 1b	9	0	0	0	0	0	0	.000
W. Kirby, of	8	1	0	0	0	1	0	.125
J. Castro, 2b	5	1	1	0	0	0	1	.200
D. DeShields, 2b	4	0	0	0	0	0	0	.000
R. Martinez, p	3	0	0	0	0	0	0	.000
B. Ashley	2	0	0	0	0	0	0	.000
D. Clark	2	0	0	0	0	0	0	.000
C. Curtis, of	2	0	0	0	0	0	0	.000
D. Hansen, 3b	2	0	0	0	0	0	0	.000
I. Valdes, p	2	0	0	0	0	0	0	.000
H. Nomo, p	1	0	0	0	0	0	0	.000

Errors: T. Wallach

Individual Pitching

ATLANTA (EAST)

	W	L	ERA	IP	H	BB	SO	SV
J. Smoltz	1	0	1.00	9	4	2	7	0
G. Maddux	1	0	0.00	7	3	0	7	0
T. Glavine	1	0	1.35	6.2	5	3	7	0
M. Wohlers	0	0	0.00	3.1	1	0	4	3
G. McMichael	0	0	6.75	1.1	1	1	3	0
M. Bielecki	0	0	0.00	0.2	0	1	1	0

LOS ANGELES (Wild Card)

	W	L	ERA	IP	H	BB	SO	SV
R. Martinez	0	0	1.13	8	3	6	0	0
I. Valdes	0	1	4.26	6.1	5	0	5	0
H. Nomo	0	1	12.27	3.2	5	5	3	0
T. Candiotti	0	0	0.00	2	0	0	1	0
A. Osuna	0	1	4.50	2	3	1	4	0
P. Astacio	0	0	0.00	1.2	0	0	1	0
S. Radinsky	0	0	0.00	1.1	0	1	2	0
T. Worrell	0	0	0.00	1	0	1	1	0
D. Dreifort	0	0	0.00	0.2	0	0	0	0
M. Guthrie	0	0	0.00	0.1	0	1	1	0

1996 NATIONAL LEAGUE DIVISIONAL PLAYOFFS

LINE SCORES	PITCHERS (innings pitched)	HOME RUNS (men on)	HIGHLIGHTS

St. Louis (Central) defeats San Diego (West) 3 games to 0

GAME 1 - OCTOBER 1

SD	W	000 001 000	1	8	1
STL	C	300 000 00x	3	6	0

Hamilton (6), Blair (2)
Stottlemyre (6.2), Honeycutt (0.2), Eckersley (1.2) **SV**

Henderson
Gaetti (2 on)

Gaetti gave the Cardinals the lead with a three-run homer in the first, and Stottlemyre made it stand up with relief help from Honeycutt and Eckersley. Henderson homered for San Diego's only run.

GAME 2 - OCTOBER 3

SD	W	000 012 010	4	6	0
STL	C	001 030 01x	5	5	1

Sanders (4.1), Veras (0.2), Worrell (2), **Bochtler** (0.1), Hoffman (0.2)
An. Benes (7.0), **Honeycutt** (1), Eckersley (1) **SV**

Caminiti

Cardinals pushed across the winning run without a hit in the bottom of the eighth. Jordan walked, moved up a base on a groundout, advanced to third on a wild pitch and scored on Pagnozzi's infield out. Gant drilled a three-run double that gave St. Louis a 4-1 lead before Padres tied it.

GAME 3 - OCTOBER 5

STL	C	100 003 102	7	13	1
SD	W	021 100 010	5	11	2

Osborne (4), Petkovsek (2), Honeycutt (1.0), Mathews (1), Eckersley (1) **SV**
Ashby (5.1), Worrell (1.2), Valenzuela (0.2), Veras (0.1), **Hoffman** (1)

Gant, Jordan (1 on)
Caminiti, Caminiti

Jordan hit a tiebreaking two-run homer in the ninth to give the Cardinals the series clincher. Caminiti's second homer of the game had tied the score in the eighth inning for the Padres, who earlier relinquished a 4-1 lead.

Team totals

		W	AB	H	2B	3B	HR	R	RBI	BA	BB	SO	ERA
STL	C	3	94	24	3	1	3	15	14	.255	13	23	3.33
SD	W	0	105	25	3	0	4	10	9	.238	4	28	5.40

Individual Batting

ST. LOUIS (CENTRAL)

	AB	H	2B	3B	HR	R	RBI	BA
B. Jordan, of	12	4	0	0	1	4	3	.333
T. Pagnozzi, c	11	3	0	0	0	2	.273
L. Alicea, 2b	11	2	2	0	0	1	0	.182
G. Gaetti, 3b	11	1	0	0	1	1	3	.091
R. Gant, of	10	4	1	0	1	3	4	.400
J. Mabry, 1b	10	3	0	1	0	1	1	.300
W. McGee, of	10	1	0	0	0	1	1	.100
R. Clayton, ss	6	2	0	0	0	1	0	.333
O. Smith, ss	3	1	0	0	0	1	0	.333
An. Benes, p	2	1	0	0	0	1	0	.500
R. Lankford, of	2	1	0	0	0	1	0	.500
T. Stottlemyre, p	2	0	0	0	0	0	0	.000
M. Sweeney	1	1	0	0	0	0	1	1.000
M. Gallego, 2b, 3b	1	0	0	0	0	0	0	.000
R. Honeycutt, p	1	0	0	0	0	0	0	.000
D. Osborne, p	1	0	0	0	0	0	0	.000
M. Mejia	0	0	0	0	0	0	0	—

Errors: L. Alicea, W. McGee
Stolen Bases: R. Gant (2), B. Jordan

SAN DIEGO (WEST)

	AB	H	2B	3B	HR	R	RBI	BA
T. Gwynn, of	13	4	1	0	0	0	1	.308
R. Henderson, of	12	4	0	1	2	1	.333
C. Gomez, ss	12	2	0	0	0	1	.167
S. Finley, of	12	1	0	0	0	1	.083
J. Reed, 2b	11	3	1	0	0	2	.273
K. Caminiti, 3b	10	3	0	0	3	3	3	.300
W. Joyner, 1b	9	1	0	0	0	0	0	.111
B. Johnson, c	8	3	1	0	0	2	0	.375
J. Flaherty, c	4	0	0	0	0	0	0	.000
A. Cianfrocco, 1b	3	1	0	0	0	1	0	.333
G. Vaughn	3	0	0	0	0	0	0	.000
C. Gwynn	2	2	0	0	1	0	1	1.000
S. Livingstone	2	1	0	0	0	1	0	.500
J. Hamilton, p	2	0	0	0	0	0	0	.000
A. Ashby, p	1	0	0	0	0	0	0	.000
S. Sanders, p	1	0	0	0	0	0	0	.000
L. Lopez	0	0	0	0	0	0	0	—

Errors: K. Caminiti (3)
Stolen Bases: S. Finley, T. Gwynn

Individual Pitching

ST. LOUIS (CENTRAL)

	W	L	ERA	IP	H	BB	SO	SV
An. Benes	0	0	5.14	7	6	1	9	0
T. Stottlemyre	1	0	1.35	6.2	5	2	7	0
D. Osborne	0	0	9.00	4	7	0	5	0
D. Eckersley	0	0	0.00	3.2	3	0	2	3
R. Honeycutt	1	0	3.38	2.2	3	1	2	0
M. Petkovsek	0	0	0.00	2	0	0	1	0
T. Mathews	1	0	0.00	1	1	0	2	0

SAN DIEGO (WEST)

	W	L	ERA	IP	H	BB	SO	SV
J. Hamilton	0	1	4.50	6	5	0	6	0
A. Ashby	0	0	6.75	5.1	7	1	5	0
S. Sanders	0	0	8.31	4.1	3	4	4	0
T. Worrell	0	0	2.45	3.2	4	1	2	0
W. Blair	0	0	0.00	2	1	2	3	0
T. Hoffman	0	1	10.80	1.2	3	1	2	0
D. Veras	0	0	0.00	1	1	0	1	0
F. Valenzuela	0	0	0.00	0.2	0	2	0	0
D. Bochtler	0	1	27.00	0.1	0	2	0	0

1996 NATIONAL LEAGUE CHAMPIONSHIP SERIES

LINE SCORES	PITCHERS (innings pitched)	HOME RUNS (men on)	HIGHLIGHTS

Atlanta (East) defeats St. Louis (Central) 4 games to 3

GAME 1 - OCTOBER 9

STL C 010 000 100 2 5 1
ATL E 000 020 02x 4 9 0

An. Benes (6), **Petkovsek** (1.0), Fossas (0.1), Mathews (0.2)
Smoltz (8), Wohlers (1) **SV**

Lopez delivered a single with the bags full to break a 2-2 tie in the eighth inning. Smoltz held the Cards to five hits over eight innings to get the victory, while Chipper Jones went 4-for-4 including a bunt single that keyed the winning rally.

GAME 2 - OCTOBER 10

STL C 102 000 500 8 11 2
ATL E 002 001 000 3 5 2

Stottlemyre (6), Petkovsek (1), Honeycutt (0.2), Eckersley (1.1)
Maddux (6.2), McMichael (0.1), Neagle (1), Avery (1)

Gaetti (3 on)
Grissom (1 on)

Grand slam homer by Gaetti was the big blow as Cardinals scored five runs in the seventh inning off Maddux to tie the series. Cardinals scored twice in the third on RBI doubles by Gant and Jordan to take a 3-0 lead before Braves tied it on Grissom's two-run homer in the bottom of the inning and a run scoring single by Klesko in the sixth. Stottlemyre pitched out of a bases loaded jam after allowing the tying run to keep the game even. Lankford put St. Louis ahead with a sacrifice fly before Gaetti put the game out of reach.

GAME 3 - OCTOBER 12

ATL E 100 000 010 2 8 1
STL C 200 001 00x 3 7 0

Glavine, Bielecki (1), McMichael (1)
Osborne (7.0), Petkovsek (1), Honeycutt (0.1), Eckersley (0.2) **SV**

Gant (1 on), Gant

Gant homered twice against his former team to give St. Louis the series lead. His first homer, a two-run shot in the first gave the Cardinals a 2-1 lead, and he connected again with the bases empty in the sixth. Osborne pitched the first seven innings to defeat Glavine, who allowed both homers by Gant.

GAME 4 - OCTOBER 13

ATL E 010 002 000 3 9 1
STL C 000 000 31x 4 5 0

Neagle (6.2), **McMichael** (0.2), Wohlers (0.2)
An. Benes (5.0), Fossas (0.2), Mathews (0), Al. Benes (1.1), Honeycutt (0.2), **Eckersley** (1.1)

Klesko, Lemke
Jordan

Jordan smacked a tiebreaking homer in the eighth for the Cardinals, who erased a three run deficit an inning earlier. With Braves leading 3-0, pinch-hitter Young drilled a two-run triple with two out and scored the tying run on an infield hit by Clayton. Eckersley won it in relief, stranding the tying run at second after allowing a leadoff double by Dye in the ninth.

GAME 5 - OCTOBER 14

ATL E 520 310 012 14 22 0
STL C 000 000 000   0 7 0

Smoltz (7), Bielecki (1), Wade (0.1), Clontz (0.2)
Stottlemyre (1.0), Jackson (3), Fossas (2), Petkovsek (2), Honeycutt (1)

Lopez, McGriff (1 on)

Braves pounced on Stottlemyre for five runs in the opening inning keyed by a two run double by Chipper Jones and Blauser's two run triple. Atlanta's 22 hits set a LCS record. Lopez (four runs scored) and Lemke paced the onslaught with four hits apiece, while Jones and McGriff each drove in three runs. Smoltz picked up his second victory of the series, combining with three relievers on the shutout.

GAME 6 - OCTOBER 16

STL C 000 000 010 1 6 1
ATL E 010 010 01x 3 7 0

Al. Benes (5), Fossas (0.1), Petkovsek (1.2), Stottlemyre (1)
Maddux (7.2), Wohlers (1.1) **SV**

Braves evened the series behind an excellent pitching performance by Maddux, who held the Cards to six hits and struck out seven before being relieved by Wohlers in the eighth. Atlanta scored on Dye's sacrifice fly and RBI singles by Lemke and Belliard.

GAME 7 - OCTOBER 17

STL C 000 000 000   0 4 2
ATL E 600 403 20x 15 17 0

Osborne (0.2), An. Benes (4.1), Petkovsek (0.2), Honeycutt (1.1), Fossas (1)
Glavine (7), Bielecki (1), Avery (1)

Lopez (1 on), A. Jones (1 on), McGriff (1 on)

Glavine pitched seven shutout innings and hit a bases loaded triple to cap a six run first inning as the Braves captured their second consecutive pennant. The 15-run margin of victory was the largest in LCS history. Atlanta outscored St. Louis 32-1 over the last three games as they became the first NL team to overcome a 3-1 deficit to win the LCS.

Team totals

		W	AB	H	2B	3B	HR	R	RBI	BA	BB	SO	ERA
ATL	E	4	249	77	11	3	8	44	43	.309	25	51	1.92
STL	C	3	221	45	4	2	4	18	15	.204	11	53	6.60

Individual Batting

ATLANTA (EAST)

	AB	H	2B	3B	HR	R	RBI	BA
M. Grissom, of	35	10	1	0	1	7	3	.286
F. McGriff, 1b	28	7	0	1	2	6	7	.250
J. Dye, of	28	6	1	0	0	2	4	.214
M. Lemke, 2b	27	12	2	0	1	4	5	.444
C. Jones, 3b	25	11	2	0	0	8	6	.440
J. Lopez, c	24	13	5	0	2	8	6	.542
J. Blauser, ss	17	3	0	1	0	5	2	.176
R. Klesko, of	16	4	0	0	1	3	3	.250
A. Jones, of	9	2	0	0	1	3	3	.222
J. Smoltz, p	7	2	0	0	0	1	1	.286
R. Belliard, 2b, ss	6	4	0	0	0	0	2	.667
T. Glavine, p	6	1	0	1	0	0	3	.167
T. Pendleton, 3b	6	0	0	0	0	0	0	.000
M. Mordecai, 3b, 2b	4	1	0	0	0	1	0	.250
G. Maddux, p	4	0	0	0	0	0	0	.000
L. Polonia	3	0	0	0	0	0	0	.000
D. Neagle, p	2	1	0	0	0	0	0	.500
E. Perez, c, 1b	1	0	0	0	0	0	0	.000
M. Wohlers, p	1	0	0	0	0	0	0	.000

Errors: J. Blauser, M. Grissom, C. Jones, F. McGriff
Stolen Bases: M. Grissom (2), C. Jones, J. Lopez

ST. LOUIS (CENTRAL)

	AB	H	2B	3B	HR	R	RBI	BA
R. Gant, of	25	6	1	0	2	3	4	.240
B. Jordan, of	25	6	1	1	1	3	2	.240
G. Gaetti, 3b	24	7	0	0	1	1	4	.292
J. Mabry, 1b, of	23	6	0	0	0	1	0	.261
R. Clayton, ss	20	7	0	0	0	4	1	.350
T. Pagnozzi, c	19	3	1	0	0	1	1	.158
W. McGee, of	15	5	0	0	0	0	0	.333
M. Gallego, 3b, 2b	14	2	0	0	0	1	0	.143
R. Lankford, of	13	0	0	0	0	1	1	.000
O. Smith, ss	9	0	0	0	0	0	0	.000
L. Alicea, 2b	8	0	0	0	0	0	0	.000
D. Young, 1b	7	2	0	1	0	1	2	.286
An. Benes, p	4	1	1	0	0	0	0	.250
M. Sweeney, of	4	0	0	0	0	1	0	.000
D. Osborne, p	3	0	0	0	0	0	0	.000
D. Sheaffer, c	3	0	0	0	0	0	0	.000
T. Stottlemyre, p	2	0	0	0	0	0	0	.000
Al. Benes, p	1	0	0	0	0	0	0	.000
D. Jackson, p	1	0	0	0	0	0	0	.000
M. Mejia, of	1	0	0	0	0	0	1	.000

Errors: R. Clayton (2), L. Alicea, M. Gallego, W. McGee, M. Petkovsek
Stolen Bases: R. Clayton

Individual Pitching

ATLANTA (EAST)

	W	L	ERA	IP	H	BB	SO	SV
J. Smoltz	2	0	1.20	15	12	3	12	0
G. Maddux	1	1	2.51	14.1	15	2	10	0
T. Glavine	1	1	2.08	13	10	0	9	0
D. Neagle	0	0	2.35	7.2	2	3	8	0
M. Bielecki	0	0	0.00	3	0	1	5	0
M. Wohlers	0	0	0.00	3	0	4	2	2
S. Avery	0	0	0.00	2	1	1	1	0
G. McMichael	0	1	9.00	2	4	1	3	0
B. Clontz	0	0	0.00	0.2	0	0	0	0
T. Wade	0	0	0.00	0.1	0	0	1	0

ST. LOUIS (CENTRAL)

	W	L	ERA	IP	H	BB	SO	SV
An. Benes	0	0	5.28	15.1	19	3	9	0
T. Stottlemyre	1	1	12.38	8	15	3	11	0
D. Osborne	1	1	9.39	7.2	12	4	6	0
M. Petkovsek	0	1	7.36	7.1	11	3	7	0
Al. Benes	0	1	2.84	6.1	3	2	5	0
T. Fossas	0	0	2.08	4.1	1	3	1	0
R. Honeycutt	0	0	9.00	4	5	3	3	0
D. Eckersley	1	0	0.00	3.1	2	0	4	1
D. Jackson	0	0	9.00	3	7	3	3	0
T. Mathews	0	0	0.00	0.2	2	1	2	0

1996 AMERICAN LEAGUE DIVISIONAL PLAYOFFS

LINE SCORES	PITCHERS (innings pitched)	HOME RUNS (men on)	HIGHLIGHTS

Baltimore (Wild Card) defeats Cleveland (Central) 3 games to 1

GAME 1 - OCTOBER 1

CLE C 010 200 100   4 10 0   Nagy (5.1), Embree (0.1), Shuey (1.1), Tavarez (1)   Ramirez

BAL * 112 005 10x   10 12 1   Wells (6.2), Orosco (0), Mathews (0.2), Rhodes (0.2), Myers (1)   Anderson, Surhoff, Bonilla (3 on), Surhoff

Four homers keyed Oriole romp. Anderson set the tone with a leadoff shot in the opening inning, Surhoff connected twice, and Bonilla's sixth inning grand slam broke the game open. Ramirez had three hits for Cleveland, including a solo homer.

GAME 2 - OCTOBER 2

CLE C 000 003 010   4 8 2   Hershiser (5), Plunk (2.0), Assenmacher (0.2), Tavarez (0.1)   Belle (1 on)

BAL * 100 030 03x   7 9 0   Erickson (6.2), Orosco (0.1), Benitez (1), Myers (1) SV   Anderson

Orioles scored three runs in the bottom of the eighth after Indians tied the score in the top of the inning. Go-ahead run scored when catcher Sandy Alomar threw wildly past first base on an attempted pitcher-to-catcher-to first double play.

GAME 3 - OCTOBER 4

BAL * 010 300 000   4 8 2   Mussina (6), Orosco (0), Benitez (1), Rhodes (0.1), Mathews (0.2)   Surhoff (2 on)

CLE C 120 100 41x   9 10 0   McDowell (5.2), Embree (0.1), Shuey (0.2), Assenmacher (0.1), Plunk (1), Mesa (1)   Ramirez, Belle (3 on)

Belle cracked a tiebreaking grand slam in the seventh inning to keep Cleveland alive in the series. Orosco walked the bases loaded before being relieved by Benitez, who yielded Belle's slam. Surhoff hit a three-run homer for Baltimore.

GAME 4 - OCTOBER 5

BAL * 020 000 001 001   4 14 1   Wells (7), Mathews (1.1), Orosco (0.2), Benitez (2), Myers (1) SV   Palmeiro, Bonilla, R. Alomar

CLE C 000 210 000 000   3 7 1   Nagy (6), Embree (0.1), Shuey (0), Assenmacher (0.2), Plunk (1), Mesa (3.2), Ogea (0.1)

Baltimore became the first Wild Card team to win a playoff series by upsetting the defending American League champs. Roberto Alomar, the subject of controversy due to a late season incident in which he spit on an umpire, tied the game with a single in the ninth then led off the 12th with a home run to win it. Orioles won the game despite setting a postseason record by striking out 23 times.

Team totals

		W	AB	H	2B	3B	HR	R	RBI	BA	BB	SO	ERA
BAL	*	3	149	43	6	0	9	25	23	.289	17	40	4.50
CLE	C	1	143	35	7	0	4	20	20	.245	15	32	5.84

Individual Batting

BALTIMORE (Wild Card)

	AB	H	2B	3B	HR	R	RBI	BA
T. Zeile, 3b	19	5	1	0	0	2	0	.263
C. Ripken, ss	18	8	3	0	0	2	2	.444
R. Alomar, 2b	17	5	0	0	1	2	4	.294
B. Anderson, of	17	5	0	0	2	3	4	.294
R. Palmeiro, 1b	17	3	1	0	1	4	2	.176
E. Murray, dh	15	6	1	0	0	1	1	.400
B. Bonilla, of	15	3	0	0	2	4	5	.200
B. Surhoff, of	13	5	0	0	3	3	5	.385
C. Hoiles, c	7	1	0	0	0	1	0	.143
P. Incaviglia, of	5	1	0	0	0	1	0	.200
M. Parent, c	5	1	0	0	0	0	0	.200
M. Devereaux, of	1	0	0	0	0	0	0	.000
M. Alexander, dh	0	0	0	0	0	2	0	—

Errors: T. Zeile (2), B. Bonilla, R. Palmeiro
Stolen Bases: E. Murray

CLEVELAND (CENTRAL)

	AB	H	2B	3B	HR	R	RBI	BA
K. Lofton, of	18	3	0	0	0	3	1	.167
K. Seitzer, dh, 1b	17	5	1	0	0	1	4	.294
M. Ramirez, of	16	6	2	0	2	4	2	.375
S. Alomar, c	16	2	0	0	0	0	3	.125
A. Belle, of	15	3	0	0	2	2	6	.200
J. Franco, 1b, dh	15	2	0	0	0	1	1	.133
O. Vizquel, ss	14	6	1	0	0	4	2	.429
J. Vizcaino, 2b	12	4	2	0	0	1	1	.333
J. Thome, 3b	10	3	0	0	0	1	0	.300
J. Kent, 2b, 1b, 3b	8	1	1	0	0	2	0	.125
B. Giles	1	0	0	0	0	0	0	.000
N. Wilson	1	0	0	0	0	0	0	.000
C. Candaele, dh	0	0	0	0	0	1	0	—
T. Pena, c	0	0	0	0	0	0	0	—

Errors: S. Alomar, K. Seitzer, J. Vizcaino
Stolen Bases: K. Lofton (5), O. Vizquel (4), A. Belle, K. Seitzer

Individual Pitching

BALTIMORE (Wild Card)

	W	L	ERA	IP	H	BB	SO	SV
D. Wells	1	0	4.61	13.2	15	4	6	0
S. Erickson	0	0	4.05	6.2	6	2	6	0
M. Mussina	0	0	4.50	6	7	2	6	0
A. Benitez	2	0	2.25	4	1	2	6	0
R. Myers	0	0	0.00	3	0	3	2	2
T. Mathews	0	0	0.00	2.2	3	1	2	0
J. Orosco	0	1	36.00	1	2	3	2	0
A. Rhodes	0	0	9.00	1	1	1	1	0

CLEVELAND (CENTRAL)

	W	L	ERA	IP	H	BB	SO	SV
C. Nagy	0	1	7.15	11.1	15	5	13	0
J. McDowell	0	0	6.35	5.2	6	1	5	0
O. Hershiser	0	0	5.40	5	7	3	3	0
J. Mesa	0	1	3.86	4.2	8	0	7	0
E. Plunk	0	1	6.75	4	1	2	6	0
P. Shuey	0	0	9.00	2	5	2	2	0
P. Assenmacher	1	0	0.00	1.2	0	1	2	0
J. Tavarez	0	0	0.00	1.1	1	2	1	0
A. Embree	0	0	9.00	1	0	1	0	0
C. Ogea	0	0	0.00	0.1	0	1	0	0

1996 AMERICAN LEAGUE DIVISIONAL PLAYOFFS

LINE SCORES	PITCHERS (innings pitched)	HOME RUNS (men on)	HIGHLIGHTS

New York (East) defeats Texas (West) 3 games to 1

GAME 1 - OCTOBER 1

TEX	W	000 501 000	6	8	0
NY	E	100 100 000	2	10	0

Burkett (9)

Cone (6), Lloyd (1), Weathers (2)

Gonzalez (2 on), Palmer (1on)

Texas won the first postseason game in their franchise history behind Burkett's complete game effort. Gonzalez and Palmer each homered off Cone as Rangers scored five runs in the fourth inning.

GAME 2 - OCTOBER 2

TEX	W	013 000 000 000	4	8	1
NY	E	010 100 110 001	5	8	0

Hill (6.0), Cook (1), Russell (2.1), **Stanton** (1.2), Henneman (0)

Pettitte (6.1), M. Rivera (2.2), Wetteland (2), Lloyd (0), Nelson (0.2), Rogers (0), **Boehringer** (0.1)

Gonzalez, Gonzalez (2 on)

Fielder

Yanks evened the series thanks to an unearned run in the 12th inning. After Jeter singled and Raines walked, Hayes bunted to Palmer, who threw the ball past first base, allowing Jeter to score the winning run. Gonzalez hit two homers to give Texas a 4-1 lead before New York rallied to send the game into extra innings, with Fielder hitting a home run in the fourth and a game-tying RBI single in the eighth.

GAME 3 - OCTOBER 4

NY	E	100 000 002	3	7	1
TEX	W	000 110 000	2	6	1

Key (5), **Nelson** (3), Wetteland (1) **SV**

Oliver (8.0), Henneman (0.2), Stanton (0.1)

Williams

Gonzalez

New York pulled it out with a two-run rally in the ninth. Williams, who homered earlier, tied it with a sacrifice fly and Duncan followed with an RBI single.

GAME 4 - OCTOBER 5

NY	E	000 310 101	6	12	1
TEX	W	022 000 000	4	9	0

Rogers (2), Boehringer (1.0), **Weathers** (3), M. Rivera (2), Wetteland (1) **SV**

Witt (3.1), Patterson (0.1), Cook (0.1) **Pavlik** (2.2), Vosberg (0), Russell (0.2), Stanton (1.1), Henneman (0.1)

Williams, Williams

Gonzalez

Bernie Williams slammed two solo homers, one from each side of the plate, as the Yankees rebounded from an early 4-0 deficit to close out the series. Williams's first homer tied the game in the fifth, and an RBI single by Fielder in the seventh gave New York the lead for good. Williams provided insurance with his second home run in the ninth. Gonzalez homered in his fourth straight game for Texas, and finished the series with five roundtrippers.

Team totals

		W	AB	H	2B	3B	HR	R	RBI	BA	BB	SO	ERA
NY	E	3	140	37	4	0	4	16	15	.264	13	20	3.46
TEX	W	1	142	31	4	0	6	16	16	.218	20	30	3.55

Individual Batting

NEW YORK (EAST)

	AB	H	2B	3B	HR	R	RBI	BA
D. Jeter, ss	17	7	1	0	0	2	1	.412
M. Duncan, 2b	16	5	0	0	0	3		.313
T. Raines, of	16	4	0	0	0	3	0	.250
B. Williams, of	15	7	0	0	3	5	5	.467
T. Martinez, 1b	15	4	2	0	0	3	0	.267
P. O'Neill, of	15	2	0	0	0	0	0	.133
W. Boggs, 3b	12	1	1	0	0	0	0	.083
C. Fielder, dh	11	4	0	0	1	2	4	.364
J. Girardi, c	9	2	0	0	0	1	0	.222
C. Hayes, 3b	5	1	0	0	0	0	1	.200
D. Strawberry, dh	5	0	0	0	0	0	0	.000
J. Leyritz, c, dh	3	0	0	0	0	0	1	.000
R. Rivera, of	1	0	0	0	0	0	0	.000
A. Fox, dh	0	0	0	0	0	0	0	—
L. Sojo, 2b	0	0	0	0	0	0	0	—

Errors: D. Jeter (2)
Stolen Bases: B. Williams

TEXAS (WEST)

	AB	H	2B	3B	HR	R	RBI	BA
D. Palmer, 3b	19	4	1	0	1	3	2	.211
D. Hamilton, of	19	3	0	0	0	0	0	.158
J. Gonzalez, of	16	7	0	0	5	5	9	.438
I. Rodriguez, c	16	6	1	0	0	1	2	.375
W. Clark, 1b	16	2	0	0	0	1	0	.125
R. Greer, of	16	2	0	0	0	2	0	.125
M. McLemore, 2b	15	2	0	0	0	1	2	.133
K. Elster, ss	12	4	2	0	0	0	0	.333
M. Tettleton, dh	12	1	0	0	0	1	1	.083
W. Newson	1	0	0	0	0	0	0	.000
D. Buford	0	0	0	0	0	0	0	—
R. Gonzales, ss	0	0	0	0	0	0	0	—

Errors: K. Elster, D. Palmer
Stolen Bases: K. Elster

Individual Pitching

NEW YORK (EAST)

	W	L	ERA	IP	H	BB	SO	SV
A. Pettitte	0	0	5.68	6.1	4	6	3	0
D. Cone	0	1	9.00	6	8	2	8	0
J. Key	0	0	3.60	5	5	1	0	0
D. Weathers	1	0	0.00	5	1	0	5	0
M. Rivera	0	0	0.00	4.2	0	1	1	0
J. Wetteland	0	0	0.00	4	2	4	4	2
J. Nelson	1	0	0.00	3.2	2	2	5	0
K. Rogers	0	0	9.00	2	5	2	1	0
B. Boehringer	1	0	6.75	1.1	3	2	0	0
G. Lloyd	0	0	0.00	1	1	0	0	0

TEXAS (WEST)

	W	L	ERA	IP	H	BB	SO	SV
J. Burkett	1	0	2.00	9	10	1	7	0
D. Oliver	0	1	3.38	8	6	2	3	0
K. Hill	0	0	4.50	6	5	3	1	0
M. Stanton	0	1	2.70	3.1	2	3	3	0
B. Witt	0	0	8.10	3.1	4	2	3	0
J. Russell	0	0	3.00	3	3	0	1	0
R. Pavlik	0	1	6.75	2.2	4	1	0	0
D. Cook	0	0	0.00	1.1	0	1	0	0
M. Henneman	0	0	0.00	1	1	1	1	0
D. Patterson	0	0	0.00	0.1	1	0	0	0
E. Vosberg	0	0	—	0.0	1	0	0	0

1996 AMERICAN LEAGUE CHAMPIONSHIP SERIES

LINE SCORES	PITCHERS (innings pitched)	HOME RUNS (men on)	HIGHLIGHTS

New York (East) defeats Baltimore (Wild Card) 4 games to 1

GAME 1 - OCTOBER 9

BAL *	011 101 000 00	4 11 1	Erickson (6.1), Orosco (0.1), Benitez (1), Rhodes (0.1), Mathews (0.1), **Myers** (1.2)	Anderson, Palmeiro	Williams led off the eleventh inning with a home run to give the Yankees the series opener. Yankees tied the game in the eighth when Jeter hit a disputed homer that appeared to be deflected over the fence by a young fan in the right field stands. The Orioles argued that rightfielder Tarasco was interfered with and had a chance to catch the ball, but to no avail.
NY E	110 000 110 01	5 11 0	Pettitte (7), Nelson (1), Wetteland (1), **M. Rivera** (2)	Jeter, Williams	

GAME 2 - OCTOBER 10

BAL *	002 000 210	5 10 0	**Wells** (6.2), Mills (0), Orosco (1.1), Myers (0.1), Benitez (0.2) SV	Zeile (1 on), Palmeiro (1 on)	Baltimore used a pair of two-run homers to even the series. Zeile's third inning blast tied the game 2-2, then Palmeiro broke the tie with his clout in the seventh to give Wells the victory. The game took 4 hours and 13 minutes to play, the longest nine inning game in championship series history.
NY E	200 000 100	3 11 1	Cone (6), **Nelson** (1.1), Lloyd (1.1), Weathers (0.1)		

GAME 3 - OCTOBER 11

NY E	000 100 040	5 8 0	**Key** (8), Wetteland (1) SV	Fielder (1 on)	Yankees scored four runs in the eighth to take the lead in the series. Orioles led 2-1 behind Mussina until Jeter doubled with two out and scored the tying run on a single by Williams. Baltimore third baseman Zeile, who earlier hit a two-run homer, then lost control of the ball faking a throw to second after taking a throw from the outfield following a double by Martinez, and Williams scored the lead run. Fielder smashed a two-run homer to complete the uprising. Key pitched eight outstanding innings to get the win, allowing just three hits and one walk.
BAL *	200 000 000	2 3 2	**Mussina** (7.2), Orosco (0.1), Mathews (1)	Zeile (1 on)	

GAME 4 - OCTOBER 12

NY E	210 200 030	8 9 0	Rogers (3.0), **Weathers** (2.2), Lloyd (0.1), M. Rivera (2), Wetteland (1)	Williams (1 on), Strawberry, O'Neill (1 on), Strawberry (1 on)	Yankees slammed four homers, two by Strawberry, to overpower the Orioles. Williams hit a two-run shot in the first to put New York on top, and their bullpen shut down Baltimore over the last five innings.
BAL *	101 200 000	4 11 0	**Coppinger** (5.1), Rhodes (0.2), Mills (1.1), Orosco (0), Benitez (0.2), Mathews (1)	Hoiles	

GAME 5 - OCTOBER 13

NY E	006 000 000	6 11 0	**Pettitte** (8), Wetteland (1)	Leyritz, Fielder (2 on), Strawberry	Yankees belted three home runs in a six-run third inning as they clinched their first AL pennant in 15 years. Leyritz led off the inning with a solo shot, then Fielder and Strawberry capped the uprising with back-to-back homers later in the decisive frame. Pettitte held the Orioles scoreless until Zeile homered in the sixth. Murray and Bonilla also homered for Baltimore.
BAL *	000 001 012	4 4 1	**Erickson** (5), Rhodes (1), Mills (1.0), Myers (2)	Zeile, Murray, Bonilla (1 on)	

Team totals

		W	AB	H	2B	3B	HR	R	RBI	BA	BB	SO	ERA
NY	E	4	183	50	9	1	10	27	24	.273	20	37	3.64
BAL	*	1	176	39	4	0	9	19	19	.222	15	33	4.11

Individual Batting

NEW YORK (EAST)

	AB	H	2B	3B	HR	R	RBI	BA
D. Jeter, ss	24	10	2	0	1	5	1	.417
T. Martinez, 1b	22	4	1	0	0	3	0	.182
B. Williams, of	19	9	3	0	2	6	6	.474
C. Fielder, dh	18	3	0	0	2	3	8	.167
T. Raines, of	15	4	1	0	0	2	0	.267
M. Duncan, 2b	15	3	2	0	0	0	0	.200
W. Boggs, 3b	15	2	0	0	0	1	0	.133
D. Strawberry, of	12	5	0	0	3	4	5	.417
J. Girardi, c	12	3	0	1	0	1	0	.250
P. O'Neill, of	11	3	0	0	1	1	2	.273
J. Leyritz, c, of	8	2	0	0	1	1	2	.250
C. Hayes, 3b, dh	7	1	0	0	0	0	0	.143
L. Sojo, 2b	5	1	0	0	0	0	0	.200
M. Aldrete	0	0	0	0	0	0	0	—
A. Fox, dh	0	0	0	0	0	0	0	—

Errors: M. Duncan
Stolen Bases: D. Jeter (2), B. Williams

BALTIMORE (Wild Card)

	AB	H	2B	3B	HR	R	RBI	BA
R. Alomar, 2b	23	5	2	0	0	2	1	.217
T. Zeile, 3b	22	8	0	0	3	3	5	.364
B. Anderson, of	21	4	1	0	1	5	1	.190
C. Ripken, ss	20	5	1	0	0	1	0	.250
B. Bonilla, of	20	1	0	0	1	1	2	.050
R. Palmeiro, 1b	17	4	0	0	2	4	4	.235
E. Murray, dh	15	4	0	0	1	1	2	.267
B. Surhoff, of	15	4	0	0	0	0	2	.267
C. Hoiles, c	12	2	0	0	1	1	2	.167
M. Parent, c	6	1	0	0	0	0	0	.167
P. Incaviglia, dh	2	1	0	0	0	1	0	.500
M. Devereaux, of	2	0	0	0	0	0	0	.000
T. Tarasco, of	1	0	0	0	0	0	0	.000

Errors: R. Alomar (2), C. Ripken, T. Zeile

Individual Pitching

NEW YORK (EAST)

	W	L	ERA	IP	H	BB	SO	SV
A. Pettitte	1	0	3.60	15	10	5	7	0
J. Key	1	0	2.25	8	3	1	5	0
D. Cone	0	0	3.00	6	5	5	5	0
M. Rivera	1	0	0.00	4	6	1	5	0
J. Wetteland	0	0	4.50	4	2	1	5	1
K. Rogers	0	0	12.00	3	5	2	3	0
D. Weathers	1	0	0.00	3	3	0	0	0
J. Nelson	0	1	11.57	2.1	5	0	2	0
G. Lloyd	0	0	0.00	1.2	0	0	1	0

BALTIMORE (Wild Card)

	W	L	ERA	IP	H	BB	SO	SV
S. Erickson	0	1	2.38	11.1	14	4	8	0
M. Mussina	0	1	5.87	7.2	8	2	6	0
D. Wells	1	0	4.05	6.2	8	3	6	0
R. Coppinger	0	1	8.44	5.1	6	1	3	0
R. Myers	0	1	2.25	4	4	3	2	0
A. Benitez	0	0	7.71	2.1	3	3	2	1
T. Mathews	0	0	0.00	2.1	2	0	3	0
A. Mills	0	0	3.86	2.1	3	1	3	0
J. Orosco	0	0	4.50	2	2	1	2	0
A. Rhodes	0	0	0.00	2	2	0	2	0

1996 WORLD SERIES

LINE SCORES	PITCHERS (innings pitched)	HOME RUNS (men on)	HIGHLIGHTS

New York (A.L.) defeats Atlanta (N.L.) 4 games to 2

GAME 1 - OCTOBER 20

ATL N   026 013 000   12 13 0
NY A   000 010 000   1 4 1

Smoltz (6), McMichael (1), Neagle (1), Wade (0.2), Clontz (0.1)

Pettitte (2.1), Boehringer (3), Weathers (1.2), Nelson (1), Wetteland (1)

A. Jones (1 on), A. Jones (2 on), McGriff

Andruw Jones, a 19 year old rookie, homered in his first two at-bats to power the Braves. He hit a two run homer against Pettitte to open the scoring in the second, and his three run shot off Boehringer capped a six-run third inning. He became the youngest player to homer in the World Series, and only the second player to homer in his first two World Series at-bats (Gene Tenace in 1972 was the first). Smoltz pitched the first six innings, allowing just two hits, to pick up the victory.

GAME 2 - OCTOBER 21

ATL N   101 011 000   4 10 0
NY A   000 000 000   0 7 1

Maddux (8), Wohlers (1)

Key (6), Lloyd (0.2), Nelson (1.1), M. Rivera (1)

Maddux pitched eight shutout innings as the Braves took a 2-0 Series lead. McGriff drove in Atlanta's first three runs with two singles and a sacrifice fly, while Lemke had two hits and scored twice.

GAME 3 - OCTOBER 22

NY A   100 100 030   5 8 1
ATL N   000 001 010   2 6 1

Cone (6), M. Rivera (1.1), Lloyd (0.2), Wetteland (1) SV

Glavine (7), McMichael (0), Clontz (1), Bielecki (1)

Williams (1 on)

Cone pitched six strong innings and received solid relief help as the Yankees broke into the win column. Williams paced New York's attack with two hits, three RBI and two runs scored. He singled home Raines with the game's first run in the opening inning, and hit a two run homer off McMichael in the eighth. Grissom had three hits for Atlanta.

GAME 4 - OCTOBER 23

NY A   000 003 030 2   8 12 0
ATL N   041 010 000 0   6 9 2

Rogers (2.0), Boehringer (2), Weathers (1), Nelson (1), M. Rivera (1.1), Lloyd (1), Wetteland (0.2) SV

Neagle (5.0), Wade (0), Bielecki (2), Wohlers (2), Avery (0.2), Clontz (0.1)

Leyritz (2 on)

McGriff

Yankees evened the Series by overcoming an early 6-0 deficit. Leyritz blasted a three-run homer off Wohlers to tie the game in the eighth, and New York tallied twice in the tenth to win it. Avery retired the first two batters in the tenth before walking Raines, who moved to second on Jeter's single. Atlanta elected to intentionally walk Williams to load the bases, but the strategy backfired when pinch hitter Boggs walked on a full count to break the tie. An insurance run scored when first baseman Klesko dropped a soft popup off the bat of Hayes. Braves jumped out to a 4-0 lead in the second inning highlighted by McGriff's solo homer and a two-run double by Grissom. The game took 4:17 to play, making it the longest game by time in Series history.

GAME 5 - OCTOBER 24

NY A   000 100 000   1 4 1
ATL N   000 000 000   0 5 1

Pettitte (8.1), Wetteland (0.2) SV

Smoltz (8), Wohlers (1)

Yankees took their third straight game in Atlanta as Pettitte, with relief help from Wetteland, outdueled Smoltz. New York scored the only run of the game in the fourth when Fielder doubled home Hayes, who reached base when Grissom dropped his fly ball for a two base error. Chipper Jones led off the Atlanta ninth with a double and moved to third on an infield out, bringing Wetteland into the game. With the infield in, he retired Lopez on a grounder to third and after walking Klesko intentionally, got Polonia to fly out to rightfielder O'Neill, who made a running catch to end the game.

GAME 6 - OCTOBER 26

ATL N   000 100 001   2 8 0
NY A   003 000 00x   3 8 1

Maddux (7.2), Wohlers (0.1)

Key (5.1), Weathers (0.1), Lloyd (0.1), M. Rivera (2), Wetteland (1) SV

Yankees scored three runs off Maddux in the third inning and held on to win their first World Championship since 1978. Girardi's RBI triple plated the first run, and Jeter and Williams each singled home a run. Series MVP Wetteland allowed a run in the ninth before recording his fourth save, a Series first.

Team totals

		W	AB	H	2B	3B	HR	R	RBI	BA	BB	SO	ERA
NY	A	4	199	43	6	1	2	18	16	.216	26	43	3.93
ATL	N	2	201	51	9	1	4	26	26	.254	23	36	2.33

Individual Batting

NEW YORK (A.L.)

	AB	H	2B	3B	HR	R	RBI	BA
B. Williams, of	24	4	0	0	1	3	4	.167
C. Fielder, dh, 1b	23	9	2	0	1	2	1	.391
D. Jeter, ss	20	5	0	0	0	5	1	.250
M. Duncan, 2b	19	1	0	0	0	1	0	.053
C. Hayes, 3b, 1b	16	3	0	0	0	2	1	.188
D. Strawberry, of	16	3	0	0	1	2	1	.188
T. Raines, of	14	3	0	0	0	2	0	.214
P. O'Neill, of	12	2	2	0	0	1	0	.167
W. Boggs, 3b	11	3	1	0	0	0	2	.273
T. Martinez, 1b	11	1	0	0	0	0	0	.091
J. Girardi, c	10	2	0	1	0	1	1	.200
J. Leyritz, c	8	3	0	0	1	1	3	.375
L. Sojo, 2b	5	3	1	0	0	1	0	.600
A. Pettitte, p	4	0	0	0	0	0	0	.000
D. Cone, p	2	0	0	0	0	0	0	.000
K. Rogers, p	1	1	0	0	0	0	0	1.000
M. Aldrete, of	1	0	0	0	0	0	0	.000
G. Lloyd, p	1	0	0	0	0	0	0	.000
M. Rivera, p	1	0	0	0	0	0	0	.000
A. Fox, 2b, 3b	0	0	0	0	0	1	0	—

Errors: M. Duncan (2), D. Jeter (2), T. Raines
Stolen Bases: M. Duncan, D. Jeter, J. Leyritz, B. Williams

ATLANTA (N.L.)

	AB	H	2B	3B	HR	R	RBI	BA
M. Grissom, of	27	12	2	1	0	4	5	.444
M. Lemke, 2b	26	6	1	0	0	2	2	.231
C. Jones, 3b, ss	21	6	3	0	0	3	3	.286
J. Lopez, c	21	4	0	0	0	3	1	.190
A. Jones, of	20	8	1	0	2	4	6	.400
F. McGriff, 1b	20	6	0	0	2	4	6	.300
J. Blauser, ss	18	3	1	0	0	2	1	.167
J. Dye, of	17	2	0	0	0	0	1	.118
R. Klesko, dh, of, 1b	10	1	0	0	0	2	1	.100
T. Pendleton, 3b, dh	9	2	1	0	0	1	0	.222
L. Polonia	5	0	0	0	0	0	0	.000
J. Smoltz, p	2	1	0	0	0	0	0	.500
M. Bielecki, p	1	0	0	0	0	0	0	.000
T. Glavine, p	1	0	0	0	0	1	0	.000
M. Mordecai	1	0	0	0	0	0	0	.000
D. Neagle, p	1	0	0	0	0	0	0	.000
E. Perez, c	1	0	0	0	0	0	0	.000
R. Belliard, ss	0	0	0	0	0	0	0	—

Errors: J. Blauser, J. Dye, M. Grissom, R. Klesko
Stolen Bases: M. Grissom, A. Jones, C. Jones

Individual Pitching

NEW YORK (A.L.)

	W	L	ERA	IP	H	BB	SO	SV
J. Key	1	1	3.97	11.1	15	5	1	0
A. Pettitte	1	1	5.91	10.2	11	4	5	0
D. Cone	1	0	1.50	6	4	4	3	0
M. Rivera	0	0	1.59	5.2	4	3	4	0
B. Boehringer	0	0	5.40	5	5	5	5	0
J. Nelson	0	0	0.00	4.1	1	1	5	0
J. Wetteland	0	0	2.08	4.1	4	1	6	4
D. Weathers	0	0	3.00	3	2	3	3	0
G. Lloyd	1	0	0.00	2.2	0	0	4	0
K. Rogers	0	0	22.50	2	5	5	2	0

ATLANTA (N.L.)

	W	L	ERA	IP	H	BB	SO	SV
G. Maddux	1	1	1.72	15.2	14	1	5	0
J. Smoltz	1	1	0.64	14	6	8	14	0
T. Glavine	0	1	1.29	7	4	3	8	0
D. Neagle	0	0	3.00	6	5	4	3	0
M. Wohlers	0	0	6.23	4.1	7	2	4	0
M. Bielecki	0	0	0.00	3	0	3	6	0
B. Clontz	0	0	0.00	1.2	1	1	2	0
G. McMichael	0	0	27.00	1	5	0	1	0
S. Avery	0	1	13.50	0.2	1	3	0	0
T. Wade	0	0	0.00	0.2	1	0	1	0